WRITTEN BY A
LAVISHLY ILLU
BRIMMING

—this is "A Dictionary of American Antiques." Whether you collect Ale Shoes or Zoetropes, you will find the explanation you need in this definitive volume. Here is what this book says about such known, and little known, items as—

- Cornshuck Seat: Chair seat, imitative of rushing, but made from twisted husks from green corn. A pioneer-type chair seat.

- Gate-leg Table: Drop-leaf table in the Gallic or Gothic style, with turned support at each corner of the main top board, but having two additional legs on each side, forming swing-out gates, which support the leaves. Legs are vase-columnar or sausage-turned.

- Queen Anne: The style succeeding the William and Mary period, developed from the same cabinet, case and seat forms, with substitutions of cabriole legs. Both are almost pure Chinese in basic style.

- Sugar Chest: Southern furniture, the product of environmental necessity of storing sugar out of the reach of slaves. Some look like slope-fall desks of the early 19th century; most are of wild-cherry wood. Date is 1810-50.

    An entertaining and extremely useful book for the antique hunter, collector, student and scholar!

Also by CARL W. DREPPERD

*ABC's Of Old Glass

Handbook Of Antique Chairs

American Clocks And Clockmakers

First Reader For Antique Collectors

The Primer Of American Antiques

*New Geography Of American Antiques
in collaboration with
Lurelle Van Arsdale Guild

*Available in paperback form from AWARD BOOKS

A
DICTIONARY
OF
AMERICAN ANTIQUES

Carl W. Drepperd

AWARD BOOKS
NEW YORK

TANDEM BOOKS
LONDON

SECOND AWARD PRINTING 1970

Copyright © MCMLII by Carl W. Drepperd

Published by arrangement with Doubleday & Company, Inc.

Library of Congress Catalog Number: 52-11623

AWARD BOOKS are published by
Universal Publishing and Distributing Corporation
235 East Forty-fifth Street, New York, N.Y. 10017

TANDEM BOOKS are published by
Universal-Tandem Publishing Company Limited
14 Gloucester Road, London SW7, England

Manufactured in the United States of America

Foreword

Dr. Samuel Johnson, great champion of English literature and father of the modern dictionary, once remarked, "Dictionaries are like watches; the worst is better than none, and the best cannot be expected to go quite true." There is another phrase, probably apocryphal, attributed to Johnson which goes like this: "Sir, no sort of book is so well calculated to earn the damnation of both reader and author as a dictionary; the former damn it for its lack of inclusion, the latter for its interminable definity." So much for lexicons and lexicon making from the most famous of compilers and writers.

"Chiffonier," assert some dictionaries, means a ragpicker and a place for rags and tags. There was once a Society of Literary and Scientific Chiffoniers which, under the leadership of one, Habbakuk O. Westman, published a *History of the Spoon*. This present work now in your hands may, if you like, be characterized as a chiffonier, filled with the rags and tags of collecting nomenclature. For, in all truth, the compilation has been a rag-picking job from first to last. Even the title, *Dictionary of American Antiques,* is cut from fabric having some elasticity. The purists will at once pounce upon it as inadequate in that the content of the volume contains much material having no colonial or Federal American provenance.

This work began in 1942 with a single drawer file of less than 500 data cards, on each of which was written a word, term, or phrase with what seemed to be its original and its current meaning. On the day the file was closed, October 1, 1951, there were over 21,000 cards in a multi-drawer file, together with a group called "master cards" referring to data which eventually must find its way into one India-paper volume, perhaps of 2,000 pages. Unfortunately, over 8,000 cards had to be dropped, their context eliminated from this work.

The space limitations of this book, established because of the present-day economics of printing, bookmaking, and bookselling, made this action mandatory. That is why, under such headings as Lithographers, Buttons, Cut-Glass Patterns, American Silversmiths and Their Marks, Gunsmiths,

Clockmakers, Historic Old Blue Staffordshire, Historic Bottles & Flasks, Engravers, Artists, Silhouettists, Miniature Painters, Portrait Painters, Drawing Instruction Books, Pewterers, and some others, you will not find definitive or even exemplary listings of names, patterns, et cetera, but will be referred directly to a standard existing work on the subject, or told where to seek further information. In most cases the Bibliography at the end of this book will list the volumes for direct reference. Had we not used this technique, this book would be a six-volume publication and not what it is designed primarily to be: a dictionary for the general collector of antiques and relics of America's past, and of the heritage of its settlers, whether colonial, pioneer, or latter-day immigrants.

Since work on this volume was started, other students have published extended glossaries, lists, "dictionaries," and "encyclopedias." Each of these volumes stands as an honest effort in response to a most important factor: the obvious need for a book of dictionary type, as definitive as possible. This, no more and no less, is the compass of this present volume. It cannot be called unabridged, for that means all-inclusive. Neither can it be called "abridged," for there was nothing, other than the tremendous file of data cards, from which abridgment could be made. So it is a first book, containing perhaps more terms and definitions than any other five volumes of categorical nature.

There is, seemingly, a reversal of the mathematics of odds at work when it comes to the chances of finding a given word or phrase in anything short of a definitive lexicon. It seems that, if there are 15,000 entries, the chances should be 15,000 to 1 that you will find what you seek. And then, having failed on a few, it seems the chances are 15,000 to 1 that you will not find your desired entry. We shall leave such speculation to the mathematicians and can recommend that you do the same. If the meaning of what you seek is not here and not in any of the works listed in the Bibliography, it must reside in legends and in colloquialisms long forgotten, unhonored, and unsung.

This compilation and its organization, from first to last, have enjoyed the good wishes and occasional or protracted services of many enthusiasts and top-level people of collecting. Acknowledgment, coupled with profound thanks, is here extended to Mrs. Marjorie M. Smith, editor and publisher of *Spinning Wheel Magazine,* and Alice Winchester, editor of *The Magazine Antiques.* The late Harry T. Peters was an enthusiastic supporter of the work, as have been Dr. John L. Ruth, Dr. Matthew Chappell, George Hay Kain, Esq., Earl Breeding, Esq., and Messrs. Mark Shannaberger, Lockwood Barr, Joe Kindig, Jr., and Joe Kindig, III, Charles and Irving Lyon, Arthur Sussel, Benjamin Ginsburg, Henry Landis, Earle Newton, Frank O. Spinney, and the late Charles Messer Stow, dean of commentators on things antique. Kathryn Kent, Vette Watson, Beatrice Crane, Jane Scott, Marcia Ray, Mildred Sahulka, Mrs. Kellock Myers, and many others were most helpful in many ways. No less than five books, none by this author, have been enriched with material from the master file from which this dictionary derives. Others, indubitably, will spring from it. The entire file will revert to a foundation engaged in American historic and antiquarian research and will be available to students engaged in writing essays, monographs, and books.

Pride is something which must be erased from the ego of all who presume to enter the field of lexicography, bibliography, or glossary compilation. This dictionary is an honest effort to preserve in one spot, between covers, definitions and explanations of words and phrases used in collecting antiques. It is just that; no more, no less. That it will be of some service to you is the heartfelt wish of the author,

CARL W. DREPPERD

Bronxville, N.Y.

A

aakin: Oaken; made of oak.

aback table: A table not standing on proper leg supports but supported wholly or in part by affixing to a wall; a console table.

abacus: (1) Flat member at top of a capital. (2) Mechanical calculating machine or device, especially the Chinese frame of wires on which beads are strung. [*An early American and a Chinese bead example are pictured.*]

abattant: Having a front that drops or lowers; falling front; slope fall.

abb: The warp yarn on a loom.

ABC plate: Children's plates of pottery, porcelain, pewter, glass, et cetera, stamped or decorated with letters of the alphabet and sometimes with appropriate maxims.

abdice: a small ax.

abele: The white poplar.

abel-whackets: A card game.

Aberdeen Cut: A pattern of cut glass. *See* Cut-Glass Patterns.

abezzo: Resin of the silver fir, diluted with oil to make a varnish.

Abraham's balm: The red willow; bark used as aromatic.

acajou: Mahogany. **acajou nut:** A flavoring nut used with cocoa beans.

acanthus: Leaf form, stylized; a decorative element much used on classic-revival furniture from the Adam period. [*Example pictured.*]

Accomac Cut: A pattern of cut glass. *See* Cut-Glass Patterns.

accordion leg: A table leg which pulls out rather than swings out.

acerra: Incense box, or censer pan.

acetabulum: A measure of goblet form.

achat: The mineral agate.

achauffe: To warm, hence achauffing dish —chafing dish.

acid-etched: Glass decorated by biting with hydrofluoric acid through a wax ground. Technique dates from 1870s.

Ackermann prints: Prints from the various color-plate books published by Rudolph Ackermann of London, from early 1800s.

à cordeline: *See* Vitro-di-Trina.

acorn: (1) Nut fruit of the oak. (2) A ribbed pattern in pressed glass. Other varieties of pressed glass in Acorn pattern are Beaded Acorn and variants having clusters of leaves, or paneled with leaves.

acorn basket: Large roofed basket fixed in the fork of a tree for storage of acorns. [*Example pictured.*]

acorn bottle: Any wide-mouthed bottle used for sprouting acorns, a parlor curiosity popular in 1840s and 1850s.

acorn butter: Acorn-shaped butter cooler of pewter on a brass base used at table. Patented 1855.

acorn lamp: Two-part glass lamp burning a small squat candle. Seems to date from 1890s. [*Example pictured.*]

acorn molding: Molding having dentils tipped with acorns.

acorn thumbpiece: Pairs of acorns forming thumbpieces on tankards, et cetera. Dutch and Swiss, 16th and 17th centuries.

acronycal: Of the evening; sunset or dusk.

acroterium: Pedestal or pediment with urn or other object upon it. Literally, the summit or top; hence any finial topping an arch, pyramid, pediment, or table.

acus: Pin or needle form.

Adam (A FURNITURE STYLE): Deriving from Robert Adam & Brothers, mid-18th-century architects, who created the classic-revival style of furniture on which Heppelwhite and Sheraton (as well as others) are based. The Adam period refers to that period of the 18th century (c. 1750–80) when classic styles by these masters were the vogue. The style never captured colonial America, as its high point coincided with the Revolution. [*Examples of Adam-style furniture are pictured.*]

Adam & Eve andirons: Wrought-iron effigies of man and woman used as decorative uprights on fire irons. The figures are in silhouette. The term is colloquial.

adamantine: Of the earth; hard; rocklike. Name given certain gesso compositions used in making decorative panels for furniture, mirrors, and clocks. **adamantine candle:** A hard candle made at Salem, Mass., from 1845 by Seccomb & Dennis.

Adam pewter: Adam-period classic garden ornaments. They are not true pewter but about 90% lead.

Adams: Name now given to a pattern of pressed glass imitative of Diamond & Fan cutting. Made by Adams & Co., Pittsburgh, from 1880s or later.

Adams, Harvey: Maker of stonewares at Longton, England, who cultivated the American market from 1875 and made several visits to study the tastes and requirements of the people.

Adams, Dr. W. F.: Violin maker of Montpelier, Vt., 1787–1859. *See* Clarinet Cremona.

Adams, William: Owner of the Greenfield Pottery, Tunstall, from 1810s, where sponge-decorated wares of brilliant colors were made for the American market. This pottery also produced white granite (ironstone) china. William Adams, Sr., was an apprentice of Josiah Wedgwood's. The mark ADAMS is on much ceramic ware now enthusiastically collected in the U.S.

Adams & Bromley ware: Jasper and majolica pottery made at Victoria Works, Hanley, England, from mid-19th century.

Adams calico: Calico prints made at Adams, Mass., where, by 1830s, two mills were printing 5,000,000 yards annually.

Adams-Chandler silver: Plated silver, made at Brooklyn, N.Y., by Adams, Chandler, Moore & Ormsbee, from 1870s.

Adams coverlets: Pattern-woven bedspreads by J. Adams of Delaware, O., from 1850s.

Adams Railroad Atlas: Elephant folio atlas with many full-page illustrated histories of American business. Published by Asher & Adams in several editions, 1870–80.

Adams silver: Early sterling silver made by Adams & Kidney, New York City, from 1850s.

Adams wirework: Bird cages, fire guards and fenders, baskets, play pens, et cetera, made by Samuel Adams of Boston from 1820s.

addice: An adz.

addorsed: Back to back, same as *dos à dos*.

adec: Milk vinegar; sour whey.

Adelaide chair: French Antique revival side chair named in honor of Queen Victoria's daughter, Princess Adelaide. It is upholstered and has a low seat, high back, and no arms.

adjustable chair: Chair for use of patients and patrons of doctors, dentists, barbers, and bonesetters. Capable of many adjustments. Made by C. H. Eccleston of Utica, N.Y., from 1840s. [*Example pictured.*]

adler: The double-headed eagle of the Holy Roman Empire. Not a mythological bird but an attempt to show both sides of the eagle on a single plane.

adler glass (adler glazer): Any glass decorated with the true adler as herein defined.

Admiral Toby: More properly, an admiral jug (the term "Toby" derives from use of effigy of Toby Philpot in jug form). This jug is in the form of an admiral's bust and shoulders. Date of originals seems to be 1790–1820.

Admiralty cloth: Dark blue Melton weave fabric.

adobe: Clay plaster, from *at-tob* (Arabic). Adobe walls are clay daubed over wattles, or packed solid.

adornments: Sheets of printed or stamped paper and cards having many small decorative elements to cut apart for use in decoration and in making memorials, valentines, et cetera. In active use from 1790s.

adularia: A variety of native American moonstone, found in Pennsylvania, New York, and Connecticut.

advertising wares: Any glassware, ceramic, iron, or other ware bearing the advertising of the maker or manufacturer, generally made as samples or souvenirs and given away or sold at low prices. Not to be confused with trademarks or other identification devices used generally by many makers.

ady: The St. Thomas palm tree.

adz: Hoe-shaped smoothing ax.

Aeolian: An attachment for pianos patented 1844 by Obed Coleman of Philadelphia and again (an improvement) in 1845 by C. Hirst of New Orleans.

aeophile: Philosophic apparatus to demonstrate the power of steam. A hollow metal ball with a vent. When filled with water and placed in the embers of a fire, the heat generated steam and the vent produced a whistle that lasted until all the water evaporated. An early idea for the singing teakettle.

aes: Bronze. Latin for alloys of copper.

aes ustrum: Copper foil laminated between layers of sulphur and ground to a powder to produce magical colored fire.

Aetna glass: The factory of Johnson Glass Co. at Frederick, Md., was known as the Aetna Glass House, and the glass was called Aetna. Bottles and window glass were made. Established 1790s. Aetna was a name favored by glassmakers, and several factories were known by this name.

Affleck, Thomas: Famous pre-Revolutionary cabinetmaker of Philadelphia who worked to 1790s. He was encouraged to come to America by Governor Penn. He worked in the Georgian and Chippendale styles and is known to have made furniture featuring the square leg called Marlborough.

affronté: Full-face positioning of carved or other decor of human figure or animalistic designs.

agalloch: The aloe tree.

agata glass: Mottled-effect glass achieved by sprinkling with alcohol before tempering; effect also achieved by mechanical means. The finish was applied to clear and amberina glass.

agate: Play marble turned from genuine agate, or imitations known as "glass agates."

agate bisque: One of Josiah Wedgwood's inventions, a hard stoneware bisque used in making mortars, pestles, chemists' wares, and flasks.

agate glass: (Not to be confused with agata glass.) A brownish-purple glass streaked with milk white, imitating rock agate. Made from 1850s to 1900, first at Sandwich and then at Pittsburgh factories.

agate-handled: Tablewares fitted with (1) handles of genuine rock agate (these are generally solid silver) and (2) pottery handles simulating genuine agate and used on Sheffield steel and plated wares.

agateware: Any pottery displaying veining and mottling in imitation of the mineral or rock agate, whether in the paste or body or in the glaze. In 1724 Rendrich & Jones (England) was granted a patent for mottling and staining woodenstone-, and earthenwares in imitation of agate, et cetera. In 1729 a patent to produce the same effects in redwares was granted. [*Example pictured.*]

aginatour: Hawker of small wares, gimcracks, and gewgaws.

aglets (aiglets): Tags or points on lace; a jewel in a cap. Sometimes also used in reference to catkins of the hazel bush.

Agnus Dei: Literally "Lamb of God," and symbolized by figure of a lamb with halo, holding a staff from which flies the pennon of the Cross of Jesus.

agricultural ware: Drainage tiles as used on farms.

aguamanile: Figural containers in form of eagles or animals. Early Gothic.

ague tree: The sassafras.

aiguiere: Slender bulbous-bodied pot with long narrow neck, having spout and cover. Oriental form, used for wine or coffee.

ailette: An epaulet of iron; shoulder armor of the Middle Ages. Also, and more generally meant by the term, a two-part hinged case unfolding to form a toilet cabinet.

air bed: The first India-rubber mattress, invented by A. J. Goodenough of N.Y., 1847.

air cane: An air gun concealed in a cane. Known from 18th century in this form. *See* Air Guns.

air-circulating rocker: Spiral spring platform rocker, the motion of which operated a bellows which conveyed a draft of air through tubes to the seat and headrest of chair. *The Scientific American* of November 6, 1847, stated this type of chair would no doubt meet with ready sale.

air cylinder grainer: Painters' and decorators' tool, a roller on which the grain of wood was impressed and transferred to other wood surfaces through ground color. Any hardwood grain could be approximated. Made from 1850s.

air furnace ware: Advertised by Air Furnace Co., N.Y., 1768. Skillets, ovens, bath stoves, stove plates, firebacks, and other cast-iron objects.

air guns: The first air gun noted was made by Liseau for Henry IV in 1408. Compressed air has been used to propel projectiles from tubes for ages (as darts from blowguns), but mechanical operation dates from this example. From thence onward pistols, rifles, canes, traps, and other devices were made.

airing horse: Frameworks of wood upon which to drape sheets, et cetera, for airing, or wet wash for drying. Known chiefly in cheap forms sold in woodenware shops in 19th century; it should be noted the prototypes were of mahogany and walnut, finely turned and fitted, some even displaying inlay. The finer cabinetmakers' examples date from c. 1750.

air jack: Another term for smoke jack, *which see.*

airplane antiques: Ideas for heavier-than-air machines to navigate the air predate the balloon. While most of the antiques on this subject are books and pamphlets (some of excessive rarity and value), there are models, prints, printed cotton scarves, handkerchiefs, and fabrics featuring such proposed machines. Hanson's Aerial Steam Carriage, printed on a cotton handkerchief, is one example. This print predicted "Through to China in 24 Hours" for heavier-than-air machines, and made that prediction in 1840.

air repeater: An air gun firing ten times "without powder" in half a minute. Advertised and sold in Boston in 1754.

air thermometer: Early-type thermometer on which the highest reading is coldest and the lowest reading is the extreme of heat registered. The column of air, expanded with heat, forced a colored liquid down in the tube; contracting with cold, the air permitted the liquid to rise.

air twist: A form of decoration achieved in glassmaking by drawing out glass containing bubbles of air into rodlike forms and then twisting to form a spiral. A similar effect was achieved by embedding bundles of opaque or colored glass rods within a parison of molten glass. Glassmakers had several other techniques for obtaining this effect, including ramming stems through a die ring having many V-shaped grooves, and then coating the ridged stem with a flashing of glass. This form of decoration is most generally found in the stems of drinking glasses.

aisyl: Any souring, such as vinegar, alegar, adec; any sour herb.

Aiton furniture: Beds, chairs, and case furniture made by Thomas Aiton of Baltimore, who advertised as early as 1783.

ajar: From "on char," meaning "on the turn."

ajouré: Openwork; pierced through, as carving, modeling, molding, et cetera, to achieve a lacelike effect.

alabaster: Somewhat translucent sulphate of lime or fine-grained gypsum. The first "toys" made of this mineral are noted during the William & Mary period and were carvings and turnings produced as chimney and table ornaments. From this vogue may derive the term "chalkware," which is now applied exclusively to plaster-of-Paris ornaments of the 19th century. The Chinese made carved figural, animalistic, and other ornaments (including pomegranates) from alabaster and colored them. These the Dutch traders imported, and thus popularized them in England and on the continent of Europe by 1680. Also known in Italy and made there, where also began the imitation of alabaster ornaments by recasting replicas in plaster of Paris.

alabaster glass: Made at Sandwich Glass Works, the invention of James Lloyd. This is an excellent imitation of alabaster and of Irish Belleek china.

alabastrum: Vial or flask turned from alabaster, this mineral being quite easily carved and shaped. It has been used for thousands of years to make images, jars, pots, vials, and ceremonial urns.

alamo: The poplar tree.

alamode: A taffeta fabric.

alarum: A clock or watch with alarm bell.

alay: To reduce; to mix; to piece out.

albani stone: Black volcanic tufa.

Albany glass: Product of the Albany (N.Y.) Glass Factory, established c. 1785, failed 1790, reorganized 1792, and operating to 1820s. Made carboys, bottles, jars, and window glass.

albarello: A drug jar.

albata: Alloy of nickel, copper, and zinc, yielding a silvery-white metal.

Albert chair: French Antique revival chair of c. 1840, named for Victoria's consort, Prince Albert.

Albert light: A heavy candle with a draft hole through which the wick was threaded.

albespyne: The white hawthorn.

albification: Making white; bleaching.

album: A portfolio, generally with blank pages for pasting in memorials, clippings, et cetera. Any series of folios tied together. Publications designed for table books, containing collections of verse, prose, and pictures.

alburn: The viburnum. When used to designate a tint or shade it means whitish brown, pale tan, or taupe.

alcarraz: Porous pottery vessel, generally of unglazed redware, used to cool water by surface evaporation.

alchemy: An alloy of copper and tin; a superior pewter used in 16th and 17th centuries for making spoons and plates. Also **alcamine.** Alchemy meant the practice of chemistry, considered a black art, or "arcanum."

Alciphron: A literary work by the Dean of Derry, Ireland, George Berkeley, who spent some time at Newport, R.I., 1729-31. His theme was "Nature is the language of God." Emerson drank deeply at this font of wisdom and saw "sermons in stone and books in running brooks."

Alcock & Hill: (Alcock's Hill Pottery.) Semi-porcelains, chinaware, and fine earthenwares made by Samuel Alcock & Co. from 1839 to 1860 at the Hill Pottery, Burslem, England, once owned and operated previously by Ralph Wood.

alcora ware: Spanish porcelain of mid-18th century.

alcove bed: Folding bed; fold-up bed; bed in box or cupboard, recess or niche. Examples date from 17th century or earlier.

Alden coffee: The first instant coffee; cooked coffee dehydrated to a thick paste. A spoonful made a cupful by addition of boiling water. American, made by Alden Co. of New York City from 1850s.

alderne: The elderberry.

Aldgate: English white pottery made at Aldgate from 1690s.

ale beam: The olive tree. Also oyle beam.

aleberry: A drink of boiled ale with spices and sugared bread sops.

alec: Any fish sauce, as walnut ketchup, quin sauce, mushroom ketchup, anchovy essence. All these advertised in U.S. from 1790s.

ale carrier: Conical vessel of glass, pottery, or stoneware, and sometimes in metal, having a top with washer to provide tight fit. The original "growler," designed to carry ale safely from alehouse to home, or from barrel to table. Most of these date from mid-19th century. [*Example pictured.*]

alecost: The herb rosemary, used to "bitter" ale in brewing.

ale firkin: Woodenware; an eight-gallon measure, also made in copper and other metals.

alegar: Sour ale; malt vinegar.

ale hoof: The ground ivy.

ale king: The winter cherry.

alerion: The tamed eagle, generally pictured with the bill of a dove, without legs and claws.

ale shoe: A shoe-shaped vessel of metal for heating ale in the fireplace. The toe of the shoe was placed in embers to heat the ale. [*Example pictured.*]

ale wood: Olive wood.

alexander: The great parsley plant.

Alexander mirrors: John Alexander of Philadelphia made many fine mirrors in the tabernacle and Constitution styles from 1790 to 1810.

alexandres: Kid gloves, imported from Paris, 1820s–50s.

alexandrin: Embroidery by the yard, imported from the Near East, from 18th century.

ale yard: Slender conical glass 36 inches tall; ceremonial ale glass to "drink a yard of ale." Date is from 18th century.

Algate hole: Niche in walls of fireplace to hold tinder, matches, unguents, and tobacco.

Alhambra vase: Copies of the famed "La Jarra" of the Alhambra, made in 1842 at Sevres and again in 1860s by Deck of Paris.

aliothus: Used by japanners in decorating their products in imitation of pearl; made from shellfish and sometimes called "pearl of aliothus." From *aliot*, seed pearl.

Alioto: Trade name used by Meriden Britannia Co. from 1850s for the white metal base of their silver-plated wares.

alkanet oil: Linseed oil boiled with alkanet root to dye it and so provide a staining furniture polish. Used from 17th century.

Allan's seven-shooter: A toy; a seven-shot peashooter, sold as a hoax in a mail-order swindle of the 1870s.

allay: Alloy. Term is Elizabethan English.

allblaze dish: Covered dish fitted with underpan in which alcohol (spirits of wine) was burned to heat contents; chafing dish.

alleageas: East Indian fabrics, printed cotton, hempen, or linen cloth.

alleluya: The wood sorrel.

Allendale: A bedspread imported from England in early 19th century. These spreads were in the counterpane or counterpoint weave. A variety of this type, pattern-woven, was produced at Colonel Rutgers' factory (N.J.) in 1820s. This mill produced a counterpane with the American eagle on it. *See* Rutgers Spreads.

Allen furniture: French Antique revival furniture now commonly called early Victorian, produced by Joseph & William Allen of Philadelphia from 1835. By 1870 this firm was the major furniture emporium of the Quaker City.

Allen gum: Isaac Allen of Albany, N.Y., made chewing gum from spruce gum in 1850s. In 1859 he offered "Jenny Lind Chewing Gum" and ladies' gum-mastic "sugar-coated in tin foil." Also made "pulmonary chewing gum."

Allen pepperbox: The famous "pepperbox" revolving pistol made by Allen Arms Co., having a huge barrel bored with six firing tubes, revolving as fired, and thus offering six consecutive shots. [*Example pictured.*]

Allen scandal: On March 24, 1811, Ethan Allen's daughter took the veil in the Convent of the "Black Nuns" at Montreal, Canada. This caused a tempest in a teapot throughout New England and was known as the "Allen scandal" and the "Allen tragedy."

aller: The alder tree.

Allerton ware: Pottery and china by C. Allerton & Sons, Longton, England. For

1, Acanthus. 2, Abacus; two types. 3, Acorn Lamp. 4, Adam-Style Cabinet and Chair.
5, Acorn Basket in Tree. 6, Adjustable Chair. 7, Agateware. 8, Ale Carrier. 9, Ale Shoe.
10, Allen "Pepperbox" Pistol. 11, Allumette Work. 12, American Oven. 13, American
Stoves (Franklin). 14, American Stove (Nott's). 15, Alphabet-Arithmetic Board. 16,
Angle-Front Corner Cupboard. 17, Angel Lamp. 18, Angle Lamp. 19, Angell (Student)
Lamp. (No. 7 from John Francis Co. and Virtue & Co., London.)

5

a century this firm produced Toby jugs and lusterwares. Date from 1830.

alley: A passageway; an out-of-bounds region in field games.

alley tor: A game marble.

All Fours table: Any table used in playing the card game of All Fours; not a special table.

alligator jewelry: Gold- and silver-mounted alligator teeth used as sleeve buttons, eardrops, and brooches. A vagary of 1870s and 1880s.

allison: The wood rose.

Allison furniture: Michael Allison of New York, 1800–33, produced exceptionally fine furniture in the Directoire and Sheraton styles that is the equal of any by Duncan Phyfe, and some connoisseurs consider it superior to Phyfe's. Allison was not the mass producer that Phyfe was, and his master's touch is perhaps on every piece from his shops. Some of his work is marked with a punch stamp.

allspice: Jamaica peppercorns.

allume scagliuolo: Talc, calcined to provide the gesso base used by gilders. This white plaster, mixed with rabbit-skin glue size, was used under most pure-gold-leaf work.

allumette: A form of fancywork using chenille yarn drawn over and around wire or wood frameworks to create boxes, vases, trays, lampshades, et cetera. A vogue of the 1840s and 1850s. [*Example pictured.*]

alluminor: Limner; original form of designation for a painter of pleasing pictures.

Allwine gloss: Quick-drying varnish invented by Lawrence Allwine, c. 1790. Two kinds were used: (1) copal dissolved in gold size and (2) shellac dissolved in spirits of wine. Pigment was added to produce the desired color of enamel. The white Allwine enamel has been used for years by furniture dealers to restore or touch up white enameled articles damaged or marred in transit.

allyson: The herb madwort.

almadine: A variety of native American garnet, much used in cheap jewelry from the 1840s.

almarie: A cupboard. *See* Ambrie, Ambry.

almodza: Tin; tinware.

almond butter: A superfine paste made from blanched almonds; superfine marchpane. A custard made from this, according to a recipe dated 1713, called for whites of 20 eggs and one pound of loaf sugar, baked in a "mild oven."

almond drops: Almond-shaped pieces of cut rock crystal or glass adorning candlesticks from 17th century.

almorrata: Early Spanish glass wine vessel having four spouts and insufficient footing for standing, hence suspended in cords.

almucanars staff: A navigating instrument of early (15th century) date. Made of boxwood or pearwood and used to determine "amplitude" by observing the rise and set of the sun.

alnage: Officially measured wool, and designated by a seal on bolt.

aloma: A red-yellow color.

alphabet-arithmetic board: An educational device made in 1840s by Edwin Allen of Windham, Conn., having the letters of the alphabet sliding in grooves to enable user to form words. A similar arrangement of figures provided for doing simple problems. [*Example pictured.*]

alphaenix: White barley sugar in sticks and crystals, sold as a remedy for head colds and sore throat in 18th century.

Alpha shaving mugs: The Alpha mark on such mugs is the vendor's, not the maker's, mark. Of late 19th-century production.

alquifou: Lead oxide used by potters for a green glaze.

alte Schweiz: Old Swiss, generally meaning old Swiss glass from Fluhli and other furnaces. It looks like Stiegel-type enameled ware.

althea plaster: Plaster of Paris to which althea root is added to retard setting and so provide better casts.

alto relievo: Sculptured work projecting at least half its natural dimension from the plane surface of a frieze or panel. Term refers to the technique and not to a motif or subject.

alum: Originally chrondine or animal glue, mixed with albumin. Now meaning sulphate of aluminum, the alum of commerce.

alum wax candles: Candles made of tallow melted in a saturated water solution of aluminum sulphate. This caused tallow to take on appearance of white wax and to set much harder than ordinary tallow. Made from 1840s.

alutation: Leather tanning.

Alyz: Early spelling of Alice, a cloth with threads of gold.

amadow: Touchwood; tinder. Fungus boiled in lye and dried with saltpeter. Also called quickfire.

Amana: A Dutch sect which migrated to Switzerland and Germany during Spanish occupation. Came to America early in 19th century, settling near Buffalo, N.Y., and finally in Iowa, where they have large communal holdings and make many articles of commerce from blankets to refrigerators.

amaranth: Purple wood.

amatorii: Portrait plates, generally of faience or majolica, with cupids and other love tokens. The plates themselves are characterized as love-token plates.

Amazon: Pattern of pressed glass that has saw-tooth bands at bottoms of openwares and also at upper rims of covered pieces. Made c. 1880.

ambergrise: Literally "gray amber," the morbid secretion of the whale, formerly used in cookery and to flavor wine. "Ambered wine be lusty" and "meats of noble sort, gris-ambered, steamed," are clues to uses.

amberina glass: An innovation most likely developed by New England Glass Co., c. 1833, but having numerous other claimants and patents to 1883. It is a good art glass, shading from pale amber to ruby red, with perhaps no two pieces precisely alike. Used in plain blown, swirled, tooled, or pressed work. Originally moderately expensive but finally a cheap dime-store-type product. The finer examples have pontils or pontil marks, ground off and polished.

amber slag: A milky-white glass streaked with pale to dark coffee- and chocolate-colored stripes and swirls.

amber sugar: Sugar from a hardy cane grown as far north as Ohio. The color of the finished crystals was amber. Much of it made in 1870s.

ambigu magique: See Magical Hodge-podge.

ambrie (Also **ambry, amry, almery, aumbry):** Cupboards in the Tudor-Gothic tradition with inner shelves and doors closing over them. Synonymous with almonry. True pieces date from 1400 to 1600.

ambrie caul: Coverpiece of fabric thrown or draped over the ambrie.

ambrotype: A more advanced form of daguerreotypy, in which the photo film was developed and floated on glass.

ambruzzi: Pottery in imitation of porcelain, belonging in the delft-majolica-faïence group of wares made of pottery or stoneware with tin glaze.

ambulante: A stand with handles for carrying.

amelcorn: A poor grade of spelt, or speltz, a grain of the wheat family. See Corn.

Amelung glass: Made at or near Frederick, Md., at the factory village of New Bremen, by John Frederick Amelung of Bremen, Germany, the promoter of the scheme, 1787–94. Many of the workers were from Bohemia. Good to average wares made, but at a cost that could not compete with England's Bristol glass laid down on the docks of Baltimore. A much overrated glass which seems to have inherited some of the Stiegel luster. Surprisingly, Amelung, like Stiegel, lived far beyond his means and was perhaps the main reason for the failure of the enterprise. He wanted to be subsidized by both the federal government and the state of Maryland. Amelung glass is in no way comparable to the fine glass of Germany, nor as good as commercial Bristol wares. A few presentation pieces were cut which show much promise and no little talent in the cutters' work, but these are the uncommon products of the factory, which turned out decanters, bottles, flasks, drinking glasses, and a general line of transparent white free-blown and mold-blown wares, and some in colors. *Two Hundred Years of American Blown Glass,* by George and Helen McKearin, contains an excellent notice of this glass with fine pictorial presentations of certain of the pieces.

amen glasses: English drinking glasses engraved with symbols of the Stuarts, especially the deposed James and the Young Pretender. *Amen* (so be it) and *Fiat* (let it be done) engraved on glasses were silent toasts of the Stuart sympathizers. Popular in some quarters of England, especially after the calling of the German George I to the throne. Thousands of generally available blown glasses of this period have been engraved with these words and sold as genuine examples.

American Flint Glass Works: Quite a few glass houses assumed this designation, from Henry William Stiegel onward. There is no particular virtue in attribution to a works by this name. Details will be found in *American Glass,* by George F. McKearin.

American kings: Lithographs, printed by Pendleton and published by Doggett of Boston, of portraits of Washington, Adams, Jefferson, Madison, and Monroe, from paintings by Gilbert Stuart. This same name is noted applied to playing cards featuring the first four named presidents as the kings of each suit. The lithographed portraits are 19¼" x 16¼" in size, or medium upright folios.

American Lowestoft: The term is not correct. What is referred to is neither Lowestoft nor American; it is oriental export porcelain from Canton and Nanking, decorated for the American market and brought here by American ships. There was a Chinese factor living in New England who advertised these wares.

American oven: An oblong metal box, open-fronted, with angular top and bottom serving as reflectors focused on the center pan or grid. Used in baking, broiling, and roasting before an open fire. Invented in U.S. c. 1790. [*Example pictured.*]

American porcelain: Several attempts at making porcelain pre-date the company which assumed this name for its product. Earlier ones were Bonnin & Morris, and Tucker, both of Philadelphia. The American Porcelain Works was incorporated 1854 with a capital of $300,000 and had its manufactory at Greenpoint, L.I. It produced a full line of tablewares, specialties, and novelties in the best French and English styles.

American stove: (1) One term by which the Franklin stove was known in England, where by far the greatest number of Franklin-type stoves were cast. [*Two examples pictured.*] (2) The Nott Pillar stove, a very decorative six-plate stove with a second and third story, made in U.S. from 1830s. [*Example pictured.*]

American System: Name given the high- or protective-tariff act sponsored by Henry Clay and John C. Calhoun, after the War of 1812 resulted in England and European manufacturers "dumping" merchandise in the U.S. and thus injuring local production and sales. Several household objects memorialized this act by carrying the phrases "American System" or "Long Live the American System." The best known is a mold-blown glass whiskey flask.

American Wing: The magnificent concept of the late R. T. Haines-Halsey and others, which resulted in the construction and furnishing of a large special wing at the Metropolitan Museum, New York City. Almost moribund from the 1930s to 1948, this storehouse of classic, rare, and authentic antiques is again intriguing the interest of collectors. Pamphlets and other literature are available from the Museum at modest prices.

Americo-Bohemian glass: Richly flashed and cased glass, cut and etched, and sometimes gilded, made at the New England Glass Works in the best Bohemian tradition. By 1850 this ware was known by the term here given.

amethysteen: A lately coined term for

any glass exposed to rays of sun until it takes on a purple-amethyst tint. Bottles so colored are decapitated by experts, ground down at fracture, and made into tumblers. Other treatment produces novelties and even jewelry. These are not antiques.

amianthoide: Mineral formation of asbestos in hairlike cords.

amianthus: Asbestos.

Amish blue: There are as many tints and shades of blue found on Amish fences, houses, and in their dress fabrics as there are shades of "Williamsburg blue." The Amish, or Omish, a Dutch sect that fled to Switzerland and Germany, and even to Russia, during the Spanish occupation of the Netherlands, came from Switzerland during the years 1701 to 1760 and settled largely in Chester and Lancaster counties of Pennsylvania. They are strict in dress and have a primitive, simple religion akin to that of the early Christians. These people love color, and blue is one of the colors they love best. The closest approximation to Amish blue can be had by adding indigo to whitewash. They use smalt, Prussian blue, navy blue, cobalt, or any other blue, pure or pasteled with white.

ammeos: Seeds of the ammomum, a grapelike berry which has an aromatic quality similar to camphor.

amorette (amor, amorini, amours): Cupids, or cherubim, as found on many ceramic plates and plaques; carved, painted, and stenciled on other objects and embroidered on textile fabrics.

ampel: A hanging basket.

ampelites: Cannel coals.

ampersand: The "&" figure designating the phrase "and, per se" and "id est." Much used decoratively in manuscripts and on signs during 17th, 18th, and 19th centuries.

amphora: In ancient liquid measure, half an urna. From this early nomenclature we derive the terms amphora and urn. The classic form is that of ovoid cylindrical jars.

amphora alabastron: The ovoid measure without footing, and with high flaring neck. Used by steadying in sand or in a footed metal ring.

amphitheater-American: Prehistoric amphitheater remains found in Florida, probably built by the Matacombe Indians. *American Antiquarian*, July 1887, contains an essay on this ancient work.

ampulla: A small flask of glass, ceramic ware, or wood, used for oils, ointments, and unguents.

amurce: Dregs, or partly concreted residue, of oil.

amydon: Fine starch, derived from wheat flour, used as a thickener for broths and gravies.

amygdalus: The almond-bearing peach.

anabaptist: A follower of the Swiss reformer, Zwingli. Became a sect in 1523 at Zurich. Believers in rebaptism and opposed to infant baptism. By 17th century the term was also applied to Mennonites and all other Baptist sects. Zwingli flourished 1484-1531.

anaclastic glasses: *See* Vexing Glasses.

anadem: A fillet worn on the hair.

anaglyptography: Machine ruling having the appearance of being raised from the surface, and used successfully to engrave reproductions of coins, bas-reliefs, et cetera, from c. 1848.

anamorphosis: A puzzle picture grossly distorted, yet assuming proper dimensions when viewed with aid of some optical device or by holding the print horizontally at eye level. Many varieties sold from mid-18th century.

anapes: A variety of fustian cloth.

anastatic work: Copying printing and engravings by soaking the paper in dilute nitric acid and then fixing it on a plate of zinc. A form of lithography later called zincography.

anatto: Yellow-orange dye obtained from anatto seeds, used in coloring butter, dyeing cloth, and in making staining oils and polishes.

anchor: A measure of 10 gallons. Remembering this, the phrases "wooden anchor," "tin anchor," "pewter anchor," and "copper anchor" make sense. Many a sea captain carried 20 wooden anchors (of rum) on a voyage.

anchor stove: A fine heating stove made by Chamberlain & Co. of Cincinnati. It was not anchor-shaped.

anchory: A foundry where anchors were cast. The Sterling Anchory of New York, burned 1767 and rebuilt 1768, made not only anchors but household hollow wares.

ancony: A pig, or bloom, of iron being made ready for the forge.

andersmeat: Afternoon luncheon.

Anderson: A pattern of pressed glass featuring an alternate fan and palmette design. Probably issued in 1870s or 1880s.

Anderson, Alexander: Cabinetmaker of New York working from c. 1770.

Anderson, Elbert: Cabinetmaker of New York, 1780s and 1790s. Produced furniture in Hepplewhite style.

Anderson, John: Cabinetmaker of Annapolis, Md., 1745-59.

Anderson carpets: Carpets sold by (and so marked) Hiram Anderson, N.Y., but not made by him. He was in business from 1640.

Anderson hammer: A curious hammer with a loop on the claw, terminating in a ring encircling the hammer. Patented in 1840s.

andirons: Any iron or other metal device to aid in the combustion of logs or other fuels on the hearth. Utilitarian andirons with spit racks and other mechanical additions were used in kitchens. Simple andirons were used on the hearths of common rooms, but from decorative to elaborate, and from inexpensive to costly, would be a fair statement of the range of andirons for important chambers, in average home and cottage, up the scale to the palace of the king, where silver and bronze andirons were not uncommon. Specific types are covered under names now commonly applied to them, such as Adam & Eve, Hessian, et cetera. Other names for these devices, such as firedogs, chenets, et cetera, are also entered in this dictionary.

Andover chest: Chests of William & Mary

style, generally with three full-width drawers and a pair of half-width drawers at the top, standing on ball or turnip feet. Decorated in the Chinese manner with outlines of houses, landscapes, floral patterns, and figures. Called Andover because most of them have been found in the vicinity of Andover, Mass. They date approximately from 1690 to 1720. The subjects of decoration, while occidental and sometimes amateurishly executed, are in direct imitation of the Chinese originals of this style we call William & Mary but which was imported from China by the Dutch. The Chinese originals are lacquered and decorated with landscapes and figural work in gold and colors.

Andrews & Meeser mirrors: Gilded mirrors in the Empire style and tabernacle mirrors made by Andrews & Meeser of Philadelphia and Lancaster, Pa., from 1830s.

Andrews organs: Parlor organs made by A. & G. N. Andrews, Utica, N.Y., 1845–60s.

Andries & Janson: Early English potters of Elizabethan period, working at Norwich and London from 1560s.

aneling spoon: Ceremonial spoon used in anointing candidates for ordination, in healing rites, and in coronation.

anemometer: Wind-velocity indicator, consisting of four cups mounted on cross-arms spinning in the wind. The arms are geared to a calibrated dial which registers the velocity.

anemoscope: A weathervane which registers wind direction on a dial indoors. In use from 18th century.

aneys: Aniseed.

angel bed: A day bed; a bed without posts; a trundle bed.

angel bread: A purgative cake.

angel-handled pitcher: See Wedgwood Memorial Pitcher.

Angelic Cut: Pattern of cut glass popular in 1880s.

angel lamp: A figural lamp designed by J. W. Bell, the famed modeler of ceramic wares, for Minton, and first made in 1848. [*Example pictured.*]

angelica: A reed instrument with bellows, crank-operated, which played tunes from perforated rolls. Made mid- to late 19th century.

Angell lamp: Roger Angell's patented St. Germain student lamp. Globe and shade were connected to the upright column of the lamp and so could be raised easily for lighting and trimming. [*Example pictured.*]

angel mark: A pewter touchmark indicating excellent quality, in use from 17th to 19th century.

angelot: A gold coin, also called a "half angel." 18th century.

angle-front cupboard: Corner cupboard, portable or built in, having frontal sections set outward at angles to provide more room within. Date is from 1750 to 1820. [*Example pictured.*]

angle lamp: Kerosene-burning hanging lamp with burner arm and burner at an acute angle with reservoir. One-, two-, and three-arm types were made, dating from 1890s. [*Example pictured.*]

angle stick: A candlestick hinged under the socket to provide adjustment at an angle. [*Example pictured.*]

Anglo-American: Generally meaning of English make for the American market.

angular cabriole: Gothic influence applied to the Chinese form of leg we call cabriole, common on Queen Anne, Georgian, and some Chippendale furniture. The angle form, instead of having the flowing, rounded contour of the original Chinese, is characterized by having a "sawed-out" look. [*Examples pictured.*]

Angulated Ribbon: Pattern of cut glass.

anguria: The common watermelon.

animal dishes: Any dishes of ceramic ware, metal, or glass in the form of animals. These generally are covered dishes, and innumerable varieties are known. The most popular were hares, dogs, lions, and birds, including swans, ducks, turkeys, and barnyard hens. Pressed-glass examples are the most common. Silver turtle-form tureens and hare and hen dishes of fine porcelain, as well as other animal forms, are known.

animal-head cups: See Head Cups.

animal-headed glass: Pressed-glass covered dishes with animal-headed knops or knob handles. Some are complete figures of animals. The knops are generally of frosted glass, but some are clear.

animalistic: Any animal form other than the human figure.

animal plant: The Venus-flytrap and other vegetation of the order Actinia. The Venus-flytrap was one of the first American plants of which a hand-colored engraving was issued.

animal ring: A piece of turning in the form of a ring shaped in the profile of an animal. When cut apart in segments the ring provided a number of wooden animal figures ready for finishing. [*Example of ring and its resulting figure is pictured.*]

anima-saturni: Vinegar and lead compound used in enameling work.

animated toy cap pistols: Cast-iron toys firing paper caps, with action caused by pulling trigger. These were made in a variety of animalistic and human figural shapes and date from 1880s. They are in the same philosophy as mechanical cast-iron toy banks. [*Several examples pictured.*]

ankle jack: Leather flaps tied around ankles over low shoes to make a high shoe; a sort of spat.

Annapolis tokens: Private silver coinage issued by J. Chalmers, silversmith of Annapolis, Md., in 1783, to offset a lack of coinage in local circulation.

Annely pottery: Made at Whitestone, N.Y., from 1750. Potters advertised eight different kinds of earthenware, sold at "Ye Fly Market."

Anne Pixley & Maud Granger glass: Pressed glass bearing likenesses of these two women of the American stage at the height of their popularity in the 1880s.

Annesley mirrors: Gilded oval, pier, and mantel mirrors, made by L. Annesley, Albany, N.Y., 1850s. The firm was Annesley & Williamson in 1853.

annulet: A small ring. **annuletted:**

Decorated with a series of free or linked rings or circles. A small ring encircling anything; the flat fillet of a column.

anta facia: When the sides of a piece of case furniture extend forward to form the equivalent of a column and there are other columnar elements across the front, the piece is said to be anta facia. Term is now used almost exclusively in architecture.

antependium: A fine textile covering for the front of a table, especially an altar.

Antes spinning wheel: A patented spinning wheel, simplified, improved, and mounted on Hepplewhite- and Sheraton-style stands for use in drawing rooms. Made 1780-1820.

anthemion: The Greek honeysuckle form, conventionalized, and used in ornamentation. [*Examples pictured.*] Also a pattern of pressed glass bearing this ornamentation. **anthemion back:** Chair back showing this same motif. [*Example pictured.*]

anthemis: The camomile herb.

Anthony portraits: Photographic portraits of famous Americans of the 1860s, produced by E. Anthony of New York.

anthracite lamp: Any lamp vase or body turned from the hard coal known as anthracite. Made from the 1830s as novelties.

anti-attrition: A lubricant used in wood turning, composed of four parts lard and one part graphite.

antico rosso: Old red, especially the color of old terra cotta.

anti-law iron: Colonial forged iron made after the 1750 law forbidding the operation of slitting mills or tilt hammers in the colonies.

antimacassar: Doilies, pads, and napkins used on upholstered furniture to protect the fabric from Macassar oil, freely used as a hairdressing from 1825 to 1875.

antiphonal: Literally meaning "against voice," from the Greek. The term is used to describe responsive chanting and the music for it. An antiphonary is a collection of hand-lettered music sheets for such singing.

antique: Ancient, old, passe, outmoded, obsolescent; any object of social history venerated by collectors and rescued from oblivion; any old objects collected for beauty, rarity, excellence of workmanship or craftsmanship. Up to c. 1850 the term was applied almost exclusively to ancient objects and artifacts—Greek, Roman, Assyrian, Egyptian, et cetera. During the past century the term has more and more been generally applied to furniture and other objects made up to within a century or two of our time. Now, under a U.S. statute, an object is legally an antique if made prior to 1830. Collecting vogues, vagaries, and pursuits take no notice of this dictum and are applied to pressed glass and many other objects, some of them made in the early years of the 20th century. In the 1840s the term "antique" was used by at least fifty American cabinetmakers to designate the Louis XV revival style we have, in error, been calling Victorian.

antiques faking: There is an axiom of commerce which observes there is always an effort made to satisfy a desire. The *Encyclopedia of Domestic Economy*, 1840, in regard to faked antiques, states: "Old furniture, seen so abundantly at upholsterers, brokers and auctions, is imported . . . and fabricated. What is portable is frequently sold as is, but carved parts are brought in and sold to cabinetmakers, who buy and dissect them, and make up the parts into objects adapted to our wants; sideboards are recomposed from fragments in which parts of church interiors are recognizable!" J. C. Cummerford, New York chairmaker in the 1840s or early 1850s, made reproductions of Brewster, Carver, and Winslow chairs "of seasoned old oak" which he sold frankly as copies. These chairs, however, were so well made and were copied so faithfully that Cummerford is probably the maker of nine tenths of the "originals" now owned. It should be remembered these three types of chairs, together with the so-called "Harvard" chair, were indeed scarce and rare items 100 years or more ago. They are not nearly so scarce now as they were then, perhaps due entirely to Cummerford's replicas. There is considerable antiques faking done today in furniture, glasswares, plaster wares, and Fraktur pieces, to mention a few. The fake and the faker we have with us always. As collecting antiques becomes more and more a universal pursuit, we can be sure faking will increase. Collectors can protect themselves only with the armor of education and knowledge.

antiquity: The state or status of being antique. Generally now used in connection with ancient times, from the Flood to the Renaissance.

Anthony & Cleopatra: These romantic and historic personages were made popular during the classic revival dating from 1750. Enoch Wood, c. 1790, produced a pair of Staffordshire reclining figures of the famed lovers which reflects their popularity. These figurines were produced in quantities as ornaments and were not expensive. [*Example pictured.*]

aouta: Paper mulberry; the cloth beaten from the inner bark of this tree was brought to America from the Orient by clipper ships from the 1840s.

apatite: Phosphate of lime.

àplomb: Upright; stiff; angular.

apocryphal: Aristocratic term for a fake; anything questionable. An apocryphal mark is a faked mark; apocryphal décor is decoration applied some, and generally many, years after making, as today's activity in decorating old and honestly marked plain white or gold-banded china with designs and legends that make it ten times more valuable.

à pointes de gâteaux: Diamond forms divided into triangular sections by insertion of a cross reaching from point to point.

Apollo: Pattern of pressed glass made by Adams of Pittsburgh, c. 1870s, having a band of bosses and wedges at bases, rims, and terminals. Some examples have etching or engraving. A desirable pattern, known only in clear glass.

apolonicon: Pipe organs on omnibus bodies for use in carnival parades and cir-

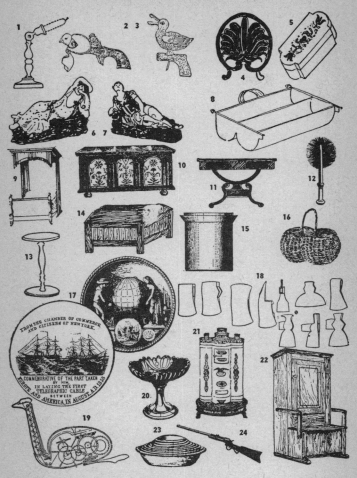

1, Angle Candlestick. **2–3,** Animated Cap Pistols. **4,** Anthemion. **5,** Apsed Box. **6–7,** Anthony & Cleopatra. **8,** Apple Trough. **9,** Arabian Bedstead. **10,** Architectural (Lancaster) Chest. **11,** Arcuate Table. **12,** Aspergillum. **13,** Arm Stand. **14,** Ark. **15,** Arthur Can. **16,** Ass Basket. **17,** Atlantic Cable Medals. **18,** Axes: Yankee, Kentucky, Double Bitt, Fireman, Ship, Broad, Spanish, Claw, Lathing, Bench. **19,** Automaton (swan). **20,** Bacchus Pressed Glass. **21,** Backus Stove. **22,** Bacon Cupboard. **23,** Bakers. **24,** Ballard Breechloader. (Nos. 2 and 3 from W. F. Ferguson, Esq.: 10, from Wallace Nutting.)

cuses. Apparently an American invention by Erben of New York, 1849. The famed omnibus builder, Stevenson, made the bodies.

apophoreta: Lozenges of marchpane with verses. These date from 16th century. Pressed-sugar wafers of 19th century were in same philosophy.

Apostle antiques: The twelve Apostles were memorialized on silver spoon handles as early as the 16th century. Reproductions, new patterns, and revivals were made to 1850. *Apostle Spoons*, by Charles G. Rupert, should be studied by collectors or students of these antiques. **Apostle mugs:** Mugs displaying the twelve saints in procession, molded in low relief on the body of the pottery mugs. Some show the figures in colors. **Apostle pitchers:** Made by Meigh of Hanley, England, c. 1840–50 Eight of the famous twelve are featured. These pitchers were produced for many years and are still obtainable, or were up to 1940.

apparat (d'apparat): Important, as a table *d'apparata*—a showpiece, a masterpiece. Also an *apputus*; a machine.

apparatus: Complete toilet cabinet; kneehole-type desk with many conveniences, including lavabo, bidet, powdering well, et cetera. **Appaumée:** The hand displayed with palm in full view, fingers and thumb extended. Term is heraldic.

apple dish: Properly applied only to dishes or bowls in the shape and form of an apple, naturalistically colored. Examples made at Chelsea, Derby, Bow, Worcester, Sèvres, Meissen, and other famous porcelain works.

apple door: Cupboard door panel drilled with a series of air holes for ventilating interior, or with a panel of rattan or cane work, or a sheet-iron panel punched with a series of holes, generally in a pattern. Apples stored in a cupboard required ventilation, hence the term "apple door." Some sideboards of pioneer type were made with large ventilated center drawers called apple drawers.

apple green: Pale green.

apple hoglin: An apple turnover. "Fold apple slices with sugar in a coarse crust and bake without a pan."

applejack: Cider brandy. Hard cider let stand in the open to freeze all but the alcohol, which was then tapped off.

applejohn: The everlasting apple, a variety that would keep two years without withering.

apple-moise: Apple mousse; applesauce. Apples boiled, drawn through a fine sieve, with almond milk and egg whites added, and again cooked. This dish dates from c. 1390.

apple parer: Mechanical device for paring apples, of which there are many varieties and innumerable patented examples. The basic idea is a forked spike to hold the apple which, rotating against a blade, was pared. Examples in cast iron, wood, and other materials are on record. Most patented examples were made commercially from 1840s; earlier home- and shop-made examples date from 1800s.

Appleton furniture: Nathaniel Apple-

ton and Appleton & Ives, cabinetmakers of Salem, Mass., working from the 1800s, produced fine cabinet and seat furniture in early Federal styles, with emphasis on Directoire and Sheraton.

apple trough: A cast- or sheet-iron kitchen utensil looking like a cake pan and often so used, but designed for baking apples. [*Example pictured.*]

applied decoration: Any separately carved, turned, or shaped elements applied to other objects as decoration, such as bosses, half pillars, moldings, rosettes.

applied handle: The handles of any vessel, especially of pottery or glass, not cast as an integral part but applied separately, although securely. In pressed-glass wares all handles were applied prior to 1865, when a patent for integral pressing was granted.

apprentice's desk: Narrow desk boxes, with slope toward the user, mounted on turned or square legs, the writing board lifting to give access to cavity in box. A prototype of school desks. The latter, after 1840s, were made with cast-iron supports.

apres: From Ypres, now in Belgium but originally in the Low Countries or Netherlands; a woolen suit and dress fabric.

apricot luster: Mustard-yellow luster with a faint pink tinge. This is the *lustre apricosa* of Europe. A metallic luster applied to redwares, stonewares, et cetera.

aprilled: Soured.

apron: Any skirt or skirting; a valance. Closestools (toilet chairs) generally have a deep valance or apron to hide the chamber jar under the seat.

apsed: Having apses or projections, generally semicircular in plan or form. Popular in Italy and the alpine regions from 11th century. [*An apsed box is pictured.*]

aquaeduct: An outer covering for a pump to prevent freezing in winter season. Term is 18th century.

aquamanile: (1) Eucharistic water jug, often with animalistic or figural handle and decoration, made of silver, gold, semiprecious metals, fine glass or pottery. (2) Water jugs for table use in form of cows, horses, lions, dogs, goats, sheep, and other animals, of common and precious metals and of pottery (ancestor of the cow creamers). Many of both varieties were made of a sort of pewter alloy. *See* Aquamanilia.

aquamanilia: Original term for the alloy of tin and copper later known as *dinanderie*, and originally used in making ceremonial jugs and ewers.

aquatic boquet: A "mystery" bouquet of the 1850–80 period. "Arrange the bouquet, tying it to stones or lead weights in a deep dish. Submerge the dish with bouquet in a deep tub of water. Submerge a glass shade, bringing it over the bouquet and its dish. Then remove the entire ensemble from the tub. The shade holds all its water and thus the bouquet is in suspension in the water of the shade. Atmospheric pressure holds the water in the shade."

aquatint: Literally, "water tint," a form of acid etching on metal plates from which prints were made. Finely powdered resin was dusted over an oiled plate and fixed by application of heat. To this finely spotted ground the etcher applied dilute acid, then covered sections with varnish, again applied acid, and so on, and in many stages arrived at an etching which, when printed, yielded a fair approximation of a water color in the tone of the ink used. Hand coloring was sometimes applied to aquatint prints. Many aquatints were issued uncolored, and many of these have been colored later to add value to the print as an antique.

aquavivarium: An aquarium.

arabesque: Any geometrical or stylized figure from the Arabic or Saracenic peoples, whose Koran forbids, as does Mosaic Law, making the likeness of anything in the heavens above or on the earth beneath. Therefore, no true arabesque can show the human figure or any bird, flower, animal, et cetera, but must be an invented figure or subject. Also a pattern of pressed glass by Bakewell-Pears, featuring as décor a series of arabesque doorways, sloping uprights topped with a circle, almost in the form of a keyhole.

Arabian bedstead: Mid-19th-century term for a canopy or tester of full size, supported only by the headposts of a bedstead. [*Example pictured*.]

arack; arrack: The original toddy distilled from coconut-palm sap. Goa-arack was made from this. Batavia-arack was distilled from rice and sugar. Almost the exclusive base of colonial "punch."

arbitration mug: Beer mug of pressed glass, picturing a high-hatted employer shaking hands with a laborer. Word "Arbitration" appears on the mug. Date is c. 1888.

Arbor Group: Ceramic figural group similar to Pew Group (*which see*) but having the figures posed in an arbor.

arca: A chest.

arcade; arcaded: A series of arches; an object trimmed with a series of arches, no matter if in miniature or monumental.

Archer & Warner lamps: Chandeliers, girondoles, and other fixtures made by this firm at New York and Philadelphia from c. 1840s. An "Archer lamp" was a lard-oil lamp made by this firm.

archil: Violet dye obtained from lichens and the herb archil. Also archilla, called by the French *tournesol;* crimson violet.

archimedeal phaeton: a balloon.

architect's scales: *See* Scale Case.

architect's table: A desk or table having a rising flap, sloping upward from the user, adjustable as to angle.

architectural chest: Any chest having arches, panels, and form achieved by structural means and not by applied décor. Tudor-Gothic architectural chests of finest quality are known as Nonesuch chests, and were made under the patronage of Henry VIII. The American counterpart is found in what are wrongly called Pennsylvania-Dutch chests, an example of which is pictured. In these chests, mostly from Lancaster and Chester counties of Pennsylvania, there is evidence of copying the inlaid work of Nonesuch chest panels in painting. The chests are architectural in construction.

architectural whatnot: A unit of furniture composed of two or more tables arranged as a pyramid, mounted on a square or circular platform, with a circular tray on a pillar in the center of each table top. Such whatnots were parlor pieces, made from the late 1810s or 1820s.

architrave: Properly, any elements surrounding a square opening.

archivolt: Material or members surrounding an arch.

arcuate table: A fold-over top console or pier table in which base and top are joined by a perfect arc of wood. The genesis of the style is Directoire, but most of these tables are of c. 1830s. [*Example pictured*.]

argal: Cream of tartar found in wine bottles, deriving from seeds of the grape.

Argand lamp: The lamp principle invented by Aimé Argand of Geneva, 1783. This type of lamp has a tubular wick which provides for air combustion from inside and outside, confines the area of wick, and at the same time provides at least three times as much wick surface. The light created was brighter, smokeless, and safely enclosed within a clear glass chimney. This was the first genuine improvement in lighting in all history. Prior to the Argand lamp all lighting was from candles or crusie-type lamps. With the invention here considered as its start, every improvement in lighting must date. Thousands of lamps on the Argand principle were made every year from 1783. Later varieties included fans to improve air draft, mantles to provide brilliant incandescence, et cetera. With the refining of kerosene, an Argand-type lamp (popularly known as the Rochester) was in almost every American home. Over fifty known American lamp manufacturers prior to 1850 made lamps of the Argand type. This was, beyond any doubt, the most efficient lamp for domestic use until the coming of electricity and improved electric light bulbs. There are many examples of lighting devices, including Argand lamps, in this dictionary.

Argand student: A St. Germain student lamp using the Argand wick, as most student lamps did. [*Example pictured*.]

argentine: A white metal alloy, most of which is white brass. Tablewares of this metal were advertised from 1810.

argentum mosaicum: Pure tin, bismuth, and mercury, ground with albumin and varnish, and used to provide a silver coating on fancy papers, plaster casts, and some porcelains and glasswares.

argent-vive: Mercury.

Argillo: Clay-base glazed doorknobs, drawer pulls, et cetera. Argillo is a process of ceramic work. Knobs or pulls of this substance, in finished form, look like marble, Rockingham-type redware, and agate. Many varieties of finish were produced at the Albany Argillo Works from 1840.

argol: Cream of tartar.

argus: A pattern of pressed glass similar to Ashburton.

argyle: Vessels of any sort, from plates to teapots and gravy boats, having an internal heating element, whether using hot water or a pre-heated slog of metal.

ark: A chest, particularly of ark shape,

fitted with rollers for ease in moving. These date from at least A.D. 1000. [*Example pictured is Tudor-Gothic, c. 1580.*]

armadio: An armoire; a huge piece of case furniture having the dimensions of a closet; a small room of cabinetwork. The *garde-manger* was the same thing.

armesin: A stiff taffeta.

arm lantern: Standard kerosene lantern with a band of tinned sheet iron forming a ring to fit the arm. Used by railroad conductors and brakemen.

Armenian stone: Blue ocher, a pigment.

armillary dial: Sun dial made up of rings forming the skeleton of an orb. The shadow of the gnomon falls on a curved surface and so is more accurate. *See* Sundials.

armille: A necklace; a bracelet.

Armitage Sheffield: Sheffield-type silverplated ware made at Philadelphia from 1797 by George and Robert Armitage, who migrated from Sheffield. Their wares were fine but are now rare, as their production was limited.

armoire: A portable closet; a wardrobe.

armor: Protective wear for man and steed, used from the days of the Crusades. Planished iron so finely wrought and fitted that entire suits, articulated, were made by experts. The fine craftsmanship demanded caused an uplift in all crafts and advances in all forms of metal smelting and refining. Certain specific types and kinds of armor are listed under their popular or proper names.

arms: Weapons, particularly now firearms, but including pikes, swords, daggers, and other cutting weapons. *See* Gunsmiths and Swordsmiths. Various types of firearms are listed under their proper alphabetical position.

Arms mirrors: T. A. Arms, successor to Arnaud & Coombes, Boston, made framed mirrors and also dealt in specialties such as "Potchumania," Grecian and oriental painting materials, stencils and paints.

arm stand: A miniature table consisting of two 10-inch-diameter disks joined with a turned pillar. Used in churches to support one's arm. [*Example pictured.*]

armure: A fabric with chain warp and linen woof, preferred by soldiers, especially to wear under a suit of armor.

Arnaud & Coombes: Mirror makers of Boston. They produced many tabernacle, pier, and overmantel mirrors to 1840s.

arnut: Pig nut; earth nut; groundnut; peanut; goober.

aroleo: Colonial weight of 25 pounds.

aromatic candle: Tallow candles, the fat impregnated with lavender oil, thyme, or rosemary. Perfume was released when candle burned.

aroph: Saffron.

arpeys: A resinous lubricant made of sheep and beef tallow and tar.

arrachis: The peanut or groundnut.

arras: Tapestry, quite frequently hung in folds as drapery; decorative wall insulation used from 14th century. The town of Arras, France, was a center of manufacture. *Arazzo* is the Italian term for the same heavy fabric. A powder of orrisroot,

used in hairdressing, was also given this name. Early wallpaper is sometimes called "Arras paper."

arrow back: Chair backs spaced with flattened spindles having arrow points or arrow-feather end-shaped sections.

arsedine: Ornamental tinselwork. Also called assad, assaden, orsaday.

arseling pole: Bakers' pole used to fling hot embers around the oven in the preheating.

arsenal Pikes Peak flask: A mold-blown whiskey flask memorializing Pikes Peak, but bearing the legend ARSENAL GLASS WORKS, PITTS. PA.

arsil: Alloy of arsenic and copper.

arsmart: A yellow dye.

art: (1) Properly, any one of the seven arts: painting, drawing, architecture, sculpture, poetry, music, and drama; expression of fine quality in these media by practitioners and adepts. When not the avowed professions of the practitioner, the art is amateur. Art, as a collector's item, is generally confined to paintings, drawings, sculpture, architecture as reflected in furniture, and in replicas of originals, produced in quantities, by experts.

Art: Pattern of pressed glass of quite heavy quality, featuring loops and diamond lozenges, yet claimed to be similar to "Moon & Star." Many pressed-glass pattern names seem to have been selected without rhyme or reason; probably the makers selected them at random.

art glass: Any specialty, from the cheapest novelties to the finest examples of cameo, latticinio, and cased glass, fall within this general category. *See* Novelty Glass. Many special glasses of art quality are listed under their proper alphabetical place.

Arthur cans: The beginning of the American food-canning industry is marked by the preserving can of tinned sheet iron invented by Dr. Robert Arthur of Philadelphia, 1854. This can had a lid which fitted over the top and below the line of the groove formed by an outstanding flange. In this groove was sealing wax or cement which hermetically sealed the can. Top was removed by heating the flange. [*Example pictured.*]

articulus: Articulated paper toy assemblies picturing crafts, trades, et cetera, and tasks of homely significance and sports, et cetera. Parts which move are connected with wires to axle of a warming-air flywheel or spinner. When toy is placed over a warm-air-register or beside a stovepipe, the current of warm air spins the wheel and the toy goes into action, running as long as the current of air is active. 1840-90.

artifact: Any relic of human making of any period in time, but especially the relics of early social history as found in tombs, kitchen middens, rubble piles, ruins, mounds, et cetera.

artificial crinoline: *See* Crinoline.

artificial stone: Any concretion, such as lime, sand, and gravel. Any ceramic product in imitation of stone, such as brick, terra cotta, and architectural pottery. Similarly, castings of special kind, of metal, treated to resemble stone; aggregates of stone, powdered or in particles, mixed with cement; wood painted to re-

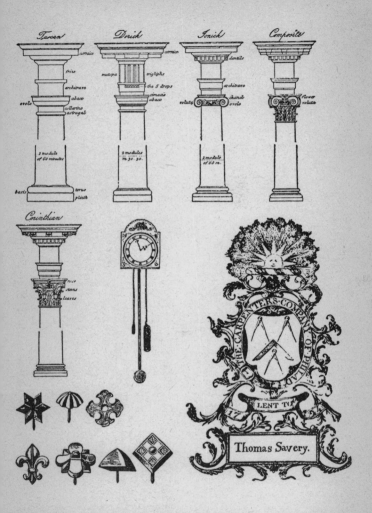

ARCHITECTURAL ORDERS: Tuscan, Doric, Ionic, Composite, Corinthian. **Center:** A Wag on Wall Clock. **Bottom left:** Seven examples of upholder's or upholsterer's nailheads. **Right:** Engraved book plate page of the earliest American book on architecture, published by the Carpenter's Company of Philadelphia, c. 1750. This volume contained engravings of the orders of architecture. By Permission of The Metropolitan Museum.

semble stone; wood painted and then sanded or coated with powdered glass.

artillerie: Archers in mass formation.

artisans: The masters of crafts and trades, such as cabinetmakers, glassmakers, pewterers, silversmiths, potters, engravers, block cutters, iron founders, braziers, decorators, japanners, sign painters, lithographers, printers, watch- and clockmakers, silhouette cutters, hair workers, et cetera.

artists: For the purpose here considered, collectors include the following craftsmen as within the category of artists. This was not always the case; in 17th-century New England a portrait painter was lower than a tinker in the scale of productive worth! Portrait, landscape, and historic painters; miniature painters; silversmiths; goldsmiths; sculptors; engravers, etchers, and wood cutters; lithographers; glass engravers and cutters; china decorators.

artists, American: The limitation of space makes it impossible to list American artists by name, place of working, and dates of activity. These may be found in comprehensive works devoted to this one subject, such as *Dictionary of American Artists, etc.*, by Mantle Fielding. Most libraries can supply books on this subject.

artists, itinerant, pioneer & amateur: Perhaps wrongly designated as "primitive art" and "primitive artists," these practitioners and their work fall into several well-defined niches. *See* Bibliography for books of reference.

artists, portrait, landscape & miniature: Space does not permit even exemplary listing of the men who painted in the academic tradition in America, colonial and Federal, from the mid-17th century. Books of information, listings, and pictorial examples of their work are in Bibliography.

artist's drawing table: Not a table upon which an artist drew sketches but a side table for paraphernalia, having canted legs, heavy stretchers, and a drawout extension piece in the top.

Art Union: A lottery for distributing works of fine art. The first one of record was conducted by M. Hennin, Paris, 1810. The first in the U.S. was the American Art Union, established 1839. By 1849 it had 18,960 members. Paintings, drawings, and sculpture by American and other artists were distributed to the lucky winners each year.

arval: A funeral feast. **arval bread:** Currant bread served with the funeral meats.

aryballo: A flask.

ash brick: A brick made from clay and coarse ashes, used as a polishing agent. A form of bath brick, meaning a brick of metal polish.

Ashburton: A pattern of cutting, and a pattern of pressed glass sometimes called Colonial. The pattern is a series of looped and curvate planes, sometimes concave. Many variants are known and listed in Ruth Webb Lee's *Early American Pressed Glass.*

ash cake: Any cake baked under the ashes of the hearth.

ashet: A platter, sometimes of wood, but any large platter or service salver, generally oblong in shape.

Ashley beater: A wire screw turning in a block, the end fitted with a whisk for beating egg whites. Patented 1860.

ash oven: A baking or warming chamber, separate from the hearth, heated with embers from the hearth fire.

ash trug: A hod or scuttle for both fuel and ashes.

ash wain: A cart or wain made of ash wood and/or for hauling ashes.

asparagus globe: A spherical frame of wires upon which the asparagus plant was trained to form a growing green globe; a garden ornament.

asparagus trough: China dishes in the form of troughs made especially to hold up to six pieces of asparagus for individual service at table. This vegetable, known colloquially as "sparrowgrass," was a luxury item much enjoyed from the 1750s.

aspergillum: asperges: Brush, or container with finely perforated top, used in the rite of sprinkling holy water. [*The brush type is pictured.*]

assady: Tinsel. *See* Arsedine.

assay cup: A cup-form wine taster. While assays of wine from 17th century have been for quality, from 13th to 16th the assay was for poison. Some of these cups were made to serve as covers for standing cups and goblets.

ass basket: Our ancestors called it so, even though colloquially. Woven of straw, withes, or willow, a pair of globose baskets made as one and imitating the human posterior. [*Example pictured.*]

ass' skin: A heavy parchment used in erasable memo books or tablets, from 18th century or earlier.

Astbury ware: Pottery produced by John Astbury, early 18th-century English master, famed for raised figural decoration on colored body, later developed as classic figural jasper ware by Wedgwood. Astbury figural wares include complete statues or figurines. He also obtained access to the Elers redware secret and produced this ware. Astbury was a famous potter, as was his son Samuel, an uncle of Josiah Wedgwood. Astbury ware, as a subject, would require at least a half dozen pages of this work even under strict abridgment rules. Students should consult any standard work on early English pottery for further data. John Astbury died in 1743.

astragal: Small convex or torus molding or beading, used as muntins to form a pattern for placing glass panels. The strips are rabbeted and glass is fixed with brads and putty. Known in a wide variety of curvate, saltier (X), and mathematical forms. Often seen on bookcase and cabinet doors. **astragal molding:** A small torus molding.

astragal mirror: A mirror made up of sections framed in astragals, or beaded molding. *See* Astragal.

astral lamp: An invention of Count Rumford, having a central reservoir for fluid conveyed to tubular arms terminating in Argand burners. This enabled the user to get the light directly over a subject, without shadows. **astral oil:** Lamp fluid for the Astral lamp. The Pratt Refinery of New York (est. 1770) made it to 1870 or later.

astrolabe: A transit for shooting the stars, an early navigating instrument invented by the Persians.

astronomical clock: A highly complicated timepiece designed to indicate phases of moon, sunrise and sunset, aspects of the heavens, and other important data for scientific-minded observers. The finest example in America was made by David Rittenhouse, our most famous clockmaker, who flourished in the last half of the 18th century at Norriton and Philadelphia, Pa.

astroscope: A philosophical instrument consisting of two cones on which the various known stars are marked.

as-you-like-it chair: A convertible armchair that unfolded into a reclining chair, a couch, or a bed. C. 1850.

athanor: A magazine furnace, holding a supply of fuel to last several days.

Athol furniture: Any cabinetwork from the various factories and shops of Athol, Mass., from 1830s.

Athol porridge: Two parts whiskey and one part honey. Scottish.

Atlantic Cable souvenirs: The successful laying of the Atlantic Cable sparked the making of medals, snuffboxes, pipes, handkerchiefs, glass novelties, and many other souvenirs. Tiffany & Company in 1859 designed the gold medals for Cyrus Field and various officers of the laying steamer. [*First- and second-class gold medals are pictured.*]

Atlantic glass: John Huffsey's Glass Works at Crowleytown, N.J., were called the Atlantic Works. He made bottles and flasks from 1850s.

Atlantic Neptune (prints): This publication was actually a captain's chart book, but in addition to its many charts of harbors, shoals, banks, et cetera, it contained a comprehensive collection of American views. Issued 1774–82, it was valuable to the British Navy in the Revolution, of which it was said: "Even with the *Neptune* we had them at a great disadvantage." Now prints from this rare large folio volume are highly prized and considered rare. Few complete copies of the *Neptune* are privately held.

Atlas: A late pattern in pressed glass, made in 1890s in red and clear glass. The pattern is a row of ball-like bosses at bottoms of hollow wares and at edges of covers. Also, a rich silk fabric of 17th and 18th centuries.

atmopyre: A room heater burning gas, as made c. 1850. The burner was a pottery tube pierced with many vents.

atmospheric lamp: A non-explosive, kerosene-burning lamp for halls, churches, and dwellings, made from 1870s by Tilden & Co., Boston.

Atterbury Duck: Pressed-glass duck-covered dish named for its designer, Thomas Atterbury of Pittsburgh, 1887. He designed other animal dishes, including the Bull's Head mustard pot and the Rabbit button.

Attleborough buttons: Brass buttons made by several factories at Attleboro, Mass.

aubergine: A small sofa. Also the color purple, or the eggplant tint thereof.

Aubusson: Carpets and tapestry from the factory at Aubusson, France. The present artistic standard of carpets from Aubusson is maintained by a national school of decorative arts, founded 1869. This factory seems to have begun work, with the aid of immigrant weavers from Flanders, about the 16th century. It is thought possible that the famous tapestries of the "Lady of the Unicorn" were woven here. The factory was placed under royal patronage in 1665, but the standard of craftsmanship never quite equaled the royal tapestry factories of Paris.

Audubon: John James Audubon, American artist and ornithologist, was born 1785 and died 1851. Obsessed with a desire to picture American birds in their native habitat, he made a series of magnificent water-color drawings which were first published in elephant folio size in England, in 80 installments, from 1827 to 1838. The octavo edition was published in America 1840–44. In addition to his famous bird prints, he also did a series of the viviparous quadrupeds of North America. All prints from the famous portfolios and volumes made from Audubon's original drawings are now classified by collectors as "Audubon prints." Innumerable reproductions are in circulation, some of them dating as late as the 1930s and 1940s.

Augur figures: Sculptures by Hezakiah Augur, the American self-taught sculptor, who worked at New Haven, Conn., 1791-1858.

au pochoir: By stencil; stencil-decorated.

Aurene glass: Made by Frederick Carder at Corning (Steuben) Glass Works from 1910. Gold and blue examples with highly iridized surface were made in limited quantities, and manufacture was discontinued c. 1934. This glass is now scarce and is collected by specialists.

Aurene-Haviland: Aurene glass made by Corning for distribution by the Haviland Co., famed American porcelain company with plants at Limoges, France.

aureola: Halo; nimbus. Correctly, the aureola should surround the entire body, while the nimbus surrounds only the head. The aureola is of Christian derivation; the nimbus is pagan.

à auriculaire: Scrolled carving after the form of a human ear.

auricular: Ear-shaped, as carvings, developed in Netherlands c. 1600.

autograph mugs: Shaving mugs bearing facsimile autographs of owners. Date from c. 1880s.

autoharp: A zither with chord mufflers to make playing easy. The instrument had 20 to 44 strings. Made from 1850s.

automatic fire lighters: Platinum sponges sprayed with hydrogen gas generated in a small container. Made in France and Germany from 1820s. Early examples are quite rare.

automaton: Mechanical effigies of people, animals, and birds, so constructed as to have lifelike action, controlled by clockwork. [*An automaton of a swan is pictured, showing mechanism.*]

automaton drawing machine: The physionotrace. It projected a profile portrait for easy outline and had a pantograph for reduction to any size desired. Made from c. 1800.

autoperipetikos: Automaton dolls. Clockwork in the body caused them to walk and make gestures. 19th century.

autophone: A hand-bellows instrument which, when squeezed, caused a perforated sheet to move over a roller and play a tune. The device was limited to three tunes and had a range of 22 notes. Made from 1875. [*Example pictured.*]

autoplastic: A process by which natural leaves, plants, and flowers are impressed in soft metal and impressions made from it on paper. The Swedish artist, Hessellus, used this process in the colonies of America from 1707.

avian vitrine: A glass case for the display of stuffed birds.

awmry: Ambrie; also a pantry or food closet.

axes: A class of tempered iron and steel cutting tools responsible for much of our advances in pioneering. The various ax types are Yankee, Kentucky, double bitt, fireman, ship adz, broadax, Spanish, claw, lathing, and bench. [*All these types are pictured.*] Others not here mentioned were not in general use in 18th century.

axhammer: Heavy hammer with triangular face forming a cutting edge.

Axminster: A type of hand-tufted carpet made at Axminster, England, from 1750. Made by machine loom weaving after 1820 and very popular in 19th century.

ax-mortise chisel: Coined word, invented by H. C. Mercer of Doylestown, Pa., for the Swedish mortising chisel with handle set at angle. This tool was introduced to America c. 1640 by the Swedes, and used by them in their log house construction.

Axson furniture: Pre-Revolutionary Southern furniture made at Charleston, S.C., by William Axson.

azoon: The house leek; also sempervive.

azur d'Hollande: Holland cobalt, fused with glass to create a vitreous mass, and then pulverized to make the pigment "smalt." Also called Smarts and Zaffer.

azure: Sky blue; clear blue.

azure-pressed: Mid-19th century collectors' term for the porcelains of Kaising, which display their décor only when filled with a liquid.

B

babeury: An ornament, or ornamentation.

Babul: Goldsmith's work, a process of soldering grains of gold into a desired form. A technique of the East Indian craftsmen of Babul.

baby beaker: A jigger; a small shot glass; a tot glass.

baby clout: Rag doll.

Baby Face: Pattern of pressed glass with knops in form of three frosted baby faces on stems and as cover finials.

baby feeders: Nippled tubes of S-shape for insertion in small bowls made of glass, pewter, silver, and gold. Used from 16th to 19th century.

baby wing chair: A 17th-century child's chair with wings similar to settle ends.

Baccarat: French glasswares of excellent quality. The fame of this glass in America is based largely on the beautiful paperweights made from the late 1840s. Dated paperweights were made in 1846, 1847, 1848 and 1849, and overlay weights from 1870. The Baccarat factory was founded in 1765 and has produced fine glasswares of all kinds, including elegancies in lighting fixtures.

Bacchus pressed glass: Superlatively fine pressed glass made by Bacchus & Son, Birmingham, England, from 1840s. Considerable quantities were shipped to the U.S. [*Example pictured.*]

bachelor's button: A button fixed to the head of a safety pin.

bachelor's chest: A chest of drawers for a man's use, having a pull-out board under its top to provide space for toilet-making functions.

bachelor's pot: A small teapot.

bachelor's wish mug: *See* Sentiment Mug.

Bache silhouette: Any silhouette cut and signed by William Bache, who worked at Philadelphia and Wellsboro, Pa., New Haven, Conn., and points between from 1795 to 1820s.

Bachman furniture: Made by the Bachman family at Lampeter Square, Lancaster, Pa. Jacob, 1766–90; John, Sr., 1790–1820s; John, Jr., 1816–50. The work of Jacob was for years thought to be Philadelphia Chippendale by Affleck or Gostelow. Jacob Bachman did not work in the Chippendale style but in the French style which Chippendale introduced to England. This early American maker learned his trade in the Grand Val, Switzerland, and so had the style first- and not secondhand. The Bachman family continued in the cabinet-making and furniture business in Lancaster County to the 1880s or later. Their chief pieces of early date are tilt-top tea tables, bureaus, chests of drawers, desks, clock cases, and chairs. The second and third generation worked in the prevailing popular styles of their day—Hepplewhite, Directoire, and French Empire.

backboard: Woodenware. A thin board about 20 inches square, cut crosswise in kerfs or grooves. Batter or bread dough remained fixed by contact with the cuts and so could be placed before the fire and baked.

backbron: Backlog of a fire.

back drop-leaf: Any table with a drawer front having a drop leaf on the opposite side. These tables stood with leaf to back and drawer to front, hence the term. Shakers favored this form of table, but they were known in several 18th-century styles.

back friend: A stool with a back; a high-backed chair.

back lamp: A wall lamp.

back painting: Painting on glass as a form of art, either direct or by glued-on prints, rubbed thin to the printing and then colored from the rear.

backpanner: Basket for carrying on one's back; back-pannier.

back portrait: (Also called a "hind-sight.") When the daguerreotype was a generally available method of making portraits, some superstitious people thought having one's picture taken would steal something from them. When finally persuaded to go to the daguerrean gallery, they often insisted upon having their backs photographed instead of their faces. Examples are quite scarce.

backstone: A slightly dished iron disk on a hanger, used in the fireplace for baking. Hence the phrase, "Walk like a cat on a hot backstone."

Backus & Bruck furniture: Sofas, chairs, beds, and case furniture made by Backus & Bruck, Columbus, O., from 1830s. Styles are Directoire, Grecian, and Empire.

Backus stoves: Stoves, particularly room heaters, fashioned of cast and wrought iron under the patents of Backus & Co., N.Y. They also made Franklin types, some with gas logs or asbestos-fiber flames. Some Backus stoves are noted for beautifully designed castings. Date from 1840s. [*Example pictured.*]

Backus ware: Papier-mâché trays, tables, chairs, et cetera, japanned and decorated, made by G. H. Backus, 44 Fulton St., New York City, from 1840s. This firm also made papier-mâché buttons.

bacon cupboard: Case-furniture piece having aspect of a high, one-door wardrobe, with an armed settle at its lower front. The seat of the settle lifts to reveal storage space beneath, or there are doors under it. The "wardrobe" part was used to store sides of smoked bacon, hams, et cetera. [*Example pictured.*]

bacon dish: Covered oval or rectangular dish of silver, Sheffield plate, silver plate, fitted with wood handle, for serving broiled bacon at table. Date is from 18th century.

bacon settle: See Bacon Cupboard.

bactile: A candlestick.

bactrian: Humped.

Bader drawing table: A refinement of the old drawing table, made by A. Bader of New York from 1850. This was an extension dining table using a principle known from 16th century.

badger: A peddler.

Badger flower prints: Prints from *Floral Belles*, published in 1867, and from *Wild Flowers*, 1859, both works by Mrs. C. M. Badger.

Badger rocker: Platform rocker operating a bellows to fan the sitter as he rocked. Date is from 1847.

Baer ware: Stoneware made by Anthony Baer Pottery, Cleveland, O., 19th century.

bagamon: The game of backgammon.

bag lamp: Lard-oil lamp invented by L. A. Beardsley of New York, 1848. A bag held lard within the reservoir and a reel of cotton cord provided a sort of perpetual candlewick. Rare. [*An example showing device and its working is pictured.*]

Bagneux shades: Glass domes, or dust shades of glass, made at Bagneux, France, and imported in considerable quantities during the years that displays of wax and other work under glass domes were popular, to the 1880s.

Bagot cut glass: Wares from the establishment of Joseph Bagot of New York, who was an exceptionally fine glass cutter, working from 1810.

bag sewing table: Directoire-, Sheraton-, or Empire-type sewing stand with a cloth bag suspended from bottom of lower drawer to hold work in progress.

baguette: Made up of many jewel or gem forms, or shapes and forms of glass. **baguette mirror:** A mirror framed in a banding of alternate small forms of glass, often in varying colors.

bahut: A coffer; a strongbox; an iron chest; a safe.

bail brasses: Any furniture hardware or drawer pulls with bail handles (that is, a drop or pull in the style of a bucket handle) of bowed shape affixed to bosses at either end, frequently mounted on a flat brass escutcheon plate. This style of handle for drawers supplanted the single droop at the beginning of the 18th century. It appears on late William & Mary case furniture and on practically all Queen Anne, the Georgian and Chippendale eras. The style continued through the Georgian and Chippendale eras.

baile: A series of bowed elements, usually of bentwood, supporting a canopy.

Bailey & Batkin luster: This firm, beginning 1800 or earlier with William Bailey, merged with William Batkin in 1808. Patented a process of silver lustering but also made all kinds of gold lusterware, and lustered for the potting trade generally. Firm dissolved c. 1827. Located at Lane End, Longton.

Bailey cut flowers: Cut paper work by Harriet Bailey of Wisconsin, sold at the Centennial of 1876 as an art novelty. She specialized in cutting flowers and bouquets of flowers. Many of her works have been framed as prints. [*Example pictured.*]

Bailey's delineator: A precision drawing instrument, invented 1846, and made at Abbeville, S.C.

bain: A bath, or bathing tub.

baize: Cloth of the serge family, generally green, and often used as table covers. Napped to look like felt, the cloth was also made in white, taupe, maroon, and brown. of blue, yellow, maroon, and brown.

Baker-Cushman Hollands: Stiffened muslin roll shades for windows, with fine painted decoration, including gold- and silver-leaf borders. Made by Baker & Cushman, Baltimore, from 1840s.

Baker furniture: Made by the John A. Baker Co. of Milwaukee, Wis., from 1840s.; the first furniture manufactory in Wisconsin.

Baker lamps: Camphene and other fluid lamps made by Baker & Von Phul of Cin-

1, Animal Ring, showing contour of cow; imposed on a ring, an Autophone. **2,** Bailey Cut Flowers. **3,** Bag Lamp. **4,** Baking Iron. **5,** Balloon Lamp. **6,** Ball-Jointed Stand. **7,** Ball Stopper. **8,** Ball Urn. **9,** Ball Vase. **10,** Balmoral Lamp. **11,** Banana Dish. **12,** Baluster Jug. **13,** Barnum's Museum Toy. **14,** Barnum Buckle. **15,** Bar Butter mold. **16,** Basin Sundial. **17,** Barrel Kettle. **18,** Barrel Decanter. **19,** Banvard Panorama.

cinnati from 1830s. They had an extensive manufactory supplying the Ohio Valley and the South.

Bakers: Trade name for any ovenware, but especially hard-fired oven stonewares. [*A nest of "Bakers" is pictured.*]

Baker sheffield: Silver plate made in the Sheffield manner by William Baker, who migrated to New York from England, 1840. He also made albata spoons.

bake stone: Same as backstone. Both terms derive from the ledge of stone built across the rear of the hearth and used for baking.

Bakewell Block: A pattern of pressed glass, one of the finer, rarer patterns featuring a petaled pattern on heavy flintware with outswelling knopped stems.

Bakewell cameos: Clay cameos embedded in glass and known as sulphides, made by Bakewell, Pears & Co., Pittsburgh, from 1830s. This fine technique in glassmaking was for many years attributed wholly to England and continental European factories.

Bakewell glass: Made at Pittsburgh in the factory established by Benjamin Bakewell, 1807, which operated to 1882. This firm made fine cut-glass services for two presidents and for Lafayette; pressed glass from 1825, and pressed furniture knobs, clock wheels, and other unique items. The Pears perhaps had the greatest and most versatile glassmakers in American history and had an enormous output. This glass is more deserving of a definitive study than either Sandwich glass or the glass of the New England Glass Co.

baking iron: A shallow iron pan, open at one side, to which a loop handle is affixed. Coals from the hearth were raked under it to provide heat for baking anything placed on top of it. It dates from the 17th century and was made to c. 1830s. [*Example pictured.*]

balance coffee machine: A pair of tanks within a carrying frame, one fitted with a spirit lamp. Steam forced the hot water through freshly ground coffee from one cylinder to the other. Made from 1830s to 1880s.

balanced steps (ARCHITECTURE): Treads of winding or curved stairs cut at angles at inner side to offer more substantial foot purchase.

baldachin: Canopy fastened to wall over a bed or chair. Made from the Gothic era, when a stone frame was used, down to 1850s, when a wire frame was used.

baldachine: An umbrella; in 17th century covered with leather or parchment.

Baldwin hinge: *See* Secret Joint Hinge.

Baldwin lamp: Any fluid lamp made by C. A. Baldwin, N.Y., 1840s–60s. He made table, mantel, and hanging lamps.

baleen: Whale bone or whale ivory, used in making buttons and scrimshaw. Said properly to be the heavy bone-hairs from the mouth of the whale—the "strainers."

ball alley: Any ball used in alley bowls, whether indoors or on the turf. *See* Skittle Ball.

ball & claw foot: This style or form of footing for legs of tables, chairs, and case furniture is most emphatically not the mark of the Chippendale style. Chippen-

dale did not use the ball and claw; he used the French foot of the Louis XV style, or a block, plinth, and other footings on his square-legged pieces. The ball and claw, or talon and ball, is a footing deriving from the Chinese and from Roman classic styles. It is found on Georgian furniture from the end of Queen Anne's period through to George IV, and in modified form on Empire and some Directoire furniture. [*See page of furniture-footing illustrations.*]

ball & collar: A type or pattern of turning found on the finer examples of early banister-back, slat-back, and Windsor chair stretchers.

ball & sausage: A type or pattern of wood turning.

Ball & Swirl: A pattern of pressed glass with ropelike swirl handles, bases, stems, et cetera, and ball-shaped bosses in rows at base rims and bottoms of hollow wares and rims of covers. A rather rare Midwestern pattern of the 1880s.

Ballard breechloader: Rifles, carbines, and revolving pistols of Ballard make, or made under Ballard patents, loaded at breech with cartridges or with powder, ball, and primer. Made from c. 1860. [*Example of rifle pictured.*]

Ballard Rockingham: Pottery of Rockingham type made by A. K. Ballard, Burlington, Vt., from 1850s or later.

Ball, Black & Co.: This name or mark on silverwares of mid- to late 19th century is that of the successors to Marquand & Co., famed silversmiths and jewelers of New York City. Solid and plated silver made on factory-production basis. Also Tomkins & Black in 1840s.

ball caster: A ball in a retainer fastened to bottoms of furniture legs for ease in rolling on floor. Date is from 1830s.

ball cover: Huge glass globe said to have been used as milk-pan cover. This usage is doubtful.

ball cushion: Pincushion of ball shape up to six inches in diameter, often decorated with needlework. Date is from mid-18th century.

ball flower: Gothic ornamentation from Tudor England; a ball centered within a series of petal forms, enclosed in a circle, used singly and in rows as borders.

ball foot: Any leg terminating in a ball, or any footing on case furniture consisting of a ball-shaped element. [*See page of furniture-footing illustrations.*]

ball-jointed: Any adjustable stand, embroidery ring, et cetera, mounted on a turned upright having a ball-and-socket joint. [*Example pictured.*]

Balloon: A pattern of pressed glass with alternate panels of hearts, lyre forms, and a balloon in rising-flight position. Quite rare; only a covered bowl is known. Date is c. 1870s or 1880s.

balloon frame (ARCHITECTURE): A type of quick timber construction with upright elements and roof rafters completed as a balloon frame before siding, flooring, and roofing are applied.

balloon lamp: Glass lamp mounted on marble base, the reservoir in the form of a balloon and its shrouds. From 1860s. [*Example pictured.*]

ball stopper: Pouring stopper with a ball

enclosed in a crownlike framework. When pouring, ball falls into top of crown; when upright, it seals the bottleneck. Date is from 1830s. [*Example pictured.*]

ball urn: A novelty urn of ball form, introduced about 1850 in silver-plated ware. [*Example pictured.*]

ball vase: Globular footed vessel of glass, some clear and some in colors. Also known in silvered, double-walled form. Made at Bristol, England, from c. 1820. [*Example pictured.*]

Balmoral lamp: Classic column lamp, topped by a deep bell shade, the column serving as a fluid reservoir or to hold a Palmer candle. Invented by Warner & Sons of London, c. 1840, this type of lamp was made by at least five American lamp factories. [*Example pictured.*]

balsam: The balm of Gilead; a yellow gum substance with the odor of lemon.

balsamaria: The original incense burners in which balsam gums were burned. Some ancient examples from Jewish and pagan temples are in circulation.

balsam bottle: Bottle with cuplike cover which serves as stopper.

Baltimore chair: Chair of spool-type turned work said to be peculiar to the Baltimore area.

Baltimore glass: This can mean products of: (1) A. Furnival and Frederick Amelung, the younger, trading as the Baltimore Glass Co. from 1799 to 1802. A Mr. Freise operated the factory to 1804 and had an interest in it to 1819, when Reppert Brothers took over and continued to 1840s. It was under other management to 1900 and later. (2) Baltimore Flint Glass Works, in operation from 1820 to 1840s or 1850s. (3) Maryland Glass Works, Baltimore, from 1850. The Furnival-Amelung wares were clear glass and yellow, green, and black bottles. Flint glass of all kinds was made at the Baltimore Flint Glass Works. The Maryland Glass Works exhibited at the London Crystal Palace, 1851.

Baltimore nursing bottle: Small chestnut-shaped flask of glass made with long neck and narrow mouth, to which nipple was affixed. Made at Millville (N.J.) Glass Works.

Baltimore Pear: Pattern of pressed glass featuring a pear-shaped fruit that is actually a fig. The pattern is known as "Fig" until the modern renaming of many pressed-glass patterns.

Baltimore tokens: Silver tokens of threepence value made by the silversmith, Standish Barry. They were stamped "Baltimore Town" and dated 1790.

baluster: Any turned, carved, or shaped element of vaselike form used as a leg, support, column, stem, or architectural member. Term said to derive from balustra, the pomegranate flower. **inverted baluster:** Any baluster form used invert, or upside down. **baluster back:** Baluster cut in half lengthwise, the flat sides used in chair backs, showing outline of the baluster form.

baluster jug: Any vessel of which the body is in imitation of baluster turning. Early ones have flaring necks of inordinate height. Popular in France, the Nether-

lands, Switzerland, and Rhinish provinces. Date is from 1500s. [*Example pictured.*]

baluster stem: Any stem of a vessel, of any material, having baluster form in imitation of wood turning or classic stone turnings. Especially noted on glasswares and silverwares, and in candlesticks of all sorts, from silver through ceramic wares to glass, stone, slate, wood, et cetera.

baluster table: An arcade of balusters on a foot member, set in pairs to support a long plank table top, under which there is an arcaded stretcher joining the two end supports. An early type of 17th-century Gothic table, it is now rare.

balzarine: Textile fabric displaying narrow stripes of finely woven stuff alternating with stripes up to an inch wide having only 40 threads to the inch. Various color combinations.

bambino: A baby wrapped in swaddling clothes, upright, with arms and shoulders bare. Andrea Della Robbia favored this form of depicting the Christ Child, and used it to such an extent the figure is now identified with Della Robbia plaques. He used it on medallions, tiles, chargers, basins, bowls, et cetera, of majolica. This is one of the best-known Renaissance art forms.

bamboes: Bamboo.

bamboo chair: Any chair made up of actual lengths of the wood of the bamboo cane, or hard- or softwood turned to simulate bamboo. Such furniture is noted from the 1750s down to 1900. Many bamboo chairs were very daintily made and either covered with gold leaf or bronzed.

bamboo revival: A phenomenon of the 1870s and 1880s, when much commercially produced furniture made of bamboo-turned sections was sold. Chairs and tables were the main items made. Many were gilt-bronzed.

bamboo-turned: Wood turning or carving to simulate the contours and ridges of bamboo cane. Chippendale used it; and it was used extensively by furniture makers in a revival lasting from the 1870s to 1890s.

bambury: From *bain-marie*, a large pan for hot water in which other vessels were immersed to keep contents warm. Also used as a bathing tub.

Bamper glass: Loderwijk Bamper of the Netherlands retired to the colony of New York, c. 1725, richly endowed. He introduced the tulip to the colonies and, after living in retirement for some years, was one of the organizers of a group who purchased the old Newfoundland Glass Co., New York City. This they operated from 1752 to 1767 and had a branch at New Windsor, N.Y., which operated from 1755 to 1782. The works purchased by Bamper were actually organized in 1732, and he may have had a hand in that enterprise as well.

Bamper statues: Effigies of wood made for Loderwijk Bamper to decorate his house and garden and which, though mentioned in his memorials, were declared a fiction by some experts. However, the statues were not fiction, and two pairs survive, one in the Museum of the Hudson Valley at Yonkers, N.Y., and the other in the possession of one of Bamper's descendants. The statues are life-size fireside figures, carved in outline of the human form and painted realistically in full color.

banana dish: Glassware (pressed, blown, and cut) and ceramic ware with open end, curled sides on stands and bases to hold bananas. These, quite definitely, were common elegancies of the 1850s to 1880s. The banana dish was first popular in the South, and most early examples were found originally south of Charleston, S.C., and Memphis, Tenn. When the fruit became common, the use of the dishes spread. [*Example pictured.*]

banco: A seat somewhat like a casapanca, *which see.*

bancone: A writing table; a small desk.

Bancroft-Miles furniture: Sofas, secretaries, bedsteads, case, and seat furniture made by Bancroft & Miles of Greenfield, Mass., from 1830s. Grecian sofas by this firm were almost a standard item in New England during 1830s.

Band: Pattern of pressed glass with rows of beveled bulls'-eyes and latticed bands encircling the wares. Probably made prior to 1860.

bandana: From Bandhana, an Indian fabric printed with a repeat pattern of large squares. These were cut apart and sold as Bandhana kerchiefs, from the 17th century. Any printed cotton handkerchief of large size, especially in gaudy colors.

bandbox: Any box to hold bands used in early dress, but particularly a box of thin split or sawed wood, generally oval or round, frequently decorated, but also often plain. Later examples were of cardboard covered with fancy paper. It is a collecting error to decorate plain old bandboxes. Within a short while an undecorated bandbox will be rarer than a decorated example!

band-door: A hinge.

Banded Diamond Point: Pattern of pressed glass with angular or zigzag banding at top of an over-all pattern of small diamond points.

Banded Star: Pattern of pressed glass with shell-form footing and dainty bands of star motif. One of the rare patterns. The name is inadequate; it should be named for its shell-form footing.

bandege: Table with two tiers, the upper one a tray.

banding: Veneering or inlaying of a band or strip around table rims or edges, chair seats, drawer fronts, et cetera.

bankkit: Woodenware. A large vessel used in salting or pickling.

bandolier: Shoulder belt of 16th- and 17th-century soldiers to which 10 to 12 small turned wooden bottles, holding charges of powder, were affixed with cords. These powder-charge cases are rare today in spite of the fact that every 17th-century soldier of Smith's company, the Dutch and Swedish soldiery along the Hudson and Delaware, and New England and French soldiers were so equipped.

bandoline: Lacquerlike dressing for the hair made from quince seeds or Iceland moss, boiled to provide the jellylike base.

bandy-legged: Bow-legged; also swivelhipped, the two disfigurements being related. The hip movement compensated for the bowed legs. The cabriole or Queen Anne style curative leg, which was known in China for centuries and is found also in Roman and Greek furniture.

bangle charms: Bangle bracelets of the 1880s, the equivalent of charm bracelets of today. The charms were many and various, being miniatures of all sorts and types of household goods, furniture, lighting fixtures, et cetera. Made of plated silver or gold.

banian, banyan: The *Ficus indica,* a variety of fig which develops downward, growing tendrils which eventually become additional trunks. Also called strangle tree and strangle vine.

banister: Same as baluster, when used as "banister back" for a chair type. [*Example pictured.*] Also the railing (corruption of balustrade) of a staircase.

banister roundabout: A baluster-back corner chair. [*Example pictured.*]

banjo barometer: Wall barometer in casing of banjo shape.

banjo clock: Clock movement, weight-driven, generally time only, in the famous casing of banjo shape attributed to Simon Willard. He did not invent this casing but merely put his excellent movement in the case. The banjo barometer case is earlier than Willard's banjo clock case.

banker: Ornamental cloth cover for a bench or chair.

bank-note jewelry: Tie pins, eardrops, breast pins, and cuff links of colored enamel on engraved gold, imitating in miniature national bank notes of $5 denomination and $20 U.S. Treasury notes. A vagary of the 1860s.

Banko: Thin-walled stoneware teapots of Japanese 19th-century make, a specialty of the potter, Banko Inetsu.

bank runner: Fisherman's reel with the spindle vertical, affixed on a post or upright rod. [*Example pictured.*]

banks, mechanical cast-iron: See Mechanical Toy Banks.

Banks furniture: Sometimes quaint and curious combinations of the graceful Directoire style and heavy Empire, made by John Banks, New York, 1820s–30s.

Bankson furniture: Fine furniture made in the Georgian and classic styles by John Bankson of Baltimore from 1770s, and later by partnership of Gordon & Bankson from 1780s, and Bankson & Lawson from 1785. Made town-house and plantation-mansion furniture.

banner stand: Wood or metal pole on firm, portable base, on which a screen in banner shape was hung at any desired height.

banquet lamp: Original name for kerosene lamps now called "Gone-with-the-Wind." Banquet lamps in the 1800s and 1890s sold, without shades, from $1 to $10 each. The shades cost $1 upward. Also the same type of lamp on a high standard.

banquette: Day beds were called by this name in the 1820s. Originally the word designated a long, low stool, generally ornately carved and well upholstered. Some are only 12 to 14 inches high but are 6 feet long.

Banvard panorama: The world's longest

panoramic view, painted by John Banvard and displayed as a wonder for many years both here and abroad. Banvard painted the banks of the Mississippi from source to mouth, and the panorama was a sensation in the 1840s and 1850s. [One element of the panorama is pictured, in its display machine.]

baptismal bowls: High footed bowls generally made for other purposes but used on occasion in the rite of infant baptism. Also low footed bowls of similar size, of glass, pottery, porcelain, and silver. Any occasional bowl used in baptism, and special bowls as made for the rite in churches.

baquet: Woodenware. A tub or bucket.

Bar & Diamond: Pattern of pressed glass featuring blocks and lozenged bars set at an angle, terminating in a four-faceted diamond point. This ware was available with plain upper section which could be etched or wheel-engraved in patterns to order. From 1880s.

bara-picklet: A small cake or cookie.

barathea: Pebbled-weave silk fabric, sometimes part wool.

barb: To dress or trim the hair; to cut a lobster apart for serving.

bar-back: Any chair or sofa back composed of vertical or horizontal bars.

Barberini vase: Now known as the Portland vase, a Greco-Roman vase of cameo glass, reproduced by Wedgwood, which made his two-color cameo ware a success. Also reproduced in cameo glass. Northwood made the glass replicas in a limited edition from 1870. Wedgwood's examples date from 1790 and were made for many years. The firm is said still to own the molds.

barber-pole banding: Spiral two-color banding. The technique derives from old-time barbers and bloodletters keeping the utensils of their trade in public view —a white pole (which was grasped by the patient) with a bloody napkin twisted spirally around it and topped by a brass basin.

Barber paperweights: Paperweights featuring a rose, made by Ralph Barber to the 1900s, and by other and equally dexterous workmen at the Dorflinger Glass Works, White Mills, Pa. Barber's rose weights are also known as the Millville rose weights.

Barberry: Pattern of pressed glass in the so-called leaf group, featuring barberry leaves and fruit, with knops in the form of sea shells. Also called Pepperberry. There are many varieties in the leaf group.

Barbers: Patented, strike-anywhere matches, made by George Barber, from 1847, in Ohio.

barber's chair: Any chair made for use of barbers or adapted to such use. Previous to 1850s it was customary for the barber to go to his customer, and haircutting and shaving were done in the home or office, using the most convenient chair available. The wig-back chair is a form of barbering chair most generally used in the home. [An example of a crude early type of barber's chair is pictured.]

barbershop wares: Glass, china, metal, and other wares used extensively in barbershops include: shave-paper vases for disposal of the tissues on which the razor

was wiped of lather and hairs while shaving; stand bottles for essences, waters, et cetera. Tonic bottles, unguent pots, and patrons' shaving mugs, sometimes (in some shops) displaying the symbols of the patrons' work or business.

barbiton: A lyre, or lyre form.

Barbizot-Palissy: Imitations of the famed pottery of Palissy, made from 1860, the imitations being more perfect than the originals. Not fakes; a revival of Palissy faience.

barbola: Gesso work done on finished pottery; a homecraft.

barbotine: Potters' slip; creamy white or colored liquefied clay.

bar butter mold: Woodenware. A folding hinged mold to press a bar of butter. In spite of all opinions to the contrary, these molds were made and sold, to produce butter in bar form, from the 1840s. [Example is pictured.]

barbwig: A variety of periwig.

Barcheston tapestry: Barcheston, England, was the site of the tapestry-weaving studios established by Queen Elizabeth during the second half of the 16th century. A specialty was map tapestry.

bardings: Horse gear or trappings, generally charged with heraldic bearings.

barège: Originally a wool worsted fabric, but in 19th century woven of silk and cotton warp with wool woof.

barge (IN ARCHITECTURE AND FURNITURE) **:** A beamlike member framed into another. **barge course:** A row of tile, shingle, shake, or flag, projecting beyond the eve of a roof. **bargeboard:** Boarding at gable ends; seen also on ark-shaped chests. Some bed testers had elaborately decorated bargeboards.

bargère: A farmer's chair; a primitive type; a rustic style. Also any chair from the rural districts made fashionable, as the bargères of Marie Antoinette.

baril; barilette: Barrel-shaped flask.

barilla: Soda derived from ashes of seaweed of same name.

Barker's mill: A water motor based upon the principle of Hero's early steam engine. Water under pressure was piped to a cylinder having two extending hollow arms with nozzles at right angles; water forced from nozzles caused cylinder to rotate.

barker ware: One of the products of the Don Pottery, Swinton, England. See Don Pottery.

barking ax: An edged tool used in stripping bark from logs.

barking-off: Killing small furred game, such as squirrels, by rifle fire which, aimed at the bark beside the animal, stunned the game with a blow. Expert marksmanship was required, and by this practice both meat and pelt were preserved intact. This kind of shooting is not a tall tale.

bark mill: Any type of shredding technique for preparing bark for use in tanning. Specifically, a huge circle of flat stones with a continuous groove cut in them in which a great heavy sharp-edged wheel runs, its axle pole fastened to a post in the center of the circle. A horse or team of horses or oxen pulled the wheel over piles of bark in the track and so

1, Bank Runner. 2, Basket Spit. 3, Basketwork Pottery. 4, Bear Jug. 5, Base Firedogs.
6, Bed Bench. 7, Beecher Bottle. 8, Beehive Crocus Pot. 9, Bellarmine. 10, Beeny Mirror
Label. 11, Benedict Stove. 12, Berry Pins. 13, Bible Stand. 14, Bickford Knitter. 15,
Biddenden Bun Mold. 16, Bideford Ovens. 17, Bill Hook. 18, Binders Rolls and Flowers.
19, Bird Spit. 20, Blake Lamp. 21, Block Carpet and Block Coverlet Patterns. 22, Blanching Pot. 23, Bird's-Eye Coverlet Pattern.

shredded it. This same general type of mill was used by potters to prepare clay. While few such mills now remain, or even vestiges of them, they were once a common sight in many regions of the colonies and in our Federal era to c. 1860s.

barlep: A barley basket.

Barley: Pattern of pressed glass featuring a vine definitely not barley, with dewdrops. A very delicate pattern, dating from c. 1870.

barleycorn: Linear measure; one third of an inch; a weight equal to 1/24th pennyweight.

barley-sugar turning: Wood turning or carving imitating the spiral twist of barley-sugar sticks. Imagine a common building lath twisted into a spiral. [*Example pictured.*]

bar lip: A heavy ringlike lip on a glass bottle said to have been designed for use at bars in taverns. Late 18th century, but used in 19th century and to comparatively recent date.

Barlow knife: A large jackknife of sturdy type; the whittler's knife; the pocketknife of our ancestors.

Barlow lusters: Copper and other metallic lustered pottery made by Thomas Barlow, Longton, England. It is marked with a "B."

Barlow Planetarium: An astronomical display device built by T. H. Barlow of Lexington, Ky, c. 1850.

barm: Any ferment used in baking; yeast.

Barnes delft: Drug jars, pots, fireplace tiles, octagonal plates, and dinner services of tin-glaze delftwares made by Zacharias Barnes, Liverpool, England, from 1760s.

Barnett desks: Rosewood and mahogany desks in the Louis XV "antique" style, made by John Barnett, N.Y., from 1840s or 1850s.

barn-symbol chests: Importations of continental European antiques, mostly from Sweden and Switzerland, and some from Spain. These chests have scratch-carved, shallow-gouged, or painted decoration of geometrical star forms resembling those painted on the Swiss barns of Pennsylvania. The term as here given, it may be suspected, is used to connote American origin for these chests.

barn symbols: Painted symbols on the Swiss-type barns of Pennsylvania, which are of Swiss ancestry and comparable to those found painted on similar barns and bridges in Switzerland. Most are geometrical or star form, made up of straight and curvate lines, and painted in gaudy contrasting colors. Emphatically not hex marks, as some commentators have suggested. These painted symbols are imitations of carved bargeboards on gable walls of the Gothic age. The fine prototypes are still found, carved in oak or stone, on churches and cathedrals of the 14th and 15th centuries.

Barnum buckle: P. T. Barnum's own product—an elastic band and buckle combination made by the master showman after his New Haven Clock Co. adventure. Patented in 1860s. [*Example pictured.*]

Barnum's museum toy: A paper panorama operated with drawstrings and knobs, made by C. C. Shepherd Co., c. 1876. Shepherd also made wooden model toys of the first New York elevated railroad, and transparent writing slates. [*Example of Barnum toy pictured.*]

Baroque: From the Portuguese *barroco*, an irregularly shaped pearl. Term now commonly used as a synonym for rococo, meaning rock and shell motif decoration; anything overdecorated, gaudily luxuriant. **Second Baroque:** The more correct name for the style we have called Victorian.

Baroque block front: *See* Block Front.

Barred Hobnail: Pattern of pressed glass featuring angular or oblique placing of rows of lozenges (bars) and dots (hobnails), the entire pieces having frosted finish.

Barred Oval: Pattern of pressed glass featuring large ovals as panels with bars bisecting them horizontally.

Barred Star: Pattern of pressed glass featuring an all-over design of stars within diamonds formed by a crisscrossing of bars.

barrèges: Tissuelike textiles with printed designs. From 1849 immense quantities were imported from France in plain form and printed in U.S.

barrel-back: The backs of club chairs, rounded in contour and conforming to the shape of the inner side of a barrel. Often upholstered in leather; made from mid-18th century.

barrel barns: Circular-shaped cattle and crop barns having a large silo in center filled from upper levels. Traditionally built round so the devil couldn't find a corner to hide in! Most examples are quite late.

barrel bookcase: Drum-shaped two- to four-tier stand of shelves for books, rotating on a stand or fixed without stand.

barrel casket: A gruesome piece of woodenware, carried on shipboard for transportation of human corpses, sometimes preserved in rum. It looks like a high, small-diameter cask, coopered, but is lead-lined and capable of hermetic sealing. [*Example pictured.*]

barrel cradle: A coopered cradle; a cradle made up of staves, rounded like a barrel, the head end complete, and cut away to serve as a hood. Regular cradle rockers were fitted to this casing. Said to date, as a type, from medieval period, when barrel ceilings were commonly used in house construction and the work of the cooper was of considerable commercial and domestic importance.

barrel decanter: Any liquor or wine decanter in the general shape of a barrel or the lower half of a barrel, curving inward to necks generally encircled with a series of rings and fitted with mushroom or other glass stoppers. [*Example with enameled decoration is pictured.*]

barrel glass: Blown tumblers of clear or tinted glass in barrel shape. Made to as late as 1885; many of that date have pontil marks.

barrel-head chair: Chairs with backs of circular shape, looking like the head of a barrel. Some, designed by the Brothers Adam in the classic style, date from 1750s. Late examples are Louis XVI revivals made as late as 1880s.

barrel kettle: Teakettles or serving

kettles of barrel shape, with hoops inscribed or simulated, having S-shaped spouts and handles set at right angles to spout. Known in silver, copper, and brass, these are rare items, dating from c. 1725. [*Example pictured.*]

barrel organ: Mechanical pipe or reed organ, the tunes deriving from a huge drum with wooden or metal pricks to operate keys or stops. Made in France, Switzerland, and Italy, and some said to have been made by London, New York, and Philadelphia organ builders. The street organ is a barrel organ.

barrel stove: Any cast-iron stove having a fire pot of barrel shape; the potbellied stove. Not to be confused with cannon stove, *which see*.

barrel table: Variant of drum table, and generally meaning a drum table with a very deep drum section.

barrel tankard: Straight- or slightly sloping-sided tankard with clusters of ribbing placed at hoop points, made of silver or pewter. 18th to 19th century.

barrel-vaulted: A ceiling or interior roofing of barrel shape. Early Gothic ceilings were actually staved in the barrel-making tradition, with huge oak staves laid over hooplike girts.

Barrett woodenware: S. M. Barrett of Cincinnati produced thousands of pieces of willow ware for home and dairy from 1840s or 1850s which were once thus designated. Much of it is marked with a brand.

barrister inkwell: One of the many "mug" inkwells, or human-face wells, made at the Bournes Pottery, Lambeth, England, from the early 1800s. The open mouth of the face was the well orifice, and there were two quill holes in which to stick the pens. [*Example pictured.*]

Barry, Sir Charles: Designer of the new palace at Westminster, England, and of much Gothic-revival furniture for its many rooms. His is the truly Victorian style, dating from 1840s.

Barry-Calder furniture: Excellent cabinetwork by Barry & Calder, Philadelphia, working from the 1790s or early 1800s. Joseph Barry did work in Directoire and Sheraton styles.

Bartholomew baby: A gaudy doll.

bartizan: A turned ornament applied to the surface of furniture, especially at corners. The original bartizan was the small tower projecting from a main tower, in which a defender was protected while at watch; a turret projecting from a corner of a wall.

Bartlett-Collins glass: Glass made at the Liberty Glass Works, Sapulpa, Okla., and originally at Coffeyville, Kan. 20th-century premium pressed glass.

barway: Openings in walls or fences fitted with bars to discourage or prevent ingress or egress of cattle.

bar window: Closely set rods of clear glass functioning as a pane, permitting passage of light but not vision. Made from 1850s.

barytone: A musical instrument of viola shape, made from 1680s.

basaltes: Black stoneware, the result of mixing iron and other oxides with basic clays. One of the world's oldest hard potteries. The finer pieces were lathe-polished. Ancient cameos of this ware are known. Wedgwood and other famed potters of England produced basaltes wares, including teapots.

baseball stool: A four-legged folding stool with canvas seat. Made from 1860s and popular with early baseball fans when there were no grandstands or bleachers for spectators. [*Example pictured.*]

base dogs; base andirons: A heavy wrought-iron three-sided frame upon which supports and stops for logs are mounted. A mid-19th-century invention. [*Example pictured.*]

basel-pot: The only references seem to indicate an earthenware pot used in cooking calves' heads. Reference dates from 1587.

basenet: Woodenware. A small bowl. French *bassinet* is the same, although now the meaning is a small basket for a baby.

Basham ware: Plaster ware—roosters, animals, bustos, and other effigies for mantel ornaments. Made in quantities by F. Basham, New York, from 1850s.

basilicon: Officinal ointment; black, yellow, and green basilicon sold in pots by pharmacists as late as 1820s.

basin dial: Sundial with concave surface, officially a hemicyleum. Known to Vitruvius. [*A true basin-shaped dial of 18th century is pictured.*]

basin stand: Square, round, or triangular stand with drawers, generally with an open space for ewer at bottom, and a ring on upright supports. Most frequently miscalled a wig stand, these stands were made exclusively for a rimmed basin placed on, over, or within the supporting ring. Much used in 18th and 19th centuries as bedroom furniture.

basket bed: A flower or herb-garden bed banked by a series of heavy stakes over which basketwork is woven as a support.

basketry: Baskets of woven withes, willow, wire, or any other reedlike material.

basket salt: Finest table salt, derived from salinas or salt springs, and obtained by evaporation of the water in baskets.

basket sleigh: Basket of cradle shape on snow runners. A Midwestern invention of the 1870s.

basket spit: A spit with a basket of light wrought-iron straps in the middle. It was placed on andiron spit hooks and turned to roast a bird or cut of meat placed within the basket. 18th century. [*Example pictured.*]

basket swivel chair: Infant's school chair. A stick chair seat and back mounted on an iron support with baskets at side of chair for books and slates. 19th century.

basket ware: Plates, chargers, dishes, pots, et cetera, of china, Parian, and earthenware in basket-weave patterns.

Basket Weave: Pattern of pressed glass featuring a design looking more like a Shaker chair tape seat. Known in several colors and clear white.

basket-weave papier-mâché: Chinese lacquer work on paper, the final layer of which is laid on in basket or tape-woven style of strips. This shows through the lacquer as a basket-weave patterned surface.

basketwork pottery: Generally majolica, porcelain, or china, the piece woven or worked from long round strands of potter's clay or tapes of clay. [*Example pictured.*]

bas-relief: When raised figures project less than half their normal diameter from a plane, the work is in bas-relief, or *basso-relievo*.

bassel bowle: Bowling ball.

basse-lisse: Tapestry weaving with horizontal warp and the weft thrown with a bobbin called a flute.

bassetaille; basse-taille: Unique effect achieved with transparent enamels laid in engraved lines on metal, and fired to fix enamels.

bass-kit; bast-kit: Basket. This term derives from the use of bast or basswood strips in weaving "kits" for carrying goods. Webster credits derivation of "basket" from *bascauda*, a brass or bronze vessel.

bass melodeon: A separate foot-pedaled instrument of a complete octave, sold as a working unit to place on the floor and play with the manually operated melodeons of the 1850s. The bass section had hose couplings with the bellows of the major instrument. The bass played with left foot as right foot operated the bellows pedal. Sounds complicated, doesn't it? But some of the instruments survive.

bast: A pack saddle of woven bast.

basting ladle: A long-handled ladle with a round bowl, having a perforated half cover.

basting spoon: Large spoon or ladle.

basswood: Soft white wood of fine grain. Bast, the inner bark, was stripped for making baskets, chair seats, and other woven work, including huge sieves and evaporators for salt, et cetera. A bass-bottomed chair is one having seat or "bottom" woven of bast.

Bataille: Tapestry by Nicholas Bataille, a weaver and merchant of the 14th century.

batant: Uprights; battens; sections of wood applied vertically on lock or latch side of a door and frame.

bath brick: Soft fired or unbaked abrasive bricks used for scouring powder.

Bath coating: Flannel, or double baize; a light woolen cloth sometimes called duffel; a coating cloth popular at Bath, famed English watering place and resort.

bath metal: A variety of brass; an alloy of copper and zinc.

bath slipper: A huge metal slipper-shaped vessel used as a bathtub. The bather sat in the heel and had head and chest out of water. Pewter, tin-plated sheet iron, brass, and copper examples are known. Used from 18th century to 1840s or later, in homes and public bathhouses.

Bath stove: Ornamental chamber grate made popular at hotels in Bath, England.

bathtub: The first bathing tubs were staved, coopered, or hollowed from blocks of wood or stone. Zinc-lined and other variants came into general use by the 1830s. The ancient trade of pewterer evolved into that of plumber, and many bathtubs of the 1830s were pewter set within a wooden form. In residences the bathtub was at times placed under a trap door level with a first-story floor.

batik: Resist-dyeing through wax; also pattern-dyeing by tying fabric and plunging in various dye baths.

batiste: Sheer linen fabric.

batlings: Twigs and limb clippings used as kindling wood. Bundles were kept near fireplace for quick lighting of fires.

bat printing: Transfer printing from intaglio copperplates with metallic ink or thick linseed oil on "bats" or sheets of glue or gelatin, and offset from the bat to the surface of chinaware. Metallic oxide powders were then dusted on for specific coloration. A variant of transfer printing.

Batso ironware: Made at the Batso furnace in West New Jersey from 1776. Fishpots, cooking pots, Dutch ovens, skillets, and other cooking wares, "superior to those heretofore imported from England."

battens: Narrow flooring boards; beading strips nailed over joints in woodwork.

battered; battering: Sloping inward from a base.

batter jug: Spouted jug of any kind, for pouring batter.

Battersea enamel: Generic term for English-made enamels, the majority of which are not Battersea products. Most English enamels are actually of Staffordshire make and better than the original Battersea. Unbreakable porcelain; white or tinted enamel fused on a metal base and then decorated in the porcelain style, in imitation of Sèvres, Meissen, et cetera. Snuffboxes, candlesticks, patch boxes, trifle boxes, pill cases, door and cabinet knobs, et cetera, were made. *See* Enamel-on-Metal. Battersea Works was started by Theodore Janssen, c. 1750. The factory failed in 1756, but Janssen is reputed to have worked at his craft for some twenty more years.

Battersea loaf: Loaf sugar from Battersea.

battery: Hammering by repeated blows to shape block tinwares, copper, and other ductile metals. Method not used much after 1851, when spinning was perfected as a refinement of the old "skimming" or shaping by lathe turning; "skum" work.

battleship wares: Pressed-glass trays, boxes, et cetera, mostly with covers, in form of ironclad battleships of the U.S. Navy, popular after our war with Spain. Notable ships such as the *Wheeling, Oregon*, and others were named examples. These were inexpensive novelties.

batwing brass: William & Mary period escutcheons for bail or drop drawer handles. The batwing is Chinese and is more probably a representation of a dragon wing.

baudekin: Rich textile fabric with warp of gold threads and woof of silk.

Bawo & Dotter: This name appears on labels and on some glass and china. It is not the mark of the maker but of the importers, who were located in New York City from 1850s. They imported French porcelains, Bohemian, lava, and Belgian glass (including hyacinth vases), potichomanie vases, and Dutch delftwares.

baxter: A wide board for strapping on feet in walking over sand and mud; a heavy shoe; a bake-maid.

bayberry: A native shrub yielding a wax-coated berry, used extensively for its wax in candlemaking.

bay salt: Red-brown salt obtained by evaporation of sea water in clay-lined pits.

bay shilling: The pine-tree shilling of New England.

bay soap: One of the earliest homemade soaps of the colonies; any animal fat boiled with bayberries and leaves, and saponified with leechings of wood ashes.

Bay State glass: Glasswares made at the manufactory of the East Cambridge Glass Co., established 1854. Vials, lamps, bottles, silvered glass, plain and cut glass, molded glass, and fine flintwares were produced to 1877.

Beach furniture: Household furniture of all sorts made by Moses Beach at his factory, Northampton, Mass., from 1819.

Beaded Dewdrop: Pattern of pressed glass featuring a series of stippled ovate loops beaded with tiny droplets and rows of dewdrops.

beaded edge: Any edging finished with a narrow, round-edged molding known as "bead," or an edge finished with a continuous series of small hemispherical dots or bosses. The former is general on furniture and cabinetwork; the latter is often met with in metals, especially tablewares of silver or plated silver.

Beaded Grape: Pattern of pressed glass featuring panels of grape leaf and fruit clusters marked by lines of beads, pressed from clear and green glass as late as 1920. Beaded Grape Medallion and the same with a band are variants of grape pattern. See also Pressed Glass Patterns.

Beaded Loop: Pattern of pressed glass displaying a series of loops of beaded outline enclosing a flattened diamond pattern.

bead molding: Any small, half-round molding projecting or flush with the surface it finishes as a rim or border. (When it projects around edges of drawer or door it is sometimes called cockbead.) Any edging displaying carved or applied beading flush, sunken, or level with adjacent surfaces; any inlaid band of similar motif. Almost any simple molding can be a bead molding; the term "bead" derives from contour of cross section and not from hemispherical elements in rows, as small balls or beads.

bead patterns in pressed glass: While an effort is made here to list all major patterns of pressed glass, space does not permit specific listing of all variants. In the beaded pattern group are Beaded Mirror, Beaded Oval, Beaded Scroll, Beaded Band, Beaded Swirl, Beaded Tulip, and perhaps others of more recent naming.

beads (glass): The first glass made at Jamestown, Va., was glass beads for use in trade with the Indians. Glass beads are made by two basic processes, (1) blowing and drawing rods of glass which are cut into small sections and rolled while plastic into bead form, and (2) by blowing from glass tubes in a blowpipe, the beads falling off and cooling rapidly. In the 19th century glass beads of commerce were called "Commons," "Hollows," "Bugles," and "Dolls' Eyes."

beaker: From Byker, meaning a bucket with cover. Now any tall drinking mug of any substance, generally without cover.

beaker candlestick: A metal mug-shaped holder with pierced sides, having candle socket and a straight or flaring high chimney of clear glass. Many of silver and Sheffield plate made in late 18th and first quarter of 19th century. Revived c. 1840s in plated silver and made throughout 19th century. [Example pictured.]

beaker splat: A chair-back splat in beaker form; a form simpler than the vase or fiddle-shaped splat.

beak head: Actually bird head; carved devices of bird head and beak form used as terminals of chair stiles and arms.

Beale furniture: Directoire, Sheraton, and some Empire furniture made by Gustav Beale of Georgetown, District of Columbia. Some of his pieces are labeled.

beam: A candle.

beani: A freshman; a newcomer.

bear bottles: Glass bottles, made in pre-Communist Russia as containers for kümmel, in clear and black glass. At one time, owing to wrong attribution, these bottles were said to be "early Pennsylvania German" or "eastern Pennsylvania glass." It is not known how many imitations of the early bear bottles were made after the end of Prohibition, nor where they were made. It is likely some were made in Russia. Also a globular bottle bearing the effigy of a walking bear and the legend "California Fire Extinguisher."

bear jugs: Glazed stoneware ale jugs in the form of bears, made at potteries in Nottingham, Chesterfield, and Brampton, England, in some quantities. Some were made as tobacco jars. These jugs are creamy white or brown. Early 18th century. [Example pictured.]

bear tankard: Staffordshire tankards depicting the Russian bear grasping a caricatured Napoleon. Some are labeled "BONY." Relics of Napoleon's Russian campaign.

beath: To heat green wood to drive out sap; kiln drying.

beat the dust: Said of horses with a fault, or failing to make headway or gain ground in a race.

Beatty Honeycomb: Pattern of pressed glass in all-over waffle pattern.

Beatty Rib: Pattern of pressed glass featuring heavy vertical ribbing.

Beau Brummel: A man's fitted dressing table having a fold-back mirror and other conveniences, made throughout the 18th century in all the prevailing furniture styles. The true Beau Brummel is a more important piece than a bachelor's chest, which is sometimes given this name.

beaufat; buffet: Strictly a corner piece, as a corner cupboard, corner chair, corner table, et cetera. Never a sideboard table as designated by its later meaning.

Beauvais: A pottery and weaving center of France from 15th century. The tapestries woven at this town since 1664 are classics.

beaver tail: Leaf tobacco, after curing pressed into parcels the shape of a beaver tail, flat and ovate. This is the traditional American Indian's way of storing the leaf. French Canadians still pack it this way under the names Rose Quesnel and Petit Canadient.

becker: Woodenware; a dish.

becket: Rope handle.

bedasshed: Splashed or adorned with color.

bed basket: Infant's wickerwork crib.

bed bench: Settee or bench with fold-out or pull-out extension of the seat to convert it into a bed. [*Example pictured.*]

bed-bolt cover: Brass or other metallic medallion suspended from a single screw or nail, hiding the orifice in which the bolts of a bed are sunk. Not correctly designated as a bedpost cover.

bed casters: Corner or side plates of metal holding a swiveling pin with roller caster.

bed chair: A bedside chair; a legless chair made up of seat, back, and arms, used in bed; a chair extensible into a narrow bed or couch. Certain of the latter date from 1700.

bedder: An upholder; an upholsterer.

bedding-down candle: A very short candle, burning for less than half an hour, lit upon deciding to retire and going out of its own exhaustion no matter where placed. Generally, candle ends were used up in this way.

bed key: A large wrench carried by firemen to unbolt bedsteads when saving furniture from burning buildings.

bed moss: Spanish moss, not really a moss but an epiphyte. Plucked from trees and retted like flax to bare the dark inner fiber, which was used as bed stuffing. Now used in automobile upholstery.

bed pole: A long wand for smoothing sheets on the bed; a pole over a bed upon which to drape a tester.

bed rafe: Bedclothing.

bedroom chair: Any of the lighter fancy chairs of the 1810–50 period made with rush, rope, or tape seats, the wood being plain, stained, lacquered, japanned, stenciled, or otherwise decorated. Some were made of bamboo turning and some of papier-mâché.

bedroom scale: An invention of Merlin Lord, London, 1786; a forerunner of the bathroom scale.

bedside carpet: Strip or section of rug, carpet, or other floor matting used at bedside to protect bare feet from cold floors. Bearskins, lambskins, and other furs were so used.

bed sprays: Woven fabrics printed with sprays and sprigs of roses. If not specifically made for bedspreads, at least generally adapted for that use.

bedstead-washstand: An Eastlake-style piece of case furniture looking like a secretary-bookcase. The frontal section pulled open to reveal a washstand and the bookcase section opened into a full-size bed. This triumph of gadgetry was made by Hale, Kilburn & Co., c. 1875 to 1880s.

bed steps: Short flights of stairs, sometimes on rollers and some with railing on one side, used for getting into high beds.

bedstock: Bedstead; framework of a bed.

bed top: A canopy or valance; a tester.

bed wagon: A rolling or sliding framework holding a pan for burning charcoal. Used to aerate long-unused (or longused!) beds; not a warming device. An 18th-century invention.

bed warmer: Properly, any long-handled pan with perforated lid, for filling with live coals and passing between the sheets, or a similar device with a flat flask at end, filled with scalding-hot water and similarly used. Brass, silver, copper, iron, and pottery and glass (flask type) varieties of record. Sometimes called a bed airer.

bee box: Small wooden or horn boxes for segregating and transporting queen bees.

beech bed: A sack stuffed with beech leaves, used as a mattress.

beech butter: Beechnut oil, churned to thicken.

Beecher, Henry Ward, bottle: Glass portrait bust flask of this famed 19th-century Brooklyn, N.Y., preacher. Made in 1880s. [*Example pictured.*]

beech mast: Beechnut.

bee glue: See Propolis.

beehive chair: Chair built up of woven rushes in the beehive weaving technique. Cottage chairs made by rush plaiters in 17th and 18th century. Revived as a fashion in early 19th century, especially as a summer chair. [*Example pictured.*]

beehive crocus pot: Pottery jar in beehive form, pierced for bulb growing. [*Example pictured.*]

bee liner: Traps to imprison bees and then release to note direction taken and so lead to the hive and the honey.

Beeny, Edwin: Mirror maker of Syracuse, N.Y., who shipped many to the West. Empire and French Antique styles, all gilded or parcel-gilt. [*His label pictured.*]

beer bread: Frostbitten persimmons and wheat bran baked in huge loaves, as bread. A slice soaked in hot water and cooled made a measure of table beer.

beer firkin: Woodenware. A measure of nine gallons.

beer jar: Large pottery container with cover, and taphole for spigot.

Beers ax: A pioneer's and lumberman's ax made by Beers of New York from 1800s to c. 1840.

beeswing: Cream of tartar deposited in wine as a scum or gathering.

beetle: a calking tool.

beetle carving: Colloquial for the furrows and ridges left in wood by beetles. Some amazing panels were preserved as curiosities.

beetled: Hammered, as beetled yarn; pounded out of the round for use in weaving damask.

beetle iron: A wedge used in splitting logs.

Bellamy eagles: Eagles carved by John Bellamy of Kittery Point, Me. He was a ship's carver and made many eagles for hatchways, over-doors, and figureheads. His most imposing figurehead was the gigantic eagle for the U.S. frigate *Lancaster*. Bellamy was born 1836 and died 1914.

bellarmine: Stoneware jugs bearing the face of a bearded man, supposed to represent Bellarmino, the fanatic Jesuit cardinal, created 1599. The jugs are caricatures and jests at his memory, and not in honor of the man. Also Bearded Man, Greybeard, and other names not so nice. [*Example pictured.*]

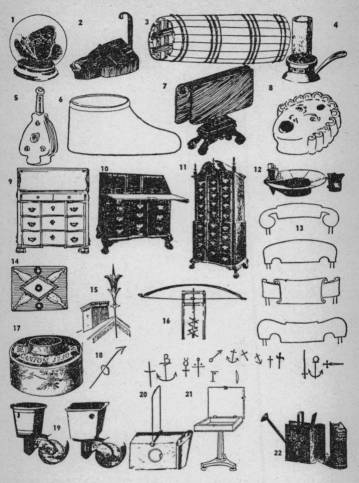

1, Barber's "Millville Rose" Paperweight. **2,** Betty Lamp. **3,** Barrel Casket. **4,** Beaker Candlestick. **5,** Bellows Bottle. **6,** Bathing Shoe. **7,** Bible-Back Table. **8,** Barrister Inkwell. **9,** Baroque Block-Front Desk. **10,** Block-Front Desk (American). **11,** Block-Front Chest-on-Chest. **12,** Boston Bathing Pan. **13,** Boston Rocker, back rail types. **14,** Bottle & Ball Motif. **15,** Bouquet Lightning Rod. **16,** Bow-Beater. **17,** Bow China (New Canton Works) Inkwell. **18,** Marks Attributed to Bow Pottery. **19,** Box Casters. **20,** Box Lamp. **21,** Box-on-Stand. **22,** Book Sprinkler. (Nos. 17 and 18 from Virtue & Co., London.)

31

bell beaker: Ancient pottery vessels of bell shape, made by the people called Beakers. Actually prehistoric pottery and found in antiques marts only on rare occasions.

bell braces: Straps studded with button-type bells.

bell can: Bell-shaped vessels with spouts, from the Zurich region of Switzerland.

bell carriage: Housing for an alarm or church bell; fancy covered spring and box for use with house call bells and doorbells. These were standard articles of fine cabinet hardware manufacturers from 1790s. Other items for domestic bells were bell cranks, also with fancy tops.

bell dial: Sundial invented by Abbé Galais, Paris, 1780, consisting of a burning glass poised over a linen thread, which burned through when the rays of the sun were focused upon it at noon, sun time. This released a gong bell hammer and caused the bell to sound. An idea similar to sundial gun, *which see.*

belled bowl: Plated-silver slop bowls of tea-service sets having a call bell affixed. Made by Reed & Barton, U.S., probably in 1870s.

Belleek: Irish porcelain having an iridescent shell-like quality. Now a generic name for any such ware.

Belle Vernon glass: Tablewares, bottles, and flasks made at Belle Vernon, Pa., glassworks, 1834 to 1880s.

Bellevue porringers: Shallow cast-iron bowls with single pierced ear-shaped handhold with foundry name "Bellevue" cast on handle. 19th century.

Bellflower: Pattern of pressed glass with all-over vertical ribbing and graceful bellflower design imposed. One of the group of patterns known as Ribbed, and one of the oldest patterns of record.

bell hood: Chimney-flue top in form of a cone of sheet iron fixed on struts at its apex, permitting it to cant with wind direction and prevent downdrafts. Made from 1830s.

bell-marked Sheffield: Samuel Roberts' Sheffield plate ratio of two pounds of silver sheeting to eight pounds of copper core, marked with a bell. This quality ware was made from 1780s.

bell metal: Copper-bronze alloy producing sonorous tone and used in casting bells. When used in making utensils and objects, the term refers to the quality and sheen of the metal. Often used in making mortars, measures, standards, and technical or philosophical objects.

Bell of Glasgow: Wares made by J. & M. P. Bell & Co. at Glasgow pottery from 1842. White earthenware, plain and printed; china- and granite wares, and decorative artwares. One of their marks is a bell.

bellows bottle: Any glass or pottery bottle in the shape of a hand bellows. Novelty bottles made by several potters and many glass houses from 1800s to 1860. [*Example pictured.*]

bellows flask: Standing glass bottle in the form of bellows. This is the prototype of the violin, Jenny Lind, and calabash group of mold-blown flasks. The bellows flasks of standing type (not to be confused

with bellows bottles) date from 18th century.

bellows stand: A fireside stand of any kind, to hold a bellows. Sometimes called "blower stand."

bellows toys: *See* Squeak Toys.

Bell pottery: American redwares and stonewares made by (1) Solomon Bell of Waynesboro, Pa., (2) Peter Bell of Hagerstown, Md., (3) Samuel Bell of Strasburg, Va., and several other potters of the same name, from 1820s to 1880s. This is Shenandoah Valley pottery, so called, admirably covered in *The Shenandoah Pottery,* by A. H. Rice & John Baer Stoudt, 1929.

bell pulls: Hands, faces, fruits, animals, and formalized classic motifs cast as movable or pull-out elements mounted on a plate, used as doorbell pulls. Made in silver, Sheffield plate, brass, iron, Britannia, et cetera. These objects date from mid-18th century. Some plates are engraved with name of residents.

bells: Bell collectors generally are interested in (1) temple and ceremonial bells, (2) cow and sheep bells, (3) table and call bells, (4) horse and harness bells. Many such bells are of considerable age. Horse bells and cow bells were used in colonies from 1700s, and several factories for production started in 1790s. Table bells of glass and china are known, but the most collected bells are of metal.

bell salt: High-standing formal saltcellar, often of silver, in separable elements, two or more of which are for salt, topped by a handled bell-form device for dispensing pepper through perforations in its ball finial.

bell top: Clock tops of casket form, not of metal but cabinetwork. Also the dome-shaped top of early-type clocks, which was a bell suspended from a crossed framework.

bell turning: A variety of early classic or fancy turning found on William & Mary period furniture, somewhat similar to trumpet turning but more bell form.

belly board: *See* Lapboard.

belly flagon: A barber's basin, held by customer across his belly as a catch-all. Of same general purpose as the neck basin.

beloit: Arrow-shaped.

belomancy: Fortunetelling with arrows; the Chinese box of sticks is this type of hocus-pocus.

Belper ware: Salt-glaze brown earthenware, figural bottles, and inkwells made at Belper Pottery, Derbyshire, England, from 1790s. One mark is "Belper & Denby, Bournes Potteries, Derbyshire."

bel-tein: Enriching and blessing the earth with ceremony of laying down food and drink at a feast. Scottish practice.

Belt furniture: Cabinetwork of good to fine quality made by Benjamin Belt of Washington, D.C., from 1820s.

Belter furniture: Work of John Belter, New York City cabinetmaker, who produced much Louis XV revival-style furniture in sets from 1840s. In 1847 he patented a machine for sawing out arabesque chair backs. Original name was Beltier and is sometimes so spelled in early references.

Beltznickle: German equivalent of Belle Nuit, a figure who cut capers on Christmas Eve.

belvedere: An observation tower or nook; a gazebo. Often on sea and river-boat captains' homes as a lookout, and even used as a lighthouse. By 1850s it appears as an architectural elegancy on many pretentious residences.

bema: A reader's desk, especially in a church.

bench cloth: A carpet for a bench seat.

Benedict stove: 19th-century 10-plate stove with decorative cast doors, invented by Philip Benedict, Lancaster, Pa., 1835. [*Example pictured.*]

bene oil: Sesame oil (properly benne), expressed by a process perfected by John Movel of Savannah, Ga., 1769. A colonial product used in soapmaking.

bengaline: Silk-and-wool fabric for women's dress; a heavy faille.

benger: A grain chest.

Benham & Stotenborough: Extensive manufacturers of japanned tinwares at Glen Cove, Long Island, N.Y., established 1840 as Andrews & Benham. Made great quantities of painted, stenciled, and decalcomania-decorated tinwares. As late as 1870 they employed 60 people. Another parent firm was Benham & Whitney. All these wares have been called Benham tinwares.

bénitier: A holy-water font.

Bennet pottery: Rockingham and ironstone types of ware made by Bennet Brothers (E. & W. Bennet) at East Liverpool, O., Birmingham, Pa., and Baltimore, Md., at various dates in 1840s to 1860s and later.

Bennett views: Nineteen aquatint views of American cities, engraved by Bennett from various paintings, and published 1836–38 by L. P. Clover. Size, approximately 18″ x 24″, plus margins. Places pictured include: Charleston, S.C., New York City, Washington, Richmond, Buffalo, Boston, Baltimore, Philadelphia, Albany, and West Point. Also Niagara Falls and the Natural Bridge. The Charleston view is scarcest.

bennin; properly hennin: High conical hat for women, generally worn with a draped veil affixed to the top of the cone. Worn in 14th, 15th, and 16th centuries.

Bennington: One of America's famous potteries or pottery centers. The production was chiefly Rockingham-type glazed wares and stoneware dairy and kitchen utensils. Tremendous quantities were made over several decades. *The Potters of Bennington* by John Spargo may be helpful to students.

Bennington book flask: A liquor flask in form of a book, made at Bennington, Vt., potteries. Made of the characteristic mottled flintware.

benny cake: Sesame-seed cake, the seeds boiled in syrup and then toasted.

bent arm: Generally refers to a chair, the arms of which are bent continuations of back stiles.

Bent ironware: Cast-iron chairs, vases, and other elegancies from the foundry of S. F. Bent, N.Y., from 1840s.

benzoin: Dried sap of the benjamin tree.

berdash; burdash: A neckcloth.

Berean, The: A series of lectures on various subjects by Ralph Waldo Emerson.

Bergama: Oriental rug of geometric pattern in vivid colors and of loose weave.

bergamot: An oil expressed from a species of mint. Also an oil expressed from peel of the Bergamo orange.

berger: A style of women's hair arrangement, shepherdess-fashion. The mode dates from 1690s.

Berger & Walter: Glassmakers of Williamsburg, N.Y., who made French-style tablewares and fancies from 1840s.

bergère: Farmhouse chair; upholstered armchair.

berhegor: Soured beer.

Berkeley: Pattern of pressed glass featuring modified lotus-form elements.

Berlin iron: Wrought and cast trinkets bearing the legend, "*Ich gab geld um eisen.*" Rings, crosses, and other objects were made and are relics of the gifts of gold by the German people to their rulers to arm against Napoleon. In exchange, they received the iron memorials. The originals date from 1809, but the foundry continued making the objects. Some parts were so small they ran thousands to the pound.

Berlin jewelry: Black glass imitations of natural jet, in cheap settings.

Berlin ware: Tinware made at Berlin, Conn., from 1740 to 1850. Plain and planished tin-plated utensils of every kind were in the Berlin list of products. The industry was started by the Pattison Brothers. *Hawkers & Walkers*, by Richardson Wright, offers a good essay on this industry.

Bermuda dovetail: Said to be typical of this island's cabinetmaking, but seldom seen. The dovetails, instead of being solid fans, are cut in open V-shape. Since this type of dovetailing appears on furniture of the 1690s, it can be assumed the style is ancient, even if peculiar to Bermuda, and perhaps developed because of the climate's effect on solid dovetailing. [*Example pictured with other dovetail patterns.*]

Bermudian broom: Broom of cane, on a stick.

bernier: An 18th-century stump puller, a large wrought-iron jack, invented by P. Sommer of Berne, Switzerland.

Berry cases: Cigar cases of various types, some painted with scenes and portraits, made by G. G. Berry, North Stafford, N.H., from 1850s.

Berry furniture: Plain and carved black walnut and chestnut bedroom furniture, painted and grained cottage furniture, and "knock-down" furniture for low-cost transportation by water, made by Berry & Co., Charleston, S.C., from 1840s.

berry pins: Needle-pointed steel toilet pins with glass bead heads, known as berry heads. Various colored "berries" in packs sold for half a century to 1900. The little packs with colored heads were arranged to look like mulberries, blackberries, et cetera. [*Examples pictured.*]

Berthe: A neckpiece.

besom: A red hearth broom; any household broom of cane, rush, birch, corn, et cetera.

bespoke: Made to order.

Bessarabian carpets: Oriental-type carpets woven by non-Mohammedans and consequently free from the Koran inhibitions as to subject. These carpets display many natural flowers and birds as well as geometrical forms. Thousands sold in 19th century to American home owners.

bestiary: Any treatise on beasts. The illustrated ones are a source of many pottery, glass, and metalware designs and decorations.

Betsy Ross plate: Pressed-glass tea plate showing Betsy Ross making the first official Stars and Stripes. Date is c. 1880–90.

betty: An oil cruse.

Betty lamp: Small fat lamp with vertical handle, often used to lower into cook pot to note condition of contents. Millions were in use in colonial period, as this was a common lamp in cottages. Term derives from *betynges* or *betyngs*, the crude oil and fat used to drench fuel used in cressets. Said also to derive from *petite*, but this is doubtful. *Betynges lampe* would seem to be the source of Betty lamp. Examples known in sheet iron, copper, tin-plated iron, brass, white metal, and, it is reported, silver. [*Example pictured.*]

betyng candle: A candle made of resin and pitch.

betyng rod: A beating rod.

beveled glass: When the bevel of bevel plate glass is so flat as to be almost imperceptible, it is genuine old glass, most likely dating from 1670s and made at Vauxhall Works of Buckingham or one of the factories of France or Italy. The acute beveled plate is later glass; the more pronounced the bevel, the later the glass. When the bevel is sharp, having the appearance of cutting, it is late 19th or early 20th century.

beveled H hinge: Brass hinges of the H and HL form (strap-hinge type) having beveled edges. Brass H and HL hinges were the aristocratic form of hinge, never painted. Iron H and HL hinges were never painted black or left unpainted when originally used; they were painted the same color as the woodwork on which they were mounted. [*Hinges of various types are pictured.*]

bever: Between-meals liquid refreshment; beverage.

beverage: Liquid refreshment; money paid to workmen to buy drink. Common beverages of colonial days were ale, cider, beer, perry (pear cider), milk, rum, and punch.

beverage board: *See* Middle Post Sideboard.

Beverly cotton: Cotton fabric woven at the first cotton mill in America at Beverly, Mass., established 1787 by the Cabot family.

bevygrease: Fat rendered from tallow of the roebuck; deer fat.

Beyers prints: Illustrations by Edward Beyers from *The Album of Virginia*, published 1858. Plates were printed in Berlin and Dresden, Germany. The work was issued from Richmond, Va., and has 40 scenic views of the Old Dominion. Prints are now scarce to rare.

bezel: The ring or retaining border sur-rounding a gem, or a protecting glass as on watches, clocks, et cetera; the frame of a cartouche.

bezoar: Gallstone of a ruminant, as domestic cattle, used as antidote for poison; any poison antidote.

bibelot: Any small and valuable curio; a cabinet item.

biberon: A suckling vessel; a water fount of metal, pottery, or glass with sucking straws, used for convenience of young children. Of ancient Swiss origin. Also a glass-spouted vessel with spout being the only opening.

Bible-back table: Two-leaf table without a top, the leaves falling from a cylindrical section which is completely covered when leaves are up. Term derives from its likeness to a book or Bible when leaves are down. Made from 1790s to 1870s in various furniture styles, including Georgian, Directoire, Sheraton, and Empire. [*Example pictured.*]

Bible box: Plain or carved box to hold a Bible, sometimes with sloping lid. Of Tudor-Gothic style and provenance. Never made with a lock, and if what is considered a Bible box has a lock, it is a desk box or coffer. The Bible was never locked up. Those from 17th century are most revered.

Bible stand: An open-ended box with shelf, mounted on a stand for use in storing and using the Bible in meetinghouse or home. Known in every furniture style from Tudor-Gothic to Empire. [*Example pictured.*]

bibliopegy: The art of binding books.

bibliothèque: A bookcase.

bice: A fine smalt blue; a copper-based color or dye, both blue and green.

biche: Furred doeskin.

bicker: Woodenware. A small staved dish; a miniature shallow tub. Also becker.

Bickford knitter: A machine for knitting made in 1860s. A home machine mounted like a sewing machine on fancy cast-iron supports, operated by a pair of foot treadles. [*Example pictured.*]

Bickham books: Calligraphic or writing exercise books (some are books of maps) published by or for the great calligrapher, John Bickham, whose *Universal Penman*, published 1743 at London, is a classic.

bicorporate: Heraldic; two bodies with one head.

Biddendens: The original charity buns or rolls distributed under the will of the Chulkhurst twins, Elisa and Mary, born joined at hips and shoulders at Biddenden, England, in 12th century. Effigies of the twins were impressed on the buns. [*A mold used 16th to 18th centuries is pictured.*]

biddery: A ware fashioned from an alloy of copper, lead, and tin, inlaid with silver and blackened with salt. Made at Biddery, near Hyderabad, and sold in U.S. from 1830s or earlier. This was a clipper-ship trade item.

Bideford ware & ovens: Pottery ovens and coarse earthenwares from Bideford Pottery, England, especially the portable ovens. These are traditional and were made from 17th century to 1890s. [*Examples of portable ovens pictured.*]

bident: Two-pronged; two-tined.

Biedermeier: A German style of furniture and decoration of the period approximating Empire, Regency, and Second Baroque, 1825–50. The name is that of a comic character created by a German caricaturist.

Bigelow papers: Wallpapers made by J. R. Bigelow of Lynn, Mass., in the 19th century.

biggin: A drip coffee-making device invented by M. Biggin, c. 1800.

Bigler: Pattern of pressed glass in what Ruth Webb Lee calls the colonial group or the Ashburton tradition. Large ovate and rounded panels, slightly convex, with barred separation elements.

Bigler lamp: Hexagonal glass font fluid lamp in the Bigler pattern.

bigney: A charm or fob.

Bihn pottery: Redware and stoneware made at Andreas Bihn's pottery, Cincinnati, from 1850s.

bijouterie: Jewelry.

Bilbao work: Veneering with sheets of marble. Mirror frames, picture frames, table tops, et cetera, were made. 18th and 19th centuries.

bilberry bounce: Fresh bilberry juice mixed half-and-half with rum.

billet: Thumbpiece on a tankard or covered cup, generally in some decorative style or form such as a shell, flower, figure; thumbpiece on pot and kettle handles; small piece of wood; a club.

billet (of paper): A folded piece of writing paper 6 x 8 inches; French letter papers; fancy note paper.

billeted: Decorated with pieces cut from turned, squared, or triangular-cut strips, arranged alternately as a border.

bill hook: A pruning hook. [*Example pictured.*]

billies: Forged medals and coins of pewter, sometimes silver-plated. Name derives from notorious Billy and Charlie, counterfeiting team of English forgers active in mid-19th century.

Billings ware: Transparent salt-glaze ware made after 1722 by Thomas Billings, English potter.

billon: An alloy of copper and silver.

bill yard (bale yard): Tapering rod of 50 or more inches, used in probing bales of wool, cloth, et cetera, the pointed end being called the cue or "q" (questioner). A game played with balls on cloth-covered tables, using these same yards as propelling sticks to strike balls, hence the game of billiards and the naming of the bill yard as the "cue."

bilsted: Sugar-gum wood; the sugar-gum tree. The wood of this tree is somewhat like mahogany and is often found used in early American cabinetwork thought to be mahogany.

Bilston enamels: Brilliant glass glaze on copper enamels made at Bilston, Staffordshire, and Wednesbury, England. Shops at both places made enameled wares and objects from 1750s to 1830s or later. *See* Battersea Enamels. Bilston enamel knobs for curtains and mirrors are well known among connoisseurs. When decorated with such subjects as "Washington's Tomb," "Highlands of the Hudson," and "American Commerce," they were made for the American market.

binders rolls (and flowers): Brass rollers and stamps for bookbinders' use in embellishing leather with blind stamping (with bare dies) or gilt stamping (through gold leaf). J. R. Hoole of New York City was a maker of these dies from 1830s. [*Examples of patterns from his catalogue are pictured.*]

bine: A stem; in ornamentation, an open twist or spiral turning. Any vine was known also as a bine.

Bininger bottles: Specifically, the cannon-shaped bottle for Biningers Bitters; actually any bottles used by this firm of wine merchants from 1810s, New York City.

binnacle: Metallic casing of the compass on shipboard.

binnacle lamp: Lamps used in pairs to illuminate the interior of the binnacle on board ship in order to make the compass card visible for night navigation. Also lamps used in staterooms, affixed to a rod fastened to the wall, providing for sway. [*Examples of latter pictured.*]

birch broom: Shredded birch sticks, the shredding folded down from one end to form a broom, the uncut core being the handle. A native American broom much used by colonists and New Englanders down to late 19th century, and still made and used.

birched ale: Clarified ale, further flavored with birch sap. Not birch beer.

Birch views: Views of Philadelphia and American country seats, scenery, and culture, painted and engraved by William and Thomas Birch, from 1800s. Both plain and hand-colored aquatints are known. They also did some naval battle scenes and were well known in the American scene, 1793–1851.

bird-back: Any chair back having a vase splat so shaped as to reveal a reverse silhouetted outline of birds in pairs, facing. [*Example of chair with such a splat is pictured.*]

bird bottle: Blown-glass bottles with figures of birds, in glass, affixed within; curiosities of glass blowing. One known maker of such fancies was Schlernitzhauer of the Oneida Glass Furnace, mid-19th century.

bird boxes: (1) Music boxes enclosing the animating machinery and bellows to give realistic movement and sound to a bird perched upon the box. (2) Blisted or other enamel boxes with bird figures on lids. Both are 18th century. (3) Glass, pottery, porcelain, and silver boxes in form of birds, generally natural size or smaller, such as hens, ducks, swans, bird-on-nest, et cetera.

bird cage: (1) A structural element of cabinetmaking, the unit of spindles, blocks, and hinges by which a turnable tilt-top table is operated. (2) Wire, rattan, or netted cage for captive birds. (3) All-brass clock of early type, with fretwork finials, brass spindles, and large dial covering the entire façade. (4) A type of Windsor chair with very thin wood or wire spindles.

bird dame: *See* Lady Bird Cage.

Bird-in-Hand: An early tavern sign picturing a hand holding a bird. The significance of this sign is seldom appreciated. The earliest-known tavern sign was a green bush. The bush became anything from a bush to a green tree, as a traditional sign. The Bird-in-Hand sign connoted not only good entertainment but of a quality "worth two in [any] bush." A village in Lancaster County, Pa., is named for a tavern with the Bird-in-Hand sign on the Old King's Highway. Here, from 1820s, Jacob Swope, a potter, made clay pipes which became famous along the Pennsylvania turnpike as favored by Conestoga wagon drivers. These pipes do not bear the sign or device of a bird in the hand.

bird lime: Thick glue used in trapping birds by making them unable to fly. The stuff is made from fermented holly-tree bark, from any of the Ficus trees, and from mistletoe boughs.

Bird-on-Nest compote: Actually, glass Robin-on-Nest, made originally by the Vallerysthal & Portieux Works, Alsace-Lorraine, and copied in blue opaque glass by a Grapeville, Pa., factory. This piece, in the original, is really exclusive pressed glass. It is a butter or sugar dish, and is so designated by Vallerysthal, which made the dishes from 1880s through 1910s.

Birdsall fireboards: Boards to block fireplaces in summer. Decorative paper-covered examples on wood panels made by the thousands by Z. M. Birdsall, N.Y., 1840s to 1860. Birdsall woodenware was not produced by same concern but by D. M. Waters, Cincinnati, trading as Birdsall Co. This latter firm also made fireboards, but chief products were brassbound buckets and tubs, butter churns and butter stamps, in red and white cedar. Worked 1840s and 1850s.

birdseye: Coverlet pattern popular from 1810s to 1840s. [*Example pictured.*]

birds eye: A yellow mottled cloth of 17th century. Pepys' diary, May 14, 1665, states: "A yellow birds eye hood as the fashion is now." Maple wood marked with innumerable fine points, or birds' eyes.

bird spit: Footed drip pan with upright frame having hooks upon which to impale small game or birds for roasting; 17th to 19th century. [*Example pictured.*]

biretta box: Hatboxes of tooled leather made to hold ecclesiastic headgear from service to service.

Birmingham glass: Pressed, free-blown, cut, and fancy (art) glasswares made at the Birmingham Glass Works of O'Leary & Mulvaney, near Pittsburgh, from 1832 to 1860.

Birmingham silver: Fine silver made at Birmingham, England, and shipped to London for marking and sale, to 1773. After that date Birmingham had its own assay office for official marking of silverwares.

bis: A silk fabric, probably of half-silk content.

biscotin: Baked confection of flour, sugar, jam, milk, eggs, and spices.

biscuit: Twice-baked breadstuff. Later usage embraced any quick-baked breadstuff.

biscuit prickle: Small wood stamp with a face having metal pricks to puncture biscuits before baking. These biscuits would be the beaten varieties, or ships' breads.

bishop: A punch made of roasted oranges and lemons in wine.

bishop'd milk: Scorched in boiling.

Bishop furniture: Cabinetwork made by Dwight Bishop, N.Y., established 1825. John Bishop, cabinetmaker of Pittsburgh, made furniture so designated in that region of Pennsylvania from 1830s.

Bishop Hill: Swedish community in Illinois, founded by settlers from Bishops Kulla, Sweden, under leadership of Eric Janson, 1846.

bishop's finger: A signpost.

bishop's size: A portrait size, 58 inches wide and 95 inches high; a half bishop is 56" x 45".

bisque: Unglazed ceramic ware, especially porcelain and stoneware.

bisque doll: Baby or play doll or manikin, made of bisque or Parian parts, articulated; doll with a bisque head.

Bissell ornaments: Molded plaster ornaments, with sawdust or other tempering material, made by the Bissell Co., Hartford, Conn., 1850s–70s. Quite frequently such ornaments were produced from traditional and often very old molds.

bit: Mouthpiece of riding and driving harness. A wide variety of early forms has sparked the collecting of these objects by horsemen and horse lovers.

bitters: Any bitter principle of non-poisonous vegetable origin used as a tonic. Quassia, orange peel, lemon peel, aloe, cascarilla bark, gentian root, ground ivy, walnut husks, hops, rhubarb, byrony, et cetera, were used. Any concoction of alcoholic base with the bitter principle. This was the alcoholic drink of the Prohibitionists and White Ribboners of the 19th century. It is said that most of the teetotal lecturers took big drinks of bitters before and after lecturing.

bitters bottles: Any bottles for bitters, but particularly the odd, special, and curiously shaped bottles made and sold by the millions in the U.S. from 1840s to 1890s. There are 450 recorded examples already identified as to bitters or makers. *Early American Bottles & Flasks*, by Stephen Van Rensselaer, and *American Glass*, by George S. & Helen McKearin, contain additional information.

bittlin: Woodenware. A milk bowl. Pewter, glass, and pottery milk bowls were also designated as bittlins.

black ball: Boot dressing in ball form.

Blackberry: Pattern of pressed glass featuring a wide band of berry and leaf décor. The pattern was issued in milk glass, or "hot cast porcelain."

black boys: Effigies of black boys used as cigar- or tobacco-shop signs in Netherlands and England from 17th century.

black glass: True black glass, in imitation of jet, is rare; the common black glass is not black but deep red and deep green.

blackjack: A leather drinking pot, also called bombard and giskin. The original figural ale pots were of modeled leather; these were ancestors of the pottery Toby jugs.

blackjacks: Molasses candy of a type made at Salem, Mass., from 1830s; sold the world over.

blackletter: Gallic or Gothic type; sometimes called bastard Gothic, sometimes German text, and sometimes Old English.

black metal: Cheap pewter.

blackstrap: Dark amber glass. Probably this term for the color of glass suggested the term also for dark molasses, or vice versa.

black teapots: Early 19th-century term for Jackfield and other teapots of basaltes, jasper, et cetera.

black walnut stain: The early kind was asphaltum dissolved in turpentine.

Blackwell rustic: Rustic piazza and garden cane furniture made by John Blackwell of Brooklyn, N.Y., from 1840s.

blackwood sofas: Imported richly carved sofa frames of Chinese make, made of black or blackened wood imitating ebony, and imitations, generally uncarved, by American cabinet factories. The imports date from 1840s. Some may have been genuine Chinese antiques.

blades: Rafters of a roof frame.

Blake furniture: Trade and customary term for furniture made by Kitteredge & Blake, and by James A. Blake, Boston, mid-19th century.

Blake lamp: Variant of the St. Germain student lamp, patented 1875 by A. M. Blake, Canton, O. Fuel font was hinged to base, enabling user to tilt it to fill. The burner arm extended from bottom of font, to which a strut was also fixed to hold the shade-ring. [*Example pictured.*]

Blakeslee mirror: Looking glass made by E. Blakeslee of Cincinnati, from 1840s. In 1850s this maker produced 2500 mirrors a week. Many are labeled. Various mid-19th-century styles.

blancard: Linen woven from bleached thread.

blanc de chine: All white, undecorated porcelain from China. Made in all the dynasties, but that of Ming period is considered finest.

blanc de sore (blanc desire; blaun-desore): A tasty dish made of blanched almonds, minced capon, and rice flour cooked in wine.

Blanchard, M.: Famed early aeronaut and proprietor of automaton shows from the 1790s.

Blanchard busts: *See* Blanchard Lathe.

Blanchard lathe: One of the great basic inventions of the early 19th century; a lathe that turned irregular shapes such as decoy ducks, shoe lasts, gunstocks, oblong bowls, and hexagonal and square woodenwares. Some of the amazing products of this lathe were busts of wood and *marble*, made in 1840s. Daniel Webster, Judge Woodbury, and other notables were honored with busts turned on the Blanchard lathe.

Blanchard papers: Wallpapers, stained and block-printed, by Blanchard & Haley, Philadelphia, from 1820s. W. F. Slaughter continued the business from 1832.

Blanket, Thomas: The first weaver to loom heavy woolen cloth, said to have worked from c. 1338. His cloth was called "blanket," and that is what we call it to this day.

blanket chest: Any chest having a cavity under a lift-up top or lid, whether with drawers or without. Traditionally, the cavity was used to store blankets and other bedding.

blanket crane: Long tapering arm swinging in heavy wood or metal sockets, generally placed in pairs at either side of a fireplace. When not in use they were folded against chimney breast. In use they were "driers" for clothing, blankets, et cetera. Used also in severe weather as draft stoppers, after the manner of bed curtains.

blanket roller bed: Any bed with a heavy, free-turning roller set between the foot posts. Made from late 18th century to mid-1850s. One tradition is that the roller provided for easy drawing up of blanket. As late as 1900s, however, housewives used the rollers primarily to support the chaff bag, or other mattress, when cleaning and airing the bed.

Blaze: Pattern of pressed glass having vertical ribbing in various lengths, forming a pleasing pattern.

bleaching pot: Redware or stoneware dome with many perforations. Not a sieve, but a blanching cover to place over endive and other garden succulents. [*Example pictured.*]

bleeding bowl: Authorities of the 20th century have asserted that what we call a porringer in America was a bleeding bowl in England. The British antiquarian authority, Edward Wenham, states it is fallacious to designate any single-eared porringer a bleeding bowl unless it has within the bowl a series of numbered ring marks by which the surgeon, or leech, could tell the ounces of blood he was taking from a patient. Dr. J. H. Tilden, a keen student of the curative properties of bleeding, stated in 1932: "Bleeding was a way of causing the patient to fast without his being aware of it. Taking 16 ounces of blood from a sick man was the equivalent of a week of total abstinence from food."

Bleeding Heart: Pattern of pressed glass featuring the leaf and flower of the old-fashioned garden plant. The plant was introduced from China c. 1856.

bleu céleste: Turquoise blue; sky blue.

bleu de ciel: Sky blue.

bleu de roi: Royal blue; cobalt; lapis lazuli.

Blew papers: Domino, flock, and panel wallpapers from the now-famed warehouse of Blew, Aldermanbury, London, established 1689.

blind butts: Concealed hinges.

blind door; blind drawer: Sham door or drawer used to achieve symmetry or divert attention from a secret compartment.

blind fret: Carving imitative of fretwork on solid-wood surface.

blind hinge: A hinge for blinds or window shutters. The Talbot blind hinge, introduced 1846, made operation of outside shutters possible from within without opening window sash.

blind pins: Standard toilet pins with heads of various shapes. Many surviving curiously headed pins of 18th century were most likely blind pins; pins used to enable the blind to read, the heads forming a sort of Braille method.

Bliss & Creighton: Makers of ship chronometers at New York, Boston, and Baltimore from 1840s.

Bliss bulb vases: Hyacinth vases made for, and not by, B. K. Bliss of Springfield, Mass., 1865–75, and marked with his name.

Bliss furniture: Cabinet furniture and chairs by Edward Bliss of Springfield, Mass., 1815 to c. 1835 or 1840. Also work of Pelatiah Bliss of Springfield, 1795–1820s.

Blitz, Signor: French magician who came to U.S. in 1833 and, after making many appearances, settled at Philadelphia, where he conducted a shop and, it is said, made magical paraphernalia.

block: A pulley, in navy parlance.

Block: Pattern of pressed glass made up of evenly spaced, bevel-edged blocks in all-over application. There are variants, such as Block with Fan, Block with Thumbprint, et cetera.

Blockade: Pattern of pressed glass featuring geometrical blocks with fans and lozenges.

block & card matches: Two forms of same style of early friction matches. The block form was a square cube of wood almost cut through lengthwise to form many upright splinters, all tipped with the firing substance. The card form used thin sheets of wood, almost cut through, to form rows of matches, similar to modern book matches.

Block & Panel: Pattern of pressed glass featuring hexagonal blocks in all-over pattern, broken vertically with narrow plain panels.

block carpet: A coverlet and carpeting pattern popular from c. 1810 to 1340s. Various forms of basic pattern are known. [*Two examples pictured.*]

blocked linen: Linen cloth decorated by block printing. Fast dyes were applied in a pattern from wooden blocks.

block foot: The block terminal of furniture legs when larger than the leg proper; any square end on a furniture leg; a spade-type foot without slope or taper.

block front: Alternate projecting and recessing surfaces, rounded at junctures, on drawer, door, and framed parts of cabinet or case furniture, yielding a magnificent façade. The most famous exponents of the style were Goddard and Townsend of Newport, R.I., working from 1740s to 1780s. When the blocking is elegant and pronounced, terminating in shells or fans, furniture of this type is perhaps the most desirable in the American scene. The style, however, is now known to have originated in China, reaching the colonies through either the Netherlands, Italy, or France. An example of the Newport block-front work of c. 1760 is pictured, together with the prototype in Baroque style (Venetian-made) dating from c. 1700–25. The continental European block-front cabinet furniture was generally japanned or lacquered, and decorated in gold.

block tin: Generic name for pure tin cast in blocks; any utensil or object made from block tin. Block tinware is not tin-plated sheet ironware.

blond lace: Fine lace made from silken or linen threads. Much used during 1750–70 period on women's and men's clothing. Most of it came from Buckinghamshire, England.

blood alley: A red-colored play marble; a red ball.

blood of Christ: The fuchsia flower.

bloomers: Baggy, ankle-length drawers designed for wear under a short skirt, a style developed and advocated by Amelia Bloomer in opposition to crinolines and hoop skirts in the mid-19th century as part of the "equality for women" movement.

bloom of roses: A rouge that wouldn't rub off, made by Hunt, perfumer of Philadelphia, from 1850s.

bloom vase: Double-walled blown-glass vase, generally clear but sometimes with enamel decoration. Has a very short receptacle or' well to hold the stem of a single flower. Made from 1850s. Some claim these were made to hold quill pens and not flowers. [*Example pictured.*]

Blossom: Pattern of enameled glass of the 1890s; the décor is stem, leaf, and blossom on clear glass.

blotter butter: Rich cream poured on blotting paper, which absorbed the liquids and left the fat, sweet butter as a deposit. This was spooned or scraped off and used.

blow accordeon: Known also as "melodeonette." A ten-key bellows instrument.

blown mold: Reference is generally to the method or technique of blowing glass in forming molds which, made in from two to seven or more pieces, unfolded to permit removal of finished object. Also, glass pattern and form achieved in part by blowing a parison of glass in an open mold, and then expanding and so enlarging the pattern impressed by the mold.

blown-mold lens chimney: A lamp chimney blown in a three-piece mold which impressed over a thousand small lenslike forms within the flame-covering area of the chimney.

blown salt: Late 19th-century term for a fine table salt. Now generally meaning any salt cellar of blown glass.

blowpipe: Glass blowers' most important tool; an iron tube, one end of which acted as the gathering rod to hold a parison of hot molten glass and the other end as a mouthpiece through which the glassmaker blew to expand the parison of glass for working into form or shaping in a pattern mold. Also the small pipe used by chemists, jewelers, and silversmiths. Blowing through the tube directed a flame on objects to be melted, soldered, calcined, or softened.

blowpipe lamp: Metal lamp with spout and wick, generally burning alcohol or spirits of wine. Used in blowpipe soldering, testing, et cetera. *See* Blowpipe.

bludgeon gun: An all-brass bludgeon with a concealed hammer and trigger, firing a charge through a one-inch bore barrel in the handle. Made from 1830s. Sometimes called a Billycock pistol.

blue & gold Lowestoft: Oriental export

porcelain brought home by our early commercial traders after 1790s. Generally found with blue decoration and some gold stars or other gilding.

bluebird potter: Probably deriving from "jaybird" or "bird," meaning a part-time worker at a trade. Generally a farmer who operated a pottery on the side, firing but a few kilns a year.

bluebottle blue: The blue field flowers, half dried and kneaded into a paste with gum arabic, pressed into sheets, dissolved, and strained. The remainder, after evaporation, was used as a blue pigment.

blue-dash charger: Early tin-glaze plate decorated with tulips, other flowers, or figures, generally further embellished with a rim of dashes in blue pigment, hence blue-dash chargers. Many so-called Pennsylvania-German designs are lifted from blue-dash chargers as made in England from the 1660s. Most of the examples found seem to have been made in and around Bristol.

blued white: Any white pigment, to every hundred pounds of which was added one ounce of lampblack and one ounce of ultramarine blue.

blue earthenware: Mottled and streaked blue-glaze earthenware made at Staffordshire or Lambeth from the Elizabethan period. Some examples have silver-banded lips and covers. Now quite rare. This type of ware is earlier than the German tigerware-glazed pots of somewhat the same size and shape.

blue resist: A term generally meaning resist-dyeing in blue color; a form of batik, using only Royal Dutch blue dye. Patterns are generally of Chinese or Far Eastern influence, some Javanese.

blues songs: Properly "bi'you" or bayou plaints and tunes, popularized into blues songs. The originals were the singsong of New Orleans street peddlers.

blue spatter: Staffordshire spatter said to have been made for the U.S. market. A spatter of blue begins at the edges of the ware, shading to natural toward centers, where additional and different décor is placed, such as birds, flowers, houses, et cetera.

blue stoneware: Stoneware pottery which generally, if decorated, is embellished with blue figures, scrolls, et cetera.

blue wood: Wood dyed blue on the surface before varnishing.

blunderbuss: Pistol or gun with barrel having a slightly outflaring mouth or muzzle. The exaggerated bell- or trumpet-mouthed gun of many late pictures of 17th-century colonial days never existed, and examples looking anything like them are not considered authentic.

Blunt instruments: Edward and George Blunt, instrument makers, produced nautical barometers and other devices which are often thus referred to in nautical collecting circles.

Blyth furniture: Cabinetwares made by James Blyth of Lafayette, Ind., from early 1850s. Surprisingly, a great deal of his work was in the Greek-revival and Empire styles.

board chest: Any chest made, simply and without pretense at design, from boards nailed or mortised to stiles and ends.

Many 17th- and 18th-century chests were plain board chests.

board cloth: Tablecloth or table carpet. Shelf cloths, often with a ruffle or other valance. Used from 16th century or earlier.

Boardman & Gray pianos: Musical instruments made by this firm at Albany, N.Y., which seems to date from 1840s.

Boardman Britannia: Hard alloy utensils known as Britannia, made by the Boardman Co. of Hartford, Conn., from 1850s or earlier. They produced many thousands of tea sets and other items in French Baroque and French Empire styles. Frequently marked.

boards (BOOKBINDING): Stiff book covers which originally were thin boards of wood but which, by 1700, were generally of binder's board (a kind of cardboard) or paperboard.

boat cradle: A small boat, large enough to serve as a baby's bed, properly built with ribs, stern, and prow, of clinkered or leap-streaked planking, suspended on supports to swing as a cradle. Rare but not unique, and dating from last half of 18th century. [*Example pictured.*]

boaters: Flat-brimmed straw hats originally worn by gentlemen punting on the Thames, or yachting. Popular from 1880s as a man's summer hat for all occasions. Replicas in glass, porcelain, and so on, were sold as souvenirs and novelties, often with name of resort on or inside the hat.

boat stand: Silver or Sheffield-plate tray in form of a boat, having wells to hold decanters or wine bottles.

Boaz tea set: Lusterware tea utensils featuring Boaz, the biblical character.

bobbin frame; bobbin-turned: Both terms refer to turned framing (as a chair), the turnings simulating rows of bobbins separated by rings. Names of turning for the objects simulated are entirely sound; wood turners could turn actual bobbins, spools, and button forms. [*Examples of bobbin turning pictured.*]

bobêches: Flat or slightly dished saucer-like rings placed around candles at bases to stop wax drippings. Examples of silver, brass, pewter, tinned sheet iron, japanned iron, china, glass, and wood are known. Some have rims drilled with a series of tiny holes to which pendent prisms were affixed.

bocage: Same as boscage, *which see.*

bocasin: Buckram.

Boch porcelain: American porcelain made by William Boch & Bros., Brooklyn, N.Y. In 1850 the pottery produced door and furniture knobs, pitchers, mugs, vases, and fancy wares—"porcelain lambs, images and decorative objects for home and cemetery."

bocking: Carpet lining or cheap carpeting.

Bodmer, Karl: Swiss artist who made drawings to illustrate Maximilian of Wied's *Travels in the Interior of North America*, a large book of splendid views, ranging in size from 10" x 12" to 17¼" x 23¼". The prints were made by Ackerman of London, and the work published in 1840.

Boerums: Occasional century-old reference of this term seems to mean cigar box and tobacco labels produced for most manufacturers by S. Boerum of Philadelphia, 1840-60.

bogie: A pair of trailing wheels; a wagon made up of a set of cart wheels and a bogie with extending connecting pole, used in hauling lumber of any length. Sometimes the meaning is a lambskin (*see* Bogy).

bog oak: Oakwood immersed in bogs as a seasoning process; a medieval technique that rendered the oak almost impervious either to dry or wet rot.

bog shoe: A platform of thin boards worn on the feet in traversing marshes, bogs, and fens. [*Example pictured.*]

Bogue furniture: Cabinetwork by John Bogue of Alexandria, Va., made from 1790s. Some fine Hepplewhite- and Directoire-style work is reported.

bogy; bogie rug: A lambskin.

Bohemian figurines: Often mistaken for Staffordshire; chinaware figurines of comic, satirical, sentimental, and trade subjects marked F&R, CF, and F&M were made in Bohemia (Czechoslovakia) in 19th century. After 1892 they are marked with country of origin.

Bohemian glass: Bohemian techniques of glassmaking derive not from Germany but from Venice and the Orient. Practically all fine German glassmaking and cutting techniques derive from Bohemia. Famed for its overlaid or color-flashed glass, which was richly cut and gilded, its ruby red is perhaps the best known of the flashed cut Bohemian glass. This country also produced green, blue, yellow, black, and other color-flashed and cut wares, plain (clear) crystal wares, cut crystal and engraved wares. A considerable quantity of Bohemian glass was imported by U.S. firms from 1820s. Much imitative "Bohemian" was also imported from Germany, England, Switzerland, and other countries, to sell "cheap."

bohemianism: Lackadaisical, unorthodox living in an atmosphere of wine, women, and song. Term derives from poor Bohemian art students in Paris who lived this life. Often imitated by the successful as a device to escape from orthodoxy. Also the term used to designate the ghost writers of a century ago.

boiled wood: Lathe turners preferred woods previously boiled in wood-ash lye water, as it provided better timber for turning.

bois durci: Wood filings, sandings, and raspings mixed with ox blood or animal gelatins, molded in forms to imitate medallions, carvings, and to make drawer handles and pulls.

Boker's Bitters: Medicated cordial of the 1830s. Bottles marked with name of contents.

bolder-bottomed: Rush-seated.

bole: Viscid earths of soft, oily character, as "Armenian" bole, Bohemian bole, French bole, et cetera. Used in medicine, the arts, and the crafts.

bolection molding: Literally, the molding on the outer edge of a panel. Now, generally, a heavy molding used to frame a wall section, a fireplace opening, or an archway.

bolled: (From *bollynged.*) To cause to swell or extend, as bolled flax.

Bolles, D.: A marble sculptor of Cincinnati who enjoyed some fame in the 1830s.

bollicky: Bare; naked; nude.

bolts head: Glass vessel with long neck, terminating in a conical shape.

bombace; bombast; bombays: Raw cotton or stuffing. Hence bombastic, stuffy, a stuffed shirt.

bombard: A leather drinking mug; a blackjack; a piece of ordnance.

bombax: Silky cotton.

bombay: Same as bombé.

bombazine; bombazet: Plain twilled unglazed cotton cloth, generally dyed black. Also a fabric of cotton and wool, or silk and wool.

bombé: To bulge, swell out, or extend; kettlebottomed. [*A bombé cabinet is pictured.*]

Bonaparte birds: Small folio bird prints from the L. Bonaparte supplement to *Wilson's Ornithology.* There are 27 hand-colored prints from drawings by Peale and Ryder, engraved by Lawson. *See* Wilson Prints.

bonbonnière: Sweetmeat box or candy container.

boncours: Tapestrylike fabric of 17th century.

bone china: English ware, neither hardnor soft-paste porcelain, and in many ways superior to both. The Meissen discovery was a solving of an old secret held by the Chinese. Soft paste is a good imitation of Chinese porcelain. English bone china is neither imitative of soft paste nor the true porcelain; it is the Western world's own discovery and invention.

bone glass: Alabasterlike milky glass achieved by addition of calcined animal teeth and bones.

bone lace: Lace made with bone bobbins.

bonesetter: Specialist in hip, joint, and fracture reduction; early osteopath; sometimes also medical practitioners. Dr. Job Sweet was still practicing bonesetting at New Bedford, Mass., in 1857. Dr. Still became famous as a successful physician in Civil War practicing without the needed drugs. He founded science of osteopathy.

bone soup: Animal bones cleaned and crushed, then cooked into a rich gelatinous soup. Cox, of Edinburgh, Scotland, first made a commercial product by dehydrating the soup; his product was Cox's gelatin.

bonheur du jour: A small intimate cabinet on stand, with shelves, drawers, and top.

Bonner's Boston: A view or prospect (plan) of Boston by Bonner, engraved by Francis Dewing, 1722. A rare print of colonial America.

bonnes craces: Narrow panels of fabric, preferably ornamental in weave and color, used as hangings for the head section of a high post bed.

bonnet chest: The true bonnet chest is a cupboard for millinery. Term is now sometimes applied to 19th-century cottage toilet cabinet used in bedrooms, the proper name of which is toilet stand.

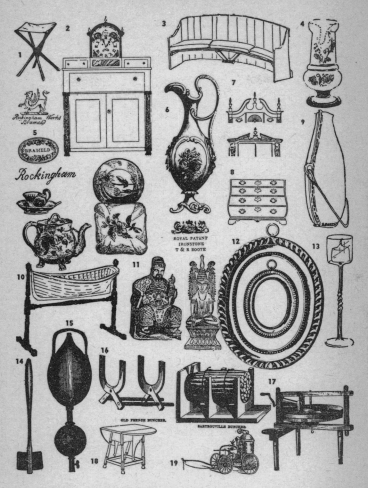

1, Baseball Stool. 2, Bureau Clock. 3, Bow Settle. 4, Bloom Vase. 5, Brameld "Rock-ingham" Marks; shell cup and saucer, teapot and two plates. 6, Boote, T & R, Pottery Mark and Ewer. 7, Bonnet Tops. 8, Bombé Form. 9, Bootleggers' Bottle. 10, Boat Cradle. 11, Boodhs. 12, Brass Oval Mirror Frames. 13, Burglar's Horror Night Lamp. 14, Bung Starter. 15, Bonnet Filter. 16, Bunchers. 17, Butter Wheel. 18, Butterfly Table. 19, Buckman Steam-Toy Fire Engine. (Nos. 5 and 6 from Virtue & Co., London.)

bonnet cupboard chest: Generally a Hepplewhite-style chest-on-chest, the lower section of which is fitted with a bonnet cupboard.

Bonnet filter: Portable filter designed to be affixed to a faucet, consisting of an India-rubber bag with fastening strap, flannel filtering cloths, and terminating in a porous globe of earthenware pottery. Invented by Louis Bonnet of the *Courier des Etats Unis,* the French-American newspaper, in 1849. [*Example pictured.*]

bonnet paper: Cardboard made up of four to six sheets of paper, laminated with glue size, and used to make bonnet forms. Date of use seems to be 1790-1870.

bonnet top: Any broken arch or pedimented top, or any scroll top, converging on a central finial urn, flame, et cetera. Also hooded top, scroll top, swan-neck top. [*Several examples pictured.*]

Bonnin & Morris: Proprietors of the Southwark porcelain works at Philadelphia, 18th century, professing to make porcelains as good as Bow. Known mark is small capital "P." Exceedingly rare, only a few pieces known.

bonspiel: The Dutch term for the Scottish winter sport of curling, in which ovate granite stones, highly polished, are slid to a marker on ice. This sport was indulged in by gentlemen of New Amsterdam in 17th century.

Bonte mirrors: A. P. C. Bonte of Cincinnati, 1850s-70s, made hundreds of thousands of mirrors for the Ohio-Mississippi Valley trade. Many examples were marked with a lithographed label bearing a picture of the factory.

booby sleigh: Coupé body on skids or snow runners.

Boodhs: Effigies of Gaudama Boodh and the Chinese Boodh were highly prized by connoisseurs of the 18th century. They were generally called pagoda, a term now reserved apparently for the nodding figures of Eastern gods and prophets. They are known in porcelain, jade, bronze, tutenag (white brass), teak, ebony, palisander, and other woods. Some examples of japanned papier-mâché are known. [*Two examples pictured.*]

bookbinder's calico: Thin cloth, gluesized, printed decoratively in colors from wood blocks for use in covering books.

book-bottomed: Bases of toilet stands or the cabinets of same, having a rounded section similar to back spine of a book.

book box: Japanned and decorated tinned sheet-iron boxes in form of books, used primarily as school lunch boxes from 1860s.

book carrier: Long tray with handles and colonnade at back, serving as a portable book rack. Date is from 18th century.

book desk: Lectern; a stand with steeply sloping top to hold a book for reading. Used from early 15th century; many in Gothic style.

book label: A small tag of bookbinder's leather with gilt-stamped border and name of owner, generally purchased by the hundreds for gluing on one's own book covers. Many lawyers still use this device for marking books in their law library.

book matches: An idea dating from the 1850s, when issued as sheets of thin

wooden matches in a cover. Patented as a new idea in 1892 and produced by Diamond Match Co. about 1897. The first one issued was an advertisement of Mendelssohn Opera Co.; second, Pabst Brewery; third, American Tobacco Co. Since then at least one million different advertisers, local and national, have used them. The feature match (with matches in form of tube of tooth paste, a banana, a chef, et cetera) was patented on the notching of the top, which made it possible for a row of matches to lie flat. This notching was a feature of early matches. These flatlying, notched-top, sheet-type matches were issued in the 1860s and are known with printed advertising impressed on the sheets of wood making up the rows of matches. The only book on the history of matches in America now current is that issued by the Diamond Match Co. about ten years ago.

book mirror: Personal small mirror in a book-form case, generally of leather but sometimes of hardwood, metal, horn, ivory, et cetera. 17th- and 18th-century bibelots.

book press: Artisan's device generally used to press books after binding, or to take the curl out of bindings affected by humidity. Large personal libraries had them of walnut or mahogany, but most are of oak or maple and were used by bookbinders in their shops.

bookrack: A cabinet piece with shelves set at an angle, but with a flat top.

books about glass: *See* Bibliography.

book sprinkler: Decoratively japanned sheet-iron container in the shape of a book, the spine opening to hold the tube and nozzle of a sprinkling can, the body serving as a water container. Used in homes to water house plants. Made by D. R. Browlow of Middletown, Conn., from 1860. [*Example pictured.*]

book stand: A sloping board with wings affixed at angles, mounted on a pedestal or four-legged support having shelves, for use in supporting a large volume (as a dictionary) kept open constantly for reference. Early examples date from 1770s. Also called a wine stand or wine rack, *which see.* [*Pictured under that term.*]

book stops: Pairs of cast-iron figures of dogs, fish, and other animals. Each half is flattened on one side, so that standing together they make a complete figure. Used as book ends or book stops. Some were made in cast glass. A novelty of the Godey era, from 1845.

boom town: Any town springing up rapidly to house employees and merchants, gamblers and other hangers-on attracted by intense activity in mining, lumbering, oil drilling, cattle raising, fishing, et cetera.

boondoggling: Engagement in idle pastime, whittling, pottering, hanky-panky, amateur craftsmanship activity. Now generally meaning useless effort, stupid waste of public funds, overemployment of stupid personnel. Term was used to connote all such political employment from mid-19th century.

Boone pottery: Stonewares produced by Thomas G. Boone & Sons Pottery at

Brooklyn, N.Y., from 1830s. Pots, jugs, pitchers, and general housewares.

boorslaps: Coarse linen.

booson; bushon; boozings: A manger for cattle.

boot & shoe bottles: Cheap perfume bottles of novelty form in shape of boots and shoes, popular as cheap wares in 1870s and 1880s. Also called leg bottles.

boot airer: A wire mesh rack or stand to hold and dry boots by the fireside.

Boote china: T. & R. Boote acquired the Waterloo Potteries, Burslem, England, in 1850. Shortly thereafter they perfected and patented a method of stenciling on pottery by pouring colored slip over paper patterns which, upon setting, was covered with other colored slips, all within a mold, which was finally filled with clay and the whole fired. This firm made many varieties of wares of decorative nature, using various patented processes, and a complete line of plain and decorated granite (sometimes called ironstone) for the American market. [*Certain of the wares and some of the marks are pictured.*]

boot glass: A drinking glass in the shape of a boot. Some examples date from 1600s. Some are engraved and cut. Later examples from 19th century were made as match and toothpick holders.

bootjacks: Cast-iron bugs, pistols, naked women, lyres, and other objects, all having arms or tentacles extended to grasp the heel of a boot and "jack" it loose from the wearer's foot. Examples in brass are also known. Said to date from 1750s in the forms here noted. Many examples of all wood, or wood and metal, date from an earlier period. All sorts made down to 1880s.

bootjack splat: A chair-back splat in the general shape of a bootjack. Some Swedish chairs of 17th century display this splat, as do many all-wood kitchen and cheap dining chairs of the 1840–90 period. [*Examples pictured.*]

bootleggers' bottle: Flat leather bottle carried in one's boots as a place of concealment for illicit trade in or the smuggling of ardent spirits. Noted in general use along the English coastal areas from 1690s, when the spirits tax encouraged this form of beating the King's excise men. Origin of term "bootlegger." [*Example pictured.*]

bootwear glasses: Drinking glasses in the form of slippers, shoes, and boots, traditionally a glassmakers' vagary from 17th century, but made commercially in quantities in 18th and 19th centuries. A tremendous number made from 1860 to 1900.

Booz bottle: E. G. Booz, liquor dealer and rectifier of Philadelphia, used a glass bottle in the form of a log cabin as the commercial container for his Log Cabin whiskey. Probably origin of colloquial term "booze" for any strong drink.

borachio: A leather or pigskin bottle.

borax: Garish, imitative, trashy, junky, or faked merchandise; cheap goods; poor taste, concerned with outward show and gaudiness. Therefore, "borax" shop or "borax" furniture are terms of derision.

borax gliding: Gold leaf powdered with mineral borax and gum arabic, used as a pigment with water and painted on glass. When dry, this was fired at low temperature, which fluxed the borax and thus cemented the gold to the glass.

borde: A portable or knock-down dining table consisting of a board or boards placed over trestles or saw bucks.

Bordesly: A tapestry woven in England at a branch of the Barcheston Works, Warwickshire.

borel: Coarse woolen cloth.

borler: A clothier.

borne: A circular divan or sofa.

borning (borning room): The mistress's room; a winter bedroom. **borning party:** A jollification held in a mother's bedroom after successful childbirth.

borstels: Bristles.

boscage: Woody verdure, shrubbery, planting, trees, woodland. Also bosc, bosky.

bosom bottles: Miniature bouquet holders of silver, glass, and other substances, fastened to busks or suspended between the breasts of women wearing the 18th-century version of a plunging neckline. Glass ones were advertised in Boston, 1756.

Bossi work: Marble inlay. Technique is of ancient origin, but one Bossi, of Dublin, in late 18th century revived the art and so earned the use of his name to describe it.

Boston bath: The Multum in Parvo bath pan, which had a pump operated by occupant that sprayed water over the body. In use from 1840s. [*Example pictured.*]

Boston chair: Cheap maple chairs, not of the period, in Queen Anne and Georgian styles, made in quantities for sale by cabinetmakers and upholsterers. Sometimes also designated by the term "New England" chairs. Both terms should be abandoned, as they do not clarify, but confuse.

Boston crown glass: Product of the Boston Crown Glass Co., organized 1790 and continuing in operation to 1820s. Hollow wares and window glass were made.

Boston glass (Cambridge): The Boston Porcelain & Glass Co., established 1814, produced fine plain-blown, cut, and engraved wares within two years and then, before Sandwich, made fine pressed glass —Amberina, mercury, and other specialties and novelties. Moved to Ohio, 1888, under Libby management. Other companies making glass at Boston and in the Boston area were: South Boston Flint Glass Co., from 1825; Boston Flint Glass Co., from 1830; and American Flint Glass Works from 1848. In 1847 the Boston Directory listed the following as manufacturers of glass: Boston & Sandwich Co.; Thomas Cains, Jarves & Cormerais; Joseph H. Lord; New England Glass Co.; John A. Preston, J. K. Dunham and G. L. Mitchell were listed as glass-cutting establishments. Students should refer to Books about Glass for further data, and particularly to *Cambridge Glass* by Lura Woodside Watkins.

Boston Newsletter: Name of Boston's (and the colonies') first newspaper, established 1704.

Boston rocker: Mass-produced stick,

plank, and board chair developed as a rocker, perhaps in Connecticut, but now generally known as "Boston." It is related to the Windsor chair and is therefore in the Gothic tradition. Early examples are best in terms of shaped roll-front seats, good bends or rockers, and fine stencil and free-hand decoration on various background paints. Developed in the late 1830s, this chair became one of the most popular items in the American home. Scores of companies made Boston-type rockers to the 1890s. It seems certain that all Boston rockers were factory-made. There are variants called Salem rockers. Production was not limited to sale in the U.S. Exports to the West Indies, Central and South America, Australia, Africa, continental Europe, Asia, India, Turkey, and the Scandinavian countries are of record. [*Examples pictured, with some of the features detailed.*]

Boston silver glass: Vases, chalices, goblets, elegancies, doorknobs, curtain hold-backs, mirror bosses, and similar objects made in the mercury technique, by which the silvering was sealed between double walls of glass and therefore could not tarnish. Great quantities were produced between 1850 and 1870s.

Boston terra cotta: Decorative and architectural wares of the hard-fired red stoneware generically known as terra cotta, by the Boston Terra Cotta Co., from 1870s. Only the decorative vases, figural forms, and garden ornaments are collected and are often considered older than the actual date of manufacture.

botano: Blue linen cloth.

boteler: A "butler"; the server of bottles and custodian of the salt. Also called a "panter," meaning pantry attendant.

botenyngs: Probably a variant of "buttonings" or "buttony," meaning aids, assistants, helpers.

botijo: An apothecary's jar.

Böttger, Johann Friedrich: An alchemist and faker who, professing to know the secret of making gold from base metals, found the secret of making true porcelain in the Chinese manner while experimenting to make a better crucible. The result was the establishment of the Meissen Porcelain Works. The secret was kept for seven years, but thereafter Sèvres, France, took the leadership in European porcelain production. Other factories were set up in Germany, notably the Royal Works at Berlin.

bottle & ball: A vagary of the Carolean era; a decorative form of carving and inlay featuring a diamond, upright within a rectangle, with bottle forms at corners and three balls across center. [*Example pictured.*]

bottle bird: Colloquial 18th-century term for a baked apple dumpling.

bottle box: Turned container of hardwood in the general shape of a bottle, made for use as protective covering. Maple, holly, and boxwood were favored. These boxes generally part at the shoulder, have a screw turned in the base section and a thread in the top section. 19th century.

bottle collector: A gatherer of old bottles and glassware shards who sold the broken stuff to glass companies as cullet and the whole bottles for reuse. So common was this practice that a federal law was enacted prohibiting the reuse of wine and spirit bottles. There were active bottle collectors in operation to the 1880s. Some had so extensive a business they advertised in local directories.

bottle asparagus: Not preserved, but grown in bottles placed over the shoots or spears as they appeared. The vegetable grew inside the bottle, often filling it. The bottles were broken to remove the succulent.

bottled ceiling: Empty bottles embedded in the plaster of a ceiling to act as a sound deadener. A 19th-century acoustical practice.

bottle glass: Two bottles of same size, one filled with fine sand, joined mouth to mouth with wax, fixed within a frame, and serving as a time-measuring device. "Glass" means hourglass.

bottle molding: A round molding.

bottle pitcher: A glass pitcher formed in a bottle mold, the neck expanded, and a pouring nose achieved by tooling.

bottle slider: A wheeled tray or coaster for bottles, used to slide one or more bottles across or around a table. Advertised in the colonies as early as 1770s.

bottle tickets (labels, tags): Small labels on chains to hang around necks of bottles, bearing the name of contents, such as sherry, sack, madeira, rum, gin, et cetera. Known in ivory, silver, gold, pewter, Sheffield plate, enamel, tin, and other substances. 18th and 19th centuries.

bottle tray: Rimmed or galleried tray used to hold bottles in service at table.

bottom-marked spoon: A fad or fancy of last quarter of the 18th century. Bottoms of spoon bowls were engraved or chased in design or pattern. All are believed to be English. According to Arthur Sussel of Philadelphia, the vogue for these spoons was not general, and it is doubtful if it reached America. Some few American silver spoons of early 19th century do have decorative marks on underside of bowls and at juncture with handles.

bouche cup: A shell for creamed meats or fish, generally of metal or hard-fired ceramic ware.

bouclé: A burl; a buckle or ring; a yarn having loops which, in weaving, produced pleasing irregularities in the cloth.

boudoir match safe: A tin dispensing box for matches patented 1865 and distributed free with a box of matches by Universal Match Co. The dispenser is marked "Boudoir."

Bouffioux ware: Stoneware of the Netherlands made at Bouffioux, now in Belgium, from early 1500s. The original bearded-man, or Bellarmine, jugs were made here. Potteries were at Bouffioux until 19th century.

bough pot: Decorative china pots with perforated lids arranged to support boughs of flowering and budding shrubs.

bouillote lamp: A gaming-table lamp; sometimes a holder for pairs or threes of candles. Bouillote is a French card game, somewhat similar to poker. The same name is applied to, or may derive from, the name of a kettle or boiler. **bouillote table:** A gaming or card table.

boul: An iron hoop.

boulden: Swollen.

boule: A bowl, especially a deep bowl for serving wine, ale, and beer; a drinking bowl of silver, pewter, wood, brass, et cetera.

Boule (Boulle), André Charles: French cabinetmaker who either invented or perfected the metal and shell inlay known as Buhl or Boule work. Born in 1642, Boule, at 25, was a member of the Academy of Arts. He had four sons and several pupils who carried on the work. It is achieved by cementing thin layers of metal and shell together and then cutting out the design through all the layers with fine band saws. Since the cutting was accurate, the various parts fitted together. The metal was either the outline or the background; therefore the terms "Buhl" and "Counter Buhl" are applied to pattern and background respectively.

boultinge: A cloth or haircloth strainer; a hair sieve.

boulting hutch: A box into which flour was filtered through a boulting temse, or sieve.

Boulton Sheffield: Plate made by Matthew Boulton & Co., Sheffield, of fine-quality silver sheeting over copper. Registered mark was a "sun." 18th and 19th century.

bouncers: Iron play marbles.

bounder: From *Boundee.* Indentured servant or redemptioner.

bouquetier: Vase of classic form, often with niches and figural décor. Also a ceremonial drinking glass somewhat like a *tazza* or large champagne cup.

bouquet lightning rod: Copper leaf and flower finials used on lightning rods. Examples cut from tops of old rods have been used decoratively without the original use being suspected. [*Example pictured.*]

bouquet table: Any small marble-topped table or stand, but particularly the Baroque-revival small tables with marble tops generally called Victorian.

bourbonia: Bronchial and pulmonary disease nostrum of 1850s, made from Kentucky bourbon whiskey.

bourette: Raw-silk cloth woven from knotty floss and having a delightful pattern effect caused by the knots. Also linen and cotton fabrics woven in the same style.

Bourne furniture: Cabinet, case, and seat furniture made at the factory of Joseph Bourne, Indianapolis, Ind., from 1850s. Mostly Baroque-revival styles.

Bourne pottery: Biscuit-colored, brown, and cream stonewares of low cost, produced by J. Bourne & Son at Denby, near Derby, England. Hunting jugs, bottles, breadbaskets, flower stands, cheese dishes, and many other objects.

bout: A bend, or curvate section; a "round."

Bouvier furniture: Michelle Bouvier was a French cabinetmaker of Philadelphia in the first quarter of the 19th century. His stock was sold by T. B. Freeman, Oct. 31, 1833, and included 30 hair-seated sofas, two wardrobes, 13 pairs of tables, 10 worktables, 24 music stools, 50 easy chairs, 8 pairs card tables, 9 pairs dining tables, 3 sideboards, et cetera. 300,000 feet of veneer were also sold. Freeman issued a catalogue for the sale.

Bovey Tracey: Pottery center in Devonshire producing wares similar to the commoner wares of Staffordshire. Among the potteries active to mid-19th century were Indiho, Bovey, Folly, and Bovey Tracey.

Bow: An early English porcelain of really fine quality, now collected by specialists and connoisseurs. *See* Bow China & Porcelain.

bow & arrow tea set: Lusterware tea sets having the bow and arrow as a decorative element.

bow beater: Egg beater of wood operated by pulling a stringed bow back and forth. Used in making syllabub, whipped cream, and as a swizzle stick. [*Example pictured.*]

Bow china & porcelain: First recorded china establishment at Stratford-le-Bow is that of Heylyn & Frye in 1744, who obtained patents to make, decorate, and vend china- or porcelain ware equal to that obtained from abroad. Weatherby & Crowther appear to have been the owners in 1750, and the pottery was known as New Canton, evidence that the wares were considered to be in the Chinese taste. In 1753 a warehouse and shop were opened in Cornhill, London. In its heyday the Bow works employed 300 people, 90 of whom were china painters. In 1775 it was sold to William Duesbury of the Derby works and merged with the latter potteries. [*An example of dated New Canton and other pieces of Bow china, together with certain of the early marks, are pictured.*]

Bowditch sofa: Sofas of mid-19th century with reversible seat; one side was upholstered and the other fitted with a mattress to convert to a bed. Made by E. B. Bowditch, New Haven, Conn., and by several other licensed manufacturers. A sofa bed.

bowed settle: High-backed settles that are actually sections or arcs of a semicircle, originally made for use in meetinghouses and churches. The date may be as early as 1660s. The fashion continued throughout 17th and 18th centuries, especially in the Non-Conformist meetinghouses. [*Example pictured.*]

Bowen, Abel: Prolific wood engraver who flourished in late 18th and early 19th centuries. He engraved innumerable wood blocks for book, newspaper, and poster illustrations and is known to have engraved the now exceedingly rare copperplate of the U.S. frigate *Constitution.* So desirable is this print that facsimiles issued in 1904 had a sale record of over $100 each.

bower: A bedchamber. Also elided to bure or bo'er.

Bowers ware: Pottery made at the Jacob Bowers pottery, Philadelphia, from c. 1790s.

bow kit: A large can with cover.

bow knife: Sharp sickle-shaped knife carried in the bow of a canal barge to sever tow ropes wrongly handled by passing craft.

Bowknot Cut: Pattern of cut glass, patented 1886 by W. Leighton. The bowknot is actually a shell form of cutting with fans, lozenges, and diagonal ridged panels.

bowler churn: Butter churn having a tin cylinder turned by a pendulum movement; a mechanical churn.

Bowles Toby: Engraving of the character Toby Fillpot, published by Carrington Bowles, print seller of London, 18th century.

bowl salt: Goblet-shaped saltcellars of glass; many made in 18th century, and some in American colonial glasshouses. The shape seems to have originated at the Bristol, England, glasshouses.

bowl turning: Same as cup turning, as found on cabinet furniture of the William & Mary period.

bow-shanked: Bow-legged.

bow stave: The choicest of straight-grained yew wood, hawthorn, or hazel, reserved for making the longbow, *which see.*

bowtel: Convex molding.

bow tongs: Sugar tongs introduced in late 18th century; a tong fitted with cups at ends for lifting a piece of broken cane sugar from a bowl or dish. Some have cupped hands, some fingers, and other terminals. Ancestor of today's sugar tongs.

bow wheels: Pairs of baskets used in trapping lobsters and crabs.

bow window pier glass: High, narrow decorative frames for mirrors used between the sash of bow windows. 18th century.

box & board table: Two boxlike cabinets with drawers and doors, spanned by a long board, permitting knee room between the boxes. The board was removable and the two boxes were then used separately. Chinese invention which became the occidental kneehole desk.

box casters: Boxlike cups, generally of brass, made to fit over legs of chairs and tables, cabinet furniture, et cetera, and carrying a roller wheel on a pivot. Made from 1770s to 1840s and later. [*Examples pictured.*]

box comb: A hair comb fashioned from boxwood.

boxiana: Any memento or relic, print, et cetera, dealing with boxing or the prize ring.

Box-in-Box: Pattern of pressed glass featuring angular impressions resembling formalized cutting of the Tudor rose.

Boxing Day: December 26. So called because on this day, and not December 25, Christmas boxes were distributed to tenants, servants, and other employees.

box iron: Smoothing iron with hollow chamber to hold hot coals or a slog of hot metal. Sometimes called a slog iron.

box-iron urn: Hot-water urn with a slog-iron socket into which a large element of red-hot iron was introduced to keep the water hot. The element in the larger urns was as large as a sashweight. Date is from c. 1750–60.

box lamp: Hanging or side-wall lamps of boxlike form, fashioned of brass, copper, or japanned sheet iron. Wicks were in flat slots. Popular shop and store lamps of 1790–1830. [*Example pictured.*]

boxman: Sandwich men who paraded the streets encased in conical boxes reaching from shoulders to knees, bearing advertising signs and posters all around. Typical street characters in the American scene to 1860s.

box-on-frame: 17th-century pioneer furniture; a plain or carved box of the proportions of a small chest, placed upon a separate turned frame; an early chest-on-frame piece. Now exceedingly rare.

box-on-stand: Pedestal stand on which is placed a writing box, sewing box, or book box. The lid of the box functions also as a table top. Style is generally Empire. [*Example pictured.*]

box ottoman: A low stool with boxlike frame having an upholstered top.

box secretary: Box-form cabinet with falling front (approximately 3 feet wide by 5 feet high), having an interior compartmented like a desk. Date is from 1830s.

box tenon: Angularly cut tenons used at corner posts of case furniture.

box toilet mirror: Small boxlike case with drawers and a pair of uprights between which is fixed a mirror arranged to tilt forward or backward. Said to have been made in all styles and periods from William & Mary to late Empire. The mirrors vary in shape with the periods. In many examples the case is not a box but a small cabinet in the style of its period.

Boyce chairs: Windsor and fancy chairs made by John Boyce of New York, 1830s–50s.

Boyd beds: Bedsteads by Henry Boyd, Cincinnati cabinetmaker, who began the manufacture of bedsteads exclusively in the 1840s and, employing 20 workmen, produced thousands of beds for the people of the Ohio Valley. Some are marked with a cold brand or stamp. Actually Boyd also made parlor furniture, but his specialty seems to have been French beds.

braceleted foot: Ankleted foot would be a more appropriate term; a raised ring or ridge around the footing of a table or chair leg.

bracelet holder: Glass novelty; a base and stem of glass surmounted by a horn, a swan, or some type of finial on which to hang a bracelet. [*Example pictured.*]

brace molding: Molding which, in profile or cross section, is a pair of ogival curves.

brache: Breach.

bracket clock: Any clock designed to stand on a shelf supported by brackets. Specifically, a weight clock with only the movement cased, the weights and pendulum suspended from the cased movement on the bracketted shelf. Many clocks called bracket are not authentic examples of the type, regardless of age; they are true portable clocks not requiring a shelf for suspension.

bracket foot: Cabinet or case-furniture footing projecting somewhat beyond the body of the piece, with shaped curvate or winglike sides. [*Example pictured.*]

bracket rules: Trivets for holding bread toasting before an open fire.

brackets: From *braguette, brague.* Any

projecting support, generally a triangular frame, whether open or solid. Some brackets have specific names, such as corbel, modillion, console. All are bracket forms, whether in masonry, wood, or metal.

brackle: To break bread or cake into chocolate, milk, soup, coffee, or tea.

brades: Necklaces; pendent ornaments.

Bradford Blackberry: Pattern of pressed glass featuring a fruiting blackberry vine horizontally applied over a series of panels.

Bradford furniture: Cabinet and seat furniture by Thomas Bradford of Charleston, S.C., made from 1790s. Hepplewhite and Directoire styles.

Bradford lamps: Oil lamps made by Samuel Bradford, Philadelphia, late 1790s, of brass and glass, and brass and other materials. Said to have worked to 1820s.

Bradford pewter: Cornelius Bradford of Philadelphia, pewterer, advertised his wares in 1765 "at the sign of the dish," as follows: "dishes, plates, basons, tankards, measures, tumblers, salt sellers, spoons, milk pots, close-stool pans, block tin and pewter worms for stills, candle molds and bottle cranes."

Bradley chairs: Superior fancy chairs, some gilded and some inlaid, made by Joseph Bradley of New York. American Institute in 1848 awarded the chairs a silver medal for excellence. Bradley's inlay work was done by G. A. Backus, whose shop was at 144 Fulton Street. Bradley's shop was at 317 Pearl Street, and manufacture may have begun in 1830s.

bradwardine: A bear-shaped jug, especially the Nottingham type of bear jug.

braid loom: A narrow fabric loom of small size, often used in the home. Scores of varieties, generally of wood construction and some of mahogany and walnut.

braid patterning: Process of stamping fabrics for fancy braid work. The equipment generally comprised a series of stamps of bent strips of brass fixed in wooden bases, each bearing a part or element that could be used singly or in a series for a continuous or all-over pattern. These stamps were dipped in wash-off inks, such as blueing and starch water, and then applied to fabric. These blocks are often mistaken for wallpaper-printing units. Most of them date from 1860s, when complete outfits were sold for homecraft work.

Braintree glass: Colonial glass, made at the factory located at Braintree, Mass., 1750s. It is believed only bottles, and possibly window glass, were made.

braising pan: A shallow pan with flaring rim, fitting over another deeper pan with straight sides, both units having handles. Used in cookery process known as braising. [*Example pictured.*]

Braithwhite carving: Probably a term of derision, as it refers to burning or charring patterns in wood with a red-hot poker or with red-hot cast-iron molds. The latter process was commercially used; the charring was brushed off the surface, which was then shellacked and painted. It is the latter process from which the term derives.

braken: The fern. Also a hemp dressing

tool, a wood trough, bread trough, and a mortar were designated by this term in early New England.

bramage: Heavy cloth used in making bedcoverings and bed carpets.

bramble net: A net for snaring birds.

Brameld: Mark found on certain Rockingham wares made at Rockingham Pottery, Swinton, England, after 1813, when the Brameld brothers took over the works, which they operated to 1842. The traditional Rockingham glazed wares, queen's ware, green-glazed wares, creamwares, white stonewares, and fine semiporcelain or English chinaware were made by Brameld. Earl of Fitzwilliam was a partner in the enterprise. [*Examples of wares and marks are pictured.*]

Brampton stoneware: Posset pots, puzzle jugs, and other early stonewares made at Brampton, Chesterfield, England, a potting center dating from mid-17th century. No one pottery can claim leadership, as four or more were in production down to 1870s, according to Jewitt, English pottery authority.

branch cross: The X-shaped cross of Burgundy, with five branches at the ends of each of the four arms.

branching sawbuck (table): Double trestles canting about 20 degrees from the vertical, supporting a long table board. Of Gothic style, dating from 15th century. Certain examples now in U.S. are imports from Östergötland and other provinces of Sweden, brought here in the 1920s.

brand: A sword; a spark; to roast; to mark with an iron. An iron or other metallic form used cold (cold-branding) or hot, to mark hides of living animals, criminals, boxes, bales, et cetera. Also to mark in red and black.

brandied candles: Tallow and mutton boiled in brandy or any spirits of wine. This clarified the mass to a point of waxlike consistency. Many commercial candles were so produced to 1800.

brandreth: Iron tripod for supporting a pot, kettle, or cauldron over a fire. Also brandiethe and brandlet.

brandy fruits: Trade term for glass bottles used as containers for fruits preserved in brandy.

brandy warmer: Miniature saucepan of silver, and sometimes of brass or copper, used in warming ardent spirits of wine.

Brandywine arch: A curved door lintel peculiar to the Brandywine Valley of Pennsylvania and Delaware.

brank: An iron framework placed over the heads of common scolds; a 17th-century punishment used in the colonies, along with stocks, pillory, and cucking stool.

bran-newing; branning; bran-tinning: A "secret" process of giving sheet iron a brilliant surface, bright and white. The sheets were made red hot, plunged in bran water, bathed in sal ammonia water, and then polished dry with more bran. 18th-century planishing method.

brasero: An open brazier; a shallow pan on feet, having a broad rim and carrying handle. Some of brass, of copper, and of iron.

brasiery: Brasswares of all kinds.

brassely buttons: The campion flowers; bachelor buttons.

brasses: Brass cabinet hardware, drawer pulls, escutcheons, et cetera.

brass foot: Ornamental or plain cast-brass footings affixed to legs of chairs, tables, and cabinet furniture. Adam, Hepplewhite, Directoire, Sheraton, and Empire furniture were at times brass-footed.

brass inlay: Buhl work. *See also* Patterned Brass.

brass mirrors (frames): Stamped or cast-brass moldings, usually ovals, but some rectangular and square. These are generally the product of various Birmingham, England, brassworks and date from 1760s. Sizes vary from a few inches to over a foot in major dimension. [*Several examples pictured.*]

brass tape work: Ribbons of brass inlaid edgewise in rollers and in blocks to form plates for printing calico, chintz, wallpaper, domino paper, and other fancy printed stuffs. Some plates were made with lead base, and some (to print solid) have interstices between ribbons of brass filled with felting. The roller types are now sought for use as lamp bases and columns. Brass tape work was also used in furniture inlay, in which case the tape was considerably narrower, laid in cut grooves, and hammered flush.

brasyll; brasey: Fish sauce.

braughwam: A large dish for a concoction of boiled eggs, cheese, bread, butter, and sauce.

brawde; brawdery: Sculptured work; raised needlework.

brayer: A roller for applying ink or other color to a surface, as a printing plate, the roller mounted in a two-pronged holder.

Brazen Lady; Brazen Huzzy: A mechanical walking doll made by the Waterbury Clock Co. in 1850s–60s.

brazier: Covered bucket of conical shape, used to carry hot coals. Also a footed pan for braising or browning. Similarly, any pan or receptacle for carrying hot coals; a small portable stove. The term is very loosely used, and originally meant a brass vessel.

Brazilian Cut: Pattern of cut glass patented 1889 and popular in the 1890s. Chief characteristics are an alternate cutting of the strawberry diamond and fans, forming a serrated, scalloped rim. Centers are cut in a series of facets comparable to the work of gem cutters.

Brazilian: Late pattern of pressed glass imitative of the best cut glass of its period of introduction, the early 1900s. A thirty-two-piece set was priced at $2.35 in 1905.

brazilwood: Dye- and cabinet wood (*Caesalpinia sappan*) yielding a red color. *Brasiletto* is either the same or an allied word. Actually Brazil did not give its name to this dyewood; the country was named Brazil because the dyewood was found there. Brazilwood was allegedly discovered on an island in the North Atlantic in the 14th century. There were at least six spellings of the name.

brazing tongs: Scissorslike tool with blocks of iron at ends used by jewelers and silversmiths. Ends were made red hot

and article to be brazed compressed between them. Tool ranged from 9 to 36 or more inches. [*Example pictured.*]

bread & cheese cupboard: 17th-century low cupboard on four legs, looking almost like a sideboard, and used as one. Generally of oak or yew wood, with a series of three or more cupboard doors. Term is modern.

bread-boarded: Any plane surface, as a table top, having cross boards forming the ends.

break: Four-wheeled vehicle with two or more sets of seats and a luggage compartment.

breakfast bowl: Porridge bowl.

breakfront: An important piece of cabinet or case furniture having a façade with two recessed sections and a projecting one, or the reverse; or with two recessed and three projecting sections, or the reverse. Mostly of English origin, 18th and early 19th centuries. Breakfront bookcases, wardrobes, sideboards, vitrine cabinets, and other case pieces are of record.

breast: A pot cover composed of two pieces of metal or ceramic material.

breast button: Pottery bottle with side or top having a swell and nipple suckle, simulating a woman's breast. Not an obscenity but a form of pilgrim's bottle.

breast warmer: *See* Stomach Warmer.

brechites: A wetting device for distribution of holy water. Not necessarily an asperges or aspergillum.

Breeden mantel: Wood mantelpiece for fireplace opening, made by the Breeden Co. of Louisville, Ky., from 1850s.

brerewood: A hatbrim.

Brewe, Lucy: Author of a monograph in which she is pictured holding a bayoneted gun. Her work, published 1816, claimed she was the only female ever to join and serve as a U.S. marine.

Brewer pottery: Products of the Jonas Brewer pottery at Cincinnati; stoneware and redware, made from 1850s.

brew-house vinegar: Sour ale or beer, sold by most early breweries. Advertised and sold to 1850s. Malt vinegar.

Brewi desks: J. Brewi & Co., New York City, trading as the American Desk Co. to 1860s or 1870s, made parlor and sitting-room desks, ladies' desk-tables, bookcases and commercial desks.

Brewster & Baldwin prints: Both firms were carriage makers of national repute who had large prints of famous horses made for them. These were premiums given to dealers, agents, and buyers. Brewster's, from a painting by Attwood, featured the horses George M. Patchem, Lady Suffolk, Princess, Ethan Allen, and Flora Temple. Brewster & Baldwin (combined) issued a print of "Celebrated Horses." Baldwin issued "Celebrated Flyers of the Trotting Turf," 1850s–60.

Brewster bed: Named for Elder Brewster, a bed of four roll-turned posts having turned cross members joining head and foot posts, spaced with upright spindles. Such beds were made to 1850s and later. It is doubtful if any were made in 17th century.

BRASSES, **top row,** William & Mary Period; **2nd row,** Queen Anne Period; **3rd** and **4th row,** Georgian and Chippendale Periods; **5th row,** Federal Period. TURNINGS: Old "Spool" from 1730s; New Spool, from 1830s, and "Cannon Ball." (From *New Geography of American Antiques*, Doubleday, 1948.)

Brewster chair: A Tudor-Gothic-style turned stick chair, named Brewster because Elder Brewster owned chairs of this type. [*Example pictured.*]

Brewster chest: Pine chest, popularized as reproduction in 1850s, made after the original said to have been owned by Elder Brewster.

Brianchon: Nacre glazed ware, of which Belleek is one and Brianchon the other. Bismuth luster. The process was discovered in 1850s.

bric-a-brac: Actually any antique of decorative quality or purpose; not necessarily a ceramic piece.

brick: Fired clay building blocks. Sammen or Samuel bricks are soft bricks. Stocks are hard bricks. Bivois are misshapen bricks. Clinkers are hard-fired Dutch bricks. Also bough pots of faïence, delft, or majolica, of brick shape, with orifice for filling with water and small holes in which to insert twigs and boughs—a household ornament of 17th and 18th centuries.

bricknogging: Timber framing filled in with brick to form a wall.

brick-oven stove: Kitchen range of cast iron having an oven lined with hard brick. Patented 1859 by Jewett & Root, Buffalo, N.Y.

brick-penciled: *See* Penciled Brick.

bride lace: Broad ribbons.

bride's quilt: Patchwork quilt (not hit-or-miss or crazy pattern) of superior quality, made for a bride-to-be.

Bridge furniture: Cabinet furniture made by John Bridge, Chelsea, Mass., from 1840s.

Bridgeport glass: Glasswares made at Bridgeport, Pa., from c. 1812 to 1840s.

Bridgeport knockdowns: Furniture made of well-fitting parts, knocked down for ease in transportation, by the Furniture Mfg. Co., Bridgeport, Conn., in mid-19th century.

bridges: Thread.

Bridgeton glass: Bottles, vials, and flasks made at Bridgeton (N.J.) Glass Works from 1836 to 1870s.

Bridgwood: Opaque porcelain made by Bridgwood & Sons, who also made china and earthenwares, at the Anchor Pottery, Fenton, England. The specialty of this firm was the ware also known as Parisian Granite, which was stamped LIMOGES! The white graniteware was extensively sold in U.S. 19th century.

bridle rosettes: Buttonlike bosses of colorful glass, brass, pottery, and plated iron used extensively to trim bridles. Most date from 1860s.

brigade: A train or string. In early railroad parlance the assembly of locomotive and cars was called a brigade, not a train, of cars.

Briggs & Vickery furniture: Enameled and japanned furniture, richly decorated, made by firm of this name, New York City, from 1840s.

Briggs mirrors: The specialty of Briggs & Co., mirror makers of Buffalo, N.Y. Mirror frames richly ornamented with composition arabesque figures.

Briggs ware: Richard Briggs of Boston, from 1850s, advertised china and glass, largely imported, and that his firm was established 1798. He was agent for Sèvres, Dresden, Wedgwood, many French potteries and glasshouses, Bohemian glass, et cetera. He decorated all sorts of china and cut glass to order.

Bright & Dark Side '49er: Staffordshire figure of a prospector, modeled in the round, one side of dark glaze and the other in brilliant color. It is suspect of late production, probably 1880s–90.

brightsmith: Whitesmith; planisher. Term used in 18th century.

Brinner furniture: John Brinner of New York City in 1762 advertised fine carved cabinetwork: "Done with the help of six London artificers, to-wit: sofa settees, field bedsteads, sofa beds, couches, easy chairs, bookcases, chests of drawers, girandoles, writing and reading tables, et cetera." He was also famed as a chairmaker by 1762.

Brislington ware: Drab-colored pottery with plum-colored glaze and a feldspar glaze with blue décor. It is redolent of Turkish and Persian ware and was produced by several 18th-century potters at Brislington, Bristol, England. [*Example pictured.*]

Bristol glass: English glasswares made at Bristol, England, by several glasshouses. The most famous glassware of the 18th century and the prototype of much so-called genuine and imitative Stiegel. Imported in considerable quantities from the early 1700s by Philadelphia, Boston, and New York importers, and sold generally throughout the colonies. Up to the 1830s, much Bristol ware was still imported. It was this importation that caused the failure of the Amelung Glass Works in Maryland; Bristol was laid down at the docks of Baltimore to sell for less than Amelung ware. Much Bristol glass now masquerades as American products of our early glasshouses; we imitated the ware to perfection because many Bristol glassmakers were emigrants to the U.S. The sapphire blue, amethyst, and milk glass of Bristol are famous, as is the cut ware.

Bristol old brass: High-yellow-color brass made at Bristol, England, in 18th century.

Bristol pottery: Delftwares (Bristol delft) were made at Bristol, England, from 1700. Memorial wares with names and dates are known. Chinese-style wares, English chinawares by Cookworthy, Champion, and others, all of Bristol, constitute a subject worthy of a monograph or book. Student is referred to *Ceramic Art of Great Britain*, by Jewitt. Figurines of the seasons and the elements, plaques, and other Bristol wares are highly regarded. There were many Bristol potteries whose products fall within this general designation of "Bristol pottery." A variety of hard porcelain was made from 1770, and with this works the old Plymouth Pottery was merged in 1780s. [*Examples pictured.*]

Bristol Rose: Pattern of cut glass featuring a large seven-point-star center with a rim of intricately cut bosses which presumably are imitative of a rose. Between each of these is a fan cutting in an almost complete circle, poised on the points of the stars.

Bristol shoes: Pottery-ware shoes made at Bristol, England, from 1703. Early ones are of delft with blue décor. Also glass shoes made at various Bristol glass factories.

Britannia: Alloy of 10 parts tin, one part antimony, and a minimum of zinc and copper. This is the hard pewter of the 19th century often used for tablewares, hollow wares, et cetera. It takes a high polish, which it holds for a considerably longer period than does pewter. It was also used extensively as a base for plating.

Britannia mark: A silver mark, consisting of a figure of Britannia, used from 1697 to 1720, when the silver standard of England was raised to a higher level. Any silver so marked is 958/1000 pure. It was relinquished as being too soft for silversmiths' working.

Britannia medals: Rewards of merit in medal form, made of Britannia metal.

Britanniaville: Colloquial name for the section of Taunton, Mass., where Reed & Barton Britannia and albata-ware factory was located in mid-19th century.

Britting pianos: Pianofortes made by John Britting of Cincinnati from 1830s.

broach: The wand or lath upon which wicking was affixed in candle-dipping. Wick broach or candle broach.

broad glass: Cheap window glass.

broadside: Any single-sheet poster, regardless of size, but generally an important sheet approximately 11" x 17" or over.

Broadwood piano: Pianoforte made by John Broadwood, London, son-in-law of Tschudi, the Swiss maker of London, to whose business this firm succeeded in 1769. Said to have been the finest pianos ever made in England.

brocade: Pattern-woven fabrics of rich quality, made by hand manipulation of the shuttle until invention of the Jacquard loom.

brocatelle: Fabric in imitation of brocade and of hand-tooled leather. Much used in upholstery and for ceremonial capes and gowns, and generally woven of silk and wool or linen and wool. Suites of furniture endowed with this name were made in the 1890s and so called because of their upholstery covering, skirted to the floor line.

broché: A loom-woven shawl in the India print philosophy, woven generally in Scotland. It was a branch of Paisley weaving activity, and popular in the U.S. from 1850s. Term is said to derive from the Indian *pudcha,* meaning the bestowal of flowers.

brochet cut: Glass cutting imitative of the ovals found on broché and Paisley shawls and the Indian shawls of Cashmere (Kashmir).

brodenail: Hand-forged nail used in building.

Broderers work: Embroidery by the Broderers Co., workshops of which were established in England by Flemish and other refugees between 1570 and 1600.

broderie anglaise: Embroidered muslin imitative of Honiton lace. Made mostly 1840s–50s, and sold widely in the U.S.

brokell: Shards; rubbish; rubble; trash.

broken cabriole: Perhaps the original

Chinese form of the cabriole or cyma curvate leg. It has a heavily accented knee from which the leg proper continues. A very early form of the cabriole, dating from the 1670s.

Broken Column: Pattern of pressed glass featuring a series of vertical columns broken with large beads or bosses. A late pattern of the 1890s, and not a product of the Portland Glass Co., as has been averred.

Broken Swirl: Blown-glass pattern achieved by blowing parison in forming mold which impressed vertical ribbing, and then twisting the plastic glass into a swirl. Parison is the term for a blown bubble of molten glass.

Bromley & Moulton beds: Patented bed bottoms made at Pawtucket, R.I., from early 1860s. The bed frames were button-, ball-, and spool-turned.

bronze argent: White bronze; originally Chinese, and sometimes called German silver.

bronze doré: Gilded bronze. *Doré* is from *d'or,* of gold.

bronze plant: Actual plant reproduced in bronze. This was done by packing the original plant in casting sand, firing it to reduce the plant to ash, filling the mold with mercury, which washed out the ashes, and then pouring in liquid molten bronze. The result was a perfect replica. Most of these elegancies date from 1840s.

Brooklyn glass: Brooklyn, N.Y., was an 18th- and 19th-century glassmaking center of considerable importance. Gilliland, Stouvenal, the Brooklyn Flint Glass Co., and other plants were in operation. Each factory of note is mentioned in this volume.

Brooks & Blackstone furniture: Cabinetware and upholstered seat furniture produced by a firm of this name in considerable quantities at Brooklyn, N.Y., in 1830s and 1840s. It is in the Directoire, Empire, and Louis XV style. Brooks made mahogany and rosewood furniture "equal to any made in New York."

Brooks-Grover gridiron: Oblong, round-end grid with side handle made to fit the two-lid and centerpiece stoves or ranges developed in the 1850s.

Brooks pottery: Marked H. BROOKS, made at Goshen, Conn., from 1820s. Pans, jugs, jars, and plates. Some pieces are dated.

broom dasher: Maker or vendor of brooms and fire faggots.

Broomhead & Blythe furniture: Fine early American cabinetwork made by a partnership so named at Charleston, S.C., from 1730s. Quality furniture in the Georgian style.

Broseley pattern: The willow pattern as depicted and used first by Thomas Turner, Broseley, England.

Broseley pipes: Tobacco pipes of clay made from 1640s at Broseley, England, to mid-19th century. After 1850s made glazed pipes with transfer décor. The early pipes were sent to colonies in huge quantities. Shards and fragments are found at many restoration excavations.

Brosius pottery: There were several potters named Brosius, generally making utility housewares and dairy wares of red clay. One pottery was near Andrew's Bridge, Chester County, Pa., and another was at Kennet Square, Philadelphia. Student is referred to the work on Chester County potters by Dr. Arthur E. James.

brottus: The Savannah, Ga., equivalent of lagniappe—something extra, a bonus, such as 13 buns for a dozen.

Browe lamps: Lard-oil, solar, camphene, and other fluid burners, chandeliers, and girandoles made by William Browe, Newark, N.J., in 1850s.

Browne harp: Six-octave "grand" and "semi-grand" harps made by John F. Browne of London and New York from 1830s. The factory in the U.S. was established in 1850s.

Brownfield ware: White-glaze, blue-printed, and sponge-decorated earthenwares, gilded wares, et cetera, of English china made at Cobridge Works, established 1808 by Bucknall & Stevenson and taken over by James Clews, *which see.* In 1836 works were taken over by Robinson, Wood & Brownfield, and was finally W. Brownfield & Sons. [*Examples of wares by Brownfield pictured, with marks.*]

Brownhills ware: The Hindu, Milan, and Pekin patterns of vases, toilet wares, redwares, et cetera, made at Brownhills Pottery, Longport, England, by various firms who owned and operated the works. George Bowers operated the pottery to 1850s; his son, Frederick, continued to 1870s, when others took over.

Brown's baby tender: A chest surmounted by a canterbury that could be converted into a cradle, a hobbyhorse, a crib, a chair, et cetera. The style is of the 1830s, but manufacture began c. 1850. Gadgetry at its best.

Brownsville glass: Bottles and hollow tablewares made at Brownsville, Pa., Glassworks from 1820s. Failed in 1880 and became a co-operative works to 1900s.

Brown Washington: A print in facsimile of the Stuart portrait of Washington, issued by Henry Brown of Boston, 1861.

brow square: Linen binding for a baby's head.

browthy bread: Light, spongy bread.

Bruen carving: Mechanically produced wood carving, patented by J. T. Bruen, 1850s.

Bruff, James: Mid-18th-century china decorator working in colonies.

Bruges stove: A drum-shaped cooking range.

brule parfum: Perfume pastilles which, in burning, released delightful fumes or odors. From *brûler*—to burn.

Brummagem: Colloquial for Birmingham (England).

Brunstrom pewter: Jules Brunstrom, Swedish pewterer of Philadelphia, working in 1780s in Pewter Platter Alley, made a full line of pewter wares. His ware is now scarce and desirable.

Brunswick waxes: Wax modeled figures, busts, and figurines, made by H. Brunswick of New York City from 1850s. He made objects for museums, for display, and for the home.

Brunt, Bloor & Martin wares: American ironstone potters of East Liverpool, O. An advertisement of record is dated 1876.

brush bath: A Chinese water coupé; any large vessel shaped like an inkwell and used to wash brushes, which were once known as hair pencils.

brush pan: A dust pan with a round box-like section attached in which brush was kept. Fancily japanned and decorated. Made in quantities by Benham & Stoutenborough, Glen Cove, L.I., as late as 1870s. Examples now scarce.

Brussels (Bruxelles): Carpeting, rugs, and tapestries made at this ancient town of the Netherlands, now in Belgium. Industry said to have started in 16th century.

Bryant furniture: Nathan Bryant, Boston, as early as 1820s, manufactured a variety of Grecian couches, card tables, bedsteads, worktables, et cetera, and advertised in the newspapers. He was also an extensive dealer in veneers and cabinet woods.

Bryce: Pattern of pressed glass featuring twisting ribbon in loops. Named for the makers, Bryce & Co., Pittsburgh, established 1850s.

bucchero ware: Early Etruscan pottery, 200 B.C.–A.D. 200.

Buchanan's Banner: Quilt pattern of 1850s, originating at Lancaster, Pa., during the "Buchanan for President" campaign. A border of swags or drapes with floral sunbursts surrounds a centerpiece in form of American eagle.

bucket brigade: *See* Fire Bucket.

Buck furniture: For some years in limited circles of collecting this term was considered a contraction of "buckeye," meaning gauche or crude. Actually, O. C. Buck & Co., Madison, Wis., operated a furniture factory from 1850s, making Louis XV revival-style chairs and case pieces.

Buckle: Pattern of pressed glass featuring a series of diamond points in the flattened ovate form of a buckle, with ovate boss. Variant is Banded Buckle, the same pattern surrounded by a band. Also Buckle with Star, not a variant of Buckle, but a device remotely resembling a buckle or brooch with star center.

Buckley & Bancroft: Labels bearing this name appear on much New England furniture of the mid-19th century. The firm was in Boston, producing parlor and drawing-room furniture and mirrors in the Louis XV or French Antique style.

Buckman toys: Live-steam toys, operated by miniature boilers, made by Buckman Mfg. Co., New York City, from 1860s. Steam fire engines, 8 to 10 inches high and 15 inches long, threw a stream of water 20 feet. Buckman also made model side-wheel steamboats. These fine toys sold at from $5 to $15 and are considered the finest steam toys made in America. [*Fire engine and steamboat pictured.*]

buck-mast: Beechnut.

Bucktrout furniture: Made at Williamsburg, Va., by several generations of Bucktrouts from 1720s. They are said to have imported London workmen. A corner cupboard, signed, and a chest of drawers in Hepplewhite style are owned by Mrs. Virginia Houghwout of Williamsburg.

"Bucktrout Group," a collection of reproductions of recent years, should not be confused with the originals. These are reproductions sponsored by the Williamsburg Restoration, but are excellently, and even meticulously, made.

buckwheat dye: Buckwheat stems and blossoms, used fresh, produce a brown dye. When dried and steeped, they produce a green dye.

Budd furniture: John Budd, New York City, from 1810s produced cabinetwares in the Directoire and Empire styles. His work compares favorably with that of Duncan Phyfe. Budd sold much furniture to Southern customers.

Bude lamp: A variant of the Argand, with two, three, and even four concentric wicks, designed to yield a brilliant and powerful light. Some Bude lamps were fed with pure oxygen to promote combustion.

budget: A small iron coffer.

bud glass: Any receptacle to hold a single bloom. Some were in shape of small tumblers with a well only large enough to hold a short stem. Some say the latter were made for use as quill-pen holders.

Buffalo rags: Colloquial for rag carpeting woven in quantities at Buffalo, N.Y., in 1850s. One lady weaver, Susan Simpson, had a considerable output.

Buffalo Willow ware: When the bridge scene on a willow-pattern plate is changed to that of a child astride a buffalo, the variant is called Buffalo Willow.

buffet à deux corps: Cupboard on cupboard; a two-piece cabinet.

buffet bas: A low cupboard; a sideboard.

buffet chair: A corner chair.

buffet stand: A medieval piece; a covered low stand. Also a sort of lectern. [*Example pictured.*]

buffet stool: Low stools or stands with slots in top to serve as handholds.

buffit: A joined stool. *See* Scabeau.

buff jerkin: A leather jacket.

buffon glass: Burning glass. Some are of concentric-lens type and have silvered mirrors to focus on objective. 18th century.

Bufford, J. H.: American lithographer of early status. Students are referred to *America on Stone*, by H. T. Peters. Bufford-Russell whaling prints were done by Bufford and published by Russell, 1870. They are hand-colored and are a series of prints on whale fishery.

buff skin: Tanned buffalo hide.

bugasin: Buckram, in calico prints.

bug eye: A large canoe peculiar to the Susquehanna and Chesapeake, fashioned from long sections of hollowed-out logs. Some were big boats used in carrying freight.

bugle: A small candle or candlestick.

bugle candlesticks: Actually bugles, with mouths fitted with sockets or prickets to hold candles. The occasional use as a device developed into actual candlesticks of bugle shape. Not to be confused with bugle.

bugle pot: A vase form made in the shape of the belled end of a bugle. [*Example pictured.*]

bugle work: Properly, "bead and bugle," a form of fancywork of the 1850s in which tubular beads, called bugles, and round form beads were used. Fringe, lace, and fabric covers made. [*Example pictured.*]

bugloss: The dye made from alkanet root.

Buhl, André Charles: The inventor of Buhl work. Also Boulle, Boule, Bulle.

Buhl saw: A fine-toothed fret saw.

buhr mill: Flour or gristmill using buhr (burr) stones. Buhr stone is the original term. The finest of these stones were mined at La Ferte-sous-Jouarre, France.

bulb bowl: *See* Lily Bowl.

bulb stretcher: Chair- or table-leg stretcher, either lathe-turned or spoke-shaved, having an elongated bulb in center.

bull broadside: Papal bulls, or pronouncements, printed on one side of very good paper, captured in great quantities from Spanish ships in our Southern waters and sold as useful paper for broadsides. Advertised for sale in Boston papers 1740s.

bulldog pitcher: Figural pitcher of squatting bulldog, made by the Haig Pottery, Philadelphia, 1825–35.

bullion: The thickened center of a crown of glass; the pontil section of a crown of glass, commonly called a bull's-eye.

bullions: Dress fastenings.

Bull mirror: Any of the thousands of tabernacle and other types of mirrors made by Reuben Bull of New York City from 1830s. Bull sold thousands of mirrors to dealers in South and West.

bull-nose tinder: Actually the dried membrane from the noses of slaughtered cattle. The most prized tinder of the 17th and 18th centuries.

bulrush jug: A jug decorated with a bulrush pattern, issued 1849 by Ridgway, the Staffordshire potter.

bull's-eye: The center piece of glass cut from a crown of glass, having the scar of pontil and a thickened section. The very cheapest cut from a crown of glass; now the most prized. Formerly used only in church windows, overdoor lights, and skylights. It distorts vision to such an extent it is not useful as windowpane. *See* Crown Glass.

Bull's-Eye: Pattern of pressed glass featuring large, bold, circular prismatic ribbing with center in form of round eye. Many variants, such as Bull's-Eye with Fleur de Lys, with Diamond Point, Pillar & Bull's-Eye, Bull's-Eye & Loop, Bull's-Eye & Rosette.

Bull's-Eye Cut: Pattern of cut glass featuring a series of rondels, or roundels, cut intaglio as a series of depressions.

bull's-eye mirror: Circular convex mirrors of small size, 6 to 12 inches diameter.

bulter: Meal bag of fine cloth. The meal was placed in the bag, shaken, and so bulted, or sifted, to obtain fine flour.

bultingark: Chest in which flour was bulted.

bulto: Carved and painted effigy of religious significance. Many made in Spanish Southwest, some by native Indians. Now considered a form of popular art, as a considerable number are homemade.

bumalady (b'mylady): An elision of "by my lady," often used in roundelays and other songs of the people.

bumarol: See Bumroll.

bumper stretcher: An oddity seldom found, but once a popular vagary. On H-stretchered chairs there is a strut set to the rear engaging a curvate or S-scroll from the seat rail, forming a bumper which prevented the chair from being pushed back against a wall. [Example pictured.]

bumping glass: Heavy-stemmed and -bottomed wineglass used to bang or bump on the table to applaud a speaker. Hence a "bumper" was not a large glass but any glass, whether small or large, made in this form. A bumper of ale would be a measure of ale in a bumper glass, and a bumper of brandy a tot of the ardent spirit in a small bumper glass. Also called firing glass.

bumroll: False hips or bustle pads, used to swell out petticoats as a substitute for the farthingale.

bunchers: A wooden U-shaped device for bunching asparagus. [Examples pictured.]

bung starter: A special mallet used to open the bung of a barrel. [Example pictured.]

Bunker Hill bottle: Glass bottle in the form of the Bunker Hill Monument. It is 15 inches high with ground-glass stopper. Date is c. 1876–80s.

bunting: Originally fine linen, but finally came to mean cheap and loosely woven woolen fabric much used in making flags.

burato: An early woolen cloth.

Burbank infant bronze: Nude boy with baby's cap on head, garland of roses on shoulders, and rose in hand, called the infant Burbank. Cast c. 1905 by Roman Bronze Works, New York City, from the original by Herbert Adams. Only a few casts were made.

Burch furniture: Cabinetwork by Joseph Burch, one of the first cabinetmakers working in Washington, D.C., from c. 1810.

Burch tin: Solid or block tinwares and japanned tin-plated ironwares produced by John Burch, New York City, from 1770s.

bureau: Slope-fall secretary with a case of drawers; slope-fall desk.

bureau à cylindre: Tambour-type roll-top desk.

bureau à dos d'âne: Writing bureau with top sloping away to each side; French slope-fall of special construction, peculiar to the country.

bureau à pente: Slope-fall desk.

bureau clock: A case of drawers in which pendulum and weights of a tall clock are encased, the hood mounted on top of the case. Rare. [Example of American make pictured. Shown through courtesy of Mr. and Mrs. John Myers, New Oxford, Pa., and the owner, William Whitman, Shellsburg, Pa.]

bureau de dame: A lady's desk.

bureau desk: Bureau means desk, hence term is an error in spite of widespread use. Generally accepted meaning is a slope-fall or slant-top desk with case of drawers below, fully encased. But at times it is supported on four legs, looking like a desk-on-

frame, but made in one piece. Made in periods from Chippendale to Empire.

bureau plat: Writing table-desk; flat-top desk. French types are generally found en suite, with pairs of Serre-Papiers, which see.

burean sideboard: A large commode; a high and wide sideboard with drawers. The deep drawers at top (bottle drawers), with shallow drawers below, indicated sideboard usage.

burean table: Term used by Chippendale in his Director to designate a flat-top desk of the kneehole type.

burel: See Borel.

buret: A drinking vessel.

Burgess furniture: The work of Joseph Burgess, cabinetmaker of Baltimore, Md., from 1789 or earlier. Hepplewhite style and other classics, some with painted-glass-panel décor.

Burgin glass: Green and colored glasswares and perfume bottles made at the Millville, N.J., factory of Dr. G. H. Burgin, who later owned the Kensington Glass Works, Philadelphia.

burglar's horror: A small thick candle which burned for eight hours in a tall, high-stemmed glass holder. A light could be kept burning in any or all rooms all night long. A burglar was supposed to be horrified by a lighted house, hence the name. [Example pictured.]

burgoin: The part of any headgear covering the hair.

burgomaster's chair: Dutch adaptation of the six- and eight-legged palace chairs of China, generally made with round marble seats, and some with revolving seats. Most likely the ancestor of the roundabout or corner chair, and of the swivel chair. [Example pictured.]

burl: The knotty protuberant growth often found on hard and semi-hardwood trees such as maple, walnut, mahogany, ash, and birch. Highly regarded for turning of fine bowls and other woodenwares, and for veneering. Burl walnut, burl mahogany, and burl ash were extensively used in fine furniture.

burl bowl: Any woodenware bowl, from small to immense, turned or hand-shaped from a wood burl. Also a mazer.

burlet: A hood; headgear.

Burley & Lyford furniture: Enameled, painted, and decorated cottage furniture and ornamental furniture, made in great quantities at Cincinnati from 1840s by this firm. This was in thousands of Ohio and Mississippi Valley homes.

Burling furniture: Excellent seat, case, and frame furniture made by Thomas, Samuel, and William Burling of New York City from 18th century. In 1802 Thomas advertised dissolution of the firm effective June 23, the new firm being Samuel & William Burling.

Burmese: One of the finer "peachblow" types of glass, said to have been colored by uranium. Made by Mount Washington Glass Co., New Bedford, Mass., from 1885, in shades from rose pink to yellow. While in the "peachblow" tradition (an imitation of a highly touted Chinese porcelain

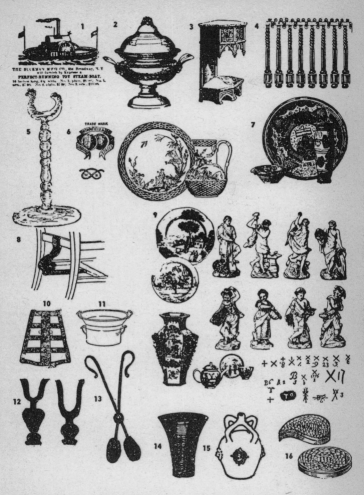

1, Buckman Steam Toy Boat. **2,** Butter Cooler. **3,** Buffet, Medieval Period. **4,** Bugle Work. **5,** Bracelet Holder. **6,** Brownfield Ware Toilet Set and Marks. **7,** Brislington Ware. **8,** Bumper Stretcher. **9,** Bristol Ware; dishes, the elements, vase, the seasons, teapot, cup and saucer, and marks. **10,** Bog Shoe. **11,** Braising Pan (Brasing Pan). **12,** Bootjack Splats. **13,** Brazing Tongs. **14,** Bugle Pot. **15,** Crown Jug. **16,** Cutlet Cutters. (Nos. 6, 7, and 9 from Virtue & Co., London.)

glaze of the same name), the Burmese variety was individualized by this name. This company also made a Peachblow.

burn: A brook.

burnet: Brown woolen cloth.

burnt ware: 18th-century term referring to pottery or china. A "burnt bowle" meant a china or pottery bowl, rather than one of metal or wood.

burnt wood pictures: See Hot-Poker Pictures.

burnwin: A blacksmith.

bur'n yard: Burial ground.

Burrage, Thomas: Joiner of Lynn, Mass., credited as a cabinetmaker by some and as a housewright by others. 18th century.

Burr bed: A folding bed in a standing cabinet. Date is 1880s.

Burr baby bottle: Glass nursing bottle with MEDALLION NURSING BOTTLE blown in the glass around a portrait bust of Mr. Burr, c. 1875.

Burslem: Town in the Staffordshire district of England. Wares made by various potters at this place are sometimes called Burslem wares.

Burt furniture: Made at the Joseph Burt factory, Worcester, Mass., from 1850s.

Burt mirrors: Moses Burt's products made at Cincinnati from 1830s. A variety of styles of framed mirrors.

Burton mirrors: Pier, mantel, wall, and small oval framed mirrors made at factory of James Burton & Co., Albany, N.Y., from 1830s to 1870s. Many sold in the West.

Burt sugar glaze: See Walker Glaze.

bury: A house.

burying a wife: Feast marking ending of an apprenticeship.

bush hammer: A mason's stone-dressing hammer.

busk: A stay used in early corseting. **busk point:** A lace tag securing the free upper end of busk.

buskin: High boot or shoe; corseting for the ankle.

buss: To kiss. Also a large pitcher.

bustanoby: A large globular or spherical bottle.

bustle: A crinoline roll worn over the nates, sometimes having a fine wire or wickerwork frame; a foundation used under skirts of elaborate drape.

busto: A statuary bust.

busybody: An assembly of prisms and mirrors in a bracketed frame, affixed to sill of an upstairs window, enabling people in room to see who was at front door. Also called "know-all," "see-all," and "Bo-Peep." Popular in London, Paris, Philadelphia, and Berne, Switzerland. These devices were used in many American cities, but Philadelphia was famous for the number used there. Said to date from the 1700s.

Butler furniture: Gamaliel Butler, merchant of Annapolis, Md., from 1750s had various cabinetmakers produce articles of seat and case furniture for his warehouse. Perhaps the first American furniture store.

Butler pottery: Earthenware made at New Brunswick, N.J., from 1810 by Potter Butler. Mullen & Connoly succeeded to the works in 1860 and operated them to 1880.

butler's cabinet: Chest of drawers with a rollback cylinder or tambour top. The dates seem to be from 1750s to 1830s.

butler's serving board: A high-legged chest of drawers with closets at sides or ends, used in storing table linens, carving tools, et cetera. Most date from 1780s to 1830s.

butler's sideboard: Small sideboard with the top center drawer fitted as a desk for use of the butler. Generally in classic style and dating from 1750s. Also called a butler's desk.

Butler silver: A justifiable term of derision for the Southern coin and solid silver stolen by General ("The Beast") Butler and his army in the War between the States. Butler was called "Beast" Butler and "Spoons" Butler. His looting of Southern homes was the least of his bestial traits.

butler's table: A fold-up table with X or some other collapsible legs. Top generally has two narrow falling leaves. Late 18th and early 19th centuries.

butler's tray: A series of bins, open or fitted with folding or uptilting tops, set on four to six legs, often castered.

Butler tin: Block-tin and japanned wares made by Thomas Butler, Philadelphia, from 1850s.

Butler-Wiswell furniture: Case and seat furniture produced by a partnership of cabinetmakers so named, working in Chicago from 1850s.

butter bit: Straining cloth for packing pats of butter for transport or safekeeping in springhouse.

butterboard: A wooden trencher, often covered with a bowl or dome, for service of butter at table.

butter boare or bore: A testing-tasting iron which, plunged into a crock or firkin of butter, withdrew a quantity for test of goodness. Used from 17th century.

butter boat: Actually a pouring vessel for melted butter, sometimes addled with lemon juice, salt, and spices. This, in most cases, was the "sauce" used at table.

butter box: Covered pottery or porcelain dish for keeping butter in service at meals. Also a woodenware or pottery box in which butter was kept.

butter cooler: Silver, Sheffield-plate, glass, porcelain, or pottery dish with well for ice or cool water under a platform, generally perforated or pierced. Many varieties made. [*Example pictured.*]

butter cupboard: From 15th century. A cupboard with pierced doors, used in storing butter, cheese, et cetera. Really early examples are of carved oak, with pierced work in the carving. The latest version, made in the 1880s, had pierced tin doors like a pie case or meat safe.

butter curler: Hook-ended knife which, when warmed and drawn across a roll of cold butter, produced curls and cornucopia forms for dainty service.

butter dishes (GLASS & CHINA): In the 19th century innumerable patterns of pressed glass were made into covered butter dishes, and many special, curious, and unusual ones in the form of a kitchen stove, a watch, a fish, et cetera, were produced. Practically all china tableware sold in sets and patterns had a covered butter dish in the service.

butter dish package: A glass dish with a fancy paper top or cover and holding a pound of butter. Used extensively by stores from 1850s in retailing butter.

Butterfly: Pattern of pressed glass with butterfly-wing-shaped handles. This is perhaps one of the patterns that did not meet with success. It is scarce, not eagerly sought, and not generally known. A variant, Late Butterfly, is pressed with bands of elements that look like butterflies. Date is 1880s.

butterfly motif: An ancient Greek device of religious origin. The butterfly was the symbol of the soul of man escaping from the chrysalis of corporeal existence.

butterfly paper: Domino and roll wallpapers displaying squares or repeat patterns of butterflies on a blocking of oak leaves.

butterfly table: Drop-leaf table with canted legs, the leaf supports being roughly triangular-shaped wings. Highly esteemed as furniture of the Pilgrim Century, and once thought to be a colonial invention. However, this type of table was used in England during the Tudor-Gothic era. [*Example pictured.*] A variant is the trestle butterfly table, having only two turned legs on platform feet, the legs joined with a stretcher near bottom and a narrow board top piece from which the leaves fall. The butterfly leaves are pivoted between top and stretcher and swing outward to support the pair of drop leaves.

butteris: A farrier's knife, used in paring the hoofs of horses for shoeing.

butter molds: Woodenware. Properly, butter stamps. Hollow-cut patterns for impressing a raised design on a pound pat of butter. The impression was called a "print," and from this derive the terms "print butter" and "butter-print." Round, ovate, rectangular, square, triangular, and octagonal patterns are known with cows, eagles, birds, flowers, tulips, hearts, and other devices, including a sheaf of wheat. Most are commercially made, but the prototypes were perhaps hand-carved by or for the individuals using them. Some of the stamps are without handholds, but most have them. Generally turned from hard or semi-hard woods and then carved, but many homemade examples were whittled from pine. Date from 1750s; still made and used.

butternut catsup: A condiment made of green butternuts pierced with needles, blanched to remove fuzz, pickled in brine and then in vinegar, boiled, and sealed for a year before use. A sort of walnut catsup or soy sauce.

butter printer: A dairy-house machine operated by a pedal which pressed the mold or print on a pound pat of butter.

butter scale: Balance scale with flat porcelain platforms used in weighing butter.

butter stamps: *See* Butter Molds.

butter stand: A butter dish.

butter taster: Thin disks of silver, bone, shell, or hardwood, carried by housewives to scrape a tiny taste of butter from firkins in the market places.

butter tester: Hollow silver tube, coneshaped, which, plunged into a firkin of butter, brought a sample from the center.

butter wheel: A mechanical butterworker to remove surplus moisture from a mass of butter. [*Example pictured.*]

butterworker: Any platform with roller or other device to serve as a means of removing moisture from butter.

buttery: Not, as is generally assumed, a place for butter storage and for dairy products. Originally the closet or room for storing butts of wine, barley water, and ale for household or tavern consumption. **buttery bar:** The service shelf attached to the lower half door. **buttery hatch:** The lower half of the two-part door usually set up as the entrance to the buttery.

button (CABINETWORK): A rectangular element turning on its center, used as a fastener for doors. Many are of wood in various sizes, ranging from three or more feet (on barn doors) to tiny ones on miniature cabinet doors. Some are of brass, wrought iron, and cast iron. 19th-century term was "turn-button," not "turn-buckle."

button bed: A bed of turned sections in the patterns used by turners of button molds. 19th century. Almost always, in error, called a spool bed. *See* Spool Turning.

button boxes: Wooden cases used by housewife or seamstress to hold a collection of buttons. Small cases to hold studs and collar buttons.

button brush: A brush of round form with stiff bristles graduated to a point, used in cleaning buttons.

button foot: A flattened ball of considerable size used as a foot on turned legs from early 18th century. The button accented the slender leg immediately above it. [*Example pictured.*]

button rug: Canvas-base homemade rugs displaying clusters of small woolwork circles within larger circles, forming an all-over pattern. Also braided rugs made up of innumerable circles of braiding, or of many large braided circles from 8 to 14 inches in diameter, mounted on canvas. Where circles meet the canvas, the area is filled in with woolwork. These seem to date from around the 1820s as a vogue. Still made in 1920s.

buttons: The various categories, subcategories, and classes of buttons are so vast an array within the field of interest in these items that no attempt can be made to list them here, by either name or class. *The Complete Button Book,* by Albert & Kent, is the most comprehensive guide obtainable, with 5700 illustrations. But even that amount of data can make the book no more than a complete *introduction* to button collecting.

button turning: The form used by turners of button molds.

Buttre chairs: Fancy chairs made by William Buttre of New York City from c. 1810.

butts: Leaf hinges.

butts; backs: Toughest and heaviest section of a hide.

Buxton Washington: A design by Dr. Charles Buxton, Perth Amboy, N.J., c. 1790. Urns, obelisk, and Washington on a pedestal, with a view of Fort George. Used as a textile-printing pattern in early 1800s.

Byam match: A "strike-anywhere" match made "with and without brimstone" by Byam of Baltimore, from c. 1845.

by Godfrey!: A congratulatory phrase offered by partisans to an elected official. Said to derive from Godfrey of Boulogne (Buillon), a popular leader in the First Crusade.

bylig: A bellows.

byssinel: Fine silk fabric or floss.

C

C: This letter is an abbreviation for *circa*, meaning around.

cabaret: A tray with matching service consisting of a pot for tea, coffee, or chocolate, sugar basin, cream jug, bowl, and two cups with saucers. Generally in china, but some have pots and trays of silver. It is the ensemble to which the term applies and not to the separate parts.

cabas: A work bag; a basket woven of rushes.

cabbage cutter: Long, broad board with shallow sides and fitted with a metal blade set at an angle across the wide board. A head of cabbage slid back and forth over this board was cut into shreds, or slaw. Since "cole" was a general name for cabbage, the term "cole slaw" describes the cabbage product of these boards. [*Example pictured.*] Larger ones, with boxes or frames to hold the cabbage, were used in cutting the slaw destined for preservation by salting to make "choucrou," the French invention that crossed the line and the Rhine and became the national dish of Germany, sauerkraut.

Cabbage Leaf: Pattern of pressed glass featuring three cabbage-leaf forms of realistic quality and, among them, the heads of rabbits.

Cabbage Rose: One of the late Imari pattern forms of decorated china, first issued by Adams, the English potter, c. 1840. It is akin to the other Imari patterned wares miscalled Gaudy Dutch and Gaudy Welsh. Also a pattern of pressed glass featuring a dainty rambler-type rose twining the objects as decorative bands.

cabbage tureen: A soup tureen in the form of a cabbage head, known in faience, majolica, porcelain, china, and redware, white-glazed. These date from 1730s and were made to 1880s or later.

cabbage ware: Pottery, whether majolica or porcelain, et cetera, imitative of the leaves or the head form of cabbage. Cauliflower was also imitated and sold generally as a novel form of tableware.

cabin candlestick: Two-part candleholder in form of a six-sided cabin, the roof supporting a chimney that is the candle socket. It is a product of the Vallerysthal Works, Lorraine, France, and not an American product.

cabinet armoire: *See* Armoire.

cabinet hardware: Drawer pulls of all kinds, hinges, escutcheons, locks, and other metalwork applied to cabinetwork. Often these are a guide to the age of the piece. Antique furniture having its original brasses (as the hardware is usually called) is always preferred by connoisseurs. [*A page of cabinet hardware is pictured, with approximate dates of use given.*]

cabinetmakers: Some cabinetmakers' names appear in this dictionary as names only, other names are followed by the term "furniture" or "chairs." But no effort has been made to include the many masters mentioned in the various books on furniture and chairs noted in Bibliography. What is important in this volume is the great number of 19th-century furniture manufacturers listed. The same applies to lists of chairmakers.

cabinetmakers' models: Furniture in miniature, sometimes one-half size, sometimes one-fourth size, or even smaller. It was always meticulously made and, it is believed, generally represents a masterpiece by which an apprentice proved his worth to be a journeyman cabinetmaker. Some were used as salesmen's samples, especially the small pieces made after 1825.

Cabinetmakers Price Book: Illustrated manual issued by the master or employing cabinetmakers of a community, giving prices paid for the work and each step of the work, prices asked, et cetera. New York, Boston, Philadelphia, Baltimore, Pittsburgh, and Cincinnati cabinetmakers issued several editions of price books. All are now scarce and valuable relics of early cabinetmaking in America.

cabinet pedestal table: An awkward Georgian-period (or later) tilt-top table having three cabriole legs fixed to a triangular hollow column, with a door giving access either to a small closet or a tier of small drawers. Dates from 1760s, and made in various forms to 1850 or later.

cabinet piano: An upright piano.

cabinet piece: A fine example of anything; a bibelot; an object of artistry by any artisan. Comparable to the now generally misused term "museum piece."

cabinetta bedstead: A folding bed made up of fourteen X members, seven on each side, folding up scissorslike and extending to a length of over six feet when opened.

A sack cover over the members supported a mattress. Made as late as 1920s.

cabinet woods, American: Cabinet- and chairmakers, from 1620, used native woods as follows: ash, beech, blisted gum, black birch (the bark, not the wood, is black), black cherry (black wild cherry), chestnut, coffee tree, cypress, loblolly pine (Southern pine), longleaf (yellow) pine, oak (white, golden, and live), pitch pine, poplar, red maple, red gum, red cedar, silver maple, sycamore (buttonwood), tulip wood (candlewood), white cedar, white pine, white walnut, walnut, yellow pine, and yellow birch. These are of re- corded use. There may have been others. Of course mahogany was used in increas- ing amounts from 1725, and other cabinet woods were imported. Holly, apple, pear, hazel, magnolia, Osage orange, spruce, and others may have been used regionally.

cabinet writing table: A cabinet mounted on a table and having a pull-out writing board. Date is c. 1820–40.

Cable: Pattern of pressed glass featuring panels divided by cablelike sections, said to have been made at completion of the famed Atlantic Cable. Cable with Ring is a variant displaying sections of cable bent through rings.

cable band: A cord hatband.

cabochon: An oval convex section en- closed within a frame or border.

cabriole: Bowlegged, bandy-legged, cur- vate. Used on late William & Mary style furniture and on some Flemish furniture of 17th century. The design is from the Chinese. For almost 80 years the cabriole leg in some form or other, plain or or- nately carved, was used on Queen Anne, Georgian, Chippendale, Louis XIV, and Louis XV furniture. It was revived in 1830 in the French Antique or Second Baroque style often miscalled Victorian.

cachemere: Cashmere; the neck-down hairs of Angora goats, spun and woven into fine shawls at Kashmir, India.

cachepot: Ovoid, globose, bulbous china jars or pots used as hiding places or catch- alls.

cachet: Metal cylinders, sometimes of sil- ver or gold, to hold seals used to validate documents and letters. Size range is from 4 to 8 inches long and from ½ to 1¼ inches in diameter. Used from 17th to 19th centuries. Term today means a special designating cancellation on a letter, hav- ing some philatelic significance.

cad: Diminutive of caddy; a helper; an apprentice, clerk, or office boy.

Cadalso glass: Spanish glass made at Cadalso, near Toledo, Spain, from c. 1540s. This works continued in operation for centuries. Certain of the glass was mottled like Nailsea and some Dutch and Flemish wares.

caddis: Woolen fabric; tape or dress cloth.

caddy spoon: Spoons made specifically for removing tea from a tea caddy, often with fancifully shaped bowls, as a fish, a paw, a fan, a cup, a shell, et cetera. Gen- erally of silver, although some were of porcelain, having broad stubby handles and deep, ovate bowls.

cadeau: A betrothal or wedding gift.

Cadmus pottery: Abraham Cadmus was

the proprietor of the Congress Pottery at South Amboy, N.J., from c. 1848. Rocking- ham and yellow-glazed wares were made. [*The mark is pictured.*]

cadnat: A canopy.

Cadogan: A lidless teapot filled from a vent in bottom. Made as a style or type by several English potters, including Spode, from 1780s.

café au lait: Coffee with milk; the color of this beverage.

cafetière: A small coffeepot used in after- dinner service.

cage jack: A globose cage of metal, some- times of silver, to hold a coil of taper threaded through a nipple at top, where it was burned as a means of melting seal- ing wax. A desk piece.

Caire, Adam: Stoneware potter who made many pieces embellished with rooster- pecking-corn motif. From mid-19th cen- tury.

cake charms: See Pudding Charms.

cake roller: Wooden roller carved intaglio with designs which were impressed on dough. In general use throughout 19th century. [*Example pictured.*]

cake table: A device to facilitate the frost- ing of a cake; an elevated stand generally contrived by tinsmiths by soldering two pans together, bottom to bottom, and then putting a cover on top. [*Example pictured.*]

calab: Same as chalab; iron or steel.

calabash: Any container imitative of the elongated globose, ovate shape of the gourd called the calabash. Sometimes of glass or pottery, forming bottles and flasks.

calamander: A rare black- and brown- striped cabinet wood from the East In- dies. Sometimes, in error, called Coroman- del.

calamine: Spongy zinc ore.

calash: A folding bonnet, or covering of cloth, over wire stays. Also a wheeled vehicle with a folding bonnet top.

calathumpian: A participant in a shiva- ree or charivari; a serenader making noise and nuisance. Generally active only in serenading newly wedded couples.

caldron: Globular pots with bails and spout lips; generally large, and known made of copper, iron, and brass.

calèche: A wheeled vehicle of the 18th and 19th centuries, seating four in the body with driver on a box.

calico: Originally a coarse cotton cloth made at Calicut in India; then printed in colors from blocks, and finally, in its most popular form, boiled in oil to give it a glaze, hence "oil-boiled calico" or chintz. The art of calico printing in colors from wood blocks was practiced in England by Huguenots, who established a factory c. 1680.

California belt: A money or purse belt, primarily made to hold gold dust, nuggets, and coin.

California birds: Color prints from John Cassin's *Illustrations of the Birds of Cali- fornia*, published by Lippincott of Phila- delphia, 1856. They are small folio litho- graphs, hand-colored. There are 50 subjects.

California glass: Bottle factories were in operation in California from 1855 to 1859. Pacific Glass Works was established 1861, and later became part of the San Francisco Glass Works.

California lounge: A lounge opening out into a double bed, made by Joseph Meeks of New York from 1849, and by him named the "California."

California pants: India-rubber coveralls combining boots and trousers which enable miners to stand dry in water up to their hips.

calimanico: Calico.

caliper press: Huge screw press having long downcurving arms from the screwhead somewhat like the jaws of a caliper. Used in making cider, perry, et cetera, and in baling cotton and tobacco.

calling spoon: A spoon with a whistle in its handle.

calliope: Greek name of the Muse of eloquence and epic poetry. A steam-powered pipe organ; a musical instrument of pipes; a 10-note wood whistle.

callopying: Mending.

callot: A skullcap or coif. A block of unhewn stone.

calorifere: Metal pot or scuttle on wheels, filled with hot embers and wheeled around a room to provide heat.

calsons (calzoons): Tight-fitting trousers of linen.

caltrap: Four-pointed device of spikes, so placed as always to fall with one point upward. Thrown in front of charging horsemen, the caltraps injured the horses' hoofs. Used in battle to c. 1600.

calumet: American Indian ceremonial tobacco pipe—the pipe of peace.

camaïeu: Properly, *en camaïeu.* Painting in monochrome, in various hues and shades of one basic color. Example, *en grisaille,* or in tones of gray.

camaïlon: The giraffe. Also camelopard.

Camargo papers: Wallpapers made at the Camargo Mills on the Conestoga River near Lancaster, Pa. Thousands of tons made for the Western trade, 1840s–60s.

Cambrian: A pottery at Swansea, England, established c. 1775 and operating to c. 1870 under various managements. Earthenware, creamware, hand-painted ware, opaque china, and Etruscan wares were made. The various marks include Cambrian; Cambrian Pottery; Dillwyn & Co.; Hanynes, Dillwyn; Swansea; Dillwyn Etruscan Ware; and tridents, single or crossed.

cambric: Fine white cotton or linen, originally from Cambrai, France.

Cambridge glass: Products of works established 1814; plain-cut, engraved, and the first pressed glass made in the U.S. Plant was at Cambridge, Mass. Student is referred to *Cambridge Glass,* by Lura Woodside Watkins.

Cambridge jug: Potbellied ale jug with handle and pouring spout, made c. 1850 by Wedgwood.

Cambridge lamp: The first student-type lamp, made from c. 1790 by Huntley of London. Also sometimes called a watchmaker's lamp. [*Example illustrated.*]

came: H-shaped bars of lead used as muntins in early windows, the panes fitting in the H-grooves.

camelard: An ointment derived from the fat of camels.

camel-back chair: Any chair with a curvate or curve-cut toprail having two humps. Probably a late and invented term.

cameline: Cloth woven from camel's hair.

camelopard: The giraffe. When first exhibited, this animal was a sensation and was thus named because it was said to resemble a camel and a leopard.

camel teapot: Salt-glaze teapot in form of squatting camel with palanquin or howdah on its back. 18th century.

cameo: (1) Opposite of intaglio; figural carving with background cut away, generally in two or more colors but not necessarily so. (2) Pattern of pressed glass displaying a small bust en cameo within a dotted medallion or oval frame.

cameo cup-plate: Cup-plate or butter chip of pressed glass containing a pottery bust or other decorative element. It is believed that many of these made in the U.S. used imported cameos. *See* Sulphides.

cameo glass: Rich cut glass in the true cameo technique, generally cut from blanks heavily flashed with another color, like the original Portland vase. The Wedgwood reproduction of the Portland vase is not glass, but other reproductions by expert cutters are. Webb of London made much cameo cut glass in the 19th century. At the Morgan sale, New York City, March 12, 1886, the "Pegasus Vase," which had been five years in the cutting by Webb, sold for $10,000. Other pieces of Webb cameo glass sold for from $13 to $690 each. A 224-piece set of decanters and various-sized wine and cordial glasses sold for $18,000.

cameo lava: Cameos cut from stratified lava. *See* Obsidian.

cameo Parian: Pottery cameos. Molded with white relief figures and tinted background; some are in very high relief. Some, it is said, were made at Bennington and other American potteries.

cameo vase: Any vase of glass cut en cameo. There are ancient and modern examples. Some cameo vases of glass may have been pressed or otherwise molded to reduce the time and cost of cutting.

camera box: A photographic device on the Daguerrean principle.

camera lucida: An optical machine, predecessor of the photographic camera, used as a drawing aid; the image was reflected on a glass screen over which paper was laid and the image traced. Used extensively by artists to achieve true perspective and to draw outlines of features of sitters posing for portraits. Many types [*one of which is pictured*].

camis: A thin diaphanous robe; hence the term "camisole."

camlet: An early fabric, generally of wool, but originally of goat's hair.

Camp, William: Cabinetmaker of Baltimore, 1802–22. His label, similar to that of Joseph Berry of Philadelphia, pictures ornate furniture having something of Adam, Hepplewhite, Sheraton, and Hope

CABINET FURNITURE.

THE subscriber presents his thanks to the public, for the liberal share of patronage they have been pleased to favour him with; informs them he continues to manufacture every article in the Cabinet Business. The several years experience he has had as a workman, in some of the first shops in Europe and America, enables him to supply those who may favor him with their custom, with furniture of the first taste and workmanship.—The public's most obed't serv't: CHRISTIAN, Cabinet-maker.
June 7   73 Broad-street.
An Apprentice wanted—apply as above.

1, Cleft Cabriole Leg, front view. **2,** Clap-Harp. **3,** Cinderella Pie Tool. **4,** Chromatic Envelopes. **5,** China Boy. **6,** Chippendale Style (so called); seat, wing chair, armchair, chest-on-chest, sofa, and three illustrations of chairs from Chippendale's design book. **7,** Christian Furniture, advertisement of 1802. **8,** Camera Lucida. **9,** Cambridge Lamp. **10,** Cake Table. **11,** Cake Roller. **12,** Cabbage Cutter. **13,** Candle Mold. **14,** Candlestick Vase. **15,** Chinese Must Go, mechanical cap pistol.

style elements. A super-classic exposition of taste.

Campaign: Pattern of pressed glass, having several variants, memorializing campaigns of the U.S. Army. Military symbols and emblems such as cannon, guns, flags, et cetera, are impressed on the glass.

campaign handkerchief: Souvenir squares of printed linen or cotton, generally issued in connection with a political campaign or presidential race. The first of record in the U.S. seem to have been made for the Harrison campaign of 1840.

campana vase: Bell-shaped, flaring-mouthed vase on knop stem and square base. Also called Krater vase.

Campbell, William: Said to have been one of the early cabinetmakers of Davenport, Ia., working from 1840s. Furniture attributed to him is in the French Antique style called Victorian.

Campbell mirrors: Mirrors of every description and size made by C. G. Campbell & Co., Newark, N.J., c. 1850. The production was largely tabernacle and Louis XV revival styles.

Campbell Pottery: Operating in New York from 1770s, this pottery made red-wares in the "Philadelphia style," including pantiles for roofing.

Campeachy wood: Dyewood; logwood. West Indies product used in 18th century.

camphene: Lamp fluid composed of turpentine and alcohol, mixed in proportions of 1.25 and 6.75. Made in quantities by local vendors from 1835. This fluid produced a brilliant flame but was highly explosive. All so-called "camphene lamps" were made to burn this mixture. Some types of camphene contained other oils, such as citron, lemon, valerian, balsam, juniper, et cetera. Makers tried to hold the mix to 5 parts carbon and 8 of hydrogen. It is said the "Vesta" lamp was the first camphene-burning lamp.

camphire: Camphor.

camphor glass: White cloudy glass having general appearance of gum camphor in lump or block form. This kind of glass was blown, mold-blown, and pressed. It was a specialty of some of the glasshouses of Pittsburgh, Wheeling, and Ohio.

camphor jug: A small glass jug made specifically as a container for spirits of camphor.

camp mug: Metal drinking cups carried by soldiers. Copper, brass, pewter, horn, silver, iron, wood, and tin examples are known.

camp paper: Paper coated with pigment suspended in wax or coated with graphite. An early form of carbon paper.

cam-wood: A dyewood yielding a yellow-red color.

Canadian: Pattern of pressed glass having arched top panels with scenic sporting views and faint stipple with ivy fronds.

canalate: Having grooves or channels. More properly, canaliculated.

canalboat furniture: From the 1820s interior travel by water, including travel on canalboats designed primarily for passengers, caused the making of some special furniture such as two-tier, bunk-type beds, small cases of drawers, and toilet stands. Hundreds of thousands of fancy chairs, generally miscalled Hitchcock, were made for furnishing river steamboats and canalboats.

canalboat lamp: Tinned sheet iron in form of a boxlike sconce made to hold three or more candles and having a tinned iron ring for hanging. The flat bottom of box permitted lamp to stand on table. [Example pictured.]

canal horn: Any horn used by canalboatmen to signal approach to lockkeeper. No special type seems to have been developed, and conch shells, long- and short-tube dinner horns, and even post and hunting horns were used.

canapé: A sofa or couch.

canary resist: Deep yellow luster with pure-white decoration achieved by the resist process. Staffordshire, from early 19th century. It should be remembered that all lusters and resist wares were made as low-cost wares for mass or middle-class markets and as much, or more, was exported by the potters as was absorbed by home markets. Lusters and resists of Staffordshire, generally unmarked, had considerable sale in South and Central America as well as North America.

canary wood: A species of mahogany from the Canary Islands.

canboard: A rack or shelf to hold drinking mugs, cans, et cetera. Some have pegs upon which to hang handled mugs.

canchalagua: Medicinal herb from California, promoted as better than sarsaparilla, 1840s–50s.

Canchester burner: 20th-century rival of the Rochester burner lamp. The Rochester was a form of Argand burner with circular wick; the Canchester was a double flat-wick burner with flame constricted within a meshed mantle, which became an incandescent cone of light. Made in parlor-, kitchen-, hanging-, table-, and student-lamp forms.

cancography: Engraving on brass.

candelabra vase: Vase of pottery, porcelain, majolica, pewter, silver, or other substances, fitted with arms to hold candles. Usage seems to have begun c. 1750s and continued to 1850s. Some vases have from five to seven arms. Known to have been made at Meissen, Sèvres, Chelsea, Derby, Bow, and Worcester. Numerous examples are unmarked.

candle auction: Auctions where bidding was timed by a burning candle having annular marks. Bidding continued, or was accepted, until the candle burned to a ring mark.

candlebeam: Chandelier; a candle tree; a rod or bar fitted with spikes on which to affix candles.

candle board: A low stool upon which are mounted in X formation five adjustable supports, the center one for a burning candle and the others to hold blown-glass globes filled with water. These served as magnifiers of the single candle flame, enabling four workers to have sufficient light.

candle bomb: Tiny hollow glass bead filled with water. Placed in the flame of a candle, the bead exploded in a few seconds. 18th-century "philosophical amusement" gadget.

candle case: A tube of clear glass mounted on a ring which, in turn, is mounted on a movable upright rod sliding in a slotted boss readily affixed to any candlestick. Promoted as an important invention to protect the flame of a candle from drafts. American, dating from 1787. Invented by the famed Francis Hopkinson.

candle cone; candle thimble: Conical-shaped extinguisher, always a part of a chamber candlestick. Generally of metal, such as silver, brass, copper, or iron, but some reported made of pottery. Also used mounted on rods to extinguish candles on beams, in sconces, chandeliers, et cetera. Not snuffers, *which see.*

candle dip stick: A slender wand to which candle wicking was tied for the repeated dipping in hot wax which formed the dipped candles.

candle d'outer: A scissorslike device with ends of blocks of metal to pinch out a burning candle.

candle dowse: Candle cone.

candle drawer: Long, narrow, shallow drawers made to serve as pull-out supports for slope-fall desk section. Used, it is said, to store a few candles. A scarce feature in early slope-fall desks and desks-on-frames.

candle inkwell: Any inkwell incorporating a holder or socket for a candle. Not to be confused with inkwells having a taper reel or holder for use in melting sealing wax.

Candle Lamp: Metal candlestick with an imitation metal candle in socket. These devices burned oil and had a narrow flat wick. [*Example pictured.*]

candle mirror: Very narrow, upright wall mirror, somewhat like a sconce. An elegancy of the Queen Anne and early Georgian period. Some have wood frames; others are of metal. Some have arms with sockets for candles; others apparently were made without candle arms and were hung to reflect light of a candlestick on a stand. [*Example pictured.*]

candle mold: A series of hollow metal or pottery tubes in which candles were cast by pouring hot wax into the tubes. [*Example pictured.*]

candle-molding candlestick: Device with hollow base and shaft in which suet or other hard fat could be pressed to mold a candle for immediate use. Invented and made at St. Louis from 1840s.

candle nozzle: The socket of a candlestick.

candlepins: A game similar to bowls, the pins being candle-shaped.

candle pull: Small, sliding flat board in case or seat furniture to provide pull-out support for a candlestick.

candle shears: Snuffers; wick trimmers with a box to catch the clipped-off wick.

candleshield: Small shield-shaped shades of horn, paper, or metal, supported by a clip that gripped the candle.

candlestick: The old rhyme about "Jack be nimble, Jack be quick . . . jump over the candlestick" in no way refers to the candleholder we now designate as a candlestick. The stick Jack was supposed to jump was the candle dipping stick. Properly, any upright device to hold a candle is a candlestick. Two major ways of holding the candle in or on such a support were in use: (1) the candle end was impaled upon a spike, and (2) the candle end was fitted into a socket. Candlesticks were made of all kinds of wood and metal, of glass, pottery, china, stoneware, horn, bone, papier-mâché, et cetera.

candlestick lamp: A three-element lighting device, generally of pressed glass but sometimes made of pottery or china. Composed of a candlestick with a large socket containing a knob fitted with a small oil reservoir. A shade, resting upon the flange of the socket, is pierced with three air vents. A late, cheap elegancy of c. 1870s–90s. Generally used in pairs.

candlestick vase: Double gourd-shaped vase of Chinese design but frequently of continental European make, serving as an ornamental vase and a candlestick. Made from 1750s. Sometimes the candle socket is of metal. [*Example pictured.*]

candle thimble: An extinguisher, generally a cone-shaped dowser of metal.

candle trow: A tree for candles, especially for Yuletide illumination. The candle trow, or tree, is ancient English. The original use of a small evergreen, the branches serving as arms on which candles were placed, gave way to the use of a wooden form of central trunk and crisscrossing bars.

candle trumpet: Candlestick in the form of a trumpet with handle, imitative of the occasional use of an actual trumpet as a candlestick, the bell of the horn being the base and the mouthpiece the candle socket.

candlewick: Cotton wicking for candles; used also as a heavy yarn or cord in decorative needlework and knotting. Also the name given a woven cotton fabric upon which candlewick work is done. Early candle wicking was twisted cotton roving, not thread. It is said that cotton was not commonly used until the mid-18th century, prior to which hemp, tow, and silk down from the milkweed were used in making wicking for candles.

Candlewick: Pattern of pressed glass featuring crisscrossing and ball forms imitative of knots. A late pattern.

candlewick measure: Block of wood with an upright peg and a wire hoop or arch. Candle wicking was looped around the peg and drawn taut to the arch, and there cut. The measure varies with different candle lengths.

candlewood: Citronwood; any wood rich in resin, used for lighting.

candy paperweight: Glass paperweights encasing canes of colored glass resembling twists of stick candy, barley sugar, et cetera.

Cane: Pattern of pressed glass resembling woven cane seating.

Cane & Rosette: Pattern of pressed glass featuring panels or panes of cane weave, with alternate clear section embellished with oval rosettes.

cane-back: Chair or settee back of woven cane.

cane chair: A chair having seat or back, or both, of woven cane.

Cane Cut: Pattern of glass cutting composed of horizontal and vertical cuts, crossed by left- and right-angular cuts, thus achieving a design similar to that of cane weaving in chair seats and backs.

canephorous: A basket made for carrying upon the head. The ancient Greek depiction of the female figure carrying a basket upon the head (*Kanephoros*) was used by the Brothers Adam and by the Greek-style revivalist Hope as a decorative element painted, and even inlaid, on furniture.

cane seating: Originally a sieve weaver's or temse maker's task, the making of cane backs and seats for chairs became popular in the 17th century. In cabinetwork, the caning was woven through holes drilled around the edges of seats and backs. In 1845 Haywood Brothers of the U.S. developed a loom for weaving cane seating, and thereafter many cane seats and backs were of this unique fabric, tacked on instead of woven on the chairs.

cane ware: Pottery of fine quality, or true porcelain, of a buff-yellow color approximating the tint of seasoned bamboo. *See* Piecrust Ware.

can hook: Pairs of free-swinging clamps to attach to the chimes or stave ends of a barrel for hoisting. Not a cant hook, *which see.*

canions: Puff rolls on breeches, arranged just below the knee.

Cann & Dunn ware: Silverware, generally marked COIN, or COIN STANDARD, or STERLING, made by this firm at Brooklyn, N.Y., from 1850s.

canne; can: Metal drinking vessel.

cannette: Drinking vessel. Stones or steins were sometimes called cannettes. Also, any canne for wine.

Cannon & Drum dish: Covered dish, one of the many pressed-glass examples made from 1870s to 1890s, and including kitchen stoves, flatirons, watches, et cetera. This example is composed of a receptacle in the form of a drum with cover, displaying a wheeled cannon and pile of shot.

Cannonball: Pattern of pressed glass also known as Atlas & Crystal Ball, featuring rows of marble-size glass balls at base, rim, and junctures of cover.

cannon cane: Walking stick, the handle of which is a small brass or iron cannon, bored and having touchhole. The bore is .22 or .25. Date probably c. 1810–50.

cannon handle: Cannon-shaped handle of knives, forks, and other tableware.

cannon stove: 18th-century stove in the general shape of a cannon of huge bore. These stoves stood upright and were made by several early American iron founders, including H. W. Stiegel at Elizabeth Furnace, Lancaster County, Pa.

Cannon Street Parian: Any unmarked Parian statuary is often designated as "Cannon Street" because this 19th-century pottery made over a hundred different Parian busts, statues, groups, et cetera, none of which was marked. The pottery was at Hanley, Staffordshire.

canoe cup: Oval-shaped cup without handle, looking somewhat like a canoe.

canotype: Paper prints of early photographic plates.

Canova: Classic revival sculptor, 1757–

1822, who executed the Roman gladiator statue of Washington for the North Carolina capitol. Canova's portrait appears on certain pottery and Staffordshire china by Mayer, Clews, Wood, and others.

Canschut pianos: Pianofortes made by Michael Canschut of New York, late 18th century.

canta galli: Italian majolica or faïence made at Florence, Italy, from c. 1850.

cantaro: Double-spouted glass vessel of Spanish origin; one spout is used in filling, the smaller one in pouring.

canted: Inclined; tilted; slanting; bent.

canted candlestick: Candlestick having socket mounted at an angle with the base. These rare sticks were made for use on sloping surfaces, such as a desk top, and when so used the candle was upright. One's first thought on seeing one is that the candle would drip if burned in that stick. [*Example pictured.*]

canteen: A portable container with a spigot for dispensing liquids. This same term was used in 18th century to designate a service of plate, a tea set, et cetera.

canteen pitcher: Pitcher in the form of a flat-sided, drum-shaped canteen with raised eagle on the sides. It was footed and handled, with a pouring spout in the form of a Continental soldier wearing a three-cornered hat. Made at Phoenixville, Pa., Majolica Pottery c. 1880. Porcelain, creamy white, with gilding.

canterbury: A compartmented rack for newspapers, periodicals, music, portfolios, and papers, generally of cabinet wood but known in wirework and papier-mâché. Made in many sizes, shapes, and styles; most of them have a handhold for carrying.

cantering horse: A super-hobbyhorse mounted on four large wheels and arranged to convert the up-and-down motion of the horse into power to propel the wheels. An advertisement, dated 1863, states "it runs rapidly over the ground by weight of the rider."

cant hook: Long bar having iron spike and hooking lever at end. Used in lumbering and in handling timber. Not a can hook, *which see.*

canting lamp: Lard-oil lamp with tilting reservoir, balanced so that it tilted forward as oil was consumed and so ensured burning until all fluid was exhausted.

cantle: Edge, corner, or rim.

canton: French for "corner"; a political division equivalent to a state or province in Switzerland, such as Uri, Berne, Appenzell, et cetera.

Canton bistre: The Chinese export porcelain commonly called Canton, decorated in bistre brown instead of the conventional blue.

Canton carpeting: Straw-mat floor covering imported from Canton in huge rolls —plain, pattern-woven, and painted. Also known as Nanking carpeting.

Canton china: The blue-and-white Chinese ware of commerce. This was low-cost porcelain made up in innumerable pieces of dinnerware, generally in blue, frequently unmarked, sometimes with rice-grain indentations which show up as translucent spots in a pattern. Also the ware used for ginger pots, tea caddies, and preserve jars. Imported first by Dutch and Portuguese traders in the 17th century, it became a staple of the clipper-ship trade of America. It was a stock item in most china stores up to modern times. Production was resumed after World War II and continued to end of Nationalist regime in China.

Canton flannel: Soft cotton fabric of natural beige color, fleecy on one side, smooth on the other. The original was woven in China and imported from Canton.

Canton trencher salt: Porcelain salt dishes of Canton-style ware, molded in one piece and often mistaken for small soap dishes. Made in China for the English and American market, and many imported during clipper-ship era. Once sold in nearly every china store.

cant spar: Fire pole.

cant window: Bow window.

canvase; canvasse: Prior to 1650, linen used as bed sheeting, bolsters, and beers (pillowbeers).

caoutchou: Gum elastic; rubber.

cap case: Hatbox; bandbox; traveling bag; wallet.

Cape Cod: Pattern of pressed glass similar to Canadian but with a water view believed to represent Cape Cod. It is more reminiscent of the Butterfly Fleet in the harbor off Monomoy, Nantucket.

Cape Cod glass: Any glass made on the Cape, such as Sandwich, is, of course, Cape Cod glass; but the particular ware often designated by this name is the product of the Cape Cod Glass Company, established 1858 by Deming Jarves after his withdrawal from the Sandwich Works. Among the objects of virtue made at the Cape Cod works were pressed and cut glass, paperweights, canes, Vasa Murrhina glass, and specialties. Dr. Flowers operated the plant to the 1880s.

Cape Cod salt: Salt from evaporation of sea water, produced at Dennis, Eastham, Wellfleet, and Yarmouth, on Cape Cod.

Capewell glass: Flint glass made at works of John Capewell, Philadelphia, from 1825.

capha: A variety of damask-weave fabric.

capillaire: An essence added to water to make a palatable drink. The recipe: Mix 6 well-beaten eggs with 14 pounds loaf and 3 pounds coarse sugar; add 3 quarts water, boil twice, skim well; add ¼ pint orange-flower water, strain through jellybag; bottle. Add one or two spoonfuls to a glass of warm or cold water.

Capillary Pabulum: Vegetable hair tonic invented and sold by James H. Howe of Boston, who styled himself "high priest of taste and fashion, and renovator of beauty." Made from 1829. Original bottles with name of product blown in are now scarce.

capital: See Entablature.

Capitol coverlet: Pattern-woven coverlets displaying a repeat pattern of the U.S. Capitol at Washington. Examples signed by weaver and unsigned are generally available. Some dated as early as 1830s, others as late as 1850s.

capo di monte: Italian porcelain made from 1743 to 1759 or 1760, and again from 1770 to 1820s. These data refer to the early wares and not to subsequent production attributed to this source, or to signed or marked wares made after 1820s.

capped night lamps: Rare lamps of brass that look like fine inkwells. The tilting lid served as a reflector when opened. Used chiefly as chamber lamps. Most known examples are marked as the product of Shelton Lamp Works, London and Birmingham, England, c. 1820.

cappercalizee: Large game bird of the grouse family. Term said to be Scottish.

cap pistols (MECHANICAL): Cast-iron novelty pistols contemporaneous with mechanical cast-iron banks. Displayed movement of figures, birds, animals, et cetera, as percussion caps were exploded. Many varieties. "The Chinese Must Go" and "Hatching Egg" are scarce examples. [Both are pictured.]

capstan: The drum upon which an anchor chain or cable is wound. In the arts, a decorative, concave-sided barrel form.

cap stand: Wood stand upon which to perch a cap. Most were made from two pieces of fret-sawed thin boards, joined in X form. [Example pictured.]

capstan table: A revolving drum table.

capstick; capstock; captree; capgallows: Racks, rows, or tiers of pegs. Costumers' clothes trees, or any other clothes or hatracks. These various terms were used during the 18th century.

captain's chair: See Chairs, All Kinds.

captain's decanters: Probably a modern term for any glass decanter engraved with a ship and name. To be properly a captain's decanter the container should be of ship-decanter shape, having a very broad base and a somewhat squat or conical body.

captain's desk: Desk box with two drawers on a high frame, with fold-out leaf to provide writing surface. The term may be suspect of invention to glamorize any high desk on frame.

captain's dresser: Small chest of drawers with lidded top, side bails, fitted trays, folding mirror, and other conveniences. Generally used on shipboard but not exclusively by captains.

captain's trumpet: A megaphone used by commander of a vessel to call directions from the quarter-deck. Silver examples are generally ceremonial or presentation pieces. [The example pictured was presented by grateful passengers to a captain whose bravery saved them from shipwreck in 1853.]

caput flask: Glass or pottery flask in form of a face or head, often of a saint or holy man or pagan idol. These objects date from pre-Christian Era down through Middle Ages to 19th century. Some of the earliest-known mold-blown glass is represented in caput flasks of Greece and Rome.

caqueteuse: See Chairs, All Kinds.

carafe: Ovoid or globose vessel for beverages, without stopper.

carambole; cramball: A sort of billiard game.

carameli: See Chocolate Glass.

carat: Actually a weight equal to 4 grains used in measuring precious stones. Also the measure of purity of gold as follows: 24 carat is pure gold refined and all alloy or dross extracted. Any deviation therefrom, such as 22 carat, 14 carat, and so on is indication of the gold content and not the alloy. The term carat is generally represented by the letter k, as 14k, 22k, et cetera.

carberry: The gooseberry.

carbon oil: One of the early names for kerosene, in use at least ten years before Colonel Drake's well was drilled. Samuel Kier of Pittsburgh refined petroleum seepage from salt wells and streams and sold the product as carbon oil, superior to whale oil as a lamp fluid, at 75 cents a gallon. This new lamp fluid became so popular and desirable that the price per gallon rose to $2 in the 1850s. This may well have influenced Drake to drill for the crude oil. It is therefore an error to assume, as have some experts, that a coal-oil or kerosene-burning lamp must date from after the Drake well was drilled in 1859. Actually thousands of lamps, and perhaps hundreds of thousands, were converted to coal-oil or carbon-oil burners after Kier began his refining of crude oil from seepage. There is also record of crude petroleum being traded in 18th century as "Seneca Oil" and "Rattlesnake Oil." This oil came from the place in Pennsylvania designated on the 1755 map of the province as "Petroleum."

carbon paste mold: A modern pattern-mold technique used in glass blowing. Iron molds are lined with carbon in paste form, and in these glass can be blown and show no mold marks.

carcass floor: The joists, girts, or beams upon which the floor planking is nailed or pegged.

Cardan lamp: 17th-century improved lamp of cast brass or iron with fuel fed from bottom wick tube.

cardenium: An organette; a small organ.

cardinal: A color, red-scarlet or red-purple. Also a punch similar to bishop, made with roasted oranges, sugar, and claret.

Cardinal Bird: Pattern of pressed glass, sometimes called Bluejay, featuring a large bird on a twig. Some pieces display two or three birds.

carding: The act of carding dyed or natural wool in preparation for making roving.

card matches: Early strike-anywhere matches made in flat wood sheets, almost wholly split through in matchstick width, the ends notched and dipped in the ignition mixture. From 12 to 16 matches made up a flat card.

cardoon: A vegetable of the artichoke family, commonly used from 1600s. Also used to curdle milk in cheese making. Not the great cactus of Mexico and South America.

cards: General term for playing cards of all sorts, also games in which the cards are used. Card names extended to games include piquet, lanterloo, loo, hazard, basset, et cetera. In addition, many other names of cards were invented by the makers. Several decks of cards used in occult practice were in general use in 17th and 18th centuries. One of these was the tarot. The cards mentioned in early New England records and inventories were not playing cards but wool cards, brushlike affairs with wood backs and handles, having wire bristles with bent ends. These were used in making the roving or round fluff from which wool yarn was spun.

card table: Any table of a size and shape permitting placement of four people, the top square, octagonal, or round, sometimes folding or tilting and sometimes permanently fixed, made for or adaptable for use in playing cards. Known in every period of cabinetmaking style from William & Mary through Second Baroque or Victorian. Some card tables have two narrow flaps which raise and are fixed by wings or swing boards beneath them. Many breakfast tables were used also as card tables.

card writer: A writer of calling cards, generally an expert in calligraphy. A sign writer or painter, especially of show cards and window signs.

carecloth: A square of fabric held over the bride by four attendants. A 17th- and 18th-century ceremonial at weddings.

carer: A sieve or temse.

Carey & Young lamps: Coach lamps made by a New York firm of this name from 1850s.

cark: A measure of wool equal to 40 tods. Since a tod weighed 28 pounds, a cark was practically a one-horse load of wool.

carl-cat: A tomcat.

carlet: A comb maker's file.

Carleton House desk: Modern term for a Sheraton-style desk of table form, having superstructure of drawers and cabinets at each side with writing space in front center. Sometimes inlaid and sometimes painted with elaborate scenes, panels, et cetera. Others display a pierced gallery of brasswork on the superstructure.

Carl Fisher figures: Carl Fischer or Fisher was a master modeler of Bohemia, and his initials appear on china figurines made from 1840s to 1850s as "C.F."

Carlile furniture: Reference is most likely to the cabinet and seat furniture made by John Carlile of Providence, R.I., after 1785 to 1830.

carlings: Peas steeped in water and fried in butter. A sort of ceremonial breakfast dish for Palm Sunday, which was often called Carling Sunday.

Carmen: Late pattern of pressed glass featuring curvate diamond pressed panels with large diamond centers, alternating with clear panels.

Carmen Cut: Pattern of cut glass featuring large diamond panels filled with smaller diamond cuts, alternating with four-pointed stars and fans.

Carmer, Nicholas: Cabinetmaker and furniture dealer of New York City who advertised as early as 1767.

carmines: Red ink bottles fitted with ground-glass stoppers. This is the 19th-century trade term for all red ink bottles.

carnauba: Wax of a South American palm of the same name, often called the wax palm.

1, "Chalk Ware" Originals, of Chinese Porcelain. 2, Cresset on Top of Andiron. 3, Cresset Fire Lighter. 4, Cone Lantern. 5, Cup and Saucer Lamp. 6, Cream Skimmers. 7, Cotton Bow, in use. 8, Cupboard Table. 9, Chimney'd Fat-Lamp. 10, Captain's Trumpet (ceremonial). 11, Carter Chandelier. 12, Cylindricum Speculum. 13, Diamond Reflector Lamp. 14, Derby China; examples of ware and marks. (No. 14 from Virtue & Co., London.)

Carnes, Burrell: Extensive printer of wallpaper panels pasted together in rolls, Philadelphia, from 1789. His business was not in his name but was called Le Collay & Chardon.

carob: Pulp of the pods of the carob trees. The seeds were the standard of weight from which the term "carat" derives.

Carolean: Pertaining to the reigns of Charles I and Charles II of England, and the furniture styles of this period in the Stuart regime. Sometimes called Jacobean in error; Jacobean refers to reigns or periods of James I and James II.

Carolina flower prints: Small folio prints of flowers, all colored lithographs, eleven in number, issued by the Episcopal Sunday School Union, 1859. The flowers are identified as from the Carolinas, and all are native American wild flowers.

carols: Broadsides of Yuletide songs or roundelays. Date from 1520s in England, when the printer, Wynken de Worde, issued sheets of festive chansons for enlivening Christmas celebrations.

carol window; carrell window: A bow window, often used as a cubicle for study. Any bow or bay window.

carpet: Originally a hanging or garniture for cabinet and case furniture, tables, and chairs. Use as a floor covering seems to have begun in the colonies c. 1750. Painted floor cloths were in use by 1680. Oriental carpets were not infrequently used as hangings rather than as floor cloths to about 1750. Thereafter floor carpeting became a general practice, and by 1790 the Carpet Manufactory of Philadelphia was weaving rugs and carpets in the Aubusson tradition. By 1800 the Quaker City was the American center of carpet weaving.

carpetbag tub: A folding bathtub affected by travelers in the days when rooms with private baths were practically unprocurable at hotels. Most of these items were of waterproofed canvas, folding within a frame of heavy wire.

carpet ball: Heavy glazed pottery balls about three inches in diameter, in many different colors, with cross striping somewhat like play marbles. In recent years these have been called carpet layers' balls and alleged to have been used in laying carpets. Actually these are bowling balls or carpet billiard balls.

carpet cutters: A form of rocker on a rocking chair, of wide thin boards cut in the shape of food choppers. [*Example pictured.*]

carpet loop: A tool used in looping rag tapes in making rugs and carpets. [*Example pictured.*]

carquenet; cancenet: A necklace.

carrot tobacco: Natural leaf tobacco twisted while pliable into carrot form, steeped in wine, and then aged in casks. Buyer could grate a carrot into snuff, break it into pipe tobacco, or cut it into quids for chewing.

carrousel figures: Any animal or human figures used on carrousels, or flying carriages. Most of them date from 1870s, but some were made in 1840s. Zebras, giraffes, swans, flying angels, and similar figures are of some rarity and much sought after for interior-decoration purposes.

Carruth clays: Clay pipes for smokers sold by Carruth & Co., Boston, mid-19th century.

Carruthers, George: Founder of the Wheeling, Va., Glass Works, 1820.

carrying desk: Portable desk, often with bail handles.

carry-us-all: Mid-19th-century term for the carrousel, flying horses, or merry-go-round.

cartel: Drum-shaped clock in ornate casing and mounting.

Carter, John: English architect and designer of mid-18th century who published *Specimens of Ancient Sculpture & Painting*. His contributions to furniture design are in the Adam tradition, the neoclassic.

Carter chandelier: An excellent elegancy of 1850; a gas-burning lighting fixture with pipes, globes, and all else hidden within a series of rings festooned with innumerable cut-glass pendants hung closely. [*Example pictured.*]

Carter furniture: In Eastern New England it probably refers to furniture made by Charles Carter of Chelsea, Mass., from c. 1838. In central and northern Illinois it means the machine-carved French Antique furniture made by H. S. Carter of Chicago in 1870s.

Carter japanned ware: Probably the wares made commercially by Carter of New York from 1850s. Tinned sheet-iron wares dipped in black japan lacquer and stencil-decorated.

Cartesian bottle or imp: Bottles or tubes filled with a liquid and capped with a flexible top. In the liquid an airtight hollow figure of colored glass would rise or fall according to pressure or release of pressure on flexible top. Named for René Descartes, 17th-century philosopher, who discovered the principle by which the toy operates. Imps of glass for such bottles were advertised by Demuth, specialty glass blower of New York, in 1871.

cartonnier: A stand or case of small boxes or drawers. A box for holding paper and envelopes, used separately or as part of the fitting of a desk.

carton Pierre: A plastic of macerated paper, similar to papier-mâché, used to mold ornaments and objects of decoration. Certain kinds were made of heavy cardboard and molded into furniture elements.

cartouche: Ornamental scroll or label; a tag, an oval, et cetera, inlaid, applied, impressed, painted, stamped, carved, or etched. Also table tops of symmetrical curve, reverse curve, or scrolled outline, often found in Hepplewhite and Sheraton styles. Term derives from name of a scroll or roll of paper.

Carver chair: Named for Elder Carver of the Pilgrim Company. See Chairs, All Kinds.

carving: (1) The art of sculpturing in wood to achieve ornament, decoration, or three-dimensional effects. (2) The method of formal slicing of a roast of flesh or game. Many special terms, such as "break a goose," "thrust a chicken," "spoil a hen," "pierce a plover," et cetera.

carving tools: Any of the various chisels

and gouges used in the practice of wood or other carving. Special knives for slicing or dismembering meats at table, together with allied appurtenances, such as steels for sharpening, shears for disjointing, skewers, and knife rests.

carwater: Water impregnated with mineral iron. Sometimes called chalybeate water.

Carwithin, William: Early cabinetmaker of Charleston, S.C., known to have been working by the 1730s.

Caryatids: Images of the ancient priestesses of the Temple of Diana or Artemis. Any representation in glass, china, metal, stone, or wood, as used after 1750 and popularized in the classic revival. Caryatid bowls, candlesticks, andirons, pillars, et cetera, are known. A draped female figure with a capital on the head to support an entablature.

casapanca; cassapanca: Seat-high chest fitted with low back and arms, serving also as a seat. Tudor and Gothic forms in use from 14th century, sometimes with a cushion. Variants of this basic idea are found in chest-bottomed settles, bacon cupboards, and other case furniture. This same name was given to wide thronelike chairs placed on a dais, which were confined almost exclusively to use of royalty, the nobility, and high officials in 15th and 16th centuries.

Cascade glass: Principally barroom glasswares, but also pressed, blown, and cut housewares made by Cascade Glass Works, Pittsburgh, from 1850s.

Case & Green: Lithographers and color printers of Hartford, Conn., from 1840s.

case bottle: Bottles blown especially for fitting in cases, whether singly, in pairs, fours, sixes, or brigades of twelve or more. Triangular, square, rectangular, octagonal, round, or cross-section shapes, specifically made to fit compartments in cases. Generally of fine thin glass, but sometimes cut, etched, enameled, or gilded. Most case bottles with the cases or trays are of English, Dutch, French, Swiss, and Swedish origin. It is doubtful if blown case bottles were produced in the colonies or in any early Federal glassworks, unless at Amelung and certain of the early Pittsburgh houses. Case bottles in original trays and cases are now scarce to rare items.

cased glass: Any basic blown element in any color, coated with one or more layers of contrasting colored glass. Highly decorative effects were achieved by cutting or etching through the layers of casing. In recent years cheaper kinds of plated glass, not cut or etched, have been called "cased," while the cut and etched wares have been designated as "overlay" glass. A considerable amount of cased and overlay glass was made in the U.S. at the New England glasshouses and at Pittsburgh, White Mills, Pa., Brooklyn, and Wheeling.

cased seat: "Slip seat" is the modern term. Frames, either upholstered or caned, rushed, roped, basket-woven, et cetera, fitting within a chair to form a seat. Some chairs were made with two cased-seat elements, one being the proper seating for a closestool or night chair.

case furniture: Strictly speaking, any piece of furniture that is a cabinet or any piece that is useful as a container, repository, place of safety or security. Furniture in general is divisible into three general classifications: case, seat, and stand. *See* Seat Furniture and Stand Furniture.

Casella instruments: Casella of London was a 19th-century manufacturer of barometers, hygrometers, sundials, thermometers, et cetera, for use in the home, farm, cottage, and dairy.

case of drawers: Any item of case furniture that developed from a simple chest, as follows: single large cavity chest with lid; the same with one drawer at bottom; then two and three drawers with evershallower chest cavity; and finally a fourth drawer under the lid, the lid fastening down to become a permanent top. Thus the steps from chest to case of drawers. When the piece has several drawers but retains a chest cavity, it is sometimes called a blanket, bedding, or linen chest.

casetta: A marriage chest, usually made in pairs.

cashaw: The red pumpkin or squash.

cashmere: Soft woolen fabric made from the neck wool of Kashmir goats. This is the wool used in the intricately woven yarn-dyed shawls imitated in Paisley and brochet.

cashoes: Netherlands term for mahogany.

cask bars: (Sometimes chime, or chimb, bars.) Heavy shaped and sometimes carved bars for inserting inside the grooves at the heads and bottoms of barrels to provide additional support when barrel or cask was filled. Some used to brace the manhole of a wine tun. French and Swiss examples are often intricately carved in mermaid, dolphin, and figural forms, stained and gilded. These were made in pairs and sometimes framed.

casket; casque: A large box, generally decorative but sometimes wholly utilitarian, ironbound.

cassa ligna: An aromatic bark similar to cinnamon.

Cassidy lamps: Portable, bracket, sconce, table, and ceiling lamps made c. 1870–90. Some are made to burn gas and some kerosene. They are sometimes marked, but there is no place designation on those examined.

cassie paper: Imperfect paper, soiled, wrinkled, or damaged in making.

Cassin prints: Prints of California birds, found in Volume 8 of *U.S. Exploring Expedition*, a government publication issued in 1858. The prints are royal folio and 42 in number.

cassolette: Ovoid spherical casket or other shaped vessels, generally with pierced lid or cover, used as perfumers or pastille burners.

cassone: A casket or chest, generally quite large in size, footed or on skids, often richly carved and with fine wrought-iron work. 15th and 16th centuries. Sometimes called cassoon.

Castel Durante: Famed Italian majolica ware made from the Renaissance period. Some of it is luster-glazed, some of armorial, portrait, and scenic decoration. Some of this ware is excessively rare, especially the early examples.

cast glass: Figural and shaped glassware cast in open or closed molds of dry plaster and clay.

casting bottle: Any bottle with a sprinkler top.

castle candlestick: Metal representation of a square tower with four corner turrets or bartizans, having five candle sockets. Italian and traditional; may be of any date from 18th to 20th century.

castle cupboard: Perhaps a 20th-century trade term for the Gallic- or Gothic-style clothes closets, from 14 to 24 inches square and to 6 feet tall, the tops corbie-stepped or crenelated, doors fitted with fine decorative wrought-iron hinges and latches and often with carved pilasters, and doors pierced for airiness. These date from 1400s and were most likely set up in rows, as are modern lockers, and used in churches, monasteries, castles, wardrooms, and halls.

Castleford: All wares made at Castleford Pottery near Leeds, England, from 1790s. There were many proprietors of this works from the days of its founder, David Dunderdale. White- and cream-glaze, embossed-design ware, some salt-glaze, Parian, black Egyptian ware, et cetera, were made. Very decorative teapots, jugs, pitchers, sugar basins, and American "historic" wares featuring Liberty, Arms of the U.S., Washington, and Franklin in relief with bands of color in the creamware are known. This pottery exported wares to the U.S. from the days of its founding to 1870s or later.

castor: A beaver; also a beaver hat.

castor bottle: Caster bottle; casting bottle.

castor-oil candles: Oil of the castor bean, refined and hardened by a secret process, was made into candles which sold at the fabulous price of 12½ cents each in the 1840s. Only one manufacturer, E. Morse, Alton, Ill., seems to have produced them.

cast porcelain: Opaque white glass; milk glass. The Bristol variety is often decorated in the Chinese taste and has the appearance of true porcelain. This term was used to describe milk glass by makers from the early 19th century.

casuers: Broad, wide sleeves.

cat & dog lamps: Deep figural-form dishes of glass, Parian, bisque, and other translucent wares. Cats, dogs, owls, Cupid faces, and other forms are known. Fairy-lamp candles burned in them provided a dim night lamp. They were also used for window illumination. Date is probably from 1870s.

cataract: An early laundry machine consisting of a wooden drum revolving in a deep trough, operated by a crank.

catenary: In antiques parlance, half of a perfect oval, divided on its minor axis. Galileo considered this the perfect form for an arch of equilibrium.

caterpillar work: Stitched-on fancy-work using chenille yarns, frayed braids, and similar fuzzy tapes to create rugs, mats, tidies, and cushion tops.

Cathedral: Pattern of pressed glass featuring pointed arches with crisscross filling alternating with open sections marked by groups of upright fronds. Also called Orion.

cathedral-back: A rare style of back found on some Windsor chairs of loop-back type. The loop is bent to form a Gothic-style arch. [*Example pictured among chair illustrations.*]

Catlin prints: George Catlin, famed artist, sportsman, and student of the American Indian, produced many paintings from which prints were made. These include the following publications in portfolio: *North American Indian Portfolio, 1845,* 25 prints; *Views of Niagara, 1831,* 3 prints; *O-Kee-Pa, 1867,* 13 prints; and a series of sporting views published by the Colt Co. advertising their famed rifle. Also any print from a painting or drawing by Catlin.

catmallison: Chimney cupboard to store smoked and dried meats.

catoptricks: Drawings made with aid of reflecting mirror; an optical toy of the 18th century which made seemingly confusing drawings appear in proper order.

catshead bank: Pottery bank in form of a cat's head, said to have been made at Bennington Works.

Catskill moss ware: Product of Ridgway & Co., Hanley, England, for sale to U.S. market. Historic views of Albany & Schenectady Railroad; the Hudson River; Boston; Wyoming Valley of Pennsylvania; Tomb of Washington; New York Bay; et cetera. Term derives from the border of the ware, which is of a pattern imitative of mosses and ferns.

catsup: Originally an Indian sauce. In England it was the brine in which green walnuts or fresh mushrooms were pickled. Around 1835 the love apple, or tomato, was sliced and pickled, the resulting liquid being tomato catsup. Finally the entire pickle was cooked and strained to a purée.

cattails: Heads of rushes used with flocking (raveled wool) to fill bed sacks and pillows in 17th and 18th centuries.

catted: Crisscrossed billets arranged to support heavy clay daub work, as in "catted chimney" construction. A pioneering technique of building.

cat trough: Cut-stone, pottery, or cast-iron troughs of small size.

catty: Caddy; a container.

caudern: Cauldron.

caudle: A pottage; a sort of thin gruel. Also a hot drink of wine, eggs, and milk.

caudle cup: Any cup used in serving caud or caudle, some of pottery, pewter, or silver.

Caughley: Pottery in Shropshire, established c. 1750. Made porcelain decorated at Worcester, and made first reproduction of the willow pattern in blue. Also made the famed Salopian wares.

Cauldon Place: The Ridgway Pottery, founded 1794 and in the Ridgway family to 1850s. Later operated by Brown-Westhead, and Moore & Co. Many kinds of wares produced.

cauldron; caldron: Large globular pot of cast iron, brass, or copper.

cauliflower bowl: Replica of a head of cauliflower in natural colors in form of a porcelain bowl. Produced by the Chelsea Pottery as early as 1750s. Cauliflower teapots and cauliflower ware in general are in the tradition of imitating the natural form of this cream and green vegetable of the kohl family.

causeuse: See Chairs, All Kinds.

cavetto: Concave, quarter-circle molding.

cavill: Caul or coif. A hairnet.

cayenne bottle: Small glass bottle with metal top to which a small spoon is attached. A dispenser of that potent condiment, cayenne pepper.

Cayenne woods: Any of the tropical hardwoods from the Island of Cayenne.

C-curve: One of the favorite decorative forms of the mid-18th century, used extensively by Chippendale, Ince & Mayhew, and other designers. It derives from the Chinese, and the curve resembles the form of the Roman letter C. [*Examples of the form pictured.*]

ceiling carpet: Decorative felting designed for tacking to ceiling beams of newly constructed cottages, eliminating the necessity for lath and plaster and providing better insulation. Made from the 1850s. Used also by owners of many old 17th- and 18th-century homes with exposed beams. It is doubtful if any examples survive. When used in inventory or other commentaries, the term means what is here described.

celadon: The clear, green-glaze, gray-bodied stoneware of Lung Ch'uan, Sung period. Also sea-green color, generally applied to porcelain.

celadon fleur: Flowered porcelain with green ground.

celery: Glass vase, made in many varieties, used to hold stalk celery at table. Any vase of other substance put to same use.

celestina: A mechanical organ playing from perforated paper rolls. Also called a dulciana. Made 1850-90.

cellar (bed cellar): A canopy.

cellaret: A cabinet or case of portable nature holding bottles, decanters, and glasses. The early portable bar.

celure: Same as bed cellar; a boxlike frame fastened to side wall over head of a bed, with rods to hold tester curtains. Any canopy over a bedstead, supported by means other than the bedposts.

cendrée de Tournay: Lime cement or mortar, aged before use.

censer lamp: Globular metal device, the lower half a fuel reservoir and the upper half pierced to shield the lamp flame. Used at times to burn perfumed oils. Known in brass, Sheffield plate, and silver. Some are quite small.

census mug: Liverpool transfer-printed mug displaying the first U.S. census figures (1790) for the states and territories.

Centennial: Pattern of pressed glass by Gillinder, Philadelphia, made in 1876. The platters have either Independence Hall, Carpenters Hall, or bust of Washington. Other pieces have bands of large overlapping circles with fine diamond beading in the lap and large diamonds tiered in circle centers.

Centennial bookmarks: Jacquard-loomed silk ribbon bookmarks woven at the Centennial Exposition by the Phoenix Silk Co., displaying portraits of Washing-

ton, Lincoln, Grant, and other notables. Fifty-five hundred punched cards were required to weave the intricate patterns.

Centennial glass: (1) Wares made and sold at the Centennial glassworks of Gillinder & Sons, including lovely souvenir busts in frosted glass. This was a complete glassworks, producing free-blown, mold-blown, pressed, and cut wares, all of which were for sale and many of which were souvenirs of the exposition. (2) Novelties memorializing the Centennial, generally patriotic or historic, made by dozens of glass companies and sold throughout the nation from 1875 to 1880 or later.

Centennial inkstand: Bronze figure of Liberty with an eagle perched on her uplifted right hand. It had an ornate base with the U.S. shield and a crystal inkwell covered with a bronze lid dated 1776. Made by Muller & Sons, New York City, 1876.

Centennial lamp: Deep cup or tumbler-shaped shade of colored glass, some mold-blown and some pressed, used as holders for squat candles which, when burning, illuminated the shade. Used in rows and tiers to light up window ledges for celebrations. Once quite inexpensive articles of carnival taste, they are now collected by glass enthusiasts.

Centennial sofa bed: Sofa extending to bed size, made as a specialty for many years prior to the Centennial but revived and named as here. Advertised extensively in Philadelphia as a good piece to have to accommodate guests for the exposition. Reeves & Eastburn, Philadelphia, were the makers.

centripetal chair: See Chairs, All Kinds.

century vase: Silver display piece made by Gorham for exhibition at the Centennial. It was valued at $25,000 and contained 2000 ounces of solid silver.

Ceraglioli ware: Plaster ware of the sort erroneously called Pennsylvania Dutch. Bartholomew Ceraglioli was a manufacturer of plaster chimney and mantel ornaments, busts, statues, et cetera, in New York City from 1840.

cerecloth: A plaster for bruises, sprains, et cetera, consisting of cloth covered with wax saturated with arnica or some other balm.

Ceredo Pikes Peak: A mold-blown historic flask memorializing Pikes Peak, made at Ceredo Glass Works near Huntington, Va.

Ceremenati & Bernardo mirrors: This firm of Italian experts, Boston, from c. 1810, made many fine tabernacle mirrors of the type miscalled Sheraton. The firm was also Ceremenati & Monfrino. Advertisements of both firms, apparently at the same address, 3 State Street, are of record.

cereograph: A process of making plates for printing which deserves explanation. The artist or sketcher made a drawing on a plate coated with wax. This, in turn, was dusted with graphite. A copper-deposit shell was achieved by galvanic battery and copper bath, after which the thin shell of copper was backed with melted lead, cooled, and mounted on a wood block. Many maps were made by this process. Some plates for printing a limited number of copies were made by casting in the wax with plaster of Paris. Still another method of quick plate-making was to coat steel sheets with a layer of plaster. The artist drew through the plaster down to the hard metal. Then hot lead was poured over the plate and a cast was made from which printing could be done.

certosina: Marquetry or inlay in tile form of alternate squares of black and white, often of ebony and bone. Also any geometric-pattern inlay work.

cerule chair: See Chairs, All Kinds.

cerus (ceruse): White; white lead.

Chace pottery: Hard glossy stoneware, impressed "L. & B. C. CHACE," made at Somerset, Mass., from c. 1839. Clark Chace, Jr., and brothers Benjamin and Leonard were of this firm.

chaff bag: A bed sack stuffed with dried cornhusks.

chaff cutter: Machine for chopping green cornstalks and other vegetable fronds, invented by Sharp of London, c. 1750, and used extensively on large estates in the colonies. The first ensilage cutter.

Chaffers delft: Delftwares made by Richard Chaffers of Liverpool, one-time apprentice of Alderman Shaw. Chaffers began making delftwares in 1752. The "hourglass" pepper shakers, at one time reputed to have been sold by the thousands in the colonies and to have had colloquial expression in the phrase, "He's as hot as Dick's pepperbox," are now known to have been pounce or blotting-sand boxes, not pepper shakers, in spite of the fact that many were used as both salt and pepper shakers. Chaffers made many plates, mugs, canns, beakers, bowls, and other objects of delft.

chafing dish: Any dish with an etna or small stove under it. Not primarily a dish for table cookery, but a dish to keep stews, ragouts, gruels, et cetera, hot. Many early examples used small braziers for charcoal as heating devices. These have a spark and ash pan under the heating element. Later examples had lamps burning spirits of wine (alcohol) with various muffling or turn-down devices. Iron, brass, copper, Sheffield-plate, and silver examples are known. Sizes range from small 8-ounce bowls and dishes to large ones with a dish from 8 to 18 inches in diameter. The ensemble is usually on a stand with 3 or more feet.

chagrin: Shagreen, a leather.

Chagrin bowls: Woodenware bowls turned at the turnery at Chagrin Falls, O., from 1840s.

Chain: Pattern of pressed glass featuring a series of diamond-marked ovals in a chain, the joints superimposed on rayed circles. A variant, Chain with Star, breaks the line of ovals with a small starred circle that looks more like a formalized representation of the sun. These are late patterns, 1880s-90s. Chain & Shield is not a variant but a different pattern displaying a series of loops in shield form, inside of which is a twisting chain.

chain decanter: A blown or mold-blown decanter with a belt in center or middle of raised chainlike pattern.

chained: Threading of molten glass applied in chain form as decoration. Also called guilloche.

chain handles: Lengths of chain, passed through ears of buckets and jugs of metal, and serving as handles.

chain pump: A well pump composed of a pair of chains running over a drum, fitted at intervals with buckets or scoops.

chair-bottom cut: Pattern of cut glass imitative of chair caning.

chair button: (1) Ball-like terminal on arms and legs of chairs. (2) The thong attached cuplike container of rear legs of chairs made by the Shakers, called "tilting chair."

chair fire screen: Willow work or rush mat, hung on back of a chair to screen the sitter from heat of a fireplace. Used generally on dining-chair backs placed near fireplace at mealtimes.

chair-frame spinning wheel: A compact spinning wheel, the wheel, spindle, treadle, cords, et cetera, being housed in a framework somewhat like that of a chair, without seat or side stretchers. Said to be a refinement of the North Irish wheel. Date is presumed to be from 1730s, but most likely, in regions where popular, this type of wheel was made to 1835.

chairmakers: See Cabinetmakers.

chair nails: Upholstery nails, often with fancy heads.

Chairs, All Kinds: Two books about chairs, *The Rocking Chair*, by Esther Stevens Frazer, and *Windsor Chairs*, by Wallace Nutting, were the only sources of collectors' information until the author's *Handbook of Antique Chairs* was published in 1948. However, all general books on antique furniture have one or more chapters devoted to chairs. The best information on the peerless chairs of 18th-century Philadelphia is found in *Blue Book, Philadelphia Furniture, 1682-1807*, by W. M. Hornor, Jr. In this dictionary for antiques collectors we shall not attempt a listing of chairmakers in spite of the fact that we have collected over 3,500 names of such artisans, working from 1620 to 1875. What space can be allocated will be used for a listing of various types of chairs, with special reference to terms now generally used to designate a chair which in many cases is not the original designation. The list is as follows:

Brewster: A many-spindle-turned chair of 17th century, reproduced in 1840s. Many variants. Named Brewster because Elder Brewster is said to have had one. [*Example pictured*.]

captain's lounge: A long-seated, rush-bottomed chair for lolling. [*Example pictured*.]

captain's Windsor: (1) A Windsor horseshoe armchair with a low-set comb. [*Example pictured*.] (2) Any Windsor with high legs, somewhat like a weaving stool, for use in the wheelhouse.

caqueteuse: An early armchair, narrow-backed, seat widening at front, and with horseshoe-form arms. Dates from 1350s to 1550s.

Carolean: Turned and carved hardwood chairs with caned seats and backs; crested and with carved and scrolled stretchers. Date is 1600s to c. 1680s. [*Example pictured*.]

Carver: One of the Pilgrim Century type chairs of New England. Turned stick chair,

Like the Brewster chair, it is of Tudor heritage. [*Example pictured.*] Also reproduced in 1840s.

cathedral-back Windsor: A loop-back side chair with a distinct double curve and hump in the loop. [*Example of back only pictured.*]

causeuse: A club-type upholstered chair of France.

centripetal: A cast-iron chair on flat springs. 19th century, probably from 1850s.

cerule: A chair made up of a series of X-shaped members forming a seat; also called Dantesque chair and Savonarola chair. Italian, dating from 1500. Some made in Switzerland and France.

chair-on-chair: Child's high chair made by mounting a small chair on the leg and rail frame of a larger chair. [*Example pictured is of Queen Anne period.*]

chair table: Table with round, oval, oblong, or square top mounted on an arm-chair framework, and convertible from table to chair by tilting top upward. 17th-century style, of Tudor heritage. [*Example pictured.*]

chaise à capucine: French phrase meaning chairs of the country.

chaise bonne femme: Upholstered-back, rush- or rope-seated, open-armed chairs with arm pads. Generally 18th century, of Provence, France.

Charles II chairs: *See* Carolean chair.

chicken-coop: Colloquial for any stick chair, especially a Windsor.

Cleopatra's Barge chair: A fancy chair, rush-seated, with fine gilt and color decoration. Name derives from the chairs of this type used on the Crowninshield pleasure yacht, *Cleopatra's Barge.*

Cleveland rocker: A platform-type rocker with a stamped leather panel of Mrs. Grover Cleveland. This dates it.

closestool: Any night chair. The Elizabethan "jakes" of late 16th century are not the oldest of these. There are examples reported dating from c. 1300. Some authorities claim that many corner chairs, especially those with deep valances, were night chairs, or closestools. Some had pewter, brass, tin, or even silver pans. [*Examples pictured.*]

club: Any chair with a seat 21 or more inches high is generally suspect of having been designed for club use. However, in 18th century, leather-upholstered chairs for library and men's retiring rooms were often designated as club chairs.

coaching: (1) Folding chair for coach or post chaise. (2) Sometimes a folding seat on a cane.

cockfight: A long-seated chair with an upholstered back and a padded front bar on extension of the leg; the seat was a saddle form. The chair often called a cock-fight, with upholstered seat and back and a padded rail across back, is a gentleman's room chair, or club chair. [*Both types pictured.*] Some of the second noted chairs have a reading board set at an angle over the back. All of these chairs were designed for use of occupant sitting facing the back, straddling the narrow section of the seat.

cockfight stool: A different sort of seat; a cage for the fighting cock, the wire or mesh cage fitted with legs and a cushioned seat, permitting use also as a stool. Some have drawers for spurs, alum, arnica, et cetera. These are generally of classic style, made in 18th century.

comb-back roundabout: An English Windsor chair with a comb back.

comfort rocker: Wicker or rattan rocker woven to conform to the contour of the human form. Modeled from a snow-bank impression of a body. Made by Heywood & Co. from mid-19th century. Still made.

common-sense: Bamboo-turned Windsor-type chairs and settees made at Mottville, N.Y., by The Sinclair Shops. Seats and backs are tape. [*Example pictures from an advertisement.*]

compass: (1) A perfectly round seat chair. (2) Chairs having seats of molded leather having impress of a compass card.

Connecticut Pilgrim: 17th-century chair with turned stick frame and paneled back, with rush or rope seat.

conversation: The S-shaped seat chair for two, seating them side by side but facing. [*Example pictured.*] There is a French chair, known also as the voyeuse, which is a modified balloon or saddle-seated chair with a caned back and a padded top rail.

corner: The roundabout chair; the chief characteristic of this type of chair is that the angles of the seat are at front and back and at sides. This puts the front leg directly in center, with legs at either side and another at rear. This chair fits into a corner but is seldom now so used. Popular as desk chairs. Said by some commentators to have been the general closestool, or night chair, of 18th century, and seldom seen out of bedrooms. Type derives from a Chinese mandarin's chair of 16th century. Queen Anne, Georgian, Adam, Chippendale, and many other period styles. [*Examples pictured.*]

Cromwellian: Turned frame, generally of hardwood, upholstered with turkey work and trimmed with fringe. A chair of 17th century, reaching its high point of popularity in Cromwellian era. [*Example pictured.*]

crook-footed: A chair with rockers. In spite of all claims for the American (or colonial) invention of the rocking chair, it just isn't so. The crook-footed chair of England was in use by 1660. While not popular, and confined, perhaps, to children's chairs, the evidence of "prior art" exists. Evidence is given in *Spinning Wheel Magazine,* March 1950.

cupboard chair table: The base is a boxlike member with a door. Four uprights over the cupboard support arms on which rests the tilting table top, convertible to a high-backed chair. [*Example pictured.*]

Cupid's-bow Windsor: The reference is to the shaping of the comb on a comb, or fan-back Windsor; it is in the outline form of a Cupid's bow, or the human upper lip.

Dann: A camp chair with carpet seat. Many made by Dann Brothers of New Haven from 1850s.

decrowned: Said of any chair of 17th-century England, or the colonies, from

CHAIRS, all kinds: Top row: Mandarin's, Hogarth, Exercising, Voyeuse, Bird-Back.
2nd row: Brewster (2), Thrown, Beehive, Carolean. **3rd row:** Wainscot, "Modern" of
1850 (2), Turned, Common-Sense Settee. **4th row:** Joined Stool, Shaker Rocker, Closestool,
Scoop, Burgomaster's. **Bottom row:** Fancy chairs (2), with advertisement, Boston Rocker,
Rocking Stool.

CHAIRS, all kinds: **Top row:** Quadrant, Faldestool, Martha Washington, Sgabelli. **2nd row:** Three corner chairs and turnings as follows: Early Pennsylvania, Standard Pennsylvania, New England, Virginia, Rhode Island, Bamboo. **4th row:** Salem Chair Back, English Windsor, American Windsor (Comb-Back Armchair), Horseshoe Windsor. **Bottom row:** Banister-Back, 9-Spindle Bow-Back Windsor, Adam-Period Armchair, Banister-Back Corner Chair.

CHAIRS, all kinds: **Top row:** Barber's, Brewster, Captain's Lounge, Cathedral-Back, Chair-on-Chair, Cradle Rocker, Draught. **2nd row:** Cupboard, Cromwellian, Electric-Treatment, Gothic, Jenny Lind, Prince of Wales. **3rd row:** Round, Shell-Backed Throne, Standing Stool, Square Windsor, Sleigh, Wig-Back. **4th row:** Threshing, Sleepy-Hollow (with leg stool), Figure-8 Chair Backs, Cockfight (true variety). **5th row:** Cockfight, properly Club, Glastonbury, Chair Tables (2), Winslow Chair. **Bottom row:** Carver (2), Music-Room (2), Conversation, Upside-Down Windsor, back of Ribbon-Back.

76

which the crownlike cresting has been removed; a chair of the type made without the carved cresting. The cause is laid to indignation of the British people over the treaty with France against the Dutch Republic.

double bow-back: Said of Windsor chairs having an extra bow, with connecting spindles, over a standard bow back.

draught: A chair fashioned from a large tree trunk. Tudor country style. Some made by pioneers up to 1850s in U.S. Others of even later date made as novelties. [*Example pictured.*]

drunkard's: Any chair with a double-width seat; a love seat.

easy inclining: Directoire- or Sheraton-style chair with adjustable back; grandfather of the Morris chair.

electric-treatment: Chair fixed on an insulated dais or platform. [*Example pictured dates from 1836.*]

elbloe (elbow): Any armchair was once so designated.

Elysian rocker: Trade name of a late Directoire-styled rocking chair of 1870s and later.

Empress: Term is English for a turnip-footed "Victorian" upholstered chair.

English willow: Imported chair woven from willow fronds.

exercising: Massive Empire-Grecian-style chair with mechanical movement giving the equivalent of a horseback ride when sat upon and the motion levers pulled. [*Example pictured.*] Halstead of New York made these chairs from 1840s. Other manufacturers had similar chairs in production.

faldestool: The *Chanson de Roland* calls this "the seat of Princes." A chair of state. Any chair on which cushions and rich fabric drapery were laid. Term is origin of *fauteuil*, or upholstered chair. The faldestool is an early chair, dating from c. 1200. There are many varieties, including the Dantesque chair. [*The curvate X-sided example pictured has wrought-iron stretchers and four carved "polls," or "heads."*] When in use this chair would have a cushion and a drape over the back rail.

fancy: The painted or gilded chair of classic-revival style, revived by the Brothers Adam c. 1750 and made continuously since then, each decade providing lower-priced examples. The culmination is the cheap turned and shaped-form chair with rush seats, painted, stenciled, or freehand decorations, commonly and erroneously called "Hitchcock." Original fancy chairs were often embellished with scenic and other painting by experts and were meticulously fitted. All fancy chairs were designed primarily for the boudoir, the chamber, the music room, or the ladies' salons. By 1825 the fancy chair was found in every home and cottage, in canalboat and river-steamer cabins, in theater loges, et cetera. [*Examples pictured.*]

fancy-back Windsor: A combination of French styling in the Windsor tradition; turned legs, saddle seat, pierced bow, and fancy laddered panel back.

fan rocker: A faddish invention by a New Orleans gentleman; a rocking chair patented 1847. When used, the chair im-

parted motion to a cooling fan. These chairs were also made in Philadelphia.

fauteuil: Upholstered armchair. Term derives from faldestool.

fiddle-back: Queen Anne and Georgian chairs having back splats somewhat imitative of the contours of a violin. It must be confessed that many so called are not fiddle-shaped, but vase form.

figure-8: Any chair with a back element having the Arabic numeral 8 as a major part of the design. [*Examples pictured, backs only.*]

five-legged: A rarity of great excellence and genuine quality; the extra leg is in the center of the front seat rail. Generally of classic styling, French examples are almost the only ones now found, but it is said the Brothers Adam also designed such chairs for their clients.

foolscap: A Victorian conceit of English style; a fool's cap is made a part of the back upholstery.

foot-rest: Any chair with a narrow shelf or board attached to the front legs about 4 to 6 inches above floor line. This was a device to make any chair a nursing chair, or to provide special comfort for short-legged people.

French: Any chair of Directoire styling was once so named by cabinetmakers. Obviously any French-styled chair of any period is so designated.

garden-tool: A conceit of the 1790s; a chair made up of elements imitative of rakes, spades, hoes, and other garden tools.

Glastonbury: A simple variant of the X-supported chair; the original is 15th century, preserved at Glastonbury Abbey. [*Original pictured.*] Many varieties, down to the folding camp chair.

glass: A chair with frame of metal rods, tubes of glass covering the rods.

go-chair: Any wheeled chair, for pushing or self-propulsion. The self-propelled variety was made and advertised by William Long, cabinetmaker of Philadelphia, 1785.

gondola: English Victorian chairs of considerable elegance, upholstered in shell form and other tufting, said to be imitative of the comfortable seats of private gondolas of Venice. Also the long, slender upholstered lolling chairs of the same period; a sort of short couch.

gossip: The slipper, or nursing, chair.

Gothic: (1) Any chair of the Gallic era called Gothic, dating from 13th century to the Renaissance. (2) Revivals of the style or elements of any age or period, but especially the 18th and 19th centuries. Some hall chairs were directly imitative of the early forms. [*Several examples pictured.*]

gout: (1) Any wide-seated chair. (2) Armchair with a matching long stool, both upholstered. Together, such pieces were used as a day-bed. These date from Georgian era, c. 1720s. **gout stool:** A cradlelike stool, upholstered, to ease a leg afflicted with gout. Also called a poodle lounge.

Grecian: All Greek-revival chairs, of which there are some hundred or more varieties and sub-varieties. They enter into every quality class of chairmaking from 1750s, and more generally from 1790s. Mostly, however, made as cheap chairs, cottage chairs, and fancy chairs from 1820s.

green: Colloquial for Windsor chair, often, but not always, painted green.

groaning: "A chayer of comfort for ye bearing downe paines of childbirthe" and "ye suckling of infants." The nursing chair, as called in 17th century. Some had "rockers" or bends as early as 1680s.

hall: Generally show chairs, usually uncomfortable. Also a chair for the hall porter of a ménage or club, often hooded, like a one-seat settle.

harratine: Reference is to an upholstered chair covered with the fabric harratine.

Harvard: A turned chair of Tudor style, called "Harvard" in America because the president of that institution has such a seat or throne. [*Example pictured.*]

herculaneum: Fancy chair in the classic style.

high roundabout: Corner chair on high legs; probably a barbering or hairdressing chair.

Hogarth: A super cabriole-legged chair with tiered back. Hogarth pictured but did not design it. [*Example pictured.*]

hoop-back: Classic chair with looped back; Windsor chair with loop or hoop back.

horseshoe: The low-back Windsor armchair. Chair with back in horseshoe shape.

Horst fan: A rocking chair whose movement put a fan in motion to cool the user and shoo away insects.

hunter: Adjustable easy chair. Library chair with horseshoe arms.

incroyable: Directoire chair somewhat like a reading, club, or cockfight "sit-facing-the-back" type.

Jenny Lind: Any fancy chair of the mid-19th century named for the singer. [*One example pictured.*]

Kelley: Fancy chairs made by Kelley & Co. of Cuyahoga Falls, O., from 1830s.

Kimball: Fancy chairs made by Kimball of Salem, Mass., from 1840s.

king: Patented reclining chair. Also called "as-you-like-it chair."

lacemaker's: High-legged narrow-back chair. A stick chair.

ladder-back: Any chair the back of which is made up of two upright stiles crossed with flat pieces, some shaped and formed in contour. Can be pioneer, ropeseated, or very fancy Georgian and Chippendale.

lady: A small armchair, not upholstered; also a low, upholstered wing chair, very narrow in the seat.

Lady Pepperel: A high-back chair with upholstered seat and back panel.

légère: Papier-mâché chair of French Antique style.

lobby: An anteroom or hall chair.

locomotive: Three-wheel chair with treadle propulsion. Any rolling chair.

Lord rocker: A platform rocker.

low comb-back: Horseshoe Windsor with a low comb over the arm rail.

mandarin: Chinese chair of regal quality, sometimes (originally) covered with gold leaf. [*Example pictured.*]

Manhattan: Bamboo-turned folding chair with carpet seat.

Manwaring: Reference is to chairs of design by Robert Manwaring, shown in his design book of 1765.

Manx: A stick chair of the Isle of Man; said to be one of the ancestors of the Windsor.

Martha Washington: Sheraton-style ladies' upholstered armchair with all-wood arms. John Short of Salem made chairs of this type, labeled with his name, from 1790s. [*Example pictured.*]

master roundabout: Superior corner chairs, some very ornate.

morning-glory: Cast-iron chair with morning-glory design on back.

music-room: Chairs of classic style with harp-form backs. [*Examples pictured.*]

Newmarket: Chair with round seat, late Windsor type, with ball-turned spindles. Made by Chapman of Newmarket, N.H. Still made at Breakfast Hill Shops, same state.

nursing: Any low chair used in feeding infants.

pocket: A Louis XV-style chair of mid-19th century, back and seat forming a perfect pocket in which to sit.

portrait: French antique chair with portrait medallions in back.

quadrant: A true corner chair with a quarter-circle-form seat. The periphery of the quadrant is the front of the seat. [*Example pictured.*]

Rhode Island: Fancy chair with four flat arrow-form spindles in back. Also a form of Windsor, primarily marked by bobbin-form spindles and special turned legs.

ringed: Early turned chair with turned rings, cut loose in the lathe, as ornament.

ringside or cockfight: A "sit-facing-the-back" chair, but more properly a chair with sitting-up desk in front and a lolling back.

rocking: Any chair on bends, date from 1660, as noted in *Spinning Wheel*, March 1950. Use in America may date from 1750s.

recumbent rocker: A reclining (adjustable) rocking chair.

round: Adam-style classic chairs of roundabout type. [*Example pictured.*]

roundabout: A corner chair.

saddle-cheek: Upholstered wing-type chair with sidepieces resembling saddle cheeks. **saddle-swivel:** A saddle-form seat of leather, over a wood base, padded, fixed to a long screw in a three-legged stool.

salamander-back: A slat-back chair with slats formed in outline of salamanders, head to head. Style is early French.

Salem: The special back of a Georgian chair that is sometimes given this name. [*Example pictured.*] Also a rocking chair of Boston type, smaller than the Boston and sometimes with flat rather than rolled seat.

Savonarola: Cerule chair; a chair or

seat of X members in a line. Often with arms and back.

scholars: A Chinese form, copied by Dutch in developing the Queen Anne chair back.

school: A late fancy type of all-wood chair, unpainted, but varnished.

Schrenkeisen rocker: Platform rocker, the platform on casters.

scoop: An all-wood, pioneer-type home-made chair. [*Example pictured.*]

scissors: Cerule or Savonarola. Also called Dantesque and Voltaire.

sewing: Adjustable-back swivel chair.

sgabelli: Italian Gothic chair, persisting in general style to 1800. All-wood chair with plank seat, 3 or four-legged, with a plank back piercing rear of seat. [*Early example pictured.*]

slat-back: Any chair with cross slats in back, anchored in rear stiles or posts. Particularly the rope- and rush-seated ones with as many as five or six cross slats, shaped and bent.

Sleepy Hollow: An easy, or lolling, chair with conforming footrest. [*Example pictured.*]

sleigh: Chair seat, often of basketwork, mounted on runners. [*Example pictured.*]

stabellen: Same as sgabelli.

state: Thrones; important chairs for officials.

stepped Windsor: Windsor with chair-back top rail with steplike rather than curved ends.

stick: The Windsor; any chair made of wood sticks.

stove: Any chair, but especially a child's high chair, with a stove or heater in the front.

straddle: The cockfight, ringside, and similar chairs, straddled and sat in facing the back.

straw: Chairs woven in the beehive tradition of straw work. [*Example pictured.*]

stump: Windsor-type all-wood chair with stumpy turned spindles; so called from 1840s, when introduced as cheap chair by Windsor makers.

Suellen rocker: A lullaby rocker; a folding upholstered rocker of the late Victorian era.

swinging writing arm: Chair with writing arm, as on a Windsor, pivoted in or on the supporting spindle and on a platform, permitting easy entry into the chair. A rarity.

three-tier comb-back: Windsor with comb on comb over an arm rail. It is a rare type.

threshing: Heavy wood chair on heavier skids with rollers between; actually drawn by oxen to thresh out grain; some sectarians in U.S. preferred this to the flail in threshing wheat. [*Example pictured.*]

thrown: A chair made up of turned parts. [*Example pictured.*]

tilting: A Shaker chair, the rear leg bottoms with bowl-shaped sockets and a strap fixed to a block with ball turning that fitted in the leg hollow. Chair tilted on the ball.

Trafalgar: Fancy chair commemorating Nelson's victory.

tulip Windsor: Misnamed; actually an Eastlake chair, all wood, with tulip carving on ears of top rail.

umbrella: A hall chair with a back compartment for umbrellas.

unfolding: X-support chair with tapestry or carpet seat. Also an ancient type made up of many X forms, one element of the X's made long to form the back.

upholstered Windsor: Windsor chair with upholstered seat. When first reported by this author in 1946 it was called an "invention," but this is not so. These chairs were made. Recently a set of six with both maker's and upholsterer's original labels was found.

upside-down Windsor: A grand idea; why it isn't made today is a mystery. A Windsor-type garden chair with horseshoe-shaped arms, made precisely the same on both sides of a double-sided saddle seat. Leave it out in the rain if you like; you just turn it over for a dry seat. [*Example pictured.*]

Varangian: 15th-century turned chair.

Vienna rocker: Bentwood and cane rocker of 1880s.

voyeuse: A form of the straddle chair. [*Example pictured.*]

wainscot: Tudor-style chair of solid wood with wainscot back. [*Example pictured.*]

walnut Windsor: All-walnut stick chairs, advertised in 1766.

weavers: High-legged stool or four-legged type chair with backs and sometimes with outflaring arms.

Winslow: A Tudor-type chair, used by Pilgrim Father Winslow. [*Example pictured.*]

chaise: A two-wheeled carriage used from 17th century.

chaise à capucine: See Chairs, All Kinds.

chaise bon femme: See Chairs, All Kinds.

chaise carpet: Floor coverings and robes used in chaises.

chalcography: Engraving on copper. Term should be used only in describing copperplate work, as *chalkos* is Greek for copper.

chaldron: A measure of 36 bushels.

chalk: Porous limestone formation, very compact yet light, and readily softened when dampened.

chalker: Derisive term for a milkman.

chalk silhouettes: Solid profile portraits painted or mounted on light slabs or panels of chalk.

chalk ware: Misnomer for plaster-of-Paris ornaments, busts, and even classical figures. What is generally meant by chalk ware is the gaudily colored plaster imitations of Staffordshire and other figures, sold by street vendors from c. 1810 to 1870, and also in cheap stores, crossroads and country stores, and by peddlers. Now exalted considerably beyond its once lowly station largely because of the mistaken idea that it was once a "folk art" expression of the Pennsylvania Germans. This is not true; the stuff was sold everywhere. It was cheap ornamentation enjoyed by the poorest families. It was never tolerated in its gaudy form in any home making a pretense at distinction, although plaster busts of classic quality were in such homes from the 18th century. Most so-called chalk ware was made by Italian immigrants. All sorts of animals, figures, fruits, flowers, et cetera, are found in this cheap plaster. Every one found thus far is a copy of a bit of china, porcelain, redware, or some other model.

chalk ware (true): William Hutchinson of London, 1848, invented a technique or treatment by which sculpture in soft chalk could be made as hard as marble. This was a boon to sculptors, and from this probably came the canard about chalk ware being "carved from the native chalk." Hutchinson's process was also applied to hardening Bath stone and other soft mineral earth. Finally plaster-of-Paris casts were hardened by the process. See the *Scientific American* for 1848 for comment.

Challinor: Pottery and china made by various members of the Challinor family, which, in the person of Edward Challinor, in 1819, bought the Overhouse pottery established by Thomas Wedgwood, brother of Josiah. Fifty years later the same Edward Challinor rebuilt the pottery. In 1883 this comment was made in respect to it: "Ordinary ware, shipped in large quantities to the U.S." Challinor also acquired the original Mason's Ironstone Pottery and made white and cream granite wares, printed, plain, and sponged. Also made the patterns Ceres or Wheat, Paris Garland, Barberry, Lily, Missouri, Lotus, and others. Marks are E. CHALLINOR and E. & C. CHALLINOR. Wood & Challinor were conducting a pottery at Tunstall in 1842. Ford & Challinor acquired the Lion Pottery, Sandyford, in 1862.

Challinor-Taylor & Co.: Glass manufacturers of Tarentum, Pa., who made the pressed-glass rooster, hen, duck, and swan dishes of opalescent tablewares. Last half of 19th century.

Challinor Thumbprint: Pattern of pressed glass made by Challinor-Taylor, featuring large ovate depressions in an all-over pattern. Quite late in date.

challis: Soft featherweight woolen fabric, printed or hand-blocked, later imitated in linen and cotton. Originally East Indian, name deriving from *shallie*, meaning soft.

chalybeate: Impregnated with iron.

chamber candlestick: Candlestick fitted to broad saucer or dish, always with a handhold, and generally with extinguishing cone. Sometimes there is a snuffer in a slot under the candle socket. Pewter, brass, Sheffield-plate, silver, pottery, and porcelain examples known. In 18th and early 19th century they were generally placed on a table at foot of stairs at nightfall (one chamber stick for each bedroom) along with a burning candle. Anyone desiring to retire lighted his chamber stick, and so to bed.

chamber clock: (1) A clock in a chamber or case, generally meaning the 30-hour "bird-cage" clocks of early date. (2) Any clock for use in a bedchamber. (3) Any clock, especially illuminated ones, for use by night in a bedchamber. Many varieties.

chamberings: The furniture of a bedroom or of a bedstead.

Chamberlain lamp: Self-canting lamp of c. 1850 which tilted as fuel was consumed, causing remaining fluid to reach wick end. [*Example pictured.*] *See also* Porter Lamp.

Chamberlain-Worcester: Fine Caughley and Coalbrookdale wares decorated by Robert Chamberlain from 1786, when he also established a pottery at Worcester. The Chamberlain works became extensive and famous. [*Examples of the ware and the marks are pictured.*]

chamber pedestal: Housing for the chamber pot or thunder mug, slop jar, and other unmentionables. Some are merely drum-shaped covers, while others verge upon the beautiful or are unquestionably classic. [*An example of the latter type is pictured.*] Some, of the 1820-70 period, have tambour slides.

Chambers-Agnew glass: Flintwares, especially vials and bottles for the drug trade, made by a firm so named at Pittsburgh from 1840s to 1880s.

Chambers, Benjamin: Engraver of American historic prints working in Washington, D.C., from 1820s.

Chambers pottery: W. Chambers' South Wales Pottery wares. White granite, printed and flow-printed, made for the U.S. market from 1850s.

Chambers, Sir William: Publisher-author of *Designs of Chinese Buildings, Furniture, Dresses, et cetera,* 1757 (London).

chamber stick: *See* Chamber Candlestick.

chamber table: Dressing table. As early as 1690 this term was applied to what we now call a lowboy.

chamblet (camblet, camlet, chambray, camelot, etc.): A variegated woven fabric.

chamfer: To bevel the angle of a square column, stile, or leg; to pare down the angle where two plane surfaces meet. Also chamfret; chamfretted. Sometimes used to denote channeling or grooving.

champagne jug: A cut-glass, cameo-glass, or other rich pitcher with silver cover and ice compartment, used in serving champagne at table. Any wine pitcher with a compartment for ice.

champion match safe: Japanned tin-plate match safe patented 1865 by J. S. Henry, Manheim, Lancaster County, Pa.

Champion ware: The fine Bristol ware, fathered by Richard Champion, perhaps the one truly great English potter, whose progress Josiah Wedgwood envied and strove to ruin. Made from 1770s under ownership of the Cookworthy patents. Imitations of Chinese wares considered by many connoisseurs as better than the wares imitated. Champion became a citizen of the U.S. in 1785 and died at Charleston, S.C., 1791. [*Examples of his fine porcelain pictured.*]

champlevé: A technique and type of enamel work on metal, finer than cloisonné, in that the partitions between the areas are made so thin as to serve only as a preventive of fusion of the enamel colors.

Champnoine: Pottery, probably redware, possibly stoneware, made near Boston,

Mass., prior to 1738 by Curtis Champnoine, listed as a potter of Boston to c. 1738.

chandelier: Candle fixture of few or many branches, holding from five to fifty candles for brilliant illumination, and always suspended from the ceiling. Many varieties and makeshifts, one of which is the now commonly revived "wagon wheel," with candles set on the spokes. [*Several examples pictured.*]

Chandos table: Charles W. Elliott, furniture manufacturer, in 1876 reproduced an antique Spanish-footed gate-leg table he had purchased at Warwick, England. This reproduction he called first a "Chandos" table and finally a "ladder-legged" table. He cashed in on the Centennial-year surge of interest in antiques. [*Example pictured.*]

chandry: Storage place for candles; box, closet, or drawer. **chandler:** A candle-maker.

changeables: "These be such kinds of paintings whose lights are of one colour and whose shadows be of another colour, which is delightful to the eye." Richard Blome, 1686.

changes: The technique of ringing a diatonic chime of bells. An ancient practice from which derives the phrase, "ringing the changes." Certain of the changes were named hunting, bob, grandsire, caters, et cetera.

chanoyu: The ceremony of tea drinking.

Chantilly: French porcelain, made from 1725.

Chapin furniture: Fine furniture, clock cases, mirrors, et cetera, by the famed Eliphalet Chapin, who worked at East Windsor, Conn., to 1780s and thereafter at Hartford to c. 1810. In New York State the designation may be reference to late Sheraton-style furniture made 1820-40 by Silas Chapin of Big Flats, Tioga County.

chaplet: A head ornament; a wreath of natural vine, oak, or laurel, with flowers, or of artificial foliage, fabric, straw, et cetera. Once a popular headgear of women in 17th and 18th centuries.

chaplet bead: A decorative form deriving from the beads or berries traditionally trimming a chaplet. Small bubbles of glass in chains or strings, as in a wineglass stem or paperweight.

chapman: Contraction of cheap-man, meaning a vendor of cheap wares.

Chapman portraits: Profile likenesses cut by an itinerant profile and silhouette cutter named Chapman.

char: A kind of variety of trout or salmon. A job, generally menial, hence charwoman or chore woman.

character blanks: Engraved mortuary certificates issued as memorials were so designated in early 18th century. New England.

charge: Decoration applied to a shield. Sometimes used to designate certain inlay patterns on table tops.

charger: A large dish or platter; a voider.

chariot moons: Glass or mica-paned globes enclosing lamp or candle used on coaches or "chariots" in 17th and 18th centuries.

charivari (shivaree, Calathumpian, etc.): Serenade of noise, generally good-natured bedevilment of newly wedded couples. An American custom prevalent to at least the first decade of 20th century, from southern Pennsylvania southward to Florida.

Charles II chair: *See* Chairs, All Kinds.

Charles X: Of or pertaining to the reign of Charles X of France, 1824-30, in which year this King abdicated and the Chamber of Deputies elected Louis Philippe. In the Charles X reign the final phase of the Directoire-Empire style was enjoyed. After 1830 this style was abandoned and the revival of Louis XV we now call Victorian began. During the reign of Charles X the simple turned-leg drop-leaf dining table was developed and was made in great numbers in the U.S. of maple, pine, walnut, mahogany, cherry, apple wood, poplar, chestnut, and other woods.

Charleston iron: Reference is to the architectural wrought iron produced by the blacksmiths of Charleston, S.C.

Charlestown ware: Reference to this ware is found in early New England inventories; the meaning, while not definite, is presumed to be earthenware made at the potteries of Charlestown, or Charlestown Neck, Boston area. Potters are said to have worked here from 17th century.

Charleville: Smoothbore musket used in the Revolution by all troops other than the Pennsylvania and Virginia lines. These, rather than rifles, were made at Continental arsenals. The rifle which really won the Revolution was a Pennsylvania product, made chiefly in the vicinity of Lancaster and the Conestoga River Valley.

char pot: Shallow earthenware pans in which the small salmon called char were baked or broiled. Also pots used to preserve char.

charqui: Jerked dried beef.

charred: Said of posts, piles, and "plates" of buildings when partially burned before laying on or in earth to prevent rot.

charta bombazine: Paper made from cotton.

Charter Oak pitcher: Product of the Bennington Pottery, a pitcher bearing a design of oak leaves and acorn clusters, with rustic handle. Some all white, some blue and white. Said also to exist in Rockingham glaze.

Chase furniture: Cast-iron furniture for lawn, cemetery, and veranda, made by Chase Brothers and other firms named Chase at New York City, Boston, Buffalo, and Chicago from 1840s and 1850s.

chase mortise: A gouging tool with sloping side, used where space for insertion of tenon is constricted.

Chase pottery: *See* Somerset Pottery.

chasing: Decoration of metal achieved by small shaping punches and modeling tools. While often accented with engraving, chasing is not a form of engraving or cutting, but a cold modeling process.

chasuble: An ecclesiastical garment.

chatelaine: A clip with a chain to which a purse or etui was attached. Often of silver, but sometimes of gold.

chaudern: Sauce; gravy.

Chandron & Rasch: Philadelphia silversmiths who were also dealers in fine china and cut glasswares from 1820s. They were among our first silversmiths to use the designation "Sterling" on silver.

chaufer: Hot-water basin.

chauffeuse: Low chair generally used by fireside.

chayere: Bishop's throne. From this term we derive the word "chair."

cheadle brass: Dark brass with a greenish tone or hue.

chebobbin: Snow runners of huge form used in logging. Sometimes spelled tarbobbin, charbobbin, and sheboygin.

Checkered Diamond: Checkered pattern spangled with diamonds within the checkers. A form popular in mold-blown glass.

cheese & cracker bowl: Tidbit container consisting of decorated china or pottery bowl with divider and a two-part lid of silver, pewter, or Sheffield plate. Cheese cut in small pieces and hard crackers were kept in the two compartments. Date is c. 1870. [*Example pictured.*]

cheese brig: Poles and crossbars to support skimming bowl over pans of cream in cheese making.

cheesecake of cards: An arrangement of six playing cards, the overlapping corners of four held taut by two crossed in center. A card trick of the 1840s, often using four kings and two aces and framed as a wall decoration.

cheese cutter: Fine wire stretched from prongs on a grid, with handle, used in cutting cheese in shops. Finer examples used at table.

cheese dish: A sleigh-shaped dish of china, silver, Sheffield plate, et cetera, supporting a round of cheese at table; a covered dish to hold a loaf of cheese, especially a Stilton.

cheese ford: Woodenware. A cheese mold.

cheese ice: Eggs, syrup, and cream, boiled to custard, enriched with grated Parmesan cheese, passed through a hair sieve, and frozen in molds. This was a great delicacy of the 1790s.

cheese knife: Silver or plated-ware knife with a blade curving up into a pointed fishtail; a knife for cutting a piece of cheese and spearing it by the fishtail to serve it. [*Example pictured.*]

cheese press: Any device for squeezing the excess liquid from curds in the final process of forming the cheese. Many kinds known, some using large stones shaped for the purpose, others with screws, and still others with a pincerlike arrangement.

Cheesequake wares: Stoneware made in the old English manner at Cheesequake Creek Pottery, N.J., from before the Revolution. Mugs, pots, and jars are known, decorated in the style of a century earlier. The pottery was revived c. 1805.

cheese safe: Cabinet frame covered with woven wire to store cheeses.

cheese taster: A probe, often of wrought iron, in the shape of a curving wand. When inserted in a cheese and withdrawn, flakes adhered to the point for tasting and appraising the cheese.

cheese vat: Wooden tank on four or more supports, with barrow holds at sides.

Cheetham carpets: Venetian ingrain and three-ply carpets woven at the looms of Cheetham and Heald, Philadelphia, from 1820s.

cheffonier sideboard: A small sideboard with zinc- or lead-lined drawers in late Regency or Empire style. A chef's food cabinet.

Chelmsford glass: Bottles (including the Lowell Railroad flask) and perhaps other wares, made at Chelmsford (now Lowell), Mass., from 1802 to 1827.

Chelsea: English porcelain or china produced at Chelsea, London, the works deriving from a china-decorating establishment for the embellishment of plain whitewares from China. When producing the ware itself, it is said the makers used petuntse, or Chinese porcelain clays brought in as ships' ballast, but this is not certain. The works seems to have started c. 1730, and critical and legendary history of this porcelain-making center is recorded in several books. Chelsea Groups are statuary toys, statuary groups, et cetera. Chelsea Moons are slight imperfections in this ware discernible as small crescent shapes more translucent than the general body of the ware. [*Exemplary marks and samples of early and late Chelsea wares are pictured.*]

Chelsea hangings: Wallpaper made by the Boston & Chelsea Paper Co. from late 1840s.

Chelsea pottery: Art pottery produced at Chelsea, Mass., by the Chelsea Keramic Art Works from 1866. Owners and operators were various members of the Robertson family (father and sons). Terra cotta or red bisque (sometimes called red Parian) in the ancient classic style, sometimes painted with appropriate decoration, colored-glaze, tin-glaze, satin-glaze, hand-hammered effects, and other good art wares were made, as well as replicas of the famous Chinese dragon's-blood red- and crackle-glaze wares. The plant moved to Dedham, Mass., in 1895.

cheminee: Screen of needlework or tapestry used before a fireplace. From 16th century.

chenets: Andirons; firedogs.

Cherokee clay: The "Unaker" of the American Indians, exported to England from 1744.

Cherry: Pattern of pressed glass featuring festoons of fruit and leaves on twigs. Paneled Cherry is a variant, with twigs over panels. Stippled Cherry is another variant, the background being stippled or finely dotted, and having broad V-shaped ridged bands.

cherry bounce: Originally cherry dram, a drink made of fresh cherry juice mixed half-and-half with rum.

cherry-red glass: A product of the Bristol, England, glass center from 18th century. This is often thought to be Bohemian, and probably is the Bristol answer to Bohemian red glass.

cherry rum: A variety of "bounce," made by soaking fresh sweet or wild cherries in rum for three months or more.

cherrystone: A black pigment.

cherry wood: The *New York Cabinet-makers Price Book* of 1834 rates cherry wood at the same price as mahogany. This is evidence that our native cherry tree was once highly regarded as a cabinet wood, regardless of the 20th-century controversy concerning its suitability for fine cabinet work. The cabinetmakers of the 1830s ranked cherry wood thus: walnut, cherry, mahogany, curly maple, plain maple.

cherubim: Plural of cherub. The cherubim were the four angelic messengers of the highest class. In early ideas of heaven seraphim took precedence over cherubim.

Chesapeake majolica: Also known as Clifton ware. Majolica made at the Chesapeake Pottery, Baltimore, from c. 1880.

chess: Ancient game of oriental origin, played on a checkered board with pieces known as queen, king, bishop, knight, castle, rook, and pawn. Considered the acme of intellectual pastime. Franklin wrote or published a treatise on the game. The *Chess Monthly* was published at New York City from 1857. Chessmen are the pieces of a chess set, and many are handsomely carved of ivory and hardwoods. Some are known in silver and in Parian.

chessel: Woodenware (but also known in pewter, copper, and sheet iron) cheese mold, often carved intaglio to form a design on top of the cheese. Also a hoop or ring used in cheese making.

chest diaper: A drawer cloth.

Chester spice cabinet: Miniature highboy with cupboard doors behind which are many tiny drawers for spices. Arthur Sussel states these are peculiar to Chester County, Pa., but others are known to have been made in the neighboring county of Lancaster by the Bachmans of Lampeter Square. The style is Queen Anne or early Georgian, and examples are exceedingly rare.

chest joint: A hinge.

chestnut bottle: Chestnut flask. Reference is to the shape, an enlarged form of the chestnut as it grows within the bur. The surface may be plain, writhen, swirled, or otherwise decorated.

chestnut-mahogany: Native chestnut of selected grain, steeped in alum water and then in logwood dye.

chestnut roasters: Brass or wrought-iron drums on long handles, having beautifully pierced lids fitted with hinge and fastener. Made from 18th century. [*Example pictured.*]

chestnut urn: Gracefully curvate, funnel-shaped urns with covers, used primarily to store chestnuts for gentle aging in the shell. Made of tole, iron, wood, pewter, brass and, it is said, of silver and Sheffield plate, for use on tables and mantels.

chest-on-chest: The simpler form of tallboy. The term is aptly descriptive because the piece is a composite of a somewhat smaller chest of drawers mounted upon a slightly larger one. Some have cabinets with doors in the bottom section. Date is from 1730s or earlier.

chest-on-frame: A chest of drawers, generally five or more, fitted within a separate frame designed to make the bottom drawer readily accessible without much stooping. Precursor of the chest-on-chest, and made from 17th century.

chest-settle: Long chest of Tudor style with lid serving as seat, fitted with settle back and arms. Date is from 16th century, and used in Virginia, New England, and probably Maryland prior to 1670s. [*Example pictured.*]

chest table: (1) The frame of a chest-on-frame. (2) A small square chest with a large top extending beyond chest walls, hinged to the chest and serving as a table. *See also* Table Chest.

chete bread: Bread made from second-best wheat. Also known as criber bread, raunged bread, and range bread.

Cheval Glass: Literally "horse mirror," so called because it is high enough to reflect a horse; a full-length mirror, large enough to reflect the height of a human being.

cheval screen: Standing screen supported on two pillars, or a folding screen of notable height. Some are fire screens. Not pole screens, *which see.*

chevon: Goat's meat.

chevron: Heraldic form deriving from the gables or roof rafters of a house. A wide V-form, with the point up.

chewer: A narrow alley between structures.

chibbol: A small onion.

chica: Extract of the *Bignonia chica* leaves, boiled in water. The red sediment formed into cakes and dried. Mixed with bear's grease or bird fat, this became the skin pigment of the American Indians, who made chica from pre-Columbian times.

Chicago furniture: Certain furniture of the Middle West now verging upon antiques status is of Chicago make. The first cabinetmakers of Chicago were Bates & Morgan, Clark Filer, and J. Rockwell, all of whom were working in the 1830s. The work is a variety of Directoire, not quite Empire, and seems to stem from designs in the *Cincinnati Cabinetmakers Price Book of 1830.*

Chicago glass: Flint glass made at the Chicago Flint Glass Works from the 1860s.

Chicago lamp: A candle lamp for decorative or celebrative illumination. Pressed or mold-blown glass in hobnail pattern in various colors. These lamps were fitted with a wire loop handle, and large squat candles were burned in them. [*Example pictured.*]

Chicken: Pattern of pressed glass featuring a Gothic molded form having a chicken emerging from egg as a cover finial.

chicken-coop chair: *See* Chairs, All Kinds.

chicken pot: A Chinese porcelain watering pot in form of a chicken with handle under tail, filling vent on back, pouring vents on either side of the bill. These were 18th-century imports, naturalistically colored. [*Example, with filling-vent stopper, is pictured.*] Some experts say it is a teapot and some a wine pot, but Chinese experts say it is a watering pot. Take your choice.

Chickering, Jonas: Pianoforte maker of Boston who was formerly a cabinetmaker. He was the founder of Chickering & Sons and started work c. 1820.

Chickering terra cotta: The Otis

Chickering terra cotta pottery at Catskill, N.Y., made various tiles, pots, architectural elements, and utilitarian objects.

chiclatton (chicklaton, ciclatoun, and other variants): A rich fabric with gold threads. Also gilded leather or brass foil.

chief plantations: 17th-century term which, collectively, referred to New England, Virginia, Bermuda, and the Barbados, England's chief plantations in the New World. New Amsterdam was held by the Dutch and New Jersey and Pennsylvania by the Swedes and Dutch. Hence the huge gap, from the Connecticut River westward and southward to the Chesapeake-Susquehanna joining, was not under English rule.

chien yao: Chinese "hare's-fur" glaze stoneware of rare type, achieved, it is said, by running of the glaze. Dark, and even black, body glaze overrun with buff or gray.

chiffonier: Literally, ragpicker. See Preface of this work. Any item of cabinet furniture designed to hold textiles, finery, and items of dress.

chiliad: One thousand.

chill: An open four-cornered lamp with wick channels in each corner. Said to derive from chall, chell, choll, and even chull, various colloquial 16th-century English terms for "square jaw." [*Example pictured.*]

chimney-back sideboard: Modern term applied at times to an Empire-period sideboard similar to a chest of drawers and having a panel of cresting at back which is silhouetted against the wall. Date is from 1825 to 1850s.

chimney'd cruse: Fat lamp of classic shape fitted with a metallic supporting frame to hold a cylinder of glass used as a chimney for the flame. Late 18th century. [*Example pictured.*]

chimney glass: Rectangular mirror in frame, permanently fixed or hung on chimney breast. From 17th century.

chimney hook: Brass or wrought-iron hook on plates, fastened to jambs of a mantel and used to hold fire tools. These were often used in pairs and date from c. 1740s. [*Examples pictured.*]

chimney safe: A length of pottery pipe extending from wall into the chimney flue, to which stove piping was connected. May be near ceiling or about three and a half feet above floor. Low placement was generally for close coupling of five-plate, tenplate, or Franklin-type stoves, or some other room-heating device.

chimney screw: A form of Archimedean screw set on chimney top to improve draft.

chimney tunnel: The flue of a chimney.

Ch'in: Chinese dynasty of 255–206 B.C.

Chin (Nu-Chen): Chinese dynasty of A.D. 1115–1234.

china (POTTERY & PORCELAIN, DELFT & MAJOLICA): To list the potters of the world and their marks is impossible in this book. Six volumes of this size might approach a complete listing. See Bibliography.

china-boy (china man): Effigies of carved wood, china, pottery, plaster, pewter, cast iron, et cetera, imitative of a Chinese coolie or even a mandarin, as signs to advertise tea, very much as the black boy, Indian brave or squaw, Punch, et cetera, were effigy signs of tobacconists. China-boys were used from 18th century to c. 1880s. [*Example pictured.*]

china doll: Any play doll with a head and body of fired china or porcelain. The best examples were made in parts and then joined. Date is probably from early Sèvres factory but may have been made at Meissen. Greatest production is 19th to 20th century.

China goods: Oriental goods in general but especially Nanking, Canton, and other porcelains, plain and decorated, shawls, paper, jade, lacquer, fans, silks, mats, carpets, lanterns, brasses, teas, spices, and preserves. American ships, from late 18th century, were in the China trade. Our first clippers—the Baltimore clippers—were in this trade from 1820s. See Clipper Ships.

china hooks: Small brass hooks with screw ends to affix to bottoms of cupboard shelves on which to hang cups by their handles.

china press: A cupboard for the storage and display of chinaware; a china cabinet. Made specifically for this purpose from c. 1760 in Adam, Hepplewhite, Directoire, Sheraton, Empire, Louis XV revival, and all modern styles.

China razor: Chinese razors with almost triangular blade, having an exceedingly sharp edge which folds into a grooved handle. Clipper-ship imports, sold quite generally in U.S. from 1830s. [*Example pictured.*]

China stone: Kaolin clay.

china stove: A stove assembled from sections, made of tile or porcelain pieces. Many are beautifully painted and formed. Swiss, Belgian, French, Dutch, and German examples are known, and are mostly 18th century. Known in all Scandinavian countries, in Russia, Finland, and Poland. Probably also made in all countries using them.

ch'in cho: A table lute or zither of Chinese style or make.

Chinese back: Chair back in the Chinese taste or style. This includes splat backs of William & Mary, Queen Anne, Georgian, and Chippendale styles, latticework backs, and backs with pierced panels imitative of jade medallions.

Chinese blinds: Holland shades painted in the Chinese taste, the design showing inside a room in daylight and outside at night when room was lit. These are generally 19th century and were painted either in Chinese ports (the blank blinds being carried there) or by native or Chinese artists in the U.S. from 1830s.

Chinese brackets: Late ebonized wood brackets with scraps of gilding or goldleaf work in the Chinese style, made in U.S. in tremendous quantities for the cottage trade, 1875–90.

Chinese Bristol: Bristol opaque white glass, itself imitative of porcelain, painted in the Chinese style in colors fired on. Made from c. 1750 to at least 1830s.

Chinese cabinet woods: Among the imports of U.S. traders with China were fur-

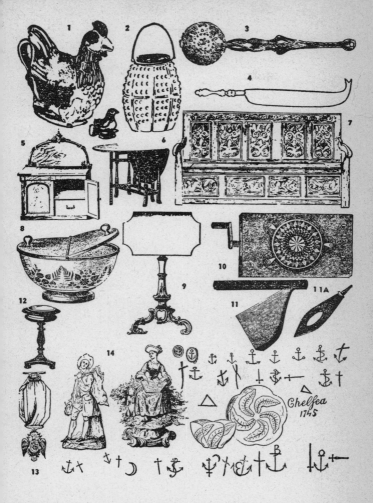

1, Chicken Watering Pot. **2,** Chicago Candle Lamp. **3,** Chestnut Roaster. **4,** Cheese Knife. **5,** Chiffonier Sideboard. **6,** Chandos (19th-century gate-leg) Table. **7,** Chest-Settle. **8,** Cheese and Cracker Bowl. **9,** Claw Table. **10,** Chromotrope. **11,** Chinese Razor. **11A,** Carpet Rag Looper. **12,** Circular Flower Stand. **13,** Cincinnati Society "Order." **14,** Chelsea Porcelain Figures, Wares, and Marks. (No. 14 from Virtue & Co., London.)

niture (and logs) of the following rare exotic woods: teak, ebony, palisander, sandal, cedar, and pear. Ebony, the finest wood (known in rose, orange, and other tints to black), was carved and polished with burnishers. From this work the French term *ébéniste*, for a fine or master cabinetmaker, derives.

Chinese chalk ware: A misnomer; it is Chinese porcelain or stoneware in humanistic, figural, and animal forms, and in fruit- and flower-form "piles" or arrangements. Copied by Staffordshire potters, and from their imitations copied by casting in plaster of Paris. The originals date from 1600s or earlier (in terms of European imports), the Staffordshire copies from 18th and early 19th centuries, and the plaster imitations from second quarter of the 19th century.

Chinese Chippendale: Any original Chinese style (but particularly the square-legged, fretted, and bamboo-turned examples) as copied by Chippendale and pictured in his *Director*.

Chinese dynasties & periods: See Dynasties, Chinese.

Chinese export porcelain: The correct name for what is generally called Lowestoft. This ware was not considered fine, or even good, in China. It was good enough only for "foreign devils" who, barbaric in taste, thought it good indeed. The first plea for correctly naming this oriental export ware was voiced by the author of *The China Hunters Club*, in 1870s.

Chinese gong: American-made dish-shaped gong bells, first offered by Isaac Williams of Philadelphia, c. 1850.

Chinese helmet pitcher: Porcelain pitchers made by Chinese potters, imitative of the tin and pewter ewers of somewhat similar shape which seem to have originated in France. Production was small, and some students believe they were made for use as night ewers. The porcelain examples known are beautifully decorated. [*General shape is pictured.*]

Chinese lantern: Folding lanterns of painted silk and of paper, gored over collapsible coils of bamboo and described as follows: "New and beautiful transparent article suitable for large rooms and gardens, are Chinese lanthorns." These were offered by J. S. Jones of Church Alley, Philadelphia, in 1833.

Chinese lustral: A washing solution for use with hard or soft water, popular in 1840s.

Chinese Queen Anne: Term sometimes applied to Queen Anne style furniture close to the Chinese original, displaying the obvious parentage. Generally lacquered, with gold-leaf decoration and inlays of mother-of-pearl. Much of this furniture is 17th-century Dutch-made. It is believed similar furniture was in New York and Pennsylvania *before* the style was popular in England. And it was indeed popular in England from c. 1700, as proved by its transition to Georgian and its domination of the scene to 1760.

Chinese Regency: The Chinese period 1898–1908.

Chinese Republic: From 1910 to the advent of the Communist regime.

Chinese silver: A slander, not Chinese but imitation silver, based on the Chinese formula for paktong, or white brass. It is made of 62 parts copper, 19 zinc, 13 nickel, and 9 iron.

Chinese strainer: Conical sieve affixed to a handle.

chinoiserie: Anything, particularly decoration, in the Chinese style or taste. Chinese objects of art collectively. Of China, by China, and imitative of Chinese décor, especially the long graceful figures, the flowers and fruits in arrangement patterns, et cetera.

chintz: Glazed printed cotton fabric; unglazed, it is cretonne. Also called toile and oil-boiled calico. The glazing was achieved by (1) boiling in oil with resins and gums, (2) by waxing, and (3) by starch. Oil-boiling was the most durable finish.

chintz furniture: In its original connotation, the chintz valance for a bed, or a window drapery. Later the meaning included chintz slip-covered furniture of any kind.

chiollagh: A stick chair of all-wood construction made on the Isle of Man. Similar to the Welsh stick chair, and ancestor of the Windsor.

chip & splinter: Colloquial for "in good order." Same as spick-and-span.

Chippendale: Furniture and other styles as advocated by Thomas Chippendale, English cabinetmaker and furniture manufacturer, in his *Director*, first published 1754. Chippendale is said to have done work for the Adam Brothers, who were advocating the new classic style and the abandonment of the all-pervasive Georgian style which had developed from Queen Anne. He may have envied the success of the Adam revolt and instituted a minor, less revolutionary shift. Chippendale simply turned to the French variant of the Georgian style and to the original Chinese sources. His revolt was successful in that it engaged the attention of the great upper middle class of England and practically all the colonies. The Great American Chippendale Error is the calling of much fine Philadelphia and New York furniture "Chippendale," when it is not and never was made from Chippendale's patterns. This does not mean there was no true Chippendale furniture made in the colonies, but what little there was can be tabulated by fairly simple rules: (1) If it *does not have ball-and-claw feet* (which were Georgian, not Chippendale) and does have the French "turn-up" or "up-scrolled" footing, or (2) has the so-called "Marlboro" square leg with an enlarged square footing or other distinctly Chinese characteristics, or (3) has backs, arms, and other major features directly traceable to Chippendale's first-, second-, or third-edition *Director*, the furniture can, with propriety, be called American Chippendale. Most Philadelphia, New York, and Boston furniture of the 18th century, commonly called Chippendale, is in the Georgian style. It is a pity that the term Chippendale (perhaps originally used to give the furniture a name from the beginning of our antiques-collecting interest, c. 1876) must now be used to give our really fine Georgian-style furniture its proper value. W. M. Hornor's *Blue Book of Philadelphia Furniture* desig-

1, Coalport & Caughley Wares and Marks. **2,** Charting Delineator. **3,** Cap Stand. **4,** Candle-stick Trumpet. **5,** Canted Candlestick. **6,** Candle Lamp. **7,** Canalboat Lamp. **8,** Chill. **9,** Chandelier (primitive or pioneer type). **10,** Candle Mirror. **11,** Coffin Planking. **12,** Chinese Helmet Pitcher. **13,** C-Curves. **14,** C-Scroll Mirror. **15,** Cadmus Pottery Mark. **16,** Chimney Hooks. (No. 1 from Virtue & Co., London.)

nates nearly all the Georgian-style pieces as Chippendale. So does practically every other book on furniture in America. This is not deplorable if we know the truth. But it is deplorable to fix firmly in any mind the erroneous belief that Georgian furniture is Chippendale in its style. Chippendale created his so-called style book in an effort to get away from the Georgian, which literally dominated England in his period of working.

Chippendale & Haig: Thomas Chippendale, the younger, in partnership with Thomas Haig, went bankrupt in 1796. The firm continued under other ownership, but not as Chippendale & Haig.

Chippendale ball & claw: "Try to find one," is the challenge of one student of the style. "If you do, it will be on a bed-post leg, for that is the only ball-and-claw footing pictured by Chippendale, and that isn't in all editions of his book." He may be right; your compilers have not studied each and every illustration in every edition of Chippendale.

Chippendale-Hepplewhite: Term used to describe transitional furniture, made in the U.S. after 1785, showing evidence of Georgian as well as classic influence. Actually, a type of furniture to be avoided except by adepts in the niceties of decoration, or museums wishing it for style demonstration.

Chippendale sideboard: Any sideboard designated as Chippendale must be just that and nothing more—a side table or "board"—used at the side of the room rather than for center placement in dining. Any piece in the so-called Chippendale style that displays cabinets, cupboards, et cetera, is a "made" piece and of late production. The sideboard was developed from three or more separate units used together. These were in the classic style, introduced by the Adam Brothers. Hepplewhite and other followers of the classic style made the former ensemble into one piece. Thus a Hepplewhite or Sheraton sideboard are genuine cabinet pieces, while a Chippendale or Georgian sideboard would be a table.

Chippendale-styled: Mirrors, trays, chairs, settees, et cetera, correctly designated if they appear as units or elements in Chippendale's *Director*, but otherwise of the style generally Georgian, or from a design book using Georgian-style elements. *The Gentleman & Cabinet Maker's Director* was first published in 1754. The third edition is considered the best. The rarest book incorporating Georgian and Chinese styles is the catalogue of Ince & Mayhew, *which see*.

chiromancy: Palmistry.

chittaroon: A bass lute. Several variants in spelling are of record; one is guittaroon.

Chittenden bedstead: Iron bedstead made by S. Chittenden of New York, c. 1850. Some are in the Directoire style.

chlamys: Greek-revival decorative form deriving from the ancient short cloak of Greek origin draped over the shoulders. A mantling of drapery, simulated in carving, painting, inlay, and stenciling. Also the white linen fabric used in making cloaks.

chocolate: Native American bean used by the Indians of South America to prepare food and drink. It was carried to Europe by the Spanish and improved upon by the Dutch, who introduced it to the North American colonies. "Chuchalette" was sold in Boston from 1678 and was known in New Amsterdam from the 1630s. Joshua Moody had a chocolate mill at Falmouth, N.H., in 1770. Walter Baker's famous mill near Boston has been in continuous operation during three centuries. The "dish" used in serving chocolate was the same small bowl or cup used in the service of coffee. Chocolate pots for serving the beverage had a hole in the lid for insertion of the "whisk" handle. The whisk was inside the pot and was whirled by the handle to keep the contents stirred up. The very best way to make the beverage is to keep whipping it as it cooks and to keep it in agitation until poured.

chocolate glass: Dark caramel glass made by the Tumbler & Goblet Co., Greentown, Ind., c. 1890s.

Choctaw stripes: Cotton fabric of alternating "nankeen" (tawny) and white bands, woven extensively at Vaulcuse, S.C., from 1840s. It weighed eight ounces a yard and sold for a penny an ounce, or eight cents a yard.

choose wagon: A dumbwaiter.

chopine: Liquid measure, one ounce less than a pint. Sometimes designated as "half of a fifth," meaning a tenth of a gallon. The designation is not clear unless gallon is specified. A Winchester gallon is a "short" or four-quart gallon, while an imperial gallon is five quarts, or ten pounds of liquid.

choppine: A high clog or patten used extensively in the 17th and 18th centuries in walking to elevate the shoe proper above muck, mud, and common street debris.

Chou: The dynasty of China lasting from 1112 to 249 B.C.

chrinsie: Any drinking vessel.

chrism spoon: A spoon used in the sacrament of anointing with blessed oil.
chrism bottle: A bottle for the oil.

Christchurch chain: Steel chains used in the fusee of early watches to transfer the power of the motor barrel (housing of the spring) to the movement. There were 500 tiny links in the average 8-inch length.

Christ cross: The alphabet as arranged in the form of a Christian cross on hornbooks (alphabet boards) of the 17th century. A and B, C and D were the top of the cross, in two rows. E to K and L to Q were the next two rows, forming the arms, R-S, T-V, W-X, Y-Z formed the base in four rows.

Christian furniture: Hepplewhite- and Sheraton-style furniture made by M. Christian, N.Y., c. 1800. [*His advertisement of 1802 is pictured.*]

Christian ware: Tortoise-shell and other earthenwares made by Philip Christian of Liverpool in the 18th century. It is difficult to identify his wares, as they are of a type similar to other Liverpool products.

Christmas balls: Decorative colored, gilded, and silvered glass balls used to trim Christmas trees. Most likely first examples were offhand pieces blown by glasshouse workers, and more commonly known as "witch balls." Other indications point to these same heavy decorative balls being made to adorn halls for Twelfth Night balls and similar holiday jollifications. The earliest advertisement of glass Christmas balls found by your editors is that of William Demuth of New York City, 1870. But it is known the balls were in use at least 25 years prior to that date.

Christmas box: Alms box carried by the poor at Christmas in which gifts were dropped. The boxes were quite large and were not primarily pennycatchers. Date is from 17th century.

Christmas glass: Pressed-glass plates with Christmas sentiments in center and alphabet around rim. Toy glassware for children's gifts.

Christmas lights: This is the term now generally used to designate the round-bottomed colored-glass receptacles in which candles are burned. They were not made as Christmas lights but as votive lights, standing in trays of sand, and used extensively in Roman Catholic churches everywhere. They may be found today in many churches in Cuba, South America, Mexico, and the West Indies, but not in churches that have already been stripped of such treasures by antiques dealers who, in the past, have purchased votive lamp shades in wholesale lots from parish priests sadly in need of funds. Some are open-bottomed, in the form of small hurricane shades. [*Examples pictured.*]

Christmas tableaux: Miniature stages of boxlike form with many changes of scene and actors, all of cut cardboard. Some figures were arranged to move in grooves on stage floor. Mostly 19th century, many made by Milton Bradley Co. from 1880s.

Christmas tree: From Yule-trow, a framework of treelike form upon the level arms of which candles were placed and burned at Christmas celebrations, especially in churches of England from c. 1410. The Moravians also used a similar device. This, coupled with the Norsemen's celebration of the return of the sun involving cut evergreen trees, resulted in the Christmas tree as we know it today. To call this a Christmas custom is an error, but it is not an error to state the custom was almost universally adopted in Germany by both the Catholics and Lutherans. The early trimmings of Christmas trees were not glass balls but comfits, sugarplums, fruits, nuts, cornucopias, candles, small gifts, et cetera.

chromatic envelope: A letter envelope printed in tint from closely ruled plates. Invariably embellished with a humorous corner insignia for the return address. Date is from c. 1865. [*Several corner cards pictured.*]

chromatic piano: Schoenhut toy piano of three chromatic octaves.

chromatrope: A motion slide for a magic lantern. By turning a crank, a kaleidoscope in motion and in color was projected on the screen. 19th century. [*Example pictured.*]

chromotypes: Prints, especially maps, printed partly in color and then finished with colors applied by stencil method.

chronophotography: Term of 1880s used to describe successive still pictures taken of motion, achieved by fast shutter speeds that stopped the motion. Assembled in proper sequence, these pictures, when projected on a screen and interrupted with a chopping movement, gave the effect of pictures in motion. The process, perfected in the U.S. by Edison, was made possible by George Eastman's "film." Prior to that the picture strip was made up of small glass panes held by side chains. *See Phantoscope.*

chronos: *See Cronus.*

Chrysanthemum Cut: Pattern of cut glass patented in 1890 by T. G. Hawkes, featuring a series of medallions cut in chrysanthemum form with chrysanthemum-like petals and a huge geometric form cut from the arcs of circles. A copy of pattern can be obtained from the U.S. Patent Office. It is #20257 of November 4, 1890.

Chrysanthemum Leaf: Pattern of pressed glass featuring a curvate leaf of Paisley-shawl pattern, with feathery edges. It is a late Sandwich pattern that dates from 1880s.

chrysanthemum plate: Porcelain plates of Chinese and Japanese make, in the stylized form of an open chrysanthemum flower. Chinese examples date from Yung Ch'eng era.

chrysos: Of gold; golden.

chrysotype: Paper positive from glass negative, in early photography.

Chubb lock: Fine period locks, with keys, and other cabinet hardware made by J. Chubb of London, first half of 19th century. Many are marked "Chubb."

chufas: A form of pea growing in the earth; a groundnut, peanut, "goober." Some amusing errors have derived from the term "ground nut." One expert seriously explained it meant nuts ground up into a sort of coarse meal eaten at Christmas parties!

church hassock: Hymnbook and hatbox with padded lid, used in church pews and kept there by the renter of the pew. So general was use that by 1840 they were factory-made.

church linen: The finest of linen, used on altars and for ecclesiastical vestments.

churchwarden (& case): (1) A long-stemmed clay pipe, and (2) a protective case made of wood covered with paper, leather, tin, or some other material.

churchwarden stand: A wooden stand for the long-stemmed clay pipes called churchwardens.

churchwort: The herb pennyroyal.

churn hod: Copper, brass, or sheet-iron coal hod looking something like a dasher butter churn.

churning chair: A rocker that operated a butter churn. Also a low-backed, high-legged chair of Windsor type for easy operation of a butter churn by occupant.

churn mill: Mechanical affairs of wood, like seesaws, tilting platforms, dog mills, et cetera, to supply power to operate the plunger of a butter churn or other light machinery. The same devices were used to operate early home-laundry machines.

churn supper: Actually the feast of hay harvest.

chyrugian: A barber-surgeon; a blood-letter, tooth extractor, or wound dresser; a leech. The word "surgeon" is derived from this term.

cia: The tea plant; same as cha. Cia is found impressed on some tea caddies.

ciborium: Covered cup sometimes called a pyx; a sacramental chalice.

cider-mill engine: A fire engine with six or eight long bars or sweeps springing from a central capstan. Men operating the engine lined the bars and ran around in a circle. Also called capstan engine and coffee-mill engine.

cider royal: Mixture of cider and brandy or cider and mead.

cierge: Wax taper.

cigarette cards: Pictures of athletes, actresses, famed people, et cetera, often in colors, inserted as souvenirs in early cigarette packages.

cigar lamp: Small silver or white metal lamps, sometimes also of pressed glass, with rope wicks and metal wick caps. Early home "table lighters" of the 1870s.

cigar-store Indians: Carved figures of life size or less, generally Indian braves or squaws but sometimes Indian queens, used as tobacconists' signs. In 17th century Dutch tobacconists first used black boys (who were supposed to be American Indians). These effigies have a most interesting history. Period of use seems to have been from 1820s to 1900s, though some 18th-century examples are of record.

Cincinnati, Order of: Badge of a society of officers of the Revolution, so named because, like the ancient Roman warrior, they returned from the sword to the plow. The order was used on china, silver, and other house- and tablewares and is now highly prized. The insignia is a bald eagle suspended on a blue ribbon with white border. Cincinnatus is displayed on the eagle's breast, receiving sword and military appurtenances. In background his wife stands at door of cottage, and beside the door are a plow and other instruments of agriculture. The motto, *Omnia Relinquit Servar e Rem Republicam*, surrounds these. The reverse of medal displays Fame crowning Cincinnatus, a seaport with ships, and joined hands with a heart. Inscriptions are *Virtutis Proemium* and *Esto Perpetua*. The society was instituted at Newburgh, N.Y., June 19, 1783. [*The badge is pictured.*] There is considerable oriental export porcelain (erroneously called Lowestoft or oriental Lowestoft) with the insignia of the society.

Cincinnati glass: Gray & Hemingway, 1848–52, produced bottles, vials, flasks, lamps, and tablewares of glass at Cincinnati. The factory was moved to Covington, Ky., in 1852. Two other glass factories were in operation in Cincinnati from c. 1815, one within the city limits and the other at Moscow, O., nearby. The city factory made bottles, flasks, and tumblers; the Moscow plant made flasks, bottles, and window glass.

Cincinnati ware: Furniture, glassware, silver, pewter, clocks, and many other objects now considered antique were made in considerable quantities at Cincinnati. In 1813 there were 13 cabinetmakers and

a clock factory, two potteries, and seve silversmiths at work. In 1836 the city pr duced $294,000 worth of furniture, $93,0 worth of chairs, and $93,000 worth of silv plate. In 1841 there were 59 furniture fa tories. The major portion of this produ tion was shipped westward via the Oh and Mississippi, and supplied the eve widening Western frontier as well as t growing South and Southwest. From 18 to 1860 Cincinnati was the furnitur manufacturing center for at least 12 stat and all the Western territories. Its on competition in sales came from Louisvil and St. Louis, and this, prior to 1860, w not important.

Cinderella pie tool: It looks like a lemo reamer but isn't; it is a pie crimper, ar what looks like the reamer is a rota crimping wheel. [*Example pictured.*]

cinquecento: Five hundred. Term gei erally used to designate furniture and a objects made from 1501 to 1601, the 16t century.

cinquefoil: Five leaves, or foils, arrange circularly or around a circle.

cippi: Low columns with memorial ir scriptions.

cipress: Neckpiece of gauze. 17th centur

circa: (Abbreviated as "c.") Around, e about the time of.

circular flower stand: An Empire period pedestal on which is mounted deep circular bowl with metal liner. planter. Date is from 1840s. [*Example pie tured.*]

circular letter: Colloquially, evidence c a ringworm infection on the forehead c cheek.

circular plane: A compass plane; an plane of concave or convex form for plai ing the inside or outside surface of curve.

circus carvings: Units or complete as semblies of carvings made to decorat circus wagons. These were figural, an' malistic, fruits, florals, agricultur: classic mythological figures, et cetera.

cisele: Chiseled, as cut velvet and othe pile fabrics.

cissus: The wild native grape.

cistern: (1) A metal or pottery containe for water. (2) A pit or covered cavern fc holding an accumulation of water.

citole: Stringed musical instrument.

citrine: Kiln-roasted black quartz yield ing a yellow stone imitative of topaz an a yellowish-red colored stone called "rhubarb."

citrons: Crystallized rinds of large lemon Also a type or variety of small melo somewhat like the watermelon.

citron water: Cordial made of lemo peel, orange peel, nutmeg, elder flower and other flavorings, steeped in wine.

cittern: Same as citole; a guitarlik stringed instrument.

clabber: To thicken, as sour milk.

clacket: Toothed wheel under tensio from a long wood spring and turning wit a twirling motion on an axle that is it handle. This produced continuous lou clacking.

clairvoyant physician: Any quack wl

1, Christmas Lights. 2, Cupid & Psyche Figurine. 3, Crusie. 4, Crystal Bottle, or Decanter Jug. 5, Cuckoo Clock. 6, Crocus Pots (2). 7, Counter Urn. 8, Court Cupboard. 9, Court Hand. 10, Corner Ottoman. 11, Cow Butter Dish. 12, Corner Wardrobe. 13, Corner Console. 14, Corn Cutter. 15, Conjurors, one showing furnace, flat kettle, and cover. 16, Crane Bracket Table. 17, Criton Ice Maker. 18, Concertina Table. 19, Columbia Jar. 20, Colt Cartridge. 21, Cocoon Jars. 22, Coal Urns, one classic, one square. 23, Coal Tongs. 24, Chamber Pedestal. 25, Coal Scissors. 26, Candle Cone and Candle Thimble on Chain. (No. 17 from Harrod's, London. No. 16 from *New Geography of American Antiques*. No. 11 from Virtue & Co., London.)

91

professed to diagnose ills by clairvoyance, by mail, requiring only a lock of hair to establish "sympathy."

clam-broth glass: A grayish-white, semi-opaque glass.

clame bread: Buttered bread.

clap-dish: (1) Box with a sliding lid. (2) Table, generally called a klopdish, with hexagonal-shaped top and fold-under legs.

clap door: Lower half of a so-called Dutch door.

clap-harp: A half lyre, with strings on both sides and a sounding board between. A really engaging piece of furniture made by Charles Clap of Gardner, Mass., from 1840s. [*Example pictured.*]

clapholt: Boards used to form staves. Clapboard is another form of the term.

clapper: Footing tool used by glass-makers; the tongue of a bell.

clap-stile: A stile with movable horizontal ledges.

claret jug: Any ewer-form jug for serving claret wine. Since this wine is mild and was used as a table beverage with meals, the jugs held a goodly amount. Known in glass, ceramics, and various metals, especially silver and Sheffield plate.

claricord: Spinet-type musical keyboard instrument having from 35 to 70 strings. Also claricol, clarishoe.

clarinet Cremona: Pine and maple violins made by Dr. W. F. Adams of Montpelier, Vt., c. 1810-50. A revival of the original type.

clarion: A shrill-toned trumpet.

Clark: Pattern of pressed glass featuring blocking over scallops as a base, over which there is a floral and leaf-stem design. It is thought to be late, c. 1880s-90s.

Clark & Coit lamp: Clark & Coit were lampmakers of New York City in the first half of the 19th century. They made a twin-burner Argand that is quite lovely. Lamps are marked.

Clark & Hartmann (Clapville) tapestry: Tapestry carpeting, the figures being *printed* on the warp before weaving. One hundred yards a day were woven at the Clapville, Mass., looms of this firm c. 1845.

claro-obscuro: Same as chiaroscuro, a two-color presentation.

clarry: Spiced red wine.

Classic: Pattern of pressed glass featuring Gothic arches with alternating geometric (somewhat like Daisy & Button) panels and frosted classic figures.

classic tray: Papier-mâché trays, japanned and painted with classic scenes in full color.

clavel: The fireplace and its various elements. **clavel page:** A fireside ornament, generally figural and in pairs, of painted wood, metal, and wood forms covered with crewelwork and needle point. **clavel piece:** The mantel, or beam supporting chimney breast, crossing from the cheeks or stiles of a fireplace. **clavel-tack:** The shelf over a fireplace.

clavichord: A stringed keyboard instrument of the 17th century, ancestor of the pianoforte.

clavis: A key.

claw & ball: Any furniture footing in which a clawlike form grasping a ball is dominant. Opposed to ball and claw, in which the ball is the dominant element and the claw secondary. Both claw and ball and ball and claw are forms of Chinese origin and are not the earmark of the Chippendale style. Chippendale, in fact, used either the French-turned, up-carved foot, the plinth with square legs, or plain square legs, with surface carving or fluting for decoration. Claw and ball is found mostly on the Georgian furniture that is *not* Chippendale.

Clawson-Mudge beds: Cherry, sycamore, poplar, and black-walnut beds made by this firm, Cincinnati, from 1840s. It is said they manufactured 40,000 bedsteads a year.

claw table: The tilt-top candlestand with three curvate legs at base of a column, the legs suggestive of a claw. This term was commonly used in 18th century. [*A superior example pictured.*]

clay candle molds: Fired hollow clay tubes mounted in wooden frames for the casting of wax candles. Some molds had as many as 196 tubes. These were used by chandlers for mass production.

clay grenade: Explosive shells of clay pottery used in warfare from 17th century.

Claypool, Joseph & Josiah: A famed father-and-son combination of cabinetmakers, working at Philadelphia from 1710. Josiah advertised in 1740s.

Clayton glass: Made at Clayton, N.J., by Moore Brothers from mid-18th century.

Clay tray: Clay, of Covent Garden, London, is the maker; clay is not the substance. The tray is of papier-mâché, beautifully japanned and decorated. Made from 1800s.

Clay ware: Henry Clay of Birmingham invented laminated paper (not papier-mâché) ware. His method consisted of full sheets, dampened with glue size between each sheet, formed over molds, and then baked in ovens. The ware was unbreakable and exceedingly rigid. Many objects, from plates to trays, fans, and fire screens, were made.

Clear Diagonal Band: Pattern of pressed glass featuring clear bands encircling the pieces, with a stipple of open dots between. It is a late pattern.

cleat & pin hinge: An early chest hinge or hinging device, operating thus: The cleats or end pieces under the lid are enlarged at rear and terminate in back of the chest and lid. A block at the back of the chest is set on a level with cleat which is bored with a hole to take a pin which, in turn, is fixed in the block. This made an excellent wooden hinge.

clee boards: Flat boards strapped on feet over shoes to facilitate walking over mud wallows, swamps, and sloughs.

cleft cabriole: The knee of a cabriole sofa leg, when not at corners but between corners as an extra support, presents a problem in symmetry solved by early Georgian cabinetmakers by the introduction of this nicety of design. The inordinate breadth of the knee was relieved by a cleft. [*Example pictured.*]

Clematis: Pattern of pressed glass featuring a stippled vine with drooping flowers. Late pattern.

Clementon glass: Bottles and window glass made at factory located at Clementon, N.J., from early in 19th century.

Clements puzzles: The Rev. E. J. Clements, in 1880s, produced cutout maps of the U.S. and states, cut on boundary lines. Back of maps carried advertising.

Cleveland flower prints: Small hand-colored engravings, issued 1849 as illustrations for *Flowers Personified* by N. Cleveland. J. B. Gimbrede and other engravers made the plates.

Cleveland glass: Any glassware made at Cleveland, N.Y., at two factories: the Cleveland Works, 1840, and the Union Works, 1850s. Bottles, pitchers, paperweights, vials, and general wares were made. There is a notice of this works in *ABC's of Old Glass.*

Cleveland rocker: *See* Chairs, All Kinds.

clew: A ball of warp yarn.

clewkin: Twine or cord.

Clews: British potter, owner of the Cobridge Works, Staffordshire. James Clews' mark is well known in the U.S., as his product was imported in considerable quantities, 1819–29. Clews issued the Landing of Lafayette pattern, in what we now call Historic Staffordshire, in 1824, and the famous States pattern with its border of 15 swags with the names of the states. He issued many other American-view patterns, made the Syntax, Wilkie, and Don Quixote patterns and a general line of other tablewares. J. & R. Clews (James and Ralph) seem to have continued potting operations in Staffordshire to the mid-1830s. In 1836 James, having in mind the great sale of their wares in the U.S., came here to establish a pottery at Troy, Ind. His lack of competent workmen and adequate clays caused this venture to fail. Among the views issued by Clews was a comprehensive set of Hudson River Valley views from original sketches by W. G. Wall.

clichés-verre: Etchings made on photographic plates and prints made on photo paper by solar light. The etching was done on the plate by the artist, free hand. Developed as a process at Arras, France, c. 1854. Durand, Leutze, Kensett, Darley, Gifford, Dana, and other American artists used the process to produce prints.

Clichy: French glass made at Clichy (France) Glassworks and imported in some quantities to U.S. from 1840s. The paperweights are superb and well known to connoisseurs. This plant also made many perfume bottles and preserve jars.

Clichy glaze: Silicate of soda glaze for pottery developed at the Clichy (France) Glassworks.

Climax: Pattern of pressed glass featuring rows of double bars set vertically, and sometimes etched floral details on the clear sections of surface. Late pattern.

climax basket: Fruit baskets of thinly sawed wood (veneer weight) tacked to solid-wood bottoms.

climax blocks: Toy building blocks.

clinquant: Brass foil, a cheap substitute for gold leaf.

Clio: Pattern of pressed glass, clear and in colors, featuring a geometric star design paneled by vertical spears and broken by horizontal bands with oval bosses. Also Greek muse of history and epic poetry.

clipper ship: In spite of allegations that clipper ships were not known prior to the 1840s, this type of craft was developed almost immediately after the Revolution and by the 1800s was known as the Baltimore clipper. (See *The Baltimore Clipper*, by Henry Irving Chapelle.) During the early decades of the 19th century any swift ship was a "clipper." In the 1840s the size of the Baltimore clipper was increased and, amazingly, the resulting craft became more profitable than steam for cargo carrying. The fuel requirements of a steamer meant departure with bunkers full and arrival at destination with bunkers almost empty, with much cargo space wasted. The American clippers sailed without fuel other than for cooking and heating, so all cargo space was full of goods. In many cases the clipper outsailed steamers crossing the Atlantic. The Baltimore and the larger American clipper brought most of the oriental goods to our ports prior to the Civil War.

cloamware: Earthenware.

clobbered: Reworked; redecorated; recovered. Said of the delicately decorated or all-white wares from China which were redecorated in the Netherlands, France, and England in much gaudier styles. This work is being done today. Scores of advertisements are being run by people for plain white marked or unmarked china (but marked preferred). These should be investigated by collectors' organizations, as it is quite easy to decorate and refire this ware and come up with a *marked* example! Of course this is faking, but it is within a pattern of faking as old as the 17th century.

cloche: Glass bell or dome, fitting over a base, to provide dustproof display of a clock, work of art, waxwork, et cetera. Also the early term for clock.

clock bottle: Any container imitative of a clock, generally of glass but also of pottery and china. There is a bitters bottle (Bininger's) and several whiskey flasks imitative of clocks. Some are quite rare. Variants are "watch" bottles in the shape and form of a pocket watch. There is also a pressed-glass butter dish in watch form.

clock case: Any casing or cabinet for a clock movement. A glass case or bell dome to cover a clock movement.

clock-eyed: Same as cockeyed; eyes which apparently do not focus properly.

clock-face varnish: Mixture of alcohol, gums benjamin, mastic, and sandarach. A fine shellac.

clock fan: An air-circulating and insect-chasing fan operated by clockwork. Later models operate from a spring while early examples operated by weights. The spring-operated type was made from 1840s in U.S., one of the earliest being made by T. C. Schaffer of Portsmouth, N.H. It ran for two to three hours at one winding.

clock line: The weight cords in weight-driven clocks.

clockmakers (American): There are many published lists of American clockmakers, compiled by Hudson Moore, Phillipse R. Greene, Willis Milham, Brooks Palmer, Wallace Nutting, and others, some

CLOCKS, all kinds: **Top row:** Dutch Hanging Clock with Bob Pendulum, Lantern Clock, Lantern or Bird Cage with Pendulum Wings, Hooded Hang-Up, "Closeted" or Tall Case Clock. **Center three:** Sheraton-Cased Tall Clock, Mural or Wall Clock, mid-18th century (ancestor of the Banjo), "Half-Clock," wall type, c. 1760. **Bottom row:** Fine "Grandfather" or Tall Case, mid-18th century, Candlestick Clock under Glass Bell, OG Molding Cased Clock, made 1830s–90s, Lyre-Form Clock, Grandmother-Type Clock.

94

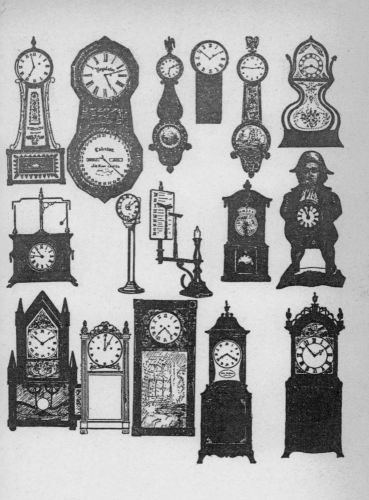

CLOCKS, all kinds: **Top row:** Banjo, Calendar, Lyre, Wall Regulator, Round-Bottom Banjo, Acorn. **Center row:** Flying Pendulum, Candle Clock, Candle Dial, Solar Clock (Timby's), Blinking Eye. **Bottom row:** Wagon Spring (Ives), Mirror Door, Wall Hanging Mirror Clock, Kidney Dial Clock (Willard), Case-on-Case Clock.

CLOCKS, all kinds: **Top row:** Lighthouse, Pillar & Scroll (Terry), Pillar & Scroll (8-day), Early Pillar & Scroll by Heman Clark (earlier than Terry's use of this form of case; Terry's patent was not on the case but on the low-cost/ all-wood, 30-hour movement, time & strike). **Center row:** Pennsylvania Pillar & Scroll (Custer), Pillar & Scroll, (Boardman & Wells), Washington (French; bronze), Columbus, of 1892 (not 1492 as marked; it was a cheap souvenir clock). **Bottom row:** Merriman "Grandmother" Case Clock, New Hampshire "Grandmother," four late Banjo types.

of which have been published. The best abridged list is in *American Clocks & Clockmakers*, published in 1947. The complete list from which this is abridged is being published in parts by Antiques Publications, Inc., of Frederick, Md., in *Antiques Digest*. All important clockmakers are noted in the first-named volume.

clockmakers (Foreign): A voluminous, though incomplete source book of names is *Watchmakers & Clockmakers of the World*, by G. H. Baillie, republished in 1947. The list of English makers in this work is the important and most nearly complete list extant. The American list is elementary.

clock-mill glass: A drinking glass with base in form of a mill with a clock face, operated by a blow tube. The base is a silver toy which stands right side up when the bowl of the tumbler is down. Dutch, perhaps early 17th century, and rare.

clock reel: A device for reeling yarn for hanking, with a counter operating by several wooden gears.

clock wheel: (1) The gears of a clock, whether of brass, tin, iron, wood, or (rarely) glass. (2) Misnomer for clock reel.

clock winder: The keeper of a public clock; a tradesman-clockmaker who wound clocks of patrons for a fee, calling at office, factory, or home for the service.

clockwork toys: Mechanical toys of all kinds, but generally of thin tin-plated sheet iron, operated by a spring and gears. Innumerable varieties. Francis & Francis of Philadelphia made them as early as 1830s.

clock urn: A finial of urn shape often used on clock cases.

Clodion: Name given a pewter pitcher depicting cupids in relief, so marked. Reference is to the French sculptor, 1738–1814, who is famed for his work in terra cotta.

clog: A heavy wooden sole and heel fixed to regular shoes for walking in wet weather. Often worn by ladies to traverse path from door to carriage or chaise. [*Example pictured.*]

cloisonné: Enamel inlay work on metal, within areas separated by fine ridges of metal which form the outline. Imitative of oriental work.

clome pan: A milk pan.

close bed: A press or folding bed.

closed arm: The upholstered section of a chair between arm and seat.

closestool: A toilet chair enclosing a chamber pot. Many chairs were converted for this purpose. In the 18th century the corner chair was a favorite chair for this usage. Wing chairs with valances were also put to this use. One authority claims such chairs were used only in bedrooms. He is indubitably right, especially in respect of all nice households. *See* Chairs, All Kinds.

close-stove: An enclosed stove; a stove of plates of iron, tile, or soapstone, fully enclosing the fire.

clothes bar or crane: A long pointed wooden bar on a hinge, used in the home for drying clothes.

clothes oar: A paddle used to stir laundry in a wash boiler.

clothes pestle: A device similar to clothes oar, sometimes stone-tipped, to beat laundry.

clothespress: A portable closet; a wardrobe or kasten.

cloth portrait: Prints or drawings with figures dressed by pasting on actual fabrics.

cloudy cedar: Improperly seasoned cedarwood which has "fogged" under the varnish because of moisture in the cells. Any such fogged wood can be cured by refinishing, as the fog is on the varnish.

clough: Draught allowance in commodity transactions, often expressed in such phrases as "and two pounds for the scale in every hundredweight."

clout: A poultice cloth.

clove: (1) Aromatic bud. (2) Seven pounds of wool. (3) A weight; eight pounds of cheese was designated as a clove.

Clover: Pattern of pressed glass, actually a Daisy & Button variant, but named as here because the clear button is impressed with a cut star facet. There are also vertical clear, or plain, narrow panels.

clover cart: An early reaper with cutting fingers, used in harvesting clover seed. It preceded the grain reaper.

club chair: *See* Chairs, All Kinds.

club decanter: Actually any club-shaped decanter, more bottle form than bulbous or ovate.

clum buzza: An open earthenware pot.

cluster column: Any support made in the form of a series or cluster of rods or slender columns. **clustered pier:** A similar arrangement of squared upright members. Sometimes simulated by carving, gouging, reeding, et cetera.

clustool: Tool used in stringing musical instruments.

Clyde glass: Offhand glass objects blown at the Clyde, N.Y., Glass Works, established 1827. This plant made commercial window glass and bottles.

clyster: A syringe.

coach: Four-wheeled enclosed traveling carriage with two facing seats in the coach and seats for two on the box. Often with extra seats on top, with luggage racks.

coach bed: Three explanations of the term seem to reside in old documents: (1) A shake-down contrived within a coach during night travel by certain folding seats carried by the passenger. (2) Another term for a sleigh bed in an alcove. (3) A bed on wheels, as the Dutch *schlap-bank-op-rollen*.

coach candle: The long and sometimes two-wicked candle used in coach lamps. Made and sold quite generally to 1910.

coach horn: Copper or brass horn used by coach drivers to sound their coming, turns, and stops. The motor horn is a relic of the coach horn. The true coach horn is straight, not coiled like the hunter's horn. From 20 to 54 inches in length.

coaching chair: *See* Chairs, All Kinds.

coach lamp: Signal lamp carried to designate the route and destination of a coach or diligence. These running lamps were red, yellow, and green, in various combinations. Regular road lamps had globes of clear glass. Made and used from 17th century.

coachman bottle: Figural bottle in glass or pottery, molded in the general form of a high-hatted coachman These are sometimes called bishop bottles. Pottery examples were made at Fenton Works, Bennington Some glass examples are quite late in date.

coach table: Small folding table used for collations, lunches, playing games, et cetera, in coaches.

Coade ware: Stoneware and terra cotta pottery made at Lambeth, England, from 1760s. It is said the Coade works shipped packet-boat loads of this ware, including terra cotta figures, to America after the Revolution

Coalbrookdale porcelain: Actually Coalport ware, made from 1780s by Rose & Co. and others.

coal can: Brass, copper, polished steel, gun metal, japanned iron, and even papier-mâché boxes to hold coal at fireside. Some are of a lovely shape [*Example pictured.*]

coal cauldron: Large three-legged iron pot used to hold coal at fireside and, at times, used as a retort stove for burning coals in fireplace.

Coalport: Porcelain-type English ware, almost a twin of Caughley, marked SALOPIAN. Rose, Blakeway, Johnson, Winter, Pugh, and other owners were successive proprietors. This works finally absorbed the Caughley Pottery and those of Swansea and Nantgarw Made the Rose du Barry ware. [*Examples and marks pictured.*]

coal scissors: Scissors-form tongs for lifting hot coals from fire [*Example pictured.*]

coal-scuttle mug: A shaving mug, dating from c. 1870s, original form issued as a container of soap by an American firm. Many varieties produced for separate sale by potters and plated-silverware makers. Chief characteristic is an open spoutlike protuberance on the lower half of the mug. In figural, or "face," examples this becomes a grotesque protruding lip.

coal tongs: (1) Large hinged iron devices for handling coals and embers in a fireplace (2) Small examples of same used in lighting fires. The large examples are quite frequently trimmed with brass, gun metal, polished steel, and sometimes silver or Sheffield plate, but many are all iron or with small finials of brass. The smaller tongs are frequently all brass, all steel, or all silver or plated. [*Examples pictured.*]

coal urn: The ultimate in fireside coal containers; a classical urn form on a tripod base. [*Example pictured said to date from Adam period.*]

Coates pottery: Redwares and stonewares made by Levi Coates of Chester County, Pa , from 1800s. Said to have reproduced a Wedgwood hunt pitcher in green-glazed ware. Coates was a part-time potter.

coa vestis: Diaphanous garment worn by courtesans, dancing girls, and other ladies of pleasure. Antiquarian comments about "taking the Coan robe" connote this choice of life.

cob: Colonial plaster made from clay, water, straw, and thatch. Such plaster was frequently used in 18th-century construction

to at least 1760. It was brushed over with thick slaked lime to whiten it.

cobalt glass: Glass made with oxide of cobalt to achieve a blue color or, with the addition of other metallic oxides, greens, purples, et cetera.

cobberde: Not to be confused with clobbered. Cobberd, coobert, cubbert, et cetera, are early spellings of cupboard. The original cup board was an open shelf (a board) on which to stand a range of cups. Now the meaning is an enclosed cabinet.

cobbet's corn: The native American maize, or Indian corn, was given this name when grown in England early in 19th century.

cobbler's candle: Another name for the double-wick candle of 18th century.

cobbler's candlestand: A stand with top, with threaded pole above the top on which an arm holding candles was fixed and adjusted by turning to suit the light-level needs of a workman. Why it should be designated as a cobbler's candlestand is a question unanswered. Many are of pioneer or homemade type. [*Example pictured is maple.*] Others are of pine, poplar, walnut, cherry, and mahogany.

Cobb reel: The only satisfactory definition would seem to be the silk reel invented during the American silkworm craze by J. H. Cobb, c. 1830.

cob iron: The first (the original) andiron or chenet. It is a one-piece wrought-iron bar, footed at each end to maintain an upright position. The bar is flattened in its lateral dimension, humped in contour, with serrated upper edge. Logs were piled from both sides, one end resting on hearth. This type of iron never stood across the hearth but was set in the middle, front to back. Date is from 13th century, when the hearth was often in center of room with nothing but a louvered smoke vent to serve as a chimney. The transitional piece, still a cob iron, shows high end supports for a turnspit. Sawed in half in middle of cob bar, such cob irons at once suggested andirons in pairs. [*Examples pictured.*]

Cobweb Cut: Pattern of cut glass featuring vertical-, horizontal-, and angular-band cutting, the interstices filled with fine cutting simulating a spider's web.

cocaine tablets: Advertised in one of America's ethical magazines of the 1880s as a substitute for morphine and alcohol! This dangerous drug, sold openly, was a twin to hasheesh candy, *which see.*

cochineal: Insect yielding a scarlet dye. From the Aztec *nochezli.*

coch-leary: Spiral, screw-shaped, air-twisted (as in glassworking).

Cochrane rifle: Predecessor of the Colt; a rifle with a revolving chamber carrying nine to eleven charges. Exhibited 1836 at Mechanics Institute Fair, New York. Invented by Cochrane, a native of New Hampshire.

cockade: A fan or brush used as a hat ornament. Noted as a style from 1710. A military cockade is fan-shaped; the brush shape is the civilian type. Used on dress uniforms by U.S. troops to c. 1850.

cock bead: Fine rounded beading noted as a projection around drawer fronts, and similar elements used in fine cabinetmaking from 1680s.

cockchafer: Caterpillar.

cockfighting chair (and stool): See Chairs, All Kinds.

cocking cart: Two-wheeled sporting vehicle with a rumble seat.

cockle pot: Earthenware pot used in cooking cockles (bivalve mollusks), such as clams, mussels, et cetera. From 17th century.

cock metal: Alloy of copper, lead, and antimony; a sort of pewter. See Pot Metal.

cock's-head hinge: Reference is to the outline or silhouette of the hinge form. Each prong of the hinge leaves has the appearance of a cock's head. The entire hinge looks more like a headless leaping frog. Known in wrought iron and brass. [Example pictured.]

Cockson ironstone: China- and granite ware made by several firms at Cobridge, Staffordshire: Harding & Cockson, 1836, to Cockson & Chetwynd and Cockson & Seddon. After 1866 made granite ware exclusively, and much for the American market. Mark is the royal arms, lettering IMPERIAL IRONSTONE CHINA, and the maker of the date of issue.

cockspur lamp: Reference is to early gas lighting, when burner tips created jets of flame in form of cockspurs. Date is from 1815 to 1830s. Found on early portable (flex tube) gas-burning table lamps.

cockspur mark: The burr or scar on underside of china caused by the separators or stilts used in the kiln.

cockstone: An early cure-stone taken from the bladder of a cockbird. Most of them were smooth gizzard stones.

cocktailings: The tail ends of all kinds of liquors drawn from casks, collected in another cask, and sold cheap to tipplers. This is the mixture technique from which the modern cocktail derives. William S. Gleim, a student of early commercial and trade customs, asserted in 1920 that within his memory bars and taverns of low repute even added the tailings from bar glasses left by customers to their bottle of dregs and resold this liquor cheap as cocktailings. This explanation would seem more plausible for the derivation of cocktail than one recently advocated, "deriving from the potent spiked ale, called cockale."

coconut candle: Made from the stearin remaining after expressing the oil from dried coconut meat (copra). These candles burned without odor. Made after 1830.

coconut cup: (1) A cup made from a coconut shell, with silver or brass mountings and rims. (2) Any cup in the general form of a coconut.

coconut dipper: (1) Coconut shell fitted to a lateral handle. (2) A coconut-shell-shaped ladle affixed to a lateral handle, the bowl made of Sheffield plate, silver, brass, or white metal. These were made in U.S. by Mix, Yalesville, Conn., as late as 1875. Actual coconut-shell dippers were made by Chapman Maltby, Northford, Conn., from 1840s. A by-product of his dipper manufacture was coconut meat, which he shredded, dried, and sold as a food product.

coconut oil: Lamp fluid and toilet oil made from copra. The oil was sold as a luxury lamp fluid from 1830s.

coconut pearl: Not a tall tale told by the early clipper captains who reported "pearls from coconuts and man-eating clams." Actually the rarest and finest pearls grow in coconuts. This phenomenon is due to the occasional development of a coconut without the soft sprouting eyes in its shell. The minerals concrete within such nuts at what should be the sprouting end and form a large pearl. This calcium-carbonate pearl was so revered in the Orient that the rajah received every eyeless coconut, and these were opened in the presence of his agent. Only one nut in 10,000 develops without eyes, and only one of these in 10,000 forms a pearl of perfect form. It is said that only three genuine coconut pearls are now in the U.S. but that hundreds are in the collections of the rajahs of India.

cocoon jars: Urn-shaped glass jars with conical lids, used generally by confectioners and druggists. These were also used from 1830s as storing jars for silkworm cocoons during the silk-culture mania. [Examples pictured.]

cocos: Bulb of the caladium or sweet manioc. Used as a yam or sweet potato.

cod: A pillow. **codpiece:** Stuffed gussets in the crotches of trousers and over the breasts. Pin cods were worn by women and used as pincushions. This may well be the origin of what are today called "falsies."

Coddington furniture: Any cabinetwork or chairs produced by the fabulous George Coddington of Cincinnati, who in 1850 boasted he had made 180,000 chairs annually, priced at from $4.25 to $22 a dozen. Cane- and rush-seated chairs, painted and gilded, were sold principally in the South and West.

coddlings: Green peas. Coddling cream was a concoction of peas cooked in rose water and served cold with cream.

Codman doll: Medical student's manikin, made by Codman & Shurtleff of Boston from c. 1860.

Codnor Park: A pottery, at place so named, Derbyshire, England, founded 1820. Here were made beer, cordial, and other bottles of two-tone (brown-and-cream) stoneware. It merged with the Denby Pottery and was then known as Denby & Codnor Park Works. These potteries were, in the main, operated by Joseph Bourne. Paperweights, inkwells, and figural bottles, bread trays, and other objects made by this pottery are collectors' items.

coffee: This beverage, originally from Arabia, took Europe by storm and was the one competitor of tea. Introduced to the colonies in 17th century. Coffeepots were mentioned in New England records in 1686, and coffee dishes (wide, shallow cups, similar to bouillon cups) in 1683. The coffee cup always had an underdish, now called a saucer, but not a saucer (which see). The coffeepot is known in every form peculiar to each and every period style, in all metals from gold to pewter, and all ceramics from redware to porcelain. Millions of cups with underdishes were made for serving this beverage, which appealed to the people of the U.S. more than tea, perhaps because our Revolution started over the tea tax.

Coffee, William: English sculptor who came to the U.S. c. 1816 and who modeled busts of Jefferson, Van Cortlandt, and others.

Coffee busts: Thomas Coffee, sculptor, of New York City, c 1840, began commercial production of plaster-of-Paris busts and other ornaments which he sold in considerable quantities. He preceded Rogers by some quarter of a century and was perhaps motivated by the success of Italian vendors of the cheap wares known now as chalk ware.

coffee furniture & appurtenances of service: Coffee tables, coffee cans, coffee jars, coffee stools, coffee dishes, coffeepots, coffee spoons, coffee grinders, coffee roasters, coffee makers, and many other items of collectors' interest fall within this general category of objects. Some of the applications are local and some regional. It is not thought necessary to describe or picture these generally recognized and known things. At one time a coffee roaster was in every home, together with a grinder, a pot, and cups Finally coffee roasting became a manufacturing process and grinding of the roasted bean was done by the grocer or coffee dealer. But the true lover of coffee still roasts and grinds for each brewing of the beverage.

coffee tree: American forest tree, native to Kentucky and some states of the Mississippi Valley, bearing nuts or berries which yield a drink similar to coffee The buckthorn tree.

coffered: Rounded at sides and lid; shaped like a coffer.

Coffeyville glass: Made at Coffeyville, Kan., by the Pioneer Flint Glass Co., which moved to Sapulpa, Okla., 1905. Pressed and blown wares were made, dating from c. 1903.

Coffin & Hay: Glassmakers of Winslow, N.J., from c. 1838. This firm also had a works at Hammonton, N.J., from 1814. They made historic flasks as a part of their production, some of which are marked with name and place.

coffin cupboard: Tall narrow cupboard with one or two (upper and lower) doors, looking somewhat like a coffin. The name is not contemporaneous, as the cupboards date from c. 1700s, while the style of coffin they resemble was a development of the late 18th century.

coffin planking: A type of flooring, useful when tapering planks were common, made by cutting in old coffin shape, bisected longitudinally, and laying in a pattern. This style of work is said to be peculiar to the arkwrights or shipbuilders from the 15th century. [*Example pictured.*]

coffin stool: Sturdy turned-leg stools of 17th and 18th centuries, designated by this term because, in pairs, they were used to support a coffin or bier at funeral services.

coffin tray: Said to be an American shape; octagonal or octagon-ended tray of japanned tinplate, decorated and striped in the carriage-painting style.

coffre-fort: A strongbox or case.

Coggeshall ware: Tin- and copperware made by Coggeshall & Co., Detroit, from c. 1835. Kitchenware and utensils for bakers, tradesmen, et cetera, were the main items.

coggle: A potter's tool; a toothed or ribbed wheel rolling in a handle, used to finish the edges of ware, especially redware dishes.

cognate: Relatives on the mother's side, as opposed to agnate (now rarely used), meaning related from the father's side. Cognate example—related example.

cogware: Coarse worsted cloth.

coif: A net for confining the hair. Some coifs are of gold chain and jeweled, but any netting for the hair is a coif.

coiffeuse: A fitted dressing table, usually having a hinged top, folding mirror, powder compartment, and bottle drawer. This was a boudoir piece. Many examples date from 18th century and are very luxuriously fitted.

coiffeuse d'homme: A man's dresser. Some have basin, ewer, and other conveniences. Some are extensions of a commode, and others have desk compartments.

coilte: Quilt, kilt, bedcover; any warm padded garment.

Coin: Pattern of pressed glass, production of which was ordered stopped by the Treasury Department, as it was a form of direct reproduction of U.S. coins. The coin representations were pressed in the glass and frosted by etching. Many objects were made with this pattern, and most of the coins are dated 1892 in anticipation of the Columbian Exposition, but some are known with dates as early as 1878. Pattern displays coins in bottoms of tumblers and as rows of bosses on other hollow wares. Made generally by the Central Glass Co. of Wheeling, W. Va.

coin-bottomed: Reference is to insertion of a silver coin in the bottom of a silver cup, ladle, or other utensil. This was done generally to display the head of a sovereign. Examples date from the first George of England to George IV. There are said to be some Victorian ones, and many of French origin are known.

coin cabinet: Special cabinet with very shallow drawers, made for use of coin and medal collectors.

coin card: Engraved card upon which appear coins and their values. Nathaniel Hurd of Boston issued a coin card in 1765.

coin china: China with designs from coins, such as busts, impressed on or applied as transfer printing. 18th and 19th centuries.

coin glass: Blown glassware with actual coins embedded or imprisoned within base or stem. The date of the coin cannot be held as evidence of the age of the glass enclosing it. Forgeries made in 20th century have genuine coins of the 18th century in them.

Coin Harvey: Nickname of W. H. Harvey, the originator of "Free Silver" and pioneer in the silver-standard school of money. He was active in Midwest from 1880s. It is said that Coin-pattern glassware was one of the results of Coin Harvey's campaign.

coins, colonial: The coins current in the colonies were many and various. Chief ones were the English guinea, French guinea, johannes (worth $16), real johannes, moidore, doubloon (worth $14.93), Spanish and French pistoles, French

1, Champion Wares; vase, cup and saucer, and plaque. **2,** Worcester Pottery; examples of ware, the manufactory, and later marks under Chamberlain and Barr, Flight, Barr management. **3,** Carpet-Cutter Rocker. **4,** Chamberlain Lamp. **5,** Clog, affixed to a shoe by toe hold and heel clip. **6,** Cobbler's Candlestand. **7,** Cob Irons, the lower one with spit hooks and turnspit. **8,** Cock's-Head Hinge. **9,** Crane Plate. **10,** Cotyledon Form. **11,** Cool Iron. **12,** Craniological Shorthand (the marks form the facial representation in circle). **13,** Cradle Spit. **14,** Creedmoor Bank. (Nos. 1 and 2 from Virtue & Co., London.)

crown, Spanish dollar, English shilling, pistareen, and colonial issues, including the famous pine-tree shilling. Silver coinage was often converted into silver plate by silversmiths. Coin was the most readily available silver; sheets and merchant bars were scarce.

coir: Coconut fiber from the nuts proper, used in mattresses.

coirboully: Molded and tooled leather.

colbertine: An early lace, said to have been made at factory set up by Colbert, Intendant of Finances under Louis XIV.

cold fire: A fire laid, ready for lighting.

cold painting: Painting on china or glass, not fired on but protected with a coating of varnish or glare.

cole seed oil: *See* Rape Oil.

colestaff: A bar or pole carried from shoulders of men walking tandem, to support a heavy load.

colla: Glue.

collage: A picture, partly painted, or a print, trimmed with cut paper, fabric, et cetera, to complete it. Glued-on decoration.

collapsion cup: A fold-up cup made of telescoping rings.

collar beam: The top beam of a building or cabinet piece.

collar of S's: Gold or silver necklace made up of a series of S-shaped elements. Also a punch made of "sack, sider, and sugar."

collector's cabinet: Any special cabinet for storing collected items such as books, coins, medals, prints, ceramics, et cetera.

college bowls: A pair of bowls; the smaller, inverted, being a cover for the larger. Date is from 17th century.

collet: A small collar. Also collaret.

collet cloth: Cloth waterproofed by boiling in linseed oil and white lead. Some chintz and toiles were so treated.

Collier revolver: Exceedingly rare flintlock five-shot revolving pistol invented by E. H. Collier of Boston, 1809. This gun was made in London in 1818. It was 'way ahead of the Colt pistol of the same type.

collinot: Imitation cloisonné of pottery, made at Paris from c. 1860.

Collins dolls: Play dolls made by J. H. Collins, Boston, from 1840s. Originals bear the mark COLLINS.

Collins furniture: Midwestern Empire- and Directoire-influenced furniture made at shops of John Collins, Davenport, Ia., from 1850s. The records show the value of the product in 1856 was $40,000.

collyflower ware: *See* Cabbage Ware.

colonial: Anything of the period (of American history) prior to 1775. The period 1775 to 1783 is called Revolutionary. Thereafter it is Federal.

Colonial: A pattern of pressed, molded, and cut glass; another name for Ashburton.

colonnette: A small column, generally in a series, as in a parapet or balustrade.

colophony: Brown resin. **colophony oven:** A pot of boiling resin in which potatoes and yams were "baked."

color discriminator: A box of 35 disks

covered with silk in standard colors and tones, each disk numbered. Sold by *Scientific American* in 1840s.

colored cut: Said of cut glass when the cutting is on blanks in opaque or transparent colors, or on glass of one color flashed with one or more layers of contrasting colors.

colored glass: The most common color of glass is green. Most glass in the pots is green until cleared or clarified to white transparent with glassmakers' soap (black oxide of manganese). Many tints and colors, opaque and transparent, are achieved in glass by addition of metallic oxides. Every color and tone from opaque milk white to black have been achieved.

colored prints: Engravings, aquatints, mezzotints, lithographs, and other pictures printed from plates, stones, et cetera, colored by hand or stencil process. Prints in color are achieved (1) by rubbing in each color on the plate and printing in one impression, or (2) by successive prints requiring a plate or stone for each printing.

colored scrimshaw: Ivory and bone scratch carving tinted with colors rubbed in the lines.

color photography: This art dates from 1854, when M. Durien of Paris achieved the effect with paper sensitized with potash, silver nitrate, et cetera, developed in soda and ammonia. People who saw the process doubted their eyes.

color printing: Printing from various blocks, each in one color, to achieve a colored picture. Invented in China, where manuals of instruction in the art were issued in 1627. Japanese color prints are in imitation of the Chinese.

colors (interior): Coffee, brown, green, mauve, pink, salmon, red, gray, and blue were the favored interior colors of the years 1650 to 1800. White was rarely used.

colporteur: A vendor of Bibles and tracts; missionary salesmen who gave of their wares to those too poor to buy.

Colt cartridge: Foil-wrapped charge of powder with bullet at one end and firing cap in other. This is the cartridge that made the Colt repeating pistol work. [*Cartridge pictured.*]

Colt Paterson: The first manufacture of the Colt revolver. Those made at Paterson, N.J., from 1836 are the rare Colt pistols. The great production occurred after removal of the factory from Paterson.

Columbia Cut: Pattern of cut glass featuring large pointed ovals of petaled outline with waffle-cut fill-in, surmounted by magnificent star cuttings with raised central bosses.

Columbia glass: Pressed and other glass produced by Columbia Glass Co., Findlay, O. Shell, Dewdrop, and Hobnail patterns were made.

Columbia jar: A glass show jar made in capacities from 1 to 39 pints. This was South Jersey commercial ware, made from 1875 to 1900 for druggists, confectioners, and sugar bakers. [*Example of type pictured.*]

Columbia tray: Daisy & Button field with 13 alternating stripes in a shield-shaped tray with bust of Columbus in oval. Date is 1892.

Columbus column bottle: Milk-glass column-shaped bottle with a metallic stopper said to be figure of Columbus. Total height is 18 inches or more. *See* Column Bottles.

column bottles: Column-form bottles with various figural trim, commemorating Nelson, Columbus, Liberty, Washington, Bunker Hill, et cetera. These date, generally, from after 1870s.

colza oil: Lamp oil pressed from a variety of cabbage seeds.

comadore: A compote or "soup" of fruit, fresh or stewed.

comallya: Irish folk songs for a group of people.

comb: A toothed implement for dressing hair, flax, and other strands. Also a measure equal to four bushels.

comb-back: *See* Chairs, All Kinds.

combed ware: A form of pottery or china decoration achieved by combing the slip after its application as a wash. Something like scroddled ware.

comb matches: Strips of matches in the form of a wooden comb, the teeth headed with ignition substance. Date is from 1838 and made to c. 1845.

comb vise: Wooden vise used by comb makers in cutting the teeth. The vise is composed of one long and one short bend, with a V-shaped wedge.

Comet: Pattern of pressed glass featuring bold swirls centering on a large bull's-eye, with three small bull's-eyes in the main tail of the swirl.

cometarium: Astronomical machine showing eccentric motion of comets.

Comet Cut: Pattern of cut glass featuring star shapes separated by curvate fans of comet-tail form.

comfit: A bonbon, confection, or sweet.

comfort rocker: *See* Chairs, All Kinds.

Commeraw pottery: Hard earthenware and stoneware made at the pottery of this name near Corlears Hook, N.Y.

commode: (1) A chest of drawers. (2) A light ribbon headdress sometimes called a fantange. (3) A night jar. **commode & glass:** A cabinet piece somewhat like a mirrored sideboard. **commode bureau table:** A table-desk with cabinets. **commode desk:** A commode with a falling-fronted desk compartment; a type of butler's sideboard. **commode desserte:** A side table for food service; a sideboard. **commode front:** Blocked front or façade. **commode mirror:** Hanging mirror with broad base for resting on a commode. **commode sideboard:** The designation of American cabinetmakers from 1785 for a long commodelike element of case furniture used as a sideboard. **commode table:** Dressing table with drawers under the top, with toilet drawer, et cetera.

commoney: Cheap white clay play marble.

common-sense chair: *See* Chairs, All Kinds.

communal cup: A common drinking cup passed around the table. A tyg, posset, boot, jug, et cetera.

communion stand: The small cupboard, often richly carved, gilt, or in a fine cabinet style, frequently Gothic, to hold the sacred Eucharistic vessels. Other period styles used, especially in Anglican churches.

communion tokens: Tokens given as mementos or records of partaking of the sacraments, or as tickets of admission thereto.

Compact: Pattern of pressed glass displaying bands of swirls.

compaigne wig: A very fine wig, c. 1700-50.

compass chair: *See* Chairs, All Kinds.

compass plane: Finishing plane for smoothing curvate surfaces. Its body is shaped like a heavy, short rocker.

compass seat: A round seat; a seat of embossed leather or other material displaying a navigator's compass card.

compass window: Circular, bay, or oriel window; sometimes called a bulk window.

compendium sampler: Modern term for a sampler combining scenic, animal, figural, and floral elements with alphabet. An "everything" sampler. Included in this category are Adam & Eve samplers, Noah's Ark samplers, Birth of the Saviour samplers, genealogy samplers, morals and maxims samplers, et cetera.

compo: Hard plaster composed of sawdust or wood flour, plaster, shellac, and alcohol. Molded as a plastic into very intricate and ornate patterns. Date is from c. 1740s, and used extensively in the Adam period. An abbreviation of composition.

compon covert: Lacework.

componé: Arranged in opposites, or differents, such as different tint or color, alternate intaglio and cameo, positive and negative, reverse and obverse, or right and left orientation.

comport: A salver; a *tazza*.

composite ironwork: Combination of wrought and cast iron to produce a railing or other architectural item, iron furniture, et cetera.

composite oil: Lighting fluid similar to camphene.

composition ornaments: Whiting, resin, linseed oil, and other ingredients, made plastic and molded in blocks to produce chimney, ceiling, furniture, and other ornaments. Also papier-mâché ornaments. Also burned ornaments, achieved from use of red-hot iron molds applied to wood. The charred background was removed by brushing and the intaglio or cameo section primed with paint and used as a carving.

compote: A shallow bowl on stand; a *tazza*. Same as comport; a carrier, or to carry; *comptier*.

Comstock frame: A quilting frame. Probably a regional name, after the maker of the frame.

concave: Opposite of convex; incurving, dished, hollowed. Concave-front furniture is made with incurving rather than swelled front.

concertina: An octagon-form bellows instrument of the accordion family.

concertina table: Ancestor of the extension table; a folding or fold-over leaf table dispensing with the gated legs and permitting a pair of legs fixed within a frame to pull out by means of a concertina action made of hinged wooden members. These tables, quite rare, date from 1740s or perhaps earlier. [*Example pictured*.]

conch horn: Dinner horn made from a conch shell. Also a calling horn used by squatters called "conches" in Southern tidewater regions. Any calling horn. The horn was used in canal transportation to warn lock keepers and passing craft.

conch pockets: Shell-form wall pockets of metal or ceramics, used as planters for ivy, greenery, flowers, et cetera. Wedgwood made many, as did Leeds, Belleek, and other potteries. Marbled, yellow, white, pink and other luster, pale green- and lavender-glazed, brass, tinned iron, papier-mâché, with tin liners, and other varieties are known. Most of them date from c. 1810.

concys: A sauce of beef stock laced with saffron, salt, and cloves, and thickened with eggs. It is from the days when cookery was called "cury," c. 1450.

condiment set: A plateau with wire or other supports to hold various condiment and oil bottles, sometimes with open dishes for tidbits.

condrack: An early lace for trimming garments.

cone-book stand: A pedestal table with a conical section top on which open books could be arranged for reference. The top revolved.

cone lantern: Lantern with globe in form of truncated cone. [*Example pictured*.]

conessi: A tree bark from the Coromandel Coast, used in colonial period as a remedy for colics.

Conestoga: The river and region of Penn's Colony (now almost wholly in Lancaster County, Pa.), which was the richest farming land in the colonies and fully appreciated by Penn. His first step was to make the Conestoga country his largest holding, including his entire grant westward from Chester County and Buckingham. This "Conestoga" land was the come-on par excellence, and its reputation, known from the days of Captain John Smith and the Dutch of New Amsterdam, caused thousands of immigrants to plan on settling in Penn's land and get a farm in Conestoga. Named for the Indian tribe whose other name was Susquehannox, and who controlled tidewater and inland hunting as far south as the mouth of the Chesapeake.

Conestoga wagon: The inland ship that is an improvement on the English road wagon of the 1720s; it is a combining of that wagon with the high-wheeled cart of the Huguenots and Flemish settlers. First example believed to have been created by John Carter of Carters Run in the Conestoga Valley near Lancaster, Pa., c. 1735. Carter was an English wheelwright. The claims of many pro-German Pennsylvania groups that the Conestoga wagon is a German invention is founded on nothing firmer than emotional postulation.

Conestoga walnut: Fine-grained black and white walnut from the Conestoga Valley.

cone sugar (cone of sugar): Cane or barley sugar originally was poured into conical-shaped molds for crystallization and draining, and came from such molds in cone shape. It was generally hung (with an insect stopper) from ceiling, and sugar was broken off as needed. Cones were wrapped in a heavy blue paper which was often used by householders as a dye source.

confect: Fruit, berry, leaf, root, or bark, boiled in syrup and preserved for use as food or medicine. From this term derive comfit, confit, confection, candy.

confidante: A sofa or settee for intimate conversation, generally semi-elliptical in shape, with the ends forming quadrantal seats, the center a three-chair settee.

conforming seat: Saddle seat; a seat formed to fit the contours of the human posterior.

congé: Quarter-round molding between major members of a façade. Also ferrules or loops on either solid or staved wooden pillars to prevent splitting. Sometimes called apophyge.

congelation: Solidification of liquids at low temperature, as ice cream, ices, mousses.

conger: (1) An eel. (2) A cucumber.

congeries: A collection or assemblage; a category.

Congress knife: A superior pocketknife with folding blades. Made for, or named for, the American market. Made by Meyer of Sheffield, who also had a store in New York City, c. 1840s.

Congress Pottery: William Hancock's pottery at South Amboy, N.J. had this name early in the 19th century It was also known as the Cadmus Pottery, the Price Pottery, and the Wooten Pottery. The product was stoneware.

conical salt: A saltcellar of glass, rising in inverted cone shape on a sturdy base, the cone having a deep valance.

conjoined: Bicorporate; two bodies with one head; in juxtaposition; side by side; tandem.

conjuror: Miniature stove ensemble with shallow kettle, small smoke vent, et cetera. Fuel was a crumpled ball of paper. [*Examples pictured*.]

Conner & Winser mirrors: Labeled mirrors, especially of the tabernacle type, bearing this name were made in quantities at New York City from 1840s.

connoisseur: One who knows; a cognizor —not the same as dilettante. The latter is one who *thinks* he knows.

Conovers: Wood-soled, iron-bladed ice skates. Name derives from a maker of such skates, c. 1850s, but this type of skate was in use for many years prior to use of this name.

conscience: A small, two-eared porringer.

conserve: To preserve; a rich soft confection of fruits, berries, et cetera, cooked in honey and rose water with spices, and kept for use as a sweet relish in jars and pots.

console: A table top affixed to a wall by brackets only. This is the original form, but later examples had additional support at front in form of legs at corners. The long narrow tables now given the name of console, having four legs and being portable, are not consoles. **console jardi-**

niere: A console table designed especially for reception of flower vases and potted plants. Some have metallic-lined wells, others marble-lined wells or dished marble tops. The term "console" is from *consolidare*—to make firm.

Constantinople case: 18th-century case of Turkish leather for cutlery, razors, and steels.

Constitution mirror: This name is now current and applied to scroll-top Georgian and other period mirrors when surmounted by an eagle. These are generally parcel-gilded (partly gilt), the eagle being always gilded. Since such mirrors were made in quantities prior to the Revolution, it may be assumed the term "Constitution" was first applied after or during the Constitutional Convention. It is more likely a 20th-century invention.

Constitution tray: Pressed-glass tray produced at Sandwich, Mass., Glass Works. It is 4½ x 7 inches in size, rectangular, flat, with a beveled lacy edge, the center impressed with a representation of the U.S. frigate *Constitution*, and so lettered. There is a tradition that a glass box with lid was issued for sale with these trays as an ensemble. This may be doubted, as covering the tray with a box hides the very thing for which the tray would have been purchased, the picture of the famed old frigate. These trays were once a low-priced item for the masses; today they are quite scarce and highly prized.

Consulate: The short period between the end of the Directoire (1799) and the beginning of the French "Empire" (1804). This period is Napoleonic, but the general was then First Consul and not Emperor.

Conte: A plumbago pencil, generally called a crayon, invented by Conte of Paris, c. 1795. Brass and silver holders protected a length of lead (plumbago).

Continental: The "patternless" pattern of pressed glass, probably pressed instead of blown for later cutting and etching, and found marketable as plain ware akin to blown, yet produced much more economically. Made by Bakewell of Pittsburgh.

contourniated: Contoured edge, perhaps achieved by lathe turning, or shaping in a lathe-turned die. Said of certain ancient coins and medals. The term was first applied to the technique in 17th century.

conventionalize: To represent a natural form stylistically; to distort or glorify; to arrange in a pattern not found in nature.

conversation chair: See Chairs, All Kinds.

conversation piece: (1) A genre or storytelling picture, generally of familial or familiar nature. (2) Caricatures, with balloons in which conversation is written or printed. (3) Any object that arouses comment and subsequent conversation; any unusual object.

conversation room: The room spelled "plor," meaning parlor, or place of parlay; a place to talk.

conversation sofa: Any sofa with its ends rounded, partly enclosing the façade and forming the equivalent of two chair backs. French. -

convex: Spherically protuberant; outstanding or bulging outward, in regular circular shape or form. The cheek section of a sphere.

convex mirror: Convex-form glass, silvered, in round frame. The frames generally gilt, burnished, and embellished with acorns and other forms. When such mirrors also are fitted with candle brackets they are called girandole mirrors. Convex mirrors are of Flemish design, probably originally made by Venetian glassmakers working in Flanders.

convolvulus jug: The Morning Glory pattern jug issued by Copeland in England c. 1849. This jug or pitcher was prompted by the then active campaign for "art in industry."

Conwell furniture: Cabinet furniture made by J. D. Conwell & Co. of Cincinnati from 1830s. This plant produced much Empire-style furniture and some late Directoire. The factory was near the steamboat landing for expeditious shipping to all river ports. It is found in practically every state bordering the Mississippi-Ohio-Missouri River system within navigational range.

cony: A rabbit, especially a cute rabbit. Originally pronounced *kunnie*, and when still heard in that form today is considered a colloquialism. *Ko-knee*, now general pronunciation, is actually the colloquialism.

Coogan floor cloths: Painted floor coverings made by J. T. Coogan at Blossburgh, Md., from 1850s, and sold at his retail stores in Baltimore and New York.

Cooke inks: Dr. E. F. Cooke of Wethersfield, Conn., made these inks from 1840s. They were writing inks in all colors.

Cook furniture: Cabinet-ware products of the shop of Leonard Cook, Alexandria, Va., from 1830s.

Cook glass: Stained, cut, flocked, and enameled glasswares and lamp globes made at Boston by J. M. Cook from 1850s. Cook & Rindge may have been an affiliate partnership; they, too, were glass cutters.

cooking lamp: A device made by the Kerosene Lamp Heater Co. in which a kerosene lamp or a portable gas ring was used to serve as the heating element of a combined chafing dish and water boiler with spigot, the whole mounted on spidery legs.

cookle: (1) Prongs of a meat spit. (2) Axle of a meat spit.

Cookstown glass: Bottles and window glass made at a factory located at Cookstown, Pa., 1831–46.

Cook's toys: Metal toys made by Cook of Birmingham, England, from 1800.

cooler (keeler): A large wooden tub.

Cooley, Anthony: The artist-postmaster of Kalamazoo, Mich., in 1840s. Said to have painted landscapes and portraits.

Coolidge furniture: John Coolidge of Cincinnati, 1840s-50s, had a factory for the production of tables, stands, desks, bookcases, cribs, et cetera, in considerable quantities, where he employed over 40 workmen. He made Empire-style furniture, which was sold throughout the South and Midwest.

cooling bidet: Shallow pan in a stand for bathing the buttocks. Now called a "cold sitz."

cooling board couch: Period-style pieces used by early undertakers (who were generally also cabinetmakers) to compose a body for burial. Certain well-designed examples have been upholstered and sold as long window seats or hall seats.

cool iron: A laundry iron which, while used hot, was fitted with a long wooden handle which permitted use without a padded iron holder. [*Example pictured.*]

coom: Accumulation around the mouth of a bake oven.

coopered bowl: A bowl made up of small staves, hooped. *See also* Quaich.

Cooper ware: Stoneware made at the potworks of A. Cooper, N.Y., from 1850s.

copal: Gum resin used in making varnish which, upon drying, resembled lacquer work.

Copeland ware: China made by Copeland, successors to Josiah Spode's great pottery in England.

copeman: A chapman; a vending merchant; a peddler.

Copenhagen ware: Danish porcelain, made continuously from 1750s.

Copernican: An orrery or planetarium.

coppel: A crucible.

copperas: Green vitriol.

copperbottoming: Insertion of copper sheeting in or over the bottoms of cooking utensils. When inserted, the joint is generally dovetailed. Copper cooking utensils were frequently tinned on the inside, while tin utensils were generally copperbottomed.

copper-cored Sheffield: Copper was not used as the core of Sheffield plate because it is "nearest in ductility and character to silver." Its use was mandatory because copper could be detected under the silver by a test gouge, while tin, if used as a core, could not. Pure tin was used by dishonest silversmiths in the 17th century to "pad" their solid plate. The "rosy twin of tin" (meaning copper) was the only filler metal permitted in Sheffield plate. Bulsover's invention was not the laying of silver on a base metal, but the use of acceptable copper rather than the earlier-used tin.

copperplate dominos: Wall coverings in sheets, or pasted into rolls, printed from copperplates, often hand-colored. 18th century.

copper queen's ware: Copper luster.

copper shades: Holland shades, on rollers, covered with copper foil and painted with decorative designs. Date is from 1840s.

copprous: Hot alcoholic beverage made frothy with eggs and milk. A kind of syllabub.

coprolites: Spirally marked fossil or petrification of the icthyosaurus, or fish lizard.

copying (sometimes cliché): Repetitive stamping of thin metal from a die.

coquelico; cocalico: Believed to mean "many colors," but actually deriving from the Conestoga Indian word "kokalekung," meaning "place of serpents."

coquemard: A high-footed hot-water kettle.

coquila: A hard nut of Brazil, much used

in making cane, parasol, and umbrella handles.

coquina: Natural coral and shell concrete, mined or quarried in a soft state but hardening into useful building stone when exposed to air. Much used in coastal South Atlantic States, Georgia to Key West.

Coranich: The wailing chant sung at funerals by Scottish and Irish peoples.

corbel: A shoulder. Structurally, an outstanding masonry shelf to support beams or other masonry.

corbet: A wall niche.

Cord & Tassel: Pattern of pressed glass featuring horizontal bands with undulating cord work and tassels in the loops of the cord.

corded quilt: An intricate technique of quilting in which the design is stitched and then stuffed with filler by aid of bodkins.

cordelier: A train of gears within a stout frame, turned by a crank. Each train imparts a twist to a cord and, at the same time, twists the strands into heavier cord. Small ones were used in making fishing lines from flax thread; huge ones used in rope walks.

cordevan; cordovan; cordwain: Spanish leather, and the workers in same. A shoemaker or saddler.

cordial chest: A case, generally of fine cabinetwork, with a fitting of bottles. Some have pairs, threes, fours, and so on up to a dozen or more bottles. Most examples now available as antiques date from c. 1750 to 1850.

Cordova: Pattern of pressed glass featuring vertical panels over lentil edge projections. Date is c. 1890s.

cordwainer: Leather cutter and maker of purses, girdles, et cetera. Finally applied to shoemakers, as a craft.

cord wheel: (Akin to *cordelier*.) *See* Line Spinner.

Corinthian: A shape or pattern of pressed glass, by Pellat, named for the pleasure boys of London during the Regency. It is classic, allied to what we call Ashburton and, in error, called colonial.

Corinthian candlestick: A classic Corinthian column form designed by the Brothers Adam as a candlestick. Popular from c. 1760 to 1840s. Also a small candlestick for the seduction chambers kept by the playboys of the Regency period.

Corinthian Cut: Pattern of cut glass featuring magnificently cut geometric star shapes enclosed within deeply cut squares, interstices filled with fine waffle cutting.

Cork glass: Irish glass made at Cork, sometimes marked, and rivaling Waterford glass. The mark is in raised lettering. Date is from latter half of 18th and first half of 19th century.

corkings: *See* Pins.

corkscrew candlestick: *See* Helix Candlestick.

corlets: Heavy cork-soled shoes used from 16th century.

cormarye: Pork roasted after soaking in red wine spiced with coriander, pepper, caraway, and garlic. An English delicacy sometimes served in the colonies, the pork being wild pig meat.

corn: Any edible grain; wheat, speltz, amelcorn, maize, and rye were all designated as corn. Speltz is a faulty grain of the wheat family, the food grain of most European peasants.

cornamute: A kind of bagpipe.

corn ball: Parched or popped corn in taffy, molded into balls as a confection.

corn beer: Corn mash from fresh corn, covered with sweet water and fermented. Thereafter the water was taken as beer and replaced with fresh water which, within twenty-four hours, turned to beer. One fermented mash provided beer on this basis for twelve months.

corn cutter: (1) A table utensil for cutting fresh corn from the cob. [*Example pictured.*] (2) A heavy knife for cutting corn and cornstalks in the field. (3) A machine for chopping up cornstalks and cobs for fodder.

corn-ear bottle: A glass bottle in the form of an ear of corn.

cornel: The berry of the dogwood.

Cornelius & Baker lamps: Any lamp made by this firm, Philadelphia, from the 1820s. This manufactory was the largest producer of lamps in the U.S. for over 50 years, making lamps in every style from cheap lard- and whale-oil cottage types to the most expensive bronze and cut-crystal examples. Many are marked. The firm was Cornelius & Co. to 1853, and thereafter as here noted.

Cornell broadside: Reference probably is to the lurid sheets issued in connection with the murder of Sarah Cornell, Fall River, Mass., in 1830s. Rev. E. K. Avery was accused of the crime and acquitted. He had to leave for Ohio because of popular belief in his guilt.

corner basket: Baskets woven in triangular form, standing upright and fitting in a corner.

corner board or sideboard: Contrary to the allegations made by some, the corner sideboard was not an unique item in our early Federal era. Hepplewhite-, Sheraton-, Directoire-, and even Empire-style corner sideboards were made. Some were made in matched pairs and not always in quadrant-angle form; some were based upon a right angle with sides of different length.

corner furniture: Corner tables, whatnots, chairs, and other items, including bureaus or chests of drawers, were made in triangular form. The corner cupboard is a well-known form of corner furniture that was made portable as well as built in. [*Several pieces of corner furniture are pictured, including a corner console, et cetera.*] There were also corner lavabos. Corner furniture was known in the Gothic era, and examples of various kinds are known from that period down to the East-lake period. Some corner furniture is very rare. For corner chair, *see* Chairs, All Kinds.

Cornflower Cut: (Sometimes called Carnation.) Pattern of cut glass featuring magnificent fine cutting technique depicting cornflowers of unbelievably fine petal cutting and outline foliage, generally arranged within a circular cut border

and surrounded by similar foliage and cornflowers.

cornice: *See* Entablature.

cornichons: Horseshoes welded together to form an odd-shaped loop, used in a game similar to quoits.

Corning Cut: Pattern of cut glass featuring long angular bands, almost lost in the busy design, which includes bosses centered in octagonal-star cutting and other devices.

Corning Glass: The modern Corning Glass center is the result of meticulous attention to the history of glass and glassmaking, and the making of fine wares by master craftsmen. Parent of the present-day Corning activity was the Brooklyn Glass Works of J. L. Gilliland & Co., established 1822, and in continuous production for 45 years. They made lamps, vases, plain and cut hollow wares, and pressed glass equal to or better than the wares of Baccarat or Pellat. This plant was finally moved to Corning, N.Y., and became the Corning Glass Co.

corn sheller: (1) A slip-on-the-hand device of leather and metal for easing the task of hand-shelling corn. (2) A machine for shelling corn, turned by a crank and steadied by a flywheel.

cornshuck seat: Chair seat, imitative of rushing, but made from twisted husks from green corn. This is a pioneer type of chair seat, and certain seats now designated as "heavy rush" are most likely cornshuck seats.

cornucopia leg: Chair, window seat, settee, and sofa legs in the form of a horn of plenty. The style is Directoire, but it is found on some Empire furniture. Duncan Phyfe used it in its finer forms.

Cornwallis jug: Copper-luster pitcher memorializing General Cornwallis, famed for his surrender at Yorktown.

corona: A multi-jet gas fixture, or gasolier, used from 1820s to 1880s.

coronal: Original spelling of colonel.

coronation: A braid or stuffed cording of variable diameter, used to produce decorative effects in application.

Coronet Cut: Pattern of cut glass featuring very complicated design, essentially Gothic in character, looking like a section of a stained-glass window. Linked pointed ovals arranged horizontally and vertically, with distorted stars and chrysanthemum medallions.

corpse coverlet: Pattern-woven coverlets in one color, cream or white, traditionally said to have been used only as covers for the dead awaiting burial. All-white or cream pattern-woven coverlets, dated, were made at Colonel Rutgers' works, Brunswick, N.J., from 1820s. These are the earliest pattern-woven coverlets of the U.S. and predicate use of the Jacquard loom well in advance of its generally attributed usage in coverlet weaving in this country.

corquillat pictures: The work of French Jacquard loom weavers who wove pictures and portraits, including one of Washington. Date is c. 1820.

corrals: Silver-gilt and chased jewelry embellished with coral stone, advertised by at least one goldsmith of Boston as early as 1770s. There may be other definite meanings of the term, but we have not found reference to them.

corrid honey: Candied or sugared honey.

corse: A girdle of braided ribbons.

Corselius Pottery: Stoneware pottery of New York, perhaps the first, established very early in 18th century. Clarkson Crolius and John Remmey, both stoneware potters, took it over between 1730 and 1745. They divided the works, as the share of the daughters of Corselius, whom they had married. The ware is gray stone with incised and cobalt-blue decoration.

corset-back: Chair back of 18th century with splats having a silhouette somewhat like the corseted female torso.

corset bottle: A glass novelty bottle in the form of a corseted female torso.

cosey chair: Upholstered wing chair.

cosinomancy: Divination by aid of a sieve.

cosmolabe: Instrument for measuring distances by triangulation; also called the pentacosm in 1600s.

Cossarts: Linens of fine quality made by Cossart et Fils, France, from 1720s. A luxury linen of colonial days.

coster: A tester or teester; a table drapery.

costeril: A shoulder flask. **costrel:** A leather bottle for a shoulder sling.

costermonger: Originally a vendor or peddler of costers, or apples. Now any peddler, especially those wearing costumes entirely covered with buttons.

costmary: A variety of the herb tansy.

costret: Allied to costeril in name, but referring to a bottle of wood or pottery with ears for a sling. A sort of Pilgrim's flask.

costume miniatures: See Talcs.

cothurnus: A booted footing used in Greek-revival furniture.

cott: A sea bed or ship's bed; a canvas box in a frame 6' x 3' x 1', suspended from ship's beams.

Cottage: Pattern of pressed glass featuring ovate panels of imitation Star & Web cutting, alternating with narrower plain panels.

cottage press: A small home or office printing press.

cottage vase: Broad-faced, flaring-mouthed porcelain vase with raised floral décor, painted scenes, and much gilt; so named because these vases were cheap cottage ornaments of the mid-19th century.

cotter pole: A pole to hang over the fire.

cotton bow: A device for fluffing cotton for fine spinning. [*The method is pictured.*]

cotton stem: Glassware stem more properly called air twist, which see.

cottonstone: Asbestos.

Cottu, M.: Early 19th-century silhouette cutter who also painted miniatures. He worked in several U.S. cities and towns.

cotyledon: The ancient decorative form that is a stylized representation of a sprouting almond. The so-called Tulip & Heart is more likely a popular form of the cotyledon. [*Example pictured.*]

couch: (1) A day bed, or (2) a sofa with one arm and partial back.

couchant: Lying down; squatting; couched. In heraldry, an animal seated on its belly, legs naturally outstretched, head erect.

Coulter & Finagin glass: Cut glass produced by a firm of this name at Cincinnati from 1830s.

council table: Large ovoid, round, or rectangular table with falling leaves supported on swing-out gates or gated legs. Date is from early Tudor times and known in all period styles. Not to be confused with console table, which see.

counterfeit: A portrait or statue. Term current to c. 1700s.

counterpane; counterpointe: Divided into lozenge forms or diamond shapes.

counter urn: Large urn-shaped glass jar used by merchants for counter display of small goods, candy, et cetera. Used from 1830s. [*Example pictured.*]

countinghouse pins: Dressing pins used as paper fasteners, generally packed in round spirals of paper in a round wooden box or cup.

country-made: This term, at times used derisively, should be considered aptly used when designating furniture of a period style made in small towns or in the back country. Significantly, such furniture (and often silver and other objects such as clocks) was often behind the times in style—Georgian when Hepplewhite was the city rage, Hepplewhite when Directoire was the rage.

County of Illinois: The vast western lands of Virginia, later the Northwest Territory, designated as Illinois County from 1778 to 1784.

coupé: (1) Basket; a coop. (2) A deep dish on stem and footing. (3) A four-wheeled coach, fully enclosed.

couped: Cut. Any part of a body (as a bust) depicted with sharp cleavage is said to be couped. If ragged, it is "erased."

courant: Running.

courbe: To bend or stoop. The stoop of a walk, the curb.

courrone de fer: High-standing branched candlestick of iron.

court chest: A questioned piece of furniture having the appearance of a lowboy with an imposed chest, the surface of which is carved in the early 17th-century style of court cupboards, while the legs of the stand are in the William & Mary or Queen Anne style.

court chimney: Small fireplace of portable nature.

court cupboard: A cupboard on open framework of Tudor style, used in Virginia, Maryland, New Sweden, and New England prior to 1660s. These pieces are often of oak, although some are known in white and yellow pine. Heavy turning, often quite ornate, plus gouge and scratch carving and applications of split turning are generally a feature of true Tudor pieces. Some have tulip carving on the door panels. Believed to have been of Spanish origin. [*Examples pictured.*] See also Press Cupboard and Livery Cupboard.

court dish: A fine drinking vessel of

carved glass, gold, or silver. A fine dish of any kind.

Courtenay carvings: Hercules Courtenay, carver and gilder of London, emigrated to Philadelphia c. 1760, where he advertised his profession. He is believed to have worked for Benjamin Randolph.

Courtesy Book: A book of deportment, especially for lords, ladies, and gentry. Issued from c. 1550 through 1700s.

court hand: Medieval script, retained as official calligraphy for documents of importance relating to the court. [*Example pictured.*]

courthouse chairs: Late low-backed Windsors with turned spindles and a writing arm. Used from 1840s by law clerks in courtrooms.

courting mirror: A clipper-ship trade item, a mirror framed with bits of colored glass, the frames usually crested. Should be in original box to have full value. A very much overrated object which was once quite common. It is said every sailor in the China trade gave one to his girl. One girl? You know how sailors are!

courting mug: Pitchers bearing décor of love tokens; posset pots and other loving cups.

Courtney & Willets furniture: Cottage furniture made by a firm so named, Philadelphia, 1830s–60. The makers were famed for mass production and selling cheap, for cash.

Court of Death: Rembrandt Peale's painting, reproduced as an engraving for "parlor use" in a size 23″ x 31″. In 1859 100,000 copies of the print were made.

couvrechief: A square of silk or linen used as a bedcap.

couvrepied: A foot quilt or stool quilt.

Coventry glass: Glassware made at Coventry, Conn., from 1813 to 1840s. Much of the ware is amber or olive-amber color. Inkwells, chestnut flasks, historic bottles, including the famous Lafayette-De Witt Clinton flask, were made.

cover: A tool (properly cove-er) to put a cove in a plasterwork molding. Also a plane to cut a cove in woodwork.

covercle: Potlid.

covered bucket: An oval metal kettle with lid.

covered ware: Containers of any substance, fitted with a cover.

coverlet (couvre-lit): A bedcovering. Term is now generally applied to pattern-woven bedcovers of the early to mid-19th century. Best examples are dated, signed by the weaver, and often marked with name or initials of the owner, and other data. There are many patterns, and all pictorial and figural examples are Jacquard-loomed. They are emphatically not Pennsylvania German as some claimants aver. *Heirlooms from Old Looms,* published by the Coverlet Guild of America, contains much information and many illustrations.

covert: A married woman; a *femme couverte.*

cow & calf candlestick: It isn't a candlestick at all, but a vase. Staffordshire pottery figure of a cow and calf at a tree trunk, the trunk being a hollow vase form.

cow butter: A butter dish of Liverpool delftware in the form of a recumbent cow. Upper part of body, with head, is the lid. [*Example pictured.*]

Cowen desks: Rosewood, mahogany, and papier-mâché fancy desks of the 1840s, named for one of the makers of this novelty.

cow-horn tips: Brass tips to cap the horns of a cow, in popular use with dairymen from c. 1750s to 1850s. Not rare, but seldom recognized for what they are.

cow lines: Batter poured from a batter jug into hot fat, making a hot cake in linear form. Term is most likely colloquial.

cowlstaff: Staff thrust through the ears of a basket for carriage.

cowntery: A desk; a counter.

Cowper candlesticks: Wrought-iron candleholders bearing the mark COWPER are known and considered American, of mid-18th century. No locale has been established for the maker.

Cowperthwaite chairs: Fancy and specialty chairs made by J. K. Cowperthwaite and his successors, N.Y., from c. 1815. Also made many Windsor chairs. The firm remained in business for many years.

Cowpland mirrors: Fine mirrors, some reflecting the Queen Anne style, made from 1840s by Joshua Cowpland, Philadelphia.

cowries: White sea shells used in decorating and in making wampum for Indian trading.

cowsatewery: 15th-century term for a lectern or manuscript writing desk.

cowtail pump: Any water pump with a wrought-iron handle curved in its length and ending in a tasseled knob.

Cox woodenware: Pails, tubs, churns, bowls, curl (burl) bowls, butter stamps, kitchen and dairy wares, spice boxes, et cetera, made by Gideon Cox of Philadelphia, sold wholesale and retail, from 1820s.

coyman: *See* Kooijman.

Cozzens stopper: Screw stoppers made for bottle closure, from c. 1850s.

C.P.: This mark, found on American arms such as rifles, has been thought to mean "Continental Property" or "Commonwealth of Pennsylvania." It means neither; it designates "City Proof," and is the mark of the proving house of the gunsmiths of Philadelphia. Used from c. 1770.

crab: An iron trivet.

crab cider: Juice of crab apples.

crab stock: A cudgel, formed from an apple seedling. **crab-stock handle:** Jug handle of pottery formed in imitation of apple wood, sometimes of several elements entwined. Used also on fine porcelains and china.

crachoir: A cuspidor or spittoon.

crackel: A flax break.

cracker: (1) Any colonist who, as an imprisoned debtor, petty thief, or slanderer, agreed to migrate to Oglethorpe's colony of Georgia, and by this act win pardon, freedom, and land. These unfortunates who "cracked" jail were designated as crackers, and the name remains in application to poor whites, white trash, poor farmers, and yokels in the South. Chances are the original crackers provided most of the top-flight families of the colony, while the later emigrants provided the later crops of crackers. (2) A small baking dish. (3) A hard biscuit; ship's bread.

cracowe: Long, pointed shoe much used from 14th to 16th century. In France called *poulaine*.

cradle, barrel: *See* Barrel Cradle.

cradle bench or settee: A bench or settee fitted with rockers and having removable bars on struts to form a cradle end. Thus the mother could rock and work while lulling the infant.

cradle coverlet: Pattern-woven cover of small size, approximately 24″ x 38″. Some are dated and signed. Not weavers' samples, as is sometimes believed.

cradle rocker: A rocking chair of gadget type with seat and arms extending laterally to form a cradle bed, with special bars and rails to provide complete enclosure. Date is c. 1840s–70s.

cradle spit: Basket spit; a wrought-iron basket on a spit, with hinged door to permit insertion of a whole bird or cut of meat for roasting before an open fire. [*Example pictured.*]

Crafts pottery: Brown earthenware, black-glazed ware, and stoneware made at Crafts Pottery, Whately, Mass., 1802–40s. The former wares were made by Caleb, Thomas, and other members of the Crafts family, who also operated potteries at Troy, N.Y., Portland, Me., and Nashua, N.H.

Craig & Ritchie glass: Glass made at Wheeling, Va., from 1829, by firm so named. Plain-blown, cut, and pressed wares.

cranberry rake: A toothed tool for gathering cranberries from the stalks.

crane bracket: Open-frame, wing-shaped supports for leaves of tables; swinging brackets similar to the bracket crane. [*Example pictured.*]

crane head: A half tester frame for a bed, made of two open brackets affixed to the head posts.

crane plate: Flat iron pan having a gooseneck handle at one side, extending upward. [*Example pictured dated from 1660.*]

craniological alphabet: A system of shorthand, the various word-sound symbols being units of a sketch of the human cranium. [*Example of system pictured.*]

cranny: Glassmaker's tool used in forming bottle necks and stems of goblets and wines.

crap: Buckwheat, darnel, speltz, and other inferior grains.

crapestone: Black stone used for mourning jewelry.

cratch: A manger.

crater: Doughnut-shaped device of sheet metal, placed over the glass chimney of a kerosene lamp to form a small stove.

Crawley tinware: Wine coolers, cellarets, bathing tubs, portable kitchens, conjurors, spring jacks, coffee biggins, block tin, japanned tin, and other utensils, trays, et cetera, made by D. Crawley, N.Y., from 1790s.

crazy work: Odd and freakishly shaped patches stitched together to form a crazy-quilt top. Also the work of "touched" or "crazy" artisans and artists, some of whom worked in confinement and produced quaint, curious, and sometimes monstrous work.

cream ewer: Cream jug or pitcher.

cream pail: Tublike container for clotted cream. Many are of silver or plated ware with glass or porcelain liners.

cream posset: *See* Syllabub.

cream skimmer: Shallow shell-like device with strainer holes, made of silver, pewter, brass, pottery, wood, horn, and other materials. [*Examples pictured.*]

crèche: A Nativity scene in miniature, originating with Nestorian Christians or the Greek Church. The figures and objects were carved from wood, cast in plaster, made of clay, et cetera. The custom is very ancient.

credence table: The fold-over-top table of the Gothic era, noted as early as 14th century.

credenza: The credence table extended and enlarged to incorporate cupboards. The equivalent of the court cupboard popular in Italy and France.

Creedmore bank: One of the early and desirable mechanical cast-iron banks, a memorial of the Creedmore range, 1877. [*Example pictured is original advertisement of the maker.*]

creel: (1) An osier basket. (2) A butcher's stool. (3) A ball of wool yarn.

creem: To shrink or to pulp. Creemed potatoes were pulped (mashed) potatoes. Creemed apples were what we call applesauce.

creepers: Small andirons used between the large ones, frequently in cooking as supports for pans, small spits, et cetera.

Crehore cards: Playing cards of early 19th century made by a firm of this name.

creil faïence: Transfer-printed tin-glaze wares bearing scenes in the classic or romantic tradition. French, of early 19th century.

crenelated: Decoration imitative of the outline of a serrated leaf; notched; loopholed.

crepe: Silk woven before scouring out soluble gum from the yarn, and taking on a crinkled appearance when scoured in the cloth. Considered rich and rare.

crepine: A caul of netting for the hair; a fringe on a hood.

crescent: A crescent-shaped gorget worn over the breast. "Impudent lasses turn up their crescents by moonlight," is an early phrase that needs no explaining.

crescent sideboard: A kidney-shaped sideboard with concave front and rounded back, fitting into a curvate alcove. They generally have six legs and are in Hepplewhite, Sheraton, or Directoire styles.

cresset: A framework of iron or other metal in which fuel for heat or illumination was burned. Cressets were used as street lamps, were carried on poles to light the way of pedestrians and coaches, and as tops of andirons and variations of the simple "fire basket" used to carry fire and coals from house to house and room to room.

Cressey & Hanson lamp: A tallow or grease-burning lamp of the 1840s; an artisans' and cottage dwellers' lamp. Actually this firm made lamps under the Jones patent for a lamp that melted its own non-liquid fat fuel.

crest: The ornamental designation of rank originally fixed to the top of a helmet. Ladies other than the Queen (and Her Majesty only by courtesy) did not own and therefore did not display a crest or cresting. Their badges were known as ciphers. It is an error to say, "The crest of Lady Montague," or "Mistress Saltonstall was so and so . . ." Ladies just did not have crestings.

crested frame: A frame having an elevated, and sometimes decorated, central element on the top. This sometimes carries a bird or animalistic figure, a head, acorn, et cetera. Sometimes the cresting is of fretwork.

crest tile: Roof-ridge tile.

crève-coeur: Two curled locks on the nape of the neck. Ladies who sported them were called heartbreakers.

crewel: Coarse embroidery stitch used in making decorative fabrics. Said to have been imitative of the Bayeux tapestries. Silk or wool yarns were used, in all colors. Very popular in 17th century, when gowns as well as hangings for walls, table covers, chimney cloths, and furniture coverings were made of crewelwork.

crib: (1) A strainer or colander. (2) A measure of flat window glass, 100 square feet in area.

crib cradle: Crib on rockers.

crib drawer: (1) A drawer compartmented to hold various items in segregation. (2) Colloquialism: a deep drawer in a commode or chest, pulled out and used as a crib for an infant.

cricket: (1) Kneeling stool used in churches. (2) Small jointed stools set by the hearthside, often as a footrest. (3) A stool table. Term "cricket" derives from Anglo-Saxon *crice*, a crutch.

Cridland mirror: T. W. Cridland, Philadelphia, 1820-35, and Lexington, Ky., from 1835, produced many mirrors of tabernacle and gilded-frame type. He also manufactured picture frames.

criers: Of London, New York, Paris, Philadelphia, et cetera. Portrayals of the street vendors and peddlers of goods and services on the streets of towns and cities. The sellers of dominos (early wallpaper in sheets), chimney sweeps, knife and scissors grinders, orange, violet, oyster, and other sellers, soup vendors, crab vendors—all these were depicted as street criers.

crimcon: Illicit relationship.

crimmle: To pleat or plait.

crimper: (1) A crimping mold used in glassmaking. (2) Any mechanical device (roller, board, et cetera) to achieve crimping of fabric. (3) An iron for crimping linen.

crimper socket: A ring of crimped metal with a short flat handle, used in burning candle ends and in making a candle fit a socket.

crinoline: Originally cloth woven from crin, or horsehair. Hence crinoline is the original horsehair covering. Used as a stiffener under gowns. Artificial crinoline was glue-sized linen or tow cloth. A 19th-century version of crinoline was the hoop skirt. These hoops (once called *vertugadin*) were used in place of the expensive crin cloth as early as 1550.

crinolined figure: Portrayal of a woman in the bell-skirted gowns of 17th and 18th centuries. Meissen figures and early French porcelains depict such styles.

crinze: A drinking cup or mug.

crisling; crizzling: Term applied to glasswares developing a fine crazing. This is often noted in lead or flint glass that has been improperly cooked or worked.

Crisp china: Wares produced at the Crisp Pottery, Bow Churchyard, Lambeth, England, from 1740s. The famed sculptor, John Bacon, worked at this pottery for a time.

crispels: Fritters.

crisper: A wire frying basket.

Crispin & Crispianus: Medieval cobblers elevated to sainthood by the Church of Rome. Patron saints of cobblers, cordwainers, slipper makers, and leatherworkers.

criton: An ice-making machine for the home, manually operated. Made in 19th century and probably still made for use on frontiers and in primitive countries. [*Example pictured.*]

crochon: Fuel for cressets, generally of pitch, tar, tow, resin, and wood chips.

crock: Originally a drinking jug, sometimes silver-mounted.

crocker: A potmaker.

Crocker toys: Miniature chamber and parlor furniture in sets, tin toys, banks, et cetera, made by J. F. Crocker of Valley Falls, R.I., from c. 1858.

crockery: All potted work.

crocketed: From *croquet*, the end tines of a deer's antlers. The projecting ornamentation, often in foliate form, of a façade, used from medieval times.

crocodile leg: A hideous furniture leg and footing, imitative of the legs of a crocodile. Empire-period styling. [*Example pictured.*]

crocus: Coarse linsey-woolsey (linen-wool cloth). Also a polishing powder.

crocus pots: Commode-shaped round-fronted pots of porcelain fitted with small cups over holes for sprouting crocus bulbs. An 18th-century "planter." Also animalistic or hive-shaped planters of 19th century for the same purpose. [*Examples pictured.*]

Croesus Cut: Pattern of cut glass featuring crossed angular cuttings imitative of sheaf of wheat, interstices filled with daisy-and-button cutting.

croft: A close; an enclosure. Also a bleachery for linen cloth.

crokinole: A game played on a circular field mounted on an octagonal board. Counters are snapped from approved position to dislocate and eliminate others on the board. Date is late, from c. 1880s.

Crolius ware: *See* Corselius Pottery. Wares made by succeeding generations of the Crolius family of potters to 19th century.

Cromwellian: Of the period of English history known as the Commonwealth; the mid-17th-century style of England. **Cromwellian chair:** *See* Chairs, All Kinds.

Cronus; Cronos: Superior Greek divinity, the Lord of Creation and the Reaper of Souls. Generally pictured with a scythe and, almost invariably, wrongly presented as Chronos or Father Time. The correct term is Cronus or Cronos; not *chronos,* meaning sequence, as of time.

crook chain: Iron chimney chain fixed on a spike or spikes to hold pots.

crookey: Cheap pottery game marble.

crook-footed chair: *See* Chairs, All Kinds.

crook pot: A pothook.

croquant: Four-parted, as a partitioned dish or four-part dish.

croquetries: Croquet sets.

Crosley mosaics: Lengths of yarn, built up carefully to form a picture in full color, glued on a canvas backing and imitative of needle point or *gros point.* The pictures were made by building up the yarn similar to the technique used in making glass canes; every slice of the block of yarn, made with a razor-sharp knife, produced a picture. Some are 13" x 16" in size. Made in 1840s and 1850s in England.

Crossbar: Pattern of pressed glass featuring angular-lined borders, crossing to form a decorative design. A late pattern.

cross-baited: Checkered.

crossbill: A name given to double flasks with crossing necks to provide pouring from either without spilling from its twin. Glass, pottery, and metal examples. Gemel flasks.

crosse cloth: Knitted kerchief, worn crossed over the breast.

crossed swords: The mark used on Meissen porcelain from 1724 to 1940.

crosseted: Mitered broken joints in the application of molding to a flat surface to provide a patterned enclosure.

cross-garnet hinge: The T-form hinge; a horizontal strap hinged to a vertical strap in its mid-section.

cross-gartered: Tapes crossed in support of hose.

cross lyre: Pedestal of a table or stand made of lyre forms crossed at right angles to form four prongs.

cross-wick lamp: Lamp with a cruciform wick slot taking a cross-form wick. This was achieved by feeding four narrow wicks in the arms of the cross-shaped holder. A patented kerosene burner made at New Orleans c. 1858–60.

crotch wood: Timber cut from the V of a forked section, valued for its vein and grain. Crotch walnut and crotch mahogany veneers were much used.

crouch ware: Earliest stoneware of England, made at Critch, Derbyshire. The true crouch, or critch, is salt-glazed stoneware.

croud: A violin. Also called a crouder or crowder.

croud pie: Apple turnover.

crouke: A pitcher, generally of earthenware.

Crowfoot: Pattern of pressed glass featuring a surface of circles with a fan-shaped element springing from the rim of each. A late pattern.

crowfoot: The simple ball-and-claw foot. Also a bar of iron with two or three prongs at end.

Crowlet ware: Tinned and japanned wares made by Crowlet of New York from 1790s to 1820.

Crown Cut: Cut-glass pattern of 1890s featuring deep X-cut panels and immense star-cut crowns.

Crown Derby: Porcelains made at the Derby pottery from 1770s under the management of Duesbury, Bloor, and others. Derby ware marked with a crown as part of the mark is called "Crown Derby." [*Examples of the marks pictured.*] The Derby Crown Porcelain Company is a much later Derby works, established 1877. [*Its mark is also pictured.*] Crown Derby Gaudy is the Imari pattern ware made from 1790 to 1800. This is the prototype of the later gaudy wares of Staffordshire blithely labeled as Pennsylvania German!

crown glass: Window glass made by blowing huge bubbles of glass, puncturing, and spinning into large circular disks by whirling the pontil rod. The bull's-eye, at the pontil, was the cheapest cut from such disks; now it is the most prized. Complete crowns were sold for circular window lights, skylights, et cetera. The bull's-eyes were most frequently used in church windows and in similar situations where light, but not transparency, was desired.

crown handle: A flat handle on porringers and basins, pierced and shaped in imitation of a crown.

Crown Jewel: Pattern of pressed glass featuring rows of square or emerald-form facets with shaped pendent droops as wide borders below clear sections, lightly engraved. Handles are rope form.

crown jug: Ceramic jug with top handle of four bent tubes forming a crown, joined at a common orifice. This jug was passed from hand to hand in company, each user taking his draught from the opening. Early stoneware or redware. [*Example pictured.*]

crown paper: Handmade paper watermarked with a crown.

crow parsnip: The dandelion plant and root.

crow's-nest: Wild parsley.

crozier: Crook form; a bishop's crook. Coiled; circinate.

cruce; cruche; crusie: A jug.

crucifix stick: Candlestick in form of a crucifix; a candleholder for a private shrine.

Cruden, Thomas: Publisher of *The Cabinetmaker's Darling,* 1765; *Carpenter's Companion for Chinese Railings,* 1770; and *Chimneypiece Maker's Daily Assistant,* 1776. All are English publications for craftsmen and designers.

cruit: Scottish harp.

crumb cloth: Linen drugget.

crumb mortar: A wooden mortar for making crumbs from stale bread.

cruse: A pot-shaped vessel with tubular spout and handle; sometimes called a krug. Also cruskin, crusekyn, crulsken. Name seems to date from 14th century.

crustade: A pie of eggs and milk with flavorings—so sayeth an early book on cury, or cookery.

crusy (crusie lampe): An open shallow bowl of triangular shape with upstanding handle and hanger, used with floating wick to burn oil. A betty lamp without covering over the fuel. [*Example pictured.*]

crybe: A bed.

Crygier papers: Domino wallpaper panels, pasted together in roll form, made by C. & J. Crygier, N.Y., from 1790s. Green, blue, pink, and gray were advertised as the colors available in 1802.

cryptochylon: Classic name given to a plated silver pitcher with wooden lining, made from 1850 at Boston, probably by Stedman & Co.

Crystal: Pattern of pressed glass that is a variant of Ashburton.

crystal bottles: The decanters first made by Ravenscroft, the first English maker of flint glass, were so named by the maker, 17th century. [*A Ravenscroft crystal bottle (decanter) is pictured.*]

crystal butter kettle: Metal kettle of oval shape with crystal-glass liner within a space filled with cold water. A late type.

Crystalina: Pattern of pressed glass featuring graceful volute panels with ruby-red edging.

crystallized lamp: Any early lamp fitted with glass globes or shades. Specifically a night lamp with a tilting cover that served as a reflector. These were made by Shelton Lamp Works, London and Birmingham, England, from 1800s.

crystallized tin: Sheet tin or tin-plated iron, the surface sponged while hot with spirits of salt. This developed a crystalline surface.

crystallo-ceramie: Unglazed pottery elements such as busts, figures, et cetera, embedded in glass. Also called sulphides. The glass casing gives the pottery form a silver appearance.

crystalomancy: A tableau, painted on thin linen with transparent oil paint, moving within a framework and illuminated. Sometimes several sheets were made to move in opposite directions and at varying speeds, giving a curious effect of lifelike motion. Many cities and towns, from 1810s, had more or less permanent crystalomancy exhibits. Sometimes the showman (often the artist) had a stock of six or more shows to display.

Crystal Wedding: Pattern of pressed glass featuring large loops, upright and invert, as a border under engraving on clear glass. Late.

C-scroll: A decorative scroll, painted or carved, often found on Restoration furniture between the Cromwellian and William & Mary periods. It is an early use of the C-curve. There is a C-scroll mirror type attributed to the William & Mary and Queen Anne periods, the frame of which shows this C-scroll. [*Example pictured.*]

cubberd: Cupboard. Originally a Tudor-period piece that combined a closet and chest.

Cube & Diamond: Pattern of pressed glass featuring a checkered pattern, the alternate squares being impressed with a diamond form. Late.

Cube with Fan: Pattern of pressed glass featuring a ground of small faceted cubes with triangular-pointed edges and a fan-shaped pattern, imitative of cut glass, in the V's of the edge. Late. Several varieties.

cubit: A linear measure of approximately 18 inches.

cucking stool: Stool or chair seat with arms and back, having a locking bar mounted on the end of a beam that is pivoted for seesaw movement on an upright column on rollers. Offending public nuisances, such as scolds, slanderers, and gossips, were locked in the seat, hauled to a convenient slough or hog wallow, and cucked in the mire as many times as the magistrate designated. Improperly called ducking stool. Also called treebucket, gumstool, and castigatory.

cuckoo clock: A rustic-type clock originating in the Grand Val of Switzerland and made in quantities in the Harz Mountains, Bavaria. The feature is a cuckoo or other bird that called the hours. Not all of these clocks are 19th and 20th century; some were made in the 17th and 18th centuries. [*Example pictured.*]

cucumber wood: Wood of the American magnolia tree, preferred for making pump bodies and water pipes, and also for dairy woodenwares.

cucurbit: The watermelon.

cudgel work: Heavy embroidery.

cue rack: See Drum Cue Rack.

cuir: Plaited or woven thongs of leather, sometimes used as chair seating.

cuir-bouilli: Ornamental leatherwork.

cuivre doré: Gilded copper; allied to bronze doré.

cullet: Broken glass, as used to start the pot mix in glasswork. It is often cullet, and most likely from other sources, that is misjudged the shards of original work in glasshouse excavations.

cullodion: Guncotton and ether, mixed to produce a viscous liquid used as a dressing on wounds. Invented by S. L. Bigelow of Boston c. 1848. This is the original spelling.

culvertail: Joining by cutting and fitting that precludes disjoining; dovetailing throughout. Used in some shipbuilding and cabinetwork.

Cunningham coverlets: Term derives from name of the weaver, who seems to have worked at New Hartford, N.Y., in 1840s.

Cunningham glass: (1) Glass made at Cunningham & Ihmsen Works, Pittsburgh, from 1850s. (2) Wares sold at store of I. S. Cunningham, Boston, from 1820s.

cup andirons: Cresset-top andirons.

cup & saucer: This elegancy, born of the popularity of tea, coffee, and chocolate, is primarily an 18th-century development. The original teacups of China were not supplied with saucers or handles. Most oriental export porcelain "sets" (commonly, though in error, called Lowestoft) had cups without handles and underdishes called saucers. The term "saucer" was originally for a small dish in which melted, spiced, or lemoned butter was served at table as a dressing for foods. Cups and saucers in sets, or as part of a dinner or tea service, were made by practically all English and some American potteries.

cup & saucer lamp: Dutch or Swedish-type open fat lamp in form of a cup with pointed spout, fixed to a saucer and fitted with a handle. Date is from 17th century and in use to 1800s. [*Example pictured.*]

cupboard: Originally a portable service board or shelf; also used for display and storage of cups. Finally an enclosed cabinet with solid or glass doors. The first mention of a "cuppeboarde" appears in 1344.

cupboard chair: *See* Chairs, All Kinds.

cupboard chair-table: A table convertible to a high-backed chair, the hutch of which is a closet with door rather than a lift-up seat.

cupboard table: A gueridon tea table or candlestand, having a cupboard section instead of a turned column. [*Example pictured dates from c. 1740s.*] Another variety of cupboard table is the deep-skirted fold-over-top table with lock and key. The top opens to a cupboard cavity. This table is more properly a coffer table.

cupboard turn (or knob): A turning knob for cupboard doors having a fixed stem turning a fastener at back of the door. There are many varieties, some homemade, some contrived by the cabinetmaker, and some of brass or iron, manufactured in quantities. Even factory-made ones were in production from the 1750s.

Cupid & Psyche: Mythological classical figures revived by the Brothers Adam c. 1750 and used decoratively as statues and paintings on walls and furniture. This pair of lovers was a favorite subject among artists of the early Republic. [*An American version of the 1830s is pictured.*]

Cupid & Psyche ware: White, pink and white, and blue and white china ware depicting Cupid giving a message to Psyche. Made from 1840s and some attributed to Bennington.

Cupid & Venus: Pattern of pressed glass which, like many others, should be renamed. Pattern features a large oval medallion in which there is a classic adult female figure and a winged infant. It is said this pattern is sometimes called Guardian Angel and sometimes Minerva.

Cupid lamp: Cupid's face molded in a deep dish of glass, Parian, or bisque china. Used as a holder for fairy-lamp candles. Date is late 1870s–1900s.

Cupid's bow: Any twin curvate form springing from a center, as the human upper lip. This is supposed to be the form of the bow carried by Cupid. It is found on chair rails, seat valences, and in other elements of cabinet- and chair work.

cup jug: A large pitcher for serving any of the mixtures once characterized as "cups" —mint cup, lemon cup, rose cup, et cetera. Same as shrub jug.

cupped caster: Furniture leg roller having a metal cup seating, the cup fitting over the leg of the chair or table.

cup plate: (1) The underdish of a coffee bowl or teacup before saucers were provided. (2) Small dishes used as butter chips, coasters, and other odd table purposes. Many of the latter were made in pressed glass, especially at Sandwich and Pittsburgh. There are a number of historical-subject cup plates of pressed glass, and some are being reproduced. *Glass Cup Plates*, by Rose & Lee, is the definitive work on the subject.

cup rose: The poppy.

cup stopper: *See* Vase Stoppers.

cup-top kettle: Dinner pail, the lid of which is a flask for coffee or tea, the vent topped with a round tin cup.

cup turning: Wood-turning form noted from William & Mary period; an inverted cup topping the taper of the main section.

curd cutter: A curd knife of four or more flexible parallel blades fixed in a handle for the cutting of curds in cheese making.

curd white: Milk curds, whiting, and slaked lime, combined to make a white water paint. Milk paint.

curfew: Cone of pierced iron or brass, used in fireplace to hold a fire of coals overnight. When the coals were raked and the curfew set over them, it was bedtime.

curiosities: Puzzle mugs, banks, busts, grotesques, whimseys, et cetera, are often designated by this term. Generally applied to glasswork and on occasion to pottery.

curiosity shop: Any antiques shop of late 17th or early 18th century.

curious: Nice; fastidious; careful. These are the 17th- and 18th-century meanings of the term.

Curling glass: The glass made by Curling & Price at Fort Pitt Glass Works from 1827. Several reorganizations developed new corporate names, all including Curling. Marked examples of early pressed creamers and bowls are known. Firm was in operation to 1900s. Made pressed, blown, cut, and molded wares.

curling stone: Polished granite pudding-shaped stones with gooseneck handles at top, used in the ancient Scottish game of curling on the ice; a game related to bowling on the green. Said to have originated in the Netherlands.

Currant: Pattern of pressed glass featuring clusters of leaves and berries under a band of cord.

currant punch: The "true punch," meaning the drink with a punch of authority, made of 1 gallon whiskey, rasped yellow of half a dozen lemons, 2 gills honey, 5 pounds bruised currants, and 2 ounces ginger, steeped for a day and strained.

currente calamo: A system of handwriting or calligraphy, invented by one McLauren, c. 1850.

currier: A dresser of skins, hides, and parchment.

Currier & Ives: Lithographers and printmakers. Producers of single-stone hand-colored lithographs in such immense quantities that surviving examples dominate the American 19th-century-print market. The firm was established by N. Currier, 1835, and did not become Currier & Ives until 1859. So great was the output of Currier and of Currier & Ives that no complete catalogue has been compiled, but thousands of subjects are tabulated, including prints made to sell at from six cents up to one dollar, and such items as trade cards, rewards of merit, book illustrations, advertising folios, et cetera. Any edition of *Currier & Ives*, by Harry T. Peters, is recommended for study. No producer of what are called American antiques enjoys as much published documentary material as Currier & Ives.

Currier engravings: N. Currier, in his early days as a lithographer, also reissued plates of George and Martha Washington and Bennett's views of West Point and Trenton Falls. Others may exist with the N. Currier imprint. These are not lithographic reproductions but plate-printed restrikes made after the original issue.

Curtain: Pattern of pressed glass featuring an all-over design of drapery swags in wide panels, broken by narrow panels of angles flanking oval bosses. Bases are spirally ribbed.

curtain knobs: (1) Knobs, plaques, or other devices to hold back curtains. The curtain holdbacks of other days include examples of pressed glass, mirror glass, gilded glass, brass, pewter, Sheffield plate, painted and japanned tinware, papier-mâché, bronze, pottery, porcelain, and carved and painted wood. (2) Knobs used at ends of a curtain pole as decorative accessories.

curtain paper: Paper printed to simulate curtains and used in many homes and cottages. These cheap elegancies were sold from the 1840s. The term was also used to designate wallpaper.

curtain pin: Any screw rod or nail topped with a large decorative head and designed for use as a curtain holdback.

Curtis-Newton mirrors: Found in Kentucky, Tennessee, and Missouri, these mirrors of tabernacle form are named for the makers who started production at Louisville, Ky., c. 1830.

Curtisville plate: General line of electroplate made in great quantities at Curtisville and Hartford, Conn., from 1850s. This was effective competition for electroplated Sheffield.

Curtis ware: Pottery produced at Philadelphia from c. 1790 by John Curtis. Stone- and redware.

cury; curry: Early form of our present word "cookery."

Cushing vanes: Weather vanes of modeled copper, gilded with pure-gold leaf. Cushing's works was at Waltham, Mass., and was established in 1850s. The Angel Gabriel is the most delightful example, but Cushing made eagle, figural, and object vanes in great numbers and variety.

cushion: A wedding dance.

cushion frame: Molding with an upcurving center which, in cross section, is of cushion form. Used from 17th century.

cushion on frame: Actual cushion work applied to a picture or mirror frame.

cusped: Having teeth or points, caused by a sharp reversal of a curve or scroll. The points of a crescent moon are its cusps.

custard glass: (1) A piece of glassware designed for the service of custard. (2) A kind of glass of off-white opaque body, imitative of the color of milk-and-egg custard.

Cut Block: Pattern of pressed glass featuring a rather narrow band of decoration in form of diamonds with square in center and with diamond-lined background. A late pattern.

cut carboys: Huge cut-glass decanters.

cut card: A form of ornamentation used by silversmiths and other craftsmen to achieve raised decoration. The process involves cutting a pattern from card-thick substance and welding or gluing to the main surface. Said to date from 1650s.

cut-flower pot: Reference is to the flowers; any pot for cut-flower arrangements.

cut glass: One of the earliest forms of ornamenting and utilizing glass. The technique of cutting, or carving, dates from pre-Christian times. The cutting technique in general use for many centuries involved use of rapidly rotating small wheels of soft ductile metal, with a hard abrasive such as emery or diamond dust, and final polishing. There is one popular book on cut glass, *Cut & Engraved Glass*, by Dorothy Daniel, and several very scholarly works on the cut wares of Venice, Central Europe, and England.

cut-glass patterns: Some few early patterns are described in this volume, but for data and pictures of late patterns student is referred to *Cut & Engraved Glass*, by Dorothy Daniel. *See* Bibliography.

Cut Jewel: Pattern of pressed glass imitative of diamond cutting.

cutlass pistol: Percussion pistol with a cutlass, fixed bayonetwise, under the barrel. Made at Amherst, Mass., from 1837. Only a few hundred were made.

cut-leather pictures: Art in cut leather, by glovers, bookbinders, and allied craftsmen. A form of découpage. **cut-leather frames:** Picture and mirror frames made of cut-leather work in form of leaves and flowers.

Cutler furniture: Sofas, Grecian couches, and chairs; claw, pier, and card tables, et cetera, made by Abner Cutler at Buffalo, N.Y., from 1820s. Noted in western New York.

cutlet cutters: Tinned sheet-iron crimpers, originally in nests of from 4 to 16, to cut flesh or paste into cutlet shape. [*Examples pictured.*]

cut-off oven: A cooking range of cast iron with dampers and checks to cut off the heating of the oven when not required for use. Made from 1830s.

cutteaux: Small swords; also carving knives.

cutter: A sporting sleigh.

cutwork: Fancywork on fabrics, involving embroidery and cutting out to achieve a lacy effect.

cutwork paper: Tissue or standard-weight paper, die-cut or hand-cut, arranged in form of decorative panels, landscapes, portraits, etc.

cycloidotrope: Mechanical lantern slide with device for tracing a rose engine (*which see*) turning on a smoked-glass surface, while the lantern projected the effect on a screen. Thus, on the screen, the pattern was developed in a seemingly magical manner, in brilliant white on a black ground. These devices originally sold for $10. They are now rare items in the realm of toy collecting.

Cyclone: Pattern of pressed glass displaying an all-over effect of swirling flutes. An excellent pattern, but quite late.

cydon: The quince.

cylerie: Ceilerie; effective treatment of wall space with drapery.

cylinder press: A power-driven printing press that produces impression by rolling over the paper.

cylindre: French term for hurricane shade.

cylindrical salts: Early silver standing salts of really imposing stature, some a foot tall. These are very rare and date from 16th century.

cylindrical speculum: Tubular mirror which, standing upright, condensed to normal any grossly distorted pictures laid flat around it. An optical toy dating from 17th century. [*Example pictured was published 1676.*]

cyma: The double curve; the line of beauty; the line of the cabriole leg; curvature similar to the italic S. **Cyma reversa:** The same curve in reverse. **Cyma recta:** The normal, right, or proper cyma.

cypress: A crape; the death notice; the bough of mourning.

cypress-knee bucket: Southern woodenware, a bucket made from the natural knees formed in root growth of cypress trees.

cypress wine: Wine of the elderberry.

D

dacian: A wall and upholstery fabric printed in metal ink. Invented 1850, and made by Bannerman, Manchester, England.

dackles: Dewdrops; glass pendants in imitation of dewdrops.

daddick: Tinder wood; touchwood; punk.

dadestring: A lead string, used in teaching children to walk.

dado: The facet of a pedestal; the longitudinal section, as base of a wall.

daduchus: Female figure bearing a torch. Greek-revival form.

daffadowndilly: The daffodil flower.

daffer: Small crockery.

daffle: Oven mop or swab.

daffling iron: Hearth scraper for a bake oven.

dag: Firearm of the type now called a pistol.

dag-prick: Triangular-bladed spade.

dagswain: Rough textile used as a bed-cover.

daguerreotype: The first photographic pictures by a process invented by Daguerre, 1839. The action of light on silver salts produced the picture, which was under glass and was visible as through a mirror. The camera obscura was used to focus the object. Commercial daguerreotype cameras, much smaller than the camera obscura, were advertised in U.S. as early as 1840s.

Dahlia: Pattern of pressed glass featuring dahlia flower and leaf design on flowing stem, on stippled ground. Not to be confused with Primrose, a similar pattern.

Daisy & Button: Pattern of pressed glass essentially geometric and imitative of a similar pattern of cut glass. The daisy is the cut (pressed) portion; the button is an uncut boss. There are many variants, including Daisy & Button with Panel, Daisy & Button with Single Panel, Daisy & Button with Cross Bar, Daisy & Button with Thumbprint, Daisy & Button with V-Ornament. Date is from 1880s. Pattern did not originate at Sandwich, but was made in such quantities as to indicate nationwide popularity.

Daisy & Cube: Pattern of pressed glass imitative of cutting, with a cube-shaped boss rather than a button.

Daisy Band: Pattern of pressed glass featuring imitative cutting around the bases of pieces in form of ovate bands of daisy form over which there is a band of bosses in lozenge shape. Upper parts are clear glass, sometimes etched.

daisy cats: Mechanical toys operated by a crank, giving motion to cats in costume.

Daisy-in-Diamond: Pattern of mold-blown glass featuring petaled forms arranged in diamonds. A similar pattern, **Daisy-in-Hexagon,** features daisy petals in hexagonal form, sometimes within a border.

Dakota: Pattern of pressed glass featuring bands of thumbprints with large clear areas above which are generally etched, but some are plain.

dale: A common field for the people; a small valley.

Dale Hall: Pottery producing excellent utilitarian and decorative wares, operated by T. J. & J. Mayer, Longport, England, 19th century. Much ware from this pottery was exported to America.

dallop: Smuggled tea.

dalmatic: Ecclesiastical gown with wide-flaring skirt.

damask: Fabric woven in pattern by shifts in warp and weft threads, imitative of the damascening on metal. Originally from Damascus and first imitated in Flanders linens.

damask coverlet: This term, found woven in some Jacquard-loomed coverlets, was used by American weavers to lend quality appeal to their products.

Damask Diaper: An early coverlet pattern (pre-Jacquard) of varying rods, squares, rectangles, et cetera.

damaskeening; damascening: Inlaid metalwork, or lathe engine-turning imitative thereof. Process originated at Damascus.

damnified: Damaged.

dancing plateau: A vibratory toy in the form of a large disk on which many miniature figures were placed, attached by a rod to the frame of a piano. Playing or strumming the instrument caused the figures to dance. Originally dating from 1870s, this toy was revived in the 1930s to attach to radio and phonograph sets.

dandy chair: Hands and arms of two persons, clasped, to provide a seat for an invalid or a child.

danglespit: A hanging spit with turnbuckle or swivel to permit turning. Sometimes fitted with crossarms, weighted with heavy balls at ends to cause long rotation. By 1820s such spits had spring-driven clockwork to keep them in rotation for a half hour or more.

D'Angoulême ware: Porcelain made at the factory patroned by the Duke of this name, Paris, 18th century.

dannack: A buskin.

Dann chair: See Chairs, All Kinds.

Dannemora: Fine iron used in making pens, buttons, and stamped items.

Darby & Joan settee: 19th- or 20th-century name given to two-chair-back settees of any period or style.

dariol: A custard baked in a deep dish.

darlsilk: Damask.

darnel: False wheat; speltz.

darnell: Linen cloth, also known as darnix, dernil, et cetera. The original name was darnex or dornick, designating a coarse damask made at Tournay for bedcovers and tablecloths.

darning: Lacemaking.

darning egg: Any ovate form used to provide a mending surface for a sock or hose. Known in glass, pottery, metal, and natural forms such as gourds and even blown eggshells filled with plaster. Not laid by sewing birds, as the one-time jokesters said.

Darragh furniture: James Darragh was one of the first cabinetmakers of Pittsburgh, working as early as 1800. The reference is probably to his work, which is said to have been in the Hepplewhite style.

dashelfink: Thistle finch. Term was common in England during 16th and 17th centuries, as was distelfink, meaning the bird painted on oven doors or stoppels.

date mark; date letter: Reference is to what are properly assay marks on English silver, the date being indicated by a letter of the alphabet. Birmingham, Sheffield, Chester, Cork, Dublin, Norwich, Edinburgh, Exeter, Glasgow, London, Newcastle, and York all had date letters, many of them beginning in the 17th century. Any good book on English silver will contain tables of the date letters used.

dating antiques: This is a matter of analysis, based upon knowledge and accessibility of documentation. For example, this description of an antique contains a statement that makes its claim of age ridiculous: "Toy pianoforte, opening to expose a toilet mirror, and playing the Blue Danube Waltz. Date is c. 1800." Strauss, composer of the waltz, was born 1825. Ergo, the piece is dated 50 years before its most likely point in time. Saw marks, nails, decorative forms, woods, glues, and many other items are considered in the dating of pieces. Styles of lettering, numerals, quality of paper, and innumerable other details must be studied. The dating of antiques is not a task for tyros.

dauber: A plasterer.

davenport (FURNITURE): (1) A long upholstered sofa. (2) Cabinetwork produced by A. H. Davenport, Boston, in the French antique-revival style.

Davenport ware: White, cream, and blue printed wares, some with openwork rims, made from 1790s by John Davenport at the Longport potteries. Later bone china was produced, much of which was exported to the U.S. One pattern, an adaptation of the old willow, was enriched with gold. Most of the ware is marked and readily identifiable.

David's staff: A quadrant.

Davis box: Shaved-wood, fancy paper-covered boxes with identifying labels of Hannah Davis, the maker, active at East Jaffrey, N.H., 1800s–50s.

Davis ware: Reference may be to (1) brasswares made by Davis, Boston, from late 18th century, who made andirons, shovels, tongs, et cetera. (2) Tinware made by Isaiah Wood, Nathan Brightman, and Henry Davis, New Bedford, Mass., c. 1840s. A number of Welshmen named Davis, Davies, or Daffyds were artisans in metal. Therefore, "Davis ware" can be a purely local designation for a product made and sold locally. This same thing is true of any and all named wares of a place or region.

davonport; devonport; devenport: A desk box with sloping lid, on a stand, the box sometimes galleried. A Regency-era desk made in considerable quantities. [Examples pictured.]

dawns: An early lace.

Dawson luster: Sunderland-type luster-wares bearing the impressed mark DAWSON. The dates of activity of this potter are 1780–1815.

day bed: A couch, canapé, chaise longue, long chair, and other names are given the chair-backed (sometimes adjustable as to angle) piece of seat furniture with a seat extending forward five to six feet, and designed primarily as a repose piece for daytime use. Said to derive from pastors' use of a cushioned bench to rest upon between church services, from early Gothic era. Actual day beds or couches are known in all period styles from William & Mary through to Eastlake. [Example pictured.]

day lamp: An Argand-burner kerosene lamp with tall chimney and globose shade, having a reservoir holding sufficient fluid to keep lamp burning twenty-four hours —a full day. [*Example pictured.*]

daytaleman: Day laborer.

Dayton pictures: Engraved and colored in oils, made by Dayton & Co., the subjects included Titian's "Venus" and many patriotic scenes and personages. Made from 1850s.

d'commodité: Any piece of seat furniture with writing arm attached.

deal: Originally any timber cut into planks or boards; finally, any wood of the conifers or evergreens.

Deans, Robert: Cabinetmaker of Charleston, S.C., working from mid-18th century.

Dearborn prospector: Drawing board designed for perspective drawing, made by Benjamin Dearborn of Portsmouth, N.H., prior to 1800. Mahogany board with brass mountings.

Debain player: Mechanical piano player introduced from France, c. 1850.

De Baviere, Jacqueline: Frenchwoman who taught the art of stoneware-making to the Germans in the 16th century.

debruised: To cancel, but not erase; to cross out. In heraldry, decorative defacement.

decalcomanie: The process of printing on a gelatin film, in reverse order of colors, so that a transfer in right order can be achieved by simply wetting the substance on which the gelatin is laid. Most of the work was—and is—done on paper. By this process decoration in gold, silver, and colors can be transferred to glass, china, wood, stone, or any other smooth surface.

decanter jug: Wide-mouthed glass jug with stopper; an early vessel in the Venetian technique of blowing and decorating; some known to have been made by Ravenscroft. [*Example pictured.*]

decanter stand: A bottle holder or slider; a boat-shaped, circular, or other form holder of silver, Sheffield plate, cabinet wood, et cetera, to hold several decanters. Many varieties known. Date is from 18th century.

deception-bed: The formal term for a folding bed hidden within a case or cabinet, especially those of some antiquity and beauty. Deception-chairs (mostly night chairs in fact), deception-night cabinets, deception-toilet cabinets, et cetera. The late Bishop Darlington's collection of antique pianos and organs included a deception piece that was both keyboard musical instrument and complete toilet table.

decoct: To boil or seethe; to reduce or extract by boiling.

DeCoudres ware: Copper, brass-, and tinware made at shops of Thomas De-Coudres, Newark, N.J., from 1825. Said to have made andirons and fireplace tools.

decoy: Carved and turned-wood effigies of waterfowl, painted to simulate actual birds, and used in flocks to decoy live birds within gun or net range. Many varieties. Student is referred to *Wildfowl Decoys*, by Joel Barber. Every type of bird from reedbird to goose and swan is known in decoy form. Decoys, when turned, were turned on Blanchard lathes.

decressant: Final quarter of the moon.

decrowned chair: See Chairs, All Kinds.

Dedham pottery: See Chelsea Pottery.

Dedham pottery patterns: The standard decorative patterns of this late 19th-and early 20th-century artware, made at Dedham, Mass., are: Rabbit, Duck, Grape, Azalea, Magnolia, Snow Tree, Horse Chestnut, Iris, Water Lily, Butterfly, Turkey, Polar Bear, Clover. The following were made to order: Elephant, Swan, Dolphin, Lion, Birds in Orange Tree, Chicken, Crab, Lobster, Turtle, Owl.

Deer & Dog: Pattern of pressed glass featuring a body, plain or impressed with hunter, dog, and running deer, topped with lids on which there is a standing dog in frosted glass.

Deer & Pine Tree: (Sometimes Deer & Doe.) Pattern of pressed glass having panels depicting deer (and doe) standing before a pine tree.

deer fats: Reference is, we believe, to candles made from rendered suets of deer and other ruminants.

deer-foot spoon: A hoof-handled spoon; a silver or other metallic spoon with a split hoof form at end of handle. An early device.

deet: The sealing plaster around an oven door when oven is charged with a complement of loaves for baking.

DeGraff furniture: H.P. DeGraff, manufacturer of New York, produced Empire and French Antique furniture in rosewood, mahogany, and walnut. Firm finally became DeGraff & Taylor. Operation extended from 1850s.

déjeune: An official or stately breakfast or luncheon. Literally, hungry.

déjeuner: A tray with pot or pitcher and cup and saucer.

del.: Abbreviation for *delineavit*, meaning "drawn by."

De La Plaine, Joshua: Early New York cabinetmaker working from 1738.

delawned: Unfrocked; deprived of the right to wear the lawn, the surplice, or the bands of lawn. Delawned was probably a temporary matter; unfrocking was final discharge from priestly privilege.

delft: The faïence of the Netherlands, tin glaze over earthenware, with blue décor, sometimes in the Chinese taste. Delftwares, as a type, were duplicated at Lambeth and Liverpool, England, from early in the 18th century. Delft is substantially the same ware as the other European efforts to approximate the porcelains of China, known to traders from the days of the Crusades, when Chinese wares that had reached the Near East were noted in the Saracenic countries, which were also making imitations of Chinese wares. The tin glaze, sometimes called stanniferous enamel, is the secret of majolica and other faïences. Delftwares more nearly approximate the Chinese décor of Canton and Nanking. There is a woeful lack of popular knowledge concerning the finer delftwares; most knowledge is confined to acquaintance with the commoner wares and with tiles. Many people think of delft only in terms of a blue tint or color. There are delftwares decorated in green, brown, black, sepia, yellow, and red, as well as varicolored delft; the product of several hundred different potters. Records of potteries in the Netherlands date back to the 14th century. In 1650 over 7000 people in the Netherlands were engaged in making this ware.

delft cage: Base and top elements of a cage of delftware, the bars being threaded wires. 17th to 18th century.

delftwares (by prefixed name): Dublin delft, Liverpool delft, Lambeth delft, and similar names refer to the type of ware made at these places.

Delhi work: Gem cutting and setting as practiced at Delhi, India, where jade was used as a setting for precious stones.

delineator: Perspective drawing machine invented by Allen Judd of Chicopee, Mass., 1849. A spyglass was focused on the scene, and a pencil point followed movement of the glass. The same name was given to a surveying instrument invented by E. S. Bailey of Abbeville, S.C., 1844.

deliten: To give delight.

Del Vecchio Mirror: Any mirror, including plain, tabernacle, and Constitution types, made by James del Vecchio of New York, early to mid-19th century. It is indeed doubtful that he made the Constitution type, but others are known marked with his label.

Demarest: A sink and toilet-bowl combination made by Mott Ironworks, probably named for Madam Demarest, a one-time fashion expert of New York City.

demi-lion: Bust of a lion rampant, generally used as a handle or finial.

demilune: Halfmoon. Tables in pairs, each a half circle, are called by this name.

demountable table: A board used as a table, mounted on boxlike members or other supports, the complete ensemble being readily dismounted and stowed away.

demy: A size of paper. *See* Paper Sizes.

demycent: The stay piece of a girdle.

Denby & Codnor Park: Two potteries, operated by Bournes in England, making many varieties of two-tone creamware, bottles, figural flasks, bread trays, et cetera. Flourished in first half of 19th century. [*Examples and marks pictured.*]

denim: Colored warp, white woof fabric, woven at Nimes, France. Originally *fabrique de Nimes*, hence denim.

denizen: Naturalized, but not native.

Dennis, Thomas: Late 17th-century joiner (furniture maker) of Ipswich, Mass., who worked in oak.

dentelle: With teeth; serrated. A series of small toothlike elements in a row, regularly spaced, as in a cornice or border. Also notched. **dentate; dentiled:** With dentils.

Derby: Pattern name of pressed glass once used for Pleat & Panel.

Derby: Pottery center in England noted for its porcelain and for other and earlier potmaking at Cock-Pit Hill Works (1720). William Duesberry of Longton, 1756, entered the business at Derby. Derby gold

and blue porcelain or china had achieved some fame by 1772. Duesberry also owned the Chelsea Works (purchased 1769). To the letter "D" mark of Derby this owner added the Chelsea anchor. In 1815 the grandson of Duesberry leased the works to Robert Bloor. Subsequently other managements and ownership carried on the famous works. [*Examples of the wares and marks are pictured.*] In 1903 certain old Derby items were restored to production (the Seasons, the Gardener, Falstaff, pig groups, et cetera). This late ware, marked ENGLAND, is known as Modern Derby, Larcomb Derby, or Paget Period Derby.

Derbyshire ironstone: Buff, cane-colored, and yellow stoneware by various potters of Derbyshire, England, are so characterized as a group.

Derby silver: Silver-plated nickel-base ware made at Derby, Conn., from c. 1870s.

Derby slip ware: The redware potters of Derbyshire molded or cast common red potter's clay in molds with engraved patterns. The clay carried the design as raised lines or ridges. White and colored slip was poured on the ware between the lines and then fired with a glaze.

Derby spar: Semi-precious spar streaked with blue and purple and metallic flecks. This was turned and otherwise fashioned into bowls and trays, usually in ormolu mountings. This is natural spar, not a ceramic ware.

Derr lamps: Betty-type fat lamps of brass and copper, made by Peter Derr, c. 1830s-60s, generally marked. The maker was a rural artisan who was a jack-of-all-trades and master of a few, working in the Lebanon-Berks region of Pennsylvania and doing business with farmers and villagers, and especially with late immigrants.

Deruta: Italian majolica pottery of the 16th century, some in luster and some in colors, bearing portraits, trophies, and grotesque décor. Now highly prized by collectors and originally a ware for connoisseurs of the period. The yellow luster is famous.

desart: Table decoration of mid-18th century, sometimes of molded sugar but also made from assemblages of china, glass, et cetera.

Desborus: Emperor of the barbers and surgeons, and legendary dictator of men's styles and fashions.

descated: Dried.

Desell, Charles: Cabinetmaker of Charleston, S.C., said to have worked in late 18th century.

deseret: Land of the honeybee; a beehive. A place of communal work.

Deshon bath: A shower bath in a cabinet. The user stood on a rocking platform within the cabinet, swaying from side to side, thereby pumping water from bottom to a top nozzle from which it sprayed on the bather. This device was made from 1840s and sold generally to the fastidious throughout the U.S.

desk: From *deske, desca, desco*—a writing table.

desk box: Box with sloping lid, used on a table or stand. Most examples date from 16th and 17th centuries and are carved or decorated in the manner of the period.

Desk-box-on-frame is the beginning of the desk-on-frame, generally a two-piece item of furniture, the desk box at times fitted with brass or iron bail handles. [*Examples pictured.*]

desk drawer: Any drawer in any kind of case furniture fitted with a drop front, pigeonholed compartments, and other writing-bureau appurtenances.

desk highboy: When the base or stand of a highboy has a pull-out board, most likely designed for use as a dressing tray, the piece is sometimes designated by this term.

desk-in-table: 18th-century table with deep skirting and sometimes false drawer front, sliding panel, or some other mode of access to a desk compartment within the skirting. Scarce item.

desk-on-frame: A frame that is of table form, surmounted by a slope-fall desk section. Made from 17th century or earlier. [*Example pictured.*] Some present-day antique rectangular tables with molding around edges are most likely desk frames that have lost their desk cabinets.

desk pulls: The pull-out slides, drawers, or boards that support the leaf of a slope-fall desk.

desserte: A tiered serving table with two or more platforms.

Dessoir furniture: M. Dessoir, French cabinetmaker, established himself in New York in 1840s and produced work in the French Antique revival style now called Victorian.

dessus de porte: Literally "above the door." Any over-door decoration.

devant: An apron.

devil: Shredding machine used by upholsterers (upholders) to make furniture stuffing from old cloth, hemp, tow, and other fibers.

devil & pope cup: Figural cup made by Ralph Wood, famed potter, featuring a smiling devil on one side and a frowning pope on the other. Cover of the cup has an orb and cross finial.

devil nose; mask nose: Any pitcher, such as the Bennington Daisy pattern, having a mask or devil's face under the pouring spout. A relic of the early "mug" drinking vessel, or perhaps of the Bellarmine jug.

Devon butter: Sweet cream, scalded, and set to clot for 24 hours. The clot, worked with bare hands in a bowl, turned to butter within a quarter of an hour. Fresh butter was so made to at least the 1840s in many households.

Devonport: A desk box on a cabinet of drawers; 19th century. The invention of a Mr. Devonport.

Devonshire Cut: Pattern of cut glass featuring star, fan, and other devices as a border or banding, with large star center.

Dewdrop: Basic or generic pattern of pressed glass constituting a group with many variants. Dewdrop is a band of fine dewdrop spots, closely set; Paneled Dewdrop is the same décor arranged in vertical panels. Variants are Dewdrop & Raindrop, Dewdrop with Star, et cetera. Variants of the Dewdrop group are listed under their now generally accepted pattern names. See also *Early American Pressed Glass*, by Ruth Webb Lee.

dewed flax: Bleaching by re-retting flax on the grass, where it is dampened by the dew.

Dewey glass: Late commemorative pressed and blown glass produced in honor of Admiral Dewey, all dating after 1898. Bowls, bottles, tumblers, trays, pitchers, busts, et cetera, are known in so many varieties that no complete list has been assembled as yet.

Dewey prints: Fruits and flowers and ornamental trees and shrubs pictured by D. M. Dewey at his stenciled-print coloring establishment, Rochester, N.Y., from 1850s. These prints were originally made for sale to florists and nurserymen as pages for their catalogues. Size is 8½ x 11 inches or less.

Dewing calico: Francis Dewing of Boston advertised his calico printing in 1715 and also that he cut blocks for such printing.

dexter: Heraldic term for the proper right side of a bearing or what, to the observer, is the left side. Opposed to sinister, the proper left side, which appears as on the right side to the observer.

dey house: A dairy, a cheese house.

DeZouche hangings: Wallpaper in rolls, sold by McAusland & DeZouche of New York from 1850s. They were also importers of composition ornaments for interior decoration.

D-front: Any cabinet piece having an extending or bowed front in the form of the bow of the letter D.

dhakas: Fine Bengalese muslins from India.

Diagonal Band: Pattern of pressed glass featuring bands of floral devices arranged diagonally. A variant is Diagonal Band with Fan.

dial mold: Brass molds for casting clock dials and sundials in pewter or tin.

Diamond: Pattern in glassmaking, used in mold-blown wares, by which forming or contact molds impress a diamond pattern on the parison of glass. Used in glass pressing to form diamond patterns, small or large, on the wares so made. A standard form used in glass cutting whereby diamonds are formed by diagonal cuttings with the wheel. Ruth Webb Lee lists a pressed-glass pattern known as Diamonds. This features a series of small diamond forms, faceted, grouped in large diamonds, arranged in bands with alternate diamond-shaped areas of clear glass.

diamond "A" matting: Floor covering woven from rattan yarn, introduced by Wakefield of New England c. 1863.

Diamond Band: Pattern of cut glass featuring a belt of small diamond cuttings. Also a pattern of pressed glass, imitative of the cutting, featuring a wide band of diamond indentations providing a raised diamond surface. Many variants in both cut and pressed wares, including Diamond Block, Diamond Cut with Leaf, Diamond Medallion, Diamond Point, Diamond Point with Panel, Diamond & Sunburst, Diamond Thumbprint, and Diamond Quilted.

diamond cement: A commercial adhesive popular in the 1820s–40s for home repair of china, glass, and furniture.

diamond head hooks: Brass clothes hooks for wardrobes, the heads being dia-

VITREOUS STONE BOTTLE
BOURNE & SON
PATENTEES,
DENBY POTTERY
NEAR DERBY.

J. BOURNE & SON
PATENTEES
DENBY POTTERIES
NEAR DERBY.

1, Desk-on-Frame. **2,** Desk-Box-on-Frame. **3,** Binnacle Lamps. **4,** Marks, Inkwell, and Urns from Denby & Codnor Park Potteries. **5,** Devonport Desks (2). **6,** Day Lamp. **7,** Decanter Jug. **8,** Dog Grate. **9,** Double-Topped Table. **10,** D'Outer. **11,** Dow, Lorenzo. **12,** Down Hearth Warmer. **13,** Duck Lighter. **14,** Dust Pan. **15,** Duette Bench. **16,** Draw, "Drawing," or "Draw-Out" Table. **17,** Dovetail Hinge, sometimes called Butterfly. **18,** Dolphin Candlestick (glass). (No. 4 from Virtue & Co., London. No. 8 from Harrod's, London.)

121

mond-block-faceted rather than smooth, ovate, or round.

diamond reflector: Lamp shade and reflector of bright metal pressed into a series of brilliant diamond-shaped facetings, made by Goetz & Co., Philadelphia, from 1850s to as late as 1880s.

diamond reflector lamp: An Argand-burner kerosene lamp with slender chimney and polished parabolic reflector, made from 1870s. Mrs. Jack Brantley of Savannah, Ga., states these lamps were popular as pulpit lamps; they were advertised as excellent lights for home or office.

Diana: Term for the "philosophic tree," which grew from an ounce of silver dissolved in niter, added to a pot of water and mercury. To grow a Diana was still a popular home experiment as late as the 1840s.

diapendion: An electuary; drugs in syrup or honey.

diaper: To paint in colors is the original meaning; now it is descriptive of decorative geometric patterns painted in colors. Diaper pattern means imitative of textile work, especially a cloth woven in diamond weave, such as Ypres stuff, favored for cardinals' robes as early as 16th century.

diaphanie: Translucent or transparent paper printed in colors to imitate stained glass. These were mounted on panes of clear glass. First offered in 1840s, it is still made.

dibble: A pewter plate.

dice vase: A dice cup in vase form.

Dickinson: Pattern of pressed glass made at Sandwich, featuring wide volutes with crisscross ribbing on half of each lobe.

dickpot: A petticoat stove; a perforated earthenware pot holding hot embers and placed under skirts to warm feet and body.

Dickson rifle: American rifles made at Louisville, Ky., by M. Dickson from 1830s.

diemen; diewomen: Gaming dice in the form of squatting men and women. These date from 16th century and are generally obscene and always vulgar.

Dietz lamps: Lamps and lanterns made by Dietz & Co., N.Y., founded 1840. They made an infinite variety of lighting fixtures, including candlesticks and candelabra, and many of the early lamps of quality are marked.

dilettante: A casual collector who thinks he knows. Compare with connoisseur, one who knows.

Dillwyn: Perhaps best known for Etruscan ware, the Dillwyn pottery was really the Swansea Cambrian pottery, established c. 1750 by Coles & Haynes and by 1785 producing Swansea porcelain. Dillwyn acquired the pottery in 1802 and by 1814 was making a ware like Nantgarw. Dillwyn retired in 1852, but the works continued in operation for some years. Among the noted wares were the porcelains or china decorated by Billingsley, Beddoes, Evans, and others. [*The various marks and examples of Dillwyn Swansea are pictured.*]

Dimick furniture: Late Sheraton-, Directoire-, and Empire-style seat and case furniture in mahogany and cherry made by H. E. Dimick of Lexington, Ky., from 1830s.

dimity: Linens woven first at Damietta, but ultimately a very fine fabric. The true dimity has a raised figure pattern that is an embossed weave.

dimpled: Said of the gathering of glass molded or tooled for expanded pattern blowing. Dimple molding is said to have originated at Liège, now in Belgium, but once a glassmaking center of the Netherlands.

dinanderie: Brass and bronze grotesque vessels, such as the cow creamer and figural pitchers, made at Dinant, formerly in the Netherlands, from c. 1350. The name is applied to the objects and to the alloy which, it is asserted, was the forerunner of pewter. [*Examples pictured.*]

dinner wagon: Three-tiered food tray on corner posts, castered. [*Example pictured.*]

diograph: An instrument for drawing landscapes in true perspective, used by amateurs and professional artists. Invented 1810 by Simeon DeWitt of Albany, N.Y., and first made by Abraham Randall, cabinetmaker of that city, in the same year.

diorama: Extensive paintings on long sheets of fabric, fed from rolls to an opening, and illuminated. An 18th-century show technique revived in 19th century by Daguerre, inventor of modern photography.

diorama of ornaments: A series of china groups, boscages, et cetera, arranged across a mantel.

diorascope: A drawing machine with a scanning screen divided into 20 rectangles by cords. Invented by Simeon DeWitt of Albany, N.Y., c. 1810.

dipped horseshoe: When the horseshoe-shaped arm and rail of a Windsor armchair is higher at its ends than its center, it is referred to as dipped. Most good examples are so made.

dipped jasper: Wedgwood and similar jasper wares, dipped to achieve biscuit coloring.

dipped seat: Any slanted, tilted, or curve-cut seating, whether solid, plank, or upholstered.

dipping cup: A ladle; a dipper.

dipsack: Colloquial for dipsacus, a teaseling burr used in raising nap of cloth as it comes from the loom.

dipstick: See Candlestick.

diptych: Tablet or book of two leaves.

Directoire: (1) The furniture style originated by the artist Louis David and by Percier, which achieved its high point of acceptance during the four-year period of the French Revolution, 1795–99. The Directoire is both simple and lovely, dominated by sweeping yet restrained curves. Sheraton copied many Directoire forms, and Directoire is the chief style of Duncan Phyfe. The entire Directoire period embraces the years 1790–1804, the latter five years being the Consular era of French history, before the elevation of Napoleon as Emperor. The Directoire style and its forms were popular in the U.S. to at least 1830. The style is sometimes called "Directory." [*Examples pictured*]

Disbrowe, Nicholas: Joiner or arkwright, born in England in 1612 or 1613, who emigrated to America and in 1639 was a property owner at Hartford, Conn. Disbrowe made tulip-carved chests which derive directly from similar chests and forms of décor in England. His most famous chest is the one he made for Mary Allyn, which he signed. [*Example pictured.*]

dise (dysun): To fix the flax on the distaff or "rock" for spinning.

dish: Any plate, shallow, or shell-like receptacle, trencher, et cetera, of any substance, primarily used in preparation and service of food but also as a protective base or stand for other objects.

dish covers: Specifically, domed covers of silver, Sheffield plate, glass, china, et cetera, made for separate sale and not originally a part of an ensemble. These were designed to keep viands hot in service at table.

dish cross: Folding metal X-shaped members with feet at extremities, used as coasters or trivets, and sometimes fitted with a spirit lamp at the juncture of bars to serve as a heater. Often the bar ends are adjustable. Many metals, from wrought iron to silver, were used. Dates range from 1780s to 1850s.

dish drawer: The drawer of a cabinet containing a washbowl or basin. A drawer having a carved front "dished" or hollow-gouged.

dished: Flattened, as the rim of a bowl.

disher: A potter.

dish flask: Pewter flask of flat type, achieved by soldering two deep dishes together, edge to edge, and fitted with a neck and stopper.

dish meat: Spoon meat.

dish ring: Capstan-form hollow ring to elevate a dish or bowl. Sometimes called a potato ring as, probably, the objects were used to hold baked potatoes in a napkin. Made from mid-18th century in many varieties, of silver, Sheffield plate, brass, and iron.

dish seat: Chair seat slightly hollowed as a dish.

dish timber: Burls of the white ash, sugar maple, beech, walnut, birch, and other timber trees, saved for the express purpose of turning bowls and dishes.

dish top: Table top slightly hollowed from the solid of the board, providing a distinct rim. Tea tables, as early as 1690, are known with this feature, although most examples in collections date from 1740s to 1820s. Tops generally are round, and the dishing is achieved by turning. The pie-crust table top is the aristocratic variant of the dish-turned top. These, too, were first turned, then carved.

disk box: Music box playing from perforated disks having burrs on the undersides. Said to be an American invention of 19th century; first ones seem to date from 1860s.

dispensary bottle: Commercial liquor and wine bottles marked with insignia of states and sometimes with the word "dispensary." These were the bottles used by state liquor-control boards of the late 19th century. Also any bottles (generally marked) used in free dispensaries, military post exchanges, and other publicly owned places.

dissected maps: Early jigsaw puzzles in the form of cut-up maps. Many made from 1820s to 1880s and later.

distaff: The thread-spinning aid used so universally by women of all classes that the term now means the feminine line of a family. Also the device to hold flax that is a part of every spinning wheel. The true distaff was a cloth-yard-long staff with a forked end, used to hold the flax or other fluff. The spindle, one third the length of the staff, also had a forked end but was used primarily as a winder for thread spun off the staff by the fingers of the spinner.

distelfink: Railbird, field finch, thistle finch. This term is said to be South German and introduced to the colonies by immigrants from Swabia c. 1720. Dishel fink, as a term, was known to thousands of Yorkshire people in the colonies prior to 1700. Theirs was the usage that probably implanted the term in America. (1) Dishel fink, meaning thistle finch, and (2) distle fink, meaning an oven stopper decorated with a bird said to be a finch. (3) Dashelfink: Field bird.

distemper: Opaque water colors used extensively for many years in wall painting and in the arts. There were many recipes for making these opaque colors. Wallpaper is generally printed in distemper colors. Term derives from *tempera*.

disteyne: To dim.

ditten; dittle; distel: Oven-opening stopple.

diurnalary: News crying and vending of newspapers on the streets, and the women who did it, prior to the advent of newsboys.

Divided Heart: Pattern of pressed glass featuring a broad band of hearts in outline, divided vertically with a lentil or shuttle form.

Dixon, Robert: Cabinetmaker of New York City, said to have worked from 1780s.

Dixon grate: Hearth grate for burning coal with a fireback for reflection of heat, a damper, and a drop ash pit.

Dixon pewter: English pewterers named Dixon produced wares from c. 1750. Not to be confused with Dixon Britannia and Sheffield plate.

Dobell furniture: This term may mean: (1) Breakfast, dining, circular, extension, and other tables made by Dobell & Hughes, Cincinnati, from 1840s and sold generally throughout the West, and (2) E. B. Dobell chairs, also made at Cincinnati, from 1850s or earlier. The latter was also an extensive maker of mirror frames.

Dobson flower stand: A multi-container stand of glass for use as a series of vases, or a planter. Imported from 1870s, it is possible that several American glasshouses duplicated the novelty. Named for Dobson, the originator.

Doccia: Italian porcelain made near Florence from 1730s to modern times.

dockery: Weasels' furred skins.

doctor's desk: Slope-fall bureau desk with an upper section divided into from 20 to 60 small drawers for storage of essences, herbs, drugs, and vials. Made from mid-18th century to mid-19th. Consequently the style range is from Georgian to Empire. By 1850 several furniture manufacturers were producing such desks as stock items.

document box: Any box made specifically for the storage of valuable papers, from the carved desk boxes of late Gothic and Tudor styles to the painted iron letter boxes with hasps and carrying handles. [*One of these is pictured.*]

dodecagon: See Polygons.

Dodge lamp: All kinds and styles of lamps for home, store, and shop lighting as produced by J. F. Dodge, Boston, 1830–60s. Many were made to burn camphene and whale oil, a few kerosene.

Doe & Hazleton furniture: French Antique revival furniture, commonly called Victorian, for every important room in the home, made by a firm so named at Boston from late 1840s.

Doe delft: A rarity in delft-type ware made by J. Doe, who committed suicide in fear that transfer china printing would end his livelihood as an enameler. Dated pieces, prior to 1797, were all made at the High Street Pottery, Lambeth, England.

Doflein, Philip: Glass mold maker who, in engraving his name on the mold of the Kossuth-Frigate Mississippi flask for the Bridgeton (N.J.) Glass Works, achieved it as a record on every bottle blown in the mold and provided the late E. A. Barber (1900) with the first clue to how and when these historic flasks were made. Doflein is listed as a mold maker in the mid-19th-century directories of his home city, Philadelphia.

dog bed: See Poodle Lounge.

dog cart: Two-wheeled sporting vehicle of 19th century. Also the small carts of Brabant used especially by milk peddlers, drawn by large dogs.

dog foot: Furniture leg tip of brass, socketed to receive the leg and finished in imitation of the foreleg and paw of a dog. Probably imitative of the now rarely seen earlier examples with this same feature, nicely carved, a part of the leg proper.

dog grate: A basket grate set between the firedogs but on its own footing. [*Example pictured.*]

dog power: A small treadmill in which a sturdy, well-trained dog was tethered; generally in the form of a large slatted drum and some, made for Newfoundland dogs, were 12 feet in diameter. Dog power was used to run light machinery in the dairy and washhouse, such as butter churns, washing machines, et cetera. There were also quite small drums made for spaniels, and these were frequently used to keep the turnspit going. The dogs for this work were called spit dogs, and the reference is to the live dog and not to firedogs fitted with turnspits.

dog's nose: Porter, laced with gin and sugared.

dog's tooth: A small burnisher made from a hound's tooth, used in burnishing gold leaf on vellum. Also any small agate burnisher of dog's-tooth shape.

dolce campana: An attachment for the pianoforte, offered in 1849 by Boardman & Gray, Albany, N.Y. The device had a series of pressing and muting hammers.

dole cabinet: Cabinet of sorrows, from

doloroso. An imposing piece of Tudor cabinetwork of oak, carved, and somewhat like a court or press cupboard. Said to derive name from the keeping in it of food and clothing for doling out to tenants and serfs. Usage dates to 14th century. This name is sometimes applied to a hanging cupboard, aerated by an open arcade of spindles in the door, yet such pieces are really pantries (*paneterie*—a place for bread or a breadbox). Therefore, any food cabinet may at times be meant by this term, even the food safes of the 19th century.

Dole furniture: E. & A. Dole of Bangor, Me., produced much case and seat furniture from 1850s or earlier. Their product may be meant by this term. Styles are Empire and French Antique.

doll: Any effigy in miniature. Made from prehistoric times to the present day for the enjoyment of children. There were innumerable kinds and types, of all conceivable substances, imitative of people of all classes, from slave to king and queen, and often in infant form. Some were mechanical and walked, talked, cried, sang, played musical instruments, drew pictures, et cetera. Much literature on the subject is available; almost every library has at least one book on dolls. Some special kinds are mentioned by their current names in this dictionary.

dollar sign ($): Said to have been devised and first used by the accountant Chauncey Lee, and appearing in his book published at Lansingburg, N.Y., 1798. Dollar is derived from *thaler,* which, in some languages, is pronounced "dahler."

Dollars Toby: A rare Toby jug in the form of a sailor seated on a chest marked DOLLARS. The flagon in the tar's hand is marked SUCCESS TO OUR WOODEN WALLS—referring to the wooden ships of the British Navy.

doll bust: Doll heads of porcelain, Parian, or china, made to top a torso of stuffed kid.

doll's-head waxer: Beeswax in a cloth casing, surmounted by a doll head. The head served as a handle when waxing hot laundry irons.

Doll toys: Generally this phrase refers to wooden toys of all kinds made at Philadelphia to at least 1876 by John Doll.

dolly: (1) A plunger with a flat round head and three or four pegged-in nipples used in stirring wash in a boiler or washtub. The staff of a butter churn is also sometimes referred to as a dolly. (2) A low cart for easy handling of heavy objects.

Dolphin: Pattern of pressed glass having small dolphins as a base and stem, and with finials of dolphin form on covered pieces. The other decoration is a series of petals arranged in a distorted diamond-oval form.

dolphin candlesticks: Pressed glass candlesticks in the form of a sporting dolphin, tail up. The tail supports the candle cup; the head rests on the base. Made at both Sandwich and Pittsburgh. Bases are of one or two tiers or steps. Square-based sticks are said to be Sandwich, and hexagonal-based ones are attributed to Pittsburgh. [*Example pictured.*]

dolphin console: A solid rectangular-form base with block or ball feet, having a columnar upright in the form of a carved dolphin, head down, the tail supporting a larger rectangular skirted top. Since some of the tops examined are oval, it may be assumed these were not made primarily for console use. There is a true dolphin console in which a table top is supported by brackets in the form of curvate dolphins.

dolphin creamer: Cream jugs in the form of a dolphin, the spout or lip being its open mouth, the handle its curvate tail; made in pottery, silver, pewter, *din-anderie*, and other metals. Ralph Wood, English potter, made them at his pottery. The form is somewhat grotesque.

dolphin epergne: Large shallow bowl, generally of glass, from the center of which a dolphin form supports an upper tray.

dolphin foot: Properly, although awkwardly, this term means a dolphin's-head foot; a footing for furniture ending in a dolphin's head. Chippendale used this, and it is very rare. [*A dolphin leg with the head at the foot is pictured.*]

dolphin hinge: Federal American-design hinge, the exposed leaf of which is dolphin-shaped in outline. In 1830 the labor charge for applying these hinges was 37 cents a pair.

dolphin lamp: An improvement on the dolphin candlestick in that the tail supports a lamp oil font. Some examples have a trio of dolphin supports. Date is from c. 1840s.

dolphin pier: A table with fold-over top, properly a card table, with carved dolphin supports. Many consider it a monstrosity.

dolphin slats or splats: Chair-back slats in the form of dolphins in pairs, head to head, and sometimes called salamanders. The style comes from the French Jura via Canada and is met with in upper New Hampshire, Maine, and Vermont. An early type of shaped slat. Examples known in France from late 1500s.

dome bed: Any bed with a dome-shaped canopy or tester.

domed saltire: Any example of the X-form (saltire cross) stretcher made with curvate upsweeping members or bowed members. Found in some Hepplewhite tea tables and Pembroke-type breakfast tables. Sometimes called tented stretchers, rising stretchers, and domed stretchers.

Domenech: A hoax of great importance in anthropological circles, 1860. The work of a schoolboy, published at Paris, 1860, edited by Domenech, and called by him a valuable contribution to knowledge of the American Indian. The hoax was disclosed immediately after publication; sold copies were repurchased and the edition suppressed. It is now a scarce item but not very valuable.

Domesday characters: Shorthand characters used in the first real property inventory of record, made in England after the Norman conquest. So definitive was this appraisal of the people's lands, goods, and chattels that the record was called the Domesday Book. [*Certain of the characters most used are pictured.*]

dominecker: Colloquial for the Domi-

nique breed of fowl, developed finally as the barred Plymouth Rock. Any hen was once called a dominecker.

dominical letter marks: Silversmiths' guild or class marks. Usage for a year was arrived at by the fall of the first Sunday in the year. If January first fell on a Monday, then the dominical letter was G. If the first day of the year was a Sunday, the dominical letter was A. The letter was used through that year as the date mark of silver. The dominical letters were A, B, C, D, E, F, G. The count was always from the first day of the year as A, to whatever letter would designate the first Sunday thereafter. The city of Baltimore used this system of date letter marking at its assay office from 1814 to 1830.

domino paper: Fancy paper in sheets for application as wall decoration. When first made, this was vended on the streets. The makers were known as *dominotiers*, and the most famous and successful was Jean Papillon, active in Paris in the 17th century. His son carried on the making of domino papers, which were hand-blocked in one color and then hand-colored. The sheets were small, something over 10" x 14". This is the original wallpaper. When pasted end to end and sold in rolls, the application was more difficult and so the trade of paper hanging was born. Paper was not made in continuous rolls until after 1803.

donarkiel: Literally, stones of Donar; a superstition of the ancient Norsemen, carried to America by the Swedes. Round stones, saved as found in the fields, and heaped in piles or placed singly atop fence posts. On some Pennsylvania farms to this day round stones, when found, are placed on fence posts.

donketh: To make dank, to dip in water. Ancient English.

Don pottery: Wares made at the pottery founded at Don by John Green and carried on from 1807 by Greens, Clark & Co., and from 1834 by the Barkers, father and son. The famous and now rare "Jumper Jug" was made here. In the early 19th century the product was imitative of Leeds ware, but fine china was also made. Sometimes called Barker ware. [*Examples and marks pictured.*]

don't-touch-me ware: Any glass, china, or pottery lettered or impressed with a phrase, in any language, meaning "do not touch me." The vagary seems to have originated in Italy c. 1450s. All potters appear to have made offhand pieces with this device. Some examples were made in Pennsylvania redwares as late as 1870s.

doofpot: Bell-shaped vessel of brass or copper, having a domed cover. Some stand 20 inches or more high.

door dern: Doorcheek or doorpost; the sides of a doorframe.

doorframe bookcase: Regency- and Empire-style cases set within a pair of pilasters and surmounted by a pediment, somewhat in the form of a doorframe.

door knocker: Metal assembly of pivoted hammer engaging a fixed striking block, the ensemble mounted and shaped in a style popular in the period of manufacture. Used on front doors for the convenience of callers. Made in white brass,

Sheffield plate, silver, copper, cast and wrought iron, pioneer types of heavy wood, et cetera.

door panels: (1) Wood panels, generally fielded, set in the stiles and rails of a door. (2) Embroidered or cross-stitch work on fabrics as a decorative element to hang on a door. These are known from all of the colonies, and from 17th century in New England, Virginia, New Amsterdam, and New Sweden (Pennsylvania).

door pistol: One-shot pistol and special trigger catch. When screwed into a door-jamb, the pistol fired and killed or wounded anyone attempting to enter. A deadly burglar trap, patented 1857 and made by or for a Springfield, Ill., firm.

door porter: A heavy figural, animalistic, or other style element of metal, pottery, glass, et cetera. Doorstop, made in some quantities from 1790s. Some have upright rods for ease in handling.

dopplewand glass: Gold- and silver-decorated glass, the décor flashed over with clear glass. Made in Bohemia.

dorado: Gilded.

Dorchester furniture: Reference is most likely to the furniture made at Dorchester, Mass. In 1830s there were ten chair factories in this town employing 120 people.

dorfer: A banker, *which see.*

Dorflinger glass: Christian Dorflinger of Alsace-Lorraine, born in 1828, learned glassmaking at the St. Louis factory, Lorraine. He migrated to the U.S. in 1846 and worked at Philadelphia. He became a partner in the Long Island Glass Works, 1848, built a glassworks at Plymouth, L.I., 1858, and another at Greenpoint, L.I., 1860. He retired to White Mills, Pa., but erected a small shop for the production of fine cut wares, which shop, according to the late Constance Houghton Frew, remained in operation to 1921. There is now a museum at this last glasshouse site in the old glassmaker's mansion. All the plants made fine lamps, bowls, stemwares, and rose and other paperweights. There was a New York salesroom which sold the product generally throughout the U.S. to the best stores and shops.

Doric: An order of architecture, named for the simplest of the classic Greek forms, developed in the province of Doris by the Dorians. One of the popular orders of the Greek revival of the early 19th century.

Doric fireplace: Greek-design open Franklin-type fireplace stove, invented by Oliver Evans, c. 1825.

Doric stove: A cast-iron space heater with four Doric columns at corners, solid-plate side walls and back, solid-plate doors with a grilled front. Made from around the late 1830s by Williams & Wheeler, Worcester, Mass.

dorin: A powder and patch box, the first "compact." Examples are known in gold, silver, plate, papier-mâché, pearl shell, et cetera.

dormand: Permanently fixed. **dormand beam:** The main beam of a structure. **dormand table:** Table with a fixed top. Also dormant.

dormond: Dressing for a bed. (Also dorsered.) Hung with fabric and cushioned.

dorrock: Coarse damask or diapered linen.

dorry; dorryle; dored: Seasoned, endorsed, especially in cookery.

D'Orsay: Long-spring, four-wheeled brougham.

D'Orsay work: Wall painting by J. Stanley D'Orsay that was a waterproof "fresco." His was a true fresco in that he colored the final or finish coat of plaster.

dos-à-dos: Back to back. A figure in early square dancing; a sporting carriage seating four, back to back.

dossil: Lint or scraped linen.

Dot: Pattern of pressed glass featuring closely spaced large circles or drops. *See also* Spotted Glass.

dot Meissen: Meaning seems to be late, quick "dot-decorated" and sprigged German porcelain.

double bead: Two-line beading or a double cock beading, often found banding drawer fronts of William & Mary and early Queen Anne style furniture.

double bow-back windsor: *See* Chairs, All Kinds.

double chest: Chest-on-chest.

double corner cupboard: Reference (somewhat confusing) is to any corner cupboard made with separate lower and upper sections.

double cruet or flask: The gemel or twin flask. Oil and vinegar bottles fused together with spouts or necks pointing in opposite directions to provide pouring from either without spilling from the other. Known in glass, stoneware, china, and horn.

double-dipped: Said of flashed glassware, with the inner layer being of one color and the outer of another, or clear.

doublé d'or: Gilt jewelry made from plates of copper with a layer of gold in the ratio of 11 to 1. Gold plate on the Sheffield principle. Tablewares are said to have been made of the same metal, and stamped DOUBLE D'OR.

Double Fan: Pattern of pressed glass imitative of cut glass, featuring horizontal, pointed, interlocking ovals in which fan-cut elements are posed in up-and-down position, forming a sort of wheat-sheaf effect.

double-gated table: Any gated-leg table having two outswinging legs on either side to support leaves. This is the rarest type of gate-leg aside from the multi-gated examples of the late 16th century with gates supporting four falling leaves.

double-geared bed: Reference is to the method of assembly and cording; a windlass principle was used to make them tight and stable.

Double Greek Key: Pattern of pressed glass displaying Wall of Troy bands with one of interlaced circles.

double-keyboard melodeon: Goodwin & Baldwin of New Haven, Conn., introduced a two-keyboard melodeon in 1852 and claimed it had all the qualities of a "grand organ." A two-manual melodeon, some with foot pedal super bass.

Double Loop: Pattern of pressed glass featuring upright loops over stippling, the lower loop not complete.

1, Dillwyn (Swansea) ware and marks. **2,** Dinanderie. **3,** Dinner Wagon. **4,** Disbrowe Chest. **5,** Document Box. **6,** Dolphin Vase (sometimes called Dolphin Pitcher). **7,** Directoire Furniture; sofa, love seat, triangular table (Rinconera), and chair. **8,** Don Pottery (Green & Barker) Ware and Marks. **9,** Double Spectacles. **10,** Desk Box. **11,** Eagle Chimney. **12,** Eagle Jar. **13,** Eagle Mustard Pot. **14,** Eagle-Top Table (antiques status not authenticated). (Nos. 1 and 8 from Virtue & Co., London. No. 7 from *New Geography of American Antiques.*)

127

double og (oog): A double ogival curve, or double S-curve, found in broad wood moldings and in profiles of glasswares, china, and metallic items.

double-pressed: Any manufacture of pressed glass, such as decanters, requiring two separate and distinct pressing operations. Further data will be found in early books on pressed-glass manufacture, the method not being mentioned by present-day writers.

double-S garland: A decorative S-form, entwined at lower bulge with a similar element in reverse; S's, facing and garlanded. The early Windsor, Conn., cabinetmaker, Rockwell, is said to have used this element carved on his lowboys and highboys. It is of the Queen Anne and early Georgian periods.

Double Spear: Pressed-glass pattern featuring a series of X's in circles, the outlines of which, between the circles as panels, form a spearlike element.

double spectacles: An innovation of the 1840s, a superior bifocal eyeglass having two lenses for each eye, hinged at nosepiece to provide positioning for use. Invented by J. Shaw, Hickley, O. [*Example pictured.*]

double stretcher: Stretchers in pairs, set rather close together, used sometimes for added strength and sometimes for decorative effect.

double-topped table: Two dished circular tops, the upper one raised above the lower on three turned spindles, the two mounted on a three-footed pedestal stand. Made from c. 1780. [*Example pictured.*]

double wall fireplace: Fireplace lined with soapstone or slabs of cast iron, with an air space between lining and walls. Outside air was introduced into this sealed section, heated, and conveyed in a duct through a grille to room above. Date is from late 18th century.

dough trough or tray: Deep slope-sided box for kneading, setting, and raising bread dough, often on a frame but sometimes separate, with canted turned legs and stretchers. These are really Gothic in origin.

Doughty prints: Hand-colored lithograph illustrations from the *Cabinet of Natural History & American Rural Sports,* published in parts, 1830–33, by J. & T. Doughty. There are 54 plates in the series; they are fine, and now scarce, American sporting prints.

Doulton & Watts: Potters of Lambeth, England, making pottery bottles, culinary and tablewares, inkwells, et cetera, of two-toned cane glaze and a very hard-bodied ware known as silicon, which was polished after firing and at times decorated in the *pâte-sur-pâte* technique.

d'outer: Pincers of brass or iron with rather heavy circular disks at jaw ends, used for squeezing out a candle flame. Also any extinguishing cone. Not a snuffer. [*Example pictured.*]

Dover wagon: See Conestoga Wagon.

dovetail: Method of joinery providing the most permanent of joints in woodwork; angular-shaped cuts and mortises which, fitted together, provide a juncture as strong as the solid plane of the timber.

The term derives from the shape of the mortise and tenon sections, which are fanlike, imitative of a dove's tail. [*Various types and styles pictured, with approximate dates of use.*]

dovetail hinge: Iron or brass cabinet hinge with leaves that flare from hinge pin outward in form of a fan or dove's tail. Sometimes called butterfly hinge. [*Example pictured.*]

dovetail key: Key blocks, set in mortised seating of same shape, extensively used to prevent glued boards from parting at the joint. Used in cabinetwork, shipbuilding, and house building to key planks, girts, and floor boards together.

Dow, Lorenzo: Itinerant powerful speaker and preacher, born in Coventry, Conn., October 16, 1777. Antiquarian interest today centers on woodcuts, silhouettes, oil portraits, pastels, carvings, et cetera, featuring this man, considered famous by his followers. [*One portrait pictured.*]

dowdruff: A huge bowl or dish, sometimes with handles and cover.

dowel: A wooden peg, fitting into bored holes in two elements of cabinet or joinery, to strengthen a juncture.

dower: A widow's portion of her husband's estate; the legal vested interest of a relict in the estate of her lord.

dower chest: There is no such thing, unless it be a widow's chest. Hundreds of painted Pennsylvania blanket chests, two-drawer chests, and others have been designated as dower chests by dealers, owners, and imitators of the first stupid designation of these chests as "dower." If they were chests made to hold a widow's portion after the death of her husband, then they are correctly named. But they were apparently made as "hope" chests, to hold the accumulation of nice things in advance of marriage. Therefore, they are dowry chests. *See also* Pennsylvania Chest.

Dowesborough glass: Albany-area glass made at Dowesborough, N.Y., from 1780s to 1820s. Snuff jars, pocket bottles, vials, and window glass. This was called the Albany Glass Works after 1792.

dowlas: Linen shirting, sometimes quite coarse.

down hearth warmer: Crescent-shaped open-ended box of pierced or punched sheet iron, copper, or brass, used as a plate warmer and placed flat on the hearth. [*Example pictured.*]

dowry chest: Correct name for all the chests now called dower.

drageoir: Bon-bon dish.

dragon claw: The probable source of all ball-and-claw and claw-and-ball footings. The device is Chinese, and in the original usage a five-clawed dragon's foot indicated imperial rank and four claws a class of subjective rank.

dragon's blood: Incense or resin derived from the fruit sap of certain Far Eastern shrubs. Used also in the arts.

draisiana; draisine: The pedestrian hobbyhorse, a two-wheeled fore-and-aft vehicle ridden straddle and propelled by a sweeping motion of the feet on the ground. Made in U.S. from 1810s, it is the ancestor of the bicycle.

drake foot: A furniture footing that is simply a large duck-foot form.

dram: See Scruple. "Dram" was a generic name for ardent spirits.

dram cup: A small, shallow, circular cup, sometimes with side handles, made to hold a tot of ardent spirits or a dose of medicine. Silver, Sheffield, horn, ceramic, glass, turned-wood, and mineral examples are of record.

drap d'argent: Silver cloth; drape of silver. **drap d'été:** Summer-weight fabric. **drap d'or:** Cloth of gold. **drap de laine:** Woolen dress fabric. The word *drap* preceding another is indicative of cloth or drapery.

Draper, Dorothy: The first human being to be photographed. Her visage, it is said, was the first taken by daguerreotype, 1839. Her brother, Dr. J. W. Draper of Boston, was the photographer. This is a reporting of data believed to be correct, yet it would seem almost impossible that Daguerre himself had not attempted portrait photography with success prior to this American achievement.

Draper buttons: Draper & Co. of North Attleboro, Mass., is said to have made "paperweight" and other fancy types of buttons. Few buttons will be dealt with in this volume as there are too many varieties and kinds. The student is referred to *The Complete Button Book*, by Albert & Kent.

draper shield: A shell-form-faced safety pin used in fastening drapery to rods.

Drapery: Pattern of pressed glass featuring shield-form valances with scalloped edges and pendant tassels. Originally called Lace. A variant has a change in the shield form and elimination of a small draped band.

drapery chain: Fancy link chains of brass, gold plate, silver, and other alloys, about 30 inches in length and used generally as a confining band for 19th-century window draperies.

draught chair: See Chairs, All Kinds.

drawer cloth: A decorative or protective rectangle of fabric used as a cover on a chest of drawers. Also called a chest diaper.

draw handle: Any drawer pull. Originally drawers were called draws. Another term for these objects, when made of brass, is "brasses."

drawing (and painting) instruction books: Listing of the hundred or more now of record is impractical here. See Bibliography.

drawing table: A 15th-, 16th-, and 17th-century extension table having what appears to be a triple-plank top with the center plank pulling out at each end from a central support, thus extending the table considerably beyond its normal length. Gothic in origin. The elements of these table tops are so arranged that wedges and falls bring the draw boards out to a common level with the plank top. Depressing the end boards lifts the top sufficiently so that the extensions can be pushed back into place. American examples are known but are rare, and these few are either New England, New York, or Pennsylvania. Undoubtedly many were used in all the colonies having early 17th-century settlement. Some examples of the Tudor era have immense turned balls on the legs, generally carved, and heavy flat stretchers. Not a table used for drawing or by artists. [*Example pictured.*]

drawn butter: Not browned or black butter, but stewed butter, the recipe for which is as follows: To 1 pound of butter add, by rubbing, 1 tablespoon of flour and ½ tablespoonful of salt. Stir into ½ pint of boiling water. Simmer for 15 minutes, stirring constantly.

drawn work: Fancywork on textiles achieved by "unweaving"; by drawing threads from warp and woof, crossing, and tying.

drawt room: Drawing room; withdrawing room; private room.

dreadnaught: The woven "bearskin" of the 18th century, a long-pile, heavy woolen cloth for greatcoats.

dredger: (1) A shaker-topped box for dusting (dredging) any foodstuffs with flour, spices, salt, et cetera. (2) A shallow pan for this same sort of culinary activity.

dredge salt: Salt mixed with pepper and other spices or treated for additional flavoring, as smoking, cloving, adding onion juice, et cetera. Also fine salt for use in a shaker.

drenching horn: A funnel or flaring tube for administering medicine to animals.

drepee: A rich dish of small game birds, highly spiced, fried in onions and almonds.

Drepperd guns: Early American (Federal) rifles, originally flintlocks, but many converted to cap-firing, made by John Michael Drepperd, Andrew, Henry, George, John, William, and five others, who operated a cartel at Lancaster, Pa., beginning 1780 and continuing to 1845, when two apprentices, Henry Leman and Henry Gibbs, separately, acquired the business, boring engines, lock molds, et cetera. This combine also made shotguns, goose guns, bellmouthed and military pistols, military, hunting, and frontiersmen's rifles. Among their customers were Daniel Boone and David Crockett. They had agents at Greenup, Louisville, and Lexington, Ky., Vincennes, Ind., St. Louis, Mo., and other points. Many of the arms survive. A. M. Carey, Esq., is preparing a monograph on this gunmaking cartel, all members of which signed their guns in the same way "DREPPERD LANCASTER." One member made all the gunlocks. Variants in spelling, however, occur as Derbert, Trebert, Dreppard. Some few rifles marked HENRY DREPPERD are known. This member, it is claimed, insisted that, being named for the No. 1 gunsmith of Lancaster, William Henry, he should include that name with his family name on his pieces.

Dresden: See Meissen.

Dresden catgut: Fancywork on muslin or gauze; a form of fine drawn work.

dresser: (1) Board to hold the plate and china to dress a dining table. (2) Dressing table.

dresser bidet: Rare item of luxury cabinet furniture made for the fair sex in 18th and early 19th centuries. A deep top lifts up to reveal a folding mirror and nests for powder, perfume flasks, rouge box, et cetera. Beneath there is a compartment behind doors holding basin and ewer. Under this is a cased bidet, sliding forward on castered legs.

dressing box: (1) Small slope-fall-fronted desk box compartmented for cosmetics, with mirror and other accessories. These date from 17th century and are known in styles from Tudor to Sheraton. (2) Chamber tables with box tops. (3) Small portable vanity cases.

dressing bureau: Chest of three or more drawers on four legs, providing knee room beneath, surmounted by recessed cabinet of small drawers and frequently with a mirror.

dressing glass: Vanity or shaving mirror mounted between posts for tilting, placed over a base having drawers.

dressing table: What we call a lowboy was originally given this name in the 18th century.

dressoir: A sideboard.

Drew bellows: Most likely the standard hearth bellows made by John Drew, or Drew & Hixon, Boston, in early 19th century. Marked examples are of painted, japanned, and decorated wood with leather collapsing sides.

drill: Twilled linen.

drilling: A saucer or small dish was so called in the 17th century.

drinkel: A dessert doily; a table towel, serviette, or napkin. These were long narrow guest towels used at table.

Drinker, John: One of the early cabinetmakers of Penn's colony, working at Philadelphia from c. 1699. Cabinetmakers from Sweden were at work in this region at least sixty years prior to Drinker.

drinking table: Semicircular horseshoe-form table, sometimes with trap doors on top giving access to wine coolers beneath, and other gadgets, including netting to hold empty bottles. Drinkers sat around periphery of table, drawn up near a fireplace for winter festivities or near an open window in summer. Also a serving table for wines and liquors.

Drinking Washington: Lithograph by N. Currier depicting Washington, posed with glass in hand and bottles on table, drinking farewell to his generals. First issued in 1848, reissued in 1876 with the wineglass erased and the bottles missing, showing Washington with hands on coat lapels. Undoubtedly this issue was a sop to the anti-liquor crowd, even then calling for prohibition and its attendant evils, not the least of which was the insincerity of advocates who were avoiding liquor as such but consuming bad whiskey spiked with herbs as a "tonic." Most of the ranters against strong drink were half tight on their lecture platforms.

drinks, colonial: While a few of the unique or unusual beverages favored by our ancestors are given separate listings in this volume, drinks in general are here defined and explained. **beverige:** Cider, water, and rum. **black strap:** Molasses and rum. **canary:** Fortified light wine from Canary Islands. **ebulum:** Elder and juniper-berry juice. **flip:** Ale, warmed, with lemon peel and spices, brandy, beaten

eggs, and other oddments, poured from one vessel to another until creamed, then reheated with loggerhead. **negus:** Light wine and water punch. **punch:** Rum, brandy, water, sugar, and fruit juices. **rumbullion:** Original name for rum. **sack:** Any variety of sherry. **sack-posset:** An egg, milk, and sherry custard with spice, served hot, generally at weddings; a sort of rich syllabub. **spruce, birch, persimmon, sassafras & root beer:** The botanicals brewed in a beer achieved from pumpkin and fruit peels, molasses, rye crusts, et cetera. **toddy:** Hot rum and water with any flavor or spice.

Drinkwater delft: 18th-century delft-type pottery made at the Pot House Lane works of George Drinkwater, Liverpool, England. Huge chargers and pitchers were among the objects made.

drip stick: Candlestick with a broad, thin flat or dished circular disk placed between base and socket around the shaft. Much in vogue on sticks of the 17th and early 18th centuries.

driving the nail: A marksmanship achievement with the Conestoga rifle. Nails, partially set in pine board, were driven in by hitting them on the head with the rifle ball from 40 paces.

drollery: A puppet show.

drop: Liquid measure—1/16th of an ounce.

drop blade: Table knife with blade offset below the horizontal to provide easier cutting.

drop crystal: Pendants of cut crystal in various prismatic and rectangular shapes, used in groups, clusters, and other forms as decoration for lamps, lighting fixtures, candelabra, candlesticks, et cetera. Modern nomenclature for the forms include Coffin, Spear, Leaf, Pear, Chain, and so on.

drop-leaf dumbwaiter: A tiered table on a central shaft with circular tops, the sides of which are made in sections to drop when piece is not in use or a particular section is not required.

drops: Applied decoration, generally made from split turnings, of egg, pear, pineapple, thistle, turtle-back, acorn, vase form, and other shapes, and frequently dyed or stained to contrast with the surface to which they were applied. One Pieter Koeck, architect and painter, is credited with the invention of this form of furniture and interior décor.

drowsen light: A tallow dip or tallow candle.

drug: A dolly, or wheeled or castered platform.

drugget: Any heavy fabric used as a bed-cover. Term finally was applied to cheap rugs.

druid-head pitcher: Rockingham-type glazed figural pitcher made by Bennett Brothers, Birmingham, Pa., c. 1845. The face is probably a variant of the Bellarmino caricature appearing on many Dutch jugs of the 17th century.

drum: The drum shape—a deep or shallow circular frame or framing for a tightly drawn skin or bladder over the end or ends—was popular as a form for many objects of furniture and decoration and even utilitarian items. Certain of these are here listed. **drum bookstand:** Circular stand with firm base and three or more shelves for insertion of books, each section broken with a cupboard angled to provide parallel book arrangement within the circle. Generally with four cupboards and four book recesses on each shelf. **drum cue rack:** Low drum table with top bored with a series of holes to hold cue butts. From the center rises a column supporting a serrated wheel to hold the cue tips. Drawers in the table valance hold billiard balls. **drum desk:** Any large drum table with rotating top, having one or more drawers fitted with appurtenances of writing. **drum teapot:** Straight-sided cylindrical form with spout springing from near bottom, usually of silver, ceramic, or Sheffield plate, but also made in pewter. **drum toilet:** Drum-shaped table fitted as a toilet stand.

drumhead profile: Three-dimensional colored effigies displaying a distorted human face. Fashioned from the eardrum of the whale.

drum major: A pinball machine of the 1880s. A coiled chute carried the balls onto a plane with numbered pockets.

Drummond candle lamp: A candlestick having a metal tube simulating a candle which served as an oil or fat reservoir, and having a coiled wick on a reel feeding through the semi-solid fuel. The same stick could be used to mold candles from soft tallow. This all-metal gadget was one of the many patented "cheap" lighting devices sold from the 1840s.

drum vat; drume fatt: Drum-shaped barrels used as goods containers from 17th century. Some were frameworks of heavy boughs, bent to shape while green. These were used, stuffed with straw, as shipping containers for glass and pottery.

drunkard's chair: Wide-seated chairs, also called lovers' chairs and love seats. Some are two-chair width. Known in all period styles of 1680s–1820s, in wing and armchair types. *See also* Chairs, All Kinds. Included here primarily because this is actually a settee.

drunkwort: Tobacco.

dry bath: A wooden tub in which hot ashes, sand, and pebbles were placed and in which bather sat to induce perspiration.

dry point: An artist's method of line engraving on copper, using a needle rather than a graver, and working freehand. The burr, or ridge, of copper thrown up by the needle holds the ink, as does the shallow engraved line.

dry sink (dry zinc bench): A kitchen cupboard with a deep well, often metal-lined, in which dishes were washed in a dishpan. Millions made from 1820s to 1880s. Called "dry" because such sinks were not truly sinks and not connected to either pump or some other water supply or to a drain. These kitchen items have been overemphasized in late years and purchased at fantastic prices for use in dining rooms and living rooms. However, they are not primitives; the majority are factory-produced items.

D-sided: Said of tables having ovate rounded sides or ends, similar in shape to the letter D.

dual-purpose furniture: Any item of furniture made specifically to serve two or more purposes. Contrary to the general belief that gadget furniture began with Sheraton, dual-purpose items date from the 17th century and probably originated in the Gothic era. The settle table, hutch table, and chair table of the 17th century are dual-purpose pieces; the library step chair, desk drawer chests, chair-bed, divan-bed, and many other pieces were made from the Queen Anne period.

dual-spouted: Two-spouted, generally for pouring at the same time, as with vessels designed for hot milk and coffee, wine and seltzer. *See* Two-Spout Coffeepot.

dubbin pin: Pin used in fixing lace on lace pillows.

Dubble coverlets: Bed coverlets woven by Henry Dubble of Lancaster, O., working from 1820s.

DuBois ware: Factory-made silver by Philo DuBois, Buffalo, N.Y., from 1850s.

Duche pottery: Redware and stoneware made by Antoine Duche, Philadelphia, from 1692. He had four sons, all of whom were stoneware potters. His son Andrew, removed to Oglethorpe's colony of Georgia, settled at Savannah and discovered the clay he shipped to England, where it was used in the making of Bow china. Son James had a pottery at Charlestown, Mass.

duchesse: Two- or three-part ensemble of armchair, upholstered bench, and end-piece, used separately as two or three seats or together as a chaise longue.

duck boxes: Crystal and jade boxes of duck form, originally an import from China. Imitations made of porcelain and pottery in Europe from mid-18th century. Finally they were imitated in pressed glass by the Vallerysthal Works, Lorraine, France, and soon thereafter in American-made pressed glass. Many other fowl served as models for these boxes, perhaps the most generally known being the hen-on-nest.

duckfoot: Three-toed webbed footing found carved on Dutch and Queen Anne furniture.

duckfoot pistol: A pistol with four barrels, set at angles.

duck lighter: A telescopic brass tube ending in a U-form prong in which is balanced a brass duck-form container with a lid on the head. The single example examined had a blown-glass handle with air-bubble decoration. Said to have been designed c. 1780s as a candle lighter, the duck head being fitted with a wick, the body serving as a fuel reservoir. This is probably correct, as the duck is so weighted as to remain in a horizontal position, swinging within its gimbals. [*Example pictured.*]

dudgeon: Burl wood of the box tree or its roots. A rare burl.

dudgeon wood: Boxwood, walnut burl, and other unique hardwoods.

doodlesack: The bagpipe, sometimes called a musical instrument.

Dudson ware: Hanley pottery made by William Dudson, early 19th century, and by James Dudson from 1835 to 1882. Made the Fern, Argyle, Barley, Vine, Pineapple, and Wheatsheaf pattern jugs, mosaic wares, ornamented china tablewares and services, white and colored stonewares. DUDSON is the mark on such wares.

Dudy (Dudij) stoves: *See* Pillar Stove.

dueling box: A box of fine cabinetwork made specifically to hold a pair of pistols, bullet mold, screw, powder flask, and other fittings.

duette: A low-backed bench or settee for two people, made in every age from Tudor-Gothic era to Hepplewhite and Sheraton. [*Hepplewhite example pictured.*]

DuFrène ornaments: Reference must be to the plaster-of-Paris ornaments manufactured by E. DuFrène, Philadelphia, from 1840s. He also made portrait busts, life masks, fountains, scagliola or imitation marble, and cheap casts.

Dugdale grate: Probably any iron grate manufactured at the Thomas Dugdale foundry, Trenton, N.J., from 1830s.

duive-kater: Dutch term for the *deux fois quatre* of France, a Twelfth-night delicacy consisting of two square sweet cakes baked together.

dulciana: *See* Celestina.

dulcimer: A stringed instrument played with a pair of soft-nosed hammers. Introduced to America by French Huguenots. A lap instrument of 18th century, made to 19th, and favored by frontier peoples, but in the form of a banjolike instrument that was strummed instead of hammered. Sometimes spelled dulcimore.

Dulty tinware: Made at Zanesville, O., from 1830s by tinsmiths J. & M. Dulty, who were also coppersmiths. Practically every type and kind of object was made.

dum: Room fuzz; carpet lint; bed lint.

dumb Betty: Woodenware. A small tub or cooler (keeler). Same term is noted applied to a dumbwaiter table.

dumbwaiter: The lazy Susan, a tripod-footed table with tall vase-form column on which two or more circular trays are made to revolve. The trays are graduated in size, the largest being at lowest level. Best examples have dish-edged trays. **dumbwaiter table:** A round table with a single large circular tray in center, slightly elevated and turning easily from a center pivot; a lazy-Susan table.

Dummer lamps: Trade name derived from the retailers who sold great quantities of lamps made by the Jersey Glass Co. Store was in New York City, mid-19th century.

dummy door; dummy drawer: *See* Blind Door.

Du Moulin mirrors: Fine gilded mirrors in the French Antique style made by a French manufacturer of this name who located at Philadelphia c. 1850.

Duncan: Pattern of pressed glass of Gothic influence, featuring petaled panels of clear glass, sharply defined, and sometimes engraved with vine or fruit-and-flower motifs.

Duncan Block: Pattern of pressed glass featuring accented beveled blocks of rectangular and distorted diamond shapes arranged as a draped border.

Duncan furniture: Wardrobes, cribs, tables, desks, bookcases, and other case

and repose furniture made in considerable quantities by over 75 workmen of the M. L. Duncan & Brother furniture factory, Cincinnati, from 1840s. In Empire, late Directoire, and French Antique styles.

Duncan glass: Any glass produced by factories owned or controlled by the Duncans, as Duncan & Miller, George Duncan, Duncan & Sons, Duncan & Heisey, et cetera. Mid- to late 19th century, Pittsburgh area. Made flint, pressed, novelties, polka-dotted, and other specialties.

Duncan Phyfe style: A misnomer, anywhere, any time; there is no such thing. Duncan Phyfe was a much-publicized good cabinetmaker of New York City who had a furniture factory and produced a great quantity of excellent furniture, especially tables, chairs, and sofas, in the Directoire style. Other good American cabinetmakers of Boston, New York, Philadelphia, Baltimore, and Annapolis, not to mention Pittsburgh, were making precisely the same style of furniture in the same meticulous manner. Since Phyfe was a master maker and factory owner, he insisted on high-grade work from his employees. But the "style" he used is to be found in the basic designs of the cabinetmakers' price books of his day, from the early 1800s to 1830. [*Examples pictured.*]

dune: A hill; a down.

Dunkirk: Pattern of cut glass achieving conventional rose form by the imposition of a four-foil on another, with cross-laddered cutting, stars, fans, and other elements. It is a quite late 19th-century pattern and is not "colonial," as some people call it.

dupla: A clock bell.

duppy bat: A butterfly.

Duprez glass cameos: Molded glass bust portraits in profile made by Duprez of Paris from c. 1820s.

Durell ware: Pottery made at New York City from 1750s by Jonathan Durell. He advertised colored and striped wares in a wide range of items and in 1773 advertised that he made "Philadelphia"-style earthenwares. Also colored slipware made by Philip Durell, New Jersey, from 1780s, at or near Elizabeth. He made sgraffito wares in the Staffordshire tradition which are frequently miscalled "Pennsylvania" wares and attributed to German potters.

Durkee yeast: Baking powder.

Du Simitière portraits: Pierre Eugene du Simitière, Swiss artist, did a series of portraits of illustrious Americans which were published in France, England, and Germany. He worked here in the 18th century and died at Philadelphia in 1784.

dust-boarded: Completely enclosed or boarded-up orifices in which drawers are placed. A mark of good cabinetmaking.

dust pan: Originally a volder or flat scoop to gather debris from a dining table with aid of spatula or brush. Finally extended to similar voiding on the floor. [*Example pictured.*]

Dutch beech: The white poplar. Much used in the Netherlands as the carcass of cabinetware destined to be veneered. Usage seems to date from early 17th century.

Dutch chocolate pot: Pear-shaped pot

1, Dovetail, standard, solid. 2, Dovetail, split, or wedge; sometimes called "Bermuda." 3, Drinking Table. 4, Dutch Chocolate Pot. 5, Dutch Cupboard, meaning Pennsylvania Dutch, general design from Hoarkill and Schuylkill valleys and so genuinely "Dutch." 6, Day Bed. 7, Dutch Chest on Stand. 8, 9, 10, 11, and 12, Duncan Phyfe's furniture in Directoire style, with the lyre motifs he used so often in chair backs and table standards. 13, Eagle and Shield Back Chair. 14, Effigy Sign ("Golden Californian"). 15, Egg Cooker. 16, Egg Work (urn made from a goose egg). 17, Egyptian Jar. 18, Egg Joint Hinge. 19, Electric Lighter. 20, Elliot Repeater, a Pepper Box. (No. 6 from *Furniture of Our Forefathers.* No. 10 from *New Geography of American Antiques.*)

133

with side handle and whipper hole in center of top; generally of brass or copper. Used exclusively in making the beverage chocolate, which was whipped as it cooked and up to time of service. [*Example pictured.*]

Dutch cupboard: Two-part kitchen cupboard with drawers and doors below and glazed doors in top section, which is set back or made shallower than bottom section. Known in Hudson Valley, Connecticut Valley, and the Hoarkill, Delaware, Schuylkill, and Conestoga valleys of Pennsylvania. Some have unbelievably intricate cut and carved moldings and applied decoration; others are quite plain. Made in painted pine, poplar, cherry, walnut, and other woods. Date is from late 17th century to mid-19th. [*Example pictured.*]

Dutch flowered papers: Silver-, tin-, and brass-foil papers, and papers in glazed colors, embossed in an all-over pattern with metal dies. Product of the Netherlands from 17th century, and used as dominos to paste on plastered walls, as book papers, and as box coverings.

Dutch foot: Any terminal of a cabriole leg, now called Queen Anne and Georgian. These include slipper foot, drake foot, grooved foot, and club foot. Some experts suspect "club foot" derives from the similarity of the foot to the head of a golf club, the all-wood club used in the original Dutch game of "gowff." [*See illustrations of furniture footings.*]

Dutch gold: Copper, brass, and bronze leaf, used extensively in cheap gilding instead of true gold leaf, and in making Dutch flowered papers. **Dutch gilding:** Leafwork with this imitation gold leaf, originally made in the Netherlands.

Dutch Lowestoft: Chinese export porcelain made to order for the Dutch market. Dutch figures, views, and ships were painted on the ware in China.

Dutch oven: (1) The true Dutch oven, a heavy iron pot with three or four stubby feet and iron lid, used in roasting and for baking a huge loaf or cake of bread. (2) Open-faced tin or sheet-iron box with platform, sometimes fitted with a spit, for baking before an open fire.

Dutch porcelain: The Dutch had so profitable an import trade in Chinese porcelains that they made no genuine effort to duplicate the wares until the discovery of the secret at Meissen. They were content with their large share of the import business of wares they could bring to market at lower cost than any home manufacture. The only Dutch imitation of Chinese wares was their delft, to the 1760s. In that decade the Weesp pottery made porcelains, as did the Loosdrecht potteries in 1771, the works at Den Haag, 1775, Eterbeck, 1776, and Amstel and Montplaisir, 1784.

Dutch slipware: Slipware was made in the Netherlands some years prior to 1560. In 1582 a Dutch potter settled at Sandwich, England, began making slipware, and so founded the Staffordshire potting industry. The fleur-de-lis and pomegranate forms appear on early Dutch wares, as do effigies of royalty and gentry, the human figure in general, and animalistic forms. Dates of making in England and the Netherlands are from mid- to late 16th

century down to 1780s. This date, according to Solon, is in error; he claims slipwares were made in the old style at Buckley to late 19th century. Tygs and other objects in slip-decorated redware, made in the 1880s, might well be attributed to the 17th or 18th century if chipped and discolored in use. This same type of ware was made extensively by small potters in Pennsylvania, New York, New England, Maryland, Virginia, Ohio, and Indiana. The Dutch-type slipwares were also made in Switzerland. Thus Pennsylvania was fortunate in having the Dutch tradition of slipware impressed direct by Dutch colonists, by Staffordshire potters, and by Swiss potters.

Dutch standing chest: A six-boarded chest on a stand with heavy turned legs and scalloped skirting, sometimes having two drawers set side by side. Date is from 1650 to c. 1730. [*Example pictured.*]

Dutch stove; Norse stove: The five-, six-, and ten-plate stoves of colonial America, misnamed "German" by such one-time experts as the late H. C. Mercer, who, in his essay on these stoves, pictures stoves found and made in Norway, Sweden, and Denmark before any were made in Germany, and calls them German. These stoves are Scandinavian, and were made in Pennsylvania mostly by English, Welsh, and Cornish ironmasters for the immigrant German market. These people were advised by their own agents at the outset of immigration to "buy a Dutch stove in the Low Countries and bring it along to Pennsylvania." The Germanic script on the Pennsylvania stoves is atrocious; no self-respecting German would write it as it is composed, misspelled, and abbreviated. And it is in Latin characters, not the bastard Gothic letters of Germany. Unfortunately the only book on the subject is the biased and inadequate *Bible in Iron*, by Mercer. But there is another book on the ironmasters of Pennsylvania, *Forges & Furnaces of Pennsylvania*, published by the Pennsylvania Society of Colonial Dames, 1914. To assume, however, that these stoves of Dutch, Norse, and even of French origin (through Belgium) are found only in Pennsylvania is an error. Examples in northern New England may be from Canadian foundries in the Three Rivers area; others were used in New York and New England. It is also asserted that Maryland and Virginia foundries produced these stoves. The only German founders in Pennsylvania were Huber and his successor, Stiegel; and Stiegel was controlled by Charles and Alexander Stedman. Some examples of Dutch stoves were probably introduced by Flemish, French, and Swedish colonists. One, the Torqueshaff, is a single plate of decorative quality, set in the back of a fireplace to provide a radiant-heating element in the adjoining room. These were at times enclosed in closets. Some stoves were cast in the Netherlands and used in New England before 1700. Five- and six-plate-type stoves were made in New England of soapstone slabs. [*Examples pictured.*]

Dutch style: By this general term reference is made to Flemish, William & Mary, and Queen Anne styles of furniture, all of which were known in the Dutch colony of New Amsterdam and in the Dutch-settled sections of the Delaware which became Pennsylvania, before William & Mary and the cabriole-legged Queen Anne styles were popular in England.

Dutch waters: Flavored aromatic waters, such as cinnamon, nutmeg, lemon, orange, and other fruit-juiced waters, created by Dutch chemists for use with the "Guiniver, Geneva, or Hollands" spirits known to us as gin.

Duval glass: Tablewares, bottles, flasks, et cetera, made at the Duval Works, Wellsburg, Va., 1813-28.

DuVivier, Fidellé: This man is famed for his work as a china decorator at the Derby and Newhall porcelain works and as a sculptor of forms, 18th century.

Duyckinck (properly Duijkinck), Gerardus: Artist and artisan of New York, who advertised japanned and floweredlooking glasses, pictures painted, and other wares and services, 1735.

Duyckink glass: Glass made at the New York glasshouse of this family c. 1645-70. Everett Duyckink, Duycking, or Duijkink was the operator.

dwarf bookcase: Not a miniature case but a case of shelves without doors. Term was current c. 1810-60.

dwarf candlestick: Low stubby stick, often of silver but known in brass, copper, iron, and Sheffield plate.

dwarf table: A table with incurvate legs ending on a heavy platform base. Directoire-Regency styling of the heavy kind.

dwelling room: The keeping room, the great room, the main hall; often a cooking, dining, sitting, and sleeping room combined. When privacy was desired, the "withdrawing" room was used.

Dwight, Stephen: Furniture maker and carver of New York, who worked from c. 1756. He was also a painter of historic subjects and portraits, kept a drawing school, and did miniatures.

Dwight of Fulham: John Dwight, the early Fulham, England, potter who, c. 1671, is credited with the discovery of true porcelain, which he did not pursue in terms of production. He is also one of the first stoneware potters to make figures, figurines, and statuary of stoneware. His work stands among the classic antiques of English pottery.

dyett: The daily fare; boarding.

dynasties, Chinese: Since these are now considered essential antiquarian data, the following list, compiled for us in 1942 by Albert Duveen, is given in full: Patriarchal Era, 3000-2205 B.C. Hsia Dynasty, 2205-1766 B.C. Shang Dynasty, 1766-1122 B.C. Chou Dynasty, 1122-255 B.C. Ch'in Dynasty, 255-206 B.C. Han Dynasty, 206 B.C.-A.D. 280. San Tai, or three states (Wei, Shu Han, and Wu), A.D. 220-280. Lu-chao, or six dynasties: Chin, 265-420; Sung, 420-479; Ch'i, 479-502; Liang, 502-557; Ch'en, 557-589. (During part of this era, the following were also in power: Northern Wei, 386-535; Eastern Wei, 534-543; Western Wei, 535-557; Northern Ch'i, 550-589; Northern Chou, 557-589.) Sui, 589-618. T'ang, 618-907. H'sia Wu Tai (the five small dynasties), 908-959. Hou Liang, 908-923. Hou Tang, 923-936. Hou Tsin, 936-946. Hou Han, 947-950. Hou Chou, 951-959. Sung, 960-1279. Yüan, 1280-1367. Ming, 1368-1643. T'a Ch'ing, 1644-1912. This last dynasty was divided into the following periods: K'ang Hsi, 1622-1722; Yung Ch'eng, 1723-35; Ch'ien Lung, 1736-95; Chia Ch'ing, 1796-1820; Tao Kuang, 1821-50; Hsien Fêng, 1851-61; T'ung Chih, 1862-74; Kuang Hsu, 1875-1908; Hsuan T'ung, 1909-12.

Dyott glass: Any of the wares, including flasks, vials, medicine bottles, lamps, vases, tableware, et cetera, made at the Dyottville Glassworks of T. W. Dyott, who rose from bootblack to pharmacist and maker and vendor of patent medicines; achieved affluence, acquired the Kensington Glass Works, and finally crashed in a mad financial muddle. Extensive notices of this works appear in McKearin's *American Glass.*

Dyott lamps: Street lamps with cast-iron standards, made by Dyott & Co., Philadelphia, from 1870s or earlier. Not to be confused with Dyott or Dyottville glass.

d'ypre: Diaper, as originally spelled.

E

eagle & arms sugar: Pressed-glass covered sugar bowl with a footing of four eagles on shields, cannon between the eagles, and a mortar-shell finial on cover. Spanish-American War souvenir glass, c. 1898-1900.

eagle & shield back: A type of chair back and splat featuring a spread-eagle chair rail, the eagle perched on a shield that is the splat. Originally made c. 1790s in England, for the American market. [*Example pictured.*]

eagle & star: A motif of applied and inlaid decoration, generally American, and often, if the work is original, offering a clue to age in the number of stars depicted.

eagle can opener: Bayonet operated by a lever to punch a series of cuts in the top of a food can. An eagle is cast on the bayonet frame. Date is c. 1870s.

eagle chimney: Any lamp chimney etched, pressed, or cut with an eagle form of decoration. [*Example pictured.*] **eagle globe:** A similarly engraved or marked object used for gas or fluid lamp or fixture. Some of the best known were cut through frosted-surfaced globes for the Centennial Exposition.

eagle claw: A gig or fish spear composed

of seven or more fishhooks arranged in a circle. The claw grasped a fish, eel, frog, muskrat, or small waterfowl. Hardly a sporting device.

eagle console: True console table with brackets in form of eagle wings.

eagle decanter: Mold-blown eagle-form decanter with wings close to body, having a metal (sometimes silver) head and neck.

eagle desk: An early or mid-19th-century school desk with wood top and an iron frame with an eagle cast in the pattern.

eagle foot: Another name for claw and ball and crow foot.

eagle-foot shell-on-knee: The description used in 1750 for what we call the Georgian shell-faced, claw-and-ball-footed cabriole leg.

eagle gas stove: An early gas cookstove with embellishment of cast-iron eagles. We suspect a date of c. 1870 for this item.

Eagle Glass: Name of the factory at Port Elizabeth, N.J., established 1817 and still operating in 1880s. Principal products were bottles and window glass.

eagle-head foot: Confusingly correct term for a carved or brass furniture foot terminating in an eagle head, the neck and wing being the leg and bracket. An Empire-style element. [*Example pictured.*]

eagle head rail: Any top, whether of chair, bench, clock, et cetera, that is spread-eagle in form.

eagle jar: Milk-glass jars of large size, ovoid, and embellished with hand-painted and -gilded eagle and flags. Made as druggists' display jars from 1850s by Millville Glass Works of South Jersey. [*Example pictured.*]

eagle mustard: Pressed-milk-glass mustard pot, produced commercially as a container c. 1890s. The eagle is stylized and almost modernistic in form, the head forming the jar cover. [*Example pictured.*]

eaglestone: The aëtites, a natural flinty crustation containing a nucleus in the form of a pebble rolling loose within the accretion. The superstition once was that these were found only in eagles' nests.

eagle sucket: Rockingham syrup pot displaying eagles in low relief.

eagle tankard: Properly, an eagle-billeted or -thumbpieced tankard. Made from c. 1660s.

eagle-top table: A curiosity not yet authenticated but, if original, possibly unique. Pedestal-type Directoire-style table with top in eagle-and-shield form and falling leaves in wing form. A drawer of conventional type is under the shield end. [*Example pictured in a drawing of the one known example.*]

eared back: The juncture of top rail and stiles of a chair, flared outward, is called an eared back or eared joint, as opposed to rounded.

Earl & Buckingham furniture: Important from its locale or production, Pittsburgh, where this partnership, formed about 1788, resulted in making the first Hepplewhite-style furniture west of the Alleghenies.

Earl of Coventry: A pattern, sometimes called Blind Earl, because it is in low relief and can be felt with the fingers. It was

so enjoyed as a design by the blind Earl of Coventry. The pattern was produced before this Earl was stricken. It is noted on Worcester, Chelsea, and Bow china as a design of full-blown roses, buds, and leafy stems.

Early carpets: Reference is to the weaver, R. W. Early of New Bedford, Mass., who made rag and fancy carpets from 1850s.

early nutmeg: A variety of peach popular in 18th century.

Earps mirror: Any mirror made by Earps & Co. of Philadelphia from 1830s or 1840s. Tabernacle types and gilded examples, many of Baroque or French Antique revival style.

earth flax: Asbestos, also called rock alum, salamander hair, and other names. Chief colonial use was in making everlasting lamp wicks.

earthstar: A fungus, a geaster, which has leaflike starry sections that are formed by the splitting and peeling of its sensitive outer membrane.

earwhistle: Ear trumpet.

Easter cross: Wood crosses covered with plaster of Paris, decorated with wax and paper flowers, and used as an Easter ornament. Often displayed under a glass bell.

Easterling: A tribe of metalworkers of eastern Europe who excelled in smelting and tempering. A group of them were invited to England to assist in the refining of silver, and the quality of metal they achieved was known as Easterling silver. This finally was contracted to "sterling silver" and was the standard established by law for the coin of the realm. Hence the pound sterling and the sterling mark.

East India fabrics: Innumerable names were given to East India fabrics by importers and their customers, all probably being imitative of the true names. See Fabrics of India.

East India mirrors: Classic Hepplewhite- and Adam-type toilet mirrors on multi-drawered stands, the latter lacquered and sometimes decorated in gold. Made in or near Eastern treaty ports for the traders having factories (offices and warehouses, not production plants). These seem to date from 1780s but were sold in many American cities after 1800s.

Eastlake: Jacobean and Gothic styling wedded in a woeful misalliance to French Antique, in an effort to escape the total French Antique influence. This finally developed into Eastlake's own admitted "good taste," which, in the opinion of many, was wholly bad. He wrote *Hints of Household Taste* in 1866 and *History of Revival of Gothic Furniture* in 1872. The Mott Iron Works of New York City made an Eastlake-design cast-iron sink in 1875. This style of furniture, made in the U.S., seems to date mostly from 1880s to 1900s. [*Some examples pictured.*]

East Liverpool ware: Mottled tortoiseshell glazed wares from the East Liverpool, O., potteries, 1839–70s, and sometimes called East Liverpool Rockingham. Some 20 potteries are said to have made this ware. It is imitative of the Swinton pottery glaze which was called Rockingham because the works were on the estate of the Marquis of that name.

1, Carved Wainscot Chair. 2, Pennsylvania Turned Chair. 3, Harvard Chair. 4, Captain's Windsor. 5, Ferat. 6, Felt-Center Table. 7, Felt Carpet. 8, Fate Lady. 9, Fairy Lamp. 10, Excelsior Tiehold. 11, Embroidery Frame. 12, Enameled Handles (3). 12A, Conjuror. 13, Evaporators (2). 14, E Pluribus Unum Drawer Pull. 15, Elers Ware (3 pieces). 16, Eight-Shaft Coverlet Pattern. 17, Empire-Style Furniture; chairs, stands, stools, tables, bureau, and beds. [12A also called an Etna.] (No. 15 from Virtue & Co., London.)

easy reclining chair: *See* Chairs, All Kinds.

ébéniste: French term for a master cabinetmaker who could work in ebony, hence *ébéniste*, or ebony worker.

ebonized furniture: Cheap mass-produced whitewood furniture painted with a thick black gloss. Some have groove carving lined with bronze gilding. Date is from 1870s.

ebony: A hard fine-grained wood of the Orient, first brought to Europe by Dutch traders in 1600s, but known to Greeks and Romans. Black, violet, green, brown, yellow, and pink ebony woods are known. It is an error to consider all ebony as black.

ebony fingers: Human hands stained dark brown by hulling walnuts.

ecce homo: Latin for "Behold the man."

ecclesiastical furniture: Lecterns, pulpits, baptisteries, fonts, altars, ambos, pews, benches, stalls, chairs, thrones, and the appurtenances of all services of all churches and creeds fall within this general category. Some early American churches had settle benches, some had Windsor benches, some had fancy chairs and settees. Many had silver communion flagons, chal'ces, and patens, and those which did not owned pewter. The same is true of candlesticks and lighting fixtures. After the mid-19th century nearly all church furniture was either Gothic or classic. The art of church decoration and its study is often termed ecclesiology.

echinus: Term now often applied to egg-and-dart molding, but original meaning was the molding, not egg-and-dart, used in the Doric order. Egg-and-dart is from the Ionic and ịs derived from the Latin *echinus*, for hedgehog. The sea urchin is also called echinus, and its shell form is reproduced in a named pattern of Irish Belleek ware.

Eck-Durand: Bronze founders of Paris, who exhibited at the New York Crystal Palace and exported their artwares to the U.S. in some quantities.

Eckstein glass: Looking-glass plates imported by Eckstein & Son of Philadelphia from immediately after the Revolution to early 19th century.

écran: A screen.

écran à éventail: Fan-shaped screen.

écuelle: Covered cup, generally with handles, and sometimes decorated.

Eddy & Arnold furniture: Cabinet furniture of the period, made from 1830s at West Stafford, Conn., by this firm.

Eddy Copyer: An early typewriter invented in 1848 by Oliver Eddy of Baltimore. That authoritative paper, *The Scientific American*, said of it in 1849: "We do not believe any printing machine can transcribe as fast as a good penman; the pen can travel an entire word while the hand is changing from one key to another...." The Baltimore *American* hailed the invention. This machine puts Baltimore, and not Milwaukee, in the lead for the first mechanical typewriter. The Eddy machine was used in several government offices in 1849.

Eddystone Light form: Eddystone was the original lighthouse or beacon at Eddystone, England. Representations of it, as

objects for use in service of food, clock cases, et cetera, date from Tudor period to 19th century.

Edgartown woolens: Any woolen goods from the Edgartown, Martha's Vineyard, shops where blankets and flannels were woven and mittens and caps knitted from the 1830s.

Edison electric pen: A pen vibrating from a small motor in the handle, powered by an Edison battery; used in cutting through the wax of a stencil for duplicating. Invented and made by Thomas A. Edison from c. 1876.

Edkins Bristol: May be Bristol delft or Bristol milk glass decorated by Michael Edkins, 1760s-90s.

Edson writing books: Penmanship books issued by A. Edson, c. 1815-20, ruled to guide student in line and angle. Eventually this system became the Spencerian.

Edwards & Darley: English cabinetmakers working in the Georgian period and perhaps the first advocates of furniture in the Chinese taste and style. They issued a book of designs in 1750, and they, not Chippendale, were the first Chinese-style cabinetmakers whose work became popular.

Edwards glass: Irish glass made at Belfast. Decanters marked in the forming molds are known.

Edwards lamps: Hall lanterns, signal and street lighting fixtures made by H. Edwards, N.Y., from 1840s.

Edwards portraits: Enlarged paper prints from daguerreotypes, overpainted with oil and water colors, made by Edwards of Louisville, Ky., and then by Harris & Co. of the same city from 1850s.

Edwards Ware: White granite wares of James and Thomas Edwards, later the T. & R. Boote pottery, at Kiln Croft, Burslem. The Edwards ownership was from 1825.

eel tongs: Wood and wrought-iron pincers to hold the slippery fish known as morays or eels. Some tongs are two or more feet long.

eeny: Full of holes.

effigy signs: Properly, a figural sign used by taverns, hotels, or tradesmen. Humanistic, animalistic, and natural forms in wide variety, including all objects, and kinds of workmen and vocations, such as firemen, chimney sweeps, Indians, smiths, boots, shoes, explorers, famous men and women, mermaids, et cetera. The "Golden Californian" [*pictured*] was the sign of Jenkins Jewelry Store opposite the Revere House, Boston, in 1849.

eftirtemsin bread: Bread made from the coarse wheaten or other flour that remained in the temse or sieve after sifting. Welsh and Yorkshire settlers in American colonies used this term.

Ege, Walter: Cabinetmaker of Gilmantown, N.H., 18th century, making excellent Georgian- and Chippendale-style pieces.

Egerton furniture: Hepplewhite, Sheraton, and Directoire furniture made by three generations of cabinetmakers named Egerton, New Brunswick, N.J., from 1760 to 1837. Matthew Egerton, Sr., worked from 1760 to 1800; Matthew, Jr., and his son worked from 1785 to 1830s.

egg & dart: See Echinus. A molding that is a row of egglike oval bosses with a series of dart points between each boss. [*Example pictured.*]

egg cooker: Copper or sheet iron covered oval vessel with a lifter in the top which raised a platform within from the boiling water. [*Example pictured.*]

egg cup: (1) Any special cup made to hold a cooked egg for service at table. (2) Collapsible drinking cup in an egg-shaped container.

egg drainer: Silver, plate, horn, porcelain, or wooden spoon with deep bowl having draining holes, used in lifting poached eggs from a pan.

egged: Fortified with an egg, as egged ale, egged stout, egged milk. Also ale to which, after brewing, a dozen eggs were added to the cask for clarification.

egg hinge: The easy-to-lift-off door hinge having an oval bearing of egg shape. Used from 1750, and generally of brass. [*Example pictured.*]

egg pan: Large iron pan with four to eight shallow depressions in bottom to hold eggs while frying.

eggshell blue: Pigment achieved by burning and powdering eggshells, mixing with vinegar, and fermenting in a dung heap.

eggs-in-moonshine: An early dish of eggs cooked in butter in a chafing dish, keeping yolks soft. Served with a dressing made of vinegar, spice, and onion fried in butter. 17th-century cookery.

Eggs-in-Sand: Pattern of pressed glass featuring rows of egg-shaped bosses placed at an angle on a stippled ground. Original name was Bean or Beads.

egg table: See Melon-Bottomed Table.

egg tree: The Easter equivalent of the Christmas tree, and very probably the older of the two. Of pagan Norse origin, the custom was introduced in U.S. by both Swedes and Moravians. A bare tree was trimmed with colored eggs in celebration of the coming of the new fertile season. By the 18th century the eggs were blown or sucked and the shell filled with wax or plaster. Thus the egg tree was used over and over again at the paschal season.

egg whisk: Any egg beater used to froth the white or "lemon" the yolk.

egg work: Fancywork involving use of complete eggshells of pullets, chickens, ducks, and geese to make vases, urns, and cups imitative of Parian. Mid-19th-century homecraft work. [*Example pictured.*]

eglantine: The rose of the sweetbrier. It is not true (or is it?) that graduates of Sweet Briar College for women in Virginia were dubbed "Ladies Eglantine," unless locally by wags and wits.

Egli furniture: The only plausible reference is to furniture made by Antoine Egli, or Egly, at Richmond, Va., from 1840s. The style is French Antique revival.

eglomise panel: Glomi, a decorator of France, started this style by coating a sheet of glass with gold leaf, drawing upon it with a series of scrapers, making a line engraving, and then coating the open lines with black and colors. Now the term is applied to any painted glass panel used in

mirrors, clocks, furniture, or picture frames. This technique of décor is oriental in origin, probably Chinese.

ègre-douce: Any dish made "sweet-sour," as with sugared vinegar, limed honey, or lemon and barley sugar. Also used in confects and candies.

Egyptian: Pattern of pressed glass. See Parthenon.

Egyptian-Empire: Much Empire-style furniture has an Egyptian motif, influenced by Napoleon's Egyptian campaign.

Egyptian fruit jar: Black-glazed hard redware, almost like Jackfield, forming a preserve jar with flaring lip having slots for fastening and sealing cover. Date is from c. 1850. Also a glass display jar made at Millville, N.J., from 1850. [*Example pictured.*]

Egyptian mirror: Not precisely the correct term, but used to designate polished bronze disks mounted on handles and used as mirrors. These were made in Egypt as early as 2000 B.C., but were made also in China from the same or an earlier period. Also a name given Empire-style mirrors reflecting certain Egyptian motifs.

eidograph: A drawing machine for enlarging and reducing from another drawing or print.

eidophusicon: A rapidly moving diorama displaying successive scenes which gave the illusion of motion. Dunlap, artist and historian of American art, was proprietor of such a show. See also Zoetrope.

eight immortals table: A square table seating eight, two persons at each side.

eight-inch man: Said of pewterers who specialized in making the eight-inch-size pewter plates.

eight-leg table: Any table standing on four legs, having falling leaves supported by additional swing-out, or gated, legs, two on each side.

eight-shaft coverlet: Simple pattern of coverlet weaving deriving from the number of loom wings or shafts used in its weaving. Made from 1810. The small rectangular blocks seem to come alive when the coverlet is moved ever so little. [*Example of the pattern pictured—pre-Jacquard.*]

eight square: Octagonal, an early table form. **Eight Square School:** The octagonal schoolhouse. The interior arrangement seated older pupils at a continuous desk facing the wall and younger ones facing the center, where the stove was set. Said to have been designed by Fowler & Wells, the phrenologists, who also designed many homes on the same time-, space-, and money-saving plan.

eimer: Probably from *omer*, a Hebrew measure, 18 gallons, 58/100ths of a standard barrel.

Eismann, P.: A mark found in gold on bottoms of occupational and shop shaving mugs, barbers' bottles, et cetera. Name is that of a distributor located at Lancaster, Pa., operating from 1880s to 1920.

elaboratory: Same as laboratory; a chemist's workshop.

elder flower powder: An early insecticide made from the flower of the elder.

Eldorado metal: A white brass or bronze

made by L. Cruckshanks of London and fashioned into fanlights, cabinet doors, and architectural elements. The catalogue of this maker, issued prior to the first book of Sheraton, displays many designs which Sheraton shows in his book. If they were his own, he also designed for Cruckshanks, a service not acknowledged by this maker of metallic elements.

eldritch: Ghastly, ghostly.

election coffee: The cup of coffee offered to voters on Election Day by Democratic candidates. There was always a gold dollar in the bottom of the cup.

electric clock: From the 1840s many springless clocks were made, using the magnetic principle to keep the pendulum swinging. Earth batteries were used to power the clocks for years without replenishment. Most earth batteries were made of layers of coke and zinc laid in a deep pit in the earth. One was made extensively in the U.S. by Daniel Drawbaugh of Eberly's Mills, Cumberland County, Pa., who also invented a telephone for voice transmission coincidentally with Bell. He lost out in the litigation, which many now consider to have ended in an unfair or biased opinion. Drawbaughs' telephone became the basis for the Independent telephone lines which, before absorption into one system, were competitive with Bell at many points. Clocks and telephones were made in the 1870s.

electric lighter: A wet battery on a stand with a removable zinc rod. Plunging in the rod set up a current which heated a platinum wire, igniting a wick drenched in kerosene. Made and sold in 1870s. [*Example pictured.*]

electric oil lamp: A brilliant kerosene burner otherwise known as the Rochester burner. One such lamp was more brilliant than a single Edison incandescent carbon-filament bulb.

electric pen: See Edison Electric Pen.

electric quilt: Anticipating the electric blanket by half a century, the electric quilt had coils of insulated wire bound in the quilt, operated from the then direct current distributed to homes. Patented 1894.

electric toys: Any magnetic philosophical apparatus is actually an electric toy. They were made first for laboratory use, then for schools and for men interested in science; there are surviving examples made for drawing-room mystification as early as 1760s. These are magnetic toys. There are battery-operated mechanical toys dating from 1840s, including an electric arc light. From the 1880s the number of electric toys increased as to type and volume. Toy electric trolleys date from 1890s and trains from c 1910. Toy lamps were made by Edison in 1880s.

electric-treatment chair: See Chairs, All Kinds.

electrometer: Quadrant with wooden upright and dial of ivory, and a light wooden rod tipped with a ball of pith. Placed in contact with a charged body, the index rod rose on the scale.

electrum: Alloy imitative of silver, 8 parts copper, 4 nickel, 3½ zinc.

elephant mark (SILVER): Hamilton & Co. of England used this mark from 1808 at

their silversmithing shop in Calcutta, India.

elephant oil: Practically every refinery of whale and lard oil also refined elephant fat for use as lamp oil. Practice dates from 1850s.

Elers ware: Hard redware, imitative of Chinese porcelain and a black basalt which Wedgwood copied many decades later, made by the Elers brothers, Dutch potters who migrated to England on the election of William of Orange to the British throne, 1688. In 1710 they moved to Lambeth, and then to Chelsea, where they became interested in the Venetian glassworks established in the 17th century by the Duke of Buckingham. The redware is pinkish and has raised decoration applied with stamps and seals. Some authorities claim it is porcelain and pre-dates the Böttger discovery at Meissen. [*Examples pictured.*]

Elfe, Thomas: Cabinetmaker of Charleston, S.C., working from 1750s in the Georgian style.

Elford, J.: Scientific instrument maker of Charleston, S.C., who worked early in 19th century. Some say he made fine clocks or regulators; he did make nautical surveyors and instruments.

Eliaers furniture: Fine French Antique furniture made at Boston from 1845 by A. Eliaers of France. He was also an expert builder of graceful "flying" staircases, which he made to specifications and shipped anywhere in the U.S. for assembly by local talent.

ell: A cloth measure. In England 1¼ yards; in Flanders, ¾ yard; in France, 1½ yards.

ellboe chair: See Chairs, All Kinds.

Ellenville glass: Hollow ware made at Ellenville, N.Y. from 1830s to 1880s. The factory had a huge output from 1845 to 1865, making blown glass exclusively.

Elliot mirrors: John Elliot of Philadelphia was a general cabinetmaker who seems to have specialized in mirrors from c. 1750. His mirrors are in the Queen Anne and Georgian styles with fretted frames, crested, gilded elements, and other niceties. They carried bilingual labels in English and German. The firm was continued by his sons until the 1800s. Hundreds of labeled examples survive and all are considered valuable antiques.

Elliot repeater: Revolving pistol made by Elliot Arms Co., N.Y., from 1860s. This had a cluster of six small barrels revolving on a center pin and weighed but eight ounces. [*Example pictured.*]

Elliott carpets: The only credible reference would seem to be to carpets woven by Charles Elliott, Providence, R.I., 1845–60.

Elliottype: Paper photoprint made from a painted negative; not a negative achieved by chemical means and a camera. Havell is said to have used the process in 1841 to reproduce paintings by masters. Revived by Elliott in 1853.

Ellis doll: Dolls fitted with heads of live wood, pressed to form in dies when green and freshly cut. The bodies were lathe-turned and were the first indestructible dolls made in the U.S. Made by J. A. H. Ellis of Springfield, Vt., and by Mason, Taylor, Sanders, and others in Vermont from 1870.

Ellis mirror: Rustic, gilded-frame and tabernacle mirrors for the cottage trade, made by Leonard Ellis of New Bedford, Mass., from 1850s.

Ellison: See Allison Furniture.

elmen: Made of elm wood.

elm seat: Chair seats made of the inner bark of the elm tree, twisted into rope.

elm-wood root; elm-root wood: The root timbers of the elm, prized as a cabinet wood.

elsin: An awl.

Elsworth miniatures: Miniature or small-size portraits painted with a shading around the face, generally in profile. This finally became a three-lobed cumulus cloud around the features depicted and is now the earmark of the painter, James Elsworth, who worked from 1820s to 1850s in the Connecticut and Mississippi valleys and other regions. He is said to have died in Pittsburgh, Pa., 1873.

eluriate: To obtain an impalpable powder of non-solvent substances by pulverization and immersion in water, then decanting when the heaviest particles fall to the bottom, and letting stand until the impalpable settles. To decant, strain, and soak.

eluriator: A patented wine decanter that is a frame for the gentle tilting of the original bottle to fill the service carafe (decanter proper) without disturbing the lees. Patented c. 1850 and sold as an elegancy in plated silver, brass, and japanned iron. Examples of hardwood are reported.

Elwe flower prints: Fifty-three engravings of tulips, anemones, roses, hyacinths, et cetera, published by Elwe at Amsterdam, 1794, in quarto size. Engraved by Myling from drawings by Brussel.

Elysian rocker: See Chairs, All Kinds.

ember fender: Low fencelike strip of metal, usually brass, punched in decorative manner, encircling the hearth or the part of it before an open fire. Used generally from 17th century. Examples extant of gun metal and wrought iron.

embolic: Aslant; askew; on the bias; oblique.

embossed calico: The textile made by Dudding & Nelson, England, that was embossed in the dimity technique but by a series of rollers in a machine and not on a loom. The embossing was generally done on printed calicoes.

embowed: Bow-shaped; arched, bowed, or bent in a semicircle.

embroidered pictures: Precisely what the name suggests; pictures achieved by embroidery rather than painting or engraving. These were elegancies, generally homemade, from the 17th to the 19th century. Stamp work, crewel stitch, and other techniques were used in making landscapes, genre, portraits, allegorical, classic, and other subjects.

embroidered sprigs: Shop-made arrasene-cord embroidery on crinoline, sold as a decorative unit to be stitched on dress fabrics. Arrasene (from Arras, France) is a woolen cord. The flower patterns of this work included the Martha Washington geranium.

embroidery dies: Metal die stamps for printing an embroidery pattern on fabric.

embroidery frame: A rectangular frame, mounted between uprights and adjustable as to angle, on which the cloth base for embroidery work was stretched taut. There are many varieties, dating from 17th to 19th century [*one example of which is pictured*].

emegrie: A form of imagery, or the imitation of natural forms with pen, brush, or needle.

Emerald Herringbone: Pattern of pressed glass featuring long upright ovals, alternating plain and herringbone, in a dark emerald green.

emeril: Emery.

Emerson prints: Subscription prints, lithographs, and steel engravings, sold by door-to-door agents, issued by J. M. Emerson. The trio were made by Sarony, Major & Knapp from the 1860s, and included Rosa Bonheur's "Horse Fair."

emigrant: One who goes from one place to another within his nation's limits, as opposed to immigrant, a foreigner entering a new country. There were no Dutch immigrants to New Amsterdam, no Swedish immigrants to New Sweden, no English immigrants to the colonies, and no French immigrants to the French colonies. Germans, Poles, Swiss, and other settlers were immigrants; others were emigrants.

Emmet, Fisher & Flowers glass: This trio took over the works of the Porcelain & Glass Manufactory of Boston, 1815, and made glasswares to 1817, when the New England Glass Co. was organized to take over the works.

Emmoen: Reed musical instrument with bass pedals, made by Milo Lucas of Boston from 1850s.

empaistic: Inlay work imitative of or similar to Buhl work. An intarsia or marquetry technique.

empire mirror: The tabernacle mirror of the Federal period; rectangular upright mirror with (generally) a painted glass panel at top. Not Empire in style, but the American version of the French *trumeau* or transomed mirror of the Directoire.

Empire period: The era of French history, and the style developed in that era, marked by the end of the Consulate, which followed the Directory, and the election of Napoleon as Emperor. This period ended with Napoleon's banishment to St. Helena, and 1804-10 is its most proper dating. The "style," however, was eliminated in France when Louis Philippe was made King in 1830. It persisted in the U.S. to the 1850s, being displaced by the Louis XV style revived by Philippe.

Empire revival: The 1890 revival of sofas, love seats, and chairs in the Empire style.

Empire State Glass Works: Located at Brooklyn, N.Y., from 1850s, making blown flintwares, clear and in colors, to 1890s.

Empire style: The heavy, unimaginative or overimaginative style that was developed in the late Consular period of France and for which the Directoire style was scrapped. [*Examples of the style pictured. These are American-made pieces, dating from 1820s to 1840s.*]

Empire tole: Painted tinware made by

Empire Scale & Tinware Co., N.Y., from 1850s. Stencil- and free-hand-decorated ware, often on a yellow, red, or black ground. Made tea, coffee, and other cans, bins, spice boxes, et cetera.

empress chair: *See* Chairs, All Kinds.

enamel: An opaque coating applied in various ways to cover a surface. **enamel cloth:** A fabric coated with oils, varnish, and pigmented, having a glazed surface. **enameled hardware:** Furniture pulls and other brasses, enameled with pictorial scenes, flowers, et cetera. Also a generic name for enameled metals. *See also* Enamel-on-Metal. **enameled ware:** Any metal, most frequently iron, cast or wrought into utensils coated with a fired-on enamel to provide a clear pit-free inner surface. Iron enamel was composed of borax, soda, sand, tin, et cetera, applied as a paste and fired to the point of fusion which bonded it to the metal. **enamel varnish:** Tin glaze as used on ceramics; a glasslike surface achieved by firing, as on metal, et cetera.

enameled furniture: (1) Oriental imports of furniture lacquered with many coats and enriched with gold and colors. (2) Glossy painted imitation of the oriental masterpieces, much in vogue as cottage furniture from the 1820s.

enameled glass: Any glass decorated in colors with fired-on enamels. This technique was used in America from 1750s. Some Bristol white opaque glass was enameled in the Chinese taste, imitative of porcelain.

enamel-on-metal: *Pâte-sur-face, pique à jour,* cloisonné, champlevé, Battersea, ironstone, et cetera. Small pill-, pastille, and patch boxes, enameled on copper with decorated, figured, or landscape lids, are often designated as Battersea but are really South Staffordshire products. The ironstone is not to be confused with the ceramic ware made in imitation of it; it should be recognized for precisely what it is—utensils of iron, enameled to approximate the appearance of china. Tablewares were so made from c. 1800, but the price was considerably above that of china and even porcelain. The decoration was in the china-painting technique, on the enamel.

en cabochon: Uncut but polished, a form of finishing for gems and precious stones.

encaustic: Painting with hot wax, applied to plastered walls.

encoignure: A corner piece; a corner cupboard; a spandrel.

encrier: Inkwell.

en croissant: Crescent-shaped.

ende-kooij: (Pronounced *endecoy.*) A duck cage, and probably the origin of our term decoy, the effigy of a waterfowl used as a lure in trapping and shooting.

end for work table: Cabinetmakers' term current to 1820s for what we now designate as a sofa writing table.

endiron; aundiron: Specific name given a new type of fire iron introduced in the 15th century, made in pairs to serve as ends, or aunds, upon which a bridge of burning logs rested. Prior to this innovation fire irons were cob irons, not used on the hearth endwise but front to back. Thus the cob iron was a humped pier

upon which log ends rested. This was used on center hearths before the introduction of closed chimney flues, and was used on the first flued hearths until the endirons, now called andirons, were developed.

endive: The poorly executed acanthus form as used by Chippendale and copied from the Louis XV style. The appearance is that of a leaf of the curly endive plant, or chicory.

end-of-day glass: General term for the tailings of glass from all the pots at the end of a day's glassmaking, used by the glassblowers to fashion objects and whimseys for themselves. Also the cheap multi-colored and -spotted glass of the 1880s–1900s. Somehow there is a feeling among collectors that end-of-day glass is desirable, but most of it is not. And it is an error to attempt to glorify the later cheap novelty glass of this name.

end-on-end drawer: A long, single, two-faced drawer with pulls at either end, used most frequently in tables to provide access from either end. Often found in gate-legs, William & Mary, and early Queen Anne tables, and in kitchen tables of the 19th century.

endore: To coat viands or pastry with egg yolks to give a glaze in cooking.

en face: Head on; full face.

engagement cup & saucer: French, Austrian, and German porcelain demitasse cups and saucers in odd, novel, and curious shapes, richly decorated, and much used as engagement presents for brides-to-be in the last quarter of the 19th century.

engine-turned pottery: Actually pottery biscuit worked on a form of the precision lathe known as the rose engine. Adapting the rose-engine turning techniques to pottery is attributed to Wedgwood after 1763. Much engine-turned ware attributed to Eilers and other potteries is most likely Wedgwood. Unglazed redwares were made at first, but after the 1790s Wedgwood used the technique on his whitewares.

engine turning: Any work done on the rose engine, or eccentric lathe, which engraved quite lovely and intricate designs on ivory, brass, steel, pewter, silver, and wood.

England: From Angles, a racial stock related to the ancient Suevi, commented upon by Tacitus as the Angli, or Anglia. These people were also ancestors of various alpine tribes, including the Germans. The homeland of the Suevi was what is now Denmark, and they seem to have entered England to help the natives against the warring Picts and Scots.

England mark: One of the "country of origin" marks, which include those of China, Japan, France, Holland (the Netherlands), Germany, Switzerland, et cetera, all of which, under the U.S. tariff laws, had to be stamped on imports from 1892. Some wares from England and France had the "country of origin" mark on them prior to 1892, and some are said to have been so marked by the 1870s.

English china: "China" was once the generic name for all porcelain from the Celestial Kingdom. England produced some porcelains (Worcester, Derby, Chelsea, Bow, et cetera) and was perhaps the first country to solve the secret of the hard stoneware that is porcelain. But the chief contribution of England's potters was a ware more useful than porcelain, English bone china. This is a semi-hard or medium paste ware achieved by the addition of calcined animal bones to the paste. There were so many potters and potteries in England that no complete listing is attempted here. Students are referred to *Ceramic Art of Great Britain*, by Llewellynn Jewitt, and *Pottery & Porcelain*, by Warren E. Cox. *See* Bibliography for other reference books.

English Hobnail: Pattern of pressed glass with several variants. The basic is an all-over diamond-waffle impression. When the impress is in the form of panels with clear spacing between, it is English Hobnail with Panel. When the panels taper and the clear space is impressed with thumbprints, it is English Hobnail and Thumbprint.

English porcelain: *See* English China.

English willow chair: *See* Chairs, All Kinds.

engobe: White clay, such as pipe clay, liquefied in water to a creamy consistency. Used to put stripes and outlines on redwares, and the secret of slip decoration.

engraved glass: Glasswares decorated with diamond point and wheel roughing to achieve depth, outline, contour, pattern, et cetera. Not the deep-cut glass of more modern times, but an ancient process allied to cameo carving, but not so exacting. Date is from pre-Christian Era.

engravers, American: Three volumes were required to carry the biographical listing of known engravers of record in 1920. These are *American Engravers upon Copper and Steel*, two volumes published by the Grolier Club, authored by D. McN. Stauffer, and *Dictionary of American Painters and Engravers*, published privately, authored by Mantle Fielding. *See also* Bibliography.

Ennion glass: Ennion (Ηννιων), probably a Cycladic Greek glassworker of the early Christian Era who signed much of his work. He is sometimes designated as a Cyprian and sometimes as a Syrian.

entablature: (1) The uppermost section of a classic column. (2) A platform. (3) A protecting frieze or border; a cornice.

enterclose: Passage between rooms of a house.

enterprise hammock: A wood-slat hammock, made from 1880s by Woodward Co., Providence, R.I., and said to have been invented by a fence maker.

entertaille; entretaille: Woven or plaited; interlaced.

envelope table: (1) Triangular-topped table of Queen Anne style with falling triangular leaves. Often has a locked compartment in skirting or valance, accessible only through the top, which is movable on hinges or pivot. (2) A square-topped table with four triangular leaves on a square frame. The main top is pivoted on a center pin and can be turned. When turned it brings the falling triangular leaves over the corners of the table frame and thus makes a table almost twice the original size. (3) The same kind of table but with triangular leaves folding over main top.

epaulet box: Wood or cardboard box shaped to hold a pair of these fringed military shoulder ornaments and insignia of rank.

epergne: A centerpiece, especially for a dining table; an ensemble of cups and vases for holding fruits, flowers, condiments, sweetmeats, and other edible items such as cookies, et cetera.

Epiphany tree: A Christmas candle tree or candle trow; a young ash tree, the boughs lined with burning candles, carried in procession on the Feast of Epiphany or Twelfth-night. Usage is centuries earlier than the Germanic Christmas tree.

épis; épi: Pinnacle or finial. In the 19th century some collectors specialized in epis from 14th- to 16th-century houses. One New York collector boasted having 60 examples from Renaissance houses.

E Pluribus Unum pulls: Early 19th-century drawer pulls of stamped brass bearing an eagle with streamer carrying this motto. [*Example pictured*.]

EPMB mark: The meaning is electroplate on Britannia metal.

EPNS mark: The meaning is electroplate on nickel silver (after 1845).

éprouvette: Pistol grip device used for testing the power of powder, the efficiency factor of which is recorded on a dial. Only the original powder testers have antiquarian value, those "improved" to serve as table lighters have been ruined as antiques. However, there are early tinder lighters looking very much like powder testers.

equifluent lamp: Solar or astral type of lamp made by E. B. Horn, Boston, from 1840s. The chief virtue of the lamp was its factor of illuminating without casting a shadow.

equipendy: A plumb bob and line.

Erato: Greek Muse of lyric and erotic poetry.

erbolat: A soufflé of many herbs.

Erie lighter: Small triangular pocket box holding a coil of slow-match cord, with flint and steel; a pocket lighter.

Erotes: Amorini; Amors; Cupids.

escabeau: Stool with rectangular top, with raked and contoured end boards; also a bench in the same form. French and Swiss, made from 15th century.

eschekere: A chessboard.

eschelles: The laddered, laced, and beribboned stomacher of the William & Mary period, much favored by fashionable ladies at end of 17th century.

escrin: A cabinet.

escutcheon: (1) In heraldry, the field or shape upon which the coat of arms is emblazoned. (2) Keyhole plates in cabinet furniture, drawers, and doors. Escutcheon wood (holly) was used for these, also ivory, bone, brass, et cetera.

escutcheon lift: A Norfolk-type latch with a movable escutcheon. Sliding the escutcheon operated the latch.

esmouchoir: A fly whisk; a fan to chase winged insects.

esparto: Spanish grass used in making ropes and cords.

essences: Essential oils diluted with alcohol, especially those used in flavoring, as essence of lemon, orange, vanilla, peppermint, et cetera.

Essler, Fanny: Viennese ballet dancer who visited the U.S. from 1840 to 1842 and was the nation's toast. Congress adjourned to see her dance. Many objects, from whiskey bottles to bandboxes, are named for her.

estagnier: An open shelf, or series of them, for arrangement and storage of metal housewares.

estamier: Pewter.

Estes woodenware: E. B. Estes had factories at New Vineyard, Livermore, Portland, and West Bethel, Me., from 1840s to 1890s, where turned wooden boxes of various shapes and sizes were produced commercially for use as packages and containers.

Esther: Pattern of pressed glass featuring shell volutes, medallions, and accented or pointed spines. A late pattern.

estre: The back of a chimney.

estrich board: A plank or deal of any wood, but specifically of softwood.

étagère: A whatnot; a stand of open shelves, generally decorative.

étain: Tin.

etched glass: (1) Light engraving with wheel. (2) Design achieved by protecting surface of glass with asphaltum or some other wax, or by a wax transfer, and then etching the exposed surface with fumes of hydrofluoric acid. This process became general after 1875.

etching: A process of making intaglio plates without the labor of engraving. The plate is coated with a mastic or wax, and the design to be engraved is cut through this down to the surface of the plate. The plate is then immersed in acid, which bites in the lines. The "art" resides both in the drawing made through the coating and in the biting.

ether glue: Solid glue and native India rubber dissolved in nitric ether. An early form of rubber cement, dating from 1870s.

etna: A metallic truncated cone set within a deep dish and permanently fixed. Spirits of wine were ignited in the dish, and the flame heated anything within the cone. Various types, some dating from 18th century. [*Example pictured.*]

Etruria: (1) Ancient name for Tuscany, famed for its Etruscan vases. (2) The name of a Wedgwood pottery in the Staffordshire district of England.

Etruria, U.S.A.: The Ott & Brewer pottery at Trenton, N.J. White granite wares, tablewares, Belleek, et cetera, were made. The pottery was established in the 19th century and most of its products are marked.

Etruscan: Pattern of pressed glass featuring broad ovate panels alternating with three flutes, and having a scalloped edge.

Etruscan majolica: American majolica wares of considerable virtue made at the Griffen & Smith pottery, Phoenixville, Pa., from 1870s.

etui: A pocket box for comfits, *dragées*, patches, et cetera. Known made of gold, silver, Sheffield plate, pewter, delft, enamel, et cetera.

etwee: Spelling of *etui* noted in 18th-century advertisements.

Eugenie: Pattern of pressed glass, said to be early, reflecting French influence. It features a series of petals, shields, and bosses, the covered pieces having shaped lifts and some having small dolphin finials.

eugh wood: Yew wood. This spelling is noted to 17th century.

euknemidas: Ancient Greek-style thigh-high leggings, made from 1850s of MacIntosh's cloth and Goodyear rubberized fabrics, having spring clips at ankle, calf, and knee; leg gaiters.

eulogy plate: The DeWitt Clinton eulogy on the Erie Canal printed on Staffordshire plates of the historic group. Maker unknown.

euphuism: Affected style of speech and writing, noted from late 16th century. Student is referred to Lyly's *Anatomy of Wit* and *Euphues and His England*.

Eureka: Pattern of pressed glass featuring bands of beveled ovate panels. Said to date from late 1860s and originating in Pittsburgh area.

eureka coffeepot: A handsome metal pot which brewed by condensation. It is late, dating from 1880s, and was made by Excelsior Co., New Haven, Conn.

European-design Chinese porcelain: Somewhat confusing designation for Chinese porcelain in Chinese forms, but decorated to order in the European taste for Dutch and other traders. An exceedingly rare type of export porcelain.

European Potteries and Porcelain Factories (other than Great Britain): It has been found impossible, in this edition of the work, to include individual entries covering each and every pottery and porcelain manufactory of Europe. The following, however, are the chief ones, but do not include the 500 or more small potteries of the Netherlands which, from the 17th century, were producing the faïence today generally known as Delft. AMBRUZZI, a majolica type, ALCORA, AMSTEL, APREY, ARDENNES, ARNHEIM, AVIGNON, BADEN-BADEN, BASSANO, BAYEUX, BAYREUTH, BEAUVAIS, BERLIN (KPM), BOLOGNA, BORDEAUX, BRUGES, BRUSSELS, BUEN RETIRO, CAEN, CALDAS, CAPO DI MONTE, GINORI, CARLSBAD, CASTEL DURANTE, CHANTILLY, CHOISY-LE-ROI, COLOGNE (GRES DE FLANDERS), COPENHAGEN, DOCCIA, DRESDEN, FAENZA, FLORENCE (MEDICI), FRANKENTHAL, FULDA, FURSTENBURG, GENOA, GIEN, GOTHA (SAXE-COBURG), GREINSTADT, GUBBIO, HAGUE, HANAU, HEREND, HOCHS, LILLE, LIMOGES, LUDWIGSBURG, MARIEBERG, MARSEILLES, MENNECY, MOUSTIERS, NYMPHENBURG, NYON, ORLEANS, PARIS, PIRKENHAMMER, QUIMPER, ROUEN, RUDOLSTADT (VOLKSTEDT), ST. AMAND, ST. CLOUD, SEVRES, STRASBOURG, VAUX, VENICE, VIENNA, and VINCENNES. These, and many others, are given specific notice in *Pottery & Porcelain* by Frederick Litchfield, edition of 1951.

Euterpe: Greek Muse of lyric song.

Evans gift books: Annuals, comprising poetry, selected prose, essays, color plates, engravings, and sentimental verse, in a fancy binding designed for gift purposes. Evans was an extensive publisher at Philadelphia. He sold six million books to 1860.

Evans Sheffield: Reference is to the

maker, S. Evans of Sheffield, England, in first quarter of 19th century.

Evans silver: It is likely this term refers to T. Evans & Co., manufacturing silversmiths of U.S., working from 1850s. Factory was in New York City.

evaporating kettle: Conical-shaped kettle with open top and long tapering spout.

evaporators: Room humidifiers; louvered metal screens for placement before a stove or fireplace. These screens were fitted with wicks and water pans and were generally of japanned and painted tin plate. An elegancy of the 1860s and 1870s.

Evarts & Bliss furniture: Perhaps the only possible reference is to the Empire-style furniture made by a firm so named at Louisville, Ky., working from 1840s. Labeled pieces not bearing the address have been traced to Louisville.

éventail: A fan.

Eventon furniture: M. V. Eventon was a cabinetmaker working at Dumfries, Va., in early 1760s. He made Georgian-style furniture and, it is reported, taught slaves the art of cabinetmaking.

Everett bowls: Woodenware. Cut-turning work of remarkable smoothness made by various makers on the Addison Everett lathe, which enabled the mechanic to turn bowls from maple, birch, walnut, and all softwoods, as thin as one half inch. Prior to the invention of this machine in 1849, all bowls were turned either on the traditional lathe or on the amazing Blanchard lathe, both of which were somewhat prodigal in terms of wood wasted in the operation.

Everett mirror: Reference is assumed to be to tabernacle and oval-type framed mirrors by William Everett, Boston, from 1840s.

Everitt bed: A folding bed, probably of late make, produced by several manufacturers. Date of 1868–72 is the apparent beginning of production.

ewery: Keeping room for metalwares, such as ewers. Term seems to be from 14th century. Any cupboard was once so called.

ex.: Abbreviation of *excudit*, meaning the publisher.

Excelsior: (1) Longfellow's "strange device"; a coined word that found its place in the language after its use in the poem. (2) A pattern of pressed glass. *See* Ashburton, of which this is a variant, having looped beveled panels in an all-over pattern.

excelsior desk: Empire-style desk with front section and top folding back as with pianoforte cases. Fitted with a sliding writing board. Made for college girls from 1850s by R. Paton, New York City.

Excelsior glass: Blown, cut, and engraved flint glass, made at the Excelsior Glass Works, Camden, N.J., from 1841.

excelsior lard lamp: Lard or lard-oil lamp on the Argand principle; probably late 1850s.

excelsior tiehold: A small shaped panel of thin metal with springs to hold a gentleman's scarf. The device was entirely hidden by scarf and collar. Date is from 1860s. [*Example pictured.*]

Excelsior Variant: Pattern of pressed glass in which the beveled ovate loopings are reduced in size to enlarge to diamond form at juncture. Now considered a distinct pattern.

exercising chair: *See* Chairs, All Kinds.

Exeter carpets: Claude Passavant wove these floor carpets in the French style at Exeter, England, from 1755, and is reputed to have exported them extensively to the colonies, although this is not fully confirmed.

Exeter ware: Pottery made at Lamson Works, Exeter, N.H., 1830–1900. Homewares and flowerpots.

Expanded Diamond: Pattern of blown glass achieved in two ways: in a forming mold, or by tooling. The technique would seem to be traditional, and was introduced to the colonies in Bristol glass, later copied by Stiegel.

expressive: A small mechanical music box.

extending tables: Pairs or trios of leafed tables, each of use singly, but forming an extended table when joined. Known from Adam period (c. 1750) to Empire.

extension gasolier: Any gas fixture suspended from ceiling by an XXXX-laddered arrangement of piping which permitted raising or lowering.

extension lamp: A ceiling-anchored fluid lamp within a series of rods, pulleys, and counterweights, permitting easy raising and lowering to position desired.

extincteur: A tall vessel filled with alkaline water and having within it a tipple filled with acid. When acid was released, this formed gas to force liquid out of the container. The same principle is used in modern fire extinguishers.

eye bath: An eyecup.

eye douche: A fountain of water for bathing the eyes.

eyrewood: Sycamore wood stained with iron oxide. Also known as harewood.

eyrthrose: Rhubarb root treated with nitric acid to produce a red dye.

F

F & M and F & R Fischer glass: Bohemian glasswares marked F & M (Fischer & Mieg) and F & R (Fischer & Reichenbach), imported in considerable quantities. Requests for data made prior to 1939 yielded this information—the F & R mark was used from 1822 to 1846, while the F & M mark was used from 1847 to the 1870s.

fabliau: A tale, anecdote, or romance recited with gestures by one or more people for the entertainment of others. Popular from 13th century.

fabrics of India: Our knowledge of these in colonial years was not limited to a few of the named fabrics. The following have been noted in advertisements of dealers dating from 1690s to 1830s: allejars, atlases, addaties, allibanes, aubrowahs, bafraes, brawles, bejurapauts, betellees, bulchauls, bryampants, begusses, chintz, chelloes, coopees, callowpooses, cuttanees, cherriderries, cushlahs, cattantees, carradarries, chowtahs, chucklees, dorcas, deribands, dudamies, doorquees, elatches, emeritees, gorgorans, guineas, gurrahs, gelongs, ginghams, humadees, humhums, izzarees, jaindaumeles, jambwars, lookherries, moorhees, mulmuls, mamodees, mahumidatties, michbannies, nillaes, niccareens, peniascoes, pallampoors, paunchees, ponabaguzzies, rahrings, rumballs, shalbafts, seersuckers, soraguzzees, soofays, seerbetties, sannos, seccaturins, soosays, seerabands, tainsooks, tapsiels, tepoys, tanjeebs. These apparently were all cotton fabrics, although not all of them were prints. Certain of them were of curly or striped weave from dyed yarns.

faceted ball: A decorative globular form flattened in an orderly series to provide interesting plane facets.

face well: Inkwells of pottery or other substances fashioned in the form of a human face, with open mouths for dipping into the ink.

facibat: Same as *fecit*.

factory: (Original meaning.) The warehouse of a factor, or agent, primarily a storage warehouse. The factor financed the purchases in advance of shipment to importers and traders.

fagot: (1) Weight of 120 pounds. (2) A bundle of sticks. (3) A brand for burning.

fa hwa: Term used for glazed wares of the Ming Dynasty in China.

faïence: Tin-glazed redware, the same philosophy of potting as majolica and delft. While the tin-glaze secret was known to the Saracens even before the Crusades, and to the Italians and Spanish prior to the travels of the famed Polo families who brought Chinese porcelains to the West, practically all faïence, majolica, and delftwares were imitative of Chinese porcelains or were made in an attempt to approximate the quality of such wares, even though using Western decorative ornamentation.

faille: A fine dress fabric.

Fairclough-Wilson chimneys: Actually these are chimney hoods or tops of English make, introduced to the U.S. about 1840.

Fair Hebe jug: Staffordshire rustic pitcher, modeled in relief, bearing figures of two men and a girl picnicking, one man toasting the health of "Fair Hebe." Made 1840s by Copeland & Garrett after a model by Voyez.

fairing mold: Woodenware. Carved cake molds used in forming cakes sold at fairs and public affairs and spectacles. Many varieties, some featuring heads and figures of people honored. Gingerbread molds were given this name, as were the finer marchpane molds.

fairy fountain: A "contained" fountain made of hollow glass tubes arranged in a cascade, through which colored waters in globules, alternating with air bubbles, played. Motion was achieved from small pumps operated by a coil spring in the walnut base. Sold for $40 in 1870s. This item was the star of the Louisville Exposition of 1873.

fairy lamps: Innumerable varieties of tiny lamps with shades, made to burn Clarke's "fairy lamps," which were squatty one- and two-wick candles. The Clarke enterprise (England) sold these lamps over the civilized world. Glass, china, porcelain, and metal bases with similar shades, and also fabric-covered shades. The Phoenix Glass Works, Pittsburgh, was granted the sole rights to manufacture under the Clarke patents for distribution in the U.S. By 1875 Gansler, Hoffman & Co. of Philadelphia was making the lamps or selling them in quantities. This little lamp was called "fairy" from its first making. Queen Victoria is said to have ordered them by the hundreds. A monograph has been written about them, *Clarke's Fairy Lamps*, by Dorothy Tibbetts. [*Example pictured.*]

fairy pipe: Small-sized clay tobacco pipe (for the ladies) with bowl in form of a woodcock's head. Originals date from 17th century.

fakes: This subject could well be expanded into a book. The faker we have had with us in all history. The 20th-century phenomenon of the growth of the collecting vogue and the scope of interest aroused have caused the making of thousands of fakes in pressed and blown glass, plaster wares, furniture, et cetera. Iron castings from old molds or old casts are numerous. There is a business in painting genuine old plain white china with genuine marks; a business of making Fraktur work, of making new furniture look like old, and many other nefarious enterprises. From 1948 to 1950 every piece of antique furniture offered in advertisements in certain journals was studied by experts. The number of pieces that were much restored and those that were outright fakes was an amazing percentage of the total. In some cases the dealer may have known his merchandise was beyond the pale, but in many cases dealers were convinced of the authenticity of their goods. There is apparently no cure for this condition of affairs except a buyers' strike. And that is quite unthinkable. The next best thing is for collectors to study not only the things they collect but also the probity of the dealers with whom they do business. Our own experience with dealers has been most happy. We have found nine out of ten willing to make written guarantees of the genuineness of the wares they sell and to refund the full purchase price if the goods prove otherwise. The cure for the evil of faking lies as firmly upon the shoulders of collectors as of dealers, if not more so. The incongruity of the situation is perhaps best expressed in this true story: Mrs. X, upon hearing that Dealer Y had purchased a piece of Revere silver from old Mrs. Z for $100, immediately went to the dealer to see it and ask its price. Upon being quoted $2000, she exploded, called the dealer a crook, a racketeer, and said he should be sued for taking advantage of Mrs. Z. She carried her fuming all through dinner, and finally her husband said, "Why are you so upset? Do you envy the man his profit?" She calmed down and then confessed she had offered Mrs. Z $50 for the piece. She was concerned not that Dealer Y had got it, but that Mrs. Z would now know she was a cheap buyer. So it goes. A dealer is a crook if he buys something for $10 and sells it for $500. But a collector who does the same thing is merely astute.

falding: A rough cloth.

faldore: Trap door

faldstol; faldestool; faldistorium: See Chairs, All Kinds.

fall board: The falling board of a slope-fall desk.

Falstaff jug: Staffordshire jug related to the Toby, featuring a figure of Falstaff, the body on a base, and hollow. Originally, it is said, the figure was made as a tobacco or snuff jar.

famille rose, vert, jaune, noire, poudre bleu: The rose is deep pinkish to ruby red, the vert is a lovely green, and so on, all being colors used on Chinese porcelains of merit and great collecting interest. Famille rose Lowestoft is Chinese export porcelain made for the Persian market c. 1810–30 and now finding its way to the U.S.

family washer: Properly the Lukens Washer, a family laundry machine made at Philadelphia and Baltimore from early 1840s by M. Lukens.

Fan: Pattern of pressed glass featuring lily fronds and some poor elements of Eastlake character and a fanlike cornerpiece.

Fan & Star: Not a variant of the above, but a pattern featuring an imitation of fan cutting with a four-petaled star form.

fan crest: A carved or cut fan-shaped element in the cresting of a chair top rail or stretcher, or on cabinet furniture.

Fan Cut: Pattern of cut glass featuring pyramids of diamond cutting with fan cutting in the V's of the design.

fancy chair; fancy-back Windsor: See Chairs, All Kinds.

fancy settee: The painted settees of all periods from Adam to Sheraton are "fancy," but the specific examples most commonly designated by this term are the so-called Sheraton-style turned-leg settees with paneled backs, painted, stenciled, gilded, and striped. Known in all colors, white, and black. Some have plank seats, some rush seats; some have seat cushions and others are caned. The so-called Hitchcock settee is a good example of the late fancy settee.

fan mirror: A mirror glass, dating from the 1700s, cut in fan shape and used as a standing mirror on tables and as a hanging mirror on walls. [*Example pictured.*]

fan rocker: See Chairs, All Kinds.

fans: One of the oldest possibilities in collecting is this device, known in early Egypt, where the flat fan was developed, and in early China, where the folding fan was invented. It is said that fans, as items of elegance and comfort, date from 4000 B.C. In colonial America perhaps most fans were imported by Virginia planters, although very elegant examples are of recorded use in Philadelphia, Annapolis, and New York from the early 18th century. Fans are known in natural leaf forms such as palm, in *vernis Martin*, silver, lace, paper ivory, horn, silk, parchment, et cetera, painted, embroidered, carved, and enameled.

fans, hand: An accessory, luxury, and staple, depending entirely upon the type, style, and decoration. Any device which, oscillated by the hand of the user, caused a gentle breeze to blow. There are innumerable varieties, dating from ancient Egypt, China, and the Near East. Probably introduced into Europe during the Crusades. Used by ladies and gentlemen of fashion, by the nobles and royalty, and also by the yokels. The making of fans was a considerable business in the 18th century; there was an ancient company of fanmakers, and there was much controversy when plate printers began making fan papers by printing from engraved plates; this technique was said to have "worked a hardship" on the fan painters' guild, and in England a tax of thirty thousand pounds on engraved fan papers was advocated. *The Fan Book*, by MacIver Percival, is a good popular volume for study on this subject. Fans have often been collected by stage people, court beauties, king's mistresses, and other ladies of similar fame. Lady Charlotte Schreiber had a famous collection and in 1888 published *Fan & Fan Leaves*. Marcel Gabriel's *Un Eventail Historique du dix-huitième Siècle*, Paris, 1901, is also a book worthy of study. The following terms are a part of fan-collecting nomenclature. **battoir:** Fan of broad blades, folding. **brise:** Fan of sticks only, joined with tapes. **chicken skin:** Fan of accordian-fold type, the sheeting or cover of thin vellum. **cockade:** Fan of folding type, opening to a full circle. **mosaic:** A form of inlay used on fan blades. **piqué:** Fan decorated or trimmed with tiny pins with gold or silver heads. **whalebone:** A fan of baleen blades or of animal horn.

fantage: See Commode.

fantascope: A series of cards which, when flipped, produced the illusion of motion. Invented by Professor Plateau and published by R. Ackerman of London, 1833.

fan top: Half-patera forms, half circles and ovals, inlaid with from 10 to 14 segments similar to blades of a folding fan, used as a cresting and as a table-top design on furniture in the Hepplewhite style.

Fan with Diamond: Pattern of pressed glass featuring ovate petal-form oriental fans and a diamond form of the same elements.

Farley-Taylor flask: Quart and half-gallon glass flasks marked with these names and the place, Richmond, Ky., are commercial containers for this firm of liquor and provision dealers. They may have been made by Louisville Glass Works.

farmer (or sower) pattern: Staffordshire transfer-printed pattern by Adams in deep carmine red. Coffee-, tea-, and cream pots, sugar basins, plates, cups, and saucers are known. Early to mid-19th century.

Farrell, Felix: Irish glass blower, one-time employee of Stiegel, partner of the Dutch blower Bakeoven, who operated or worked with Philadelphia Flint Glass Works, Kensington, from 1777.

Farrington furniture: Enameled and grained cottage furniture made by Horace Farrington of New York City from 1848. This maker also produced Queen Anne and Eastlake styles in early 1870s.

farthingale: Padded and wired skirt of 16th and 17th centuries. Also a chair of special width to accommodate ladies so attired.

fascae: See Entablature.

fascinator: Lace, embroidery, or fancy woven scarf used as a head covering.

fashion doll: Reference would seem to be the dressed dolls of fashion used as window display pieces by milliners.

fate lady: A spinning top in form of a Turkish lady with wand, whirling on a rouletted disk. When coming to rest, the wand of the figure pointed to a fortune on the wheel. Commercial examples date from early 19th century. Homemade ones date as late as 1880s. [*Example pictured.*]

fat lamp: Generic name for any lamp burning expressed fats, as the Betty lamp.

Faulkner furniture: Reference would be to John Faulkner, cabinetmaker of New York City and Hudson Valley c. 1770s.

Fauntleroy: Character of a little lord in the juvenile book by Frances Hodgson Burnett, first issued in 1886. Any item bearing the name is of this date or later. Sometimes misspelled "Faulteroy."

fauteuil: See Chairs, All Kinds.

faverel: An onion.

favrile: (1) Anglo-Saxon for "made by hand." (2) Name of the art glass developed by Louis Tiffany in the 1890s.

faw: An itinerant potter or tinker.

Fay pencils: Lead pencils, artists' pencils,

mechanical ever-pointed pencils, penholders, and colored crayons made by A. G. Fay, Concord, Mass., from 1840s.

Fazzi plaster ware: James Fazzi of Cincinnati, from 1840s, operated a plaster-casting business. His products included busts of notables, Powers' "Greek Slave," statues of Clay, Calhoun, Franklin, Washington, Jackson, and others, as well as table ornaments.

feaberry: Gooseberry.

feasetraw: A pointer or wand.

Feather: Pattern of pressed glass featuring ovate-ended feather forms alternately faceted and clear, the clear feathers having upright column of dots. The pattern has a swirl and is late. It once was called Indiana Swirl, Swirl & Feather, Quill, and Doric.

Feather & Block: Not a variant of the above but another pattern featuring high columns of ovate petals in single and double rows of lobes, alternating with upright pairs of blocks, beveled and with petaled corners.

feather bed: Depending upon ancestry and region, the feather bed, a huge sack of feathers, was used as a bedcover, as a bed proper or cushion to sleep upon. It should be remembered that the term "bed" originally referred only to the mattress, sheets and coverings, pillows and beers, or shams. The frame of support was designated "bedstead."

feather-bed smoother: A block of hardwood with a handle, used to smooth and pat a feather bed into shape after use.

featherwork: Fancywork with naturally colored and dyed feathers and feather fronds. The featherworker was a practitioner of this minor art. Also any worker in feathers for use in beds and pillows.

fecit: Made or made by. Made it. An engraving term.

Federal lamp: A lamp having a fuel vent which permits filling while lamp is burning. This lamp seems to have entered the scene about 1820. Some call it a "feeder lamp" and state that some peg lamps (reservoirs and burners with a peg on the reservoir bottom to fit into a candlestick socket) had feeders, and date from 1790s.

Federal mirror: The more proper name for the so-called "Sheraton" mirror. Sheraton designed no mirrors, nor did he display any in his design book. These mirrors are of Directoire style and are the American version of the *trumeau*, or transomed, mirror of France. [*Examples pictured.*]

Federal style: Reference is to American furniture and furnishings in vogue from 1785 to 1820, during the early Federal era or period. Our use of Hepplewhite falls within this period, but our major style source was Directoire, with Sheraton a not too close second. The middle Federal period, 1820–50, embraced late Directoire with fancy chairs and settees being made in enormous quantities, the Empire style, and the firm establishment of the Louis XV revival now called Victorian. This latter style entered the U.S. c. 1832 and by 1840 was the high style. By 1835 it almost dominated the fine cabinetmaking scene, with many French cabinetmakers producing it in ever-increasing quantities. [*Ex-*

1, Federal-Style Furniture; cabinet, two sofas, bed, side table, two chairs, and sideboard. **2,** Half-Moon Spinet. **3,** Horseshoe Hinge. **4,** Horsecar. **5,** Hedgehog Crocus Pot. **6,** Hog-Scraper Candlestick. **7,** Hindman Sofa (Grecian style). **8,** High-Low Stretcher Table. **9,** Helmet Scuttle. **10,** Gate-Leg Table. **11,** Long Table. **12,** Hutch with Cover. **13,** Hyacinth Vases of 1770. (No. 2 from Parke-Bernet Galleries. No. 8 from *New Geography of American Antiques.* No. 11, permission of Wallace Nutting.)

amples of various Federal styles are pictured.]

feeding cup: A spouted cup; a papboat.

feet (footings): The various types of named furniture feet or footings are pictured and identified. Occasional reference is made throughout this book to colloquial and regional names for furniture footings.

felletin: A tapestry weave; a kind of tapestry.

fellmonger: Hide dealer.

felloe saw: A chairmaker's saw.

felt carpet: Pressed and printed felt, in various designs and patterns, for use as a floor covering and also as a ceiling material applied over girt bottoms instead of lath and plaster. Made as late as 1880s. [*Example pictured.*]

felt-center table: Any table, but especially gaming tables, having a center area covered with felt or baize. Made from 18th century. [*Example pictured is in Empire style.*]

felter's bow: A corded bow used in whipping clipped beaver and rabbit fur into clouds which, settling on canvas, were wet and beaten into felt for cloth and hats. Also hatter's bow.

felyoles: Endpieces, curtain holdbacks, or any holder or retarding block.

female Toby: The beldame Toby, made by Whieldon and other Staffordshire potters from 1770s.

femerol; fumerol: A smoke vent; a chimney turret.

fence viewer: Official appointed by a community to examine the fencing of the commons and keep same in repair. From 17th century the fence regulation was 20 feet of fence for each head of cattle grazed on the commons.

fenere: Early spelling of veneer.

fêng-huang: Noble crest of the Empress of China, having a peacock's wings, a pheasant's head, swallow's beak, turtle's neck, and dragon's body.

fengite: Transparent alabaster, much esteemed for windowpanes in the Renaissance.

ferat: Drum-shaped vessel of brass, copper, block tin, or wrought iron, having upright side handles. A cylindrical kettle. [*Example pictured.*]

Fernald furniture: Traditionally mentioned in Maine and New Hampshire; reference would seem to be to furniture made by a company named Fernald, operating at Biddeford or Saco, Me., or both, c. 1840. It is in the Empire style.

fern settee: Cast-iron settee in fern pattern. Date is 1870s-90s.

ferrils: Ferules.

Ferris wheel: Any name or object having this reference is of a date after 1892, when George Ferris erected a huge observation wheel at the Chicago Columbian Exposition. This wheel had 36 cars of 60-passenger capacity each. A souvenir booklet given to riders has an auction record of $20. Any object named "Ferris Wheel Pattern" of manufacture prior to 1892 is misnamed.

Ferry Bridge ware: Wares made at the Tomlinson & Co. and Tomlinson, Foster, Wedgwood & Co. pottery at Ferry Bridge, Yorkshire, England. The Wedgwood of this firm was Ralph, son of Thomas, the partner of Josiah, and a remarkably inventive genius whose experiments were costly to the pottery. (He later had his own pottery.) The Ferry Bridge works made cameos, tea and coffee services, and tablewares, granite wares, et cetera. Marks are FERRYBRIDGE, with a variant having the D in reverse; Lion & Unicorn with FERRYBRIDGE & AUSTRALIAN POTTERIES: WEDGWOOD & CO. (on some cameos) and TOMLINSON & CO.

fescule: A pointer; a section.

Festoon: Pattern of pressed glass featuring bands of fans and dots with drapery in festoon form made up of blocks and dots, with pendules on some draping points. Late pattern, but good.

feu de joie: Celebrative bonfire, often accompanied by fireworks.

feul; fewel; fuel: Any combustible matter. From the French *feu* (fire).

feuterer: Variant of pewterer.

fewster: Saddle maker.

F.F. & F. mark: Reference may be to Francis, Field & Francis, tin-plate, copper, and brass workers of Philadelphia, c. 1825-50s. The mark is often found on American-made spurs.

ffittis: Downcast or are cast down. Probably 15th-century English.

flagillet: Flageolet; a wind instrument; a musical horn.

fflock: Raveled carpeting or tapestry used as a filling for bed sacks, pillows, and bolsters.

ffloor: Floor.

ffoork: Fork.

fiat: Dictation, order, or pronouncement. Literally, let it be done.

fiat glasses: Jacobite relics, made mostly in reign of George I by supporters of the Stuart cause. They are also called amen glasses.

fiat money: Bills and low-value metal coinage issued by fiat of the ruler to offset scarcity.

fibble de dido: A gadget, a hootenanny, a dingus; any "patented" article of doubtful usefulness.

fibula: A decorative pin; a fastening pin.

fictile: A plastic, such as potter's clay. The fictile art is the art of the potter. Term derives from fictitious, imitative, a fiction.

fiddle-back stand: A candlestand with a shield in form of a fiddle back. [*Example pictured.*]

fiddle-back chair: See Chairs, All Kinds.

fiddle head: The French scroll, used as a footing on French-style cabriole legs and found on all true Chippendale legs of this kind. The phrase "fiddle-head foot" is correct in spite of its awkwardness.

fiddle spoon: Spoon with handle of somewhat fiddle shape, in profile.

fiddlestick: The violin bow.

fiddle-top table: A rare type of Georgian table, the top of which in profile or silhouette is fiddle-shaped. It is not a true fiddle contour but a reverse blocking. [*Example pictured.*]

fiddlewood: The American evergreen of the vervain family, properly the Citharexylum.

fiddling Toby: See Shipmate Toby.

Field & Clark glass: Cut glass produced by a firm so named at Utica, N.Y., from 1820s to 1840s.

field bed: Any bed with a domed, ogee-curvate canopy, or a tenting imitative of the profile and contour of a field tent. [*The various types are pictured.*] These beds were advertised in the colonies as early as the 1760s. Small wickerwork children's beds with high posts and similar tentings are known as field cradles. The Pittsburgh *Cabinetmaker's Price Book* of 1830 calls the field bed a "field post bedstead," with one parrel in headboard, circular, elliptic, or ogee top, plain footboard, and urn in center of top.

Fifield sofa: Upholstered sofa made by J. M. B. Fifield & N. W. Robinson, Charlestown, Mass., from 1840s. Late Directoire and Empire styles.

fig: See Baltimore Pear.

fig soap: Soap for washing silverware and jewelry which removed tarnish, leaving the object clean and bright.

figural: Any carving, modeling, or molding after the human figure or after legendary or mythological figures having human attributes and partial or wholly human form. *Animalistic*, generally, is the term applied to figures of beasts. A figural bottle is a bottle in human shape and form. Figural candlesticks of pewter, brass, silver, glass, et cetera; figural hornbooks (covers carved of wood) which served also as dolls; figural sconces, carvings, pottery, glass, tankards, et cetera, are known. Toby jugs are classed as figural pieces, but the Bellarmine face or graybeard jugs are not as they have the mask only and not the entire figure.

figured glass: Pressed glass. Also glass blown in a figured mold, a mold that impressed a design on the blown parison forced into the mold by the breath of the blower. There is an extensive note on this term in *Victorian Glass*, Chapter XVI, by Ruth Webb Lee.

figure-8 back: See Chairs, All Kinds.

figure flasks: The early examples are of *dinanderie* or "tin-copper" pewter and date from 15th century or earlier. The Denby & Codnor Park potteries in the early 19th century made many stoneware bottles and flasks, including King William IV and his Queen. Many German examples were made from 1900 to 1914; these include grotesques and caricatures of dancers.

figureheads: Carved effigies of people, mythological characters, goddesses, Muses, national emblems, eagles, et cetera, made to adorn the prows of ships. The finest example known in the U.S. is from the frigate *Lancaster*—a huge eagle carved by Bellamy of Kittery Point, Me. This is now in the Mariners Museum, Newport News, Va.

figure lamp: Manufacturers' term for a Greek-revival gas fixture that is in the form of a goddess or virgin, supporting a grid of perforated tubes providing many jets of gas flame. Date is from c. 1815. [*Example pictured.*]

figurines: Statuary in miniature, some-times precise as to scale. Known in all antique and modern centuries, from ancient Egypt and China to yesterday and today. Jade, metal, pottery, porcelain, majolica, ivory, bone, stone, iron, brass, silver—everything was used to make these decorative objects, even papier-mâché and pressed tin plate. Carved wood examples date from earliest times.

filature: Reeling silk from cocoons, and the place where it is done.

filbeard: The filbert bush and its nuts.

filgrained; filigreed: Open lacelike work with wire; any fine openwork. Filigreed glass is an art glass made from fusing previously prepared filigreed canes, the filigree effect achieved by various colors of glass within a core of clear glass.

Fillemier work: Figural veneering achieved by an improved machine patented by Joseph Fillemier, Philadelphia, 1848.

fillet: A thin banding; a faceting; a narrow molding.

fillister: A rabbeting plane for cutting on wood panels in the flat or beveled. Work is termed "fillistered."

filo: A silk floss of six strands made in at least 100 shades and hues.

filter cock: A spigot with a filtering device incorporated in the assembly, patented 1847.

Fine Cut: Pattern of pressed glass featuring an all-over block effect imitative of fine cutting on the wheel.

Fine Cut & Block: Pattern of pressed glass featuring an all-over pattern of blocks which are really diamond forms, interlaced, the fine cutting in the fields of the charged diamonds, with fan fronds and other busy elements. A pattern much favored by some collectors.

Fine Cut & Panel: Not a variant of the above but a baroque shape with ovate panels in several widths, the broader ones filled with this same imitation of fine wheel cutting.

fine line: A technique of groundwork in glass cutting: the cuts are almost microscopic lines, horizontal, vertical, and oblique, forming a background on which deep cutting was sometimes done.

Fine Rib: Pattern of pressed glass featuring an all-over series of fine vertical and closely set ribs.

finger-carved: (1) Two- and three-groove carving at ends of arms of various chairs. (2) The curved linear carving on the marginal woodwork of much Baroque-revival and 19th-century Louis XV furniture, and on English Victorian work. Generally a series of two grooves on either side of a curvate raised molding which, in finer examples, is carved in fruit and flower forms.

finger glass; finger basin: The object we call a finger bowl.

finger names: According to nursery myths, the fingers of the hand are named Tom Thumbkin, Will Wilkin, Long Gracious, Betty Bodkin, and Little Tit.

finial: A top piece; an *épi*—flame shape, urn, acorn, leaf, bud, spike, flower, and other forms, some figural, some animalistic.

fir (fyr): Generic name for any roughly squared log of the pine family and for plates, scants, joists, and girts cut in the squaring. Also timber of the fir tree (Abies species), differing from pines and spruces in that the wood shows no resin ducts.

fireboard: A board cut to fit the opening of a fireplace, decorated by painting, papering, carving, covering with needlework or in some other fashion, and used in summer season to cover the opening level with cheeks of the masonry or tile facing.

fireboard prints: Large domino papers, sold in considerable quantities in 19th century, printed with scenes or elaborate designs in colors. These were pasted on the fireboards with a bordering. The prints are approximately 24 inches square. *See* Steele, Richardson & Harris.

fire bottle: Small bottle containing a layer of phosphorus covered with water. Slivers of wood dipped in bottle to the phosphorus were dried and, when rubbed on a rough surface, became a kind of friction match. To present-day collectors: Do not attempt this technique of fire making without consulting a registered chemist and your physician!

firebox: Any box of paraphernalia for fire making. There are many varieties, including flint and steel, slow match and flint, tinderbox, metal boxes with compartment for wood sticks tipped with chlorate of potash for dipping in a vial of sulphuric acid.

fire buckets: (1) Canvas buckets used by lines of volunteers (bucket brigades) to convey water from a pool or cistern to a fire engine. Thousands were used in this operation to keep the engines supplied. (2) Ceremonial leather buckets symbolic of the fire-fighting companies, painted and decorated by talented artists or coach painters. [*One of the latter is pictured.*]

fire-cloud ware: Spotted or mottled red (on dark ground) pottery of the Southwest American Indians.

fire dam: Figural andirons in form of bare-breasted females or female busts. [*Example pictured found at Portsmouth, N.H.*]

fire detector: A home fire-alarm device, sometimes involving use of a fine thread which burned at the merest touch of a flame and released a spring which set off alarm. Many varieties, dating from 1700s to 1900s.

fire-extinguisher bottle: Thin glass bottles, generally globular, sometimes nested in prongs of metal that melts under 220 degrees. When dropped or thrown at the base of a fire the chemical contents smothered the fire. The "California bear bottle" is a fire-extinguisher bottle.

fire forks: Shovels of various shapes.

fire frame: Cast-iron brass-fronted frame that is a modified Franklin-type stove for insertion in a fireplace, as the Allen & Backus heater, made from 1820s to 1840s and thereafter improved for use with coal and gas.

fire holder: Hearthside elegancy of wrought iron or brass in form of a small stool or platform on legs, with a handle, having an upright rod with decorative clamp to hold a long sliver of resinous wood. 18th century. [*Example pictured.*]

fire iron: The steel piece of a flint-and-steel assembly.

fire kerb: A low fender.

fire kindler: Various ceramic or mineral sponges, soaked in spirits of wine, turpentine, or kerosene, used in the hearth instead of kindling wood. The present-day Cape Cod lighter is descended from an early form.

fire lamp: Name sometimes given to a candlestick with a hurricane type of shade fitting in a slotted holder. In brass, silver, and Sheffield plate.

fireman's ale horn: A fireman's trumpet, plugged at the mouthpiece to provide a container for ale, quaffed from the bell of the horn.

fireman's helmet: Leather and oiled-canvas headgear with peaked crown and brim narrow in front and down-flaring behind. Painted with insignia of company and rank, often with a ribbon. Date is from early 19th century.

fire marks: Early fire insurance company markers for "insured" properties. Usually made of cast iron with emblems, symbols, et cetera. Most examples are from Philadelphia and eastern Pennsylvania. These are relics of the days when an insurance company maintained fire-fighting apparatus and sponsored the firemen's company. The custom dates from the 1750s, and emblems or marks are now desirable antiques. The Home Insurance Company, N.Y., has a notable collection.

fire mill: Small mechanical device rotating a rough wheel against a flint, and directing the sparks to a drawer of tinder.

fire pan: A fire carrier.

fire picture: Fire screen, painted in design, pattern, or scene, with muriates and acetates of cobalt and copper. The painting was invisible until the screen was heated by the fire, after which the work appeared in tones of green, blue, and yellow. A conceit or elegancy of the 1840s.

fire pike: A poker.

fireplace heater: Not a Franklin or Backus stove, but a small warm-air furnace for placing within a fireplace. These devices had a coal magazine that provided for 24-hour burning without attention. Made from mid-19th century, but most generally used from 1870s.

fireplace papers: Apron-shaped fancy paper, fringed with cut paper, placed over a laid fire and extending outward over the hearth. Used in summer instead of a fireboard, 1850s–80s.

fire-polished: Glass annealed at high temperature. All glass must be annealed or tempered after making. Much pressed glass was fire-polished.

fireproof hand: Double-jawed pincers of iron, connected to act in unison, with two rods for grasping. These were used to handle hot grates, cooking utensils, roasted oysters, and other broiling viands. Made of cast iron and patented 1868.

fire sack: Large canvas sacks used by firemen to carry valuables from burning buildings. Used from mid-18th century, and many marked with insignia of fire company.

fire-screen desk: Shallow drop-front desk box set vertically between footed uprights, serving as a fire screen and a desk. These date from 1780s, and very few of American make are known.

fire-screen table: Four-legged tea table, the screen being a sliding frame attached to the two back legs and covered with a heavy fabric or a painted panel of japanned metal. Made from mid-18th century.

fire shut: A framed panel of metal fitting within the fireplace opening and having slides operating behind pierced openings or decorative shutters, to regulate draft and, at will, completely enclose the fire. Then the metal shield served as a convection heater. Made from c. 1725.

fireside figures: The clavel pages of the 16th century, imitative of carved figural fireplace stiles of the 15th century. Most surviving examples are English or Dutch; only three or four sets of authentic American figures are known. Two of these are from the home of Loderwick Bamper, the Dutch merchant who "retired" to New York and established a glassworks in 1752. A pair of the Bamper figures, a grenadier and a vrow, are owned by Armour Smith, Yonkers, N.Y. (Museum of the Hudson Valley), and a similar pair is owned by a direct descendant of Bamper. Fireside figures are known in sizes ranging from 30 to 80 inches high; most of them are profiled boards, painted in the portrait technique. One pair, of King William and Queen Mary, done in needle point or *gros point*, has the needlework stretched over a shaped flat board. There are quite a few sets of fireside figures now in America. The proper place for them is at either side of a fireplace, close to the wall or stile.

fireside settee: Three chairs, one with a single right arm, one with a single left arm, and one with no arms, designed for use around a fire. When set in a line they form a three-seat settee. Date is from c. 1810. In modified Sheraton style, these assemblies are precisely what was introduced as an entirely new furniture idea in the 1930s. [*Example of one unit of ensemble pictured.*]

fire steels: Sometimes used in reference to andirons of polished steel or irons trimmed with polished steel instead of brass. Gun-metal andirons.

fire stone: Soapstone, or any gray porous siliceous stone, cut into slabs for fireplace lining, hearths, or stove plates. Also the true flint stone and the white flint.

fire stool: Any low stool or cricket.

fire thrower: A rare 18th-century weapon consisting of a large-caliber barrel mounted on a pike, fired by flint, frizzen, and fire pan, controlled by a trigger on the pike. A charge of powder fired combustibles from the barrel.

fire torch: Large-wick brass or iron open lantern swung in gimbals and mounted on rods. At first used by firemen in answering night alarms, these devices finally became parade torches. Many varieties.

firing glass: Thick-stemmed, heavy-bottomed wineglasses stout enough for pounding on the table in "firing" a round of applause. [*Example pictured.*]

firkin: A butter weight—56 pounds. Firkin, as a liquid measure, was used for measuring ale, beer, cider, and perry.

firmament: A jeweled headdress; a star-bedecked coiffure.

fish; fishtail: The IXΘΣ (Greek for fish) symbol, from the first characters of the words "Jesus Christ, Son of God, Saviour." This belief of all early Christians resulted in the use of the fish as a symbol for the faith from the first century A.D. This usage is found reflected in fish weather vanes, fish engraved on communion flagons, cups, and glasses, and the fishtail used as a handle for porringers.

fish drainer: Perforated tiles of oblong or oval form, used on platters upon which broiled, boiled, baked, or fried fish were laid for service. Many varieties, including examples by Leeds, Wedgwood, and other famous potters.

fish eaters: Table utensils in pairs; a side-bladed, spoon-handled knife and a special form fork with wide tines, known in silver, Sheffield plate, and electroplate.

Fisher, John: The cabinetmaker of Charleston, S.C., who, in 1767, advertised indoor window jalousies or Venetian window blinds. Fisher was evidently a first-rate workman with European contacts or experience and may have been Swiss.

Fisher glass: Products of the Bloomingdale Flint Glass Works, N.Y., 1820-45, under the management of John and Richard Fisher, who also maintained a retail store for the sale of these products. Table- and housewares, novelties, et cetera.

Fisher mirrors: Baroque and oval mirror frames made by Fisher & Co., Philadelphia, from 1850s.

Fisher porcelain: Ware made at Budapest, Hungary. It is reticulated or pierced, has a glossy glaze, and is marked FISHER.

Fisherville furniture: Caldwell, Amsden & Co. and William Robinson had furniture factories at Fisherville, N.H., from 1850s, producing cottage and the so-called Victorian-style furniture.

fish flask: Fish-form flasks dating from 15th century (of *dinanderie*) were made to the 20th century. Examples in pottery, glass, pewter, silver, redware, stoneware, et cetera. There is a fish bitters bottle of glass.

fish globe cage: Globular fish bowl with an enlarged hollow bottom large enough to accommodate a small bird cage. The bowl proper, filled with water and stocked with fish, and the cage with a small bird provided a "conversation piece" in the parlor. When found these glass globes are often mistakenly called flycatchers.

fish-head plaques: Modeled porcelain heads of game fish, painted in proper colors and mounted on stands, as trophies. Chelsea and Derby potteries are known to have made such elegancies. [*Example pictured.*]

fishhook broiler: A toasting rack with hooklike holders. [*Example pictured is of wrought iron, dating from 17th century.*]

fish kettle: Covered boiling or roasting pan with an inner drainer. [*Example pictured.*]

Fish lamp: Reference is to maker, W. L. Fish, who made an attachment for a kerosene lamp to turn it into a nursery stove. [*Example pictured is of c. 1863.*]

fish of gold: Articulated scaled fish made

of gold plates skillfully joined. Imported from China c. 1680s or 1690s, it was copied in silver and gold as a precious curiosity by 1725.

fishpond table: Game tables were sometimes so called because the counters used in games were often in the form of fish, and these were placed in the shallow wells in the table tops at each player's place.

fishpool: The depressions carved or cut in gaming-table verge.

Fish Scale: Pattern of pressed glass featuring vertical panels of double rows of fish scales alternating with clear.

fish scale: (1) A Chinese pattern of porcelain decoration. (2) A form of embroidery. (3) Fish scales, dried, used in fancywork.

fish trowel: Silver slicing knife for serving cooked fish. Resembles a modern pie or cake server. Blade is usually of silver, often pierced, and handle is of ebony, porcelain, or bone. Also called a fish slice.

Fisk ironwork: Ornamental statuary, animals, fountains, furniture, and some stove and ovenwares made by J. W. Fisk Ironworks, New York City, established in 1850s or earlier.

Fisk paving: Asphaltum paving.

Fislerville glass: New Jersey Glass Works, established at Fislerville c. 1850, made flasks, bottles, and hollow ware.

Fitch, John: Button maker, silversmith, clock- and watchmaker, and steamboat builder whose life was a battle between inspiration, rum, and despond. He was born in Connecticut in 1743 and died in Kentucky in 1798. He worked at Trenton, N.J., Bucks County, Pa., and Philadelphia. He owed his steamboat experimentation and his successfully operated vessel to William Henry of Lancaster, Pa., the inventor and riflemaker who had a steamboat on the Conestoga River in 1763. Fitch had close contact with Henry during the Revolution, when Fitch operated as a sutler to the troops.

Fitzgerald furniture: Products of the Peter Fitzgerald furniture factory at Cincinnati from 1830s. Made sofas, chairs, and cabinet furniture in the early Empire style.

Fitz-Squab: Pseudonym of the first American comic-strip artist, who did the comic-section drawings for the New York *Mercury*, 1843.

five boys: The porcelain more commonly called Hirado, *which see*.

five-leg chair: *See* Chairs, All Kinds.

Five Little Dynasties: The five short periods of influence in China, A.D. 907–960.

five-post bed: High post bed with three posts at the foot and two at the head, after a French style. Late 18th and early 19th centuries.

five Stuart Washingtons: Reference is to the five duplicates of Stuart's first portrait of Washington, painted in 1795. In 1887 these duplicates were owned by William Channing, Providence, R.I.; Joseph Harrison, Philadelphia; Mrs. Rogers, Lancaster, Pa.; Beverly Betts, New York City; and an anonymous owner in Great Britain. The latter example was copied in an engraving appearing in the *European Magazine* in 1800. The portrait shows Washington in uniform, with left hand

resting on a telescope, and is three-quarter length.

flabellum: Accordion-pleated circular fan.

Flaccus glass: Pressed glass made by E. C. Flaccus Co., Wheeling, W. Va., from 1890s. Milk-white covered dishes of battleship, deer, dog, cat, and hen are known, among other late novelties and tablewares.

flacking comb: A wide-toothed comb.

flacon: A small flask; a special container.

flag & shield tumblers: Pressed-glass tumblers made as souvenirs for the Centennial celebration. They display an eagle and shield on one side and the 13-starred flag of 1776 on the other.

flag-bottomed: Seated with woven rushes or flags. Same as rush-bottomed.

flag chair: Reference is to the seat; flag-bottomed.

flageolet: Six-stop musical pipe. There is a 19th-century American example impressed with an eagle and "U.S."

flag fan: A stiff fan blade mounted on the handle as a flag.

flag-house flags: The first (it is averred) commercial flag factory in the U.S. was established in 1834 by Sally McFadden on Greenwich Street, New York City. Her shop was known as the flag house.

flambé: Mottling of pottery glaze in flame form.

flambeau sconce: Torch-form wall fixture to support candle or candles.

flame finial: A finial carved or molded in flame form.

flame stitch: The *point d'hongroise* stitch, a series of zig-zags in blending colors, usually brilliant.

flaming halo: A Chinese temple candleholder of vaselike form, having a cup form at top and another below its center section.

flam pie: A thick tart of spiced and sugared apples or other fruit, served with a dash of rum.

flampoynes; flampoyntes: Pork pies.

Flanders brick: A polishing brick of soft quality similar to Bath brick and sammen brick (*which see*). Fired from river silt or sandy clay.

flanged cover: Any cover or lid having a flange extending below its rim, fitting within the object it covers. Flanged covers on glasswares were superseded c. 1805 by the galleried rim, which is a flaring flange on the object proper.

flanging aromatiques: A series of small perforated paper boxes of graduated size, each filled with aromatic powder in cotton, strung together on elastic and suspended from a chandelier. When pulled, the elastic shook out some of the powder. Air perfumer of 19th century.

flap drum table: Any drum table having lift-up flaps as a part of the top, giving access to the drum section and dispensing with drawers.

flap fire screen: A three-footed pedestal-type table base having a high column on which is mounted a wood panel to serve as a fire screen, together with a narrow crossbar to which is fitted a falling flap. This flap served as a half-top table for

**PIKE'S
NURSERY OR NIGHT
LAMP,**
AND
**TEA AND COFFEE
BOILERS.**

Arranged for either KER-
OSENE or GAS. Water is
boiled, Tea drawn, Coffee
made, Meat fried, Eggs boiled,
Farina and Gruel cooked, and
all done by the same flame
that lights the room.

1, Barberini or Portland Vase. 2, Dutch Stoves, one of 1750 (left) and one of 1850. 3, Egg and Dart Molding. 4, Fan Mirror. 5, Federal Mirrors (2). 6, Fiddle-Back Candlestand. 7, Fiddle-Top Table. 8, Figure Lamp. This is a gas burner of c. 1825. The figure is a traditional Vestal holding up her "sieve" full of water. 9, Fire Dams. 10, Fire Holder. 11, Fish-Head Plaque. 12, Fireside Settee. 13, Firing Glass. 14, Fishhook Broiler. 15, Fish Kettle. 16, Fish's Lamp. 17, Footman. 18, Four-Gore Bottle. 19, Fourneau. 20, French Revival Chairs. 21, Flower Shell.

155

reading and writing. Credited to Thomas Hodgkins of Salem, Mass., as maker, 18th century.

flashing; flashed: Coated with another color. True flashing, as on glass, is an exceedingly thin coating fixed by fire, but wearing off in time. Casing, sometimes called flashing, is a technique using a thick coating of another color.

flasket: (1) A basket. (2) A small flask.

flask-lens: Lens-shaped flasks with screw-thread necks, sometimes considered to be flasks made for screw caps, but originally fitted with a screw cap and turned wooden handhold. The glass section was filled with alcohol or water and the lens used in either classroom work, in the lithographing business, or some other photographic or drawing pursuit. Examples marked "Babbits Chromo-Lens, Patent App. For"· are known. Some of the examples are of very soft glass.

Flat Diamond: Pattern of pressed glass featuring alternating panels of clear glass with panels of a flat diamond impression.

Flat Diamond & Panel: Pattern of pressed glass featuring an oval panel set vertically, alternating with a crisscross diamond pattern.

flat joint: Said of tables with leaves, having both top and leaf edges flat, without the early tongue-and-groove or rule joint. Actually this flat joint is the oldest, but few connoisseurs seem to like it.

Flat Panel: Pattern of pressed glass of simple design, featuring a series of ridged panels set vertically, alternating with clear glass panels.

flat teapot: A low teapot, squat and curvate.

flattened pear: Another, and more apt, term for the glass bottle shape generally known as violin.

Flattened Sawtooth: Pattern of pressed glass in which the sawtooth design is truncated or flattened, and hence has a flat diamond faceting.

flaun: A custard.

flaut: A roll of wool for spinning; a roving.

flax damask: Jacquard-loomed linen-and-silk dress fabric of 1840s.

Flaxman chessmen: The chess set of 17 figures modeled by Flaxman and produced in black, blue, green, and white jasper ware by Wedgwood.

flea-bitten: Dark speckled coloration.

fleazoo: A small fur collar much affected as dress by wantons, who first had this term applied to their collars and then, by a twist of the term, it was changed to "floozle."

fleckstone: The small stone used in spinning.

Fleeson hangings: Domino papers, pasted together and rolled, made by Plunkett Fleeson of Philadelphia from c. 1760s. This is said to be the first wallpaper made in the colonies.

Flemish front: Carved chest fronts executed in Flanders and shipped to England for incorporation in finished chests. This was an early use of the parts-assembly method, dating from 17th century.

Fleur-de-Lis & Drape: Pattern of pressed glass featuring a flower form more Greek in style than imitative of a fleur-de-lis. This element is impressed on the juncture of vertical panels, bisected by a swag of drapery. A really good design.

flexible inkstand: Made of what Daniel Webster called "elastic metal," Goodyear's vulcanized rubber. A vertically ribbed round receptacle with a glass cup. Squeezing the ink-filled well caused the ink to fill the cup.

flexible statues: Early term for articulated wood manikins used by artists as models.

Flight & Barr: Worcester porcelain made after the Dr. Wall period under the management of these gentlemen, from 1783

flint: Natural silex.

flint cutter: A maker of gun and other striking flints.

flint enamel: Pottery glaze containing calcined flint.

flint glass: Originally glass made from the natural silex that is flint. Finally lead was added, and lead glass and flint glass are now synonymous except to advanced collectors of genuine antique glass, made from 17th century and prior to that age.

flintlock: Any firearm using flint in a jawed hammer, hitting a frizzen and sparking into a firing pan covered by the frizzen before firing. It is an improvement on the wheel-lock firearm, in which a wheel spun, hitting the flint and causing the ignition spark. All Conestoga or Lancaster rifle-barreled guns of the 18th century were flintlocks. Many have been converted to cap type, and in recent years certain of these have been reconverted to flintlocks.

flintware: Any ceramic ware having a flint glaze.

flip: A beverage of beer, rum, and sugar, lightened with a slice of buttered toast. Served hot or cold. Hot buttered rum is a quick flip, dispensing with the toasted bread and using water instead of beer. *See also* Tiff.

flip glass: The generous-sized full-bodied tumblers used in serving flip.

flitch: A smoked side-meat section of hog.

flitter work: Iridescent painting achieved by use of a colorless tacky varnish and a dusting of bronze powder. A coarse form of luster painting.

float-boarded: Said of filled buckets when fitted with a float of wood to prevent spillage in handling. Generally used with fire buckets in the bucket brigade.

floating glasshouse: An Ohio river boat fitted up with a glass furnace and housing accommodations for managers and workers. Operating from 1842.

float lamp: A hollow disk of metal with an airtight wick hole. The disk floated on oil and the flaming wick consumed the oil. A chamber or night light. Date is c. 1790.

flocked: Ground or scraped felt or other fabric, reduced to fuzz and blown on a design painted in adhesive gum. This formed the raised felted pattern called flocking.

floor billiards: Carpet billiards, a game played on the floor.

floor carpets (ENGLISH): It is said these date from 1740s, when Peter Parisot set up a carpet loom at Paddington and then at Fulham, patronized by the Duke of Cumberland. Passavant purchased the mill in 1753 and moved it to Exeter. Exeter carpets were exported to the colonies and were among the first floor carpets other than the examples then used by some royal governors.

floor cloth: Heavily filled canvas painted in tessellated patterns resembling marble flooring. Used under tables and to cover the entire floor of a room, these coverings were the beginning of linoleum. The filler was wood dust, cork dust, and jellied linseed oil. At London, England, in 1739 John Carwitham published a guide titled *Various Kinds of Floor Decorations, represented both in plano and perspective, being useful for ornamenting the floors of halls, rooms, &c., whether in pavement of stone or painted floor cloth.* Printed oilcloth and linoleum are cheap imitations of the original floor cloth, which was hand-painted. Paintings and portraits of most of the interiors of our 17th- and 18th-century colonial mansions show what looks like a tessellated or tiled marble floor. It isn't—it is a painted floor cloth. These cloths, in all likelihood, were on the floors of the original Governor's Mansion at Williamsburg, Va. We know that Governor Burnet of New England and New York had them. Some are mentioned in his inventory. The Henry Francis duPont Winterthur Museum displays a piece of original floor cloth in precisely the proper manner—under a table.

floor lamp: Any lighting fixture, whether for illumination by candles or by a wick and oil font. Wrought-iron floor stands for candles pre-date the Renaissance. These devices were used in every century from the 14th, and perhaps they descend from similar stands used by Romans, Greeks, and Egyptians of pre-Christian Era. Known in all period styles, and of types varying from torch holders to electric lights.

floor skates: Roller skates. Early examples have four rollers set in a line, approximating the single broad-bladed ice skate. Made from 1850s in the U.S.

floral Tucker: Reference is probably to the semi-porcelain wares, made at Philadelphia by Tucker and by Tucker & Hemphill, which were decorated with flower sprays and gold banding in the French style.

Florence Cut: Pattern of cut glass featuring bold fans, stars, and lozenges of fine crisscross cutting. A so-called "brilliant" pattern, dating from 1889. American.

Florence flask: The non-standing oval wine bottles of Italy, generally fitted with a straw-work case that also provides the base for standing.

florentine: (1) A rich custard. (2) A rich embroidered fabric.

Florida bird prints: The Maquard prints from *Birds of Florida*, issued in small folio, in parts, 1872–78. There are 18 in all.

florin: Generally an 18th-century term for a monetary unit of various countries, current in the colonies and worth, in today's coinage, from 50 cents to $1.50. The Dutch guilder was called a florin; so was a two-shilling piece.

flounder house: A residence with the back building or L constructed first and the fore-structure never added. This type of construction, while not common, was not nearly so scarce as some authorities have thought. What is now rare is survival of such houses. In 1940 examples were still standing, and occupied, at Alexandria, Va., and Lancaster, Pa. These "flounders" stood from 20 to 40 feet back of the normal building line of the street.

flour chest: Ancestor of the kitchen cabinet, a large enclosed hutch with vent for flour within a compartmented chest having many small drawers for spices and a cupboard for woodenware. [*Example pictured.*]

flow-blue: Staffordshire and other wares decorated with a blue that maculated (smudged or ran) in the firing. There are purple-, green-, and sepia-decorated wares with the same flow of the color. Examples are known from the potteries of Adam, Mayer, Challinor, Dilwyn, Wedgwood, Ridgeway, and from potteries at Maastricht in the Netherlands. Patterns displaying this kiln flow include Scinde, Kyber, Tonquin, Whampoa, Pellew, Kinshaw, Temple, Oregon, et cetera.

Flower & Panel: Pattern of pressed glass featuring broad vertical panels of cane weave with a large daisy form imposed top and bottom. The broad panels alternate with plain ones. Said to have been made in mosaic or marbled glass.

Flower Band: Pattern of pressed glass featuring a broad band of what looks like modeled flowers.

flower case: Sheet-iron-framed glasssided box having a perforated platform within and a bed of sand beneath it. Used from 1840s for carrying cut flowers.

flower cutters: Actually the petal cutters, of which there were at least 30 different shapes, used in making wax flowers.

flowered feet: Brass footings for chair, table, and cabinet furniture legs. Used from 1745 or 1750 and now rarely seen. American hardware makers manufactured this style of footing to 1840s.

flowered furniture: (1) William & Mary style lacquered furniture decorated with flowers and scenes in the Chinese taste. (2) Any flower-decorated, painted or stenciled, furniture.

flowered handle: The openwork ear of a porringer is so called. Even the brackets used to strengthen the handles of porringers seem to have specific names among advanced collectors, who speak of linguiform, circular, triangular, quatrefoil, et cetera.

flowered knob: Any door or cabinet knob of china or porcelain painted in floral pattern. These seem to have been used quite freely from 1835 to 1855, but most of them have been replaced with brass or glass knobs.

Flowered Oval: Pattern of pressed glass featuring a ring or band of large ovals with patera-like forms within them.

flowered paper: Wallpaper or fancy paper.

flowered shade: A lamp shade of ornate

"home" workmanship, draped with artificial flower sprays, some of which dropped from rim of shade.

flowered tabby: Flowered silk fabric.

Flower Garden Riley: A late Imari pattern of Staffordshire ware now called Gaudy Dutch. This pattern is of flowers and leaves in the rust, red, green, and other brilliant colors of the old Imari. The impressed mark is RILEY.

flower horn: Cornucopia-shaped vessel for cut flowers, growing plants, and bulbs. Some made for hanging on wall.

flower-of-mustard: Mustard-seed flour.

Flowerpot: Pattern of pressed glass featuring a large stippled panel on which, in relief, is imposed a ribbed vase with a symmetrical spray of flowers in the textile technique of decoration.

flowers (EARLY NAMES): Coronation was our carnation; sops-in-wine, the striped pink; pawnce, the pansy; chevisaunce, the wallflower; flowre delicl, the fleur-de-lis; daffy-down-dilly, the daffodil.

flowers (of the seasons): In ceramic and textile décor, after the Chinese, these floral motifs denote the seasons: summer, lotus; autumn, chrysanthemum; winter, plum flower; spring, peony.

flower shell: Actual shells or pottery replicas, suspended on cords and used as flower holders and planters. [*Example pictured.*]

flower stand: Turned posts or columns on footings in various styles. The uprights are about 4 feet 6 inches tall and have a cupped top to hold securely a vase, urn, or pot of flowers. There was a considerable production of these elegancies from 1820 to 1850.

flower troughs: Trays or troughs of pressed glass in various shapes, made to assemble into centerpiece arrangements, borders, et cetera, at pleasure of user.

flower-vase screen: Actually a crocheted yarn or other holder of fabric or paper to cover an earthern flowerpot and make it decorative. A homecraft of the 1850s, probably sponsored by *Godey's Lady's Book.*

fluid lamp: Any lamp burning a hydrocarbon or true liquid illuminant, as opposed to fat lamp, which burned semisolid fuels or thick greases.

flummery: Hulled oatmeal boiled until gelatinous, served with sugar and whipped or clotted cream.

flush handles: Cabinet handles set into a conforming brass plate, with a finger slot or index for ease in lifting up or out for use. The plate or escutcheon was inlaid, flush with the wood surface.

Flute: Pattern of pressed glass allied to Ashburton and a variant thereof, called by Ruth Webb Lee "the Colonial Group." The patterns, however, are not of colonial date; they were made from 50 to 100 years after the colonial era. The chief characteristic is a series of panels of varying width with flat or ovate ends. All are imitative of late 18th-century and early 19th-century cutting techniques.

flute cut: A style of glass cutting achieving a series of concave vertical cuts lapping to form ridges, and varying in width to conform to contours of object cut.

fluted molding; fluting: Intaglio round channel grooving on any substance to provide a band, fillet, or decorative effect in a column. Fluting is thus the opposite of reeding, in which the round sections are in relief, imitative of bundles, or fasces, of reeds.

fluting frame: A slotted frame fitted with round cross rods. Fabric wound back and forth over the rods and fixed in the frame took the form of fluting. These devices were much used to provide the bonnet edging in vogue from 1760, and are still used in some religious costumes purporting to be severely plain.

fly bracket: Wing-shaped, wing-out support for a leaf, as the fly or flying bracket of a butterfly table.

fly-go: A fly-shoo, attached to a chair. Generally an upright rod or staff turning to and fro, to which a horizontal fringed rod is attached. Occupant of chair operated the device by a treadle and so chased all flies from around his head.

fly legs: The swing-out legs of a table supporting the drop leaf.

fly market: From the Netherlands Dutch *vleigh*, meaning valley. The terms "fly market" and "flea market" do not refer to insects.

fly's-eye mirror: Decorative reflectors, convex in shape, faceted in imitation of the cellular structure of a fly's eye. Date of vogue seems to have been 1825–60. These often have an ebonized frame with a gilded cable border.

fly stone: Arsenate of iron, dissolved in water to make an insecticide.

flytrap: Various devices to capture flies, but generally referring to the glass globes with conical bottoms having an opening to permit entrance of flies attracted by sugar, syrup, or honey, and from which they could not escape. Bottom of device was raised on a footed ring. Made in considerable quantities from 1840s.

fodder: A parcel of 1950 pounds of lead; a weight.

Foddy, James: Advertised mirrors, pier glasses, and sconces in the New York *Gazette,* 1729. Also olive-wood-framed mirrors and a resilvering service.

foil: (1) A shield or device for protection. (2) Thin hammered metal such as gold foil, silver foil, tin foil. (3) A decorative segment of a circular or semicircular section, as the foils of a fan, a shell, et cetera.

foins: Skunk furs.

foison: Elizabethan English, meaning plenty.

folded: Lapped over, as a folded foot, folded rim on glassware. *See* Linenfold. Earlier form of the word is folden.

folding bed: Gadget furniture of the late 18th century, improved in 19th and made in many forms, all of which provided a bed by night and an article of furniture by day. Made as fold-out sofas, folding desk-bedstead, pull-out lounge bed, cabinet bedstead, wardrobe bedstead, cot bed settee. [*Examples pictured.*]

folding candelabra: Central post with connected arms, each of which has a candle socket. This fixture permitted bringing the lights from all candles to the spot desired. [*Brass example pictured has three arms.*]

folding stereoscope: Lens and photo-holding sections of stereoscope, joined by an accordion skeleton of flat pieces, permitting close folding when not in use.

fold-over & turntable: Pedestal table with oblong top frame on which a pivoted two-piece fold-over top is placed. When turned to right angle of the frame on the pivot, both leaves rest on the frame and so double the size of table top. Made in considerable quantities from 1820s to 1860s in Greek-revival and Empire styles.

foliated: Leaf form, or of foils.

foliating: Coating with tin foil, with mercury as the binding agent.

folio: A paper size. Small folio is any size from 11" x 14" to 11" x 17". Medium folio is 14" x 18" to 15" x 20". Large folio is 19" x 24" to 23" x 27". *See also* Paper Sizes.

folio stand: Any stand to hold prints, drawings, et cetera; a standing case in which these could be stored as the pages of a large book; a stand of drawers for filing flat. Many varieties.

folk art: Every immigrant (and many emigrants) to the American colonies came here to escape the thralldom of mind, body, and conscience that was his lot in Europe. One of the badges of this control was the "folk art" of Europe, all of it a blurred, feeble, or fair copy of elegancies enjoyed by the ruling classes and the merchant guilds. This folk-art tradition was one of the evidences of imposed menial position which the immigrants did escape. It is amazing how quickly the majority (excepting only the ignorant Germanic groups, called "boors" by Benjamin Franklin) threw off this influence and became users of forms more closely allied to the popular arts, and forms known to the custom weavers, lacemakers, master potters, silversmiths, blacksmiths, and other artisans, including the limners. Now any homemade piece of iron, woodwork, embroidery, furniture or wall painting, weather vane, et cetera, that is documentary evidence of freedom from folk tradition and of pioneering spirit is decried by emotional promotion as "folk art" by certain self-appointed leaders of public taste. The entire situation is ridiculous in that, having failed to use the term "popular art" first, these dilettantes now persist in using the term "folk art" and are perhaps accepting, as best they can, the charge of their own unimaginativeness and failure to grasp the true significance of the pioneering spirit that seems to have inspired at least 98% of the immigrants and emigrants to the Atlantic colonies from 1620 to 1800. There are numerous "folk art" groups, all of whom boom the work of national immigrant stocks as folk art. The most active, biased, and befuddled are the pro-German groups of Pennsylvania who, in almost every case, claim as German folk art the *arts populaires* of Switzerland, Sweden, and the Netherlands, made by nationals of these countries working in Pennsylvania. The ridiculous phase of this lies in the fact that what they claim is German is repudiated by German scholars as emphatically not German.

Folkart jewelry: Solid-gold jewelry made by Folkart, Schall & Co., Hartford, Conn., from 1855.

folt: Fold.

Folwell, John: Philadelphia master cabinetmaker and chairmaker who worked in the Georgian and Chippendale "Marlborough" style.

fondu: Cast.

fondus: A technique of color application in stripes which blended into each other.

fonge: To fondle; to take between the hands.

fontaine: Fountain. Also used to describe spigoted urns.

Fontainebleau embroidery: A form of needle-point work of Louis XV period.

Fontana: Italian art pottery often classed with Castel Durante, made from c. 1500. Faience or majolica.

food carriers: Deep metal pans with liners and pierced domed covers, resting on charcoal embers. Used in conveying food from distant kitchens to dining room. Not used generally in America, and known only of actual usage in Virginia and the Carolinas.

foo dogs: Chinese lion-form effigies, known in porcelain, pottery, jade, carved crystal, and various hardwoods, some polychromed.

foolscap: Paper size 12½" x 16". Term derives from the common watermark of this size paper—a fool's cap.

foolscap chair: *See* Chairs, All Kinds.

Foong Taou: Chinese Minister of State, c. A.D. 966, who invented printing by transference to paper of inked impressions of carved wood blocks.

football lamp: Entry or hall lamp with ovo-globular or globose shade.

foot banke: Foot stove. Also, and more properly, a footstool.

foot dresser: Low three-drawer cabinet for keeping stockings and shoes. Top is upholstered for pedicure work. Size is approximately 20 inches square and a foot high.

footed decanter: A standard decanter of glass mounted on three glass feet. Any footed ware, whether in the form of a plateau or actual feet, is sometimes designated with the prefix "footed."

foot jug: Pottery jug with impressions to fit the feet. Filled with hot water, it served as a foot warmer at the foot of the bed, under the covers.

footman: A high-footed brass or iron trivet to hold a hot-water jug or teakettle by the tableside. Also a footed tray of brass and wrought iron with handle for ease in carrying. [*Example pictured.*]

foot measure: Sliding rule with a snub at end and a sliding gauge. Used by boot and shoemakers to establish size of the foot. Fine examples have the toe snub carved in slipper form and the sliding element carved in figural form.

foot muff: A felted or fur-lined overshoe.

footpace: A dais, a stair landing, and the captain's walk on a housetop were designated by this term.

footrest chair: *See* Chairs, All Kinds.

forcer: A chest or coffer.

foredge painting: Scenic or other painting on the front edges of a book, often done so that a slight twist displays another scene. Sometimes the painting is done on an exposed portion of the pages only, a hairline wide, so that when book is fully closed the painting is invisible and returns to view only when the book is so manipulated as to expose the precise surface on which the decorator worked. Said to have been invented by Edwards, bookbinder of Halifax, England, but actually a much older art.

forelow: Aslant, askew, awry.

foreshot: The "faint," or first and last, runs of liquor from a still; generally full of aldehydes and furfurals. Rotgut was made from this potent stuff, rectified with alcohol and rain water.

Forget-Me-Not: Pattern of pressed glass featuring the flower and leaves of this plant of sentiment. Many variants, called Stippled, Forget-Me-Not in Snow, Barred, Paneled, Forget-Me-Not in Scroll, and Ribbed. All are fully described and pictured in *Early American Pressed Glass*, by Ruth Webb Lee. Forget-Me-Not porcelain is studded or encrusted with forget-me-not flowers in relief, or is painted with the flower and leaf.

fork staff: A hollowing plane.

form; forme: Framework of trestles upon which boards were laid to form a table or a long stool.

formatif piece: Carved stone or wood fireplace or mantel jamb. A fireside figure.

former: A gouge.

form piece: A muntin, the divider of a window or other glazed frame.

formulus: A stencil, theorem, or poonah, *which see.*

Forster furniture: Jacob (father) and Charles (son) Forster of Charlestown and Boston, Mass., from 1816 made scroll-arm and Grecian sofas, Partington and Dolphin chairs, Salem rockers, and other specialties.

Forsyth silver: The product of George H. Forsyth, Louisville, Ky., working in 1840s. This 19th-century silversmith's name is not in Ensko III and so is entered here.

fortage paper: Light ruled and lined paper or parchment as a preliminary of engrossing or writing upon it. Made commercially from c. 1616.

fossil marble: Marble containing fossil forms, esteemed for turning stands, *tazze,* and bowls.

Foster set: A pocket writing set of brass.

fotmal: A weight of some 70 pounds.

founday: A space of six days.

fountains: Hydraulic displays of "waterworks," spouting from stone or metal pipes under pressure.

four-column table: A pedestal table, the pedestal being four slender columns springing from a triangular platform which, in turn, has three cabriole-type legs. The top is round and tilting.

four-gore bottle: A specialty of Irish cut glass; an assembly of four triangular bottles having quadrant sides on which the cutting is done. When fitted together

the four look like one stout bottle. [*Example pictured.*]

fourneau: A small pottery stove burning charcoal in an arched opening and topped with a covered pottery dish. 17th to 19th century. [*Example pictured.*]

Four Petal: Pattern of pressed glass featuring geometrically arranged circles and centers, the arrangement forming petals. It is a wonder it was not called Hex Mark or Barn Symbol.

Four Roses: A coverlet pattern of c. 1830 having four roses arranged in a geometrical group, repeated in squares.

foursquare: Absolutely square.

Fox cracker: A hard biscuit made by Fox of Lansingburg, N.Y., from 1815 and sold almost everywhere as a great delicacy, especially for travelers. Fox cracker boxes of tin, painted and paper-covered, are of record.

foxed: Discolored by microscopic fungoid growth. Said of timber and paper when brown stain appears.

Fox glass: H. C. Fox glassware is a line of perfume bottles and druggists' vials. Said to have been made at Reading, Pa.

fox-head creamer: Grotesque fox-head-shaped cream jug, pouring from the mouth. Known in Pratt ware and said to have been made as early as 1500 in pewter and later in silver. [*Example pictured.*]

fox-head cup: Glass, earthenware, china, and silver cups in the form of a fox head, the snout being the handle. Having no bases, these are generally displayed inverted. Some varieties are made with extended ears which serve to steady the cup. In some both snout and ears form a sort of stand support. Made from c. 1740s to 1840s.

frailejon: South Andean plant with hairy stems and leaves; a heavy felted hair cloak.

Fraktur; Fractur: Meaning *Fracturschriften* or *Vorschriften,* generally in the bastard Gallic character called Gothic. Some authorities claim the Gallic script called Gothic is a form of Arabic cursive learned in the Crusades. *See* Script Hangings.

framed seat: *See* Cased Seat.

frame gauze: A gauze cover for picture and mirror frames.

frame table: A permanent or dormant table, as opposed to form and demountable trestle-type tables.

Francis Ware: Painted and decorated tinware by Henry & Thomas Francis, Philadelphia, from 1830s.

François vase: An original Greek-form crater vase found in 19th century by Alphonse F. François, and now in the Florence (Italy) museum. It is considered by some as more important than the Portland vase so ably reproduced by Wedgwood.

frangipani: The fragrant buds and blossoms of the native American *Plumeria,* found in the early 16th century by the Spanish in Mexico and southern Florida. This tree was introduced to the Orient via the Philippines. The incense made from the tree is generally considered oriental.

Frankfort black: Charred lees of wine, providing an excellent black pigment.

Franklin County wampum: Not a joke. Franklin County, N.J., people bored and strung shells, selling them to agents at 12½ cents a string. The agents sold this wampum to Indian traders, who bought furs and blankets with it from the ignorant Indians. The wampum was made to the 1840s.

Franklin-Dyott flask: Glass historic flask made by Dyott at his Kensington Glass Works, and revealing the egotism of the man in thus associating himself and his portrait in glass with Franklin. Known in several varieties, in quart and pint sizes. Fakes reported in 1946.

Franklin emblems: Reference is probably to the emblem book, *Wahren Christendom*, printed for B. Franklin, Philadelphia, 1751. Said to be the most ambitious illustrated book printed in colonial period. The emblems are obscure in meaning but deal with common things. Dr. Christopher Witt, an English mystic, is believed to have financed the venture.

Franklin glass: (1) Hollow ware and bottles made at Franklin (Pa.) Glass Works from 1812 to 1816. (2) Glass made at the Franklin Glass Works of Gillinder, Philadelphia, from 1860s. (3) Also glass made at a works named Franklin, Warwick, Mass., 1812, operating in that decade. (4) Glass made at the Franklin Works, Malaga, N.J.

Franklin maxim plate: Any plate of ceramic, glass-, or tinware featuring the maxims of Poor Richard and the author, Benjamin Franklin. Many varieties, some round, some octagonal in form.

Franklin pottery: See Quigley Ware.

Franklin stove: The ventilating cast-iron fireplace invented by Franklin as a simplification of the "mechanical fire" of the Sieur Gauger, first advocated in France c. 1710. Many varieties. Franklin did not patent his idea, and thousands of his stoves were made in England and sold as American or Pennsylvanian stoves.

Franklin Toby: The snuffing Toby, first made in the late 18th century by Staffordshire potteries, and alleged to be the face and figure of Benjamin Franklin taking snuff.

frayel: A basket made of rushes.

Frazee: American sculptor who worked in stone from c. 1810 to his death in 1852. He rose from apprentice bricklayer to mantel maker and stonecutter, and began carving busts in 1810. He is probably the first American to make a marble bust and is represented in the Boston Athenaeum by seven busts.

Frearstone: Artificial stone made from sand by a formula developed by A. A. Frear, Chicago, c. 1870.

freckled: Mottled.

free-blown: Glass blown with the pipe, modeled with shears and pontil. Hand-blown glass—not mold-blown or blown-molded.

freedom box: Ceremonial box, adaptable for tobacco or snuff, but made to enclose a scroll or keys to the city and given to visiting personages. Much used in England, Ireland, and the U.S. in early days and to 1840s at least.

freedom quilt: Term is loosely used. (1)

A quilt made as a presentation piece to a young man on attaining his majority. (2) A coverlet given to graduating apprentices. (3) A quilt bearing patriotic emblems of freedom.

Free Loves: Sect which settled at Berlin Heights, O., in 1850s, professing free love for all women and their right to have as many lovers as they wished. Artemus Ward wrote a scathing satire on this sect in 1861.

Freeman & Smith iron: Ornamental flowerpots, aquaria, brackets, ferneries, window boxes, et cetera, made by Freeman & Smith Iron Works, Racine, Wis., from 1870s.

freeman sugar: Abolitionists' sugar; they had it shipped in from La Guaira to avoid purchasing it from Southern makers who owned slaves. But the imported sugar was also grown by slave labor. At this distance in time we can appreciate the fact that the rabid abolitionists were tools of the greedy economists who wanted the South's cheap labor destroyed, even though the South was planning its own emancipation program.

free stool: The sanctuary stool or chair in a church from which an offender could not be taken.

Freetown ax: American-shaped bezeled ax made at Freetown, Mass., from 1820s.

Free Will glass: Glassworks named Free Will was located at Williamstown, N.J., from 1835, making bottles, flasks, and vials. Merged with Washington Glass Works 1850.

frein; freyn: Woodenwares made from ash wood.

Freis furniture: Only reference we have found likely is the furniture made, and then sold at auction, by L. Freis of Cincinnati in 1840s.

Fremington: Potting district or town of England where clay ovens, kitchenwares, redwares, and dairy utensils were made from 1830s.

French chair: See Chairs, All Kinds.

French chalk: Steatite; soapstone.

French Cuban furniture: Retired sea captains and wealthy traders of South Florida, from 1830s, had chair and settee frames made in France and then sent to Cuba for caning backs and bottoms. The frames are of walnut, rosewood, and mahogany. The style is Louis XV revival. There is still some of this furniture to be found in Key West, Key Largo, Tavernier, and Coconut Grove. Caning was preferred to upholstery, as it was free from attack by mold, mildew, and insect pests.

French foot: An upscrolling foot, imitative of the headpiece of a violin. See Furniture Footings. Also a curvate bracket foot [*an example of which is among the illustrations*].

French oyster press: A large pincerlike device with a slot in one jaw to hold an oyster and a wedge in the other to open the bivalve. These were made and sold by Picault of Paris from 1840s. Imports to the U.S. were popular among gourmets along the Atlantic oyster coast. [*Example pictured.*]

French polish: Varnish. A derisive term originating in England, where there was considerable contempt for a gloss achieved by a brushed-on liquid. The English idea was linseed oil and beeswax rubbed to a polish.

French porcelain: Soft-paste ware of Rouen, St. Cloud, Lille, Chantilly, and other centers. It is said that soft-bodied porcelain techniques were kept secret for many years and divulged only after Meissen hard paste was developed. Other true porcelain factories were Sceaux, Tournai, Orleans, Arras, St. Amand, and several potteries at Paris. All are 18th century.

French Provençal: Incorrectly designated "provincial," by which term the French would mean *mobilier rustique*, or country furniture. The furniture of Provence is high style and the source to which Paris turned for inspiration. Traces of the true Provençal styling are found in America in the work of Huguenot cabinetmakers and some Swiss *ébénistes* from the Grand Val. Notable among these are the Bachmans of Lancaster, Pa., from mid-18th century.

French pump inkstand: A barometric inkstand which protected the entire content of ink from air and dust but maintained a small pool for use at all times.

French revival: The mode miscalled Victorian in the U.S. is a French Antique revival, whether of Louis XV or Louis XVI styling. This term, however, would seem to stem from England and the attempt of Morant, a cabinetmaker of Bond Street in 1850, to revive the styles of Louis XIV. This was unsuccessful in that little or no difference was discernible between the prevailing French style of Louis XV in England and the more correctly termed Victorian. Some of Morant's pieces were shipped to America, and some of our cabinetmakers, including Quervelle and Henkels of Philadelphia, made it. The latter advertised the Louis XIV style in 1855. [*Examples by Morant are pictured.*]

French tallow: Pottery boxes bearing this name are from the shop of Mrs. Sciple, 23 Ann Street, New York City, who made a hairdressing of this name.

frescade: A cool refreshment.

fresco: Painting on wet plaster. Wall decoration done in any other way is not fresco work.

fresco papers: Wallpapers of scenic type made by Hart, Montgomery & Co., Philadelphia, from 1850s.

fret-carved: Carving that is pierced through; openwork carving.

fret-sawed: Openwork achieved with a fret saw. [*Operation is pictured.*]

fretwork mirrors: Wrongly designated as Chippendale, these mirrors are Georgian and Queen Anne in styling. [*Examples pictured.*]

Frey furniture: Susquehanna Valley Chippendale or Georgian furniture, made 1790–1810 by Jacob Frey, Milton, Pa.

frickle: A fruit basket.

friendship quilt: A handmade quilt, fashioned from blocks or squares borrowed from or made by friends. There was a veritable craze of making these from 1840s to 1860.

frieze: Properly, the mid-section of an entablature. A border placed at any point on a wall between floor and ceiling.

frig: The attempts at blowing and forming glass made by apprentices. The source is from the Greek φρηγω, *phrigo*, to parch. Hence the term is also found used for frying pans and spiders or for pans on feet. There is probably enough material within this one entry to encourage an essay.

frigger: An oddment of glass made by workmen for their own use from remains of metal in pots. Frigging meant doodling with tools and materials by one capable of serious usage.

frit: Dried sand, destined for use in glassmaking. Pulverized calcined flint.

frizz: To raise a burred curly nap on cloth; to crimp, crisp, or curl; to crinkle.

Frizzell glass: Reference is to framed mirrors made at Baltimore, by J. W. Frizzell in the mid-19th century. Some late tabernacle and many French Antique styled examples are attributed to this maker.

frizzen: The movable spring-tauted grater on which the flint of the hammer of a flintlock struck. When struck, the frizzen yielded and uncovered the primed fire pan into which the sparks flew, igniting the primer and so firing the gun. Other methods of firing include such items as the wheel-lock, snaphance, miquelet, and matchlock.

Frobisher, Benjamin: Silversmith of Boston who, in 1829, advertised the ware called Britannia. These data would seem to refute the claims of experts who state Britannia is of a date after 1835.

frog lamp: A Betty lamp.

frog mug: The joke mugs having a molded or painted frog in the inside bottoms, exposed after consuming the ale, beer, or cider in them.

froise: A pancake.

fromard; frow: A splitting tool; a knife mounted at right angles to the handle and hit with a mallet.

front (or out) gate: Said of the supporting gate-form frame of a gate-leg table when the gate does not swing out as a hinge but pulls out straight from a slotted run. [*Example pictured.*]

frontlet: Any band, scarf, or item of jewelry worn on the forehead.

Frost, Edward Sands: The first known commercial producer of hooked-rug patterns. His designs, full size, were applied to the burlap on which the hooking was done. Born in Lyman, Me., 1843, he started his rug-pattern business as a peddling sideline c. 1866 at Biddeford, Me. After 1870 he stenciled his patterns in full color. He sold many thousands, and eventually owned over 7000 pounds of metal stencils. *See* Hooked-Rug Patterns.

frost conductor: Loosely twisted thick ropes of hemp and straw, wound around boles and branches of early-flowering trees, with the lower end of rope drenched in a tub of water. This was called a frost conductor in the 1780s, and presumably it protected the tree blossoms from damage by frost.

Frosted Artichoke: Pattern of pressed glass featuring an artichoke form with well-defined pointed ovate petals. Ruth Webb Lee noted these variants: the petals frosted, other areas clear glass; petals

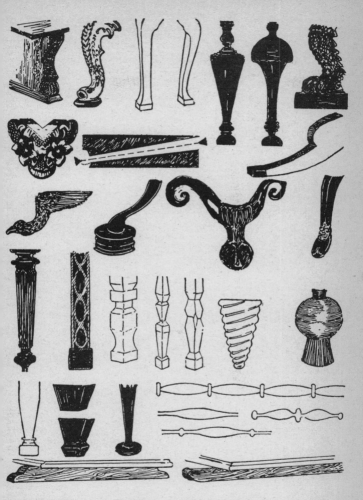

FURNITURE LEG AND FOOT FORMS: Top row: Gambrel, Dolphin, Angular Cabriole (2), Trumpet-Turned, Cup-Turned, Alligator. **2nd row:** Flowered Foot, (brass), method of "turning" a cabriole leg by mounting block off center in lathe, Leg of Mutton Leg. **3rd row:** Eagle Head, Pillbox Foot, Ram's-Horn Foot, Slippered or Sabot Foot. **4th row:** Malbro' Leg, 1820s, Marlborough leg of 1770s, "square-turned" legs; not turned but sawed out, Spiral foot, Thistle Foot. **5th row:** Stock Toe, Stub Feet (2), Button Foot, examples of bobbin turning. **Bottom row:** Shoe Footing on a chest, Skid Footing on a chest.

163

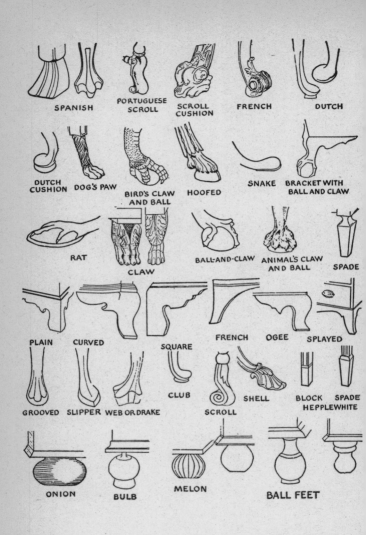

Furniture footings of various types, each identified by its generally known and used name. From *Primer of American Antiques* and other sources, including *House and Garden* and Walpole Society Publications, by permission.

frosted and clear; and the entire pattern in clear glass. **frosted circle:** Features a fan in cornucopia shape, curling from a frosted circle with an impressed daisy-form center. **frosted fruit:** Featuring all-over pattern of grapes, pears, apples, et cetera, on basket weave. It is not frosted or stippled, but gives that effect. **frosted stork:** A stork or crane within an oval medallion with fronds, the bird frosted on clear glass. Covered pieces have a stork-form finial, looking as much like a pelican as the baby-bringing bird.

Frost prints: Sporting subjects, lithographed in colors from paintings by Arthur Burdette (A. B.) Frost. Scribner's issued the first series in 1895, and another series was issued in 1903. The prints are 12" x 19½", mounted on cardboard.

Frothingham & Cross ware: Tin-plate, sheet-iron, and copper utensils made by a firm of this name at Salem, Mass., from 1830s.

Frothingham furniture: Made at Boston and Charlestown, Mass., by Benjamin Frothingham, who worked 1754–1809. He made really excellent cabinetwork of great repute among advanced collectors. He was a major in the Continental Army.

frounce: A wrinkled ornamentation.

frow: A hoe-shaped cutting tool on a short handle, driven with a club or bat, used in cutting clapboarding, shingles, and lath.

frozen Charlotte: Rigid dolls, unarticulated. Name said to derive from the tale of Charlotte, the proud girl who refused to dress warmly for a five-mile ride on a cold day and arrived stiff.

fruggan: An iron used to stir ashes in an oven.

fruit basket: (1) Silver or Sheffield-plate wire baskets with bail handles to hold fruit at table. Real silver examples date from early 1700s. (2) Any chip, willow, or straw basket for cartage of fruit. (3) Willow-work baskets to hold fruit at table.

fruit caddy: Apple-, pear-, pineapple-, or melon-form tea caddy turned from fruit wood.

fruit coolers: Urns, generally of ceramic ware but known also in turned and staved wood and in metalware, designed to hold ice or cold water in a well within the piece, under a dish to hold fruit. Some have openwork covers.

fruit knife: (1) Silver-bladed knife for table use. (2) Silver-bladed folding knife carried in one's pocket. (3) Glass knife for peeling and cutting fruit.

fruit paperweight: Glass paper holder, now called a paperweight, encasing clusters of fruit forms in natural colors. Some are attributed to New England Glass Works, Cambridge, Mass., c. 1850s.

frumenty: Hulled wheat, boiled in milk.

Fryer mirrors: Tabernacle, ogee-molded, oval, and overmantel framed mirrors made by Elijah S. Fryer, Baltimore, from 1830s.

frying-pan candlestick: A perfect name for the object—a chamber candlestick in the form of a small, handled frying pan with a socket in center. Noted in copper, brass, and tin plate.

Fry latch: Cabinet or door latch of oblique form, invented by Robert Fry of Spring Garden, Pa., c. 1840s.

Frytag ware: Pottery made by Michael Frytag, Philadelphia, from 1795. Utilitarian house- and kitchenwares.

Fuchsia: Pattern of pressed glass featuring a floral banding of fuchsia flowers, leaves, and stem. There is also a Square Fuchsia, with a larger flower in vertical panels on square-form pieces, and a Goblet with Fuchsias, displaying frosting.

fuchsine: Red aniline dye.

fuddling cups: Six cups arranged in a triangle form, bound together. Generally of pottery, the three corner cups having handles. When filled it was impossible to drink from any one of them without spilling contents of the others. Experts filled any one of the cups and drank with ease.

Fulda porcelain: German porcelain made from 1765 at Fulda, in Hesse. Operation ceased in 1780s. Marks are a pair of crowned swash F characters and a cross. Landscape-, figure-, and bird-decorated. It is rare.

Fulham carpets: Parisot woven carpets made at Fulham, England.

Fulham ware: Now generally applied to any wares made at the potting center of Fulham, England, over several centuries and by various potters. Specifically, brown stoneware with raised decoration, from which it is assumed many items of Pennsylvania art, especially the stove plates, were copied, at least in part. This is probably true, as every ironmaster other than Huber, the German, would most likely have had some Fulham ware. [*Example pictured*.]

fuller's earth: Soft gray clay having an affinity for oil and grease and used as an absorbent of lanolin in woolen fabrics. Operation was called "fulling the cloth."

full-molded: Said of mold-blown glasswares when blown in a full-size mold, thus requiring no further blowing for expansion of the piece. Most historic flasks and three-mold pieces were so blown. The process would seem to date from c. 1810.

fuming box: A pastille burner.

funeral kerchief: Reference is to the memorial printed kerchiefs dedicated to the great and near great, printed in black and in colors on cotton and linen squares.

funeral ring: Gold or silver ring given mourners attending a funeral. Generally engraved with name of the departed. Also hairwork rings, woven from hair of the departed.

funeral spoon: Another early type of memorial gift, used when eating the funeral meats served after the burial and generally engraved with the name, age, and death date of the departed.

funerary piece: Any object buried with a body in grave or vault.

funk: Same as punk—touchwood or tinder. Also a word for a bad odor.

furbelow: Ornamental fringe.

furniture bruise remover: A technique of wetting a bruise or broad gouge with thicknesses of drenched blotting paper and applying a hot flatiron. This caused the wood to swell and fill the bruised spot, from where the refinishing process took over. Deep bruises require several applications. This process was used from 1820s and was probably traditional.

furniture check: Crossbarred pattern of textile, used generally in making slipcovers for upholstered furniture. From mid-18th century or earlier.

furniture fender: A buffer-tipped screw affixed to bedsteads, sofa and chair legs to prevent backs or other parts from scraping wall.

furniture "for": A phrase meaning, in almost every case, fitment, covering, or garniture, as furniture for a mantelpiece, a chest, et cetera.

furniture knobs: Any pull of knob form for drawers, doors, et cetera, of wrought iron, wood, brass, copper, silver, plated metal, glass, horn, or ivory.

furniture lift: Not hardware, but a screw and socket of wood for adjusting the height (lifting) of any case or cabinet furniture. [*Example pictured.*]

furniture making & manufacture: Cabinetmakers *made* furniture; manufacturers produced it in factories. Actually, shops like A. Hepplewhite's, T. Chippendale's, and Duncan Phyfe's were factories, using every known cost- and labor-saving device, but having a peerless standard of excellence.

furniture patterns: Full-size patterns of thin metal or paper used as guides for cutting and carving. Many paper examples were made in the U.S., 1845–70s.

furniture styles: All furniture of antiques status derives from one of these three basic sources: (1) Gallic or Gothic, (2) oriental, and mostly Chinese, and (3) classic, from Egypt, Greece, and Rome. The Spanish, Portuguese, and Dutch traded via sea routes with the Orient years before the discovery of America. Columbus' voyage was not to find a continent but to find a new route to the East by going westwardly around the globe. The spice trade was the chief purpose of these many commercial voyages. But the wrappings of spices and the porcelain and other exotic containers established a new vogue for the wares of the Orient, and soon furniture was arriving at various European ports. By the late 16th century the Chinese styles began to replace the Gallic, or Gothic. To digest all of the information within the three groupings of style source is impossible here. Generally, the following should suffice for most students: Gallic, or Gothic, embraces the furniture of importance made from c. 1200 to 1560 and all its variants, which includes most of what we have been calling Pilgrim Century furniture, such as settles, forms, drawing tables, gate-leg tables, ladder-back chairs, wainscot chairs, Windsor chairs, et cetera. Chinese styles are reflected wholly or in large part in William & Mary, Queen Anne, Georgian and Chippendale, and, with variants in carving, mostly rococo, in Louis XIV and Louis XV styles. Classic furniture was revived chiefly by the Brothers Adam in the middle of the 18th century. Adam, Hepplewhite, Directoire and Sheraton, Empire, all derive from the classic. Victorian, so called, is actually French Antique revival, chiefly Louis XV and XVI styling. Eastlake is an attempt to return to the Gothic, as is the work of William Morris. Swedish modern is Chinese in its derivation, as is nearly all of the simple furniture of the Shakers. To accept these data as truth will require considerable study by some skeptics. But with such pursuit of the subject, the truth will be revealed. One other kind of furniture, based upon natural forms and sometimes called natural or rustic, is furniture framework made from natural wood, with or without the bark on it. This is a very ancient form of furniture, restored to popularity in the 18th century, when rustic living was revived as a fashionable vagary.

Furnival china: T. Furnival & Sons, a firm of the 19th century at Hanley, England, made white granite and ironstone wares, dinner services, and toilet sets, some very charming and delightful.

Furstenburg porcelain: German ware made from 1750; during the Napoleonic era, under direction of Jerome Bonaparte. Became a corporation in 1880s and continued manufacture from the old molds and patterns, actually creating reproductions with a tinge of legitimacy. Unwary collectors, not knowing the fine quality of the old ware, are often fooled by the poor imitations. Marks are italic *F*, some dated, and a running horse.

fusil: Flint and steel—a fire-making tool.

fusion: The melting point of a metal or alloy. Lead melts at 600°, bismuth at 500°, and tin at 442°. An alloy of these three metals melts at 200°. Trick "pewter" spoons of this alloy were made in the 1800s They melted in hot tea!

fustian: Velveteen or corduroy; the lesser velvets.

fustic: West Indian mulberry wood used in making a yellow dye.

futchel: A bent timber used in carriage making; the bend is a mild S-curve achieved by bending in a frame.

fyke: Funnel-shaped fish net, introduced by Swedes and Dutch and used on the Hudson, Delaware, Susquehanna, and Schuylkill rivers from 17th century.

fylot: The swastika form, of Indo-Chinese origin. Somewhat like that of the Nazi party in Germany, except that the fylot's right-angle bars point in the opposite direction.

fynlina: Faenza ware; faïence or majolica, made from c. 1475 at Faenza, Italy.

fyoll: Woodenware. A cup. Also name given an iron cook pot.

G

gabbo: Three-card loo; a card game.

gabie: A collander.

gad: Measuring rod ten feet long.

gadnail: A long wrought nail.

gadroon: Properly, godroon—ruffling or pleating. Sometimes incorporating the fruit of the olive tree. Used as a form or style of edging and ornamentation in furniture, ceramic, glass-, and metalwares. At times it is a quite simple series of convex curves.

gad steel: Flemish steel made in small pigs called gads.

gaesa: A shafted scramasax; a fighting halberd. A weapon of war.

gaffle: The bend or power section of a crossbow.

gage: A square yard of slate tiling, laid with its lap not counted.

gail: A wooden tub. Also gaildish, gailclear, gailpot.

gailage: Same as galosh—a clog, patten, or galosh worn as a lift to avoid snow, mud, et cetera.

Gaiter Berry: Berry of the dogwood tree.

gaiter bottle: Bottle in form of ankle-high shoe, generally with a stopper. Known in glass, pottery, china, metal, and leather. Often used as shoe warmers; filled with hot water and inserted in one's shoes, it warmed the insides before the shoes were put on for the day. Most examples date from 1840s, except the leather ones, which were really bottles made by cordwainers as early as 16th century. [*Late example pictured.*]

galash: To cover one shoe with another shoe form for protection.

galenicals: Herbs and tinctures of herbs.

galentine: An aspic jelly containing meat or fish, with spices, bread crumbs, and crusts.

Gale sterling: Silverware by William Gale & Son, New York City, established 1821, who were early users of the sterling mark of purity.

gall: Impurities in glass, also called sandiver, which were generally cooked out and skimmed off before using glass in the melting pots.

galleried: Any low railing, arcaded, fretted, pierced, gadrooned, or fenced. A device of decoration and of practicality in usage for furniture, especially tops of tables, trays, stands, desks, chests, silverware, and service objects. **galleried rim:** A rim around the container in which a cover is placed. **galleried tray:** Tray with rim at an acute angle, from 60° to 90°.

galley balk: The beam in a chimney to which pots and other containers were fastened. Generally of green wood; when finally of iron, on a hinge, this device became the crane.

galley door: Second-story doorway similar in style to the main doorway of a house, and placed directly over it. Often opening to a balcony that is the roof of porch or portico. Sometimes called funeral door or casket doorway.

Gallier work: Papier-mâché work as done by John Gallier of New York City from 1850s.

gallimaufry: The hash of viands, so called in 17th century, became our New England boiled dinner.

gallipot: Vase-form pot with narrow neck, from "gleypot," or grease pot; pot for unguents and ointments.

gallonier: A four-quart jug or pitcher.

galloon: A sort of lace used in dress trimming and fancywork. Also the fancy tape used in upholstery, much used in 17th century; a tape for shoestrings.

Galloway-Graff ware: Terra cotta vases of classic form made by a pottery of this name, Philadelphia, 19th century. Made the Washington memorial vase from 1876.

galls: Wood tumors, used in making dyestuffs. Galls of oak were used in inks. These tumors are caused by wasp stings on leaves. Animal galls (bile sacs) were used for fine pigments for artists.

gall soap: A soft soap made of olive oil, coconut oil, caustic soda, and turpentine.

galluchat: Sharkskin leather.

gallybagger: A scarecrow.

galoche: High boot.

galvanic necklace: Copper and zinc beads or blocks on a metallic chain. Same device was used for garters, bracelets, and belts. Dr. Christie, in 1840s, said these were electric and healthful.

galvanized furniture: Chairs, settees, stools, tables, and stands of fancy cast iron, galvanized to prevent rust. Made from 1870s.

galvano-plastic: Shells of copper, deposited by electroplating, the surface tinned or silver-plated and the shell backed with lead. This process was used to make many plaques and other decorative objects after 1850.

Gamage piano: Pianoforte made at Boston by O. A. Gamage, established 1833.

gamashes: Gaiters. Also gamogins, gambadoes.

gamboge: A yellow gum of vegetable origin, much used in the arts.

gambreled roof: A peaked roof, expanded to provide more area under it by breaking the slope with a high hip. This roof was apparently first used in Flanders and is found in the colonies as early as 1636.

gambrel leg: *Gamba* means leg. In furniture, a *gamba* is a solid end support, carved or shaped, used on some tables, chairs, and benches. [*A section of a* gamba, *or* gambrel, *is pictured.*]

Gambrinus: The jovial patron saint of brewers. A jolly Saxon giant, often portrayed as an effigy sign on breweries and porterhouses.

game cart: Four-wheeled sporting vehicle, a *dos-à-dos.*

game pie dish: A casserole of pottery or china cane ware made to simulate fancy pastry decoration. Wedgwood made such items, as did many potteries on the Continent. These are covered dishes of oven-ware.

game plate: Generally a service plate decorated with gaming scenes or pictures of game birds.

gander: To look about furtively, as in fear of surprise. Said to derive from "gander moon" of pregnancy, when a husband going out of the house was said to be "gandering."

gantree: A stand for barrels.

gapestick: A large wooden spoon.

garbelled: Impure, adulterated. A spice garbeller was an examiner for impurity or adulteration.

garde du vin: A wine bin, preferably also a cooler, generally in a special cabinet, zinc- or tin-lined, or within a compartment in a sideboard.

garde-manger: Originally a small room for storage of viands, finally a large closet. Also, *garde-ménager.* The finest examples are architectural, simulating a chapel or house. The entire kitchen was once known by this term.

garden engine: A small-size hand-pumper fire engine for use in the garden to spray flower and vegetable beds. [*Example pictured.*]

garden ginger: Hot peppers.

garden prop: Heavy pottery, terra cotta, or artificial stone basin set on three or four sturdy stubby supports of columnar form, resting upon a heavy foundation block. These are imitative of ancient Greek and Roman forms. Placed in gardens of some pretense for planting of rare flowers, ferns, sedums, and succulents, from 1840s. [*Example pictured.*]

garden-tool chair: See Chairs, All Kinds.

Gardner-Decker furniture & mirrors: Any mirror made by a firm so named from 1850. Large-style tabernacle and oval-framed rococo styles. Frames marked "Gardner" only are not of same manufacture but are picture frames. Also a perforated veneer furniture with solid frames and veneer seats and backs, made by Gardner & Co., N.Y., from 1870s.

Gardner lounge: An extensible chair, generally a rocker, unfolding to couch form, the rockers supporting the head of the piece.

Gardner furniture: This reference would be to the various chairs and cabinet-network made by some 25 factories at Gardner, Mass., which, prior to 1840, employed over 350 people.

garet: The watchtower of a castle or château; the top story of a house, under the peak of the roof. Garret.

garf angyl: An eel spear.

Garfield Drape: Pattern of pressed glass with dotted drapery swags, so called because there is a Garfield memorial plate with a somewhat similar series of swags around the edge.

gargarisme: A mouthwash.

Garibaldi plaster: Images of plaster of Paris made in quantities by Garibaldi & Co., Boston, from 1840s. Ornaments in variety that included some now called Pennsylvania chalk ware.

Garnet wheel: Early type of roller-bearing axle invented by John Garnet, New Brunswick, N.J., c. 1800.

garnish; garnishing; garniture: Decorative sets, suites, and assemblies of plate, china, vases, et cetera. "A garnish" was the 17th- and 18th-century name for a set of china. Also any decorative group for the mantelpiece, a chest, or top of a highboy.

garreted: Masonry wall, mortared or dry joint, having spalls or splinters driven in the joints.

garrison house: Any early residence used also as a garrison to which neighboring families repaired in times of danger and alarm. The Little House near Newbury-port, Mass., is a garrison house; so is Sellier's Fort (Zeller's Fort), the ancient French *petit château* that was built in Lancaster County, Pa., by Madame Clothilde Sellier. Hundreds of frontier residences of importance were so used.

garrons: Large spikes of wrought iron.

garter loom: Narrow fabric or tape loom.

garth: An underclose, especially of a church or chapel structure.

garwindle; garnwyn: A yarn reel.

gas bag: India-rubber bladders to hold illuminating gas under pressure for portable lanterns. Made from 1840s.

gas candle: Gas jets imitative of candle form. These were among the first gas illuminating fixtures and were made and used in U.S. from 1820s.

gaslight parasol: A pink parasol used indoors under brilliant illumination. The pink cover of thin silk imparted a delicate rouged hue to the faces of the girls who carried them. No matter how silly this may sound, it was a vogue of the 1840s.

gate-leg desk: Slope-fall desk with baluster or trumpet-turned legs, the support of the desk board being a pair of gates. Carolean and William & Mary styles, but known also in Tudor, which is indicative of the Gallic, or Gothic, source of the piece.

gate-leg table: Drop-leaf table in the Gallic, or Gothic, style with (in its general style) turned supports at each corner of the main top board, but having two additional legs on each side forming swing-out gates (sometimes draw-out gates) which support the leaves. Legs are vase-, columnar-, or sausage-turned, with turned or plain stretchers. Exceptional examples have double gates at sides, and even rarer examples have a series of top flaps, all supported with gates, sometimes having as many as 24 legs. It is from these we derive the term "thousand-leg table." [*Examples pictured.*]

Gates & Parran furniture: Made by cabinetmakers so named, London, 1780s.

Gatling gun: J. R. Gatling of Indiana, 1861, invented this gun, a repeating small cannon, ancestor of the machine gun.

gaubert: An iron rack for pots and pans, used in or at the fireplace.

gaud; gaudy: A toy or bauble; cheap display stuff, as mantel and chimney ornaments of pottery or plaster; any cheap finery.

gaudy Chamberlain: Chamberlain Worcester porcelain in the Imari style. *See* Gaudy Dutch. The Chamberlain Imari is very fine.

gaudy Dutch: A design copied from the Chinese and Japanese ware known as Imari, applied to English porcelain, soft paste wares, and ironstone, the first examples being by the Royal Worcester works prior to 1780. A revival of the pattern was attempted, apparently simultaneously, by several English potters in the first decade of the 19th century. The ware did not appeal to the lower-income-bracket families, for whom it was made. Much of the ware remaining on hand was literally dumped into the U.S. market after the War of 1812. It was such dumping that caused the "American system" of high tariff laws. None of these wares was made for the Pennsylvania German market, as has been asserted time after time. The name "gaudy Dutch," which is justified, does not mean gaudy German but refers to the Dutch importers who introduced this gaudy Imari ware from China and Japan to the northern European markets and to England. The pattern names for the ware now current are sheer inventions by 20th-century collectors and dealers. Single Rose, Double Rose, Urn Flowerpot, Sunflower, Carnation, Butterfly, Dahlia, Oyster, Grape, War Bonnet, Love Bird, Primrose, King's Rose, and so on, have no antiquarian significance as names. Many potters making the ware did not sign it. Riley was one of the potters who did. Therefore, the ware was once called "Rileyware." This gaudy ware was once very plentiful and was, on introduction, the cheapest good china obtainable. We have seen records of a Boston firm that imported it by the hogsheads and sold the dishes—bread-plate or tea-plate size—for 12½ cents. In all, two attempts to revive the Imari pattern were made by English potters, the latter attempt resulting in ironstone and granite ware being decorated with this delightfully gaudy pattern. The colors usually are rust-red, brilliant blue, luster blue, green, yellow, pink, luster pink, and gold.

gaudy fat: Excessively fat meat.

gaudy ironstone: F. Morley & Sons (successors to Mason) attempted, in 1851, to make popular their plain ironstone by adding Imari decoration in all the gaudy colors of the original. This failed to capture a market and was sold at cut prices to clear it out.

gaudy Welsh: The name given late Imari-pattern wares in England from 1820s.

gaudy Worcester: *See* Gaudy Chamberlain.

gauffered; goffered: A surface displaying manipulation with an iron to achieve a raised, patterned effect.

Gautier furniture: Cabinet furniture made by Daniel Gautier, French cabinetmaker of New York City, from 1730s. It is in the French style *later* advocated by Chippendale. It is not generally appreciated that certain French cabinetmakers in the colonies were as well acquainted with the Louis XV style as was Chippendale, and were using that style before the now greatly promoted English cabinetmaker adapted the French style and made it the chief source of the patterns in his famed *Director*.

Gautschi music box: One of the widely distributed Swiss music boxes, made by a firm established 1824 and having a branch assembly plant at Philadelphia from 1870s. The main factory was at Sainte Croix.

gauze fire screen: Ormolu- and brass-framed screens, fitted with fine wire gauze, and seldom now found with the original gauze intact. Generally of French make or styling. [*Example pictured.*]

gavel: A ceremonial mallet, generally with a striking block. Known in ivory, wood, stone, silver, et cetera, and not, originally, in what we would call mallet form.

gay: A painted picture.

gayetty paper: Medicated paper binding for minor cuts, wounds, and sores.

Gaylord mirror: Made by W. M. Gaylord, Utica, N.Y., from 1820s. Tabernacle, gilt and mahogany, and plain carved frame mirrors, many of which were shipped to lake ports.

gay pole: A Shropshire term for a chimney pole or galley balk.

gazul: A variety of barilla. Soza and salicor are also varieties. Burned, the plants yielded alkali.

geburtschein: Birth certificate, generally hand-lettered, but some partially printed for filling in with data. Much used in Flanders, the Netherlands, the Provinces, and Switzerland. Said to be of Scandinavian origin. Examples known in New England, Pennsylvania, Ohio, New York, Maryland, and Virginia.

'Geechee lime: Preserved limes of olive size, a delicacy of the Ogeechee River Valley of South Carolina.

Geldowsky furniture: Louis XV revival furniture made at factory of F. Geldowsky, East Cambridge, Mass.

gemel: In pairs, as adhering bottles; a joined hinge; twinlike. From the Latin *gemellus*, twin. Gemini, gimbal, et cetera, derive from this root. Also gimmal, and even "Jimminy."

gem pan: Multi-celled pan of iron or sheet iron for baking the dinner biscuit called a gem.

Gendar instruments: Barometers and thermometers made by W. T. & T. V. Gendar, N.Y., from 1840s.

Genesis: Perhaps the original name for the pressed-glass pattern now known as Daisy & Button.

Geneva: Guiniver, the flavoring agent of the botanical alcoholic beverage now called gin, Hollands, et cetera. Also name of a town in New York, locale of Geneva Glass Works, where bottles and hollow wares were made from 1810 to 1840s or later.

genre: A style of painting, said originally of the Dutch school, depicting scenes of everyday life; the life of the people, high, middle, and the lowly; a storytelling picture. The term is now considerably misused. Also a type or kind of thing, especially relating to technique or manner, style, et cetera.

gentlemen glassmakers: Sponsors of glasshouses who, on occasion, worked with the fascinating metal.

geometrican: The improved pantograph or drawing machine for enlarging or reducing. Invented 1840s by George Earl, who toured the U.S. selling it and giving instructions in its uses.

geometric turning: Face engraving with the lathe known as a rose engine.

George & Martha Washington teapot: Leeds-made bulbous pot of queen's ware, transfer-printed with medallions of the Washingtons. The handle is (or was) of yew wood, bound with raffia, fitting in pierced ears on the pot. [*Example pictured.*]

George japanned ware: Reference seems to be to the japanned tin-plated wares made by Thomas George, Chicago, c. 1850s, and sold generally in Wisconsin, Iowa, and Illinois.

George Rex jugs: Round-bellied stoneware jugs with cylinder-shaped tops, scratch-decorated, or molded with a round medallion in which GR appears. These are blue and gray, made in the Germanic style. Common ale pots, manufacture of which was encouraged so that the common people of England would be praising their imported German kings and so come to accept the new line and forget the Stuart pretenders.

George Washington breeches: Not a canard or a cheap joke. A man named George Washington was a breeches maker of London from 1750. Old bills or orders for a pair of Washington breeches should not be confused with any patriotic style, but simply orders for breeches from this maker.

gerb: A clay mortar used in fireworks.

German boor: Redemptioners who sold themselves into service for payment of passage money. Some Philadelphia merchants had ships under charter to transport German immigrants by the hundreds to Penn's colony. Before they were accepted for passage they sold themselves for seven or more years, and were in turn sold for cash to any buyer on arrival. Since the trade was entirely in Germans, most of whom were illiterate, the seven years of servitude gave them an education of sorts, taught them English, and prepared them far better for citizenship than others of their countrymen. Private research indicates that such immigrants were taught clockmaking, cabinetmaking, silversmithing, and other exacting crafts by these masters, who owned them for a term approximating an apprenticeship. While in servitude, these immigrants were called boors.

German coffee: Chicory roots, dried and roasted.

German Luster: Copper lusterware made in German potteries to 1900, imitative of the kind of copper luster made earlier at

Staffordshire. Some of this ware is banded with sand embedded in the clay. Not made as a fake but as cheap ware, and sold by cheap stores everywhere, including Woolworth's.

German porcelain: This designation is generally given to wares other than the true porcelains of Germany; the softpaste wares of Thuringia, Basdorf, et cetera, from 1750s. Much of it is quite lovely.

German student lamp: A misnomer; this type of lamp with oil font and burner joined by a pipe sliding up and down on a rod was called the Saint Germain student lamp. The first effort to call it German was by C. F. A. Heinrichs of New York in the 1880s, who advertised his lamps as Saint Germain or German. The lamp originated in France.

Germantown glass: Made at Braintree, Mass., by Joseph Palmer, who employed German workmen (they were probably Swiss, as Germany was not releasing good glassmakers for migration), c. 1755–60. General line of wares for the home, bottles, and hollow wares were made, or so it is alleged.

Gerz pottery: Yellow-glaze earthenware, so marked, was made at Lancaster, Pa., from 1850 to 1880.

gesso: Plaster coating of ornamental nature, generally painted, sometimes stiffened by wire and used in ornamentation of mirror frames. It is composed of refined plaster, chalk, whiting, fire clay, and other mineral earths, combined with a gelatinous or gluey water. This same material was painted on wood before application of gold leaf and other foils.

gesting: Staying with; being a visitor for entertainment and lodging. Gestony is another form of the term.

Gettis mirror: Made from 1840s at Milwaukee by William Gettis; tabernacle and rococo types.

gewgag: Geegaw, gee jaw, jew jay. Corrupted to Jew's harp. Term is really jaw harp.

Geyer furniture: Papier-mâché tables and stands, cabinetwork in fine woods, cheap cottage furniture, Grecian sofas, chairs, marble-topped tables, et cetera, made at Cincinnati by John Geyer, successor to McAlpin Furniture & Cabinetworks (established 1834) from c. 1850.

Giannini sculptures: J. Giannini was a marble sculptor working in Cincinnati in the 1850s, He executed hundreds of busts, ornaments, and elegancies for the adornment of mansions in the Ohio Valley.

Gibbons, Grinling: English designer and carver, appointed to the Board of Works, London, 1670, and patronized by royalty, He became famous and taught Watson of London, Drevot of Brussels, and Lawreans of Mechlin.

Gibbons glass: Reference is to either stained glass or objects of antique glassware sold at the Gibbons studios, Philadelphia, from 1850.

gibby stick: A stick with a hook on one end, known in iron and wood.

gibcroke: A pothook.

gibs: Hard candy, also called rocks and Gibraltars, made from 1820s by Mrs. Spen-

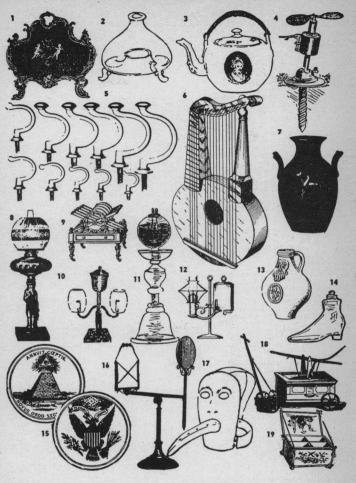

1, Gauze Fire Screen. **2,** Glass Flytrap. **3,** George & Martha Washington Teapot. **4,** Gyro Pigeon and Spinning Device, with Anchor. **5,** Gun Hooks. **6,** Guitar Lute. **7,** Greek Ware, by Copeland, Late Spode. **8,** Greek-Slave Lamp. **9,** Grecian Music Stand. **10,** Gray Lamp. **11,** Goblet Lamp. **12,** Graydon Lamp. **13,** Greybeard Jug. **14,** Gaiter Bottle. **15,** Great Seal of the United States. **16,** Graphoscope. **17,** Gossip Mask, or mask brank for punishment of scolds. **18,** Garden Engine. **19,** Glasswork Toilet Box. (No. 1, from Harrod's London. Nos. 7 and 13 from Virtue & Co., London.)

cer of Salem, Mass. This lady is said to have invented the candy known as black-jacks.

Gibson plate: Doulton of Lambeth, England, plates decorated with pen drawings by the famous American artist, Charles Dana Gibson. The 24 drawings titled "The Widow and Her Friends" make up a set of plates.

Gien faïence: French faïence made at the Gien potteries from 1860s.

gig: A two-wheeled vehicle with a seat or shoe set forward of the wheels.

gig; gigged up: Drawn to a point; hence the phrase "the gig is up," now generally phrased "the jig is up."

gigg mill: A fulling mill.

Gilbert, Sir Humphrey: Author of the discourse on the discovery of America, published 1576, and half brother of Sir Walter Raleigh.

Gilbert piano: T. Gilbert (originally Guilbert) made pianofortes at Boston from 1820s. After 1827 it was Gilbert & Currier.

gilded glass: Gold oxide used as a decorative paint on glass which, when refired, displayed the pure-gold work. Popular in U.S. from 1850 but used as a process at several 18th-century glasshouses, including, allegedly, those of Stiegel and Amelung.

gilding wax: Copper flakes, red chalk, and verditer in wax, used to deepen color of annealed goldwork.

gill-ale: Not a measure, but ale flavored with ground ivy.

Gillerland glass: The proper name is Gilliland, *which see.*

Gillette woodenware: Ash-wood cups and saucers, also made of ash burl; white-ash knot bowls, et cetera, made at Henniker, N.H., from 1817. Much of this ware is credited with at least a century more age than it has. Platters, chargers, churns, and dairy wares were also made.

Gillies furniture: Iron furniture from the shop of T. J. Gillies, New York City, established in 1840s. Made chairs, sofas, settees, beds, stands, tables, and stools.

Gilliland glass: Fine flint tableware, colored, cut, and plain, made by John Gilliland and R. & J. Fisher from 1820. This plant became the Brooklyn Glass Works, which moved to Corning, N.Y., and became the Corning Glass Co.

Gillinder busts: Pressed, frosted glass busts by Gillinder & Sons, many (of Washington, Franklin, Lafayette, Lincoln, Jackson, et cetera) made and sold at Centennial Exposition of 1876 by this firm, which had a complete glassworks on the grounds. Also made busts of Dewey, Schley, McKinley, and others during Spanish-American War period.

Gillinder glass: Pressed, blown, frosted, and lamp wares made by Gillinder & Sons, Philadelphia, from 1860s, and also known as Franklin Glass Works. They originated the "Westward Ho!" and other patterns, and made figural candlesticks in the techniques of Vallerysthal and Portieux. Other products were cameo and camphor glass. The pressing department moved to Greensburg, Pa., in the 1880s and finally merged with the U.S. Glass Co.

Gillingham, James: Master cabinetmaker of Philadelphia who worked in the Georgian and Chippendale styles. From 1750s to 1768 he was in partnership with Henry Clifton.

gilloche: Interlaced circles, used as ornamentation; chained decoration.

Gillow, Richard: Cabinetmaker of London who invented the telescoping extension dining table. Member of a firm in business from 17th century, first at Lancaster, removing to London in 1765. Exported to Bermuda and the colonies, and some Virginia, Maryland, and Carolina furniture was undoubtedly from the Gillow shops. The firm is still in business.

gillyflower: The clove pink, esteemed for its blossoms used raw in salads and as a spice in cookery.

gillypot: Gleypot; a pot for ointment.

gillyvine pen: Lead rod pushed through the pith duct of a gillyflower stem; an early lead pencil. A plumbago stick.

Gilman instruments: Nautical and scientific devices made by B. C. Gilman of New England, working from late 18th century.

Gilpin, John: Character invented by W. Cowper and pictured by Cruikshank. Issued as prints and appearing on cheap pottery.

gilt latten: Gilded brass.

gimblet: Gimlet, a small boring tool.

Gimbrede, J. N.: Proprietor of a fancy store, print seller and engraver of New York, mid-19th century.

gimcrack: The works of a watch; any small machine.

gimlin: Woodenware. A salting tub.

gimmal: Twin; a dual flask; an oil and vinegar flask. **gimmal ring:** Same as gemal ring; joined circles of laminated gold or silver elements terminating in clasped hands.

gimmew: A wooden hinge or joint.

gimp: Narrow fabric ornamentation; fancy tape of silk, linen, or wool, interwoven with metallic thread.

gin: A snare or trap; a catching device. Hence cotton gin to trap seeds. Said to derive from small engine.

ginchawder: Chowder of fish, diced, spiced, and laced with wine.

ginger horse: Ginger cake, shaped by cutters in outline of a horse, iced with lemon-flavored white sugar. The term was applied to all ginger cookies cut to any shape. The small round ones were called gingernuts and, finally, when baked crisp, gingersnaps. Often sold by street vendors from 1800s.

Ginna tin: Painted, decalcomania-decorated, and stenciled tea, coffee, and other boxes, made mostly for use of retail stores by Ginna & Co., New York City, in the last half of 19th century.

Ginori: Art pottery and faïence of Italy, made at the Ginori Works, established c. 1820s. It is in imitation of capo di monti and other fine Italian wares.

gipse: Woodenware. A mortar for pounding spice and sugar.

girandole; girondole; girondella:

Reference, generally, is to the circular concave or convex mirrors with gilded frames and side brackets for candles. From *gyro*, to turn. Properly, any turning bracket. Originally a Catherine wheel. Made in innumerable varieties. Bernard & Jugiez of Philadelphia advertised "girondels" in 1766. The proper spelling is girandole, not girondole.

girandole banjo: A banjo-type clock having a circular bottom element. A rare type, but made in U.S. from c. 1800s.

gird: A griddle.

girdbrew: Flummery; oatmeal jelly.

Girlingite: Name given the sect we call Shakers.

girt; girtled; girted: Broad tapes arranged on a bed or couch frame; an upholstery technique.

gispen: A leather pot; a blackjack. Some are modeled in figural forms; the original Toby-form jug.

gittern: The early zither.

Gitti chalk: Plaster ware made by Joseph Gitti, N.Y., from 1850s.

Giustiniani: Neapolitan faïence or artware of the 19th century.

glacier: Pottery or glass vessel with an ice pocket.

gladwyn: The iris foetidissimi, esteemed for its seed pod, which opened and displayed orange and red seeds. Spellings include glaydon, gladden, glydwyn.

Glasgow delft: Tin-glazed redware made at Delft Lane Field, Broomielaw, Scotland, from 1750. After 1770 the works made queen's ware and finally became potters to the Prince of Wales. The delft is in the Dutch style and tradition.

glass: To attempt any historic listing of glass and glassmakers would be fatuous. For history of American and other glasswares, the student is referred to the Bibliography.

glass: in novel uses: The following are grouped because of necessity for saving space. **glass inlays:** Glass panels, painted, used as inlays on furniture. From 1780s to 1820s this device was used on fine classic-style furniture made at Baltimore. Examples are rare. **glass keys:** Piano key covers of glass. **glass knife:** Made from 1850s, the early examples having crystal blades and colored handles. **glass knobs:** Furniture knobs of pressed, blown, and cut glass and doorknobs of glass in the paperweight philosophy of making are of record from 1810 to 1870s and even later. **glass knockers:** Glass-headed beaters used in laundry work, made from 17th century. **glass lamps:** Contrary to general belief that glass is a 19th-century lamp material, these objects were advertised in the colonies as early as 1719. The vast majority made in U.S. date from the kerosene era, but prior to 1850s many glasshouses produced lamps in blown and pressed techniques for other lamp oils. **glass mains:** Water pipes of blown and cast glass, patented by W. T. DeGolyer of Schenectady, were laid in New York City in 1850 to extent of 12,000 feet. **glass marbles:** Clear and tinted glass balls for play in sizes ranging from ¼ inch to 3 inches in diameter. Most popular from 1870s.

glass agate: A play marble of glass imitative of agate.

glass beds: Decorative glass cylinders strung on iron or brass rods, and forming bedsteads.

glass boater: A glass hat in the shape of the hard straw or stiff-brimmed hat popular since 1880s.

glass boots & shoes: This form of glassware, as bottles, flasks, and drinking vessels, has been made from 17th century. In 19th century the idea was revived and millions of novelty boots and shoes were made of glass. See *Victorian Glass*, by Ruth Webb Lee, and *Spinning Wheel* magazine, April, 1952.

glass busts: Blown- and pressed-glass busts of people, some bottle form. The most important pressed-glass bust in the entire glass-collecting scene is almost never mentioned. It is of the man who made the greatest advance in glassmaking in 5000 years: Michael J. Owens (1859-1923). The bust, pressed in a three-part mold, was issued 1923. It is of finely frosted glass. There are modeled glass busts of Wellington, Wesley, and other notables, innumerable pressed-glass busts (some used as bottle stoppers) both classic and historic, among them Washington and Franklin, made by Gillinder of Philadelphia during the Centennial of 1876. There is a mold-blown bottle bust of Henry Ward Beecher and other notables. Many mold-blown busts made in France were not bottles but hollow busts used as bottle stoppers, often as large, or larger, than the bottle proper which served as a base.

glass caps: Variants of glass hats; some blown, some pressed. Even fine-cut examples are of record. Mostly 19th-century novelties.

glass cement: (1) Transparent cement used in mending broken glass and in the restoration of important but damaged pieces. (2) Caustic soda and resin boiled to soap, mixed with plaster of Paris and used to bind parts of glass elements together, as lamp reservoirs on bases, et cetera.

glass chair: *See* Chairs, All Kinds.

glass china vase: The potichomanie vase, which was a craze of mid-19th century. Made by pasting colored pictures inside glass vases and cementing with a binder of white or colored cement after application, imitative of Chinese porcelain.

glass cloth: Wall hangings and drapery fabrics woven from fine spun-glass threads; made as early as 1830 by Olivi of Venice and in 1837 by M. Bonneil of Lille, France. In 1873 it was considered a "lost art." Now made in quantities for substantially the same uses. Brunfant of Paris was engaged in spinning and weaving glass fabrics in 1860s.

glassed-in-paste: The crystallo-ceramie, or casing of ceramic busts and other objects in glass, the result being imitative of silver in glass. Also called sulphides.

glass everlasting inkstand: The magical inkstand. Glass container housing a solid dye from which ink was produced by adding clear water and shaking. The process could be repeated over and over again. Guaranteed to produce enough ink for a page a day for 100 years. Made from 1870s.

glass factories: Many are listed by name in this dictionary, but complete data may be had from certain of the volumes listed in the Bibliography.

glass fire screen: Stained glass in metal frames used as fire screens from 1850s to 1900s.

glass floor tile: Squares of heavy glass, made and sold by Hewins of Hartford, Conn., from 1840s. Later development was a prismatic round, fitting in metal frames bored or cast to hold the pieces, and used as sidewalks over extended basements.

glass flytrap: A revolting table piece made of pressed glass, looking like a covered butter dish with interior truncated cone. Made by Co-operative Flint Glass Works of Beaver Falls, Pa., from 1890s. This, however, was not the first glass flytrap; blown examples, footed, looking like squat bottles with stubby necks and open upcurving bottoms, were made from 1830s. [*Example pictured.*]

glass hats: Whimseys of blown and pressed glass, some examples (blown) dating from 18th century, all of various hat forms and shapes. Most examples are 19th century. *Victorian Glass,* by Ruth Webb Lee, pictures many of them.

glass money: Properly, glasshouse money in form of paper notes exchangeable for goods at company or other stores. Also glass coinage, some very ancient, and bearing evidence of being pressed in forming molds.

glass mortar: A mortar of heavy metal for pounding glass to powder and making smalt. Also decorative druggists' signs of glass in form of large mortar and pestle.

glass novelties: Any whimsey or toy of glass.

glass paper: (1) Sandpaper. (2) Thin paper transfers for decorating glass.

glass pen: Hollow glass tube with a point.

glass pipe: Hollow tube of glass.

glass pot: The melting pot of a glass furnace.

glass powder horn: A novelty, of powder-horn shape, blown from glass. It is doubtful if these were ever actually used in the field; so breakable a receptacle for powder would be impractical for the hunter. The examples of record date from 1800s to 1850s.

glasswork: Parlor art of pasting colored prints on panes of glass, backing with whiting, and then forming into boxes. [*Examples pictured.*]

Glastonbury chair: *See* Chairs, All Kinds.

glatton: Welsh flannel; some woven in province of Pennsylvania to 1720s.

glaze: To ice; to put a transparent or other coating on ceramic ware.

glaze cap: Patent-leather (glazed kid) or oilcloth cap in military fashion.

glazure: Glazing.

Gleason carving: Machine carving, done with rotating chisels guided by a master pattern. Machine invented 1840 by W. B. Gleason, Boston.

Gleason krater: A small device to place on a kerosene-lamp chimney to make it a miniature stove.

gleeman: A singer.

gleewood: A harp.

gleypot: Ointment pot; gallipot.

gliddered: Coated with tough varnish.

glimstock: A candle.

globe back: Cast-iron bank in shape of terrestrial globe.

globe clock: A solar clock rotating a globe and having a pointer or hand for time-telling. A novelty clock of the 19th century, popular to 1890s. At least four different types were made by American clockmakers.

globe inkwell: Globose-shaped inkwell, generally of silver, with slide cover.

Globe iron furniture: Fancy chairs of cast iron made by Globe Iron Works, N.Y., from 1860s.

globe jar: Any round-bodied jar of pottery or glass.

globe lamp: Originally the "moon" or globose transparent-glass-shaded lamp advertised in the 1700s by several colonial dealers. Also a bulbous lantern of pierced sheet iron, generally made up of six gores, one of which was the door.

globe Liberty compote: Covered dish of pressed glass in form of terrestrial globe, displaying continents and oceans, surmounted by a Liberty head, made c. 1892.

globe teapot: Globose-shaped teapot.

globe writing table: Terrestrial globe of large size on a tripod stand, the shell of the upper half folding into lower and exposing a writing table or desk section.

glocken kan: Bell can; bell-shaped drinking vessel.

glockenspiel: A scale of bells to make music; chimes. A zylophone.

Glomi work: Eglomise panel or painting on glass, originally in gold and a solid color. Invented by Glomi, an artisan of Paris, 18th century.

gloria: Melodeon.

glory hole: Reheating furnace of a glasshouse.

glory lamp: Small disks of wood supporting a bit of taper. Floated in a bowl of water, these tapers, when lit, provided light for a few moments and were generally used in bedchambers. Millions sold from first half of 19th century.

glost: Preliminary glazing kiln in a pottery, preparing ware for decoration.

Gloucester ship: Schooner-type vessel developed at Gloucester, Mass., as early as 1715.

glove chaplet: A mourning piece, said to have originated in Glamorganshire, Wales. A wax wreath or paper flowered piece with a glove in center.

glum pot: Ointment pot.

glyphograph: Etching done on plate glass for printing on paper. Said to have been used by Cruikshand.

gnomon: A pointer; the shadow-casting rod of a sundial.

goat & bee jug: Chelsea porcelain jug of c. 1745 featuring seated goats in bocage and a bee in high relief. This jug was pear-shaped, had a rustic handle, and practically duplicated a similar type of jug first made in silver c. 1724.

goat & monkey glass: Match holders in form of carts drawn by goats and monkey, made by Tiffin Glass Works, Tiffin, O., late 19th century.

Gobelin: Tapestry made at the Royal Works, successors of the old Cooman Works, operated by the Gobelin family. Flemish. The factory was in operation from 1443, and the Royal Works took it over in 1667.

goblet: A standing cup, or cup on a base.

goblet lamp: A handled cup form having an orifice in which a peg lamp was placed. [*Example pictured.*]

gobstick: Same as gapestick; a wooden spoon.

go-chair: See Chairs, All Kinds.

goddard: A covered cup or chalice of the type sometimes called pokal.

Goddard block front: John Goddard, with Job Townsend and Goddard's sons, Townsend and Stephen, made the superlatively fine block-fronted furniture of Newport, R.I., from mid-18th to mid-19th centuries. Most books on furniture of American make contain material on this furniture.

Godefroy prints: Prints of American Revolutionary interest, issued as a portfolio, 1783–84, at Paris, France, with text in French. A reissue was published in 1918.

godet: A mixing tile or saucer, used by artists.

goffering iron: A fluting or crimping iron. **goffering stack:** Wooden slats set between uprights, used in pleating or crimping.

golab danee; g'lobdane: Rose-water sprinkler. The term is East Indian.

Gold, Standard: The 1796 standard for U.S. gold was 11 parts gold, 1 part alloy, or 11 to 12. This is the same as 22 carat.

goldbeater's skin: Parchment made from intestines of oxen, used in beating out gold to microscopic thinness in making gold leaf.

Golden Age stove: A beautiful cast-iron box stove for the parlor in the Louis XV style, also convertible in a few minutes to a cooking range. [*Early 1850s example illustrated.*]

Golden Dog pitcher: French pottery akin to Quimper ware, advertising the Shop of the Golden Dog, an important trading post in Quebec, Canada, established by Nicholas Philibert, 1736. There are late replicas in circulation.

golden walnut: A finish of walnut wood employing copal, rubbed to achieve a golden sheen. Found only on unrestored pieces of the Queen Anne period.

Golden Wedding: Pattern of cut glass featuring ovate panels and serrated edge; a curious technique of cutting not generally used. Within the panels are various devices and some geometric cutting. Made from 1894.

gold-leaf profiles: Gold leaf mounted on glass, etched with fine needles and profiled as a portrait of a sitter. Very rare, dating from c. 1780s. A phase of eglomise work, but not to be confused with 19th- and 20th-century imitations done by photo-chemical processes.

gold-on-glass: The true eglomise panel

work of gold leaf laid on glass, fixed only by wetting the glass with the tongue and then (1) drawn upon with hair pencils dipped in asphaltum and surplus gold wiped off when dry, or (2) etched with fine needles and chisels, exposing the glass, and then painted over, giving the effect of gold and color on the face. Process used to 1870s.

gold-on-silk: Painting on silk with nitro-muriate of gold, exposed when finished to hydrogen fumes. The gold deposit remained on the silk. Process dates from 1840s.

gold pens: The non-corrosive pen point of pure gold, said to have been invented in U.S. c. 1825. Over 1,000,000 a year were made in late 1840s.

gold scratch: Wood, coated with gum arabic and fine sand, rubbed with soft gold which transferred to the sand. Silver was also applied in this manner.

Goldsmith pictures: Deborah Goldsmith, amateur itinerant artist, worked in New York and Connecticut from 1808 to 1836, making portraits in oils and water colors. She married in 1832 but still signed her work D. GOLDSMITH.

gold stick: A rod of gold or gilded metal carried by officials as a badge of office.

Gold Street luster: Copper luster which looks like gold (and was gold), made at the Gold Street Pottery, Longton, England.

gollossians: Galoshes; go-low shoes. Pattens for bad weather.

Gombron: The first port opened to the East India Co. and from which porcelain, originally called Gombron ware, was shipped to England.

gondola: Same as sleigh bed.

gondola chair: See Chairs, All Kinds.

Gone-with-the-Wind lamp: A late term of no meaning, but passing as proper for the kerosene lamps of the 1870s and 1880s (and some even as late as 1920s) with glass shades and various types of reservoirs and stands. It is a device to give some glamour to lamps made by the million and sold at from $1.50 to $5 each by every type of store, shop, and mail-order house at the tail end of the 19th century. Named for the famed novel of the War between the States.

gonfannon: Pennon fastened to a lance.

Goodell furniture: Reference most likely is to the chairs and cabinet pieces by David Goodell of Pomfret, Conn., last half of 18th century.

Goodell parer: Apple parer made by Goodell Co., New Hampshire, from 1870s, who also made cherry stoners and seeders, potato peelers, and other gadgets.

goodfellow Toby: Jovial character in theatrical pose, pot on hand, forming a Toby-type drinking pot or pitcher.

Goodwin furniture: Cabinetwork and chairs by Joseph Goodwin, Charlestown and Salem, Mass., who advertised in 1771.

Goodyear buttons: No attempt is made in this volume to designate buttons by type, substance, or name of maker. This entry is merely to point out that in the hard white pewter button shop of A. Goodyear & Son it is asserted the first experiments in vulcanizing rubber were carried on.

goose basket: A conical basketwork device, open at each end, having a horn or funnel shape, made to slip over the head, neck, and forebody of a goose when plucking.

Gooseberry: Pattern of pressed glass featuring the gooseberry, leaf, and stem as a banding under a single row of very small dots.

goose gun: A long-barreled shotgun, a flintlock originally, but many converted to percussion-cap firing. The barrel has a swelling at the firing end to give additional strength to what is otherwise a thin barrel. American makers generally stamped their names on the locks and sometimes on the barrels.

gooseneck arm: A chair or settee arm that is more properly a swan's neck, sometimes having a terminal in the general form of this bird's head.

Gordon & Bankson: Cabinetmakers of Baltimore from 1780s. Makers of much of today's fine Maryland antique furniture, but said also to have made considerable furniture for the wealthy planters of Virginia.

Gordon & Taitt: London cabinetmakers of record, working from 1750s.

Gorgas clocks: Any clock made by any member of the Gorgas family, one of whom taught David Rittenhouse. Most Gorgas clocks now surviving were made by Jacob Gorgas of Ephrata, Lancaster County, Pa. All are excellent timepieces, beautifully cased. Gorgas was the first pre-Revolutionary clockmaker of record to issue an advertising brochure. Jacob Gorgas, a grandson, had first a clock-case shop and then a furniture factory at Ephrata.

gorge: Narrow-base big-bellied bottle of pottery, often with some device (such as a Bellarmine mask) impressed upon it.

gorget: A breast kerchief; a breastpin; a plate for the breast held on a necklace.

Gorgonism: Overemphasized, exaggerated writing, especially in respect to art, and generally minor art. The voluminous twaddle and humbug written about Pennsylvania art, especially about German sectarians, church groups, et cetera, are in the nature of Gorgonisms.

Gorham & Webster: The silversmithing concern which in 1843 became the Gorham Co. This firm in the 1880s published the first American book on silver collecting. Jabez Gorham was a mass producer of silver spoons in the 1820s. Some Gorham silver is now of antiquarian status, so the marks, generally lacking in books on silver, are reproduced in this volume. Note that one of the marks is found only on the electroplate, the Gorham Co.'s own approach to making Sheffield, or non-solid, silverware.

Gorham Washington: Replicas in bronze of the full-length Houdon statue. Cast in 1931 by the Gorham Co. and signed by the makers.

gorse berry: Gooseberry.

gossamer hat: A summer-weight hat.

gossip chair: See Chairs, All Kinds.

gossip mask: A brank or scold's gag, placed on slanderers and gossips as public punishment. Many offenders were left free to go about their duties, but the gag prevented speech. Some gags were sheet-iron masks covering the entire face, with eyeholes and a grotesque tongue protruding. [*Example pictured.*]

gossip pot: A two-handled mug.

Goss ware: Scent bottles, jewel boxes, and artwares of terra cotta and ivory porcelain made at Stoke-on-Trent by Henry Goss's pottery from 1858.

Gostelowe, Jonathan: Philadelphia cabinetmaker of Swedish ancestry, working 1744–95. Second only to Savery and Randolph and, in the opinion of many, the peer of these men. His work was labeled.

gotchbelly: A rotund spouted jug.

Gothic: A term that is an ancient error in that it is applied to the medieval style, owing nothing whatsoever to the Gothic; it is Gallic and is considered a variant (originally) of Greek architecture. The style was spread generally over ecclesiastic and secular Europe by the Guild of Freemasons.

Gothic: Pattern of pressed glass, sometimes called Cathedral, featuring a series of rayed arches.

Gothic back: Chair back with splats pierced in a decorative form called Gothic. Also chair backs made up of turned wood, arched in the style of church seats. *See also* Chairs, All Kinds.

Gothic Chippendale: Furniture featuring legs carved in shallow Gothic arches and pierced splats.

Gothic clocks: Steeple clocks; pointed arch clock cases, carved or plain.

Gothic Cut: Pattern of cut glass featuring star, fan, and geometric cutting, with serrated edge and some pointed Gothic arch terminals; hence the name. It dates from 1888.

Gothic end table: Table with solid end supports carved in Gothic style or a series of arcades of Gothic arches.

Gothic filter: A water filter made by Doulton & Watts, Lambeth, England. The cistern is in the shape of eight Gothic arches with figures of saints in low relief. Date is c. 1850.

Gothic fire screen: A five-sided frame of pointed hinged arches filled with wire screen. Date is from 1850s.

Gothic furniture: Properly, furniture of the age miscalled Gothic, really Gallic, A.D. 1200–1500. Revivals of the style, generally only of elements, occurred in 17th, 18th, and 19th centuries. Eastlake is a Gothic-revival style. In the U.S. an *Album of Gothic Designs for Cabinetmakers* was published in 1868 by Henry Baird, Philadelphia. It features objects of furniture later shown in Eastlake's book.

Gothic tray: A curvate-edge tray, sometimes called a Chippendale tray.

Gothic Windsor: Said of a comb-back chair having either arched framework or an arch on the fan piece.

gouache: Thick water color.

gouff (golf): Game played with crooked sticks and a feather-stuffed ball as early as 1620s in the Dutch colony of New Amsterdam. Governor Burnet of New England died possessed of a "sette of gouf clubbes and several dozen balls."

gouged: Scooped out; carving on two or more levels, but having a flat effect.

Goupil & Co.: Art dealers who sold many things, including materials for home-crafts—wax for flowers, things for Grecian painting, et cetera.

Gouroud: This name on a container of any sort applied to the contents; generally cosmetics by Dr. Felix Gouroud of New York, made from 1840s.

gout chair: See Chairs, All Kinds.

government job: Work done by craftsmen for themselves or others on their employers' time, or using the master's materials on their own time.

Governor Winthrop desk: There is no such thing; this is a modern trade name for a hybrid made commercially since 1900.

gower: Woodenware. A large platter.

graal: A large basin of wood, pewter, brass, pottery, or other material.

Grace fire: A Franklin fireplace as cast by Robert Grace of Philadelphia from 1740s.

grace hoop: A large rolling hoop used by girls as an exercise to develop grace in movement.

Graham ware: Salt-glazed stoneware from the Graham Pottery, Brooklyn, N.Y.

grain: A weight, approximately ¼ carat; $1/7000$ of a Troy pound.

grain brandy: Whiskey.

Grainger Worcester: Thomas Grainger, nephew of Chamberlain, established a pottery at Worcester, England, in 1800. After 1812 it was Grainger & Lee, then Grainger & Co. They did an extensive business with the U.S. See Perforated Parian. [Pottery mark pictured.]

grain jar: Large containers of pottery or wood to hold bread grains.

grain tin: The finest of pure tin, achieved from the ores by a granulation of pure particles. In 19th century it sold for $25 per cwt.

gram: The chick-pea.

grammalogue: A word sign or symbol, as in shorthand.

grammercy: Contraction of Grammer Zee, not of "God have mercy."

grandfather chair: Any important comfortable chair may be so called by people who must have a tag name for everything.

grandfather flask: Any flask holding a quart or more; some hold a gallon.

Grand Rapids ware: White-glazed kitchenware, flowerpots, urns, vases, et cetera, sold by mail-order and other shops from 1870s. Many potteries made such ware, and the name Grand Rapids has been traced to a Michigan pottery; the ware sold by the Leonard Co.

Grange lamp: Any lamp marked GRANGE was made by Grange & Co., Philadelphia, from 1860s. This company manufactured glass lamp wares, lard oil, and kerosene burners, and assembled lamps of plain and fancy types. Also imported much ironstone and queen's ware, some of which, it is alleged, is marked with company name.

However, we have not seen examples so marked.

Granger glass: Made near Saratoga, N.Y., under management of Oscar and Charles Granger. The factory was at Mount Pleasant, a branch of the Mount Vernon Glass Co., which finally became the property of Congress Springs interests, making bottles and flasks for mineral waters.

granite glass: (1) Wares made at Stoddard, N.H., at the Granite Glass Works. Bottles and flasks were made from 1840s to 1870s. (2) Glass made from powdered granite, rich in silica, feldspar, and lime. Said to have been developed as a process in Finland.

granites: Ices or cream sherbets, et cetera, with fresh fruits added. An 18th-century dessert elegancy.

granite ware: The more proper name for all the heavy ware that masqueraded as ironstone. True ironstone is not heavy; that is, not thick and clumsy.

Granville purse: A pocketbook. Many were made at East Granville, Mass., from 1830s, when the entire town was dependent on the manufacture.

Grape Band: Pattern of pressed glass featuring a band of stippled grape leaves and modeled bunches of grapes. A late pattern.

grape bottle: The secret of keeping grapes fresh after cutting for as long as nine months. The bunch was cut with a section of the vine, and this section, with proper support for the grapes, was passed through a cork into the grape bottle, which was filled with pure water over a lump of charcoal. The other end of the cutting was sealed with wax. The result was grapes all the year round—sold at very high prices in the winter, especially February through May. [Example pictured.]

grape settee: Cast-iron settee with elaborately cast grape-leaf and -bunch forms on back and sides, with foliated legs and trim.

grape shears: Short-bladed, long-fulcrumed shears for cutting grapes.

grape table: Vineyard table for sorting and packing grapes for market. Round, oblong, and in many other varieties. Date is from mid-19th century, and much used in New York State. Many have rotating center plateaus and look like oversize lazy-Susan tables.

grape tongs: An elegancy of silver or gold for picking up and eating grapes served as a dessert. Date is from mid-18th century. Small shears were sometimes placed with the tongs at table.

Grapeville glass: Name for the glass made at Grapeville, Pa., by Westmoreland Glass Co., including hen- and rooster-covered dishes as mustard containers. Some of the glass is marked. The factory is still in operation (1952) and, since 1948, has been making a line of cup plates.

Grape-with-Thumbprint: Late pattern of pressed glass featuring lightly stippled foliage and modeled grape bunches in arched panels surmounted with a row of thumbprints.

graphoscope: A single lens mounted in a frame for viewing pictures. [Example pic-

tured.] A folding one to view a single small picture was made as a watch charm.

grapho-stereoscope: A framework fitted with a single lens for graph viewing and a double lens for viewing stereoscopic pictures.

graspers: Tongs.

Grasshopper: Pattern of pressed glass featuring this insect in high relief over a cluster of foliage. Since this same foliage pattern is known without the grasshopper, the name to come for it will be Triangular Foliage Cluster without Grasshopper—or perhaps a name like Spivik, or Copse, or November.

grate apron: A fireboard; an apron to place over the laid fire; any solid screen to close up a fireplace opening.

Gravel Lane ware: Gray and brown stoneware and white salt glaze made at the Gravel Lane Potteries, Bankside, London, from 1670s. Many Bellarmine jugs thought to be of continental European make were produced here.

gravures découpés: An engraving or drawing, generally figural, dressed in cutouts of fabric, lace, gilt paper, et cetera.

Gray & Hemingway: Proprietors of the Cincinnati Glass Works from 1850. Lamps, decanters, apothecaries' vials, and perfume bottles were made.

Graydon lamp: Student lamp of the St. Germain type, having a fuel feed passing directly from reservoir to an oversized Argand burner. [*Example pictured.*]

Gray furniture: Southern French Antique furniture made from late 1840s by John D. Gray, Atlanta, Ga. D. M. Young was the retail agent in the 1850s.

Gray lamp: Gas lamp with generator a part of the ensemble. Patented 1860, the lamp is a beauty, looking much older. A brilliant lamp with marble base and heavy brass or bronze metal parts. [*Example pictured.*]

grease base: Said of candlesticks having round, oval, or square saucers or galleried bases to catch wax drippings.

Greatbach, Daniel: Pottery modeler and artist who worked at Bennington and at the Jersey City pottery. He was English-born and -trained.

Greatrakes, Valentine: A successful psychic or psychological healer born at Waterford, Ireland, 1628. Creatorex, Greatrex, and other variants in spelling are found. The term "no Greatrakes" is said to have degenerated to "no great shakes," and was applied to imitators of this man who, it is alleged, cured hundreds by the laying on of hands.

Great Seal of U.S.: Official seal of U.S. [*An early engraving of the obverse (main) and reverse sides is pictured.*]

greaves: (1) Tallow refuse from candlemaking. (2) Boots. (3) Buskins. (4) Leg armor. All, at some time or other from 1500s, were known by this name.

Grecian: Many and various items termed Grecian were made from the classic-revival period sparked by the Brothers Adam and pointed by the specific Greek designs of Thomas Hope. Greek-revival architecture was the dominant style of our early Republic. Among the items of general interest termed Grecian were: music stands [*example pictured*], sofas, worktables, lamps, chairs, settees, case furniture, trivets, china shapes and patterns.

Grecian cane back: See Chairs, All Kinds.

Grecian Cut: Pattern of cut glass featuring bold star cutting with looped points and small all-over star cutting.

Greek revival: About the sixth decade of the 18th century the Brothers Adam began using Greek forms in furniture and residence design. They worked only for the nobility and the wealthy. Thomas Hope, a Dutchman retiring to England in the late 18th century, was the popular champion of Greek revival, although his designs were also beyond the purse of the common man. Marco Bozzaris, Greek patriot fighting for the freedom of Greece in the 19th century, gave Greek-revival styles a new lease on life. By 1830 all America could buy Grecian-styled things. Greek-revival architecture seems to have been part and parcel of our early Federal days. It appears to have influenced the designers and planners of all sorts of structures in the new state of Ohio. Greek styles were incorporated in buildings of brick, stone, and wood. Some so-called museum experts still do not believe this was the case. They have failed, perhaps, to study the *Historical Collections of Ohio*, by Henry Howe, issued in 1850. This book, illustrated with hundreds of woodcuts, depicts Greek-revival architecture existing in public and private buildings in every Ohio village and town. New structures in New England, Pennsylvania, Maryland, and Virginia also had elements indicative of the Greek revival. American architects included it in their books of designs. It was grafted on Empire styles and is reflected in the wallpapers and textiles of the period.

Greek slave: A sculpture of a nude figure by Hiram Powers, the American sculptor, reproduced as a statuette in Parian by Minton in 1848 or 1849.

Greek-slave lamp: A marble-based bronze figure lamp with cut-glass oil font made by Meriden Malleable Iron Co., West Meriden, Conn., c. 1883. It is far superior to the Gone-with-the-Wind models which, in the main, are of later date. [*Example pictured.*]

Greek ware: Trade name for the Grecian-style vases by Copeland. This is late Spode, made from 1866, and is mostly toilet wares in various sizes. It was a luxury item and not common. [*Example pictured.*]

Green, James: A cabinetmaker of Alexandria, Va., working there in 1823 and at Washington, D.C., from 1831. His sons established a furniture factory at Alexandria which was operating in the 1880s.

Green & Co. Minerva: The Minerva Pottery at Fenton in 1812 was owned by C. J. Mason, the producer of true ironstone. Thomas Green of Burslem joined the firm in 1833. In 1859 the firm became a stock company trading as Green & Co. From 1851 the production was mostly dinner- and other tablewares, toy sets, and trinkets.

Greenaway, Kate: English artist famous for her colored drawings of children in what might be called Empire- or Regence-period dress. Born 1846, died 1901. Tiles, paper dolls, prints, books, calendars, chinawares, fans, toys, valentines, and dolls of Kate Greenaway provenance are avidly collected.

Greenbank glass: Made at a town of this name in New Jersey by Scott & Rapp from 1870s. Glass buttons were made at this plant.

green chair: See Chairs, All Kinds.

Greene, Anna Katherine: Lady publisher of the *Maryland Gazette*, 1767–75. Lady publishers are not unique in the American scene; Clementine Rind published the Williamsburg, (Va.) *Gazette*, and Anna Goddard published the Baltimore *Advertiser*. There were several other lady publishers in the newspaper, book, and periodical fields.

green glass: (1) Common glass made from sand, soda, and potash, colored by impurities which are always present if not clarified. Generally made into cheap bottles, vials, flasks, et cetera. (2) Glass in various intentional green tints, shades, and colors, achieved by resourceful use of metallic oxides. These are good to fine wares.

green-gown: To tumble or make love play on the grass, which usually stained the dress.

green gum: The best cloth for roller shades, similar to Holland's, but heavily impregnated with gum.

Greenleaf wirework: Meat safes, bird cages, window and fire screens of woven wire and wirework, made by Greenleaf & Co., Providence, R.I., from 1845.

greenling: A codfish.

Greenocks: Textiles and embroideries imported from Greenock from early 1800s.

Green pottery: John Green's works at Swinton, England, the Don Pottery, produced the famous "jumper jug" in colored glazes and with verses, much ware imitative of Leeds pierced wares (and which, in the absence of marking, are generally attributed to Leeds), dinner-, tea, and tablewares with some plates flowerpainted in great fidelity to nature, cane ware, black ware, and Rockingham glazed ware.

Greentown glass: Agate and chocolate-colored glass, in pressed patterns and forms, made at Greentown, Ind., from 1890s to 1900s.

Greenwood furniture: Cast-iron and cast-brass frame and body hatstands, stools, glass frames and vanity stands, table frames, bed frames, ottoman and chair frames made by M. Greenwood & Co., Cincinnati, from 1850s.

Gregorian wig: A head of false hair designed by Gregory, a barber-surgeon of the 17th century.

Gregory, Mary, glass: While it is now definitely established that a woman named Mary Gregory worked at the Sandwich glassworks, during its final decade of operation, as a glass enameler, this person had nothing whatever to do with the creation of the product to which her name is in error applied. What is meant is clear and colored transparent and opaque glass, enameled with figures, flowers, et cetera. This ware is believed to have been first made either at Bristol or St. Louis, in direct imitation of the luxury ceramic ware known as pâte-sur-pâte. This ware, of which Solon (who worked at Sèvres and with Minton's) was the most famed artist, was achieved by painting in slip on colored biscuit. Each piece was the work of an artist. Some Solon vases sold for $10,000. The cheap imitation of pâte-sur-pâte in glass captured the imagination of the masses. Pâte-sur-pâte reached its point of highest favor in the 1870s. The imitations in glass date from c. 1880 and were in continuous production to 1910 and later. The glass was made in Bohemia, France, Italy, Germany, Switzerland, England, and the U.S. Articles from tiny vases to punch bowls, including barbers' bottles, shaving mugs, et cetera, were made. Many water sets, toilet sets, and night sets are of record. Bristol made toilet bowls and ewers. The cheapest is simply tin white enamel on the glass. Refinements are tintings of flesh on faces, rouge spots, and tints on garments. Sandwich, in its final years, made some of this glass, and Mary Gregory was *one* of the young women hired to do the production-line enameling.

Gregory paper: Wallpaper manufactured and imported by S. H. Gregory, Boston, Mass., from 1840s.

greine; greined: Not grained, as has been assumed, but greened or made green; stained green; painted green. "A pair of firedogs, greined," means brass covered with verdigris. "A greined chair" means a chair painted green.

Greiner doll: American-made molded doll heads marked GREINER on neck. Louis Greiner worked in Philadelphia from 1850s.

grenade lamp: A cigar lighter in the form of a hand grenade, under three inches in diameter.

Grendly, Giles: The only conceivable reference would be to the London cabinet-maker of this name working in middle years of the 18th century and said to have exported furniture to the American colonies.

gres de Flanders: Gray salt-glaze stoneware, much of which was made in Flanders from 14th century.

Gresham lamp: R. H. Gresham had a lamp works at Jeffersonville, Ind., from 1850s and made fancy and plain lard-oil, fluid, and phosgene lamps. The factory also produced japanned tinwares.

Grey & Hemingway glass: See Gray & Hemingway.

greybeards: Potbellied stoneware jugs with bearded face and other applied or molded ornaments. These were commonly called Bellarmines, as they were first made in mockery of this cardinal. 17th century. [*Example pictured.*]

greyhound inkwell: Rockingham greyhound and rabbit on a blue-tinted oval base, within which is a well for ink. Date is from 1820s.

greyrusset: A coarse gray cloth.

greystones: Coarse millstones.

gridiron; grid: Grills of wrought iron or other metal for broiling foods in a fireplace. Not a griddle, this being a solid piece for baking and grilling, made of soapstone or talc, smoothed wrought or cast iron, potstone, or fired clay.

Gridley pitcher: Pressed-glass pitcher featuring bust of Captain Gridley, to whom Admiral Dewey made the remark, "You may fire when ready, Gridley," that opened the battle of Manila Bay.

Grier eagles: Reference is to the eagles carved in hardwood, naturally finished, and of poplar, rouged and gilded with gold leaf, by Dr. Robert S. Grier (1790–1865) of Taneytown, Thomes Creek, and Emmitsburg, Md., from 1812 to 1850s. Dr. Grier was a Presbyterian minister who owned a farm bisected by the Mason-Dixon line, lying partly in Pennsylvania. He carved eagles, statuettes, whimseys, and cane heads in the academic tradition, almost professionally, but as an amateur from first to last. His are the eagles which, owned by many fortunate possessors in the Gettysburg region of Pennsylvania, were imitated in jackknife carvings by the hobo, Shimmel. Dr. Grier's eagles and other carvings are now excessively rare.

griffin: Mythological figure with body of a lion, head of an eagle, and wings of a bird. A heraldic device, and also used in decoration. This beast was supposed to lay eggs!

griffin cup: In the 16th century ostrich eggs were esteemed for their shells, which were made into cups and sold at fabulous prices. "Laid by a giant bird akin to the griffin" was the popular belief; hence the name.

Griffin furniture: Hepplewhite- and Directoire-styled furniture made at Pittsburgh from 1790 by Griffin & Morrison to 1800, and then by Griffin & Thorn.

griffin hook: A mechanical needle for swift rug hooking. Needle carries the tape or yarn with it, in a sort of sewing-machine action. Some varieties are double and work even more swiftly. A device scorned by professional rug hookers in traditional techniques. Made from 1890s.

Griggs furniture: Thomas Griggs, Sr., from 1754, and Thomas Griggs, Jr., from 1760, are listed as cabinetmakers of New York City, making chairs, tables, and case pieces in the Georgian style.

grimace: A caricature.

gringo: Origin of this term for U.S. soldiers derives from a popular song they sang in the Mexican War—"Green Grow the Rushes."

Grinnell mirror: Tabernacle mirror imitative of the French *trumeau*, made in considerable quantities by Peter Grinnell & Son, Providence, R.I., from early 19th century. These mirrors are not in the Sheraton style—they are French. Sheraton designed no mirrors.

gripe: A three-tined fork. Also grope and grip.

grisaille: In tones, tints, and hues of gray; grizzled.

gris de lin: Purple-gray; the hue or shadow of purple. *See* Purple.

groaning chair: *See* Chairs, All Kinds.

grosgraine: Coarse ribbed taffeta.

grooved drawer: Any cabinet drawer with deep grooves in sides fitting in tongues of wood in the drawer orifice. Generally found in cabinets made prior to and during first half of 17th century.

gros bleu: Deep royal blue.

groshandeseer: Vulgar for *grosse chandelle de cire*, a large wax candle.

gros point: Embroidery in points, imitative of woven tapestry. When done in wool it is *gros point;* when in silk or fine thread it is *petit point;* but the *gros point* was the first technique. Sometimes used as a term for *point de Venise*, a Venetian lace.

grotesque: The original meaning was a painting in a grotto or catacomb. Now means distorted, whimsical, capricious, or just plain ugly.

grotto; grot: A natural or artificial cool cave. Built of arched stone, often over a spring, these were the refrigerators of early homes and mansions, castles, and châteaux. Also an artificial den, elaborately contrived, to provide coolness in the heat of the day.

groundnut: The goober, ground pea, or peanut. Also the glycine apios, found by the Swedes on the Delaware and used by Conestoga Indians, the Delawares, and Susquehannox as food. Also the St. Anthony's nut or European sedge, bearing small tubers and raised for pig feed. This extended information is mainly for the lovely lady who, lecturing on the Christmas customs of our ancestors, said, "And they served ground nuts as goodies, but I have been unable to find the recipe for them." The peanut or groundnut was also called a chufa.

grout: Liquid mortar.

Grove piano: A close-coupled Empire-style piano of the 1840s, looking somewhat like today's miniature piano, made by D. B. Grove, Philadelphia.

growme: A stretcher for woolens.

growsome: Good growing weather; weather excellent for crops.

guelderose; guelder-rose: The snowball, or *Viburnum opulus*.

gueridon: A round-topped occasional table, often used as a candlestand.

guglet: Drinking jug with nipplelike spout.

guikmon: Conventionalized chrysanthemum flower.

Guild miniatures and portraits: Signed ones must exist. The artist, James Guild, was a farmer's helper who became a peddler, then an itinerant silhouette cutter, then a miniature painter who walked the highways seeking custom, and finally did large portraits. In 1824 he went to London to study. His home was at Tunbridge, Vt., but he worked at Albany, Syracuse, Buffalo, Lancaster, Baltimore, Richmond, Norfolk, Philadelphia, New York City, and intermediate points.

guild pitcher: Any pitcher or jug bearing arms, insignia, or emblems of a craft or guild. Similar to trade pitchers. Glass, china, stoneware, delft, silver, gold, pewter, and wooden examples are reported.

Guilford chest: Reference is to the painted chests of Guilford, Conn., and vicinity. The painting is imitative of carving on earlier English chests—hearts, crowns, roses, tulips, birds, et cetera.

Guilford toys: Hand-propelled four-wheeled velocipedes, hobbyhorses, pull-wagons, and other expensive wood toys made by Crandall of New York City at his Guilford, Vt., factory from 1850s.

guilloche: Decorating in form of a chain; a series of interlaced or overlapping rings. Often noted on early and late art glassware in form of threading.

guinea pockets: Carved depressions in the rims of game tables where the player kept his store of stake money. Quite frequently small counters were used—not the gold coin comparable to our $5 piece.

guipure: Openwork lace of geometric design and pattern.

guitar lute: [*An example is pictured from the patent papers issued in 1881.*] It is quite an instrument.

guitarpa: Instrument invented by Don José Gallegos of Malaga, combining in one instrument the tonal qualities of the harp, cello, and guitar.

Gullah: Dialect spoken by natives of the Carolina-Georgia coastal area. It developed in the littoral in the 16th and 17th centuries.

gully mouth: Small pitcher.

gum flowers: Wax flowers, used in decoration as early as 1660.

gum hive: Beehive cut from section of the gumwood tree.

gumshaver: Cask made from a section of the gumwood tree.

gumstick: A teething stick for babies, known in gold, ivory, jade, coral, silver, whalebone, and other "safe" materials.

gun-butt handle: The pistol handle used on knives and forks of early type.

gundalow: Longboat with lateen rig, much used along New England coast in 18th century.

gun hook: A brass holder, affixed to the wall in pairs, to hold guns in place. [*Examples pictured are often mistaken for fireplace hooks.*]

gunpowder punch: Actual gunpowder dissolved in ale and in wine, as a he-man drink. A frightful discovery was made when the results of the saltpeter in the powder affected the he-man who boasted taking this drink.

gunsmiths: It has been found impossible to include the names of American gun-, pistol-, and rifle makers in this volume, and there is as yet no definitive book available. There are lists, admittedly incomplete, recorded in the Bibliography. Over 1500 names from this dictionary file have been given to A. M. Carey, Esq., who is working on a complete listing of American gunsmiths, scheduled for publication in 1953.

Gurran (Juran): A Scotsman from or of the Hebrides Isle of Jura. The MacIlvoys, MacRaines, MacEvoys are from Jura.

gutta-percha: The Malayan sap related to rubber that was used extensively in making plastic molded goods from 1840s.

guttae: Plural form of gutta; a conical-form ornament, or finial, often used in rows or series.

guttus: A boot-shaped jug or drinking vessel. Originals were of leather.

Gwenedd, Madoc Ap Owen: Welsh explorer credited with discovery of America before Columbus. Sir Thomas Herbert mentions this in his *Relation of Some Years Travels,* published 1634.

gymp: *See* Gimp.

gymp head: Properly, gymped head. A dimity bed canopy with fringed gymp trimming. The same treatment was used around the rails of the beds in 18th and early 19th centuries.

gypsy rose: The corn rose.

gyron: A heraldic form; a tapering triangle terminating in a point, an oval, or some other form. Also a technical term used in describing inlay work. The gyrons of an inlaid table top can be a series of tapering triangular forms or wedges joining a center oval.

gyro pigeon: A steel propeller of two blades, stamped from quite thin metal and fired by a heavy spring. The flying object became a target for wing shooters, the slightest hit rendering it impotent and causing the spinner to fall. [*Example pictured.*]

H

habdalah: Ceremonial chargers of gold, silver, brass, pewter, bronze, or other substance, used in Hebrew synagogues.

haberdyne: Dried salted codfish.

habiliment: Decoration of garments with rich borders of gilt thread, seed pearls, and silver.

Habsburg: Literally "Hawks Castle." The royal family of this name came from Switzerland. *See* Hohenzollern.

hacienda silver: American-mined silver refined in the haciendas of Mexico, Peru, and other Spanish colonies. The word "hacienda" is said originally to have meant "work to be done."

Hadley chests: Carved stile and paneled chests of the region around Hadley, Mass. They are 17th-century chests in the English Tudor tradition, generally tulip-carved.

haematinon: Black glass imitative of the natural form, obsidian. The secret of making it was rediscovered in 1848 by Pettenoffer of Munich, Bavaria.

Hafner ware: Stoneware made at Nuremberg, Germany; generally polychrome with figural and swirl décor. It is 16th century, and rare.

haggaday: Wooden door latch.

Haggerty glass: Made at Brooklyn, N.Y., from 1850 to 1890s at Haggerty Glass Works. Green glassware, bottles, hollow ware, flasks, and carboys.

hagstone: Witchstone; a stone bored for a cord and hung on bedpost to prevent nightmares or bad dreams. Probably Norse or Swedish.

Hague & Redfield: Britannia-ware makers of New York City from 1840s. Also makers of japanned wares.

Hague (Den Haag) porcelain: The mark is a stork or crane standing on one leg with fish in beak. Made at The Hague, Netherlands, c. 1775–78.

ha-ha: A sunken fence; a retaining wall.

Hahn sofas: Sofas or seat furniture by J. C. Hahn, New York City, working from 1840s.

Haig & Chippendale: Firm succeeding Thomas Chippendale, made up of his son, Thomas, Jr., and Thomas Haig. Haig withdrew in 1796, and Chippendale died in 1823. At one time, after 1771, the firm was Chippendale, Haig & Co.

Haight carpet: Floor carpets woven by the Haight Mills, New York City, from 1830s. Printed felt, dyed-in-the-yarn, and printed-pattern carpets.

Haig ware: Red- and yellow-glaze earthenware and stoneware made by the Thomas Haig pottery, Philadelphia, from 1813. Plant was still operating in 1876.

Haines calculator: An adding machine of wooden disks, internal gears, and registering tabs, made by W. H. Haines, Rochester, N.Y., from 1849.

Haines furniture: Early Federal- and Empire-styled furniture made by Ephraim Haines, Philadelphia, from 1805 to 1835. He made really fine chairs.

hair bottom: A chair or settee seat made of horsehair or other haircloth.

haircloth carpet: Matting of horsehair, used generally; from mid-18th century for halls and stairways. Said to have been vermin-proof.

hair jewelry: *See* Hairwork.

hair oil: Bear's grease, pomades, coconut oil, et cetera, often emulsified with cologne water, used as a hairdressing.

hair painting: (1) Delicate stitchery with human hair as thread. (2) Human hair pounded in a mortar, the pigment mixed with gum-arabic water and used to paint mourning pictures!

hair pencil: Any painting brush for artists' use, made of badger, sable, squirrel, or other animal hair, fitted in quills. Quills from crows and nearly all other birds, including swans and ostriches, were used. The type of quill was the size indication of the pencil.

hair-rope pump: Water pumps of a cable of hair worked on a drum with a pulleyed weight at bottom. The hair rope entered water and retained a considerable quantity. Upon reaching the surface, the rope was passed through a wringer, the water squeezed out and caught in a trough.

hair wood: The dwarf boxwood. The leaves and stems were used in an infusion as a hair tonic. Not to be confused with harewood.

hairwork: Human hair woven into flowers, fruits, portraits, foliage, boscage, et cetera, as a remembrance, but not necessarily of a deceased person. These were often used

as love tokens and were often made from baby hair. This fad is responsible for much jewelry of the 18th century. The custom is not Victorian, but dates from the early 18th century and remained in vogue to the 1880s.

halberd: Pick and ax blades mounted on either side of a pointed steel head, the ensemble set on a pikestaff. A weapon dating from the Crusades.

halcyon: The kingfisher. When this bird flies the water there will be no storm—hence halcyon days.

Haldane furniture: William Haldane is perhaps the founder of the Grand Rapids furniture industry. He opened a cabinet shop in 1836 and in 1848 began manufacture by machinery. A general line of Empire-style house furniture was his first production.

Hale copper: Copperware and utensils made by Jacob Hale, Newburyport, Mass., from 1835 to 1850.

Hale pottery: Early Philadelphia redware and stoneware made by Samuel Hale from 1730s.

half canopy: Half tester; a bed canopy attached only to the headposts, or from wall at head of bed.

half chest: (1) A lowboy; properly a dressing table. (2) Lower half of a chest-on-chest, sometimes made specifically as a low chest of drawers. This is an 18th-century term.

half doors: Doors arranged as two swinging sections; the Dutch door. Purpose was to provide a door to keep children in and animals out, while providing light and air, which was achieved by closing lower half while leaving upper half open. Such doors had fasteners by which the two halves were fixed firmly together when desired.

half-headed bed: Descriptive of the first beds to lower the height of the headboard and substitute posts at head to hold the tester frame. The full-head beds had a headboard as high as the foot posts.

half joe: Portuguese coin worth about $8.80, issued from 1722 to 1835. The true "joe" was the double johannes, worth 72 shillings.

half legs: The parts of a split leg, one half of which turns out on a gate to provide a support. Seen on some gate-leg and other tables. A device in Gothic- and Tudor-style furniture.

half-minute glass: Small sand glasses with large orifice to permit what was called "forty winks" or thirty-second timing.

half-moon chair: A corner chair. *See* Chairs, All Kinds.

half-moon gate leg: William & Mary style side table with a double semicircular top, the standing half supported by four turned legs, joined by flat stretchers spaced around the semicircle. Two gated legs pull out from side to support the other half-moon leaf, thus providing a full round table when required.

half-moon sideboard: Semicircular sideboard with a bow front extending outward a distance equal to one half the length. Generally in Hepplewhite style.

half-moon spinet: It looks like a large,

deeply valanced half-moon table in the Hepplewhite style, but it conceals a spinet frame and a keyboard of five octaves. A rare type. [*Example pictured.*]

half-peck loaf: Loaf of bread weighing 8 pounds, 11 ounces, ½ dram.

halfpenny styles: Not a derisive term but a reference to the styles and patterns in William Halfpenny's *Book of Designs*, published 1750.

half tester: A canopy over the head section of a bed. Same as half canopy.

half tops: A confusing term meaning pairs of shallow trays folding over to form the top of a stand, serving as catchalls when extended. Seem to date from the Adam period.

Hall, Jonathan: Potter of Roxbury, Mass., from c. 1760.

Hall, Peter: Cabinetmaker of Charleston, S.C., from 1760s.

Hall, Thomas: Producer of many magic-lantern slides, some having movement, as the chromatrope. One was a picture of Washington within a revolving wreath from which rays of light would flare. Worked in Boston from 1835.

Hall Boardman Britannia: Philadelphia-made metalware by a firm so named, from 1840s. Lamps, ladles, bedpans, beer and ale mugs, coffee sets, church wares, and "music plates," which might mean metal plates for printing music.

hall chairs: *See* Chairs, All Kinds.

Mallet & Davis: Pianoforte makers of Boston from 1850s.

Hallett, William: Master cabinetmaker of London, 1730–70.

Halm furniture: Divans, cases, chairs, sofas, et cetera, in the Directoire, Empire, and French-revival styles made at Columbus, O., from 1840s by M. Halm.

hallmark: Actually the approval stamp of the Guild Hall or governing body of a trade, as the silversmiths. Equivalent to a college of heraldry for artisans stamping the wares made. No American silver is hallmarked, as we had no guild. There are assay and class marks, but these are not hallmarks.

hallotype: Positive photo prints achieved by sunlight.

Hall sanders: Turned wood boxes for holding and sprinkling sand on writing in ink, as a blotting device. Made by a firm labeling them as here noted.

hall seats: Benches used in hallways. Any bench so used, but specifically the uncomfortable plank-seated Greek-revival and Empire examples.

hall sideboard: A sort of imitation console standing on four legs and having a backboard. Used in hallways as a table, sometimes flanked by costumers. Date is late, probably from 1840s.

Halvorson case: Daguerreotype cases made of wood flours, shellac, and other gums, molded in hot dies. Named for the American inventor, Halvor Halvorson, working from 1840s, who also is credited with inventing a spring shade roller, a two-wick lamp, and a haircloth loom.

Haman clapper: Haman, the one who

was hanged high, had this ritualistic clapper named for him.

Hamilton: Pattern of pressed glass featuring a band imitative of Irish cutting, with rays of flutes. When the rays are not shown and the space devoted to a band of pressed leaf forms it is called Hamilton-with-Leaf.

hammer cloth: The cloth covering the box seat of a coach.

hammered nails: Wrought nails; the work of the nailsmith before the advent of machine-made nails, 1788–92.

Hammondton glass: The Coffin & Hay glassworks at Hammondton, N.J., makers of many flasks, including historic examples, hollow wares, and offhand work. Established 1814 and in operation to 1850s.

hamoke: A hammock or hanging bed.

Hampton grate: The grate devised by Adam Hampton, founder, for open burning of anthracite fuels. New York, 1850–60.

ham stand: Two flaring cones, joined point to point with a sturdy collar, one with a spike upon which a ham was impaled. A piece of kitchenware of sheet iron now seldom encountered.

Han: Chinese dynasty, 206 B.C.–A.D. 280.

hanap: A silver cup, from Anglo-Saxon *'hnaep.* From this we derive hamper. Also hanaperium, the chest in which silver drinking cups were kept.

Hanau ware: Early pottery made by Dutch settlers in Hanau, 1660s.

Hancock, Henry & William: Henry Hancock, who retired from the cabinetmaking business at Boston, 1831, was advertising canterburys, night chairs, pier tables, secretaries, wardrobes, lolling chairs, and other items in the 1820s. These were in the Directoire or Regence styles. William advertised substantially the same line of wares in 1829.

Hancock luster: John Hancock of Etruria, the Staffordshire district of England, was a specialist in luster application to pottery and is said to have done work on Spode ware. He is believed to have developed the steel or gun-metal luster. Date is assumed to be after 1810.

Hand: Pattern of pressed glass named for the finials, a hand with fingers clenched on a short baton. The pattern is one of alternate clear and diamond panels. Its makers, O'Hara of Pittsburgh, in 1880s, originally called the pattern Pennsylvania.

hand cannon: The first firearm; a short-barreled bell-mouth cannon mounted on a stock, fixed with cording, and fired from a touchhole with a piece of smoldering rope. Date is c. A.D. 1200.

hand cooler: Ovate balls of ceramic or glass, the glass examples being made in the fancy paperweight tradition. Some hand coolers are of onyx, agate, or veined marble.

hand crane: A drum on which a rope was wound by cog-and-handle action, thus pulling the cording, which was reaved through pulleys on a gantry, or lifting apparatus.

hand glass: (1) A hand mirror. (2) A glass-covered or all-glass box for starting plants.

H & HL hinges: These are the common form of wrought-iron hinges, but they are known also in brass. The H hinge is made of two upright straps with a single clasp joint. The HL hinge is really a single upright strap with another having an L shape, also joined with a single clasp. The L strap was always on the door, not on the frame. The added strap was for additional support of the door. [*Both types, in iron and brass, are reproduced.*]

handiron: Same as andiron.

handled cup: The cup, a small bowl used in drinking tea, coffee, and chocolate, was apparently first made with handles from c. 1780. With this innovation the under-dish, also a shallow bowl, was extended and flattened to somewhat the proportions of the piece today.

handler: The workman in a pottery or other shop who affixed handles on hollow wares; not the packer or carrier of finished ware or work in process.

handles, wood: Many varieties of carved and pressed-wood handles or pulls were applied to French Antique revival furniture from 1830s. These include forms imitative of birds' wings, eagles, fruit clusters, leaves, shells, books, hands, et cetera.

Handley: Pottery made at the Kiln Croft Works, Burslem, England, later owned by T. & R. Boote. Handley had the works from 1800 to 1825. Made whitewares.

handmade screws: One of the earmarks of old cabinetwork is the use of hand-filed wood screws, without a constant pitch and having no points, whether made of wrought iron or brass. They did not penetrate the wood but were screwed into bored holes. Machine-made screws, dating from 1825, were also made without points to c. 1850.

hand pumper: Wheeled fire pump operated by hand by groups of men manning the pumper bars on each side of the machine. The water well was filled by brigades of bucket carriers passing lines of buckets from a cistern, stream, sump, or other repository. Many of the early hand pumpers did not have hose lines but a long nozzle, which was aimed at the fire and the stream of water thus directed. Therefore, the engines had to be pulled close to the blaze.

hand screen: A fan.

hand spit: A fork-ended rod turning on a prong that fitted over a spit rod. A slice of bread, apple, potato, or other comestible was impaled on the tines and turned until done to the liking of the user. A parlor spit. [*Example pictured.*]

hand tapestry: *Gros-point* embroidery.

hand warmer: A silver ball with a small basket within to hold a coal ember. A 17th-century elegancy, generally about two inches in diameter. Sometimes mistakenly called tea ball, witch ball, and pomander ball.

hanger table: A console with two legs in front, the rear supported on wall hangers. Sometimes called a hangore table in old inventories.

Hangest: Henri Deux ware, the faïence made by Madame Hélène de Hangest at the Château Oiron.

hanging cupboard: Any cupboard affixed to the wall without floor support, whether flat or corner style. Known in pioneer type as well as sophisticated period styles.

hanging vase: Term is variously used to describe any vase suspended on chains or cords from stand or ceiling, and any vase having loose handles within a supporting ring or boss.

hanging wardrobe: The piece did not hang; it is a cabinet piece in which robes were hung, rather than folded and placed in drawers.

hankwinder: The niddy-noddy, a device used to wind yarn from spindles. It consisted of a center bar with crosspieces set at right angles in their plane. It turned in a quasi-rotary motion.

Hanley Dresden: Raised flower china ornaments in the Dresden style, made at the Dresden Works, Tinkersclough, Hanley, England, from 1843. Not marked. Much of this ware was sold in the U.S. and considered to be of continental European make.

Hanover: Pattern of pressed glass by a Tarentum, Pa., factory, featuring beveled panels of clear glass with star pressed panels.

Hanson house pump: If there ever was a device to fool experts, this is it. It is a house pump, but not for a well or cistern. It is a water-powered pump operating from a city water supply which, in many cases in the early days, was not of sufficient power to force water higher than the first story of a house. So bathrooms, lavatories, et cetera, were supplied with city water by this booster. An example may be seen in Volume II, page 225, of *Manufacturer & Builder* magazine, a periodical in most large public libraries.

Hanukah: A ceremonial lamp used in the Jewish Feast of Dedication, having a battery of eight reservoirs with wicks. Also an eight-branched candelabrum.

hapharlot: A coarse coverlet.

Harbeson, B.: Pure tin and copper utensils so marked are the work of Benjamin Harbeson, Philadelphia, working from 1790s.

hardanger: Embroidery in the Norwegian style; fine stitchery with cutwork on voile or linen.

hard gold: Alloy of gold and bismuth, or gold and zinc.

hard metal: The right, or high-tin-content, pewter.

hard paste: The true porcelain; the kind that will turn a file; body and glaze are closely bound. This porcelain feels cool to the touch. Only three factories in England —Plymouth, Bristol and New Hall—made hard-paste wares.

hard pine: Southern yellow pine. Hard pine may look soft but isn't. It has considerable natural gum, visible in its grain. Rift-sawed, it makes excellent flooring. *See* Heart Pine.

hards: Coarse flax used as bed stuffing.

hard white: Button pewter.

hare motif: The hare is supposed to represent the soul of man going over the great divide.

harewood: Stained sycamore.

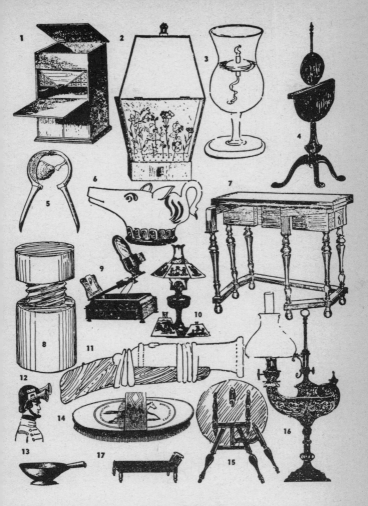

1, Flour Chest. **2,** Flower Case. **3,** Float Lamp. **4,** Flap Fire Screen. **5,** French Oyster Knife. **6,** Fox-Head Creamer. **7,** Front-Gated Table. **8,** Furniture Lift. **9,** Grapho-stereoscope. **10,** Hartshorn Lamp Shade. **11,** Hand Cannon. **12,** Hearing Cap. **13,** Holdfast Washbowl. **14,** Horse Brush. **15,** Hindenlooper Klaapdish. **16,** Harvard Lamp. **17,** Hydraulic Bed. (No. 7 from *New Geography of American Antiques*.)

Harford mirrors: *Trumeau*, tabernacle, and Constitution types of mirrors reported made by Charles Harford, Philadelphia, from 1790s. He is listed in the 1797 directory.

Harlem plate: Reference probably is to the J. L. Harlem factory at Hockanum, Conn., operating in 1850s and making plated snuff- and tobacco boxes.

Harlequin & Columbine: Popular name for a mechanical cast-iron bank which, priced at around $100 in 1943, is said to have sold in 1951 for $1500. The action is by a pair of figures, Harlequin and Columbine, who do a short turn or *pas* when lever is pulled. *See* Mechanical Toy Banks.

harlequin furniture: Trick furniture having concealed writing cabinets, bottle drawers, or having a dual purpose achieved by rapid transformation. Mostly 18th century.

harlequin pattern: Any diamond-diapered pattern in contrasting colors.

Harlequin's sword: A folding fan.

harmonica: Musical glasses. **harmonica gun:** A pistol firing a moving row of ten cartridges in a frame, traveling across the barrel orifice. This reference is to the later meaning of the term—a mouth organ.

harmonic telegraph: The telephone was so called prior to 1868. In 1869 the name telephone was adopted. The device was not invented by Alexander Graham Bell; Bell invented *one* of three telephones. One was marketed almost simultaneously with Bell's, but the other preceded Bell by seven or more years.

Harmony glass: Product of the Glassboro, N.J., works known as the Harmony from 1813 to 1837, after which it was known as the Whitney Glass Works.

harp: (1) The lyre or any multi-stringed instrument within a frame played by plucking with fingers. (2) Pattern of pressed glass featuring six panels, each impressed with a lyre form. Said to be an early lampshade. (3) Framework to support a lampshade.

harpitted: Hooked, as a rug. 17th-century term.

harpsichord: Ancestor of the grand pianoforte. The true harpsichord has three or four strings for each note, plucked by a quill moved by the keys. The Dutch name is *staarstuck;* the French, *clavecin à queue.* Not to be confused with the spinet, developed from the harpsichord, the strings hit with a hammer and only one string for each note.

harratine chair: *See* Chairs, All Kinds.

Harris & Zoiner: These names, cast on stoves, are names of the designers, not the makers. They worked in Cincinnati from 1850s.

Harris fireboards: Prints in form of large dominos or squares of wallpaper for passing on boards set in fireplace opening as a closure in summer. Also manufactured curtain paper, *which see.*

Harrison log-cabin pitcher: Believed to have been made by Ridgways; transfer-printed, black with green tracery and luster bands. Made for Robert H. Miller, Alexandria, Va., 1841, while that city was still within the District of Columbia. Pitcher displays portrait of Harrison, flags,

label HARRISON & REFORM, and log cabin marked TO LET IN 1841. Arriving after the election was won by Harrison, the pitchers were enthusiastically received and practically all were sold. The remainder was stored at the Miller St. Louis store and found many years later.

Harrison table: Dining table with rack-and-pinion extension action. American, and made from 1853.

Harrison terra cotta: Garden and home statuary and vases, made from 1850s by S. A. Harrison, Philadelphia.

harrs: Hinges.

Hartley: Pattern of pressed glass featuring imitation diamond star cut surmounted with fans, with alternating clear panels having leaf engraving on some.

Hartley crown glass: Glass made by a process using a hollow pontil rod which greatly reduced the bullion, or bull's-eye, with its coiling wavy lines. Made from 1835.

Hartman patterns: Embroidery patterns printed on fabrics from wood blocks, produced by T. Hartman, N.Y., from 1850s.

Hartshorne: Derbyshire ironstone pottery, cane ware, and Rockingham glazed wares made at the Hartshorne pottery from 1790s. Black luster was also made. Still operating in 1880s.

Hartshorn shede: Reference generally is to a lamp shade of printed paper on a wire frame, made to sell for 25 cents and used with kerosene lamps. Date is from 1860s. Most surviving examples are exceedingly brittle, age-stained, and scorched. [*Example pictured.*]

Harvard chair: *See* Chairs, All Kinds.

Harvard Cut: Pattern of cut glass featuring cutting imitative of cane seating, with the "holes" cross-hatched. There are several varieties.

Harvard lamp: Boat-shaped classic lamp on an upright rod, adjustable as a student lamp. Designed by Tiffany c. 1885. [*Example pictured.*]

Harvard rower: Child's exerciser or "participation toy." This is a rowing machine in the form of a wooden car on rails, moving backward and forward by pulley and cords. Date is 1880s.

Harvey-Latham ovals: Mirror frames of oval shape were made by a firm of this name at Providence, R.I., from 1840s. Some are said to be very ornate examples.

hash dish: Generally a hollow-walled and covered dish of Sheffield plate, but known in Chinese export and other porcelains, stoneware, et cetera, for service of various hashes. The hollow-wall construction was for filling with boiling water in the manner of a hot plate. Date is from 1780s to 1880s.

hasheesh candy: Drugged candy, sold as an anti-spasmodic and remedy for confusion of thought and melancholia. Made by Gunja-Wallah Co. of New York and widely advertised in 1860s. The drug was hasheesh (or hashish), Indian hemp, or *Cannabis indica.*

hash spoon: Large-bowled spoon with tapering tubular handle.

hasp: The leaf of a hinge, or fastener.

hassel; hackle; hetchel: Flax beater;

flat beveled paddle for breaking or hetcheling flax in the preparation for spinning.

hastener: A tin-plated mirror used in the roasting of meats. Placed opposite the fire, it reflected the heat and thus hastened the roasting process. Used when spit was not available.

hasty pudding: Oaten, corn, or wheaten meal (not rolled oats or corn flour) poured into boiling water and stirred to a thick paste. Eaten salted or sugared, with milk.

hat bottles: Probably inkwells. Glass hats, blown hollow, with a short-necked orifice in crown.

hatch bed: Sack-bottomed bed attached to rails with coil springs.

hatelet: A skewer.

hats, glass: The earliest varieties appear to be hennins, or conical-shaped hats used as candle snuffers. In 18th and 19th centuries innumerable glass hats were made as novelties, as containers for matches, toothpicks, spills, and splinters.

hatter's bow: A bow with handle, used in whipping hair of animals into a sort of fog which, settling, became the base of felt as used in hatmaking.

hat tip: A leather band for a hat. Work on such was called hat-tip work.

hat tree: A many-branched stand having pegs for hats. **hat rail:** A long board set horizontally on a wall and having pegs for hats.

hauchee paucher: Mashed potatoes.

Hauel, Jules: Perfumer of Philadelphia, 1830-60s, who packed his products in transfer-printed and hand-painted porcelain boxes, now avidly collected.

Hauksbee, Francis: The physicist whose work influenced Franklin. The work on physics, issued 1709, gave Franklin ideas for his electrical experiments. The Hauksbee pump was invented by this man.

hansmaler: (1) House painter. (2) One who did painting or decorating at home instead of at a factory or atelier. **hausmalerei:** Painting at home. Many of the decorators for Meissen, Sèvres, Chelsea, Derby, et cetera, worked at home. Same as *termineered:* produced at home for assembly or finishing elsewhere.

haustment: Corsets and braces worn under the dress.

hautboy: An instrument similar to the oboe.

haut-lisse: Facsimile tapestry weaving; the cartoon was set behind the work, the warp threads set vertically, and the weft interlaced by workers according to the pattern.

haut-relief: High relief.

Haviland china: The ware made at Limoges, France, by the Havilands of Westchester County, N.Y., who revolutionized the porcelain industry of France and achieved mass production of fine wares at prices appealing to practically all classes of people in the U.S. Several branches of the family held and operated potteries and conducted wholesale distribution in U.S. Now all branches are again compacted within one organization. Today considerable Haviland is made in the U.S. from original molds. The story of the various Havilands is told in *Haviland-Limoges,*

by Serry Wood. All Haviland ware is 19th century, dating from 1840s, and has been in continuous production for over 110 years.

Hawkes ware: Tinned sheet-iron wares made by Ezra Hawkes, Boston, from c. 1825.

Hawkins, Armand: Antiques dealer extraordinary of New Orleans, patronized by all visitors, including Eugene Field. Flourished 1825-1900s.

Hawkins, James: Cabinetmaker of Charleston, S.C., in 1790s.

hawk irons: Cauterizing irons used in falconry. [*Examples pictured date from 1670s, and are exemplary of tools that have challenged many collectors as to their original use.*]

Hayburner: Cast-iron stove used much in the prairie states, burning twisted wisps and billets of dried grass (hay), corncobs, and cornstalks. Some have pistons with mechanical action to feed charges of fuel to the firebox. Examples having the name HAYBURNER cast on the plates are not uncommon. 19th century to 1900s and later.

Hay candles: Hard pressed candles made by Allan Hay, N.Y., from 1840s.

Hayes lamps: Hamilton Hayes of Brooklyn made girandoles, chandelier, table, and mantel lamps of the prevailing period styles from 1840s.

Hays' easy chair: Adjustable upholstered rocker in Empire style, having a side lever to adjust to desired positions. Invented 1834 and made from that date.

haystack measures: Jug-shaped measures (generally pewter or brass) having wide belly, narrow neck, and funnel mouth. Made in sets from a gill to a gallon.

hay-ward: A watcher of the meadows.

Hazard furniture: French Antique style furniture made by Simeon Hazard, Newport, R.I., from 1850s.

head cup: Any cup in the form of a human, animalistic, or bird head. The face Toby is properly a head cup. Originally of modeled leather, later made in silver and other metals and pottery. Rabbits, foxes, and other animals, adult men and women, children's heads, et cetera. There are two kinds: the proper cup type with opening at top of the modeled head, and the upended kind, displayed with the open rim down. These appear to be finished bustos when displayed. Headpieces of glass, pottery, and metal are of great antiquity, probably of Greek origin. Many varieties from mythology, heads of heroes, gods, goddesses, et cetera.

head scraper: Slender rods with dulled rake or knop, used by fashionable ladies to penetrate an elaborate coiffure and scratch the head without disarranging the hair. 18th century.

heald: A heddle; an eyed leader for the vertical thread of a loom.

healings: Bedclothes.

Healy-Buxton desk: Secretary desks made by a firm of this name at Worcester, Mass., from 1840s. Also made washstands and other bedroom furniture. Cottage Empire styling.

hearing horns: Worn by mariners, lookouts, sentries, et cetera, to enable them to hear sounds over great distances. Sometimes called a hearing cap. [*Example pictured dates from 1848.*]

hearn: Coarse linen.

heart & crown: A cresting in the form of a cutout design of a crown over a heart, typical of Connecticut chairs of early 18th century.

heart-back: A form of chair back, generally of Hepplewhite style or influence, the general outline being a single heart or a pair of interlaced hearts.

heartbreaker: Twin curls at back of neck. *See* Creve-Coeur.

hearth garniture: Sets of andirons, tools, screens, fenders, pages, et cetera.

heart pine: This phrase, often heard from Virginia southward, is often mistaken for hard pine. The meaning is precisely as spoken—heart pine, or wood from the heart of the pine tree. Heart pine can be from a white or yellow pine. If yellow, it is fine-grained; if white, it is straight and free from knots.

heart wing: A tuck-away table with a large top folding on a single frame like a section of two-rail fencing and mounted on bottom braces. A heart-shaped element mounted between top and bottom rails stands parallel to the top when it is tilted. Swings to right angles as a support when top is horizontal. [*Example pictured.*]

Heart-with-Thumbprint: Pattern of pressed glass, called by some Heart & Bull's Eye and by others Bull's Eye & Heart. Pattern is a rococo band of hearts, upside down and right-side up, the rightly positioned ones having a large thumbprint.

Heart Divided: A pattern of hearts bisected vertically with a bar.

heater drawer: Sideboard drawer lined and capped with sheet iron. A small charcoal brazier or alcohol stove in drawer kept plates warm, and at times drawer was used also to keep foods warm.

Heathcote ware: Made at the Heathcote Pottery, Fenton, England; blue printed and hand-painted wares, gilded services, and ornaments. Made from 1790s to 1880s and later. Mark is three feathers, with C. HEATHCOTE & CO. over and CAMBRIA in a label beneath.

Heath ware: Earthenware made at the Heath pottery, Tunstall, England. The marks are the lettering H & S (for Heath & Son) in a label under a spread eagle and on the body of a crock surmounted by a crown. 19th century.

heat light: Huge Argand-burner kerosene lamp of 1890s designed to provide heat as well as light. [*Example pictured.*]

Heavy Jewel: Pattern of pressed glass with stippled background and beaded jewel-like bosses.

heddles: Eyed wires or slotted reeds used to hold the warp of a loom.

hedgehog crocus pot: Bulb pot, popular from late 1860s. Some made at Bennington potteries. [*Example pictured.*]

hedge marriage: Illicit intercourse. "She hae been hedge married to many a man but ne'er belled and booked."

heel tap: Round-bottomed cups that will not stand. In service they stood on sand in trays or were filled while held by the tippler. A "tumbler."

heel tipping (heel tippling): Pouring proffered liquor into one's boot or the gutter of a boot top.

Hegan mirror: The only possible reference found is a mirror made by F. Hegan, Louisville, Ky., working from c. 1840. Tabernacle and ovals of record are labeled.

Helene: Pattern of pressed glass made up of distorted diamond and star elements imitative of heavy cutting. A late pattern.

heliac spring: Helical coiled spring as used in fine timepieces.

helic candlestick: Helical coil of wrought iron or spring wire to hold a candle. Date is from 1650s to 1750s, with some examples of frontier and pioneer make of 19th century.

heliograph: Photo positives printed by sunlight.

hellenstein: Imitation Greek marble. Same as thiel.

helling: Boiling gilt metal in a vile concoction to obtain a certain finish.

hell oil: Water from olive-pressing vats was left to stand and the more rancid oil skimmed from it, to be used as a lamp oil. It had a bad odor when burned.

Helmet Ewer: Helmet-shaped pitcher. [*Example pictured is oriental export porcelain.*]

helmet scuttle: A coal hod of helmet shape. [*Example pictured.*]

hemicycle: Half circle. **hemicycleum:** Sundial with hemispherical cavity on which the shadow of the gnomon falls.

hemiglobular: Half global in shape.

Henderson pottery: Made by D. & J. Henderson, owners of New Jersey Porcelain & Earthenware Co., 1828. In 1830s firm name was changed to American Pottery Co. Flint-glaze stoneware, Parian, whiteglaze redware, buff and yellow ware, and Rockingham glaze ware. Made relief-decorated, hunting, hound-handled, Apostle, and other novelty pitchers. Marked Henderson prior to 1833. This pottery made a now rare Toby jug.

Hendrickson, Doll & Richards mirrors: Tabernacle and other mirrors, some with Boston-made crown glass, made from 1830s by a Boston firm of this name.

hendy: Gracious; nice.

hennin: High conical hat, generally topped by a long gauze veil or valance. Popular among women from 14th century and variants worn by colonial women in early 17th century. *See also* Bennin.

Henri Deux ware: Pottery of pipe clay, molded and stamped, inlaid with colored clay, and fired with a thin glaze. Excessively rare; made at Touraine in period of Henri II.

Henrietta: Pattern of pressed glass imitative of heavy cutting in large diamondform blocks with wide facets.

Henshaw of Boston: Pottery and glass importer, one-time partner of Deming Jarves, 1814–19. This man imported tons of the ware now known as "Gaudy Dutch" and distributed it wholesale. Data documented by his account books.

Hepplewhite: Furniture style in the classic tradition, after the style introduced by the Adam brothers. The *Guide* from which the style named Hepplewhite was copied by cabinetmakers everywhere was not published by the cabinetmaker but by his widow, Alice, trading as A. Hepplewhite & Co. Hepplewhite is credited with being the first to produce a sideboard as a complete cabinet piece instead of an assembly or cortege of three pieces. This master did his best work from 1770s. The style was practically unknown in the colonies until after the Revolution. The earmark of the style is a square tapered leg, classic sweeping curves, and cyma-curvate façades. He did feature some French cabriole legs and also designed fancy chairs, mirrors and sofas of great elegance, tables, Windsor-type chairs, and dual-purpose furniture. The design book, published in 1788, has been reprinted several times, and facsimile copies are in most large libraries. [*Examples of the style pictured.*]

hepatizon: The Corinthian "liver color" somewhat similar to aubergine or eggplant color. Term derives from the Greek and Latin. As here given, the ancient term referred to the color achieved on bronze and other metals.

herald chaser: A chaser in metalwork who specialized in ciphers, crests, and coats of arms.

heraldic: Of or pertaining to the art of heraldry, or the symbolism of the age of chivalry, during which practically every family of any importance whatsoever in Europe was granted a coat of arms. Student is referred to Burke's *Irish Heraldry* and especially to Rietstap's *Planches de l'Armorial Général*, which contains thousands of coats of arms of European families and from which most of the present-day "experts" get the coats of arms they profess to find after great research and sell for from $25 to $100. The mysteries of heraldry, the meanings of the many terms for colors, metals, and other field insignia will be found in any standard work on this subject.

heraldic positions: Many writers, early and late, seen to use certain heraldic terms for the positions of animals displayed according to practices of the College of Heralds. Rampant: erect on one paw, looking to left. Gardant: same position, looking down. Regardant: same position, looking right. Salient: on two paws, looking left. Statant gardent: four paws on ground, head looking outward. Passant: three paws on ground, looking left. Sejant: squatting, forelegs stiff. Couchant: down on all fours. Dormant: down on all fours, head in paws.

herald painter: Sign painters of 17th and 18th centuries were so called because most signs were pictorial, stylized, or heraldic in some form.

herblade: A sweet jam cooked from herbs and sugar with fruit.

herb mortar: Woodenware; a mortar in which to pulverize dried herbs.

Herculaneum: A term of classic-revival significance, applied to the Abbey & Graham Pottery (established 1793) in the reorganization in 1796. Located at Liverpool, the pottery was the largest in that community; the product was chiefly queen's ware, on a parity with Leeds and Wedgwood. Blue printed wares, punch bowls, mugs, dinnerwares, and specialties were produced. Terra cotta was also made. The products are stamped Herculaneum. [*Several marks are pictured.*]

Herculaneum chair: See Chairs, All Kinds.

herle: A twist, or fillet; part of a peacock's tail.

herlots: Tie garters.

Hermstadt gold: An imitation that rapidly became more valuable than the gold it imitated; an alloy of 16 parts platinum, 12 zinc, and 7 copper. First made in 1850.

Hero fountain: A fountain employing a hydraulic principle discovered by Hero, the great scientist of Alexandria, Egypt, c. A.D. 50. Two globes are poised, joined at their necks, on a crossbar within a frame, topped by a small basin and spout. The upper globe empties its contents into the lower, and the force of the falling water or other liquid is made to propel a part of the stream upward and escape through the nozzle of the fountain as a small spouting flow. Fountain will play as long as the globes are reversed. Made as a parlor curiosity and elegancy from 1870s to 1890s.

herringbone: (1) A pattern imitative of the back and rib bones of the herring; a form used in inlay, with a pattern laid diagonally on each side of a spine. (2) A pattern of pressed glass displaying alternate narrow panels with diagonal ribbing, with bands of diamonds, ovals, and other mish-mash.

herse: Stretching frame, often used by parchment makers.

Hertz pen: A writing pen of an alloy of iridium, zinc, and platinum, which did not corrode in any ink.

Heslops water: Bottles marked or labeled Heslops "Fly Water" were containers for an insecticide popular from 1780s to 1840s.

Hessian maps (of colonies): Maps printed at Nuremberg for use of Hessian troops sent to America to defeat the colonial bid for freedom. Titles are in German.

Hetherington & Netterfield Pottery: A stoneware pottery of New York City operating to at least 1855.

Hettinger shade: A window shade of fabric covered with paper. The maker is listed as doing business from 1840s at New York City.

hexafoil: Six-leaved or -segmented; six-scalloped, -sided, or -luned.

Hexagonal Block: Pattern of pressed glass imitative of the cheapest cutting, in broad panels with narrow clear foils. How it got this name is one of the 1001 mysteries of pressed-glass pattern nomenclature.

hex square: Six-sided.

Heyl copperware: Kettles, pots, pans, and saucers in all sizes, usually marked with stamping on handle, made at Columbus, O., by Heyl & Mason and by J. K. Heyl from 1840s.

Heyne, J. C., pewter: The rarest pre-Revolutionary American pewter, made at Lancaster, Pa., by John Christopher Heyne. The store and shop he owned (but did not found) were established in 1744 and are still in business. Originally a trading post for pioneering parties going westward (with a branch at Vincennes, then in Illinois country), the firm is now the Steinman Hardware Co. Heyne pewter is not particularly fine metal, nor is the workmanship superior; it is simply the scarcest pewter in the American scene and so has had greatness thrust upon it. It is said less than 50 marked pieces are known.

Hicks copperware: General line of cooking utensils made at Ware, Mass., by S. D. Hicks; mid-19th century.

Hidalgo: Pattern of pressed glass imitative of cutwork, featuring large blocks and curved sweeps. The considerable expanse of non-cut area on each piece was either left plain or was wheel-engraved.

hieroglyphic mica: Natural mica in which small particles of iron oxide have discolored the lamina, forming spots looking like hieroglyphs. At one time gullible ones believed these sheets to hold hidden messages and lost testaments, as those plates of gold allegedly found and translated by Joseph Smith. The mica is known in Pennsylvania, New York, and Ohio. The fault probably occurs in all deposits of the mineral, but not in all of the blocks mined.

higdon pickle: The true recipe for this colonial delicacy is as follows: Chop green love apples and cabbage fine with onion and green pepper. Put in a jar and salt for a few hours. Press out liquid and cover with vinegar. Again squeeze, and put in stone jar with ground and seed mustard, cinnamon, and horse-radish; cover with vinegar and let stand for a week.

Higgins linen: Fine linen, woven by nuns and parish scholars, sold in U.S. from 1830s. Finest kerchiefs were made of this linen.

higgler: A huckster; a bargainer.

highboy: A 19th-century term for what was originally called a high chest. From William & Mary period through Queen Anne and Georgian to Hepplewhite styles, often with bonnet tops and (in Georgian period) with beautifully carved and shaped cabriole legs. Generally made in two pieces, a lowboy form with a superimposed chest of drawers. There is also a single-piece high chest of drawers that is sometimes called a highboy chest.

highboy secretary: Modern term for an unusual piece of the William & Mary period. The base is a trumpet-turned six-leg lowboy, the top a cabinet with a large falling front (obviously modeled after the Spanish vargueno). Of Dutch make. The interior of the upper cabinet is fitted with drawers, closets, pigeonholes, and other desk necessities. [*Example pictured.*]

high chest steps: A run of three steps, made up in box form, used to reach the top drawers of a high chest and kept under the chest frame (lowboy section) when not in use. Sometimes also placed upon tops of flat-top highboys for display of plate and ceramic wares.

high-low: A high shoe with leather thongs tying in front.

high-low stretcher table: 17th-century table modeled after a Tudor-Gothic form, with four turned legs (usually button or ball turning) joined at ends with low stretchers and with a high-placed front

and back stretcher, often with a cross stretcher. These, in the colonies, seem to date from c. 1660. Sometimes called Cromwellian table. [*Example pictured.*]

High Rock bottle: Saratoga Springs bottle used as a container for the waters of High Rock Spring. The date, 1767, on the bottle is not the date of making (which is from c. 1870) but that of the year of the spring's discovery.

high roundabout: See Chairs, All Kinds.

High Street delft: Lambeth, England, delftware, made at the High Street pottery operated by the Welshman Griffiths from c. 1750.

Hill china: Reference is to the Hill Pottery at Burslem, where a beehive mark and a hand mark were used by various ownerships; 19th century.

hillier: A thatcher, a roofer, and a tiller of the soil were all so designated at various times in 17th century.

Hill's views: Folio engravings of American views published in 1820 as a portfolio titled *Picturesque Views of American Scenery*, with plates by Hill from drawings by J. Shaw, or engravings from books such as *Drawing Book of Landscapes* (1821), *A Series of Progressive Plates of Flower Painting* (1818), and others. Most famous of Hill's plates are the magnificent views from the *Hudson River Portfolio*, 20 colored aquatints from paintings by W. G. Wall.

Hinckle Pottery: There was a pottery at Philadelphia owned and operated by a man of this name in 1790.

hind: A female deer, improperly called a roe. Roebuck means a red deer. Doe is the correct term for the female deer. Hind was the most generally used term to 18th century.

Hindenlooper klaapdish: Folding table of Netherlands pattern, with folding turned legs nesting under the top. The underside was also generally painted in elaborate style. [*Example pictured.*]

Hindman sofa: A Grecian sofa with one end contoured for the repose of the body and the other fitted as a footrest. Made by Caldwell Hindman of Boston from 1820s. This man also made equally unusual rocking chairs. [*Example of sofa pictured.*]

hind's-foot spoon: Reference is to the handle, which has a trifid, or three-cleft, end of tulip form. Popular from Restoration period, England (from 1660s); a style that persisted to end of Queen Anne period. French *pied de biche*.

hindsights: Back portraits, *which see.*

hinged-man bank: A 20-pound pair of castings fastened with a hinge at back and held together with a coin-slotted plate on the skull pan. These were made from 1840s and are the first of the cast-iron toy banks. [*Example pictured.*]

hinges: Any elements in pairs, joined with movable clasp, serving as joined leaves to permit swinging of a door, table top, slope fall, or other occasional access cavity. There are many varieties. All considered worthy of attention by collectors are mentioned in this volume. [*Some are pictured.*]

Hinkley bed: Reference is to the combination of rods and slats of wood and

1, Domesday Characters. 2, Gorham sterling and electroplate marks. 3, Golden Age Stove. 4, Grape Bottle. 5, Fret Sawyer. 6, Engine Turning. 7, Hunting Goblet. 8, Heart Wing-Table. 9, Knife Boxes. 10, Highboy Secretary. 11, Eastlake Styles, Chest and Table. 12, Ice Pocket Decanter. 13, Iron Pump. 14, Inkwell Teapot. (No. 10 from *New Geography of American Antiques*. No. 11 from *Art Decoration Applied to Furniture*, by H. P. Spofford, Harper & Brothers, 1878.)

metal, patented c. 1850, to make a bed comfortable. There were many licensed bedstead makers who used the Hinkley method of supporting the mattress or bed sack.

hippocras: Wine spiced with botanical drugs, let stand, and then strained. A tonic dedicated to the Father of Medicine.

hippogriff: Fabulous beast having the body of a horse and the head, wings, and claws of a griffin.

Hirado: Fine Japan porcelain with soft blue décor of children at play under pine trees. The best Hirado displays seven boys at play, the medium grade pictures five boys, and the ordinary ware has three boys. The pottery was sponsored by the Lord Mastura, Prince of Hirado, 1751. Data vouched for by Heromichi Shugio of Tokyo, a Japanese expert and connoisseur.

histiodrome: The line of a ship's course. Term dates from 17th century.

historical glass: This category includes political- and military-campaign glasses; memorial and souvenir objects of glass; memorial plates of presidents, theatrical figures, circuses, business, et cetera; flasks, bottles, glasses, dishes, boxes, whimseys; pressed, molded, engraved, and cut.

historic American-view china: A collector's item since the 1870s, when its present-day value was prophesied by Prime. The complete history of this ware, featuring views of American cities and memorials of people, events, places, and states of the Union, has been attempted by several authors, including Barber and Halsey, but the final book, an amazingly definitive volume, is *American Historical Views on Staffordshire China,* by Ellouise Baker Larsen. First published in 1939, the book was practically unobtainable until a new, enlarged, and revised edition was published in 1950. This ware should not be confused with English wares from the Staffordshire district characterized by some as "Anglo-American" but bearing views of historic nature, such as memorials of Mexico, Cuba, and several South American countries, Canada, et cetera. The original ware of truly historic interest was made from the 1820s (if not earlier) and continued to the late 1840s. Thereafter the product is of different quality and is to be classed with other "late" wares made by English potteries for American importers. Among these were Jones, McDuffy & Stratton of Boston, who had over 100 different views made; Mellen & Hewes of Hartford; Bawo & Dotter of New York; Van Heusen & Charles of Albany; Wright, Tyndale & Van Roden of Philadelphia. Some of this so-called "historic" ware was produced as late as 1900. With the passing of time it will undoubtedly become a collector's item. It is also worthy of study if only to avoid being fooled unmercifully by it in terms of value or sums paid for it in the belief it is the genuine old historic ware.

historic bottles & flasks: These exist in such numbers as to make inclusion of most of them impossible here. The best illustrated check list is in *American Glass,* by George S. and Helen McKearin. Other volumes on this subject are mentioned in the Bibliography.

historic "old blue" Staffordshire: It isn't all "old blue," but the entire listing of historic China is to be found in *American Historical Views on Staffordshire China,* by Ellouise Baker Larsen. Other books on the same subject are mentioned in the Bibliography.

hitching step: A combination of hitching post and mounting steps (or carriage steps), generally of cast iron. Many varieties, including some figural posts displaying a jockey, a groom, a stableboy, et cetera.

hoarding: A billboard or expanse of wall dedicated to the use of bill posters. Aubrey Beardsley, the tragic genius of black-and-white art, wrote a monograph which he titled *The Art of Hoarding,* in which he made a plea for beautiful advertising.

hob: (1) The sides or side of a fire grate. (2) A constricted open fire serving also for minor cookery.

Hobart bell: Any church or tower bell cast by Aaron Hobart of Abingdon, Mass., where bells were cast from 1769.

hobble: An ankle lock or stopple for domestic cattle, to prevent straying.

hobby: An avocation or part-time pursuit, not necessarily antiques collecting. Gunning, sailing, canoeing, butterfly chasing, anthropology, languages—any study can be a hobby.

hobbyhorses: Large play toys; small effigies of horses on wheels, tracks, rockers, et cetera. [*Several examples pictured.*]

hob crane: Small metal crane or hinged pot holder for use on hob grate. The hob grate was never popular in colonial or Federal American homes.

Hobe furniture: Excellent French antique revival furniture of mid-19th century; some labeled Hobe are traced to C. F. Hobe, a custom furniture shop of New York City, active in the period.

Hobnail: (1) A pattern of pressed glass featuring a series of bosses in an all-over pattern. There are some 15 major and minor varieties of record, including hobnail with ball feet, with ornamental band, with panel, with bar, flattened hobnail, and so on. One pattern is still made. (2) Blown glass worked in a series of upstanding blobs of glass simulating hobnail heads.

Hobson's choice: (1) The inns of Old England patronized by the famous carrier, Hobson, active from 1690s. When an inn advertised it was "Hobson's choice" it was speaking well for itself, as Hobson demanded good food, good bed, good quiet, and good service. (2) Choice made by Lieutenant Hobson, U.S.N., to sink the collier *Merrimac* in the entrance to Havana Harbor during the Spanish-American War. He attempted to bottle the harbor and prevent the escape of the Spanish fleet within. His brave attempt failed in its purpose. The fleet escaped for a few hours and then was totally destroyed or disabled by a U.S. naval squadron.

hocchee: A chicken stuffed with fresh seeded grapes, parsley, and sage and stewed in water and white wine or in a court bouillon.

Höchst: A Porcelain made in Germany, at Höchst, from mid-1740s.

hockleberry: Original spelling (or one of them) of huckleberry.

hocks: Tall-stemmed, fancy blown glasses for ceremonial drinking of the wine hock, properly Hochheimer. Examples may date from 18th century or the 20th. **hock stand:** A stand for a bottle of this wine.

hodden gray: Cloth of natural gray tone woven from the wool of black and white sheep.

hodgepodge: From hot pot, a meal cooked in one pot.

Hodgetts tin: Domestic tinwares, planished and plated varieties, made by Hodgetts, Taytor & Hodgetts, New York City, from 1840s. Coffee urns, nurses' lamps, egg coddlers, and other tablewares, as well as stove wares.

Hoffman bed: A folding bed within a cabinet imitative of a low case of drawers. Date is from 1850s.

Hogarth chair: See Chairs, All Kinds.

Hogarth cup: Fulham pottery mugs with raised Hogarth figures. Made from c. 1690s. Hogarth was an English artist famed for his caricatures of the foibles of society, the law, and other professions.

hog maw: Pig stomach, stuffed with sausage and vegetables and roasted.

hog reeve: Official swineherd of a community.

hogs: Bristled dusting brushes.

hog-scraper candlestick: Iron candlestick with long shaft serving as a handle, the base being round with a sharp edge. Actually used to scrape hogs at butchering time. Most date from 1800 to 1850s. [*Example pictured.*]

hog yoke: (1) A bracket or brake; a framework fitted on hogs to prevent rooting and straying. (2) The backstaff of mariners was also called by this name.

Hohenzollern: Swiss family of feudal days who became the ruling house of Germany, parlaying the Duchy of Prussia into the German Empire by absorbing various independent German states, stealing territory from Poland, Denmark, and France. The entire pattern seems to derive from the jealousy of Prince Federick of Prussia over the Prince of Hesse's election to the throne of Britain as George I to succeed Queen Anne. Frederick wanted to be a king himself, so he created his kingdom. Strangely enough, the Hohenzollern, or "high-measure," castle was near that of the Hapsburgs in Switzerland.

hohokam: Pertaining to the native American Indians of the plains and the pottery they made.

hoiden (hoyden): An animal of vivacity and spirit in motion; a young hare. To romp indecently, exposing the unmentionables.

holder: Any device that is an extension of, or protection for, the hands, as pads, tongs, et cetera.

holder quill: See Quill Points.

holdfast: Iron tool in form of inverted L, the long stem driven in a hole, the short stem used to hold a piece of timber for cutting or carving. The short stem is generally slightly bowed.

Holdfast Bowl: A washbowl with rimmed foot and hollow handle; often mistaken for a culinary utensil. [*Example pictured.*]

hole book: The artist, Peter Newell, invented this style of book. He pictured, for example, the path of a ball fired from a gun, and each page had a hole in it where the ball had gone through. Newell made several such books; all are now collectors' items. They date from 1890s or 1900s. The first book with holed pages made in U.S. was Dunigan's multiplication-table book for children, with cutouts on each page.

Holland & Green: Successors of C. & W. K. Harvey, proprietors of the Stafford Street potteries, Longton, England, in 1853. Made much printed granite ware for the American market.

Holland-Fox Philadelphia: Collector's term for the now excessively rare engraved view of Philadelphia by Gilbert Fox, after a drawing by John Holland, c. 1796. Hand-colored, 15.4" x 21.1" in size.

Holland-painted Dresden: Actual Dresden porcelain made plain at the pottery and decorated in the Netherlands, from 1740s.

Holland prints: Wood-block prints in oil colors after the Baxter and LeBlond technique, made at Boston, Mass., by A. Holland. Date seems to be after 1850.

Hollands: A fine Dutch linen of the sort which, filled with wood flour ground in oil, was made into roller-type window shades.

Holling: Epiphany eve, when the Epiphany tree, later used as the Christmas tree, was displayed.

Hollis: Pattern of pressed glass featuring imitation lattice cutting with mitered joints.

hollowed pediment: The reverse of scroll. [*Example pictured.*]

hollow prisms: Triangular or prism-form framed boxes of wood or metal, fitted with panes of glass and made watertight with cement or putty. All have an orifice for filling with water. When filled, these were large prisms used in philosophical experiments and demonstrations of the colors in light. Date is from 18th century; many were homemade to 1850s. Often called beeliners, which is incorrect.

hollow relief: The ancient Egyptian style of carving, neither intaglio nor cameo. The object is outlined by a deep cutting, often on one side only, and modeled from that side.

hollow seat: A slip seat; a removable seat.

hollow stopper: Glass bottle and decanter stopper blown hollow, and often with a hole at the blowpipe end. Blown without use of pontil rod.

hollow ware: Any ware, of any substance or material, for use as a vessel or container. All saucers, pitchers, cups, bowls, et cetera.

Holly: Pattern of pressed glass featuring a band of holly leaves, stems, and berries. Leaves are stippled lightly.

holly maze: A garden labyrinth of clipped holly bushes.

holm: The holly tree. **holm oak:** An oak bearing holly-like leaves.

Holmes, Stonier: Potters of Hanley who produced much late granite ware for American market after 1870s.

Holmes furniture: French Antique revival and Eastlake furniture made by Holmes & Co., Boston, from c. 1850. A catalogue was issued 1868. Also made reproductions of late Sheraton-style furniture.

holosteric barometer: Circular disk-dialed barometer having a recording hand, with another hand that could be turned, by means of a knurled knob in front of the glass over the dial, to the same position as the recorder. By this device, the rise and fall from the tabulated point could be computed.

Holt & Co. furniture: There was a furniture factory at Bangor, Me., by this name, operating from 1850s.

holyrop: Wild hemp.

Homan Britannia: American-made hard pewter, some plated with silver, made at Cincinnati from 1840s.

Honan stoneware: Chinese stoneware from Honan Province; that of the Sung Dynasty has a purple-black glaze and is quite rare.

Honetsie flowers: Poor spelling of the name of seedsmen, Honna et Cie., of Brussels, who, from 1840s, sold exotic seeds and corms, bulbs, et cetera, in U.S. from their store in New York City.

Honeycomb: A basic pattern of pressed glass with enough variations to satisfy, if not confuse, a cataloguer. The pattern is imitative of facet cutting of surface to yield a hexagonal pattern looking like the cross section of an enlarged honeycomb. Student is referred to *Early American Pressed Glass,* by Ruth Webb Lee, for variant details.

honeycomb counterpane: Coverlet weave, generally in all white or cream yarns but some reported in red, blue, and yellow, imitative of a honeycomb in cross section.

Honfleure: A style of painting for amateurs whereby imitation of japanning and china painting was achieved in six easy lessons. Mr. & Mrs. Honfleure were the teachers. They were active at Boston from the early 1820s and sold painting kits for the work.

hong: A factory, or a factor's warehouse.

Honiton: A popular homemade lacework, patterns for which were sold in fancy stores from 1850s.

Hoock, William: One of the members of the Sanderson Furniture Sales Co. of Salem. *See* Sanderson Furniture.

hooded chest: (1) The scroll top of a high chest. (2) The barrel-topped deep chests having semicircular ends above the square section. Probably Swedish.

hooded washstand: Stand with splash-board to prevent spotting the wall.

hoof foot: Queen Anne and Georgian cabriole-legged furniture, the leg end being in the form of a hough, or hock, below which is a hoof, at times on a pad, or shoe. Also any other foot imitative of the foot of a hoofed animal.

hooked rug: Burlap or coarse linen base with pulled hookings of colored tapes, generally cut from fabric and later sheared or cut. Innumerable patterns are known, the most famous being those by Frost, which were stenciled in color on the burlap and sold to women for homeworking.

hoop: Staved wooden tankard with hoops marking its three drink contents. "I don't give a hoop [whoop]" is said to derive from this vessel.

hoop-back: *See* Chairs, All Kinds.

Hooper lamp: Camphene and lard-oil lamps in considerable variety of all popular types, made by H. N. Hooper of Boston from 1830s.

Hooper mirrors: Pier, mantel, and wall mirrors in gilded frames, also oval and tabernacle forms, made by Hooper Brothers, New York City, from 1840s.

hooter: Colloquial for a vessel to make the hot drink, hooter; chief ingredient was elderberry wine.

hop cauldron: Potbellied copper cauldron with cover, standing on iron legs. Used in steeping hops to make "wort," or hop tea, used in making beer. Swedish, from 17th century.

hop jug: Pitcher with hop-vine design issued by Minton Pottery c. 1849.

Hopkins prints: Lithographs, particularly from the *Vermont Drawing Book of Flowers,* a series of 10 flower drawings reproduced in medium folio and the first flower prints of important size issued in America. Issued by Bishop Hopkins of Vermont, 1846–47. Prints inscribed "Hopkins Lith, Burlington, Vt."

hopniss: The native American Apios, or ground pea. In 19th century also called the Dakota potato. [*Example of Glycine tuberosa, a variety, is pictured.*]

hopping-john: Cow or pigeon peas cooked with rice and bacon.

horizon (ART): Many artistic horizons are false, and made so by following art-instruction books. The natural horizon is the observer's eye level. For example: Sit before a multi-paned window and note the horizon in relation to any of the horizontal muntins. Rise, keeping the horizon in view. It rises with you! In 1849 Dr. Burton laid down the rule that the horizon of a picture should be between the eyes and shoulders of the topmost figures in the composition. Burton pointed out that Leutze's "Washington Crossing the Delaware" made Washington a giant because of the false horizon. This, of course, is the trick used by certain artists who are said to have the gift of making small figures look big.

horizontal freezer: An ice-cream maker of the 1870s, looking like the small barrel churn used in dairies.

horizontorium: A machine for drawing horizontal perspectives, invented in 1821 by W. Shires. There is a curious lithograph issued in 1832 by Hobson of Philadelphia that has puzzled many print collectors. It is the Philadelphia Bank Building, drawn by this machine to demonstrate the perfection of its work. The proper way to scan a picture made by the horizontorium is by reflection in a tilted mirror. Shires also invented a machine called the perspective delineator in 1832.

hornbeam: The *Carpinus caroliniana,* a tree of firm white wood, smooth bark, with leaves somewhat similar to those of the beech.

horn breaker: A peeler or shaver of horn in sheets for use in lanthorn panes, watch crystals, and wherever non-shatterable transparency was desirable. Sometimes used instead of glass in windowpanes.

horn carving: Scratch-carving, also called scrimshawing, done on horns used as drinking vessels, powder containers, et cetera.

horn cup: (1) Drinking vessel made from a whole horn. (2) Non-shatterable cup made from pared horn.

horn dish: A dish made from thickly pared horn, shaped by molding after steaming. A tortoise-shell bowl.

horn gunflint: Colloquialism for poor goods, deriving from the phrase: "Connecticut peddlers sell wooden nutmegs and horn gunflints."

Horn lamp: (1) Lamp with a horn globe, shade, or pane. (2) Camphene-burning lamp invented by a mechanic named Horn. Made by J. O. Fay of New York from 1840s. (3) Any lamp from the emporium of Edwin B. Horn, 64 Cornhill, Boston, from 1840s. Pulpit, girandoles, and table lamps, including the equifluent, which burned without casting a shadow.

horn lattice: Lattice windows (diamond-paned) fitted with horn panes.

Horn of Plenty: Pattern of pressed glass featuring concentric ring and cornucopia forms from a center. Ends are alternate thumbprint and waffle elements.

horn paper: Thin paper soaked in an oil solution to give it transparency.

hornplast: Objects pressed in molds, the plastic being made from boiled parings of animal horns. Snuffboxes, cases, lockets, et cetera.

horn salts: Saltcellars made of a section of animal horn, with pegged-in wood bottoms.

horn silver: The luna cornea of the alchemists. Silver dissolved in nitric acid and precipitated by muriatic acid, forming a white curd which, fused, is translucent and flexible. This is the basis of the legend that certain alchemists could make flexible glass. They did—only it was horn silver. Since it is really a muriate of silver, it blackens on exposure to the air.

hornsmith: A worker in horn.

hornsponge: Plastic made from rasped cattle horn treated with lye. The resulting paste was colored and molded into forms and shapes.

horn white: White pigment made from ashes of horn.

horography: A term for the art of making sundials.

horologe: A clock; from *hora*, hour, and *logos*, word. Literally, hour word.

horse & cart railroad flask: The "Success to the Railroad" flask on which the representation of a horse-drawn cart on rails is impressed by mold blowing.

horse bean black: Charred beans pulverized or levigated and mixed with gum arabic to make a black ink.

horse bells: Metal arches fitted with three or more bells (sometimes two) and fixed over the collars of horses. Other bells used with conveyances were on strips for attachment to shafts, body straps, saddles, et cetera.

horse brasses: Brass fittings for harness and driving rigging.

horse brush: Grooming brush for stable use; many varieties. [*One example pictured.*]

horsecar: Any car used on street railways before the advent of cable pull or electric drive. [*Example pictured.*]

horse fire screen: Screen suspended between two high poles.

horseflesh mahogany: Bahamian mahogany; it has a coarse fiber and dark color. Name in use from 1780s.

horsehair: The almost everlasting fabric, originally made in various patterns of weave and in colors. The all-black horsehair of plain weave is the last phase of its use in 19th century. The hair was not always horsehair.

Horse-Head Medallion: Pattern of pressed glass featuring a horse's head within a circle of dots, with crossed palm fronds.

horse knife rest: Pairs of horses' heads or rearing horses joined with bars to serve as rests for carving knife. 19th century. Generally electroplated silver.

Horseshoe: Pressed-glass pieces having a horseshoe-pattern finial or handles. The rest of the pattern is Eastlake and terrible.

horseshoe chair: *See* Chairs, All Kinds.

horseshoe flask: Perfume flask by Whitall-Tatum in general shape of a horseshoe with the device impressed on both sides.

horseshoe hinge: A rare and very good type of hinge as made by blacksmiths. [*Example pictured.*]

horseshoe Windsor: *See* Chairs, All Kinds.

horseshoe wine table: A table shaped somewhat like a horseshoe. Much used in taverns and eating saloons from 1850s.

Horses of America: Forty prints of American turf and track horses published by Moseman & Brothers, harness manufacturers, in 1870s. Prints measure 9" x 12". The book was an advertising device and sold for 50 cents. In 1950 copies sold at around $25.

Horstman furniture: Mostly lodge, fraternity, military-hall furniture, et cetera. The firm dealt primarily in woolens, uniforms, and regalia but also sold this furniture from 1830s to 1860s.

hot cast porcelain: Cryolite, or fine white glass, cast into panes, forms, and figures from mid-19th century. Milk glass.

hotchpotch: A measure of beer, made hot and laced with rum. Probably from hot pot.

hotel silver: While the so-called Victorian age resulted in a mass of utterly outlandish silverware designs for the home, especially in plated wares, the heavy plated silver for hotel use was modeled after the simple and often classic forms in vogue prior to 1820. This silver from every point of view is more desirable as a collector's item.

hot-poker pictures: The pyrographic art at its best; excellent landscapes having tonal qualities, and even portraits, were "painted" by expert workmen who did their work on basswood, scorching it with a red-hot poker. Art practiced from 1850s to 1870s as a novelty, but the technique was used as early as 1790.

hough: The ankle joint in an animal's leg.

hound handle: Figure of a coursing hound used as a handle on pots, jugs, pitchers, et cetera.

hound-head cup: It looks like the model of a dog's head until you lift it. Then it is revealed as a hollow drinking cup. Similar to fox-head cup, *which see.*

hourglass: (1) The time-measuring device made up of hollow ovate globes joined at the neck and filled with fine sand. (2) Pattern of pressed glass imitative of fine cutting.

hourglass salt: Hourglass-form standing saltcellar, generally silver; from 15th century.

house pot: A teapot in the form of a house.

house sagen: Mottoes, precepts, axioms, and biblical quotations, generally scribed in the bastard Gothic characters invented in northern France. Pieces identified by this term were done by Swiss, Flemings, Swedes, and other immigrants to the New World. House sayings (literal translation) were used in New York, New England, and other colonies and states. Most surviving examples date from late 1790s and are known dated as late as 1880s.

housesmith: The ironsmith who made railings, hinges, gratings, and other hardware for housebuilding.

Hovey fruit prints: C. M. Hovey, from 1852 to 1856, issued a two-volume work titled *Fruits of America* in small folio size. There are 96 different fruit subjects. The work is often found bound but was originally issued in parts.

Howard, Timothy: Joiner (cabinetmaker) of Lynn, Mass., from 1760s.

Howard banjo: Late-type banjo-shaped clock casings for very fine movements, made by the Howard Co.

Howe mirrors: Tabernacle and other types of mirrors popular in 1840s, including full gilt frames of massive proportions to decorate steamboat saloons and hotels. Made by the Howe Co. at Louisville, Ky., from 1842.

Howe pins: Machine-made pins manufactured by Howe Co., Birmingham, Conn., from 1840s. Solid-headed pins in five sizes.

Howe tinware: Products of William Howe, Boston, from 1820s. Housewares, candle molds, and kitchenwares.

Howe woodenware: Considerable production of dairy wares, butter stamps, tubs, buckets, bowls, and pails. First made at Fitzwilliam, N.H., from 1832. After 1850 firm was Wakefield & Howe.

howf: A porterhouse, or beer saloon.

H.P.M. china: French-type semi-porcelain made by Holmes, Plant & Madew at Burslem, England, from 1876.

Hsia: Chinese dynasty, 2205–1766 B.C.

Hsien Fêng: Late Chinese period, A.D. 1851–61.

Hsi Wang Mu: The fairy goddess of China who rides a crane.

H-stretcher: Any underbracing of a chair, table, or stand having stretchers from front to back legs, braced midway with a cross stretcher.

Hubbard, Charles: Painter and decorator of glass vases and druggists' furniture (bottles, flasks, jars, et cetera), working in Boston from 1825.

Hubbard horse prints: J. R. Hubbard, Boston, 1882, issued a portfolio of 24 celebrated horses in full color, with each print mounted.

Hubbel & Patterson: Cabinetmakers of New York City who dissolved their partnership in 1774. Makers of important furniture in the Georgian style.

hubbin: An anvil for nail makers.

Huber: Pattern of pressed glass featuring narrow vertical convex panels.

huchière: A chest maker.

huckleberry bottle: A quart-size bottle resembling a milk bottle but really made as a container for huckleberries. The neck is long, with an interior diameter of approximately one inch, and the mouth is ringed. Made from mid-19th century.

huckster: A higgler, a peddler of provisions.

Hudson furniture: Empire and French Antique revival-style furniture made by B. & W. Hudson, Hartford, Conn., from 1850s.

Hudson River Portfolio: Landscapes in aquatint of the Hudon Valley in a series of 20 fine prints with engraved surface, approximately 14 x 21 inches. Hand-colored. Most plates engraved by John Hill. Now rare as a complete set.

hugger-mugger: Done in secret.

Hughes ironstone: Granite ware made for the American market at the Waterloo Road Pottery, Longport, England, by the Thomas, Stephen, and Thomas, II, Hughes interests, 1820–80. The mark is THOMAS HUGHES IRONSTONE CHINA. The firm was succeeded by Mellor, Taylor & Co., who continued to make and export the same wares to the U.S. Their mark is the Royal Arms in plain shield, with crown and wreath, with name of the potters and the words, "Warranted Stone China."

Huguenin, Georges: Toymaker of Pennsylvania, Bucks-Montgomery County region. Several members of family, of which Georges was a grandson, seem to have indulged in this work. Carved wood animals and wool-covered sheep are known. Colloquially, Hugin toys.

Huguenot: Any member of the French Reformed Church, or the Reformed Church of Flanders, Switzerland, or the Netherlands. Origin of the term resides, or is said to reside, in one of these sources: (1) Hugonots, named for Hugo, Comte de Tours, whose ghost walked at night because the reformers met at night. (2) *Huguenon* (Flemish), meaning Cathari, or Puritan. (3) *Huguenote,* meaning a large pot. (4) *Eidgenotten* (Dutch), partaker of an oath. (5) William Tell and other Swiss were called Eidgenessi because of their oath of opposition to Austria in 1308. The confederation of Uri and Appenzell and those who took the oath of allegiance were known as the Eidgenossenschaft.

Huguenot chests: Bird-and-tulip-deco-

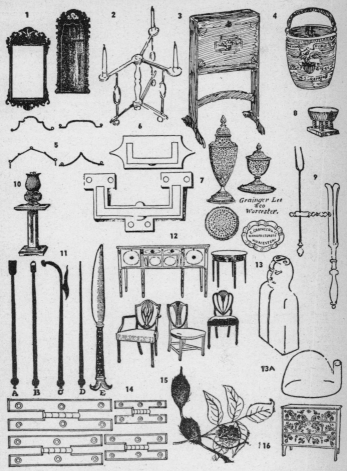

1, Fretwork Mirrors (2). **2,** Folding Candelabra. **3,** Fire-Screen Desk. **4,** Fire Bucket. **5,** Field Bed Canopies, four of some eight known types. **6,** Flush Handles. **7,** Grainger Worcester (pierced Parian) and mark of this works. **8,** Garden Prop. **9,** Hand Spit. **10,** Heat Light. **11,** Hawk Irons: (a) Head Iron, (b) Nare Iron, (c) Sear Button and Nare Knife, (d) Nare Iron, (e) Cauterer. **12,** Hepplewhite-Style Furniture. **13,** Hinged Bank. **13A,** Humpback Inkwell. **14,** H Hinges, beveled edges. **15,** Hopniss (Apios) Leaf and Fruit. **16,** Huguenot Chest. (No. 7 from Virtue & Co., London.)

rated chests, made wherever a Huguenot settlement occurred in the colonies; especially in Taunton region of Massachusetts, Lancaster County, Pa., Central Hudson Valley, and New Rochelle region of New York. The chests of Taunton are two- or three-drawer, with entire façade painted. [*An example is pictured.*] Others seem to have been made with two small drawers at bottom and a large chest cavity under lift-up lids. The chests of Lancaster, Pa., region are architectural. These facts would seem to indicate the typical Huguenot chest is a case piece in the cabinet style of the region with painted décor deriving from France, Flanders, Switzerland, Brabant, and the Netherlands.

Huguenot silver: Silver in the English or French style, sometimes of Dutch influence, made by masters who migrated to the colonies. Pantin, Archambo, De-Lamerie, Revoire (Revere), and many others are of record. This term is used only in collecting circles as a minor or sub-designation. It is early American silver.

Hull & Stafford toys: Made at Clinton, Conn.; toy furniture of metal, toy japanned wares, wheel toys, trains, and fire engines.

Hull glass: The one logical meaning is the glassware produced at Hull, England, from 1750s or earlier. Not a particular kind or style of glass.

Hull lights: Term was in use in the South prior to 1860 and most likely referred to candles "imported" from J. C. Hull of New York, who conducted an extensive business in manufacture and coastal distribution of white candles.

Hull ware: Cream-colored, green-glazed, and blue transfer-printed wares made from 1802 at Hull, England, under various famous owners: Ridgway, Hipwood, Bell, and others. [*The mark is pictured.*]

Humiston & Warner: Stoneware potters of South Amboy, N.J., from 1840s. A fine "eagle" pitcher was made by them and marked with their names.

Humiston candle mold: A continuous candle-molding machine made by Homan & Co., Cincinnati, from 1850s.

Hummingbird: Pattern of pressed glass falling within at least one unique category: it is sensibly named. It features a recognizable hummingbird poised in the air, tapping the honey from a flower on a leafy stem. Not content with the simple term "Hummingbird," some collectors of pressed glass call this pattern Hummingbird and Fern!

humming top: 19th-century spinning toys of metal having open ports that cause a rising and falling whistling or humming note when the top is in motion.

hummums: Turkish bathhouse, especially those catering to women.

humpback inkwell: An atmospheric inkwell having a hemispheric reservoir with a narrow-necked orifice or vent. Atmospheric pressure kept the ink supply in the well. [*Example pictured.*]

humped bow: Said of chair and settee backs having a bow or bowed rail with a hump or bend, giving a Gothic effect.

humpen: Ceremonial beaker, generally of glass, enameled, inscribed, and sometimes

dated. Mostly Swiss, some German, late 16th and early 17th century, and therefore quite rare and much esteemed. Some have unbelievably fine miniature paintings in enamel. The German examples are the finest ones, the Swiss being less meticulous in execution of the décor. Sometimes called a wilcommen glass. In spite of the place of manufacture, it is indicated the workmen who produced these glasses were Venetians, not Swiss or Germans.

Humphrey chimney: A tubular chimney for lamps, made of mica sheets in a metallic framework. Date is from 1850s.

hundred: This term, when used in early manufacturing inventories and invoices, generally meant 100 gross, or 14,400 pieces.

Hundred & One (101): Pattern of pressed glass featuring alternate dewdrop panels of elongated ovals and extended narrow cartouche forms set vertically, as 10101010, or 101.

hundträ: The *hund-tra*, or dog tree; Swedish name given the American dogwood growing profusely in the forests of what is now Pennsylvania.

Hungary water: Ardent spirits flavored with rosemary, thyme, and sage. A form of gin. Known from 17th century and sometimes mentioned in punch and cordial recipes.

hungrels: Rafters.

Hunneman brass: William Hunneman, Boston, 1790s–1850s, was a brass founder and sheet-brass worker. Said to have done business with Paul Revere. All sorts and kinds of wares and parts are attributed to his foundry.

hunt board: The term, of late, has been wholly a snobbish appellation for what, in 90% of the cases, is a homemade or backcountry shop-made sideboard popular in the highlands west of the tidal plains of the South. The original hunt board was a high side table for the service of a collation taken standing: a hunt breakfast, generally of sausage cakes, small steaks, chops, et cetera, on bread or biscuits, with hot spiced wine and other drinks, prior to setting out on a ride to hounds or on the return. Now applied to any Southern-made high sideboard, many of which were in homes not concerned with the ceremony of the gentleman's sport of fox hunting. Some sideboards with apple drawers and potato drawers are now called hunt boards. Mahogany, walnut, cypress, cedar, and pine examples are known. Sometimes called a hunt table. [*Several examples pictured.*]

hunter's chair: *See* Chairs, All Kinds.

hunting cup: Any cup or beaker of metal, horn, china, glass, et cetera, without footings, given to riders in the saddle. These date from 16th century or earlier. Many are of military significance. It should be remembered that fox hunting, steeplechasing, and allied sports were indulged in largely by gentlemen who went to war as officers and were required to be excellent horsemen.

hunting Derby: (1) Derby porcelain decorated with hunting scenes. (2) The bowler-type hat worn by riders to hounds.

hunting objects; hunting goblets: Goblets of glass engraved with hunting

1, Hurricane Trumpet Shade. **2,** Hurricane Chimney. **3,** Hurricane Mammoth Lamp. **4,** Hurricane Hanging Lamp. **5,** Hurricane Footed Lantern. **6,** Hurricane Snuffers. **7,** Hutch. **8,** Hollowed Pediment. **9,** Helmet Creamer. **10,** Hull Ware Mark. **11,** Herculaneum Ware Marks. **12,** Fulham Stoneware Bottle. **13,** Hyacinth Vases (3rd quarter 19th century). **14,** Hobbyhorses. **15,** Hunt Boards or High Small Sideboards. **16,** Franklin Stoves (early type).

scenes. Some have six panels, overlaid. This form is attributed to Germany, but all goblets of this type were made by Rice-Harris of England from 1840s. [*Example pictured*.] **hunting pitcher:** Beverage pitcher with hunting scenes in relief, transfer-printed, or painted, often with hound handle. Numerous objects preceded by the designation "hunting" may refer to the sports of fox hunting or some form of gunning for game; i.e., hunting clothes, hunting shoes, et cetera.

Huntington pottery: Reference generally is to the stone- and redwares produced at the Huntington, L.I., pottery from early 19th century. One of the products was thousands of redware pie plates with white slip curlicues, traded in now as Pennsylvania German slip ware.

hunt table: An ensemble of tables, each having a top in the form of a twelfth segment of a circle, with segmental leaves of same size on each side. With leaves up, each table was a quarter circle. Two made a half circle, and so on to a complete circle. Generally the point is truncated to provide a hole in the center of the complete ensemble. Often now used in two sections to place before a window. Scarce to rare. Found in Virginia, eastern Pennsylvania, Eastern Shore of Maryland. All are probably of English make. Same name is also given a long narrow table with curvate drop leaves, forming a large round table with leaves up.

Hun Yock: Now popularly believed to be a variant of "hunky," but not so. It is an early 19th-century Pennsylvania expression for any foreigner, especially a Chinese. It was the name of the first Chinese laundryman and cook in Lancaster, Pa. His name was given to any foreigner.

hura: Cream-white to yellow-shaded softwood.

Hurdle furniture: Hurdle Brothers of Alexandria, Va., from 1830 advertised Grecian, Windsor and fancy chairs.

hurdy-gurdy: A mechanically played violin or cello, a crank giving bow movement and a keyboard fingering the strings. Played by street entertainers and strollers called Savoyards. Original Swiss or Italian term was *hurdi-gurdi*. Played on streets of colonial towns in 18th century. Examples survive. The early term did not mean what the same term means today, a grinding organ.

Huret doll: A doll of molded gutta-percha. Made from c. 1850.

hurricane chimney: Glass protector of candle flame, first made in chimney form, sometimes called trumpet form, from c. 1735. [*Example pictured*.]

hurricane footed lantern: Actually a brass or japanned iron candleholder consisting of a matching base and cap for a hurricane shade or globe, the bottom piece generally footed. 18th century. [*Example pictured*.]

hurricane hanging lamp: China saucerlike element and top, designed as base and cap for hurricane shade, joined with chains and suspended from ceiling by a chain on top of cap. [*Example pictured is 18th century*.]

hurricane mammoth lamp: Huge hurricane shade of glass, double OG in con-

tour, with brass or iron base and cap, the latter punctured with air holes. Some as high as 44 inches. [*Example pictured*.]

hurricane shades: Burning candle protectors, often of handsome proportions, made of clear glass, either plain, engraved, or cut, and a few types flashed with color. Generally 14 to 22 inches in height, and used in pairs. However, quite small examples are known, and one use for these, in quantities, was as votive light shades, *which see*.

hurricane snuffer: The rarest type of candle snuffer, designed to snuff a candle burning within a hurricane shade. A tubular extension of the scissors handle carries the snuffer at its lower end. [*Example pictured*.]

hurricane trumpet shade: The bellform hurricane shade, used in exactly the opposite position from the hurricane chimney. Proper position of usage can be determined by the welted rim, or bottom. [*Example pictured*.]

hurst: A thicket; a bosky spot. Often added to place names, as Gracehurst, Allenhurst, Brookhurst, et cetera.

hutch: A cabinet with lidded compartment for bulk storage of grain, meal, et cetera. Date from early Gallic (Gothic) era. [*17th-century example pictured*.]

Hutchinson furniture: Made at Springfield, Ill., from 1850s; solid and veneered heavy Empire-style examples, many of which survive as now treasured antiques of the region.

Hutchings woodenware: Parley Hutchings of Worthington, Mass., manufactured wooden bowls and plates and patented the lathe he developed for speedy, economical work. He cut the bowls on lathes with curvate knives and so made many from a single block of bowl wood. His platemaking was done by the same process. The patent is dated September 25, 1847. Students can procure copies from U.S. Patent Office for the usual fee.

hutch table: A box-on-frame, with lid, topped with a tilting board to convert the piece to a table. Pioneer furniture, frequently homemade, and dating from 1660s. The piece persisted as an item of cottage furniture to the 1880s. [*Example pictured*.]

huttches: Lidded board chests; hutches.

hyacinth glass: The contemporaneous name for what is now called a hyacinth vase; a glass vase with bulb-holding lip. Filled with water, the vase was used to raise bulbs indoors. Many colors from clear glass to deep purple, greens, blues, amethyst, ruby red, et cetera. Date is from 1760s or earlier, and made in France at that time. Revival of use is a part of the French Antique furniture and elegancy revival we now call Victorian. [*Examples pictured*.]

hyalith: Bohemian glass imitative of basalt and other minerals, often with enameled decoration.

hyalography: Engraving on glass; properly, engraving glass plates for printing.

Hyde roaster: Coffee roaster. A revolving crank turned a cylinder with a fire bed underneath.

hydraulic bed: (1) A bed bath. [*Example*

pictured.] (2) **A** water-filled mattress of India rubber.

hydria: A water vessel.

hydria-kalpis: Tautological term for a water jar, since both *hydra* and *kalpis* are ancient terms for precisely the same thing.

hydrolator: Mechanical conveyor of water in buckets from well to house, operated from within the house.

hydromel: A beverage made of water and honey.

Hydrophant: Trade name for a thermometer and humidity indicator combined in one device. Popular in 1860s–70s.

hydropult: A stirrup pump; a small fire engine.

hydrostatic balls: Gauges in the form of small glass balls, used in testing the spirit content of wines and liquors. Early 19th century.

Hypso polish: Silver polish made from hyposulphite of soda.

I

ice accumulator: A spraying device for use in winter, to produce ice for home needs by solidification of the fine particles. Made from 1840s by John Dutton, Delaware County, Pa.

iceboat: The sturdy brother of the sporting ice boat; a craft with runners, mast, sails, and bunkers for passengers and goods. Said to have been used extensively on Northern rivers from early 19th century.

icebreaker: An ice pick or chopper.

ice-cream dish: Covered cup with wide lip and two handles, on an underdish, used for service of ice cream at table. Known in pottery, porcelain, and Wedgwood white jasper ware. Made from 1760s.

ice-cream freezers: Many varieties, including the prototypes of all freezers now considered modern. Early ice-cream makers included some magnificent porcelain jars with liners around which ice and salt were packed to freeze the cream. These are often mistaken for fruit and wine coolers.

ice-cream jar: *See* Ice-Cream Freezers.

ice cutters: Platforms with gangs of serrated-edge knives or saws for the even cutting of ice from rivers and ponds. If you find a platform with up to 12 knives, all equally spaced in one row, blades forward, that is a single-row cutter.

ice glass: Novelty glass, crystal-clear, with hairline crackle over the outer surface. Ice bowls, ice-cream dishes, plates, stands, coolers, et cetera, are known. Imported from Austria. Date is from c. 1865.

ice hook: A picklike tool with spike set at 70° angle. Used in handling river and pond ice.

Iceland crystal: A sort of soft fluor spar or murrhine of the consistency of talc but as transparent as rock crystal. A scientific natural curiosity much esteemed in latter half of 18th century.

ice maker: *See* Criton.

ice pitcher: Any pitcher or jug with a compartment for ice, whether permitting ice to touch contents or in a special pocket filled from outside the vessel. Some are said to date from 18th century, but most surviving examples are 19th century. Many are of electroplated ware or Sheffield plate. **ice pocket decanter:** Same philosophy of cooling contents of a vessel. Certain examples of 1790s are attributed to Irish glasshouses. These have the ice cavity in the base, the opening corked when decanter was in use. [*Example pictured.*]

ichthyocolla: The true isinglass; gelatin of culinary grade, made from fish.

Icicle: Pattern of pressed glass imitative of icicle forms of unequal length, forming a delightful undulating margin, or verge. Known in both opaque and clear glass. The pattern is early.

Ihmsen glass: Any glass made at the Ihmsen factory, Pittsburgh, from 1810. Cut, engraved, pressed, and blown wares in wide variety. This plant became the Pennsylvania Flint Glass Works and remained in operation for almost a century.

ikats: A technique of dyeing yarns by resist and tie methods. In weaving, these formed a pattern. Of Malayan origin, although Diderot describes a similar method of pattern-dyeing silk threads used at Lyons, France, in 18th century. Sometimes called yarn-dyed patterning. The Incas, Aztecs, and Mayans in the Americas also used this complicated method of dyeing to achieve a pattern in the simplest of loom work.

IL hinge: The original and proper term for what is called the HL hinge. The appearance of an H formed by the joining hinge leaf gave rise to the term HL.

Illinois parrot: Now called the Carolina parakeet, but originally common in the Ohio Valley and perhaps noticed first by French explorers in that region.

illuminary: A sconce of wood or metal.

illuminated glass: Heavy lead glass cut from the underside and the cutting silvered. Kidd of London, c. 1850, made this ware in considerable quantities. Imports by U.S. dealers were sold as elegancies at high prices.

illuminated heater: Four-burner kerosene lamp which served also as a heater. Made by Ansonia Brass & Copper Co. from 1870s and called Truesdell's Illuminating Heater.

Ilmenau porcelain: Thuringian ware (German), made from 1771. The works continued through the 20th century.

Marks are a clover leaf, a large I, a crossed X with curled ends, and (modern) a bird on a peak, with letters FNJ in a crude circle.

imagerie: Painting, especially a portrait.

Imari: The pattern name of Japanese origin for the original Chinese K'ang Hsi multicolor ware. This is the original of so-called gaudy ware of all kinds. Ceramic historians say it was first made by the Korean potter, Ri Sampei. The Chinese are said to have called the ware Wan Li. Japanese imitation began in 1648. Called Hizen and Arita by the Japanese, it was sold in huge quantities to Dutch traders. In Europe the ware was called "Gaudy Dutch," while the Dutch called it "Old Japan." Thus the present-day term "Gaudy Dutch" is exactly in line with 17th-century nomenclature but is entirely in error when subscribed with the tag line "so called because it was made for the color-loving Pennsylvania Germans." That is pure fiction. It is not generally known that some of the finest wares in this category of décor are neither Japanese nor imitations made by any English potter; reference here is to the Wan Li patterned oriental export porcelain wrongly called Lowestoft. The patterns include citrons, pomegranates, flowers, and citrus-fruit forms.

imbostment: Sculpturing.

imbowed: Looped.

imbricated: Overlapped, as tiles on a roof, birds' feathers, or fish scales. Any decoration imitative of such forms.

imitation Dresden: Not fakes by other potters, but homemade work imitative of the original Dresden wares. Sealing wafers, the colored sheet paste used to fasten folded letters, was cut into leaf and petal forms in suitable colors and affixed, by wetting, to a piece of plain white china. This gave the effect of raised work. [*Example pictured.*]

imitation pastels: Printed, generally lithographed, subjects imitative of pastel drawings. McLoughlin Brothers, late in 19th century, published many subjects.

imitation steel: Found stamped on some buttons of a very hard pewter alloy made 1800–20s. Obviously the buttons were imitative of cut steel ones.

immigrant: One entering a new land from a foreign country. An emigrant is not an immigrant; the emigrant is a resident of one state or province entering another within the same country, or from the mother country to a colony of that country.

immortelle: The strawflower.

imobste: Embossed.

imp: Engraving term, meaning the printer of the edition.

impasto: Thick application of pigment, sometimes pressed or molded into special shape or form. The early wares of Florence, Italy, have an impasto blue decoration. Many paintings show impasto in the application of color to canvas, or of *gouache* colors.

Imperial Lambeth: Green & Co. Lambeth wares made at the Imperial Pottery, late 18th century to 1850.

imperial ottoman: Circular or oval-shaped sofa with many cushions, generally in George IV and Regency styles.

imperial water: Cream of tartar, sugar, and sliced lemons in iced water. This was served after standing for several days.

imperial yellow: Citron yellow.

imports, of furniture: Numerous evidences of unimpeachable documentation are extant proving that much furniture was imported by proprietors, wealthy traders, royal governors, and others from the 17th century. In 1685, before coming to his colony, William Penn wrote, "A Dutch joiner and carpenter is coming; let him make Wainscot, tables and stands; we shall bring much furniture."

imprimus: In the first place. Often this word begins wills, documents, inventories, and official communications of 17th and 18th centuries.

imp't: Elizabethan English, meaning "grafted with new feathers."

Incan jugs: Pottery from Peru, made by the Incas, some bearing resemblance to Egyptian wares, some to Greek classical wares, and some not far removed from the appearance of Toby jugs. [*A grotesque example is pictured.*]

incardine; incarnation: Red color.

Ince & Mayhew: London cabinetmakers who issued a catalogue in 1762 showing the elegant furniture they made and sold. Either Chippendale copied from the work of this firm, or they copied from him. The catalogue is far rarer and more desirable than Chippendale's *Director.* It is asserted by some that it was issued in parts from 1759. The firm was in business from 1758 to 1810.

inch pins: The sweetbreads of the deer.

incised: Cut below the surrounding surface; carved, etched, or gouged.

incroyable chair: *See* Chairs, All Kinds.

incroyable hat: The exaggerated cocked hat affected by the fops and dandies of 18th-century Paris.

incubus: The nightmare.

inde: Indigo.

Independence Hall: Properly, the Pennsylvania State House, where the Continental Congress met and signed the Declaration of Independence. Represented in numerous memorials, prints, pictures, embroideries, effigies, including penny banks of iron, tin, glass, pottery, et cetera.

Independence toile: Sepia brown, terra cotta, and dark blue representations of Trumbull's painting of the Declaration, printed from copperplate on cotton, as a handkerchief.

India crackers: Firecrackers were once so called.

India houses: Curiosity shops which traded goods from India and China for cash, new merchandise, or secondhand stuffs.

Indiana: Pattern of pressed glass imitative of cutting of shell, star, and faceted boss forms.

Indian goldwork: Pure, or 18k, gold, beaten as thin as cellophane and formed into hollow balls, cubes, and blocks for necklaces and other jewelry. East Indian work.

Indian-head pitcher: Pressed-glass novelty pitcher in form of Indian head with feathered headdress, a back fin of feathers forming handle. Said to be Sandwich.

Indian loomed fabrics: Prints and plain cotton goods from India, imported from 17th century and most popular in 18th and 19th; no less than 99 different names, from allejars to ruckerees, are of record.

Indian queen: (1) Bennington pottery statue of buxom lass with fillet-bound flowing hair, flaring skirt, and Indian apron and sash, made from c. 1850s. (2) Effigies of the Indian women used as tobacconists' signs. (3) Inn signs featuring Indian maids.

India-rubber furniture: Not a canard. Sofas, tables, chairs, stools, bedsteads, and other items of furniture made by Charles Goodyear from his newly invented hard rubber. Made from 1850s in the style now called Victorian.

indigo: A shrub, the infusion of which yields a yellow dye, in turn oxidizing to a rich blue. One of the chief proponents of its culture in America was Andrew Turnbull, who laid out a vast acreage in Florida in the 1760s, where he and his Greek wife planned to live as king and queen of a huge indigo empire. They imported a large colony of Minorcans, who were to be their leetmen, and laid out New Smyrna as their capital city. The Minorcans revolted; Turnbull fled to Charleston, where other indigo planting was done. Here he lived from 1781 to 1792. The Minorcans finally traded shaddock (grapefruit) for secondhand furniture from New England and so acquired a considerable holding of 18th-century antiques when they were merely household discards. These, rediscovered in early 1900s and purchased for small sums, were the chief stock in trade of several now famous galleries. Descendants of Minorcan serfs are now found in the region of Florida between Saint Augustine and New Smyrna. Ruins of early indigo mills are said to be observable at Fort Orange and New Smyrna. The early term for the plant was indigoffer.

industry tea plate: Pressed-glass plate with industrial scenes, or allegories of farmer plowing, with log cabin in center. May be Sandwich or Ohio glass.

infallible kindler: The first lighter on the "Cape Cod" principle; a porous stone element on an iron rod, kept in a can of kerosene. Made commercially in great quantities by R. P. Smith. Used to start fires in stoves as well as fireplaces.

infare: A bride's welcoming dinner.

infloriated: Blossomed, in a pattern.

infusion pot: A pottery pot for still-brewing, or infusing, as wine with herbs, water and teas, et cetera. **infusor:** A variant, in form of a vessel with a pocket or cavity to hold herbs or tea.

ingle: The fireplace. Hence inglenook, ingle cheek, et cetera.

Inglis furniture: Made by Thomas Inglis of New York in 1770s; probably also earlier. Georgian-style items.

Ingols jewelry: Early costume-souvenir jewelry made by A. B. Ingols of Denver, Col., from 1870s.

Ingraham, J.: Cabinetmaker of Boston, 18th century, working in Georgian and Chippendale styles.

ingraved: Inlaid as well as carved work was once so designated.

initial stem: Stemmed glasswares which incorporate the initials of owners in the stem work. Mostly Murano glass, made to order.

inkhornism: Expression of scholarly quality not generally understandable to others.

inkle: Tape or braid, lace- and crewelwork were once so designated from 16th to 18th century.

ink stick: Chinese black and colored inks in solid sticks, ground in water on slabs having collecting well, to produce the best ink. Importation evidently began as early as 15th century. Now generally called India ink. Ink was non-acid, long-lasting, and very finely divided. As late as 1900 the sticks sold for from $1 to $10 for the best varieties.

inkstones: Small balls of mineral earth and concentrated color, soluble in water.

ink vase: Generally the glass liner of the inkwell in a desk set.

inkwell: Any container for ink into which the pen was dipped. Innumerable varieties of every known substance survive the years. There are collections having as many as 500, all different. Some are quite valuable, as the "paperweight" type of glass inkwell and the silver examples by 18th-century silversmiths.

inkwell teapot: Eight-sided, squat, conical teapot of red stoneware or black and brown glaze, made from 1700s. Some are Meissen. [*Example pictured.*]

inkwell tumbler: Tumblers of glass blown in a forming mold which was used primarily for blowing inkwells. These are quite rare.

inscription rug: (1) Oriental rugs inscribed in Sanskrit, Arabic, Bessarabian, Chinese, and other Eastern characters, certain of them being signed by the maker. (2) Inscribed hooked rugs and other similar pieces. (3) Inscribed woven rugs from machine looms or from tapestry looms.

Insmore-Batchelder furniture: There was a firm of cabinetmakers so named at Brunswick, Me., working from 1790s. This is the logical reference, unless it would be to a store of the same name in another locality.

insprung comb: Said of comb-backed Windsor chairs and settees in which the spindles spring inward by constriction within a narrow top piece. A rare vagary of chairmaking.

insufflated: A phrase promoted as descriptive of blown glass by enthusiasts of the 1920s.

insurance marks: Fire-insurance-company marks; large badges placed on an insured property to identify the structure for the fire companies sponsored by the insurance company. Practice was most widespread in Philadelphia from 1750 to 1840. Many varieties. Mostly cast iron, but some of lead or wood.

intaglio: A gem engraved by deepening, to

form an impression on a seal. Cut in, as opposed to raised or en cameo.

intarsia: Inlay of woods of various tints and values to represent a scene or view. Large areas were done by this method. An art rising in the Venetian district of Italy. Term is now applied (but wrongly) to any inlay work.

interlaced: Two or more elements of the same nature, overlapping, as hearts, circles, ovals, diamonds, et cetera.

invected: Indented, cut into, serrated, or scalloped.

inven.: Abbreviation for the Latin *invenit*, meaning conceived or invented by.

inverted bottle: Any bottle designed to be filled, closed, and stood on its mouth or neck. Bottoms usually rounded. Generally display bottles, used by confectioners, druggists, and other merchants.

Inverted Fern: Pattern of pressed glass displaying fernlike fronds on vertical ribbing.

Inverted Thumbprint: Pattern of pressed glass, often in colors, with many variations of the thumbprint in reverse; that is, as a series of round bosses.

invisible ink: Oxide of cobalt dissolved in aqua regia and suspended in water is one such ink. Writing is invisible until the paper or other surface is heated. Many people made an invisible ink of lemon juice and salt.

Ionic: One of the classical orders of architecture, revived as a general decorative theme in mid-18th century. **Ionic candlestick:** A candleholder in form of an Ionic column.

Jowa: Not out of place here; this is the form used to denote the Jowa district of Wisconsin Territory that became the Iowa Territory and eventually the state. The letters I and J were used interchangeably.

I.P. (J.P.) flask: The Keene, N.H., Masonic flask initialed I P and standing for Justus Perry, operator of the Marlboro Street Glass Factory.

Ipswich bellows: Fire blowers made by the syndicated bellows makers of Ipswich, Mass., who seem to have worked from the mid-17th century.

Ipswich lace: The same community as above gave its name to lace made here from 1785 in considerable yardage. Finally the Boston & Ipswich Lace Co. located here.

iridescent: Lustered. The glass commonly called by this term may be a fine product from Webb, Lobmeyer, Tiffany, or some other master makers, or cheap carnival ware. There are many varieties. The term is correct but not appropriate for all.

iridescent painting: *See* Flitter Work.

Irish butter: Fine creamery butter imported from Ireland. Importation seems to have started c. 1750.

Irish Chippendale: Name given to ribbon-back Georgian chairs and other seat furniture, some made of oak with mahogany veneer. Tape and ribbon backs, intricately carved, and very deep aprons characterize the chairs. Actually it is not Irish, but made in Lancaster and Yorkshire, England, from 1730s. Said to have been made for absentee Irish landlords. It is gorgeous Georgian furniture.

Irish delft: Tin-glaze redware in the delft tradition made at Dublin, Ireland, from c. 1710. Similar ware made at Belfast from c. 1680s.

Irish glass: The glassware of fine quality made at Cork, Waterford, Dublin, Belfast, Londonderry, and other points in Ireland, and especially the cut and engraved wares from such manufacturing centers imported by a dozen or more wholesalers in U.S. from late 1780s. Some idea of the quality imported by the U.S. may be had from the Pennsylvania and Virginia totals in 1802: 130,000 drinking glasses. Some recent commentators have belittled the Irish imports as insignificant. This is most likely an error in appraisal of the situation as a whole. Student is referred to Bibliography for names of works on glassware that include information on this fine glass.

Irish glue: Seccotine; a glue size developed for linens and damasks. Also used as a library glue. It is now quite scarce.

Irish porcelain: Belleek ware. The most stupid remark made concerning this shell-like ware was by Eastlake, who called it "a detestable ware, glistening like wet barley sugar." If there be any who need further evidence that Eastlake spoke like an arrant fool, a study of Belleek ware is recommended.

Irish Windsor: Stick chairs of elm and oak, having spool- or ball-turned legs and rush seats. Date is 1760s–1840s.

iris stone: The moonstone.

iron, ornamental, cast & wrought: Domestic and architectural items of wrought and cast iron are now entering into a new phase of popularity in the world of collecting. While many objects are mentioned in this dictionary, the full scope of the subject can be grasped only by reference to the works listed in the Bibliography.

iron button-turned bed: Bed with cast-iron frame in the pattern of button or ball turning popular in the 1850s. Only the posts had the castings imitative of the turning. Made at Boston.

iron dust: A speckling technique applied to gold luster or other metallic glaze by dusting with particles of iron.

iron hat: A high silk hat or topper cast in iron. Sizes from small, used as match and spill holders, ash receivers, et cetera, to full size, used as slop jars. Generally with a white lining. [*Example pictured.*]

ironing table: Name given any stretcher or other rectangular table used also for ironing of laundry. The Shakers made such a table for dining and ironing.

iron men: *See* Bouncers.

iron piano: Reference seems to date from 1837, when Chickering began using cast-iron rather than wood frames for the piano strings. This eliminated the almost constant tuning required when the wood frame was used.

iron porringer: Cast-iron vessel of the conventional American porringer shape, with pierced, crest-shaped flat handle or ear. Often cast with name of founder on handle. Bellevue, Colebrook, Mary Anne, Curtis Grob, and others names are of record. Made from 1780s to 1840s. Some have white enameled lining.

1, Imitation Dresden. 2, Incan Jug. 3, Iron Hat (spittoon). 4, Jug Heads. 5, Jack Bed.
6, Janus. 7, Jenks Flytrap. 8, Jumble Gun. 9, Kettledrum. 10, Key Check. 11, Key
Pistol. 12, Knee Trays. 13, Knickknack Saw. 14, Lady-Form Bird Cage. 15, Lacemaker's
Candlestand.

iron pump: Cast-iron well and cistern pump, with some wrought iron parts, made from 1820s by several manufacturers in U.S. [*Early example pictured.*]

iron sleigh bed: Cast-iron sleigh bed imitative of the carved wood examples of the period, made from 1840s by a Boston foundry.

ironstone: Originally ironstone ware was a shell of cast iron with a heavy tin glaze, decorated as china. This was indestructible tableware, but it was too expensive for the mass market. When C. J. Mason, after some years of testing, perfected a china body containing scoria from iron furnaces as part of the clay body, he called this resulting hard but thin ware "ironstone." This ware he patented in 1813. Mason's patented ware was made and sold for years, not primarily as whiteware, but as good specialty ware of unusual strength, decorated and some having embossed patterns. Today, owing to the pirating of the term ironstone by many potters and its application to wares emphatically not in the Mason tradition, there are many who call the thick ware, properly "granite ware," by the term made famous by Mr. Mason. Many shapes of the true pottery ironstone reflect the silverware styles of the period. Mason is known to have made bedposts, huge bowls, vases, and decorative wares in addition to a full line of tableware. Many of the potters using the mark sold goods in the U.S. Among these were Pankhurst, Elsmore & Foster, Alcock, Corn, Boote, Ford, Challinor, Baker & Co., Meakin, Wedgwood, Turner, Goddard, Shaw, Ridgway, Turner, and Tomkins. Some ironstone is decorated in the gaudy colors of Imari; this was produced from c. 1825 to 1835.

Isaac's foot bath: An actual foot tub or deep japanned pail decorated in color (some stenciled). The piece was shaped to accommodate the feet and calves. I. A. Isaacs of New York was the maker.

Isabella glass: Wares made at the Stanger-owned Isabella, N.J., glassworks, 1848–68. Bottles and flasks.

isinglass: *See* Ichthyocolla.

Islington glass: Fine glasswares by Rice Harris; pressed, blown, cut, and engraved. Made at Islington, England, from 1840s. Considerable quantities imported by U.S. jobbers from c. 1845.

Italian heater: A large loggerhead.

Ivanhoe: Pattern of pressed glass featuring imitation cutting in diagonal block pattern with melon elements.

ivorytype: Hand-colored photographic portrait, some actually on sheet ivory or an imitation. Made from late 1840s to 1860s.

Ivy: Pattern of pressed glass featuring ivy leaf and vine imposed on vertical fluting, or ribbing. Many varieties, including Ivy in Snow, Budded Ivy, Stippled, Spiraled, et cetera.

Ivy House ware: The first pottery owned outright by Josiah Wedgwood was the Ivy House works, where he produced his striped, dappled, and all-green-colored ware from 1759.

ivy screen: A long trough on wheels or casters, with a high slatted trellis on which ivy, planted in trough, grew and provided a living screen. These were popular in ultra-smart homes from 1850s.

I. W. & Co. ware: Reference is to wares made by Isaac Wilson & Co. at Middlesboro Pottery at Tees, England, from 1852. Prior to that the pottery ownership was of another name. Creamware, dinner, tea, and toilet sets, flowerpots, lusters, and similar wares. The mark is I. W. & Co.

Izon-Whitehurst hinge: *See* Secret Joint Hinge.

J

jacinth: The hyacinth.

jack: (1) A lifting device. (2) A measure of a quarter pint. (3) A turnspit, operated by gears from a clockwork or from a treadmill, crank, or weight and pulley.

jack bed: The one-post bed, rails from post to walls. This bed was a corner piece. Date is from 17th century. [*Example pictured.*]

Jackfield ware: Black-glazed pottery, plain or decorated. Jackfield, England, has been a potting center since 1630. From 1763 this center also produced yellow-glazed ware.

jack-in-pulpit vase: Glass vase form in the shape of this wild lily of the field and woods. Many colors and combinations of colors. Date is from c. 1850.

Jack o'Hoop: Jacques Androuet, a designer who copied from the Italian Renaissance styles.

Jack o'Lent: Effigy of Judas Iscariot, carried by a company of mummers for pelting by all and sundry. A ceremony of Holy Week, known in Florida, Louisiana, and Maryland in 18th century.

Jackson & Baggott glass: Cut glass, made by a New York firm so named from c. 1815. Firm had a retail store and an extensive cutting establishment.

Jackson brasses: Colonial brass door knockers, warming pans, candlesticks, stirrups, spurs, skillets, basins, et cetera, made at Boston by Jonathan Jackson prior to 1730s.

Jackson glass: (1) Bottles and hollow wares of clear white, pale green, and blue glass made at Jackson Glass Works, Waterford, N.J., from 1850s. The works was established in 1820s. (2) Any glass memorializing Andrew Jackson, especially the Jackson-Mantua flask made at Mantua, O., glass factory displaying the vagary of a recutting of the line "A. Jackson," which in the original mold marked the glass in reverse.

Jackson grate: Fireplace grate and other fireplace equipment as made by Nathan H. and other Jacksons from 1820s. There were Jacksons in fireplace-equipment business at Philadelphia who removed to New York. Nathan worked c. 1820s–50s at New York city.

Jackson press: A dining-room piece now often called a hunt board, which it is not. The styling is of the early Empire period, and it is a cabinet-piece sideboard with bottle, silver, and linen drawers or cupboards. Date is from 1820s, and many were used from Louisiana to Georgia in both town and plantation homes.

Jackson silver: Plated silver with molding and stamping imitative of chasing of scenes identified as Andrew Jackson's birthplace at Waxhaw and his residence, the Hermitage. It is in the Baroque style, dating from c. 1850s, probably made by Meriden or another Connecticut manufacturer. The two above-mentioned scenes occur on a teapot; there is also a bowl displaying Jackson's Forest Home and his tomb.

jack tar: A Toby-type jug featuring the figure of a sailor. Made in this form from c. 1810 to 1830 or later.

jack towel: A roller towel.

jacobak-anetjes: Stoneware pots made under the direction of Jacqueline, Countess of Hainault and Holland, who taught the Germans along the Rhine the art of making stoneware pottery.

Jacobean: The period of James I, Charles I, Charles II, and James II, roughly 1605–85, including the Cromwellian era of England. Another name for Carolean. Reference is to the Flemish, Dutch, classic, and other furniture and elegancy styles of the period.

Jacobite glasses: Ceremonial glasses affected by Stuart sympathizers after the abdication of James II and the reign of William and Mary. Quiescent during the reign of Queen Anne and revived after the coming of the German King, George I. These are often "firing" glasses with heavy bases and stems, or fine goblets, generally engraved with certain symbols or phrases, as "Amen" (meaning so be it—may the Prince return), "Fiat" (let it be done), "Redeat" (may he return), "J.R." (James Rex). If any Jacobite glasses were made in the colonies, the one logical maker would have been H. W. Stiegel, at the Lancaster County, Pa., glassworks in the glassmaker's village of Manheim. The sponsors of the Stiegel enterprise were Charles and Alexander Stedman of Philadelphia, Jacobite refugees who were in the last rebellion which was crushed at Culloden. There is no documented record that Stiegel did make such glasses, but then, such glasses were always made in secret and used at secret gatherings. By 1750 the use of the glasses was largely a matter of sentiment for a lost cause. There are many fake Jacobite glasses; the "fake" being late engraving in the old style on old, plain glasses.

Jacob music box: Jacob & Sons of New York, with factory facilities in Switzerland, imported and sold thousands of prick-roll and steel-comb music boxes from mid-19th century.

Jacob's Coat: Pattern of pressed glass displaying panels of crazy or patch quilting.

Jacob's Ladder: Pattern of pressed glass imitative of cutting; a cross-cut diamond pattern with panels of horizontal prisms; these are the "ladders."

Jacob's staff: (1) A surveying rod with cursor mounted on top. (2) A sword cane. (3) The mullein plant. (4) A pilgrim's staff.

jaconet: An Indian cotton fabric was so named in the 18th and 19th centuries.

jacony salt: Saltcellars of hyacinthine shape or color, so named by H. W. Stiegel. One writer assumed the phrase to mean a basket salt. The term, however (jacouny), was used in 18th century for the hyacinth. The color, depending upon whether the flower or the gem stone was meant, would be pale amethyst for the flower and yellow for the gem.

Jacquard: A weaving process by which pictorial, damask, and tapestry patterns were achieved, invented by J. M. Jacquard of France. One of the most important loom inventions in all history. This process made automatic tapestry and pattern weaving possible.

jade: The semi-precious pyroxene mineral revered in Burma and China and much used for carving panels and sculptured objects, idols, et cetera. While chiefly of greenish hue, other tonal varieties occur, many far rarer than the green, as mutton fat, milk, camphor, gray, purple, rose, lavender, agate, yellow, black-green, and mottled.

jaggery: Palm sugar; from it the potent beverage called arrack was distilled; also called palm rum.

jagging iron: A crimping tool. Small ones were used in crimping pastry; large ones, to make and restore cloth frilling.

jalap: Powdered purgative root.

jalousies: Slatted wood shutters, the original idea of the Venetian blind. First use was outside the window; by mid-18th century the jalousie was arranged inside and controlled by tapes and cords.

jamb hooks: Metallic hooks, often of brass, on iron screws or spikes, fastened in masonry or woodwork of a fireplace jamb to hold fire tools upright.

jam dish: Open dish, or covered jar with domed lid, to hold jellies, marmalades, conserves, and other delectables generally known as jam.

Jamestown glass: Beads and probably hollow wares and bottles made at the tile, brick, and glass furnace erected by the first settlers at Jamestown, Va., from 1610. Erection of factory is authenticated by documents of the London Co. A second glasshouse was built in 1617. This was called the first mint in America, as the beads made were traded with the Indians as wampum, or money.

James ware: Japanned sheet iron and stamped tinwares, decorated, as made by N. E. James of New York from c. 1850s.

jamills: Gauze netting, plain and in colors, sometimes in printed designs, used chiefly as mosquito netting and fly screening, often on tester beds.

Jammock: A weight used to bruise or press fruits; also the jar or tub in which the bruising was done. Jammocked strawberries were berries crushed in sugar.

Jams: Buttons made from coiled or woven wire of any kind from steel to pewter.

Janus: The two-faced god of mythology, used in classic and grotesque decoration. [*Example of original, from a Roman coin, pictured.*]

Japan earth: Cachou; a breath sweetener.

Japanned ware: (1) First name of the mirror-black-glazed china made by Whieldon, Wedgwood, and other early potters. Jackfield ware and allied black glazes and lusters. (2) Sheet iron, tinware, tinned wares, pewter, papier-mâché, wood and non-fictile objects, coated with a quick-drying oil-based varnish with colored pigment, and further decorated with fine to amateur painting, stenciling, and even transfer printing. There has been a great revival of interest in this and allied decorative arts by publication of many and various instruction books in recent years.

Jardiniere: A garden pot for shrubs and flowers; an outer vase to hold a potted plant; also a pot filled with wet sand to hold cut flowers.

Jargonium: An element allied to zirconia, isolated in 1869.

Jarrah wood: Wood from an Australian timber tree.

Jasmine stem: Tobacco pipestem made from a length of jasmine stalk.

Jasper ware: Excessively hard stoneware achieved by adding barium sulphate to the clay. Dense, non-porous, it requires no glaze. This is the ware developed by Wedgwood and is the secret of his cameo blue and white, plain-colored and varicolored cameo ware in the classic tradition.

Jaunty: Genteel.

Jeanne d'Arc bottle: One of the many stupid misnomers prevalent in blown-, molded-, and pressed-glass collecting. It is not the famous Maid of Orleans depicted in this mold-blown bottle, but a damsel of the Baroque revival customarily called Victorian. Marked examples of the bottle with "D. D. Deposee Lorraine" would indicate manufacture prior to 1870, when Lorraine was taken by Germany and called Loringthen, or manufacture after 1918 when Lorraine was restored to France.

Jeffersonian style: The Empire style is meant, under the quite erroneous impression that Jefferson favored it at Monticello. Actually Jefferson had four dozen Windsor chairs and much fine furniture in the styles of the Directoire, Sheraton, and Hepplewhite.

Jefferson silver: Silver-plated Britannia ware with molding in clever imitation of chasing, depicting views of Jefferson's Mill and Monticello. Teapots, water pitchers, and bowls are of record. Style is Baroque, and date is after c. 1840. This plated silver, as well as that in memory of Jackson, Washington, Webster, and others, is now almost unknown to collectors.

Jeherekooshon: From the Persian, meaning "delightful poison," and applied to a wine tube or bottle. The Persian tale is

that a noble attempted to preserve grapes fresh. The liquid turned to wine and he kept the fluid, marking it poison. An inmate of the harem, mad with toothache, attempted suicide by taking the poison and lo, wine was discovered.

Jenks flytrap: A boxlike patented trap promoted in 1850s. [*Example pictured.*]

Jenks shades: Window shades of transparent Hollands, painted with landscapes, castle ruins, arabesques, Gothic scrolls, and interior views, made in quantities by W. O. Jenks of New York from 1840s. When drawn, these shades provided a picture within the room by day and, when lamps were lit at night, an illuminated picture for the delectation of the passer-by. Very, very chic. Many of the shades are now mounted on white cloth, put in stretcher frames, and offered as "primitive paintings."

Jennens & Bettridge: English manufacturers of japanned wares and pressed paper, including papier-mâché. Much of this ware was sold in U.S. from 1818 to 1870s. Many of the objects are stamped with makers' name. The factory was at Birmingham.

jenny balk: A small beam.

jenny coat: A child's nightgown.

Jenny Lind: Swedish singer whose concert tour in U.S. was sponsored by P. T. Barnum. The country went mad over this girl's voice, and innumerable statuettes, wallpaper, elegancies, candlesticks, lamps, et cetera, were made and sold. Most of the souvenirs date from 1850s. Practically every chairmaker in America made a chair he called Jenny Lind. Henckle of Philadelphia made a bed approved by Miss Lind herself. It was *not* a button- or ball-turned bed. *See* Chairs, All Kinds. There were Jenny Lind dolls, buttons, gloves, laces—everything.

jenny quick: A pressing iron.

Jensen, Gerrit: Dutch marquetry worker active in London from 1630s.

jeroboam: Any large container or bottle.

Jersey City glass: Flint glass, cut, engraved, gilded, and plain; druggists' wares, vials and perfume bottles, pressed wares, and general line, made from 1820s to 1860s at Jersey City, N.J.

Jersey City Toby: *See* Henderson Toby.

Jersey Lily furniture: Named for Lily Langtry, the "Jersey Lily," famous actress of 1880s. Eastlake style.

Jersey porcelain: Made at Jersey City, N.J., by subsidiary of the glassworks. Made for a short time, 1825–28, it pre-dates Tucker ware, the famed Philadelphia porcelain.

Jersey tea: Leaves of the red root shrub, used prior to the Revolution as a protest against taxed tea.

Jersey terra cotta: Busts and other objects and wares attributed to south and central New Jersey potteries from early 19th century. One example is an excellent bust of Washington.

Jessup, Jared: A wall painter who worked in Connecticut from 1820s.

Jesuit bark: Quinine.

Jet: Natural black mineral. Imitated in black glass and in hard black wax. Jet jewelry and buttons may be of the mineral, or glass.

Jevens lamp: Lamps for camphene, lard oil, and sperm oil, made by J. W. Jevens of Brooklyn, N.Y., from 1840s. Baroque styles. Some lamps are marked in the metal or with a small metal label.

Jewel Band: Pattern of pressed glass featuring simple bands of chain and dot work.

Jewel Cut: Pattern of true cut glass featuring bold deep prismatic divisions within which are tiny faceted areas, and large crowns of cutwork with fans.

Jewel with Dewdrop: Pattern of pressed glass displaying vertical bands of stippling, edged with dewdrops, and with round and oval bosses in the banding, alternating with clear bands.

jeweled tole: Decorated japanned tinware, having flecking of colored beads anchored in the mastic.

jewelry: Adornment for fingers, wrists, breast, brow, neck, and dress, made of any precious or semi-precious metal studded with precious or imitation gem stones and other mountings. The precious stones of the 16th to 18th century were the diamond, emerald, ruby, sapphire, beryl, topaz, jacinth, peridot, turquoise, moonstone, garnet, rock crystal, cat's-eye, amethyst, pearl, coral, and amber. Diamonds were not cut in present-day style but were usually flat. Contrary to common belief, they are not worth more, unset, than present-day stones. Today there are several promotional names given to old stones, used largely to establish a fictitious value beyond that indicated by the weight and water.

Jew's pitch: Natural asphalt or bitumen found floating on the Dead Sea.

jiffer: Earthenware cheese toaster.

jigsawing: Fret sawing, often by amateurs of 19th century, imitative of the fretwork on early mirror frames and also in many curious designs. Many Georgian mirrors have fret- or jigsawed cresting, bottoms, and sidepieces or cheeks. The late jigsaw work, done by thousands of hobbyists, is, as a general rule, not worthy of collecting, except as a quaint curiosity and vagary of homework.

jig's up: *See* Gig; Gigged Up.

Job's-tears: The *Coix lacryma-jobi* from which a white sheathing derives, used (1) in fashioning ornamental work and (2) for use as a teething or gumsticks for babies.

jockey scale: Ceremonial beam scale for weighing in riders. Often graduated into stones, pounds, and ounces. The scale is often of brass or steel, having a padded leather seat attached to one end of the beam.

jockle: A small clock in a carved case, somewhat in the style of a cuckoo clock.

jogging: Wriggle work.

johannes: Gold coin of Portugal, much circulated in colonies in 17th and 18th centuries. Worth about $8.80.

John Bull: The first steam locomotive used in U.S. Made in England and used on Camden & Amboy Railroad from 1832.

John furniture: French Antique style (Victorian) furniture made at Cincinnati from 1840s or early 1850s by S. J. John.

Johnnycake: From journey cake. Shawnee cake. Thus did two experts of the 1830s take opposite sides. Take your choice. Both were breadstuffs to take along on a journey, one fortified with ginger and sugar, the other with bear's grease!

Johnny Green bank: A clockwork mechanical bank of the 1880s. Deposit of a coin causes a boylike figure to ring a bell and "Jack Stout" pulls a kitten from the well.

Johnson, Thomas: Designer, cabinetmaker, and carver of London who in 1750 published a book of designs. Probably the man who gave Chippendale his "style" source, as Johnson was a master of the rococo, from the French of Louis XIV. Published a book of design for girandoles, another on designs for tables, frames, lamps, et cetera. In 1750s his work was considered "modern" style. Published printed patterns, turnery patterns, clock-case designs, and many other aids to the furniture trade.

Johnson bookcase: A four-sided framework with open shelves on each face, mounted on an iron axle set vertically on a heavy cast-iron base. The frame revolved. User could bring his choice of books readily to hand. The date is from 1870s.

Johnson embroidery: Homemade embroidery done on the Johnson sewing machine, mostly from the 1870s. It is a good imitation of handwork on tulle, canvas, and beaver cloth, in metallic and colored threads and flosses.

Johnson furniture (MIDWESTERN): John Johnson was established c. 1849 at Davenport, Ia., making furniture in the Empire and French Antique styles. This is probably the reference. However, this is not to say there were no other cabinetmakers with sufficient production to warrant applying their name to the goods they sold.

Johnson glass: Reference is probably to the Johnson-owned Aetna Glass Works at Frederick, Md., established in 1790. Nothing definite is known about the quality of the product, but certain old residents of the locale, interviewed in 1949, stated "they made glass like Amelung." This is a tradition worthy of exploration, but that is all. It cannot stand as fact until proved.

Johnston, David Claypool: American artist and caricaturist; publisher of *Scraps*, which earned for him the name of the American Cruikshank. *Scraps* was published annually for many years and then reissued. Any copies are desirable collectors' items. First half of 19th century.

Johnston, Brooks lamps: Astral, sinumbra, and other specialty lamps bearing this stamp or plate are of London make, probably from 1790 to 1830s. Bemis & Vose of Boston were importers of these lamps.

Johnston, John: Cabinetmaker of Marlboro, Md., from 1760s. Georgian styles.

Johnston ironware: Franklin stoves, kettles, griddles, Rittenhouse stoves, Canada ten-plate stoves, firebacks, and clock weights made by or for Robert Johnston of New Haven, Conn., from 1785 to c. 1800.

Joined chest: Any chest, but primarily those of the 17th century, made by a joiner, a user of the best techniques, such as dovetailing, mortising, rabbeting. The term "joined" used in connection with stool, chair, table, form, et cetera, refers to the quality and kind of workmanship.

Jonathan: Iron hearth item; a four-footed stand having hook on its top. A toaster used at hearth level, or suspended from crane or spit.

Jones, Inigo: Eminent English architect and designer of first half of 17th century. He is responsible for the first classic revival in England. Jones was King's Surveyor of Works from 1615. He died 1652.

Jones, William: Furniture designer of England who published a book of patterns in 1739: *The Gentleman's or Builder's Companion.* Some commentators claim this is the first book to show furniture designs.

Jones & Rammelsberg: Grecian- and Empire-style furniture manufacturers of Cincinnati from 1820s. This firm made much of the furniture, now antique, found on plantations of Tennessee, Kentucky, Alabama, Mississippi, and even Texas. The distribution was not direct, but through agents and stores, furniture-store boats, and factors throughout the Ohio-Mississippi Valley.

Jones (BALTIMORE) **ware:** Black luster-, stone-, and earthenware tea- and coffee-pots, chocolate pots, tankards, pitchers, and bowls made at the Jones Pottery, Baltimore, from 1840s.

Jordan: A chamber pot.

Joshua tree: A tree-form yucca growing in Southwestern U.S. The phrase "Don't Josh me" was originally "Don't Joshua-tree me."

Joslin combs: Tortoise-shell combs of the 1840s, made in Boston by W. A. Joslin.

Journal des Scavans: Early scientific magazine with many illustrations of looms, instruments, tools, flying machines, et cetera. Published in last half of 17th century.

Journal rack: Fanwise-arranged series of dividers on a stand to hold magazines and periodicals. The dividers may be slatted or fret-sawed. Made in this style from c. 1790s to 1840s. Not a true canterbury, *which see.*

Joyned: Work done by a joiner; a cabinet-maker. *See also* Joined Chest.

Jubbe: A large jug.

Judy: Name once used to designate what is now called a Betty lamp.

jug decanter: The term is completely descriptive; a decanter in jug shape.

jug heads: Pottery stopples, some in bust form. These small effigies at times were imitative of the heads of famed people. Some made in U.S. by local potters, allegedly of heads of Washington, Adams, Jefferson, and Madison. From these small stoppers derives the application of term to people with small heads, or addlepated folks. [*Examples pictured.*]

Jug yeast: Hops and potatoes boiled together, strained, the liquor poured over mashed boiled potatoes, sugared, and let work in a jug.

Ju-I form: Chinese Ju-i head decoration on porcelain and japanned ware, cut in jade, et cetera. Derives from the idol of long life.

juju: A toy or amulet.

Jukes Mount Vernon: Aquatint engraving of the home of Washington issued by Jukes of London, 1800, from a drawing by Alexander Robertson of New York.

julep cup: A short beaker of silver; actually a silver tumbler, as made by silversmiths generally from early 1800s, but glorified by naming it a julep cup and so perhaps enhancing the value or at least establishing a reason for overpricing. Such inexpensive cups were given as trophies at local race meets, which in most cases were simple trials of horses' running ability. A considerable number of these silver tumblers survive, suitably engraved with name of owner, winner, and date. Many were so used in Kentucky, made by Kentucky silversmiths.

jumbal: A rich biscuit of sugar, flour, eggs, butter, cream, and almond paste flavored with rose water. Now "jumble."

jumble gun: A forcing syringe of tinware with handholds and plunger, to force the batter above mentioned through a star-shaped opening. The plunger was pushed by the diaphragm of the operator. [*Example pictured.*]

Jumbo: Pattern of pressed glass that is also dated "Patented September 23, 1884." The glass features a frosted representation of Barnum's famous elephant as a finial of some size. Incidentally, the patent does not specify or picture Jumbo.

Jumeau dolls: French imported doll, first made in 1840s and achieving considerable importation by 1880s, when Wood of New York offered them to dealers everywhere at from $16.50 to $72 a dozen. Obviously these were not cheap dolls, the normal retail price being $2.50 to $10 each.

jumper jug: Don, England, pottery jug featuring the "orange jumper," a red-coated and otherwise luridly dressed character bearing a card lettered "Milton Forever." There is a verse under the jug spout.

jumps: Stayed bodices of the 18th century.

jussel: The dish also called salamigundy (salmagundi) and salami. Grated bread with eggs and herbs, boiled.

just: A vase-form flagon, generally of silver. Term is from *justa,* meaning a proper measure.

Justice pottery: The probable reference is to the redwares and stonewares made by John Justice of Philadelphia, working in 1790s.

justicia: The malabar nut.

juvenile mugs: Straight-sided mugs in various tints and colors by various potters, some in luster, some transfer-printed, molded, scratched, and hand-painted, but all issued as mugs for children. Many have maxims and mottoes. Most of production from 1790s to 1850s.

K

Kager bell: Not a type of bell. Bells cast by W. Kager of Louisville, Ky., from 1840s and much used on steamboats and plantations. Kager also cast church bells.

kail pot: A cooking pot for cabbage.

Kakiemon: The "patchwork-quilt" pattern originally on Chinese porcelain, as a series of geometric elements in various colors, and in textile patterns. Imitated by English and continental porcelain makers, the design was copied by resourceful housewives and from it developed the crazy-quilt work which many believe to be an American invention. It is quite possible this was the first Imari pattern. The potter Kakiyemon is credited with first making, c. 1650.

Kaldenberg pipes: Meerschaum pipes, shaped and carved by Julius Kaldenberg of New York, active from 1850s.

kaleidoscope: (1) Glass with tinfoil backing. A technique used much in making buttons. Some have eglomise decoration. (2) Optical tube viewer having prisms and tumbling bits of colored glass which formed an endless series of patterns.

kalemdam: A case to hold a quill pen for carrying on the person. The cover section has a slot to permit the feathered portion of quill to protrude from case. Many are of japanned iron. Others are pewter, brass, or silver.

kaligraphic ornament: Penmanship used as a decorative theme. Some Bohemian glass is cut with the swirls and curls of fine calligraphy. These pieces of cut glass may date as early as 1710s.

kalpis: A water jar.

kamptulicon: Insulating compound made of ground cork and India rubber. Also a mixture of ground cork and oxidized linseed oil, used as a filler on canvas to make floor cloths. Really the precursor of linoleum.

kane backing: Cane webbing used on chair seats and backs. The Portuguese spread this Far East technique over Europe.

kangaroo: The so-called Psyche sofa. Style is Directoire. [*Example pictured.*]

K'ang Hsi: Chinese period, 1661–1722.

kao-ling; kaolin: Same as petunse. Porcelain clay.

Kaplan desk: A satchel or attaché case with desk facilities, compartments, et cetera. Made by one Kaplan from 1870s.

kast; kaas; kasten: The huge portable closet of the Dutch; a case or press for clothes. Many varieties, dating from 15th century. Most examples in America derive from Dutch settlements in Hudson, Connecticut, and Delaware valleys from early 17th century. These are frequently of late 16th- and contemporaneous 17th-century making. Much credit has been assumed by one of the journals of collecting for revealing that *kast* or *kasten* is the proper term for what has been called a *kas*. Esther Singleton, in *Furniture of Our Forefathers* (1898), terms the piece a *kast*. *Kaastel*, or *kastelen*, while referring to this item of furniture, means a garniture of vases and beakers as used on a *kast*.

kasten makker: Casemaker; cabinetmaker.

kate: A Malayan weight equal to 11.73 ounces. Known to us because tea was sold by the kate. Our ancestors pronounced it *katde*, and that's how the term was used until it became "caddy"—hence tea caddy.

katniss: The sagittaria, or arrow-leaved swamp root. The roots are edible and are potato form. 17th-century Swedes on the Delaware found this root used by native Indians as food and so used it themselves, finally cultivating it.

Kauffman, Angelica: Swiss-born artist who captured London and all England, achieving fame and fortune as a portrait and decorative painter; did work on china, porcelain, furniture, and walls. Her figure work is superb. Worked in latter half of 18th century.

kay; kai: Early name for what is now called a Betty lamp.

kealer; keeler: Woodenware. A cooling tub; a shallow coopered tub.

keech: Tallow.

keel: To cool.

Keene glass: Reference is to the glass made at two factories at Keene, N.H., the Keene Works and the New Hampshire Glass Works. Flasks, bottles, and cut and polished wares. Flasks are generally marked.

keep: A food safe; a meat safe. Generally with perforated panels. 19th-century examples have sheet-iron panels perforated in pattern form. Early examples are of wood, with lattices, arcades, and other vents.

keepand: Keeping. **keepand room:** The general living-dining-cooking room.

keffekil: Meerschaum; meerschaum; Stella Maris.

keg stove: Small potbellied stove. Some are really tiny ones, looking like toys, but they're not. They are small-room or cabin heaters.

Kehew, John: Navigation instrument maker of New Bedford, Mass., active from 1840s.

Keim ironwork: Superlatively fine cast iron made at the Keim "Windsor Furnace" in Lancaster County, Pa., from 1825. Full flask castings in panels, one of St. John, 12½" x 15½"; one of the Last Supper; another series of Apostles, 4" x 5" and several sizes of crucifixes.

kell: A caul, a cover, and sometimes undergarments are so designated.

Kelley chairs: *See* Chairs, All Kinds. Kelley of Cuyahoga Falls, O., also made bedsteads. He was active from 1830s.

kellis: A hood.

Kelso, John: Cabinet- and chairmaker of Philadelphia from 1760s, and New York from 1770s.

kelsop: Rennet; the milk jellifier made from peptic section of cattle.

kelt: Cloth of natural black and white wool.

Kennedy chairs: Reference is to the maker, Samuel Kennedy of Fallston, Pa. Kennedy had a wheel factory where he made chair parts and finally duplicated the technique of Hitchcock and began production of chairs from his own parts. These are fancy chairs. Factory in operation from 1830s.

Kennedy coverlets: Coverlets from the factory of David Kennedy, Steubenville, O., operating from 1830. Kennedy made rugs, carpets, and coverlets. The latter are generally marked and sometimes dated.

kennen: A half-bushel measure.

Kensington glass: Actually an 18th-century glassworks at Philadelphia, operated by Robert Towars in 1771, by Elliott, the mirror maker, from 1772 to 1777, and by Thomas Leiper from 1780. In 1804 James Rowland renamed the works Kensington and operated it to 1824. In 1825 Thomas Dyott operated the plant, continuing to 1838. In 1840s it was owned by Henry Rapp. House- and tablewares, mirror and windowpanes, mineral-water and drug bottles, historic flasks, and other products were made; also cut glass.

Kent, William: English furniture designer, architect, and artist of note, 1684-1748. Chippendale borrowed from Kent, as did many other Georgian furniture makers. Kent's designs were published as a book in 1744.

kent cob: A bush filbert of large size.

Kent glass: Ohio glassware, featuring vertical ribbing between bands of diamond diapering. Kent, Wells & Co. made bottles and hollowware at Kent, O., from 1850s. Edmunds & Parks were the makers of the mold-blown and patterned ware first mentioned, from 1820s to 1830s.

Kentucky: Pattern of pressed glass featuring segmented fans or swags with curvate ends, between which are panels imitative of crosscutting.

Kentucky cowbell: A named bell, paper-labeled Kentucky, made by Sargeant of New Haven, Conn., from 1840s. On the label is a bovine scene.

Kentucky glass: Bottles, flasks, demi-johns, and other containers made by Taylor, Stanger & Ramsey and other proprietors of the Louisville (Ky.) Glass Works from 1850s. Some very rococo bottles are credited to this plant. Also a term for the cut and engraved glass made at Louisville and other points, using Wheeling and Pittsburgh blanks.

kerchief press: A small linen press of screw-down type for pressing handkerchiefs and neckerchiefs. Some have small drawers under the press proper. Generally of all-wood construction.

kerf: Channel, cut as a series, on boards (1) to prevent warping, (2) to hold any plastic laid upon the board when set upright, as a kerfed baking board.

kermes: A species of dye allied to cochineal; dried *Coccus ilicis*, used in making a vermilion color. The sulphuret of antimony or mercury supplanted kermes in many fields after 1600s. **kermes oak:** The oak with prickly leaves on which the kermes insects feed.

kermesse: A temporary cot; a shakedown for the night. Kermesse bed.

kerosene: Rock oil; petroleum. Used generally as a lamp oil after the successful sinking of the Drake well in 1859, but known for centuries and even by the ancients. In 19th century, Trinidad asphaltum was distilled to capture a lighting fluid called kerosene. Lamps for its use were made in England and France. Kier of Pittsburgh made a lamp oil (and medicine) from surface petroleum prior to the commercial output resulting from drilling for the oil.

kerosophane: Wax impressions imitative of the porcelain elegancies known as lithophanes.

Kerr porcelain: Reference is to the decoration, not manufacture, by Joseph Kerr, Philadelphia, from 1850s.

kerse: To cover with flags of slate.

Kershaw, J. M.: Engraver of St. Louis from 1840s or 1850s.

Kerwood, William: Furniture maker of Trenton, N.J., who sold his own output. Working from 1800s to 1850. Surviving labels indicate he made sofas, easy chairs, desks, tables, clock cases, bureaus, bookcases, and Venetian blinds.

Ketcham japanned ware: E. Ketcham of New York was an extensive manufacturer of japanned and polished tin-plated wares from 1850s. His goods were sold by many dealers throughout the country. He shipped to every state from Maine to California. Some of it is marked with a small stenciling. All sorts of kitchen-, dairy, house-, and tablewares, and decorative objects.

Ketchum glass: Ornamental and decorative glass made by Daniel Ketchum, one-time expert from the Gilliland works, Brooklyn, N.Y.

keter: A Torah crown.

kettle, apartmental: Four-section cookers or food carriers, some with heating element under, all parts joined with a long looped handle engaging ears on all kettles. Tin-plated ware.

kettle body: *Bombé;* bulging; imitative of the contours of a kettle. Noted on desks, chests of drawers, and other cabinet pieces from 18th century. Imitations of the style or technique made in 19th century are in the Empire style.

kettledrum: Hemispheric drum body of the 18th century, much used by military companies. [*Example pictured.*]

kettle stand: Galleried and tray-topped stand made specifically for service of tea from the kettle, some having tops of two levels. All styles from Queen Anne through Georgian and Chippendale, Adam, et cetera, to Empire.

kettle tilt: Metallic frame with lever and

handle so contrived as to tilt a large kettle for pouring. A fireplace hot-water supply system.

kewbas (sometimes kewblas): Novelty glass of 1890s, color-flashed over milk white, with coating of clear over the color. Made at Union Works, Somerville, Mass.

key basket: Stamped leather basket for keys (seldom recognized for the intended usage), used extensively on plantations to hold keys to the various offices, storerooms, et cetera. Some are of wood and some woven from twigs. Usage dates from 17th century to 19th. Some are very elaborate.

key box: Shallow wall cabinets with glass-panel doors, in which keys were hung on hooks. Some are very fine, of shield shape, or rectangular with broken pediment or Gothic tops.

key check: Identification check or tag of metal, much used from 1840s, the owner's name die-stamped on reverse of a decorative tab. One of the objects collected by girls of the 1840s and 1850s as souvenirs of various beaux. [*Example pictured.*]

Keyes, Royal: Cabinetmaker of Jamestown, N.Y., working from 1815.

keyhole piercing: Keyhole-shaped orifices in a series, as on the rim of a galleried tray. This piercing is known on metal and wood objects.

key pistol: A rare firearm; the shaft of a huge key bored and serving as a pistol barrel, fitted with matchlock. Examples date from 15th century. [*Example pictured.*]

kibble: Woodenware; the bucket of a draw well.

kibosh: Plaster coating. Wooden framework, with wattles, coated to produce hollow statues, arches, et cetera, for short-term usage. Derived from the Arabic and used as a means of covering infidel statues in churches and buildings captured in the Moslem wars.

kick-up scale: A small scale used to weigh money. Counterfeit would not activate the scale; sound money would. Some are said to date from 17th century. Nearly all available examples today are of the 19th century.

Kidder & Carter mirrors: Tabernacle-type mirrors made in considerable quantities by a firm so named at Charlestown, Mass. This firm also made tin-foil mirror backing, which it sold wholesale.

kidderminster: (1) A type of woven carpeting. (2) Coarse linen and woolen fabric.

kid doll: Reference is to kidskin doll bodies, stuffed. Generally with a porcelain, china, wood, or Parian head. Made from 18th to 20th century.

kidney table (table à rognon): A table having a top contoured as a curved oval or kidney shape. Underbracing generally conformed to the top contour. An early chair-side or occasional-table form.

kier: A boiler for bleaching cloth.

Kilbrunn, Lawrence: Portrait painter of colonial New York, working from 1750s. Advertised as a "limner from London" in 1757.

kilderkin: Woodenware. A container holding one eighth of a hogshead, or 16 to 18 gallons. Generally coppered, but some of hollowed tree trunks, especially cypress, were used in the South.

killikinick: Dried inner bark of the red willow and the upland sumac, added to smoking tobacco for fragrance. An American Indian discovery used extensively in all early tobacco recipes and by manufacturers to 1870s and later. It may still be used by some.

Kimball furniture: French-revival and other styles of last half of 19th century, made by J. Wayland Kimball and Kimball and Co., Boston, Mass. In 1876 Mr. Kimball issued a book of furniture and drapery designs in important format.

Kimball-Whittemore mirrors: Plain and ornamented gilt mirrors in the Empire style, made by this firm from 1840s to 1860s.

kinetoscope: The first motion-picture projector for home use as made by Thomas Edison. The first home examples date from 1890s. Some had glass-pane films, not celluloid.

King, William: 18th-century cabinetmaker of Salem, Mass.

King cameo: The marble sculptor, J. C. King of Boston, also cut cameos from 1840s. He was the sculptor of the bust of Dr. Woodward made for a group of citizens at Worcester, Mass., in 1848.

King chair: See Chairs, All Kinds.

King furniture: The product of the Horace King furniture establishment at Hartford, Conn., from 1840s. Empire and French Antique styles. Also rustic furniture of laurelwood.

King Hal jug: Ralph Wood and other Staffordshire potters made figural jugs of good King Hal. The Wood example displays the Prince of Wales, later George IV, masquerading as King Hal.

King profiles: Not silhouettes, but profile portraits in water color, imitative of similar cheap portraits as done by James Ellsworth and others. Done by Josiah King, working from 1840s.

king's bloom: The peony flower.

king's cup: The marsh-marigold flower.

Kinnear lamp: Lard lamp, patented 1851 by Delamar Kinnear of Circleville, O. Ufford of Boston leased patent and made thousands, advertised as "smoke-consuming patent lamp." Priced at from 67 cents upward to $1.25 each. Cast iron and tin bases.

kino: Gum-resin astringent used in 18th century.

Kinsey plaster ware: Ornaments of plaster, miscalled chalk ware, made by P. & C. Kinsey of Cincinnati, 1840–60.

kinsy-winsy: Restless; uncertain.

kip: A half-ton measure or weight.

kipper nut: The peanut, or goober.

kirble: Windlass of a draw well.

kirimon: The paulownia flower, used as a decorative element by Japanese.

kish: A basket for sod or turf.

kisilm; kilm: Persian fabrics; rugs woven without a pile, with orifices, to serve as wall hangings, permitting passage of air. These were used in 1890s as part of the hanging of a Turkish nook in many homes.

kiss comfit: 17th- and 18th-century breath sweetener.

kissing bridge: Any covered bridge was once so called.

kist: A chest.

kit: Woodenware. A small pail; a milking pail.

kitchen caster: A large-size casting box or can with handle. Known in all metals from tin to silver. Some are of wood.

kite keyhole: Reference is to the kite-shaped escutcheon of ivory, bone, brass, or wood, through which a keyhole was pierced. Usage was quite common from 1810 to 1860.

Kit Kat: A London club of early 18th century. Pictures of members, all famed or important men, were painted the same size, 28" x 36". This size canvas is still called Kit Kat size.

kitt: Pickling tub or pail.

Kittredge furniture: See Blake Furniture.

kitty fisher: Bed hangings of gauze or fish netting of very fine weave. "Kitty" was a quite common name for any night-flying moth in 18th century. See Mosquito Bar. [*Example pictured.*]

kmt.: Abbreviation of a standard, of exchange used by the Swedes on the Delaware prior to 1660. It referred to *koppar mynt thaler*, fifty of which were equal to one English pound sterling.

knag: A peg upon which to hang clothes. **knagg board:** A row of pegs on a hanging board, fixed horizontally on a wall or in a closet or case.

kneading table: The top of a dough trough. The first kneading was in the trough proper; after raising, the second kneading was on the board, from which dough was shaped into loaves, put in pans, and let rise again before baking. Sometimes the entire ensemble is called by this name.

knee carving: Carving on the knees of cabriole legs began in the Queen Anne period and continued through the entire Georgian era, including Chippendale. The same nicety is found on the French Antique revival furniture of the 19th century which, of course, derives from precisely the same style source as did Chippendale's French designs. There are various decorative elements incorporated in knee carving, the most general being leaf and flower-petal forms.

kneehole: An opening in any case furniture to permit the introduction of the knees of a person seated before or at it. Said generally of the cabinet-form desks which, having neither failing front nor open underpinning, had to have kneeholes. The true kneehole desks (sometimes called dressing tables) are small pieces. The large library desks are more properly pedestal desks, although there is extensive knee space between the pedestals.

Kneeland & Adams: Cabinetmakers of some prominence at Hartford, Conn., working from 1780s. Partnership dissolved in 1795. Made fine case and seat furniture, mirrors, and clock cases in the prevailing styles of their period.

knee tray: A tea tray shaped like a lapboard, often of papier-mâché, japanned.

Majority are 19th century, best examples being by Jennens & Bettridge, but many by other concerns from 1840s. Generally of French styling. [*Examples pictured.*]

Knell sofa bed: Extensible sofa, forming a full-size bed, made by George Knell of Philadelphia from 1850s. French-revival style. They are not common.

knickknack work: Jigsaw work was so called in the early 19th century. Homework of all sorts throughout the early Federal period was called domestic economy. [*The jigsaw outfit pictured was recommended for homework.*] The open circular table, frame, and treadle permitted working from any part of the periphery, flat, or at an angle.

knife boxes: Sideboard cabinets in classic style, as urns or shaped cases, having slotted interiors to hold not only knives but all sorts of table silver. [*Example pictured.*]

knife cleaner: (1) An enclosed rotating box in a frame turned by a crank. Knives placed in it were thus cleaned. (2) An open compartmented tray fitted with bath brick or some other polishing agent for more easier hand polishing. Most knives were steel-bladed.

knife rest: Properly a carving-knife rest; a trestle upon which to rest the knife. Many of silver, plated ware, glass, pottery, tile, et cetera, in some decorative form.

knife tray: Deep bevel or slope-sided tray of fine wood, with middle partition and carrying handle (sometimes of brass) or handhold. These were made throughou 18th century and are mentioned in cabinetmakers' price books to 1830s.

Knight mirrors: Robert Knight of Brooklyn conducted a manufactory of gilt and mahogany mirrors from 1840s. The style is Empire and French Antique revival.

Knights of Labor mug: A beer mug of pressed glass made to catch the corner-saloon trade of the early union calling itself the Knights of Labor. Late 19th century. A similar beer mug was made featuring Arbitration.

Knipe, William: Bedstead manufacturer of New York City working in 1840s and catering to the visiting buyers from the South. Empire and French Antique styles. Said to have made sleigh beds and ball-turned beds.

knobs: Drawer pulls and door pulls as used in cabinetmaking. Many varieties, generally further named for the subject of décor on the face, as Washington knob, eagle knob, dove knob, floral knob, et cetera.

knocker latch: Door latch with a hinged handle serving also as a knocker. 18th century.

knodden cake: Cake baked from enriched bread dough.

Knole sofa: A sofa made in 1870s in imitation of the 17th-century sofa at Knole Castle, England. It is noted for its adjustable arms. [*Example of the reproduction pictured.*]

Knolton, David: Cabinetmaker of New York, working from 1770.

knop: A swelling or ball form on a stem, a in glasswares.

Knostman-Timpke furniture: Empire-style, factory-made furniture made at Davenport, Ia., from 1850s.

knot glass: The cheapest panes of crown glass; the square with the pontil blob, or bull's-eye. Now the most highly prized of old windowpanes.

Knowles, Taylor & Knowles: Potters of East Liverpool, O., from 1870, prior to which the firm name was Knowles & Harvey. An extensive production of all sorts of wares. The pottery began operation in 1852.

Knowles ware: This reference is not to the above pottery but to the Matthew Knowles & Son Potteries at Brampton, England, operating from 1830s as successors to the Welshpool and Payne potteries of Mr. Blake, founded in 18th century. Knowles made spirit kegs, fruit jars, punch jugs, tobacco jars, puzzle jugs, posset pots, grotesque smoke pipes, brown-and stoneware, jam pots, filters, et cetera.

knuckle duster: A combined equivalent of the brass knuckle and revolver. It had no barrel and was fired directly from the cartridge chamber. Invented in 1865 and marketed as "My Friend."

knuckle joint: Another term for tongue-and-groove joint; the table joint that is found on most 17th-century drop-leaf tables.

Kohlenkamp lamp: Street, carriage, and home lamps made by Nicholas Kohlenkamp of Philadelphia from 1820s. His lamps were used in the first illumination of Chestnut Street in the Quaker City. The lamps generally are of classic or neoclassic style.

Kollner, Auguste: German artist who made 54 Views of American Cities, published as a series in 1848-51, in 8" x 11½" size (or slightly larger), as colored lithographs. These prints are destined to be increasingly scarce.

kooi; koey: Decoy. Rudolph Hommel, Ph.D., once asserted this term derives from the American Indian term "kooee," a call. The learned doctor was probably in error. The Dutch on the Hudson, Delaware, Connecticut, and other rivers probably gave the Indians the term. See also Decoy.

kooijman: Keeper of decoys. Term is Holland Dutch. See also Ende-kooij.

kooker: A small box for sand. Probably a blotting-sand box.

Koonz coverlet: Any coverlet marked "Abram Koonz," or "AK," is probably by this maker, who had a factory at Albany, N.Y., from 1840s and advertised extensively as a wholesaler and retailer.

koro: An incense burner.

Kosciusko, Thaddeus: Lithuanian educated at Warsaw and Paris, came to America in 1777 and took part in American Revolution. Returned to Poland, was imprisoned in Russia, returned to U.S. in 1797, and retired to Switzerland, where he died in 1817.

koss: Same as kast, which see.

Koster: Flemish printer of block books from or before 1430. Working at Haarlem, the Netherlands, he used movable type before 1440. His apprentice, Johannes Gans-fleish, extended the master's experiments and, under the name Gutenberg, has been credited with being the inventor of printing. Koster did not "invent" his techniques; he borrowed them from the Chinese, and from there the step to cutting a block book apart and using the letters over and over again in other combinations was natural.

kou-chu: The lacquer gum of China, derived from a lac-bearing sap of native shrubs. Originally designs were drawn in the sap, as with ink, gold leaf laid on, the surplus wiped off. The work and the gum were imported by the Dutch from 17th century.

kouri: New Zealand gum used in waterproofing; 19th century.

kouthon: The original puzzle mug, made by Greek potters in pre-Christian Era.

kovsh: Russian vessel of silver similar to an American porringer.

kowl (cowl): A large vessel carried on a pole by two men walking tandem.

Kramer, M.: Boston importer of Dutch and French clocks, hobbyhorses, and play toys. Store and warehouse seem to have been established in 1820s and continued to 1840s or later.

Kramer furniture: Made at Cincinnati from 1840s at the steam-powered factory of the concern. Empire and French Antique revival styles commonly called Victorian. Largest production was in 1850s.

krater: Wide-mouthed jar with pronounced up- and outflaring lip, often wider at top than any part of the vessel. Some of the 19th-century pieces called "crater vases" have bell mouths, handles on the central bulb, and stand on pedestals. Examples from practically all famous potteries are of record.

kraut board (crou board): Oblong board with cutting blade set at an angle, often fitted with a sliding box to hold a head of cabbage. A kraut cutter. "Choucrou" was the original French name for salt-pickled cabbage.

krug: A cruse.

ku: A goblet or chalice.

Kuang Hsu: Chinese period, 1875-98.

kuan mao: The official cap with curvate bands at sides that is found as a top rail and cresting on many chairs imitative of Chinese styles; Queen Anne, Georgian, and Chippendale.

Kuan Yin: Goddess of mercy, longevity, and maternity. Statues of this Chinese mythological figure were imported in quantities from late 17th century.

Kyanize: To treat timber against decay. Named for the discoverer of the process, John Kyan of England, 1830s.

kyathos: Ceremonial drinking cup of ancient status.

kylin: Mythical Chinese figure; single-horned dragon head on deer's body covered with scales and having an oxtail.

kylix: Ceremonial drinking cup of ancient status. Also cylix, a tazza-shaped drinking vessel.

L

labarum: A banner pendent on a cross-staff.

labeled: Identified by a paper or metal label, as furniture with printed or engraved labels pasted under drawer bottoms, on door backs, et cetera. Some marks called labels are actually brands, applied hot, charting the wood surface in the pattern of the branding iron.

Labhart ware: A potter named Martin Labhart was operating in Milwaukee, Wis., and Chicago, Ill., from 1850s. This ware is most likely the kind referred to.

Labrador stone: Feldspar having jewel-like encrusting.

laburnum wood: European cabinet wood of hard quality and mottled appearance.

lace: Thread work producing designs and patterns of gossamer quality. Innumerable weaves, ties, forms of knotting, and patterns. Pillow lace is woven on pillows; bobbin lace, with the aid of small bobbins, et cetera. Earliest kind is point lace. Student is referred to *Seven Centuries of Lace*, by J. H. Pollen.

lace: To fortify, as a soup or beverage, with brandy or wine.

lace box: Decorative wooden box, sometimes oval, used by women to hold lace or other finery. A bride's box. Some have a ball handle. Also a workbox for the homecraft of lacemaking.

lace edge: Fancy edging, as on trays, pierced in lacelike pattern. Noted on silver, Sheffield, tin, and some wood trays. Also a technique in Ceramics and Pressed Glass.

lacemaker's candlestand: An upright, footed, pedestal stand having four arms supporting magnifying globes and a center candle socket. Like lace globe, used in shops where fine work was done. Some are reported with up to six candles and twelve globes. [*Example pictured.*]

lacemaker's chair: *See* Chairs, All Kinds.

lacemaker's globe: Globular vessel of glass on a stand or frame. Filled with water, these served as a concentrating lens, focusing the light of a candle to the spot desired by the worker. [*Standing example pictured.*]

lacemaker's table: A lapboard-shaped table top, generally on four cabriole legs, the abdominal cutout enabling the worker to sit very close to his work. Date is from late 17th century and apparently made through 18th century to 19th. Generally imported from France, Flanders, or Belgium.

lace pin: Item of luxury jewelry, often diamond-studded. Used to pin lace jabots or lace points.

laces: (1) Livery braiding, as on uniforms. (2) Ties for trousers, dresses, and other garments, shoes, et cetera.

Lachenmaier iron: The only logical reference is to the cast-iron settees, chairs, beds, and stands made by a founder of this name, active in Philadelphia first half of 19th century.

lackaboys: Thin-soled shoes.

lacmus: A Dutch dyestuff imitative of orchella.

lacture: When used as "today supped on a lacture, beef, cheese, and toasted crusts," this term means a salad of mixed greens.

lacwork: Japanning. The early recipes did not mention solution of the lac in a carrier, but recommended application from the lumps in any color desired, heating the object to be covered and rubbing with the lac.

lacy glass: Generally pressed glass with fine stippling and lacelike patterns or elements. One of the attributes of certain examples made at Sandwich glassworks. See Ruth Webb Lee's *Sandwich Glass*.

ladder-back: *See* Chairs, All Kinds.

ladder leg: *See* Chandos Table.

ladder stand: A pair of miniature ladders fixed in an inverted V form, the rungs with wire platforms on which to stand perfume and cosmetic bottles.

lade gorn: Woodenware. A pail with one long stave serving as a handle; used primarily for drawing water from a shallow well.

ladgen: To calk the seams of coopered work.

ladies' exerciser: A device looking like a loom frame, with an invalid's cot and a large wheel set in the tester joists at top. Advocated in 1830s as a home exerciser for ladies. The lady pulled cords and tensed herself, no doubt.

ladies' friend: Anything from a needle-threader thimble to a cooking range may be meant by this general term, applied to scores of objects, particularly in first half of 19th century.

ladies' twist: Dainty rolls of dental tobacco; actually for chewing by ladies. This method was considered most proper for ladies, 1750s–1850s.

ladle arm: A chair or settee arm which, in the flat, displays a sort of ladle-form outline.

lady bird cage: Large doll body, generally a carved wood head and torso only, fitted with a cage bottom to hold pet birds. This was an elegancy of the 17th century. Not a cage for ladybirds. Most examples appear to be from Netherlands. [*Example pictured.*]

Lady Jane: A large covered bottle, generally with wicker basketwork. Also Dame Jane, from Dame Jeanne. Demijohn is a variant.

Lady Pepperell chair: See Chairs, All Kinds.

lady's chair: See Chairs, All Kinds.

Lafayette glass: (1) Brass- or pewter-rimmed case having a print of Lafayette on one side and a mirror on the other. (2) Any glassware memorializing the visit of Lafayette, 1824–25, such as the boat-shaped saltcellars marked SANDWICH and "B & S Glass Co."; tumblers, blown, with the lettering WELCOME LAFA-YETTE; flasks or whiskey bottles impressed with bust portrait, et cetera. There is also a Lafayette fruit jar having a bust of the hero impressed upon it.

Lafayette hat: A waterproof hat developed by Joseph Juel, French hatter of New York, 1824. It was boxed in a case having a label depicting the landing of Lafayette at the Battery, N.Y., 1824.

lagen: A large measure of liquid. The measure was a coopered "lagen," which some say is the origin of "flagon."

Laird, Joshua: Mold maker for pressed and blown glass, working at Pittsburgh, 1830s.

lalanti: Pendent ornament, hanging loosely from a joint. Also necklace of paper-thin gold ornaments.

Lalique: A French art glass of the 20th century, made by René Lalique, Paris, from 1906. Originally concerned with the making of unique and unusual perfume flacons, Lalique became the foremost maker of art glass, combining frosting, cutting, molding, pressing, and free blowing. A vogue of the post-war period, 1918–28. Some of the pieces are of huge size.

lamb-black: Lampblack derived from burning sheep suet.

Lambert & White: This name found on painted fire buckets is that of an extensive maker of firemen's equipment and military items from 1820s at Philadelphia.

Lambert pine: The sugar pine.

Lambeth delft: Tin-glaze redwares made at Lambeth, England, from 1630s. It is genuine delftware. It should be remembered that "delft" as a name does not refer only to the Dutch faïence made at Delft, but is a generic term for a type of faïence. Hence the term "Lambeth delft" is not out of order. **Lambeth ware:** A different product, from the Doulton & Watts Pottery at Lambeth. This is a glazed stoneware in cream and brown and in cane color. It is generally marked. Lambeth was a potting center from 1600s, when the Rous & Cullyn pottery was in operation. Coade, in 19th century, made terra cotta wares and specialties at this place.

lambskin: (1) A small sheepskin with its wool, used as a rug. (2) The mother formed in vinegar.

lamb's wool: A drink made of crab or tart apples roasted with sugar, pulped, spiced, and added to ale. A winter drink, used especially in the Christmas season.

lamhog: Woodenware. A drinking pot with solid block handles.

lamp: Any light source other than a candle. Innumerable varieties. The first and only genuine improvement in lamps was made in 18th century by Argand, the Swiss scientist who devised the round, or tubu-

lar, wick which had a draft of air inside as well as on its outer surface. From 1780s all fine lamps were fitted with Argand-type wicks or burners.

lampas: Damask or other fine fabric, sometimes of silk, used in wall decoration, upholstery, and as table covers.

lamp boiler: A metallic urn designed to enclose a kerosene lamp. Fitted with a tap, flue, and auxiliary heating stand over the lamp chimney. Date is 1860. [Example pictured.]

lamp enameling: Glass blowing from rods of enamel glass; generally small novelties. Itinerant glass blowers gave demonstrations, using only a Bunsen burner to melt the rods. Resort places still have groups of such workers making demonstrations, generally charging an admission and putting on a show.

lamp filler: Reference may be to a spouted can used to facilitate the filling of any lamp with its burning fluid. Early examples are small open troughs with pointed filling end. Some are quite small, about three to four inches over all. [Example of early type pictured.]

lamp fluids: Lard oil, whale oil, olive oil, palm oil, rendered fats, combinations of alcohol and turpentine, kerosene, and other oils, from nuts, fruits, fish, animals.

lamp holder: Bracket with adjustable fork; a safety device to hold a kerosene lamp.

lamp iron: Confusing term, used to specify a two-burner kerosene stove-lamp, used to heat a laundry iron.

lamplighter: (1) One who contracted to keep in order, and lighted at specified times, lights outside any home. Also any civic employee engaged to keep the street lamps of a community filled, lit, and in order. (2) Device to facilitate the lighting of lamps in the home.

lamp mat: Leather, fabric, or metal mat to place under a lamp.

lamppost candlesticks: Solid metal sticks imitative of lampposts, with newsboy and bootblack figural decoration and colored globes. These burned lamp oil (generally kerosene), not candles, in a taper wick. [Examples pictured.]

lamp scissors: Straight or curved-blade small scissors, some having one broad blade, made to trim lamp wicks of flat and round types.

lamp screen: Paper, cloth, or metallic shield to hang on a lamp chimney.

Lampson, Goodenow: Steel table-cutlery makers of Shelburn Falls, Mass., from 1850s.

lamp teapot: Squat, small teapot in the general form of an ancient Roman lamp.

Lanay-Hautin glass: French glass, made at Paris, including a variety of quality of fine pressed glass in lacy patterns, often mistaken for Sandwich. The spelling is a variant of Launay-Hautin.

Lancaster butter box: A large wooden carrier, fitted with up to 48 cups of pottery or turned wood, each holding a pound print of butter. [Example pictured.]

Lancaster chests: Reference is primarily to the 18th- and early 19th-century painted chests miscalled dower chests, but possibly dowry chests, as made in the Conestoga Valley of Lancaster County, Pa. These chests are actually imitative of the "nonesuch" chests of Tudor England. They have architectural panels, not merely painted-on panels, and the decoration is one in philosophy with the nonesuch chests. Dates from 1730 are reported. Similar chests were made in South Jersey, dating from 1640s. [*Example of Lancaster chest pictured.*]

Lancaster glass: Flint- and green wares for druggists, lily-pad pitchers in the philosophy of South Jersey glass in the Dutch style, also jugs, bowls, et cetera; private mold work and offhand pieces. Made at Lancaster, N.Y., from 1840s. Continuous production under various managements, including a co-operative, to 1900s.

Lancaster quilts: (1) Quilts woven at Lancaster, Mass. Considerable production from 1840s. (2) Coverlets made at various factories, but especially the Schum enterprise at Lancaster, Pa., also from 1840s.

Lancasters: Imported bedspreads or counterpanes, known from 1810s, said to have been woven in Lancashire, England.

Lancaster wares: Redware and stoneware pottery from various kilns set up at Lancaster, Pa., from 1750s. Marks include Weidel, Gast, Fritz, Ganse, Harrison, Martin, Hardy, Swope.

lance: A steel-pointed staff. **lanceolate:** Lance-shaped or lance-pointed.

lancet top: Pointed, as a Gothic arch.

Landis Washington: A crude lithograph from a painting by John Landis, picturing Washington at prayer in his study at Mount Vernon. Published at Lancaster, Pa., in 1840s.

Landon, Felix: Perfumer of Paris, established 1830s, who exported many bottled perfumes to U.S. from 1840s. Innumerable fancy bottles in figural and rococo style are old Landon containers.

Landreth prints: Flower prints from a now rare commercial periodical, *The Floral Magazine & Botanical Repository*, published by the D. & C. Landreth seed and nursery establishment, Philadelphia, from 1832. Hand-colored lithographs after drawings by Kennedy and Lucas, after drawings by William Albright.

landscape rugs: Now rare. Landscape-pattern rugs were featured by Hiram Anderson, N.Y., from 1845. Also called scenic floor rugs.

landscape shade: Window shades of Holland cloth painted with landscape designs. Advertised as "Chinese" by J. Jones of Philadelphia from 1830s. Some of the landscapes are Chinese scenes.

landscape variable: Invention of James Peale, the artist: a glass panel partially painted at bottom and sides with boscage, rocks, figures, et cetera, behind which moved a continuous strip of landscape on rollers. A sort of miniature panorama. Made about 1878.

land yard: Measure of 18 feet.

Langdon candles: Commercially made candles by John Lang of Boston from 1770s. Made spermaceti candles.

lange leizen (lang lijzen): The exagger-ated long figures of Chinese art. Term is Dutch, meaning "long body."

Lang prints: Printed calico fabrics in dull and glazed finishes. Printed by William Lang, Philadelphia, from c. 1790s.

Lannoy, Cornelius: Reputedly the first glassmaker in England, sponsored by Queen Elizabeth.

Lannuier, Honoré: French cabinetmaker of New York, 1780–1818. Worked in the Directoire style and most likely inspired Phyfe. His work is on a par with Phyfe, and undoubtedly much unlabeled furniture attributed to Phyfe is by Lannuier. Said to have made some of furnishings of Federal Hall, c. 1790.

lantern case: (1) A glass bell. (2) Any glassed case for display of objects.

lanthorn: Framework or body of wood or metal with apertures fitted with transparent or translucent horn panes. Some date from 14th century.

lapboard: A work board "cut to fit the contour of the torso in a plane at or near the navel." Vulgarly "belly-button board."

lap dovetail: Hidden dovetailing.

lapel striker: A small corrugated metal tab pinned under the lapel of a coat to provide a convenient place for striking matches.

lapis blue: Lapis lazuli blue, from the mineral lazurite. Lapis is an early term for calico printing.

lappeted: Embroidered or needleworked in a zigzag pattern. Also a similar pattern achieved on the loom.

lap secretary: A secretary (desk box) of standing type with a fall front to rest on the lap of the user.

lapstone: An anvil used on the lap of the worker. Generally of stone, but also of lead, iron, brass, et cetera, depending upon the type of work done on it. Leather dressers, shoemakers, and other artisans used lapstones.

lap wire: Tin-coated thread of reindeer sinews, made in Lapland.

laque: Lacquered.

lärda tidningarne: Spruce beer.

larder: Originally the room for storing lard. Then called the pantry, the buttery, the food-storage closet. Pantry, of course, was originally the bread room.

lard head: The burner of a lard lamp.

lard lamp: A very economical lamp for burning lard.

lard-oil lamp: Any lamp using an oil expressed from lard; it was true oil, not melted lard. Many varieties are known.

lard squeezer: Wide-jawed wood pincers for squeezing fat from fragments in the rendering kettles.

Large barometer: Reference is to the name of the maker of post-form barometers, Joseph Large of New York, from 1840s.

last: Measure of 80 bushels.

lasting: Fabric woven from multiple threads in double warp. Prunella cloth is a lasting, as is Florentine, drawboy, and Amens cloth.

Last Supper fireplace: A cast-iron fireplace front featuring a modeled represen-

1, Lacemaker's Globe. 2, Lamp Filler Dropper. 3, Lavabo, with Two Taps. 4, Leg caliper. 5, Leather Bottle. 6, Long Bellows. 7, Leaf-Scroll Handle. 8, Lincoln-Mask Jug. 9, Lily Bowl. 10, Leather (female) Toby-Type Jug. This is the prototype; preceded potted examples by a century or more. 11, Liberty Mug. 12, Lemon-Squeezer Atomizer. 13, Lincoln Lamp. 14, Loo Table. 15, Lamp Boiler. 16, Knole Sofa. 17, Lamppost Candlesticks.

tation of the biblical scene. Date is c. 1840s.

Last Supper tray: Pressed-glass tray featuring the Last Supper as conceived by Da Vinci. Date from 1870s or 1880s.

latch pan: Dripping pan.

Late Buckle: Pattern of pressed glass with oval panels, clear-centered in imitation of star cutting.

lathe bow: The bow and cord used to operate the miniature lathe used by jewelers.

laton: Latten; brass.

Latrobe heater: A late-type Franklin fireplace fitted with doors. Date is from 1840s.

latten: Brass. When covered with gold leaf it is gilt latten.

Lattice: Pattern of pressed glass with irregular angular panels and crisscross work. Late pattern.

latticino: Crossed, curved linework in paperweight decoration.

Launay-Hautin: See Lanay-Hautin. This firm issued a catalogue in 1840, picturing glass looking so much like Sandwich that one wonders no longer about the source of some Sandwich patterns.

laundry stove: Potbellied stove with a rack or belt to hold laundry irons for heating. The top of the stove carried a wash boiler.

laureate: Crowned with laurel.

lavabo: A hanging wall cistern with one or more taps and a fitted bowl. Toilet ensemble for bedroom or closet. Used from 16th century. Brass, pewter, and other metals, stone, pottery, delftware, et cetera. [Example pictured.]

lava glass: (1) Art glass made by Mount Washington Glass Works, some engraved, enameled, and gilded. (2) Black glass made from c. 1850s by W. A. Smith of Philadelphia. Bowls and bottles were made of it.

Lava ornaments: For these, "Lava" was a trade name. The ornaments are plastics, molded to shape and form. Date is from 1870s.

Lawrence portraits: Tinted portrait photographs.

Lawson, Richard: Cabinetmaker of Baltimore, 1780–85. In 1785 he had a partnership with John Bankson. Lawson was London-trained.

lay'd work: Inlay. Also a form of fancy embroidery.

Lazerville glass: Bottles and vials made at a glassworks of this name at Wellsburg, Va., from 1840s.

lazoo: Lasso.

lazyboy: A broad two-edged knife mounted on a Y-shaped handle; used in cutting brush and weeds.

lazy Susan: Any rotating tray on a central staff for ease in self-service at dining table. Some round tables have a rotating platform in center. Lazy Susan may have up to five rotating trays of graduated size.

leach: Calves'-foot jelly, spiced and sliced cold as a savory.

leaching: Lye making, by draining water through wood ashes in a stone, pottery,

or coopered vat. The resulting liquor was run off into channels, where some of it crystallized and became what we now call baking soda. The liquid was lye.

lead back: Any chair, settee, or sofa back with medallions of cast metal, usually of pewter. Portrait busts, fruits, flowers, and carved element were produced by this method, the medallions tacked on the furniture and often finished with it, or painted.

leaded diamond: Lead-camed, or -muntined, window frames, the pattern being in diamond form. Some early ones had sheet-mica panes; others, horn panes. Most were of glass paning, the glass being in tints of green, amethyst, violet, rose, and yellow.

lead glass: Glass made of a mix containing 40 to 60 parts lead (galena) to 100 parts clean sand. Also called flint glass. Original flint glass had genuine calcined flints in it. Lead glass is considered superior to line-and-soda glass and even to the flint stone glass. Some uninformed people call the double-walled mercury glass "lead" because it looks thick and heavy and is as brilliant as freshly cast lead.

lead mirror: Sheets of glass backed by pouring hot lead upon them.

lead saucer: A graphite deposit in gum water, collected on china saucers and used as a "dry" pigment in certain homecraft stenciling.

lead Shakespeare: Now excessively rare because the bust was a device by which dutiable lead from England entered duty-free because it was cast into bust form, memorializing Shakespeare, and entered as a work of art. On arrival, some 500 tons of these busts were melted down and recast into common lead ingots. All this hocus-pocus occurred in the 1840s.

lead string: Bands to lead children, often made from the mother's wedding garments.

lead ware: It isn't a "ware" in terms of household use; reference is to lead garden ornaments such as vases, boxes, statuary, et cetera.

Leaf: Patterns of pressed glass featuring a leaf with other elements: Leaf & Flower, Leaf & Loop, Leaf & Dart, et cetera. Leaf & Flower is a vine-form band; Leaf & Dart is a frosted panel pattern with droops of a dart form dividing the panels and of leaf form imposed upon them. Arched Leaf, Frosted Leaf, and others are noted in the various reference books published by Ruth Webb Lee.

leaf-scroll handle: Drawer pull of Georgian period anchored in leaf-form supports. [Example pictured.]

leaf silhouette: A large leaf, bearing a scene in silhouette on the surface of the leaf itself. Such work was achieved by removing the fleshy part of the leaf not required by pricking it out with a needle point. This was the method to 1850s. Thereafter acid was used. Few examples survive.

Leake ornaments: Stamped leather used in the same manner as paper plastics, papier-mâché, et cetera; molded décor for affixing to wood in place of carving or as décor on walls or other surfaces. Most examples are found on oak paneling and furniture. Date is from 1840s. English-made.

leams: Tools.

leao: Fine blue-painted porcelain.

leaping steamboat: Shallow-draft river steamers that could be made to leap sand bars by sportive captains who slowed down on approaching a bar and then started going full steam ahead.

Learned, Elisha: Cabinetmaker of Boston, Mass., who worked in first three decades of 19th century and made Sheraton- and Directoire-styled furniture.

Leary & Sanderson: Pewterers, tin-smiths, and coppersmiths of New Orleans, working in 1840s and 1850s.

leather bottle: Leather container for liquid in shapes contrived by the cord-wainers or leatherworkers, called bottles by virtue of purpose and use, not actual shape. [*Example pictured.*]

leather lambrequin: An embossed, dyed, and gilded cornice for placing over window and door draperies. These may date from 1850s, but greatest production was from 1865 to 1885.

leather tapestry: Art leather, die-stamped, molded, gilded, et cetera, used as a wall covering and as a furniture upholstery fabric.

leather Toby: Figural pot of molded leather. The first real Toby jugs. Date is from 16th century. [*Example of a Dame Philpot pictured.*]

leatherwork: (1) Homecraft work in leather. (2) Tooled and wrought leather objects made by professionals. (3) Book-binders' and art leatherworkers' products, ranging from bibelots and boxes to wall coverings, shields, et cetera.

Leavitt ware: Woodenware made at Chicopee, Mass., from 1830s by B. Leavitt.

Lee: Pattern of pressed glass featuring large down-pointing ovals.

Lee, D. & W.: Chairmakers of New York City working in 1840s. Fancy and late Windsors, some marked.

Leeds ware: Queen's ware; the output of the pottery that gave Wedgwood real competition and captured a huge European market. Reticulated, punched, and basket-ware, made from 1780s and covered completely by only one antiques publication in America: *Antiques Digest*, published at Frederick, Md., from 1951. All Leeds patterns, by name, and all punched and other wares are illustrated in full in this journal.

Leffert stove: A carriage stove, burning alcohol; a warm-air generator. Date is from 1850s.

Leffingwell & Williams: Potters of Norwich, Conn., from 1771. Produced earthenware, some of which has been called Pennsylvania redware.

leg caliper: A leg-shaped caliper used by machinists. Date is from 1840s. Sometimes carried for suggested use as a broad form of humor. [*Example pictured.*]

légère chair: See Chairs, All Kinds.

leg-of-mutton leg: Curvate-shouldered leg of a pillar or pedestal. Directoire styl-ing. [*Example pictured.*]

legs (FURNITURE): Bandy, concave, cerule, reeded, cabriole, and other leg forms are pictured, with proper or generally accepted names for them.

Lehman, Benjamin: Cabinetmaker of Philadelphia from 1780s. He wrote a manu-script price list, published 1930, in the *Pennsylvania Magazine*, issued by the Pennsylvania Historical Society of Phila-delphia.

Lehne ware: Painted woodenware made at or near Litiz, Pa. It is decorative, not utilitarian, ware.

lehr: A glass furnace.

Leicestershire bottle: A sauce bottle for a condiment made in U.S., not Eng-land, from c. 1870s.

lekythos: An oil flask.

lemonade can: Early term for pitcher used in service of this beverage, which, incidentally, was often made without sugar and taken as an anti-scorbutic tonic.

lemon razor: A tool for skinning the de-sired paper-thin yellow derma off lemons for flavoring purposes.

lemon-squeezer atomizer: It is an atomizer, not a lemon squeezer. The ac-tual name is Lennox sprinkler, and it was used to sprinkle clothes. [*Example pic-tured.*]

lemon top: Any finial of lemon form; often on andirons and of brass.

Lenox glass: Vials, druggists' wares, bottles, plate glass, and paperweights made at Lenox, Mass., from 1850s to 1870s.

Lent barometer: Reference is to the maker, M. Lent, of Rochester, who made rosewood, black-walnut, mahogany, and plain cased barometers of the pillar type from 1850s.

lenticular: Lenslike; shaped like a lentil seed. Lentil molding displays sections of lens edges. Some looks like a section of true spool turning.

lentil: A shape, as of a lentil seed. The word "lens" is derived from this.

Leominster combs: Millions of hair combs were made at Leominster, Mass., from 1770s. Horn, ivory, shell, and box-wood examples are credited to this pro-duction center, the first comb-manufac-turing locality in the colonies.

Leonard, Elisha: Cabinetmaker of Boston in first quarter of 19th century, credited with perhaps more production than he achieved. Directoire and Empire styles.

leonine: Lion form; of lion style.

leontine: A broad ribbonlike chain worn with a watch.

leopard's bane: Arnica.

leopard's-head mark: It isn't a leopard, but a lion, used as a class mark of assay or proof by the Goldsmiths & Silversmiths Company of London from A.D. 1300. Still the final mark of quality.

Le Prince & Marcotte: Cabinetmakers of New York City from 1850s. French An-tique revival styles.

Leslie table-bed: A gadget which started, c. 1840, as a table that could be converted into a bed. In 1849 the patentee improved the device by adding a washstand! Frank

Leslie, Upper Rahway, N.J., committed this gadget.

lestage boot: The seamless-top boot; the boot that was seamed only at the juncture of upper with sole. Secret was peeling the round hide from legs of cattle, tanning, and then shaping into boot uppers having no seams, visible or invisible.

letelorye: The super omelet of the 18th century. The recipe: Strain fresh eggs through a hair sieve, mix with butter and cream, cook; when cooked, whip until it stands.

lettered can: Generally any china mug or metal container with motto, name, verse, or legend impressed or painted upon it.

letter values (of alphabet), old: In compiling this work the author has found as many as ten variations of spelling of some of the entries. Student is advised to study letter values (to be found in most unabridged standard dictionaries) in pursuit of further information. The Dutch, French, Swedish, and English uses of certain letters, in terms of values, with special critical, diacritical, and accent marks, are required study for antiques research workers. For instance, there is no *y* in the Dutch alphabet. But the letters *ij* have the same value. So the name Van Rijn is pronounced Van Ryn. Iohn is the same as John. *Ia* and *ja* have the same power as *hya*, et cetera.

letterwood: Snakewood.

Letton silhouette: Profile likeness, as cut by R. Letton, who traveled in U.S. as an itinerant cutter from c. 1805 to c. 1825.

leuwin (lewin): A tablecloth.

lever slide: Reference is to early magic-lantern slides having motion imparted by a lever attached to gears. There are very complicated examples of record. [*Example of simple lever slide of seesawing scene is pictured.*]

Leverton, Thomas: Contemporary of the Brothers Adam who favored Etruscan antique sources for his classic designs and cabinetwork.

levys: Folding doors; jalousies and Venetian blinds were so called.

Lewis, W. K. & Bro.: This was a firm of food packers at Boston from 1830s, and any container bearing their mark should be so considered. They did not make the containers.

Lewis Britannia: Isaac Lewis and Lewis & Curtis wares, made from 1830s to 1850s in Connecticut.

Lewis mirror: Fancy and tabernacle mirrors made by Robert Lewis' factory from 1840s.

Lewis prints: Lithographic prints, hand-colored, from J. O. Lewis' *Aboriginal Portfolio*, containing Indian subjects, 80 in all.

ley cask: A wooden cask for leaching lye.

ley metal: Cheap pewter; the very poorest is an alloy of lead and antimony. Some authorities quote ley metal as 80% tin and 20% lead. This is an error. Any pewter with 80% tin was of the very highest grade.

Leyniers tapestry: Brussels tapestry woven at establishments of Urban, Gaspar and Daniel Leijmers, and Henrik Reijdams from 1700s.

Liao: Chinese dynasty, A.D. 907–1125.

libation vase: Ceremonial vase for liquors poured in honor of a deity.

Libbey hats: Frosted-glass souvenir hats of the Columbian Exposition, 1893, also marked "Libbey Glass Co., Toledo, Ohio." The Libbey interests owned a famous glassworks at Toledo, where they produced blown, pressed, and cut wares in great quantities over many years. This factory was originally located in Boston.

liber: The inner bark of a tree. Also called "volumen" when such bark was rolled. From *libra*, book and volume.

Liberty Bell: Centennial pressed-glass pattern with Liberty Bell and legend, "100 Years Ago." Originated by Gillinder & Son, and some made on the Centennial grounds. Covered butter dishes, compotes, goblets, tumblers, and a pressed-glass bank are known. Several varieties, having snake handles, dated pennants, and other features.

Liberty glass: Cut glass of late type made at Liberty Glass Works, Egg Harbor, N.J., from 1899 to 1901.

Liberty Glass Co.: Not to be confused with works noted above; this plant was located at Sapulpa, Okla., and at Coffeyville, Kan., from 1900s. Pressed glass. Student is referred to *ABC's of Old Glass.*

Liberty mug: Opaque white glass, probably Bristol, with painted (fired on) décor of spread eagle within a wreath and 15 gold stars surmounted by word "Liberty." Now quite rare; reproductions noted. [*Example pictured.*]

Liberty urn: Carelessly used term applied to any ovate or globose covered vase with handles. Some are of pottery, others of metal or even turned wood. Proper term is Campagna, or Campaña urn.

library steps: Portable steps, sometimes folding within a stool or cabinet. Generally three to five steps, for reaching high bookshelves. Sometimes a part of a library chair.

licensed bellman: Public crier who called news, advertising notices, et cetera, and who rang a hand bell to attract attention.

lidded lip: Any vessel having both a lip for pouring and a cover screening the top and lip.

liddle table: A gadget for the kitchen; a table with crank-powered knife grinder, scourer, rotary brush, spice mill, apple parer, food chopper, et cetera. Made from 1847 and popularly called a kitchen mechanic.

Liége bottle: A tulip-engraved glass bottle, made in sets for enclosure in cases. Many elements other than tulips, such as fuchsia, pomegranate, and pink, are noted. Much of this décor derives from Spanish occupation of Netherlands, and its counterpart is found in Mexican glass of 18th century and of course in Spanish cut and engraved glass. To call such wares "Pennsylvania German" is utterly ridiculous. The bottles here considered were made at Liége, now in Belgium.

lien erh: Chinese term for the side table or altar copied by Dutch and English cabinetmakers. **lien san:** Chinese term for a sideboard table.

lift handle: (1) Stout handles as used on

chests and trunks for ease in handling. Many varieties, of brass, are found on 18th-century pieces. (2) Handles generally called "drop" and meaning having loose bails that "lift" for use.

light & heat lantern: A hand lantern convertible to a foot stove. Date is 1870s.

Lightfoots: Reference is to the first pins made in America, by Richard Lightfoot, N.Y., from 1770s.

lighthouse (FORM): The term is a late application to a form with some quite early usage. Tapering, upright coffeepots, teapots, chocolate pots, clock pedestals, bottles (late examples actually in form of a lighthouse with lenses defined), and other objects.

lightstand: Small topped table with four legs, or with pedestal, to hold lamp or candlestick. Known in all styles of furniture from Queen Anne through Eastlake.

ligneous marble: Imitation marble, made of wood. Table tops, wall sections, and columns were made of it. Extensive manufacture by Freund & Co., N.Y., from 1850s.

lignum vitae: Excessively hard wood, heavy enough to sink in water. It is tough enough to turn an ax blade. A rare, exotic wood, esteemed for mallets, chocolate cups, paperweights, and box sanders.

lillikin: A small pin.

lily bowl: A bulb planter; a shallow bowl, clear, pale blue, or amethyst in tint, with pontil mark. Date is from mid-18th century. [*Example pictured.*]

Lily of the Valley: Pattern of pressed glass featuring a stem, with ivy or oak leaves, and lily-of-the-valley florets.

lily-of-the-valley cut: Realistic cutting of glass in leaf, stem, and flower form of the lily of the valley, with panels of star cutting. Attributed to H. C. Fry Co.

lily pad: Glass-decorating style in which a coating of glass is flashed over a formed piece and the coating tooled into looping called lily pad. A Dutch form of glass decorating, first noted in South Jersey glass of 18th century.

lily pot: Cup with cover.

limbeck: An alembic; a distilling vessel.

lime-ash: A cement made of slaked lime and wood ash.

limed: Polished.

lime seat: Seats for chairs, made of a cord or rope twisted from the inner bark of the linden tree.

lime stove: A portable stove yielding heat from controlled slaking of lime. Patented 1856.

lime wood: Linden-tree wood. Reference is seldom if ever to the wood of the lime-bearing tree, a citrus-fruit tree. Grinling Gibbons favored lime wood—i.e., linden wood—for his carving. When the citrus-tree wood was used it was in place of box, as this wood is hard and can be burnished.

Limoges: (1) Enamel work, on metal, famed from 16th century. (2) Porcelains of various potteries, notably those of the Havilands, who were not a French firm, but an American family who introduced mass production to the potteries of this French city. Late in 19th century an excel-lent imitation of oriental export porcelain. miscalled Lowestoft, was made at Limoges.

limpsey: Soft and pliant.

Lincoln, F. W., Jr.: Scientific instrument maker of Boston, working in first quarter of 19th century.

Lincoln Drape: A pattern of pressed glass displaying traditional mourning drapery and festoons, assumed to have been issued in memory of President Lincoln. A variant or two are noted by experts, including Lincoln Drape with Tassel.

Lincoln lamp: Oil lamp with a reservoir in form of a horizontal tank, burner at one end, filling orifice at other, the entire device adjustable on an upright rod, firmly based. A student-type lamp, made by Bridgeport Brass Co. from 1870s. [*Example pictured.*]

Lincoln-mask mug: Actually a satyr-mask mug but called Lincoln because of the resemblance to the features of Abraham Lincoln. [*Example pictured.*]

Lincoln plate: Reference is to plated silver, made as late as 1870s, by D. B. Lincoln of Brooklyn, N.Y. Barrel pitchers, mugs, chalices, flatware, and hollow ware. The firm was established 1840.

Lincoln rocker: Reference is to a walnut- or mahogany-frame rocker with up-holstered seat, arm pads, and back, said to be the type of chair Lincoln occupied when assassinated by Booth.

Lind (Lynd), Michael: Swedish cabinet-maker of Lancaster, Pa., working from 1750s to 1790s, who is known positively to have made Queen Anne styled chairs of walnut. There are six chairs by this maker in the Du Pont collection, from one of which a label by Michael Lund was removed c. 1855 by a great-grandson of the original owners. This label, with a recitation of how it was removed, was found in a family Bible. The label is privately owned. Lind is mentioned in the civil records of Lancaster.

linden seat: Twisted rope made from strands of the inner bark of the linden tree.

Lindsay, John: Cabinetmaker of London, 1785, who migrated to Norfolk, Va., and entered into business there. He worked in the style of Adam and Hepplewhite, and considerable fine Virginia furniture was made by him.

line carving; linear carving: Groove carving; flat carving.

line engraving: Intaglio engraving, cut into any plate, generally copper, for the printing of replicas on paper. The lines are filled with ink, the plate surface wiped clean, and dampened paper laid on the plate, both being forced through a press somewhat like a clothes wringer. The dampened paper is forced into the lines and of course picks up the ink. The same process is used in steel engraving, the engraving done on soft steel, hardened after the work, for long-term use.

linen chest-on-frame: William & Mary and Queen Anne piece; sturdy chest on low frame or stand. Date is 1690–1740.

linen fold: A form of panel carving displaying a formalization of the folds of line drapery. It is early English, from the Gallic or Gothic era, and was generally used on fine wainscoting and furniture of Tudor period.

linen glacé: A polishing starch used in laundering fine linen.

linen press: (1) Wooden screw press for use in pressure-folding of household linens. (2) A case of drawers and cupboards for the keeping of linens. (3) A two-door cupboard for keeping linens.

linen tester: (1) A tester, or set of bed curtains, of linen. (2) A thread counter for ascertaining the quality of woven linen.

Lines & Augur: Most likely reference is to a firm of cabinet furniture and chairmakers of this name, working from 1840s at New Haven, Conn.

line spinner: A small rope-making machine used in households for making all sorts of light cord, fishing line, et cetera. The device has various revolving wheels, and hooks to which thread is fastened. By turning a crank these threads were spun into one cord.

Lining, Thomas: Cabinetmaker of Charleston, S.C., working from 1740s.

Link hairwork: Not a technique, but any hairwork done by Robert Link & Brother of New York City, working from 1840s. Hair jewelry.

Link toys: Sand toys with the high-sounding name "Mechanical Box with Automaton." A lithographic scene, with articulated figures, moving by the fall of sand on fan wheels in the box proper. Date is c. 1850s. Robert Link of New York City was the maker.

Linnel Brothers: Reference probably is to William & John Linnell, wood carvers, frame and furniture makers, London, England, from 1720s.

linset (linseat): A spinner's stool.

linsey-woolsey: (From *lysle-wulse.*) Cloth of wool and flax.

Linthorpe wares: Mid-19th-century ceramic wares noted for their special glaze, which produced accidental effects, never two precisely alike. Vases from the tiniest to huge size, trays, plaques, *tazze*, bottles, et cetera. Mark is LINTHORPE, alone, or on the outline of an urn.

linting bee: A frolic; a cotton-seeding party of days prior to the cotton gin.

Lion: Pattern of pressed glass featuring frosted lion finials, bases, and stems. It is quite late—from 1880s.

lion beam: The main beam of a ceiling.

lion coverlets: Probable reference is to pattern-woven coverlets of 1830s which display a poorly designed lion in two corners, with initials K or C VB. Said to be those of Katherine Van Buskirk.

lioness: A sportswoman.

lion passant: The mark often called leopard—this being the lion passant mark used as an English silver mark since 1544. The lion always faces to the left.

lipper: A dilating tool used by glassmakers to flare out a lip.

Lippiatt plate: Late 19th-century silver plate by a firm so named. Specialty was satin-finish ware.

liquid bread: Rich extract of malted grain; strong porter, or stout.

liquor chest: A cabinet for bottles of liquors or for cooling wines, et cetera. Generally in Hepplewhite, Directoire, or Sheraton style.

Lisbon ware: Portuguese majolica. Sold in Boston as early as 1650.

list: A frame, as for a picture. A "list" in cabinetmaking is a narrow strip. In weaving, it is the selvage of any cloth.

Li Tai Po: Chinese poet of the Tang Dynasty. There are representations of him on Chinese wares.

Litchfield ware: Any pottery made at Litchfield, Conn., from 1750s. Several potters, John Pierce, J. Wadham, and H. Brooks, were working, probable production being slip-decorated redwares.

lit de repos: A day bed; a sofa.

litharge: Red lead.

Lithodipyra: Classic name for stoneware used by the Misses Coade for the product of their pottery at Lambeth. One of the products were imitation carved stonework. Noted sculptors were employed, including J. Flaxman.

lithograph: Any print from the stone process discovered by Senefelder; actually a chemical offset technique requiring a porous stone as the carrier of the original design. See *America on Stone* and *Currier & Ives,* by Harry T. Peters. These books list processes, makers of American lithographs, and are lavishly illustrated.

lithographers, American: Harry T. Peters' *America on Stone* and *California on Stone* contain the most comprehensive biographical lists of lithographic firms and publishers ever compiled. Student is referred to these volumes and to others listed in the Bibliography.

Lithophane: Porcelain pane cast in wax molds, depicting scenes, portraits, and genre subjects with the soft quality of mezzotints when light is transmitted. The secret is depthing the mold to achieve perfect tonal quality by the passage of light. Made from 1830s; invented and developed in France, but also made in Germany, Austria, and, it is claimed, in the U.S. at the Majolica pottery, Phoenixville, Pa. There are records of many lamp shades, candlestands, historic panels, et cetera, made of lithophanes. Some are further embellished by transparent coloring.

lithophone: Faïence tile impressed with designs and fired with glaze having varying depths, forming a shadow picture. Not to be confused with lithophane.

Little, E. C.: Chair- and cabinetmaker of New York City working from 1840s.

Little Harry night lamp: A toy lamp, only 1½ inches high, but it worked. "One firefly power" was its light-giving factor.

little pot: A pint jug.

Little Rest silver: Any silver made at what is now Kingston, R.I., but which once rejoiced in the name of Little Rest. There were several producers of early Federal wares in this community in late 18th century, including one who turned counterfeiter, was condemned to death, escaped, and was never heard of again.

Little Scissors Pictorial: House organ or company publication of George E. Nesbitt & Co., lithographers and printers of

LIGHTING DEVICES & LAMPS: **Top row:** Early Chandelier, Oil Lamp, Astral Lamp, Moon or Punched-Tin Globe, Jamb Hook Betty in Candle-Socketed Holder. **2nd row:** Queen Anne Period Rushlight Holder, Standing or Hanging Candlestick, Street Lamps, Argand Lamp, Flat-Wick "Lighthouse" Lamp, Two-Wick, Tin Lamp. **3rd row:** Cone Lantern, Argand Lamp, "Gone-with-the-Wind" Lamps (3), dating from 1880s, Spirit Gas Lamp. **Bottom row:** Double Candlestick, Watchman's Lantern, Tin Lantern, Blown-Glass "Moon." (All from *New Geography of American Antiques* and *Pioneer America, Its First Three Centuries.*)

New York in 1850s. One issue contains a catalogue of the famed clipper-ship cards issued by this firm.

littmose: "A fair blew colour," says an early lexicographer. Probably litmus blue.

Liverpool lamp: Patented lamp with two flat wicks fitted in semicircular slots, forming a round burner. Made by Shelton Lamp Works, Liverpool, from c. 1810.

Liverpool ware: Any ceramic wares made at Liverpool, England, from 17th century, when the first potteries were established. Famed for its delft-type tin-glaze redware, its transfer-printed wares, char pots, mugs, dishes, labels, butter pots, bird cages, and many other items of fired clay. All important Liverpool potteries are listed individually in this volume.

livery: Originally a badge worn by gentlemen, but by 16th century the meaning changed to denote the uniform worn by menials, servants, and lackeys.

livery cupboard: Same as press cupboard, *which see.* An open, or partly open, stand of the Tudor period. An early comment on the piece reads, "in ye facyon of livery, yt be without doors." Said to have been a food-storage cupboard.

living vase: Vase form of terra cotta or china, covered with a flannel jacket, sowed with grass seeds, germinated in a dark room, and then left to grow. This conceit has its counterpart today. A late-19th-century variant was a sponge in a tumbler, sowed with flaxseed.

LL hinge: Cabinet hinges for small doors. Much used from 1750s to 1820s. [*Examples pictured.*]

Lloyd, William: Springfield, Mass., cabinetmaker, working from 1790s to 1820s in Hepplewhite, Directoire, Sheraton, and Empire styles; also made clock cases. Some labeled pieces survive. Died in 1845.

loaf sugar: Cone-shaped loaf of crystallized sugar. *See* Cone Sugar.

lobby chair: *See* Chairs, All Kinds.

lobby chest: The original term from which "lowboy" derives. A low chest, not over 36 inches wide and high, with two top drawers, side by side, and a tier of three drawers under, on a stand. Cabinetmakers' dictionary of 1803 defines lobby chest substantially as here.

loblolly: The field pine; the Gordonia pine. Same term was used for boiled oatmeal, "thick spoon meat."

lobscouse: Soup made of meat stock thickened with browned whole onions. Used as food for seamen to prevent scurvy. The French "turlutine" is substantially the same soup.

lobstock: Fat candles of Chinese origin, generally of white wax with a coating of color and a wick of cotton wound around a sliver of bamboo.

Lock, Matthias: London designer of furniture and elegancies who issued these books and manuals: *Drawing Book of Ornaments,* 1740; *Six Sconce Designs,* 1744; *Six Table Designs,* 1746; *A Book of Ornaments,* 1748; *A New Book of Ornaments,* 1752 and 1768; *A New Book of Pier Frames,* 1769.

Locke, Joseph: Patentee of the novelty glass called amberina.

Locke tinware: Made at New Orleans from 1850s by Samuel Locke and sold generally in the South.

lock horn: The canal navigator's horn of warning, sounded on approaching locks.

Lockport glass: Made at Lockport, N.Y., on Erie Canal; product including private mold bottles, table- and hollow ware, fruit jars, hyacinth vases, glass bells, et cetera, 1840s–70s. Various ownerships. Plant remained operative to 20th century.

Lockwood-Hannington mirrors: Firm so named established a factory at New York City c. 1810. Tabernacle, gilded, and carved mirrors. Eventually imported mirrors from France and Germany and became large wholesalers.

locofoco: (1) A strike-anywhere match, from *locus,* place, and *focus,* hearth. (2) A political party of the 1830s.

locomotive car: A combined steam-power plant and passenger coach, made from 1850s. Used on city street lines and on extended railways.

locomotive chair: *See* Chairs, All Kinds.

Lodi carpet: Ingrain carpets woven from 1830s at Lodi, N.J., by J. Cass, who also made carpet looms.

Logan, John: Plate of glass, memorial of Logan, vice-presidential running mate of James G. Blaine, made 1884 by Gillinder of Philadelphia. A portrait plate of political character.

Loganberry & Grape: Pattern of pressed glass featuring sprigs of berry clusters and fragments of vine with grapes.

Logan pottery: Cream-glazed wares, some with clumsy molded decoration in the Leeds tradition. Made at Logan, O., 19th century. Most pieces marked in color through a stencil before firing.

Log Cabin: Pattern of pressed glass in which the hollow ware is in the shape and form of a log cabin, frosted.

log-cabin bottle: There are several types, perhaps the most famous being those in memory of Tippecanoe and North Bend; political bottles of log-cabin shape, made by Mount Vernon Glass Works. The E. G. Booz "Old Cabin" whiskey bottle is cabin-shaped, as is the Jacob's Cabin Tonic bottle. These were made by Whitney Glass Works. There are modern reproductions which should give most collectors pause in purchase of any cabin-form glass bottles.

loggerhead: A lozenge of iron on a rod, with either decorative or utilitarian handle, used to heat a drink by plunging the hot iron into the liquid. Some loggerheads have a stone heating element.

log house; log cabin: *Danckaerts Journal,* 1679, gives a clue to the introduction of the log house, blockhouse, and log cabin to the American colonies. The Swedes, either direct, through Dutch settlers, or by representation in ship companies, introduced the log construction. A revival occurred after the Revolution, when border pioneers and newly arrived immigrants resorted to log construction to provide cheap, good houses constructed from readily available materials. Student is referred to *The Log Cabin Myth,* by Shurtleff.

log on frame: A type of construction of French origin, involving a structure of framed timbering covered with hewn logs. This type was original with the Mississippi Valley. Most restorations and rebuilding of structures originally of this type are now made as log type and are historically incorrect.

logrolling: Co-operative, neighborhood clearing of land for a settlement or farm. Later, political chicanery.

logwood: The imported dyewood which yielded blue, violet, and black dye.

lohan: Of or pertaining to the sages and scholars devoted to Buddha.

Lollards: Followers of John Wycliffe, the first Protestant reformer, who died in 1384. The French reformers, the Moravian Huss, and the German priest, Martin Luther, were followers of this man's basic ideas. The term Lollard was derisive and applied to all followers of Wycliffe, whether preachers or converts.

lollipot: A sweetmeat. Origin of lollipop.

London pewter: Reference is to the imports, from 17th century, cried or advertised, by inference, to be better than local wares. Any English pewter was once called "London" in the colonies.

London Pottery: A works at Lambeth, established in 1750s, which made delft-type wares, brown salt glaze, white stoneware, and cream- and tan wares. After 1860 the pottery specialized in water filters.

Long, William: Wood carver, toymaker, and cabinetmaker of Philadelphia from 1780s.

long-barrel bottle: Bourbon whiskey bitters bottle in the form of a long barrel or cask.

long-barrel rifle: Reference is to the American rifle developed in the Conestoga Valley of Pennsylvania by French, Dutch, and Swiss gunsmiths who taught many others, including English gunsmiths, the art of snailing, or rifling, a gun barrel. Many of these gunsmiths, from 1750s, bought servants from the Palatine, taught them the art, and these Germans, after seven years of service to pay their passage money, became proficient gunsmiths and added to the production of the precision rifle that aided materially in winning the Revolution.

long bellows: Long-handled hearth bellows. [*Example pictured.*]

longbow: Military and hunting weapon used prior to the advent of firearms. The American Indians' best bows were fashioned from the wood of the Osage orange. The French called forests of this bow wood *bois arcs*. We retain the name for one such wooded section, the Ozarks. English bows were of hazel, hawthorn, or yew wood. All bows were made from billets split, not cut, from the wood.

long bullets: A game of tossing small cannon balls. The balls weighed from one to ten pounds.

long clock: A tall case clock.

long cradle: A cradle balanced on rockers parallel to its sides, not at right angles.

longipes: A berry of ovoid shape tasting like a super-cherry. A native of the Orient, introduced by Charles A. Dana of the N.Y. *Sun.* Proper name is *Elaeagnus longipes.*

long lady: A tall candle.

Longport: *See* Davenport.

long-sup: A sling.

long-tail sugar: Ship's molasses.

Longton: A region of England famed for its potteries (Jewett lists at least a dozen), all of which shipped goods to America.

Longton Hall: A porcelain-type ware made from 1750 to 1758 at this place, in England.

looking-glass clock: (1) Clock dial and movement set in the upper panel of a wall mirror. (2) Clock for mantel use, having a mirror in lower door panel.

loom basket: Properly a shuttle basket. Term often used to designate any basket used in weaving, spinning, knitting, or even sewing.

Loop: A pattern of pressed glass similar to Ashburton, *which see.*

Loop & Block: Pattern of pressed glass featuring colored diamond blocks, drapery, and balls. Loop & Dart, Loop with Diamond, Loop with Round, Loop and Dewdrop, Loop Drag, Loop with Jewel, Loop and Fan, and other loop patterns are mentioned in the various books of Ruth Webb Lee. All are Loop variants.

loop handle: Carved pearwood handle fitted in anchoring cups, on hollow wares of silver, Sheffield, copper, and pewter, especially coffee- and teapots.

loopuijts: A special Dutch "Hollands gin."

loosdrecht: Dutch porcelain made from 18th century.

loose-bodied gown: A loose gown as the only covering of a body.

loo table: Round table for playing cards. 19th century. [*Example pictured.*]

lop fence: A sort of hedge fence, grown from saplings trained to form both posts and rails.

lord's rocker: *See* Chairs, All Kinds.

Lord Ward bottle: The true early bottle for the sauce called Worcestershire, as originated by Lord Ward.

Lorenz glass: Pittsburgh glass made by Frederick Lorenz, who, having learned glassmaking at the O'Hara works, became owner of that and other plants.

lorimer: A maker of spurs.

Loring Ward Co.: Furniture makers of New York in 1840s.

l'Orme, Philibert: 17th-century French designer.

losset: Woodenware; a trencher.

lotus ware: The KTK ware by Knowles, Taylor & Knowles, made at East Liverpool, O., from 1870s. Named lotus because it resembles the bloom of that lily.

Louis Philippe: The royal restoration furniture period of France, from 1830. We miscall it "Victorian."

Louis Trieze, Quatorze, Quinze, Seize: Reference to reigns or periods of Louis XIII, 1610–43; Louis XIV, 1643–1715; Louis XV, 1715–74; Louis XVI, 1774–93, et cetera.

Louis XIV Cut: A pattern of cut glass that is a classic but erroneous representation of a compass card, with fleurs-de-lis and ten-pointed star.

Louisville furniture: Louisville, Ky., made furniture from the founding of the community. The 1844 directory lists 37 cabinetmakers.

Louisville glass: Wares made at the Kentucky Glass Works at this city from 1850. Small violin flasks, private mold-marked and other bottles, flasks, and utility wares.

lounging chair: *See* Chairs, All Kinds.

loutrophoros: Bath-water jar of ancient Greece.

love knot: Double bowknot, or knot of crossed loops. Any secure knot, used decoratively.

love-letter ink: Disappearing ink; it faded within a few weeks. A conceit of the 1840s.

lovers' chair: Actually a settee for two people.

lowboy: From lobby and lobby chest. A low chest of drawers on high legs; also the lower half of a highboy or tall boy. Various period styles, from William & Mary through the Georgian period to Chippendale. [*Example pictured.*]

low case of drawers: The 18th-century term for what we call a bureau. A case of three or more drawers. Not a lowboy.

low comb-back: *See* Chairs, All Kinds.

Lowden porcelain: Ware from the works which preceded the Worcester, England, porcelain pottery.

low-down grate: A Dixon grate, made by Dixon of Philadelphia from 1850s.

Lowestoft: Village in East Anglia where delftwares and some imitative porcelains were made from 1760s. Mostly carnival ware or souvenir goods; some imitative examples show purely local or regional personal names, et cetera. Another ware is given this name by virtue of a great error, still persisted in by many, of calling the trade porcelains of Nanking, Canton, and other treaty and factors' ports of China "Lowestoft," which it is not. Certain self-professed guides to collecting taste have of recent years taken sides in this naming controversy and have caused hybrid names, such as "oriental Lowestoft," "oriental export porcelain," and other terms. The true collectors of the 1870s arrived at the conclusion that what they had been calling Lowestoft was, in fact, cheap Chinese porcelain. The bulk of what has been called Lowestoft was imported from 1790s to 1890s. Some so-called "historic" Lowestoft, with scenes of American importance, were made in China within the past 60 or more years for missionaries who, when disposing of their China-made ware, realized fantastic prices for it. There is even a hush-hush trade in redecorating sparsely decorated examples with coats of arms, initials, et cetera, of a wealthy and likely customer. Such "sets" are often sold from a "sample" piece.

Lowestoft true: Actual ware made at Lowestoft, England. [*Example pictured.*]

low lamp: A bedchamber oil lamp, generally compactly made and not high-standing. Term was much used in early 19th century.

low poster: A bed with four low, rather than high, posts.

Lozenge: An early cut-glass pattern featuring a series of deep cuts at angles, to form groups of four faceted lozenges. Erroneously called Large Diamond.

lucarne: A dormer window or a skylight.

Lucca ware: Plaster ware; the ware generally miscalled chalk ware. Lucca, Italy, a center of plaster-image making, trained hundreds of men in the art who migrated to U.S. These Lucchese immigrants were to be found making plaster ware in every city of importance from 1830s.

lucerne: A rich clover seed.

lucifer: A strike-anywhere match. Slow to ignite, they released a pungent, sulphurous odor. Also called hell-sticks. The true lucifers were not rigid stick matches but flexible flat shavings impregnated with sulphur and tipped with antimony and potash. They were ignited by pulling through a fold of sandpaper.

Lucky oil: Bleached sperm oil. The preparer was named J. L. Lucky.

Ludlow glass: Product of the Ludlow (Mass.) Manufacturing Co. from 1810s. Traditionally bottles were produced.

Ludlow toys: Children's wheeled toys, such as express wagons, baby carts, barrows, et cetera, made from 1870s at Ludlow, Vt.

ludoscope: A type of zoetrope (*which see*) providing direct vision through a scanning disk.

luffered: Boarded, as a louver; a series of slats set at an angle within stiles, to permit air circulation, and arranged to permit closing when desired. Louvered; jalousied.

lug handles: Projecting knobs, or bosses, on various wares of glass, pottery, and metal, to which cords or thongs were tied to form a carrying loop.

Lukens, T.: Quaker cabinetmaker of Pittsburgh who worked from 1790s. The history of this man has been researched to the point of indicating production of Hepplewhite- and Directoire-styled furniture, and fancy chairs.

lukes: Velvet cloth.

Lukey silver: Product of an American *lady* silversmith working in Pittsburgh from 1830s; her shop was located on Fifth Street, between Wood and Market.

lune stick: Calendar of moon phases, engraved on a rod or baton.

Lupton, William: A cabinetmaker of Charleston, S.C., working from 1740s. Georgian styling would be indicated.

lure: A face.

Luristan bronze: Bronze of 1st and 2nd centuries B.C. found in the Luristan district of Persia. Student is referred to *The Luristan Bronzes*, by Phyllis Ackerman.

luster dish: Not an item of lusterware, but a cast-iron bowl with a handle and a shallow trough, used as a container for stove luster, a polish of lampblack, graphite, and resin. The bowls survive in various shapes; production seems to have started in 1830s and continued to 1870s.

lustered glass: Glass stained with oxide coloring of thin quality, fired on.

luster painting: Prismatic painting.

lusters: Chandeliers of glass, hung low to

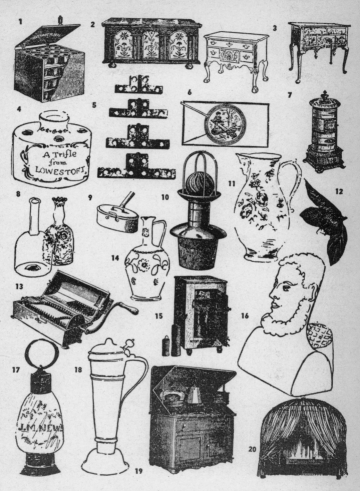

1, Lancaster Butter Box. **2,** Lancaster Chest. **3,** Lowboys (2). **4,** Lowestoft. **5,** LL Hinges. **6,** Lever Slide. **7,** Madeira Stove. **8,** Mallet-Shape Bottle and Vase. **9,** Mackerel Kettle. **10,** Marbled Cork. **11,** Mask-Spout Jug. **12,** Medlar, Fruit and Leaf. **13,** Meat Cutter. **14,** Minorcan Jug. **15,** Milk Cooler. **16,** Mirror Rest. **17,** Name Lantern. **18,** Mortar Jug. **19,** Musgrave Stove. **20,** Mosquito Bar, or "Kitty Fisher." (No. 2 from Wallace Nutting.)

give maximum light. Temporarily out of fashion during the era of high headdresses, as they ignited so many creations of this nature. Lusters was also the name given to glass pendants and prisms, some of which were silvered.

lusterware: Originating in either China or Persia, the first luster was imitative of jade, ruby, and other precious stones. The techniques of lustering were improved by adding metallic oxides and so were imitative of metals. Italian and Moorish potters seem to have had knowledge of the processes by 14th century. The lusterwares of general antiques trading and collecting are the wares made from early 19th century by various English potters, of whom some twenty or more were in active production. Only two metallic oxides were used, gold and platinum. Platinum was used for the silver luster. Gold produced all other metallic effects from deep bronze to pale copper, the pink, the moonglow, mottled Sunderland, deep purple, et cetera. The lusters here considered are of coarse coatings or glaze stains of opaque quality on redwares, pottery, and various other chinas of England. Continental European lusterwares of late 19th century were sold generally by stores and shops to 1900.

lustrage: The gum finish on silk, originating at Lyons, France, from 1650s.

Lustral Ware: Trade name of wirework by Woods, Sherwood & Co. of Lowell, Mass., from mid-19th century. Breadbaskets, stands, toasters, racks, caster frames, et cetera. Wire was plated with a white metal which did not oxidize.

lute: A cement or glue, popular in 18th century. Herewith one "secret recipe" for its making: Dissolve gum arabic in "chamber lye" over a chafing dish, mix with flour, and cook for a quarter hour, or until it becomes a jelly-like paste.

lute: A stringed instrument of great antiquity; ancestor of all plucked string instruments. **lutestring:** A string for a lute; also a fine fabric named for lutestrings. A thin silk.

Luther, William: One of the Salem, Mass., cabinetmakers in the Sanderson Furniture selling cartel. *See* Sanderson.

Lutheran Church: This church was planted in the American colonies by the Swedes who embraced Luther's doctrine and made it the state church of Sweden long before similar action by the various Germanic principalities. The legend that Muhlenberg, the German Lutheran minister, founded the Lutheran Church in America is sheer nonsense. The Swedes had Lutheran churches in what is now Pennsylvania and Delaware by 1640s. The Swedes also supplied a Swedish minister for the first Lutheran church at Lancaster, Pa., Old Trinity. His name was Nyberg. He later became a Moravian.

Lutz, Nicholas: Glassblower of Sandwich plant who made thread-twist and other fine artistic wares. Lutz came from Lorraine, France, and was a graduate of the St. Louis factory. He worked also for Dorflinger and the Mount Washington Works. His was the Venetian technique. At one time the work of Lutz was attributed to specific plants, but this is now regarded as an uncertain attribution; the glass is Lutz type, no matter whether made by him at Dorflinger's works, Mount Washington, Boston, or Sandwich. He made cane and threaded wares, paperweights, and other elegancies, and was an inspiration to his employers.

luzerne: The cloverlike legume now called alfalfa, from the Arabic, *Al-Facfaca.*

lye leach: Any device for leaching lye from wood ashes, the leaching being drenching with water and the filtration thereof through the ashes, carrying the strong alkali with it. There are quite small kitchen lye leaches which provided a means of getting fresh lye in a few moments from hearth ashes, and there are hogshead-sized leaches for an annual or semi-annual leaching to provide gallons of lye. The small devices were sometimes called "lye drops."

Lyell, Fenwick: Back-country cabinetmaker of New Jersey, working from 1780s at or near the Butswamp region. A linen press by him was sold at auction in 1945 for $700.

Lyon, Dr. Irving W.: Author of *Colonial Furniture in America,* the first book on American antiques, published 1891. His grandson is now proprietor of the antiques business founded by Dr. Lyon's son, C. W. Lyon.

Lyon, W. C.: Cabinetmaker of New York who persisted in the custom tradition as late as 1850s. It is said his pieces included objects that are today credited or attributed to Phyfe.

Lyon & Maginnes: Cabinetmakers of Ohio, "11 miles from this place [Cincinnati] on the Hamilton Road," working in 1800, when they advertised "escritoires and dining tables, plain and veneered."

Lyon glass: Pressed glass that Deming Jarves admitted was the best in America, made by Lyon & Co., Pittsburgh, successors of the O'Hara works.

lyre-back: Any seat furniture having back displaying a lyre form as a major feature. This element was introduced by the Brothers Adam c. 1750.

lyre bed: Iron bed displaying lyre-form castings in head and foot sections.

lyre clock: Lyre-form casing, related to the banjo form in that the general shape is in the banjo tradition. The sides of the throat are curvate, and there are generally brass rods imitative of lyre strings. Both wall and shelf examples were made.

lyre form: Any element imitative of the shape of a lyre.

lyre-gate table: Table with narrow top supported by lyre-form end and having very deep drop leaves on gate supports. A dining table folding down to a very small unit.

lyre sofa: Scroll-curved-end sofa. More particularly a sofa with end arms having lyre panels.

lyre stove: Cast-iron decorative parlor stove with an open lyre-form pair of S's rising from firebox to smoke chamber, the firebox proper having doors to expose or enclose the fire. Date is from 1830s and made to 1870s.

M

macaron; macaroon: Diminutive of marchpane; an almond-meal biscuit.

macaroni: A fop, addicted to exaggerated fancy dress or uniform.

macassa; macassar: Striped wood, sometimes called zebra wood.

Macauley carpet: A painted floor cloth made from 1830s in various patterns by Isaac Macauley of Philadelphia.

Macbeth Cut: Cut-glass pattern patented 1890, featuring repetitive cuts fanning outward from a central star. Found on flat dishes and bowls. Some commentators call this a rare pattern. It might be well to consider this fact: any pattern of any kind of the 1890s that is now "rare" is in that category only because the pattern was not accepted and did not sell even in the era of poor public taste that was the 1890s. It is always wise to know a thing is rare; it is wiser still to know *why* it is rare.

mace: Pickled and/or sun-dried membrane of the envelope of the nutmeg.

MacFerran bed: An iron bed of any style cast at the MacFerran foundry, Philadelphia, from 1830s. This foundry also cast many iron deer, lions, dogs, eagles, and other ornaments for lawns and building decoration.

machine chair: An invalid's chair on rollers; properly an item of interest to doctors, nurses, et cetera. Not mentioned in chair section.

mackerel kettle: Properly a fish kettle; an oval saucepan for stewing any fish. Known in copper, tin, and iron. [*Example pictured.*]

Maddock, T. & Son: Potters of Trenton, N.J., and publishers of an excellent book on American potters and marks.

macrame: Knotted work; a fringe or tape.

Madeira stove: A round space heater of decorative type, dating from 1840s. [*Example pictured.*]

Madeira wood: Swamp wood of cedar or mahogany genre found in Florida and Louisiana and used from 1780s as a cabinet wood. Sometimes spelled Maderah, Madra, et cetera. Also canary wood.

madia: A bread case; a pannetierre, *which see.*

madura: (1) High-tin-content pewter. (2) A shade of tobacco leaf after curing.

madwort: The alyssum plant.

maeser: Dutch term for knotty wood; hence "mazer" for a burl bowl.

Magasin Japannaise: An early antiques and curio shop of New York, owned and operated by A. H. Pakker of Amsterdam from 1840s. Paintings, lacquers, porcelains, and antique furniture, some 300 years old.

magazine pistol: Pistol invented by Orville Percival of Connecticut, 1840s. It had a powder magazine and a ball magazine. Twisting and manipulating loaded the hand gun.

magenta: Aniline red.

magical hodgepodge: A fascinating toy of 18th century, duplicated in U.S. to 1820s. It is a picture book of various subjects, the page margins having variations imperceptible to the eye. When the pages are flipped, pictures of one category only show up. Change of holding position causes other pictures to show. Originally called Ambigue Magique.

magic gold: If you care to make it, here's how (recipe not tested by the author). Dissolve gold in aqua regia and let it crystallize. Next dissolve crystals in vinegar. Let crystallize, remove, and dissolve in rain water. Crystallize again and grind to impalpable powder. Put in a hard-boiled egg from which yolk has been removed. Let stand until a "water of gold" or "oil of gold" forms. Paint any silver with this oil and it turns golden.

magic inkstand: Inkwell charged with a lozenge of ink concentrate. Repeated fillings with water created ink. London imports of this novelty continued for many years in mid-19th century.

magic metal: Mercury or quicksilver. It actually "melts" at 36° F. below zero. It is a solid metal at 38°. At 80° below it can be wrought like iron. Plates and other objects hammered from the metal while solid melt as if by magic at 36°. Magicians can make coins that turn to liquid in your hand, but they need dry ice for the trick.

magic mirror: Highly polished metal mirror with embossed back. The back embossing, while not perceptible to the eye in viewing the polished side, none the less sufficiently influences the other side to cause reflection of any bright light from the mirror to take the form of the back embossment. Chinese and quite early.

magic table: Gadget furniture of 1840s. This table was convertible to a bedstead, settee, or sofa, with a built-in musical instrument. A few were made by P. M. Droyer of New York City c. 1850s.

magnesium lamp: Brilliant lamp feeding a ribbon of magnesium through a slot over a flame of a spirit lamp. 1850s.

Magnet & Grape: Pattern of pressed glass featuring what are supposed (we presume) to be magnet-shaped panels in which a grape leaf is displayed upright and a bunch of grapes pendent. Varieties are according to finish of the leaf, frosted or stippled.

magnetic belts, chains, etc.: Electrical hocus-pocus of quack medicine; chains of copper and zinc links, encased or exposed, worn for cure of any- and everything. The types known by this name were made at Jefferson, Wis., from 1840s.

Magnin-Guedin music box: Swiss prick-roller and comb-type music boxes were made by a firm of this name having a store in New York City in mid-18th century.

magniscope: Early home moving-picture machine. Made from c. 1896.

magnum candle: A large Palmer candle with coiled double wick. One yielded sufficient light for a large room. Used in a special lamp which pushed the candle upward through a tube as it was consumed.

magnum decanter: Any extra-large decanter or wine bottle.

mahanamala: A garland of jewelry. Some think the term is Hawaiian, others that it is East Indian. Take your choice.

mahoganize: To make a surface finish imitative of genuine mahogany. Most attempts are imitative of old, not new, mahogany, which is quite pale. Wood surfaces were treated with acid, then varnished with dragon's-blood shellac, stone-rubbed, and varnished again.

mahogany: (1) West Indian and American wood of rosy tint, heavy, and fine-grained, known from 17th century and used as a cabinet wood from c. 1690s. Height of popularity was reached c. 1740s and maintained from thence onward. (2) A drink made of two parts gin and one part molasses.

mahogany-armed: Any settee or item of seat furniture of any wood other than mahogany, but having arms of the rare wood. Much painted seat furniture, including Windsor chairs, showed wear first on the arms. The finest examples of such were fitted with unpainted mahogany arms. Some Windsor chairs had mahogany seats.

maid: The iron frame of a back stone; an item of hearth furniture.

maiden-head spoons: Silver spoons of 17th century having stick stems topped with the bust of a woman—originally, it is said, a portrait bust of the virgin Queen Elizabeth. Reproductions were made in smaller size in 19th century. Originals are 7 to 9 inches long. Examples known in pewter and in brass. Some experts assert it is the "Virgin" spoon of the Apostle spoon sets.

maiden's blush: Pressed glass imitative of cutting with bosslike pendants. The name derives from a flashing of pink color between the pendants and over the entire lower area of the hollow-ware pieces. It is quite late—some made in 20th century.

Maid-of-the-Mist cup plate: Butter chip or cup plate having what has been called the suspension bridge at Niagara with a steamer under it presumed to be the *Maid of the Mist.*

mailbox bottle: Novelty bottle in form of a mailbox of the 1890s, with a long neck.

Maine: Pattern of pressed glass with floral panels, said to have been issued plain or in colors, and with fanned flutes, upright T-headed panels of balls, and other features.

main line: An established mail route.

maize glass: Art glass by Libby Co.; pressed glass in form of maize ear (corn ear), probably dating from 1890s and appealing to the great corn states.

majolica: Glazed redware imitative of porcelain, the glaze being stanniferous—that is, containing tin as an oxide. There are some people who resent any definition of majolica, faïence, or delft (all the same basic wares) as "imitative of porcelain," but resentful or not, such is the case, and without decrying majolica one bit. This ware, because of the attempt, developed into an excellent thing in itself. The majolica plaques by Della Robbia are unequaled in terms of beauty and have no counterpart in china. Majolica wares were of three classes: fine, general, and cheap. We should not judge the entire production by study of any one. Majolica was made in U.S. in Pennsylvania and Maryland and perhaps at several other locales. *See* Delft and Faience.

majolica, Italian: The original early potteries of Italy which produced fine majolica were Gubbio, Urbine, Castel-Durante, Faenza (from which the term faïence for the same ware derives), Forli, Deruta, Caffaggiolo, Venice, and Castelli.

makke: Minced bones and onions marinated in wine and fried in oil, as a sauce.

malachite: Soft green mineral of semi-precious quality.

Malaga glass: Reference is to Malaga, N.J., site of the Franklin Glass Works, established 1810. Bottles, flasks, and hollow wares.

Malbro' leg: Heavy turned and reeded leg, dating from c. 1810. The term as here given is correct. It is a contraction of Marlborough, but in no way does this leg approach the true Marlborough leg of 18th century. [*Example of Malbro' leg pictured.*]

malefactors' cage: A cage of iron bars, cramped as to space, in which culprits were confined and exposed to public view. The original hoosegow. 18th century and earlier.

Mallard, P.: Cabinetmaker of New Orleans from 1830s. Said to have worked in Louis XV revival styles. Prudent Mallard finally established a furniture factory in this famous city for the production of French Antique furniture made in the grand manner, to 1860, for Southern planters and city tycoons.

malle-molli: Muslin from Bengal, India.

mallet shape: Said of bottles of glass or pottery and of any vessel of any material when formed in shape of a mason's maul or mallet. [*Examples pictured.*]

maltha: Mineral pitch; asphaltum.

mämm: Quick beer, made of sugar, a double jigger or dram of rum, and water. Swedish, dating from 1640s in America.

mammoth: (1) The beast called the elephant. (2) Any great object. (3) Any large object of advertising usage, as "the mammoth knife of Cincinnati."

mammy chair: Actually a bench on rockers with a cradle compartment in the form of removable fencing at one end.

Manchester toys: Tin toys, toy furniture, tin bank clocks, and other juvenile novelties made at Pawtucket, R.I., from 1860s by Cyril Manchester. For the benefit of unconvinced skeptics, these dates are verified by advertisements of record and by mention in *New England Business Directory* of 1867.

manchet: A loaf of fine white bread, made small, as a roll.

Mandan corn: A native American maize found growing in profusion west of the Mississippi and cultivated by Indians. Named for Mandan in Missouri Territory.

mandarin chair: *See* Chairs, All Kinds.

mandeglore: The mandrake.

mandoline: Originally a mechanical music box.

mandorla: A decorative form; an oval pointed at both ends.

mangel-wunzel: A huge turnip, often raised for cattle fodder.

mangle board: A flat board with handhold, often beautifully carved in some popular pattern or form, used in flattening and squeezing wet laundry. Also any wringing or twisting machine for more effective mangling. Most true mangle boards in America were of Swedish, Dutch, Swiss, or French origin or tradition.

Manhattan chair: *See* Chairs, All Kinds.

Manila shawl: A shawl of Canton, China, not the Philippines; embroidered silk with floral and fruited borders and a central pattern somewhat reminiscent of the design on so-called willow ware.

Manning furniture: There are several cabinetmakers and manufacturers of record having the name Manning; oldest of our 19th-century records is Isaac Manning of New Brunswick, N.J., working from 1840s.

Mann pottery: Most likely reference is to wares made by Jairus Mann, West Amesbury, Mass., from mid-19th century.

manomin: Native wild rice.

manrope: The rope railing of a closed stair, or as an extra railing for the closed side of an open stairway. Also used on ship's ladders.

Mansfield (O.) furniture: Any cabinetwork produced by the several early-to-mid-19th-century workmen of this Ohio community. Schroers, Grove, Heldman, Beard, and Niman are names our researchers have reported. Since few other towns in the U.S. are mentioned in this volume in terms of artisans, it should be noted that records of early workers in any craft, in any community, are usually found in tax rolls and other county courthouse records and in directories. Such research is properly the task of students seeking specific information of this kind.

mansion-house dwarf: Staffordshire figurines of merry little men. Imitative of dwarfs in livery, a favorite 18th-century occupation and craze; any dwarf could have a sinecure if he would go into livery for a lord or lady. Negro dwarfs were especially desirable as messengers.

manteltree: Actually a drying rack standing or swinging out from wall and having branches; most examples used before a fireplace. Also the beam over the chimney upon which the breast rested. Finally, the mantel proper. Manteltree sets were garnitures of delftware, porcelain, plate, et cetera, consisting of from three to five pieces; vases, pots, and jars. Manteltree mirrors, or mantel mirrors, designated any mirror designed specifically for use on a chimney breast. These are generally two or three times as wide as they are high. Known in all period styles, but most general in the heavy turned section, carved, and gilded frames of Empire style.

Mantoon: A large robe; a cover-all.

man trap: Huge spring traps set to catch poachers. Made for and used by the privileged landowners of Europe from 15th century. A single poacher could not escape from one but could be released by a fellow poacher.

Mantua glass: Made at Mantua, O., by David Ladd from Connecticut at his glassworks, established 1821 and in operation from 1822. By 1823 he had established another glasshouse at what is now Kent, O. Flasks, blown wares of considerable collector's interest, window glass, bowls, et cetera. There are extensive notices of this glass in *American Glass*, by George S. McKearin.

manumotive car: A carriage propelled by gears and levers, by hand action of the occupant.

Manwaring chairs: *See* Chairs, All Kinds.

Manx chair: *See* Chairs, All Kinds.

many-face doll: Doll head molded with two or three faces. The head was mounted to rotate and display a desired face within a frame of bonnet or hood.

map horn: (1) A powder horn scrimshawed with map of a region. (2) Horn case for charts.

Maple Leaf: Pattern of pressed glass featuring a rim of frosted grape leaves. Why it is called Maple Leaf is just another of the mysteries of pressed-glass pattern names and naming.

maple-matted: Term is found used in connection with chair seats and is presumed to mean bark fiber or split withes of maple wood, woven green into a chair bottom.

map sampler: A needle-worked sampler with a map as part of the decorative scheme. Maps on samplers are usually in outline.

maquette: A room in miniature, generally in a glass case, with furniture and fitments. A play toy for grownups.

marble: A kind of glass, also called onyx, slag, and agate; it is imitative of marble veining and structure, in colors and with milk-white, cream, and pale tinted base mixtures, blown and pressed. A play-toy ball.

marbled cork: A liquor-bottle cork with a glass agate marble in a dome of wire. Tilting bottle caused marble to leave its center and permit pouring of liquid; restored to upright position, the marble again covered the pouring vent. [*Example pictured.*]

marbled mirror: The Bilbao mirror, the frame made up of thin veneer of marble.

marble-slab table: True sideboard table, the marble slab used as top being stainproof, cool, heatproof, and a good carving base. Marble tops for tables of all sorts, but especially those used in service of beverages and foods, were in general use by 1710s. Such a top, in almost every case, is a badge of fine quality. Slate was the topping on the tables of the middle class. It is asserted that marble-top tables were used in the colonies as early as 1700. Style revived c. 1835, when the new French Antique revival furniture now called Victorian was a luxury. Marble tops were placed on library tables, flower stands, sewing tables, and bedroom pieces. Some of the latter were marble-lined.

marbleized: Made to appear imitative of marble, as stained paper, cloth, spotting and painting on walls and floors, and painting on iron and slate mantels.

marble soap: Reference is not to appearance of the soap, but to a "soap" used to clean marble. It was a paste of lye and whiting, laid on marble and left on for a few hours, then washed off with clear water.

marche pied: A footstool. In 1870s Walter Duryea invented an elegancy he called a *marche-pied crachoir*, meaning a footstool containing a spittoon.

marchpane (marzipan, messepain, marci-panis): A sweetmeat made from almond meal and honey, molded in wood forms, and often decorated with vegetable colors. Many are of ceremonial nature and quite large. Molds as early as 16th century are known; a dated example of 1563 is in the writer's collection. Nuts other than almonds, as kernels of apricot pits, filberts, hedge nuts, et cetera, were used.

Marcolini: A period of production at the Dresden or Meissen works, 1780s-1800s. Count Marcolini actually directed the works from 1774 to 1814. Mark is a star between the crossed swords, and sometimes the figure 4.

Marden shades: Fancy painted and gilded window shades or blinds made by George Marden of Boston from mid-19th century.

mare's nest: Tiresome repetition of an old tale.

margarine: Originally a butter substitute made from olive oil; a vegetable butter made by M. Mauries, Paris, c. 1860.

Marieberg: Swedish porcelain made from 1750s.

marine glue: Crude rubber, naphtha, and shellac, first combined by M. Jeffery, 1842, and used extensively in cabinetwork and the arts as well as boatbuilding.

Mariolatry: Literally, idolatry of the Virgin Mary.

marked pontil: The pontil mark, so called, is the point of pontil-rod detachment on blown glassware, generally a fracture within a dimple or a protuberance. In order to eliminate the sharp fracture but not the thickening, some glass blowers impressed a star or circle over the fracture. This is a rarely noted occurrence. However, some Irish and English glass blowers affixed the name or initial stamp of the factory on the large pontil in the center of a crown of window glass, the "bull's-eye."

Marks, Davis: A cabinetmaker of Cleveland, O., working in 1830s. Nothing is certain as to his style, but it was probably early Empire and late Directoire.

Marlborough leg: Name given by some commentators to the square leg adapted by Chippendale from the Chinese. Not to be confused with Malbro', *which see*. The name derives from a drawing made by an

apprentice and designating a square legged chair as Marlborough.

marly: A flat edge or rim of a dish.

Marot, Daniel: French cabinetmaker who worked in the Netherlands and in England. His style was that of the Louis XI period, pictured in a design book issued by him in 18th century. Marot worked as an architect and designer at the court of William & Mary and was a successful blender of the Baroque with the Chinese styles imported by the Dutch.

marquetry: Ornamental inlay; wood on wood. Design may be geometrical, floral, scenic, et cetera, in vari-colored woods. A form of intarsia. Marquetry is an extensive sheet or area of work. Inlay is generally the letting of a colored band into a gouged line or groove.

marquise: A love seat, generally upholstered. A double-width chair. Made from 1680s in all period styles. The same wide type chair is noted in Gallic or Gothic period as a throne or seat of state, generally with cushions. The same term is applied to ornamental hoods over doors and to valances. When the usage is not clear it is sometimes assumed that marquise (as a hood) refers to outside or exposed usage, while valance applies to indoor usage.

marquise d'alcove: A corner chair for two, upholstered. A corner sofa. Style is usually Louis XV.

Marquisette: Pattern of pressed glass featuring arched panels of meshed stipple.

marriage coffer: Dowry (not dower) chest of oak, often with linen-fold carved panels. Date is from 16th century; none of American colonial construction. Flemish, Swiss, French, Dutch, English, and Swedish. The latter examples may be of pine or other coniferous wood.

married-off: Said of assemblies of elements, as of stands, chests, et cetera, not originally paired, but brought together by dealers or collectors. A form of faking that may be unintentional deceit. Some early collectors assembled such pieces in the belief the practice was legitimate. Certainly it has the benefit of tradition. If any early owner put two pieces together to create one, as a small chest on a larger one to make a high chest, and the piece has survived, chances are it is accepted today as genuine by some collector or dealer.

Marseilles: Pertaining to the French city, of the same name; carpets, embroidery, and other objects, including faience ware made from 1700s by several potteries.

Marshallville glass: Hollow wares and window glass from the Cumberland Glass Works, Marshallville, Md., made from 1810s.

marsh sled: A drag on broad ski runners used in transporting goods and cropping salt hay from marshes and fens.

marten pole: Stripped high tree with top branches intact, hung with holed gourd to provide nesting for martens.

Martha Gunn jug: Ralph Wood "Toby" figural jug in the form or caricature of Martha Gunn, bath-woman of Brighton who dipped George IV as a babe in his first sea bath.

Martha Washington: The widow who became George Washington's bride and our first "first lady." Many objects are rightly or wrongly named for her. *See* Chairs, All Kinds, for one of the correct namings. **Martha Washington plate:** Canton-ware plate with chain of state labels and a center circle bearing initials MW. Made for Martha in 1793. **Martha Washington sewing table:** Sheraton-type worktable with flap-lidded side pockets, drawers, and reeded legs.

martial ball: A tonic ball of iron filings and cream of tartar. Dropping a ball in a tub of water caused the acid to attack the iron and produce "chalybeate water," or iron water approximating that of various tonic springs.

Martin's Ferry glass: Reference is to Martin's Ferry, Va., glass made from c. 1850s. Bottles and pressed wares. This place was in West Virginia after the partition of the state.

Martin's ring: A finger ring of gilt latten, or gilded copper, imitating gold. Bracelets were also made of this cheap metal.

marver: Polished stone or metal slab on a frame. Used in the arts and especially in glassmaking.

Maryland: Pattern of pressed glass featuring down-pointed oval panels with fans under the panels.

Maryland Pottery: Recommended to some earnest student as a brochure subject. This pottery, established 1815 at East Baltimore by David Parr, shipped goods by water to all ports in the Chesapeake and as far south as Charleston and Savannah. Stoneware and earthenware. James L. Parr was managing the works in 1845.

Mary's Lane glass: Irish glass from the Mary's Lane works, Dublin, established 1746. Diamond-molded jelly glasses and decanters, a number of which survive in U.S., either from the volume of original imports or of recent importation as antiques.

marzipan: *See* Marchpane.

mascaron: Decorative element of mask form.

Mascotte: Pattern of pressed glass featuring a band imitative of lozenge cutting and a clear upper section that is sometimes etched or engraved with a leaf-and-vine motif.

maselin: An alloy used in making cups, from the same term used in 17th century to designate a maser, a wooden bowl.

maser: A wooden bowl, often of maple or burl.

mask cup: Mask jug; not a Toby, but a jug displaying a face mask. An American example features the face of Daniel O'Connell. English mask cups or jugs are known featuring Admiral Rodney, Nelson, et cetera. Some classic ones of goddesses are of record. There is a mask cup of "Old Rough & Ready."

mask spout: A beaked or headed pouring spout imitative of swan, dragon, eagle, duck beaks, et cetera; an animal-head form and, rarely, a human face. [*Example of the human form pictured.*]

Mason, Miles: Potter of England working from late 18th century. In 1797 he made blue dessert wares, melon wares, Mankin wares, et cetera. Owned or had in-

terests in potteries at Liverpool, Fenton, and Daisy Bank. His son, Charles James Mason, was the originator of ironstone.

Mason & Slidell: Reference would be to souvenirs of this pair who caused an international incident in Civil War period. James Russell Lowell issued a pamphlet.

Mason ironstone: Charles James Mason's famous ware, originated prior to 1813 and patented in that year. Made by Mason and by Morley; later by Ashworth. An Imari pattern, called Gaudy Ironstone, was made. It should be remembered that Mason's ironstone is not heavy, thick granite ware, but a strong standard-weight ware. The original ironstone was not pottery but cast-iron shells coated heavily with fired-on enamel.

mason's joint: A stonework technique like coping, eliminating one miter.

Mason stove: Cast-iron stoves bearing this name or that of John Mason & Co. are not of manufacture by these several people, but indicative of their designs as pattern makers. Iron founders made the stoves. Firm was in business from 1840s at Providence, R.I.

Massachusetts clock: Shelf clocks of a design taken from a chest-on-chest form. Sometimes called "half clocks." [*Example pictured.*]

Massachusetts desk: Name given in 1890s to a banker's or countinghouse table with six bulbous reeded legs. Long enough for side-by-side work of two or more people.

Massachusetts glass: Properly any glass made at a Massachusetts glass factory, whether in Boston area, Cape Cod, or inland. Actually the glass made at Massachusetts Glass Works at Charlestown: amber, green, and black bottles, flasks, hollow wares, and private mold work. Operating to 1870s.

massicot: An ocher color derived from lead oxide.

Massillon stamps: Reference is believed to be to stamped linens for embroidery, and the stamps for the work, as made by several producers at Massillon, O., from 1850s. A. Pierce and S. P. Borden were makers of these devices.

mast: A weight, 2½ pounds.

Master Mason: Architect and builder who designed both houses and its furnishings. William Adam, father of Robert and James Adam, was a master mason. The term is also significant in this ancient secret order to designate a fully accepted member.

master roundabout: *See* Chairs, All Kinds. Any object name preceded by word "master" should be either a large, extra-fine, or noteworthy example, as "master's Windsor."

mastich: A mastic.

mastings: Tall pine poles suitable for ships' masts. An act was passed in 1711 "for the preservation of white and other pine trees" in Her Majesty's colonies, to insure the masting of the Navy.

match: A lighting or fire-making device. **matchbox:** Any safe or container of any material for the keeping of matches. **match-light box:** Cased bottle of acid to ignite slivers tipped with chlorate of potash. **match pad:** A table pad of thin metal or wire work for easy striking of matches. **match safe:** Any container for matches, particularly the strike-anywhere matches of 19th century. Some are for pocket carriage. Many varieties of innumerable materials, some very elaborate ones of china with figural lids. **match stamps:** U.S. revenue stamps affixed to packages of matches, indicating a tax paid.

matchlock: A type of firearm having a lock or firing device which transported the tip of a smoldering wick match to the priming pan. Followed by (1) the wheellock and (2) the flintlock.

matelassé: Embossed fabric or leather.

matted: Pitted or dotted.

Matthewman flask: Powder flasks made by John Matthewman, New Haven, Conn., from 1840s. Had a considerable production.

maulkin: A swabbing pole used to clean an oven hearth.

maund: A container.

maw glass: English ware, especially for druggists' display, and merchandise jars of large size, imported by Van Schaack & Sons, Chicago, from 1870s.

Maw majolica: Made at Maw Pottery, Broseley, England, from 1850s.

May apple: Fruit pod of the mandrake plant.

May dukes: Maddox, a variety of cherry.

Mayer: Brothers in the pottery business, owners of the Dale Hall Pottery, Burslem, from 1830s. Made exceptionally fine vases, urns, pitchers, and tablewares.

May pops: Fruit of the passion flower. Not May apple.

May queen (& king): Parian groups modeled by John Bell and produced by Minton from c. 1848. Psyche and another winged figure support the king; two angels support the queen.

Maysville glass: Flasks, bottles, vials, and philosophical wares, made from 1810s at Maysville, Ky.

Maythe, Smith: Notorious Ohio-Kentucky highwayman of the Robin Hood persuasion. Published his memoirs in 1841.

mazarin; mazer: Any deep dish of burl or maple. Also a porringer. In 19th century, a deep dish fitting within a shell or framework of silver or other metal. In Elizabethan age mazer meant a maplewood bowl.

McAlpin furniture: Product of the McAlpin Furniture Factories at Cincinnati from 1835. This factory made an immense amount of furniture sold generally throughout the Midwest. Empire and French Antique revival, fancy chairs and settees, sleigh and post beds.

McCormick-reaper platter: Pressed-glass platter featuring the reaper of Cyrus McCormick, which incidentally was not the first American reaper, but incorporated the basic ideas of the earlier reapers made by Obed Hussy and his associates, originating in the Taneytown region of Maryland. McCormick's first activity was in Virginia, not far from the Hussy locality.

McCully & Co.: Owners of various Pittsburgh glass factories, including the Sligo,

the Phoenix, and the Empire works. Produced wares of blown, molded, pressed and cut glass. 19th century.

McCully ware: Probable reference is to the stone- and redwares of the McCully Pottery, Trenton, N.J., founded 1750s. The redwares were in the Staffordshire tradition: combed, spiral, and tulip slip decoration. Some early ware is marked with an impressed stamp.

McFarland pottery: Earthenware made at Cincinnati from 1790s. James and Robert Caldwell were owners of works in 1800s.

McGraw furniture: Cabinet, case, and seat furniture by McGraw & Co., New York City, working 1815-35. Directoire and Empire styles. Also fancy chairs. Extensive exporters and coastal shippers.

McGuffey Readers: Early schoolbooks made up of collections of "suitable texts" compiled by William Holmes McGuffey of Kentucky while teaching school at Ashland. Millions of McGuffey Readers were used in American schools. Early editions are valuable.

McIntire, Samuel: Architect, carver, and housewright of Salem, Mass., from late 18th through early 19th century. Designed and supervised execution of many palatial mansions and carved innumerable elements for their interior and exterior decoration. He also made sofas and other items of furniture, or so it is alleged. Carved work on some surviving sofas of the Salem region is almost precisely like the work of this great American master builder and artist. He is known to have worked as a carver for the Sanderson cartel of Salem. He died in 1811. A son, Samuel Field McIntire, also did carving for the Sandersons and advertised as a furniture carver in 1815.

McIntosh cards: Reference is to holiday greeting cards sold wholesale by W. C. McIntosh of New Haven, Conn., from 1880s. Chromolithographed cards.

McKee, J. & F.: Proprietors of glass factories in Pittsburgh area from 1834. Full details of their operation will be found in *American Glass*, by McKearin.

McKee-mark jar: Preserve jar of glass. Blown, with wide lip, ground flat, and a tight-fitting cover. Cover is marked "F. & J. MCKEE, PITTSBURGH." Date is from 1850s.

McKenny prints: Colored prints from *History of Indian Tribes of North America* by T. L. McKenny and J. Hall. Portraits of Indians issued 1836-44 as a folio, in parts.

McLaughlin Brothers: Publishers of children's books, toy books, novelties, valentines, et cetera. Established 1828. Also made card games: Old Maid, Punch, Logomachy, et cetera.

McLewee lamps: Advertising lamps and fixtures made by F. McLewee of New York City from 1830s. One of his specialties was a druggist's mortar, studded with colored bull's-eyes and illuminated by gas.

McQuate Pottery: Henry McQuate was a potter of Lancaster County, Pa., who in 1840 began the manufacture of redwares decorated with green-tinted slip. His pottery was at Myerstown.

mead: (1) A meadow. (2) The metheglin or

fermented drink of honey, malt, and water. Hydromel.

Meader ware: Products, most likely, of the Meader potteries at Cleveland, Ga., operating from 1825.

Mead plate: Silver-plated wares made by J. O. Mead & Sons, Philadelphia, from 1840s.

Mead porcelain: Soft-paste wares made by Dr. Henry Mead, Jersey City, N.J., c. 1816. Only one piece is believed to survive.

Meakin: Extensive manufacturer of ironstone china from 1840s, much of which was exported to U.S. Firm was J. & C. Meakin. J. Meakin also owned a pottery at Longton and another at Cobridge, Staffordshire.

meal ark: A hutch for flour of any corn (that is, any bread grain). Also bulting-ark, cornark, and probably flowersarca. Such pieces of furniture were common by the year 1500.

meander: In architecture, brickwork in pattern, as "Wall of Troy."

measure, beer: 2-quart and 4-quart cans, of copper or plated tin, with glass insert at side, and ventilated covers. Glass indicator enabled user to know content without opening the measure. Many are as late as 1900s. A standard item of brewery and saloon equipment.

meat chopper: A machine for dicing meat by turning a crank. A drum of cutters within a case did the chopping. [*Example pictured dates from 1830s.*]

meat ware: Vegetables, the "proper" cooking of which was commented upon in manuscripts of pre-Christian Era. The best cooks invariably cooked vegetables in alkaline water before finishing cooking in clear water. Hence the British tradition of cooking with baking soda.

mechanical match safe: Cast-iron device with a well for wood-stick matches, exposing only one in a slot. Pushing a lever caused a bird figure to pick up a match in the beak. Popular from 1880s.

mechanical secret drawer: Rarest of the rare-type "secret" drawer in slope-fall desks. Wooden gears, ratchets, metal springs, and other machinery, operating from secret buttons and in certain sequence, permit the pushing of an entire section backward, opening a cover at back of piece for access. Some even have brass serpent heads showing. When the machinery operates, the serpents "strike" at any hand tinkering with the mechanism. Probably a clockmaker's addition to a cabinetmaker's masterpiece. The few examples of record date from 1750s.

mechanical toy banks: Reference generally is to the cast-iron toy banks having articulated and movable figures put into operation by a lever (some with springs), adding a small show when a coin is deposited in the bank. Some mechanical banks are of tin and some have wood parts. See Bibliography.

mechanical watch: Of course any time-telling device is a mechanism; reference here is to watches with such features as barking dogs, mill wheels, singing birds, and even tableaux. Some of the latter are so hush-hush that a curtain is parted to expose the scene, generally obscene or pornographic. Most of these date from 1660s to 1780s.

mechanical window pieces: Store-window display pieces with motion, made generally from 1870s, but imitative of much earlier and similar devices. All sorts of genre scenes in action, from Santa Claus to St. Valentine, and baseball games to sailing ships.

Mechanic Glass Works: The only record is a quart flask impressed with this name and the place, "Philada." Date is estimated at from 1840 to 1860.

Medallion: Pattern of pressed glass with almost nothing to recommend it but a range of colors: amber, green, yellow, blue, et cetera. It might be designated as Eastlake style, with curving bands on some pieces, a medallion of overlapping pie wedges, and Gothic blocks, bumps, and roof edges. A medallion bottle is described under Burr Nursing Bottle. It has no relationship to this pattern save in name.

medallion wafer: A sealing wafer having pressed bas-relief designs, sometimes as cameos, in two colors.

medder: From meader; a quadrangular cup of woodenware, footed and with handles, traditionally used in serving the beverage mead.

Medford glass: Tablewares of glass made at the co-operative glassworks at Medford, N.J., from 1840s; under other management from 1860s.

medicine (bottle) hats: Glass hats blown in bitters or medicine bottles or flask molds.

medicine horn: Any container with a spout or neck for introducing medicine into the mouth of horses and domestic cattle. Some of genuine horn, others of metal, pottery, and glass. Glass examples have a heavy, deep ring or valance on neck.

medicine spoon: A covered spoon with sucket or other lip-lap. Used to feed medicine to invalids. Some have graduated scales in bowls to aid in measuring doses. Some have hollow handles for sucking the dose. Brass, pewter, glass, and silver examples of record.

Medici porcelain: Imitation Chinese wares made in Italy c. 1470–1510. Some authorities assert it was real porcelain.

medlar: A small fruit of the apple family (perhaps the "rose apple"), generally eaten "rotten-ripe." [*Since this fruit is seldom properly presented in any antiquarian essay, an example is illustrated.*]

Meed, Stats: Cabinetmaker of New York City, said to have worked in 1810s.

Meeks, Joseph: Cabinet manufacturer of New York, 1805–40s. Extensive producer of Directoire-style furniture to c. 1820, and thereafter Empire and French Antique revival-style furniture. Sold to agents and dealers in all coastal states, Gulf states, and in the Gulf and Atlantic coast countries of South America. Issued illustrated catalogue posters.

Meeser mirrors: George Meeser manufactured tabernacle, mahogany, and gilt-frame mirrors at Lancaster, Pa., from 1830s to 1850s. After 1850 he (or another of same name) was operating in Philadelphia. Firm at one time was Andrews & Meeser.

megascope: Magic-lantern projector using actual objects, prints, et cetera, instead of slides. Date is from 1820s.

megelp: Oil drier used in the arts. The necessary drier for good impasto. Many variants of spelling, such as meglip, gumption, et cetera. Meglip, a drier used with water colors, is from the same term.

megillah: Case for a sacred roll. Silver, brass, and even gold examples are known.

Meher sundials: Patented gnomon dials made from 1860s; they cast a shadow indicating time of various places. George Meher of Philadelphia was the inventor.

Meigh: Pottery family of Hanley, England, operating from c. 1770s until in 1861, when the plant became the Old Hall Earthenware Co. Blue-printed, plain, and fancy decorated tablewares, Parian wares, jet-ware. Makers of the well-known but late-19th-century patterns of tableware known as Buckle, Richmond, Perth, Exeter, Verona, et cetera. Spill cases, stonewares, novelties.

mei-ping: Chinese term for what we call a gallipot; an oviform jug shape.

Meissen: The ware that most closely approximated Chinese porcelain and claimed as a German invention, but actually a chance discovery by E. W. Tschirnhausen and J. F. Böttger, the latter an alchemist and fakir who, under the pretext of requiring "better crucibles" for his secret of making lead into gold, found the crucibles he made were porcelain. He had achieved perhaps what Dutch potters had achieved half a century previously and did not know they had porcelain. Tschirnhausen did know it, and so in 1709 the Meissen Porcelain Works was formed. Date given is approximate. Some claim 1708 and others 1710. Italy, England, and the Netherlands had potters who achieved porcelain and rejected it. There is some excuse for the English, no excuse for the others. So to Germany or, properly, to Saxony, should go the credit. Many of the original productions of the works to 1756 were reproduced from 1825 to 1850s. Uninitiated collectors are easily fooled, as there was no appreciable letdown in the quality of the production. Most present-day authorities (including German connoisseurs) agree the first products of Meissen were stonewares and that true porcelains were not made until 1713. Early Meissen, 1710–14, is either red-brown stoneware or faïence. By 1720 the Meissen Works had developed a fine underglaze blue, but by then the "secret" had also escaped to France and the Sèvres works had knowledge of how to make porcelain. The greatest production years of the factory were during the first half of the 19th century. The plant is still in operation. Some wares, made for the Near East (Turkey, Arabia, and Persia), are noted for the decoration on the face, including designated contents of the dishes, as flesh, fruit, vegetables, melons, et cetera.

Meissonier: French furniture designer of 18th century from whom Chippendale borrowed his French styles and designs.

melamotype: Photographic positive print often colored by hand.

melapep: Cucumber-seed oil.

melhegor: Soured honey water. A souring akin to vinegar.

mell: A warming pan.

mellifluid: Word coined by John Adams to describe the character of the writing of Thomas Jefferson.

melliot: A musical instrument of the 17th century.

Mellor: Pattern of pressed glass with a décor of ovate melon forms, segmented and arranged horizontally in two bands with upright sections at junctures. Named for T. W. Mellor, designer for Gillinder of Philadelphia and Greensburg, Pa. Date is c. 1878–80.

melly: The cucumber. Introduced to the colonies by the Swedes on the Delaware and said to have arrived from the Near East via Turkey, Russia, and Finland. Pickled cucumbers were called poke-melly.

melodeon: Reed instrument played from a keyboard. Hundreds of thousands were made in U.S. from 1830s, some having only four octaves and others as many as seven with bass played from foot pedals. Two major types were made, one playing by suction of air through the reeds to the bellows, the other by pressure from the bellows through the reeds. Some of the cases are quite charming and some had been stripped of their reeds, keyboards, et cetera, and converted into what are called "spinet desks." At one time thought to have no traditional existence, these conversions are now known to be imitative of actual desks, with cast-iron frames and melodeon-style cases, made in quantities for schoolmaster's desks. *Spinning Wheel*, the antiques publication founded 1945, seems to have been the only publication noting this truth. The reed organ superseded the melodeon as a parlor musical instrument shortly after or during the War between the States.

meloharp: A lap instrument of the zither type. The casing is ovoid in shape, fitted with from 26 to 68 strings. Played with a pick. Late 19th century.

melon-bottomed: Said of any table or stand of Directoire styling having (1) a tray secured by legs about 12 inches above floor line and (2) a top under which there is a segmented half-melon form for use as a catchall.

melon foot: Rare-type ball foot, the ball carved in segments imitative of a melon form.

melon shape: Ovoid, globular, in the general form of a melon, not necessarily segmented. Most Liverpool transfer-printed pitchers are said to be melon-shaped. Sizes from miniatures of only 2 inches up to 18 inches are of record.

melophine: An improved melodeon of the 1850s.

Melpomene: Greek Muse of tragedy.

Melton: One researcher reported a French pressed-glass automobile plate with a happy-faced driver being called a James Melton plate in North Carolina. Actually a pattern of pressed glass having an imitative band of cutting topped with Gothic pointed or rounded arches and an acorn finial. Date is c. 1874.

memento mori: Mortuary memento, as a watch movement in a skull-form case. Anything to remind the owner and observer of his mortality.

Mendelssohn figurine: Gentleman seated, said to be a companion piece to one of the many Jenny Lind figurines. Felix Mendelssohn-Bartholdy (1809–47) would seem to be the person figured.

Meneely bell: Any bell founded by Meneely of West Troy, N.Y., from 1825.

meneld: Spotted black and white.

menhaden: Fish somewhat similar to the shad; the mossbunker. Esteemed for its oil, often sold as olive oil!

Mennecy: French soft-paste porcelain made under the patronage of the Duke of Villeroy. Often called Mennecy-Villeroy. Date is from 1730s to 1770s.

Mennonite: Member of a true primitive Christian sect, founded by Menno Simons, a former Catholic priest of the Netherlands, 16th century. One museum official has called Menno a "Swiss émigré," which is entirely in error. The man was Dutch; his converts were Dutch and English. The Spanish occupation drove the members of the sect to Russia, Germany, Switzerland, and France. They were among the first continental Europeans to migrate to William Penn's colony.

menu: Catalogue of viands; bill of the day's fare. Many are elaborate, especially those printed (some engraved) for formal and ceremonial dinners.

menusier: Master cabinetmaker. Abbreviated M.M. (*maitre menuisier*). A title comparable to *ébéniste*.

menyver: A cover of skins; a fur cape or throw.

mercery: Originally mirrors, combs, curlers, toiletries, and cosmetics were designated as mercery. Finally the mercer became a dealer in cloth.

merchant candlestick: Early-19th-century Chinese tutenag (pewter) candlesticks in form of top-hatted, frock-coated gentlemen of the Occident holding vases with prickets. Probably made in sets.

merelles: Game played on a scribed board with 18 counters, 9 to each player. Playing field is laid out in 3 rectangles within each other, joined and bisected between angles. Player getting 3 counters in a row was the winner. Date from 15th century. Sometimes called "fig-mill."

merese: A pad or button of glass between bowl and stem of a vessel, or between parts of the stem.

Meriden Britannia: Made from 1850s by Meriden Britannia Co., Meriden, Conn. A hard type of brilliant pewter, generally plated with silver. Meriden made two kinds of plated ware: the Britannia-based and nickel-based. Marks were nearly the same, but a star in the mark indicates the Britannia base.

meridian: A before-dinner drink, generally a strong punch.

merino: (1) Fine twilled wool fabric. (2) An upholstery and drapery fabric, often called merino damask.

merletto: Lace pattern after the form of crenelated battlement.

Merlin chair: Invalid's self-propelled chair.

mermaid bottle: A flask with volute tail coiled as the tail of a sea horse. Blown in the Venetian glass technique with applied frilling and prunting. A variety of this flask was made of pottery at Bennington.

mermaid motif: "The force of evil in alluring form" is said to be the ancient explanation of this mythological figure. Used as a motif in heraldry, on pottery, rarely on furniture, and popular as a waterside tavern sign.

Merriam mirrors: Wall, pier, and mantel mirrors in Regency, Empire, and French Antique revival styles, made by B. W. Merriam; some so labeled.

Merrill, G. B.: Designer and engraver of calico printing blocks, working at Lowell, Mass., for the chintz printeries, c. 1850s.

merry-man plate: Dutch and Lambeth delft plates with inscriptions, making up a set of six or eight, with a "master" plate bearing effigy of Charles I, Charles II, or William of Orange. Verses range (1) What is a Merry Man (2) Let him doe what he can (3) to entertain his guests (4) with wine and merry jests (5) but if his wife does frowne (6) then merriment goeth downe (7) so Ho! to a Wife well willed (8) and guests wie merriment filled.

merry night: A country party; a rustic ball. A cantico or spree.

Merry's Museum: Magazine for children first published in 1840s and continued to 1860s.

merrythought: The wishbone of any cooked bird, with its meat.

Mesmer, Franz Anton: Pseudo physician whose treatment was preferable to the genuine drugging doctor's practices. Mesmer used autosuggestions and direct, hypnotic suggestions for the cure of what are now called psychosomatic (body and soul) conditions of disease. Marquis de Lafayette purchased Mesmer's secrets and attempted to introduce a cult here in late 18th century. He was amazed to discover, on his famous visit of 1825, that a book on metaphysical science, titled *Alphabet of Thought*, had been published by Hugh Hamilton of Lancaster, with a Harrisburg imprint (Pennsylvania), 1825, and that the Shakers were practicing certain simple formulas of autosuggestion. The truth that mind is of the essence of life and that matter is its servant is of proved cosmic significance. That all present-day practices fall far short of being satisfactory in every case is beside the point. America has many memorials of the Mesmer era, of the Louis XVI period, and the Directoire, of France. Certain of Mary Baker Eddy's ideas are found in *The Alphabet of Thought* here mentioned.

mess; messing: Two people eating from one plate or bowl.

metal collar: Thin steel or brass sheets cut into collar form and enameled white; the cleanable collar of the 1850s-60s.

metallochromy: Metal coloring by galvanic plating. Method used from 1845.

metallophone: An xylophone-type musical instrument with metal bars.

metal polishes: The early "natural" polish was the Dutch rush, or *Equisetum hyemale*; a stem carrying fine particles of silica or silex. Tripoli was pulverized silica. Rottenstone, whiting, and oxide of tin were also used. Soft or "sammen" bricks, bath bricks, were for metal polishing.

metal-top chimney: A metal device fitting over a flaring glass chimney, forming a constrictor. The date is 1860s.

metamorphic chair: A library step chair.

metamorphosis: A folding paper toy which, in folding, displays changes of figure or scene. Also harlequinade. Made in colonies from 1770s, but of much earlier dating in England, where in 17th century morals by John Bunyan were so displayed.

mete-form: A bench for seating at dining table.

metheglin: (From *meddyglynn*.) A drink of honey and water, fermented, or honey and wine.

mether: A goblet-shaped vessel of wood.

metropolitan ware: Dark redware, slip-decorated, made at London potteries from 1600s. Much of it was brought to colonies by settlers. It is one of the prototypes of the redwares of Pennsylvania.

metzelsuppe: From *metzeln*, to kill and cut up. Samples of meats from a hog butchering.

Metz tin: Tinwares made by Christopher Metz, Chicago, from 1850s.

Meyer & Warne: Manufacturers of silver-plated wares, Philadelphia, from 1840s.

Meyer ware: Reference would seem to be to the product of any potter named Meyer, or Mayer; no less than six are of record, the earliest being Henry Meyer, Philadelphia, 1790s.

Mezetti, P.: Maker of plaster ornaments, New York, 1850s.

mezuzah: Ritualistic vessel or container, sometimes gem-studded.

mezzograph: Daguerreotype positive, printed on paper.

mezzo-relievo: Middle-relief carving or molding; higher than bas-relief.

mezzotint; mezzotinto: A form of engraving using a plate with crisscrossed all-over hatching, and achieving tonal gradation of velvety smoothness by work with burnishers. The invention of the process is generally credited to Prince Rupert, by Evelyn in a work titled *Sculptura*. Actually developed by a German engraver in 17th century. In 18th century mezzotints were printed in colors by rubbing the colors into the plate. The first mezzotint engraver in the colonies was Peter Pelham of Boston, working in first half of 18th century.

mica reflector: Actually a metal reflector covered with sheet mica.

micmac: The common tobacco pipe of the native Indians; distinguished from the calumet, which was the ceremonial pipe. Walnut-shaped bowl fitted with reed stem.

microscope table: Round, revolving-top table mounted on a central column having three legs. Used primarily by gentlemen scholars for microscopic study. Rosewood, mahogany, oak, cherry, and other examples survive in styles from Sheraton and Hepplewhite to Victorian.

middle interest; middle patent: The middle class; the fairly well-to-do.

middle-post sideboards: Rare-type Hepplewhite- and Sheraton-styled cabinets having five legs, one on each corner and one squarely in the center of front. Some have marble tops. Said to be a beverage board; in other words, an early "bar" for the home.

Middletown plate: Silver-plated white metalwares made at Middletown, Conn., from 1870s. Mostly tea sets.

Middlesex cut: Eight-pointed star cutting with fans. It is of late usage, probably 1880s.

mier: A device for crumbling bread.

mildernix: Sailcloth, used also as the canvas for floor cloths.

milk bench: An open cupboard or stand used to hold crocks, bowls, and other dairy utensils.

milk cooler: (1) Cabinet with ice or circulating water, in which milk was cooled. (2) A small springhouse with pools or canals of cold water in which milk pans and cans were placed. The cabinets were fitted with tinned copper cans. [*Example pictured.*]

milk glass: Opaque white glass. Originally made as imitation porcelain, and so decorated. The present-day habit of calling any opaque glass "milk" is fatuous; green, black, blue, yellow, brown, and purple milk glass are not milk glass, but opaque wares of the color designated.

milk paint: Fresh curds of milk with slaked lime, linseed oil, and color. A good interior paint.

milk polish: Fresh, whole milk used as a furniture polish.

milk wood: Willow wood, esteemed for making dairy woodenwares.

milkydown: Silk of milkweed pods, used in quilt padding. The down from one pod was just enough for a square inch of padding.

Millard & variants: Patterns of pressed glass. (1) Millard displays large volutes in fan form. (2) The variants show color (amber or ruby) flashings, sometimes engraved.

Millard furniture: Reference probably is to the furniture made by W. C. Millard & Co., Providence, R.I., from 1840s.

millefiori: Flower-pattern canes of glass and the cuttings of same used in making the body of objects, paperweight centers, et cetera. "Many flowers" is the meaning generally accepted.

Miller, Joaquin: Often considered of Pacific Spanish ancestry, this man was born in Indiana and named Cincinnatus Heine Miller. Family moved to Oregon in his boyhood. Law clerk, newspaper writer, poet, author of *Songs of the Sierras*. He assumed the name Joaquin.

Miller bronze: Lamps and statuary by the Edward Miller Co., originally the H. N. Howard works, established 1843 at Meriden, Conn. The art bronzes date from 1867, the lamps from the date of the firm's founding.

Miller furniture: Reference may be to any furniture produced by a maker named Miller, as George Miller of New York, from 1820s; George Miller of Philadelphia, from 1730s; Henry Miller of Lancaster, Pa., from 1830s; Jacob Miller of Savannah, Ga., from 1820s, and so on.

Miller glass: Reference is to wares produced at Franklin Glass Works and Harmony Glass Works, both in New Jersey, when owned by D. H. Miller, glass merchant of Philadelphia, during the 1830s.

Miller luster: American lusterware made at Philadelphia by Abraham Miller. Miller acquired the molds of Tucker porcelain works in 1838 and made some wares from them to 1840 or later. The Miller pottery was founded by Andrew (father), 1790. The luster made by Abraham was silver.

Miller waxes: Wax portraits by George Miller, modeler, of Baltimore, working from 1820s.

millet mill: (1) A mill for grinding millet seeds. (2) Mill for grinding coffee, spices, et cetera, made by Edward Millet, Philadelphia, from 1835.

Millet yellow: The color, a rich yellow, used by the French master, Millet. Used also by several potters to produce an all-over yellow ware.

Milliken stencils: Stencils for home-craftsmen made by John Milliken, Lawrence, Mass., from 1850s.

Mills, J. K. & Co.: Furniture manufacturers of Davenport, Ia., from 1850. Empire-style cabinet furniture and chairs.

Mills & Deming: Cabinetmakers of New York City from 1790. Worked in Hepplewhite style.

Mills dominos: Wallpaper panels made by Zechariah Mills, Hartford, Conn., from early 1800s. Also made lined trunks and covered boxes. Panels, pasted at edges, were made into rolls.

Millville glass: New Jersey center of glassmaking, the major plant of which was Whitall-Tatum, still in operation. Rose paperweights, novelties, special blown wares, druggists' wares and display bottles, tablewares, et cetera. James Lee had the first factory at this place, 1806. F. Schetter of Baltimore had a factory here in 1832. Whitall interests took over both plants prior to 1854. From 1880s made half a million or more "atmospheric fruit jars" and milk bottles. Plant is still in operation as a division of the Armstrong Cork Co. of Lancaster, Pa.

mimosa: A cabinet wood resembling mahogany. The tree bears sweet-scented flowers and beanlike pods.

mindal wood: Wood of the almond tree.

mined shingles: (1) Slate shingles. (2) Wood shingles made from bog cedar, found preserved in mires, detected by probing and recovered by surface mining.

Minerva: Pattern of pressed glass featuring the warrior goddess within a pearl-studded medallion.

Ming: A Chinese dynasty, 1368–1644, and having these subdivisions or "periods" applied to ceramics, jades, and other elegancies: Hung Wu, 1368–98; Chien Wen, 1399–1402; Yung Lo, 1403–24; Hung Hsi, 1425; Hsuan Te, 1426–35; Cheng T'ung, 1436–49; Ch'eng Lua, 1465–87; Hung-Chih, 1488–1505; Cheng Te, 1506–21; Chia Ching, 1522–66; Lung Ch'ing, 1567–72; Wan Li, 1573–1620; T'ai Ch'ang, 1620; T'ien Ch'i, 1621–27; Ch'ung Ch'eng, 1628–44.

Mingel bellows: Any bellows by John Mingel, Philadelphia maker working from 1780s. Some are beautifully painted and stencil-signed.

miniature folio: Prints 5" x 7" or within those limits.

miniature lamps: (1) Salesmen's

samples of lamps in miniature, including some very charming student lamps. (2) Any small lamps, preferably burning oil, but also any of the novelty lamps using the Clark candle, a short squat reservoir of solid wax fitting into various glass and other containers, and known generally as fairy lamps. These are London-made, late 19th century. (3) Small novelty lamps, as the Nelly Bly, the Jules Verne, et ectera, travelers' lamps.

minifer: The smallest size of toilet pin.

minium: Red lead. Litharge. Originally the red mercury oxide, vermilion.

Minorcan jug: A Mediterranean jug form; globose body with high neck and slender handle, derived from ancient Greece. Found in northern Florida in the hands of Minorcans who came here as serfs to work on indigo plantations. The jugs were either made at or near New Smyrna or were brought to Florida by the settlers from Minorca. [*Example pictured.*]

Munster jug: Tudor-style ceramic-ware jug displaying a Madonna in relief and architectural panels.

minstrel harp: A small harp (not lyre form) under 40 inches high and 26 inches wide. 18th century. Some are marked "J. Egan, Dublin."

mint jalop: Probable source of "mint julep." Mint water, distilled, mixed with rum, and laced with jalap, or jalop, a purgative root of the ipomoea vine.

Minton: English china, made first by Thomas Minton from 1796 and continuing thereafter as a most successful pottery. Made bone china, tablewares, vases, statuary, tiles, Della Robbia wares, and a host of other ceramic products. All good books on English china give attention to this ceramic enterprise down through the years.

Mioton: Pattern of pressed glass featuring pressed panels with semicircular tops. A barroom glassware.

miquelet: The French or Flemish improved firing mechanism for a gun; prototype of the American flintlock and indubitably brought to the colonies by French gunsmiths. A piece of flint, set in the jaw of the hammer, struck a barrier which retreated and uncovered the primer in the priming pan.

Miranda: Title of a Minton Parian figure modeled by Bell and sold at the New York Crystal Palace Exposition, 1853.

mirror: (1) Any looking glass. Mirror glass originally had a faint bevel, tooled on. Plate glass was required because of the distortion yielded by mirrors of crown glass. Mirror frames of olive wood in the Italian (Venetian) style were used in early 17th-century colonial homes. Frames of every period style are of record and many are pictured. Perhaps the two most common errors in respect to mirror terminology are (a) "Sheraton" mirrors, an error for tabernacle mirrors. These derive from the French *trumeau*. Sheraton designed no mirrors. And (b) "Constitution" mirrors, which are Georgian, not Chippendale, and have gilded eagle ornamentation. They have no relationship whatsoever to the Constitution. (2) Pattern of pressed glass relating to the Ashburton group of simple pressed planes imitative of early cutting. (3) Glass cut in the so-called "mirror" pattern. **mirror black:** The shiny black glaze on certain ceramic wares. **mirror knobs:** Caps of decorative quality tipping the nails or screws supporting the bottom of a hung mirror. **mirror rests:** Busts of ceramic ware or carved stone, having deep angular cuts at rear to support a mirror. [*Example pictured.*] **mirror silver:** Tin foil floated on the glass over a film of mercury. **mirrorsmith:** The maker of all-metal mirrors, and the polishers of same.

mirror-back: French Antique revival-style chairs having oval backs, looking very much like the molded oval mirror frames of the same period.

mischianza: The grand ball given by General William Howe when occupying Philadelphia during the Revolution. It was a Loyalist and Tory party of lavish quality. Some of the decorative elements were marked for (and of) the ball and were cherished by Tories as souvenirs. The affair was given in 1778.

mission style: An invented name, probably by an antiques dealer or by some borax furniture maker of Grand Rapids, used in 1890s in an attempt to cash in on the somewhat general interest in the missions of the Southwest and California. What most people mean by mission style is the simple style of William Morris, the English reformer of taste.

Missiquoi: A spring at Saratoga; its waters were bottled in containers identifying the contents and made at Congressville, N.Y., glassworks.

Mississippi pocket rifle: An Allen pistol for target use is marked with this name. It has its hammer on underside. Allen also invented a "pepperbox" type of revolving pistol.

Mississippi table: Reference seems to be to gaming table of 1740s and related to the Mississippi Bubble scheme. A sort of bagatelle table. Not a gaming table from a river steamboat, as some collectors believe.

"Miss" Toby: Jug in the form of a female figure, perhaps of the brewhouse girl who married the brewer, inherited the brewery, married the counselor who settled the estate, and had a daughter who became Queen of England. The figure wears a mobcap, topped by a tricorn. Late 18th century.

mistletoe yellow: A fabric dye for home use, made from mistletoe berries.

Mitchell & Freeman plate: Advertising plate for the American firm of china and glass merchants so named, at Boston, by the famed William Adam pottery, contemporaneously with historic Staffordshire.

Mitchell & Rammelsberg: Furniture manufacturers of Cincinnati from late 1840s. Mass-produced pieces in lots of 200 or more in a six-story factory. Employed 250 people. Sold furniture all over the Midwest.

Mitchell lamp: Ornate hanging lamp made by Mitchell of New York from 1830s. The reservoir, above the burner, was of highly polished metal and served as a reflector.

Mitered Diamond: Pattern of pressed glass imitative of cross-diamond and ball

cutting, with angular wedges of clear glass.

mixing table: A small sideboard, butler's cabinet, or a cabinet often called a "hunt board," with compartments for liquors and wines and a mixing area, sometimes marble-topped. Examples with sliding tambour fronts are known. Mostly from the South and not in any great numbers. Examples from England are more plentiful and in infinitely better taste and style. Much Southern furniture, made on plantations by traveling cabinetmakers, bears evidence of special making to suit the whims of the owners, who were seldom well versed in good design.

Mizpah: A watchtower. A parting salutation; a blessing.

M'nite: Father Jogues, 1643, comments on presence of M'nites, or Mennonites, on Manhattan Island.

mob; mobble; mop; mopple: The singular refers to a close cap with lappets. The verb means to veil or turban the head.

mobles; meubles; moebles: Household furniture. Mobile items.

mob pistol: The multi-barreled duckfoot pistol.

mocha ware: Reference is to mottled and banded creamware in mocha, buff, mustard, orange, and other tintings, daubed, mottled, and haphazardly applied. Date range is said to be 1800-50s. Bowls, jugs, plates, mugs, tankards, and pots.

mock tapis: Cloth painted in imitation of tapestry.

model books: Pattern books for home use and guidance in many of the arts, textile, fictile, and metal. Earliest known is *Tractat de la Noble Art de le Guille*, by Vosterman, Anvers, 1527. Peter Quentel issued a book the same year at Cöln. So did Tagleinte, at Venice. English, French, Swiss, Italian, and German issues are of record in an imposing array. The Royal Library at Berlin issued a bibliography of all known pattern books.

model cannon: Miniature working models of naval and military cannon. Mostly of brass, bronze, or iron, but some are of silver. May date from 17th to 19th century. The type is not always indicative; some early types were reproduced as models many years later.

moderateur: A Carcel lamp, using a spring-driven piston to drench the wick with oil. Early 19th century. Imitations are of record, called "moderator," using two flat wicks and burning kerosene. Date is from 1865.

modern: Of the moment, the hour, the day, or the era. In collecting, anything made after 1893, when the country of origin had to be stamped on imports. The "modern kitchen chair," for example, dates from 1835; it was very modern in its day; made of castings, metal pipe, wire, and wood, requiring only cushions for complete comfort. [*Examples pictured are as modern as 1952.*]

modillions: Brackets or blocks arranged in a series under a cornice; correctly only under a composite, Corinthian, and sometimes an Ionic cornice.

moeg: Sledge used at threshing time.

mogador: Handkerchief.

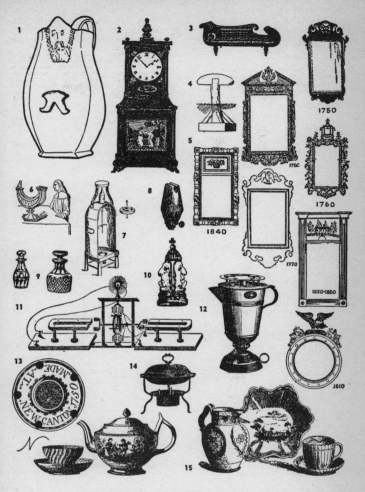

1, Old Man Pitcher. **2**, Massachusetts Clock. **3**, Kangaroo or Psyche (one type). **4**, Mushroom Stool, showing underpinning. **5**, Mirrors (seven varieties, all dated). **6**, Nef. **7**, Niche Screen Roaster. **8**, No-Chimney Lamp Burner. **9**, Noggins. **10**, No-Popery "Janus" Mug or Cup. **11**, Norwich Light. **12**, Nursery Lamp Heater. **13**, New Canton Inkstand Top. **14**, Oyster Chafer. **15**, New Hall Ware; 5 examples and "N" mark. (No. 1 from Mrs. Virginia Houghwout. No. 15 from Virtue & Co., London.)

mohair: Angora goat-hair fabric.

moiré metallique: Tin plate with a pink crystalline finish, lacquered for protection. Date is from 1830s.

moise: To improve.

moku-me: Japanese, meaning "veins of the wood." A pattern found on ceramic and metalwares.

molasses: Treacle from sugar crystallization. Kinds, from light to dark, depend on the cane, the length of cooking, and the utensils used. **molasses gate:** A faucet for use on a molasses barrel. **molasses jug:** A syrup jug with drip trap under spout. Many varieties, some patented.

molded: (1) In cabinetwork, carved or shaped on the bench, with tools, not turned. (2) In other arts, casting or forming in a mold, as molded glass, molded china, et cetera.

moldings; mouldings: Shaped lengths of wood or any other substance used by application to frame an area or serve as a border. Among the better-known names for such moldings are ovolo, scotia, cavetto, cyma, ogee, torus, astragal, bead, fillet, apophyges, and flat. The terms have significance in architecture and in cabinetmaking. There are many variants of the basic types.

Mollthorpes: A family of waxworkers who sculptured and cast portraits in wax, working at East Haven, Conn., from 1760s. Reuben was the most famous. He died in 1814.

molly cot: A male who interferes with women's work.

Molucca: Wood of the catalpa tree.

Molyneux brass: Reference is to the brass foundry of this French family at Boston, where in 18th century they cast fireplace equipment.

Monahan, John: A famous maker of steamboat furniture; maintained factory at Louisville, Ky., from c. 1838.

mon-ami: May butter, eggs, sugar, sweet curds, and boiled cream made into a standing dish, trimmed with fresh violets.

money boxes: Rare items from U.S. Treasury; boxes in which paper moneys were shipped to banks. Cardboard, with ornate posters indicating contents. Also any till, drawer, or strongbox for coin.

money buckle: Shoe buckle of coin silver.

money button: Costume button of silver or gold.

money-changers' tables: Merchants' and bankers' tables, often elaborate, with carving, having hidden tills, wells, and compartmented drawers. Swiss or Italian. Date is from as early as 15th century.

money vase: Crater-type vase with cover, used as a hiding place for coins.

monkey spoon: Silver spoon of late 17th and first half of 18th century, with figure of a monkey carved or worked on handle. At funeral of Philip Livingston, 1749, the pallbearers received monkey spoons, gloves, and mourning rings.

monks' table: Generally a refectory table of simple but early type.

monstrance: A vessel to contain the Host; usually with a crystal or mica window for display of communion bread.

Montague chairs: Reference is not to type but to place of making, Montague, Mass. Late fancy chairs and Boston rockers. Richardson & Dike were the makers.

Montague Cut: Real cut glass of late 19th century featuring a 15-pointed star, X-elements, and fans.

Montauk Cut: Cut-glass pattern featuring bold palmate fans and 4-point stars in diamonds.

monteith: Serrated-edge bowl, often with removable rim, and of silver. Also small cooler for wineglass; small punch glass looking very much like Stiegel-type saltcellar in expanded diamond pattern.

Montgolfier: Iron stove of Franklin type, made for fitting in fireplace opening to reduce the opening size and correct faulty draft. Late 18th and early 19th century.

monumental: Large, important. **monumental candlestick:** A high footed columnar stick. **monumental rug:** A full room-size rug.

monument lamp: Lamp with conical glass reservoir and heavy base. Made by New England Glass Co.

moon: A large globose frame fitted with panes of mica or horn, enclosing a torch.

Moon & Star: Pattern of pressed glass featuring moon disks in rows, one row being impressed with a star.

moonlight luster: Splashy pink luster, sometimes called Sunderland.

moon-quarter sideboard: The crescent-front sideboard. Sometimes also refers to the quarter-segment or corner sideboard.

moonstone glass: A variety of semiopaque milky glass; also the glass tint known as "clam broth."

Moore & Waterhouse iron: Statuary of cast iron, made at a foundry of this name, Philadelphia, in 1840s and 1850s.

Moorehead tin: Tinware made by R. H. Moorehead, Cincinnati, from 1830s. A general line of house- and dairy wares and lanterns.

Moorehead ware: Possible reference is to terra cotta and other clay-ware vases, statuary, and urns made by a pottery so named at Philadelphia, from 1860s.

Moorehouse, William: Cabinetmaker of Cincinnati, working in 1830s, making cabinets, sofas, tables, and chairs. The styles were Directoire and Empire.

Moore ware: English china breakfast, tea, and dinner wares; decorative objects and the "camel teapot," made by St. Mary's Pottery, Mount Pleasant, Longton, from 1830s. Moore & Hamilton, Samuel Moore, and Moore Brothers. Some of the ware also bears the mark of T. Goode & Co., London. The Glasgow Pottery, Trenton, N.J., is also a possibility within this nomenclature, makers of Moore centennial china. A whiteware was made by Moore Brothers at the Bleak Hill Pottery, Burslem. This ware, from 1850s, was exported to the U.S.

mooting ax: A grubbing ax.

moquette: Loose-pile velvet carpet.

Moran Westerns: Reference is to Prang

chromos from Moran's views of Yellowstone and Rocky Mountain scenery, from 1870s. Fifteen views are of record.

Moravians: (1) Members of the Unitas Fratrum sect of Moravia who found exile on the estate of Count Zinzendorf in East Germany and migrated in companies to the colonies, one great settlement being at Bethlehem, Pa., another at Litiz (now Lititz), Pa., and others in Virginia, the Carolinas, et cetera. (2) Candies, generally flat crystallized sugar flavored with mint, originally designed as a wafer of medicinal value to put in scalding water and drink as peppermint tea! Now, and for many years, esteemed as a candy.

mordant: Any etching or fixing agency or coloring material.

moreen: Originally a watered-silk damask (moiré); also a non-watered-effect damask or thick worsted. True moiré was of angora.

Morey-Ober lamp: Britannia bell-shaped lamp with two wick burners for whale oil. Makers, at Boston, were pewterers, blocktin smiths, and Britannia-ware makers from 1820s to 1850s or later.

Morgan-Wood wares: English china made at Hill Works, Burslem, from 1860s. Morgan, Wood & Co. and Wood & Baggaly. Printed and green-glaze wares.

morgengabic: Same as morganatic, a half marriage, excluding wife or spouse from equal status, title, or inheritance, but giving children full status. The term as here given is Germanic.

morise: A pinch ornamentation on blown glassware.

Mormon prints: *Antiques Digest*, published at Frederick, Md., is the only publication in the antiques field to deal with this subject at any length. There are innumerable fine prints of the places and people involved in the movement of the Church of Latter-Day Saints from New York State through Ohio, Illinois, and Missouri to Utah. There is a most engaging small folio lithograph print of Hyrum and Joseph Smith, shown full length in profile on one plate, with the Temple at Nauvoo, Ill., in background, published at London in 1847.

Morning-Glory: A pattern of pressed glass displaying this flower, stem, and leaf.

morning-glory chair: Cast-iron chair with back in form of this flower; also an iron chair of latticework with the vine and its flowers cast on it.

morning-glory horn: Early cylinder phonograph horn in the form of a morning-glory flower.

morrice: The "fig-mill game" played on a board of concentered squares.

Morris chair: The adjustable reclining chair invented by William Morris (1834–96). He was a reforming designer who advocated a "return to simplicity" movement and to functional design. Wallpapers, rugs, lamps, beds, carpets came from his pencil as a design for better living.

Morse pistol: A toy air gun shooting darts. Made from 1860s.

Morse tin: Japanned tinwares made at Providence, R.I., by three makers named

Morse. Catalogues indicate activity as late as 1870s.

mortar & pestle: Metal, stone, ceramic, or wood bell-form vessel with pounding rod, used in pulverizing and powdering all kinds of substances. Roasted coffee was originally "ground" by pounding in a mortar. Many varieties and sizes of mortars, some beautifully decorated in the casting. Examples from 15th century are of record.

mortar jug: Pewter or tin jug of cannon form. Flemish, Swiss, Dutch, and Germanic examples of 16th and 17th centuries known, the latter known as "roerken." [*Example pictured.*]

morteotype: (1) Daguerreotype of deceased persons. (2) Daguerreotype inserted in frame on tombstone.

Mortlake: (1) English tapestry works founded by James I, 1619. Any tapis made at this works. Rubens and Van Dyck made designs; Flemish weavers were employed. Works ceased operation in 1665. (2) A ceramic ware designated by this name, made at the same locale from late 1680s. It is delft-type, tin-glaze ware, the works established during reign of William & Mary, c. 1688–89.

Mortlock's china: Wares sold by an 18th-century dealer, John Mortlock of London, who had great prestige; had name impressed and stamped on wares ordered in quantities from Rockingham, Nantgarw, Coalport, Swansea, and other potteries. The Mortlock teapot is the "Cadogan."

mortmain: "Killing off the maine, or debt, by amortization"; considered a new technique of mortgage repayment, but mentioned as a common practice of property purchase from Chaucer's days.

Morton glass: Cut glass by T. W. Morton of Baltimore, in business from early 1830s.

Morvan: A Burgundian.

mosaic glass: Purple and white bicolored glass pressed in fluted design is one product designated by this term. Actually any glass pattern or design contrived by assembling tiny pieces or rods of glass, cut into thin sections and encased, to form walls of vessels, plates, paperweights, et cetera.

mosaic gold: Sulphuret of tin, used in giving a gilt luster to plaster, stone, and other substances.

mosare: Pickling jar.

Moscow glass: Made at Moscow, O., 1814–30s, including Lafayette, Clay, and other historic flasks and general utility wares. Plant was near Cincinnati.

Moses furniture: Generally a derisive term in southern Illinois. Moses Phillips and Evert Westervelt conducted cabinetware establishments at Vandalia from 1830, making "modern and elegant" mahogany Directoire- and Empire-styled cabinetwork.

mosquito bar: A tenting for a tester bed, or a special tester on a wirework rod, made of fine netting. A "bar" to mosquitoes and night-flying moths. A "kitty fisher." [*Example pictured.*]

moss bed: A bed sack stuffed with dried moss.

moss rose: This popular garden rose, named for the mosslike fuzz that is peculiar to it, became a craze not only with indoor and outdoor gardeners from early 19th century, but was used as a decorative element on all sorts of objects, painted, stenciled, cast, molded, etched, et cetera, on everything from glass to silver. A Bristol milk-glass vase with moss-rose décor in color, made in 1830s to sell at 10 cents, sold in 1910s as "Stiegel" glass at very high prices. Any moss-rose ware can safely be dated 1808 at the earliest and 1898 at the latest.

moss ware: Coarse brown decorated wares made by the delftware potter, Thomas Spencer of Liverpool, at his Prescott pottery from 1790s. Cheap wares with a décor imitative of mossy growth. Made by other potters when it became popular in the cheap trade.

mote spoon: Any spoon with perforations in the bowl, used in "moting" or crumbling. Some spoons without perforation, used ceremonially at certain assemblies, were called "motes," which, it is suspected, were originally called moot spoons, or moot-hall spoons, the moot hall being a place where "moot questions" or controversies were settled by an arbiter.

Mother Goose: Traditionally this character is said to derive from Elizabeth Vergoose of Boston, a 17th-century baby-sitter who lulled tots to sleep with ballads. Thomas Fleet published the rhymes, and so "Mother Goose" achieved immortality.

mother-of-pearl: Nacre. The inner shell enamel of certain bivavle mollusks, as oysters, mussels, clams, et cetera. Any pottery, glass, or composition imitative of this glaze, or the actual thing, as used in button making, et cetera.

moth silk: Properly, raw silk. The term was much used during the American silkworm craze of 1830s–40s.

motion: A puppet show.

motley: A professional or court fool's dress. Also a fool's cap. Said of some chairs having a fool's-cap cushion or decoration.

Mott iron ornaments: Garden statuary, settees, tables, chairs, fountains, et cetera, of cast iron, made by Mott Ironworks of New York from mid-19th century.

mold marked glass: Generally glass marked identifiably by the maker with his name or symbol, or to order for a customer, or in honor of a patron. The marking may be in blown or pressed glass. Of course any mold-blown or pressed glass owes its decoration to mold making.

moulding plane; molding plane: Term applied to any plane with a shaped cutter or cutters, used to produce various mouldings, or moldings, in wide variety. The name moldings, such as fillet, fascia, ovolo, torus, et cetera, are traditional and have changed little through the years. All of them derived from the classic orders of architecture, either directly or through the guilds of Freemasons, who carried on in the Gallic traditions, which also derived from classic sources.

moultan: Light muslin woven in a pattern imitative of embroidery. Originating commercially at Glasgow, Scotland, from 1840s.

Mount Pleasant glass: Olive and dark green, amber and yellow-amber flasks, bottles, and hollow wares credited to the glassworks at Mount Pleasant, N.Y., from 1840s. A horse-drawn railroad flask, the

Townsend Sarsaparilla Tonic bottles, and some Saratoga-water bottles were made here.

mounts: Furniture fittings, as drawer pulls, escutcheons, knobs, handles, turns, hinges, latches, and hardware in general for the cabinet trade.

Mount Vernon glass: Made at Oneida County, N.Y.; the original factory moved to Mount Pleasant (*see above*). The Mount Vernon "mark" sometimes mentioned is an impression on a prunt, reading MT. VERNON GLASS CO. There is a space for insertion of name of party for whom the prunt-marked bottles were made; this was also impressed on the prunt.

Mount Washington glass: Blown, pressed, and cut glass made at South Boston, the Mount Washington Glass Works, established 1837. Merged 1894 with Pairpoint works.

mourning locket: Locket of personal jewelry, designed as container for miniatures, hair, nail parings, et cetera, of departed loved ones.

mourning quilt: Bedquilt of mid-19th century, when sorrow was a sweet emotion; a quilt of memorial patches, or a quilt of only black, white, and gray cloth patches.

mousseline: Light wool (*de laine*) fabric of fine quality. Lana muslin.

Moustiers: A French faïence of considerable fame; six potteries produced wares at this place from 17th to 19th century.

mouth mirror: Early types of this dental instrument were ornate, sometimes gold- or silver-mounted, and very decorative. The utilitarian type dates from c. 1850s.

moving bookshelves: Shelves between decorative post ends, mounted on castors. Popular from 1820s to 1860s.

moving sideboard: A sort of large tea-cart or "wagon table" to wheel from kitchen to dining place. Open shelves are arranged between broad end posts.

moving slides: Magic-lantern slides with rotary or jump motion.

mower's ring: A ring-form bottle for carrying on arm or shoulder. Generally pottery or stoneware. A farm field worker's bottle.

Moyer ware: Reference would seem to be to the products of the Moyer, or Meyer, pottery, Harrisburg, Pa., from 1858. The kilns were set up at a much earlier date by a potter named J. Young. Stoneware.

mozil: A wine cup.

muckender; mucker: Handkerchief.

Mudge inhaler: Presumed to be a misnomer. A genuine "puzzle mug" in form of a pewter tankard with hollow handle having two holes at top which, if not covered by thumb of drinker, spilled contents. This name derives from an example found engraved with name "Mudge's Inhaler." The vessels are actually 18th century; the engraving on example found is of 19th century.

mudgejar: Inlay pattern of Moorish style, found on Spanish chests and cupboards and noted on court cupboards of Tudor style.

mud-hook-footed: Said of the clawlike supporting feet of pedestal-type tables.

muffetee: A wrist muff.

muffineer: A tall shaker-topped vessel for dusting sugar on muffins. Also used as a salt shaker and spice shaker. Examples of silver, Sheffield plate, brass, pewter and wood, pottery, glass, et cetera. The form dates from 17th century or earlier. Also called a muffinen.

muff pistol: A very small pistol with a two-inch barrel.

mug: A drinking vessel, originally in form of a "mug" or human face. From this term all handled drinking vessels were finally called mugs.

mugger: A dealer in crockery, especially a peddler, or gypsy.

mug-lock: Padlock in form of grotesque body, with arm forming the hasp. Key was inserted at bottom of torso.

mugwort: Wormwood.

mull: Mill, especially a small hand or pocket mill.

Mullen, J.: Extensive seat-furniture manufacturer of Cincinnati from 1830s. Fancy and Windsor chairs were his specialty.

mullica: A window glass; probably a trade name of early 19th century.

mullion: The element of a panel or window assembly other than stiles and rails. Of a paneled door, the upright sidepieces are stiles; the top, bottom, and middle crosspieces are rails; the uprights between rails are mullions. In windows, the uprights, straight or curvate, separating the whole into paned (paneled) parts, are mullions.

multi-color well: Inkwell with a revolving top rotating to reveal various wells in which colored inks were kept. These date from as early as 1800. There is also a well with fixed top, having 3 rotating wells.

multi-winged table: Said of any falling-leaf table having three or more leaves, all supported on gates or butterfly supports.

multum-in-parvo bath: A metallic bathtub of sheet iron, tin, or zinc, of chair shape, serving as sponge, hip, and sitz bath.

mundungo: Tobacco.

Munn boiler: An egg cooker with built-in sand-glass timer. Date is from 1840s.

muntins: Dividing bars for panels of glass in doors and windows. Some are arranged in lacelike tracery. Generally of wood, from 17th century, but also of lead work when of earlier date. Lead and other metallic muntins are of traditional usage and have never been altogether outmoded.

mural crown: A crown pictured as a series of battlements, or of 9 to 13 "walls" of varying height. Greek-revival-style element.

Murano: An island in the Adriatic, near Venice; site of the famed Venetian glasshouses from 13th century. From these glassworks the art of fine glassmaking spread over Europe.

murraine: The black briony.

murrhine: Fluor spar; the murrhina of the ancients. Also art glass imitative of natural murrhina. There is a pottery of calcined stones, imitative of glass, mentioned as having this name.

Muscipula: Figurine by Spode, after the painting by Sir Joshua Reynolds, picturing a young girl with mouse cage in hand and a kitten at her feet.

musette: A bagpipe.

museum jar: Glass jar for hermetic sealing, used to preserve museum specimens, generally in alcohol.

Musgrave stove: An Empire-style cabinet of hardwood, made to accommodate three early, permanently installed "gas burners." Originally this luxury was priced at $75. So many were sold that the price dropped to $40. Made in 1850s at Cincinnati by H. B. Musgrave. [*Example pictured.*]

mushroom: A shape imitative of the natural fungus; a sort of rounded pancake or biscuit form. Found on chair arms, footings, and as turning terminals.

mushroom paperweight: Glass paperweight with umbrella-like form embedded in the casing.

mushroom stool: Heavy wooden garden seats formed like a large mushroom. These were popular in American gardens of 1870s and may well be popular again. [*Picture in form of a working drawing of 1870 example is shown.*]

mushroom stopper: Curvate-top, umbrella-form stopper of blown, pressed, molded, and cut glass.

musical glasses: Bowls of glass selected for a chromatic scale and mounted in felted frames. Played by rubbing rims with wetted fingers. Popular from 17th century and made commercially in 19th century with oak and mahogany cases. Also tumblers, wineglasses, glass tubes, et cetera, in chromatic scale, played as a musical novelty.

musical spits: Kitchen music, achieved by placing a mechanical music box in the spring or weight motor of a turnspit. Swiss, for the Italian restaurant market; some known in U.S. as 19th-century curiosities.

musical toy: Any plaything, whether for children or sophisticated adults, delivering music mechanically or by playing with hammers, keys, or bells. An infinite variety of examples date from 17th to 19th century.

music box: Specifically the Swiss pricketroll, tune-comb, mechanical box operating from spring motor. Many varieties. But also any motor-driven or cranked mechanism yielding music from pipes, reeds, tuning forks, bells, et cetera.

music chair: Adjustable-height, swivel, and any other special chair or seat for a musical performer at or with an instrument.

music cover: Engraved and lithographed pictorial covers of sheet music. Thousands of different titles covering every human activity are of record.

music-room chair: *See* Chairs, All Kinds.

musket: A short-barreled smoothbore gun. Term is often loosely used.

Muskingum glass: Reference is to glass made in Muskingum County, O., at various works, as Zanesville's Sullivan Works, White Works, et cetera.

must: Variant of "mast," any ground or mashed pome fruit.

mustache cup: An elegancy which followed the war with Mexico, when men of the Army and Navy, from lowest to highest rank, cultivated the hair growth of the upper lip. Curlers, oils, dyes, brushes, combs, and the mustache cup followed. Some were actually made for use of left-handed men. It is safe to assume any mustache cup is of a date after 1850. What is not generally known is that mustache glasses and beakers were also made, some of Sturbridge glass and some of Belleek porcelain.

mustard coffee: Coffee fortified with a pinch of mustard.

mustard pots: Any commercial or "boughten" container for the sauce, mustard, invented by Mother Clement of Durham, England, 1729. She sold her sauce in pots, carried in stock by several colonial apothecaries (who were also dealers in condiments) of Philadelphia, New York, and Boston. Silver, Sheffield plate, glass-lined, plain glass, pottery, and wood examples.

mutton ham: Smoked lamb legs, "salted in brine, reeked in smoke of corncobs and sweet hay." The original "ham-lamb" or "lamb-ham."

muzzling: Muslin.

myrobalane: A dried aromatic fruit somewhat similar to the date or prune.

mystery: In antiquarian parlance, (1) the secret of a craft or trade or (2) a religious drama or play. A mummery. "Master" and "mister" both derive from knowledge of the mystery of an art or craft.

mythological group: Classic figures: Zeus, Cronus, Venus, Adonis, Jove, Juno, Ceres, the Seasons, et cetera. Generally of china, pottery, or porcelain, displaying two or more figures, popular from the Adam period to mid-19th century. There were several revivals thereafter.

N

nabeshima: Japan porcelain made at the private pottery of the Prince of Hizen from 1716. Enameled decoration; famed for a red-orange color.

nacre: Mother-of-pearl.

Naderman harp: The large harp with pedals, developed by H. Naderman of Paris c. 1776.

naïf: True native luster or gloss.

nail: A linear measure of 2¼ inches.

nail penny: A nail length measure, the size range being three penny, the smallest, to twenty penny, the largest. The length in inches varied somewhat with the decades or eras of manufacture.

Nailhead: Pattern of pressed glass made up of imitative cutting that is a criss-crossing of X-patterns with bossed junctures.

nailhead globe: Lantern and lamp globes of glass with oblong protuberances in a series of rows.

nail naper: A gimlet or gimblet.

Nailsea: English glass made at place so named in Somerset, near Bristol. Factory was in operation from 1788 to 1873. Most of the products were of the same nature as Bristol wares, but famed for a bicolored, swirled glassware, generally dark green and white.

name box: Sewing box, decorated inside and out, with various stock names, as Anna, Helen, Margaret, et cetera, painted or printed inside the lid. Date is from 1840s.

name pitchers: Reference is to pitchers and ewers commemorative of some famed person or place, with representations and names molded, transfer-printed, or painted on.

name scissors: A stock name device of marking a scissors with female names of all kinds. Popular and advertised in U.S. from 1825.

name stoves: Any cast-iron stove with the name of the founder and any special name of the model. No less than 250 named stoves are of record. Mayflower, Kentucky, Indiana, May Queen, Boston, Etna, Grecian, et cetera, are representative of the names.

named wallpapers: Reference is to name of scenic design or the pattern. Rising Sun, Washington, Constitution, Bay of Naples, Nanking, et cetera, are some of the names.

name lanterns: Reference is to ceremonial patterns with names of individuals cut or engraved on the globes. [*Example pictured.*]

nameless: A certain pyriform glass pitcher on a flat base that has been named "nameless" somewhere, at some time, by somebody, also nameless. A late model has been more properly designated as "Queen Anne" by some authorities and as "Georgian" by others. Our sympathy, of course, is with the nameless one who, not recognizing the source of the design, was content to name the pattern or design "nameless." These collectors of late glass seem to have a kind of fun of their own.

nankeen: Fawn-colored fabric of naturally tinted cotton. Woven in China and India; it is recorded as a popular breeches fabric.

Nanking: (1) An export porcelain of China; finer than the export ware erroneously called "Lowestoft." (2) A woven straw matting, also from China.

Nantgarw: Porcelain from the pottery at this place in Wales, founded c. 1810; highly glazed soft-paste ware of considerable merit, made to 1820s. There is an extensive notice of this ware in *Ceramic Art of Great Britain*, by Llewellynn Jewitt.

napery: From *mappa*, a cloth, or from *knappa*, the nape of the neck. Either or both may be correct. Napery means (1) table linen, and (2) neck linen.

naphtha lantern: A self-generating gas lantern, the fluid naphtha in a reservoir above the lantern proper. Heat from flame generated naphtha gas. Date is c. 1880s.

Napier bones: Rods of bone or cardboard bearing sums of multiplication and forming a calculating device for mechanics. Invented by Lord Napier.

napkin press: A small screw press for table linens.

Napoleon bottle: Reference is to a figural bottle of a French soldier, definitely *not* Napoleon. The date is c. 1850s.

Natt mirrors: Thomas Natt, the maker, was working at Philadelphia in 1840s. Traditionally said to have made tabernacle and fancy mirrors for the hotel and steamboat trade.

nature prints: Outlines of leaves, flowers, fibers, lace, et cetera, pressed in soft lead plates to make an impression, then electroplated and printed.

Nautilus Cut: Pattern of cut glass featuring three large rings, joined like the famous Ballantine trade-mark, with a shell-form fan cutting in each from the center.

nautilus jug: Shell-form jug by the Davenport works. A ceramic pitcher.

naval mirror: Reference is most likely to the tabernacle-form mirror which frequently has a naval or marine scene painted in the upper glass panel.

navette: (1) A nef; a boat-shaped vessel of ecclesiastical usage for holding incense. (2) A sweetmeat box of ship form for the table. Some have clock movements and dials. Date is from 15th century or earlier.

navigation: (1) The art of sailing the seven seas. (2) A series of locks and dams on a stream to make it navigable. Not a canal. Most notable error is on U.S. stamps designating the locks and dams on the Ohio River as its "canalization." It was not that at all; it was the creation of a better navigation.

necessaire: A toilet case; a vanity box; a grooming kit.

neck basin: A barber's vessel used in shaving; patron held the basin, which was notched to fit the neck closely.

neck bottle: A crescent-shaped glass or pottery bottle to hold hot or cold water for application on the neck.

neck seal: Prunt of glass on bottles at or near the neck.

nectar: The recipe speaks for itself: Boil 2 gallons of water for ½ hour; add 1 pound of raisins, seeded and chopped, 4 lemons, sliced thin, the yellow rind of 2 additional lemons, and 2 pounds of loaf sugar (Muscovy is best). Boil 10 minutes. Let stand 4 days, stirring twice daily. Strain through linen; bottle; and let stand a fortnight (2 weeks). Serve in wineglasses with ice.

needle gun: Any "modern" gun of 19th century firing metallic cartridges with a needlelike hammer.

needle house: Any needle case.

needle lock: A patented five-ward lock, operated by five needles on the key.

needle-painted: Art achieved with the needle and varicolored silk threads; stitched pictures. Not needle-point work. The art dates from 15th century.

needle point: Point or single-stitch work, using threads of silk and wool. If silk, the work is *petit point;* if wool, it is *gros point.* Both are needle point.

Needles, John: Cabinetmaker of Baltimore, working in 1840s in Empire and French Antique styles.

Neeves, James: Glass cutter of New York, working from 1850s.

nef: *See* Navette. [*15th-century example pictured.*]

Neff, Joseph: Violin maker of Philadelphia, working from 1840s.

Negro cloth: Linsey-woolsey; half-and-half cloth.

neighborhood: Originally a small settlement or village. Sometimes several were incorporated into a town.

Nelly Bly: The woman who beat Jules Verne's eighty-day schedule for a trip around the world. Novelties and gadgets of 1890s were named for her. There is a pressed-glass platter picturing her in traveling dress. The name was a pen name of Elizabeth Cochrane. She made the trip in 1889.

Nelson & Hardy jug: A Staffordshire jug with low-relief busts of Admiral Nelson and Captain Hardy, who was with Nelson when the Admiral died at Trafalgar. The decoration is colored.

neo-Chippendale: Said of the 1840s in England, when Johnson's designs, reissued, were labeled Chippendale. Allowing for the compromises necessary to apply machine production to the designs, the so-called Victorian style might be called a Chippendale revival in that his styles were drawn from Louis XV sources.

neo-classic: New classic, or classic revival.

nephite water: Carbonated water, sold as a "health julep" in 1800s by Townsend & Speakman. These druggists added syrups to the water and so vended the first "soda water."

ne plus ultras: Writing papers for use when traveling. Date is from 1840s.

neroli: Oil of orange.

nests of drawers: Cabinets with tiers of drawers, especially a number of small drawers.

net for the night: A tatted or knitted nightcap.

netherstocks: Short stockings.

netsuke: A decorative fastener of button-like character. Many are carved of ivory, jade, et cetera. Japanese.

Nevers figures: Glass toys made at this town, especially figural toys for crèches.

Nevers ware: Early faience of France, produced at the town of Nevers. By 1700 there were twelve potteries in operation.

nevin: A fur; an animal skin.

New Albany glass: Reference is to

product of a plant at New Albany, Pa., 1812-90s. Bottles in wide variety.

New Amsterdam glass: Early glass of New York City from (1) the Smedes works, from 1650, and (2) Duyckinks, from 1652.

New Bedford lights: Candles, millions of which were made at New Bedford, Mass., from 1800s. Many fine spermaceti candles were made here. **New Bedford glass** was also made at this place; up to 1870 there was a factory making blown, pressed, and cut wares.

Newbold glass: See Risley Glass.

New Boston glass: The factory was at Perryopolis, Pa., from 1810s. Hollow wares and bottles.

New Bremen glass: Amelung glass, which see.

New Bridge ware: Ironstone china made at New Bridge Pottery, Longport, England, from 1877. One possible other product is the crayon-decorated ware, a technique originated by F. J. Emery, who was a partner in the New Bridge enterprise.

New Canton: (1) The china and porcelain ware produced at Bow works. (2) The contemporary name of the works itself. [Example pictured.]

Newcastle bottle: Any bottle, but especially the standard (English) quart bottle, made at Newcastle-on-Tyne from 1680s. The glasshouses of this vicinity made blown, engraved, and cut wares which were imported and sold by merchants in colonial, and early Federal days.

Newcastle ware: This reference, if not to glass, is to ceramics made at Warburton works or other potteries of the region; known also as Tyne wares. The pottery district was established in 1730s.

newel finial: Decorative épi placed upon the newel of a stair-railing assembly. Clear and "paperweight" types of glass, carved wood, turnings, statuary, et cetera.

Newell lamp: Safety lamp made by Newell-Willard of Boston from 1850s. Glass reservoir (said to be Sandwich) on pedestal base. Lamps burned camphene within a mesh or screen around the flame. Also any lamp mounted on a newel post.

Newell portraits: Colored photographs made at Philadelphia, 1850s, by a photographer-artist of this name.

New England glass: Products of the New England Glass Co., founded 1817. Early pressed glass. Also made paperweights, the artist being M. Pierre from Baccarat. An enormous production of fine wares, as good as any from the Stiegel and Amelung glassworks, plus cut and engraved wares, and the wholesale and retail distribution of imported wares frankly advertised as such. Student cannot appreciate this glass enterprise or its products without reference to *Cambridge Glass*, by Lura Woodside Watkins.

New England Pineapple: Pattern of pressed glass featuring a pineapple-form panel, saw-toothed to represent the surface of the fruit, with a looping probably to represent the foliage, the entire units of this form separated by a three-petaled lily form. Knowing what we do about pressed-glass pattern names, one wonders why this one was not called Tulip &

Pomegranate and even claimed as "Pennsylvania Dutch."

Newfoundland glass: Bottles, flasks, and offhand production at a works named "Newfoundland being within four miles of this place [New York]" in 1758.

New Geneva Glass: Works founded at New Geneva, Pa., by Albert Gallatin, of Swiss-French ancestry, who taught French at Harvard, fought in the Revolution, was elected to Congress, and became Secretary of the Treasury. This saga of a glassmaker who made good begins with the glass factory here considered, established 1797. He withdrew from active management in 1803, when partners purchased his interest. Free-blown, pattern-molded sugar bowls, jars, bottles, and tablewares. Plant moved to Greensboro in 1807.

New Granite glass: Stoddard, N.H., glass, made at New Granite Works, 1865-71. Snuff jars, bottles, and hollow wares.

New Hall ware: True English china, the result of the Cookworthy and other patents and the collaboration of famed potters. Bagnall, Champion, Keeling, Palmer, Hollins, Warburton, and others established the New Hall Works at Shelton, Staffordshire. Hard-paste china with the famed "composition" glaze made to 1810, thereafter bone china. Works closed 1825 and reopened 1826. In 1842 the plant was moved to Joiner Square and ceased to be New Hall. Only early mark is a swash letter N. Later mark is "New Hall" in a circle. [Examples of the ware pictured.]

New Hampshire tops: Trellised cornices on cabinet pieces, such as highboys, instead of the more general pillar-and-scroll or broken pediment, are now credited to a "school" of New Hampshire cabinetmakers working in latter half of 18th century.

New Haven copper: Made at Seymour, Conn., from 1849 by the New Haven Co. Manufactured braziers and acted as dealers in block tin and ingot lead. Patented a permanent gloss for copper utensils in 1876.

New Haven folding chairs: Tuck-away seat furniture, camp stools, self-propelled invalids' chairs, et cetera. Made from 1870s.

Newhouse furniture: In Alabama this was fine furniture; made by B. Newhouse, Mobile, a branch of the Newhouse enterprise in New York City, from 1840s. French Antique and Louis XV revival furniture of a quality appealing to Southern planters. Found from Mississippi to Georgia.

New Jersey foot: Trifoliate foot; variant found on Queen Anne style cabriole leg, said to be peculiar to New Jersey—with exceptions, of course.

New Jersey spatter: Said of the spatter-decorated wares of the American Pottery, Jersey City.

Newland mirrors: Prize-medal winners at the Crystal Palace, N.Y., 1853; important mirrors and stock examples made by Newland of Philadelphia, operating from 1840s. Gilded pier and overmantel, wall, oval, and tabernacle types.

New London glass: Bottles, flasks, and vials made at New London, Conn., from 1850 to 1870.

Newman flower prints: These are book illustrations from Dr. J. B. Newman's *Botany*, 1846, with 46 colored plates by Whitefield, and *Boudoir Botany*, 1847, with 60 colored quarto, or small folio size, prints.

New Orleans "character" prints: Small folio prints of street characters from set of 16 issued by Pychard & Garcia, 1876.

New Orleans iron lace: The cast-iron balconies of New Orleans have intrigued thousands who were not aware that many of them were made at Philadelphia by Wood & Perot, who shipped so much fancy ironwork to this city that a huge branch foundry was established right at New Orleans as Wood, Miltenberger & Co. If there be any die-hards who would seek further proof, the foundry was at 57 Camp Street and 247 Tchoupitoulas. Foundries of Pittsburgh, St. Louis, Cincinnati, and Baltimore sold some iron lace to New Orleans builders, but the major business went to the firms here mentioned. The New Orleans Ornamental Iron Works was another local trading firm made up of the Baumiller, Goodwin, Bennett, and Lurges foundries.

New Philippines: Texas, when a state of Mexico and an independent nation, was sometimes so named.

new tenor: Silver within two pennyweight alloy in the pound pure. A coin standard established 1697 to discourage use of silver coinage by silversmiths as a source of commercial metal. The new tenor was of too high a value for such use, and the smiths bought the lesser-value, higher-alloy metal. The standard was maintained to 1720, when old tenor was again issued, the ratio being 11 ounces 2 pennyweight pure silver and 10 pennyweight alloy to the Troy pound.

Newton, J.: Miniature painter and drawing-school proprietor, Pittsburgh, Pa., from 1830s.

Newton Britannia: Made by Orrin Newton, Pittsburgh, from 1834 to 1863.

Newton gun: Product of gunsmith P. S. Newton, Hartford, Conn., established 1843, still active in early 1860s. Made the "attached muzzle" rifle.

New Windsor glass: Made at New Windsor, Ulster County, N.Y., 1750s–80s. Window glass and bottles.

Niagara Falls: The number-one natural wonder of colonial and Federal America and one of the world's natural wonders. Innumerable prints, paintings, engravings, lithographs, and book illustrations were made, with the result that no picture of the Falls is considered rare or highly desirable. There is a pressed-glass platter with the Falls frosted and the sky clear.

niche screen roaster: Commercial name for a bottle-type roasting jack with a clockwork turnspit. An excellent roaster; date is from 1830s. [*Example pictured.*]

nicho (nekko): A frame or shadow box of wood or sheet metal, housing a holy figure. Spanish Southwest, 1800–50s.

Nicholson cards: Advertising cards, some marked with this name (others may be marked "Central"), produced at Baltimore from 1850s. This enterprise developed a press that printed 10,000 cards per hour.

Nickel & Suffa "antique": This subject seems to have been neglected by all commentators. The firm manufactured a new "antique" style of chamber and cottage furniture at Providence, R.I., from 1850s.

nicknacktory: A private museum devoted to housing a varied collection of curiosities.

Nicoll Liverpool: One of the unbelievable phenomena in the American scene. John Nicoll of New Haven, Conn., was a wholesale dealer in Liverpool wares from the end of the Revolution. His imports were of huge total and included Staffordshire wares, "eanemel'd, pencill'd, and blue."

niddy noddy: Wooden winder used in hanking yarn. It has slender parts and is shaped like a double-ended anchor, with the flukes at right angles.

niello: The decorative art from which intaglio engraving for print making developed. Niello is deep-line engraving on gold and silver, filling the lines with copper, lead, and sulphur in borax, forming a kind of black enamel, fired in the lines, and then polished. In button making, the niello-metallic examples were not made by this artist's process but by etching, filling the lines with galvanic deposit of other metal, and polishing. This same thing was done on watch cases, sword blades, pistol and gun barrels, et cetera, from 1840s.

nigger: A term applied to black-skinned people, originally was not a derogatory term; it derives from Nigra, pronounced *knee-gra*, not *knee-grow*. The Southern usage as knee-gra, or negra, became nigger.

niggered: Pertaining to logs cut by firing standing or fallen timber.

nigger linsey: Cotton ticking.

night clock: Any clock or timekeeping device having illumination, through an aperture or by projection. All types are rare. One is literally a candle dial, casting a shadow that lengthens as the candle diminishes. In this type, the burning candle is the clock.

night crow: Chamber pot, thunder mug; in colonial Virginia, "Oliver's skull."

night-jar steps: Bed steps of two tiers, the top one covering the night jar.

night stand: A closed cabinet for night jar and other unmentionables, generally at or near the bedside.

night-watchman jug: In the Toby tradition but not a true Toby. This jug is a squatting watchman with lantern and, viewed from the front, appears as a figurine. At rear there is a pouring spout. When used as a jug, the arm of the figure serves as the handle. Late 18th century. [*Example pictured.*]

Nilsson: A hoop-skirt form named for Christine Nilsson, a famed lady of the stage and heartbreaker of the 1870s.

nipp'd diamond waies: A form of glass decoration; the phrase is 17th-century English and not generally understood. Read it "nipped diamond-wise," meaning the plastic hot glass is nipped with a tool into diamond form. The nipp'd diamond form of decorating plain glass by nipping with the puncella, a sort of shears, is an ancient technique.

Nixon, T.: Silhouetter or profile-likeness

cutter of New Haven, Conn., and other localities, working 1800–20s.

nobile: Well known.

Noble engine: Internal-combustion engine predating the "Otto" of Germany by many years. Made by Butler Noble of Dexter, N.Y., 1836.

nob thatcher: Wigmaker.

no-chimney burner: Perforated metal shield for any kerosene-burning flat-wick lamp, eliminating need for a chimney or for use if and when a chimney broke. [*Example pictured dates from 1860s.*]

nocturnal: A sort of circular slide rule with sighting bar for telling time at night from the stars.

nodding figures; nodders; pagods: Porcelain figures with separate heads and hands, poised and wired to nod and wave when given a push and continuing in action for a long time because of delicate poise or balance. Many are of Dresden or other continental European ware, some of delft. Imitative of Chinese examples, some of religious significance. [*Example pictured.*]

nog: Strong beer; heady beer.

noggin: Potbellied drinking vessel, originally with a face or head (noggin) on it. Finally a small stoppered decanter for individual service of rum, whiskey, gin, et cetera. [*Example pictured.*]

nola: A choir bell.

nonagon: *See* Polygon.

nonchalantes: Heelless slippers, braid-trimmed, from 1840s.

nonesuch: The superlative intarsia-paneled chests of Henry VIII period, from which, believe it or not, the architectural chests with painted panels found in Pennsylvania, derive. The name is from Henry's palace, the "Nonesuch."

Nonnemacher ware: Pennsylvania German pottery from the center of Germanic settlement, Allentown; made late 1840s–80s.

Nonpareil: Pattern of pressed glass made up of diagonal bands forming large diamond panes in each of which is a heraldic cross-form element.

noon house: Where the nooning was eaten on Sundays by churchgoers of 17th and 18th centuries. Often the nooning was a break between halves of a four- or five-hour sermon.

Norcross, Otis: Crockery merchant of Boston from 1810; firm became Jones, McDuffee & Stratton. In the years of operation this house sold gaudy Dutch, so called, Staffordshire, Wedgwood, and many other wares.

Norfolk latch: Similar to the patented Suffolk latch, but with handle mounted on an escutcheon. Made from 1770s and still obtainable as a cast-iron or brass item.

Noritake: Japan porcelain, made in 20th century, at the largest porcelain factory in the Far East. Exported to every country on the globe, including U.S. Marked "Nippon," or "Made in Japan." Pronounced "Norah-tah-kee," not "Norah-take."

northern Virginia: New England.

North pistol: U.S. naval sidearm made by S. North of Berlin, Conn., from 1808.

Northwood glass: Reference is to the product of the English glassmaker, Northwood, who settled in U.S. in 1880 and worked for several different works (LaBelle and Bridgeport, O., among others) and finally had his own factory at Indiana, Pa., where he made late pressed wares, custard glass, and some novelties, all of which are now items of collecting interest.

Norton Pottery: Bennington; the pottery originally established by John Norton, 1793. Christopher Fenton became a partner in 1845. He started his own, the United States Pottery, in 1847.

norway: A whetstone.

Norwich shawl: Silk and wool shawls as woven at Norwich, England, from 1797. Stripes, checks, and three-color 'broidered effects.

Norwich-Thomas electric light: W. S. Thomas made this light, with its own dynamo and arc. Examples made at Norwich, Conn., 1847, as scientific apparatus. [*The inventor's own drawing is reproduced as illustration.*]

Norwich ware: The pottery wares of Norwich, Conn., made from 18th century. See *Early New England Potters and Their Wares*, by Lura Woodside Watkins.

nose basket: Hickory muzzles for oxen who tramped out the grain; a direct violation, by religious New Englanders, of the biblical injunction, "thou shalt not muzzle the ox when he treadeth out the corn."

nosing: A projecting round or half-round molding.

nostrum: From Nostradamus, who called his plague elixir "nostrum," hence any cure-all.

Nottingham stone: A ceramic ware. Brown stoneware with decoration, also called Brampton ware and Chesterfield ware. Made from c. 1700 to 1800 or later.

nove: Bassano porcelain and faïence, made from 1750s. Italian.

novelty: Any new or cheap object of any substance: toys, whimseys, doodads, gewgaws. Glass, pottery, metal, plastic, and other novelties, memorials, cheap commemorative and other objects.

Noyes, W. J.: Cast-iron-ware producer of Albany, N.Y., mid-19th century. Made marked kettles, pots, pans, and hollow kitchenwares.

Noyes & Morrill: Furniture manufacturers of Worcester, Mass., from c. 1840s. Cabinet furniture, stuffed rocking chairs, including the so-called "Lincoln" rocker; sofas and fancy chairs in Empire styles.

nubie; nubia: Originally "nubian," a piece of lightweight turban material wound into a headdress by men and women of 17th and 18th centuries. Called a nubie during most of last half of 19th century and early 20th.

nulled: Knurled, or irregularly ridged. Imitative of the structure of a burl. Also make-and-break moldings, bead-and-wheels, et cetera.

number mugs: Shaving mugs with gold or luster numerals on them instead of names. Numbered mugs were used in the high-class barbershops, where the mug of a specific number, assigned to a patron,

1, Night-Watchman Jug. 2, "Nodder," properly a "Pagod." 3, Ox Yoke. 4, Onion Jar. 5, Overpanel Mirror. 6, Orrery. 7, Orguinette. 8, Old Abe, the Wisconsin eagle. 9, Paint-Scraping Furnace. 10, Pantograph. 11, Parrot Filter. 12, Paste Cutters. 13, Peg Jug. 14, Pen Card. 15, Phoebe Lamp. 16, Pew Group.

253

was used for none other than the client. The less exclusive shops paraded occupational and named mugs of patrons.

nuncheon: Nooning; lunch; midday bite.

Nunns piano: Made by R. & W. Nunns of New York from 1820s. This firm invented the diagonal-strung frame and the square (really oblong) piano of the 1840s-90s.

nuphenbecker: A vessel with cover, of ceramic ware, glass, or metal. The term has various spellings; one researcher suggests it derives from "novena-becker," meaning a covered bowl holding relics displayed at a religious ceremony (in France and Italy) during medieval times. There is a Germanic variant (reported from Switzerland) naming the object neuppenbecker. There are probably other spellings. The use, originally, as a reliquary would seem to be questionable.

nuptial cup: Bridal cup.

nursery banners: Colored banners of chintz or linen with nursery subjects printed or hand-worked upon them. Some in the 1870s were of architect's linen cloth, line-embroidered and hand-colored. The cloth was used to provide easy tracing from the subject desired.

nursery heater: Generally a device fitting over a kerosene or some other fluid lamp providing a quick stove for heating milk and gruel. [*Example pictured.*] Late examples used Clark "fairy-lamp" candles.

nursery refrigerator: Often mistaken for a converted night stand or even a wine cooler, these are ornate bedroom refrigerators holding a cubic foot of ice. The interior was lined with zinc or sheet tin; the casing was of walnut. Here is an idea for a present-day maker; a really small electric bedroom refrigerator.

nursery yacht: A pair of quarter-circle rockers with a seat at each end, a cage in center. Two youngsters could run this yacht on the nursery floor and entertain another in the center caged cabin. Date is from 1850s.

nursing chair: *See* Chairs, All Kinds.

nutcracker night: Halloween.

nutmeg graters: Small graters, of various shapes and sizes, for grating the aromatic nut of the mace. Many people carried pocket graters to spice their own food and beverages. Incidentally, the same graters were used to pulverize pressed (tail or plug) tobacco into snuff. These were favored by many who professed to abhor tobacco but used it in secret.

nutmeg lamp: A very small night lamp, of the same philosophy as the acorn lamp, the fairy lamp, sparking lamp, et cetera. The nutmeg was an oil-burning lamp, not a candle lamp. The glass reservoir is marked NUTMEG. Made to 1900s.

nutmeg spoon: A grater-handled spoon.

nut peeler: A nutpick.

nutto wood: Hickory wood.

Nyon ware: Swiss porcelain, made 1780s-1810s. Some of it is gold-banded, with colorful floral décor and scenic effects. It looks like American Tucker porcelain, and most likely some has been sold as such.

O

Oaken Bucket: Pattern of pressed glass in imitation of coopered woodenware. Various colors and clear.

Oakes furniture: Cabinetwork by Andrew Oakes of Brooklyn, one of the first to advertise furniture made of "blisted," the gumwood that looks like mahogany. Worked in 1830s and 1840s. Advertised bureaus, tables, "curled and plain."

Oakes spoons: Silver spoons made at Hartford, Conn., in great quantities by Henry Oakes at his "manufactory" in 1830s. He advertised his spoons "pure as dollars."

oak gall; oak apples: The gall is a leaf excrescence, the apple formed on the tree proper. Both were used in making inks and dyes.

oak opening: A copse.

oast: A hop kiln.

oatmeal: True meal, stone-ground, from oat grains; not rolled oats.

obelisk: Square form tapering to an angled point or a finial.

oble: Thin ceremonial wafer. **oble iron:** The forming iron used in making obles.

oblique braces: Angle-set braces joining chair seat and leg, or table top and leg.

The Chinese styles are of various shapes and forms.

obsidian: Volcanic glass; cooled lava. Generally black, but stratified colors are not uncommon.

obsquare: Oblong.

obverse: The right or main side of any coin or medal. The recto or right-hand page of a book.

occasional table: Any small table of good style or taste; a sofa table.

occupational mug: The term is almost universally applied to shaving mugs with actual or emblematic scenes of the occupation of the owner, whose name is generally also on the mug. These mugs are all late 19th century and bespeak not an exclusive barbershop but a general one. The finer shops used only numbered mugs without names. There were drinking mugs, sometimes painted with emblems of the occupation of the owner, made by several Staffordshire potteries. These are much earlier than the shaving mugs.

O'Connell pitcher: A mask jug made by Bagnall Beach Pottery, Philadelphia, c. 1848, and by the Haig pottery, from the same molds, from 1855 to possibly 1900. It is a mask of the Irish patriot, Daniel O'-Connell.

oco snuff: Advertised as dental snuff but actually a dipping or chewing snuff, much used by ladies from 1800 to 1860.

octafoil: Geometrically impossible, as a "foil" is a 120° segment of a circle, or one third of a circle. What is meant usually is a circle of eight scallops.

octagon drum table: A drum-type table with an octaform head instead of a proper round one. Date is from 1800s to as late as 1840s.

oddfellows' knife and fork: Thick-handled device with two prongs, one a two-tined fork, the other a knife.

'ods-pitikins; 'ods-bodikins: Mild oaths, meaning "God's little pity" and "God's body, friends!"

oeil-de-boeuf: Ox eye; an oval boss. Found on much Tudor furniture.

oeil de perdrix: (Partridge eye.) Grain-of-corn-shaped.

oelost: Hot syllabub-like drink of whole milk and beer.

oenochoe: A pitcher or pouring-type vessel; wine pitcher of ancient Greece.

o'erfret: Adorned.

offhand: Work out of regular routine, but contracted for; custom-made ware by a glassmaker or potter.

offuskit: Darkened; smoked; clouded.

ogee: A cyma curve or cyma-curvate element, in plan or section. An ogee molding, mitered, forms the outer edge of the ogee foot. Oog means a double-cyma curve; og, a single one. The cyma curve is the S-curve.

ogival: Same as ogee; also ogive.

O'Hara glass: Cut, engraved, blown, and pressed glass of the Pittsburgh region in several factories owned by or being of the O'Hara interests. In 1870s a consolidation of factories was named the O'Hara Works.

Ohio: Pattern of clear pressed glass made plain, for etching or wheel engraving. The name is said to have been bestowed in honor of the U.S.S. *Ohio.*

Ohio glass: Any glassware made in Ohio, especially at the factories of Kent, Mantua, Portage, and Zanesville, the latter place boasting a glassworks from 1815.

Ohio antiques: The state of Ohio enjoys an unique status in national history in that it was settled mainly by "emigrants" from other states. Virginia, Maryland, Kentucky, New York, Pennsylvania, and Connecticut provided the most settlers. Not until after 1850 was there a surge of German immigrants. The popular arts (in error called "folk" art) of this state are a blending of the popular forms of all its settlers. The early architecture (other than log and blockhouses and stone garrison houses of the pioneer settlers) was Greek revival. The history of Cincinnati in terms of its production of furniture, artwares, clocks, sculptures, et cetera, is deserving of a book of several volumes.

Ohmer furniture: Made at Dayton, O., from 1838 by M. Ohmer, who was still working in 1876. Empire and French Antique revival styles.

oil-boiled calico: Chintz.

oiled paper: (1) Tracing paper of early kind. (2) Early substitute for glass: heavy paper soaked in linseed oil.

oil for lamps: These oils were used as lamp fluids: elephant oil, whale oil, lard oil, camphor oil, turpentine, olive oil, expressed animal fats, and fish oils.

oil-gilded: Gold leaf attached with varnish size.

oil neroli: Orange oil.

oil stand: A household reservoir for lamp oil. Often with a small tap. Advertised as here named from 1830s.

oil tankard: A tankard-shaped vessel with a slender spout; a lamp filler.

oinochoe: Ancient handled and spouted vessel with pear-shaped body and long neck.

ojas: Unglazed redware water jars. Evaporation kept the contents cool.

O.K.: An endorsement said to derive from word of appraisal of Martin Van Buren when he was a presidential candidate. He was "Old Kinderhook," or O.K. Substantiated by opinion in *Saturday Review,* 1941, by Allen Read. The late tutor, Luther Willig of Lancaster, Pa., stated that his grandfather, a music publisher, issued the "O.K. Gallop" in honor of Van Buren.

Old Abe: The Wisconsin eagle that was carried as a live standard in many battles of the War between the States. Many photographs, prints, and effigies were made. [*Old Abe is pictured.*]

Old Bridge Pottery: James Morgan and Jacob Van Winkle operated the Old Bridge (N.J.) Pottery, 1785–1820. The Bissett Pottery was also located at this place from 1815. Both made stonewares and probably redwares with slip and sgraffito decoration.

old cabin bottle: The Booz whiskey bottle; it is not log-cabin but smooth-walled cabin style with neck forming the chimney in center of roof. Address of store on side and name on roof. Several varieties and many reproductions. Jacob's Cabin Tonic was sold in a similar bottle. One variety of Booz bottle has date 1840 on roof, name and designation of contents on side, and lacks the marks of door and windows on front.

Old Dominion: The historic name for Virginia. Old Dominion coffeepot; Old Dominion stove, et cetera, are names used in reference to Virginia. Such named objects were not necessarily made in Virginia.

Oldfield ware: Made at Brampton, England, by Oldfield, Madin, Wright, Hewitt & Co. from 1810. Brown and cane-colored salt-glaze and slip-dipped stonewares. Stilton cheese dishes, game pots, pipes, and other novelties made to 1880s.

Old London Dock bottle: A gin bottle with the name mold-blown in the glass. One of the products of A. M. Binninger & Co., established 1778, N.Y., dealers in all sorts and kinds of alcoholic beverages, tonics, and bitters. The bottle dates from c. 1840s.

old man (of the woods, or mountains) pitcher: Rockingham glaze pitcher of broad front, six-panel form, having a pouring spout in form of bearded man and a pouring rest on the front panel. A gallon pitcher. [*Example pictured.*]

old-mine diamond: Diamonds from mines in operation before the African fields were discovered. Use of term is antiques-trade snobbery; an old-mine diamond is generally rose-cut, flat, has less fire and is less valuable than modern cut stones. The term "rose-cut" is also a phrase used largely with intent to connote rarity or high desirability.

Old Sachem bottle: A bitters bottle said to have been made from 1840s.

Old Scripture ware: The logical assumption would be biblical-scene ware, but the reference would seem to be to japanned sheet-iron wares made at the Old Scripture Factory, Mason, N.H., 19th century.

Olds pie: Parian advertising imitations of pies, top crusts impressed with anchor and arrow points and "H. O. & Co." The pies were made by Olds & Co., New Haven, Conn.

Old Will Jug: Lambeth stoneware jugs featuring "Old Will," a Toby-like drinking character, sitting astride a keg.

O'Leary, Mulvany & Co.: Glass manufacturers of the Pittsburgh area, 19th century.

oleographic paper: Marbleized paper.

oleostatic lamp: A patented lamp which maintained the fuel oil at the proper level at all times.

Olive glass: (1) Product of the Olive Glass House, formerly a Stanger Enterprise, Glassboro, N.J., 1808–24. (2) Glass of an olive-green color.

Oliver's skull: Facetious term for a chamber pot, popular in the Virginia colony during Oliver Cromwell's reign, as a manifestation of derision.

ombre; omber: (1) A striped fabric with gradual shifting of one color into another. (2) A three-player card game played on a triangular-shaped table, preferably. **ombre table:** Any three-sided table.

omnigraph: A reducing-enlarging drawing machine. A pantograph.

omphalos: A rounded knob or boss.

Oneida glass: (1) Glass made at several factories in Oneida County, N.Y., as Durhamville, from 1840s; Dunbarton, same period. (2) Blown and cut glass made at the Oneida Glass Works, Vernon, N.Y., from 1809.

onion foot: A flattened ball foot of onion form.

onion green: A glaze color on ceramic ware, approximating the tone of a green onion stem.

onion jar: Footed pottery jar with 8 to 12 circular orifices or spout holes. Onions kept in the jar sprouted through the holes and so provided savory relish and sauce material. Probably Swiss. [*Example pictured.*]

onionskin: A surface or glaze quality of ceramic ware. Especially American Indian pottery of Southwest which has a surface resembling onionskin.

Onslow: A named pattern or style of flat silver, said to have been made first by Hester Bateman of London. Chief characteristic of the pattern, on spoon handles, is a backward curve or curl at the top.

onyx Wedgwood: Another, and contemporaneous, term for jasper ware.

ooze: Strong tannic acid. **ooze leather:** Derived from hides tanned in this potent acid.

Opal: Pattern of pressed glass of opalescent body and heavy vertical or swirled ribbing. Opal was the original name for what is now called milk glass. In the trade, opalescent glass was a body imitative of the opal gem, not milk white. The confusion of terms is due to trade and factory names and claims. In *ABC's of Old Glass*, opal glass is correctly designated as dense white.

Opaque Scroll: Pattern of pressed glass featuring rococo scrolls, made only, so it is said, in opaque glass in several colors.

opaque white: Glass looking like porcelain; said to have been the first type of glass ever made, before the secret of transparent glass was discovered.

open arm: A chair arm that is a framed arm rest, not upholstered or otherwise closed.

open back: Any seat furniture having a framed back, not covered or upholstered.

open-book pull: Drawer pulls in the general form of an open book.

open border: Any rim or edging with piercing or openwork.

open-pot Toby: A type of Toby jug in which the figure of Toby holds a true miniature jug of himself, open at top, and fillable with a jigger of liquor.

Open Rose: Pattern of pressed glass featuring rose sprigs with the blooms full-blown.

open-scroll cupboard; open cupboard: Any open-faced or doorless cabinet for keeping of hollowares, with scroll-cut stiles and rails.

open thimble: The original thimble; a metallic finger stall. All sorts of metals from gold to iron were used in thimble making, many of the examples engraved or molded. The closed thimble came into general use in early 18th century.

open twist: Spiral turning of two or more bines or stems, with the interior section cut away, thereby presenting an open spiral. Rare and early, from William & Mary and Carolean periods.

openwork glass: Said of pressed or blown wares having decoration in form of a series of apertures, or openings.

ophicalce veinée: Veined serpentine limestone, sometimes used as a table or sideboard top.

opodeldock: A cure-all. The recipe: Castile soap, camphor oil, oil of rosemary, origanum, and rectified spirits.

optical glass: Historically, any lens. Now any glass of fine quality, fit for lens making.

optigraph: Magic-lantern attachment to show the early "motion picture" films of the 1890s.

optique: A viewing device; a large lens in a wooden frame. The lens reversed orientation of the subject. Therefore, all views made for use in such devices were engraved with lettering in reverse. These are the optique prints. The optique viewer in its simplest form is sometimes miscalled a lace mirror.

orange bishop: Wine spiced with roasted oranges that have been pricked with cloves.

orange buds: Dried tiny oranges falling from trees and esteemed as a flavoring.

orare: This phrase, preceding the name of an individual, means "pray for." Variant of *orate*. Early English.

orbevoi: A Gothic seat, or chayere, with high back.

orbicular: Of orb or globe shape.

orcel: A small vase.

orchella: A lichen used to make a purple dye.

Orcutt ware: Reference would seem to be to the New England pottery at Ashfield, Mass., founded by Walter Orcutt, and to the wares made by any of this clan of potters at Whately, Mass., St. Johnsbury, Vt., and Ashfield, from early 19th century. Redwares and some stonewares.

Oregon: Pattern of pressed glass featuring beveled blocks, fans, and narrow panels.

oregrund iron: Reference is to its quality; the finest Swedish bar iron.

orfevrerie: Goldsmiths', jewelers', and silversmiths' work, collectively.

orfrays: Gold-embroidered cloth; damask with threads of gold; gold and silver embroidery.

organ-accordion: Four-octave reed organ mounted on a bellows, with keyboard of standard form. Made by Bartlett of Concord, N.H., and others.

organette: Self-playing table organ, crank-operated, using perforated paper rolls.

organize: Raw silk of middling quality.

organs: See Pianos & Organs.

orgeat: Orange-flower water and almond flavoring, with barley sugar. Also barley water, in which almonds and oranges were steeped. A flavoring agent and a beverage.

orguinette: The original organette. [*Example pictured.*]

Oriental: Pattern of pressed glass in Eastlake style. Fans, flower vases, marine views, fish, et cetera, are pressed on it.

oriental-occidental figurines: Reference is to Chinese export porcelain figures of European personages of 18th century.

oriental rug: Any rug woven in China or the Near East; properly, now, the rugs of Persia, Bessarabia, Turkey, et cetera. Oriental rugs as floor coverings in the American scene date from c. 1750 or possibly 1730.

Orient lamp: A cheap all-metal lamp for kerosene, made in 1870s. Patented 1869.

oriflamme: A banner of royal status. From *ore*, gold, and *flamme*, purple.

origanum: Oil of wild marjoram.

Orion ware: Faïence made at Orion, France, from 1525. It is rare.

oripment: Yellow dye derived from arsenic and sulphur.

Orléans ware: Faïence and porcelain made at Orléans, France, from 1750s.

ormolu: Alloy of copper and zinc; a brass

of golden quality. The meaning is milled gold.

Orphean: A reed melodeon of superior quality. Trade name of Lucas & Co., the makers, at Boston, Mass., from 1850s.

orphion; orpharion: A lute-like instrument of 17th century.

orphrays; orphreys: *See* Orfrays.

orpimen: Gold paint.

orr: A wood ball.

orrery: A mechanical planetarium. [*Example pictured.*] David Rittenhouse made the first one in America, 1750s. The first one of record was made by Thomas Tompion or George Graham, London, 1705, for the Earl of Orrery. **orrery stand:** Any table to hold such a device. [*Example pictured.*]

orvieto: A medieval faïence of France.

Osage orange: Native American wood much used in making the longbow by our Indians. French term for wood of this tree was *bois arcs*, from which we have our "Ozarks." Osage orange was used as a hedge plant for natural fences in some Southern colonies and states.

Osborne-Wilson dials: These are clock dials, imported in considerable quantities after the Revolution and used by many American clockmakers. All are painted dials with a cast-iron underplate, generally marked.

Osceola: A Georgia Creek Indian who became chief of the Seminoles. He was a noble character, mistreated by the government, and betrayed. There are now scarce lithographic prints of this great Indian. The rarest is the full-length one from a painting by Catlin, published 1838.

oschive: Bone-handled knife, from *os,* bone, and *chivvy* or *chive,* a knife or blade.

osier: The weeping willow; fronds used in basket making. So popular was the annual cropping of osier twigs or fronds that an acre of osier was considered as valuable as an acre of wheat.

Oskamp, Clemens: Silverware manufacturer of Cincinnati from 1842. Not a custom silversmith.

ostades; osnabrigs; osnaburgs: Netherlands and Flemish woolens and mixed textile fabrics.

ostensorium: A container, generally with a glass panel, to display the communion bread. A monstrance.

Ostrander, Charles: Britannia manufacturer of New York from 1840s.

ostrich cup: A chalice made from an ostrich egg, mounted in gold or silver.

ostylment: Furniture.

otaheite: The dwarf flowering and fruiting orange used as a house plant.

Otaphone: Trade name for sound deflector worn by the deaf. Made from 1830s.

otcyrd: Orchard.

Ott & Brewer: Potters of Trenton, N.J., who made the American imitation of true Belleek Porcelain, aided by imported workmen from the Belleek works.

otta; otyr; attar: Essential oil.

Ottawa glass: Reference is to the glass made at Ottawa, Ill., from 1880s, when four companies were in production. The

Peltier works made novelties and paper-weights from 1890 to 1910. Lily flowers, glass tulips, and many whimseys.

ottoman couch: (1) A three-sided couch; a long divan with ends in form of a continuation of the piece at right angles. (2) Any oriental-style couch. (3) A large hassock.

Otton furniture: J. H. Otton of Philadelphia in 1835 advertised "antique and modern style petite furniture, girandoles, stands, stools, carved busts, and candelabra." This cabinetmaker also conducted a fancy turnery establishment.

oude Loosdrecht: Dutch porcelain made at Loosdrecht to 1784, after which the factory was removed to Amstel. Formerly the Weesp pottery.

oudenaarde: Dutch tapestry of Brabant and Flanders, woven from 16th century.

Oukey furniture: French Antique style furniture made by J. Oukey, one-time foreman for Anton Roux. Oukey was in business from 1855 in New York City.

outcurving leg: Square leg with an outcurve, giving greater stability to stand, table, or chair. Style is Directoire.

outshot: Overhanging, as an upper story of a house.

oval brass: Cabinet drawer pulls mounted on oval bases; the handles are bail form. The era of greatest usage was 1780s to 1830s. Many of the ovals are stamped in patterns, with eagles, scenes, ships, et cetera. Some are of classic style.

oval convex mirror: Advertised as early as 1770s in New York, "in colors to suit the furniture of a room." Oval in shape, convex in surface. Not a girandole.

Oval Miter: Pattern of pressed glass in the Ashburton style, imitative of broad cutting, having pointed oval panels.

ovals: A contraction referring to oval picture frames made in a wide range of sizes, plain, carved, molded, gilded, et cetera, of French Antique style, and dating from 1830s to 1880s.

oven broom: A cornhusk broom for the hearth of an oven.

oven fork: Pie fork.

oven-polished: Said of wood turning, baked in an oven, and burnished in its own oil on a lathe.

overflap: A fold-over top.

overlap: Said of the edge of a door or drawer when it has a flange or lip overlapping the opening into which the door or front fits.

overlay: A type of glass; properly a casing of one color over another. When the layer is quite thin it is called "flashed" and is not overlay.

overmantel: The panel above a mantel or chimney breast.

overpanel mirror: A tabernacle-type mirror or *trumeau* with the upper panel smaller in width than the mirror glass. [*Example pictured.*]

overshot: Glass with a sharp crystalline finish.

overupholstered: Term does not mean overstuffed, but refers to any seat furniture with upholstery fabric carried over the edges of the seating and nailed to the frame, as opposed to slip-seating.

ovo-: Prefix denoting oval form, as ovo-cylindrical, ovoglobular.

Owl & Possum: Pattern of pressed-glass stemware, the stem a tree trunk branching over bowls, with an owl on one branch and possum on another. Variants are without the tree trunk for stem.

owl-head spoon: 16th- and early-17th-century spoons with round bowl and straight stem topped by an owl's head.

owl jug: A pitcher in the form of a squatting owl, the cover an owl's head in the true round, emphasizing the eyes of the bird, and turnable in any direction. 18th-century Staffordshire.

owl pepper: Silver pepper shaker in owl form; late 19th century.

oxbow front: Curvate in façade, in the form of an oxbow. Said of chest of drawer fronts and other case or cabinet pieces. Sometimes called ox-yoke front. There are two outswellings on either side of a center incurve. **oxbow serpentine:** A less emphasized curve of similar pattern.

ox marrow: A hair pomade of 1850s, introduced commercially as a product by X. Bazin of Philadelphia. The Staffordshire pots for this product have transfer-printed lids.

ox muzzle: A nose basket for cattle.

ox shoe: Concave curvate plates of wrought iron, used in pairs in shoeing the cloven-hoofed oxen used as draft animals.

oxybaphon: A wine jar.

ox yoke: The essential part of ox harness. [*Example pictured is for a pair of oxen.*]

oyez: Hear ye!

oyster chafer: Charcoal-fired chafing dish for the low-heat cooking of oysters. [*Example pictured.*]

oyster chevvy: A small pan for the pie of spiced diced oysters. Date is from 1700s.

oyster cracker: A large pincers with a pocket in one jaw to hold an oyster shell for opening. Date is from 1830s.

oystering: Veneer work, using bias-cut sections of hardwood burl displaying oyster-shell markings. Oyster-shell walnut.

oyster Toby: A Toby-jug figure of an oyster vendor carrying tub of the bivalves on head. Both male and female figures of this Toby were made.

oyster tree: A fable based on fact. Oysters and other shell fish attach themselves to mangrove roots in water and are exposed at high tide.

oyster tub: Earthenware tub in which oysters in the shell were brought to table for opening and eating by the diners.

oyster white: Properly the pigment derived from the lime of calcined oyster shells. Now any off-white tint.

ozokerit: Mineral wax.

ozone soap: A toilet, shaving, and dental soap of 1850s. It imparted a violet odor to the body and overcame unpleasant breath.

P

Paas: Easter; the paschal season. Celebrated by Dutch colonists from 1620s with gaily colored boiled eggs. This practice was not introduced by Moravians, as has been asserted.

Pabst furniture: Made by one D. Pabst of Philadelphia from 1860s. French Antique with a German accent. German Baroque.

pachyderm: Thick-skinned; any animal with a thick hide.

Pacific glass: (1) Glasswares made at Potrero, Cal., from 1867. (2) Any glasswares from several plants in California.

Pacific R.R. cup: A collapsible cup.

packstaff: A peddler's long staff, sometimes used in carrying his pack.

padauk: Vermilion-red mahogany.

padusoi; paduasoy: Silk originally woven at Padua, Italy.

Paddington carpet: *See* Parisot Carpet.

paddock cheese: The asparagus.

paddocks: (1) Frogs. (2) Frog cheese; asparagus.

pagod: Any grotesque Chinese figure or idol, especially those having nodding heads and waving hands. Imitations made at Dresden are preferred to the Chinese originals. [*Example pictured.*]

paid: Painted over; coated; erased by coating.

Paillard music box: Pricket-drum and tuning-comb type of Swiss music boxes made by Paillard, who had a New York store from 1850s.

Paine furniture: Boston-made quality furniture of last half of 19th century. Eastlake, Morris, and art styles, including pedestals copied from Dutch stoves.

paint chest: Jasper-ware or bone-china case to hold bladders of artists' and decorators' colors. Wedgwood made them from 1780s.

painted cote pailey: A painted dress fabric of 1820s.

painted Dutch: Term for the 19th-century gaudy Imari pattern. Term used by J. L. Cunninham, merchant of Boston, 1826.

painted floor cloth: Sailcloth, filled, and painted in tessellated and other patterns, from mid-17th century. Used as an all-over covering for floors or under tables and stands. This is the original luxury floor of the colonies and was used in the finest homes, governors' palaces, et cetera. The early equivalent of linoleum. If rugs were used, they were laid over the painted floor cloth. Later variant was "oilcloth."

painted-panel furniture: Any rich furniture, generally of Hepplewhite style, having painted underglass panels.

painted parson: Signpost.

painted pewter: Pewter wares japanned and painted. The Dutch started the vogue c. 1650.

painted satin: Hand-painted satin, generally in rococo or Baroque patterns, used in upholstery in 18th century.

painted valance: Board covering for drapery heads or Venetian shades, painted in decorative manner, sometimes stenciled.

painted wall: The wall painting of America is imitative of (1) the domino papers used as wall coverings in France, England, and other countries, or (2) of the Chinese paper wall hangings imported from 17th century by wealthy Europeans. Our wall painting was not true fresco work. In most cases the painting was done on dry plaster. Many examples of original wall painting survive; most of it is early 19th century or late 18th. Many painters used stencil patterns. The best work is freehand, scenic, and imitative of scenic paper.

painted window shades: When the Hollands shade of filled muslin replaced the Venetian shade in popularity, the best ones were either stock-painted or painted to order. Painting was in transparent colors, providing a picture indoors when shades were drawn in daytime, and a treat to the passer-by in evening when lights were lit.

paint-remover furnace: A device that has challenged quite a few experts. It is a triangular-shaped frame of closely set wires on a handle. Filled with embers of charcoal, it was held near paint for removal. It blistered the paint and softened it for easy removal with scraper. [*Example pictured.*]

pair-of-birds chests: Huguenot chests painted with pairs of birds, sometimes called lovebirds (sometimes distelfinks), curvate flower stems and tulips. Most found in and around Taunton, Mass.; some in and around New Rochelle, N.Y., and Lancaster, Pa. In Massachusetts these are rightly called "Taunton chests."

Pairpoint glass: New Bedford glass factory of this name produced blown and cut wares from 1860s. Merged with Libby in 1880. Also made silver-plated caster frames and other holders for cut-glass cruets, bottles, boxes, et cetera.

Paisley: Pattern woven at Paisley, Scotland, imitative of cashmere shawls. Student is referred to *The Paisley Shawl and the Men Who Produced It*, by Matthew Blair.

Paisley ware: Ceramic ware made at Paisley, Scotland. The Ferguslie pottery made most of the wares: garden vases, flower boxes, statuary, et cetera. One product of Paisley was an earthenware bathtub 5½ feet long.

paktong: White brass. Also called tutenag.

palace carpet: Any oriental rug over 15' x 25' is generally called a palace carpet.

palimpurs: Hand-painted and resist-dye chintzes and calicoes. The "tree-of-life" design first appeared in the Occident on palimpurs.

palisander: Violet ebony.

Palissy ware: 16th-century faïence by France's master potter, Palissy.

pall: A robe embellished with a Y-form. A religious vestment of priests. Sometimes called a pallium.

pallade: A rich cloth cover.

pall-mall; palle-maile: A game played with boxwood ball and mallets in an alley, scoring through an iron arch in the fewest possible strokes. 17th century.

palma Christi: The castor bean.

palmate: Palm-shaped.

palm candle: Candle made of palm wax.

palmer: (1) One who had made the pilgrimage to the Holy Land. (2) A paddle to spank children on the palm of the hand.

Palmer, William: Fancy-chair maker of New York City, 1790s-1800s. Black and gold chairs with rush and cane bottoms.

Palmer candles: Philosophically, "a reservoir of solid fuel with its proper wicking, made for use in certain lamps." Palmer candles were made with double-twisted or helically coiled wicks. Some had four wicks. Could be burned as candles, but made specifically to burn in lamps, the candle hidden in the column of the standard, forced upward by a spring. The Palmer magnum candle gave as much light as an Argand burner. Early 19th century to late 1880s. Palmer candles and various fixtures for use were not cheap items. From c. 1856, one Samuel Clarke took out a "patent," which Palmer could have made invalid, as it was nothing but the Palmer basic idea applied to short, stubby candles for use in what are known as "fairy lamps." These became the cheapest lighting elegancy ever offered to the English people, and fairy lamps were in use from Hoxton to Windsor Palace. These "too, too sweet lamps" appealed to Victoria, who had them everywhere. Clarke made a night lamp which he called "burglar's horror."

Palmer-Hanley: Ceramic ware made by Henry Palmer, 18th-century potter of Hanley, England. Basalt ware, jasper ware, and other products resembling Wedgwood. So closely did he approximate Wedgwood that an injunction was issued against him. The matter was compromised. Palmer's seals and intaglios were also a thorn in the Wedgwood side.

palmer tester: The 19th-century "kitty fisher," a textile screen "more durable than wire," woven at Middletown, Conn., as late as 1890s.

palmette: A small palm leaf, or a formal representation of one. Also a pattern of pressed glass featuring a palm-leaf design. There is a chairback featuring a carved palmette found in some 18th-century seat furniture and again in early 19th century through the Regency period.

paly: Decorated with pales.

panache: A plume of feathers.

panada: A jelly made from toasted bread boiled in water.

pancheon: Earthenware or metal milk pan. Also known in woodenware.

pan cupboard: Shaker furniture; a low kitchen cupboard for pots and pans.

pandaemonium: A horror show in a museum.

Pandean pipes: Musical pipes in batteries of from fourteen to twenty.

pandora: From *pandura*. A stringed musical instrument. More properly the pandore.

Panel & Flute: Pattern of pressed glass of narrow and broad vertical fluting.

Panel & Rib: Not a variant of the above, but a different pattern, featuring bands of diamond-form décor with fluting between.

panel back: Said of late Windsor-type all-wood chairs having a central panel instead of all spindles. Made from 1840s.

paneled patterns: In pressed glass there are many variants of basic name designs described as "with panel" or "paneled." Daisy & Button with Panel, Paneled Daisy, Dewdrop, Diamond, Diamond Point, Flower, Grape, Grape Band, Ovals, Rib, and Thistle are some of them. Student is referred to *Early American Pressed Glass* and *Victorian Glass*, by Ruth Webb Lee, for details.

paneled vase: A blown-glass form of vase made from 1760s to 1860s, and at one time credited solely to Stiegel factory. It is now doubtful if Stiegel made many of these; most examples are credited to New England glasshouses. The panels are sunken or raised, and rise one half to two thirds of height of vase. Necks are outflaring. Range is from 8 to 18 inches high.

panel papers: (1) The true domino paper for wall decoration, printed, stenciled, or hand-painted, measuring from 12" x 15" to 18" x 24" (approximately). (2) Upright panels of 19th century, in sheets 2½'-3' x 8½'-9', imitative of gilded leather, velvet, wood, marble, et cetera.

pane parchment: Animal parchment soaked in lye until transparent or translucent. Used as window lights instead of glass or mica.

Pankhurst stone china: J. W. Pankhurst & Co. made this ware at the Charles Street Works, Hanley, as successors to William Ridgway. It is white granite ware.

penner: A pen case; sometimes a kalemdam.

pannetierre: A wall cupboard with a ventilated front, used for keeping bread.

pannier: (1) A container made somewhat like a basket, but sometimes of spindles with solid bottoms and domed cover. Used as breadbaskets originally, then as baskets for any commodity. (2) The whalebone-framed puffs worn at the hips on 18th-century gowns of extreme fashion.

pannikin; pankin; pancrock: An earthenware pan or a metal equivalent; a small pan.

pannuscorium: A tough woven fabric used in boot- and shoemaking as a substitute for leather, from 1840s.

panoply: A grouping of ancient arms, as

axes, lances, shields, helmets, drums, et cetera, used as wall decoration or as carved décor on mirrors, clocks, et cetera. Trophies on display.

panshon: Pan with insloping sides.

pantaloon eagle: The American eagle displayed or pictured as having leg feathers looking like pantaloons.

pantiles: Roofing tiles of overlapping pan shape; tiles for similar usage, but of S-shape, forming ridges and gutters when laid in vertical lines.

pantins: Articulated paper dolls of the 18th century. Many were made to move by pulling a thread.

pantograph: Drawing machine for enlarging or reducing. Also, in 19th century, known as the Smithograph. [*Example pictured.*]

pantoufle: A house shoe; a slipper.

pantry: Bread room.

papanjay: Membrane of the sponge cucumber. Used as a washcloth. How this name, a variant of popinjay, meaning parrot, was applied to a gourd membrane, Webster saith not.

papboat: Small pear-shaped vessel with a tubular spout or stem, for feeding infants and invalids.

paper blind: Wallpaper pasted on scrim and used on a roller to shade or screen a window.

paper carpet: Cloth, stretched to cover a floor, and properly seamed, sized, pasted over with two or more layers of cartridge paper, then decorated with cutouts from wallpaper, bordered, dried, glue-sized, oiled, and varnished. These were asserted to be "durable" floor covering if kept varnished. The idea dates from 1820s.

paper domino: (1) A single sheet of paper, flatcap size (14″ x 17″), block-printed, stenciled, hand-colored, or blocked in a single color, made for decorating walls. Generally of a simple repeat pattern. Sold by street vendors and in fancy stores. The original wallpaper. (2) Play dominos, printed on cards instead of wood or ivory cubes. Many soldiers carried sets of paper dominos in their kits.

paper filigree: Coils of various colored paper tape, the size of a watch spring or smaller, arranged flat to display the coiling and glued to a surface in a pattern. A single box covering required a thousand or more coils. Art sprang into being in 17th century. French and English examples are best; American examples are considered crude. Tea caddies, mirror frames, picture frames, fancywork boxes, et cetera, of this intricate paper work are of record. Some are quite late, from c. 1870s.

paper fireboard: A wood or wire frame covered with heavy paper, used as a cover for fireplace opening. The area was further covered with a decorative paper print or with paper cutwork in imitation of Wedgwood pottery, Sèvres porcelain, or Della Robbia subjects.

paper flakes: Cut-paper work imitative of the geometrical pattern of a snowflake. Effect was achieved by folding the paper into quadrants and cutting with knife or scissors. Experts used only their fingers

and tore the paper into the design. Popular from 1840s.

paper glass: An early flexible transparency anticipating cellophane, invented by the Swiss scientist Schonbein, the inventor of guncotton, 1847. The announcement, made prior to 1850, was that the product was tough, flexible, could be formed into bottles and flasks, and used for windowpanes. He subjected papier-mâché to a catalytic.

paper hanging: The Chinese luxury wall covering; the painting of scenes, montages, et cetera, in full color, on large sheets of paper, and affixed to walls with an adhesive. The "paper" was sometimes the finest silk, mounted on paper, the art work done by hand. Later the work was done by block printing in colors, a technique used by the Japanese in their smaller color prints and imitated in Europe first in domino papers and finally, after the invention of the continuous-roll paper machine, 1803, printed in rolls. Any roll wallpaper prior to 1803 is made up of dominos, pasted together. Paper hangings were advertised by several fancy stores in the major cities of the colonies from mid-18th century. William Appleton of Boston advertised them in 1771.

paper house: Not a dealer, but a dwelling constructed from heavy waterproof paper "boards." The Rook Co. of Chicago offered the boards and the idea in 1869.

paper mosaic: Fruit, flower, landscape, and genre pictures composed of small-shaped bits of colored paper in the technique of colored stone inlay.

paper sizes: When paper was handmade in frames dipped into the vat of pulp, the sizes all were named, sometimes for the watermark, as follows: foolscap, 12½″ x 16″; demy, 15″ x 20″; medium, 17″ x 22″; royal, 19″ x 24″; super royal, 19″ x 27″; imperial, 21″ x 30″; elephant, 23″ x 27″; Atlas, 26″ x 33″; columbier, 23″ x 34″; double elephant, 26″ x 40″; antiquarian, 31″ x 52″; double imperial, 30″ x 44″; emperor, 47″ x 68″. These are printing and artists' paper sizes, in use from 16th to early 19th century. Commercial blanks and note papers had sizes by name as follows: letter, 10″ x 16″; packet note, 9″ x 11″; ladies' bath, 7½″ x 11″; octavo, 7″ x 9″; billet, 6″ x 8″; packet post, 11½″ x 18″; packet note extra, 11½″ x 18½″; bath note, 8½″ x 14″. The sizes commonly called "folio" as used in the making of prints are as follows: Small folio is any print sheet size from 11″ x 14″ to 11″ x 17″; medium folio, 14″ x 18″ to 15″ x 20″; large folio, 19″ x 24″ to 23″ x 37″. Other paper sizes sometimes mentioned are: census, 18″ x 26″; check folio, 17½″ x 24½″; crown, 15″ x 19″; flat cap, 14″ x 17″; or 13″ x 16″, or 12″ x 15″.

paper toys: Cut paper, trick paper work, pantins, paper dolls, paper furniture, card games, game boards, in infinite variety. Cutouts for the making of sand toys (meaning paper toys operated by falling sand) and "articulate" or paper toys operated by a flywheel or paper turbine running in a draft of warm air, all fall within the category of paper toys.

paper ware: Compressed paper in sheets, with waterproof glue sizing, formed under prodigious pressure in presses. Not papier-mâché but pressed from sheets of cartridge paper. Made from 1840s. Fruit boxes, pressboards, pails, buckets, cuspidors, slop jars, bathtubs, and even car wheels were made of this material. It is a fact that Pullman-car wheels were made of this substance. Paper can be compressed to the hardness of iron and the density of lignum vitae.

paperweights: Originally called paper holders, the fancy glass paperweights which are today a major collector's item were first noted in print in the *New York Illustrated News* of July 16, 1853, thus: "Ancient Egyptian Glass Globes filled with colored flowers precisely like the paper holders now sold in the shops." The comment was in reference to the then current display of Egyptian antiquities. These elegancies are examples of good glass blowing. The maker assembled a nest of small blown flowers, coils, et cetera, slices of decorative canes, air and alcohol bubbles, air twist, thread twist, and other decorative devices, encasing the assembly in a large blob of clear glass. The technique was not used exclusively in making paperweights; it was used also in making inkwells, perfume bottles, glass stoppers, doorknobs, newel-post finials, buttons, studs, and other elegancies.

papier-mâché: Macerated paper, or paper pulp, with glue size, molded into decorative elements and objects, furniture, boxes, et cetera.

papier-mâché portraits: Square or oval plaques with a modeled portrait in profile and a bordering that serves as the frame if desired. These plaques are painted naturalistically. Date of first making seems to be mid-18th century. A cheap elegancy, generally portraits of kings, queens, and notables.

Papillons: Domino wallpaper panels, named for a master maker named Jean Baptiste Papillon.

papiro-graphia: Glazed black paper cutwork mounted on light-tinted or white paper. Signor Gamberine, an art instructor, promoted this parlor art in 1840s. It was a revival of work done in 17th century.

papyrography: Printing through a fibrous stencil, as in today's mimeographic process.

papyrotomia: Hubbard, the silhouette cutter, so named his art.

papyrus ware: Papier-mâché wares sold in the white for home decorating.

par: In full. **parfurnished:** Completely furnished.

paradise apple: The pearmain, grafted on the quince, produced this fruit.

paragon couch: A lolling couch of the 1850s. French Antique style.

paraments: Church cloths.

parapluie: An umbrella.

parbunkle: A rope sling.

parcel: Part. **parcel gilded:** Part gilded.

parched corn: Popcorn.

parchemin simples: Frames of linenfold carving, each fold in a pane.

parchment fold: Panel carving that is a variant of linen fold.

Pardessus: (1) A glass dome or bell,

named for the maker, Pardessus, of New York. (2) A short coat with flowing sleeves, a rage in the 1850s.

parfum: A stand with burner and pan, used in burning incense to perfume a room. Date is from 17th century, and in constant use, each age having its own version.

parget: Plaster. **pargeted decoration:** Plaster decoration, molded or contrived by various heads, noses, or nozzles attached to a bag containing wet plaster, applied by the artist-workman.

Parian babies: Table ornaments, box lids, et cetera, displaying naked babies disporting on drapery. Made of Parian.

Parian jewelry: Mary Brougham, the designer, collaborating with Minton's pottery, produced brooches and other jewelry elements in a Parian that resembled carved ivory. Date is said to be from 1830s.

Parian ware: Unglazed porcelain in the light biscuit, imitative of Parian marble.

Parisian: Pattern of cut glass featuring a central multi-pointed star and a cut band star, with fans and grid cutting. Made by Dorflinger.

Paris lamp: A ring lamp, the ring being the reservoir for oil and support for shade.

parison: A globule or dip of hot glass on the blowpipe.

parisot carpet: Woven floor carpets, imported by colonial dealers from 1750s. Made from 1740s at Paddington, England, at the mill patroned by the Duke of Cumberland.

Paris porcelain: There were at least ten porcelain factories in Paris, making either soft-paste or hard-paste wares. Most of the factories were designated by street names, as Rue de Boudy, Rue St. Giles, Rue Amelot, et cetera.

Paris whiteware: Is not Paris porcelain but plain white, or fluted white, glazed kitchenware.

Parker lamps: (1) Bronze table lamps, chandeliers, and wall brackets made by Charles Parker of Meriden, Conn. (2) Sinumbra (shadowless) lamp patented 1830, having the oil reservoir above the flame, in a hollow tube encircling the glass chimney.

Parker lens: A huge three-foot-diameter burning glass, weighing over 200 pounds, made for the purpose of fusing metals by concentrated heat of sun's rays. Parker lens melted ten grains of platinum in three seconds. These lenses were made in the 1780s in England.

Parker mottoes: Paper patterns, punched for woolwork, and used as overdoor decoration. "God Bless Our Home" is the most common one. There were many others, ranging in size from 7" x 10" to 10" x 24".

Parliament hinge: A two-leaf hinge, each leaf carrying one segment of the joint.

parlour; parlor: The parley room; conversation room; "withdrawing" room.

Parnell figures: Modern porcelain paste sculptures by Gwendolen Parnell. One of a kind; generally of 18th-century flavor or genre.

parocheth: Elaborate curtain for the Torah.

parrel: Chimney piece.

Parrot filter: A mystery piece of glassware, often dismissed as "philosophical" but not that at all. It is a filter used by travelers. Sand was placed in the horn-shaped tube [pictured] and water poured in the upper end. The liquid filtered through the sand and came out fit or safe to drink—or so claimed the maker, M. Parrot of Paris, in 1800.

Parrot-Gilbert furniture: Made by a firm so named at Dayton, O., from 1860s. Some of the chairs are of late Directoire style, others in French Antique style. Some pieces carry paper labels.

parrot pitcher: Pressed-glass novelty pitcher of 1880s; made at Dalzell glassworks, Findlay, O. The form is a perched parrot, the handle on the back of the bird.

Parr toys: Velocipedes made by G. Parr, Buffalo, N.Y., from 1860s.

parson's quilts: Quilts made by the ladies of a congregation for presentation to a pastor, especially a bachelor parson. Inscribed in needlework by the ladies who made it. A fashion in vogue in rural communities from 1840s or earlier.

Partheimuller wicker: Furniture of woven willow fronds, made at Boston from 1850s by F. Partheimuller. He imported the English willow chair.

Parthenon: The pressed-glass pattern more generally called Egyptian. Bosses of clusters of seven dots, arranged in daisy form, framing a paneled impression of the Parthenon, Athens (or, more probably, the Temple at Karnak), or the figure of an Egyptian woman holding wheat fronds in her lap.

parti-gold: Sheet of silver with a thinner sheet of gold, welded and then beaten into leaf. Proportions were one third gold and the balance silver. 18th-century low-cost gold leaf.

Partington soap: An illiterate woman, Ruth Partington, even though unable to write her own name, was clever enough to boil up a beauty soap, which she sold from 1815. B. T. Babbitt made her soap to 1850s.

partisan: A spear with a lily-form head of sharp steel.

partners' desk: Flat-topped pedestal desk with drawers in both sides. Some have adjustable writing boards. Date is from 18th century.

Partridge toys: Toys sold by a Boston firm of this name. Controlled sale of some cast-iron mechanical banks, Noah's arks, panorama toys, et cetera, from 1870s.

part service: Limited sets of dinnerware, silver, et cetera.

parure: A set of jewelry, as a necklace, bracelets, earrings, and brooch.

Pasch eggs: Colored and decorated eggs, of the edible variety or of china or glass.

Pas-de-Calais: A section of Flanders, famed in 17th century for its stoneware production by many potteries.

pasigraphy: A universal system of signs and symbols for common, world-wide understanding. Promoted in 17th century.

passager: Curled or ruffed lock of hair worn in the center of the forehead.

passementerie: Trimmings, as laces, beadings, fringes, and tapes.

passe partout: Thin gummed tape, used in binding a backing and a pane of glass with a picture between. The best framed pictures were passe-partout bound before the wood or other frame were inserted. Also a print with a special border to fold over a glass front and paste down. The Aldine Co., art specialists of New York, issued such prints in 1870s. Several American genre subjects and landscapes were in their list.

passe temps: Pastime.

Passmore tin: Tinware for the household, made at Philadelphia by Thomas Passmore from 1790s through 1800s.

paste: (1) Imitation gems of borax or glass, sometimes of clear glass with colored foil backing. Also called "strass." (2) Any vegetable-base adhesive.

paste cutters: Brass pastry wheels; nearly all of those used in America were of English make. Also called paste marker. [Examples of 1770–1800 pictured.]

paste papers: Colored paste decoration on paper; a sort of paper fresco or paper mural. A vogue of 18th and early 19th century.

paste royal: Wafer dough, made from 4 ounces sugar, 1 ounce cinnamon, 1 ounce ginger, beaten in a mortar with gum dragon, rolled thin, molded, dried, and kept boxed.

pastiglia: Relief designs in plaster, painted and gilded.

pastilles aromatiques: Briquettes or cones of perfumed tinder, for burning as incense to perfume a room. Pastille burners were often in cottage form. Both pastilles and burners date from mid-18th century. The idea is probably from China.

pastry: (1) The oven room of an establishment; the bakehouse. (2) Shortbread or crusting. **pastry board:** A wooden board, carved intaglio, used as a mold to provide a raised design on pastry. Marzipan molds were sometimes used, but the true pastry mold was generally circular.

patand: Any sill timbering, as of a partition.

patch box: (1) Decorative, enameled, jeweled, and molded porcelain box for the beauty spots called patches. (2) The cavity in the butt of the American rifle in which the greased patches for wrapping the ball were kept.

patch quilt: Any quilt or bedcover, the display side of which is contrived by stitching various designed patches of the same size, or proper-fitting sizes, in various colors and sometimes different fabrics. There are many star-form patterns, conventionalized flower patterns, tree forms, et cetera. Student is referred to Old Patch-work Quilts, by Ruth Finley, in which 100 patterns are pictured. Quilting parties, quilting bees, and other community-of-interest parties for making quilts were held as a mode of entertainment during first seven decades of 19th century. The patchwork quilt is not to be confused with "crazy quilt," which, while made of patches, was a form in imitation of the patchwork variety. The crazy quilt was made from any odds and ends, in various colors, joined by various lock and cross stitching; these are more properly "harlequin quilts."

patented furniture: The files of the U.S. Patent Office contain an amazing array of papers dealing with patents issued for curious chairs, tables, sofas, rockers, library steps, beds, cabinets, desks, et cetera. The entire collection was one time scheduled for inclusion in this dictionary, but it was found impossible to include in a one-volume book. The compilation will probably be published separately as *Patented Furniture of the U.S.A., 1790–1890*.

patera: (1) Round or oval-form drinking vessel of ancient Greece and Rome; a saucerlike bowl with handles. Also called aleison, sphagon, and spondeion. Of bronze, silver, gold, pottery, and shell-like glass. (2) Any ornamentation in imitation of a patera, carved, inlaid, or painted on furniture, mirrors, chairs, lighting fixtures, or on woodwork. Generally embellished with some conventionalized or classic form of flower or figure. Introduced by Adam in his classic revival of 1750s.

paterna ware: Hispano-Mooresque faience; a rare medieval pottery decorated with figural, symbolic, and architectural forms.

Paterson Colt: The original Colt revolving-chamber pistol made at Paterson, N.J., sold with all its appurtenances in mahogany boxes. These are the rarest Colt revolvers and now have an amazingly high value in arms collecting. In 1950, $3000 was not an unheard-of price for a complete Paterson Colt with all accessories, in original box.

pâte-sur-face: Enamel on metal, as on some clock faces, most watch dials, and on the Battersea and other enamels. Decoration by painting or transfer and refiring.

pâte-sur-pâte: Paste on paste; porcelain-clay painted on porcelain body to achieve extraordinary fine decoration, with tonal modulation owing to varying density of paste. The work of Solon in France and England was largely in this technique. Only accomplished artists could do this work.

patience dock: Not a pier, a place of punishment, or a bar of justice. Reference is to a leaf vegetable, called winter spinach, usually cooked with sorrel.

Patna: A chintz made at Patna, India.

patriae pater: A crude woodcut of Washington issued in 1776. It predates other appellations, as *"des Landes Vater,"* naming Washington as father of his country.

Patricia: Pattern of pressed glass imitative of cutting, with bands of diamond form.

patriotic cover: Any envelope for letters with patriotic symbols printed upon it. Date is from Civil War period, but there are Confederate examples of considerable rarity.

pattens: Lifts, or low stilts, of wood or metal, worn under soles of shoes for walking over mires, mud, and filthy gutters.

pattern brass: Brass wire, used in inlay. Used from 1720s on some English furniture, but more common on the Continent.

pattern mold: A mold for blowing pattern glass. No matter how small the mold or its pattern, a parison of glass expanded within it retained the marking with any further expansion, out of the mold.

pattern paper: Flowered and pattern-printed paper, made from 16th century; some used as wall covering and much used in fancy paper work, bookbinding, et cetera.

Patterson & Hubbell: Cabinetmakers of New York City, working in 1770s. Georgian styles are assumed.

Patterson iron: Sadirons and stands, hearth grates and tools, firedogs, trivets, et cetera, made at Cincinnati by Patterson Foundry from 1850s or earlier.

patty pan: (1) Pan in which the patty shells were baked. Also the shell itself. (2) Galleys of patty pans, so called, which are more generally gem pans.

Paul & Virginia: Plates and pitchers memorializing this romantic couple, some by Wedgwood in his cameo ware. Bennington made a Paul & Virginia pitcher. Most of the plates are French.

Pauline art pottery: Made at Chicago and at Edgerton, Wis., in 1880s by Pauline Jacobus and associates. Sold through jewelry stores.

Paul Pry Toby: A dram cup in form of bust of Paul Pry, wearing a high beaver hat. The piece is less than 4 inches high. Staffordshire, made from 1790s.

pavior: A paver; a layer of flags, blocks, and cobblestones.

Pavis: A body shield for a knight. **pavisor:** Servant-carrier of the shield.

Pavonia: Pattern of pressed glass displaying diamond-form knops and finials, and engraved floral-spray décor.

paw caster: A roller caster, or castor, fitted in a paw-shaped brass holder. Many varieties.

paw foot: Cast-brass end for furniture legs in form of animal paw; any furniture footing of paw form, attached or carved on the wood.

pawnbroker's chairs: The chairs of elaborate quality made for the Medici family of Italy, who were descended from a family of usurers.

Pawtucket print: Printed cotton fabrics made at Pawtucket, R.I.

pax: Peace. Also the holy picture or object kissed by worshipers.

pax wax: Beeswax.

Peabody plate: Pressed-glass plate of English make, with registry mark, displaying sixteen stars around a crown and the name GEORGE PEABODY. This is a memorial to an American, born at Danvers, Mass., who became a famous London banker and philanthropist. Bread plates, butter chips, mugs, goblets, and other vessels reported. *Magazine Antiques* carried a notice of this man and ware June 1937.

Peabody pottery: Any ware made from 1640s to 20th century at various potteries operating down through the years at Peabody, Mass.

Peacedale shawl: Reference would seem to be shawls woven at the Peacedale, R.I., mills mid-19th century.

peach blend: The mineral earth or ore from which Klaproth isolated uranium. The substance is now called pitchblende.

peachblow: Novelty or art glass imitative of the peachblow vase which sold at the Morgan sale, 1886, for $18,000. The imitation is not good, and there are varieties, as several glass factories made peachblow glass. There is a good essay on this glass in *Victorian Glass*, by Ruth Webb Lee. An imitation of the Chinese porcelain vase by Hobbs-Brocunier and other objects in peachblow were made by them and other firms. The glass, while collected, is not yet valuable or rare. Some has a satin finish, achieved by an acid bath. Some is white-lined. A variety of peachblow is "Burmese," patented by the Mount Washington Glass Co., 1885; this glass was in advance of the furor and publicity of the peachblow vase sale.

peach-leaf leaven: A yeast made of boiled peach leaves, potatoes, sugar, and salt, set to fermentation by a small dash of baker's or brewer's yeast.

peach-leaf yellow: A dye color made from soaked and rotted peach-tree leaves.

peachy wood: A dyewood, shipped from San Francisco de la Campeche, at times used to adulterate Brazil wood.

peacock: This bird, sometimes considered ill-omened, has been an inspiration in much popular art. **Peacock Eye:** A pressed-glass pattern of Hungary. **Peacock Feather:** An American pressed-glass pattern that bears only the faintest resemblance to a feathering, but does have a resemblance to the pointed ovate "eye" of such feathers. Other uses of the bird motif and its gorgeous tail should be obvious to the observer when found.

peal: A set of bells covering a major scale.

peanut: The groundnut, or goober.

peanut carving: Sometimes called "Philadelphia Peanut," this is a carving vagary in the form of raised elements of peanut shape.

Pear: Pattern of pressed glass featuring spray, leaf, and two pears, the covered pieces with acorn finials. Not Baltimore Pear which, originally and rightly, was called "Fig."

pear ice: Grate 4 large pears (juicy variety) into juice of 3 lemons. Add 2 gills syrup and ½ pint water. Pass through a cloth or hair sieve and freeze.

pearl: An element of decoration in carving, ceramics, metalwork, and glass. Generally a pear-shaped dot.

pearl ash: Water passed through wood ash, evaporated, the alkali deposited in the form of pearls.

pearled rug: Tufted rug achieved by use of a metal spreader, covered with tapes of rags, laid on base material and stitched, generally by machine. Date is from 1870s or later. Popular in the late 1880s and early 1890s.

pearlins: Coarse bone-knitted lace.

Pearl River ware: Canton-china imitations made in Staffordshire.

pearls of fish scale: A bead maker of France named Jacquin, in the reign of Henri IV, filled bubbles of glass with scales of the bleak fish and achieved an imitation of natural pearls.

pearmain: A variety of apple, advertised in the colonies as early as 1760. It is said the variety dates from 12th century.

pear pitcher: Pressed-glass container sometimes called "sweet pear," displaying leaves and fruit.

pearwood book: Memorandum tablets of polished pearwood from which notes in pencil could be erased.

Pease oil: Signal light oil made by Pease Refinery of Buffalo. Much used for home lighting when obtainable.

peat bucket: Any bucket for the fuel, peat.

peat reek: Peat smoke, and the trace of it in certain distilled spirits of Scotland and Ireland.

peau de pêche: Peach bloom.

peavey: A canting hook; a clawlike iron head on a stout pole.

pebbles: Lenses cut from rock crystal or quartz.

peck loaf: A big loaf of bread, weighing over 17 pounds.

pectin putty: The althea plaster.

pedal base: An attachment for the melodeon, having bass pedals and notes, all within the apparatus, connected to bellows on instrument with a flexible tube. Made from 1850s.

peddler: A vendor with a basket or bag of goods, from *ped*, a bag or basket.

pedelion: The winter rose, or *Helleborus niger*. It is not a rose, but an alpine winter-blooming plant of the buttercup family with large, pale rose-tinted petals.

pedestal: A closed stand or a solid support; a small sideboard, made in pairs, with side doors. Date is from 1820s.

pedestal & claw: Said of certain tables having a pedestal on four short outcurving legs fitted with brass claw ends, castered.

pedestal basin stand: A bowl stand without cabinet.

pedestal desk: Flat-topped desk on two pedestals, with kneehole space between. Best examples disassemble for ease in transportation and handling. Mostly of English make.

pedestal gate table: A table with drop leaves. The top proper is supported by heavy columns fixed to a footed pedestal. The leaves are supported by gates at either side.

pedestal leg: The turned leg form introduced to England by Daniel Marot, a French Huguenot, 1685. It is an inverted-cup turning.

pedestal sideboard: Two pedestals, joined by a center drawer section, its top on the same level as pedestal tops.

pediment: An ornament over a cornice; scrolled, broken, crested, rolled, waved, et cetera. The scroll pediment is the one most generally used in our colonial furniture. The broken pediment is classic and not scrolled.

pediux: A reticulated foot armor.

pedobaptist: Member of any church practicing infant baptism.

peel: (1) A flat paddle for handling bread in ovens, to place and remove the loaves.

(2) A pillow or bolster, as peel bere, a pillow cover.

peep show: Miniature theaters presenting tableaux, sometimes with motion, or a succession of views. You peeped through a lens to see the show, illuminated by top windows, candles, lamps, et cetera.

peer glass: Thought to be a variant of pier glass, but others believe it meant (17th century) any looking glass.

Peerless: Pattern of pressed glass imitative of cutting, with bands of diamond-form decoration and fan patera, oval and round.

pegboard: A board run around a room or across one or more walls, studded at regular intervals with pegs upon which to hang clothes or other objects.

pegging: Extra-heavy crocheting.

peggypoker: Short fire poker.

peg jugs: (1) Drinking vessels with a series of pegs marking levels inside the vessel. When used as a communal cup, the drinker took the level down a peg. (2) Soda-water glasses of the 1850s, in various shapes, with handles. Clear glass. [*Examples pictured.*]

peg lamp: Lamp reservoir of glass, with a stubby peg for fitting in a candlestick.

peg-leg teapot: A Staffordshire teapot in the form of a jovial wooden-legged man doing the "split"; his peg leg serving as the spout of the pot. It is colored naturalistically. The piece is in the philosophy of Toby jugs of the same era, first quarter of 19th century.

peg tankard: *See* Peg Jugs.

pelican bank: Cast-iron mechanical bank in form of a well-modeled pelican. The only action is the bird opening its mouth upon insertion of a coin. Within the mouth is a red imp.

pelice: Oil or wine jar.

pelike: Woodenware. A bowl.

pelisse: A twilled woolen cloth and a garment made of it.

Pellatt, Apsley: English glass expert, manufacturer, and historian. Made pressed, cut, and artwares, including the Pellat lusters, or cut candlesticks with double rows of cut pendants.

Pelletier, John: French cabinetmaker who worked in London in last decade of 17th century and first decade of 18th. Made fine carved furniture.

pelis work: Leaves and flowers stamped and modeled from leather. The leather was formed in iron molds.

pillow bere: Pillowcase or cover. In 19th century sometimes called a plowber.

pelmet: A shallow valance used to conceal the cords, rod, or pole, et cetera, of a curtain hanging.

Pelton japanned & Peltor ware: H. A. & E. A. Pelton of Albany, N.Y., made this ware from 1848, japanned in various colors and decorated. A general line was made. Sometimes confused with Peltor ware, which is not a japanned ware, but Britannia, made at Middletown, Conn., from 1850s.

Pembroke table: A breakfast table with drop leaves, named in honor of Lady Pembroke, who delighted in dining and entertaining guests at such tables. Various

styles from Adam to Sheraton. One authority says it is named for the Earl of Pembroke, for whom Chippendale made but one table of the type. However, now a Pembroke table is any 18th- or early-19th-century drop-leaf breakfast table.

pen card: A fine wire brush (a section of wool card) used for cleaning steel pens. Date is from 1840s. [*Example pictured.*]

pencil'd china: Painted china.

pencilled brick: Painted brick walls with the joints outlined in white.

pencilled calico: Printed calico.

pencil post: A very slender post. **pencil-post bed:** Generally of Queen Anne and early Georgian periods.

pendant: Pennant. Also any drooping element, as pendant crystals, pendant post, or simply pendants; small elements approximating finials in reverse.

pendant turn: A cabinet hardware item; keylike handle on a shank, moving a catch at the back.

pendalogue: Precious stone, cut pear shape, and used as a pendent ornament.

penitentiary carpet: Rag carpets woven by prisoners in penal institutions.

penitentiary mill: Millstones cut and fitted by convicts. These are reported made in Southern prisons in early 19th century.

penmaker: A small die cutter, encased in gold, silver, brass, or hardwood, designed for cutting a pen point on a quill.

Penn Glass Works: Mentioned as in operation at Philadelphia in 1683; products, other than window glass, not known.

Pennington: Ceramic wares made by three potters, brothers, of this name, at separate potteries. Delft, common earthenwares, and china; beakers, vases, and garnish sets in the Chinese taste. Seth Pennington seems to have been the most active potter. All worked in 18th century. [*The mark and several examples pictured.*]

Pennsylvania chests: Reference is to the painted chests imitative of the "nonesuch" chests of Tudor England, and of the farm and village chests of Switzerland, the French Jura, Sweden, and Flanders. Finest examples are the architectural chests of the Conestoga Valley, Lancaster County, Pa. All are painted, some dated. This statement, however, is not meant to include the traditional hardwood chests, sometimes inlaid with name, sentiment, and date. These are not typically Pennsylvania. Most of the painted chests are *dowry* (wedding, or "hope") chests and not *dower* (widow's portion) chests. [*Examples pictured.*]

Pennsylvania Dutch: More misinformation, erroneous claims, and wrong beliefs are current in respect to the meaning of this term than any other phrase pertaining to American social history and objects that survive. What is now Pennsylvania was colonized by the Swedes and the Dutch half a century before William Penn was granted the land, and became the spearhead of England's determination to brook no "foreign" colony between New England, New York, and Virginia. With Swedes, Dutch, and some Finns in residence on his arrival, Penn offered haven, freedom, and land to the harassed yeomanry of Europe. Innumerable French

Huguenots, Swiss Mennonites, Amish from Flanders, Rhinish Palatinates (many of whom were not from Germany but were refugees who had found temporary haven there), Swabians, Danes, Dutch, Walloons, Swedes, and Flemings arrived in the colony from 1680s to 1760s. These people required a dialect for communication. They had one thing in common: they were Protestants. The churches became the language fusing centers, not the courthouses. The Swedes had planted the Lutheran Church; the Dutch, the Reformed Church. The Mennonites were followers of a Dutch reformer; the Amish were a branch of the Mennonites. These people were Anabaptists, or believers in adult immersion. So was born the lingua franca of Penn's Colony, now called Pennsylvania Dutch. It is a mixture containing roots from Yorkshire, Lancashire, Cornwall, Wales, Scotland, Ireland, the Netherlands, Sweden, Germanic Swiss, Swabia, France and Flanders. Many of the Reformed and Lutheran ministers were bilingual. The term "Pennsylvania Dutch" derives from the New York Dutch peoples, who so designated their fellow settlers in the Delaware Valley. It is a far more proper term for the lingo than Pennsylvania German. Several societies exist for the spread of propaganda proving that Pennsylvania is all Germanic in terms of its popular arts and crafts. The result of these activities has been emotional rather than an analytic approach to research. Seventy-five years ago a Pennsylvania historian stated that the errors began with Penn's agents, who, in passing immigrants for entry at Philadelphia, designated them all as "Palatines" when, as a matter of fact, they had come from the various European countries above mentioned. Thus has fancy about Pennsylvania been promoted as fact, and outright falsehoods made to appear as truths.

Pennsylvania iron: Instead of referring to the altogether inaccurate, biased, and sometimes stupid allegation in respect to Pennsylvania iron and ironwork, we refer to Acrelius, the Swedish historian, who covers the period 1638–1758 and who stated "the workmen at the iron furnaces and forges (in 1758) are partly English and partly Irish, with a few Germans." Work is carried on in the English fashion." The few Germans were laborers bought for a term of years (redemptioners). Huber, a German, had an iron furnace, 1750, which Henry Stiegel got hold of. The total tenure was less than 26 years. The Pennsylvania stove plates were made (with exception of Huber and Stiegel) by English and Welsh ironmasters. These were made for the immigrant German market and saved the immigrant from buying such stoves in the Netherlands and transporting them. The inscriptions are in very poor German and in Latin characters. The stove of plates is of Norse origin, introduced by the Swedes and Dutch.

Pennsylvania Glass: General reference is to the Pennsylvania Flint Glass Works of Whitehead, Ihmsen & Phillips, Pittsburgh. In 1835 this works employed 2 engravers, 15 cutters, 3 molders, 12 blowers, and 37 helpers. Any glass made at any factory in Pennsylvania, at any time, is of course Pennsylvania glass.

Pennsylvania (other designated

items): pottery: Reference usually is to the Swiss and Staffordshire types of sgraffito and slip-decorated wares. The earliest dated piece (18th century) is by a former Staffordshire potter, Smith. Considerable Swiss wares of the type called Pennsylvania were imports. However, there were no less than 50 potters in eastern Pennsylvania alone who made such wares. Student is referred to the works of Edwin Atlee Barber for further study. **slatback:** A chair back with four to seven slats, curvate and shaped to fit the back of the torso. Its counterpart is found in the Netherlands and the Swiss Jura. **trestle table:** X-ended long tables, or solid-ended with board stretchers, of Swedish style, dating from 1660s and as late as 1800. Many of genuine age were imported as antiques from Sweden c. 1922 and sold by unscrupulous dealers as "Pennsylvania." They are frequently of pine. [*One example pictured.*]

penny foot: In metalwork, any round, disk-form foot about the size of a large penny.

pennystone: (1) A round, flat stone. (2) A game of toss played with such stones.

Penrhyn marble: Painted slate.

Penrose glass: Irish glass, made by Penrose at Waterford; it is very fine cut glass; many pieces have the name of makers molded in the bases.

Pensilvanian stove: The Franklin stove in its original and all-18th- and early-19th-century forms.

Pentagon: A late pattern of pressed glass in angular form, with square knob finials and flute and honeysuckle fan decoration.

pentagon shape: Five-sided. *See* Polygon.

pepper box: (1) A shaker-topped container for pepper. (2) A revolving pistol with all the barrels in the revolving unit. (3) Salem, Mass., because of docking of ships loaded with cargoes of pepper; also Pepper Port.

Pepper floor: Early linoleum made at New York, c. 1880s, by C. H. Pepper.

pepper squatter: A candle snuffer.

pepper water: Swiss-Alpine tonic water (*pefferwasser*).

perambulator: A distance-measuring device; a single wheel within a forked handle, with gears to registering dial.

perce: To pierce.

Percier & Fountaine: French architects of the Empire period who, in 1809, published a book of designs. Charles Percier of this firm designed furniture, draperies, wall coverings, and lamps. His designs are reflected in American Empire styles of such objects.

perdu: Hidden, or partly hidden. Also meaning in a desperate state. **Profile perdu:** A profile turned partly away from the observer.

perifocals: The better-vision spectacle lenses as ground by Brigham Optical Works, North Oxford, Mass., from 1840s.

perforated Parian: Parian ware done in the Leeds technique of punching out a pattern with individual dies. Grainger of Worcester, England, made a considerable quantity of it from 1850s. [*Examples pictured.*]

perforated veneer: Laminated wood as used in panels and chair seats, perforated by multiple boring or drilling. Last quarter of 19th century.

perfume casket: Any box, of any material, holding bottles of perfume. Some have pincushion tops. 19th century, generally of French style, dating from 1830s.

perfumed match: The luxury match, made by Charles Partridge of New York from 1850s; it was non-sulphurous and had a perfumed ignition mixture. High-priced parlor matches in elegant packages.

perfumes, 17th-19th century: Essences, or spirits, were the perfumes; "waters" were the equivalent of our toilet waters. Of the essences, there were bergamot, lavender, ambergris, musk, rose, jasmine, mint, benjamin, Venus, millefleurs, tuberose, cassia, violet, citron, clove, goujak, jonquil, pink, lys. Of "waters," there were lavender, rose, honey, Hungary, Portugal, myrtle, Cordova, mousseline. Jockey Club was one of the popular perfumes, sachets, and toilet-water odors of the 1850-90 period.

perfume shell: Porous sea shells impregnated with perfume. A resort novelty of 19th century.

pergola hangings: Luxurious needlepoint hangings for use in outdoor grottoes, glens, and pergolas.

Pergolesi, M.: Italian artist, designer, and decorator working in London from 1770s who, with Ciprani, worked with and for the Brothers Adam. One of the classic-revival artists. Was author of a book on decoration.

perhigor: Pear vinegar, especially soured perry, similar to champagne vinegar.

perkin: A cheap drink made from cider-mill mash and water. Other names were cyderkin, puree, and purkings.

Perkins beds: This may have been a derisive term for the mattresses made by the inmates of the Perkins Institution and Massachusetts Asylum in 1840s.

perpetual oven: Sheet-iron oven connected in series to flue from any fire in common and constant use. Hence the oven was always ready for baking. Offered about 1790. Advertised in 1800.

perpetual paste: Mucilage of gum tragacanth and water, with a corrosive sublimate preservative.

perpetuana: Everlasting cloth; a tough wool fabric.

perquer: Thoroughly; completely.

perry: Fermented pear juice, yielding a drink very much like champagne.

Perry mirror: A gold-stenciled portrait on glass of Commodore Perry, mounted as a plaque between gilded dolphin forms topping a framed mirror. Date is c. 1814-20s.

Perry stamps: Butter molds, made in quantities at Reheboth, Mass., from mid-19th century. Most of the so-called Pennsylvania-German butter molds were made by Perry and sold everywhere.

Persian Squash: Pattern name applied to Persian print design displaying a melon form that looks like a decorated pear.

persimmon beer: Made from frostbitten persimmons, lemons, and bran, baked in loaves, the resulting "bread" soaked in water and a house beer brewed from it.

perspective delineator: A drawing aid for work in perspective.

perspicillum: A telescope. The first one was not built by Galileo, but by the Dutchman Janssen, 1604.

Pert: Pattern of pressed glass featuring a sort of holly leaf and inverted heart or pointed oval panel. All pieces are petite in size.

peruke: A crested style of hairdress and a false hair wig in imitation. Now applied to wigs generally. Periwig is a contraction of peruke wig.

Peruvian cortex: Jesuit bark. Quinine.

Peruvian silver: The native silver of Peru wrought by European workmen in Peru, in styles of the period.

pestles: Legs.

Petal & Loop: Pattern of pressed glass, originating at Sandwich. Of the Ashburton group, featuring large petals surrounded by a border or loop.

Peterboro glass: Window glass, bottles, and flasks made at Peterboro, N.Y., from c. 1790s to 1820s.

Peters, Gustavus: Printer of Carlisle and Harrisburg, Pa., who, with J. B. Moser, from 1820s, issued broadsides and children's books printed in colors from wood blocks. Peters may have been the first American printer to publish books with illustrations printed in colors, not hand-colored. German and English texts.

Peters medicine chest: Made by James Peters of Lancaster, Pa., from 1765. Fitted chests of from 3 to 50 pounds capacity, for private families, ships, plantations, and exploring expeditions.

petite chaise longue: Decorator's term for a single-end sofa or settee, from 4'6" to 5'6" long. Often used at either end of a fireplace. The style is Directoire.

petite commode: A small chest of drawers.

petite console: A miniature but true console, generally used in pairs. [*Example pictured.*]

petit point: The finest of needle point, simulating tapestry weave. Originally done in silk floss with small stitches, or "little points."

petrin: A dough trough.

Petry lantern: Petry Brothers were lantern manufacturers of New York City from mid-19th century. Ship, railroad, house and barn lanterns, pole lanterns, et cetera.

petticoat lamp: Any lamp with an oil reservoir of a conical form imitative of a standing petticoat. Pewter examples may have been first ones. Glass, pottery, brass, and pewter examples known.

petticoat valance: The full-gathered valance, in the style of garment drapery, used anywhere, but often on testers and bedrails and across a mantelshelf.

petum: Tobacco. First so named by Acosta, 1588.

petunse: (Various spellings.) Feldspar melting at 2000°. The secret of Chinese porcelain. Combined with clay, this provided the stoneware body.

1, Perforated Parian. **2,** Pennington Ware and Marks (six examples). **3,** Présentoir. **4,** Press Cupboard. **5,** Pressure Scale. **6,** Pouring Toby. **7,** Psalterium. **8,** Pudding Charms. **9,** Premium Fountain. **10,** Propeller. **11,** Pincer Rushlight. **12,** Poke. **13,** Pocket Rifle. **14,** Poodle Lounge. **15,** Pot-au-feu. **16,** Powder Horn, engraved type. (Nos. 1 and 2 from Virtue & Co., London.)

pew group: A conversation group of ceramic ware, posed against a backboard or on settles. Astbury, Dwight, Wood, and others made them in 18th century for mantel and table ornaments. [*Example pictured.*]

pewter: Originally an alloy of tin and copper. Finally any alloy of the low-melting-point metals, including bismuth and antimony, lead, and tin. Sad pewter is the heaviest but not the best. The higher the tin content, the better the pewter.

pewter cupboard: Any open cupboard is now subject to this naming. It is doubtful if cupboards were made specifically for pewter, which was used because of the lack of china and pottery and because of its more serviceable, non-breakable quality and its lower cost.

pewterers: Biographical listings of the name of American pewterers appear in several excellent volumes of record. These are mentioned in the Bibliography.

pewterers' marks: The London pewterers in 1534 were given permission to mark their wares. American pewterers generally used their own stamps and did not always add the equivalent of a class mark. See Bibliography for books of pewter interest and information about makers and marks.

pewter grid: Any examples are signs, as of the London Pewterers Co. The melting point of pewter precludes its use in any grid.

pewter press: A term in the same category as pewter cupboard, but referring to a cupboard with closed or glazed doors.

phaeton: High carriage, invented in 1760s, with seat sometimes as much as 12 feet above the road. [*Example pictured.*]

phancered: Variant of fancied; made fancy, as decorated.

phantoscope: A metal box containing a flipping mechanism through which still pictures, each with a slight variation in position, are passed and viewed through an aperture. An early motion-picture machine of c. 1890s. Also the name of the Jenkins projector for motion pictures, 1898. The film was in "chronophotography," from the experiments of the 1870s and 1880s by Muybridge.

pharmacy jars: Porcelain, pottery, metal, or glass jars for tinctures and simples, herbs, and other drugs, often with the names lettered directly upon them, or on labels affixed to the jars. Some, of majolica, date from 14th or 15th century. **pharmacy wares:** Any dish or container, decorated or plain, for use in a pharmacist's store.

Phelan table: Game table, especially a billiard table, made by Phelan & Co.

Phelps-Kingman furniture: Case and seat furniture of 1840s, made at factory of firm so named, New York. Victorian styles, so called, and some fancy chairs and cottage furniture.

Phelps mirror: Reference most likely is to products of the mirror works of G. B. Phelps, Wheeling, Va., operating from 1830s. Tabernacle and oval-frame mirrors.

phenakistiscope: See Zoetrope.

phiale: Ancient term for a shallow dish or bowl; not a bottle.

Philadelphia: This city, founded by the Swedes as Wicaco, 1640s, was selected as the site of his capitol by William Penn. From 1690s there were excellent clock-, chair-, and cabinetmakers at work. There is no finer 18th-century Georgian colonial furniture than that of Philadelphia, which, by 1750, was America's "first" colonial city. Here was developed (1) the Philadelphia chair, meaning the American Windsor, and (2) the Philadelphia school of fine cabinetmaking with many outstanding practitioners of the art. Here also were glassworks of various kinds and sorts from 18th century, rug factories, wallpaper factories, et cetera. All before 1800. The Philadelphia dressing table is of classic design (Adam, Hepplewhite, Directoire, and Sheraton) and looks like a small sideboard. There is also a pattern of pressed glass called Philadelphia, featuring plain looplike petals alternating with horizontally reeded ones.

philatory: A sacred relic.

philippic: An impassioned, emotional outpouring; a speech.

Philip-Wynne woodenware: Turned and carved butter stamps, bowls, et cetera, made by a firm so named, New England, in 1840s.

philom.: Abbreviation for philomath, a lover of mathematics. An almanac compiler.

phillamot: Dead leaf color; a raddle or rouge of 1680s to 1700s.

philographer: A penmanship artist; a calligrapher.

philopena: Any twin-kerneled almond. A game at nut-shelling parties in which the lucky finder of a twin-kernel nut was awarded a wish or a kiss. Finally any pairing, as of cards, dominoes, et cetera.

Phoebe lamp: A double-bowled, open-topped Betty lamp, sometimes used with two wicks. Arrangement was one bowl over the other. Name is said to derive from Phoebus; the moon. [*Example pictured.*]

phoenix: Mythical bird which nested in flames. Often used decoratively as an element or feature.

Phoenix art glassware: Opalescent, cut, etched, and pearl glassware made by the Phoenix Co., Pittsburgh.

Phoenix glass: The product of any glassworks named Phoenix, as the M'Cully Works, Pittsburgh, from 1830s, and others too numerous to list. '

Phoenix iron: Product of Savery's Foundry, New York City, from 1840s; housewares of cast iron, including andirons.

Phoenix majolica: See Phoenixville Majolica.

Phoenix mirrors: Phoenix was the name of the large factory of H. V. Sigler of New York in 1850s. He made thousands of tabernacle, pier, overmantel, and other mirrors, bronzed and gilded.

Phoenixville majolica: The faïence made at Phoenixville, Pa., from 1867, by a plant under various ownerships, including Schrieber & Co., Beerbower, and Griffen, Smith & Hill. Mark is ETRUSCAN with initials of makers.

phonoharp: A small autoharp; a miniature zither.

phosgene: Liquid gas, released by heat. Used as a fluid in special lamps from 1830s.

photo-cameo: Photographic likeness on shell, made to resemble a cameo. Reported from 1840s.

photo dioramics: Motion lantern slides in which a scene was used as a drop for passing of figures. Date is from 1860s.

photogenic drawing: High-sounding name for a daguerreotype. Not content with this term, they invented another for oil-colored photos: the "photo-prosopon"!

phrenological inkwell: When the vogue of reading character from cranial structure was at its height, many professionals and amateur "bump-readers" affected this inkwell in the shape of a head marked with the areas of character; transfer-printed on white china on an inkwell base of oblong shape, with dipping well at front. Marked, sometimes with name of phrenologist. Rare.

Phyfe, Duncan: Now-famed cabinet-maker of Albany and New York who was the chief exponent of the Directoire style in the Hudson Valley. Noted for his cabinetwork of great excellence, his mechanical-leg tables, lyre-back chairs, et cetera. Learned trade at Albany. Born in Scotland, 1768; died New York City, 1854. **Phyfe chair:** The only genuine example would be a chair known positively to have been made at the factory of this man. It is an error to call any style, especially the Directoire style, by the name of this maker. His work was not in "his" style. **I. M. Phyfe & Phyfe & Co.:** Extensions of the Duncan Phyfe factory and in operation to 1858. Seem to have been interior decorators.

physiognotrace: The variant spelling of physionotrace (*which see*) used by Lemet of Albany from 1810. He did a portrait profile of a lady for $35 and of a gentleman for $25. This price included reduction in size, engraving on a small plate, and a dozen impressions.

physionotrace: The pre-photographic-era portrait miniature invented or widely promoted by Saint Memin. A good chalk drawing in profile, reduced in size by a pantograph, engraved on a copperplate, and prints made. Most are quite small. A complete set of all made in America by this artist is on file at the Congressional Library. From first decade of 19th century, or earlier.

piano engine: Fire engine with a pump and well, somewhat in the form of a pianoforte case.

pianoforte: Keyboard instrument which employed hammers to strike the strings. Made in U.S. after 1780s. Ancestor of the modern piano.

piano harp: An early upright piano; the frame was perpendicular, set as a harp. Made at Philadelphia from 1790s, and at New York from 1810s.

piano lamp: A high lamp, achieved by making stand or table and lamp base as one fixed assembly. A vagary of the last quarter of 19th century.

pianos & organs: Since there is great demand for a list of American makers, the following is given, covering the mid- to late-19th-century makers who produced

90% or more of the surviving instruments. This list, while comprehensive, is not claimed to be complete.

Aeolian Co.: Founded 1887, Meriden, Conn.

Ahlstrom, C. A.: Jamestown, N.Y., from 1875

Allemendinger: Ann Arbor, Mich., from 1872

Andrews, Geo. N.: Waterville, N.Y., from 1834

Antisell, T. M.: San Francisco, Cal., 1866

Bacon & Raven: New York City, c. 1890s

Bauer, Julius: Chicago, from 1857

Baus & Co.: New York City, from 1882

Behning & Sons: New York City, from 1861

Behr Brothers: New York City, from 1881

Bent, George P.: Chicago, from 1870

Bent, R. M.: New York City, from 1870

Biddle, J. & Son: New York City, from 1860

Black & Keffer: New York City, from 1890

Blasius & Son: Philadelphia, from 1855

Bloomfield Organ Co.: Bloomfield, N.J., 1890s

Boardman & Gray: Albany, N.Y., from 1837

Boedicker, J. D. Sons: New York City, from 1857

Bourne & Son: Boston, Mass., from 1837

Braumuller Piano Co.: New York City, 1880s

Bridgeport Organ Co.: Bridgeport, Conn., n.d.

Briggs, C. C. & Co.: Boston, Mass., from 1877

Brown & Simpson: Worcester, Mass., from 1883

Bush, W. H. & Co.: Chicago, from 1885

Cable & Sons: New York City, from 1873

Calenberg & Vaupel: New York City, from 1858

California Piano Co.: San Francisco, from 1882

Carpenter, E. P.: Organs, Brattleboro, Vt., from 1850

Century Piano: Minneapolis, Minn., from 1883

Chase, A. B. Co.: Pianos and organs, Norwalk, O., from 1875

Chase Brothers: Grand Rapids, Mich., from 1880s

Chicago Cottage Organ Co.: Chicago, from 1880

Chickering, S. G.: Boston, Mass., from 1884

Chickering & Sons: Boston, Mass., from 1823

Clough & Warren: Detroit, Mich., from 1850

Colby Co.: Erie, Pa., from 1888

Conover: New York City, from 1870

Cornett & Co.: New York City, from 1890

Cornish & Co.: Washington, N. J., from 1875

Decker & Son: New York City, from 1856

Decker Bros.: New York City, from 1862

Dunham & Co.: New York City, from 1834

Dusinberre & Co.: New York City, from 1884

Dyer & Hughes: Boston, from 1866

Earhuff, J. G.: St. Paul, Minn., from 1880s

Emerson: Boston, from 1849

Estey: Brattleboro, Vt., from 1846 (organs) New York City, from 1885 (pianos)

Everett: Boston, from 1883

Farrand & Votey: Detroit, Mich., from 1881

Fischer, J. & C.: New York City, from 1840. (Also Nunns & Fisher)

Fort Wayne: Fort Wayne, Ind., from 1871

Gabler: New York City, from 1880s

Gordon, S. T. & Son: New York City, from 1854

Guild: Boston, from 1854

Haines: New York City, from 1851

Hallet & Cumston: Boston, from 1833

Hallett, Davis & Co.: Boston, from 1839

Hardman, Peck: New York City, from 1842

Harrington, E. G.: New York City, from 1873

Hazelton Bros.: New York City, from 1850

Hemme & Long: San Francisco, Cal., from 1875

Henning: New York City, from 1880s

Hilstrom: Chesterton, Ind., 1880s

House, S. L.: Chicago, from 1883

Ivers & Pond: Boston, from 1880

Jacob Brothers: Brooklyn, N.Y., from 1879

Jardine: New York City, from 1835

Jewett: Leominster, Mass., from 1860

Keller: Bridgeport, Conn., from 1876

Kellmer: Hazelton, Pa., from 1883

Kimball: Chicago, from 1857

Knabe: Baltimore, from 1836

Krakauer: New York City, from 1870

Kranich: New York City, from 1864

Kurtzman: Buffalo, N.Y., from 1856

Lindeman: New York City, from 1836

Loring & Blake: Worcester, Mass., n.d.

Lyon & Healy: Chicago, from 1865

Mason & Hamlin: Cambridgeport, Mass., from 1854

Mathusek: New York City, from 1834

McPhail: Boston, 1884

Meyer, C. & Sons: Philadelphia, from 1823

Miller Organs: Lebanon, Pa., 1873

Moline: Moline, Ill., 1888

Morgan: Jersey City, N.J., from 1860

Morris: Boston, from 1846

Needham: Connecticut, from 1847

Nelson: Muskegon, Mich., from 1891

Norris & Fletcher: Boston, 1873

Nunns, R. & W.: New York, from 1820s

Pease: New York City, from 1872

Peek: New York City, from 1850

Prescott: Concord, N.H., founded 1836

Rice-Hinze: Des Moines, Ia., from 1886

Roosevelt: New York City, from 1872

Rosche: Elmhurst, Ill., from 1879

Schubert: New York City, from 1880

Schumacker: Philadelphia, n.d.

Shoninger: New York City, from 1850

Smith & Barnes: Chicago, from 1884

Sohmer: Astoria, L.I., from 1872

Staderman & Fox: Buffalo, N.Y., from 1877

Starr: New York City, from 1884

Steck: New York City, from 1857

Steinway: New York City, from 1853

Sterling: Derby, Conn., from 1868

Stieff: Baltimore, from 1842

Story & Clark: Chicago, from 1880

Stultz & Bauer: Brooklyn, N.Y., from 1882

Sturz Bros.: New York City, from 1873

Stuyvesant: New York City, from 1886

Taber: Worcester, Mass., from 1875

Vose: Boston, from 1851

Walters: New York City, from 1847

Waterloo: Waterloo, N.Y., from 1861

Weaver: York, Pa., from 1870

Weber: New York City, from 1852

Wegman: Auburn, N.Y., from 1883

Weser: New York City, from 1879

Western (Cottage Organ Co.): Ottawa, Ill., n.d.

pica: A measure equal to one sixth of an inch.

Pickard ware: China made at Antioch, Ill., and decorated at the factory. Date is from 1879.

Picket: Pattern of pressed glass, the decoration of which is in the form of picket fencing.

Pickhardt secretary-bed: A folding bed, hidden within a secretary desk cabinet. Strangely enough, this is late in time, patented 1860. Made at New York.

pickle caster: A silver or plated frame with loop handle and one or more pickle jars, with a fork or tongs, or both.

pickle leaf: A china side dish in natural leaf form, for service of pickles with a meal. Made from 18th century.

pickles: Any delicacy preserved in brine or soured wine, as mushrooms, walnuts, onions, gherkins, peas, olives, peaches, limes, greengages, citron, cucumbers, and love apples.

pickwick: Slender pointed spike, often on a chain, used with Betty lamps to "pick" the wick. Often of iron, but brass and even silver examples are reported.

picnic: A gathering at a tavern to which all comers brought a contribution of food for a common feast.

picot: An edging of small points and loops. Needlework allied to lacemaking.

pictorial portrait flask: Said of glass flasks, mold-blown, displaying portraits of individuals having historic significance, as Jackson, Franklin, Washington, De Witt Clinton, Lafayette, et cetera.

picture knobs: Porcelain, pottery, or other knobs with screw threads, affixed to nails after they were driven in wall, and used to hang pictures and support them at bottoms; also called mirror knobs.

picture sampler: A specific kind of fancywork sampler; one with a picture done by needlework.

pictures on glass: *Polygraphice*, published in 1700, gave instructions in this art, originating in China and displayed at its best in the interior paintings on crystal snuff bottles. The painting was done on the back of the glass, in reverse order of color application, to provide a good frontal view. Later, engravings were pasted on glass with varnish and washed off to the bare lines. The color was then applied. Also done in gold leaf as a complete cover, the picture then cut out of the leaf with points, and those exposed portions of glass covered with paint. Now called "eglomise panels," whether in the Glomi technique or not. The gold and color technique was used in Italy from 15th century. Many pictures on glass were painted to order in China for factors who shipped to European and American markets. One should not forget that South America was a buyer of such minor elegancies from the early 1800s.

picture tube: A metal tube used in viewing pictures and diorama exhibitions. Looking through tube gave the effect of concentrated illumination.

piecrust: A form of carving and dishing, achieving a piecrust effect, on a table top, tray, or stand top. The carving is generally in a series of short and long curves, imitative of the paste work done with a pastry gun. Piecrust tables are the finest pedestal tables of the Georgian era. **piecrust tazza:** A serving tray, often of Sheffield plate, resembling a miniature piecrust table. **piecrust ware:** An unglazed cane ware of a tint like piecrust. Often made to imitate a game pie. One of the products of the Belleek pottery was piecrust ware. Many potters made it.

pie fork: Two-pronged, spring-tined fork for lifting hot pie dishes from oven.

pie-plate clock: Clock casing for wall hanging, of pie-pan or piecrust form. Date is from 1860s, generally of hardwood, carved or machine-turned. The Ingraham Co. of Bristol, Conn., was the originator.

pier: The space between windows in a structural wall. Tables, stands, glasses, baskets, lighting fixtures, et cetera, designated as "pier" ware were designed for placement against such piers.

pier basket: A wall basket; some are of true basketwork, others of brass, painted iron, et cetera. Many were used as planters, first half of 19th century. Hung between windows against a wall, so called "pier." There are 17th- and 18th-century examples of record. [*Example pictured.*]

pierced back: Said of chairs when the carving is deliberately pierced through to enrich the design or accentuate a pattern. Date of the technique is from 17th century. Said also of fret-carved and fret-sawed settee and chair backs.

Pierce flower stand: Mary Pierce of New York, 1870s, invented this planter for use on window sills. It is cast iron with moss bed, drip pan, and saucer.

piers' porters: Workmen imported from the Netherlands by the Earl of Ormond to work at Kilkenny in 16th century.

Pietà: A portrayal of the human form at prayer with folded hands.

pietra dura: A much-esteemed marble, the "durable rock" used in furniture inlay and trim, for tops and other purposes.

pigeon basket: Split hickory basket in the shape of large ovate jar with cover. Used in transporting live pigeons.

piggin: Woodenware vessel used in dipping water from a tub. A shallow-bowled ladle on a handle. Also made in metalwares and in pottery. Some cream pails were called piggins.

pightle: The back yard of a house. A working place in the open.

pigtail: A small candle, sometimes burned at an angle to create a better light for short space of time.

Pike instruments: Philosophical and scientific instruments of professional quality made or sold by Benjamin Pike & Sons, N.Y., from 1830s. Some of their electric toys, including an arc lamp, are now rare items.

Pikes Peak flask: Mold-blown glass flask commemorative of Pikes Peak. There are some thirty subvarieties. Student is referred to McKearin's *American Glass* for details.

pilaster: An architectural or cabinet-making element composed of base, column, shaft, and capital. Also any flat upright member. Some clock cases of pilaster form, with tall case movements, are called pilaster clocks. So also mirrors and some decorative cast-iron staves.

pilaw: Fustian cotton cloth of olive drab or lead color.

pilcher: A flannel wrapper.

pilchpin: A large pin.

pilcrow; pilcroft: Paragraph mark, or pointing hand.

pilgrim bottle: (1) Flask with holed ears for carrying cord. (2) A pilgrim-form bottle of silver used as a banquet decanter.

Pillar: Pattern of pressed glass with panels of large thumbprints. Also a type of molding in which a double parison of glass is pillar-marked on the outer parison.

pillar & claw: Another term for ball and claw.

pillar & scroll: A pediment of two facing scrolls with finials at center at either side, over pillars from below. A feature of clock casing much favored by Eli Terry for his famous $15 wooden-movement clock.

Pillar Cut: A form of glass cutting featuring faceted pipes in a series of vertical ribbings. The style originated in the 1550s.

pillar dining table: Pairs, or threes of pedestal tables with drop leaves, made to assemble into long trains. Examples date from Georgian period, c. 1750. Any table supported on a single pillar, with footing or pedestal base.

pillar stoves: Cast-iron stoves by Dudy of Leeuwarden, the Netherlands, imported from 1820s. They are very beautiful stoves, upright, and some with open grates. [*Example pictured.*]

pillbox foot: A rare-type Queen Anne period footing which is in fact a circular shallow boxlike form upon which the pad of the cabriole leg terminates. The "pillbox" is an integral part of the leg. This term was first used in 1870s or 1880s. [*Example of the footing pictured.*]

Pillement, J.: A furniture designer of the 18th century who was an exponent of the Chinese style.

Pillivuyt ware: French porcelain, made at Foecy and Noirlac, with a big wholesale and retail depot in New York in 1840s. Great quantities of the ware sold in U.S.

pill-lock: A gun lock eliminating flint and steel and substituting a pill of fulminate of mercury for firing. Date is from 1810. Invented by Forsyth of London.

pillow beer or bere: A pillow cover or pillow case. Sometimes, when a single sheet of fabric, also called pillow sham. Inventory of Captain Tyng, Boston, 1653, mentions pillow beers. Earlier spellings are noted as "pellow beris," originally "pilve-vere."

pillow lace: Bobbin lace woven on a hard cushion.

pill slab: Stone, delft, or porcelain slab used as a base for rolling pills. Some, not square but of shield shape, decorated with armorial bearings, are mistaken for wall plaques. In fact, some have hang-up holes and were hung as plaques in early apothecary shops. Date of decorative examples is from 16th century.

pilve: A pillow. **pilve-vere:** Pillow cover. Origin of pillow beer.

pincer rushlight & candlestand: A wrought-iron stand on spidery footing (or a sturdy block of wood), having an arm fixed in a tension slide, the arm end fitted with a candle socket; arm broken in center with a hinged pincer form and jawed holder for a piece of rushlight. [*Example pictured.*]

Pinchbeck: An alloy of twenty parts copper and four of zinc; imitation, or "chapman's," gold, named for Christopher, or Oliver, Pinchbeck, born 1670, who made peddlers' goods from this alloy. By 1750 the term was current for any cheap imitation jewelry. Pinchbeck was a Fleet Street clock- and watchmaker from c. 1712. He died 1732. His son called himself "senior clockmaker to the King." **Pinchbeck paperweights:** Glass domes covering embossed thin copper-zinc alloy sheets in various forms. Date is from 1850s.

pinch-hole snuffbox: Snuffbox, generally circular, having a rotating lid with a figure-8-shaped opening and inner lid with same orifice. When these coincide, they reveal the snuff and provide a perfect "pinch hole" for insertion of finger and thumb tips.

pinch-me rocker: A standard chair form with four legs set firmly on floor, the seat arranged to rock on the side rails.

pincushion seat: Any upholstered seat having a domed or high, rounded effect. Noted from Queen Anne period through Georgian era.

Pinder & Bourne Burslem: A Burslem pottery, once the property of Messrs. Riley, owned and operated by the Pinder Brothers to 1880, when it was taken over by Doulton of Lambeth. The products were decorated vases, spill pots, flowerpots, et cetera, and a terra cotta ware.

pinders: The groundnut, peanut, or goober.

pineapple: The fruit emblematic of hospitality. Pineapple forms were popular as a decorative element. **pineapple bedstead:** A high- or low-post bed with carved pineapple finials. **pineapple cloth:** A drapery fabric woven from retted fibers of pineapple leaves. **pineapple egg cup:** A lidded egg cup of the fruit form. **pineapple jug:** Pouring vessel of pineapple form or pineapple décor. **pineapple lamp:** Fluid lamp with oil reservoir in the fruit form; candlesticks with socket housed in or over a pineapple form. **Pineapple-Pressed:** A pattern of pressed glass having the fruit impressed as a decorative form and as pressed finials. Clear and milk glass. **pineapple teapot:** Pot in pineapple form, eyed as the fruit, and realistically colored.

Pine Orchard House ware: Reference is to the Enoch Wood Staffordshire blue-printed ware featuring view of this Catskill Mountain resort.

pine-tree money: The shilling and other denominations of coinage struck in New England by officials of the Massachusetts Bay Colony from 1652. Originally they bore only the NE indicia on obverse and value in Roman numerals on reverse; a tree was added to the die, first a willow and then an oak. Finally, in 1663, the tree was made a pine. Jonathan Hull, silversmith, was the coiner, with his partner, Robert Sanderson.

pinkster: Spring festivity.

pin kuo hung: Peach bloom.

pink wood: Naturally pink- and rose-tinted yew wood. Any naturally pink-tinted wood, often a heartwood.

Pinney, Eunice: Early 19th-century amateur water-color artist whose copies of English prints and attempts at originality resulted in many portfolios of engaging crudities and quaint "pieces." One of the first promoted "primitive" painters. The work is amateur art by a woman who had fun doing her painting. Eunice worked around Windsor, Conn.

pins: Dressing aids, which in colonial period were really expensive items, as each pin was handmade. Priced from seven shillings a dozen in 1770s. Sizes, from smallest, were named: lillikin, lace, short white, mourning, middling, corking. Machine-made after 1830, and then sold in curious and quaint papers, boxes, and nests.

pintongs: Heavy pins of gold, silver, or plate.

pin-up lamp: Any lamp with angular base to form brackets for fastening to wall. Some have a bayonnet or spike to fit in a wall fixture.

Pinwheel Cut: Pattern of cut glass, more properly "buzz star," featuring star cutting with points at angles rather than radiant, and space-filled with fan cutting.

pinwheel plate: A plate rim pierced with openings placed as though from a whirling circle.

pinx.: Abbreviation for *pinxit*, painted it.

pinxter: The Whitsuntide season, celebrated with a fair or festival.

pinxton: A soft-paste porcelain and an enamel made in East Derbyshire, 1790s-1810s.

pione: The peony seed, used as a spice.

pioneer art: Paintings and drawings of a strictly amateur quality, the result not of a pioneering in techniques, but of pioneering in instruction by itinerants and private "school" and self-instruction books. The more proper term is "amateur art." Reference is to the American art work by millions of free peoples as a pastime, or in an effort to achieve a degree of proficiency to earn decorators' wages; today in error called "primitive" and "folk" art.

Pioneer Flint Glass: The glass factory at Coffeyville, Kan., 1903.

pipe: A measure or container holding 126 gallons. Half a tun.

pipe clay: Fine white clay, used in making

smoke pipes and also as a white dressing for breeches and other military wear.

pipe dryer: A wrought-iron stand for racking washed clay pipes for drying. Hoops, connected with uprights, or loops, with bands.

pipe head: Pipe bowls in form of human and other heads. Some are of political significance, as the "Clay-Clay" pipe.

pipe kiln: A carrier or stand for clay pipes, especially the long-stemmed variety called churchwarden. A kiln for firing pipes.

pipes: (1) Reeding, generally vertical, and sometimes fluting are so called. (2) The tubular sections under the barrel stock of a musket, carrying the ramrod. (3) Receptacles for burning tobacco in smoking.

pipe stand: A flat cabinet with drawers, with a metal tray and upright in which long-stemmed clay pipes were racked within upper curvate arms. [*Example pictured.*]

pipe tongs: Tongs of miniature size, used in lighting pipes with a small ember.

piping: Cording, in sewing. Cords used for stringing fruits for drying.

pipkin: A saucepan, a brandy warmer, a coal hod; all these, at various times, have been called pipkins.

piqué: (1) Minute inlay work, often in gold or silver. (2) A form of needlework. (3) A kind of fine corded fabric.

Piranesi, J. B.: Italian exponent of the classic revival.

pistol bootjack: Dummy pistol of cast iron, made in halves, hinged, opening into a bootjack.

pistol grip; pistol-handled: Knives, forks, and other utensils with the long, slightly curvate handles of the type used on early pistols.

pit-bottomed: Said of iron- or other stove wares having extended round bottoms fitting the standard stove holes of the cooking ranges made generally after 1830s.

pitcher: Any pouring vessel with a handle. Innumerable pressed-glass examples in an amazing array of patterns are of record in illustrated pamphlets by various collectors, including Mrs. Minnie Watson Kamm, whose many booklets list over 1200, all different!

pit coal: Stone coal; mined coal.

pithos: A large earthenware cask, some dating from pre-Christian Era. Generally decorated or sculptured.

Pitkin flasks: Once used to designate what were imagined to be flasks made at Pitkin Works, East Manchester, Conn., from 1780s. The flasks are ribbed and swirled and were made at various plants, the attributions of source being based on the general form and contours. The glass is green, amber, and other colors. **Pitkin glass:** Made at factory here named, in olive green and amber. Flasks, inkwells, snuff jars, bowls, and the famous Jared Spencer "Manchester" mold-blown flask. **Pitkin silver:** Coin silver, mass-produced by W. L. & H. E. Pitkin of Hartford, Conn., from 1850s. Table flatwares. Marked.

Pitman, Benjamin: Britannia-ware maker of New Bedford, Mass., in mid-19th century. Earlier, from 1830s, he was a silversmith.

Pitman, Marc: Cabinetmaker of Salem, Mass., from c. 1799 to 1820s.

pit saw: Oblong frame with a saw blade in center; in use, the frame embraced the timber and the blade cut it. A lengthwise cutter, not a crosscutter. A two-man saw, each man working saw from the frame ends, one generally in a pit beneath the timber being cut.

pitsche: A wine can, of Swiss origin. Examples of silver, tin, copper, iron, and brass are known.

Pittsburgh: (1) One of the great glass-making centers of the U.S. from 1790s. (2) Pattern of pressed glass featuring prismatic fluting over bands of cup forms looking like lily-of-the-valley flowers.

Pittsburgh Steamboat: A pressed-glass cup plate, or butter chip, featuring a steamboat and marked UNION GLASS WORKS, PITTSBURGH, 1836.

pit'ung: A brush jar.

pivot hinge: An early chest hinge, generally an extension of a stile or rail, bored to fit a pin. Sometimes of metal.

Place's ware: Fine pottery made at York, England, from 1660s. It is imitative of the true china, then excessively rare.

placket: Several definitions are of record: a slit in a gown; the pocket in a gown; the pudendum in breechings.

plaid: (1) A long shawl. A Scottish plaid is a shawl, not the crossbarred fabric generally, in error, called plaid. The cross-barred fabric is properly a tartan. (2) A pattern of pressed glass imitative of fine crosscutting, in squared or fan-shaped panels divided with ridges.

plain flute: A style of glass cutting that is not a fluting but a series of broad facets, somewhat like Ashburton in pressed glass.

Plain mirrors: Bartholomew Plain is listed as a mirror maker of New York from 1790s. Labeled examples include gilt-framed girandoles, tabernacle, pier, and (it is reported) Constitution types. Son John continued the manufacture to 1840s or later, while another son, Edward, became a silversmith.

plancer: The visible underside of a cornice.

planish: The technique of beating metal to a polish; form-hammered.

plank bottom: Any all-wood seat of a chair or settee; Windsor chair and settee seats are saddle-shaped, or contoured to fit the derrière. Later examples are scrolled, or rolled, as the Boston rocker and the all-wood side chairs popular in 19th century.

plantation bell: The call bell of a large farm, often mounted in a tower or belfry, to signal work hours, call to meals, et cetera. Priestly & Bein of New Orleans were large distributors of such bells from 1840s. Many also were made at Troy, N.Y.

plantation desk: Generally a misnomer, elevating the quality of the piece. Reference is to table desks, made from 1840s, having a sloped writing board, cupboard for ledgers, and pigeonholes. Used in schools, countinghouses, offices, banks, and by farmers, storekeepers, and planters.

planter's Toby: A Toby-style jug depicting the English version of a planter in the colonies.

plaster ware: Erroneously called chalk ware, and at times said to be "carved from native chalk." Ninety-nine per cent of the production was simply castings of plaster of Paris, decorated crudely with colors in imitation of the original pottery or porcelain ware. Often the forms were cast from such originals without benefit of permission. All of the plaster ware (called chalk ware) claimed to be Pennsylvania Dutch or Pennsylvania German was made by itinerant vendors in small shops from plaster or metal molds. The makers were generally of Italian or French extraction. Nearly all forms made are traceable to (1) Staffordshire figures and figurines; (2) Chinese figures and figurines, tomb markers, such as the pomegranate pile and fruit piles; and (3) classical figures or figurines, busts, et cetera. Made in every community in the U.S.; all but the classic examples are most likely 19th century. It is known that classic busts of plaster were sold as early as 1725. Term "chalk" probably derives from the invention, 19th century, of a chemical compound that hardened plaster casts to the consistency of alabaster.

plata: Spanish term for silver; from the Latin. Probably origin of "plate" as a term for silverware of solid-silver content. To say silver plate is really to say "silver silver." Argent is the heraldic term for silver.

plateau: A footed metal tray, generally over 15 inches in one dimension. Rarest are of solid silver; commonest of brass or of Sheffield plate.

plate back: Reference is to a chair or settee back splat, similar to the spoon back. Found in Queen Anne style furniture.

plate carrier: Straight-sided bucketlike device of fine cabinet wood, with a broad stave left out from top to bottom, and a bail handle. Dinner plates were stacked in it for carriage to and from pantry. [Example pictured.]

plated glass: Overlay glass.

plated silver: Reference is generally to electroplated ware; a thin deposit of silver on base metal. Not Sheffield plate.

plate-etched glass: Intaglio engraving on plates for making transfer prints on tissue paper. Not common practice until late 19th century. Generally plate engraving on glass was from metal plates to paper, with fatty ink, and the "engraving" done on glass with corrosives. Sometimes the ink carried a corrosive to bite lines in the glass.

plate-lettered: In mold blowing of glass, a removable and interchangeable metal plate with lettering to mark bottles for any customer, especially a druggist or vintner.

plate stand: A pedestal stand, tri-footed, with a "top" made up of notched, outflaring arms. A fireside plate warmer of Queen Anne and Georgian period, now quite rare. [Example pictured.]

plate top: Table top with round depressions around its rim. Sometimes the top is scalloped to conform to the plates.

plate trencher: Woodenware. (1) A square of wood with a shallow bowl-form gouging and sometimes a saltcellar. (2) A

trivet block to serve as a stand for plates, pots, pan, et cetera, at table.

plate wagon: A deep tray on legs, castered or wheeled. The ancestor of the teacart.

plated silver (Sheffield & electroplate): Makers of these wares have only exemplary listing in this work. See Bibliography for books containing lists, marks, and illustrations of the wares.

platform rocker: A "non-creeping" rocker. Popular from late 1860s. The chair's rockers engage flat surface rails, which are made a part of the chair by bracing, springs, and leather thongs.

platinum mirror: Mirror glass with a film of platinum deposited on it, the front being the metal deposit, serving as the mirror. From the rear, these mirrors can be seen through; the original one-way glass. Made in 1850s.

plat ménage: A standing centerpiece of ceramic ware, metal, or glass, with arms, plats, hanging baskets, et cetera, for comfits, flowers, tidbits, et cetera. Examples known as Wedgwood, Leeds, and other wares, Irish, Stourbridge, and Bristol glass, French glass, Sheffield plate and silver. [Example pictured.]

playing cards: Volumes have been written on the history of these aids to gaming and pastime. The variety is infinite, many types having specific names.

Pleat & Panel: Pattern of pressed glass featuring stippled panels with fluting above and between.

pleasaunce: A delight.

pleuvarre: Imitation marble (see plaster ware) achieved by soaking plaster casts in a solution of alum until surface crystallization was noted. Polished, the plaster looked like marble. Made from 1830s.

Plimpton: An item of gadget furniture; a toilet table, secretary desk, with a bedstead folded within. Some examples are not folding, all the elements are joined!

plique-à-jour: A form of cloisonné, the outline of form being in fine wire, the enamel between.

plow: A tool for gouging the groove of a tongue-and-groove assembly in wood.

plumassier: A featherworker. A feather merchant.

plumbago: Graphite. Pressed into sticks, it was a pencil used in drawing on paper, parchment, and thin panels of holly wood. Plumbago portrait; plumbago miniature.

plumbeotypes: Daguerreotypes printed on paper, invented as a process by one Plumbe of Philadelphia, 1845.

plumber: Leadworker. Pewterer. The pewterers of the 1830s seem to have graduated into the trade of plumber, or sanitary lead worker.

Plume: Pattern of pressed glass featuring feathery plumes with round lobes as panels and borders.

plumpers: Cheek "falsies" worn inside the mouth to plump out the cheeks.

plum-pudding mahogany: Rich, dark mahogany, with markings resembling boiled plum pudding.

Plumstead, Charles: Cabinetmaker of Philadelphia who is reputed to have worked in the William & Mary and Queen

Anne styles prior to 1715. If this finally is established it will refute the dicta that no furniture in the Queen Anne style was made in America during her reign, 1702–14.

plunket: Coarse woolen cloth.

pluviale: An ecclesiastical cape; a vestment.

Plymouth Cut: Pattern of cut glass featuring a basic star design filled with multi-pointed stars and grid cutting imitative of cane weave.

Plymouth Rock weight: Paperweight of pressed glass, in form of the traditional rock, made by (or for) The Inkstand Co., Providence, R.I. The date, 1620, on the piece is commemorative of the landing of the Pilgrims.

Plymouth ware: Reference is to the ceramic wares of Plymouth, England, by Cookworthy and his successors, at Coxside and other locales. The industry began in mid-18th century. Products were table-wares, vases, candlesticks, Madonnas, stands, figures, and trinkets. The factory was removed to Bristol and conducted by Champion. [*Examples pictured.*]

poacher's gun: A light fowling piece, or shotgun, convertible to a cane. A shotgun-cane.

pocket chair: See Chairs, All Kinds.

pocket globe: Miniature terrestrial globe in a pocket case.

pocket gymnasium: An early Goodyear rubber novelty; an elastic band of great strength, used in exercising. [*Advertisement of early 1870s pictured.*]

pocket rifle: A working model, miniature rifle, made by Stevens Arms Co., 1870s. Sold in a mahogany case with 250 rounds of minicaliber ammunition. Also, any rifle-barreled pistol. [*Example in use pictured.*]

pocket sewing machine: A 12-ounce sewing machine without wheels or gears; worked by springs. Operated by clamping to a table; hand- or foot-operated.

pod: (1) A box sleigh. (2) As a suffix, as tripod, the meaning is foot, or footed.

podger: A pewter plate.

pogie: (1) A poor farm. (2) A small fishing boat.

pogmoggan: An Indian stone hammer; not a tomahawk or axe.

poikilographia: The art of penmanship.

point: One seventy-second of an inch.

point d'esprit: Cotton netting with square dots.

point device: With exactness; precise.

point d'Hongrie: Zigzag embroidery or point work, in bands, of various colors blending into each other. A favorite upholstery trim.

point lace: Tag lace; lace with long points. Lace woven with a needle in contradistinction to pillow lace.

poison bottle: Cobalt-blue bottle with sharp diamond-point cutting or pressing. You knew it was poison from color in the light, or from the points in the dark.

poitrel: The breastplate of armor; a "falsie" of the 17th and 18th centuries.

pokal: A tall covered goblet, generally elaborately decorated.

poke: A restraining iron or wooden halter or stopple worn by cattle to prevent straying. Animals "poked" could not breach a fence. [*Example pictured.*]

poke-melly: Pickled cucumbers, soured in raspberry, black currant, or other aromatic vinegar and salt, with spices. Introduced by Swedes in 1650s or earlier. Said to be a delicacy they had from Muscovy.

poker picture: Picture achieved by use of a hot poker on wood.

Poland bottle: Reference is to glass bottles for Poland Spring water. Mold-blown in shape of bearded man.

Polar Bear: Pattern of pressed glass featuring an ambulant polar bear.

pole: A measure of distance, 16½ feet.

pole bed: A low-post bed, the tester frame of which is a single pole from the room wall, from which two-swag drapery falls to head and foot.

pole end: Finial for a standing flagpole, or for ends of curtain pole.

pole lathe: A turner's lathe operating from treadle and cord, the latter affixed to an overhead pole, acting as a spring.

pole screen: A high pole on a footed pedestal, on which a fire screen is fixed, adjustable as to height. The cheval fire screen. When the device is also fitted with a shelf to hold a candlestick it is designated as a pole-screen candlestand.

police candle: A folding planished tin box, when open serving as a lantern with candle, the inside of box being the reflector.

police baton: The billy club. The weighted staff of office, used also to make peaceable the obstreperous. Some have stilettos, and some have pistols concealed in them. Generally of hard, heavy wood, turned and polished, sometimes painted, and identified as to police district, owner, et cetera.

polished bottom: Said of pontil-marked blown wares in which the pontil is ground off or out, sometimes leaving a dimple.

Polish teakettle: A small samovar. Properly a water heater.

political glass: Any glassware bearing portraits, symbols, and names of candidates for office.

Polka Dot: Pressed imitation of overlay glass; in two colors, with the dots clear on the colored ground.

pollard: To decapitate; to take off the poll, as a tree. Hence pollard oak, pollard elm, et cetera. Decapitating caused the tree to grow a new set of limbs around the cut bole and to develop peculiarities in grain. The fine-grained oak today, often characterized as "pollard," is from normal trees. In 1840 a London paper stainer, Robert Horne, issued a wallpaper imitative of pollard oak, which was pasted on the wall and then varnished, giving the effect of paneling.

poll evil: A rash on the scalp under the hair; a neck rash on horses. A skin disease affecting the scalp. "Evil on the poll."

polleys: Play marbles of the "commony" variety, but glazed.

polonaise: A draped overskirt.

polyautography: The original term for what is now called lithography. Examples so called were issued 1799–1800, reproducing work of several artists.

polygon: Balanced geometrical form imitative of the perfect circle. Pentagon is five-sided; hexagon, six-sided; septagon, seven-sided; octagon, eight-sided; nonagon, nine-sided; decagon, ten-sided; undecagon, eleven-sided; dodecagon, twelve-sided.

Polymnia: Greek Muse of sacred and serious song.

pomace: The residue from fruit pressing to extract juice.

pomade (pomatum): Creams, unguents, greases, such as lanolin, coco and palm oils, olive oils, suets, waxes, et cetera, made into perfumed or medicated specialties.

pomander ball: An orange punctured with whole cloves over the entire skin, then powdered with orris, cinnamon, and rose ashes, wrapped in paper and corded for hanging or carrying, enclosed in a perforated metal case. **pomander case:** A globular two-piece hinged case of perforated metal, for carrying a pomander ball. **pomander chain:** A necklace of small balls of perfumed stuff. The material, called "diapasm," was aromatic herbs and spices reduced to a coarse powder and molded into large pills with gum arabic.

pomcitron: Preserved pear-citron, or citron-pear.

pomedorry: Pork meat paste with egg white, formed into balls, boiled slightly, and then spit-broiled.

pomegranate: "A bunch of tiny aromatic grapes within a firm, leathery shell." A magnificent fruit of the Orient, with berry-filled red fruit having a pronounced blossom end. The fruit was the inspiration for many decorative forms, as were the bud and flower. Grown in U.S. as a garden tree from Virginia southward, and as a house tree, protected in winter, in the North. Best way to eat the fruit is to suck, after squeezing like an orange, through the blossom end. The syrup grenadine is from this fruit. **pomegranate teapot:** Of pomegranate form, filling from the bottom. **pomegranate thumbpiece:** Dutch and Swiss pewter flagons have this delightful design of thumbpiece. The German examples have ball form. From 16th century.

Pomeroy paste: A honing paste used in sharpening cutlery.

Pomeroy pistol: The truly early American firearm of 17th century, made by Eltweed Pomeroy, a gunsmith of the Pilgrim Co.

Pomona glass: Late novelty glass of 1880s; it is pebbled, parti-colored, etched, and sometimes pattern-decorated. New England Glass Co. originated the ware.

pompadours: Fabrics, hair and dress styles, pomades, jewelry styles, et cetera, named for Madame the Marquise de Pompadour, mistress of Louis XV.

pompier: Single-pole ladder with rungs extending on either side, generally with hook at top. Firearms ladder.

pompillon: Ointment made from black-poplar buds.

pompoons: The original, and preferred, spelling of pompon. A ball or pome form

of feathers, fronds, cords, silk floss, et cetera.

ponce print: See Godefroy Prints.

pond lily: Water-lily form, as the famed "pond lily" pitcher made at Bennington pottery; blue-and-white and all-white Parian.

Pond patterns: Hooked-rug patterns imitative of those of Edward Sands Frost, made at Biddeford, Me., from 1877 by D. Pond & Co.

pongee: Coarsely woven silk, from coarse floss. Term is from the Cantonese dialect, *p'un-ki*, meaning homemade. The Chinese radical *ki* means table or bench.

pontil: Glassmaker's fixing and working rod; affixed to bottom of work in blowing, it left a scar—the pontil mark—when detached. Also called a punt or punty. Some pressed glass, removed from mold with a pontil rod, carries the pontil mark.

Pontipool: Japanned tinware, beautifully painted, advertised by this name as early as 1760s. Derives from an early place of manufacture, Pontipool, Wales. Any fine-painted sheet-iron ware.

poodle bottle: Figural bottle in form of poodle with a barrel front between paws of the dog. **poodle lounge:** Chaise longue or couch for poodles. A decadent vagary of the royal mistresses and court courtesans who had repose furniture for their poodles made in the same style as their own couches. Sometimes called gout stool. [*Example pictured.*]

Pool barometer: Weather forecaster made by Charles Pool of New York after 1819. Styles are classic, Directoire, and Empire. This same maker produced a number of types of scientific instruments.

poonah: A theorem, or stencil.

poor man's press: Probably a late term for a crudely made press cupboard of pioneer quality, made up of plain board case or carcass and with simple paneled doors and plain drawer fronts. [*Example pictured may be 18th-century Pennsylvania or Swedish.*]

Popcorn: Pattern of pressed glass with all-over dewdrops and panels of ovate "corn-ear" form.

Pope bird prints: Chromolithographed prints from *Upland Game Birds and Water Fowl of the United States,* published 1877–78 by A. Pope, Jr. Prints are folio size.

pope's-head brush: Brush heads in form of the papal headgear, mounted on long slender pole, for dusting walls and ceilings.

pope's mug, face, nose: Colloquial for the Bellarmine mask jug.

popinjay: (1) The parrot. (2) Individuals who were parrotlike in walk, talk, and gaiety of garb.

poppy finial: Carved forms imitative of the curly-leafed poppy, petals down, and capped with an acorn or ball. Form dates from Middle Ages.

popskull: Southern name for cocktailings, or remainders and dregs of wines and liquors; sold cheap as tipple. Strong enough to pop your skull.

porcelain: The fine stoneware impregnated with its glazing agent, as discovered in China and imitated in Europe by the tin-glaze wares, faïence, majolica, and delft, until the accidental discovery of how to make the Chinese ware at Meissen, 1710, and England, 1690s (the latter discovery not recognized or exploited at the time). In Europe these several factories produced porcelain: Meissen, Dresden, Hochst, Frankenthal, Berlin, Vienna, Saxe, Ludwigsburg, Vincennes, Vieux Paris, Sèvres, Carlsbad, Rosenthal, et cetera. In England: Bow, Chelsea, Derby, Bristol, Caughley, Coalport, Liverpool, Pongton, Minton, Nantgarw, Pinxton, Plymouth, Spode, Swansea, Worcester, Wedgwood, et cetera. Most of the English porcelains are of soft paste. See Bibliography for listed books on subject. **porcelain mirrors:** Mirrors with porcelain frames; small ones of one-piece framing, large examples in parts, assembled. **porcelain buttons:** Innumerable varieties of fired porcelain blanks, decorated and refired. Some are underglazed. **porcelain thimble:** Actual thimble of fine porcelain.

porcellena: First name used to designate porcelain, or China ware.

porcupine wood: Wood of the coconut palm.

porphyry: Igneous rock embedded with feldspar and quartz crystals.

porringer: Original definition was a small pan. Now a double- or single-eared small pan of silver, brass, copper, pewter, iron, or even wood.

porringer table: An eared-top table, the ears at corners or midway between corners. Early examples have scalloped skirting and cabriole legs. Later examples have canted legs, and fret-scrolled tops. Origin of term is not clear.

Portabella ware: See Porto Bello.

portable barometer: The invention of Daniel Quare, one of the world's great watchmaker-scientists, London, 17th century. The casing is very much like a street-lighting standard. Wall barometer, some examples made for table use.

portable desk: Any desk case that is portable is properly described by this term, but specifically a three-drawer and bookshelf arrangement with a carrying handle. These date from 1750s.

portable divan bed: A couch folding into a trunk.

portable melodeon: Small melodeon with fretwork panel, folded-under supports, detachable bellows and pedals. [*Example pictured.*]

portable wainscot: Actually portable hardwood marquetry flooring, glued on canvas and rollable for carriage to the point of use.

porte-crayon: Metallic holder for a plumbago stick. Used as the writing aid we call a pencil, but not called a pencil when invented; at that period pencils were hairbrushes.

porte-lamp: A framework of open circles of metal for carrying a burning fat-lamp. Said to date from 12th century.

porte-monnaie: Handbag or purse.

porte-manteau: A standing costumer, or clothes tree. Not a trunk.

Port Elizabeth glass: Made at Port Elizabeth, N.J., from 1810s by the Strangers and other famed Jersey glassworkers.

Porter, Rufus: Itinerant decorator, amateur scientist, and man of parts, jack-of-all-trades who mastered every one and finally founded that great periodical, *The Scientific American.* Published, 1826, a now rare homecraft book, *Valuable and Curious Arts,* which included all sorts of recipes and instructions (with illustrations) for wall painting.

Porter Britannia: Made by Porter Co., Taunton, Mass., from 1859.

Porter lamp: A canting lamp, tilting in a cradle, or on pivots, to ensure complete usage of all fluid in reservoir. **Porter lamp fluids:** Camphene.

Porter lamps: Lamps by H. Porter of Boston, from 1830s; hall lanterns, table and mantel lamps. Successor of shop was R. H. Spaulding, who had an extensive manufactory (or arrangements with other makers) and an imposing retail establishment.

Porteus-Phillips lamps: Product of a partnership of this name at Philadelphia, from 1840s. Camphenes and lard-oil lamps for table, mantel, and for hanging.

port-fire: Matches, tinderboxes—any portable fire-making apparatus.

portfolio stand: A case with drop doors, to hold prints, maps, et cetera. Some leaves form a table for viewing specimens and proofs. Also with latticework wings or dividers. Imposing items when designed for library or drawing room, generally in classic or Sheraton style.

portico: Classic entrance porch. Miniatures in porcelain, china, pottery, and plaster ware, often to hold a watch.

Portland glass: Pressed glass; patterns include Shell & Jewel, Shell & Tassel, Tree of Life, Loop & Dart, Roman Rosette, et cetera. Made at Portland, Me., 1864–70s. Sometimes marked P. G. Co.

Portland vase: The cameo glass vase, named for the Duke of Portland, who secured it from the Barberini family. This ancient and classic example of cameo overlaid glass cutting is of Greco-Roman Provenance. An extensive notice appeared in the *Magazine Antiques* (see Index of that periodical). The vase was reproduced in 1790 by Wedgwood, in his jasper-cameo ware, and c. 1870 by Northwood in the original technique of glass cutting. This vase is the prototype of all genuine modern cameo glass.

Porto Bello ware: Astbury's ware memorializing the victory of Admiral Vernon, 1739, when he captured Porto Bello from the Spanish. Lawrence Washington served under the admiral and, when building his mansion on the Potomac, named it Mount Vernon. The Astbury ware has molded relief decoration of the six-ship fleet of the admiral, harbor view, et cetera. Advertised in colonies from 1760s. Also a more or less generic term for Astbury's red or tawny fauncolored ware with white clay figures.

portpane: Bread-carrying cloth. Often embroidered and decorated in cross stitch. The so-called "door panels" and towels of New England, New York, New Jersey, and Pennsylvania were most likely portpanes.

portrait; portraiture: Graphic presentation of the human face.

portrait chair: See Chairs, All Kinds.

portrait of ceremony: Classic art phrase meaning a portrait painted in the most perfect manner, displaying the consequence or importance of the subject. Sully, Eicholtz, Peale, Pine, and other American painters did portraits of notables in this manner.

portugals: Sweets, pastilles. Also the punk pastille, perfumed, for burning to deodorize a room. Time is 17th century.

poshai: Soft goat's hair spun into silky threads. The secret of the cashmere shawls, which are so fine they will slip through a wedding ring.

posnet: A small skillet; a tri-footed pot with handle.

posset: Hot milk with wine and spice. **posset pan:** The pan used in heating milk and mixing posset. **posset pot:** A tyg, pot, or cup, with cover, for serving posset as a going-to-bed drink, often carried to the bedchamber and taken upon getting into bed. Also a large cup, used communally, for drinking posset.

post augur: A screw augur, invented 1760 by William Henry, gunsmith, of Lancaster, Pa. A screwhead attached to a rod with crossbars, used in boring post holes in the earth.

postiche: A fake; an imitation. A deliberate effort to create and dispose of a fake antique.

post paper: Paper watermarked with a post horn. See Paper Sizes.

post spoon: A spoon-bladed long-handled shovel, used in digging post holes and wells.

post-Victorian: Not after Victoria's death, but after the age of popularity of the style named for her. Eastlake, Morris, and other designers started the post-Victorian era.

post wood: Any wood, such as locust, cypress, cedar, which resists moisture.

pot: A jug or pitcher. Originally a one-quart vessel.

pot & kettle: In spite of all attempts to describe these two vessel forms, this would seem to be the true status: Pots are cooking vessels for foods, boiled or slow-baked, simmered or roasted. Kettles are for boiling water or other fluids.

potager: A soup dish.

potato beer: A yeast of potatoes boiled with hops.

potato bowl: A 19th-century wooden bowl, turned and carved, for service of baked or boiled potatoes at table. Mostly imported from England. Date is from 1840s.

potato cutter: A small bowl-shaped cutter to cut small balls of potato flesh.

potato kettle: A secondhand and useless teapot, used as an "oven" for baking potatoes.

potato pasty: A two-part pan with liner for baking and serving meat pies with mashed-potato crust. [Example pictured.]

potato ring: See Dish Ring.

potato scoop: A shell-form, perforated element, mounted on a wand, to lift potatoes baked in fireplace embers. [Example pictured.]

potato-soup glaze: Said of imperfectly or cheaply glazed oriental export porcelains. Glaze which crawls in rivulets, developing pits and blisters.

pot-au-feu: An earthenware covered cook pot, fired and used on the hearth, amid embers. [Example pictured.]

potbelly: Said of any curvate, ovoid form with pronounced bulge, as potbellied stove. Barrel-shaped.

pot brake: A pothanger, potcrook, pothook, trammel.

pot brush: Cleaning brush for kitchen wares, bottles, et cetera.

pot button: Brass button made from the brass of old pots.

pot cake: A dumpling.

pot claw: Same as pot brake, which see.

pot cradle: A baby cradle made entirely of pottery. Generally Staffordshire; some are 17th century, or so it is said.

pot dog: Fire irons to support pots over coals.

pot fowling: Wholesale slaughter of wild fowl for meat and market.

pothook: Southern meaning said to be a slave collar of iron. Also any hook, claw, or brake to hang pots.

potiche: A temple jar; Chinese. Any fine jar of porcelain used for ornamentation.

potichomanie: A homecraft of decorating the interior of glass vessels with paper cutouts pasted flat against the inner wall, then coated with paint or plaster. 19th century. Many with all or part of original décor have been stripped and the glass vases, et cetera, used in original form. Most of the glass is blown and has pontil mark. Potichomanie jars were advertised in 1857 by W. P. Walter of Philadelphia, as made by Philadelphia Glass Co. "for making imitation china vases." **potichomanie balls:** Glass balls of large size, decorated inside with cut paper applied through a small opening.

potlids: Reference is to the decorated lids of pots used as commercial containers for shaving soaps, pomades, et cetera. Innumerable varieties, some of American firms, but made in England.

pot marigold: Spicy marigold flowers used to flavor soups and stews.

pot metal: Alloy of copper and tin, or lead. Also "cock-metal."

pot paper: Any paper watermarked with a jug or pot. Made from 1540s.

potpourri: Flower petals dried in a covered jar. **potpourri jar:** Covered jar designed specifically for preserving dried flower petals.

pot sittin: Foods burned to the pot.

potster: A potter; a pot maker. Also called a crocker, tilester, and some others not so nice.

potstone: The lapis ollaris of the ancients. The soapstone used in turning pots usable in the fire. Steatite.

pottage tongs: Fork-ended tongs to grasp a pot. [Example pictured.]

Potter & Bodine glass: Philadelphia-made; mineral-water, porter, and milk bottles, from 1850s.

potter's "dozen": The smallest unit made

1, Pottage Tongs. 2, Potato Scoop. 3, Platt Ménage. 4, Portable Melodeon. 5, Potato Pasty Pan. 6, Petite Console. 7, Pipe Stand (for long-stemmed clays called churchwardens). 8, Plate Stand. 9, Pier Baskets. 10, Plate Carrier. 11, Poor Man's press. 12, Plymouth Ware, three examples. 13, Pillar Stove. 14, Pennsylvania Stretcher Table. 15, Pocket "Gymnasium" of gum elastic. 16, Phaeton (original form). (Nos. 3 and 12 from Virtue & Co., London.)

at a pottery was the standard of capacity, and 12 pieces was a dozen. The same type of piece, of twice size, was not a dozen of 12, but a set of 6 pieces. Other sizes ran from one to 9 to a dozen.

Pottersville: The Somerset pottery region of Massachusetts.

Potterville: Wisconsin region settled by people from Staffordshire, 1840s, under the auspices of the Nottingham emigration society.

pottery picture frame: Clay-ware frames, glazed and fired; some square and rectangular, but most are ovals, probably cast in molds made from an original carved wood oval frame. A cottage-type frame. Some made in Shenandoah Valley of Virginia and in western Maryland.

pottery pies: Game-pie dishes of cane ware, looking like baked piecrusts, and deliberately imitative of such pastry work. Made by Wedgwood and other potters in England and on the continent.

pottery pillow: (1) Chinese porcelain pillow forms, rectangular and square, beautifully decorated. Actually used as head supports while sleeping. (2) Decorative pillow forms of European, English, and American make, decorated. (3) Sometimes the hot pillow bottle; a pottery container for hot water, to add comfort to the ill or for warming a bed. (4) Lawn seats, made by the Norton Pottery, the saddle-form cushions resting on a pottery stand imitative of a tree stump.

Pottier furniture: Made by A. Pottier of New York City from 1850s; elaborate French Antique revival in style, of ebony, rosewood, walnut, and oak, with gilt-bronze and porcelain decoration.

pottle: Two-quart measure.

pottle pot: Any bottle form of pottery, glass, leather, or metal; a two-quart jug.

Potts tea caddy: Japanned sheet-iron tea caddy made by William Potts of New York from 1850s. Many styles and sizes, some of "store size."

poudre marchant: Powdered or pulverized spices.

poudrette: Fertilizer for the soil, endorsed by Daniel Webster in 1840s.

poudreuse: A dressing table; a powdering table. Lowboys were sometimes so called.

Poughkeepsie ware: Reference is presumed to be to the stoneware made at this town on the Hudson by Adam Caire.

pounce: Blotting and parchment-surfacing powder, made from powdered cuttlefish bone and resins. **pounce box or bag:** Containers for the pounce used in dressing a parchment for writing. Also the sand boxes of writing sets. Any container holding blotting pounce or fine sand.

pounced: Perforated.

pour Toby: A quaint Toby form, one arm crooked, one raised. The crooked arm is the handle, the raised arm the pouring spout. [*Example pictured.*]

Powder & Shot: Pattern of pressed glass having stipple background with powder-horn emblem and beading representing shot.

powder bowl: A face-powder box, with cover, often equipped with a feather or fluff-puff applicator.

powder bucket: Heavy canvas bucket-form bag, usually decorated with insignia of the service, used on line-of-battle ships and other naval vessels by the "powder monkeys," or boys who carried powder from below-deck magazine to the gunners. Some are of wood, others of leather.

powder flask; powder horn: The container for powder carried by hunters, soldiers, and sporting gunners. Infinite variety of horn, bone, metal, leather, and wood. (Never of glass or easily shattered substance.) Map horns were used by pioneers, the map of the region engraved on the horn or flask. Late examples of painted and japanned tin plate were commercial containers in which powder was sold. These are known with Hazard, Du Pont, and other manufacturers' labels. There were many artisans who followed the trade of powder-flask making. [*Engraved map horn pictured.*]

powder fort: Pepper shaker; peppered. "Powders" almost invariably, in early household sense, meant ground spices, pepper, salt, et cetera.

powder-horn bottle: Long slender bottle *not* used as powder flask or container. A sort of boot bottle, probably for carrying "liquid powder" for the inner man, rum or whiskey.

powdering table: The *poudreuse*. Also a true wig stand with an apron; any fitted toilet table or stand. Latter are of Directoire, Hepplewhite, Sheraton, or Regency style.

powdering tub: A salting tub.

powder tube: Blow tube of wood with metal tip, used to blow powder on a wig.

powdringe: A fur marking, a natural spotting or powdering of light fur with dark.

Powell, Joseph: Furniture maker of New York City, working in 1760s. Georgian styles.

Powers, Hiram: American sculptor of world fame. Born at Woodstock, Vt., 1805, and taken to Cincinnati, O., as a child, where he was apprenticed to a clockmaker. Made modeled figures for a clockwork automaton. Financed by Nicholas Longworth, he studied sculpture in Italy. Died at Florence, Italy, 1873.

Powhatan pipes: Red clay tobacco pipes made in Virginia and so marked. 19th century.

pow-wow: A conference. Also the term used vulgarly for ancient faith-healing procedures and the use of simples, introduced by the Dutchman Helfenstein in 1740s.

poyterl: A wood buskin or stomacher.

prairie schooner: See Conestoga Wagon.

Prang, L. & Co., prints, et cetera: Louis Prang, operating from mid-19th century at Roxbury, near Boston, had by 1870 become the world's largest chromolithographer, devoted to the production of popular art objects; prints for the people. Prang reproduced fine art by well-known professionals. His habit was to purchase the art with rights to reproduction. Bierstadt's "Sunset in California," Tait's "Chickens" were reproduced in full color and sold up to 30,000 copies each. Prang employed Winslow Homer as a young man.

"Cards" of album size were issued by Prang in a catalogue of subjects. This firm also produced many educational cards and prints in series. The Prang prints and other specialties are destined to become a collecting item as all-pervasive as Currier & Ives. What the subject needs is a definitive book and illustrated check list.

Pratt & Auchmoody furniture: Milwaukee "Victorian" styles made by a firm so named, as early as 1840s.

Pratt cloth: Flannel incorporating flocking in the weaving.

Pratt furniture: Probably direct reference is to black-walnut furniture made by D. G. Pratt of Boston. It is recorded this man also produced parlor and lawn croquet sets and stock carvings. This may cover the term "Pratt eagles" sometimes heard as descriptive of walnut eagle carvings used as wall brackets, et cetera.

Pratt lids: Commercial potlids, generally of soap and cosmetic boxes of ceramic ware, transfer-printed in colors. These were made at the Fenton works of F. & R. Pratt from late 1840s. This firm made some boxes for American manufacturers and also produced a now rather rare inkwell-shaving-soap potlid picturing John Bull playing chess with the Pope.

Pratt ware: Staffordshire pottery with raised figural and other decoration; also figurines. The décor and the figures are vividly colored in tones of orange, blue, purple, green, and black. Made by Felix Pratt at Little Fenton, England, from 1770s to 1800s or later. Pratt ware is often used generically for any ware falling within the category and philosophy of the original.

prawlong: A praline. "Toasted filberts, boiled in syrup to a caramel."

Praxis Catholica: *The Universal Practice; an early Doctor's Book,* printed at London, 1680, for Robert Couch, sometime practitioner in Boston.

preacher's lamp; pulpit lamp: Any reflector lamp, designed to illuminate the minister's notes.

premium fountain: A cast- and wrought-iron fountain made specifically for private lawn or garden by Farnum of New York in 1840s. Named "premium" because it won a prize at American Institute, 1847. [*Example pictured.*]

prene: An iron pan.

prenette: Lifts, of tripod form, to support porcelain on kiln shelves in firing. **prenette mark:** The fine points in the glaze of finished ware indicating use of the device.

Prescott: A revolving pistol of the 1860s; a six-cartridge and ball pistol firing from a revolving cylinder through one barrel, as did the Colt.

Prescott furniture: Made by Levi Prescott of Boylston, Mass., from c. 1800. Sheraton, classic cabinetwork and fancy chairs.

presentoir: An elaborate *tazza.* [*Example pictured.*]

preserving cement: Beeswax, resin, and brick dust; used as a seal on early preserving-jar tops and bottles.

president cups: (1) Tucker & Hemphill, Philadelphia, porcelain coffee cups on which are painted representations of a U.S. president. Washington, Adams, Madison, Monroe, J. Q. Adams, and Jackson are reported. Made c. 1832–34. They are now rare. (2) Any drinking vessel of any material, displaying portrait or name of any president.

press bed: Any folding bed.

press cupboard: A Tudor-style, Gothic- or Gallic-influence item of case furniture known and used in the colonies in 17th century. The dates may be from 1560s, and even the most careful documentation of ownership is not proof of making in the colonies. Generally of oak, with some (of Swedish make) in pine. Two-decked, solid cupboards, tulip- or floral-carved, sometimes with applied ornamentation of split turning. They are very rare. [*Example pictured.*] Also sometimes called a livery cupboard. *See also* Court Cupboard.

pressed azure: Kai-tsing porcelain of unique decoration between two thin walls of porcelain clay. Invisible unless the vessel is filled with liquid.

Pressed Block: Pattern of pressed glass featuring bevel-edged blocks of cartouche or lozenge shape, conforming to contour of the pieces.

pressed candle: An extra-hard candle, especially favored in the South. Packed in conforming, slide-cover boxes of walnut, cherry, or maple. Made from 1830s; the boxes are now a collector's item.

Pressed Diamond: Pattern of pressed glass imitative of cutting, displaying a faceted fine "cutting" producing diamond forms.

pressed glass: The patent of Enoch Robinson, 1826, for pressing door handles, furniture knobs, and similar solid objects would seem to be the beginning of a parade marked by the pressing, in 1830s, of drinking glasses and other hollow objects, within ten years causing a revolution in glass manufacture. Some experts say decanters could not be pressed, but it was done thus: The body was pressed in a mold with a plunger, then the piece was reheated and the neck drawn out. Decorative window panes were pressed, as were all sorts of tableware, liquor and beverage services, et cetera. Many pressed-glass pattern names are inventions, some being changes of original names and many being recent appellations bestowed because, in the mad race of pattern production, many makers just gave a pattern a number. "Pressed inside and out" is a technique of putting pattern on both the outer mold and the plunger which did the pressing. Very little glass was so made. "Pressed-on handles" is the term used to describe the method of pressing handle forms separately and attaching them to pressed bodies, the handles adhering because of joining while glass was hot and semi-plastic.

pressed (& molded) glass: Made from 1890s, when combination molds yielded pressed work and molding in same operation. Molds were partitioned and had vents to enable workman to blow a part of the piece while other elements of it were being pressed.

pressed-glass patterns: Utterly impossible of inclusion here are the pattern names for pressed-glass designs in addition to the master lists compiled by Ruth Webb Lee. Student is referred to *Sandwich Glass, Early American Pressed Glass,* and *Victorian Glass,* by this painstaking author. Other and lesser volumes are listed in the Bibliography.

Pressed Leaf: Pattern of pressed glass featuring oak-leaf decoration and acorn finials on clear glass.

pressed quilt: A thinly stuffed quilt, very tightly stitched.

pression lamp: A Parisian lamp introduced in U.S. by C. Ducreux of New York; a standing lamp of 1840s, with certain "patented" features and very ornate appearance. It is in the French Antique style.

pressure scale: Sheet- and cast-iron base, with a sliding tube having a platform at top. Tube is calibrated and is pressed into base by object placed on platform for weighing. A home and office scale. [*Example pictured is 19th century.*]

prestcut: (1) Glass of pressed type deliberately made imitative of cutting. (2) Pressed glass designed to be touched up by wheel cutting in pressed pattern, thus saving 75% of the cutting. Both date from early 1890s and presaged the end of true cut glass popularity with style and fashion leaders.

Preston, Alfred: Manufacturer of cabinet furniture at Middletown, N.Y., from 1850s.

Prestonpans: Potteries (2) at place so named, in Scotland, working prior to 1838 and another, established 1836, by Belfield & Co., for production of Rockingham wares, cane wares and, it is alleged, glazed, decorated white wares. The earlier works are credited with varied production, including figural pieces. Latter data not verified by compilers of this present volume.

pretzel: A representation of "folded arms over the breast" as a hard-baked bread. Noted in Switzerland and North Italy from 14th century. There is some belief that the pretzel was introduced in America c. 1849 by the German immigrants to Pennsylvania. We have discovered use of the pretzel and its commercial baking in New Orleans previous to any in Pennsylvania.

pretzel back: A fatuous term; reference is to a ladder-back type of chair with scrolled, pierced slats, the form in no way resembling a pretzel.

Priam stove: An airtight cast-iron range first made in 1840s.

price books: Cabinetmaking reference and that of other trades is to the price books published by associations of cabinet-, chair-, clock-, tinware, and other makers of a community, listing the costs of each operation of production in full detail. Cabinetmakers' price books are often illustrated. Issues by many groups are of record. All dated before the 1840s are valuable items of reference.

Price ware: Pottery from the George Price pottery at South Amboy, N.J. Proper name was Congress Pottery.

pricked: Point-punched, or stabbed lightly and repeatedly in a pattern to delineate a form or motif. **pricker:** Any pointed tool used in prick work on paper, leather, metal, et cetera.

pricket stick: Candlestick with a pointed bayonet in the center of a platform on which to impale, rather than socket, a candle. Often on church candlesticks; the original candlestick form. **pricket plug:** A unit in the form of a short candle end, but of metal, fitted with a pricket; a device used to convert a socketed candlestick to a pricket stick. **pricket socket:** A candle socket with a conforming cavity in its bottom to impale on a pricket stick and so convert it to a socketed candlestick.

Prickett grate: Iron fireplace grate of 1850s, made at Chicago in quantities for the Western trade by G. W. Prickett.

prickle ware: Willow or wicker basketry.

prie-dieu: A prayer stool, a home pew, with kneeling cushion and standard for prayer book. "Pray-to-God" is sometimes used as the term.

primavera: White mahogany; any fine-grained wood of creamy or pale yellow color. Also an allegory of spring or the spring season.

prime: The hour of 6 A.M.; the standard; of good quality.

primer: (1) A first book; a beginner's book, as the *New England Primer.* (2) A quantity of anything supplied as encouragement; the liquid necessary to start a pump in action.

primitive: Literally, "of the beginning," as a form of art; the first evidence of a springing into being. The beginning of fine art which sparked the Renaissance. A term used loosely to designate the immense production of amateur art in the U.S. from the 1790s, but particularly the production sparked by itinerant instructors and self-instruction books, 1820s-50s.

Primrose: Pattern of pressed glass featuring primrose sprays and flower finials, with stippled background.

Prince of Wales back: Any chair back displaying the three feathers that are the badge of the Prince of Wales. In stylized form the device sometimes resembles a large fleur-de-lis. Also a Victorian chair named in honor of Victoria's first son; it had five, not three, upholstered feather forms. [*Example pictured.*]

Prince Rupert's drops: Small pear-shaped gobs of glass formed by dropping molten glass beads in water. When cold, pinching off the tail caused the entire object to fracture, or "fly." The disintegration was accompanied by an explosive report.

Prince Rupert's Metal: White brass.

prince's metal: Nickel or white brass, as used in metallic non-rusting window frames, fanlights, panels for glazing, et cetera. Cruckshank of London designed many fan- and other lights which were used by Sheraton in his design books.

Princess Cut: A very "busy" pattern of cut glass having an all-over star form with various diamond cuttings and planes, fans, et cetera. It is a late pattern of the 1890s.

Princess Feather: Pattern of pressed glass, sometimes called Lacy Medallion; feather forms with pyramidal diamond pointing on a fancy stippled ground.

print colorer: An employee of a print establishment who worked at laying water coloring on the prints and lithographs.

printed: Indicative of impression of design, by pressure, as printed handkerchief, printed carpet (a plain-tone Brussels carpet printed in a huge press, or from rollers, with a colored pattern), printed calico, printed rubberized fabrics, aprons, et cetera.

printed burlap: Carpet weave patterns printed in various colors on burlap. A cheap carpet or drugget of mid-19th century. The designs are after the French styles of 18th century.

Priscilla: The lady of Pilgrim days who made up John Alden's mind for him. **Priscilla syrup:** A syrup pitcher with metal top named for the lady.

Priscilla Pressed Glass: A pattern featuring petal-like panels with rings and florets.

prismatine painting: Luster painting, using a palette of gold, silver, and colored bronzes. A homecraft, allied to chair painting and other decorating. It was popular from 1860s and again revived by Esther Brazer in 1930s–40s.

Prism Cut: Cut-glass pattern featuring central multi-pointed star surrounded by a wide band of cane cutting and prismatic fan cutting.

Prism-Engraved: Pattern of pressed glass with narrow prismatic bands and somewhat elaborate engraving of grapevine, feather, fern and bead, ivy, and other designs. Prism is an altogether different pattern of prismatic flutes, pressed in the body to the shoulders or nearly to rims of the various pieces. Variant, Prism & Crescent, displays narrow panels of prisms spaced with panels of cross prisms and rounds. Prism & Flute and Prism with Diamond Points are other varieties, fully described and pictured in the works issued by Ruth Webb Lee.

prison coverlets: Pattern-woven coverlets of all types, unmarked, and made generally in prisons and workhouses under direction of a master weaver. Sold wholesale by a county or district to help defray expense of prison operation. The unmarked coverlets of 1850–80 period were generally so designated by the housewives who bought them.

prison furniture: From 1790s to 1840s, cabinet furniture and chairs made by prisoners in our jails were sold at auction and at wholesale to shopkeepers. Chairs were made and sold in this manner to the 1880s.

prison goods: Any commodities, as coverlets, furniture, chairs, cloth, nails, horseshoes, et cetera, made by prisoners in jails and workhouses. Baskets, shoes, cordwood, mortars, and other objects were prison-made.

probang: A medical applicator for throat and lung treatment; a slender whalebone wand, sponge-tipped. Date is from 1840s.

problem globe: An armillary or skeleton sphere used in early classroom study.

prod: A bow sling, for throwing a ball or slug.

profile perdu: Partial profile, of the face turned somewhat away from the observer. Not noted in silhouettes, but in drawn profiles.

profilograph: A mechanical aid to silhouette cutting, invented by or contrived by Charles Wilson Peale. Also a silhouette cut by aid of the device.

promethean: A roll of paper with a fire cap at end. Hitting the cap with a hammer caused the paper to ignite (sometimes) and so serve as a match. The fire cap was a glass bead containing a drop of sulphuric acid embedded in chlorate of potash.

proof: (1) Evidence, documentary, substantiated by such or by other witness. (2) In original condition, unused, pristine. (3) The measure of alcoholic content of a liquid; 200 proof being 100% alcohol. (4) Of a print or engraving, an impression of the plate or stone as originally prepared and contemporaneously printed, as opposed to, "restrike," a later—generally much later—impression.

propeller: (1) The Archimedes screw principle applied to a bladed shaft driven to propel boats through water; any boat so driven. (2) Any method of propulsion and the device by which it is applied. (3) A child's toy cart operated by hand levers. [*Example pictured.*]

propolis: The bee glue of ancient usage. Not the wax of the comb, but a resinous cement used in comb construction and to seal the bodies of insect invaders killed within the hive.

prospect door: The door in the kneehole compartment of kneehole desks. Also the upper section of a two-part "Dutch" door.

prospect glass: A spyglass.

protean stone: A gypsum imitation of ivory.

Prouty, A. T.: The first cabinetmaker of Kalamazoo, Mich. He set up shop in 1835. Furniture was in Empire style.

provenance;provenience: The"whenceabouts" of a thing; its origin, subjectively.

Providence glass: Pressed glasswares produced at the Providence, R.I., glassworks from 1831–35.

Providence shell: Clafian & Bowen, 1827, established a shell works at Providence, R.I., which remained operative for many years, making, it is asserted, combs, jewelry, buttons, pins, et cetera.

Prud'homme, J. F. E.: An American engraver of the early 19th century who became an early daguerreotypist with a gallery at New York City to 1850s.

prune oil: Illuminating oil made from plum and cherry stones.

prunt: A gob of glass applied as a decorative element, tooled or pressed. The same device used to impress identification, label, name, et cetera, on bottles and other glass objects.

psalterium: A breast harp, played with hammers. [*Example pictured.*]

pshu: Wild rice.

Psyche: (1) The soul, or spirit, exemplified as a lovely butterfly-winged maiden.

(2) A Directoire-style sofa of a curvate form to fit the human frame. Also known as the "kangaroo." The style persisted throughout the Empire era to the French Antique revival called Victorian.

Psyche & Cupid: Pattern of pressed glass featuring a classic medallion connected with bands and covered pieces having floriated finials.

P. T. B. armorial china: One of Barnum's antics. He purchased the porcelain service of a Russian prince initialed P. T. and had the letter B. added and fired on. This was done in 1846, after purchase of the huge service at a Paris auction.

Puck lamp: A tiny metal lamp not over 4 inches high, burning a perfumed fluid. Date is from 1890s.

pudding cap: An infant's padded cap.

pudding charm: Small sterling-silver figures and tokens for baking in ceremonial cakes and puddings. A custom that is centuries old. [*Examples pictured are of late 19th century.*]

pudding plate: A dinner-plate size, now called luncheon or supper plate.

pudscha: The East Indian term for what we call a broché or broshay shawl. Most examples within our collecting ken are of English make, after the Indian originals.

Puebla: Mexican glass, made at Puebla from 1648 to the present century. Engraved wares with tulip decoration are often mistaken for Stiegel and Amelung. The motifs on Puebla glass are from Spain.

puff box: Any powder box with a puff applicator.

Puffer-puffs: A term apparently local to Lowell, Mass., and referring to refinished and repainted second- and third-hand furniture from the shops of one Puffer, an early dealer in antiques, in business from 1845.

puggen: A gable; the gable end of a structure.

Pugh & Teater: Makers of glassware at Moscow, O., from 1820s. Blown glass.

pugil: An approximate measure "as much as can be held between the four fingers and the thumb."

Pugin, Augustus Welby: English designer, born 1811, who published *Designs for Gothic Furniture*, 1835. He was considered a madman mistaken for a genius.

Puggley Gothic: Reference is to the Gothic church-type furniture made from mid-19th century by Robert Puggley of New York City.

pulk: A small stool or cabinet.

pulkara: East Indian fabric with orifices in the weave, designed as a wall and window hanging to permit passage of air. Some are studded with small cut fragments of mirror glass. Imported from 1880s.

pulpit shell: The sounding board over a pulpit, often in shell form.

Pulsifer carpet: Painted floor cloths as made by Pulsifer of Salem, Mass., from c. 1790s. **Pulsifer furniture:** Made at Salem, Massachusetts, from 1790s. Hepplewhite and classic styles; also Sheraton, much closer to the originals than elsewhere in U.S., or so it is stated.

pulwere: A pillow.

pumpernickel: A black bread, "*bon pour Nichol,*" or "good for my horse Nichol," is the legend of naming this coarse peasant bread by an officer of Napoleon's army.

pumpion: A squash or pumpkin.

pumpkin hood: A framework of wood, wire, or bone, collapsible, like a calash top, cloth-covered.

pumpkin twist: Coils of fresh pumpkin wound on poles and dried.

pumplemoes: The shaddock or grapefruit.

pump pitcher: Pressed-glass pitcher imitative of a tree trunk, with handle and a spout set midway in the bole; not operative. A novelty of 1890s.

pump tree: The bole or main body of a pump, originally of solid wood, bored. A standing pump.

punch: A beverage of water, sugar, fruit or berry juices, and ardent spirits and wines.

Punch & Judy jugs: Relatives of the Toby in philosophy, but displaying the puppet characters in face and form. Made from c. 1820s.

punch decoration: Decoration on wood, metal, leather, et cetera, achieved by dies or punches having a design on them, and punched in a pattern. Some unusual furniture of walnut, made in Southern states, was decorated with such work, and, strangely, is not mentioned or noted in any of the so-called inclusive displays of Southern furniture. The work seems to be of 18th century.

puncheon: A vessel of 84-gallon capacity.

punch'd tin: Not punctured or pierced tin, but tinware modeled by hammering the sheets in molds or forms.

punch font: Glass vessel in form of a huge wineglass with domed foot, the bowl fitted with a tap. Used in service of wine punch. Believed to be Irish and of Irish glass.

punch ladle: Large bowl with pouring lip, holding a cupful; generally on a long handle of ebony, bone, or horn.

punch pot: Ceramic vessels looking like teapots but bearing on them as decoration convivial scenes or symbols of drinking beverages other than tea. Some, for service of hard cider, have handles imitative of apple wood.

punctured tin: Pierced tinware, generally lanterns, graters, or raspers.

pung: (1) A rough sledge on plank skids. (2) A settle bench.

pungents: Bottles for smelling salts.

punkah: A broad vane or fan suspended from ceiling and kept in motion by servants manipulating cords. Much used in the South as an insect shooer. The same sort of fan mounted on a long handle.

pupitre: A scholar's desk.

purcella; pucella: A glassmaker's tool looking like a pair of garden shears.

purfled: Decorated with a border or a banding.

Purington (also Purinton) ware: Both names are apparently found in connection with potteries in the Swansea-Somerset region of Massachusetts, and so

1, Pennsylvania Painted Chest. **2,** Queen Anne Style Furniture (seven examples). **3,** Quenelle Mold. **4,** Quill Buncher. **5,** Quill holder. **6,** Quilt Pattern Stamps. **7,** Rabbit Grill. **8,** Ravenscroft Glass Goblet. **9,** Raeren. **10,** Roach Trap. (No. 1 from the late Wallace Nutting's *Furniture Treasury*.)

the logical reference is to the wares produced here.

purpain: A napkin; a serviette.

purple: The rich red, originally obtained from a small shellfish, at one time reserved for royal or noble use. **purple-gris de lin:** A red-gray. The deep purple; deep red.

purple camaïeu: A monochrome in purple tints and tones.

purple luster: A lucious red luster obtained from gold oxide.

purple stoneware: A variety of Lambeth stoneware, mottled with the color popularly called purple (red-blue) or "eggplant" color.

push-boat: A barge or longboat propelled with poles.

Putnam bed: A spring-supported bed invented, made, and sold by John Putnam, founder of the publishing house of that name, c. 1845. The bed frames have pronounced button turning.

putto: Nude cherubic figure of a boy.

putz: Swiss-German for *crèche;* a Christmas display with figures. The various high festivals, including Easter and Whitsuntide, also were marked with special putzes or *putzen.*

puzzle teapot: The Cadogan teapot, solid-topped, filled from the bottom.

puzzulana: Volcanic earth which, when reheated, sets as a plaster or cement under water.

pybot: A quarter bushel.

pye: A printed text of biblical nature.

pygarg: The moose.

pyked: Pricketed; pointed. Piked.

Pyle caddy: A tea caddy made by James Pyle of New York City from 1840s. Plain and fancy japanned examples by a merchant who also supplied tea-store window images of Chinese figures and tea-store signs.

pyramid: The square, squat, conic form which, with many variations, is used in architecture, cabinet, and other furniture. Flower stands, tables, lamp stands, shelves in tiers, et cetera, are known in pyramidal form.

pyriform: Pear-form; pear-shaped.

pyro: Fire. **pyrophorus:** A dry fire powder. **pyrotechnics:** Fireworks.

pyrope: Polished red garnet or carbuncle.

pyx: (1) A case or chest for the host (bread) of the communion. (2) The coin chest of the assayer. (3) Any jewel case or coffer.

Q

quacksalver: A charlatan; a faker. A vendor of salves and simples.

quad bottle: A four-separate-section bottle; a bottle of four parts.

quadrantal: Quarter-circular.

quadrant chair: The true corner chair, the seat a perfect quarter circle, periphery at front. *See* Chairs, All Kinds.

quadrig; quadriga: A rig or car drawn by four horses, whether a Roman four-horse chariot or the swank "four-in-hand" of the 19th century.

quadrille pool: A game box, opening to become the board of play for the game quadrille, played with fish and counters. **quadrille table:** A table for playing the same game.

quadrilobed: Four-lobed; having four lobate extensions. A square table with four semicircular drop leaves would be a perfect quadrilobed top with all leaves up.

quaich: Woodenware. A drinking cup with two ears. Any coopered bowl or drinking cup. Also any ceramic or metal cup.

Quarre prints: Embellishments in form of pictures with lacy borders, made by Quarre for *Godey's* and other journals. In 1845 he entered lamp-shade manufacture.

quarrier: A square wax candle.

quarry; quarrel; quare: A square pane of glass.

quarter: A measure of eight bushels.

quarternion; quaternion: Fourfold, four-part.

quartern loaf: A four-pound, five-ounce loaf of bread.

quarter round: A molding, precisely quarter round in section.

quartetto tables: Nests of tables, generally four.

quassia: Wood of the bitter ash, esteemed as a tonic. **quassia cup:** Woodenware. A cup turned from quassia wood. Water or wine let stand for a few hours or overnight became impregnated with the bitter principle. Root of the tree also used as a tonic bitter and a bittering agent in beer brewing.

quatrefoil: Four-lobed tracery; a Gothic or Gallic form.

quatuors: Small mechanical music boxes.

Queen Anne: The style succeeding the William & Mary period, developed from same cabinet, case, and seat furniture forms, with substitutions of cabriole legs. Both are almost pure Chinese in basic style and, in their first occidental forms, were lacquered and decorated with Chinese motifs. In the Queen Anne period the four-leg "roundabout" or corner chair was developed from the Chinese chair of many cabriole legs which, in first European version, was almost a duplicate of the Chinese chair now called "burgomaster's." The Queen Anne style became Georgian in England and Louis XV in

France. Chippendale is Frenchified Georgian with some original Chinese styling. [*Examples of Queen Anne furniture pictured.*]

Queen Anne scale: Not necessarily of the period; an elegant balance scale with polished brass, copper, or silver scoop and pans, used extensively by confectioners, spice and tea dealers, and apothecary shops in 18th and 19th centuries.

queen's metal: Alloy of nine parts tin, one bismuth, one antimony, and one lead. The finest pewter made.

queen's ware: Creamware of 18th century by Leeds and other potters. By 1840, eight potteries of Liverpool, O., were making creamwares called queen's ware.

quenelle mold: A metal or pottery form for shaping poached meat paste. Many forms. [*One pictured.*]

quercitron: Yellow dye obtained from inner bark of the black oak; also any lemon color.

quern: A miniature burr mill for grinding bread grain to flour in the home. Upper stone generally operated over the nether by a wooden rod, anchored at top in a sling and fitting in a dimple in the top of the moving stone. Very elaborate examples with hardwood stands and cabinet housing a temsing drum (bolting device) were made as early as 1750. The typical colonial examples were open, exposing the stones.

Querville furniture: American-made Directoire, Empire, and French Antique furniture produced by Anthony Querville at Philadelphia from 1820s. Said to have made White House furniture for Andrew Jackson. Querville is reported to have been apprenticed to Christopher Marshall, Jr., son of the Lancaster and Philadelphia diarist of the Revolution. In 1830 the Querville establishment was known as "United States Fashionable Cabinet Warehouse" and advertised so in *U.S. Gazette*, December 1830.

queue back: Said of chairs having a deep curve or cleft in the top rail as a neck rest, the queue or club of a gentleman's hairdress falling over it.

quezal: Novelty glass, said to be named for the quezal bird of South America. Made 1890s–1900s; it is vari-colored. Quezal Art Glass Co. of Brooklyn, N.Y., believed to be first producer. Other makers said to have copied the ware.

quhile: While, as spelled in 15th century.

Quiche: Guichee; a district of South Carolina.

quickbeam: Any fast-growing tree.

quick-fire: Amadou; a sort of punklike tinder chemically treated.

quickstep: (1) The Army fast march, 110 steps to the minute. (2) Any music for this speed of march; also music for the dance, similar to the gavotte, called the quickstep.

quick varnish: An insect-repelling glare laid over fresh painting; made from egg white, brandy, and onion juice.

quiddity: A phrase conveying the same meaning as provenance, or provenience; the essential nature of a thing and its projection in understandable terms. The what, why, and wherefore of a thing. Not an oddity.

quietsol: A sunshade; a parasol.

Quigley ware: Dark glazed redware, made at S. Quigley's "Franklin Factory," a pottery at Cincinnati from 1820s to 1840s. Cookie jars, snuff jars, kitchenwares.

quill buncher: An adjustable metal stand for the quick bunching of bird quills for commercial use as pens, brush ferules, toothpicks, et cetera. [*Example pictured.*]

quilled: Fine bands pinched into wavy form. A favorite form of glass decoration; threads of glass pinched. Also a form of applied needlework decoration. Turned into bobbinlike forms, in a series.

quill holder: Hollow cylinder of sheet metal (painted sheet iron, brass, copper, horn, and silver examples known) with a cap, the main cylinder slotted to permit exposure of feathering, to hold a writing quill for carriage in the pocket, case, or safekeeping in a desk. The kalemdam or kalendam. Used from 1700s or earlier to 1860s. [*Example pictured.*]

quilling: (1) Arrangement of ribbon or lace in fluted folds simulating a row of quills. (2) Stitching fabric to fabric in bands over a quill to achieve a sort of fluting. (3) Fluting achieved by an iron or other press.

quilling wheel; quiller: The wheel device for threading bobbins, in early days wound on a feather quill.

quill pencil: Actually a brush. All brushes were once called "hair pencils."

quill picks (marked): The transparent lettering on quill toothpicks of 1840–80 period, distributed by hotels and cafés as souvenirs. This was achieved by warming quills in hot sand and stamping with cold dies.

quill points: Ready-cut quill pens, usually pointed at both ends, made and sold in bundles or boxes, for insertion in penholders. The ancestor of the steel and the gold pen point.

quill string: Significance lay not in the size or quality of the string, but in the color. Cords used in tying commercial bunches of quills indicated the quill size, thus: red for smallest, No. 8; green for No. 10; orange for No. 20; deep red for No. 30; red and green for No. 40; pink for No. 50; pink and blue for No. 60; pink and yellow for No. 70; pink, blue, and yellow for No. 80. In 1840 the price of 1000 No. 80 quills was $40.

quilt: Any padded covering for a bed. From the Latin, *culcita*, a bed sack. Patchwork quilts are decorative top coverings of quilts, made in geometric patterns from square-cut and pattern-cut fabrics in colors. Crazy quilts are top covers in hit-or-miss form, made from odd sizes of fabric. The magazine *Spinning Wheel* has published extensive notices on quilts. See also books noted in Bibliography. The subject of quilts must include these data: The padding was either (1) a napped wool fabric, (2) raw or washed wool, (3) cotton, (4) bran, (5) flax, (6) hemp, (7) milkweed down, (8) thistledown, (9) eider or swan's-down, (10) other down feathers, (11) ravelings, (12) bombast or raw cotton. This listing is perhaps not complete. Some qualities and records indicate use of cattail fuzz, catkins, boxwood leaves, needles from hemlock fronds, et cetera.

Not only were bedcovers quilted, but also petticoats, dresses, jackets, and upholstery fabrics. The actual stitchery of quilting held the sandwich of fabric and padding together firmly and prevented bunching or lumping of the padding.

quilting chairs: Not a special kind of chair, but any four chairs of the same height in the back. The quilting frame was supported on the four chair backs. Also the chairs seating the workers as they stitched a quilt.

quilting patterns: (1) Any of the traditional patch patterns used in assembling the top cover of a patch quilt, often named, the name not infrequently having local application rather than universal. (2) Metal stamps looking like cake cutters, made specifically to stamp the stitchery pattern on the quilting fabric. When impressed on colored fabric, the stamps were dipped in starch water. When on white fabric, the starch had a drop of laundry blue added. The starch not covered by stitchery was brushed off. [*Examples pictured.*]

quilting pocket: An apron, the front of which was a huge pocket for paraphernalia used in quilting.

Quimby rods: The lightning rods of A. M. Quimby, maker and super-salesman of the 1830s to 1850s.

Quimper ware: Faïence of Finistère, France, made by Henry Quimper, decorated in colors, picturing natives of the region in colorful dress. The original ware of the Finistère potteries from 1740s was in the Chinese style of decoration. The pottery industry was started c. 1690s. Since 1900 Quimper ware has been a favorite fancy-store and gift-shop item.

quince cream: A delicacy made from boiled, pulped quinces and heavy cream, whipped, wined, and sugared. The same mixture was used in filling quince tarts.

quincunx: An arrangement of five elements in a square, with one in center.

quincy: A beverage of hot rum and quince jelly.

Quincy railroad flask: Any historic glass whiskey flask commemorating the first "railroad" in the U.S., that of the quarries at Quincy, Mass., running through Milton to Tidewater, a distance of three miles. Started operating October 21, 1826. Many varieties.

Quincy railroad map: Actually a map of the region showing the railroad. It is 6" x 8¼" in size, lithographed, and was issued by James Eddy, 1826. A copy was offered in 1949 at $250, an indication of its rarity.

Quinlan, J.: Custom glass blower making reservoirs, shades, and bases for the lamp trade, New York City, from 1860s.

Quinn ware: Terra cotta pottery from the works of E. H. Quinn, New York City, established 1850s.

quirk: (1) A diamond form or shape; a diamond pane of glass. (2) The V-shaped groove in or between moldings. (3) Embroidery on stockings (now clocks). (4) A rhomboidal shape.

quinshon: A cushion.

quintuple dish: A dish in quincunx form; four fitting parts around a central dish.

quoniam: A drinking cup.

quotidal: Daily; every day.

Q.V.: Abbreviation for *quod vide,* "which see." Also "see also."

R

rabbet; rabbeted: Edged by planing; notched to fit. Rebated.

rabbit-eared: With flaring or upstanding ovals imitative of, or having the general form of, rabbits' ears, as stiles of chairs.

rabbit-head cup: A stirrup cup in form of head of a wild hare, with long ears. Cup is a hollow "bust." Upended, it is a drinking cup. Fox, hound, stag, bear, and other animals' heads made in same style, for use as cups.

rabbit grill: A sheet-iron or other pan with spikes on which to impale halves of a rabbit for broiling. Generally on a frame. [*Example pictured.*]

rabbitskin glue: Parchment glue made from rabbitskins, used extensively in gilding and gold leafing. Also a gelatin glue pulled to approximately rabbitskin size.

rabit: A woodenware drinking cup.

race bell: The prize generally awarded to race-meet winners prior to 1670s, instead of the later silver and gold cups.

race knife: A hook-ended blade for scribing or marking.

raceme: A silver or plated clip, generally to hold a napkin in place.

race meet: A sporting event, the chief attraction of which was a series of running or trotting races.

rack: A cob iron.

racking crook: A pothook.

raddle: Rouge. Also the ocher dye used in marking or branding sheep.

Radford furniture: Grecian sofas, sideboards, fancy and bird's-eye maple chairs, all kinds of tables, in late Directoire and Empire styles, made by H. Radford, Brooklyn, N.Y., from 1830s.

Radiant: Pattern of pressed glass made at Findlay, O., imitative of "moderne" cutting, with bowed elements, stars, fans; some engraved on a clear band, others clear glass.

radiates: Tapering rays converging to a common center, generally noted in inlay of two tones of wood.

radiometer: The philosophical sun engine in miniature; a series of tiny metal-foil vanes poised by suspension and encased in a glass bulb. One side of each vane is blackened. Any radiant energy, as sunlight, causes the vanes to turn. A favorite 19th-century display piece in jewelers' windows.

Raeren: A stoneware of Flanders (not Germany) made at Raeren, near Aix. Brown, yellow, and gray ware, made from 1500s. The object called a Raeren is a baluster-form jug. [*Example pictured*.]

raffles: Subdivisions of leaf forms, used in a decorative element.

rafraîchissoir: Wine table, with slots for decanter bottoms. A table for refreshments.

rag carpets: Carpets woven from cord-chain warp and rag woof. Carpet rags are balls of tape, properly cut and stitched together, with as many colors as possible. A popular cheap carpet for the homes of America, 1810–1910.

rag doll (poupée en chiffons): A doll made of cloth and stuffed with fine-cut rags and tags of textile fabric. Frequently the form is printed, stenciled, or painted.

rag gold: Tinted gilt.

ragman's roll: Any official paper or document with many seals, tapes, and ribbons; also a game of chance in which rewards and forfeits were tied to wax-ended tapes, the tapes pulled to get the message.

raik: Range; roam.

railroad chair: A metal plate to hold rail to ties.

railroad clothes washer: A laundry machine for the home, having a "train" of corrugations within.

railroad flask: Any historic, mold-blown flask picturing a horse-drawn or steam-propelled railroad locomotive or car.

Railroad Glass: Pattern of pressed glass featuring railroad trains.

Raindrop: Pattern of pressed glass somewhat like inverted thumbprint, the prints being of greater diameter.

raised chest: Any chest-on-frame.

raised willow: The traditional willow pattern in raised decoration and then blue-tinted; noted on some Doulton-Lambeth wares of yellow-brown, or mustard color.

raising: A structure of framework erected by a community of effort, as a barn-raising, schoolhouse-raising, et cetera.

raked: Turned outward; canted; sloping; at an angle.

Rake's Progress: Transfer-printed ceramic-ware pitcher featuring scenes from Rake's Progress, an 18th-century Hogarthian moral story in pictures.

rake steel: We are advised it meant rake handle, not the steel head of the rake, the logical assumption.

ramekin: A cheesecake baked in a pottery dish; finally the name of the dish.

ramification: Timber cut from the bole of a tree, above the root and below the

branches; frequently odd figurations occur in this bole wood, even internal burls. A tangent cut of curly bole wood produced "bird's eye," and a crosscut produced "tiger."

ramillie: A tie wig of Georgian era.

rampant: Heraldic term, meaning erect, one foot on ground, other limbs elevated, head facing to left. Counter-rampant is same pose, facing right.

ram's foot: Cloven-hoof foot, topped by wool-fringe carving.

ram's-head bowl: Any bowl with curling horn-form handles.

ram's-horn arm: A chair or settee arm, springing from stile in the flat, then down- and upcurving to a down-curl and ball.

ram's-horn foot: Claw-and-ball foot springing from a shell carving, flanked by ram's horns. [*Example pictured*.]

ram's-horn support: A horn-form support between seat and chair or settee arm.

Randle, William: Cabinetmaker of Boston who advertised desks, bookcases, tables, and mirrors, with japanned work, from 1715. Queen Anne style may be assumed. Interesting also that japanning is mentioned in connection with the furniture, predicating possibility of colonial-made japanned Queen Anne, or in the Dutch style, from the original Chinese.

ranger stone: Lime and sand, molded in forms and dried.

range table: A pair or threesome of drop-leaf tables, leaves of which, raised and locked together, formed an extensive "range" of table board.

Rannie, James: The almost unheard-of one-time partner of Thomas Chippendale. He died in 1766.

Ransome: Ironstone and other extremely hard ceramic ware by Frederick Ransome. His mark at first was a genius sharpening an arrow point on a grindstone made of Ransome ware. This potter did actually make such grinding stones of hard pottery. [*Example pictured*.]

Ransome stone: Flints, boiled in caustic, and pressed in molds to form decorative objects.

Ransome stove: Any of the hundred or more designs of fancy cast-iron stoves made by the Ransome Co. of Albany, N.Y., from 1840s.

ranter: A large beer mug.

rantree; roan tree; rowan tree: The mountain ash tree. *Not* Roanoke, the meaning of which is white shell wampum.

rap: A minimum-value coin of Ireland. Hence the phrase, "I wouldn't give a rap."

rape: Coleseed; cabbage seed. **rape oil:** Oil extracted from the seeds. Same as coleseed oil.

rapper: A door knocker.

raspasses berry: The original term for what is now called the raspberry. Sometimes, in early usage, the raspis berry.

ratafia: Liquor distilled from broken fruit pits.

ratchet: Source of term is *rocko*, the distaff. A mechanical device using notches in or on a wheel or board, fixed or moved by a pawl or detent. A sort of trammel.

ratchet candlestand: A stand with ratchet to raise or lower the height of the burning tapers. [*Example pictured.*]

rateen: Coarse woolen cloth used in garment lining. Ratteen is variant spelling.

rat foot: A variant of claw and ball, the claw fine and tenuous, the ball an oval pad. [*Example pictured.*]

rattail spoon: Spoon handles displaying a tapering extension of handle reaching to almost tip of bowl.

rattail hinge: Hinge with one leaf, generally mortised in the moving element joined by the hinge, the anchor being an extension of the hinge pin bent away from the joint and anchored in the stile. [*Example pictured.*]

Rattan Cut: True cut-glass pattern displaying Persian-form arches in alternating imposition, the points filled with rattan or cane-seat cutting, with fan cuts between. Not neat and very gaudy. You can be sure it is of the 1890s.

rattan rug: Fine shavings of the rattan reed, spun into cord and woven into rugs. This is not an oriental type of rug, but made and woven in U.S. by William Houston of Wakefield Brothers, New England, 1860s.

Rauschner, Jan Christian: Danish wax modeler of profile portraits, working in U.S. from 1800s. Made wax portraits of many notables.

ravedore: Tapestry.

Ravenshead: Plate glass made at Ravenshead, Lancashire, England, from mid-19th century.

Ravenna glass: Made at Ravenna, O., from 1850s. About 1880 this factory made American lily paperweights, doorstops, et cetera.

Ravenscroft: Early English flint or lead glass by George Ravenscroft, from 1670s. Mark is a raven's head on a prunt. [*Example pictured is from historic Steuben Glass Collection.*]

raven's duck: White canvas; sailcloth.

Rawson furniture: Reference is to Hepplewhite- and Directoire-style cabinetwork by Joseph and Robert Rawson of Newport, R.I., from 1790s.

Ray: Pressed-glass pattern featuring a rayed-form plate center and oval-ended petals, a sort of tulip form and other wiggles and waggles.

Raymond & Alfred furniture: Empire-style cabinetwork by a partnership so named, made at Warren, O., from 1830s.

raynes: Rennes sheeting; a fine linen sheeting made from 16th century.

Raynes silver: Reference is to manufactured solid silver by Joseph Raynes of Lowell, Mass., from 1850s. He promised new spoons for old and offered jewelry of California gold. Paid a premium on silver coin in 1852 to supply his factory with coin silver.

razor box: A hang-up box for razors, generally for two, but sometimes for more. Often of pioneer workmanship—meaning homemade—and decorated. [*Example pictured.*]

reactionary lifter: An exerciser; decorated cast-iron base and springs, acting as a weight for weight-lifting exercises.

Reader, A. W.: Cabinetmaker working at Columbus, O., in 1840s.

reading chair: Any lounging chair, not a special chair as to type or style.

reading screen: Folding circular fan adjustable on a stand to screen direct or interfering light from a page.

reamer: A cream pot.

reaper: A machine for reaping grain, eliminating the scythe and cradle; the first examples of record by Obed Hussey of near Taneytown, Md., made in early 1830s. Patented by Hussey, June 1833. McCormick "improved" the Hussey reaper and patented the improvement.

reaper tray: Pressed-glass tray displaying a reaping machine of 1890s.

rear: Underdone.

Reaumur porcelain: The original oven glassware; regular glass reheated at very high temperature after forming.

rebate: The proper and correct form of the term now generally spelled "rabbet."

Rebecca candlestick: Figural stick of a woman with jar on shoulder, the jar being the candle socket.

Rebecca-at-the-well compote: Standing dish, the baluster of which is a figure of a woman with water jar on shoulder. Pittsburgh Glass, c. 1876–86.

Rebecca-at-the-well pitcher: Eight-sided ceramic-ware pitcher with deeply molded scene of Rebecca at the well, and so marked in lettering. Made at Bennet Pottery, Birmingham, Pa.

Récamier: The kangaroo sofa of Directoire style named for the famous madam of that period, as pictured in the painting by David. Also a long glove of stocking weave.

recessed stretcher: The H-form stretcher, with the crossbar just a shade back of the front legs.

records: Generally phonographic records, large and small cylinder, and disk. The first records were neither, but sheets of tin foil wound around a brass cylinder for playing.

recreant: One who yields to an adversary.

recto: The right side; the obverse. Verso is the opposite of recto; reverse, the opposite of obverse.

recumbent rocker: See Chairs, All Kinds.

red block: Hexagonal blocks and red flashing in a pressed-glass pattern.

redded wood: Wood dyed with a red water stain, dried, and then varnished.

reddy-up: Refurbish.

Redford glass: Made at Redford, N.Y., from 1830s; mostly offhand work; primarily a crown-glass factory.

red haw: A variety of hawthorn.

Redgravian tray: A papier-mâché lap tray with shallow wells for bottles. Made from 1840s by Jennens & Bettridge, England.

Red Jacket ax: A pioneer's and farmer's ax, trade-named Red Jacket from 1850s.

red maple: The common maple.

1, Ransome Urn and the famous grindstone mark. 2, Ridgway plates and one of the potter's marks. 3, Rockingham; three examples, early, middle, and late. 4, Rattail Hinge (showing the leaf, always in a mortise, and the spike, always driven in the stile). 5, Razor Box. 6, Refracting Stereoscope. 7, Ridgewood Smoking Case. 8, Ring Handles. 9, Ring Scissors. 10, Road Glass, or Pocket Glass. 11, Rochelle Pitcher. 12, Rogers Japanned Ware. 13, Rolling Cart, ancestor of the Conestoga Wagon. 14, Royle Teapot. (Nos. 1, 2, and 3, from Virtue & Co., London.)

Redoute roses: Lovely stipple-engraved prints of roses in color, from drawings by Pierre Joseph Redoute, 1759–1840. Some printed in colors and some editions hand-colored. This artist also did a series of lilacs and other flowers. Redoute was from Brabant and studied flower art under Van Spaendonck.

Redwood glass: Made at Alexandria, N.Y., by John Foster from 1850s; lily-pad wares and others somewhat like South Jersey glass.

Reed & Barton: Manufacturers of pewter, Britannia and electroplated silver, Taunton, Mass., established 1824. Millions of pieces bear this mark.

reed blind: Reed slats, bound with cord-chain stitching, rolling up like a stage curtain, and sold plain or painted. A substitute for Venetian blinds from 1840s or earlier.

reeded: Decorated with outstanding molding, properly vertical, close-set, and fine; opposite of fluting, which is a recessing of similar motifs. Any reedlike corrugation of a surface.

reeded rug: Similar in appearance to a hooked rug, but made in different manner, thus: the decorative material was stitched after pulling over reeds.

Reed pen: A retractable gold pen sliding into its holder. Made from 1790s, by Isaac Reed & Son, Philadelphia.

reed stitch: The rug-making technique of pulling material over reeds, stitching, removing reed, and cutting the loops into tufts.

Rees Limoges: The wares made by Thomas Rees at Limoges and marketed through a New York warehouse. White-ware, gilded and decorated in colors. Dinner and other services, druggists' wares, and perfume pots and bottles.

refectory: An eating room. **refectory benches:** The long benches used at sides of refectory tables. **refectory porringer:** Any table porringer or eared utensil, but specifically those having solid ears, stamped with insignia of a monastery or nunnery. **refectory table:** A large table; examples date from Gothic or Gallic era, 13th century. A dining board.

reffus ware: Rejects, as unfit for sale as standard, of a pottery. Often sold cheaply. From the "reffus box." Discolored, over-done, misshapen, blistered, and cracked.

reflecting chandelier: A large mirror-lined shade over a ring of gas jets, completely screened by five tiers of crystal prismatic droops. Made in various sizes from 1850s, but most popular in 1870s.

reflector grate: A small coal grate burning in a Franklin-type fireplace, completely surrounded by a polished round copper reflector frame. Made from 1850s in England.

Reformed Church: This church was established in America by the Dutch on Manhattan Island and in the Hudson Valley. The German members and their ministers, under the synod of Amsterdam, severed relations and formed a dissenting group, now claiming original establishment. The original Reformed Church in America was the Dutch. Many French Protestants were affiliated with this church.

refracting stereoscope: The adult phase of the prismatic-lens toy to view pairs of images in three-dimensional aspect. The term stereoscope means "to see [in the] solid." This type preceded the open form, most commonly known. [*Example pictured.*]

regatta carriage: Three-wheeled horse-less carriage, self-propelled by hand cranks on the vehicle. Often used on large estates to view the scenery and take mild exercise. [*Examples pictured were made from 1840s.*]

Regence: The epoch or brief period between the death of Louis XIV in 1715 and the coronation in 1723 of his grandson, Louis XV, who was only five years of age at the monarch's death.

Regency: The English period, 1811–20, when the King, George III, was completely insane and placed in limbo, the rule centering on the Prince Regent, later George IV, who ruled to 1830. On his passing, William IV was made King, ruling to 1837. On his death, without issue, a daughter of the cadet branch of George III, the Duke of Kent, was "elected by selection" as Queen Victoria. The English Regency period, by interior decorators, is stretched considerably beyond its true limits to include a great deal of what should be designated as George IV and William IV. The style, properly, is not Sheraton, but Directoire, comparable to what we have been erroneously calling "Duncan Phyfe style."

Regency plume: The three-feather crest of the Prince of Wales.

Regester, S. B.: French Antique furniture maker of Philadelphia from 1840s.

Regout, Peter: Potter of Maastricht, the Netherlands, from 1840s. Ware generally marked "Petrus Regout," or "PR." Rope knot of pretzel form is also a mark. The ware is still made in quantities.

regulus: Fined, but not refined, metal; the first reduction of an ore.

Reid Liverpool: English china made from 1750s by Reid & Co. of Liverpool. Painted, decorated, and blue and white wares for export.

Reifsnyder furniture: Reference may be (1) the antique furniture from Reifsnyder collection, certain items of which still hold the all-time auction record from 1930, or (2) Buck, Bossart & Reifsnyder furniture, made at Philadelphia from 1840s in French Antique style.

Reilly lamp: Possible reference is to examples of lard-oil and camphene lamps marked "Reilly" and made by S. S. Reilly of New York from 1840s.

rein round: A round leather thong. These were "drawn" from flat-cut thongs in a machine. Many used on early sewing machines.

Reisner work: A metallic inlay imitative of the Buhl technique.

relict: A widow.

reliquary: A container for a relic, generally a sacred relic, often of precious metal with rock-crystal panes, and sometimes gem-studded. Date is from 12th century. Many forms, some carried on the person, others wall-hung, and some on standards.

Remick view: Christian Remick, artist of

Boston, did six views of the harbor in 18th century, one of which sold for $790 in 1889. This view was engraved by Sidney Smith in 1904 on a plate 1½′ x 5′. Prints of this view are now rarities.

Remington andirons: Patented andirons in form of iron draft boxes with ventilators and other features. Made from 1840s by S. Cariss of Baltimore. [*Example pictured.*]

Remington pepper box: Big five-chambered, five-shot, barrel-revolving pistol by E. Remington & Sons, Ilion, N.Y.; made from 1860.

Remmey ware: Stoneware made by (1) three generations of potters of this name at New York, 1744–1831, (2) Henry Remmey, Jr., Philadelphia, from 1825. Water jars, bowls, chemical wares, et cetera.

Renaissance: The period of revival of culture, following the medieval, roughly bracketed as from 15th century. In this period all the arts flowered again and the mind of man was released from many of its self-, church-, and politically imposed restrictions.

Renfrew sprig: The Prince of Wales' crest, three plumes.

reniform: Kidney-shaped. Two circles, joined.

rent table: Revolving drum table with many drawers in periphery of skirting, each drawer labeled with name of tenant and containing the rent records of the renter.

repairer: In potteries, the assembler of parts of cast figures into the finished ensemble for firing. Any general repairman.

repeint: To limn or depict in paint.

repose furniture: Any bed, couch, divan, settee, long chair, day bed, et cetera, of sufficient size and shape to permit repose position by user.

repository: A large cabinet of drawers, closets, et cetera, to contain all the paraphernalia of a lady or gentleman. Some are "break-front" pieces up to ten feet wide and eight feet high.

repoussé: Design formed in relief by punching light or very ductile metal against soft wood or leather, without piercing. Brass, tin, copper, and silver objects were so decorated. During the last quarter of 19th century, brasswork of this nature was a homecraft indulged in by many ladies. They used as a punch block a small bed of pitch, or of brick dust, resin, and tallow. Many shallow *repoussé* bowls, plaques, and picture frames of this period still survive.

republican calendar: A Directoire calendar which eliminated all pagan and Christian terminology from names of days and months. Abandoned in 1805.

reredo: (1) A screen or tapestry behind the altar of a church. (2) A fireplace without a grate; a fireback.

rere supper: The third supper of the evening. The first evening meal was called supper, the second banquet, and the third "rere." The midnight feast from which partakers, often called Roaring Boys, left to make a noise on the streets.

reserve: (1) Supporting or protecting elements. (2) A resist-dyeing technique.

reservoir stove: Any stove equipped with a water-heating element in form of an oval or square tank encircling the smoke flue. From 1840s, "water backs" were incorporated in many kitchen ranges.

resist: A process of achieving design or pattern by transfer or painting with substance that would resist a dye bath or painting coat. Resist-dyed fabric, resist-luster, resist-engraved. **resist-luster:** The silver (platinum) luster with white or colored resist décor, and similar techniques in the gold lusters such as copper, Sunderland, et cetera.

resonator: An ear trumpet.

ressaulted: Having projections, as bulges and blocking, said of case furniture having this elegancy of design and construction.

ressaunt: The OG, or OGG molding; the S- or double-S-curve molding.

restrike: A second printing from a metal plate or from a lithographic stone. A form of faked old print. Innumerable Currier & Ives lithographs were restruck by a dealer who obtained certain original stones; similarly many early-19th-century-engraved plates were restruck from 1870s to 1890s and later.

resurrection plant: The *Anastatica hierochuntina*, which, revived in water, blooms. Commonly called rose of Jericho. The plant now generally sold as resurrection plant is not the true variety, but bird's-nest moss of California.

retablo: Wood panel painting of religious nature, commonly a *santo*, done by amateur and untalented artists of Spanish North America from 16th century to mid-19th.

rete: The movable disk of an astrolabe.

reticella: Cutwork in linen, often in bird, beast, flower, and human form, centered in lace squares. Done from 15th century to 19th. The best patch quilt is a poor imitation of reticella work.

reticulated: Pierced; foliated; a network.

retinned: Any ware made of tinned sheet iron and retinned after making. Very bright and handsome, long-lasting tin plate.

reverse: The minor side. See Obverse and Recto.

reversible seat: Chair or settee backs hinged to the seat in such manner as to permit pulling over, so "reversing" the seating; generally the seats are fixed, as in a carriage, omnibus, streetcar, or railway coach. Made from 1850s.

Revitt, Nicholas: English architect and designer who did much for the Greek-revival movement by publishing, with James Stewart, *Antiquities of Athens* in 1762.

Reynolds & Tummel furniture: "Parisian and antique" cabinet furniture, advertised in mid-1840s by a firm so named, Brooklyn, N.Y. It is what we have called Victorian style.

Reynolds mirror: Any mirror made or sold by J. Reynolds of Philadelphia, working from 1780s. Fretwork mahogany and walnut-framed mirrors with gold-leaf decoration; classic mirrors and early tabernacle forms. Also, it is asserted, made

Constitution mirrors. It is not clear whether this man was a dealer or both dealer and maker.

rheiocline: Seat furniture and mattresses with coil springs and hair padding. Term refers to the dual conical-form wire springs. Date of general use is from 1840s.

rhinoceros horn: The great horn of this beast was turned into "poison-proof" cups, vases, et cetera. Popularly this beast's horn was called unicorn (unihorn) horn.

Rhode Island chair: See Chairs, All Kinds. **Rhode Island Windsor:** See Chairs, All Kinds.

Rhodes silver: Reference would seem to be to silverwares manufactured by Rhodes, Anthony & Carley of Cincinnati from 1830s.

rhodium: Non-tarnishing white metal of the platinum family; salts of the metal are rose-colored, hence its confusing name. Rhodium was advocated as final plating for silver to prevent all tarnishing. Seldom used because of high cost. In 1840s rhodium pens were a rage; the tip only was of the metal. The "unalterable" pen.

rhombus: Parallelogram or square with oblique-angled sides; broad diamond form. Why this term was once applied to a six-sided bottle is a mystery.

rhyton: Handled figural cup in form of male or female head. Ancient form.

Ribbed: Pattern of pressed glass with beautiful all-over vertical ribbing, contoured with the shape of the pieces, and with ovate ends.

Ribbed Grape: Pressed-glass pattern featuring ribbing, with grapevine, leaf, and fruit. **Ribbed Palm:** Variant, ribbing with palm-form panel. **Ribbed Pineapple:** Variant, with a thistle form, called pineapple, impressed.

Ribbing: A technique or style of surface decoration displaying ribs of various widths, raised, defined by grooves, et cetera. Carved, molded, chased, pressed and otherwise achieved.

ribbon: Pressed-glass group featuring pressed ribbon forms, alternately frosted and clear; variants are "frosted," "fluted," and "clear." See Ruth Webb Lee's *Early American Pressed Glass.*

ribbon back: Chair or settee back with interlacing bands carved in ribbon form. A very elegant 18th-century chair of Georgian period. [*Example by Robert Manwaring pictured.*]

ribbon edge: Rippled edging on glass- and ceramic wares, and sometimes carved on furniture tops, lids, and door and drawer fronts.

Ricardi cut: Cut glass made by Passquale Ricardi of New York from 1810. His work was famed in early 19th century. It is not marked.

Rice & Revere: Lamp makers of Boston from 1830s; hanging, sideway, table, and mantel lamps of brass and japanned iron.

Rice-Harris glass: Rice-Harris, England, made pressed, cut, and engraved glass of fine quality from 1840s.

rice grain: Reference generally is to Chinese porcelain of the Canton variety, blue-decorated ware, with rice grains embedded in the paste, producing translucent pattern of spotting. The original technique is said to be Persian, 13th century. Kilns of the Ch'ien Lung Dynasty produced masterpieces in this ware.

Rice-Johnson glass: Lily-pad-decorated blown wares and other South Jersey technique glasswares made by Rice & Johnson at Harrisburg, N.Y., from 1840s.

rice paper: There isn't a particle of rice in it; the "paper" is shaved pith of the tungtsau tree of Formosa; achieved by turning boles of the pith in a lathe against a long, razor-sharp knife blade.

Richards glass: Colored, plain, enameled, and figured glass made by Richards Brothers at Jackson, N.J., 19th century.

Richardson Cut: Pattern of cut glass featuring a checkerboard, with alternate squares star-cut and plain. Date is from 1889.

Richardson prints: Block-printed paper in colors for window hangings and in squares for fireboards; sometimes used also as "squares" for wall decoration. Made from 1840s at Albany, N.Y.

rich-flower: The peony.

Richmond: Pattern of pressed glass displaying curvate pointed panel at base, over square-form footing and sections of pineapple pressing.

Richmond bed warmer: Copper hot-water pan on rod, made from 1830s by H. D. Richmond of New Bedford and Boston.

Ricker, Henry: Cabinetmaker of New York, working in 1770s.

Rickets bottle: Any high-kick-up-bottom bottle blown in a mold, patented 1822 by Henry Rickets of Bristol, England.

riddles: (1) Devices for sifting. (2) Bed curtains.

rider's bottle: Doughnut-shaped bottle of stone- or redware, for carrying on arm or shoulder. Often called harvester's bottle. Date is from 1790s.

Ridgewood case: Soldier's pipe, tobacco, and match case of metal, with various martial scenes and emblems, c. 1860. Some have metal top and leather pouch. [*Example pictured.*]

Ridgways: Family of English chinaware manufacturers noted for the various kinds of ceramic wares made by them and exported to the U.S. during the entire 19th century. Job Ridgway, father, from 1800s, and his sons, John and William, from 1814. Owned the Cauldon Place works, Hanley, Staffordshire. Earthenwares, chinaware, eggshell ware, Rose du Barry ware, some china in various patterns, et cetera. [*Examples of ware and marks pictured.*]

riding saw: A crosscut saw for logs, operated by a bicycle movement of operator, perched on a beam. Made from 1860. [*Example pictured.*]

Ridley plums: Sugar-cured fresh plums, packed in decorated boxes of the sort often called "brides' boxes." Produced by Ridley, confectioner of New York City from 1800s.

rifflers: Curvate-shaped files or rasps used in fine woodwork, as block fronting, violin making, clock-case making; in all fine and carved cabinetwork.

rifle: A gun with rifled barrel. **rifle-cane:** A firearm with rifled barrel concealed in a walking stick.

rifling: Snailing within the barrel of a gun to impart a spinning motion to projectile, the line of flight being the axis. Believed to have been an idea of Leonardo da Vinci. Rifling of gun barrels was known to Swiss artisans in 15th century. Swiss and French gunsmiths introduced the art to the American colonies, first near Lancaster, Pa., early in 18th century. The original gunsmiths taught many apprentices. Thus developed the remarkable accurate Pennsylvania rifle, which, in the hands of soldiers of the Pennsylvania line in Revolution, caused havoc with the British forces in battles.

Rigali, Gaden: Extensive maker of plaster-of-Paris ornaments, New York, from 1850s.

rigaree: Glass ornamentation of tapes or bands of glass, sometimes in contrasting colors.

Riggs banjo: Banjo-cased clocks by Riggs of Philadelphia, who made many in various sizes for the stations and depots of the Pennsylvania Public Works, later the Pennsylvania Railroad. Noted here because these are a distinct type of fine clock in the Willard tradition, but not of New England make.

right: Proper; genuine; authentic. **right line:** Straight line. **right tinware:** Block tinware; not plated. **right whale:** The baleen filter-mouthed, two-spout whale, as opposed to the fin-back whale.

Riley ware: Any pottery by Riley, the famed English potter, but particularly his late Imari pattern ware which is now generically designated as "gaudy Dutch." At one time in early collecting circles all this Imari ware was called "Riley ware." Riley's ware of this genre was made 1810-20. Much of it was "dumped" at low prices in U.S., as the ware did not sell in England.

rimon; rimonim: Finials on the rods of the sacred scrolls.

rincinus oil: Castor-bean oil.

ring brasses: Drawer pulls consisting of a boss or medallion, with ring-shaped drop pulls. Period of original use 1780s-1830s. Many old types are reproduced. Some of the plates are ovals. [*Examples pictured.*]

ringed chair: *See* Chairs, All Kinds.

ringed knop: Any knop in the stem or finial of glassware that is banded with a ring of glass, of same or other color.

Ringgold: A major in U.S. Army who was hero of Palo Alto; his name or bust portrait appears on flasks, coffeepots, cup plates, et cetera.

ring gold: A gold-silver-copper alloy, mostly gold, used in making rings.

ringleader: He who opens the dancing at a ball.

ring-leg: Any table, chair, or other furniture leg turned in a manner said to be ringed; a variety of button turning, *not* spool turning. Date is from 1830s.

ring scissors: A folding scissors with ring holds, blades folding into shank. [*Example pictured.*]

ringside chair: *See* Chairs, All Kinds.

ring tree: A small tree form of metal, pottery, or glass, with branches upon which to hang finger rings.

Ringwood iron: Hollow ware, named for

the furnace in New Jersey where cast, from 1760s.

Ripple: Pattern of pressed glass with bands of rippling, or weave pattern, stippled.

rippons: Spurs.

Rippowam stove: A fancy parlor stove of 1850s, made by a company so named at Stamford, Conn.

rising desk table: Deep-skirted table with three fold-over leaves, manipulation of which caused a desk box to rise from the skirting. Gadget furniture of 18th century, probably French.

rising hinge: Hinge with spiral rather than flat bearings on the pin joint. Movement of door causes the hinge to "lift" the door, by the rise of the hinge part, to clear a carpet or other floor obstruction. Also lifting hinge. Made from 1750s, generally of brass. [*Example pictured.*]

rising pan: Pan for rising of bread dough.

rising panel table: Architects' table with a sloped writing board rising and adjustable on trammels. "Rising writing table" was original cabinetmakers' and designers' term for the piece. Made from 18th century.

rising screen: A screen frame in slender uprights on either side. Sometimes fitted on back legs of a table desk to prevent drafts. 18th century.

rising table: Pedestal table with three round tops of graduated size rising on tubular center post to form a lazy Susan or dumbwaiter. Early 19th century.

Risley glass: Cut glass made by William Risley from 1820s to 1833, when Newbold & Trotter purchased the business.

Ritchie & Wheat glass: Made at Wheeling, Va., from 1820s by firm so named. Made pressed glass from 1829.

rithmimachia: A very early board game, invented c. 1494, by Shirwood, and much preferred to chess by scholars of several centuries. The game was offered *en tabula* from 16th century.

ritorto: Glass with delicately colored striping.

Rittenhouse, David: American clockmaker, astronomer, and scientist of 18th century. He invented a Franklin-type stove. Famed for his "orreries."

rived (riven): Split, not sawed.

Riverside: Pattern of pressed glass with diamond and fan decoration between oval centered panels.

riveted hose: Water hose of leather, riveted at seam.

roach trap: A pottery cup with beveled top. Some examples are marked "Roach Trap." [*Example pictured.*]

road glass: A flat drinking glass, rectangular in shape and section, fitting in one's pocket. Blown with pontil mark. Said to have originated in Spain. [*Example pictured.*]

Roanoke: Pattern of pressed glass somewhat like Sawtooth.

rob: A beverage made of preserved fruit or jelly.

Robb figures: Full and three-quarter life-size figures of Indians, et cetera, used as tobacconists' signs. Also carved figurehead and carrousel decoration and trim, animal figures, et cetera. New York from 1860s, made by Peter and S. A. Robb.

Robbins furniture: (1) Robbins & Winship, Hartford, Conn., in 1850s, made furniture in French Antique style. (2) H. F. Robbins made the same-style furniture at Madison, Wis., from 1850s.

robble: Woodenware. A dough paddle, sometimes chip-carved.

Roberts, Thomas: London cabinetmaker, working in William & Mary period. Richard, son, worked in Queen Anne period to Georgian, 1730.

Roberts-Cadman Sheffield: Plated ware, probably electroplated after 1840s, by firm so named, from 1780s. They used a "Ball" mark.

Robertson ware: Bean pots, redware planters, flowerpots, et cetera, made at Robertson Pottery, Chelsea, Mass. This pottery finally made artwares, dragon's-blood wares, and moved to Dedham, Mass., near close of 19th century.

Roberts silver: Manufactured solid silverware by E. M. Roberts, Hartford, Conn., from 1850s.

Roberts stoneware: Made at Utica, N.Y., from 1820s; gray-glazed stoneware with scratch and blue decoration.

robin-nest dish: A sugar dish, the form of which is a bird on nest. Pressed glass, the bird being the cover. There is a Vallerysthal dish of this genre and several American variants, one in all blue.

Robinson, Edward: Painter of transparent window shades, fireboards, et cetera; Philadelphia, from 1850s. Factory operation.

Robinson coverlet: Named for the weaver, James Robinson of Pittsburgh, Pa., who signed many. He is listed as working from 1830s. Signed examples are dated in 1840s.

Robinson glass: Reference is probably to window or other glass made by Robinson of Zanesville, O., from 1836.

Robinson pencil: Pencil cases of gold and silver by B. Robinson of Philadelphia, from 1830s, are sometimes called thus. Maker also made pen cases. The "case" was the barrel in which the pencil (graphite) or penholder retracted.

Roby lamp: Joseph Roby of Boston, from 1786, advertised "new invarated lamps of one hundred candle power." Oil-burning, Argand-type lamps.

rocaille: Rococo; rock and shell forms, flowing curvate leaf forms.

Rochelle: An iced-water pitcher with a dam inside spout to stop ice pieces. Many varieties, some inscribed ICE WATER in gold. [Example pictured.]

Rochester Glass: The Rochester, Pa., glassworks, the largest tumbler factory in the world. Operating from 1870s to 1901. Blown and pressed tumblers in infinite variety—million made each year.

Rochester woodenware: Product of the flat-stave works, Rochester, N.Y., from 1820s. Coopered woodenware.

rock; rocko: The distaff, the original spinning device. Later meaning the charge of flax on the distaff of a spinning wheel.

rock crystal: Properly, only pure transparent quartz. In the trade, the best lead glass is sometimes called crystal and rock crystal. The term is also applied to elegant bottles, vases, et cetera, carved from the true rock crystal, and to table cutlery with handles of the natural quartz. These are of quite early date, from 15th century.

rockee: A bench with rockers.

rocking chair: See Chairs, All Kinds. **rocking cradle settee:** See Cradle Settee. **rocking stool:** A stool with rockers, used by occupants of rocking chairs as a leg and footrest. [Example pictured.]

Rockingham: A brown-glazed ware originating at the Rockingham pottery, Swinton, Staffordshire, about 1790s. Fine, compact earthenware body, with brown, red-brown, or chocolate glaze. Various partners owned the pottery at Rockingham, makers of the original ware. Now a generic name for any good mottled or plain brown-colored glaze. Made the first "cadogan" teapot, other specialties, Leeds-type wares, et cetera. Certain of the Rockingham wares are pictured.

rock-oil lamp: Patented by Deitz of New York, 1857; a flat-wick lamp for rock oil, the prototype of most early kerosene lamps.

rococo: Rocaille; rock- and shell-form decoration.

rod gas lamp: Stationary lamp fixture, screwed to floor, with rising rod supporting one or two Argand gas burners with hurricane shades. Date is from 1820s.

rods: Any tubular or solid section of any substance, but particularly the rods of glass which, in cross section, display decorative forms in colors, silhouettes, portraits, flowers, fruits, and other objects, even initials, dates, and lettering. These, sliced apart, were used in making (1) walls of vases, bottles, et cetera, cased in clear glass, and (2) paperweight nests.

Roe-Camblin lanterns: Hall lanterns and lamps for the home; made of stained, cut, and engraved glass panels, metal-cased, by firm so named, from 1850s.

roemer: A display piece, especially of glass. Term is Dutch. Most examples are probably glassmakers' masterpieces.

rogerian: A type of wig.

Rogers groups: Plaster statuary groups reproducing the excellent genre sculptures of John Rogers, American, dating from mid-19th century. The complete listing of Rogers groups with contemporary illustrations of many will be found in Antiques Digest, compiled by Earl Breeding, Esq., an attorney working with the firm founded by Henry L. Stimson, who once posed for John Rogers. Rarest of Rogers groups are the salesmen's samples in miniature, of a size less than 4 inches high. Only three subjects are known.

Rogers lamp: A "non-explosive" round-wick, open-flame burner lamp with dousing cap on a chain. Safety feature was keeping the camphene fluid in a sponge of rock wool. First half of 19th century.

Rogers tin: Large and small objects of japanned tinned sheet iron, made by Cincinnati Tin & Japan Works, owned by M. Rogers & Co., working from 1840s. [An ex-

ample of an ornamental tea caddy is pictured.]

Rogers ware: English china by John Rogers & Son, early 19th century. One pattern displayed scenes from the English drama.

Rohrman tin: Japanned commercial containers and fixtures, marked with embossed stamps, made by J. Hall Rohrman & Son, Philadelphia, second half of 19th century.

roleau: Cylindrical form.

Rolfe, Eden: Advertised 1846 as successor to H. Seidenburg, cabinetmaker of Newburyport, Mass. In 1847 the latter was still advertising under his own name. The furniture was in the French Antique style. Both men had factories, and the transaction may have involved sale of premises and not the retail business. There is also a tradition the firms made cottage furniture; cheap furniture.

roll-back top: Reference is to chair backs of Directoire style, especially noted in Baltimore-made examples, the back rail curving in a scroll, as did the ends of sofas of this style. Date is from 1800s.

rolled paper work: Paper fillgree.

roll-end bench: A low seat on four legs, with rolls at either end of the seat proper. Esteemed for coffee-table use. Empire and Regency styles. [*Example pictured.*]

roller organ: Mechanical reed organ playing from a toothed roller. Some four hundred different rolls were available and interchangeable. Middle to late 19th century. Sometimes called the celestina.

roll hangings: Wallpaper printed in squares, or rectangles, called dominoes, pasted together into rolls; after 1803, printed on continuous rolls.

rolling lamp: A lamp suspended in gimbals. 18th-century novelty. Some could be rolled on the floor.

rolling-pin bottle: Actually hollow glass rolling pins readily filled with hot or cold water at pastry cook's choice. Not designed as a bottle, but possibly so used.

rolling stone: A stone lawn roller of 18th century.

rolling wagon: Ancestor of the Conestoga wagon; a boat-shaped wagon on four wheels of roller type. English, from early 18th century. [*Example pictured.*]

rollipoke: Coarse hempen cloth.

roll spring: A coil spring so constructed as to roll up for carriage.

rolly-polly can: Tin tobacco cans, lithographed. They are shaped in roly-poly figural form of sports, policemen, Negro mammies, et cetera. Mayo's Cut Plug was packed in them c. 1900.

Roman cement: Lime slaked in beer, mixed with tallow. Good waterproof cement or plaster. Also any American gypsum-base cement as used in construction and statuary casting.

Roman glass: Reference is to the glass of ancient Rome, from factories established in the reign of Tiberius, employing workmen of various nationalities expert in making glass.

Roman Key: Pattern of pressed glass featuring borders in the "Wall of Troy" design.

Roman Rosette: Pressed-glass pattern featuring whirling 11-petaled swastika forms on a band of stipple, with ribbing above and below.

Roman vitriol: Blue stone.

Romayne work: Carved portrait medallions within circles as found on Renaissance chests.

Rome porcelain: Reported as porcelain made at the Eternal City from 1790s to 1830s.

rommer: Globular-bowled thick-stemmed wineglasses; many varieties. The term may derive from or be a form of roemer. It really doesn't matter. These are European, Rhine Valley glasses, many of Dutch make.

rood: (1) A cross. (2) A measure of area; forty square poles.

Rookwood pottery: Art pottery made at Cincinnati by Mrs. Bellamy Storer and other enthusiasts; no two pieces alike. Established 1879. Often signed by the artist and always marked with the RP signature and flames.

rooster Betty: French or Swiss Betty-type lamp with round pad-form reservoir, suspended from a U-shaped support. A rooster effigy stands back of the wick hole.

rooster fight: The mechanical toy depicting two fighting roosters; manually operated; sometimes with pendulum.

rooster finials: Misshapen swan finials on glassware, and actual representations of roosters (with pinched tails) also used as finials of blown and tooled glass.

rooster pitcher: The "Chanteclair pour La France"; a pitcher of rooster form with the handle a curvate tail feather. 19th century.

root pot: A planter for sprouting bulbs. Bulb pots for crocus, hyacinth, and tulips date from 18th century. The root pots of popular 19th-century use date from 1870s.

root walnut: Root wood of the walnut tree, esteemed for burl-like markings; used as veneer.

rope bed: Any bed having the mattress or bed sack suspended in a cradle of taut ropes strung on wood buttons along bedrails.

rope bottom: Chair bottom of woven rope.

rope-turned: A style of wood turning imitative of the twist of rope.

ropewalk: A long covered arbor in which the strands of hemp and other fiber were woven into cordage. Some were 500 feet long.

Rorke lamps: Glass lamps made at National Flint Glass Works, under ownership of E. Rorke & Co. Wide variety of kerosene-burning table lamps.

Rosa furniture: Only reference found is to Victorian cabinetwork and chairs made by Rosa Brothers, Fishkill, N.Y., from 1850s.

rose blanket: Bedcover of early 19th century with conventionalized rose clusters embroidered in corners. Said to be a bride's coverlet.

rose bowl: Generic term for crimped- and ribbon-edged shallow bowls of art glass made from 1880s. Indubitably used as rose bowls when sold as glassware, but thousands used in connection with plated-silver stands and ensembles sold as berry bowls.

rose carpet: A Bessarabian rug with roses; woven by Christians of the Near East and hence free of Mohammedan restrictions on use of true flower forms.

rose cut: An early technique of cutting diamonds, imitative of the conventionalized rose form in its facets. Much overrated as to quality, rarity, and value. Nearly all rose-cut stones are shallow-pebble, old-mine diamonds. Rose diamond refers to the cut and not to tint or color. Emeralds and rubies of early cutting also display the rose-petal faceting.

rose du Barry: Deep rose color; a porcelain glaze.

rose engine: A special mandrel for a precision-turning lathe, creating magnificent engine-turned patterns.

rose glass: Clear glass flashed with gold oxide to produce rose-petal effect. New Bedford Rose; so called because made at Mount Washington glassworks, New Bedford, Mass. Made in 1880s.

rose handles: Brasses of rose form with bail handles; drawer pulls.

rose-head spoons: Early silver spoons of Henry VI period, with straight stem and flat seal of rose form. Rose of Lancaster spoon.

Rose in Snow: Pattern of pressed glass featuring clear glass rose, stem, and leaf spray on stippled ground.

rose mark: Dutch pewter mark of a Tudor-form rose.

Rosenthal: Continental European ceramic ware of comparatively modern manufacture and still produced.

Rose of Washington: Set of views of the city, lithographed in a pattern on sheets, die-cut to fold into a rose form. Date is c. 1862.

rose paperweight: Glass weights with an enclosed rose form, in red, white, or yellow. The most publicized weight is generally called "Millville Rose" and associated with Ralph Barber. Actually, these weights were first made at White Mills, Pa., at the Dorflinger Plant, by E. J. Larsen, who taught Barber how to make them. Barber later worked at Millville and made these weights to 1910. Recent rose weights and bottle stoppers by Kazian are also of excellent quality. These rose weights are among the latest ones made.

rose pompadour: Deep rose-red.

rose-shamrock-thistle glass: Wineglass with overlay panels of blue in which these several emblems are cut. Made by Richardson of London, 1840s.

Rose Sprig: Pattern of pressed glass displaying a sprig of stem, leaf, and rose bloom, in panels or between fluting, et cetera.

rose stopper: Small version of the rose paperweight, made into bottle stoppers, usually on perfume bottles.

Rosette: (1) Pattern of pressed glass featuring groups of five rosettes, one large in center and one at each corner of a square-form panel, with horizontal line border, pearl-studded. (2) Any circular-form boss of concentric rings, petal forms, or other décor.

Rosette & Palm: Pressed-glass pattern showing palmate forms on either side of a faceted element.

Rosette Medallion: Pressed-glass pattern having pointed daisy forms in circular daisy medallions, joined by diamond forms with ovate fan-shape palmettes between medallions.

rose umbrella: Umbrella-form framework for training a climbing or rambler rose plant. [*Example pictured.*]

rose-water bowl: The original finger bowl; small ewer of silver, often repoussé-decorated, filled with rose water to wash the fingers at table. New York silversmiths made such bowls prior to 1800s.

rosin glass: Bubbles in various forms, made in the glass blowers' techniques, from melted resin. Many made as a homecraft, but also commercially for necklace beads. Somehow the homecraft was practiced largely in Southern states and colonies, especially South Carolina and Georgia, before 19th century. This, probably, because of the availability of rosin, or resin.

Ross desk: A school desk having cast-iron frame and wood top.

rosso antico: (1) Natural red marble. (2) Imitation of it in red stoneware, as made by Wedgwood and other potters. Sometimes with black decoration.

Ross patterns: Hooked-rug patterns by Ross of Dayton, O., from 1880s. Imitative of the original Frost patterns. The Ross firm developed or promoted the mechanical hooker by which rugging was done rapidly. This device is scorned by true crafters, who place it in the same category as machine embroidery.

roster: A gridiron.

rotary desk: Not a drum table; a standard kneehole desk with rotating elements in the pedestals. A Wooten Desk Co. vagary, made from 1870s at Indianapolis, Ind.

rotary freezer: Cylinder enclosed within another, the interstice packed with ice and salt, the inner filled with ice-cream mix, rotating end over end in a framework, for making ice cream at the table while the dinner was in progress. A French machine. Earlier types, of china or porcelain, were assemblies of two jars achieving the same result. They did not rotate.

rotary milk shelf: Slatted wooden frames of graduated size, arranged on a central shaft and enclosed in a framework. A huge piece of woodenware to hold pans of milk. [*Example pictured.*]

rotary stove: Stove with rotating holed top enabling user to bring any apertures over the fire. Made from 1840s.

rotgut: Distillers' "foreshot," or first run from a still.

Roubillac, Louis François: French sculptor who modeled figures for Chelsea porcelain groups.

Rouen: A faience of France, made at city so named from 1540s.

Rouen cassimere: Hand-woven silk-and-wool fabric made in U.S. by Joseph Ripka.

rouge (jeweler's): Sulphate of iron, used as a polish.

rouge-de-fer: Rust of iron; rust-red color.
rouge flambé: Flaming red.

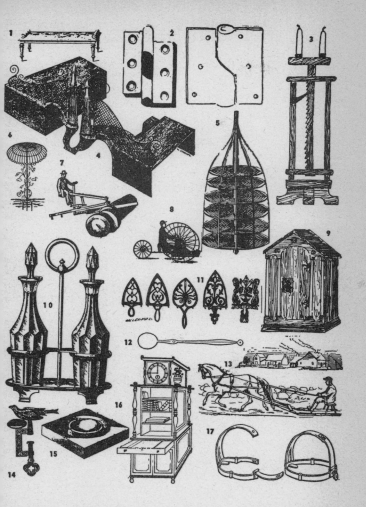

1, Roll-End Bench. 2, Rising (or lifting) Hinges. 3, Ratchet Candlestand. 4, Remington Andirons. 5, Rotary Milk Shelf. 6, Rose Umbrella. 7, Riding Saw. 8, Regatta Carriage. 9, Saddle-Roof Cabinet (Tudor-Gothic). 10, Salad Caster. 11, Sadiron Stands. 12, Salamander Iron. 13, Sapling Jumper. 14, Sewing Bird. 15, Seed Sprouter. 16, Saul's Bookcase Clock. 17, Scold's Bridle.

Rough-and-Ready Toby: Portrait jug, crudely modeled, of General Taylor Said to be of American make. Rare.

rouleau: Roll- or club-shaped.

roundabout chair: *See* Chairs, All Kinds.

round chair: *See* Chairs, All Kinds.

rounded rail: When rails and stiles, as of a chair, are joined with a rounded joint, the work is so-called.

roundel: Any round form used as decoration. Also a turned, flat trencher of wood, often carved or scratched with tulip and pomegranate forms. English and French examples date from 15th century. Some early Staffordshire slip-ware dishes are imitative of roundels.

roundel cut: A technique of cutting to achieve a flat-cut round in glasswork. Also called a kugel, a rondel, and a boss.

rounds: Rungs or stretchers.

rouse; rouze: To "warm up" a color with a red-orange tint.

roving: Carded wool, roved into a fluffy cord, ready for spinning into yarn.

roving wheel: Two wheels, mounted, rim to rim, through which wool roving was passed and measured.

Rowe bed: There was a Rowe bedstead factory at Cincinnati, in 1850s, making patent, common, and trundle beds. This is probable reference.

rowels: *See* Spurs.

rowing engine: Fire engine built like a bandwagon, with six benches. Rods were pushed forward and backward by men on benches, moving the central pumping shaft. Date is from 1840s.

rowler: A roller.

rown shawls: Rowan-tree woods.

Roxbury carpets: Any floor coverings from the looms of Roxbury, Mass. Made in quantities from 1850s.

royal crystal: Part ruby-flashed pressed glass in a pattern imitative of diamond and chain-diamond cutting.

Royall, Anne: Newspaperwoman and political blackmailer, 1769–1854. J. Q. Adams described her as "a virago in enchanted armor." She is perhaps the grandmother, in spirit, of radio commentators who snoop and scoop everything, preferably the dirt.

Royal Pottery: A works at Weston-super-Mare, Bristol region, England, established 1830s. Vases, flowerpots, figures, including the Alpine pot and Oxford pot for growing azaleas, roses, et cetera. Crocus pots and other planters. Marked with Royal Arms and lettering.

Royle teapot: Self-pouring gadget teapot; a plated-silver elegancy with a plunger force-pump that forced tea through the spout. [*Example pictured.*]

R*Port: The R with star on silver labels or Sheffield plate means Ruby Port. *See also* W*Port.

rubila: The term used by Governor Winthrop of Connecticut, who was also a Doctor of Physik, for his cure-all, or nostrum, administered to all patients.

Ruby Rosette: Ruby-flashed pattern of pressed glass, having a row of clear-glass rosettes as a scalloped band. **Ruby**

Thumbprint: A similar flashed pattern with bands of large thumbprints. We are disposed to say, "This is just the kind of gaudy glass you will like if you like this kind of glass."

Rucima: Goddess of weeds or weeding, generally represented in statuary for the gardens, cast in lead or in some form of terra cotta.

rudder table: The butterfly type of drop-leaf support, in the form of a ship's rudder, broad side of blade up. Said to have been the original form and term, and that "butterfly" is a 19th- and 20th-century term.

Rudd's table: A harlequin cabinet, pictured in Hepplewhite's *Guide*; two-drawer, tambour-fronted toilet table.

Rudolstadt: Really "Sitzendorf" ware made from 1760s. Also a late-period German ware made to 20th century.

Rue bedstove: Pottery foot warmer for hot water. Made at Rue Pottery, Matawan, N.J., from 1850s. Some potters from Bennington worked at this pottery.

ruffled pawn: A curtain or valance for the mantelshelf. A hearth curtain.

rug: To 1750, "rug" designated any fabric, patterned or plain, needleworked or felted, designed as a bed- or table cover. Not a floor cover unless specifically designated as floor rug.

rug chest: Huge chest for bedclothing, sometimes on frames. Examples of Tudor, Jacobean, William & Mary, Queen Anne, and Chippendale styles prove the general usage of this item of case furniture.

ruinated: Spoiled; damnified; in tatters; torn. In ruins.

rumble-polished: Metal objects polished by tumbling in a rotating cylinder.

Rumford, Count: Benjamin Thompson, Tory of Revolution, who fled Boston, migrated to England, and served a German prince so well as consultant that he was made a count. Scientist and general experimenter of the Benjamin Franklin type. Rumford invented a stove, a lamp, a baking powder, a pamphlet case, a tonic, and other things. Invention of stoves included a grate for burning coals, and the shallower fireplace with angled walls that is the general pattern in use today.

Rumford case: A box form, made to look like a book, used to store pamphlets, tracts, et cetera, for filing on library shelves.

rum-jug: A toddy jug. About 1900, spouted glass jugs, blown or pressed, and some even cut, were so called. Also the spouted jugs used as batter jugs, especially for making "cow-lines," the continuous round noodle of batter fried in deep fat.

rumpel: The jaw-harp, improperly called Jew's harp.

Rumpp leather: Reference is to a firm of leatherworkers of Philadelphia from 1840s, producing fine *porte-monnaies*, bags, purses, et cetera. Firm is still active.

run-about lamp: A pressed-paper fuel reservoir with a brass burner; a lamp of the 1880s.

runcible spoon: Broad-tine form with a cutting edge; ancestor of the modern salad fork.

rundlet: Measure of 18 gallons.

runge: Woodenware. An oval-form tub with two handles.

runnels: Grooves in platters and planks to catch meat juices and collect them in a well, for basting. Also ornamental grooving on wood or metal.

running pump: Spring water piped to an upright bole with an ever-running tap.

Rupert's drops: Gobs of glass dropped into water for quick cooling, taking the form of a tadpole. The head resists blows, but breaking the tail causes the entire piece to break into fragments in a mild explosion.

rural: Of the country. Often used to describe anything from homemade to crudely professional work.

rush bottom: A chair seat of woven rush. Millions of fancy chairs were so made, originally, including some few Windsor chairs in 18th century.

rush dip: A long oblong-bowled ladle for soaking pith in hot fat.

Rush horrors: Staffordshire figures of Emily Sanford, Henry Rush, and others, with pastille burners in form of Stanfield Hall, Norwich Castle, et cetera. Rush was Emily's lover who murdered several members of the Stanfield Hall family. Cottage ornaments.

rushlight: Rush stems, peeled of all but a spine, to the pith, soaked in hot fat, and used for lighting source instead of candles. **rushlight holder:** A pair of iron pincers to hold the rushlight, sometimes on an iron stand and sometimes on a wood base. Made in colonies from early 17th century.

rush ribbon: A roll of rush pith soaked in fat.

Russel & Weeks: Cabinetmakers and chairmakers of Brooklyn, N.Y., who in 1830s made sideboards, secretaries, pier, writing, dressing, and worktables, bookcases, desks, and Windsor and fancy chairs. Empire styles.

Russel furniture: Knock-down furniture for shipment to Southern ports, made by Ira Russel of Boston. Also made marble-topped tables, whatnots, dining and bedroom furniture, in French Antique style. Mid-19th century.

Russia bristles: Wild-boar bristles, many of which were shipped from Russia after the 1800s, for use of American brushmakers.

Russian butter: Butter churned from cream collected off simmered whole milk. *Family Magazine* in 1830s attributed the discovery to a "Russian nobleman."

Russian thermometer: Name given the Delisle thermometer in 1840s. The term is even more apt today in light of what we know of modern Russian techniques of thinking: this thermometer registered the boiling point of water as zero and the freezing point at 150°!

rustic: The one furniture style that is beyond the basic three great pools of derivation, Gothic (or Gallic), Chinese, and classic. Of source allied in philosophy to simple Gallic, but using the actual and natural wood in form and growth. Examples are generally from 18th-century originals. Made in quantities by several manufacturers in U.S. from mid-19th century. **rustic frame:** (1) A picture frame of natural wood, with bark, generally sawed in half, laterally, to make a sort of molding. (2) A frame of slats crossed at ends. **rustic picture:** A curiosity of homework; a painting embellished with moss, twigs, sponge, cork, bark, putty, pebbles, et cetera.

rusticated: V-shaped gouging in wood boards to simulate a masonry joint.

Rust lamp: Whale- or lard-oil lamp with leakproof feature, made by S. Rust of New York City from 1840s. Solar lamps of good quality and style.

Rutgers spreads: Pattern-woven chenille spreads made at Colonel Rutgers' factory at Brunswick, N.J., from 1820s. Dated and lettered examples are known. So scarce are these that one, in not perfect condition, changed hands at a substantial advance three times within an hour at the White Plains Antiques Show, spring, 1951.

Rutt, George: Cabinetmaker of Lancaster, Pa., from 1790s. Worked in Hepplewhite style. Marked examples are of record.

rye & Injun: A flour of rye and corn meal. Breadstuffs baked from it.

Ryves wallpaper: Squares or dominoes of wallpaper made by Edward Ryves, Philadelphia, from 1770s. Wood-block-printed, hand-colored, and -stained.

S

S & W queen's ware: Late white earthenware made at Stafford Pottery, Stockton-on-Tees, England, from 1870s. The works, however, date back to 1825 and were operated by William Smith and John Walley. In 1848 they were under injunction to cease fraudulent marking of their products as WEDGWOOD. At one time this pottery had a branch at Mons, Belgium.

saber leg: Furniture leg with a curve comparable to that of a saber. Sometimes called a scimitar leg.

sablier: The hourglass, invented by Luitprand, a learned monk of Chartres, who is credited with rediscovering the secret of glassmaking.

sabot foot: Literally, a shoed or shod foot; a metallic shoe fitting over the end of a table or chair leg. The style is French Provençal. [*Example pictured.*]

sabot lamp: The reservoir is shaped like

the wooden shoe called a sabot. Burner is placed forward, off center, the reservoir fitted with a carrying handle. Believed to have been an advertising lamp.

saboton: Armored shoe; the covering over footgear that was a part of a suit of armor.

Sabrina: A popular "name" piece of sculpture of mid-19th century. Copeland made a Parian figure after the original. A nude figure, seated, with drapery on seat.

sack: A measure of wool, "of 2 weys." A wey is said to have been 1½ bushels.

sack bed: (1) The bed sack, or mattress. (2) The sacked bottom of a bedstead to hold the bed sack.

sackbut: An early wind instrument, somewhat like a modern trombone.

Sackett card: Penmanship visiting card by O. Sackett. This American calligraphic expert wrote up to 4000 visiting cards a week, at a fair price per dozen. Made a European tour and wrote cards for many important people.

sacrament tokens: Brass, pewter, iron, and other tokens used as badges of admission to the communion table in many churches. Custom active during 18th century and to 1840s.

sacredaan: Javanese mahogany.

sacring wheel: Narrow treadwheel fitted with tinkling bells, turned by crank work, and mounted on stands. Used in Roman Catholic churches during the Mass.

sacristy chest: Church chest for storing vestments. Mostly early Gallic styles or of the Renaissance.

sad: Heavy. **sadiron:** Heavy iron. **sad ware:** Heavy ware.

sadden: In dyeing, to give a violet or bluish tinge.

saddle bottle: (1) Gourd-shaped bottle carried in sling. Actually most round-bottomed bottles called "saddle" are wine bottles, made so to stand in beds of sand or to hang on walls. (2) A bottle with an enlarged section in the neck proper. (3) A long, slender bottle carried in the boot by riders.

saddle bracket: Cast-iron hook for hanging saddles.

saddle-seat chair: See Chairs, All Kinds.

saddle swivel chair: See Chairs, All Kinds.

Saddler & Green: Inventors of the transfer process of china decoration first used at Liverpool, 1752. They conducted a pottery and printing establishment for the wares of other potters, including Wedgwood. Many Liverpool wares with printed transfer decoration came from the decorating establishment of this firm.

saddle-roofed cabinets: 15th-century closets in form of a vestibule, having façade, sides, and roofing. [*Example pictured.*]

saddy piece: A thank-you piece.

sadiron stands: Trivets of spade, star, or other shape, of wrought iron, cast brass, or cast iron, designed as stands for laundry irons. Innumerable varieties. Excellent essay appeared in *Spinning Wheel* magazine. [*Examples pictured.*]

saffaw: 17th- and early-18th-century term for the sofa, or day bed.

safflower: The saffron flower, yielding a dye and a flavoring; the dried stigmata of the autumn-flowering crocus.

sailor work: Scrimshawing or whittling bone and decorating with needle or other scratching tool, the lines filled with blacking. Also jackknife carving and some forms of needlework. Jack afloat was a man busy at such tasks when not on duty.

St. Andrew stretcher: The X-stretcher.

St. Anthony's nut: The groundnut or peanut.

St. Cloud: Porcelain made at St. Cloud, France, from 18th century. Some put the date of this soft-paste production as beginning 1677.

St. Cyr: The school founded by Madame de Maintenon of France; embroidery and fine needlework.

St. Germain lamp: The original name of the student-type lamp which somehow, for some years, was called German student lamp. The lamp seems to have been introduced in its best-known form, not its prototypes, by Richard Briggs of Boston in 1860s. Of the prototypes, American imports from Shelton and other English makers date from late 18th century.

St. Johns River antiques: J. Wells Champney, the artist who illustrated *The Great South*, was probably the first man to discover the huge storehouse of New England antiques in the St. Johns River country and the New Smyrna section of Florida, in the homes of descendants of the Minorcan immigrants brought in to serve as serfs. Freed by their own rebellion, these people traded "shaddock," or grapefruit, to New England sea captains for secondhand furniture collected in and around Boston. Since this trading went on in the 1830s, the secondhand stuff was largely Georgian furniture or earlier. By 1910 most of the store had been bought up by Boston and New York dealers. The Flagler promotion of St. Augustine in 1880s and 1890s caused many wealthy collectors to do "antiquing" in this region.

St. Louis: Glassware of France. Factory operation began in Vosges Mountains c. 1680s. In 1840s much fine pressed glass from this factory was imported and, in patterning, caused many American makers to imitate and "improve" on it. Among the St. Louis marked examples are figural pieces of great beauty. Some people are under the impression this mark on glass denoted the St. Louis, Mo., exposition.

St. Louis (American): Glassware made at factory of Nelson, Case & Eads, St. Louis, Mo., from 1840s, and by Blow & Farrel and other short-lived factories.

St. Louis Cut: A pattern of cut glass displaying pentagonal facets, sometimes called Dutch Diamond.

St. Mémin: C. B. J. F. de St. Mémin, a French artist working in America during first quarter of 19th century, made what he called "physionotrace" engravings, about 2½ inches in diameter, from chalk profiles, delivering a dozen proofs of the plate, and the large original, for $25 to $35. His collection embraced everybody who was anybody in most of the large cities and towns. Also made the lithographic drawing of the first voyage of Robert Fulton's *Clermont*, which was printed at Dijon.

sake-ju-bako: Carrying case of Japanese make, holding flask for *sake* and drinking bowls.

salad caster: Oil and vinegar bottles in caster frames. [*Late example pictured*.]

saladier: A slaw cutter; wooden board with shredding blade set at an angle.

saladiere: "Let the saladieres [sallet dishes] be of porcelaine, or of Holland's Delft Ware, not silver or pewter"—John Evelyn.

salad scissors: A scissors-like arrangement of long-handled, wood spoon and fork to facilitate service of salad. Considered "modern" and of 20th century, imports of this item are of record in 1850s. Carved wood; made in Switzerland and France.

salamander back: Chair slats so cut and shaped to look much like pairs of salamanders (or tadpoles) head to head. This style is from the French Jura, late 16th century, and entered the colonies through French Canada. Examples are found in Canadian border states. *See also* Chairs, All Kinds.

salamander iron: Browning iron used in cookery. Heated to red or orange color, the iron was used to "brown" pastry crusts, roasts, and chops. [*Example pictured*.]

salamander leg: Cabriole-shaped leg, carved in scale form, and terminating in a salamander head.

salamander marble: Cast iron, painted and dusted to simulate marble, often used in making fireplace frames and mantels.

salamander plate warmer: Brass stand, generally footed, with a valance, upon which plates were heated by the fireside. Sometimes called a "footman." [*Example pictured*.]

Salamander ware: Any ware made at the New York City "Salamander Stoneware Pottery." While no ware of record is generically designated as Salamander, any ovenware, or ware usable in intense heat, was given this name on occasion.

salamander wool: Asbestos, especially the fibered wool or spun yarn of this curious natural fireproof fiber.

Salem chairs: Name given Georgian-style chairs made at Salem, Mass., distinguished by "ears" at juncture of stiles and top rail, and by a delightfully openwork back splat. [*Example pictured*.]

Salem, Mass.: chemicals: Household chemicals, alum, saltpeter, and others, made from 1819. **furniture:** Under the guidance and sales planning of Elijah & Jacob Sanderson, a cartel for the shipping of shop- and factory-made furniture of extra-fine to average-good quality was instituted after the Revolution. Shipments were made to the West Indies, South America, and all coastal U.S. ports. Adams, Pulsifer, Appleton, Austin, Hook, Luther, Burbank, Swan, and other cabinetmakers were in the scheme. Said to have operated up to the embargo caused by War of 1812. **glass:** Tradition is that glass was made here from 1640s for about a decade. Recently discovered data document the tradition and make it fact.

Salem, N.J., glass: A factory was established at this place c. 1850. Vials, bottles, and preserve jars were made to 1880s.

Salem rocker: *See* Chairs, All Kinds.

Salem secretary: An important piece of case furniture, looking somewhat like a sideboard, but having a large center drawer unfolding into a desk compartment.

salep cup: A beverage, not a container; a tonic made from powdered orchid roots, sold generally in London to the working people of the metropolis. Only records of sale in U.S. are at Boston and New York, and these are traditions not substantiated by documentary evidence as yet.

saler: A cellar, as for salt. This spelling occurs as "siller saler" and as "birral saler," meaning, respectively, silver cellar and burl cellar.

saleried: Flavored with celery.

Salisbury furniture: Made at Norfolk, Va., from 1840s by L. Salisbury. French Antique style is assumed, not proved.

sallet; salade: Fresh uncooked leaf vegetables, herbs, and flowers, served as a table dish from 14th century, dressed with sour wine and oil. "Daundelyouns" were esteemed for sallets; also daisies, roses, borage, nasturtiums, primrose, rose, buttercup, violets, endyve, lettuce, lamb's lettuce, chyves, shallots, chickweed, et cetera. The "sallet bowle" was of china or woodenware. The terms "sallet stand," for a bowl on pedestal or three or four legs, "sallet cruet," the cruet for oil and vinegar, are found used in 17th and 18th centuries. Sallet was once the approved spelling.

Sally Snow: Anything quite small, or in miniature. The original Sally was a midget weighing only 18 pounds when 12 years old. She was exhibited all over New England at fairs and museums. Sally was born in 1810.

salon: An important formal room; an important social affair. **salon panel:** Classic panel, painted in pastel or in tones of gray. **salon suite:** A parlor suite. **salon vase:** Any important base of ceramic ware. Not to be confused with solon vase, *which see*.

Salopian: The London china warehouse of this name controlled the sale of considerable Staffordshire production; a branch of the Turner interests, of Caughley Potteries, Broseley, Shropshire. Salopian is found impressed on Turner's wares, and as a capital S in underglaze blue. The name is found on willow-pattern ware, china imitative of Royal Worcester, and other sorts. Rose & Co. acquired the Turner potteries in 1799 and transferred the business to Coalport in 1814.

salt: The term, generally, is used to designate a saltcellar; as silver salts, Stiegel salts, pressed salts, et cetera.

salt caster: A glass or pottery container with perforated head and cork-sealed bottom. No metal fittings.

saltcellar candlestick: A stick with a bell base somewhat in the shape and form of a saltcellar.

salt chair: A chair with deep well under the seat for storing the household supply of salt. Some benches had salt chests under the seats. Said to have originated as a practice in Normandy.

salt cloth: A ceremonial canopy draped

over the important table piece now called a standing salt.

Salter mirror: A mirror maker named Salter was on the tax rolls of Philadelphia in the early 1800s.

salt glaze: A pottery glaze, generally on stoneware, achieved by the chemical action of common salt vaporized in the kiln.

saltire: X-shaped.

salt ladle: A salt spoon.

salt mouth: A wide-mouthed jar.

salt pouch: A leather sack for carrying salt.

salt shovel: A shovel-form salt spoon.

salver: Literally, "saver." A dish or platter for meat which "saved" the juices. Salvers are not necessarily of precious metal. In fact many were of wood, some of tin, brass, pewter, pottery, porcelain, stoneware, iron, et cetera. Of course the finest examples are of silver and of Sheffield plate. The paten used at Holy Communion services of evangelical churches is sometimes called a salver. In 17th century a new kind of salver was described thus: "A new fashioned piece of plate broad and flat, used in the giving of beer or any liquid thing to save the carpet or cloths from drops."

samian: A red color approximating the ancient redware of Samos, Greece, which is not glazed, but a dense ware, polished by burnishing.

samite: A rich silk fabric.

sammen: Soft or underfired building and paving bricks. In error called salmon bricks.

samp: Coarsely ground grains, boiled.

Sam Patch: The first "fall jumper" of record. Sam jumped Genesee Falls and survived. Not content, he tried it again, and was lost. Hence, "mad as Sam Patch."

sampler: A square of needlework in various patterns, with examples of alphabet and numerals, figures, et cetera, to serve as a "sample" in marking household linens and other textiles. A stitchery sample piece. Innumerable variety; seldom are any two precisely alike. Early samplers are higher than wide, middle period are square, and from mid-18th century onward the style was to make samplers wider than high.

samples-in-little: Miniatures of pottery, glass, wrought or cast iron; of chairs, case furniture, et cetera, designed as samples for salesmen. Any such samples predicate factory production. There is a distinction between craftsmen's miniatures, children's furniture, et cetera, and these salesmen's samples.

samp mill: A small hand mill with upper and nether stone, for the home grinding of grain. See Quern.

sampson: A beverage; hot cider laced with rum.

Sampson's pillar: A mouse trap with a falling block which killed the little creatures. Mouse entering the trap caused the block to fall.

Samson ware: Samson & Vivinis of Paris, from 1840s, made beautiful wares imitative of various fine, earlier wares. State Arms teapots, eagle tea caddies, Washington Memorial plates, Martha Washington plates, oriental porcelain, and other fine wares were imitated by this firm so well that in some cases they are better than the originals.

Sanborn silver: Factory-produced silverware of coin quality, made by Sanborn of Lowell, Mass., from 1840s.

sanctuary lamp: Hanging lamp, usually suspended on chains, and used in holy places, burning perfumed oil. Also the votive light shades of clear and colored glass, improperly designated as sanctuary lamps. These were made by Stiegel and many other American glasshouses from colonial period. The early types of such shades are miniature hurricane globes. Clear shades are now votive to the Virgin, but the once designated color of this lamp was blue. Red is the Sacred Heart. Green and amber are also used, with varying significances, depending upon geographic locale. Probably most so-called early Christmas lights were votive shades. Most 19th-century ones are goblet or tumbler shape. Round-bottomed ones stand in a tray of sand. Flat bottoms are set on racks, in batteries of from 12 to 144 or more.

sand-blasted: Any substance, the surface of which is sprayed with sharp sand under air pressure, as sand-blasted glass, metal, or pottery.

sand bottle; sand jar: A one-time homecraft; various colors of sand arranged to display a pattern on clear glass walls of container. Some are so carefully made that portraits, scenes, figures, et cetera, are displayed. McGregor, Ia., seems to have been a center of making in 19th century; the work said to have been done by surviving members of the Sioux and Kiowa tribes of Indians. The sand is tamped tightly and the bottles or jars sealed. Most date from 1870s and later.

sanders; sand boxes: Sand was used as blotting powder for ink writing for many years after the discovery of the more convenient usefulness of unsized paper-pulp card for this purpose. Every substance was used in making the boxes, from gold to papier-mâché. All sand boxes had perforated tops through which the sand was sprinkled on the inked writing and through which the sand was poured back into the container. The device dates from medieval times to mid-19th century. A sand box was a part of all desk sets or all desk equipment to 1850s. Millions of examples survive.

sanders: Colloquial for sandalwood.

Sanders, Pittman & Dodge silver: Probably our earliest silverware manufacturers. The firm was established 1790s at Providence, R.I. May have been a cartel. Various spellings reported, including Saunders, Pitman, and Dodge. Ezekiel Burr, John Jenckes, and others were members. Employed 30 workmen, making spoons.

Sanderson furniture: Elijah and Jacob Sanderson of Salem, Mass., from 1779 and later, with others conducted an extensive shipping enterprise for the distribution and sale of fine furniture. Samuel McIntire of Salem did carving for this project. William Hoock was a member of the cartel. The Sandersons were working from 1760s. See Salem Furniture.

sandever: The scum forming on glass melting pots. Also called gall.

sand oven: Oven wall of two elements, the interstices filled with sand; single-wall ovens lined with sandstone.

sand painting: (1) Canvas or board covered with a tacky size, japan drier, or glue, on which colored sand was laid in a pattern as a painting, the surplus shaken off when dry. (2) Painting in colored crayons on sandpaper, fixed with a spray of shellac or varnish.

Sandwich Bible: Small piece of glass in book shape, some gold-flecked.

Sandwich cut & engraved glass: The variety of really fine wares produced at the Sandwich Glass Works has been screened by the publicity given the cheap pressed wares made at this works. Actually fine cut and engraved glass, on blanks blown at the same works, were made from 1820s to the very end of operation. Ruth Webb Lee, in *Victorian Glass*, devotes a chapter to recent important findings in respect to this type of Sandwich glass. The early ware, to 1840s, is cut in the traditional Bristol, Stourbridge, and Irish techniques. After 1840s the French rococo revival styles predominate.

Sandwich glass: Any product of the Jarves Cape Cod Glass Works at Sandwich, from 1820s to end of production in 1870s. Cut, engraved, enamel-decorated, transfer-decorated, molded, pressed; the scale is all-inclusive. Patterns were first identified by name in *Romance of Old Sandwich Glass*, by F. W. Chipman, 1932, and by Ruth Webb Lee in her definitive work, *Sandwich Glass*. See Bibliography for further book titles. **Sandwich Loop:** A Sandwich pressed-glass pattern displaying petaled loop forms. **Sandwich pendulum bob:** Pressed-glass bobs for clock pendulums, attributed to Sandwich, used by several Connecticut clockmakers. Use dates from 1840s. **Sandwich shades:** (1) Glass lamp shades by Sandwich Glass Works. (2) Paper and porcelain shades sold with lamps, and separately, by Sandwich Glass Works. **Sandwich Star:** Pattern of pressed glass, Sandwich-made, featuring large four-pointed stars on a diamond form, arranged in panels.

sandwich tray: A tray for sandwiches; a tray with an edge having a flat border.

San Francisco glass: Potrero, Cal., glass, and glass from the works of Hostetter, Smith & Dean. Bottles, flasks, and window glass.

sangaree: Wine, water, sugar, nutmeg, and bay leaf; a sort of cobbler.

sang de boeuf: Oxblood; a blood-red color.

Sanger, Stephen: Recorded cabinetmaker of Alexandria, Va., 1830s.

Santa Claus: Modern version of the Dutch "San Niklaus." To confuse this genial character, a saint devoted to children and their happiness, with the German buffoon "Belznickle" is an error. The two were not the same. Father Christmas of France is close to San Niklaus. But Belznickle was a clown who cut capers on Christmas Eve.

Santa Claus bottle: Mold-blown bottle

in the form of the popular concept of the figure; late, dating from 1900s.

santolina: Cotton of natural lavender color.

santos: Any effigy or painting, such as a retablo, bulto, et cetera, of religious significance. Many are found in the Southwest and in Pacific region. May date from 1600s or from 1900s!

sapling jumper: Long saplings notched for ease in bending, joined by crosspieces and a bench, and bent upward to serve as shafts for harnessing to a horse. The ensemble is a pioneer sleigh. [*Example pictured.*]

Saracenic: Of the Saracens, Mohammedans who abide by dictates of the Koran in their decoration and follow the injunction to make no image of anything on earth, in the sky, or the waters. Decorative elements are stylized, or geometrical.

sarapa: A poncho of black and white rubberized fabric, made in U.S. by Charles Goodyear. Some very fancy patterns.

Saratoga slicer: A cutter to thin-slice potatoes into a helical pattern. Dropped in scalding hot fat, the result was that popular delicacy of the Saratoga hotels— the potato chip. [*The cutter is pictured.*]

sarcanet: Thin silk fabric.

sarcophagus chest: An Empire-style chest tapering from a wide top to a narrow base, with conforming drawers. [*Example pictured.*] **sarcophagus top:** Any superstructure, especially of cabinetwork or clock casing, in the form of a classic burial case.

Sardinia: A brass foot warmer with raised wire protecting screen. So named because the type is used extensively in Sardinia, Italy.

Sargeant bells: Cow bells, some with paper labels naming the object "Kentucky Cow Bell." Made from 1850 by Sargeant Hardware Co., New Haven, Conn. [*Some of their cabinet hardwares pictured, made from 1860s.*]

Sargeant mirror: Products of the looking-glass factory of J. Sargeant, Cleveland, O., from 1830s. Tabernacle mirrors and some gilt-framed overmantel and pier glasses.

Sarreguemines: Pottery center of France, in the Department of the Moselle. A faïence works established in 1770s. Later products included cameo ware as good as Wedgwood's. Potteries continued in operation through first half of 20th century; one of the Lindbergh plates was made here.

sarsafaix: Sassafras wood.

sash-cornered: "With the corners sashed; at an angle, and carved." Some early American cabinetmakers, c. 1780s, called this work "sash connard." Examples were not only carved; many were inlaid. [*Examples pictured.*]

sash door: Any door divided with muntins, as a window sash, and glazed.

Sass, Jacob: Cabinetmaker of Charleston, S.C., working in 1780s. Said to have worked in classic style.

satin glass: White opaque glass, flashed with a color and then subjected to satining in hydrofluoric acid vapor. Many colors, made at many glassworks during the art-glass craze from 1880s.

satin paper: A specialty paper imitative of silk and satin, made by Hart-Montgomery & Co. of Philadelphia from 1850s.

satyr cup: 18th-century ceramic-ware cup upon which is a modeled satyr's face.

sauceboat: Elongated shallow pitcher for melted butter, the usual "sauce" of early days. Examples known in silver, Sheffield plate, and many kinds of ceramic ware. Some are reported made of hardwood. Many are made with a pouring spout or lip at either end. These date from 17th century. After 1730s most examples are single-spouted or -lipped.

saucepan: Bulbous vessel of metal, some of silver, with cover and side handle, for the making of sauce, a concoction of melted butter, wine, spice, salt, et cetera.

saucered cup: Made in Japan at the Imari works; a tea bowl with its underdish permanently fixed as a part of the piece.

saucer light: The cup-and-saucer lamp.

saucers: Originally individual shallow bowls at each diner's place, for dipping morsels into the melted butter sauce. Our present-day meaning of term is not the same; our saucer derives from the proper underdish of a tea or coffee bowl.

sauce tureen: Covered sauceboat.

sauer-kraut augur: A curling center bit of iron, with curvate side arms, plunged and twisted into a tub or barrel of kraut to lift out a huge wad of it for use.

Saugus iron: Reference is to the 17th-century ironworks at Saugus, Mass. Cast wares were made here from 1645. The village was known as "Hammersmith."

Saul's bookcase & writing-desk clock: An amazing piece of gadgetry in cabinetmaking; actually a tall-case-clock movement in a bookcase and desk cabinet instead of a standard tall case. [*Example pictured.*] Its equivalent was made as a bureau clock. [*Example pictured.*]

Saulson kettle: Actually a three-section round dinner pail. It is late tinware, made to 1890s at least.

saunders: Sandalwood.

sausage stuffer: Any device for forcing ground meat into a casing. Most are plunger-gun type, but some are fitted with screw and handle, feeding from a hopper.

saut bucket: Salting bucket.

save all: Small pan to hold a candle end; a small boss upon which a pricket is mounted to impale a stub of candle. Some fit into candlesticks.

Savery, William: Cabinet- and chairmaker of Philadelphia, working from 1740s in Georgian styles. Savery and Randolph are generally credited as the originators of the Philadelphia school of fine cabinetmaking. Savery worked to 1780s.

Savery iron: Tinned and enameled ironwares for kitchen use, made at Savery, or Phoenix, Ironworks, Philadelphia and New York, from 1830s. John M'Devitt designed most of the objects. Coffeepots, andirons, sadirons, kettles, large porringers, et cetera. Some are marked.

Savonarola chair: See Chairs, All Kinds.

Savonnerie carpet: Broadloom tapestry-type carpet, named for the original factory, once a Paris soap works. Now part of the Gobelin works.

Savory, Thomas: Wall painter and decorator of Boston and Chelsea, Mass., from 1840s.

Savoy chair: Gallic-era chair of barrel shape, carved and decorated. Generally of oak; some of walnut. Date is from 1450s or earlier.

sawbuck table: Any table top supported on X-members at ends. It is a style of Gallic source, and examples in America are generally of Dutch, Swiss, or Swedish provenance or inspiration. [*Simple example pictured.*]

saw marks: All straight-blade saws, of no matter what date, make the same kind of cut marks on timber. The circular saw, invented c. 1815, marked rounded or curvate instead of straight cuts. Of one thing we can be sure: no furniture made prior to 19th century can display circular-saw cut marks.

saw pit: The pit over which timber was sawed by man power with the pit saw.

saw-shaped: See Square Turning. No lathe, prior to the Blanchard Gunstock lathe of 1820, could turn square members. Therefore, such members, as chair and cabinet legs, balusters, et cetera, were sawed into shape.

Sawtooth: Pattern of pressed glass, more properly called Diamond by many original makers of the pattern; it is a series of faceted diamond forms extending outward to a point. There are many variants, including Sawtooth & Star.

saw-tooth trap: An animal trap of mid-19th century with a saw-blade element bent in a half circle which almost decapitated the rodent caught. [*Example pictured only because examples in collections have defied identification.*]

Sawyer, T. & E.: Makers of melodeons, seraphines, and harmoniums, at Nashua, N.H., from 1850s.

Sawyer shade: Transparent painted window shades, landscape, genre, and rococo, made by Sawyer of Cincinnati from 1840s.

saxhorn pitcher: Alcock of Burslem made this pitcher with low-relief sculpturing of the Distin family, famed saxhorn players.

Saxon: Pattern of pressed glass imitative of simple Stourbridge and Irish cutting; a band of square bosses between short fluting.

Saxon arch: A semicircular arch.

Saxon engraved: A simple pressed-glass form with engraving.

Saxon style: A modification of the ancient Greek rounded arch supported by decorative columns. Gallic, or Gothic.

say: Contraction of sayette, a long combed-wool fabric made at Amiens from 15th century. Also a term for silk fabric, from *soie*.

"say Moses": An old colloquial form of offering marriage. "I did say Moses to Mona and She did say me Nay."

scabeau: A buffit, or joined stool. Little

Miss Muffit did not sit on a tuffet; she sat on a buffit—which was also a scabeau.

scadle: A stand for grain in sacks.

scagliola: Plaster of Paris, glue, isinglass, copal varnish, alum, and other ingredients, forming a hard plastic capable of taking a glossy polish, in plaster pap and oil. Doorknobs, drawer pulls, columns, et cetera. There was an extensive factory manufacturing this product at Albany, N.Y. from 1850s. Invented by H. S. Farley of New York, 1840s.

scale-blue (salmon, et cetera): Scale-like application of these and many other colors.

scale case: (1) Ivory or other rules (scales) in a case. (2) A small weighing scale with pans, counterweights, et cetera, in a carrying case.

Scalloped Diamond Point: Pattern of pressed glass featuring a band of diamond pointing above a series of ovate petals, and with scalloped edges.

Scalloped Lines: Pattern of pressed glass featuring lined bands of onion-form elements.

scallop shell: A form of pottery or glassware, silver, et cetera, imitative of the natural scallop shell, used as a decorative dish.

scamasax: A dagger; sometimes spelled scramaxe.

scamel: A stool.

scarehare: Any effigy placed in fields and hedgerows in the hope of scaring off hares; motion imparted by wind.

scarn; scairn; skarn: Frame used to hold the quills for bobbin weaving.

Sceaux: Porcelain and faïence made at Sceaux Pottery, near Paris, from 1750 to the Revolution.

scenic rug: Landscape rug.

scenography: Perspective drawing.

scent apple: Filigreed metal ball or case holding strong scent. Known from 13th century. Possibly another term for pomander ball or case.

scheppel: A grain measure. Wooden examples are picturesque and quaint, conical in shape, staved, et cetera.

Scherr, Emilius: Pianoforte maker of Philadelphia from 1800s. Sheraton-, Directoire-, and Empire-styled cases. Excellent instruments, endorsed by DeMeyer, pianist to the Emperor of Austria.

Schimmel, Wilhelm: Crude jackknife carver of the Carlisle-Gettysburg region of Pennsylvania who spent most of his life as a tramp, or hobo, carving crudities for whiskey, meals, and lodging. At one time thought to be spontaneous creative efforts, all the work is now proved to be imitative. The carved eagles which have enjoyed a vogue for some years are now traceable to (1) cast-iron snowbirds and cornice ornaments and (2) originals by Dr. Grier, a Presbyterian minister with charges in north central Maryland but whose home was a farm bisected by the Mason-Dixon line. Schimmel carved his eagles, especially item 2 above, immediately after the close of the Civil War. The deciding battle of that conflict was Gettysburg. Every public house in the vicinity wanted a gold eagle for patriotic display. Dr. Grier's eagles were unprocurable from their owners, and Dr. Grier had died. So Schimmel was commissioned to imitate them. It is safe now to date the large Schimmel eagles as the earlier and his smaller items as the later product of this uncouth immigrant and ne'er-do-well. *See* Grier Eagles.

Schinna-Hannes: Correctly, Schinder-Hannes, nickname of the robber baron Hilzerlip, who was executed at Mayence. The term for a ne'er-do-well is still occasionally heard in Germanic settlements and communities such as Allentown and Reading, Pa.; Milwaukee, Wis., et cetera.

schist bowl: Culinary and apothecaries' bowls and mortars, carved or turned from the hydromica and other schists.

schmelze: Mock agate, of glass, blown into various utensil and object forms.

Schmertz glass: From 1855 the Belle Vernon Works, Pennsylvania, was operated by Robert Schmertz. This would seem to be the logical reference.

Schnader painting: For three or four generations a family of this name has painted chairs, trays, tinware, and carriages at Rohrerstown, Lancaster County, Pa.

schnappsflaschen: Swiss bladder-shaped glass flask with "stuck-on" or applied neck. Dark green ribbed, swirled, and dotted glass. Made from 17th century.

schnelle: Tall German stoneware flagons, called steins, with relief decoration in the style of 15th and 16th centuries. Old and rare.

Schnitz Creek: Brook in Lebanon County, Pa. The Pennsylvania version of "Salt River" immortalized as defeat for a politician because Henry Clay was taken up that river in error to make a political speech, 1840.

scholar's chair: A type. *See* Chairs, All Kinds.

scholar's cup: Chinese ceremonial cup awarded learned men, sages, and officials.

school chair: *See* Chairs, All Kinds.

school sheets: Writing sheets of good blank paper, for calligraphic exercise, surrounded by vignettes of historic or educational significance. Mostly English, dating from 1780s to 1840s.

schooner: Properly "skunner," from the Norse, meaning a swift ship. Also a conical-shaped high ale glass for a swift drink.

schrenkeisen rocker: *See* Chairs, All Kinds.

Schum, Philip: Proprietor of a coverlet-weaving mill and dyehouse at Lancaster, Pa., from 1852, prior to which he had a modest establishment in the rural area near the city. First weaver of the Washington coverlet and other patriotic examples, mostly from 1860s. Also made many standard and stock patterns on Jacquard attachment looms. This firm was still operating as P. Schum Son & Co. in 1920s, and still weaving coverlets in the traditional old manner.

Schuylkill glass: Robert Morris, financier of the Revolution, with others established a glassworks on the Schuylkill River near Philadelphia c. 1784. The early product included fine cut glass by the professional German cutter, W. P. Eichbaum. This man made examples of the fine cutting then practiced in Germany before the same techniques were attempted at the Amelung works, Frederick, Md.

sciagraph: Cross-sectional view, especially architectural, displaying interior of a structure.

scientific antiques: These may be toys displaying action of steam, electricity, friction, light, sound, fire, et cetera, or the philosophical apparatus from which the toy evolved. Also all fine weight-scales, measures, standards, and instruments such as barometers, hygrometers, thermometers, globes, astrolabes, chronometers, regulators, plumb bobs, telescopes, transits, et cetera. Medical and surgical instruments fall within the category, and also all adding and calculating machines.

scimitar leg: Same as saber leg; a cabinet or chair leg of curvate form, imitative of the curve of a saber or scimitar. Not an OG curve such as the cabriole leg.

scissors chair: *See* Chairs, All Kinds.

scissors pull: A drawer or door pull resembling the fingerholds of a pair of scissors. [*Example pictured.*]

scissors table: X-supported table, the X's folding as scissors.

scissors tongs: A nipping scissors, the ends being sharp-rimmed cups. Used mostly for nipping sugar from the commercial cones and to lift pieces from a bowl at table. Used from 17th century. Ancestor of the bowed sugar tongs.

scob: A school desk.

Scofield carpets: William Scofield of Danbury, Conn., was a 19th-century weaver of felt and rag carpets. This is most likely reference.

Scofield rug: Not the same as Scofield carpet; here the reference is clear; hooked rugs made from yarn, with the Scofield automatic "jigger-jagger" hooking device.

scold's bridle: Hinged wrought-iron gag in a framework, placed on the heads [*in example pictured, the V in the upright permitted nose to protrude; the lip, inside the ring, was under the scold's tongue*] of "scolds, bawds, and strumpets" from 17th century. These poor women could hide their shame indoors or could walk the streets in their gag, fastened on for so many hours as punishment for too much talking.

sconce: Ornamental wall bracket to hold lamp or candle. [*Various examples pictured in greatly reduced size.*]

scoop back: Said of chair backs with lateral conforming curvature. This term is modern.

scoop chair: *See* Chairs, All Kinds.

scoop scuttle: Helmet-form coal scuttle with glass roweled spur handle and matching hand scoop. Made from 1840s by Tyler of London. [*Example pictured.*]

scoop hod: The American version of the foregoing. [*Example pictured.*]

scorched paper: A homecraft, in which paper is decorated by scorching with red-hot irons held at varying distances from the surface. Some very pretty effects were obtained by protecting the surface with cutouts, resulting in silhouetted forms.

score: A measure of 21 chaldrons. Also 20 gross.

score marks: Scratching or scribing on wood by cabinetmakers and carpenters.

scorifier: A retort for the recovery of precious metal from sweepings and filings.

scorper: Circular or semicircular knife, with one or two handles, used in finishing insides of bowls, kegs, barrels, and other woodenwares.

scot: Assessment, or tax. Probable source of term "scot-free."

Scotch bowl: Shallow iron pot for deep frying. Flaring walls, open top, sometimes white-enameled inside.

Scotch boxes: Sycamore-wood boxes, tinfoil lined, painted with various tartans. Made at Laurence Kirk, Mauchline, and Comnock, Scotland, from early 19th century.

Scotch mull: A pocket snuff mill; a hornshaped snuffbox.

Scotch grandfather: Reference is to tall-case clocks, somewhat undersize (from 5 to 6 feet tall), seemingly preferred as a size by many English clockmakers of 18th century. Not grandmother size.

Scotia ware: Ironstone and earthenware made at Scotia works, Burslem, England, from 1850s. Various owners. Mark is a knot and SCOTIA WORKS.

Scott Pottery: This works was at Cincinnati, operated by George Scott from 1850s.

scouring rush: The Dutch rush; fine sand embedded in the fiber. Used for scouring pewter and other metals.

scrabbled (scribbled) ware: Potters' term for sgraffito, *which see.*

scratch-carved: Intentional scratching, shallow or deep, to form pattern or design.

scratch pan: Lead pan, approximately 12″ x 18″ and 3″ deep. Evaporating pans for brine, to get salt.

screed: Floated-on plasterwork.

screetore: Escritoire; secretary.

screw box: Cutter, or "tap," for making a screw thread on wood of various diameters, set in a boxlike head, with turning handles.

screw key: The monkey wrench. The invention is accredited by some to Taft & Goodman of Albany, N.Y. [*Example pictured.*]

screw nail: The metallic screw designed for use in cabinetwork and other fine woodwork. The spiral is poorly cut, irregular, and the nail is pointless. But these nails served their purpose very well, as they were not self-sinking, but were screwed into bored holes.

screw ring: A screw with a boss through which a ring is fixed loosely. Millions were used from 1750s as hangers, pulls, et cetera. Ring sizes range from ½ inch to 2½ inches or more. All early examples have pointless screws. [*Examples pictured.*]

screw tap: The cutters which gouged out the spiral on wood or metal, to create a screw. *See* Screw Box.

screw-Wedgwood: Term is confusing but of sound basis. Early two-part jasper and cameo vases were fastened together with wrought-iron bolts and screw nuts.

1, Sèvres Glassware. 2, Sewing Tree. 3, Sgraffito Ware (six examples). 4, Shaving Desk. 5, Ship's Table Wineglass. 6, Show Jars. 7, Sharpware Toby Jug and Mark. 8, Shaw "Liverpool" Delft. The bird-in-cage is a dish tile. 9, Shell Flask. 10, Saw Trap. (Nos. 7 and 8 from Virtue & Co., London.)

Later examples have brass bolts and nuts. Brass said to have been used from 1780. In 1903 one expert stated that spurious examples have the screw nut hidden under plaster of Paris.

scribane: A lady's desk or writing table.

scribe's knife: Long metal blade, one end a scraper and cutter, the other a burnisher.

scrick shoe: An ice skate, early examples being a bone fastened to a shoe sole. Introduced to the colonies by the Dutch and Swedes.

scrimshawing: Properly an occupational pastime, especially of sailors on a voyage. Unfortunately the term now, in error, designates only ivory and bone carving, shaping and engraving. Embroidery, whittling, cane making, carving, all these can be "scrimshawing," meaning time-killing, amateur workmanship.

scrinium: A writing case. A box to hold scrolls. [*Example pictured.*]

script hanging: Pen- and brushwork on a large scale, used decoratively. Done on paper, sized linen, and even on leather. A form of calligraphy but more often with pictorial scenes, figures, et cetera. Dutch and Swedish settlers in the colonies decorated churches and rooms in homes with such work. Later, Swiss immigrants introduced the Swiss version of the written congratulations and blessings, a popular art of France and Italy, also practiced in Germany and the Netherlands, England and Scotland. The loveliest *Fraktur* work, so called, is on Dutch and English colonial deeds, and this, since every immigrant getting land was given a deed, is the probable source of much calligraphic work in imitation of the flamboyant initials on the official papers.

scriptore: A desk. Scriptory, scrutoire, *secretaire*, et cetera, are variants.

scrivener's desk: A scrivener was a public writer. His desk was the tall-legged, stand-up form with sloping writing board.

scroddle ware: Agate ware; lava ware; mottled and variegated pottery, some colored in the glaze and others achieving scroddled effect by mixing clays in layers and cutting crosswise before working on the potter's wheel.

Scroll: Pattern of pressed glass showing stippled band with scrolls springing from ovals, and with acorn finials. **Scroll & Flower:** Another pattern, generally of opaque glass, featuring upright rococo panels with a fine spray of flowers, or spiral beading with flowers between. **Scroll with Flowers:** Not a variant, but a different pattern showing Star of David and stippled leaf scrolls. **Scroll with Star:** Another scroll pattern, overlapping circles around a star.

scroll cone: A cone, sometimes mistaken for a spinning top, upon which cord was wound in grooves. When wound, a pencil affixed to cord from the cone, fixed as a center, would scribe a geometrically correct scroll.

scroll foot: A type of carved furniture footing, the English type, used from 1650s, has the scroll turned backward. The French and Flemish bring the scroll forward. [*Examples pictured.*]

scroll pediment: Scrolls ending in

rosettes or other elements, flanking a central pedestal and finial. **scroll top:** The same, in many versions and varieties, some simply band-sawed.

scrowled: Carved in scroll form, as the top rail of a Tudor-Gothic wainscot chair. Scrowled, in this case, means carved, not scrolled, but the term is used to denote both carving and scrolling. A scrowled table is a table with carved, scrolled supports.

scrumbled: Painting softened in outlines by dry brushing.

scruple: Twenty grains; a weight.

scrutoire: The slope-fall-front bureau or desk, so called from 1690s.

sculp: From *sculpsit* and *sculpebat*, meaning "engraved by."

scutch: The flayer used in swingling (beating) retted flax. Also a pointed-head, chisel-peened hammer used by brick masons.

scythe rifle: An emery-coated sharpener and cleaner for scythes.

sea bed: A tiered berth of two or more beds, sometimes with struts and bedboards folding downward against the wall. Used in American homes from late 17th century. Some have a loomlike framework and, with the bedboards missing, stand unidentified as to original use.

sea-horse bottle: The more proper name for the mermaid bottle, *which see.* A scent bottle in the general form of a sea horse, made of blown, tooled, and crimped glass. Mostly from Bristol and Nailsea, but some said to have been made at Sandwich.

sea-horse ivory: Variant term for unicorn horn; the horn of the hippopotamus.

sea kale: Cauliflower.

seal: Any intaglio stamp used to make an impression in wax, on wafers, or on paper. Many varieties, some carved in precious stone, some in metal or ordinary stone. Some set in rings.

sealed glass: Glass marked by an impression of identification or emblem on a prunt.

seal spoons: Early silver, and some few brass, spoons having hexagon-form stems topped with seals. Date is from 1550s to 1650s. Seal blank on face is usually engraved with a cipher or crest.

sea-mark: A beacon, a lighthouse. Also certain church steeples, high rocks, et cetera.

sea pie: The oyster.

Sears & Wood beds: Reference would seem to be to bedsteads made by a firm of this name, Moline, Ill., from 1850s.

Seashell: Pattern of pressed glass named for shell-form finials; one of the patterns finished with wheel engraving, to the order of the buyer, in any one of a variety of available patterns. Also a pattern of cut glass featuring bold curvate fan cutting.

seat furniture: Any item of furniture designed as a single or multiple seat; chairs, stools, rockers, benches, sofas, love seats, wide chairs, tête-à-têtes, settees, et cetera.

Seaux: Pail-form tubs or receptacles; buckets; jardinieres, et cetera.

Seavy pottery: Made at Chelsea, Mass.,

second quarter of 19th century, by Amos Seavy.

seaweed: A marquetry design; also a natural pattern in walnut, esteemed as a veneer. William & Mary period.

secession quilts: Bedcovers of patchwork type with Confederate sentiments, generally produced by the patriotic ladies of South Carolina and Georgia.

Second Rococo: The period in error called Victorian, roughly 1830–70, in France. Also Second Baroque and French Antique revival. The United States accepted this style from 1830s and clung to it to 1880s.

second-size plate: Breakfast size; pudding size.

secrétaire abbatant: Cabinet with an upright panel falling outward to serve as a desk board and revealing desk fitting within the cavity exposed.

secretaria bookcase: The common form of slope-fall secretary with bookcase top.

secretary drawer: Any large drawer which pulls out partly, having falling front, the entire space designed for use as a desk. Found in bureaus, sideboards, and other pieces.

secret drawer: Any compartment hidden, and sometimes protected from accidental discovery, by curious gadgets, levers, springs, et cetera; a feature of many desks, cabinets, and other case furniture of 17th to early 19th century. Some secret drawers are in cornices, some in table valances, many behind pigeonholes or small doored sections of slope-fall secretary desks.

secret joint hinge: The Baldwin patented hinge. A two-leaf hinge with joint but no pin, and no evidence of how it worked. Made thus: One leaf was cast and finished and replaced in the casting mold to coincide with the pattern mold of the other leaf, having bosses and cups into which the hot metal ran, chilled on contact with the cold, and so provided a permanent workable joint. Patented 1783. Sometimes called the Izon-Whitehurst hinge.

section jar: Shallow glass-jar sections with rings and a closure area permitting each jar in a tier to serve as the cover of the one under it, the final jar having a domed cover. Many varieties blown at Millville, N.J., from 1850s to as late as 1900. These are display or show jars. [*Examples of blown and pressed sorts pictured.*]

sedan chair: A transportation chair in a body with doors, fitted with pairs of shafts fore and aft to permit carriage by two (sometimes four) men. Sedan-chair makers were actually in the coachmaking trade, also making the horse-drawn "chair," but they are often referred to in early documents and directories as "chairmakers." So certain ones have been listed as chair- and cabinetmakers when they were chaise makers. **sedan clock:** A clock for use in chairs and carriages, chaises, et cetera. They are fitted with dials of 4-inch diameter or less and have large watch movements. Ancestor of the automobile clock.

Seddon, George: London cabinetmaker of last half of 18th century who conducted an extensive manufactory and shipped merchandise to the Southern states.

sedelia: Altar chair; ecclesiastical furniture.

Seder: Ceremonial plate of metal or pottery; charger form; some examples excessively ancient and rare.

seed spoon: Silver teaspoon of the 1880s having, on stem, midway between bowl and tip, an openwork "basket" for deposit of seeds from canned "fruit" for conveyance to plate without using the bowl of the spoon! This "gastrocity" was designed by Mermod-Jaccard Jewelry Co. of St. Louis, Mo., as a great novelty spoon for the holiday trade. [*Example pictured.*]

seed sprouter: Unglazed tile, approximately 8 inches square, with saucer-form depression in center and a concentric canal. This was filled with water, seeds were placed in the saucer, the entire thing covered with a pottery lid or dome. By this process the germination period of seeds was established by Dr. Nobbe, who invented this gadget in 1860s. [*Example pictured.*]

seek 'em: The old cry to the hunting dog, now "sick 'em." From Anglo-Saxon *secan.*

Seelye furniture: Seth Seelye, cabinetmaker of Lansingburg and Geneva, N.Y., was working from 1800 to 1850. The styles range from Directoire to French Antique. Some pieces are said to be labeled.

seersucker: Originally an East Indian fabric of stripes with mossy frilling between. From *shiroshakkar*, meaning milk and water. Originally of silk and cotton, and all white.

segmented: Of parts, joined into a whole. Segmented generally connotes firm or fixed joining; "articulated" connoting movable or flexible joining.

segreant: Heraldic griffin posture; the figure poised for a leap, wings spread.

Seidenburg, Henry: Furniture manufacturer of Newburyport, Mass., from 1840s. Made many fancy chairs.

Seignouret, François: French-born cabinetmaker of New Orleans, working 1820s–50s. He made many armoires and was a specialist in Louis XV chairs.

seiler: A ropemaker.

Seixas: Fabrics of all sorts, a term confined to the Philadelphia region of Pennsylvania in 1770s. Reference is not to textiles woven by B. Seixas, but sold by him at his extensive retail store.

sejant: Heraldic term for a beast seated with forelegs straight, supporting the forebody.

Sekhmet: Cat-faced goddess of Egypt, sculptured on many effigies and tomb statues.

selan: High glass shade of trumpet or tubular shape to enclose a candlestick and candle. A hurricane-type shade.

self-acting chair: An invalid's sofa and bed, the back attached to seat rails by hinges, the seat proper sliding forward. The upholstery and not the frame was contoured for comfort. This chair was made from 1848.

self-pouring teapot: Teapot with a pump action which forced the hot beverage from the spout. Plated silver, of 1880 period. [*Example pictured.*]

self-threading needle: The first ones of

record in the U.S. seem to have been made at Lockport, N.Y., in late 19th century. The eye had a spring steel side with an angular cut. Pressure on the side enabled user to spring the part, and the thread automatically slipped in. Idea revived in 1940s as "new."

Sellers' riddle: John Sellers of Darby, Pa., in 1770s was making screw-form sieves for sifting grains and seeds. These were mounted in wooden cases. Surviving examples often pose a question to collectors of tools and gadgets. The screening is bent in the form of an Archimedean screw.

Sellew Britannia: Sellew & Co. of Cincinnati was an extensive maker of candle molds, pewter and Britannia wares from 1830s. Issued engraved advertising sheets in 1839 picturing tea services, ladles, spoons, and other wares. The product is marked. Great quantities shipped to South and West.

Seltzer (Selzer), John: Chest and chair painter much publicized by Esther Stevens Brazer and other researchers into early American painting, working at Jonestown, now in Lebanon County, Pa., but in Seltzer's day a part of Lancaster County. The importance given this man as an innovator, designer, and painter is not reflected in any contemporaneous reports. There is an extensive notice of Jonestown in I. D. Rupp's History of Lebanon County, in which all industries of the past and the then present (1840s) were mentioned. Concerning Seltzer, not a word is said. All designs credited to Seltzer are found in printed birth certificates. The man is said to have worked from 1770s to 1830s.

semainier: Literally "once a week"; term generally applied to cabinets with seven or more drawers, as razor cabinets. Most have slate or marble slabs. Many are in Louis XV style. The term is now used for almost any multiple-drawer cabinet.

semi-octagon: Bisected octagon form, yielding a pair of six-sided figures sometimes called "trilateral." The form was used in table tops. [The figure is pictured.]

semlokest: Seemliest. Ancient English.

sempiternum: The everlasting coin. Used extensively in 16th and 17th centuries for table covers, cupboard and chimney cloths; often fringed.

Seneca oil: Rattlesnake oil is one meaning; rock oil, or crude petroleum, gathered by Seneca Indians from surface of pools in northwestern Pennsylvania, is the proper meaning. The rock oil known as Seneca was used medicinally in 18th century.

sensitive Druidical glass: A hoax, perpetrated at the entertainment place in Cincinnati, 1840s, called the Druidical Exhibition. The gist of the hoax was the assertion that the secret of making glass that would fly to pieces when brought into contact with any poison had been solved at Pittsburgh. Drinking goblets and tumblers of this secret glass were said also to have remarkably musical tonal qualities. Many were sold, and for some years any musical glass was called "Druidical."

sentiment mug: Any mug, of any substance, with motto, emblem, sentiment, maxim, et cetera, painted, engraved, printed, or otherwise applied.

Sephardic: Of or pertaining to the colony of Spanish and French Jews who settled at Newport, R.I., in 18th century.

septagon: See Polygon.

sequence: The spelling is 18th century for the bangle now properly called a sequin. This latter term is from a very small Venetian gold coin.

seraphine: The finest melodeon; had double reeds and extensive range. Made for churches, schools, and public halls; sold from $125 to $150 each. Made by several firms at Concord, N.H. Later a small table melodeon with bellows attached to pedal by a tape.

serass: Lead, crystal, or flint glass.

serendipity: The gift of finding; of superawareness. From Horace Walpole's *Three Princes of Serendip*, who were always finding valuable things they had made no conscious attempt to locate. There is more to this than is generally within the average person's philosophy. Studies of considerable importance seem to reveal that if an individual has keen appreciation of, and longing for, certain objects, conditions, and experiences, he need not seek them; they find him.

sergeant's cloth: A tough or long-lasting fabric; a military-uniform fabric. Also the American cudweed.

seroon: A bale made of hide, used in packing dried fruits. From Mediterranean regions.

serpentine: The S-curvate hammer which was the carrier of the glowing match to the primer of the early firearm known as the matchlock. Any form that is undulating or curvately wavy. **serpentine fluting:** Twist-flute turning achieved rapidly on the Huntoon lathe, patents for which were owned by J. B. Rand of Fisherville, N.H., in 1850s. This man made piano, seraphine, and other cases, bedposts and furniture legs with this type of turning.

serre-papiers: A stand with cabinet fitted with paper drawers, pigeonholes, and orifices for writing equipment. One or a pair of these stands generally flanked a *bureau plat*, or flat-top writing table.

server: A sideboard of small size, 36-46 inches wide and 36-40 inches high. Sometimes called a hunt board. Generally in Hepplewhite, Directoire, or Sheraton style. Often the top has an upstanding rim at sides and back.

service bush: The Juneberry bush.

serving-boy: Term is probably modern for a Dutch cabriole-legged stand somewhat like a lowboy but having a top extending 4-6 inches beyond the body at front and sides. Used as a server. The actual pieces date from c. 1700s to 1750s. From Netherlands, France, Flanders, and probably also Switzerland.

serving leaves: The pull-out shelves of some sideboards, mostly in Empire style.

serving table: Any high side table used in serving or service of food in a dining room. Date is from 17th century. Adam and other classic designers flanked such tables with cabinets in three-piece assemblies; Hepplewhite made table and cabinets on one piece. Thus came the modern sideboard from the earlier serving table.

sesame: An oily seed, pressed for the oil.

set hammer: Blacksmith's tool; a heavy hammer used in flattening and swaging.

set kettle: Any kettle fixed in brickwork or other masonry, with fire chamber under it.

setl: Early term for a seat. *Setl thesel,* meaning "be seated."

settle: High-backed, board-ended, and sometimes roofed bench, often fitted with seat cushion. Colonial, from early 17th century to mid-19th; of Tudor style. Some examples of hardwood have paneled backs. The closure style of settle warded off drafts; the piece was most generally used by the fireside. Some examples are curvate. [*Example of early and late cottage types pictured.*]

setwork: Inlay work.

seven-boys porcelain: *See* Hirado.

seventy-two gold: Reference is to the mark "72," meaning 72 parts fine, or 18 karat. This is metric-system marking, in which 100 is pure. Thus 72/100 pure is said to equal 18k, which is 18/24 pure. To be precise, the formula is: 100 is to the parts pure as 24 is to x. Therefore, 72-mark gold is 17.28k.

Sèvres: The finest of French porcelains, made from 1730s. Original factory was at Vincennes. Established at Sèvres 1753 as the Royal Manufactory. **Sèvres glass:** Launay-Hautin opaque white glass decorated in the Sèvres manner. Made from 1840s. Some Baccarat overlay glass vases were also decorated in the Sèvres manner. [*Example pictured.*]

sewar: The arranger of dishes on the table of an important person.

sewing bird: Bird forms of metal (brass, plated silver, iron, et cetera), with attachments for affixing to table or stand. The objects served as holders of fabric in sewing, the material clamped in the beak of the bird. Innumerable forms and styles, not all "bird" forms. In use from 18th century, but most examples are 19th century. [*Example pictured.*]

sewing chair: *See* Chairs, All Kinds.

sewing desk: A sewing stand made in desk form. One was made by the Shakers; these are often now used as telephone stands. Some large examples have many drawers and a large working top. A dressmaker's desk.

sewing-machine doll: A mechanical toy, spring-driven, featuring a doll with china head, sitting at a sewing machine. Clockwork in sewing-machine cabinet works the treadle and imparts motion to the doll. Not a German toy but American-made, by Parminter of Boston, 1880s. There is a sewing bird on the machine.

sewing-machine secretary: (1) Manufactured item; desk box on cast-iron frame like that used on sewing machine. (2) Homemade equivalent using discarded sewing-machine frame.

sewing tree: A staff on a block having deep-cut notch to fit over edge of table. The staff carries thread on spools or bobbins. The device dates from 18th century and continued in use to mid 19th-century. [*Example pictured.*]

Seymour furniture: From 1790s John Seymour & Son, at Boston, Mass., made peerless cabinetwork and furniture in the classic styles, Hepplewhite, Directoire, and Sheraton. It is somewhat unfair to compare the work of the Seymours with that of Phyfe. The comparison should be the other way round. The Seymour workmanship standard was of the highest. One earmark of their work (since imitated by unscrupulous dealers and some owners) is a robin's-egg blue painted in cupboard interiors and desk cavities.

Seymour shears: Steel scissors of all kinds for home use, barbers, tailors, and tradesmen, made by Henry Seymour & Co, N.Y., from 1830s.

Seymour silver: Manufactured fine silverware by Joseph Seymour, Syracuse, N.Y., from 1840s. One of the first to issue tableware in patterns, as follows: Cable, Bridal Wreath, Prairie Flower, Corn, Tulip, Cottage, Plain Thread, and Prince Albert. This firm bought up much old silver for making into new and must have so destroyed tons of old Hudson Valley silversmiths' work.

sgabelli: *See* Chairs, All Kinds.

sgraffito: A technique of pottery decorating achieved by covering unfired redware with a white, cream, or gray slip, drying this, and then scratching through the coating to expose the red. Many pleasing designs so achieved, often further embellished with splashed-on green, purple, violet, and other tints on the slip. Technique originated in China and was used extensively in Italy, whence the name here given derived. The technique, along with decorating redware with lines of white slip fed through single or groups of quills (slip-decorated), was used by Staffordshire potters from 17th century and introduced to the colonies by them and by Dutch and Swiss practitioners in this art. The tulip, pomegranate, heart, bird, figural, and other wares in this style of decoration were not introduced to Pennsylvania by German or Swiss potters but by the Staffordshire potter, Smith. Original term was "sgraffimento," meaning incised outline. Doulton and Watts of Lambeth made ware in this style for many years. [*Examples pictured.*]

shadbush: The servy-tree; servy bush.

shaddock (shaddock-orange): The grapefruit.

shade cord: The decorative cord assembly which rotated the roller of early Holland shades. Now most examples have spring-catch rollers.

shadoof: Term borrowed from modern Egypt; a well sweep with a heavy stone counterweight at the butt end.

shadow: A kind of silhouette portrait, painted on a convex glass, mounted on a white background. Any light casts a shadow of the painting on the background. Probably the original silhouette, dating from 1770s. Gold leaf and black paint were used in making the portrait; in eglomise manner.

shadowless lamp: The oil lamp in which the reservoir was a ring upon which the shade rested. Thus the lampstand was a slender column and the light cast no shadow around the base area. Date is from 1800s. Generally with Argand burner.

Many varieties of style and price range. Not a cheap lamp.

shagreen: Fishskin leather, often used in covering boxes and cases. The knife boxes now well known in Georgian and classic styles, of mahogany and other hardwoods, derive from oak boxes for the same use, covered with shagreen. These date from 1680s.

Shaker blue: Properly, Amish blue. Pigment achieved by mixing ten parts of white with one part indigo.

Shaker butter: Single-skimmed cream, scalded, chilled, churned, worked, salted, and aged in casks throughout a winter before use. It did not become strong or rancid.

Shaker herbs: Culinary herbs grown, dried, and packed by the Shaker communities.

Shaker spice boxes: Tin herb boxes. (Note: The term Shaker Spice box also refers to shaker-top (perforated) spice dredgers.)

Shaker washer: A huge laundry machine, invented by David Parker of Shaker Village, N.H., in 1850s. Used in hotels, institutions, et cetera.

shalloons: Term for the textiles of Châlons, France.

shamash: The side bracket for the Hanukah lamp.

shambles: A slaughteringhouse or pen.

sham bureau: A cabinet with simulated drawers, but used as a chest or as a case for a folding bed.

shammy: Chamois leather.

Shang: Chinese dynasty, 1766–1122 B.C.

Shanghai: Chinese treaty port. Also name of a humorous weekly paper published at Baltimore from 1850s.

shank's lamp: A night lamp with a matchbox in the base.

shank's mare: Travel on one's own two legs.

shanks, button: Since certain button collectors are now carrying classification to extremes comparable to the varieties and variants hitherto believed to be the exclusive vagary of stamp collectors, it is thought advisable to treat with the shank phase of button contruction. A shank is a method of achieving a fastening for the button. Early loops fitted on the back of a button are now called "antiquarians." A "Birdcage" is a shank either applied or made a part of the button, and in the form of a crown or bell, having three or more openings. A "Flat" is a single blade of metal or other substance sunk in the button and perforated with an eye. A "Loop" is a single bent piece of material sunk in the button, forming an eye. "Pinned" refers to a loop or other type of shank fitted through the button and at times forming a boss on the face. Cutouts and Domes are shank forms molded in or formed in the button itself. A "Bridge" is a crosspiece over a ridge or groove cut in button back. A "Bridle" is a form like a miniature flat-iron handle. Cord or Gut shanks are crossed pieces of cord or gut string, through holes in the button proper. Flexibles are single loops of cord, gut, or piano wire. Cones are bumps or pyramids on the back of button, pierced for an eye.

Leathers are leather buttons, with a thong extending at back, as a loop, for fastening. "Pitches" are shanks buried in hard pitch or bitumen, within a button shell. Even these various shanks have variants, some based upon whether or not the glass of a glass button shows a swirl where the shank is inserted! Many brass and other metal buttons carry marks of makers, patent, registry, or other insignia. These, too, it appears, are now subjects of some importance to advanced button collectors. Since the author's office was the research center for *The Complete Button Book* by Albert & Kent, and these minutiae were not deemed of importance to warrant extended inclusion in that volume when published, the data here given is a digest of that research.

shanteepoor: An extra-fine muslin from Bengal. Sold for as much as 500 rupees a bolt. It is so fine that dew falling upon it while bleaching on grass renders the fabric invisible. Very fashionable in 1840s.

shape watch: Pocket and chatelaine watches in curious cases, formed like lyres, shells, scarabs, mandolins, violins, roses, hearts, et cetera.

Sharpe ware: Derbyshire ironstone ware made at Swadlincote potteries of Thomas Sharpe and Sharpe Brothers from 1821. Cane ware, mottled or Rockingham, black and lusterwares. Mark is large SB in rustic border. Extensive makers of the Toby jug. [*Example pictured, with mark.*]

Sharp rifle: American breechloading rifle.

shaving desk: Small slope-fall table desk with at most two drawers in underbody, the desk surmounted by a shaving mirror. Made in all periods from William & Mary to Hepplewhite. [*Queen Anne style pictured.*]

shaving horse: Bench fitted with clamp or vise to hold shingles for shaving or feathering.

shaving mug: Shortly after shaving soap was packed in a mug (c. 1840) instead of in the covered round boxes of great previous popularity, there was almost national acceptance of the idea. Barbershops favored the mug, and soon personalized mugs of clients began to appear in shops. After the war period, from 1865, the character, personalized, and occupational shaving mug appeared as a specialty. Innumerable trades, crafts, professions and callings, avocations, favorite sports, et cetera, of the owners were painted on the mugs in colors. Thousands of barbershops had cubbyholes filled with customers' mugs. The upper-bracket shops, patronized by gentlemen, did *not* permit such mugs on the premises. These shops had numbered or initialed mugs, all alike. The majority of occupational shaving mugs that survive date from 1870s to 1900s. The safety razor ended the barbershop shaving business, and the shaving cream in a tube began outselling the cake type used in mugs. The earliest known shaving mug issued by a soapmaker is that of H. P. & W. E. Taylor of Philadelphia, assumed to have been issued in 1840s as a commercial package.

shaving stone: Treated block of pumice stone used by ladies to remove superfluous hair. In ancient times pumice was used by men to remove face hair.

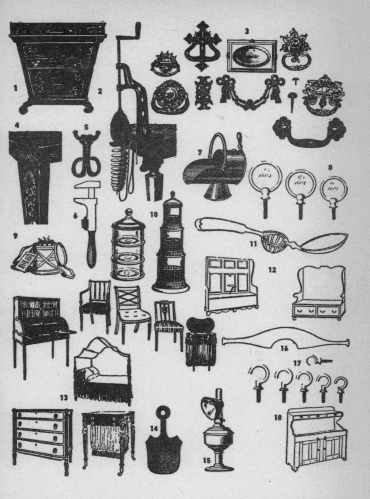

1, Sarcophagus Chest. 2, Saratoga Slicer, or Potato Quiller. 3, Sargeant Hardware (cabinet). 4, Sash Corner (on a table). 5, Scissors Drawer Pull. 6, Screw Key. 7, Scoop Hod. 8, Screw Rings. 9, Scrinium. 10, Section Jars. 11, Seed Spoon. 12, Settles (left, 17th, and right, 19th century). 13, Sheraton Furniture Styles. 14, Shield Palette. 15, Sickroom Lamp. 16, Shoulder or Stick Yoke. 17, Sickle Hooks. 18, Sink Bench (dry sink).

Shaw, Anthony: Maker of great quantities of white granite and creamware for the American market. Pottery established at Mersey, 1850. Early mark is the Royal Arms and "Stone China"; later marks are WARRANTED ANTHONY SHAW BURSLEM and WARRANTED ANTHONY SHAW & SONS OPAQUE STONE CHINA ENGLAND.

Shaw & Rettig: Cabinetmakers of Cincinnati who worked in the Directoire and early Empire styles, 1838–60. Later product was cottage furniture and French Antique style items.

Shaw-Applin furniture: Product of a Boston, Mass., firm, founded in 1790s and still in business in 1880s. The gamut of styles ran from Hepplewhite to William Morris. One phase of the production was church furniture.

Shaw burner: An astral (Argand-type) burner patented by F. Shaw of Boston, who manufactured a variety of candelabra, solar and astral lamps, from 1840s.

Shaw Liverpool delft: Delft-type and tin-glaze wares made at the pottery established by Alderman Shaw from mid-18th century. [*Several examples are pictured.*]

Shawl strap: Metal strip with rotating handle and rolls of tape strap. Straps tightened by turning handle. A bundle carrier. Book straps are of similar construction.

shawm: An early reed pipe for making music; ancestor of the fife.

Shaw stove: A gas stove of 1850s; a decorative table with burners, surmounted by a round oven.

Shaw ware: Dark brown ware with white-glaze lining and white decoration. Made at Burslem by Ralph Shaw from 1733. First kept his process a secret, then patented it and, in an infringement suit, lost both the suit and his patent's validity. Said to have moved to France, where he established a pottery operating to 1750.

shay: Chaise, "one-horse shay" being colloquial for one-horse chaise.

Shearer, L. B.: Furniture manufacturer of Boston from 1840s.

Shearer, Thomas: The forgotten man of 18th-century furniture design. He was the designer in chief of London Cabinet-makers Co. and authorized the designs in the book of prices from 1780s to 1800s. Shearer's designs are classic and were as influential in Federal America as those of Hepplewhite. Shearer is said to be the first designer to create a corner washstand.

Shearer & Pine: Furniture makers of Chicago, 1850s.

shear steel: This phrase, found on some tableware, is a guarantee of the quality of the blade of the knife.

sheathed: Covered.

shebang: Probably from *bagnio*. A groggery; a speak-easy; a blind pig.

she-billiards: The game of table croquet, probably also applied to the game as played on a lawn.

she-brick: An improperly placed paving brick which squirted water when trod upon in wet weather.

Sheeler, Taylor & Bloor: Earthenware potters of Trenton, N.J., from 1850s.

sheep mat: An entire sheepskin, used as a door mat, sometimes dyed.

sheep's-head clock: Type of clock, generally of brass, but some of iron, similar to the bird-cage or lantern clock, but with a larger dial, extending beyond sides of the sheet-metal casing. 17th and 18th centuries.

sheep-shearing chair: It is not a chair but a chairlike contraption in which a sheep was strapped for shearing.

sheet hanging: Wallpaper in rolls.

Sheets & Duffy glass: This firm operated the Kensington Glass Works, Philadelphia, in the 1850s.

sheffel (sheppel): A measure of grain, 6.117 bushels. Roughly 6¹/₁₀.

Sheffield plate: The sheet silver and copper sandwich, imitative of solid silver, made by several manufacturers at Sheffield, England. Considerable misinformation is in circulation, such as "no Sheffield was made after 1840," and so on. The idea of laying a plate or sheath of silver on both sides of a thicker plate of copper was not an original invention. Dishonest silversmiths used the same idea in 17th century, using a heavy core of pure tin. This was subject to very heavy penalty but was *legalized* when promise was made to make the center core of copper, readily detectable by assayer. Further, the makers of this ware were *not* permitted to call it silver plate, as that term was reserved for pure or solid silver of the same grade as the crown coiner's "sterling." They were permitted to call the ware "Sheffield plate," and that name only. Class marks mean little, as the standard of silver to copper varied with makers and periods. In 1760 some makers used six ounces of silver over eight pounds of copper, while others used two pounds of silver over the same weight of copper. Many devices had to be used in order to permit engraving on Sheffield plate, one of which was inlay of a heavy cartouche or panel of silver. The most general practice was to shape the ware with dies and impress the decoration with dies. After the 1840s attempts at galvanic plating resulted in electrochemical methods of depositing the silver on the copper base. This method, no less than the earlier plating by laying on silver in thin solid sheets, resulted in true Sheffield plate. The philosophy of this plate must always be kept in mind: layers of silver on both sides of a plate of copper. The modern method of putting the silver on the copper does not upset the philosophy. But plating on a white-base metal would *not* be in the Sheffield plating tradition. That is plated silver. And in this branch, American manufacturers made such strides that English Sheffield-plate imports became a small item after 1850. Further, American plated silver included spoons, knives and forks, ladles and other flatware, while Sheffield primarily was confined to hollow wares, trays, lighting fixtures, trinkets, boxes, et cetera. The rosy hue of certain old Sheffield plate is due to a wearing away of the silver. It should be remembered also that Sheffield, as a ware, has been exalted considerably beyond its true merits. It never was anything but plated ware, a product imitating true or right silver, providing a brave display for little outlay. It may come as a surprise to some to know that certain small items of furniture, including piecrust tables with two-foot-diameter top and standing two feet high, were made of Sheffield plate from 1800 to 1820s. **true, or right, Sheffield:** Does not refer to this plate; reference is to solid silver made by Sheffield silversmiths from 1773, after the place was granted its own assay office. The Sheffield true-silver mark is an anchor.

Sheldon furniture: Reference most likely is to furniture designed by one Sheldon, who in 1846 advertised his services as a designer to furniture manufacturers in the newspapers of Newburyport, Mass. He worked from 1825 to 1855, practicing also as an industrial and machine designer and as a conductor of drawing schools.

Sheldon lamps: Made by William Sheldon, Boston, from 1830s; table and hanging lamps, camphene, whale-, and lard-oil lamps.

Shell & Jewel: Pattern of pressed glass, described as Victor, *which see.*

Shell & Tassel (square): The confusing quality of this pattern when it is necessary to say that "the square shell & tassel" had "round corners" while the variant "round is smaller and has a recumbent-dog finial on covered pieces." Oh yes, the "square" has a crackle-frosted effect.

shell-back: A shell-form chair back, first noted on Elizabethan "jakes" or night chairs. The meaning, according to who gives this name to a chair, may vary from a chair with shell-carved ornament on rail or splat, to a chair with back of large shell form, invert, fluted, and scalloped, mounted between back posts. [*The Elizabethan "jakes" is pictured.*]

shell block: Wood block bored with 40 or more holes, used in loading shotgun shells.

shell box: (1) A mid-19th-century rococo idea in homemade ornamentation; a box covered with cement, plaster, or a putty of whiting and linseed oil, embedded with all sorts of shells. Made to at least the turn of the 20th century. (2) A special box for shotgun shells, sometimes of leather or metal.

shell coupe: Natural nautilus shells or similar votive forms of porcelain or pottery, mounted and fitted with covers, used as inkwells, or inkhorns, from 17th century.

shell cupboard: (1) Any corner or other cupboard with a shell-form interior top section. (2) Cupboard with exterior shell carving. (3) A collector's glass-fronted cabinet for display of shell specimens.

shell flask: Any flask, blown and tooled, blown-molded or pressed in shell form. These are mostly perfume vials. [*A pressed example pictured.*]

shell-form valance: Any valance of considerable depth, shaped to present a shell-form silhouette. Not carved. Date is from early 18th century; Queen Anne and early Georgian.

shell gold: Powdered gold.

shell sconce: Sconce having a wall plate in the form of a shell.

shell tureen: Soup and sauce tureen with cover, fluted and shaped in shell form. This form, in ceramic ware, would seem to date from mid-18th century.

Shenandoah pottery: Pottery of the great valley of this name, extending from Augusta County, Va., to Harpers Ferry, where the river joins the Potomac; potteries located at Winchester, Strasburg, Hickory, Jugtown, and Thurmont, Va., with the parent works standing at Hagerstown, Md., and Waynesboro, Pa. Redware, mottle-glazed, "buckeye," and for the common people. Swiss, French, Dutch, and other traditional decoration; some pottery picture frames cast from actual French ovals. The original operation began at Waynesboro c. 1830. The rest followed and continued to 1900 or later. The Bell family owned a number of the potteries making ware in this region and of this class. *See* Bibliography.

Sheraton: The furniture fashioned after designs shown in Thomas Sheraton's *Drawing Book* issued 1792-95, originally in parts, as a subscription publication. Mostly copies of other cabinetmakers' works and of designs by David, the artist of the Directoire. Once considered as the creator of a basic new style, Sheraton is revealed as a would-be publisher, would-be evangelist, and would-be anything; he died in impoverished circumstances and was a success in neither his work nor his life. This is a shock to most people, but it is so, and there's an end to it. His designs are in the classic tradition and, because they derive from excellent sources, are fine in nearly all points except where Sheraton himself tried to add or subtract. He was much concerned with gadget, harlequin, and deception furniture. His great contribution is said to be the "twin bed." Most of his muntin designs derive from the work of Cruckshank, the iron and prince's-metal establishment of London, 1780s. After publication of the *Drawing Book*, he later attempted a more ambitious "dictionary" of all styles but died while soliciting subscriptions. Esther Singleton appraised the man and his work in a precise manner as early as 1898. She said he appears to be the Maeterlinck of designers. The extent of error in respect to Sheraton as a stylist can be gathered from the innumerable contemporary references to "Sheraton mirrors." You will not find a mirror design in his *Drawing Book.* [*Examples of the style called Sheraton are pictured.*]

Sherburne, Thomas: Cabinetmaker of Boston who in 1765 advertised tea tables, dining tables, desks, bookcases, bureau tables, and cases of drawers. These would be in the Georgian style.

Sherman frame: A flat, grooved, or fluted molding, crossing at corners, with imposed angular cornerpieces. A variety of ticktacktoe frame. Made from 1850s or later.

Shermer, James: Mirror-frame maker of Philadelphia from 1800s-30s.

sherrisack; sherris; sherry: The fortified wine of Juarez de la Frontiera, Spain, contrived by aging the native wine of the region and then fortifying with a brandy distilled from the same wine. In 17th and 18th centuries called "sack." One of the most popular wines used by the gentry of England; its only rival was port.

shield back: Reference is to the back form and shape of a classic-style chair, generally associated with Hepplewhite; the outline of the back is shield shape with curvate top rail meeting at a point, and downcurves inside the stiles, also meeting at a point.

shield palette: Artist's palette in shield form, with handle. [*Example pictured belonged to William Hogarth.*]

shikii: A silk rep fabric.

shilli-shalli: Designating people who could not make up their minds but who wrung their hands and cried, "Shall I, shall I, shall I?"

S hinge: Any hinge having leaf supports forming opposing S's.

Shin Piece: Trumbull's painting of the Declaration of Independence, engraved by Durand, 1820. The term was invented by Randolph or Roanoke.

shin plaster: Paper currency; said to derive from *chien piastre*, meaning dog money or dog-eared money.

shinty: Game played with crook sticks and balls. Incorrectly "shinny."

ship carpenters' houses: Not houses for these officers, but knock-down houses of mahogany, pine, and other woods, made in New England and shipped in parts to Southern cities. The oldest house in Key West, Fla., is such a house, erected in 1825 by Captain Coussens.

ship chest: Wood chest, plain or covered, with sloping face and back boards to conform to the contours of a ship's walls.

ship decanter: Any decanter of glass or other material, made with a very wide base. All ship pitchers, carafes, decanters, cruets, et cetera, were made with extra-wide bases.

ship grinder: The "sow and pig mill"; a metal boat-shaped vessel with a roller fitting into the V-shaped interior of the "boat." The roller, V-edged, had extending axles on either side. The wheel was rolled back and forth by the bare feet of the operator. A spice grinder. It is a Chinese invention.

Shipman chairs: Fancy chairs made by W. B. Shipman of New York from 1844.

shipmate Toby: Sailor's-figure Toby-type jug; some display junior officers. Also called fiddling Toby.

Shippen, E. W.: Maker of cast-iron furniture, garden ornaments, and figural statues. Philadelphia from 1850s.

shippers: Name given to dealers in furniture who purchased local production and shipped it elsewhere for sale, especially where furniture was scarce.

ship sleigh: A huge boat-shaped sleigh accommodating as many as 36 to 60 passengers for sleigh rides. Mainly noted in the Boston area from 1840s.

ship's light: Not a signal or running light, but a cabin lamp, generally mounted in gimbals so the oil reservoir always had its burner right side up.

ship's ware: Any tableware made for use on shipboard; the china is often marked with name of ship or shipping-line owners. Practice started c. 1810s.

ship's wine: Wineglasses used on ship-board at dining tables. The base is extraordinarily wide. [*Example pictured.*]

ship tumblers: Drinking glasses with bottoms as wide as the side walls are high.

shirred rug: Colored strips sewed on burlap in prearranged pattern, the tapes applied by shirring. Not a hooked rug.

shirt board: A bosom-shaped ironing board; the bosoms were ironed with beeswax. A board for finishing laundering of stiff-bosomed shirts.

shivaree; sherivaree (charivari): A noisy serenade to newly married couples. Sometimes called "calathumpian music." This kind of noisemaking was indulged in to a great extent from southern Pennsylvania to Florida during 19th century. Origin of both terms is obscure.

shiver: The roller of a pulley.

shoe bottle: Glass bottle in the form of shoe or boot, et cetera.

shoe cup: Drinking vessel in the form of a slipper, shoe, or boot. Some of tooled leather, silver-mounted, some ceramic ware, some glass, silver, horn, and other substances.

shoe foot: Sometimes called skid; a base footing in the form of a runner that would slide on any floor, especially on a sanded one. [*Example pictured.*]

shoe glass: Any glass drinking vessel of shoe form.

shoe lamp: Kerosene lamp with glass reservoir in shape of a shoe; the burner fixed on the top, a handle over the heel.

shoe pac: The pac shoe; a moccasin made from a single piece of leather.

Shoninger, B.: Organ manufacturer, New Haven, Conn., from 1850s. He made the Cymbella, Paragon, Chorale, Capella, and Eureka reed organs.

shooks: Barrel staves, ready for assembly by a cooper; parts of packing cases ready-cut for use.

shoon: Plural of shoe; "a pair shoon."

shop-joiner: A cabinetmaker.

Shore porcelain: Joseph Shore, potter of Islesworth, made this ware; a quality of porcelain similar to Derby. Operating to 1800. Thereafter Welsh earthenware was made at the works.

shore whaling: Sighting whales from land and setting out in longboat to harpoon and tow the huge mammals back to shore.

Shorey furniture: John Shorey had a shop or factory at Lowell, Mass., from 1845.

short form: A jointed stool.

Shou-l'ao (L'ao-tzu): The Chinese god of longevity.

shoulder yoke: A carved and formed shoulder piece conforming to contours of neck and upper torso, with extended arms, for carrying pails or parcels. The "stick-pole." [*Example pictured.*]

shovel block: Template, or form, of cast iron, used by blacksmiths to form the bowl or spoon of a shovel. Every blacksmith had at least one.

shovel board: The original of shuffle-board, a game of puck-pushing, originally with shovels. Also the Edward VI shilling, the big one.

shovel spoon: Miniature silver shovel for lifting salt from cellar.

show bottle: Any fancy window or counter bottle, mostly for druggists' shops, but used also by confectioners, sugar bakers, and others. Supplied by glass importers, and many made by Millville Factories, South Jersey, from 1840s. Many varieties, some in tiers, the bottoms being ground-glass pegs fitting in the necks of others. Plain, blown, cut, and pressed. [*Several examples pictured.*] **show jar:** A variant of the show bottle, the vessels being jar form. Some are enameled, painted, gilded, cut, et cetera. Some are in sections composed of from three to six units. [*Examples pictured.*]

show umbrella: Large advertising umbrella. Those used in political campaigns and to advertise unusual products are esteemed as collectors' items; beer, wine, and liquor advertising, lake-ice, fresh milk, coal, wood, and other examples known. Often the covers are in color.

Shrine: Pattern of pressed glass so called because there are designs of crescents and stars in beaded ovals.

shrub jug: The jug used to serve shrub, an 18th-century beverage comparable to our "ade"; made of fruit juices, flowers, aromatics, and spices, with water and sugar.

Shun Chih: Chinese period, 1644–61.

shuttle carving: Elongated, pointed oval gouging in series, as a border or arranged as petals, circles, rays, et cetera. A style originating in Elizabethan or earlier Tudor days, continued as a pioneer form of décor in 1800s. Used on many early chests.

Siamese twins: Chang and Eng, the twins connected from birth by a heavy fibroid band, first exhibited by showman Barnum. A Staffordshire pottery group of the pair was made c. 1840s.

sick couch: Any special couch or bed with air, water, or some special mattress and having adjustable features. Ancestor of the hospital bed.

sick feeder: Spouted papboats, spoons, and other devices for feeding the ill and helpless and administering medicine. Many forms in substances from silver to pottery and glass.

sickle hooks: The cup hooks found in many cupboards. Early examples have pointless screws. [*Examples pictured.*]

sickroom lamp: This term is probably adapted; the lamp is also what is called a pulpit lamp; kerosene burner with metallic chimney and conical reflector for directing beam on spot desired. Examples prior to kerosene age are known, dating from 18th century. [*Example pictured is c. 1860.*]

sideboard: In 15th century this term referred to a series of from four to nine high steps for display of plate and ceramic wares in the dining or "great" hall (in cottages, the keeping room) of a home. Steps were covered with linen or other cloth, even cloth of gold (orphrey). The steps had significance, the highest being reserved for utensils to serve the King. In 17th and 18th centuries, to c. 1760, sideboard meant a flat-topped high table used for service of foods and always placed at the side of a room. Adam designed cabi-

nets to stand on either side of such tables. Hepplewhite, Ince & Mayhew, and other designers made the table and cabinets in one unit. Chippendale did not. In 1738 Joshua Claypool of Philadelphia advertised "sideboards."

sideboard cupboard: In 17th century and late 16th this term referred to what we call a court or livery cupboard. In 19th century the style was revived in the era of "golden oak," 1880–1900, and imitations, fearfully and wonderfully designed, incorporated certain of the general characteristics of the court cupboard and were sold as sideboards.

sideboard lamp: Argand high pedestal lamps designed for use in pairs on a sideboard. Date is from 1790s.

side chair: Not a type but a kind of chair. Though often thought to designate a chair to stand at the side of a room, the term referred to chairs without arms which were used alternately beside chairs with arms. Such an arrangement provided actual armchair facilities to every diner, yet only half of the chairs were armed. The others were "side chairs." There is another factor worthy of consideration; the original designations may have been for the chair *with arms,* the chair having sidepieces.

side hinge: Strap hinge with vertical straps on both door and stile, the hinge joint being centered. This style dates from 14th century.

side-hung mirrors: Mirrors made to hang horizontally, having endpieces matching and of the same general type as the crests on upright mirrors. Usually there are three panes of looking glass, two narrow and one wide. The date would seem to be from 1680s; the period style, William & Mary. [*Example pictured.*]

side lantern: A sconce with a globe, or any lantern form used as a wall bracket. Date is from 17th century, c. 1680s.

side meat: Bacon, salted but not smoked.

siderox: Ironwood.

side table: Any table with or without leaves, having a narrow top, and used generally standing against a wall space. Some have shaped fronts and drop leaf; some designed for use in pairs. The species seems to date from late 17th century. Also any table with folding feature, the entire piece made to stand against the wall in narrow space. The "klapdisch" of the Dutch settlers is such a table. Some 18th-century examples are very complicated, serving as half tables or as full-size tables, yet with top capable of being locked so that it stands against the wall as a large round oval or other shaped panel.

siege: A seat; the ledge upon which glass pots rest in the furnace.

sifter sugar: A spoon with a pierced bowl, used to lift sugar from bowl and sift on food at table.

sigh clout: Straining cloth.

sight measure: The dimensions of a looking glass.

Sigler mirror: Any mirror from the Eagle or Phoenix Mirror factories of S. J. Sigler, N.Y., from 1840s. Gilded pier, overmantel, oval, and other types in great variety made in mass-production quantities. Most examples carry a label of the maker, or did when new.

signal pistol: It looks like a firearm. Orthodox grip and stock, the barrel an extended iron bar terminating in a bowl swinging to one side. Flare powder in bowl was fired by trigger pull. [*Example pictured.*]

signs: Inn, shop, and other signs, whether on boards or as effigies, are today collectors' items. Carved wood, painted-panel, wrought-iron, brass, pewter, leather, ceramic, and other signs are of record.

singing teakettle: Invented 1848 by a coppersmith of Quincy, Ill., it had a whistle on the spout. Also any teakettle which had so much lime accretion in the spout that it would "sing" when the water boiled. These were prized possessions because they signaled boiling and required no watching. Probably the reason the whistle was added.

signpost barometer: Folding barometer, one arm swinging out like a signpost. Thermometers were also so cased.

Sigourney mirror: Charles Sigourney of Hartford, Conn., was an extensive importer of Dutch mirror glass from 1790s. This is probably origin of the term.

Silber lamp: Silber Light Co., Ltd., of London made this one and shipped quantities to the U.S. Glass reservoir impressed with a garland of seven U.S. shields. The firm also exported many burnished nickel reservoir lamps. Date seems to be after 1860s.

Silenius jug: Pitcher decorated with a representation of this classic figure supported by two satyrs in high relief. Staffordshire, 19th century.

silent butler: Covered dish with handle, similar to a bacon dish. Often of silver or Sheffield plate.

Silesian stem: Actually a William & Mary style of turning imitated in a glass stem.

silhouette: Anything cheap, but specifically shadow profiles cut, painted, or mechanically drawn. Named for the economical Controller General of France, 1757, for whom anything economical or cheap was named. The name survives only in the shadow profile portraits. **silhouette chair:** A chair for the subject to sit in while profile likeness was traced and cut. A lamp and a frame holding the paper were affixed to the chair. **silhouette china:** Any ware displaying profiles of genre or classic scenes or portraits. **silhouette en chiffons:** A full- or half-length figure dressing of lace and fabric under a silhouette profile likeness. **silhouette Lowestoft:** (1) China bearing silhouettes of personages; emphatically not Lowestoft and not necessarily the Chinese export porcelain generally miscalled Lowestoft, made from 1770s. (2) Rare export Chinese ware bearing a scene and a medallion, the unpainted portions of the décor displaying silhouettes of personages said to be Napoleon and others of his regime. One service plate of this ware has an auction record of $3500 achieved in 1929.

silhouettists: Listing of the many practitioners of this gentle art is impossible here. See Bibliography for further data

and books which have lists of the makers and examples of their work.

silk: Fabric woven from the spun fibers of the eria, or silk worm, spun and woven in Italy from A.D. 1100. Georgia, Rumania, Spain, Persia, Turkey, and Italy produced silk long before imports from China were in the cargoes of traders.

silk & stuff: A fine shoemaker. The cordwainer made ordinary shoes.

silk grass: The milkweed. Used as quilt stuffing and as wicking since 16th century.

silk reel: The device used in winding silk from cocoons.

Silliman inkwells & sanders: The Silliman Co. of Chester, Conn., active 1820s–80s, was an extensive maker of desk, traveling, and pocket inkwells, sanders, and other devices for writers. Made many turned-wood examples.

silver-case: Silver cupboard. Almost any Southern cupboard on frame was once so called in the antiques trade. The term is probably coined for "quality" appeal.

silver: The precious white metal of great repute, esteemed for ductility and comparative rarity. Polish smelters, known as the "Easterlings," were adepts at its early refining from crude ore. From these experts, working from 14th century, we have the term "sterling" to designate a high standard. The term was first used in England as a contraction of Easterling. Only solid silver was known as "plate" from the Spanish *plata*, meaning silver. When cunning silverworkers began making silverware with a core of tin, they were fined, punished, and the practice of "plating" forbidden. Not until Bulsover resurrected the practice and claimed honesty for it by using a core of copper did the practice become legalized. Then it was handicapped by restricting the descriptive term to "Sheffield plate."

silvered glass: Double-walled art glass imitative of platinum luster pottery, achieved by a mercurial deposit inside the glass and hence untarnishable. Substantially the mirror technique applied to cheap ornamental glassware. Made from 1840s, when it was a new vogue, to 1910s, when Woolworth stores had vases of it at five and ten cents each. These were from Bohemia and Germany.

silvered knobs: (1) Furniture brasses, silvered. (2) Silvered glass knobs advertised 1853 by Jones & Farwell, Boston, as "a new and splendid article for house, store, ship, chest, drawer, and desk locks."

silvered mirrors: Reference may be to any mirror backing, most of which are not silvered, but backed with tin foil floated on mercury. A true silvered mirror was invented 1869 by the Walker Co. of New York, whose process actually put a coating of pure silver on the glass.

silver furniture: Chairs, tables, and even beds, fashioned of silver for wealthy nobles, mostly English and French, early to mid-17th century.

silver grate: Reference most likely is to the white brass (commonly called "German silver" in the trade) grates made by Hampton of New York from 1840s, or to the earlier English grates of prince's metal, also white brass, made by Cruckshank and other founders of London.

silvering: Coating with an infinitely thin layer of silver, as clock and watch dials or surfaces well protected from wear.

silver inlay: Silver or tin leaf amalgamated with mercury, ground into a putty, and worked into undercut carving on wood, brass, et cetera. The amalgam hardened in the cut and was held in place by the undercutting. This is an 18th-century process.

silver lacquer: Collodion in alcohol, painted over newly polished silver. A thin film prevented tarnishing.

silver luster: (1) The platinum luster on ceramic ware that yields all the silver effects. (2) A silver polish made of alum dissolved in lye, skimmed, and mixed with soft soap.

silver-mold ware: Reference is to ceramic wares formed in the same molds used by silversmiths. It is said that some Sunderland luster pitchers were so formed.

silver-mounted: Part silver; silver-trimmed, -decorated, et cetera. Some iron grates were made with silver mounts. Innes & Whitehouse of Cincinnati, 1857, advertised such grates for fireplaces.

silver pipe: A tobacco pipe of pure silver. Date is from 17th century. Rare.

silver resist: Platinum luster on ceramic ware, the white body exposed where the design application "resisted" the setting of the silver glaze. The resist method originated in the Orient as a dyeing technique, perhaps before 10th century A.D.

silversmiths (American) and their marks: Several thousand names and marks were found impossible of inclusion in this dictionary. However, the most definitive single work on the subject, *American Silversmiths and Their Marks, III,* by Stephen G. C. Ensko, contains all of the authenticated names available up to the time of its publication in 1948. Other books on this subject are noted in the Bibliography.

silversmiths (English) and their marks: The same space problem which precludes inclusion of lists of American silversmiths is true also in respect to this subject. See Bibliography.

silversmiths (other): European silversmiths are represented in many hoardings and in some collections of silver in the U.S. See Bibliography.

silver standard (U.S. coin): In 1796 the U.S. coin standard was established at 1485 parts pure silver and 179 parts alloy. Hence the term 1485/1664 pure silver.

silver table: Properly a side table for the display of silver plate. Often with a fretted or arcaded gallery or rim. Date is from 18th century. True examples are of light construction.

silver tishea: A silvery silk fabric of 17th century.

Simons, Menno: Dutch reformer of 16th century who forsook the priesthood of the Church of Rome and preached simple Christianity. His work appealed to the Waldensians of Flanders, who took the name Mennonites. Menno Simons was not a "Swiss émigré," as a one-time museum curator has stated, but a Dutch native. His followers were Dutch, Flemish, Walloons, and English. During the Spanish occupation of the Netherlands, the Mennonites fled across the Rhine to the Palatine and Switzerland. Among these were many who later came to America, including the famous Rittenhuijsen (Rittenhouse) family.

Simons ware: Earthenware by D. Simons of Boston from 1750s.

simpler: An herbalist; a master of simples, meaning medicinal herbs.

Simpson salt glaze: A pipe-clay pottery, salt-glazed, made for the colonial American market by Simpson Pottery, Jackfield, England, from 1760s.

sinapis: Mustard.

Sinclair, William: Cabinetmaker of the Wissahickon section, Philadelphia, from 1800s. Researchers fail to designate styles or kinds. Hepplewhite and Directoire are presumed from the date of activity. If after 1830s, probably also Empire style.

singing dolls: Dolls 22 and 30 inches tall, with organs in the torso, playing a choice of some 14 tunes from paper rolls. Pressing the body operated the bellows and organ mechanism. The doll sang (hummed) the tunes. Made by Massachusetts Organ Co. in 1880s. Working examples are quite scarce, but most non-working models can be repaired.

single-head couch (or bed): By this term, in the mid-18th century, the master cabinetmakers of London designated what we, today, call a "twin bed" when purchased in pairs. Several authorities have stated that no counterpart of the twin bed of the 20th century exists in the antique. This is an error. Ince & Mayhew, London, 1762, featured single-head beds with field canopies, purchasable at their shops singly or in pairs. Also, from the 1830s, American bedstead manufacturers turned out thousands of single-head (narrow-width) beds which were used singly and in pairs.

singles: Finest raw silk thread.

sinister: The proper left side of a shield or bearing; the right side as you view it.

sink bench: From zinc bench; the zinc-lined washing bench used in kitchen primarily for preparation of vegetables and washing dishes, before the days of water conveyed to taps in pipes and carried off in drains. Many varieties from 1800 to 1880s. Most examples currently in circulation and sold since 1940s are the comparatively late ones, factory-made. This is not a dining-room or living-room item, and it is a decorating error to use them in such rooms. They are no more appropriate there than are cobblers' benches. [*Example of sink bench of 1850s pictured.*]

sinumbra lamp: Name is from the Latin, meaning "without shadow." This lamp had an annular reservoir for the lighting fluid which served also as a rim for the shade. The burner was of the Argand type, circular, and enclosed within a glass chimney. Two manufacturers of London made the sinumbra: Parker, from 1820, and Quarrell, from c. 1821. Quarrell's "Albion" was an improvement over the ringlike reservoir that was on a level with the burner; it placed the reservoir above and around the top of the lamp chimney. This lamp also was made in the 1820s. All sinumbra-type lamps are in themselves improvements on a French type made from c. 1810.

Sir John Robinson teapot: Oval-bodied teapot, squat and potbellied, made from 1820s, of Sheffield plate and so named as a style.

sirloin platter: Silver or Sheffield-plate platter 20 to 28 inches long; used, and named for that use, in serving roast sirloin of beef. Date is 1750s–90s.

Sir Roger de Coverley: Character created by Addison and Steele of the *Spectator*.

situla: An ancient pail or bucket.

six-board chest: Exactly what the term implies, a chest made up of two end boards, a front and back board, a bottom, and a lid. [*Example pictured.*]

six dynasties: The group of Chinese dynasties, often classed in one grouping, A.D. 220–589.

six-legged hunt board: An oddity in high sideboards, with the apple compartment reached through a lift-up section of the top. Much Southern furniture from beyond tidewater was not made for the truly aristocratic class of Southerners but for well-to-do farmers who achieved planter status. Often their furniture was made by itinerant cabinetmakers of no great talent, and this was further stultified by some of the customers' demands. [*Example pictured is country Hepplewhite, Southern in origin, rural in styling, and most emphatically not from a center of culture.*]

six marks: Reference is generally to the pottery marks on porcelains of the Ming Dynasty, China. The Dutch revered this ware and called the figural decoration *lange lijsen*, or long-bodied.

Six Nations work: Generally fancywork by American Indians of the Six Nations, sold at Mrs. Davy's store, Niagara Falls, N.Y., from 1840s. Bead, porcupine-quill, and moose-hair work.

sixteen-post bed: Said of the 17th-century beds having a cluster of six small posts around each of the foot posts of the bedstead.

size: (1) Tremulous gelatin, or glue before setting; a vehicle of tacky, adhesive, and sealing quality. Gold size, japan size, linen size, et cetera. Water sizes were of glue or gelatin base, or the albumin of grains. Animal sizes such as rabbitskin, parchment, egg white, et cetera, were also water sizes. Vegetable and mineral gums and waxes were generally dissolved in either oil or spirits of wine. (2) A measure equal to 8 ounces, or half a pint.

skane: Frame for holding the bobbin quills used in weaving. Also skarn, skan, skein.

skaters' lamp: Small collapsible sheet-iron lamp pinned to the clothing or carried in hand by skaters. Some burn oil, others a candle.

skeel: A milk tub of woodenware.

skeleton shell: Finials and other elements carved on Georgian furniture, the work imitative of a shell in pierced openwork.

skeltery: The art of making and manipulating toy theaters. Skelt of London was a maker of parts and vendor of printed tableaux, from which the name derives. Other makers were Lloyd, Park, Webb, Redington, and Pollock. Early to mid-18th century and later.

skewback: A large angular-faced stone topping the two piers of a fireplace or other opening.

skewer head: The holster of a meat skewer, often elaborately modeled. [*Example pictured is by M. Chesneau for Elkington of Birmingham, England, c. 1850.*]

skewer rack: Metal or wood panel with hooks or knobs upon which to hang sets of skewers.

skillet: The original piece identified by this name was a footed deep pan of metal, with a cover comparable to what we call a porringer. This name noted in 16th and 17th centuries. [*Example pictured.*]

skim-milk paint: Two quarts skim milk, two ounces fresh slaked lime, five pounds whiting, stirred and ground. Other coloring matter then added. This was used as any oil paint, but it dried in two hours. The recipe is authentic and documented.

skin paper: Early thin note paper, now called onionskin paper.

skins: Early usage generally referred to the skins of animals with the hair or fur upon them, the tanned leather being called 'hide.'

skirret: A root vegetable about the size of a small carrot; the caraway-seed plant.

skirret pot: The pot in which vegetables were cooked.

skirt: A frieze, a valance, an apron. Skirting. skirt lamp: The petticoat lamp.

skittle ball: The spherical ball with flattened poles used in the alley game of skittles. Any vessel of flattened spherical shape may be called "skittle ball." Skittle alleys were generally in taverns, porterhouses, and inns, often in cellars. The game is comparable to our game of bowling at pins, not like the game of bowling on the green. Skittles played on the green, however, not uncommon. [*Example of play, using cone-shape pins pictured.*]

skynn couch: A day bed covered with haired skin.

slaap bank: A bed in a shuttered alcove; a sleeping bunk. When further termed *op rollen*, it means a bed with legs slotted to receive wheels for ease in rolling, as under another bunk or other bed. Term and style of bed are Dutch. Only colonies having record of use are New York and Pennsylvania.

slab: A four-legged long, narrow, high table.

slab brackets: Metal brackets fixed into walls to support a slab of marble or slate at table height. The true console table.

slab frame: Four-legged stands of wood or metal to hold a marble slab and form an important table.

Slagenhaupt chair: Samuel Slagenhaupt of Taneytown, Md., produced many ladder- or slat-backed cottage chairs. Production began 1790. The seats of the first chairs were of twisted oak withes, not rush. Rush was the standard seating of the late production. Son John carried on the business after 1840s. It is likely that

1, Six-Board Chest. 2, Six-Legged Hunt Board. 3, Signal Pistol. 4, Skewer Head. 5, Skillet. 6, Slip-Slide. 7, Skittle Play. 8, Social-Table Assembly. 9, Soho Lamp. 10, Slut Lamp. 11, Sofa Tester Bed. 12, Smoothing Soapstone. 13, Snow Weight. 14, Spatter Ware. 15, Spring Mill. 16, Squirrel Bell Cage. 17, Spring Jack Roaster. 18, Spear Plate. (No. 1 from *New Geography of American Antiques*.)

any such chairs of this region, no matter by whom made, were called by this name.

slag glass: Agate glass is sometimes referred to by this name.

slant top; slant front: Same as slope front, *which see.*

slaps: Cuffs.

slap-stick: The later form of the stuffed club used by court fools and jesters. Striking bat with cushioned end, with a hinged section that made a terrific noise when the bat was smacked on a person's body. Late-19th-century examples, used in lodge initiations, have a device for firing a blank cartridge.

slat-back: See Chairs, All Kinds.

slate-table: This term is found in 17th-century inventories. Favored for use as meat-cutting tables and for food preparation. Also polished, for use in important rooms. Some are of Gallic or Gothic age, but the style or type was also brought in from China, where slate or stone seats (for summer use) were popular for chairs, and mineral tops fitted on teakwood and ebony table frames. **slate-leaf:** The same sort of table. The slate is of flagstone thickness, ground or worked smooth, and laid in a conforming hollow in the wooden top. Sometimes several pieces of slate were inlaid in a pattern.

slaw; slay: The dictionary of obsolete and provincial English reveals that slaw and slay mean "hinged." Therefore, the slay, or slaw, bed is a hinged bed, either folding into a cabinet or hinged to the wall, as a bunk, but capable of dropping flat. Term is not, then, a corruption of "sleigh bed," as some authorities have assumed. Further, the term "slough bed" (again, not sleigh bed) means a bed that can be slewed, twisted, turned, or folded.

slee: Properly, sley: a weaver's reed.

sleeker: A smoothing tool used by plasterers, foundrymen, and leatherworkers.

sleeping bank: A bunk; a trundle bed.

S-leg: Any furniture leg in the general shape of the S-curve.

Sleepy Hollow chair: See Chairs, All Kinds.

sleepynge chayre: An adjustable chair of 17th century. Sometimes also an arm-and-wing chair, upholstered.

sleigh bells: Harness or shaft bells used to provide a jolly jingle when traveling by sleigh. The practice would seem to date from early 18th century.

sleigh chair: See Chairs, All Kinds.

sleigh cradle: Basket sleigh.

slice: (1) A server with spade-form blade, often of silver, in use from 18th century. (2) A form of peel used by bakers for handling breadstuffs baking in oven.

Slicer furniture: William Slicer was a cabinet- and chairmaker of Annapolis, Md., in 1760s. This is most likely reference. Georgian furniture may be assumed as the style used by this workman.

slick-bone: A shoemaker's and leatherworker's bone burnisher.

slide screen: A standing screen having leaves that can be pulled out on slides, doubling and tripling the area of the screen.

sliding frame table: The early form of extension table.

sliding gate leg: It isn't a gate leg, since there is no "gate" action. Instead, the supporting framework pulls out laterally in grooved sections. It is a variant of the true gate leg, in substantially the same style and of the same period.

sling: A beverage made from some ardent spirit, water, and sugar: gin sling, rum sling, brandy sling.

slip (CERAMIC) : White clay of creamy consistency used as a coating for redware, or for application in lines, or by meticulous brushwork, as decoration. The crudest slipware and the finest pâte-sur-pâte masterpieces are "slip-decorated." **slip cup:** A small pottery bowl with orifices for insertion of one or more quills through which the slip was conveyed for application in lines, dots, wriggles, et cetera, to redware.

slip end: Type of handle or stem on early silver spoons; the stem of polygon shape in cross section, cut at an angle at its free end.

slipper bottle: High-heeled slippers of glass with crude neck and orifice; some of them may be imperfections or fakes.

slipper box stool: Generally a square high stool with a boxlike top section having an upholstered lid, used for storing of shoes and slippers. Date is from c. 1830s to 1900.

slipper chair: Actually a low nursing chair, said also to have been in favor as a seat while putting on one's shoes. Any short-legged chair. Examples date from Queen Anne period as fine chairs, and from 16th century in cottage styles.

slipper foot: Furniture footing of slipper shape, outcurving, and noted on early to late cabriole legs.

slipper glass: Any novelty beverage container of glass in the general shape and form of a slipper. *See also* Boot and Shoe Glass.

slipper warmer: Pottery bottles of slipper shape. Filled with hot water, these were used as "trees" to warm slippers and shoes. Seem to date from 1840s.

slip-slide: Magic-lantern slides displaying motion by changes achieved with slipping parts of glass. These generally are after 1850s. [*Examples pictured.*]

slip seat: Any seat which is removable from chair, stool, or bench. Usually a frame covered with upholstery and fabric, or leather, or a frame covered with tapes, rush, rope, withes, caning, et cetera.

slip ware: Any ceramic ware decorated by application of slip or liquid clays. The term is applied to early Staffordshire tulip-, portrait-, and figural-decorated wares of 17th century and to the wares made in Massachusetts, Pennsylvania, and other colonies and states from late 1760s to 1890s. A Staffordshire potter seems to have been the first slip-ware producer in Penn's colony. However, there is much Pennsylvania slip that is imitative of Swiss wares, with typically Swiss, Swabian, or other colloquial Germanic text lettering. Most of the so-called colonial or Pennsylvania slip ware is of a date after 1800. Some of it is very late indeed. Fakers were potting the crudest kinds after 1910 and getting amazing prices from unwary collectors who were avidly seeking unique and unusual pieces. The Shenandoah Valley potters, Bell and others, made much slip ware to 1900s. The Maritime Provinces of Canada had several slip-ware potteries.

slit back: Slat back; banister back.

slog iron: A sadiron with handle affixed from the nose, or front. From "slog," to lag behind. A hatmaker's iron.

slope front: Slant front; slope fall.

slop frock: A linen garment of smock form; also a nightgown.

slorried: Bedaubed. Painted with daubs or spots of different color.

slub: A candle molded in the hands by squeezing soft tallow round a wick.

slubbing: Process of carding wool into a continuous roll; roving.

sluer iron: Slur iron; a flatiron, sadiron, laundry iron.

slug iron: Laundry iron heated with a removable slug of iron made red hot in the fire. Originally a tailor's handy iron, but made also for home use.

slut: An open-cup fat-lamp, sometimes on a stand. 17th-century form. [*Example pictured.*]

Small furniture: S.C. Small, of Bramson, Shaw & Co., Boston, operating as a separate business, made French Antique style upholstered furniture in 1870s and also advertised a service of restoring antique furniture. It is not clear whether he meant refinishing the furniture then called "antique" (the currently popular style, French Antique) or genuine antiques of the Boston area.

smallwares: (1) Trade term for narrow fabrics. (2) Little items in any line of manufacture, glass, china, iron, brass, et cetera.

Smallwood furniture: Manufactured furniture, made at Newton Corner, Mass., from 1822, prior to which factory was at Charlestown, Mass. In 1855, E. A. Smallwood, son of the founder, employed 75 workmen. Made considerable knock-down furniture shipped to Southern ports and the West Indies. Sofas, settees, divans, tête-à-têtes, cabinet pieces, and specialties; styles range from Directoire through Empire to French Antique. Probably a relative of the Smallwood who advertised antique furniture in 1850s at Roxbury, Mass., but whose advertising probably meant new goods in the French Antique style.

smalt: Dark blue glass ground to impalpable powder and used as a pigment; also coarsely ground to sandlike consistency and strewed on fresh paint as a protective coating. Used from 17th century.

Smede's glass: Bottles, hollow wares, and window glass made at Smede's Glassworks, New Amsterdam, from 1654.

smetz: Cloudy glass achieved by fusing various oxides in the mix to yield a glass imitative of the carnelian or agate.

Smith, A. E. & Son: Stoneware potters of New York City from 1850s.

Smith, Ebenezer: Cabinetmaker of Beverly, Mass., working from 1800. Styles,

presumably, were Directoire or Sheraton and Empire. May have made cottage furniture.

Smith, Elia: Cabinetmaker and joiner of Hadley, Mass., from 1755.

Smith, George: Upholsterer to the Prince of Wales. In 1808, he published a book of furniture designs. The work pictures 158 items with such French names as Escritoire, jardiniere, dejune, chiffonier, et cetera. Directoire, Empire, and Greek-revival influence. *Not* to be confused with George Smith, manufacturer of japanned tinwares at Providence, R.I., from 1850s. Or with George Smith, cabinetmaker of New York City, from 1840s, who worked in French Antique style.

Smith, J. O.: Maker of japanned wares, Middletown, Conn., from 1850s. Also a modern artist and art director who was perhaps the first to call attention to the lineage of modern linoleum, descending from the painted floor cloths of the 17th century.

Smith, John Broadfoot: Early cabinetmaker of Cincinnati, working from 1810s.

Smith, William: Cabinet- and chairmaker of Richmond, Va., from 1840s. French Antique style.

Smith & Co. Britannia: Made at Boston from 1850s.

Smith & Hawley furniture: Dressers, bureaus, tables, sofas, lounges, and other items, of rosewood, mahogany, and walnut, made from 1850s at Cincinnati. French Antique style.

Smith-Burgis Harvard: Reference is to Sidney L. Smith's engraved copy, made 1906, of the Burgis engraving of Harvard College, made 1731.

Smith-Feltman Britannia: The ware bearing this mark was made by firm so named at Albany, N.Y., from 1840s. Also made "Argentina," a silver-plated white metal.

Smith mirrors: Tabernacle-type looking glasses of 1840 period made by James Smith of Philadelphia, who was also a clockmaker.

Smithograph: The pantograph.

Smith-Remington tin: This ware was made at Davenport, Ia., from 1850s; plain and japanned.

Smithson, H.: Japanner and decorator of New York City who, in 1850s, made new painted trays and redecorated old ones.

Smocking: Pattern of pressed glass featuring all-over diamond-pointed shirred bands. Also needlework of fine stitchery, producing ornamental shirring esteemed as fine garment decoration. Some textiles were treated to produce ornamental shirred effects. The original seersucker fabric featured mossy shirred effect in one stripe of cotton, and a gleaming unshirred stripe of silk.

smoke bells: Conical or flattened bell shapes, used suspended over lamps or lamp chimneys to catch the carbon and so protect ceiling from discoloration. Generally with a fastening hook on top. Known in metal, pottery, and glass, the latter of clear, colored, and opaque white with colored bands. Some have fluted, ruffled, or crimped edges, and some are painted and gilded.

smoker: A device with bellows and small combustion chamber for loading with tobacco or other fumigant. In operation it injected a cloud of smoke into beehives, ants' nests, hornets' nests, et cetera, and rendered the insects harmless by drugging.

smoke jack: An iron flywheel or fan placed in chimney above fireplace. Turned by heat, it provided power, transmitted by gears, to turn a spit. Similar vaned wheels were used as devices on chimney tops to improve draft. Advertised in colonies as early as 1750s.

smoothing boards: Long boards, some flat, some corrugated, used in flattening and smoothing wet wash.

smoothing stick: (1) Long tapered wand used to smooth sheets in bedmaking. Some are in shape of elongated bobbins, thickest in center. (2) Bat-form rod with rounded end, pillow-shaped, this section sometimes painted and decorated, used in smoothing pillows, feather beds, bolsters, and bed sacks.

smoothing stone: Soapstone laundry iron; thick piece, spade-formed, bound with iron band and fitted with handle. [*Example pictured.*]

smouch: Any adulterant used with genuine tea leaves to "lengthen" a canister of it. Raspberry, bay, and other shrub leaves were used.

Smyth grate: Thomas Smyth of New York, from 1790s, was a maker of iron-and brass-trimmed grates, perpetual ovens, and fireplace baskets for burning coal.

snail cement: A cement used to mend glass and porcelain; it is a milt, or albumin, from the mucoid sacs of slugs and snails.

snake buttons: Glass globules with snake forms painted or engraved on them. Said to be of Druidic origin.

snake chain: Scalework of gold and silver, curiously wrought and joined to form a chain imitative of the skin of a snake. Noted from mid-18th century as an item of jewelry.

snake fence: Rails piled in crisscross fashion at ends to form an angulate fence.

snake foot: The rat foot, carved without claws, and hence looking like a snake head. [*Example pictured.*]

snake-hair red: Early dyers' jargon for nagkassar buds, which yielded a red color. Not so stupid as it may sound; the East Indian *nag* means snake, and *kassar* means hair.

snake horn: Blowing horn with long tube coiled as a snake. Sometimes called serpent horn.

snake trail: A form of decoration with left and right curvate daubs of color. Also any curvate zigzag work on pottery.

snakewood: Veneer wood from South America, esteemed also for inlay work. Beautifully marked. Also spotted and mottled dark yellow or mustard-mahogany-colored wood from Far East. Some of the mottling displays similarity to letters of the alphabet, and this is sometimes called "letterwood."

snaphance: Flintlock firearm with a cover over the priming pan, snapping open as

trigger flint hit the frizzen; a refinement often found on flintlock guns.

snarl: A curvate horn found on some anvils. Usefulness was in beating the anvil, which transmitted blow to the snarl and so enabled the smith to dispense with use of the separate tool called snarling iron. This tool had an upcurving horn; used in hollowing or raising the surface of a metal. Used by hitting the shank and so transmitting the blow to the snarl end.

snath: The handle of a scythe.

sneaker: Rarely used term for a punch bowl or a "snifter" brandy glass.

snipe bell: A hanger of iron, used in pairs. "Snipe bells to hang a small chist on ye walle."

Snow & Kingman: Boston toymakers who made rocking horses, cabs, wheeled toys, and miniature or child's furniture. 19th century.

snow birds: Wrought- or cast-iron bird forms (sometimes rectangles mounted as crosses and cloverleaf forms) fastened to roof to prevent the sliding off of any layer of snow. Some are eagle form. It is a moot question as to whether the original purpose was to prevent cascading of snow to the street, or to retain the snow on the roof in order to use its insulating factor in winter. Many thoughtful students favor the latter reason. The "bird" is on an iron rod, fastened to roof before tiling or slating.

snow castle: A pure-white snuff of bleached tobacco and other irritants to induce copious sneezing. A medicinal snuff of mid-19th century.

snowdrop jug: Pitcher by Fenton Pottery having as decoration the representation of a snowdrop plant in bloom. Mid-19th century.

snow skates: Ski boards; introduced to colonies by Swedes and Dutch.

snow weights: Glass globes on bases, hollow, filled with alcohol and flakes of whiting, enclosing a cottage scene, sometimes with figures holding umbrellas. Shaking the ball causes a miniature snow flurry until all the flakes settle. Used as paperweights. Originals are of French make, introduced in 1840s or 1850s but most popular from 1880s. [*Example pictured.*]

snuff boat: Snuffbox in form of a ship's hull; the deck raises as lid. [*Example pictured.*]

snuffboxes: The pocket elegancy of men and women for carrying the ground or rasped tobacco known as snuff. Gold, jeweled, silver, enamel, horn, brass, copper, pewter, Sheffield plate, onyx, tin, iron, pottery, china, porcelain, wood, papier-mâché, some painted, some engraved, transfer-printed, stamped. Date is from early 17th century, and made to end of 19th and even obtainable as new items today. There are many historic examples of American interest. Snuff became a favored form of taking tobacco in England during the no-smoking laws of James II. *The Story of Snuff & Snuffboxes*, by M. M. Curtis, tells considerable of the story.

snuff dip: A stick of sweetwood, chewed to a brush, then dipped in snuff and rechewed. A style of snuff-taking favored

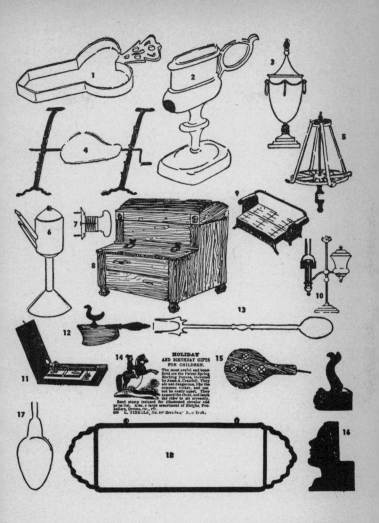

1, Snuffer Case. **2,** Snuffer Holder. **3,** Spice Urn. **4,** Spit Irons. **5,** Swift (one of various types). **6,** Spout Lamp. **7,** Spring Door Stop. **8,** Step Chest. **9,** Stone Sofa Bed. **10,** Stolpe-Walton Lamp. **11,** Stanton Desk. **12,** Sugar Cleaver. **13,** Sucket Fork. **14,** Spring Rocking Horse. **15,** Straw Split. **16,** Stove Rests. **17,** Sugar-Loaf Spoon. **18,** Side-Hung Mirror.

by many women of the South. At one time the excuse was, "This is good for the teeth and gums."

snuff dish: When found mentioned in early inventories the meaning is a tray for candle snuffers. [*Example pictured.*] Also snuffer holder. [*Example pictured.*]

snuffer: Scissors-form trimmer with catching box, used in trimming candle-wicks as the candle burned. Not an extinguisher. Many varieties, ranging from silver to wrought iron. [*Examples pictured.*]

snuff grater: Pocket grater for rasping a bit of carrot tobacco into a pinch of snuff. Some are of precious metal. Terms in use were tobak rasp, tobacco rasp, and carrot rasp. Perhaps the term most used in New England was nutmeg grater. Most of the religious and moral advocates of "no tobacco" in Massachusetts carried graters called "nutmeg" to rasp their own snuff.

snuff jars: These commercial containers, when of small size, are usually of brown or olive glass with wide mouth. The large containers are of stoneware, crock-form, with flat lids.

snuff names: In 1802 these kinds of snuff were offered by most of the snuff makers, including Lorillard of New York and Demuth of Lancaster, Pa.; both firms still in business: dePans, Macouba (Maccaboy), Strasburg, Bolligaro, Dunkirque, Morocco, Saint Omar, Sans Souci, Bergamot, Tonka, and Vanilla.

Snug Harbor mats: Table mats made by inmates of Sailors' Snug Harbors, or resting houses for old sailors. Date is from 1860s.

syntel: A snuffer.

soap griddle: Soapstone griddle; oval, oblong, or rectangular block of soapstone, or shaped pan of same substance. The griddle with the natural lubricant, perfect for pancakes, flapjacks, et cetera.

soap press: A screw press for forming rasped hard soaps into forms.

soapstone: The mineral steatite; the *lapis ollaris*, or potstone. Native to America, extensively mined in Massachusetts and along the Delaware. Used in forming turned and shaped cooking pots and pans, griddles, table tops, bathtubs, sadirons, fireplace linings, stove plates, and other objects, including some figural carvings and turned candlesticks. A paint was made of the powdered stone, or talcum powder, ground in oil and used as a preserving coating for exterior woodwork. A slab of soapstone with a carrying handle was often used as a bed warmer.

sociable: A seat for two. **sociable table:** A drum-form wine stand, with segmental tables forming a half circle or more around it. Rare. [*Example pictured.*]

sockdologer: A fishhook with a locking device preventing any "getaway" by fish. Patented in 1840s.

socle: A plain, square support or base.

soda glass: One of the non-lead-glass group; made from carbonate of lime, soda, and sand.

soda water wagon: The water wagon, often referred to as quitting alcoholic beverages. Wagons hauling soda fountains were familiar scenes on streets of American cities from 1850s. Syrup, ice, and a "fillerup" of "sodywater" made the drink.

sodden iron: Grinding, mixing, macerating, or pulping iron, used in culinary arts.

sofa britska: A sofa or couch on wheels.

sofa grate: Fireplace grate, with front imitative of a Grecian sofa. Advertised as sofa-fronted grate in 1820s.

sofa table: Any table made for use at side or back of a sofa, and at times, on short legs, in front of sofa. Low splay-legged tables are of record from 1700s. Adam period displays first genuine sofa side or end tables. Known in all periods from that time, in classic styles. Some have foldover tops used as writing tables.

sofa tester: A sofa bed fitted with a half tester. [*Example pictured.*]

soffit: Underside of an arch or lintel.

soft ground: Reference is to an etching process yielding prints looking like crayon or pencil drawings. The protective ground is soft and lifted from the plate by the pencil markings made on thin paper laid over it.

soft paste: The semi-porcelain, as opposed to the stoneware body or hard paste. The one great Western ware that is neither soft nor hard paste is English bone china.

Soho lamp: A candle-burning lamp of great excellence and beauty. Many styles, with globes and shades. The candle fitted within the columnar base and was lifted by a screw. Made by Crosse & Blackwell, London, from 1830. [*Example pictured.*]

soies: Bristles.

Solander case: A case in the form of a book. Container for papers, pamphlets, et cetera, looking like a book and so treated. Also an old book with all leaves and rear cover glued together, a large orifice cut out, similarly used. *See also* Rumford case.

solar clock: (1) Sundial. (2) Clock dialed and contrived in its escapement to display solar time. (3) Sometimes the globe clock.

solar kaleidoscope: An effect achieved in a lantern slide to show motion of corona of sun. Several thin disks of glass, properly painted, mounted in brass-ring gearing in such manner as to turn when a rod was turned. This projected the motion of the corona in colors. Date is from c. 1825–30s.

solar match: Patented strike-anywhere match with "non-sulphurous" tip.

soldiers' quilt: Generally patchwork, but some wool worked and embroidered, made by soldiers and sailors in government hospitals after 1865.

sole die: A cutting die in shape of a shoe sole.

soler: The upper story of a house.

solid-fat lamp: Any lamp having a bend or U-shaped segment of tubing near flame, returning to reservoir, can be appraised as a solid-fuel lamp. Solid fuel, of course, means any of the non-liquid fats or greases, as beeswax, mutton fat, tallow, et cetera. These lamps can be used to burn any oil, but only such lamps can burn solid fats. The flame kept the fuel melted while the lamp was in use.

solid jasper: Fine stoneware colored throughout, and not only on the surface.

solleret: Armor of the foot; articulated, pointed steel overshoe. Also any pointed toe slipper, the toe coiling upward.

Solomon's lily: The black calla, or *Aurum sanctum*. Native of Near East.

solo table: Gaming table with niches for glasses, chips, and cards. Generally felt-topped.

Somerset pottery: Any ware made at the seven or more potteries of Somerset, Mass., in 19th century, from 1830s. Specifically the company so named which made draining baskets, colanders, snuff jars, milk pans, bean pots, from 1840s. The Chase Pottery made stonewares from 1847. See Bibliography for books on New England pottery.

Sommerville glass: Made first at Sommerville, Mass., then at Brooklyn, N.Y., finally at Corning, N.Y. Glass pigs are its famed early product.

somno; somnole; somino: The item of furniture called a night stand; the case furniture in which the chamber pot, slop jar, et cetera, were hidden.

Sorrento work: Fine jigsaw work for application as decoration, and also in imitation of Buhl work. A vogue of the 1870s under this name, but done from 1840s, with hand- or foot-power jig saws, as a home- or shop craft.

soup bread: One of the products that started the Borden Co. on its successful career. Meat and whole meal, baked hard, but soluble when dropped in boiling water and cooked. Invented and patented by Gail Borden of Galveston, Tex., Feb. 9, 1850.

soupière: Soup tureen.

sour beer: The true malt vinegar.

Sourland pottery: Wares made in the Sourland Hills of New Jersey from 1780s. Glazed redwares often mistakenly attributed to Pennsylvania.

South Boston glass: A full line of good glasswares, table, decorative, and utilitarian, made from 1812 to 1850s at South Boston Glass Works, Boston, Mass., under various managements and ownerships.

Southern Cross: Battle flag of the Confederacy, a beautifully designed flag. A broad saltire or X-cross form on a field, the cross studded with 13 stars. This is not the Stars and Bars flag, which had two red stripes and one white and a field of blue with 7 stars.

Southern dining table: Pairs of tables, each having one great drop leaf, which, reaching the base of the other, gave it the appearance of a console. Supported by swing-out legs, both leaves and both tables made a long dining table. Empire style, dating from 1820s.

Southern Ivy: Pattern of pressed glass with vertical ribbing and ivy vine with leaves.

Southern sofa bed: The Royal Street, New Orleans, staple; a grand sofa convertible to a bed. From three to six were the normal thing in most plantation houses, where guests came in hordes and stayed for days and weeks. Most of these date from 1840s. [*Example pictured.*]

Southwark Pottery: The Bonnin & Morris porcelain works, Philadelphia, established in 18th century but very short-lived. Only a few pieces of the product are known.

Southwick (Wheeling) glass: Pressed and blown clear and colored flint wares and private mold work, produced from 1850s.

souvenirs: Remembrance items, relics, trifles, whimseys in infinite variety, referring to events, circumstances, areas, regions, places, people, animals, et cetera. So many different kinds of items were made as souvenirs that to list them is impossible here. Chief among the parade of souvenirs now avidly collected are fans, handkerchiefs, patch boxes, spoons, snuff-boxes, glasswares, and ceramic wares. Most of the places, people, and events can be further checked, but not always is it possible to know the maker if the item is unmarked. Certain of the American Art Unions sent a souvenir of consolation to non-prize winners in the form of a print or engraving. Sometimes the residents of a community financed making a souvenir. Of recent years the souvenir silver spoons of the 1880s and 1890s have become collectors' items.

souvenir spoons: Silver tea-, orange, table-, sugar, and other spoons, generally with specially modeled handles, bowls, et cetera, inscribed, lettered, and otherwise identified as souvenirs of a place, event, or person. A phenomenon of the 1880s and 1890s. There is only one current publication listing all such souvenirs rightly within the category of special spoons: *Antiques Digest* carries a continuing record, listing every known example and picturing many.

sovereign's-head mark: English touch mark, 1784–1890, meaning tax was paid on the item of gold or silver on which it appears.

sow & pig mill: Same as ship grinder, *which see*.

sow cup: Leather, ostrich-egg, or coconut-shell body with silver or other metal pig's head, used as a wine dispenser. Probably 16th century.

sowing basket: Broad, flat basket with ears on rim for fastening to belt of user, with handhold opposite. Used in sowing seed in the field.

Sowle mirror: Looking glass made from 1830s by Sowle & Ward, Sowle & Jenks, and Sowle & Co., Boston. Tabernacle, pier, mantel, gilded, and other mirrors.

soy cruet: A tall cruet with stopper, used for the Chinese soy sauce, or a reasonable equivalent of walnut ketchup, sold from 1770s in most American cities. A metallic holder for the cruet was called a soy frame.

spade-end handles: Brass and wrought-iron fixed bail handles, the fastening ends in the form of spade blades. [*Examples pictured.*]

spade foot: A leg end that is in the form of an enlargement of the leg in section, and square or tapered. [*Examples pictured.*]

spaderoon: A small sword, or sword shape.

spa glassware: At the world's many spas,

or health resorts where patients take curative waters, various service flasks, pitchers, vials, et cetera, were in use, all specially made and often marked. The same applies to drinking glasses. Some of the identification is enameled on, some etched, pressed, or cut. Most of these date from 1840s. Many visitors from the U.S. brought such glasswares home with them as souvenirs. The glass is French, Bohemian, Swedish, Swiss, Dutch, and German.

Spalding & Watt ware: Pewter and albata of late production, dating from 1840s. Made by this firm in New York, N.Y.

spandrel: A decorative element of any kind, generally triangular or round, occupying a corner or corners. Applied, carved, painted, molded, et cetera. The corners of a clock face are called spandrels.

spangled glass: Glasswares of the "art" variety with flakes of mica and fragments of glass embedded in the parison and covered with another before formed to desired shape. Some varieties made without recoating. Hobbs-Brocunier and others made it from 1880s.

spaniel jug: Spaniel-form pitchers, the dog erect and in begging attitude. A sort of Toby jug. Date is from 1760s to 1830s. There are many reproductions legitimately made by various English potters.

Spanish foot: A variant of the scroll foot, said to have originated in Spain in 17th century. The footing is an upright scroll, turning backward, the bend being the floor touch spot. Flemish examples reverse the scroll and bring it forward. [*Example pictured.*]

Spanish glass: (1) Actual glasswares of Spain, often diamond-point-engraved and in patterns and styles that are readily mistaken for Stiegel and Amelung. The reason for this is that the design is familiar: the floral basket, tulip, and scrolls. These typically Spanish glass decorations were impressed upon the Netherlands during the Spanish occupation, and to a limited extent upon France. Much of it was made at La Granja de San Ildefonso. (2) Similar glasswares made by Spanish people in Mexico, also mistaken for Stiegel and Amelung by the uninitiated.

Spanish juice: Licorice.

Spanish monkey: Water jug with strap handle for hanging, and small spout. These vessels are unglazed and cooled water contained in them by evaporation. Users tipped the vessel suspended from ceiling; a small stream fell from the spout and was caught in the mouth. An early sanitary drinking fountain.

Spanish style: Said to be the style grafted on Tudor furniture after the defeat and capture of many vessels of the Armada. The furniture on these ships was carved with tulips, sunflowers, and other forms, all of which appear on English furniture and some on colonial 17th-century chests, notably the Hadley and other Connecticut chests and the various court and press cupboards of Virginia and New England.

Spanish white: Ground chalk used as a pigment.

sparables: Small nails, tacks, and brads.

sparking chair: Lovers' chair; a chair big enough for two, preferably snug.

sparking lamp: Any single-wick miniature lamp giving just enough light for pitching woo. Any lamp of the "fairy" type, using a candle of squat design that is essentially a reservoir of solid fat, having one or more special wicks in an elaborate base and globe.

spatter ware: Ceramic wares, originally cheap cottage wares, decorated with a spattering (sometimes sponging) of color on bands, rims, and bodies, the plates frequently further decorated with such motifs as a cottage, sometimes called schoolhouse, an eagle and shield, a peacock, et cetera. Of recent years plain spatter ware has been embellished with additional decoration and refired, sometimes quadrupling its value. Unhappily some plain whitewares have been both spattered in color and embellished in this manner. It is astonishing how many simple advertisements for "plain white old china, preferably marked," have appeared in antiques and collecting journals since the late 1830s. One may well wonder what decoration that plain whiteware now carries.

spatulate: Attenuated in form; fingerlike or broadsword-shaped.

Spaulding stamps: Butter stamps of wood, carved with designs of eagles, tulips, cows, et cetera, made at Meriden, Conn., from 1840s. A. F. Spaulding was the manufacturer.

Spear plate: A Staffordshire willow-pattern plate bearing the "card" of Henry Spear, stationer, of New York, as a part of the design. Date is 1860s. [*Example pictured.*]

spears: Barbed, multi-pointed throwing staffs, the heads of wrought iron, used in taking fish, muskrats, otter, beaver, et cetera. Many varieties, early ones handmade, and sometimes homemade.

specie jar: Specimen jar. Generally of glass, and known in many forms; used mainly for preserving specimens of fish and other animal forms in alcohol. Also any jar for herbs, stick candy, et cetera, as used in shops. These are generally widemouthed jars with japanned sheet-iron tops.

specklebelly: A white-bibbed goose.

spectacle pulley: A pulley with a pair of rollers mounted in a pair of curvate holders, hence the name. Used in fitting early window drapes and shades. [*Example pictured.*]

speculum: Alloy of copper and tin. Also a polished concave mirror.

speech writer: A machine allied to the typewriter which printed symbols and was used to type in shorthand. Patented and made from 1849 by J. B. Fairbanks of Cattaraugus, N.Y.

spencer: A short jacket, somewhat like a mess jacket.

Spencer-Gillman mirror: Made at Hartford, Conn., from 1800s; French *trumeau* and tabernacle mirrors, gilded pier mirrors and others.

Spencerian: A system of calligraphy or beautiful handwriting; a penmanship technique originated by Platt R. Spencer of Fishkill, N.Y., about 1800 and later developed by him at Windham, N.Y., and also at Geneva, O. This system was used in almost every public school in the U.S.

Spencer work: Geometric lathe turning or engraving done on the Spencer lathe, invented by Asa Spencer, 1816.

spermacetis: The true sperm-wax candles.

spew bowls: Silver, brass, tin, and pewter two-handled porringers, covered, with a slightly dished top, pierced in center. Literally a pocket spittoon of the 17th and 18th centuries.

spheric delineator: Four quadrants of a circle, made of thin sheet iron, folding on hinges, designed to demonstrate the mathematics of a sphere. Made by Stephen Manning of Kankakee, Ill., from 1868. Some were also made of cardboard.

spherule: A small ball at the end of a fan element or unit, or used in series as decoration around mirrors, clock-case bottoms, et cetera.

spice cabinet: A multi-drawer cabinet for storage of herbs and spices. Not always a kitchen piece; some, made of mahogany and of walnut, in William & Mary, Queen Anne, and Georgian styles were undoubtedly designed as withdrawing-room pieces, the precious spices doled out by the mistress of the household. From 19th century these are usually kitchen pieces, and by 1840s some took unusual shapes and sizes. There are rotating examples, trick types which bring the spice box desired to a lidded orifice. Spice-box sets of delftware, woodenware, plain and painted tinware, et cetera, were standard items of manufacture.

spice dredge: Shaker-top metal or wooden boxes for sprinkling spice.

spice mill: Grinding device, usually for grinding pepper, cloves, and small seed spices. **spice mortar:** Metal bell or bowl in which spices were pulverized by a pestle.

spice urn: The super-spice container; a tall urn of silver with many small containers within the body. Made also of Sheffield plate, tole, and Pontypool ware. [Example pictured.]

spider-leg table: Probably a 20th-century term for gate-leg type of table with slender turned legs, some not over one half inch thick. Reported, but not verified, are examples with spool turning and with ball or button turning.

spider-web caning: Cane seating and backing in exceptionally fine weave, displaying a circular pattern somewhat like a spider web, the center usually a decorative panel. The last artist in this technique found advertising his service was W. J. Moran of New York, in 1930. The technique is noted on fancy chairs, settees, and other furniture of the classic style, from Adam to Regency. Spider web is of course superior to the crisscross "daisy-and-button" form imitated in glass cutting and in pressed glass.

spigot bowl: Any large footed bowl or urn on stand having a buttonlike protuberance with orifice in center, near bottom of bowl. A tap or spigot of silver, brass, or wood was fitted in this with a cork gasket for drawing off contents.

spill: A combustible straw, generally of coiled paper, but also long slivers of pitch pine and other matchwood, and selected twigs, natural straws, et cetera. Used as a match to convey flame from hearth to lamps, candles, or vice versa. **spill pot:** Any container made specifically for or adapted for use as a standing container for spills.

spindle back: A seat-furniture back contrived with a series of upright rods or spindles. Stick back, chicken coop, and other names are known. Most Windsor chairs are at times called spindle-backs.

spinet: Keyboard musical instrument, the keys connected with mechanism that plucked the strings with quills, or *spina*. The harpsichord. The virginal of the 17th century.

spinet desk: (1) The true spinet desk is a melodeon cabinet-form body with drawers, folding slant-top desk board, and cast-iron cabriole legs; originally made for school use, especially for teachers, from 1830s. (2) Melodeons, spinets, and other small keyboard instrument cases with keyboard and mechanism removed, converted to desk uses. The magazine *Spinning Wheel* was the first publication in antiques field to publish the facts about the true spinet desks. The first maker was the Hildreth Cabinetworks at Lockport, N.Y., which called it "combination" desk because it combined rosewood body with cast-iron legs.

Spinner, David: Swiss potter of Pennsylvania who made slip wares at his kilns in Bucks (Buckingham) County from late 18th century to c. 1810.

spinning chair: A chair adapted to use by, and not primarily a type made for, a person spinning at the wheel or using the rock, or distaff.

spinning frame: The multiple-reel machine invented by Hargreaves, 1767. The spinning jenny. The "spinning mule."

spinning visit: The annual donation party given to the minister of a church; gifts of food, clothing, furniture, et cetera, given in lieu of salary.

spinning wheel: The device that supplanted the distaff, or rock. The wheel, rotated by action of treadle, geared in high ratio to the spinner to which flax fibers were fed by wetted fingers of the operator. Spinners who spun "dry," without wetting fingers, were adepts at the work. Also the name of the magazine of collecting, published since 1945 at Taneytown, Md., an early center of silversmithing, clockmaking, and chairmaking. The name of the grant of land of this region was "Spinning Wheel."

spiraled foot: Carved or turned tapering spiral used as a footing. Style is French and sometimes found on Buhl-work cabinets. [Example pictured.]

Spirea Band: Pattern of pressed glass which might just as well be titled "spidery diamond and dumbbell band"; the band is narrow, and generally two appear on the pieces.

spirit boat: Boat-shaped holder for bottles (generally three) or decanters for ardent spirits. The boat is of hardwood cabinetwork.

spirit gas: The combination of turpentine and alcohol invented by Jennings of

New York, 1830s. The most dangerous lighting fluid ever devised, but it gave a lovely, brilliant light. Thousands of lamps were made to burn it. All "camphene" is a variant of this mixture. **spirit-gas lamp:** Any lamp designed to burn the fluid with reasonable safety. The technique was to convert the fluid to gas in a warming chamber, after which it burned without a wick, through jets. [*Examples pictured showing this detail.*]

spirit kegs: In general, any wood keg for the aging and transport of ardent spirits. Specifically the ceramic or glass kegs with taps for home dispensing of whiskey, gin, rum, and brandy. Stoneware and other examples made at American potteries in early 19th century. Some of the Staffordshire and porcelain examples are very ornate. Glass examples with cutting are quite rare.

spit cup: A cuspidor; a spittoon.

spit irons: Irons made specifically to hold a turnspit, the feet resting on hearth, the head on breast beam of fireplace. Generally with loops for insertion of spit at various heights. [*Example pictured.*]

spit stool: A low stool where the person turning the spit before the hearth was seated. Also spit chair. Some authorities claim the term was also used to designate the cage of a mechanical work for the automatic turning of a spit. A steam spit chair of this type is of record; it is of cast iron and had a heating element inserted in the hearth fire.

spittoon footstool: A stool with wood frame and upholstered top. A treadle extending from under side, when stepped upon, raised top upright, exposing a spittoon. Date is probably from 1870s.

spittoon stand: More properly a dentist's and barber-surgeon's sanitary item; rosewood, mahogany, and oak stands, some marble-topped, fitted with a bowl. Late examples have drain and running jet of water.

spitze: Pointed or peaked.

spitzen: A flagon.

splashboard: A high rim at sides and back of a stand used as a lavabo, preventing splashing of walls when in use. A bedroom piece.

splasher: The thin tile, pierced, commonly called a fish drainer, used on platters to prevent splashing in carving. Leeds, Wedgwood, and other potters made them in quantities.

splash ware: English ware with a decoration in the Imari technique; a gaudy ware. The decoration is Chinese in origin.

splat back: A seat-furniture back; a chair back featuring a splat in the back, generally set between top rail and seat rail, or between top rail and a cross rail between the back stiles, just above the seat. Splats in various forms and shapes. Not slatback.

splayed: Turned outward, raked, canted.

split back: Chair back with slats or banisters, split, the flat side generally turned inward. Some, however, have the turned side toward back of occupant of the chair. Split banister.

split brass: Colonial and early Federal technique of brass-casting round objects such as candlesticks, handles, andiron trim, et cetera. The round parts are cast in halves, hollow, as shells, and brazed together. The line of joining is fine, but it is there. An economical measure to save brass.

Spode: The ceramic ware of Josiah Spode (1733–97), peer of Wedgwood as an inventive and artistic potter. Josiah Spode made salt-glaze stonewares, red- and jasper wares, "old blue," delftwares, busts, figures, inkstands, vases, and specialties, together with fine dinner- and tea wares. Successors were Copeland, at first using the designation "Copeland, late Spode." Copeland firm is still in business. See *Spode and His Successors*, by Arthur Hayden.

sponge tree: Metal tree with many tenuous branches. A druggist's display device. Sponges were impaled on the branches and gave the frame the effect of a mossyleaved tree; a tree bearing sponge leaves. Most examples are from 1880s.

spook yeast: Yeast in its foaming stage, when the spook (spirit) is in it.

spool banjo: The traditional fine banjo-type clock case having a spool-turned device on either side of casing serving as a base for the side brasses or brackets.

spool-turned: The spool turner was a specific workman who turned lengths of wood in his lathe into long sections of spools, cut apart for use and bored for the spindle. This form of turning was rarely used in making furniture, but examples do survive, especially beds. Most objects now called spool-turned are not spool-turned at all but are mostly ball-turned and sometimes button-turned. The button turner was another specific workman who turned wood lengths into button molds. [*These various types of turning are pictured.*]

spoon back: Properly spooned back, meaning the back splat of a chair spooned in shape to fit the contour of the human torso.

spoon boat: The original spoon holder; boat-shaped, a part of a standish, tea stand, or a separate item, as "blue china and pencil'd spoon boats" advertised in 1750s. Mostly of china or pottery, but some of glass or metal.

spoon bread: The suppoon, suppawn, soopone of the Conestoga and Susquehannox Indians, reported by Rising, the Swede, and by Campinius, who translated poon and pawn as "bread." It is corn bread, boiled rather than baked. The Swedes added eggs and baked it in an oven.

spoon collector: A thief of high degree, one of the company of elegants who purloined a silver spoon from every host as a souvenir. Dr. Johnson, Macaulay, and others mention them.

Spooner, Sherlock: Cabinetmaker and manufacturer of furniture, Boston, from 1820s. Made case and seat furniture in the Grecian and Empire styles and advertised the latest London and Paris designs.

spooning chair: Lovers' chair.

spoon seat: Variant of the saddle seat; a chair seat carved in the form of a grain shovel. Some chairs were contrived by adding legs and backs to large grain shovels, part of the handle serving as an anchor for bracing the back.

spoon vase: A silver or plated vessel to hold spoons, handles up.

spoon warmer: Shell-form vessel for hot water in which spoons were warmed. This is the tradition. Another possible use has come to light; that of a rinse for spoons at sideboard, drying by servant before laying at place of dinner during service of a course requiring a spoon.

spot & dot: Trade name for any pressed-glass pattern of dots and spots, as Daisy & Button, and any overlay or imitation overlay in all-over spotted pattern.

spotted glass: Dotted glass.

spout cups: Pap cups; feeding cups; cups having flattened spouts of curvate form and covers, sometimes with an orifice for keeping contents stirred. Made from 16th century; for some reason examples of silver are highly esteemed.

spout head: The connecting element between the eave trough and a downspout; often decorative. Early examples of lead date from 14th century. Cast iron, copper, zinc, tin, stone, and other examples known. An architectural element.

spout lamp: A refined Betty lamp of Dutch origin; many variants of the basic idea. [*Example pictured.*]

spout vase: Any vase with side spouts, standing upright from the bulbous section.

Sprague carpet: Woven pile carpets by W. P. Sprague at his factory, Philadelphia, from 1790s.

Spratt prints: Caricatures of occupations and vocations; the figures are composed of objects associated with the subject: the grocer made of vegetables, the fruiterer of fruits, the shell collector of shells, et cetera. Issued at Boston from 1830s as individual prints, and at Baltimore, 1831, as a small portfolio. Lithographs, some hand-colored.

spread eagle: A favorite form of displaying the national bird; painted, blown in glass, carved, molded, and appearing as a decorative element on many objects.

spread glass: Window glass made by the cylinder method instead of by blowing in crowns.

Sprig: (1) Pattern of pressed glass displaying fan-blade panels with a sprig of fernlike quality. (2) 17th- and early-18th-century term for a corner cupboard.

sprig; sprigged ware: China decorated with painted-on, transferred, or raised decoration in form of rose and other small sprigs. Actually, the designation is proper only when the ware has the sprigs applied as raised decoration. From 1900s any ware decorated with small flowers has been designated as sprig by amateurs of collecting.

sprigs: Light cotton fabrics with printed floral décor, the flowers given a raised effect by embossing between rollers. A true sprig form. Also the basic sprigged fabric; the sprigs embroidered in colors.

spring doorstop: A bumper with spring screwed in baseboards near doors. Made from 1840s by Talbot of Taunton, Mass., a manufacturer of building hardwares.

[*Example pictured, showing details of construction.*]

Springer, Charles: The secretary to the Swedish Minister at London, 1680s. He was kidnaped and sold into bondage; lived in Virginia for five years. Escaping in 1693, he reached Philadelphia, where he became secretary to the Congregation of Swedes in Southwark.

Springfield wagons: Toy wagons made at Springfield, Vt., probably from 1870s.

Springfield ware: Reference may be to chairs or tinware made at Springfield, Mass. In 1837 up to $15,000 worth of each were made here and sold generally by peddlers of the region to the Hudson Valley.

Spring Garden pottery: Philadelphia earthenware, black-glazed ware, and Rockingham glazed ware, made at Spring Garden Pottery of A. Miller from 1850s or earlier. Sugar and candle molds, patch boxes, perfume vials, and druggists' jars also made at this works.

spring hinge: Any hinge with a strong spring enclosed which causes the door to close when released.

spring jack: A roasting oven to stand before the fire; a jack spit in a case closing all but the front, with clockwork turning mechanism. Date is from 1820s. [*Example pictured shows the operation.*]

spring mill: Shallow mortar-and-pestle mill having the pestle attached to a springboard or other reaction device. A wheat- and corn-pounding mill to make meal, based upon a Chinese form. American Indians used a hand-pull pestle attached to a tree limb, which lifted it. [*Example pictured is operated by weight of individual, plus leverage exerted by arms.*]

spring neck: Attachment for a decanter which lifts the stopper. Silver or base metal.

spring pole: A form of well drill using a large pole as a spring, with iron-tipped rods pounded into the earth by man power. First salt and oil wells were drilled thus, prior to the steam-powered drills. A gusher of oil was struck in Kentucky, 1829, by this method.

spring rocker: Chair rocking on a base that is a part of the chair assembly, and so preventing the frequent "creep" that was noted in all chairs not having perfectly aligned rockers. The seat with its rockers was kept in alignment with the base by spring clips, two on either side. In most cases the creep was exchanged for the squeak that developed in these chairs. The date of this rocker is from 1870s. Some authorities say the Shakers made a comparable chair.

spring rocking horse: A fine child's toy; a hobbyhorse having cantering motion by virtue of coil and tension spring mounted on a firm base. Date is from 1860s. [*Example pictured.*]

spring seat: (1) Any seat with flat or coiled springs hidden by padding and upholstering. (2) Seat upholstered over a base of springlike quality, whether hickory slats or a mesh covered with coil springs.

spring swing: An exerciser for small children; a coil-spring device suspended from ceiling, having cords and harness in which a toddling child could walk without danger of falling. Patented 1847.

spruce work: Dried spruce twigs, softened in water and woven into miniature rustic furniture, picture frames, box covers, et cetera.

sprung stretcher: A bowed stretcher, generally affixed to two front legs of a chair, and joined by another bow stretcher from back legs, or by straight pieces. The tension in the bow is designed to keep the leg assembly taut, or "sprung."

spud: A peeling iron.

spue box: Any receptacle used as a spittoon or cuspidor.

spun bamboo: Lathe-spun bamboo, lacquered and overlaid with gold. A Burmese lacquer.

spunge: A sponge. **spunging house:** A debtors' prison.

spun glass: (1) Glass threads drawn so fine they can be woven, as silk. (2) Glass novelties, spun from rods of glass over Bunsen lamps.

spunk: A sulphur-tipped sliver of wood; an early match. Any touchwood; punk.

spurred hook: Wardrobe or closet hook of brass having the appearance of the spurred-end umbrella handle or cane handle. Sheraton period.

spurred stick: Candlestick of tubular type with socket bottom moving by means of a spurred extension in a slot.

spurs: Rowels; goads in form of wheels with pointed teeth, rolled or pressed in horse's flank from heel of a rider. Sometimes on a whip end for use when driving. Date is from Crusades.

Spy print: Caricatures and other pictures from the London publication called *Spy*. Most of them are by Cruikshank, caricaturing high life. There are 72 prints in color.

squab: A small stuffed cushion; an upholstered stool. A pillow for a stool or chair. Also a cylindrical bolster fitting in the curve of a curl-ended sofa. **squab seat:** An extra cushion on an upholstered chair.

squam: Oilskin hat.

square ax: The American ax, having a square face, a single blade, the handle set one third back from the square face.

Square Fuchsia: Pattern of pressed glass having almost square-paneled form, each panel decorated with a fuchsia flower spray.

square halo: When the halo over a statue (originally a solid pan of metal to protect an exposed statue from rain and snow) is square in form or outline, it designated the person depicted was living at the time.

square pattern: Silverware and chinawares in hexagonal or octagonal forms. The term "square" was first used by Gale, Wood & Hughes, silversmiths of New York, c. 1830s. There is mention of it in the American Edition of the *Encyclopedia of Domestic Economy*, N.Y., 1845.

square stile: Said of the back legs and stiles of hickory chairs when they are left or finished square rather than turned. Some have crudely carved cresting on back rail or upper slat. Date is from 17th century.

square turning: A misnomer; what is meant is shaw-shaping. Square timbers sawed and carved in a pattern. Noted in newel posts, columns, chair and table legs, balusters, and pillars. Probably early Gallic, or Gothic, in origin. [*Examples pictured.*]

square Windsor: A Windsor-type chair without a single turned element in it; all spindles, rails, legs, stretchers, et cetera, are square. There is a good example in the Cape May Courthouse (N.J.) Museum. The chair type is peculiar to South Jersey. [*Example pictured.*]

squatting dame andirons: Obscene cast andirons in form of a naked, squatting woman. Late 18th century and early 19th.

squat toilet bottle: The vessel is disk form, engraved, the neck high, with a stopper. Made at Millville, N.J., probably from 1880s.

squeak toys: The bellows-bottomed toys of wax, papier-mâché, and plaster, in form of animals of all sorts, pressure on the bellows causing a squeak supposedly imitative of the call of the beast or bird. The wax ones are oldest, papier-mâché marking the middle period, and plaster being the latest period. Innumerable examples. Made from 1750s to 1920s.

squelette: In skeleton form, as an exposed clock movement or any other exposed movement or works. Also a term for a frypan.

squill: The sea onion. Also a basin or dish.

squilla: The refectory bell used to call inmates to meals. A dinner bell.

squinch: A sconce.

Squirrel: Pattern of pressed glass featuring stippled squirrels on tree branches.

squirrel bell-cage: An early-type squirrel cage with a barrel which, in turning, tripped a series of little bells. Made in colonies from 1750s. [*Early example pictured.*]

squirrel-cage chair: A Windsor chair with a revolving seat.

squirrel teapot: Salt-glaze teapot in the shape and form of a squirrel.

squylour: Ancient name for the scullery (squellery); the place for keeping pots and pans.

stabellen: Swiss term for the flat-seated, fancy-backed chair with stick legs, known also as sgabelli. *See* Chairs, All Kinds.

Stables, William: Cabinetmaker of Baltimore, late 18th century and early 19th. In 1802 he advertised for journeyman upholsterers in the New York newspapers. In 1796 Stables was in Alexandria, Va.

Stacy lamp: Home and ship lamps made by F. Stacy of Buffalo from 1840s. His lamps were used on many canalboats. The man was also a tin- and coppersmith. This is the clue to the type made. Lantern types of lard-oil lamps, with copper or tin reservoirs.

Staffordshire plate: Reference is to ceramic wares banded with silver or Sheffield-plate trim. Wedgwood and other wares were so embellished, dating from c. 1780s.

Staffordshire sanitary ware: Washbowls, sanitary toilets, bathtubs, sitz

1, Stalking Horse. 2, Stand Pan. 3, Stilt Stove. 4, Stump Quilt. 5, Summer Boiler. 6, Swedish Chest. 7, Swedish Cupboard. 8, Sussex Pig. 9, Swan Melodeon. 10, Snuff Boat. 11, Spade-End Handles. 12, Spirit Gas Lamps. 13, Southern Sofa Bed. 14, Spectacle Pulley.

baths, and allied items, decorated with blue willow pattern and gold, with flowers and other décor. Made in 19th century to 1890s. Mott Ironworks of New York were agents of some of the makers.

staggered back: Said of a chair back when elements, generally spindles, do not continue through a rail but are supplanted by another set, these placed not over but between the ends of the first. Noted in some Windsor chairs. They are rare items.

stag-head cup: Variant of the fox-head cups; tot cups in the form of a stag's head, dehorned.

stained glass: (1) An ancient art of transparent painting on glass, the work fixed by firing, used mostly in decorative windows. (2) Art and table glasswares, drinking glasses, et cetera, stained as to color and refired, some with figural, scenic, and other decoration. Some of these wares are early, but most of those surviving and generally available as antique are of 19th-century production, from 1840s. Mostly European.

stair-button: Button-headed nail, some with slip-on heads, used with rods to fix a carpet to stairs. **stair-corner:** Decorative triangular, dished element of metal, placed at the juncture of riser, tread, and baseboard, serving to prevent accumulation of dust in the corner. **stair-eyes:** Eyelets serving as holders for the rods used to keep stair carpeting in place. **stair-nails:** Same as stair-button. **stair-rod:** Metallic rod, often flat, sometimes decorative, used to fix stair carpet in place; set at the base of all risers, at inner side of each tread. **stair-rod eyes:** Same as stair-eyes.

stale: A decoy bird. Anything old, passé, outmoded, dry, or hard.

Stalker, John: The father of occidental japanning techniques based upon those of the Orient. He published a treatise of the art in 1688. This was at the apex of popularity of japanned furniture as high style.

stalking horse: Now rare but a once common item; an effigy of the forepart of a horse, life size, of canvas, straw-stuffed, serving as a screen for hunters in the field. [*Example pictured is from 1660.*]

stamnos: A wine jar.

stamped linen: Reference is to block-printed or transfer-stenciled linens for embroidery. In 18th century tin blocks, often mistaken for cake cutters, were used, the ink being starch water and indigo bluing. In 19th century most of the stamping was done with pricked transfer patterns, pounced with blue powder.

stamped paper: In rolls, it was wallpaper. In sheets, the term was domino. In quires, it was taxed paper. These definitions are 18th century.

stamps: (1) Postage-paid indicators, printed on covers, or adhesives issued by official or private postal carriers. (2) Fractional currency of U.S. imprinted with replicas of postage stamps of same denomination.

stamps, postage: Collectors' items of considerable interest and having worldwide attention on the part of devotees who are concerned with every phase of adhesive label, printed envelope, mailing

card, and stampless cover, with special emphasis on such specialties as original covers, pairs, and blocks of four, adhesives, first-day usage indicia, air-mail stamps, local stamps, carriers' stamps, postmasters' provisional issues and (in U.S.) stamps of colonies (Hawaii, Puerto Rico, et cetera), and stamps, official and provisional, of the Confederate States of America. In this connection, little if any attention has been paid to one of the most costly stamps ever issued and imposed upon a people, the British tax stamp, mandatory use of which fomented the revolt of the American colonies.

standard: (1) Element supporting a top, as a table or stand. Many shapes, sizes, and forms. Lyres, pineapples, eagles, columns, et cetera, used instead of leg supports. (2) A model or agreed-upon size, shape, or style.

standfast candlestick: Screw-bottomed candlestick, or bayonet type that stayed put until forcibly removed from position.

stand furniture: Any furniture of standing type, particularly candlestands, tables, desks, tabourettes, et cetera.

standing bookshelf: A series of shelves between posts or board ends.

standing candelabrum: The multi-candle, standing stick; a column on supporting base, holding branches or tiers of candle sockets. Known in styles from Queen Anne to French Antique revival. Silver, Sheffield plate, Leeds ware, other china, delft, porcelain, and glass.

standing carpet: Ceremonial piece of carpet for personages to stand upon.

standing cup: Ceremonial cup or important drinking vessel.

standing desk: A desk on frame; any desk unit standing on the floor.

standing kettle: Properly, a kettle on a stand with alcohol burner underneath.

standing paperweight: Glass or other weight poised on a pedestal. Some are placed edgewise, as a picture.

standing salt: The imposing saltceller of early days; often of silver, sometimes of gold, but always important. Many were draped with a carecloth of fine fabric.

standing tea chest: Footed tea cabinets or caddies, sometimes castered.

standing tray: Any footed tray.

standish: (1) A writing set, composed of inkwell, sand box, wafer box, and often seal box, taper, and other appurtenances. Later known as writing set. (2) A dish of importance on footing or stand.

stand lamp: This term was generally applied to any lamp with an extra-large lamp-fluid reservoir. Also any lamp on a stand or framework of metal, wood, et cetera.

stand pan: The pan from an umbrella stand, now used as catchalls, ash trays, and planters. [*Example pictured.*]

stand stool: Also called go-stool. A circular pen holding a toddler's body within its compass, sometimes fitted with rollers or casters. [*An example of primitive type is pictured.*]

Stangate glass: Items of glass made by Christy & Co., Lambeth, England, at

Stangate Works; enameled, pressed, milk, and other novelty wares, and colored transfer-printed glass, fired for durability of the decoration.

Stanger glass: The Stangers were one-time apprentices and then employees of the Wistar Works in New Jersey. They and their children were identified with different glasshouses, but principally the works at Glassboro, N.J., established in 18th century and continuing to 19th (1781–1824).

stanniferous: Containing tin, especially tin oxide; the secret of the opaque white and colored glazes on delft, faience, and majolica wares.

Stanton desk: A flat lap-desk especially for travelers. Date is from 1850s. Some are of japanned sheet iron, others of hardwood. [*Example pictured.*]

stanza sampler: Cross-stitchery samplers with amatory or pious verses.

Star: Pattern of pressed glass featuring a diamond-form waffle band, the center of each diamond filled with a four-pointed star.

Star & Oval: This pattern of pressed glass is an all-over effect of prisms, stars, oval bosses, with a floral band around the pieces. The maker tried to get everything on this ware.

starch bellows: An insufflator for dusting starch over foodstuffs.

Star Glass Co.: Makers of lamp shades at Norristown, Pa., from 1850s.

Star of Bethlehem: (1) A quilt pattern featuring a large star in each patch. (2) A sixteen-pointed three-dimensional star woven from bands of paper or stiffened (starched) tape, used as a Christmas-tree ornament.

Starr lamps: W. H. Starr, lamp manufacturer of New York and Providence, R.I., made many types of lamps from 1830s. Shadowless, sinumbra, Doric, parlor, lustral, pillar, and others, for lard oil, whale oil, camphene, and ethereal oil. His chandeliers had a central oil reservoir from which tubes carried oil to burners. In 1845 he boasted that over 10,000 customers had purchased one or more of his lamps. Had several burners of his own patenting. In 1840s he offered girandoles. Mostly brass. Many are marked.

star-rosetted: Entirely covered with stars, closely set. There is a pattern of pressed glass of this name that is so decorated. There are many "star" patterns of pressed glass, not all of which are mentioned in this work. All are found in the books by Ruth Webb Lee noted in Bibliography. *See also* Star.

stars (in U.S. flag): As a guide to dating objects displaying the flag, but only as a guide and not as infallible proof, 13 stars were in use on the flag from 1776 to 1790; 14 in 1791; 15 from 1792 to 1795; 16 from 1796 to 1802; 17 from 1803 to 1811; 18 from 1812 to 1815; 19 in 1816; 20 in 1817; 21 in 1818; 22 in 1819; 23 in 1820; 24 from 1821 to 1835; 25 in 1836. Students can check subsequent additions from the roster of state admissions.

starwort: The common aster.

state chairs: See Chairs, All Kinds.

State-in-Schuylkill: Reference is to the ancient fishing club, the most exclusive and oldest social club of Philadelphia. The dinnerware is embellished with a fish, as, traditionally, are the drinking glasses.

state of plate: Reference is to engravings which sometimes were changed from one printing to another. These changes are said to reveal the first, second, third, and other states of the plate. Copper engravings were not sufficiently hard or durable to withstand large numbers of printings, which is why steel was preferred, especially in 19th century.

State prison furniture: A term of derision for furniture made by or at the Forsters' shop, Boston. Some of the workers were ex-inmates of the state prison who had learned chairmaking and cabinetworking in the prison. The Forsters were supervisors of this work for the Commonwealth of Massachusetts, from 1820s.

statuary porcelain: Parian; unglazed porcelain. Another name was carraran.

Staughton, Anna: The married name of Anna Claypoole Peale. She did print coloring and considerable art work. One of the Philadelphia Peale family.

stave: A measure of nine feet. Also a unit in coopering, one section or segment of a barrel or keg. **stave-cradle:** A basket of staves suspended in a sledge-shaped frame on wheels. Invented 1870 by A. Woodward of Massachusetts.

stead: A device or means of making steady, or steadfast; a bed, steaded, means a bedstead.

steamboat kettle: A hatmaker's felting kettle, generally fixed in a fireplace and not made for general household use. They are large; miniature boilers, usually of copper or brass.

steam iron: A hollow laundry iron connected with tube to a teakettle, which supplied steam for heating. Steam escaped through a vent in the nose. Made from late 1870s, and that's how old the steaming iron is; it isn't mid-20th century after all.

steam kitchen: A steam chest with various pots, fed from a steam boiler on a stove or in a fireplace. Made from 1780s.

steam man: An American machine in the form of a robot, 8 feet tall, with a steam boiler in his "chest"; pistons moving legs, he "walked" at the rate of 30 miles per hour, pulling a carriage. Built and demonstrated 1868, an ingenious American invention.

steam sideboard: The style is Sheraton, the material cast iron, the purpose a combined sideboard and steam radiator to heat a large dining room. The top was marble. This is neither a hoax nor a unique invention. Thousands were cast and installed by the New York Steam Heating Co. from 1850s, made at the company's foundry in New Haven, Conn. A boiler in the basement supplied the steam. The company promoting this altogether sensible idea made many other clever heating elements of cast iron, including statues, eagles, et cetera.

steam sleigh: A huge boat-shaped carrier equally at home in the water or on ice, steam-propelled, invented 1836 by I. D. Corson and tried on the ice at Galena, Ill.,

Dubuque, Ia., and at Prairie du Chien, Wis.

steam toys: Toys in form of steam engines and locomotives, steamboats, et cetera, made in quantities from 1840s. There are many different types, models, and sizes, some cheap and some very expensive.

steatite: Soapstone.

Stedman: Pattern of pressed glass in the Pittsburgh-prism group, the prisms being of varied width, ovate-topped, in petal form.

Steele print: Fireboard squares of paper, printed in colors in various designs. Made by Lemuel Steele of Albany, N.Y., from 1830s. Steele, Richerson & Harris were successors to L. Steele.

steel mezzotint: The steel mezzotint plate was invented by Professor Perkins, an American, who gave one to J. M. W. Turner, 1821, who found it excellent for the purpose. Sartain engraved many of his mezzotints on steel plates. The one big factor in favor of the plate was long life in use, yielding innumerable impressions.

steelyard: The off-center balance scale with a sliding weight on the arm, or yard. In use from reign of Edward IV. Small ones were called a steel foot.

steeple cups: Steeple-form covers for important cups. Made from 15th century, generally of silver. Steeple salts are in the same philosophy. The steeple, of course, has religious significance.

steinglass: Glass imitative of marble and semi-precious stones, onyx, et cetera.

Steinman pewter & copper: Product of the oldest hardware store in the U.S., founded 1744 or earlier, once a trading post with branches as far west as Vincennes, Ind. Located at Lancaster, Pa., famed now because at one time its owner was the pewterer, J. C. Heyne, whose mark, "ICH Lancaster," designates the rarest pewter in the American scene. Pewter and copperwares made by this firm to c. 1820s, when the business was divided and the store remained a hardware store. Also made gunlocks, gun barrels, and other trade items.

stem cup: Small bowl on a stem, with flaring base.

stencil: A cutout pattern for the application of color or delineation of form to any other surface. Also called poonah and theorem.

stencilled coverlet: A bedcover decorated with stenciling.

stenger: *See* Stanger Glass.

stentorophone: A speaking trumpet; a megaphone.

step-chest: A rare Swedish-style chest noted in South Jersey and Pennsylvania, of a style dating from 1640s. Known also in Switzerland. An ideal sea-voyage chest. It is in the nature of a high trunk, with a low chest in front of it, but made in one piece. [*Example pictured.*]

Stephen, Adam: Chairmaker and purveyor, listed in the account books of General Washington.

stepped Windsor: *See* Chairs, All Kinds.

stepping stool: Shaker furniture; a stool with from three to five steps.

step rails: The iron- and sometimes brass-

trimmed rails lining the steps of a stoop, or entrance to a home. Noted in use from 1700s.

Ster. Amer. Man: The sterling mark of Chaudron & Rasch, silversmiths of Philadelphia, 1810–40. Not mentioned by other authorities on silver and so not credited with being among the first to use the sterling mark for quality of metal used.

stereopantascope: Projecting lantern for stereoscopic views.

stereoscope: Viewing device for melding the stereoscopic views to a three-dimensional scene; a bifocal viewer.

sterling: The money standard; the new money standard of Great Britain. In 17th-century new tenor, sterling was worth more than old tenor. The present sterling standard is 925/1000 pure silver. The U.S. coin standard was slightly lower, 900/1000. Scottish standard, 916.6/1000.

Sterling (Mass.) furniture: This Massachusetts town in 1830s had 24 manufactories of chairs and cabinetwares, employing 80 hands and making goods valued at $50,000 each year. No mention is made of the styles, which can be assumed as Empire and cottage, with some fancy chairs and rockers.

stern piece: The carving for the stern of a vessel, as opposed to figurehead. Often an eagle over a shield. The stern piece was in low relief and flat, or only slightly curvate in form.

Stetson lamp: There was a Stetson lamp works at Boston, Mass., from 1850s. This is most likely reference. No data available on types or kinds, but camphene, lard-, and whale-oil lamps may be assumed.

Stetzenmeyer ware: Stoneware made at Rochester, N.Y., by Stetzenmeyer and Goetzmann from 1850s. Cream pots, jugs, jars, butter crocks, churns, chamber pots, beer and soda-water bottles are of record and marked by this firm.

Steubenville glass: Reference is to the glass made at Steubenville, O., from 1830s. Blown and pressed wares, highly esteemed in Ohio as relics of early glassmaking in that state.

Stevengraphs; Stevens silks: Jacquard-loomed ribbon pictures marked "Woven in Silk by Thomas Stevens." Thousands sold during the N.Y. Crystal Palace exposition, 1850s, and at the Centennial, 1876.

Stevens, Andrew: Cabinetmaker of New York who in 1840s advertised antique furniture made to order. He was referring to the "style antique" recently imported from France, meaning Louis XV revival, now called Victorian.

Stevens, Charles: Engraver of New Orleans, working in 1850s.

Stevenson ware: There were a number of potters named Stevenson who operated mainly in 19th century and whose wares were exported to the U.S. The details are beyond the compass of this work but may be had from certain of the works mentioned in the Bibliography.

Stevens toys: The J. & E. Stevens Co. of Cromwell, Conn., was established 1843. In 1853 they produced iron toys. By 1870 their line was composed of 250 different toy items, including steam engines, mechanical banks, cap pistols, sand toys, and other specialties. Prior to 1853 the production was limited to iron housewares.

stew: (1) Slow-boiled or simmered food. (2) Hot bath. (3) A small fishpond.

Stewart box: Confection boxes, originally for gum paste and other specialties made by Stewart & Co., 1850s. Cardboard, covered with gold paper. Stewart made the gumdrops but not the boxes.

stick barometer: Any upright column housing a fluid barometer, the registering part in a hooded top. A wall barometer.

stick chair: See Chairs, All Kinds.

stick yoke: A narrow, pointed oval framework of wood with shoulder pads.

Stiegel glass: Any and all glass made at the American Flint Glass Works of Henry W. Stiegel at Manheim, Lancaster County, Pa., from 1765. Stiegel imitated two glassmaking traditions, largely because his workmen knew these traditions: the Bristol, England, and the Fluhli Swiss methods and product styles. No absolutely authenticated piece of Stiegel is known, although many examples are logically credited to his manufacture because they were at one time quite commonly owned in Lancaster County. Much misinformation is current in respect to this German immigrant, who was probably a redemptioner under contract with the Stedman combine of Philadelphia. The Stedmans owned a part of everything Stiegel attempted in iron and glass manufacture, real estate and town planning. Stiegel-type wares in colors now command fabulous prices. The best known are saltcellars, creamers, sugar bowls, engraved rummers, and enameled bottles and glasses.

Stiff coverlet: Any woven coverlets marked "Stiff" are probably by J. Stiff of New Milford, Pa., working from 1840s.

stile: Upright element of any kind, as the frame of a door, the upright columns or corners of a chest, rear leg and back supports of a chair. **stile & rail:** The uprights and the attached cross members.

stile-gated: A pedestal-type drop-leaf table with a wide center gate, pivoted at its own center to support both leaves.

Stiles desk: A reading desk looking like a cabinet but having leaves on both sides, with tuck-away legs. A late gadget invented 1870s by a Mrs. E. W. Stiles.

Stiles furniture: Probable reference, if Midwestern, is furniture from the factory of William C. Stiles, Columbus, O., established in late 1830s. Empire, cottage, and French Antique.

Stillwell grate: One possible reference is grates, fenders, and fireplace tools made by G. W. Stillwell of Brooklyn, N.Y., working in 1840s.

stilt stove: A small stove of wrought iron, cast iron, or soapstone, on very high iron legs, braced with stretchers, and connected to flue with a pipe. Dutch; a shop heater or chamber stove, dating from 1700s. [*Example pictured.*]

Stimpson frame: An embroidery frame, very complicated and gadgety, invented by a Mrs. Stimpson and sold generally in 1850s.

Stimson, Henry L.: Famed lawyer, Secretary of War in F. D. Roosevelt's cabinet.

In 1873, he posed for the boy figure in the Hide-and-Seek group by John Rogers.

stinkpot: A smudge pot; also an early poison-gas idea; earthen pot charged with powder, brimstone, and other combustibles giving forth choking smoke and fumes. A fumigating device.

stinkstone: Inelegant but correct term for a species of fluor spar which emits a fetid odor when struck, fractured, or rubbed.

Stinson prints: Souvenir pictures given as premiums with magazine published by George Stinson of Portland, Me., 1880s.

Stippled: Generic patterns of pressed glass, as follows: Stippled Band, Stippled Bar, Stippled Chain, Stippled Clover, Stippled Daisy, Stippled Grape, Stippled Grape Festoon, Stippled Medallion, Stippled Star, Stippled Woodflower. Space does not permit detailed description of all these types and variants. See books by Ruth Webb Lee in Bibliography.

stipple engraving: Engraving on metal plates achieved by innumerable dots, incised, varying in size and density, and producing all the variants in tone requisite to portrayal of the subject. Printed the same as line engraving, by filling the dots with ink, wiping plate surface clean, and passing through rollers with a sheet of dampened paper.

stirrup handle: Rigid metal handles of stirrup form affixed to jugs and other pouring vessels.

stirrups: The toe and instep rests used in horseback riding. Many varieties, some very ornamental and of overshoe form.

stitched seat: Upholstered seat, one meaning of which is overupholstered; the seat cover carried downward to the wood frame and fixed with gimp and nails. Another meaning is embroidered upholstery fabric seating.

Stitcher & Clemmens: Cabinetmakers of Baltimore from 1790s to 1820s. Said to have worked in classic styles of Hepplewhite, Directoire, and Sheraton.

stitches; stitchery: These techniques of needlework in 17th and 18th centuries were named. The most generally known were tent, purl, fern, fin, chain, bread, Rosemary, mowle, fisher, whip, cross, brush, queen, Spanish, stem, split, flat. Needle point describes (1) *petit point*, which is a stitch covering one mesh of the background fabric, and (2) *gros point*, which covers two meshes. Also, the former was often done in silk while the latter was done in wool. Cross stitch is the X form achieved by two stitches. Tent stitch is a single diagonal stitch in alternating series, not crossing, as a row of V's, points up.

stitzen: A flagon. Term is Hungarian.

stockbuckle: A buckle used with the stock collar as a fastener in 18th century. Often of silver or gold.

stocking: Originally the cloth from which hose patterns were cut and stitched. When hose were knit and formed in the making, the term stocking was also applied, although the hose were not made of stocking. Knitted hose would seem to date from 15th century. There are some excellent examples of steel chain hose, used as armor, which appear to be "knitted."

stock toe: A degenerate form of the so-called Marlborough leg; a plinth at the foot of a square or tapered square leg, having a molding around its juncture. Date is probably 1790s–1810s. [*Example pictured.*]

Stoddard glass: Glass made by any of the four factories at Stoddard, N.H., from 1840s to 1880s. Generically, any dark green glass with twist decoration; inkwells, medicine bottles, water bottles, flasks, et cetera. Some lily-pad pitchers, preserve jars, and mold-blown wares. See Bibliography for books on glass.

Stokes laundry mill: A washing machine, or mill, made and sold for household use by Richard Stokes of Philadelphia from 1790s.

Stokes mirrors: Tabernacle-type mirrors made by or for James Stokes, Philadelphia, from 1800s. May also have made other types. He is listed as a merchant in 1797.

stolen: At one time this term meant "taken from its proper place," whether by purchase or theft.

Stolpe-Walton lamp: It is a St. Germain student-type lamp dispensing with the brass knurled side regulator of the wick (which got very hot) and controlling the wick from a knob at bottom of burner. Made from 1870s. [*Example pictured.*]

stomach warmer: A three-lobed metallic bottle assembly for use in warming parts of body, such as breast or stomach, hips and the shoulder area.

stone: Weight of 14 pounds. Two cloves.

stone bee: A community party to clear land of stones.

stone boat: A sledge for moving large stones.

stone filter: Two stoneware jars, the upper having a special porous bottom, permitting water to seep through and be cleansed in the process.

stone paper: Rag-paper pulp with glue, oil, and mineral filler, used as building paper. Made in 18th century.

stone pick: A heavy three-pronged form for loosening and piling stones. Some of late date had detachable and replaceable tines.

stone scale: A weight scale divided into stones and pounds.

Stone sofa bed: A sofa that converted into a bed; Empire style, mahogany and walnut. Made by M. Stone, Charlestown, Mass., from 1840s. [*Example pictured.*]

stone table: Marble- or slate-topped table of any kind. Also called stone top.

stonie: Play marble of stone, or a pebble.

stooft: A stool.

stoop; stoep: Entrance porch.

stoplap: Needlework; "reweaving" apertures deliberately cut in linen cloth; to create a pattern.

stopper mold: In glassmaking, the mold for glass bottle and decanter stoppers; hollow dies cut in metal, affixed to pincerlike arms. Plastic glass rods, inserted, were squeezed into stopper form. Various types.

stoppers; stopples: Glass or other bottle-neck closures, often with decorative knobs, handholds, and finials.

stop-reeded: Reeding that only partially covers an area, as a chair leg, cabinet leg, et cetera; grooving to cover one half to two thirds rather than whole of an area. Some variants show shallow continuations of the grooving.

stork lamp: A fat lamp with hang-up handle, long beaklike spout, with drip underspout, the whole on a conical base, resembling a stork. It is of Netherlands ancestry. Generally brass, but some in copper and sheet iron. A refinement made by the Shelton Lamp Works, England, c. 1800, is a student-type lamp with a reservoir of funnel shape carrying two burners.

stormont: Curvate repeat pattern, and repeat and point, as the rim pattern of a piecrust table.

stoup: A font or basin; a pail or portable cask. A basin for holy water. A stoup was a measure ranging from ½ pint to ½ gallon.

Stourbridge glass: English glass made at Stourbridge, Worcestershire, England, at various factories existing since 1556. Cut and plain blown glass, novelties, lamps, tablewares, all kinds of drinking glasses, decanters, bowls, vases, and specialties. Factories here had interest in, or majority ownership of, Irish factories at Cork and Waterford. This glass and that of Bristol were the major import in colonial period. **Stourbridge (U.S.) glass:** Made at a factory so called at Pittsburgh, from 1823 to 1830s, when name was changed to T. & J. Robinson.

Stoutenburgh mirrors: Looking glasses made at Newark, N.J., from 1840s by Stoutenburgh & Day. Tabernacle, oval, and French Antique gilded and rosewood examples are of record or reported.

Stouvenal glass: Fine French-type cut and pressed ware, the finest made in the U.S., by Joseph, Francis, and Nicholas Stouvenal, N.Y., from 1837 to 1870. Their pressed wares were equal to Baccarat and St. Louis factory production.

stove bottle: Stoneware and earthenware bottles in the form of Norse iron-pipe stoves. Some date from 17th century. Rare.

stove chair: *See* Chairs, All Kinds.

stove funnel: Cast-iron smoke pipe; later, sheet iron.

stove hollow ware: Cast-iron cooking pots, pans, et cetera, with recessed bottoms fitting the stove-lid opening on a range. Also now accepted as relating to any hollow ware used on stove, whether or not recessed on bottoms.

stove-in-stove: A large Franklin or similar iron fireplace having apron hearth on which stands a smaller basket grate with a firebank. Made from 1760s to 1820s. Rare.

stove iron: Laundry iron with an internal charcoal stove, a shield for hands of user, and a periscopic smokestack on the front end. Made in England from mid-19th century. In 1940s the unsold and forgotten stock of a Long Island store was found to contain cases of these irons in original greased paper wrappings. The antiques shops of the East were flooded with these irons, the standard price being $10.

stove lifter: A stove-lid lifter; an iron prise and holder. Many types.

stove rests: Decorative blocks in bust and

bird forms, standing four to six inches high, having an offset in which cast-iron stoves were rested when set up. Cast-iron, brass, and pottery examples are of record. [*Examples pictured.*]

stoves: A number of these heating devices were used in colonial days. In New England some stoves made up of soapstone plates, ironbound, are considered early. In the Hudson Valley, New Jersey, Pennsylvania, central Maryland, and Virginia there were foundries casting the Swedish, or Norse, five-plate, six-plate and ten-plate stoves. These plates are very decorative and have been used in the past fifty years for firebacks. The Franklin-type stove was first cast in Pennsylvania, but many examples were imported. Very few torqueshaffs, or single-plate iron radiators (backing up a fireplace in another room), were used. Dumb-stoves were iron devices through which passed the smoke of another stove, often on a floor below the dumb-stove. The most ornate dumb-stoves made were those of huge, almost life-size statues of Washington and classic figures. These also had fireboxes for use as hot stoves if desired. See Bibliography for titles of books on stoves.

stove screen: (1) The cast-iron screen with tilting mirror, made by Wood & Perrot of New Orleans from 1850s. (2) Any large screen designed to hide a space heater or room stove.

stove shelves: Cast-iron brackets and plates, fastened to smokestacks of stoves, to serve as warming areas. Date is from after 1860s.

Stow & Haight furniture: It is Grand Rapids furniture, dating from 1880s, and, it is to be most fervently hoped, will never be classed by anyone as a desirable antique. One product of the firm is already in the collected class: plain drop-leaf kitchen tables.

Stow's "music plate": This phrase is questioned as being most probably a confusion. However, the one man who could right it, the late Charles Messer Stow, has passed on without clarifying the matter. Reference most likely is to the music plate advertised by Hall, Boardman & Co. of Philadelphia, c. 1840s; a plate with musical decoration, made of Britannia metal.

Strachan furniture: James Strachan and D. Davidson, from 1750s, made Queen Anne and Georgian-style furniture at New York City. Also sold mirrors and brass hardware. Name is pronounced Strawn.

straddle chair: See Chairs, All Kinds.

strain: To stretch. **straining frame:** A framework upon which canvas or other fabric was stretched. Generally fitted with wedges which were hammered in to do the straining.

strainer: A sieve used to filter liquids.

straining rails: Low-placed stretchers joining legs of tables, benches, stools, and chairs.

strangenglazer: Cone-shaped, tall, slender wineglasses of 17th century.

strap hinge: Horizontal band hinge, the leaf on the door much longer than that on the stile.

strapwork: In metalcraft, as in silversmithing, the application of straps or strips of decorated metal, punched, chased, modeled, or fancy outline, although some examples are quite plain.

Strasbourg ware: Faïence and porcelain made at this city in Alsace-Lorraine, where French and German styles and peoples meet and seem to prosper in peace.

strass: Flint glass, fused from rock crystal, borax, and arsenic. Used almost exclusively in making imitation gem stones, otherwise called "paste."

Stratford Cut: Deep-V glass-cutting pattern in outline form of six-pointed stars, the hexagons alternately barred, hatched, and floriated.

Strawberry: Pressed-glass pattern featuring bands of berries with foliage. Originally a pattern for milk glass.

Strawberry & Currant: Not a variant, but another pattern displaying alternate clusters of each fruit.

Strawberry & Thistle: Misleading name for a pattern of pressed glass featuring beehives, bees, and thistles. One of the early "experts" probably thought the beehives were strawberries.

Strawberry Diamond & Star: Cut-glass pattern of waffle-cut style with various treatments of the small bosses, and a border of fan cuts. Several varieties.

strawberry dish: (1) Fluted-edged footed dishes of glass which just happened to become popular for serving strawberries. Better known by this name than the true. (2) Shallow bowl with pierced drainer bottom to hold berries of this variety at table. (3) The rectangular silver dish, generally shallow, used primarily in service of strawberries.

straw chair: See Chairs, All Kinds.

straw floorcloth: Straw matting "cheaper than painted floorcloth" was advertised in 1800, made in Philadelphia, and sold for $1.90 a yard, 54 inches wide. English painted floorcloths in tessellated patterns sold at $4 a square yard.

straw plat: Spring wheat straw, plaited for hatmaking.

straw split: A tool having an awl with oval flat handle having four orifices, each with crossed wires inserted. A piece of straw cut with the awl point was started through an aperture and pulled, thereby being cut in four strands ready for plaiting into the hat straw usually called "leghorn." [*Example pictured.*]

straw work: Structures made of straw, by plaiting, weaving, and tying. The work, imitative of architectural structures, is of Chinese origin but was practiced in Spain and the Netherlands, France, and England from 17th century. A little-known homecraft of colonial days. Few examples of the work survive.

street light barometer: Portable barometer.

street signs (pictured markers): The original street signs, not lettered, but pictorial, symbolic, or figural, indicative of street names for those who could not read, which meant the majority of the people when these came into vogue in 17th century.

stretcher bed: A couch; a day bed.

stretcher table: An early-type four-legged table, the legs joined by stretchers at or near the floor.

striated: Striped, streaked, or banded.

strigil: (1) A hand or claw, in miniature, on a wand; a back-scratcher. (2) A pattern of pressed glass with decorative elements resembling a strigil.

strike: To set or fix a color, as in dyeing.

string box: Any holder for twine. Examples of silver, Sheffield plate, and brass, as well as pewter, glass, and cast iron, are reported. Some are table holders, others suspended, some holding as many as six balls of twine and cord. Not generally box-like in form; often ball- or reel-shaped.

Strong prints: Flower prints from Dr. Strong's works on flowers, issued 1840s-50s at New York. There are 240 colored prints in the quarto volumes of the set. *American Flora* is the title of the work, originally issued in parts as a magazine.

Strouds: Scarlet-colored wool blankets, named for Stroudwater, England, the place of making in 17th and 18th centuries.

Stuart, Henry: A master workman in the Sanderson furniture cartel, Salem, Mass., 1790s-1810s.

stub foot: A furniture footing, often as a separate block. Various forms [*some pictured*]. Especially used on chests having no other footing.

stucco paper: (1) Embossed, thick paper used to cover ceilings and then painted in imitation of fine pargetry work. (2) Papier-mâché sheets used in a similar manner, but with more pronounced relief and sharper definition.

stuck shank: An applied stem, especially in glassmaking; not a drawn stem, but one stuck on.

student lamp: Any study lamp. Name became general when it was used in connection with the St. Germain lamp for students. How this lamp came to be called a German student lamp is one of the mysteries of nomenclature. It is a French invention.

stud table: Semicircular, felt-covered gaming table with a niche cut in the straight side for the dealer, called the stud horse.

stuff: Fabrics, textiles, bolt goods, dry goods, piece goods.

stump-back chair: *See* Chairs, All Kinds.

stump foot: Any leg or stile extending to the floor, without special terminal decoration or treatment.

stump quilt: Name is from the decorative technique, said to be imitative of wood cut from a tree stump. A Miss Collins, in 1867, invented the design. It is not a patch-quilt pattern, but an all-over pattern. [*Example pictured.*]

stump work: High-relief embroidery; high-piled needlework. Popular in England and the colonies from 17th century.

sturtzbecher: Drinking bottle of figural form, molded or modeled stoneware.

Suabian: South German; Swabian. A "Swab." The language of the region is tinctured with Swiss phrases and some Italian. It is the butt of endless jokes among the German people.

subaqueous lamp: A whale-oil lamp within a glass dome and airtight base connected with tubes to a bellows to supply air, and weights to sink it. Used underwater as a fish lure for night fishing with net and gig. A commercial example with India-rubber tubes was on the market by 1850s.

submerged pump: A non-freezing pump, with the valves deep in the well and only levers and spout exposed.

sucket fork: Two-tined fork, the handle fitted with a spoon bowl. Dual-purpose tableware of 17th century. Now scarce. [*Example pictured.*]

sucrier: Sugar basin; sugar chest or case. 18th-century name.

suction organ: The melodeon and any small reed organ; so called because sound was not achieved by bellows pressure but by atmospheric pressure on the open side of the reed box, against a vacuum caused by a suction bellows. Because the bellows of a melodeon is pumped the same as that of any other organ, it is assumed by many that this is to create pressure. It isn't; it is to create a vacuum. In small instruments this method of building is by far the cheapest. The bellows of such small organs does not "suck" air in its valves; it expels air.

Suellen Lee rocker: A folding rocker frame. *See* Chairs, All Kinds.

suet: The "sweet" fat of beef and mutton.

Suffolk glass: Blown, cut, and pressed glassware made at South Boston factory of this name, first half of 19th century.

Suffolk latch: A palm-fitting handle, a thumb press and decorative plate. Examples in brass (scarce) and wrought iron. Date is from 1640s to 1880s.

sugan: Coarse rush, growing in the bogs or marshes called sugans. Soggins.

sugar: Any sweeting, crystallized. The sugar of colonial and early Federal days was cast in conical shapes, upside down, the juice draining from the apex of the cone. These were suspended almost like hams, on cords, and the sugar hacked away in pieces, powdered in mortars, and granulated on pounding boards. This was basin, or bowl, sugar. Tea sugar was served in pieces or lumps. The cone was sometimes called a loaf.

sugar augur: A device to loosen sugar in cones or barrels. The cutter is a straight center tine with two curvate-end tines set at angles, the whole on a stout iron rod with a crossbar handle.

sugar basin: A bowl for sugar, not always with a cover.

sugar basket: Variant of the basin; a glass liner in a silver basket.

sugar brandy: Jamaica, Barbados, and other rums made from sugar cane.

sugar chest: The item of Southern furniture much publicized since 1930s as a unique and unusual piece of furniture. It is simply the product of environmental pressures resulting from necessity of storing a considerable quantity of sugar out of the reach of slaves. Some sugar chests look like slope-fall desks of the early 19th century but are actually storage bins for a dozen or more cones of sugar. Most ex-

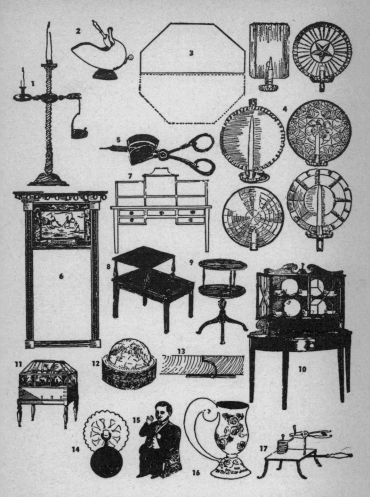

1, Swivel Light Stand. **2,** Scoop Scuttle. **3,** Semi-Octagon or Trilateral Form. **4,** Sconces (6). **5,** Snuffers. **6,** Tabernacle Mirror. **7,** Table à Gradin. **8,** Table Bed-Steps. **9,** Table with Double Top. **10,** Table Cabinet. **11,** Table Conservatory (Wardian Case). **12,** Table Globe. **13,** Table Joint. **14,** Tongue or Tablet Pull. **15,** Tammany Bank. **16,** Tantalus Cup. **17,** Taper Jack. (Nos. 4 and 6 from *New Geography of American Antiques*. No. 10 from *Furniture of our Forefathers*.)

amples are of wild-cherry wood; some have oak lining. Date is mostly 1810s-50s.

sugar cleaver: A small cleaver, steel-bladed, often with a brass or copper bird form over the blade. Also a pair of stout shears; both used to hack and cut chunks from a cone of sugar. [*Example pictured.*]

sugar cone: Conical crystallizations of sugar in forms of similar shape, made commercially in sizes from 3 to 30 pounds. Always with a heavy cord extending from tip of cone, and always wrapped in heavy blue paper, which was esteemed as a dye source by our ancestors. Barley, grape, maple, and cane sugars were all "coned" commercially. The grape sugar was very expensive, barley sugar next, then cane. Crystallized honey was comparable to barley sugar in cost.

sugar fixtures: The appurtenances of sap tapping, sugaring off, barley boiling, cane crushing, et cetera.

sugarhouse doctor: Any long blade scraping against a cylinder is called a "doctor." This particular doctor was the scraper on the evaporating drum of a sugarhouse; it doctored off the sugar for coning, or loafing. There was still plenty of non-crystalline liquid in such doctored-off sugar; this seeped from the cones as molasses, or syrup.

sugarhouse patients: Tubercular people who were ensconced in sugarhouses during the season of operation. The alkaline fumes were thought to effect a cure, and this might indeed be the case. Ground hogs eating mold from tree roots after a snakebite are no longer eating tree mold; they're eating penicillin.

Sugar House pottery: Pottery molds for candy and marchpane. So many were made at Westbury Pottery, England, that it was called the Sugar House Pottery.

sugar loaf: A cone of sugar. **sugar-loaf spoon:** A spoon with a sugar-loaf shape above the bowl as a base for the stem or handle. Many Utica silversmiths of first half of 19th century used this peculiarity of styling. [*Example pictured.*]

sugar mold: Cone-shaped pottery mold in which the hot crystalline syrup was packed to harden and drain. Made of tin-glaze pottery as early as 1660s. Any mold of small size to form barley sugar or maple sugar into pretty figures, leaf forms, et cetera. Some of the cone molds were made of metal.

sugar nips: Sugar shears.

sugar-paper dye: Blue paper, as used to wrap sugar cones, soaked to extract the desirable blue pigment, used in dying linen and wool yarn.

sugar shears: Sugar nippers; scissors-like cutters.

sugar tongs: Silver tongs with claw or shell ends to lift lumps from a basin.

sugar trammel & irons: Two separate elements are here involved; the trammel is the pot rack used in sugar boiling; the irons are andirons made to support a huge sugar kettle.

sugar tree: The sugar maple.

sugar urn: A sugar basin of urn shape, with cover.

sugar vase: Actually a shallow basin for sugar lumps.

Sui: Chinese dynasty, A.D. 581-618.

sulphides: Fire-clay portrait busts and other elements of decorative nature embedded in blown-glass balls, as paper-weights, door handles, and portrait medallions. The clay takes on a silvery appearance which remains and never deteriorates. Also crystallo-ceramie.

summer; sommer: The main transverse beam of a structure, from which the jousts (also jeests or joists) were set. Probably from *sommier*.

summer beds: Twin beds, as designed by Sheraton; two beds under one large tester, generally protected with a kitty-fisher curtain of scrim.

summer board: A fireplace board, used to block the opening in summer. Fireboard.

summer boiler: A hot-water urn of copper with a charcoal fire box underneath. Used in many kitchens for summer hot-water supply from 1820s. [*Example pictured.*]

Summers mirrors: An extensive manufactory of looking glasses was carried on by T. A. Summers of Rochester, N.Y., from 1850s. French Antique styles.

sumpter: The horse in a cavalcade that carried the provisions or parcels.

Sunburst: Pattern of pressed glass, imitative of sunburst cutting, of 1890s. There are other Sunburst patterns and variants, such as Sunburst & Bar. All are rather late products. Some are listed in Lee's books.

Suncook glass: Glass made at Suncook, N.H., from 1850s, prior to which the plant was at Chelmsford. Mostly window glass.

Sunday comics: So far as is now known, the first comic supplement of record in the U.S. was instituted by the N.Y. *Sunday Mercury* in 1843. "Fitz-Squab" was the cartoonist for all four pages of comics.

Sunderland: The luscious pink-purple-splashed luster derived from gold oxide, called 'Sunderland because this pottery made a great deal of the ware. It is now a highly prized item of advanced collecting interest. See Bibliography for books on lusterware. **Sunderland ware:** Not to be confused with the crushed-strawberry-effect luster; the "ware" is brown with a white-glaze lining. Made at Fulham by The Bailey Pottery.

sundial: The shadow timepiece, effective on sunny days, when the movement of the earth causes the shadow cast by sun on the pointer, or gnomon, of the piece to advance on the dial and give fairly accurate time. This is always "sun time" and not the standard, or zonal, time of the place. For example, the sundials of Boston and Detroit differ materially in the sun time registered on the dials when it is 12 o'clock noon by the clocks of these cities. The most correct sundials are those casting the shadow on a curved, not a flat, surface. The most interesting of the curvate dials are called armillary dials, or spheres; they are skeleton spheres of circles set at proper angles. See Bibliography for books; students should also study *Sun Dials & Roses of Yesterday*, a volume on the shelves of most libraries. The bell sundial, the sundial gun, and other mechanical devices, using a burning glass which ignited powder or fired a thread or cord at noon, are very interesting time-pieces. The bell dial has a tension spring, hammer and bell, released when the sun-glass fired a tow linen thread.

sun engine: Captain Ericsson, famed de-signer and builder of the *Monitor*, was an exponent of the "caloric" or hot-air en-gine, and once stated that the sunshine on the roofs of Philadelphia homes was sufficient to generate 100,000 horsepower. He was quite right. Ericsson attempted, as did other inventors, to produce an en-gine run by sun heat. Mirrors and lenses were a part of the equipment. All the models did run, but apparently no huge power plants were constructed.

Sunflower: Pattern of pressed glass fea-turing banded panels with the sunflower plant and flower.

sunflower chests: Sunflower-and-tulip-carved chests of Tudor style, as made in the Connecticut Valley in 17th century. See Bibliography. The sunflower, a helio-trope, or flower that turns to keep its face to the sun, was esteemed as a country-man's clock and had "tree-of-life" signifi-cance. It is found on slip ware, carved on chests, painted on tavern signs, and used in symbolic decoration, secular and reli-gious.

sunflower pattern: A modern term for the 19th-century Imari ware now called gaudy Dutch that features a flower as-sumed to be this bloom.

Sung: Chinese dynasty, A.D. 960–1279. This is Northern Sung. Southern Sung is A.D. 960–1127.

sunken panel: A pattern or form achieved in blown glass by forming the first pari-son in a mold that impressed the form. Thought to be a Stiegel type. It was later proved this kind of work was done at Sandwich Glass Co. plant as late as 1840s.

supière: A soup tureen.

suppawn: Corn-meal porridge; spoon bread.

supper dish: Hollow dish, filled with hot water, serving as a base for three or four food dishes. Silver, plated-ware, Sheffield, pottery, china, and porcelain examples known.

supreme: A banquet sherbet or compote glass. This is the container used in serving a "supreme" of anything of elaborate nature, as ices, creams, fruits, jellies, et cetera.

surcingle: A girdle tied by its ends.

surcoat: Overcoat.

surplice pins: Hangers for vestments of choristers, vergers, and other acolytes.

surtable: A centerpiece of china, pottery, glass, or silver, as container for fruits, flowers, comfits, nuts, and raisins. Some are very complicated creations. Some mar-velously beautiful ones made at Dresden, Sèvres, Chelsea, Worcester, Leeds, and other potteries.

surtout: All over; overall. Anything from a pair of levis to a calcimined wall is "surtout." A greatcoat; any over-all deco-ration or covering.

Sussex pig: A drinking vessel, not a bank. In use, the form is set on its hams and the head (top) removed. Not so early as one might think; the Bellevue Pottery, Rye, Sussex, made them as late as 1870s. They are traditional to the region. Now scarce. [*Example pictured.*]

Suzanne Franklin: Reference must be to the four-foot-high statue of Franklin, done from life by F. M. Suzanne, con-temporary of Houdon, while Franklin was at Passy. Replicas in terra cotta were made in 19th century.

swag: Decorative element imitative of droops and drapes. Carved, modeled, molded, cut, and otherwise achieved on wood, metal, pottery, glass, et cetera.

swage: Decorative border of grooves; a grooved molding. Also the tool used by smiths in shaping hot iron under the hammer.

Swan, Abraham: Neo-classic designer of the mid-18th century in England. He worked in variants of the styles of the Brothers Adam, and somehow his style seems to have been known by some of the colonial cabinetmakers.

Swan: Pattern of pressed glass with medal-lions of preening swans set in a fine waffle-weave background and with finials (on covered pieces) of a modeled preening swan.

swan dish: Oval dish with swan-shape cover. Pressed-glass dish of two parts, the whole in swan shape. There are Vallerys-thal & Portieux examples which may have been the models for American products.

swan finial: Gobs of glass tooled into swan shape (so called) but often resem-bling a rooster, cockerel, or hen. **swan lamp:** Small night lamp with reservoir in form of a swan, the burner affixed to a hump on the bird's back.

swan melodeon: A six-octave, 48-natural-key instrument with instantaneous action achieved by improved vacuum bellows di-rectly on the reeds. In 1850 the instrument was priced at $40. [*Example pictured. The style of the case is Directoire, with lyre-form supports at both ends.*]

Swansea: Porcelain made at Swansea, Wales, from 1814 to 1824. One of the little-known early-19th-century porcelains that are the darlings of advanced ceramic col-lecting. The twin of Swansea, Nantgarw ware, is another. It is said that some ex-amples marked with the latter name or symbol were made at Swansea. There were potteries at Swansea from 1750s. *See also* Dillwyn. [*Certain of the marks of this pottery are pictured.*]

swanskin: Closely woven woolen cloth.

swan's-neck sofas: The sofas of the Di-rectoire style which generally have ends gracefully curvate, some of swan's-neck form, terminating in a carved swan's head.

swatheling: Wrappings of infants.

Swedes in American colonies: The Swedish influence in pioneering, settle-ment, the popular and fine arts, and so-cial sciences of the colonies is generally and quite carefully elided by practically all of the pro-Germanic historians. This is deplorable on many counts, the most significant of which is reflected in their designating many descendants of original Swedish pioneers as of other origins. The Van Courtland and Van Rensselaer fami-lies are descended from Swedes. There are hundreds of family names in Pennsylvania that were originally Swedish. The furniture styles, glass styles, et cetera, of these northern people must be considered in any critical study of pioneer furniture and housewares. A Swedish two-drawer chest with panels and a Swedish cupboard on frame are pictured. The latter was once and may still be at Williamsburg, but no longer on view. It is of late importation, although a genuine Swedish antique. Significantly, that cupboard was discovered to be precisely what it is as the result of research for this dictionary. Joe Kindig, Jr., of York, Pa., assisted the author, and an unprejudiced editor was given the findings to pass on to the people at Williamsburg. The result was withdrawal of the piece from its place of exhibition. **Swedes Glass:** Reference is to a glasshouse presumed to have been operative on the Delaware before the arrival of William Penn.

Sweeney & Bell glass: Wheeling, Va., glass made from 1830s. Fine plain-blown, cut, and pressed wares. The firm also imported quantities of Baccarat, Vallerysthal, and Portieux glasswares, which it distributed at wholesale.

sweep-back: Chair rail of loop form.

sweep gate: The toll-road barriers which, weighted at butt ends, swung upward in the same manner as later-day railroad-crossing gates.

sweep top: A field-bed canopy having graceful, sweeping curves.

sweet bag: A perfumed glove.

swept whorl: A decorative element, applied in a sweep or whorl.

Swett & Allen: Partnership of chair- and cabinetmakers working in Cambridge, Mass., from 1840s or earlier.

swift: An adjustable reel for winding yarn prior to quilling. Known in wood and ivory. [*Example pictured.*]

swift blocks: Toy building blocks in sets of from 36 to 80, all blocks attachable to each other on all sides. Date is from 1860s.

swing bed: A sea bed; a bed frame suspended from ceiling on rods or chains.

swinging writing arm Windsor: See Chairs, All Kinds.

swing kettle: Any kettle suspended or supported in a stand that permits easy tilting for pouring. Most examples have a spirit lamp under the kettle. Silver, plated ware, and other metals.

Swinton ware: Pottery, salt-glazed stoneware, and yellow wares made at Swinton, England, from mid-18th century. Student is referred to *Ceramic Art of Great Britain,* by Jewitt.

Swirl: Pattern of pressed glass featuring a band of diamond-form quilting and bands of swirls, or curvate fluting. **Swirl & Dot:** A pattern that might well be called "French Bread & Butter Pat," in that the swirl is a twist and the dots are ovate elements.

Swirled Wheat Cut: A pattern of cut glass, not pressed, featuring somewhat stiff representations of wheat heads with fanlike fronds.

Swisher: Of Swiss origin; from Switzerland.

Swiss: The Helvetii; once a part of the kingdom of Burgundy, fell into German hands and rebelled, achieving independence in 15th century. Practically all of the so-called Pennsylvania-German "folk arts" are neither folk arts nor German; they are Swiss popular art forms. No nation on earth has had as many home workshops as Switzerland. In fact, every home and cottage seems to have served as a feeder shop for factories and wholesale warehouses over the past four centuries. The people were independent workers, making and selling their products of home manufacture at contract prices. Even fine watch and clock parts were made by this system. The Swiss also were experts in glassmaking, dairying, in textiles, and in the making of pottery. Their barns are found reproduced in Pennsylvania to this day, and in some regions bear also the decorations, wrongly called hex marks, which are a part of the Swiss tradition. Perhaps the first people to carry the Swiss traditions to Pennsylvania entered the colony as early as 1690 with the Mennonites or Anabaptists, who, having lived for over a century in Switzerland, were originally Dutch refugees.

Swiss lambrequin: A valance of Swiss lace with a cornice form, used over windows and doors.

switchell: A drink for summer prepared as follows: Steep a cup of vinegar, a cup of molasses, a cup of oatmeal, and a sprig of ginger in a gallon of water. Cool, and take as a haying drink. Generally carried in stone jugs, harvest rings, and small coopered kegs.

swivel light stand: An upright wooden screw on base, with crossbar tapped to run on the screw. [*Example pictured.*]

swivel-top sewing stand: An Empire-style stand having a rotating top with fold-over leaf. This enabled user to rest the leaf on an opened drawer and so double the area of top.

Swope lamp: Invented by the potter, Z. Swope, of Lancaster, Pa. A conical reflector heated the reservoir and enabled the lamp to burn lard. Only first examples are of pottery; the inventor made most of the lamps of sheet iron. He patented the item in 1860s.

swordsmith: A cutler; a maker of swords, knives, and daggers.

swordstick: A thin blade hidden in a sheath of wood looking precisely like and serving as a cane or walking stick.

swyre: Neck. A "bottell, swyred," is a bottle with a neck.

sycamore: Originally the fig-mulberry. Used extensively in making the carcasses of furniture destined for veneering of surface. In colonies the name was given to the plane or buttonwood tree.

syllabub: A dessert confection of whipped cream, sherry, egg whites, et cetera, achieved in a "syllabub churn" and served in glasses of various shapes, called "syllabubs." Closest approximation of the luxury dessert, the zabaglione of Italy. The first syllabub was warm whole milk, fresh from the cow, curdled with white sherris (white sherry) and sweetened with sugar. There are variants in spelling of the name, and many variants in the recipes used from early 17th century.

Symmes ware: Stoneware with blue decoration made at Symmes Pottery, Charlestown, Mass., from 1740s or 1750s.

sympathetic ink: Any ink, invisible after use, but restored to view by acid, alkaline, or heat applications.

symphona: The organette, *which see.*

synagogue chandelier: Brass hanging fixture of ancient pattern, the arms stamped or cut in animalistic forms. Because often found in temples of the faith of Moses and Aaron, the name as here given has been applied. It is in error; these are simply ancient forms of hanging candle fixtures of early Tudor style, derived from the Near East.

Synan ware: Late Somerset, Mass., pottery, made 1890s to 1910s. Stone kitchenware.

Syntax pattern: Dr. Syntax was a character invented by William Combe and made immortal by the illustrator, Rowlandson. So popular were the Combe books about the doctor, embellished by the Rowlandson sketches, that the pattern appeared on chintzes, handkerchiefs, as framing prints, and as pottery decoration. Most of the plates, generally Staffordshire, date from roughly 1801 to 1830s.

syren: (1) A musical instrument, reported as related to the zither. (2) A mermaid.

syrinx: The pipes of Pan; pastoral pipes; musical pipes.

T

tabagie collegium: "Smokers" were so called in 17th and 18th centuries; a college of smokers of tobacco, meeting in conclave, drinking and smoking. Originated in the Netherlands as a social practice.

tabard: A square-cut garment of cloth worn over armor, usually emblazoned with the arms of the knight. Also an embroidered banner hung on a crossbar. A fire screen.

Tabb, Philip: Iron founder who made cast- and wrought-iron furniture from mid-19th century. Shops were in New York City.

tabby: Coarse watered taffeta, from 17th century.

tabby floor: Tamped earth floor.

tabellion public: Official scrivener or notarial writer, exercising limited authority of legal status, appointed by royal authority.

Taber instruments: Nautical instruments made by W. C. Taber and C. Taber & Co. of New Bedford, Mass., from 1830s.

tabernacle: Miniature shrine, often a shallow cabinet with multiple-paned glass fronts, a holy or saintly figure displayed in each. A home shrine used by Italian, French, Spanish, Swiss, and other peoples from 1500s. Any niche for a statue, in cabinetwork. [*Example pictured.*]

tabernacle mirrors: Wall mirrors resembling the general shape of a tabernacle, yet more directly related to the French *trumeau*. Not "Sheraton," as sometimes claimed. There are many varieties, owing to the quality and price range. These mirrors were made by the hundreds of thousands, to retail at from $1 to $25 and more. There is one style factor common to all: there is a large mirror panel surmounted by a decorative panel, usually painted glass, generally called an eglomise panel, and varying in style and quality with the intended price of the mirror. Some have a wood panel, with carving or applied decoration. Cheap examples are of flat molding with applied reeding, applied cornerpieces, and are of painted white wood or cherry. Fine examples display gilding, have mahogany frames and additional decoration in form of gilded balls, et cetera. This mirror was popular from 1790s to 1860. [*Examples pictured.*]

tabinet: Silk-and-wool textile, esteemed for curtains and draperies as well as dress fabric.

tableau vivant: Costumed figures with facial resemblance to characters portrayed, assembled in groups to display a historic scene or event. They are miniatures, generally on bases 3' x 4' in size. American examples of Molly Pitcher and Barbara Frietchie reported. Rare.

table à jeu: (1) A game table. (2) A flat-topped chest-on-frame.

table beer: Bread beer.

table book: Any large book, especially a picture book.

table cabinet: A side table with a cabinet affixed. Used as a sideboard. [*Example pictured.*]

table case of drawers: Chest of drawers on a table; chest-on-frame.

table catches: The brass hardware item that served as a catch on tip, or tilt-top, tables. Several types; usage dates from 1750s.

table chest: Chest on a tablelike form or stand. Also a four-drawer chest serving as a base for a table top.

table clock: A rare type of clock, with dial on top of a rectangular, square, or round casing, often of brass, with glass paneling. 16th to 19th century.

table columns: Pedestal columns, often made by turners as stock items for cabinetmakers. Incidentally, they often made Windsor-chair parts, piano legs, et cetera, as stock items.

table conservatory: A table top rimmed with a trough, surmounted by a glass case or framework of glass, for growing plants, flowers, and herbs in the house during the winter season. Many cottages used them as chive, parsley, and lettuce beds! [*Example pictured.*]

table globe: A terrestrial globe rotating in a felt-lined hollow within a table case. [*Example pictured.*]

table joints: The leaves of the oldest (and also the cheapest of modern) tables were simply squared on the edges and met with similarly square-edged tops. The next type, dating from 16th century, is a tongue-and-groove joint, the groove not generally very pronounced, but nonetheless forming a closed joint. The final, most graceful type is the table joint, having a recessed half-round edge on the top proper and a similar recessed concavity on the inside of the leaf. [*Example pictured.*]

table mirrors: (1) Small looking glasses (average size 9" x 12") in very wide framing, some of painted vellum, straw work, holly wood, or yew wood, often showing genre scenes. Date is from 1500s. (2) Mirrors permanently affixed to table tops, in the frame or mounted between columns.

table-on-table: The open court cupboard is sometimes so designated.

table pans: Reference is to metallic rather than ceramic pans for night stands.

tables: The term table is from tablet, meaning a writing surface. The original term for what we now call a table of any kind was "board." The following kinds of tables are of record, explained only where it is felt further remarks are required: *Table à écran:* table screen. *Table à écrire:* writing table. *Table à grandin:* writing table with bookshelves. [*Example pictured.*] *Table à rognon:* table with kidney-shaped top, a curved oval. Bed step table: bedside table of two tiers, one larger than the other, forming a bed step. [*Example pictured.*] Table board: a table top laid upon X or other form trestles. [*Example pictured.*] *Table de chevet:* bedside table. *Table de papillon:* butterfly table. *Table de Solon:* any formal, important, marble-topped or carved table. Table desk: same as desk-in-table. *Table dormand:* a table board fixed to its supports. Double round-top table: pedestal table with two round tops, one elevated above the other on slender columns. [*Example pictured.*] Tiered writing table: pedestal of open shelves, with a round or rectangular-shaped top used for writing. Drawing table: a table with extension leaves pulling out from ends and rising to meet the fixed or main top. This is a very early form, of Gothic or Gallic origin, and dating from 14th century. Also called *table s'allongéant.* [*Example pictured.*] Lazy Susan table: dining table, generally round, with a rotating round centerpiece slightly elevated. This was sometimes called a farm table or harvest table. The grape-packing tables of 19th century also have a rotating centerpiece and are sometimes mistaken for harvest tables. Other tables of general usage were: drop-leaf, tavern, gate-leg, Pembroke (a breakfast table with narrow drop leaves). Many gaming tables have special names allied to the game played. Wine tables and other specialties are listed elsewhere in this volume under the commonly used names.

table scrutoire: A desk box for use on a table.

table setting: A "set" of anything; of silver, china, glassware, linen, et cetera. Recently applied with considerable frequency to sets of pressed glass within a pattern.

table-strut: Any support of a top member, making it useful on a table.

tablet: The ancient meaning is sheets of asses' skin or parchment, for making notes, keeping accounts and records.

tablet bottle: Druggists' screw-cap bottles, useful for carrying tablets of drugs.

tablet (or tongue) pull: Variant of the teardrop pull frequently noted on furniture of the William & Mary period. The design is also from the Chinese; a circular disk of solid metal affixed to a projecting boss and hanging pendent from a decorative plate. [*Example pictured.*]

taborette: (1) A small drum table; from "tabor," a drum. (2) A similar piece, but not tabor form; any small stand or stool. Some are upholstered and used as seats. Some made as part of a three-piece chair. The rocking tabourette was made to accompany a rocking chair.

Tabriz marble: Once believed to be petrified water; a translucent stone mined at and around Lake Ourmia, Persia, and amidst the pools of Shirameek, also in Persia, where the water is supercharged with minerals which calcify into this semi-transparent stone.

taffy-tolu: An early chewing gum.

Taft press: A cast-iron copying press. [*Example pictured is dated 1848.*]

tailor's goose: Large sadiron with gooseneck handle affixed to fore part of the iron.

tailor's seat: A portable folding chair with spring legs and adjustable back.

Taiping: The Chinese "rebellion" period, 1850–65.

Tait, Thomas: London cabinetmaker who worked in the classic style of Adam and Hepplewhite and who, it is asserted, shipped furniture to Southern ports on order after Revolution. These data not confirmed.

Talavera: The pottery of Puebla, Mexico; a fine and now rare majolica. Made from 17th century.

Talbotype: A paper daguerreotype.

talc: (1) Miniature portrait on copper or other metal, with a series of sheets of mica (the "talcs") upon which elements of costume were painted and so "dressed" the figure and provided for transformations. 17th century. (2) Soft, hydrous magnesium silicate used in making impalpable toilet powders and lubricants. A form of soapstone.

tale: The first and the last drawing of parison from a glass pot.

talent: A weight of gold or silver equal to 56 pounds, 11 ounces, 17½ grains, Troy. Thus a talent of any of these metals was a fortune. The damsel who weighed two talents silver (Captain Hull's daughter) was just a nicely stacked young lass.

talking stick: A hollow tube, such as elderberry wood with the pith removed, used as a whispering device by children and young lovers.

tallboy: Colloquial 18th-century English term for a high chest, from which, most likely, we have the term "highboy." The original reference applied only to a chest-on-chest. Research indicates that chests were colloquially called boys, or *boites*.

tall-case clock: The proper name and designation for what is now called a grandfather's clock, never known by that name until the poem *My Grandfather's Clock* appeared in the 19th century. Tall-case clocks were made from the 17th century, some converted from earlier examples of clockwork, but fitted with pendulums. The object of the tall casing, or closet, was to hide the pendulum and the weights and to give protection to the movement. Known in all period styles of casing from William & Mary to Sheraton. [*Examples of the clocks, hoods, and other details are pictured.*]

tallow dip: (1) Homemade dipped candles of common tallow. (2) A brass, copper, or iron Betty-type lamp burning tallow.

tally board: A carved wood board, one side plain, generally with Swiss, Dutch, or Swedish style of carving on the other side. These were hung by the door with tally or message chalked on the plain side. The carved side turned out when no message was on the board. Not a busk or stay as is sometimes thought. [*Example pictured.*]

tally man: A talesman or accountant. A clerk.

talma: A child's sacque.

tamarisk: Properly, tamarack; the larch tree and its wood. Also a pole pine.

tambour: Slats, glued on canvas, to form a flexible wooden partition or covering, used as a vertical or horizontal series. Also a form of fancy needlework using a tambour frame. Embroidery rings. **tambour wardrobe:** A wardrobe oval in plan, standing six to eight feet, and having tambour sliding doors.

Tammany bank: One of the better-known mechanical cast-iron banks, of which there are a hundred or more varieties. [*Original advertisement of the item is pictured, offering the bank as a premium for a subscription to a magazine.*]

tammy: Glazed fabric, also known as durant and calimanico.

Tam o' Shanter pitcher: Staffordshire white-glaze pitcher with raised figural decoration of Tom and his convivial companions at their favorite sport, drinking. Date is from 1830s. Many reissues of record, some of 20th century. The Tam o' Shanter stopper is a glass figural stopper of this Scottish character, or of his traditional hat or cap.

Tanagra: Pottery figures, glazed in colors, or painted carved figures of earlier date in the same philosophy. Said to date, as a traditional item, from 400 B.C. Made at Tanagra, Boetia.

T'ang: Chinese dynasty, A.D. 618-907. Vases of T'ang form are drum-shaped in body with tapering hexagonal or oval necks and curvate handles. These generally are attributed to the K'ang Hsi or the Yung Ch'eng periods.

tangs: The cotter-pin-like wire fasteners used to hold early cabinet hardware in place; fastened securely inside the piece, tangs lasted for centuries.

tankard: Originally woodenware, staved or turned, with cover, to carry a quantity of liquid. From 16th century, a drinking flagon with cover, known in wood, tin, pewter, iron, horn, silver, pottery, and leather.

Tantalus: Holder for liquor and wine bottles in a frame with a locking bar over the stoppers. **Tantalus cup:** A hydrostatic toy cup with a siphon that empties the contents before the cup's contents can be carried to one's lips. Metal and glass examples of record, dating from 1750s. [*Example pictured.*]

tape loom: A house loom for weaving narrow fabric.

tape pistol: Repeating pistol using a tape of percussion caps for firing.

taper: A candle. Especially a long, slender candle. Also a long, multi-thread wax-coated wick for use in lighting candles and in a taper jack, a footed platform with reel of taper and a scissors-form pincers to hold the part for burning. [*Example pictured.*] **taper stick:** A small socket candlestick to hold the candles known as tapers. **taper·cologne:** A sprinkler-headed cologne bottle with tapering sides.

tape seat: Narrow fabric or flat leather tapes woven in simple basket pattern over seat rails to contrive a chair or settee seat.

tapisserie d'Auxerre: Embroidery with a darning stitch on netting or scrim.

tappit; toppit: Meaning topped, or crowned. Lidded. **tappit hen:** A covered measure, the form being bulbous, with constricted neck and flaring at mouth. Sizes vary from a few ounces to a gallon capacity. They are very cute; known in silver, but mostly of pewter.

tarboggin: A ski-bottomed sled. Origin of toboggan.

tar boiler: Open iron kettle with a long open spout. This is neither a pouring spout nor a handle. It is a cooling device. When tar was boiled to make pitch, it had a tendency to boil over. This was discouraged by the long shallow runnel which cooled the stuff sufficiently to keep its boiling under control. Date of the boilers is from 1820s. They are made of cast iron. [*Example pictured.*]

target balls: Hollow glass balls with necks. Filled with cut paper or feathers, ribbons, et cetera, or unfilled, they were thrown from a sling or by an attendant and used as targets for marksmen. It is perhaps unfair to emotional memories of Buffalo Bill, but these are the targets he hit with the greatest of ease with rifle or pistol—when his cartridges were loaded with birdshot and not bullets! One seed of shot broke the glass target ball.

tarlatan: Sheer linsey-woolsey.

Tarpon Springs School: A school of artists at Tarpon Springs, Fla., founded by George Innes, N.A., who painted here in 1870s and 1880s. The term is somewhat silly; Innes drew practically no followers and did not care about it one bit. He did the painting.

tartan: What is in error called a "plaid"; the crisscross pattern of colors in combination, primarily the badges of Scottish clans.

tass: Ceremonial breastplate with a neck chain. Ritualistic of the Hebrews, dating from 1000 B.C.

Tassie: A cameo cast in imitation of classic examples, in glass, made by the seal cutter, James Tassie of London, 1770s-90s, and his nephew, William, 1796-1820s. So popular in their day and age, they were revived and again called Tassie gems in England's Victorian era, when Victoria was still a young queen.

tasting bowl: A porringer.

tate: A switch or tuft of hair; a transformation. A wisp of straw was given the same name.

taufschein: Baptismal certificate, printed, partly hand-colored or entirely done by hand. A form of *Frakturschriften*, or calligraphic work.

Taunton: Pressed-glass pattern featuring borders of sharp rope-twist effect. Once called Scroll. Some examples are engraved on the expanses having no pressed pattern.

Taunton Britannia: Lamps, candlesticks, nursing lamps, and general wares made at Taunton, Mass., and perhaps the best of the Britannia metals.

Taunton chest: The tulip-and-vine-painted chests with birds, in red, white, and darker tones, made at Taunton, Mass., from late 17th century. Often called a Huguenot chest. If there were any in Pennsylvania to equal them, one could be quite sure they would be called Pennsylvania German and not the French style, which they are.

tavern stick: Contraction meaning tavern candlestick, having a bell-bottomed base with a clapper, making it a table candlestick and call bell.

tavern ware: Special china for inns and taverns, generally marked with some identification. Made from 1780s by various Staffordshire potters, including Leeds, who were prepared to paint insignia on their queen's ware. Actually most of the early marked ware was made for exclusive hotels and watering places, not roadside taverns and neighborhood inns.

tawho: Root of the wake-robin plant, baked for food. Poisonous when raw.

tawing: Mild tanning for skins, not hides.

tawkee: Dried seed berry of the *Orontium aquaticum*. Used by Swedes on the Delaware as food in 17th century.

Taylor, H. P. & C. R.: Soap and cosmetic manufacturers of Philadelphia, established 1820. This firm packed certain of its products in china boxes with transfer-printed tops or lids. There is no list of all varieties of boxes or the subjects depicted on them. But over six different ones are of record. All are identifiable by the appearance of this name, or "Taylor's," as a part of the design lettering.

Taylor, John: Cabinetmaker, upholsterer, and auctioneer for the disposal of household goods, active in New York from 1770s.

Taylor bell: A doorbell, patented 1860s, having a spring-driven hammer within the gong which sounded a tattoo when the crank outside the door was turned. [*Example pictured.*]

Taylor doll: White china doll first made in 1840s. The name is that of the maker, now generally applied to any similar early-type china doll.

Taylor portraits: D. B. Taylor of Rochester, N.Y., from 1860s operated a portrait-painting factory in which any small photo, daguerreotype, or miniature was copied. Used oil techniques, water color, and even penwork. Many examples now mistakenly called "American primitive" are from the Taylor factory. Some are signed with a stencil on the back.

Taylor Toby: Any bust or figural pitcher featuring General Zachary Taylor. The one example most generally known is a pitcher and not a Toby-form jug. The maker is not identified.

Taylor & West: Plaster-of-Paris ornament makers of Cincinnati from 1850s.

tazza: A shallow bowl or circular platter on a baluster stem and broad base. Originally a large basin or reservoir for bathing. Plural of this term is *tazze*, not "tazzas."

T-Base: Any stand base in the general form of a letter T. [*Example pictured.*]

tea: The celestial herb; the hot wine of the Orient. First mentioned in Boston by allusion to a "teapot" in 1695 and "tea table" in 1708. Mentioned in connection with "tea dishes" in late 17th century. Tea was a rare item and a beverage that increased rapidly in popularity. Originally sold in apothecary shops. One of the causes of the American Revolution, when taxed by the Crown. Substitutes found useful by many American colonial families were raspberry leaves, loosestrife, strawberry and currant leaves, camomile, sage, ribwort, and thoroughwort. Innumerable items of furniture appear in inventories designating usage with, or developed for, the keeping, service, and preparation of tea, as tea table, tea tray, tea caddy, teapot, teaboard, tea bottle, tea casket, tea chair, tea dish, tea chest.

teache: A sugar pan; an evaporating pan.

tea-chest top: Any hollow deep top hinged to a cabinet, with a sliding or other small door of access to the cavity exposed when the top was lifted. These are referred to as tea-chest tops because the cavity was allegedly a chest for tea.

tea conjuror: A very low or flat teakettle fitting over a deep dish with chimney and door. Tow, tinder, or shredded paper was placed in the lower section and ignited. The resulting combustion heated the water in the shallow kettle for a cup or two of tea. This is an early-19th-century item. [*Example pictured.*]

tea connoisseur's table: An elegancy of the 18th century; a tea table with a drawer compartmented with lead- or tin-lined boxes to hold various teas.

tea dish: A bowl of small size with an underdish.

tea dust: A color described as "delicate dun."

tea Kati: Tea caddy. Also sometimes found spelled tea kate.

teakettle: Properly a hot-water kettle in which water was brought to the furious boiling point for making tea in a teapot. When of silver, the teakettle was generally fitted with stand and spirit lamp.

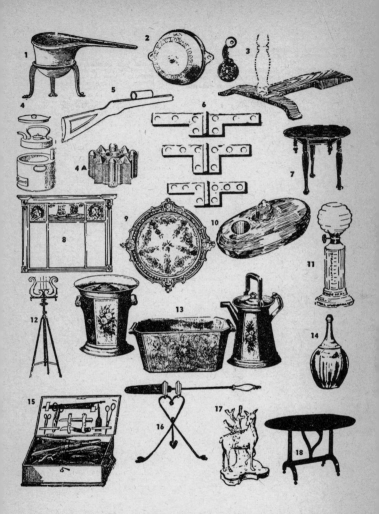

1, Tar Boiler. 2, Taylor Doorbell. 3, T-Base. 4, Tea Conjuror. 4A, Town-Mold. 5, Telescope Stock. 6, T Hinges. 7, Three-Legged Hexagonal Table. 8, Three-Panel Tabernacle Mirror. 9, Tile and Plate. 10, Toddy Warmer. 11, Time-Indicator Lamp (one type). 12, Tollie Music Stand. 13, Toilet Cans. 14, Tomato Flask. 15, Tool Chest. 16, Token. 17, Tortoise-Shell Figure (Whieldon). 18, Trestle Tilt-Top Table.

It should be noted this reference is to a silver teakettle and *not* to a silver teapot. When of brass, iron, or some other metal, the teakettle was made generally, but not always, without a stand and spirit lamp. These usually were brought to a boil on the hob grate or in the hearth. Teapots were used for the brewing of tea, thus: First the pot, of silver or other metal, or of ceramic ware, was scalded with boiling water. Then the tea leaves were added and the proper amount of boiling water poured over them. Teakettles were always used for heating the water; teapots for brewing the tea.

tea kitchen: A tea urn. Generally a hot-water urn, but sometimes used for brewing tea. *See* Tea Machine.

teakwood: An East Indian and oriental wood, esteemed for cabinetwork and flooring. Logs were imported from end of Revolution, and considerable furniture of the styles of the period was made by Chinese artisans for importers, 1800–50s. Several traders of Boston had teakwood furniture of Chinese make on hand for sale to dealers and retail custom.

tea leaf: Late ironstone ware decorated with a gold luster in form of conventionalized tea leaf, some of which look like carnation petals. English producers of this pattern, in quite a few varieties of decorative style, were: Grindley, Furnival, Wedgwood, Meakin, Burgess, Shaw, Wilkinson, Johnson, Corn, Clemson, Powell & Bishop, and Edwards. Most of this ware was produced from the 1870s. All of it is after 1860 (or so aver the English experts consulted). Importation continued to 1890s. American imitations with fictitious English marks are known to have been made at East Liverpool, O., and at Trenton, N.J. The basic ware is sometimes decorated with ribbing and other devices in the paste or in the body. Once ownership of this cheap ware was a badge of good taste and poor purse. It is now quite popular among many collectors.

tea machine: A huge central urn with spirit or charcoal heater and two taps for filling two smaller urns in which the tea was brewed, these also having taps for filling cups. A Sheffield-plate specialty made from 1790s.

tea plate: Specifically a size of plate, properly the 6-inch-diameter plate of silver, pewter, Sheffield plate, plated silver, glass, pressed or blown, and all forms of ceramic ware from redware and delft to porcelain.

tea poise; teapoy: A stand, originally for holding canisters or caddies of tea, but later designating a small tea table.

teapot stands: Trivets, generally of a metal ring, with a grill or twisted wire.

teapot Washington: The pose in several popular full-length portraits of the General and President, one arm cocking left hand on hip, the right arm extended, the body dumpy.

tear: An intentional or even accidental bubble of tear shape in glass. Intentional tears in stems, et cetera, were sometimes blown by inserting a fine, hollow, needle-like pipe through the hot metal and blowing it to size desired. Some were made by inserting a drop of alcohol, others by inserting a nail in the glass and closing the orifice after withdrawal of the piercing element.

tear box: A romantic elegancy of the 18th century; a small box of gold, silver, enamel, et cetera, enclosing a small sponge on which the tears of a sweetheart were wiped. An idea of the miniature size of the box may be had from the fact that they were carried on watch fobs.

Teardrop: A pattern of pressed glass featuring rows of small fig- or pear-shaped elements and rows of a twisting S-form yielding upright and invert shapes of the same form. **Teardrop & Tassel:** Not a variant of Teardrop, but an earlier pattern featuring the teardrop shape of fig or pear form, surrounded by a rococo feathering, stippled, and other very busy but not unpleasing motifs.

teardrop handles: Elongated pear-, tear-, or trumpet-shaped drops with rings, fixed loosely to a ring on a boss, used as furniture pulls. William & Mary and early Queen Anne periods. Chinese design. [*Examples are pictured; see* Brasses.]

teaslider: A castered trivet for sliding a teapot across or around a table.

tear spoon: Ancient form of spoon with a periform bowl, very shallow, and with a flat rim affixed to a handle.

tea sugar: Reference is to the baskets with glass liners designed to hold lumps or pieces of cone sugar. Generally of silver or Sheffield plate. The lumps were not always put in the tea to sweeten it; often the user put a piece of sugar in the mouth and sipped the tea "around" it!

teat spoon: A spoon with partly covered bowl and a suckle at end. An infant feeder and medicine doser for invalids.

tea water: Soft water was considered best for tea. Almost every town and city had public pumps, some of which were known as the tea-water pumps because they delivered the softest water. There were barrel carts driven around the towns dispensing tea water at so much per gallon. Springs yielding soft water were called tea springs.

teazel: A thistle or other burr used in raising the nap of cloth in finishing.

technicon: A practice keyboard instrument that made no sound. Often just a board with the keys painted on it; better examples have actual depressible keys.

Tecumseh: The Indian chief famed for his battle with our forces at the Indian Town. There is a mustard or honey pot in the form of a 2-inch-square blockhouse with a roof-form lid and chimney finial called Tecumseh.

teint: Color, hue, or tone.

telamone: The male figure or form used as a column, the female being a caryatid.

telegraph fan: A flirting fan; any fan with the letters of the alphabet and a pointer, enabling user to "telegraph" a message to another in the same room without uttering a word. Date is from late 18th century.

telegraph-pole effigies: In 1840s, when telegraph poles were first set up in town and village streets, they were planed, painted, and surmounted with carved effigies of doves, eagles, horses, Indians, busts of famed people, pigs, roosters, et cetera. Many such carved wood figures severed from pole tops are today revered as "primitive" carvings. Every pole in Portsmouth, O., for example, in 1848, was so embellished. This is an almost forgotten phase of street decoration and the camouflaging of what have eventually become eyesores on our streets.

telescope stock: A skeleton or solid gunstock with a metal ring to contain a telescope. [*Example pictured.*]

telescopic candlestand: A luxury trammel; a pedestal candlestand with the pedestal tapped to hold a wooden screw supporting the table or stand top. The tap and screw were of sufficient scope to permit raising and lowering the level of the top to maintain the flame level of candle at the point desired regardless of candle height. [*Two examples pictured.*]

telescopic stick: Said of a collapsible candlestick enabling user to keep the flame at same level by raising the stick height as candle burned.

Teller mirrors: From 1855, at Buffalo, N.Y., G. D. Teller was making looking glasses of various kinds, but chiefly tabernacle forms.

Tell furniture: Made by Swiss cabinetmakers at the co-operative at Tell City, Ind., incorporated 1859. One periodical in the antiques field, *Spinning Wheel*, has shown the type and kind of furniture made by this enterprise. It is to be found in the lower Ohio Valley and the middle Mississippi Valley and was made from 1858 to c. 1876. The style is French Antique, but not that which we immediately recognize as "Victorian"—it has something a trifle different about it.

tellurian: Of the earth.

telonkon phonon: A hard-rubber trumpet with tube for the ear, used by the deaf. The Grecian name is from 1840s.

tempera: Water color mixed with a binder such as beaten egg white, glue, gelatin, or gum arabic; a wall paint and an artist's medium. Tempera color does not penetrate plaster and is therefore not to be confused with fresco painting, which, properly, is the coloring of wet plaster by a penetrating pigment.

Temperanceville glass: Lewisville, N.J., glass made from 1830s and called as here because the works employed only teetotalers. Flasks, bottles, and hollow wares of blown glass.

Tempest pottery: Cincinnati yellow and Rockingham glaze ware made from 1850s. The pottery was known as the Hamilton Road Works, owned by M. & N. Tempest.

Temple & Temple Gate ware: Bristol, England, pottery wares, actually stonewares; the Temple works established 1730s and the Temple Gate works later. General stonewares, including some enormous jugs. **Temple Backs:** Another Bristol pottery making fine earthenwares, Parian, and delft glaze wares from 1780s.

Temple glass: Reference is to Temple, N.H., window glass and bottles made from 1780 to 1782. Said to have been made by deserters from British army.

Templeton furniture: Reference is probably to furniture made at Templeton,

Mass., from 1830s, when 22 people were employed in production.

temse: A strainer; a sieve.

tender porcelain: Soft-paste ware, such as Bristol, Sèvres, and other wares, including the American "Tucker" porcelain. The term is from the French *porcelaine tendre* as opposed to hard paste, such as Meissen, called *porcelaine dure*. The Sèvres works was established 1738 at Vincennes and moved to Sèvres in 1755.

tendril stem: Any stem, as of a glass goblet, entwined with applied spiral of glass thread.

Tennent, Thomas: Instrument maker of Philadelphia, 1830s and early 1840s, who moved to Newburyport, Mass., in 1845 or 1846.

Tennessee kettle: Sugar kettle of copper, ranging in size from 2 to 7 feet in diameter, variations being in 6-inch differences. Made at New Orleans, or sold extensively by J. B. West of that city to 1880s.

ten-toes: Colloquial for foot travel.

tent stitch: Diagonal stitching in imitation of tapestry weaving. Tent stitch did not involve a cross-stitch technique.

term: Stones, posts, sometimes carved and lettered, marking the boundaries of a property holding. Some are carved with effigy finials. Sometimes called carved fence posts, but properly term posts, or posts of a term fence. Also a spade foot. Making such a foot was called "terming."

terme: A human figure displayed from head to hips and from there downward as a tapering column. Small examples of metal with socket tops are properly terme candlesticks.

Terpsichore: Greek Muse of the dance.

terra coelian: Of the heavens; an ovate, globose device with hanger, displaying a map of the heavens. A device of this kind was made at Chambersburg, Pa., from 1860s by a Dr. Agnew.

terra cotta: Unglazed redware, or red stoneware. Tiny to large objects, utensils, devices, architectural elements, and stoves are of record.

terre verte: Green earth, a pigment. Green unglazed ceramic ware.

Terry & Barnes mirrors: Theodore Terry and Horace Barnes, in partnership at Boston from 1840s, made gilded clock cases and mirror frames.

Terry clock: The term generally used to designate a mantel or shelf clock in a casing of free-standing pillars at each side of the boxlike case, surmounted by a double scroll and three brass shell finials. Eli Terry did not create this case, nor was he the first clockmaker to use it. His inspiration was indubitably the similar beautiful casing used by his compeer, Heman Clark, prior to Terry's use. [*Example pictured.*] Of course any clock of any kind by Eli Terry is properly a Terry clock. His pillar and scroll dates from second decade of 19th century.

tessellated: Of tiles; in a tile form; a tile-form pattern.

test: A round or oval deep ring of iron used as a rim to hold a bed of sand or wood ashes for a crucible in refining small amounts of metal.

tester (sometimes teester): A framework for bed hangings. A headpiece. From the French *tête*, meaning head. **tester laths:** The slender wood pieces joining high posts of a bed and forming the tester frame.

tête-à-tête: A seat for two, especially one having seats facing in opposite directions. A love seat. Also a tea set for two. Any intimate seat, table, bench, or item of usage.

tetrachord: A four-string musical instrument, played by strumming. Also a keyboard instrument somewhat like a hurdigurdi, the keys pressing the strings against a revolving drum.

tetrapod: Four-footed table or stand.

Texas: (1) The independent nation which became a part of the United States. The most extensive state in the Union. (2) A pattern of pressed glass featuring a series of loops, sometimes flashed with red, and gold-striped.

textilographs: Jacquard-loomed pictorial fabrics, especially narrow fabrics used as souvenirs. Some display scenes from *Mother Goose, Alice in Wonderland*, and other popular subjects. Date is from 1850s.

Thalia: Greek Muse of comedy and joy.

thaumatrope: A variety of zoetrope, *which see*.

theabethorne: The gooseberry bush. Also theabes and thesethorn.

theatrical glass: Any blown or pressed glass, cut, etched, or formed in pressing or blowing molds, displaying names, faces, forms, et cetera, of stage and theatrical personages and even noted burlesque characters of low repute. Lola Montez, Jenny Lind, and many others are so memorialized.

thenseygnements: Thinking processes, from *thenche*, to think.

theorbo-lute: A two-headed multi-stringed lute used in 17th century to make chamber music.

theorem: A stencil; a picture produced by painting through stencils, one or more for each color.

therm: Pedestal, usually solid, of classic design, to support a bust, statue, or lamp.

Thibet shawl: A shawl of northern India, extensively imported and sold in U.S. from 1820s to 1840s.

thiel: Artificial stone. Also called hellenstein.

thimble hand: Pressed or tooled blown-glass hand with the fingers arranged as hangers for thimbles.

thimble-pie: Tapping the heads of youngsters with a finger tipped with a thimble as a rebuke for inattention.

thimble porringer: A dram or dose cup in single-eared porringer form; perhaps a bleeding bowl. Some bowls are 2 inches or less in diameter.

T hinge: A hinge of the LL form with the vertical leaves shortened, in use displaying a T form at top placement and similarly truncated LL form at bottom. [*Examples pictured.*]

Thistle: Pattern of pressed glass displaying a horizontal banding of thistles and leaves.

thistledown: The fine down from the thistle seed pod, used in superfine quilts. One square inch of quilted surface required down from 6 to 12 thistle heads.

thistle foot: A ball foot with a protuberance of round upward-tapering form, causing the foot to resemble a thistle. William & Mary period style. [*Example pictured.*]

thistle sander: A desk elegancy of silver in the form of a thistle head, footed and with a tail. A standing box de luxe. [*Example pictured.*]

thistle whiskey: Scotch whiskey bottle of 1880s in thistle form. [*Example pictured.*]

Thomas, Seth: Highly successful clockmaker of Connecticut who was once a workman for Eli Terry. A Seth Thomas clock is any clock made by him; he did not create any specific style of casing, but copied all the then popular casings from 1810s to 1850s. The business he founded is still in operation, being a part of General Time Instruments Corp.

Thomas furniture: Philip Thomas was a "Joyner & Chairmaker" of Lancaster, Pa., from 1760s. Said to have made Georgian-style furniture and Windsor chairs. A few labeled pieces survive.

Thomas mirrors: Elias Thomas of New York City, from 1810s, made tabernacle, pier, mantel, and toilet mirrors in gilded, walnut, and mahogany frames. Some parcel-gilded. Some are marked with maker's label.

Thompson burner: A patented gas jet with a cone-and-ball governor to overcome the flare and dimming owing to varying pressures. Made from 1850s.

Thompson chair: It is an invalid's chair, propelled by occupant's grasping a circular railing extending from the wheels.

Thompson mantels: Cast-iron chimney mantels, beautifully molded, made from 1840s at Lawrence, Mass., by S. J. Thompson.

Thompsonville carpets: Woven at Thompsonville, N.Y., from 1840s; three-ply Brussels types, Axminsters, et cetera, woven on hand looms in an extensive manufactory.

Thomson brush: A cup-form brush with a wheel, for cleaning the nails. Used immersed, with the hand, in a bowl of water.

Thomson glass: Double-walled glass with silver or mercurial deposit. Invented by Hale Thomson in 1840s. Many decorative objects, vessels, and utilitarian pieces made of this glass; cut, etched, or plain. Later applications of the principle involved paper-thin glass and resulted in making the ware cheaply for even the thinnest purses.

Thorps & Sprague plate: Advertising plate of rose-pink transfer-printed Staffordshire-type ware, maker unknown, for firm of this name at Albany, N.Y., c. 1825-50.

Thousand Eye: Pattern of pressed glass that is an all-over application of round disks, graduating in size suitably to contour of the pieces. There is a tiny diamond form between the rows of circles.

thousand-eye sconce: A sconce with a

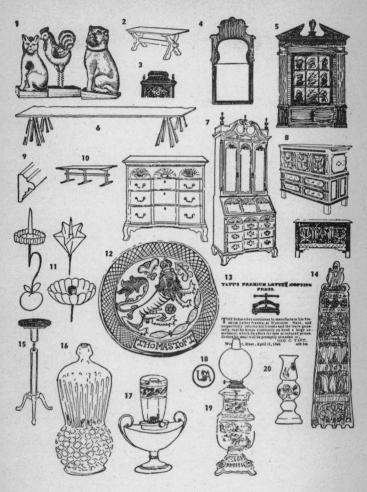

1, Squeak Toys. **2,** Sawbuck Table. **3,** Sarcophagus Top. **4,** Two-Part Mirror. **5,** Tabernacle. **6,** Table Board, c. 1560. **7,** Townsend-Goddard Block Fronts. **8,** Tulip Chests. **9,** Treacle Molding. **10,** Trestle Table. **11,** Tree Candle-Pans. **12,** Toft Plate. **13,** Taft Press. **14,** Tally Board. **15,** Telescopic Candlestand. **16,** Thistle Whiskey Bottle. **17,** Urn Lamp. **18,** U.S.A. Lancaster Button. **19,** Vase Lamp. **20,** Vase Candle-Lamp. (No. 17 from Virtue & Co., London.)

reflector made up of many tiny panes of mirror glass.

thousand-pound book: A book, published 1830 by Linsell of London, attacking (actually revealing) the morals of a high-placed member of the royal family of England. Copies in the U.S. were sought by the agent, R. B. Brown of New York, who offered to buy them back at one thousand pounds or five thousand dollars a copy. The offer no longer holds. It was made in 1831.

thrave: Twenty-four sheaves or 4 shocks of corn in the field.

threaded glass: (1) Glass with applied threading, not impressed. (2) Glass having the appearance of division into fine threads, examples of which were made at Sandwich. This same effect was later achieved by machining and sometimes in pressed wares. (3) Swirled fine ribbing which is *not* threading and should not be so called. It should be noted that some threading is of heavy character, as the rings on jars and around decanter necks. The term is now often loosely used.

three babes in a tub: A religious fantasy out of the legend of St. Nicholas (San Niklaus, or Santa Claus), who performed a miracle of restoring to life and form the bodies of three babes who were chopped up in a tub. The symbol is found on spoon handles and other silverware of 18th century. The legend, of course, is medieval.

three boys porcelain: See Hirado.

Three Face (properly Three Graces): Pattern of pressed glass with the faces of the three Graces of Greek myth pressed on the stem. All three faces are seemingly alike.

three-leg chair: See Chairs, All Kinds.

three-legged hexagon table: It is the skirting that is hex form, not the top, which is circular. There should, of course, be six legs, but there are only three; there are turned droops, or pendants, at the other and alternate angles of the hex-form skirting. A freak table. Some date from 1780s or 1840s, later ones may be Grand Rapids. [*Example pictured.*]

three-mold: Said of glass blown in three-piece iron molds.

Three Panel: Pattern of pressed glass with three panels of raised lens like protuberances, alternate ones with a flower form impressed.

three-panel tabernacle: A tabernacle-type mirror made for overmantel use, the width embracing one wide and two narrower mirror panels, each surmounted with a painted glass panel, the whole confined within a gilded framing with cornice. Miscalled "Sheraton." [*Example pictured.*]

three-tier comb-back: See Chairs, All Kinds.

threestule, threstule: A three-legged stool; origin of "trestle."

three-toed foot: Queen Anne period footing on cabriole legs, having a three-divisional carved pad, or toe.

threshing chair: See Chairs, All Kinds.

throne: Calaboose cant term for the three-tiered "ajax" or ancient prison-house

toilet which requires a Chic Sale to do it justice in terms of description; what more need be said here?

throstle-spun: Opposite of homespun; thread spun on the throstle, the spinning machine invented by Arkwright.

thrown: Turned on a lathe of any kind. The thrower in a pottery was the worker who turned the clay on a potter's wheel, a one-mandrel, vertical lathe. Throwing woodenware and all sorts of elements resulted in the early terms "thrown chair," "thrown bowle," et cetera, a thrown chair being a chair made from turned elements. *See also* Chairs, All Kinds.

throwsted: Twisted, as thread. Throstling is a corruption of throwsting, meaning spun on a throw—a wheel. The fiber turned.

thrysi: A staff tipped with a cone and vine, twined. A decorative element.

thumb Bible: Any bible in miniature. N. Proctor of Boston, 1765, issued a thumb Bible less than 2 inches square in page size.

Thumbprint: Pattern of pressed glass with all-over design of ovate depressions resembling thumbprints. There is variant with the ovate print pointed which is called Almond or Pointed Thumbprint.

thunderstone: Elongated conical fossil shell.

thurbible: A censer swung on chains.

Thuya; Thuja: A wood of the evergreen Thuya genus, as white cedar. The American arborvitae is a Thuya.

T'iao-an: Chinese for a ceremonial side table; the kind Chippendale and other designers copied.

Tice floorcloth: Painted canvas floorcloths "made to order within three months" by Painter Tice, N.Y., working 1810s–20s.

ticktacktoe frame: A style of picture or mirror frame of flat molding, sometimes parcel-gilt, imitative of rustic framing, the members crossing at corners and projecting.

tidy: A lace mat, originally to cover a marred spot (to tidy it up), but in general use during 19th century on tables, chair arms, chair backs, and even seats. **tidy pin:** A fastener to hold a tidy in place on upholstery; the pin is a curved coil, the head decorative. Once inserted, these pins stayed in place until deliberately removed.

tierce: A measure, 42 gallons.

tiered: Stacked, with interstices, as a tiered table, tiered compote, stand, et cetera. A series of levels on a common supporting member.

tie ring: A stable fixture; cast-iron or brass rings and holders, for tethering a horse.

tiff: Originally the drink now generally referred to as flip; one recipe is beer, rum, sugar, and a slice of buttered toast.

Tiffany Reed et Cie.: The Paris branch of Tiffany, Young & Ellis, the first Tiffany firm dealing in objects of art, jewelry, and silverwares.

tig; tyg: Tile; a drinking "tile," from the French *tuile* and the early English *tigel*. A handled communal cup or bowl.

tiger jug: Reference is to the glaze, imitative—perhaps originally by accident—of tiger-skin mottling in miniature. Many early tiger-ware jugs are potbellied and trimmed with silver. These may date from 16th or 17th century. The secret of the glaze is known, and there are jugs of 19th-century make in the same technique.

T hinge: Wrought-iron and brass hinges, assembled from upright straps having angular arms, to right of one strap and left of the other, thus forming a T. This term applies to the top hinges only, as the same hinge used at bottom of door has the arms at bottom and hence is called LL hinge.

Tilden inkstand: A non-spilling ink bottle in a metal stand, made from 1870s by Tilden, Hale & Co. of New York City.

tile & plate: Composite, assembled wares of Atkins Sheffield-plated frames with inserts of tiles by Copeland (late Spode). Some very fine trays, teapot stands, cake plates, and other flat pieces were made. [*Example pictured.*]

tile carpet: Any hooked, woven, embroidered, or appliquéed carpeting of tile pattern, in squares ranging from 4 to 12 inches.

tile seat: A chair seat of delft tile or tiles, early examples in wood chairs, later inserted in wrought- and cast-iron chair frames.

tilewright: A maker of pantiles. Often pantiles were the bread-and-butter product of a redware pottery.

Till ware: Earthenwares and cane wares made by Thomas Till and T. Till & Sons at the old Sytch Pottery, Burslem, from 1830s.

tilter water set: A stand holding an ice-water pitcher tiltable for easy pouring. Some in silver, but generally in electroplated ware.

tilting chair: See Chairs, All Kinds. **tilting cruet:** A stand holding two or more cruets fixed in gimbals. A ship table item. **tilting drum table:** Generally reconstructions, using old round-top tilting stands, adding a skirting and some drawers, and so contriving a drum table. All examples examined for this work showed evidence of such reconstruction, and none of them show evidence of originality in this form.

tilt top; tip-top: Round, rectangular, and other form table tops, mounted on pedestals (some on folding legged frames), the tops hinged, secured with a stout latch or other fastener, tiltable to upright or "screen" position at will. 18th and 19th centuries. Range of size is from 1 foot to 5 feet in top diameter or major axis. Most piecrust, dish-top, and bowled tables are tilt tops.

Timberlake carpet: Floor oilcloths and woven carpets made by Timberlake and Bryant, Louisville, Ky., from 1840s. In 1845 this mill was weaving 3000 yards of carpeting per month.

timber wheels: Pairs of wheels on a common axle, for carting logs to sawmill. The logs were suspended under the axle in transporting.

time globe: A clock featuring a globe with a pointer, the revolution of which told the time of a given place and of all other time zones on the earth. At least four different varieties were made in U.S. from 1860s. These are now highly desirable clocks of the sort sought by collectors. [*Example pictured.*]

time lamp: Any lamp consuming its fluid oil at a rate computable in terms of hours and fractions, indicated on the reservoir. There is a small pressed-glass lamp for the bedside, with title "Pride of America" pressed on it, that burned with a dim flame, yet showed the passing of the hours on the side of a candle-form reservoir. [*Example pictured.*]

timocracy: The ideal political state envisioned by Plato and Aristotle. The precise opposite of communism. Plato's republic was subservient to the people; in communism, all people are subservient to the state.

Timpson & Gilmore: Cabinetmakers of New York from 1780s, who were first or among the first to introduce the Hepplewhite style to America. In 1794 the partnership was dissolved, but Thomas Timpson continued making Hepplewhite-style furniture and illustrated his newspaper advertising with a Hepplewhite shieldback chair.

tin: In metalworking, the fourth precious metal, its superiors being platinum, gold, and silver. Tin plate originally was pure tin and not tin-washed iron. Block-tin ware originally was pure tinware. Painted tin is not pure tinware, but tinned sheet-iron ware. Some of this ware, however, is very fine, as tole and Pontypool wares, the painting often done by real artists, in form of portraits, landscapes, and genre subjects, classical scenes, bosky views, et cetera. Cheap painted tin is in the coach painter's style, or stenciled.

tincal: The borax used as a flux by tinners, braziers, and silversmiths.

tinder: Any quick-igniting substance, such as tow, charred linen, lint, punk, saltpeter-impregnated linen, et cetera. **tinder-bottomed:** Said of any candlestick looking like a socket on a covered pan with handle, the pan being a tinder-box with flint, steel, and tinder. [*Example pictured.*] **tinder bow:** A bow with cord, used to spin a rod in a hole in a soft block of wood, surrounded by tinder, for making fire. **tinderbox:** Any container of the necessary equipment for making a fire, with sparks in tinder, or with burning glass, or both. Many varieties, from silver pocket examples to large iron boxes.

tinder gilt: Gold, dissolved in muriatic and nitric acid (aqua-regia), then soaked into cloth that was reduced to tinder. This tinder was rubbed on metal, as clock faces, and so gilded the surface. Method used in 17th and 18th centuries.

tinder pouch: Fire-making equipment enclosed in a leather pouch, some very beautifully tooled.

ting: A footed caldron.

tin glass: Bismuth, added to tin to make it more brittle and less ductile.

Tingley bed: Any bed made at "the 3 story high, 35 x 120 foot size" factory of Tingley & Co., Patroons Creek, Tivoli, N.Y., the entire product being of the Lindley "bugproof" type. Made from 1840s.

tin kitchen: Open-faced roasting oven of

tinned sheet iron, used before an open fire, fitted with spits and hooks. [*Example pictured.*] In this the spit is horizontal. Some other examples have a vertical suspended spit, often run by clockwork.

tin putty: Oxide of tin.

tin safe: A meat or pie safe; a panneties or bread cabinet, with sheet-iron panels pierced for air circulation, often in very pleasing pattern.

tin Toby: A lithographed tin container with hinged lid; probably a tobacco box. Date is 1900 or later. *See* Rolly-Polly Jars.

tinsel picture: Minor art work or homecraft pictures, using tinsel papers cut into shapes and mounted to form a picture or montage, especially those imitative of fruit and flower pieces, landscapes and costume prints. Late 18th century and early 19th. Some are amazingly intricate and fine. **tinseled prints:** In the same philosophy, but the trim is on and over a printed picture. A *gravure découpée.*

tinsmiths: While many 19th-century tinsmiths are listed in this dictionary, others of record simply had to be dropped. The consensus seems to be that the name of the maker is not important in tin or tin-plated sheet-iron ware; the important things are the quality of the ware found and its probable usage.

tin wedding ware: All sorts of objects, such as boots, shoes, slippers, bonnets, high hats, tables, chairs, et cetera, made by tinsmiths in full or oversize, and sometimes in half or miniature size, as gifts for a tin wedding anniversary.

tippet: A neckpiece, generally of fur.

Tippecanoe-North Bend: Nickname of William Henry Harrison, who, with Tyler, was a great political and military figure. All sorts of souvenirs of these men as candidates survive, especially flasks of mold-blown glass.

tip staff: The snore staff of office, used by officials of courts and churches to waken sleepers and quiet the noisy. Some have a feather tip, others a knob. [*Example pictured.*]

tipsy musicians: Barroom ornaments of terra cotta, approximately 18 inches high, made from 1870s. Figures represent four musicians, probably what used to be called a "German band."

tip-top: Tilt top.

tirggels: Molds of wood, stone, iron, and pottery, for making the almond-meal cake also known as marzipan, marchpane, mercipanis, and mazibaume. They are carved in floral, fruit, emblematic, figural, animalistic, bird, and other forms, some actually genre scenes. Sometimes pronounced "turtle" and "turgle." The use of these molds would seem to date from 16th century.

tithe pig group: Ralph Wood pottery figure group of statuary, depicting a farmer and his wife paying their tithe with a pig to the parson. Several varieties.

toad boxes: Chinese jade and rock-crystal boxes carved in form of rotund toad (the "moon toad"), and imitations in Parian and porcelain.

Toa-kuang: Chinese period, 1802-50.

toasting fork: Two- or three-tined long-handled fork. **toaster:** A wire clamp or grid to hold a slice of bread, also on a long handle. Some are small wire fences, close-set, to hold several slices of bread, pivoted on a footed trivet and so turnable to toast both sides with a flick of the wrist. Many varieties. Generally of wrought iron and iron wire. Rare examples brass-trimmed.

toast rack: A rack for serving toast at the table. Silver, Sheffield plate, and iron examples in seemingly infinite variety. Date is from 18th century.

tobacco grater: A pocket grater for rasping carrot or twist tobacco into snuff.

tobacco pipes: These smokers' items were made in quantities from 1610s; the pipes of the wealthy were of silver and those of the yokelry of clay. Finally the wealthy smokers discovered the yokel's clay was the better pipe, and the "churchwarden" clay was devised. Innumerable varieties, shapes, and forms, in various substances from stone to paper. **tobacco stopple:** Utensil carried by pipe smokers of earlier days to tamp the glowing coals of the weed after lighting the pipe. Examples of gold, silver, ivory, wood, stone, pottery, tin, brass, et cetera, are of record, brass and iron ones being most common. Reproduction of 18th-century ones made to 1930s. These are as fascinating an item as Apostle spoons. Many are busts of famed persons. Some stopples are affixed to finger rings. [*Examples pictured.*]

Toby (the original): Paul Parnell, farmer of Yorkshire, England, who died 1810, was the original "Toby Philpot" of O'Keefe's bacchanalian songs, mentioned by this name. Parnell drank, in his lifetime, £2000 sterling worth of home-brewed Yorkshire "slingo," or strong beer. The term Toby for a figural jug depicting a genial, rotund character dates from 1760s. This date is in respect to the name "Toby" and not the figural-jug idea. These jugs were known in 17th century, and leather examples, well modeled and painted, in the shape of an innkeeper and a barwoman, are well known to experts in collecting of drinking relics.

Toby jug (American): Reference is to copies of English Tobys made at Henderson's Jersey City Pottery, or to figural jugs of American interest no matter where made. There are examples of Washington and others which may be quite late but which nonetheless are collected.

todd: Twenty-eight pounds of wool.

Todd looking glasses: There was a manufacturer of looking glasses named Todd at Portland, Me., operating in 1815 and working to 1830s. Said to have made tabernacle-type mirrors. This is most logical reference.

toddy: The true toddy is obtained thus: The flower stalk of the coconut tree (looking like a white flower-covered bush) is cut off and the sap running from the tree collected and used as a beverage. Most esteemed if the sap is permitted to ferment. This drink is a favorite of troops in the subtropics and of sailors voyaging in those regions. Thus the term entered the language and was applied to imitations of the drink, made from rum, gin, whiskey, and brandy, with sugar and fruit juices. **toddy kettle:** Small kettle, with spout and cover, mounted on a high, perforated conical section; so designed for use over a gas burner. Generally of tinned sheet iron, in capacities from half pint to one quart. **toddy lifter:** Glassware device having the appearance of a miniature bottle with quite long neck and with an orifice in the bottom. Used by plunging into a bowl of toddy, placing thumb over the neck orifice, and so "lifting" a measure of toddy from the bowl. Contents fell into a drinking glass upon release of thumb. Atmospheric pressure did the trick. **toddy plate:** A pottery dish with flat bottom and narrow upstanding rim, used as a coaster for toddy glasses. Some marked by potters; mostly Staffordshire. **toddy warmer:** A pewter or brass hot-water bottle with a well in which to stand a mug or glass. Probably a gruel warmer. [*Example pictured.*]

Toft ware: The tulip, bird, flower, and figure decorated slip wares made by Thomas Toft, Ralph Toft, and other 17th-century Staffordshire potters, the ware that was copied by Pennsylvania potters and now called Pennsylvania German. A secret but active business of reproducing this ware has existed since the 1900s, and many examples now considered genuine, in near proof condition, may be fakes. The ware (authentic) is now quite rare, but it was originally made in great quantities for the people; it was never a luxury ware. Smith, the first potter of redware in Pennsylvania, was a Staffordshire man, and probably the German potters copied his ware. It is more likely, however, that they copied a similar ware made in Switzerland and sometimes lettered with sentiments in Italian, French, and German. [*Example of Toft ware pictured.*]

toggle iron: Whaler's harpoon with razor-sharp blade and a cross barb set in a slot back of the blade to prevent withdrawal. Not to be confused with toggle bolt.

toile: Glazed chintz, especially pictorial, floral, and scenic. Most famous is the *toile de Jouy*, made by Oberkampf from 1760s. Fine prints made also at Mulhouse, Lyons, Rouen, Nantes, Agen, Orange, and other textile centers. Printed calico, many made in U.S., especially at the early Philadelphia print works. English examples of early 19th century are much esteemed. There are innumerable reproductions now available. There is no special virtue in ownership of the early originals except as specimens.

toile de Jouy: Glazed cotton fabrics printed in colors from blocks. First examples were imitative of India prints, but soon the product, while using the India-print methods for obtaining the results, featured designs of contemporaneous genre.

toilet bracket: Hanging mirror with attached tray for brush and comb. Cheap wood- and tin-framed examples made from 1860s. Many are homemade.

toilet cans: Sets of painted or plain tinned sheet iron, generally a basin, slop jar, and covered water pail with pouring spout. [*Example pictured.*]

toilet fountain: Late agateware, or enameled sheet iron, wall lavabo, one of which was made as late as 1890 by the Central Stamping Co., of New York, and Saint Louis, Mo. The reservoir of this ensemble

was also used singly, without matching bowl, as a douche. Both are marked AGATE.

toilet glass: (1) A mirror to hang over a toilet table. (2) A small case of drawers (toilet stand) with a mirror mounted between uprights. Known in all period styles from William & Mary to Victorian.

toilet set: (1) A set of bottles and powder jars for the toilet table. Known in pottery, porcelain, glass, and metal. (2) Bedroom sets of sanitary ware, generally basin, slop jar, pitcher, and chamber pot. Known in glass (sometimes cut!), porcelain, often embellished with floral and even classic scenes, and gold, china, ironstone, redware, silver, brass, and pewter. Some of the ornate slop jars are now being promoted as "banquet sugar bowls."

toiletta: Diminutive of toile, meaning a small item of textile work. This definition must be explained: Toile is from *tela*, meaning a web, in turn, it is said, related to the Greek *techo*, to weave. Toile then came to mean a dressed fabric and toilette, or toiletta, to dress with a fabric. There are many terms in collecting and cataloguing allied or referring to the art of dressing, grooming and laving, primping, et cetera. The toilette dressing case is a stand with four or more drawers, each fitted with a full-out mirror. When all mirrors were set up the user could view the effect of coiffure and rouging from every angle.

toise: Two yards, or six feet.

token: A curling iron in a sheath, on a footed stand. These, properly, should stand only by or in a bedroom or boudoir fireplace. [*Example pictured.*]

tokens: (1) Emergency money of no official status, often issued as a gibe against official or fiat money. (2) Symbolic checks of entrance or participation, as communion tokens, breakfast tokens, or passes to entertainment. (3) Evidence of right to participation in some event, as a viewer of a parade, rider in omnibus or coach, ferry, et cetera. (4) Metallic advertisements of stores and shops, generally having some trade-in value. (5) Small medals.

tole: Painted tinned sheet-iron ware. The French equivalent of Pontypool. The term actually means to lure, decoy, or bait. A ball-shaped, hollow button, painted. Sometimes used as a bead. Some chairs of Provence and Aignon have painted tole panels in the backs; these are the French equivalent of the American "fancy chair."

tollie stand: A music stand; some have a candlestick fixed near the rack. [*Example pictured.*]

Tollman woodenware: An extensive manufactory of buckets, keelers, bowls, churns, et cetera, was conducted by C. Tollman of Boston from 1830s or 1840s. Wise & Lane succeeded to the business in 1850s.

tomata: The early spelling of tomato, the love apple. Native American plant, originally the tomati. **tomato flask:** The original ketchup bottle. [*Example pictured.*]

tombac: Alloy of 75% copper and 25% arsenic—so says an ancient recipe. More generally 16 parts copper, 1 tin, 1 zinc.

tombstone pottery: Reference is to redware, true Lowestoft, and delftware lettered by incision, scratching, or painting, made into steles or memorials placed over tombs or at grave heads.

tomfoolish: Nonsensical.

Toms, W.: Wood carver and chairmaker of Bath, England, who issued a design book for 36 chairs c. 1830. Many were copied by U.S. chairmakers.

Tom Thumb lamp: A small glass hand lamp with a lever for lifting the chimney. Made by Cahoon of Boston, 1850s–60s. Probably called a Tom Thumb after Barnum's famous midget.

Tong: Pattern of pressed glass featuring beveled diamond forms and hourglass ovals. Said to be a very early pattern.

tongue & groove joint: A table joint; the tongue is on the top boards, the groove in the drop leaves. This is the joint that should be on all good to fine 17th-century tables, especially gate-leg and butterfly types.

tongued corner: A cabinet and table-top corner finish that eliminates the 90° angle by incurved cutting and a reverse, forming a rounded tongue.

Tonkin, W.: Cabinetmaker of Alexandria, Va., working from 1780s. Classic-styled cabinetwork, Hepplewhite in tradition. Advertised in Alexandria *Gazette*, 1794.

tontisse: Shorn, as to make flocking. Finely cut wool.

tonungs: Graspers; as fire tongs, ice tongs, skid tongs.

tool chest: Properly a chest fitted with its complement of tools. Many were made up for emigrants and pioneers. Examples of American make date from early 19th century. [*A pioneer's tool chest of 1830s is pictured.*]

toothed piano: The piano without strings that never needed tuning. The secret was a huge comb of tonal teeth, a sort of gigantic music-box comb, each tooth of which had its corresponding hammer. Made in U.S. by its inventor, C. B. Clap of Gardiner, Me. Owners having playable examples they wish to dispose of will please write to the author of this volume. We want one example for a museum we patronize and will be glad to tell other museums of available ones.

toothing plane: The plane with a blade that grooved a wood surface with many "teeth"—as many as 22 to the inch. Such work was done to prepare a surface for veneering.

toothkey: A turnkey with a claw, on a rod, firmly socketed. It was used in drawing teeth; the claw grasped the tooth, and slow turning lifted it from its socket. It hurt.

tooth ornament: Dentiled; rows of toothform elements used as ornament. French *violette*. It is found used from early Gallic era, 13th century.

toothpick: This much-maligned "ghastly" item was in use from Tudor times, made of gold, silver, horn. In 1867 a Boston woodenware manufacturer set up a water-powered machine that turned out four million wooden toothpicks per day. Original boxes of these are now collectors' items.

toper's pitcher: Any wine vessel or pitcher, engraved or painted, incised or cut with a sentiment in favor of drinking or in praise of drink.

top-gilded: Glass embellished with gold on its top or used side. The result was quick marring of the surface. The gilding was therefore soon applied to the underside of the ware. Top-gilded glass is the earlier variety.

top-hops: The tender fresh shoots of the hop vine, cooked and eaten with or in place of asparagus. The shoots of the pokeberry were also considered a rare treat. Warning: Use only the first, early shoots of the pokeberry bush. They are said to be poisonous when even half mature.

topiary work: Pruning foliage into fantastic, formal, or figural forms. An 18th-century garden vagary.

topier work: Road making or path construction of rough stone covered with crushed oyster or other shells.

Toppan, Abner: Cabinetmaker of Newbury, Mass., who worked in the styles of Hepplewhite and Sheraton. Born 1764, died 1836. Worked from 1785 to 1835.

Toppan, Stephen: Furniture manufacturer of Dover, N.H., from 1820s. Credited with making Sheraton and Empire styles in cabinet furniture, Windsor and fancy chairs, and massive sideboards.

torchère: Tall pedestal-form candlestand or lamp holder.

Torrey fruit jar: A black-glaze redware preserve jar of mid-19th century, more commonly known as the Egyptian fruit jar.

Torricellian barometer: The sealed-end, glass-tube barometer invented by Torricelli. With the open end immersed in liquid of the same character as the filler, the column within the tube rose and fell with variations in atmospheric pressure. Signpost barometers are usually of this type.

torsello: Obscure as to precise meaning; these have been found used: (1) A corded bale of raw silk. (2) A corbel to support a beam. (3) A pair of dice, or cubes.

tortoise-shell ware: Bowls, dishes, spoons, ladles, combs, and trinkets made from mottled and amber-colored tortoise shell. Horn ware. Any pottery with a glaze simulating tortoise shell, as Whieldon's wares. Figures and animals of this ceramic ware are now rare items. [*Example pictured.*]

torus: A bold convex molding.

Tory, Geoffroy: The Frenchman who made public the secrets of the art of printing which the Dutch had obtained from the Chinese and which Gutenberg learned in the Netherlands. He published the classic printed book, *Champfleury*, 1526.

touch needles: Small rods of gold of known varying karat, rubbed on the touchstone beside a rubbing from gold of unknown purity, to establish the standard.

touchwood: Tinder of dried fungus. Also the horizontal shell fungus growing on trees, the underside of which is white until touched, whereupon it turns brown at the point of contact.

Tournai: Tapestry made at this French

1, Triangle Tilt-Top Table. **2,** Trumpet Vase. **3,** Trunk Bed. **4,** Tulip Chalice. **5,** Turkey Bell. **6,** Turret Sideboard. **7,** Twin Cannon. **8,** Twin Tabourettes. **9,** Twisting Snake Toy. **10,** Twin-Bottle Vase. **11,** Two-Drivers Jug. **12,** Two-Seat Sofa. **12A,** Tipstaff. **13,** Two-Spout Coffeepot. **14,** Trunk-on-Frame. **15,** Tower Urn. **16,** Tin Kitchen. **17,** Tinder-Bottom Candlestick. **18,** Thistle Sander.

city, the rival of Arras after 15th century. Sometimes Touraine or Turnay. These terms do not refer to the tapestry but to the fabrics better known as dornick, darnick, doornick, and similar names.

Tourneaux, M. le: Silversmith of New York who, from 1790s, made cheap goldwashed and silver trinkets for the Indian trade.

tournesol: Archil or litmus violet color. Crimson-violet.

Towars glass: Olive-green glass made at Philadelphia. One research worker on this dictionary project reported it made from 1770s to 1900! Also made window glass, plain-blown and cut glass.

towel horse: A towel rack.

tower urn: *Dinanderie* and plain pewter urns for water or wine; they are on high footed legs, with spouts, and many are imitative of the towers of castles. Originals date from 14th century. Dutch and Flemish. [*Example pictured.*]

Towle silver: The sterling silver made at Newburyport, Mass., by the silver manufactory that grew out of the shop of A. F. Towle. It is 19th- and 20th-century ware of good quality. This firm issued some of the most interesting historic monographs about their products known in the commercial Americana scene.

town molds: Aspic, jelly, and pudding molds in the form of a medieval walled town. These are late 19th century and early 20th. [*Example pictured.*]

Townsend fenders: Fireplace fenders made by Townsend & Co., St. Louis, Mo., from 1830s.

Townsend furniture: Block-front masterpieces made by Christopher Townsend, Newport, R.I., working 1722–77. Similar fine cabinetwork by Edmund Townsend, Newport, 1760s–1811. Job Townsend, originator of the American school of block fronting, from the Dutch style, worked c. 1718–65 and taught the block-front technique to John Goddard. Job, Jr., worked c. 1750–1818; Thomas, 1760s–1820s; James, 1765–1827; Robert, 1760–1805. All these were sons of Job. A nephew, John, worked 1752–1809. And Jonathan, son of Christopher, worked 1760–70s. All of these made block-front furniture and some clock cases. **Townsend, Stephen:** Partner in firm of Townsend & Axson, Charleston, S.C., worked from 1760s. He made Georgian-style furniture but not block-front pieces.

toy furniture: Dollhouse furniture, play-toy furniture. Made of cast tin or pewter, iron, wire, wood, paper, glass, pottery, and plastic such as gutta-percha. Children's furniture is miniature furniture, generally of wood, for the use of children at play, especially playing house.

toys: Anything for play, but primarily miniatures of existing utile and other objects. Mechanical "go" and steam toys were generally miniatures of similar things in general use, but not always; sometimes the toy preceded the use, as philosophical toys using the magnetic and steam principle. Toy collecting, especially dolls, mechanical cast-iron banks, furniture, steam toys, and clockwork toys, is now a vogue. The French and Swiss clockwork toys of the 18th century, especially the singing birds, automatons, et cetera, were expensive toys for adults, some bringing fantastic prices when new.

toy weapons: Cap pistols, cannon, air guns, wooden swords, and other toys of military significance.

Tozoni, Clemente: The plaster-image and toymaker of Albany, N.Y., who made innumerable novelties, cottage ornaments, and statues, many of which were hand-colored with daubs, imitative of cheap Staffordshire china ornaments. This is what has been called "chalk ware." Many of Tozoni's pieces are now actually called Pennsylvania German and sold as such! Hudson Valley plaster ware has been carted to Pennsylvania by the ton and there sold to gullible collectors as "original Pennsylvania German chalkware." This would be laughable if it were not a minor economic crime. Some of the wisest of collectors have been caught in this net of emotional regard for a ware that is mainly 19th century and the product of Italian image makers. Some of Tozoni's original molds survive. It is also probable that some of the surviving molds are in use, creating "chalk ware" for gullible dealers and collectors.

trabeate: A beam; flat, rather than arched.

trace: A trail; not a road or highway. A fugitive path, as Howard's Trace, Huspeth's Trace, et cetera.

Tracy chairs: Reference is to makers of this name, especially E. B. Tracy of Scotland, Conn., maker of Windsor chairs. See p. 226 of *Handbook of Antique Chairs*, by author.

trade money: Trade cards or bills imitative of paper money, especially National Bank bills of 1840s–60s.

trade pitchers: (1) Pitchers, especially Liverpool transfer-printed ones, featuring the emblems and symbols of various trades and crafts. (2) Pitchers bearing advertisements of makers and vendors. There are many varieties of both, some of American significance.

Trafalgar chair: *See* Chairs, All Kinds. **Trafalgar couch:** Greek-revival-style couch with dolphin feet, shell-carved head, and ship's-prow footboard. Date is really 19th century. **Trafalgar vases:** Classic, ovoid urns celebrative of the Trafalgar victory. Glass, porcelain, pottery, and silver examples known.

train oil: Fish oil. Lamp fluid.

Trainque, Peter: French cabinetmaker working in New York from 1830s. Empire and French Antique revival styles.

trajectorium lunare: Machine delineating the path of the earth and the moon around it.

tram: Heavy raw-silk floss or thread.

trammel: Adjustable rack, generally with a hook. Also a mechanical drawing instrument for scribing ovals.

transfer-printed: Printing by offset, one of the very first uses being the transference of a print from a copper plate to china and so achieving the decoration without handwork. Metallic inks were used, ground in oil, and printed on tissue from copper plates. One engraving thus sufficed for the decoration of hundreds of pieces of pottery. The same process was used in decorating glassware. A "transfer print on glass" is not the same thing; this is a matter of fixing an engraving or print on glass with varnish and, when dry, removing the paper by damping and rubbing, then painting over the remaining picture. This is a form of eglomise painting, sometimes found in clock-case and mirror panels, also on some framed glass pictures. The next logical step was decalcomania transfer, with all the color in the transfer. This method is now used in much glass and pottery decoration.

transitional: Representing the change from one style or period to another with inclusion of certain elements of both.

transom shelf: An over-door shelf, or a shelf over the doorframe, utilizing the opening in a wall higher than the doorframe proper.

transparent items: Various items of antiquity and near antiquity fall within the general category of transparency. These are starched windowpanes, painted with emblems and illuminated from behind; similar items of linen or cotton cloth, illuminated with candles; paper work for illumination; transparent playing cards printed on a flexible glass called "people's skin" and pasted over scenes, figures, and portraits; frosted glass slates through which copy could be seen and drawn; window shades of oiled Hollands painted in scenic effects, giving a picture within by day and outside by night, when room was illuminated.

transparent rustics: Three-dimensional pictures built up from various pieces of wood, stone, shell, dried verdure, sponge, moss, et cetera, the houses having glass windows and the sky a transparency. Generally displayed in a shadow box admitting light from the rear. Date is from 1850s. Often homemade.

transpontine: Literally, "on the other side of the bridge"; derisive term for music-hall entertainers, farce actors, harlequins, et cetera.

trap; trappen: Swedish term for step or steps; stairs.

trap ball: A children's game in which the ball was put in play from a trap looking like a wooden shoe having a stout tongue that, hit with a billet, put the ball in play. If a player caught the ball the trapper was "out," but if not caught he had other tries. He who caught the ball became the next trapper.

traps: Curiosities in form of nutlike seeds having four sharp spines.

trapunto: High-relief quilting achieved by stitching first and then stuffing the area.

travisher: A tool; a shaving plane used in contouring, as in making the saddle seat of a Windsor chair.

travoise: The two-stick drag of the American Indians.

tray-topped: Any stand, table, or cabinet having a rimmed or galleried top.

-tre: Suffix meaning "of wood," as bastre, pintre, ashtre.

treacle molding: Wood molding, the contour of which, in profile, shows a nosing with an undercut, forming a "drip." [*Section pictured.*]

tree candle pans: Small candle sockets

in pans, on pins, for affixing to trunk and branch of Christmas trees, or the much earlier candle trows. [*Examples pictured.*]

tree feller: Mechanical saw operated by cranks, turned by two men.

tree of life: (1) An East Indian or oriental design of Buddhistic significance, popular as a pattern from 17th century. (2) A pressed-glass pattern of all-over mottled and veined effect, having as much resemblance to the tree-of-life motif as an egg has to a cube.

tree of Saturn: Copper wires or a single strand suspended in a fish bowl filled with water in which sugar of lead is dissolved. The lead is attracted to the copper and deposited in treelike (branched) form.

tree seat: Circular bench built around a tree, or made in sections to encircle a tree. Some, of cast iron, are made in three or four segments.

Tremain, John: A retired actor who became a cabinetmaker of New York in 1751.

trembleuse: Cup fitting into a rimmed recess in its underdish.

tremor: A hood.

trenail; trunnel: A large spike; many were made of wood. From "treen-nail."

trencher: Wooden plate or platter. **trencher salt:** (1) A wooden salt dish. (2) Depression in a trencher to hold salt.

Trent Turner & Wood: The Stoke-upon-Trent pottery of Turner & Wood, makers of Parian and majolica from 1850s.

trestle stand: A stand, sometimes with tiers of bookshelves, the underbody of the piece built like a small trestle table. **trestle butterfly table:** A trestle-type underbody with a single stretcher from which the rudders swing out to hold the drop leaves. This is a rare 18th-century table type. **trestle foot:** Reference is to the rectangular blocks of wood used as a footing on the better type X- and pedestal-end stretcher tables. **trestle tables:** Long and frequently narrow tables of one or two boards resting on stretchered trestles at either end, sometimes with a middle trestle. These are now rare items but were once in general use in the colonies from 1610s (at Jamestown) to 1750s. Some were still made as cottage furniture in 19th century, to 1850s. The very narrow ones were used as side tables or sideboards, the diners seated along one side only. Some of these tables are 16 feet long, the general run of sizes being 6 to 10 feet long. Use of the form is noted from 14th-century England. **trestle tilt top:** Not a pioneer-type table but a Directoire or Regency period table with pedestal ends and stretcher, with a "wishbone"-form brace that holds the top when raised from its tilted position. [*Example pictured.*]

Trevor & Ensell glass: Blown flintwares produced by a firm so named at Pittsburgh from 1810s.

trial piece: Pottery, porcelain, or china piece of any kind, lettered, and with symbols, blobs, and stripes of color. Such pieces were trials to test colors as fired in the kilns. Every pottery made them from time to time as standard tests. Now they are rarities.

triangle tables: A Chinese invention; tables and stands with triangular tops, four of which assembled to make a larger, square table, and in larger assemblies made various long, octagonal tables and even platforms. There are many European varieties, among which these are sometimes found, made of mahogany and walnut as drawing-room, library, chamber, and tea tables. **triangular-envelope table:** Triangular top with smaller triangular-form fold-over leaves, the whole on a triangular base, the top pivoted in center. When turned on the base the leaves can rest on the projecting angular corners of the skirting and so increase the size but do not change the shape of the top. Some have rounded leaves, and these of course convert the triangular top to a round top. Such examples have falling leaves, not fold-over. **triangular tilt top:** A standard tilt-top mechanically, but with a hollow triangular base that is a box for sewing things, the top hinged to one side. [*Example pictured.*]

triangular cabinet stand: A corner piece of triangular form having a tambour door; some were night stands, others music, sewing, and whatnot stands. Chairs, cupboards, et cetera, of triangular form speak for themselves and require no further definition here.

tribute: Contract work.

tricoteuse: A sewing table with a yarn basket made a part of the pedestal.

tric-trac: Backgammon, and the board or table on which it was played. Some idea of the age of the game may be gathered from the fact that a manual of play was published 1760, titled *Le Grand Tric-Trac.*

tridarn: A Pennsylvania three-level or three-tiered cupboard, the top level usually open, the center and bottom enclosed, with drawers and doors. Generally has shelves slotted to hold spoons, and rails to facilitate standing of pottery and plate. This is the ancestor of practically all Pennsylvania kitchen cupboards; it came to Penn's colony from Wales c. 1685; not from Sweden, France, Switzerland, the Netherlands, or Germany.

trident: Three-pronged fork or spear.

trident spiral: A sugar auger.

trifid foot: A furniture footing carved or marked into three elements or sections.

trifid spoon: Any spoon having a handle end in form of three lobes. Sometimes also a term referring to the three tines of a fork.

trifle: (1) A dessert of eggs and cornstarch, and the dish for serving. (2) Small wares of any kinds, especially souvenirs of a resort or watering place.

trifoliate: Three-leaved, three-lobed.

trifooted: Three-footed, as in any bulbous-form vessel with three steadying feet.

triglyph: A V-shaped section used decoratively in friezes.

trilateral table: Semi-octagon-topped table with a single drop leaf, supported on four fixed legs, with one swinging. Generally in pairs, with cabriole legs and arcaded aprons, for use as two side tables and together as one elongated octagonform table. Rare. Queen Anne and Georgian-styled examples known.

Trilby: Pattern of pressed glass with an all-over cane-lined background and heart-shaped panels picturing the heroine of the famed Mauve Decade novel.

trilobate: Three-lobed, as a cloverleaf or shamrock. A true triangle table with rounded leaves of half-circle form. **trifoil:** A form found in specialties of silver, china, and glass tablewares, centerpieces, et cetera.

trinoptric lantern: A magic lantern of great illuminative power, throwing a circle as great as 25 feet in diameter. Made from 1850s.

trio stove: An efficient but unlovely-appearing heating stove of cast iron, built like a huge bassoon. The bell of the horn is the fire chamber; the rest of the device is a circulator for the hot gases of combustion before conveying to chimney flue. Made from 1850s.

tripartite mold glass: Three-mold blown glass, or three-mold pressed.

triplanic portrait: Any portrait with outstanding, narrow, vertically set fins which are sections of two other portraits. An angular view from left reveals one, full-face reveals another, and an angular view from right the third portrait. Used in 20th century on advertising novelty window signs, and from mid-19th century to display political characters, as Lincoln, Washington, and some other statesman. Generally of paper or cardboard, lithographed, or tin-plated sheet iron. The genuine early examples are painted in either oils or gouache. It is said the idea derived from a mystifying picture designed to show changes in the facial expression, and that not all were made on a flat board but that some were based on curvate surfaces, as the shafts of a column. In 18th century, engraved examples, hand-colored, were in use.

triple back: Said of any chair with the back in three tiers. One is a Windsor armchair with loop back and a comb mounted on the loop.

Triple Bar: Pattern of pressed glass featuring a banding of vertical bars of varying size, looking somewhat like a piece of turnery. **Triple Triangle:** Another pattern, of ruby-flashed and clear glass, three segments of an X-form panel being in colors, hence triple triangle.

tripod candlestick: William & Mary and Queen Anne style stick composed of a shallow tray on three feet with an upright candle column and socket. Known in silver and in brass.

tripod card console: A "mechanical" table with two movable supporting legs of the pedestal swinging into tripod form when flanges to support a drop leaf are pulled out. When not in the form, the table will stand firmly only against a wall. Phyfe made such tables.

tripod gate leg: Three legs supporting a folding two-part top, and two more forming a gate for support of the leaf.

tripod tables: Any three-leg-supported tables and stands; many varieties from Queen Anne period and earlier. There are canted turned-leg tables of this type that may date from William & Mary period.

tripod ware: Any silver-, glass-, or ceramic ware with round bottoms, supported on three legs or feet.

Tripp tinware: S. A. Tripp of New Bedford, Mass., with partner, N. Gilbert, was an extensive maker of tinware from 1830s.

triptych: Three-leaved folding picture, often of religious nature. Also a mirror in the same style with three looking glasses, two wings being adjustable to any angle desired.

triskle: Said to be a Semitic device out of Carthage; a boss or round with three bent or running legs arranged around it as a common axle. Examples found in Ireland.

Triton candlestick: Triton, the merman, holding a dolphin form which becomes the candle socket. Silver luster, made by Wedgwood, modeled by William Bacon.

trivet: Properly a three-legged flat-topped stand. Innumerable varieties, and not all three-legged. Some stand a foot or more high, have box tops, and are of brass and wrought iron. Some are tiny, low, and of cast iron, made for a miniature flatiron. Some are of tile, pottery, or glass, but generally of silver, silver-plated base metal, brass, copper, or iron.

trompe: Water-powered bellows or hydraulic blowing machine.

trompe-l'oeil: A "fool-the-eye" picture. Still-life painting done with meticulous attention to every detail, often of unrelated objects so arranged to suggest a third dimension. Any form of decoration, especially intarsia work of the Renaissance, deceiving the eye of the beholder. From "trump," to nonplus. Actually derived from "triumph."

tromp marine: A one-string musical instrument of square tapering shape, played in upright position. Dutch amateur musician's instrument.

trone: A weight of approximately a pound and a half.

trophies: Decorative elements, carved or painted, cast, et cetera, dealing with the emblems or signs manual of the arts, the chase, and other sports, pursuits, and callings. May even be a display of the tools of a trade.

trophy cup: A prize cup, awarded winners, placers, and sometimes third-bests in contests. Souvenir of victory. Generally of silver, but many of porcelain and pottery for lesser events and local meets.

Trotter, Daniel: Philadelphia cabinetmaker working in first quarter of 19th century. Worked in the Directoire and Sheraton styles.

trotter glass: *See* Risley Glass.

trow: A tree or treelike form.

Troxel ware: Pottery made by Samuel Troxel, Pennsylvania, first quarter of 19th century. It is redware in the Staffordshire or Swiss tradition, sgraffito- and slip-decorated.

truck: To trade or barter.

truckle: To go under; as a truckle bed.

true pewter: Right pewter; made of 75 to 90 parts tin, the balance copper. A white bronze.

truhe: A dowry chest, not a "dower chest." Dower is a widow's portion. Dowry is a wedding portion.

Trumble furniture: Made at Philadelphia by Francis Trumble from 1750s. The shop was a true manufactory with an important production of sofas, chairs, cupboards, chests, tables, stools, and other items.

trumeau: A pier mirror of France of the Directoire period, prototype of the tabernacle mirror. Most examples have a carving or a painting in a panel over the glass. A *trumeau* is a wall space between windows, as the English "pier." Recent advice from researcher into the history of this type of mirror includes these comments: The Trumeau is a type of pier mirror imitative of a high-transomed door. The French transom or overdoor window was, traditionally, larger than a fanlight. Legends seem to indicate the French had no specific name for a transom and, during one of the German wars, when the Germans asked what the element was (by stating *vas iss das?*) the reply was "Oui, wahsisdoss" and so, to this day, in rural France one hears the term "wahsisdoss" for a transom or high overdoor light.

trumpet-mouthed: Curvate-flaring, or bell mouth. **trumpet shade:** A rare form of hurricane shade, trumpet-shaped. [*Example pictured.*] **trumpet-turned:** Any turning, especially noted in William & Mary style tables and highboy stands, in the general shape of a trumpet. [*Example pictured.*] **trumpet vase:** Glass, ceramic, silver, et cetera, vase of trumpet form on a baluster or stem and firm base. [*Example of form pictured.*]

trundle bed: Truckle bed; a low bed to roll or slide under a standard bedstead.

trunk bed: A trunk with a folding bed tucked in the lid. [*Example pictured dates from 1860s.*]

trunk-on-frame: A cabriole-legged stand with rim holding a trunk-shaped coffer. Made from 1700s and quite rare. Most examples, if not all, are English or Dutch. [*Example pictured.*]

trunk peddler: Any peddler who carried his stock of wares in a trunk on his back.

trunnel: Same as trundle and truckle, *which see.*

truss: A weight measure of hay; new, 60 pounds; old, 56 pounds.

trussing coffer: A clothes chest.

trussing cups: Pairs of cups fitting together. Generally of silver.

trusty servant jug: Souvenir of the College of Winchester, England, the trusty servant being a snouted, donkey-eared beast dressed as a servant. This figure embellishes the jug. Made from 1850s to 20th century, and may still be produced.

tryall boots: Great boots with flaring tops, prohibited in Puritanic New England. Jonas Fairbanks wore them, was tried before a judge for misdemeanor, acquitted, and thereafter anyone who desired could wear cavaliers' great boots in Massachusetts Bay.

trydarrn: Welsh for a fine cupboard.

try square: An L-shaped angular rule to "try" or test the square of work, used constantly by cabinetmakers and carpenters.

tube pan: Any baking pan with a tube or chimney in the center.

tub salt: Saltcellar in the form of a miniature tub.

Tucker & Griffin: Cabinetmakers of Boston, 1800–30s.

Tucker china: Semi-porcelain made at Philadelphia by William Ellis Tucker from 1826; first decorated in sepia only, gold and colors used after 1828. Various managements and partners, including Hulme and Judge Hemphill, to 1838. Ware as fine as Sèvres and in the French taste. It is now rare and one of the most desirable fine ceramics in the American scene. This ware deserves a monograph in which the already voluminous material written about it will be digested and compressed in one volume.

Tudor: (1) An English royal house, Elizabeth being the last of the line, 1485–1603. This "house" is descended from Sir Owen Tudor of Wales. It followed the short-lived house of York. (2) An architectural style reflecting the last phase of the perpendicular. (3) A furniture style representing the final phase of English Gothic, with admixtures of Spanish, Flemish, and Dutch 16th-century styles. The Tudor age produced triumphs of wood throwing, or turnery, and during this period the stick chairs were developed, of which the American Windsor would seem to be the most perfect form.

Tufft, Thomas: Philadelphia cabinetmaker working from 1760s to 1780s in the late Georgian and the Chippendale square-legged style now overemphasized as "Marlborough." Tufft's work is representative of what is now called the Philadelphia school, the group of master workmen who produced the finest Georgian-and Chippendale-style furniture made in the colonies.

tui: A food vessel. A ceremonial bowl, often of bronze.

tule: (1) The giant broadleaf rush. (2) Paper made from swamp tule.

tulip: The dullaband, tullebandin, or lily of Persia, brought to Europe by the Swiss botanist Gesner in 1559. Grown extensively in the Netherlands, where it thrived. Used in popular arts as a favorite theme in decoration, mainly because of the simplicity of the bloom and its exquisite beauty. Often now considered the sign manual of Pennsylvania-German art, which it is not. Tulip decoration was prevalent in New England, New York, and Maryland colonies before there was a colony of Pennsylvania. It was introduced to that region by the Dutch and Swedes on the Delaware. All Europe knew the tulip, but nowhere in Europe was it so overwhelmingly popular as in the Netherlands. The stylized or conventionalized tulip form as a decorative element preceded introduction of the lily in Europe. It was used in Italy and in Spain from 14th century.

tulip chalice: 17th-century wine cup of silver, pewter, brass, tin, and pottery; slope-sided cup on hollow conical base, with the surface of the cup scribed or embossed with tulip forms. There is little relationship between the metal and the potted forms. [*The example pictured is of silver, c. 1660; from the Biggs Collection, Maidenhead, Berkshire, England.*]

tulip chest: Any chest with carved or painted tulip decoration, as the Connecticut and Taunton chests, also the Swedish chests, Swiss chests, et cetera, of Pennsylvania.

tulip cup: Egg cup in form of open tulip; silver, Sheffield plate, plated silver, and ceramic ware.

tulip ware: Any pottery, especially redware, embellished with slip or sgraffito decoration of tulips.

tulip Windsor: *See* Chairs, All Kinds.

tulipwood: (1) The wood of the tulip tree; whitewood or poplar. (2) Variegated wood of Brazil, esteemed in cabinetmaking.

tumbler: Originally a round-bottomed cup that would not stand firm, hence "tumbler." Any flat-bottomed drinking vessel of medium height and without a special base. The high types are properly "beakers." Some early tumblers were served on sand-filled trays, the beverage in them taken in one draught or quaff. **tumbler cups:** Silver, brass, and pewter cups with heavy rounded bottoms; they wobble but will not overturn because of the weight of the bottoms. **tumbler hat:** A glass hat blown in a tumbler mold. **tumbler lamp:** (1) A lamp in gimbals. (2) A lamp reservoir attached with metal straps to a glass tumbler serving as its shade.

tumble-up: A tumbler with carafe, the tumbler placed downward over the neck of the vessel as a cap.

tun: A 252-gallon container.

Tunbridge ware: Wood mosaic, displayed in table tops, stands, and other furniture, trays, novelties, souvenirs, fans, et cetera, made in quantities at Tunbridge, England, from 1700s. Tessellate and diamond-point inlay in many colors of wood. Also wares made imitative of the inlaid work achieved by laminating blocks and sawing apart crosswise to yield a sort of inlay veneer. Tunbridge work was imitated in U.S. by some amateurs and professionals, who made inlaid tables, stands, et cetera, that are holy horrors, yet boast "10,000 pieces of inlay"!

Tung-chi: Chinese period, 1861–75.

tunged: Tongued.

Turcot, Peter: Upholsterer of New York City who in 1802 advertised bedsteads, sofas, easy, dining- and drawing-room chairs, window, field, canopy, and four-post bedstead curtains, cornices and blinds.

tureen: The soup-service bowl, name said to derive from the huge *soupière* made for Marshal Turenne after the marshal had used his helmet repeatedly as his soup dish in the field. The originals, of silver, are important pieces, dating from early 1700s. Sheffield-plate examples date from mid-18th century. Pottery, china, and porcelain examples date from 1720s.

turkey bell: Small jingle bell with strap for belling turkeys in the field. [*Example pictured.*]

turkey-breast cupboard: The angle-fronted corner cupboard.

turkey jar: Pressed-glass containers in the form of a turkey cock. These have been extensively reproduced in clear and colored glass since 1940s.

Turkey red: Fine burnt-umber color.

Turkey sofa: Low sofa, standing only a foot above the floor; a Sheraton style borrowed from the Turkish ottoman.

turkey wheat; turkey corn: The native American maize, especially our field and sweet corn.

Turkey work: Any imitation of oriental pattern achieved by point stitch, crewel, cross, or other stitchery, some almost a miniature form of rug hooking. Popular on upholstery fabrics of 17th century.

Turk's head: Metal or pottery baking dish producing a cake swirled like a turban. These are really a form of mold, with sloping, swirled ribbing, rounded or V-shaped in contour, and generally with a funnel or vent in center. Date is from 1800s. **Turk's-head mug:** A sort of Toby jug or cup displaying a hussar's head with shako, draped with swag and tassel; English and continental European, dating from Napoleonic wars. The face is depicted in full modeling, with sideburns and mustachios.

Turnai-Meissen: French porcelain using the crossed-swords mark.

turnbuckle: An open sleeve of metal, the ends tapped for a screw; used in tightening, or drawing taut, wires or rods. Turning the buckle caused the screws to draw inward.

turned: Shaped on a lathe. The various antiquarian terms affiliated with turning are: **turned cabriole:** A curvate-form leg achieved by turning on lathe, off center. The more common form of the cabriole leg which, in its finer forms, is achieved only by shaping and carving. Another variant is the sawed-out cabriole. [*Example pictured showing the line of the turnery.*] **turned chair:** Any chair made up of turned elements throughout; some, of 16th and 17th centuries, are highly imaginative pieces. *See* Chairs, All Kinds. **turned claw & ball:** A turned cabriole leg with a claw-and-ball foot. **turned cot:** Any cot bed on turned posts. **turned foot:** A bun-, ball-, or shuttle-shaped foot.

turner; turnery: The art and craft of wood turning. [*Certain of the various patterns are pictured.*]

Turner & Lane: Cut-glass makers of New York City from 1840s.

turner's polish: Beeswax, turpentine, and a coloring agent, used to burnish turned work before removing from the lathe.

Turner ware: The pottery ware of William & John Turner of Fenton, England, among the most successful of English potters from 1760s. Mark is simply TURNER, sometimes with the Prince of Wales' feathers. Stoneware, whiteware, cane ware, jasper ware, blue-glaze ware, of all kinds and shapes. To some connoisseurs, Turner's jasper ware is more desirable than Wedgwood's.

turnery tools: The various chisels, gouges, dividers, cutters, et cetera, used in the art of turning. The basic "tool" was of course the lathe itself.

turnsol; turnsole: Any heliotrope, or flower which turns its face to the sun.

turnstile: An improvement over the step stile; a heavy post with an X-member on top, and sometimes also midway down the post, joined to the upper with slats. The member turned, permitting the passage of humans but stopping cattle.

turnstool: A high stool with seat mounted on a wood turnscrew, later examples having iron screws. Date is from 1790s, and still made for certain artisans' use at workbenches.

turn-up bed: A folding bed, especially the simpler sorts which folded against a wall. These in various forms were advertised as early as 1760s.

turpentine nut: The pistachio was once so called; it is the fruit of the *pistacia terebinthus.*

turret pistol: The Cochrane pistol with multiple charges carried in a turret aligned with the barrel. Invented and patented 1837.

turret sideboard: A pair of turretlike cylinders or ovals, standing upright, joined by a table top and a backboard. Made from 1800s. Style is Directoire. [*Example pictured.*]

turtle back: Fancy chair back, the splat being turtle form. Also name given the split oval-turned bosses used on 17th-century cabinet furniture.

turtle stop: Door checks in the form of cast-iron or cast-glass turtles.

turtle to-do: The turtle frolic; a sort of feast for all and sundry when a large turtle was taken and made into stew. This sort of party was an 18th-century social affair.

turtle top: Table top, especially the mottled marble ovate tops on so-called Victorian tables.

turtle weight: Miniature glass or metal doorstop turtles used as paper holders.

tutania: Tutenag; hard pewter or Britannia; 4 parts brass, 4 tin, 4 bismuth, and 4 antimony.

tutenag: White brass; fine pewter. One formula used no tin, having 16 parts copper, 13 zinc, and 6 nickel. Also called white copper. The Chinese invented it. Owing to its whiteness and cheapness, it was finally called "German silver."

tutorial plate: Presentation silver given by students to tutors or teachers. Generally inscribed in a manner that earns it this designation. It is not a special type or form of silverware.

Tuttle, James: Cabinetmaker of Salem, Mass., who in 1796 advertised Philadelphia or Windsor chairs, common chairs, and settees.

tuyère: A bellows pipe, specifically those of an iron furnace.

twankay: A camp by a stream; especially a flagged or pebbled beach where laundry was done in the running water. Also a green tea from China.

tweefold: To double up, to fold. A saddle-bag.

twibil: A two-bladed ax; also a chisel used in mortising.

twifler: Colloquial for a trifler; a maker of trifle dishes used in service of trifle, a light pudding. A trifle was also the name given a pie dish.

twig basket: (1) A true basket woven

from twigs. (2) Imitations woven of stands and rolls of clay, fired, yielding a ceramic twig basket. Some are molded in imitation of twig weaving.

twilight: A covering cloth for chests and tables, later designating a head covering or shoulder shawl used in the cool of the evening.

twin cannon: Cannon cast in pairs, joined at the trunnions. Said to have been a Spanish invention; cast in brass, some so small they are in the model class. Cannon of this type were captured from Santa Anna's Mexican forces in the Mexican War. [*Example pictured.*]

twine box: Any container for a ball of twine or cord, almost never in true "box" form.

twin lamp: Sometimes called a wedding lamp; kerosene lamps made in pairs, of glass or metal, with a lifting hold between the joined reservoirs. A curiosity, but made in quantities, most likely as a lamp for more light and not as a wedding lamp.

twin pipe: Now a rare item; a tobacco pipe with twin bowls and single stem. Never smoked as a double-barreled load, but both filled and one bowl of tobacco smoked at a time. American, dating from 1820s. Made of ceramic stoneware.

twin-shell: A form of two shells, joined. Early examples of the form are known in silver designed by Pierre Germaine of Paris from 1740s. The form is found in various pottery and chinawares.

twin tabourette: Pairs of stool forms, joined by a platform. Date is from Gallic era of 1400s, and now here. [*Example pictured.*] Examples of 19th century said to survive in rural areas of U.S.

twisted: Carved or turned in a twist or spiral; formed by twisting, as twisted work in ceramic techniques, twisted wire decoration, ropemaking, spinning yarn and threads.

twisting snake: Warm-air toy cut spirally from cardboard, suspended by head or tail, and left to uncoil. It turned continually in any draft of air. It is of course a form of screw or flywheel. Toys of this kind are known from 1700s. [*Fine example pictured.*]

twist wringer: A footed trough with a crank and holder. Wet laundry was placed in the holder and the crank end turned to wring it out by twisting. Commercially made from 1840s.

two-back: A pair of chair backs forming the back of a settee.

two-bottle vase: Pairs of drum-form bottles joined off center; sometimes called orchid vases. [*Example pictured is Chinese, of early 19th century.*]

two drivers jug: An important pitcher by Minton; an ale jug depicting a locomotive on one side, a stagecoach on the other, with the two drivers on the front. Date is 1849. [*Example pictured.*]

two-faced doll: A doll with head having two faces, one smiling, one crying, pivoted to turn within the headdress and to bring either face to the front. See *Fascinating Story of Dolls*, by Janet Pagter Johl.

two-faced teapot: Leeds ware or other creamware teapots with faces on either side, tinted at hairline, lips, and cheeks. Last quarter of 18th century.

twofold table: The gate-leg table. These tables are seldom found inventoried as gate legs prior to 19th century; they are most generally called "twofold."

two-hearth stove: Two small open-grate stoves cast back to back, with a dumb-stove or drum immediately above, or in a room above, connected to the twin stoves with a pipe.

two mark: Said of any metalware, as silver or pewter, having one mark on the body and another, of a different maker, on lid or cover. Any such pieces are suspect of repair and rebuilding. It is doubtful if any are the original joint work of two makers.

two-part chest: A chest-on-chest, composed of a large three-drawer unit as a base piece and another, only slightly smaller, mounted upon it. Date is from 1780s. Generally in one of the classic styles, Adam, Hepplewhite, Directoire, Sheraton, or Empire.

two-part mirror: Any mirror with two plates of mirror glass, especially those of William & Mary, Queen Anne, and early Georgian periods. [*Examples pictured.*]

two-seat sofa: It defies description! [*Example pictured.*]

two-spout coffeepot: It is true; a stoneware, white-glazed giant pot, spouted to fill two cups at a time; obviously a restaurant type or refectory pot. Made at Bennington Pottery.

two-spout pitcher: A vessel with a spout and handle on opposite sides. Thus it could be passed from hand to hand, the user pouring from the spout opposite his handle. Some were made of pressed glass, others of ceramic ware.

two story: Four-sided lanterns with two panes on each side. Early 18th century.

twyford: *See* Astbury.

tyg: A wide, straight-sided pot with two, three, four, or more handles (depending upon diameter) for passing from hand to hand, and often, when full of a beverage, requiring two-hand usage. Early type of communal mug, dating, it is said, from 15th century, but especially known in its 17th-century Staffordshire redware form, decorated with slip in form of tulips, birds, and figures; often dated and with name of potter and some verse or sentiment. Tygs were also made in the Derbyshire potting district. Both kinds were brought to the colonies by settlers, and counterparts attempted in 17th- and 18th-century colonial potteries. During late 1880s and 1890s many examples of original English making were purchased by antiques collector-dealers and shipped back to England, where the objects were bringing high prices.

Tyler, H.: Coverlet weaver of Connecticut, working from 1830s.

Tyler, Wat.: Waultier le Tieulier, a leader of the common people or peasantry in medieval times. He worked in England, striving for reforms, if only for recognition of fact that the yokels were also human beings.

Tylor woodenware: Butter stamps,

bowls, and other wares made at "the Bucket factory," Marietta, O., and at Cincinnati from 1840s.

tymbr: A bale of 40 pelts or furs.

tympanum: Ornamental space over a door, usually of arch or rounded form, as a half circle. On clock dials, the space carrying the boss, the moon phase, rocking ship, or other device.

Tyne ware: Reference is to the wares made at the various potteries on the river Tyne.

type: (1) The letters used in printing, measured in 72nds of an inch, called points, but in early days designated by sizes such as pearl, nonpareil, primer, great primer, et cetera. Great type designers such as Bodoni, Caslon, and others created letter forms that are classics. The study of type is essential to a complete understanding of objects of antiquity. For example, the writer exposed a great fraud in Pennsylvania pottery before knowing a single thing about pottery as an antique. The late Mrs. A. K. Hostetter, whose collection of Pennsylvania glass and pottery was noted all over the country, once showed the author a "magnificent" charger of redware, lettered "American Independence 1776," claiming it to be the finest piece of Pennsylvania pottery known. It was. But there was something

greatly wrong with it. The lettering was *impressed* from printer's type of a style and face that were not made before 1850. She returned the piece to the dealer, threatening him with a suit at law for fraud. He admitted the piece had been made that year at a pottery near or at Honeybrook, Chester County, and that the inscription had been made with type borrowed from an old printing shop. Most of the types, prior to our own first casting of type, came from England, France, and the Netherlands. Dutch, and not German, types are the ones used at the printery at Ephrata, Pa., from which the *fraktur* patterns of that community derive. The catalogues of the Dutch type founder who supplied the Ephrata press are of record, one example being in a Chicago museum. The name of the face is Bastard Gothic. The first lettering book is not German, as has been claimed, but Italian, as is the second. The third was published in Switzerland, and its pirating is the first German book. The size of type, as is our linear measure of inches and our measure of time, is by the system of 12, not the decimal. This is called the Babylonian system of measure. It is based upon division of the circle into 360 degrees, one thirtieth of which is the major number 12.

typograph: An early typewriter, made from 1870s.

U

Ubiquitarian: A member of the first dissenters from Father Martin Luther's "reformed" service of the Church of Rome, and its doctrine.

Ufford lamp: Made by Ufford of Boston under the Kinnear patents; a lard-oil lamp of no special interest except to collectors of old lamps. Cast-iron base, tin reservoir, and broad-wick burner, without chimney or globe.

ultramarine: A blue color, originally levigated lapis lazuli.

ulva marina: It sounds important, but it is dried seaweed used at one time as a stuffing for mattresses and upholstery.

umber: Brown earth used as pigment. When burned (roasted) it turns reddish. Umbrian earth.

umble pie: Not "humble pie," but umble pie is the term; a pie made from the umbles of deer.

umbrella chair: See Chairs, All Kinds.

umbrella lock stand: An iron stand of the 1850s and 1860s, holding six or more umbrellas in locking loops.

umbrillo: The umbrella of the 1760s. Wood frames covered with silk and "oyled cloth."

Umpire jar: Measuring jar for the home, doing double duty as a celery glass. Name is from the makers, Umpire Glass Works of Pittsburgh, in 1890s. Probably an at-

tempt to steal the repute of the Empire Glass Works.

unaker: Cherokee clay, found to be an excellent pottery clay.

unbanded dish: The true Chinese plate form, a circular and exceedingly shallow bowl without a flat or beveled rim. These are far superior to the banded-rim plates in the field of export wares of Chinese origin.

Uncle Tom: The chief character of Harriet Beecher Stowe's tear-jerking novel, *Uncle Tom's Cabin*. P. T. Barnum had it dramatized and staged it with accompaniment of Negro spirituals, giving "little Eva" a big play. In England a wallpaper memorializing the novel's characters was issued; also Staffordshire statues and some furniture. The Uncle Tom & Eva statue was issued 1853 and launched at the N.Y. Crystal Palace Exposition. A clay pipe of Uncle Tom was made by Fiolet et Cie. of St. Omer, France.

undecagon: See Polygon.

under-bed: Trundle bed.

underdish: A plate used under a bowl or cup; a sort of coaster; a saucer for a cup. Practically all existing glass bowls now miscalled "baptismal" were small drinking bowls and were issued with an underdish. Drinking bowl, however, did not necessarily mean a bowl to drink from; it also meant a bowl in which a beverage was mixed and ladled out. The original Chinese teacups were small bowls with under-dishes.

under-mirror tables; skirt-mirror tables: Free-standing console-type tables with a solid panel mirror section at the back, below the top. These were useful in noting the hang of a skirt, but seldom by the wearer. The date of most would seem to be 1815–40s.

undine: A curious bit of glass or china looking like a pitcher without a handle but having a long, tubular spout with a downcurving end. Probably a medicinal item. Sold in apothecary shops in 19th century.

unfolding chair: See Chairs, All Kinds.

Ungaretti plaster: Josef Ungaretti of Boston, from 1830s, was an extensive maker of what is now called Pennsylvania chalk ware. The utter ridiculousness of pro-Germanic claims as to the source of "chalk ware" was first noted in the research on chalk ware for this volume, instituted in 1942. At that time we were told of a magnificent collection of pewter chalk-ware molds "from Nuremberg," used for half a century by a Pennsylvania German maker of the ware. We traveled two hundred miles to see and photograph the molds, only to learn "they had been stolen" the day before. Draw your own conclusions. These items were not cast in pewter molds, but in plaster molds. They were not made by Germans, but by Italians and some Swiss and French.

ungula foot: Hoofed foot, used on some fine furniture of early 18th century.

union bowl: Pressed-glass bowl made by Deming Jarves at Sandwich Glass Works, 1851; it is huge, 21 inches high and 22 inches in diameter, weighing 60 pounds.

Union fire tools: Hearth tools of loggerheads, pokers, tongs, and shovels of wrought iron with brass heads in form of a round seal bearing the American eagle and 13 stars. Made from c. 1790s to 1800. Probably Boston or Philadelphia.

union furniture: Midwestern term meaning furniture made at the co-operative works called the Cabinetmakers Union, Cincinnati, from 1850s.

Union glass: Made at the Union Works, Pittsburgh, from 1830s. Also at Wheeling, where several plants assumed the name Union. Probably others. The name of the works is of no great significance.

Union Glass Works: Philadelphia works at Kensington, established 1826. Made fine blown and cut glass.

Union playing cards: Political cards of the War between the States era, made by American Card Co. Liberty was the queen of each suit. Officers of various ranks were pictured on the other court cards.

unions: Fabrics woven of two different kinds of thread, as silk and wool, wool and linen, linen and cotton, cotton and wool, et cetera.

unique: Singular; one of its kind.

United Provinces: The Netherlands.

universal chair: An adjustable upholstered chair of 1870s.

universal commode: A self-sealing covered toilet pan made by Burslem Pottery

from 1860s; 12 inches in diameter and 6 inches high. For this reason examples are assumed to be kitchenware. Not so.

unmeddled: Pure, unmixed.

upholstered Windsor: See Chairs, All Kinds.

upholsterers' nails: A 36-page catalogue could be issued of the fancy-headed nails made for upholsterers' use in 19th century alone. If it was a usable form, it was made as a nailhead. [Some examples pictured.]

upping block: A mounting block; a doorsill.

upside-down Windsor: See Chairs, All Kinds.

Urania: Greek Muse of astronomy.

uranography: Delineation of the heavens on a map, or globe.

uranoscope: Precursor of the planetarium projector; a lamp in the center of a sphere five feet in diameter, made of tubes, lenses, and reflectors, suspended from a domed ceiling and displaying the firmament and planets. This machine dates from 1840s.

urn lamp: Argand-burner lamp of ancient, classic, lamp-urn shape; the burner is in center of top and fitted with a glass globe. Reservoirs are of Sheffield plate. [Example pictured.]

urn pot: Redware pot of classic shape with decorative ears, designed as flowerpot.

urn stands: High stands, often with cabriole legs, specifically to hold urns. Some items of this same type have a cabinet top, the purpose or use of which is now obscure. Also stands with raked legs and galleried tops designed primarily to hold a tea or coffee urn. These are often in the Hepplewhite style.

urn stove: Actually any parlor stove or space heater of the 1840–80 period having either (1) a water urn (for humidification) on top of the ensemble or (2) a larger urn for keeping coal. Specifically a decorative cast-iron plate stove of square form with a large urn above the box. [Example pictured.]

Ursinus: A Polish scholar who was concerned with law, medicine, and writing, from late 15th century to first quarter 16th. There is a college in Pennsylvania named for this Johannes Ursinus.

U.S.A. pewters: Military buttons for the uniforms made at the Zantzinger factory, Lancaster, Pa., from 1777. The buttons, not marked, were made by J. C. Heyne or by Steinman of the same city. [Example pictured.]

Useful Arts: Title of a type of book on domestic economy, or how to do many things and make many things yourself. There were at least half a dozen so titled, the best being those of Rufus Porter of New England and Reuben Chambers of Pennsylvania.

U.S. Glass Co.: Pressed-glass makers at Falmouth, Mass.

ushibdi: Carved stone or glazed pottery effigies of mummies, with hieroglyphs; when genuine, these are relics buried with mummified bodies in ancient Egypt as effigies of servants to wait upon the departed. There are many examples now in the U.S., on sale in curio and art shops.

1, Urn Stove. **2,** Wafer Dresden. **3,** Walking Balloon. **4 and 5,** Wall Lavabos. **6,** Wall lantern. **7,** Wall pockets. **8,** Wash-Hand Stand. **9,** Washington Bust Bottle. **10,** Washington Urn. **11,** Washington Pen. **12,** Washington Andiron. **13,** Watchmaker's Lamp. **14,** Water Velocipede.

Usk ware: Painted tin-plated sheet iron made at Usk, near Pontypool, England, from 1760 to 1860.

U.S. platter: A pressed-glass tray, approximately 8" x 11", in general form of U.S. flag, with stars on a circular field, starred stripes, and other features. A souvenir of the Chicago World's Fair of 1893.

U.S. Pottery: The Fenton pottery founded by C. W. Fenton, brother-in-law of Julius Norton, later characterized as the American Wedgwood because of his good taste and good products: Rockingham glaze, flintware, scroddled wares, et cetera. Pottery at Bennington.

Ustick hardware: Hinges, locks, keys, and nails made by William Ustick, N.Y., from 1760s. Some of the items are said to be marked USTICK.

Utica glass: Crown window glass, said to have been made at Utica, N.Y.

Utica stoneware: The stoneware made at the pottery of Roberts, Fields & Co., New York City, was called Utica ware; probably in connection with Erie Canal activity, as the ware dates from 1825.

utile dulci: One of the early soluble powder-"patented" drink makers. A spoonful in a glass effervesced and made water a flavorful, refreshing drink.

V

Vail globes: Celestial and terrestrial globes on stands, made by G. Vail of New York from the 1840s.

vaissellier: French cabinet, popular as a display cabinet in Louis XV period. Often the doors are fitted with a wire grille rather than glass.

valance lath: Same as tester lath; the slats spanning tops of bedposts.

valentine glass: Any glass cut or pressed with hearts and arrows. This term is rather loosely used.

Valentine views: Reference is generally to views of New York and environs from *Valentine's Manual*, an annual published yearly from 1841 to 1870 and containing many full-page and some folding views of old New York, many in color.

vallens: Valance.

valonea: A dyestuff from steeped cornhusks.

Val St. Lambert: Belgian glassworks founded 1790 by M. Cockerill, an Englishman, while Belgium was a province of the Netherlands.

van aiger; van aigre: Sour wine. Vinegar.

Van Bibber mirrors: Fashionable looking glasses, classic and Georgian, imported by Andrew Van Bibber of Baltimore from 1785. His label is on many, but he was not the maker.

Van Courtland: The family of colonial importance springing from the Courland Swede, Olaf Svenson, who, upon his service of enlistment with the Dutch West India Co., changed his name to Van Courtland and took up an immense grant of land.

Van Court silver: Manufactured silver of sterling quality by I. Van Court. Mostly specialties, such as butter dishes, basins, and fish knives.

Van Dewater furniture: Late-19th-century furniture of mass-production status, made 1850s–80s in New York City by a firm so named. Another firm of this name made house and cabinet hardware in New York City as late as 1850s.

Van Dunck Toby: It is a bottle of pottery, similar to the "coachman," as a container for Van Dunck's gin. Many are not pottery, but blown glass, molded.

vane: A banner or indicator. From *fane* or *fana*, a flag. A weather vane is a wind-indicating device of metal.

Van Hamme delft: John Ariens Van Hamme established a delftware pottery at Lambeth, England, 1670 or 1680, probably on the advent of King William. His ware, similar to Netherlands delft, is not marked.

Van Houten tin: Any tinware, japanned and decorated, with a stencil mark of this name, is from the Van Houten shops at Paterson, N.J., where the goods were made as late as 1870s. **Van Houten woodenware:** Made by G. Van Houten of New York from 1840s. Bowls, tubs, pails, churns, et cetera.

Van Loon ware: Reference is to pottery made at Ashfield, Mass., by Van Loon & Boyden, from c. 1850s.

Van Rensselaer: Lars Larsen, a Swede who settled in Rensselaer, the Netherlands, upon expiration of his enlistment with Dutch West India Co. assumed the name of the Dutch village and took up vast holding of land on the Hudson.

vapor grate: The grate invented and made by Bettoner of New York from 1840s; it was a parlor grate with ornamental andirons and a tank. Fire kept going in the grate evaporated 30 or more gallons of water a day and so humidified the air of the house.

Varangian chair: *See* Chairs, All Kinds.

vargueno: A Spanish chest-on-chest, the upper section with a falling front used as a writing desk; interior fitted with drawers, cabinets, and compartments. Date is from 14th century, and still made in Spain and elsewhere, often in the old style. These were in every state once under Spanish dominion: Texas, California, New Mexico, Louisiana, and Florida.

varnish: Lac dissolved in a volatile oil or spirits of wine; gums or lacs used were shell, resin, elemi, mastic, sandarac, gamboge, adragent, copal, and tši-chui. Fixed oil lac varnish had a linseed oil base.

vasa murrina: The varicolored semiprecious mineral fluorite from which cups, vases, bowls, and amphorae were turned and carved in ancient times, valued more highly than gold. Glass in imitation of this natural mineral, with flecks of gold, silver, mica, and pounded cullet. Made in U.S. by Dr. Flower, patent-medicine maker, at his leased Cape God glass factory. *See* Venetian Brown & Gold.

vase: Any column-form vessel of any substance. A book could be written and illustrated with 1000 different varieties without exhausting the subject.

vase & collar: A turned element, as a chair spindle or stretcher, consisting of two opposing vase turnings, separated by a wheel turning called the collar. Noted in the finest Windsor-chair stretchers, especially the cross stretchers.

vase candle lamp: A night-lamp assembly of three units of glassware. Date is from 1860s. [*Example pictured.*]

vase grater: Sometimes called an urn grater. It looks like a small classic urn, often of silver. Top hinged to one of the side elements, in turn hinged to bottom. All unfold to expose the grater for nutmeg, or perhaps for snuff.

vase lamp: A terrific (the proper word) example of Victorian styling in U.S. Frosted cut globe over a sun chimney above a reservoir. The latter fit into a vase which, in turn, was properly a receptacle for flowers submerged in water. [*Example pictured.*]

vase stoppers: Toilet and other bottle stoppers of vase form, hollow, for use as vases for single blossoms or nosegays. Some are of cut glass.

vase tables: (1) Any tilt top or other table on a vase-form pedestal support. (2) Sewing and other stands of solid or skeletal vase shape. [*Examples pictured.*]

vaso à colonnette: A Corinthian classic Krater vase, ovoid, with eared rim supported by angular columns from the body. A colonnetted vase.

vaso calice: A krater-type vase form imitative of the calyx of a flower.

vaso rotelle: A krater-type vase with volute or accented curvate handles.

vasque: A tublike jardiniere, ornately and richly contrived.

vatt: A measure of 9 bushels. Any deep tub, especially of huge size. A vat.

Vaughn, A. H.: Cabinet- and chairmaker of Le Roy, N.Y., working from 1850s. This is probably the maker of the "Le Roy chair," one time a sort of antiques oddity promoted in central New York State in 1910s. Not verified.

vaulted: Domed. **vaulted bureau:** A concave-fronted bureau; excessively rare form, dating from 1790s to 1815; reminiscent of Hepplewhite, but said to be Directoire in style.

Vauxhall glass: Primarily the slightly bevel-edged plate glass made at the Vauxhall works, established by the Duke of Buckingham c. 1660. It is said fine crystal vases and other objects were made here by Venetian workmen employed by the duke. Most of the plate-glass production was for mirrors. **Vauxhall pottery:** Made at this same watering place and garden from 1690s. Stonewares and delftwares from several potteries. Term applies to any ceramic ware made here.

vegetable ivory: Palm nut of the Peruvian Andean variety; it is a solid-meat nut, having some resemblance to ivory in color and texture.

veilleuse: An ottoman-type sofa for two. Also a stand of pottery in form of a miniature stove for heating gruel, pap, and a night draught, by means of a candle within the device.

velocambipedextrianism: Name invented for the sport of bicycling in 1860s

velours: Velvets.

venaries: Veneering in sheets, ready to use.

veneer; veneering: Application of thin sheets or slabs of rich and rare wood over a carcass of common or cheap wood. Early veneer was hand cut with a veneer saw, a refined pit saw. Some veneer is a sixteenth to an eighth of an inch thick.

Venetian blinds: The indoor jalousie; the shade of slats, tilting with cords to any angle desired. A rage of the 19th century, invented in the 18th and revived in the 20th. Slats were originally of wood, set in tapes, and sometimes on end pins within a frame. French seem to have made the first ones for indoor use, adapted from a Venetian shade or screen.

Venetian brown & gold: Glass, commented upon as "new" in 1847, designated as brown in tone, with gold spangles, used in making ornaments. This sounds like a far earlier attempt than Dr. Flower's to make vasa murrina glass imitative of the natural mineral.

Venetian curtain: Jalousied slats set upright rather than horizontally as in Venetian blinds. Also used indoors, generally in pairs, to cover the upper and lower sashes of a window.

Venetian dentil: Alternate cube and beveled blocks, the bevel from bottom to form a recess at top in a fillet or molding.

Venetian glass: Actually Murano glass, made on one of the islands near Venice and owned by that republic. Here glassmaking attained its heights; the makers were forbidden to leave the island, but their progeny were permitted to intermarry with the nobility. Glass made here from 13th century A.D. and still made. The techniques of this glass center were imitated everywhere, even in U.S. in 18th and 19th centuries, one imitation being the swan finial. **Venetian glass balls:** The fancy glass paperweights with mysterious décor within them were first so called.

Venetian ground: A paint used to cover canvas in preparation for painting by artists.

Venetian roof: A roof of slats, looking like clapboarding, but adjustable, as a Venetian blind, to air the space under it.

Venetian shutters: Indoor and outdoor window shutters with jalousies or movable slatted sections.

Venetian stove: An iron or brass stove used in a fireplace. Some are portable.

Venetian sun blinds: Under this name, in 1767, John Webster of Philadelphia advertised what we now call Venetian blinds. The advertisement appeared in the *Pennsylvania Chronicle*, December 3, 1767. He explained to perfection the usefulness of the blind in his advertisement.

Venice porcelain: Made from 1720s at Venice and almost a duplicate of Meissen in quality and style.

venison dish: Venison, correctly, means any wild meat or game. Hence this dish is not a dish for what many people think is venison, the meat of the wild deer. This is a dish of metal, used as a service platter, with heavy grooves and a well to catch meat juices.

ventilated tester: A bed top with an open trellis or gallery over the curtains, providing air when the curtains were drawn. Seems to have been in use to 1850s.

ventilating cupboard: Cupboard with ventilating sections or arcs in doors and at sides, as slatted, louvered, jalousied, or barred windows, arcades, et cetera. Forerunner of the meat safe and pie safe.

ventilating glass: Panes of window glass with angular apertures, or gills; the idea was such glass in windows would permit the room enclosed to "breathe." Made from 1850s.

ventilating stove: Any stove of the so-called Franklin type using room air in ventilating the draft and so causing the room itself to undergo a change of air as the stove burned.

ventricular: Reference is to certain late Gothic decorative details having resemblance to the lattice-form skeletons of the fossil ventriculites.

Venus pedestris: Classical name for streetwalkers, prostitutes, and ladies of easy virtue who walked the streets seeking companions. Also any woman taken in adultery and branded with an A. Also the *vivandière* camp followers who not only bedded with the soldiers but nursed the sick and wounded.

verditer: This term applies to either a green or a blue color derived from copper or green earth.

verdure: A wooded landscape and depiction thereof, as in paintings, tapestries, rugs, et cetera.

verjuice: The juice of any unripe fruit, as grapes, apples, pears. An early souring.

vermeil: Silver gilt.

vermiculated: Carved or worked to simulate open worm burrows; any worm holing.

Vermont glass: Bottles and hollow wares of glass made at East Middlebury, Vt., from 1813 to 1817. **Vermont stoneware:** Any stoneware made in Vermont, or any stoneware by potters, as the Farrars of Geddes, N.Y., who professed to make "Vermont stoneware." **Vermont woodenware:** In 1850 there were between 40 and 50 manufacturers of boxes, pails, bowls, butter stamps, firkins, and churns operating in Vermont. Boxes included everything from tiny pill size to huge cheese boxes.

vernis: Varnish. **vernis Martin:** The secret varnish of the brothers Martin of Paris from 1740, approximating lacquer of China. The secret was the equivalent of modern shellac with a spirits-of-wine base and with any desired pigment for color.

verre de fougère: Drinking glass. **verre eglomise:** Painted glass panel. **verre tachette:** Glass with spotting of enamel.

verre de soie: Iridescent or lustered glass made by Corning-Steuben works from 1905 to 1930. An art glass.

Verreville: A pottery at Glasgow, Scotland, producing many figures, porcelains, basketwork articles, and fine gilded and flowered wares. The pottery was established as a glass factory, 1777, sold to a Mr. Geddes in 1806, and converted to a pottery in 1835. Glass of fine quality was made in conjunction with ceramic wares. After 1856 only earthenware was made. No marks, other than initials of proprietors, stamped on the ware.

verrier: A small cabinet with glass-paneled front.

verso: The left-hand pages of a book; any proper left side.

vert campan: Green marble of the Italian plain called the Campagna.

vertical pierced: Said of chair splats when not solid, but pierced in, or as a part of the design. Many Georgian chairs have such splats.

vert pomme: Green-apple color.

vert pré: Vivid green; grass green.

vertugadin: Crinoline padding.

Verzilinni glass: Made by a Venetian so named, working in England in 16th century.

vesper lamp: Gas-generating lamp of 1840s, generating its gas from camphene. A no-wick lamp; the burner had vents for flame in jets.

vesta lamp: Non-explosive camphene lamp of 1840s.

vestimental essence: Made from 1780s; it is a sort of solvent for grease spots and stains in clothing.

vestment rack: A figural carving of a bust with outstretched arms, grasping a pole upon which vestments were hung. Usage in this form dates from 1400s to 1700s. Ancestor of the coat hanger de luxe.

vexing glass: Flasks of glass with bottoms as thin as an onion peel and so having a measure of flexibility. Also called anaclastic glass. Made from 17th century as curiosities.

V front: Any cabinet piece with the frontal section at angles, converging to a shallow V form.

Vibert prints: Prints sold at the galleries of Goupil, Vibert & Co. of Paris at their New York store from 1840s.

Vicar & Moses: Ralph Wood statuary group of a preacher in pulpit with clerk in his box under it. Date is from 1790s.

Vickers metal: High-tin-content ware of the general type later called Britannia. Often mistaken for silver. Marked I.V. or I. Vickers.

Vickers ware: Pottery made at Vickers pottery, Downington, Pa., from 1790s to 1830s. Utilitarian wares; glazed.

Vickery furniture: Among the earliest Kalamazoo, Mich., furniture, made by I. Vickery from 1835. Empire style.

Victorian: Pertaining to the period or reign of Victoria of England, often apostrophized as 75 years of prissiness, stuffed-shirtism, bombast, expansion, and poor taste, with peace and plenty. Also the Second Baroque or Louis XV antique-revival style.

Victoria regia: The giant water lily of the Amazon, grown successfully in U.S. and represented in a series of huge color prints of striking beauty. This is the water lily with a bloom larger than the human head.

vidame: An overlord.

vielle: A lute with a playing crank; a sort of hurdi-gurdi.

Vienna rocker: *See* Chairs, All Kinds.

Vieux Paris: French porcelain from any one of the factories named for one of the streets of the city.

view sheets: Letter sheets with views of places; souvenir stationery, dating from 1850s and very popular from 1860s to 1864, with street, city, town, and camp scenes.

vigogne: Green and blue color made from alum and stems of the bellflower.

Vile & Cobb: The superior cabinetmakers of the mid-Georgian period at London. Vile, by some connoisseurs, is considered superior to Chippendale. Evidently they had only royal and immensely wealthy patronage.

vinaigrette: Small box with pierced inner box to hold a piece of sponge steeped in aromatic vinegar. Many are in the category of fine jewelry, of gilt, gold, silver, and jewels, enameled, et cetera.

Vincennes porcelain: Made from 1738 at this French city, removed to Sèvres in 1753.

viol: A large violin; a bass violin.

violette persée: Rich violet color. **violette tin:** An alloy of tin and cobalt.

violet walnut: Heartwood of the walnut tree, often a rich dark violet color. The tone was not permanent.

violin bottle: Glass bottle in general shape of a violin; early ones are blown and tooled; later ones are mold-blown.

violin splat: Any chair splat of violin shape.

viometer: An odometer; a distance-measuring device on a carriage or cart.

virginal: Keyboard musical instrument, made from 16th century.

Virginia court cupboard: The rarest 17th-century furniture of America; a true court cupboard, of which Virginia probably had more than any other colony, but most of which were relegated to slave huts. Wallace Nutting found one in a Petersburg, Va., hen house in the 1920s.

Virgin spoon: Early silver spoon in the Apostle tradition, bearing the effigy of Mary on the handle. Date is from 16th century. Many times reproduced. Also the

spoon now called a "maidenhead" because it bears a small female bust on the handle end. Date is from 15th century.

vis-à-vis: Face to face.

visorum: A reading stand, especially for a typesetter.

vitric panel: A pane or sheet of glass. Also vitrine panel.

vitrine: A cabinet with glass front; a glass bell or cover.

vitriol match: A round wood box of tipped wood stick matches, the base containing a glass container of vitriol-soaked asbestos fiber. Touching the acid with the match heads caused ignition. Date is from 1820s.

vitro di trina: Venetian glass with fine threads of opaque white in a colored body, or colored threads in transparent body.

vitro porcelain: The term once used in preference to "milk glass."

vitruvian: Reference is to wavelike scrolls used as a band or border as a line of curled S's.

vittle: The yolk of an egg.

vivant: A tableau.

Vodrey ware: Jabez Vodrey had potteries at Pittsburgh, 1827–39; at Troy, Ind., 1840–46; at East Liverpool, O., to 1857.

vogle: Swiss term for bird, found so spelled on some bird-decorated redwares.

voider: A cachepot, a tray for clearing the dining table, a scraper with cover. Made of silver, plate, brass, paper, wicker, et cetera.

volcano: A lamp chimney.

voltaic chain: Pulvermacher, in 1849, made a hydroelectric chain of links of zinc and copper, or other electro-accumulator metals, worn as a cure for nervous ills. It was endorsed by the Academy of Medicine in 1849.

Voltaire chair: *See* Chairs, All Kinds.

volute foot: The French foot of 18th-century Louis XV period; it curls forward and upward. Noted on Chippendale and on practically all so-called Victorian furniture to 1880s.

voorhuis: The front of the house; the main hall; the front room.

votive cushion: Seat-cushion covers embroidered with religious or genre scenes. **votive light shade:** Miniature hurricane shade used on votive candles in Roman Catholic churches. Many have been found in West Indies, Mexico, and Central and South America.

Vowels furniture: Made by George Vowels of New York City from 1840s. French Antique styles.

voyder: Same as voider.

voyeuse: *See* Chairs, All Kinds.

vyrge: A mace; a pronged club.

W

wadd: Black lead; plumbago.

wafer Dresden: China decorated with fragments cut from sealing wafers in various colors. This formed a raised décor on the china. [*Example pictured.*]

wafer iron: Pairs of circular iron disks mounted on long, pincerlike arms, bearing engravings which form raised decorations on the wafers baked in them. Also name given irons for forming the huge wax seals on tapes affixed to important documents.

wagon-spring clock: A type of clock movement by Joseph Ives, inventor and clockmaker of Connecticut, first half of 19th century. A leaf spring is the power source, compressed and converted to movement by a series of cast-iron arms and chains. The finest examples were made at Brooklyn, N.Y., by Ives, c. 1820s, in cases alleged to have been made by Duncan Phyfe. The chief virtue of the clock was a possible power source sufficient to run a clock 30 days. However, 8-day and 30-hour types of wagon-spring are known. Some examples are known with wooden movements. [*Example pictured.*]

wag-on-wall: A type of clock comprising a movement with dial, sometimes with hood, but without other casing, exposing the weights and the swinging pendulum. Note well this fact: If it is not a pendulum clock, it is not a wag-on-wall. Clocks with weights and chains exposed, but with other movement controls hidden in the hood, or set over the movement, are properly Friesland clocks, in general, and can be Chinese or Japanese clocks, English clocks of the bird-cage type, weight-driven, et cetera. Without a wag, or swinging pendulum, no exposed clock should be called by the name here given.

wainscot chair: *See* Chairs, All Kinds.

wainscot chest: A paneled chest of oak.

wainscot cupboard: A paneled cupboard; a press.

wainscott: From *wagenschotte*, riven oak. Oak split into thin planks with a frow. Riven, not sawed. Term is from the Danish.

waits: Serenaders, carolers, night singers, trumpeters.

Wakefield & Howe: Extensive manufacturers of woodenware, Boston, to 1850s.

Waldensian: French religious sectarian; a follower of Peter of Lyons, called Valdensis, from Vaux, or Waldum. He rendered the four gospels from the Latin into French (the language of the people) in 12th century. He is the reformer ahead of all the others and, it should be realized, all religious reformations dealt first with putting the gospels and the missal in the language of the people instead of in the often meaningless Latin, sometimes spoken by clerics who did it by rote and who knew not what they uttered. Known also as a Vaudoise.

Walker cradle: Self-rocking cradle invented 1850s. Spring-driven or by weights and rack.

Walker glaze: The burnt-sugar glaze appreciated by some connoisseurs of American pottery. It derives from Walker lime, found near Clarksville, Ga.

walking balloon: One idea of personal air transport proposed in 1840s. You walked in 20-foot steps because the balloon made you weigh from one ounce to a pound or two, and you could hedge-hop, waft over buildings, et cetera. [*Example pictured. This is from a print that is now a collector's item.*]

walking doll: The "autoperipatetikos," or doll, 10 inches tall with articulated limbs, or with a roller device. (Either type walked.) Joseph Lyons & Co. of Boston made them before 1850s. Examples are now highly prized.

walking horse: Adult-size baby creeper for invalids.

walking-man irons: Andirons, the frontal element in the form of a walking man. Made 1790s–1820s. Cast iron, originally painted with mineral paints. [*Example pictured.*]

wall Argand: An Argand-type sconce, the wallpiece being the reservoir, an extension tube holding the burner and globe. [*Example pictured.*]

wall fountain: A lavabo, generally with a bowl, sometimes in an open cabinet or hood, with bowl shelf. Pottery, delft, pewter, silver, porcelain, brass, and other examples known, dating from 17th century or earlier. [*Example of peaché marble is pictured; also an example of porcelain.*]

Wallace furniture: Early French Antique styled furniture made at Fitchburg, Mass., by Wallace Shops, from 1830s. Also fine cabinet furniture by Robert Wallace, working in New York City from 1750s.

Wallace lamps: A "hold-or-hang" lantern made by Wallace & Sons, Ansonia, Conn., who also produced many kerosene lamps after 1870s.

Wallis furniture: Salem, Mass., is its home; made by Joseph Wallis from 1830s. Also made mattresses stuffed with palm leaf or fiber. Also furniture by William Wallis of Charleston, S.C., in 1790s. This is in the classic style of Hepplewhite.

wall lantern: Sheet-iron lantern made specifically for use as a wallpiece but usable as a hand lantern. [*Example pictured.*]

wall mirror: Any mirror, as the pier, tabernacle, *trumeau*, et cetera, designed for use on the wall, rather than over mantel or mounted on a chest or stand.

wallpaper: Paper wall covering or hanging; the finest hand painted by Chinese and imported in blocks, squares, and sheets; the common variety being the "domino" papers, hand blocked and colored, vended on street corners. This is the paper, pasted together and rolled, that became the wallpaper of commerce. See *Historic Wall Papers*, by Nancy McClelland; *Wall Paper*, by Phyllis Ackerman; *History of Wall Paper*, by Alan U. Sugden.

wall pocket: Any hanging device of any material, formed into a pocket or receptacle for suspension on a wall. Originally used primarily for cutlery storage, but now used as "planters." [*Example pictured.*]

wall table: Side table, sideboard, hunt board.

wall veil: Any material, from paneling and wainscoting to paper, fabric, tapestry, et cetera, to "veil" the basic structure of the wall. In 1870s, C. W. Spurr, of Boston, offered "patent papered wood hangings." These were a veneer of wood pasted on paper. Similar wallpapers were made in England from 1840s. The original idea seems to derive from Japanese papers covered with veneers of exotic woods.

wall vitrine: Glass-cased wall lantern or glass-cased hanging cupboard.

walnut Windsor: Windsor chairs of walnut in entire structure. These were advertised as early as 1766 in South Carolina as "imported" from Philadelphia.

Walsh lamp: Double "bull's-eye" lamps of pewter and other pewter lamps made at Boston, from 1820s, by Henry Walsh.

Walsh tinware: Plain and japanned tinwares, some marked, by W. S. Walsh, Boston, from 1840s; he was successor to A. Stevens.

Walter, Joseph: Furniture manufacturer of Cincinnati from 1840s.

Walter china: China decorated by, but not made by, Theodore Walter of Boston, 1870s. He fired china for early amateur decorators.

Walton, Henry: Itinerant portrait and landscape painter working out of Ithaca, N.Y., from 1830s. Now called a primitive painter.

Walton furniture: Made and sold from 1780s at the factory and ware rooms of Samuel Walton, Philadelphia. Late Georgian and classic styles.

Warburton: Cobridge pottery made by John Warburton and successors from 1720s. Delftwares, but famous for gold-decorated wares made after 1810.

Ward, Artemus: Pseudonym of Charles Farrar Browne, a humorist of 19th century. Beds, handbags, shaving mugs, bottles, et cetera, named for him.

Wardell grates: Fire grates made by H. D. Wardell of Boston and by Wardell & Jones, from 1820s.

wardian case: A glass-covered herbarium; a box for growing plants; sometimes a window garden.

Ward lamp: Parabolic reflector lamps by Ward of Rochester, N.Y., made from 1840s. Many of the type were enclosed in boxes and used on locomotives as head lamps.

wardrobe: Originally a ward, or room, for robes, especially women's wear. Sometimes, jocularly, a room for the keeping of china and antiquities.

Ward-Stokes furniture: Made at Cincinnati from 1820s or early 1830s; Grecian-style furniture and Windsor chairs.

Ward ware: Furniture hardwares and other imports sold by Richard Ward of Salem, Mass., from 1780s. His billhead was printed on reverse side with a catalogue of his stock.

Warham, Charles: Cabinetmaker of Boston, working in Queen Anne and Georgian styles, prior to 1730s. In 1734 he was in Charleston, S.C.

warming pan: Large, flat metal pan with pierced lid, on long handle, used to warm beds when filled with glowing coals. A "safe" type used a pan of hot water, the endpiece being a large flask. **warming stool:** A footstool with a warming pan in it.

Warne & Letts: Potters on the Cheesequake Creek in New Jersey, near South Amboy, from 1770s. Stonewares were made. Many of them marked, some lettered with slogans and mottoes.

Warner, William: Furniture maker of New York City working in 1760s.

warping: Setting the threads longitudinally to form the warp in a loom. The length of the warp established the length of the piece of cloth woven.

Warrington: English pottery made at Warrington by Fletcher Bolton from 1790s, principally for the American market; blue-and-white-printed ware, a black-glazed ware, and gold and silver luster ware.

Warwick bed: A bedstead fitted with resilient double slats.

Warwick cruet: Oval or round Sheffield-plate holders for wine, vinegar, and other bottles. Generally in pairs. Some are solid-silver holders. Said to have been named for the Earl of Warwick.

Washburn furniture: Grecian-style furniture by J. N. & S. Washburn of Taunton, Mass., made from 1820s. **Washburn pail:** Woodenware made by Governor Washburn of Massachusetts, one of the founders of Smith College.

wash hand stand: Name given an article of furniture that is of stand shape, with a fold-out, boxlike top hiding a washbowl. [*Example pictured.*]

washing bats: Decoratively carved and shaped bats for beating laundry in tub, boiler, or on stones by the brookside. Many forms, used from 17th century, are as here described. The idea is as old as the hills, or as old as laundry work.

washing dolly: A small washing machine looking like a butter churn, the dasher with blunt fingers.

washing mill: Any early-type washing machine; one was advertised by this name in 1790, made and sold by R. Stokes of Philadelphia.

Washington andirons: Cast-iron fronts for fire irons in the form of a Revolutionary officer in uniform. Doubtful if it is intended as an effigy of the general, but could be. [*Example pictured.*]

Washington bust bottle: Exactly what you'd expect: a blown-molded bottle in bust form, for Simon's Centennial Bitters. Originals are in amber and in clear glass, inscribed with name of contents. Reproductions are minus the inscription and have a pontil mark. [*Example pictured.*]

Washington vase: Cast-iron garden vase with medallion of Washington. [*Example pictured.*]

Washington Glass: Mount Washington Glass Co., factory at Boston, established 1837. Made paperweights, glass busts, and other specialties, lamps and blown and pressed wares. Merged with Pairpoint Co. in 1894. There was a Washington Glass Works in operation at Williamstown, N.J., from 1830s, making flasks and bottles.

Washington pen: Stamped steel pen with medallion of Washington impressed on it. Made from 1850s. [*Example pictured.*]

Washington Spring bottle: A Saratoga water bottle for Washington Spring water, with bust of Washington on the bottle.

Washington tea caddy: Wedgwood tea caddy (also a punch bowl with same décor) carrying profile lettered "His Excellency General Washington, Commander in Chief of the Forces of the United States of America." Probably dating from 1785 to 1790.

Washington wallpaper: Clough of Boston made this memorial wallpaper of engaging design. Date is 1800.

washing urn: A pedestal-type washstand of cast iron with projecting arms carrying soap dishes. Date is c. 1840s. [*Example pictured.*]

washstand: Primarily a toilet stand with bowl and shelf for pitcher of water.

washstand cornice: A wood valance fixed over a washstand, with protecting curtain to prevent wall splashing. It is late, of Eastlake style, probably 1870s.

wassail: From the early Anglican, *waes hael*, be well. A hot spiced drink generally concocted in a bowl, also called wassail (pronounced wassle), the best varieties being made from spiced sack or sherry. Wassail bowls were often of turned wood, sometimes with a removable silver rim. They are related in importance to the mazer bowls.

watch-bottle: Any bottle or flask of glass, pottery, or metal, in shape or form of a watch. The best-known example is a small flask for whiskey called the whiskeybury flask. **watch box:** (1) A small shelter for the watchman or policeman of a beat. (2) A wooden case simulating a clock case to hold a watch at night. **watch-clock:** An alarm clock. **watch-cock:** Balance-wheel covers of old watches, generally very decorative, engraved and cut, now often made into jewelry. **watch-dish:** A butter dish with cover in the form of a watch; pressed glass. **watch paper:** The padding paper used in old watches between the inner and outer cases, often bearing engraved or printed advertising of watchmakers; some painted, as love tokens. One, in the writer's collection, is crocheted. **watch-stand:** Any decorative device, often a figural or other group of china, in colors, with an orifice and slot to hold a watch, thus making the piece a clock.

watchmaker's lamp: An artisan's lamp of 18th century. [*Example pictured.*]

watchman Toby: Figural jug in form of a seated watchman with lantern, the spout at rear, formed from back of the chair.

Watcombe: Art pottery, made in England from 1870s. Terra cotta and bicolored wares.

water carving: An involved process. Wood cut to a predetermined shape, punched with dies, then planed to the depth of the punching and soaked in water, which caused the punched parts to swell and stand out in relief. Then kiln-dried, the embossed parts finish-carved. Invented as a process in 1830s.

water clock: The clepsydra; any timekeeping device using the escape of water in drops to register the time. An ancient device, made from the days of pre-Christian Rome to the 20th century. Innumerable types and kinds.

water coupe: A water cup. Used also for oil, colors, et cetera, by artists. An inkwell for India ink. Some are of ceremonial nature and elaborate.

waterfall: A chandelier with many cut prisms and pendants.

Waterford: The rich glass of Ireland, made at Waterford in 18th and 19th centuries. Often finely cut. Much was imported by U.S. dealers from 1785.

water gas: Water decomposed to yield hydrogen, burned in a "mantle" of platinum-wire gauze. This lamp, because the decomposition was by electric current from batteries, was also called an electric lamp. The date is from 1840s.

water-gilded: Gold leaf applied to a surface sized by floating on with a wet brush. It will be ruined if washed with water.

Waterloo glass: Irish glass made by Waterloo & Co., Cork. Some of it is marked.

waterman's badge: A badge worn by licensed water carriers, ferrymen, etc. Mostly from the London Thames-side area. Many are of paper.

Waterman tin: Marked japanned tinware made by Waterman of Boston from 1820s.

watermark: The mark left on pulp in the trays of wire which made the sheets of paper. The trademark of the maker is the chief watermark. Some bear dates. Others indicate the size, as foolscap. Earliest of record are from 1301, made in the Netherlands.

water set: Reference is to pitcher, tray, and glass or glasses for service of drinking water. Many are of pressed glass and of plated silver.

Waters guns: Pistols and guns made by Richard Waters of the New England Colonial Co. early in 17th century.

Waters pottery: Made at Lambeth from 1800s. Sheets of clay were pressed in dies to make some of the pieces. Also statuary and delft glaze wares.

water walker: The water velocipede made up of a framework with a saddle seat resting on three floats. User propelled it by treading water with paddles affixed to shoes. These devices were used by sportsmen on Eastern rivers in 1840s. [*Example pictured.*]

Watson, William: Cabinetmaker of Charleston, S.C., who died in 1736; Queen

Anne and early Georgian styles. His widow carried on the business after his death.

Wattis flask: Pocket flask, so called because made by Edward Wattis of Philadelphia from 1860s.

Wavecrest: An art glass, originally called "opal ware," decorated and distributed by C. F. Monroe Co., Meriden, Conn., from c. 1895 to 1900s. Said to have been blown and pressed glass made in France and decorated only by firm here noted. Also made a variant called "Nakara." Wavecrest mark is a cartouche of scrolls, flag with name WAVECREST over a seagull, with C. F. M. Co. and trademark.

wax bead: Necklace bead of hard wax. Sold in colonies by 1770s.

wax cloth: Decorative damasks, impregnated with wax, used as table mats.

waxed plaster: Reference is to plaster castings, kiln-dried and plunged in linseed oil for 12 hours or more, dried and polished.

wax jack: Spindle for reel of taper, on a stand of silver, brass, pewter, or iron. Used to provide easy method for melting sealing wax. Generally a desk appurtenance in 18th century.

wax lamp: The fairy lamp; any "cup-and-cover" lamp burning a squat wax candle.

wax milk: A liquid soap of 2 parts wax, 1 part potash, and 10 parts water, boiled to saponification. A furniture soap and polish.

wax portraits: Modeled or cast wax profiles, generally mounted on a dark background. Many famous makers, including Patience Wright, Mrs. Platt, Joseph Wright, Robert Hughes, and Henry Adams. Professionals and amateurs practiced this art of portrait making from 18th century to 1850s. Beware of fakes cast in wax from plaster models, in turn made from bronze medals of famous people, especially Presidents of the U.S., all but one of which are profiles on bronze struck at U.S. mints. *American Wax Portraits*, by Bolton, is recommended for further study.

wax pourer: A partly covered pan with many spouts (2 to 12) and a handle. Wax heated in pan was thus poured into candle molds. Sheet-iron utensil of intriguing design and now quite scarce. [*Example pictured.*]

wax string: Candle wicking soaked in wax, coiled on spools. Our researchers discovered it was for sealing fruit-jar and preserve-can lids before India-rubber rings were available.

Wayne & Moore: Cabinetmakers of Philadelphia from 1760s. Dissolved as a partnership in 1769 and conducted alone by Robert Moore from that date. He moved to Baltimore in 1784 and then sold his business to Gordon & Bankson. Jacob Wayne, Philadelphia, worked 1785–1805, making late Georgian and Hepplewhite or classic-style furniture.

way wiser: Mileage indicator used on carriages. Used from 18th century.

weather glass: A barometer.

weather strips: Fabric tapes and metal trim used in making windows and doors tight against drafts. Used from 1840s or earlier.

weather vane: The wind-direction indicator, acting like a flag, but of durable material, as wood, iron, copper, et cetera. Many are three-dimensional and depict all sorts of things, horses, angels, cocks, fire engines, locomotives, anvils, et cetera.

Weaver, N.: 18th-century cabinetmaker of Newport, R.I.

Weaver & Volkmar: Grate and fender makers of Philadelphia from 1830s.

weaver's chair: A high-legged stool with back, used at the loom. **weaver's candlestick:** A hanging candlestick of iron, looking like a long-stemmed tobacco pipe. Now rare items. They hooked anywhere on the loom. [*Example pictured.*]

Webb & Scott: Cabinetmakers of Providence, R.I., working from 1780s. Georgian and classic styles.

Webb cameo glass: The carved glass, revived by Webb of England as a technique, imitative of the work done anciently and of which the original Barberini, or Portland vase, is a splendid example. It is cameo carving in glass, first formed into utile or decorative objects. Tiffany & Co. were agents for Webb from 1860s. A set of Webb cameo glass, at the famed Morgan sale, 1886, brought a higher price than the much-publicized "peachblow vase."

Webb lamp: A lard-oil lamp, marked "Webb's Improved Lard Lamp." One of a hundred or more cheap lamps of the mid-19th century.

Webb molds: Candle molds by W. Webb of New York from 1850s; he was previously a candle-mold maker of London in 1830s. Marked WEBB.

web foot: A furniture footing with accented ridges and a thin pad, imitative of or similar to a webbed animal foot or paw.

Webster plate: Silver plate made by Webster Mfg. Co. of New York City; a specialty was a patented revolving and tilting coffee and tea machine.

Webster silver: Plated Britannia, with simulated chasing, picturing the birthplace and residence of Daniel Webster. The style is Baroque; the date, 1855. A complete tea and coffee service was made. The same-style ware was made in commemoration of Jefferson, Jackson, and Washington, with various appropriate scenes of historic significance relating to each personality.

wedding lamp: Pressed-glass double lamp, made from 1880s to 1910s.

wedding mirror: A master size and style of the courting mirror, of Persian origin, triptych in form, with painted glass framing.

Wedgwood: Pottery, stoneware, cane ware, jasper ware, ironstone, luster, and any other salable ceramic ware made (1) by Josiah Wedgwood and (2) his successors down through the years. Business founded 1759. Popular fame derived from his jasper ware, imitative of carved cameo glass and marbles of the classic era. Some connoisseurs of his age called the ware trash and its making a crass imitation of originals. The ware is still made, and many uninformed collectors imagine they are buying old Wedgwood, when in reality they are buying the new. Which poses this problem: Isn't the new worth as much as the old? Josiah Wedgwood classed his own products in order of importance thus: (1) intaglios and medallions, (2) bas-reliefs and medallions, (3) portraits, (4) Roman classics, (5) heads of illustrious Romans, (6) the Ceasars, (7) the 52 emperors, (8) the popes, (9) kings and queens, (10) illustrious moderns, (11) busts and small statues, (12) lamps and candleholders, (13) sets of coffee and tea and chocolate service, (14) flower, bough, and root pots, (15) vases, (16) black basalts, (17) encaustic painted wares, (18) art work in jasper, (19) inkstands and chemical vessels, (20) thermometers. There are several books and many monographs on the subject of Wedgwood. Meigh of Hanley issued a Wedgwood commemorative pitcher in 1859. It is Parian. The bust of the potter is from the Reynolds portrait. It is not generally known, but Wedgwood dabbled in photography as early as 1799 by use of camera obscura. He had everything but the developing chemical before 1800. Tom Wedgwood, by R. B. Litchfield, London, 1903, has a notice of this activity.

weed ash: A lye used in dyeing. Said to have been made of the ashes of burned grass.

Weed parer: Apple parer patented by Weed of Plainsville, O., 1849.

weeds: Mourning garments, properly spelled "waede."

Weems, Mason Locke: Born October 1, 1759, Anne Arundel County, Md., became an itinerant preacher and colporteur. Did a *Life of Washington*, in which he published his now famous "cherry tree" story

weesp: A Dutch porcelain made from 1764.

weft: Another term for woof; also the flag flown to indicate whales offshore.

weld: A yellow dyestuff made from the plant *Reseda luteola*.

well: The section of a tall-clock case from below the hood downward to the base.

Well & Provost: This name on stoneware or glassware containers indicates commercial use from 1850s by a flavor, essence, jelly, fruit, and pickle-packing concern of New York City.

well & tree platter: Any platter showing depressions in form of runnels or channels, joined laterally to a larger stem channel, in turn leading to an ovate pool or well. Not necessarily a feature of antique platters.

well-desk: Slope-fall secretary desk having a sliding panel in the fixed writingboard section giving access to the top drawer of the case section. This is a feature of the desks made from 1690s in the William & Mary style; it is considered a refinement in any desk of the 18th century.

Wellford mantels: The term is not quite correct: Robert Wellford of Philadelphia, working 1801-39, was a maker of composition ornaments for the adornment of wooden mantels and mirror frames and plasterwork of walls and ceilings. He signed his work, and so the signature is often assumed to mean making of the entire unit or piece involved. He did a wholesale and retail business, with customers in

Pennsylvania, Maryland, Delaware, Virginia, the Carolinas, New Jersey, and Ohio. He advertised from 1801 and is listed in directories to 1839.

wellhead: A coping or covering for a dug well, embracing anything from a simple iron railing to an elaborate wrought-iron-work cage, arch, drum, and lifting mechanism. Some are stone-carved, some of lead work, and some of sturdy oaken construction. The parapet of stones around the mouth of a well, sometimes surmounted with a simple hood on pillars, is a type of wellhead. However, when the term is used to denote a unit or assembly of pieces, it is probably a wrought-iron or carved-stone example of some importance.

Wellington-Hill pitcher: Reference is to a ceramic pitcher in which bust representations of Generals Wellington and Hill are painted or modeled. Various makers. English.

Wellman grate: A reflecting-type coal-burning fireplace grate made as late as 1870s by Smith Foundries, Pittsburgh, Pa.

well reel: A large reel on posts or other supports, turned by a crank, lifting the bucket from the well. [*An early pioneer type is pictured.*]

Wells & Foster: Makers of philosophical instruments, including barometers, at Cincinnati, O., working in 1830s.

Wellsburg glass: Made at Wellsburg, Va., to 1840s, first factory at Charleston, Va. Green and flint tablewares, bottles, and flasks. It is an error to designate this glass as West Virginia. These several localities were in the state of Virginia when the glass was made. There was no state of West Virginia until 1861, when the western part of the Old Dominion "seceded" and joined the Northern or Union contingent of states.

Wellsville pottery: Stoneware made from 1830s by an S. Wells at this locality in Ohio.

well sweep: A long pole, pivoted to work freely in an upright support, the butt end weighted, the long end supporting a rigid bar of iron or wood which plunged a bucket into a well and lifted it out filled. The well sweeps were counterweighted to work freely and be operable by a child. The entire old ensembles are now sought after as antiques.

Welsh dresser: Sometimes in error called a hutch; it is a cabinet-form or open-form sideboard table *without* an open cupboard above it. When there is such an addition the piece is a Welsh cupboard. **Welsh cupboard:** Most of these are distinguished by open shelves. The characteristics of the pieces are sawed and cut valances, open shelves, and general naïveté of construction rather than sophistication. This type of cupboard enjoyed considerable use in the Welsh settlements of Pennsylvania from the 1680s.

Welsh plate: Tin-plated sheet iron.

Welsh terrazzo: Coal-ash mortar; made from two parts coal ash and one part lime.

welted foot: Said of any footing in which the material of the foot is turned either up or down as a finishing lap, giving a rounded, lapped-over edge. Noted primarily in glasswares, but deriving from sil-

1, Steam Sideboard. 2, Van Dyke Cutting (profile). 3, Walking Man (Hessian) Andiron. 4, Wall Argand. 5, Washing Urn. 6, Well Reel. 7, Wax Pourer (candle-mold filler). 8, Whale-Oil Lamp. 9, Weaver's Candlestick. 10, Wimble, or Gimlet. 11, Whieldon Ware. 12, Whistling Locomotive, pull toy. 13, Wine Rack or Bookstand. 14, Wooden Lamp. 15, Wine Bibbler. 16, Windmill, interior. (No. 11 from Virtue & Co., London.)

versmithing techniques which, in turn, may have derived from the armorers' crafts.

Wentworth-DeGraff: Furniture with this name printed on paper labels or branded, stenciled, or stamped is by a New York cabinetmaking factory in operation from 1840s.

Wentworth miniatures (numbered): T. H. Wentworth was a miniature painter of considerable merit, working from 1810s in Connecticut and New York, painting many miniatures, which he numbered consecutively. This is said to be true at least of his 1815–30 activity.

Wesley cloth: Damask table covers woven with a portrait of John Wesley in the center, surrounded by vines. **Wesley ware:** Reference is to pottery, china, et cetera, featuring this eminent minister. Medallions of Wedgwood jasper, engraved glasswares, Staffordshire busts, and low-relief plaques. Warning: Some of the glasswares, while actually antique, bear engraving that is quite recent.

Westbury: This pottery town in Bristol area, England, was the home of the Sugar House pottery, so called because it specialized in making molds for sugar bakers. From 1780s the works also produced brown and cane wares. It is the early molds that have collecting interest.

Westchester County highboys: Reference is to the cupboard-top or press-top highboys, rather than those with drawers, which seem to be peculiar to Westchester County, N.Y. This is not really the case; they are found generally in the Hudson Valley from Yonkers northward to Hudson, N.Y.

Westerfield, David: Cabinetmaker of Washington, D.C., from 1820s.

Westervelt: Famous maker of weather vanes of molded copper sheeting, covered with gold leaf. Every type of figural, eagle, and effigy vane, made from 1850s to 1880s. Factory at New York City. Jasper Westervelt & Sons were cabinetmakers of New York, 1840s. They had no association with the weather-vane makers but are noted here because the name is the same.

Westfield whips: Reference is to whips made at Westfield, Mass., from 1830s. There were 13 or more makers of horsewhips in this town in 1837.

Westford glass: Amber flasks and bottles made at Westford, Conn., 1850s–70s.

Westgate furniture: Probable reference is to cottage and French Antique style furniture, mirrors, and beds made in quantities by Westgate, Baldwin & Co., Fall River, Mass., from mid-19th century.

Westinghouse: Rarely used, but reference is to a threshing machine made by George Westinghouse at Schenectady, N.Y., in 1830s.

Westlake: A Cincinnati furniture term, the phrase coined to offer competition to the "Eastlake" styles as promoted by Grand Rapids.

Westlake stove: Having no relationship to the above; a charcoal-burning stove of small size, fitted with special saucepans and teakettle, all units having flues through them. This stove was made in 1850s, and examples are now quite rare.

Westmoreland glass: (Not to be confuse.. with one of the innumerable "patterns" of pressed glass.) Glass made at Grapeville, Pa., by the Westmoreland Specialty Co., a firm established by M. West of Pittsburgh in late 1880s, which produced not only a wide variety of glass novelty containers but also the products in them, as candy, mustard, and other specialties. The milk-glass "bank" and other mustard containers, many clear and painted glass candy containers, and pressed cup and other plates were made here, and a continued production was maintained to 1910s and later. Factory is still producing a line of cup plates and pressed wares and sells its reproductions as such, at low prices, for the gift-shop trade. They are so well made that many dealers of no ethical standards sell them without blush as antiques—at the antiques price.

West Point Foundry ware: Fine cast-iron and brasswares produced at West Point Foundry, Cold Spring, Putnam County, N.Y., from 1817. Andirons, hollow wares, trivets, made as by-products of cannon and engine production.

West statuary: Imitations of Rogers groups made by the West Co. of Chicago from 1890s. Imitative only in the sense that it was popular parlor statuary of plaster, treated to resemble the Rogers; not infringements on Rogers' own sculptures, but made from original work of other artists.

Westwater cut glass: Not a pattern, and emphatically not one of the "outdo-the-others" cutting designs of the 1890s, Westwater cut wares are the product of John Westwater & Sons of Columbus, O., made from 1830s, using blanks made by other glass producers.

wet Quakers: Quakers who deviated from the orthodox in terms of dress and by partaking of spirituous beverages.

wet sweets: Preserved wet candies, such as ginger in syrup, kumquats in syrup, roses and violets in syrup, and similar dainties.

wey: Measure of 40 bushels; also 6½ tods of wool.

weymaker: An estimator of weights.

Weyman, Edward: Looking-glass maker of Charleston, S.C., also identified with firm of Weyman & Carne, and a cabinetmaker of some stature. Working from 1750s and advertised in 1764.

whale bed: A rope bed without ropes; the cords were twisted whale sinews which never lost elasticity and never deteriorated.

whalebone seat: A chair seat woven from strands of flexible whalebone instead of cane, the whalebone being more durable and of course more costly. This chair seating is said to have originated in Philadelphia c. 1840s–50s.

whale fin: Whalebone; stays. **whale candy:** The crystallization of fat known better as spermaceti. **whale harpoon:** The barbed spear thrown to makefast, on a running line. Not the killing weapon; whales were killed after harpooning with lances. **whale lance:** The razor-sharp unbarbed lance on a long shank (up to 6 feet) and mounted on a 10-foot shaft.

whale oil: Liquid fat rendered from the whale blubber. Esteemed as a lighting fluid. **whale oil lamp:** Any lamp with reservoir to burn whale oil. Made of metal, pottery, and glass. [*Several varieties pictured.*] **whale plates:** Delft plates picturing whaling scenes, made by many potters, but especially by Justus Brouwr and Widow van der Briel. Captioned in Dutch. **whale tooth handles:** Door handles of whale teeth (or other sea mammals), sometimes scrimshawed and carved, mounted on brass shafts.

whang: A shoe tie or lace.

wharrow: A small, crooked, pointed spindle, used as a distaff, especially by women walking or riding.

Whatley pottery: Stonewares made at Whatley, Mass., from 1830s.

whatnot: The étagère; a stand of many platforms, open, to display bric-a-brac and novelties.

Wheat-Price Glass: One of the factories of Wheeling, Va., noted for its flasks and other hollow and flatwares.

wheel back: Any ovo-circular chair or settee back. One of the Adam-period specialties, of classic origin.

wheel barometer: Barometer with a circular recording dial of wheel shape.

wheel cover: Curved wickerwork guard used as temporary covering for a muddy carriage wheel.

Wheeler, W. R.: Artist and landscape painter who settled at Des Moines, Ia., in 1850s.

Wheeler clock: The mystery clock which operates on an inclined plane or ramp, gravity acting upon the weight, which is the clock itself. Maurice Wheeler of Chelsea, England, was a maker of these specialties, often purchased by coffeehouses and inns as attention attractors.

Wheeling glass: Reference is to any glasswares made at the many factories of Wheeling, Va., from 1820s. There is a book, *Wheeling Glass,* of recent publication which contains much information.

wheel lock: A gunlock making its own fire, without recourse to the slow-burning match. A spinning steel wheel, spring-driven, released by trigger, hit flint and caused sparks to fall into the powder. This type precedes the flintlock, which is a simplification of the wheel lock. The wheel lock had to be wound up by a removable crank in order to get a spin from the wheel. Yet this was actually a hammerless gun, as the wheel did the work of igniting. Date is from 1500s. The winding key of this device was called a "spanner."

wheel pistol: Not a wheel-lock type, but a four-barrel pistol with the barrels formed of hollow spokes within a wheel.

wheel stopper: Decanter and bottle stoppers of glass having wheel form. They are round, rayed, and made in a squeezer, molded from the plastic glass.

Whieldon: Thomas Whieldon, master potter of the 18th century, had Spode, Astbury, Heath, and others as apprentices; took in Josiah Wedgwood as a partner. First production was mottled-ware knife handles and similar specialties in his imitation agate. Made toys, chimney ornaments, coffeepots, et cetera, melon plates, and tortoise-shell wares. His pottery started operation c. 1740. [*Examples pictured.*]

While, L.: Cabinetmaker of Buffalo, N.Y., from 1830s. Empire style.

whim: A horsepower mill; a capstan with pole to which horse was hitched for movement in a circle. The pole with underground gears and rods conveyed the power. Also called a "horse-gin."

whip churn: Metal cylinder with plunger; cylinder perforated at bottom. Worked up and down, it whipped cream and syllabub or made a serving of butter in a bowl.

whip-rack: Pendant or bracket consisting of a toothed wheel, the slots to hold whiplash ends for display or in a livery stable.

whipsyllabub: The syllabub that was most delicious; the recipe: 1¼ quarts rich cream, ½ pint white wine, ½ pint sack, juice of 2 oranges and 3 lemons, 1 pound sifted powdered sugar. Beat all ingredients for half an hour with a whisk, let stand in cool place, and serve next day. It will keep, if cold, for a week.

whisk: (1) A wire or hair beater for eggs and cream. (2) A broom. (3) The game at cards, now called whist.

Whiskeybury watch: A small round, watch-shaped whiskey flask of glass with this name and a dial on a paper label, or on a glass label cemented on the flask face.

whiskey fruits: Dried fruits, packed in layers and sprayed with whiskey at the rate of one pint to the bushel. This is an early 19th-century home recipe.

Whiskicothe: A derisive name for Chillicothe, O., settled by soldiers of Anthony Wayne's command who liked whiskey better than vittles and so reputedly made the place a sink of iniquity. The beverage sold for 50 cents a gallon and so, said Mrs. Grundy, men, women, and children drank it.

whistle-belly vengeance: A drink said to have originated at Salem, Mass., the name probably deriving from the English prototype, known as "whip-belly vengeance." The drink was mulled sour beer or home brew, spiced with rye-bread crusts, molasses, and sometimes rum.

whistling locomotive: A unique locomotive toy which ran by steam and whistled. [*Example pictured.*] Also a pull toy which did the same sort of noisemaking.

whispering stick: A shaped gag of thin wood and laces, placed on whispering or talkative children in school.

Whitall-Tatum Glass: Millville (N.J.) Glass, the original factory established by James Lee, 1806. Whitall Brothers took it over in 1840s, manufacturing innumerable drug and specialty jars, vials, special brand bottles, preserve jars, et cetera. The famous Millville rose paperweight was made here. Whitall-Tatum became the name after 1850s. Factory has been in continuous operation for over a century. Now owned by Armstrong Cork Co. In 1870s this factory made over 1000 different items of glassware.

whitby jet: A brilliant carbon mineral, allied to coal, carved and made into jewelry, ornaments, buttons, statues, busts, et cetera.

Whitcomb liniment: Faith Whitcomb's panacea, known also as Shaker liniment. Millions of bottles sold in mid-19th century.

white: To cut or planish. **white-alley:** A white play marble.

White, Barton: Cabinetware factory proprietor of Cincinnati who in 1830s was a mass producer of Empire-styled wares, merging to French Antique in 1840s.

White, Blanche: Upholsterer and maker of "kitty fishers" in 1760s at New York City. In 1750s she was in Philadelphia. Some say she moved to New York in 1767.

White, Isaac: Cabinetmaker of Buffalo, N.Y. Made French Antique furniture to order from 1860s.

white brass: The Chinese invention improperly called German silver.

white carved: This term means carving before application of paint or gilding, and usually refers to white or softwood carvings, as for frames. Also the framing after application of the plaster coating or gesso.

White chairs: Made by Charles White of Raynham, Mass., from 1850s. Decorated, all-wood fancy chairs.

Whitechapels: Needles of steel, pointed and blunt, in all sizes, made from 1740s in England and imported by colonists for many years.

white dip ware: Imitation delft. The glaze is not tin, but common lead glaze over a coating of white slip.

Whitefield views: These are flower prints of native blooms, posed against landscaped backgrounds, published by Appleton in book form, 1845. The various views are identified in the book. Prints on paper size 7" x 10".

Whitefriars glass: Made at London from 1680s; a rare, early glass.

white japan: Seed-lac varnish with a white pigment. Not frequently used, as it generally turned yellow.

white lac: An insect wax used in certain varnishes.

Whiteman jars: Milk bottles with wire clips, some bearing name of milk dealer. Distributed by A. V. Whiteman of New York from 1880s. *Ladies' Home Journal* ad offered 10% commission to any lady convincing her milkman he should use these sanitary containers in milk distribution. The jars hold a quart.

white metal: Pure tin, nickel, silver, and all-white metal alloys, white brass, albata, electrum, argentine, and other alloys.

white pepper: Regular peppercorns shorn of their black shells, which carry most of the pungence and flavor. Yet the "white" seeds, for many years, fetched a premium price.

White's Cabinet: A recipe book, published from 1660s in innumerable editions, containing many ideas and recipes which were later the basis of patents. White called himself "a lover of artificial conclusions."

whitesmith: A planishing smith; a superior workman in iron, comparable to the armorer. Also a worker in pure tin of the "block" variety, not cast, but hammered and battered, planished and "skum." Originally "whitster."

White trays: One of the jokes of antiques collecting. White (milk) glass trays of simple form, marked S. S. White. In 1940s offered by some dealers as rarities, prices ranging to $20 each, for table use. They are really dentists' trays distributed by the S. S. White Dental Supply Co.

white walnut: Any walnut other than black, ranging in color from red-brown to yellow-brown and even creamy white. Called "Virginia walnut," not because it grew in the colony later known as Virginia, but because *all* of the British colonies were once called Virginia, even the Popham Colony in Maine, a lumbering venture preceding the settlement at Plymouth Rock.

whiting: Levigated chalk, ground to a paste with water under a muller, dried and repulverized. Basis of gesso, putty, and used as a white pigment.

Whiting mirrors: Made by Stephen Whiting of Boston from c. 1770. Georgian styles.

Whitlock & Harris: Furniture manufacturers of New York City from 1840s, successors to Thomas Beal. These shops, from Beal's founding, made cabinetwork in classic, Empire, and French Antique styles.

Whitney: The rifle invented by Eli Whitney, who produced 40,000 of them for the Federal Government in Jefferson's administration.

Whitney glass: Glass made at the Whitney works, Glassboro, N.J., from 1776 and operative to late 19th century, making flasks, bottles, jars, jelly, and other containers. First products all blown and blown-molded, in the South Jersey technique.

Whiton, E.: Cabinetmaker of West Stafford, Conn., prior to 1840s. Some reports are he worked in the earlier styles rather than the contemporary ones of his day.

Whittemore wardrobe: A wooden framework covered with curtains, folding against the wall, yet portable. Made from 1870s.

Whittingham brasses: Fireplace equipment of brass, pots, pans, kettles, and other wares marked Whittingham are American-made, dating from late 18th century to early 19th. Made by R. Whittingham of New York City.

Whittington ware: Any pottery made at Whittington, England, from late 17th century, but particularly the wares of red-brown color. Bromley, from c. 1800, made whitewares, transfer-printed wares, and, with Arthur Jewitt, enameled wares.

whorl foot: The French curled or turned-up foot. Used from 18th century to 19th on original Louis XV styles by Chippendale and on French Antique revival furniture called Victorian.

whortleberry: Whortle, or whyrtle, means plant. Hence any berry from a plant. This is the name given the American blueberry.

Whyte, Andrew: Cabinetmaker of Marlboro, Md., prior to 1760. Georgian styles assumed. Probably also Queen Anne.

whythen: *See* Writhen.

wicker: Willow. Wicker-bottomed; a basketwork bottom of willow withes.

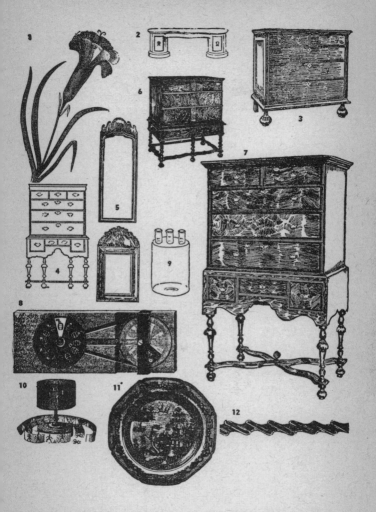

1, Wooden Flower. **2,** Wine Sideboard (the scale is microscopic; one inch equals six feet).
3–7, Examples of William & Mary Style Furniture and Two Mirrors. **8,** Zoetrope Slide.
9, Woulff Flask. **10,** Zoetrope with "films." **11,** Willow-Pattern Plate. **12,** Barley Sugar
Turning (one type). (Nos. 3–7 from *New Geography of American Antiques* and *Pioneer
America, Its First Three Centuries.*)

Wickersham bed: Bedsteads, classic and sleigh styles, made from 1790s to 1810s by Abraham Wickersham, Philadelphia. He specialized in making bedsteads and bed frames.

Wickersham tin: Davenport, Ia., japanned and plain tinware, made in 1850s by Wickersham & Williams. Product sold along the Mississippi River and inland. Produced ware to the value of $10,000 a year at wholesale.

Widmyer furniture: Made at Lancaster, Pa., by Widmyer & Ricksecker from 1830s. Directoire, Empire, and French Antique. Furniture store and factory operated to 1900s or later.

Wienker furniture: Made at Muscatine, Ia., from 1850s. Empire and French Antique, some river-boat furniture made. Firm was a company operating a manufactory.

wig back: Any chair back with a sharply defined circular cutout in the top of back, or back rail, over which the wig or the clubbed hair of a man would fall. Noted in chairs from Queen Anne to late Georgian period. [*Example pictured.*]

Wigglesworth toys: Play toys and dolls from shop of John Wigglesworth of Philadelphia, operating from 1790s. He made some toys, it is reported, and imported others.

wight: A Christmas cake in figural form, generally of a babe.

Wightman lantern: Four-sided lantern with changeable glass panes, using either lamp or candle as a light source. Invented by Daniel Wightman of New Lebanon, N.Y., and made from c. 1849.

wig stand: Not a stand with an open ringed top (which is a washbowl stand), but a stand with a rounded skull pan or boss on a short spindle, like a milliner's bonnet stand.

wig vise: A screw and jaw with skull pan on a rod; could be clamped to any table top and used to dress a wig.

Wilcox plate: Electroplated silver "superior to Sheffield," made by Wilcox Plate Co. of Meriden, Conn., carrying a mark of crossed hammers within a belt impressed with name of company. Mid-19th century.

Wilcox ware: Reference is to Wedgwood wares decorated by the china painter, Mrs. Wilcox, the daughter of Thomas Frye of the Bow China Works.

Wild, John Caspar: Artist of St. Louis and other points who instituted the publication *Valley of the Mississippi*, of which 10 numbers appeared from 1842. The prints are lithographs of St. Louis and other points of interest. He moved to Davenport, Ia., in 1845, where he painted and issued other views of Mississippi river towns and cities. He was a native of Zurich, Switzerland, and worked for some time at Philadelphia, where he did views for Atkinson's Casket.

Wildes lamp: Pewter and Britannia lamps in some variety made by Thomas Wildes, New York City, from 1830s. Also made candlesticks.

Wilkinson, Jemima: She was the "Universal Friend," having a religious sect on Seneca Lake, N.Y., from 1780s.

Wilkinson ware: Ironstone, the graniteware kind, some lustered, much of it made for sale in U.S. from 1880s; Wilkinson was the successor of Alcock. The pottery was at Burslem.

Willard clock: Generally the banjo clock, but also the kidney-dial clock, attributed to Willard as the case designer, which he was not. [*Examples pictured.*]

Willard washer: Home washing machine invented and made by Simon Willard (not the New England clockmaker) of Cincinnati, O., from 1828.

Willets china: Belleek type of ware made in U.S.

Willett, Colonel Marinus: Cabinet- and chairmaker of New York; member of firm of Willett & Pearsey. Also conducted an auction store, 1774.

William & Mary style: The Dutch style of plain case on finely turned legs, joined with shaped flat stretchers and embellished with solid lacquer finish painted with chinoiserie decoration, akin to the designs on fine porcelains of China. Called William & Mary because it entered England as a popular style with the coming of King William of Orange and his Queen, a Stuart princess. Soon shorn of its lacquer and decoration and made of natural walnut, or the décor simulated by application of burl and oystered figure veneering. The style was known in the colonies of New York, New Jersey, and Pennsylvania, and in western New England, before it was popular in England, having been introduced by the Dutch in these several parts. The style is essentially Chinese in taste and form, and its prototype was known in China from the 15th century. [*Examples are pictured.*] This is the style that developed into Queen Anne by the simple expedient of substituting cabriole legs for the turned legs and eliminating the stretchers. The first cabriole leg was achieved by quarter-sawing a heavy William & Mary style turning of either cup or trumpet shape, the effect of which was a cabriole form. Chief items of this style are dressing tables called lowboys, chests-on-frames called highboys, desks, kasten, chairs, settees, and tables.

William & Stevens: Mirror makers of New York City, selling extensively to Southern and Western dealers, advertising "Louis Quatorze, Elizabethan, Gothic & Plain" looking glasses in 1840. The firm was established in 1810.

Williams, F. A.: Furniture manufacturer of Atlanta, Ga., with retail shop on Peachtree Street. Made Empire and French Antique furniture.

Williams, John & James: Cabinetmakers of Washington, D.C., from 1820s. Made classic and early Empire-style goods.

Williams, Samuel: Manufacturer of stock furniture parts and moldings for the cabinetmaking trade of Philadelphia from 1760s. He was also a cabinetmaker working in the Georgian style.

Williams, William: Scientific instrument maker of Boston from 1760s.

Williams & Ives: Cabinet- and chairmakers of Salem, Mass., from 1790s. Classic and Sheraton styles.

Williamsburg glass: Fine colored and clear blown glass, plain and cut, made at

Williamsburg, Brooklyn, N.Y., from 1840s to 1890s.

Williamsburg restoration: Restoration and reconstruction, much of it entirely new, from old plans, of the old colonial capital of Virginia. Not essentially an American restoration; the emphasis is on the superior imported furnishings assumed to have been prevalent during the administrations of the royal governors rather than the colonists' colonial period. Many reproductions of glassware, paint colors, furniture, silver, pewter, et cetera, are made by selected manufacturers and sold with the official stamp of approval of Colonial Williamsburg, Inc., financed by John D. Rockefeller, Jr.

Williams mirrors: Fine classic, Directoire, pier, and *trumeau* mirrors, overmantels, et cetera, made from 1810 at New York City. In business for 45 years. Final production was rococo and Baroque style. Also mirrors made by Dudley Williams, Salem, Mass.; business taken over by William Everett in 1850s.

Williams pictures & frames: Probably the chromos, lithographs, and engravings published by Williams, Stevens & Williams of New York City from 1850s, and the frames they also made as a part of a mirror manufactory.

Williamsport glass: Made at what is now Monongahela City, Pa., from 1816. Finally became property of the Ihmsens of Pittsburgh.

Willington glass: Made at Willington, Conn., from 1815; bottles, carboys, flasks, and hollow wares in amber and green; working to 1870s.

Willis bed: Late-Empire-style bed without a crack or other orifice, being tightly fitted and so "bugproof." Made by many makers under Willis patents.

willkommen: Large glasses, traditionally the coming and the parting glass offered to guests. The parting glass was called the Come Again, or *wieder kommen*, glass. Some are elaborately engraved and worked. Examples date from 1500s. European and generally Germanic or Swiss.

willow ironstone: Mason's and other ironstone, and some granite ware called ironstone, printed in the willow pattern.

willow pattern: The Chinese traditional blue-decorated ware, the scene stylized, engraved, and printed in transfer. [*Example pictured.*]   **willow-pattern handles:** Chinese-form and -style brasses for cabinet furniture. [*Examples pictured.*]

Wills Euston ware: Reference most likely is to art pottery, vases and busts of delicate pink terra cotta. All marked W. & T. Wills, and made at their own pottery, Euston Road, England, from 1860s.

Willson, Miss (ARTIST)**:** Crudities by a "Miss" Willson who lived with a "Miss" Brundage, playing house in a Green County, N.Y., hut and painting very colorful smears done with berry juices, dyes, and other natural pigments. When "Miss" Brundage died, "Miss" Willson was mad with grief, fled the hut, and was never heard of again. This 19th-century tragedy leaves nothing but a lot of paintings, called "primitive" perhaps because they are almost psychopathic.

Wilmurt, Thomas: Mirror maker of New York City from 1850s. His looking glasses are stenciled with his name on the back dust board.

Wilson, D.: Cabinetmaker of Madison, Ind., working in second quarter of 19th century. There is an extensive notice of this man by Mary B. Sharpe in the *Magazine Antiques*, October 1945.

Wilson, John: Cabinetmaker of Charleston, S.C., from 1790s, who apparently moved to Lancaster, Pa., about 1805. He worked in the classic style.

Wilson coverlets: "Ingrain"-weave coverlets by Robert Wilson of New Philadelphia, O., from 1840s. His coverlets are imitative of the carpets introduced in 1830s called "ingrain."

Wilson globes: Terrestrial and celestial globes were made first in U.S. by J. Wilson as a factory operation at Albany, N.Y. A globe maker from c. 1810, Wilson started his factory 1818.

Wilson plate: Silver-plated wares bearing mark of R. & W. Wilson are of Philadelphia make, from c. 1830s. Factory at Fifth and Cherry streets made coffee urns, teapots, tankards, creamers, and services. It is asserted this firm at first made Sheffield-type plated ware.

Wilson prints: Bird prints by Alexander Wilson, the famed ornithologist who came to America from Scotland in 1794, working as a peddler, weaver, and rhymester. In 1807, while working for John Aitkens, Philadelphia, he began painting birds of America; probably gave Audubon his idea. Wilson's birds are prints of small folio or royal quarto size, 76 in all. They are the finest all American bird prints, engraved here and hand-colored. Published 1808–14. Charles L. Bonaparte's supplement to Wilson's work contains small folio prints issued in a volume published 1825–33 in parts, with drawings by Peale and Ryder, engraved by Lawson.

Wilson ware: Wares of Neale & Wilson and Robert Wilson, at Hanley, England, marked with a crown, "C," and "Wilson." Cream-colored earthenwares, decorated under these names from 1792 to 1802, then became D. Wilson and, after several other ownerships, Mayer & Ridgway and finally Ridgway & Co.

Wilton carpet: A type of weave, similar to Brussels, but with loops cut, giving a more springy pile.

wimble: A gimlet; a boring tool. [*Example pictured.*]

wimple: A head covering, with bands and collar, popular in 18th century, but now generally the style affected by nuns. Originals were of silk and linen.

Winchell tin: Japanned tinware produced on a wholesale basis by Winchell Works, Cincinnati, from 1840s. Production was enormous, covering everything from a penny whistle to a water cooler; 34 people were employed in the manufacture.

Winchester measures: Standard pint, quart, peck, bushel, and other measures approved by the market town of Winchester, England. Many are of cast brass, bronze, and some of iron bear the insignia of the town and are lettered in raised characters.

Windle tin: Planished and painted tin-plated iron made by Windle & Co., N.Y., from 1840s.

windmill: The wind-power mill requiring no damming of streams, and grinding grain efficiently though in smaller quantities, and of course at the whims of the wind. The mystery to most people is not in regard to the exterior of a windmill, but to its inner working. [*An early American interior view of such a mill is pictured.*]

window: From the Welsh, *wyntdor*, meaning door to the winds. Openings were first only curtained, then horn-paned or skin-covered, mica-covered, and finally glass-paned. Mica is said to have been used in Greece and Rome. **window blinds:** Slatted assemblies, as the jalousie or Venetian blind, the bamboo curtain, or the Holland shade. **window curtains:** Any drapery trimming, covering, or enhancing the appearance of a window opening. **window harp:** Box-form ventilator for under a window sash, strung with taut wires upon which the wind played and made harplike tones. **windowpanes:** Quarries or cuts of glass, crown-blown, plated, or pressed. **window seat:** A small backless sofa for placement at a window; some are actually replicas of Chinese altars; some are Greek-revival or other classic style. **window spring:** A substitute for cords and weights to counterbalance sash windows. J. C. Butterworth of Providence, R.I. made them from 1860s but somehow they did not supplant the sash cord and weight.

Windsor chairs: See Chairs, All Kinds.

Windsor legs: Reference is to turned legs in various styles, as found on Windsor chairs. [*Various types pictured.*]

Windsor soap: Spotted white and brown soap in various scents.

Windsor stain: An inelegant but penetrating chemical stain to achieve a red color on the wood; quicklime slaked in urine, spread on wood as a paste, dried, and brushed off.

Windsor stand: High three-legged stool with turned legs.

Windsor trays: The oval tin trays of commerce in 19th century.

wine bin: A cabinet designed to hold wine bottles, sometimes for cooling, in which case the cabinet is lined with zinc sheet or lead.

wine board: The middle-post sideboard.

wine cabinet: A cellaret; a footed cabinet with hinged-top cover to hold bottles of wine.

wine cisterns: Huge bowls for holding bottles of wine in ice, some of staves with brass hoops, some all silver.

wine cloth: Tablecloth used when the supper was "special," with wine.

wine coaster: Circular disks with galleries and sometimes footed; coasters for wine bottles and decanters. Some of solid silver, others of Sheffield plate, brass, and painted iron.

wine cooler: A cabinet or staved piece on stand, used to cool wine bottles in water or ice.

wine font: A huge decanter or urn, often of glass, to hold wine for service from a spigot or tap.

wine fountain: A pair of glass bottles with descending spouts, fitted with internal stopples. Pushing up the stopples with glass edge caused wine to flow. Late, but unusual device, the glassware engraved. Patented by Stefiitcher of Vienna c. 1870s. Also called a wine bibbler. [*Example pictured.*]

wine funnels: Silver funnels of small size used in decanting wine.

wineglass lamp: Wineglass-shaped lamp of blown glass, the bowl drawn together at top to fit a metal wick cap. A night lamp.

wine nips: Cutters for severing the wire holding corks in bottles of sparkling wines.

wine pipe: Tubular siphon for drawing wine from casks, generally of silver. Resembles a small trombone.

wine rack: An open sloping box on stand, similar to bookstand. [*Example pictured.*]

wine sideboard: A sideboard with drum-shaped supports, the drums holding rotating stands for wine bottles. [*Example pictured.*]

wine stand: A drum-shaped holder on base, often of electroplated ware, to quick-chill a bottle of wine in cracked ice. A hotel and restaurant piece.

wine tables: Stands of various types for the service of wine, some having galleried rims, some with a series of circular depressions to keep a bottle secure. Others are knee-high, for use at chairside.

wine tasters: Small bowls of silver used by experts in grading wine; some are porringer shape.

wine tester: A bottle of almost test-tube shape, with a heavy bottom, lowered into a cask of wine through the bung to get a sample for test.

wine wagon: Decanter stand of silver, holding one to three bottles and mounted on wheels for service around the table.

wine waiter: Oblong tray with galleried sides and upright central panel with handhold, mounted on a standing frame. The tray holds six to eight bottles or decanters.

wine warmer: Stand with a shield-form back, usually of metal, to hold a bottle of wine near the hearth in order to bring contents to room temperature; especially used for sherry, port, madeira, and other wines, never served chilled.

Winfield bed: Ornate brass bed of four-post and canopy type, made at Birmingham, England, from 1850s by R. W. Winfield. Advertised and sold in U.S.

wing cheek: Upholstery over a shape and form of chair or settee back that is allied closely to the back and side cheekpieces of a settle.

wing commode: A fireside wing chair used as a commode chair or closestool.

wing desk: A slope-front desk with a board divided vertically and opening outward in two wings, the writing board pulling out from the exposed cavity. Rare, and probably of a date around 1800s-10s.

winged bookcase: A breakfront with the central section outjutting, the two side sections called the wings.

winged chest: Chest of drawers with side extensions for very narrow drawers.

winged stem: Wineglass stems with tooled effects simulating wings on the stem. This may be due to legend of religious significance, as the Holy Grail; the flying cup of some saint or other.

Wingender ware: Probable reference is to the redwares produced at the Wingender Brothers Pottery, Haddonfield, N.J., in 19th century.

Winne & Abeel: Founders at Albany, N.Y., who made considerable quantity of hollow ware from 1850s.

Winne furniture: Labeled items sold by John Winne of Albany, N.Y., from 1840s, whether from his own factory or others.

winnow cob: A winnowing basket; the device used in tossing grain after flailing, to blow off the chaff.

Winship ware: The only reference found likely is the pottery made at the kilns of Norwich, Conn., from 1840s, when they were owned by Joseph Winship. More generally designated as Norwich pottery or Norwich ware.

Winslow chair: See Chairs, All Kinds.

Winslow furniture: This is probably furniture made by David Winslow of Boston from 1840s. Empire and French Antique. Or it may refer to the Grecian dining tables, ship cabin furniture, chairs, and other pieces made by Winslow & Flanders, Chelsea, Mass., from 1840s.

Winslow stoneware: Water kegs, filters, butter pots, churns, spittoons, pitchers, jugs, and flowerpots of stoneware, made at Portland, Me., at the J. T. Winslow Pottery. Marked examples are of record.

Winter: A miniature painter who signed his little portraits thus has left a trail of his work throughout the Midwest. He worked in Chicago in 1850s.

winter buds: This secret of our early-19th-century ancestors should be revealed. They cut bud stems from bush and plant in late autumn, sealing the ends with wax and storing them in a damp, dark cellar until midwinter. Then the sealed ends were cut off and the twigs and stems put in water fortified with niter or salt. The buds revived and opened as fresh flowers!

wire mattress: Any coiled or woven wire bedspring.

wire shade: A woven wire window screen. Some early examples seem to be of damask weave but aren't; they are painted in tones of gray with scenes, rococo scrolls, et cetera, a practice continued until 1920s.

wirework: Under this categorical heading falls a variety of articles and items, ranging from wirework in iron to wirework in gold and platinum. Which is to say it embraces sieves, cullers, potato boilers, drainers, screens, fenders, grilles, toasters, racks, and jewelry. Fruit and breadbaskets of wirework in silver, silver-plated wire, brass, and japanned iron are noted from mid-18th century. The iron potato boilers date from 17th century, and many are delightful baskets, ovate or globose, with constricted tops and ball-form handles.

There is no catalogue or definitive book on wirework of all sorts, but we have the assurance of *Antiques Digest* that sufficient research has been done to insure publication of data in 1953. Student is therefore referred to this publication.

Wisconsin.fence: A low parapet of lime, sand, and gravel cement, formed between boards. Said to have been introduced by Swedish settlers in 1830s. Data not verified.

wishbone stretcher: When either the back or front (but not both) legs of a piece, as a chair or stand, are X-form and the others vertical columnar form, a heavy stretcher begins at the center of the X and becomes a two-pronged element leading to and joining each of the other legs. The shape is "wishbone," hence the term. Noted from 18th-century Georgian period, but quite rare. Used also in 19th century, some on quite late items.

Wistar glass: Caspar Wistar, Dutch button manufacturer of Philadelphia, born in Netherlands, 1696, migrated to Pennsylvania in 1717 and became a Quaker. Married Catherine Jensen, descended from Reynier Jensen, first printer of Penn's colony. Established a glassworks by importing four master workmen from the Netherlands, 1739; erected factory at Alloway's Creek, Salem County, N.J., and began production of Dutch-styled glass, the first in the now-famed South Jersey tradition. See *ABC's of Old Glass*, by the author, and McKearin's *American Glass* and *200 Years of American Blown Glass*.

witch balls: (1) Hollow spheres of glass in whorls of color, said to have been made by superstitious workers in glasshouses, who used them in homes as "witch warners." From this custom came that of hanging the balls on candle trows at Epiphany, and so came the "Christmas balls." First made in England. (2) Fancy balls of glass, many in various colors and combinations, generally with a vase-form holder, for use as a decorative element and not as a witch warner. These date from 1820s and seem to have been made to 1900s as art novelty glass.

Witchet: A two-bladed turning plane to smooth poles.

witch lamp: A sheet-iron fat-lamp with single wick, swinging in a U-shaped support on a rod and base. A few are known in brass.

withy: The towering willow tree.

Witmer coverlets: J. Witmer of Manor Township, Lancaster County, Pa., set up looms for three-color damask coverlet weaving in 1830s. His coverlets are signed and often dated.

Wittinham brass: Research reveals a brazier named thus was working in New York City from 1790s. Made brass candlesticks and andirons.

wizard's purse: Morocco leather circular-form four-flap purse having a fold that defied opening except by those in the know. Form is Chinese. Many made in late 19th century.

woad: A plant yielding a violet and a blue dye.

Wolf, Charles: Cabinetmaker of Cincinnati who specialized in bookcases and bureaus, working in 1840s and 1850s.

Wolfe pottery: Made at Chillicothe, O., from 1850s.

Wolford china: White granite ware or thick ironstone "equal to any English!" made at Wolford Pottery, Washington County, Mo., from 1840s. Local clays were used.

Wolverhampton ware: Painted and japanned papier-mâché wares, including trays. Production started in 1770s, but was most active from 1830s to 1850s. Beds and chairs were made of this paper plastic.

wonder camera: The magic lantern; also a projecting machine working from any print by reflection.

Wood, Aaron: Apprenticed, 1731, to Dr. Thomas Wedgwood, potter, of Burslem, primarily famed for his raised-work molds for the ware erroneously called "Elizabethan."

Wood, Enoch: "The Father of Pottery," active from 1780s, so called because of his genius as modeler, potter, and businessman. **Wood & Caldwell:** Firm of Enoch Wood and James Caldwell. The history of these potters and descriptions of wares, marks, et cetera, are all tabulated in various books listed in Bibliography.

Wood, Lansford: Items signed or labeled by this man, working at Worcester, Mass., may include an ornamental painting, a gilded mirror, or an item of cabinet furniture. He worked from 1840s.

Wood, Ralph: One of the great potters of England, working at Burslem in first half of 18th century; made wares similar to Whieldon's.

Wood & Caldwell: Potters of Burslem, England, who made wares imitative of Wedgwood raised-figure lusters and other wares, from 1790s or early 1800s.

Wood & Hughes: This mark, or W & H, on silverware indicated silver manufactured by Wood & Hughes, New York City, from 1850s.

Woodall glass: Actually Webb glass, signed by Woodall, a master cutter.

Woodbridge furniture: Enameled and grained cottage furniture, sold in suites from $25 upward from 1850s. Made at New York City.

wood carpet: Parquetry flooring, especially the kind glued to canvas and laid down and removed at will.

wood-chest: Any board chest; any chest of wood; also a sea chest made by William Wood or Woods of New York, who in 1830s had a manufactory.

wood-cruets: Stands of rosewood, walnut, mahogany, or maple, with two circular disks, one pierced for cruets, the other flat as a support. If of fine workmanship, most likely of 18th century.

woodcut: A common wood engraving and any print made from it.

woodcock's head: The only antiques reference applicable would seem to be a clay tobacco pipe of 17th century, made in form of woodcock's head.

wooden chimney: The chimney of piled logs or billets, catted with clay inside, the wood serving mainly as a framing.

wooden clock: The term applies generally to any clock movement constructed of wood. Also, but rarely, to clocks cased, as usual, in wood.

wooden flowers: Artificial flowers made from plane shavings of pine, dyed and waxed or varnished. [*Example pictured.*]

wooden Indian: The traditional tobacconist's sign of the U.S., but descended from "black boys" used by European dealers in tobacco from 17th century. The cigar-store Indians, in male and female form, carved from wood and realistically painted. Once common, now quite scarce and valuable.

woodenware: So vast is this field, especially in respect to the dairy and kitchenwares and containers of wood, molds, et cetera, of the 19th century, that we cannot even list the categories. See Bibliography. Perhaps the most unusual item in the entire list is a wood lamp; a lamp of turned wood (cedar, maple, or walnut) with a metallic reservoir enclosed in the huge bulb turning. [*Example pictured, with typical examples of woodenwares.*]

woodenware makers: When there has been a maker's name applied to woodenwares, such makers' names are listed in this dictionary. But for further works of reference, see Bibliography.

Woodin, Thomas: Art instructor and cabinetmaker of Charleston, S.C., from 1760s. Probably worked in the Georgian style.

wood latch: Wooden door hardware; hinges and locks were also made of wood, noted not only on house doors, but also on chests and cabinets.

Woodrow & Furguson: Cabinetmakers of Warren, O., working in 1830s. Empire-style pieces reported.

Woodruff barometer: Sheraton and French Antique style barometers made by Charles Wilder of Peterboro, N.H., from 1830s to 1860s.

Woodruff furniture: (1) Cabinetwork by Woodruff of New York, contemporary of Phyfe. Sheraton and Directoire styles; early 19th century. (2) Reported as made "in the South" by an itinerant named Woodruff.

woods, cabinet: The following are of recorded usage in the American scene, from early 1600s to date: pine, maple, deal, pear, wild cherry, oak, box, elm, ash, beech, birch, cedar, poplar, walnut, sycamore, cypress, amboina, mahogany, rowan, butternut, bilsted, heart pine, southern pine, and others. This is not to say all of these were in use at any one period.

Woodsum shades: Fan-shaped lamp shades made by Woodsum, Boston, from 1850s.

wood toys: Any play toy, doll, pull toy, effigy, animal, et cetera, made of wood. Some are articulated; some show motion when pulled or otherwise manipulated. So infinite is the variety that no one volume could list and picture all known kinds, dating from earliest times.

Woodward lantern: Kerosene lantern of the type that was used on railroads, farms, and as a general convenience.

Woodwell chairs: Fancy and cottage chairs made from 1830s at Pittsburgh, Pa., by J. & J. Woodwell.

woof: Shuttle thread; the cross-weave thread in cloth.

Top and 2nd rows: View of Worcester Porcelain Works, examples of the ware, and reverse and obverse of a porcelain two-shilling coin issued by the factory in 18th century. **3rd row:** Woodenwares, as advertised in 1853; eight Tobacco or Pipe "Stopples" of brass. **Bottom row:** Urn worktables and examples of early woodenwares, including burl bowl with handles, burl porringer, nest of bowls, scoop, two spoons, and a burl mortar.

Wooley & Harris woodenwares: A large production of bowls, butter stamps, et cetera, some marked, made by a firm so named at Albany, N.Y., from 1840s.

wool-on-wool: Designation given hand-worked coverlets and other fancy pieces worked on wool, in wool yarns; an art allied somewhat to turkey work or rug hooking.

Woolsey-Jones tin: Japanned tinwares made at Syracuse, N.Y., and extensively distributed via Erie Canal. Date is from 1840s to c. 1860.

Wooten ware: Pottery made by J. Wooten at Congress Works, South Amboy, N.J., from 1850s.

Wootton, Sir Henry: Ambassador of James I to Venice, where he did a book on architecture, published 1620.

wootz: East Indian steel.

Worcester: A porcelain of England; factory founded 1751 by Dr. Wall. This works, under various managements and companies, has remained active in production of fine dinnerwares, specialties, and statuary. [*Examples pictured.*]

workbag chair: Any chair made with a sewing bag fitted to a drawer under the seat.

work holder: The sewing bird, in any of its various forms, some not bird-shaped at all.

Workman, Daniel: Cabinetmaker of North Adams, Mass., working from 1840s.

wormed glass: The air-twist technique noted in stems of wineglasses.

worm walnut: The inferior European walnut wood; antiques of walnut, looking like colonial production but literally riddled with wormholes, are suspect of importation, probably from Switzerland or Italy.

worn stretcher: Once considered a badge of genuineness of a chair in terms of antiquity; a wearing down on the stretcher from use as a footrest. Most otherwise questionable antiques so found today are suspect of "rasping down" to simulate wear.

Worthington curtains: Woolen curtains produced by various looms at Worthington, Mass., 19th century.

Worthington furniture: Produced at Washington, D.C., from 1820s by William Worthington, Jr. Directoire and Sheraton styles.

Woulff bottle: Three-necked bottle used in chemistry. Many were made by Millville, N.J., glassworks. It is an oddity now used as a three-bud vase. [*Example pictured.*]

W'Port: The W and star on bottle labels of silver or plate designate white port wine.

Wren, Sir Christopher: Rebuilder of London after the Great Fire of 1666. He worked in the classic style, which was continued in the Georgian period.

wriggling: Wriggle work, achieved by dextrous rocking of chisel on metal, or by brushwork on any surface, to achieve a wriggly line. Noted as a form of engraving on silver and pewter of 16th and 17th centuries; also on china decoration.

Wright, G. & A.: Perfumers and soap-makers of Philadelphia, packing many of their products in transfer-printed china boxes, some in colors. All Wright packages are now collected; some have historic scenes on them.

Wright, Joseph: Wax miniature modeler and maker of plaster life masks. Did a life mask of Washington, widely copied, and the prototype of most busts and cameos. Son of Patience Wright, he was born 1756.

Wright, Patience Lovell: The mother of Joseph, a wax modeler of great renown; did portraits of Franklin, Chatham, and others. Worked from 1750s in New York, London, and Paris.

Wright, Smith & Co.: This mark, on any ceramic ware, is that of the firm of Philadelphia importers who dealt in Liverpool, Canton, Sèvres, and other wares and represented Bakewell, Pears & Co. (glass) and Tucker & Hemphill (American porcelain) firms.

Wright & Bridgford iron: Kitchenwares and kettles bearing this mark cast in it were made by a firm so named at Louisville, Ky., from 1850s. They were also producers of sheet-iron and sheet-copper wares.

Wright chairs: Reference is to the maker, J. M. Wright of Oswego, N.Y., who produced rockers, Grecian chairs, and fancy chairs from prior to 1840.

Wrights, Frederick: Glass blower working in Washington, D.C., from 1820s.

Wright stoneware: Made at Taunton, Mass., by F. Wright from mid-19th century.

writer's coupe: Water cup, ink cup, color cup, some very ornate. They seem to be of Chinese origin, where ceremonial coupes were the property of poets, philosophers, and Personages. Some of jade, bronze, celadon, silver, or gold. Others of rock crystal, brass, porcelain, or pottery.

writhen: Twisted or coiled strands; in twist formation. Term is from *wuryd* and *wrethen*, to coil or twist. Said of silver spoons with strands of the metal twisted in bulb shape, open, or over a solid knop. Term is ancient English, from 16th century or earlier.

writing arm: Any chair fitted with a broad arm, flat, sometimes with drawer under, to serve as a writing chair.

writing box: Silver, brass, or pewter covered boxes holding inkwell, sander, wafer case, and pen well. The same type of box was also made of wood, some brassbound. A table writing-material box.

writing chair: Any chair made for use at a desk.

Wrotham slip: Reference is to slip-decorated pottery (redwares) made at Wrotham, England, from 1600s. Some decorated with tulips. Also early brown-glaze wares.

wrought: Done with the hands, as forged, carved, shaped, hammered, incised.

Wunderkammer: A museum room; a room of wonders. Germanic term.

Wurmski silhouettes: Standard cut silhouettes, important because cut by a Polish immigrant working at Philadelphia in 1840s.

Wyeth, Richardson & Nelson: Furniture manufacturers of Wendell, Mass., from early 19th century. After 1833, firm became Wyeth & Richardson. Chairs and cabinet furniture in the styles of their period; classic, Directoire, Sheraton, Empire, and probably French Antique.

wyrtgeard: The kitchen garden. The "wortgard" or herb garden, "for sallets and flavours."

wyvern: Heraldic winged beast; dragon-headed cockatrice without spurs.

X

xanthine glass: Yellow glass.

xenia: Greek-revival word, meaning guest or hospitable.

Y

Y: This letter, preceding a word, with or without hyphenation, or as a lower-case letter preceding a capitalized word (yTentented or y-tented, for example), is a substitution for the obsolete English letter once called "thorn" and shaped like a tailless italic *p*, having the power of *th*, meaning "the" or "ye."

yad: A pointing rod with a carved hand and extended forefinger.

Yale & Curtis lamp: Bell-shaped pewter whale-oil lamp with handle and two-wick burner. Marked with maker's name. Made at New York City from 1825.

Yale chair: A writing armchair with a cane back and seat, the writing arm adjustable. Made by Park & Lang of Lansing, Mich., from 1880s. Probably a suggestion it was in use at Yale College resides in the name.

Yale lamps: Whale-oil and other fluid lamps of the period, made by Edwin Yale of Boston from 1820.

yam: The yellow-red sweet potato.

yang-stai: Porcelain for export. We still wrongly call it Lowestoft.

Yankee bowl: Iron cook pot, open-topped and cup-shaped, without the flared rim of a Scotch pot.

yardarm barometer: Bent-tube barometer, often mounted in a mirror or within a clock dialing.

yard-of-ale glass: A 36-inch-high, tube-like drinking glass; the "aleyard."

yarn box: A box or basket form to hold yarns, often of split wood bands, painted scenically or with symbolic forms. Some have ears upon which to wind yarn in hanking.

yclept: Named.

Yearsley ware: The first Wedgwood; made at Yearsley, England, from 1600. Coarse brown ware. "At Yearsley there are pancheons made by Willie Wedgwood, that young blade."

yellow berries: The color gamboge.

yellow dog pitcher: *See* Golden Dog.

yellow glove: A dandy; a fancy gentleman.

yellow pine: The Georgia or Southern pine.

yellow ware: Creamware, queen's ware, and also the distinct yellow-glaze ware often used for mugs and teapots.

yellow wood: Satinwood. Also the *Virgilia lutea*, native to the coastal region south of Maryland.

yeoman: A landowning farmer or husbandman. Not a serf or tenant. A self-reliant man of the soil.

Yeomans, E.: Furniture maker of French Antique and Eastlake-style goods, Chicago, from 1870s.

ying yu: Another term of the Chinese for what we call Lowestoft. This is the term used in Kiang Province for wares shipped to Canton for decorating, refiring, and export. It was made to order for "foreign devils" and was not of quality or form used in China. It was cheap stuff, a dinner set of 200 pieces costing less than $4 dockside, Canton; shipmasters found it very profitable *ballast*.

yin-yang: Male and female; man and woman.

Y-ladder: A single-pole orchard ladder with rungs extended through it on either side. There is a broad Y at the end, placed on the ground to steady the pole and prevent turning while in use.

ympe: A young tree.

Ynisymudw: A terra cotta pottery not far from Swansea, Wales; the works made white and painted wares from 1850s, blue-and-white wares, and housewares.

yoke back: When the top rail of a chair or settee extends beyond the upright stiles and has a bend, it is called yoked or yoke-backed. The style is Chinese and is noted in the simpler forms of William & Mary and Queen Anne chairs.

yoke front: Serpentine in façade, or front,

especially with the curvate humps associated with an ox yoke.

yonker; jonkeer: A yeoman; a gentleman of the country.

York ware: Rockingham glazed wares made at York, England, from 1830s.

Young, Alexander: Terra cotta maker of New York City from 1850.

Young America bust: A Parian bust, symbolic of the subject, made in Europe for Cutter, Hyde & Co., Boston, 1865–76.

Young furniture; S. & M. Young: Fine Directoire-styled furniture, custom-made by these artisans at New York City from 1815. Sheraton- and Regency-styled cabinetwork attributed also to them. Firm continued to 1824, after which Moses Young continued alone to 1834. Their work is as good as Phyfe's.

Young porcelain: The only reference is found in one Edward Young, listed as a manufacturer of porcelain at Trenton, N.J., in 1850s.

Young pottery: Stoneware made at Harrisburg, Pa., from 1840s. In 1858 the pottery was acquired by a William Moyer.

yqueme: To gratify; to please.

ytented: Cloth, on tenterhooks, for shrinking.

ytizled: Teasled, or brushed with the teasel, or thistle.

ytouked: Dyed.

Yuan: Mongol dynasty of China, A.D. 1260–1368.

Yung Cheng: Chinese dynasty or period, 1722–36.

Ywain: A given name, same as Owen.

ywole: I will.

Z

zaffre: Smalt; cobalt-blue glass, pounded for a dressing, or levigated, for use as a pigment.

Zanesville glass: Any glass made by several factories at the Ohio town of Zanesville. Some of it is so well made it is mistaken for Stiegel. Flasks, bottles, sugar basins, vases, and general wares. See *ABC's of Old Glass*, by the author, and the two massive tomes by George S. & Helen McKearin.

zarf: A cupholder of metal; a glass holder. Originally used with coffee cups; probably a Near Eastern device. The type most commonly known is the plated or white metal holders used by soda-fountain proprietors in serving sodas and sundaes in glasses.

zephyr moss: An early-19th-century decorating stuff made by knitting green and brown yarns into a mossy unit, stiffening with glue or gum-arabic water, and then raveling it out.

Zerfass, John: Cabinetmaker of New York from 1840s.

Ziegler furniture: Mass-produced parlor, bedroom, library, and dining-room furniture in the French Antique style, made at New York City from 1850s.

zigzag work: *Point d'Hongroise*, or *Hongraise*. Zigzag waves of varicolored bands, blending.

Zimmerman antiques: From an antiques shop of Cincinnati, operating as early as 1877, conducted by Zimmerman & Sons, cabinetmakers. This is an entry suggesting considerably more research, preferably on the spot.

zinn: Tin, and therefore pewter. Pronounced "tsin."

Zinn, Charles: Willow-ware manufacturer of New York from 1850s; his goods still look "new" now because all his followers imitated his styles and weaves. The

techniques he established are followed to this day.

zither: A stringed lap or table instrument, popular in last six decades of 19th century as a home instrument; a shallow, harp-outline-form sounding box with 32 or more strings and four sets of chords. Plucked or strummed (on the chords). Many varieties, including the autoharp.

zoetrope: The first home-movie machine; the wheel of life. A barrel form mounted on a pedestal, free-turning, with slots along the periphery, near top edge. "Films" showing attitude or form change, position shift, et cetera, many in colors, when spun in this machine and viewed through the slots, had active motion. The films are precursors of the movie film, and some, after 1880, were photographic. The colored strips with black outline are printed from line cuts and are the first "silly symphonies." Many varieties and sizes, some with mirrors, others which must be viewed in a mirror, et cetera. The author projected a zoetrope film successfully over television in 1949.

zoetrope slide: A magic-lantern slide with zoetrope action, rotating a transparent disk carrying the figures through a chopper, the whole moved by a crank. These slides, in 1890, sold for $6.50 each. Each provided a "show" lasting four seconds. As important as the zoetrope itself in the history of motion pictures and the antiquities of the art. [*Example pictured.*]

zoetropon (traumtrope): Cards, on one side of which is drawn one element of a scene (as a bird cage) and on the other the complement. Strung on two loops from the sides and twisted; tautening the cord caused the card to spin and show the complete picture.

Zollinger furniture: Made at Sandusky, O., from 1850s; French Antique and cottage furniture.

Zuber: Wallpaper and textile printer of

Rixheim, Alsace-Lorraine, in 18th and 19th centuries. Many of the Zuber et Cie. products were sold in U.S.

Zurich porcelain: Product of the Swiss factory at Zurich, operating from 1760s.

zuurkool: Pickled cabbage, chou-crou, kraut, or sauerkraut.

Zu-Zu: A Zouave; the baggy-trousered, fez-capped soldiers with a reputation for snappy action and ginger.

zygon: A boat thwart; a rower's seat.

zylo balsamum: Extract of balsam. Bottles so marked contained a hair tonic of this name.

BIBLIOGRAPHY

Titles and authors of books consulted by the various researchers employed in the basic compilation of this dictionary. Volumes followed by a star (*) are presumed to be in print and readily available for purchase. Others may be found in large and important libraries.

ART

Fine, Amateur, Major, Minor, and Graphic

DICTIONARY OF AMERICAN PAINTERS, SCULPTORS, & ENGRAVERS Mantle Fielding
18TH CENTURY PAINTING IN NEW ENGLAND Louisa Dresser
ART IN AMERICA Holger Cahill*
HISTORY OF THE ARTS OF DESIGN IN THE U.S.A. William Dunlap*
AMERICAN ENGRAVERS UPON COPPER & STEEL D. McN. Stauffer (2 vols.)
AMERICAN ENGRAVERS UPON COPPER & STEEL Mantle Fielding (1 vol.)
AMERICAN PAINTING Samuel Isham*
PORTRAITS OF WASHINGTON G. A. Eisen* (3 vols.)
NATIONAL ACADEMY OF DESIGN, EXHIBITION RECORD Bartlett Cowdrey*
AMERICAN PIONEER ARTS & ARTISTS Carl W. Drepperd
SOME AMERICAN PRIMITIVES Clara Endicott Sears
AMERICAN PRIMITIVE PAINTING Jean Lipman*
LIMNERS & LIKENESSES Alan Burroughs*
AMERICAN PAINTING: FIRST FLOWERS OF OUR WILDERNESS James Flexner*
PRIMITIVE PAINTERS IN AMERICA Lipman & Winchester*
JEREMIAH DUMMER Clarke & Foote
INDEX OF ARTISTS, ILLUSTRATORS, ENGRAVERS, ETC. Daniel T. Mallett*
BIOGRAPHICAL INDEX OF AMERICAN ARTISTS Ralph C. Smith*
EVOLUTION OF ART Ruth de Rochemont
MATTHEW PRATT William Sawitzky
LIFE PORTRAITS OF WASHINGTON & THEIR REPLICAS Morgan & Fielding
STILL LIFE PAINTING IN AMERICA Wolfang Born*
A GRAMMAR OF THE ARTS Sir Charles Holmes
CHARLES WILLSON PEALE Charles C. Sellers
GILBERT STUART William Whitley
EARLY AMERICAN PORTRAIT PAINTERS Cuthbert Lee*
AMERICAN ROMANTIC PAINTING E. P. Richardson*
JOHN RAMAGE Frederick Fairchild Sherman
AMERICA'S OLD MASTERS James T. Flexner*
EARLY AMERICAN PAINTING Frederick Fairchild Sherman
AMERICAN MINIATURES Harry B. Wehle*
GILBERT STUART & HIS PUPILS John Hill Morgan
DICTIONARY OF MINIATURE PAINTERS J. J. Foster

SAMUEL F. B. MORSE Harry B. Wehle
CURRIER & IVES, PRINTMAKERS TO THE AMERICAN PEOPLE H. T. Peters
AMERICA ON STONE H. T. Peters
CALIFORNIA ON STONE H. T. Peters
CURRIER & IVES (abridged) H. T. Peters*
BEST 50 CURRIER & IVES Charles Messer Stow
THE SPIRIT OF AMERICA (CURRIER & IVES) W. S. Hall
ALPHABETIC LIST OF 5,735 CURRIER & IVES PRINTS F. A. Conningham
EARLY AMERICAN PRINTS Carl W. Drepperd
AMERICAN DRAWING BOOKS (A bibliography published by N.Y. Public Library) Carl W. Drepperd*
AMERICAN GRAPHIC ART Frank Weitenkampf
THE QUEST OF THE PRINT Frank Weitenkampf
HOW TO APPRECIATE PRINTS Frank Weitenkampf
FLOWER PRINTS OF 18TH & EARLY 19TH CENTURY Gordon Dunthorne
ENGRAVINGS & THEIR VALUE Herbert Slater
FAMOUS SPORTING PRINTS Romford & Kendall
PRINTS FOR THE LAYMAN Elizabeth Whitmore
SHADES OF OUR ANCESTORS Alice Van Leer Carrick
SHADES OF MY FOREFATHERS Hannah R. London
PORTRAIT GALLERY OF DISTINGUISHED AMERICANS William H. Brown
CLIPPER SHIP; SPORTING; RAILROAD, INDIAN & PIONEER CURRIER & IVES Fred J. Peters
AMERICAN HISTORICAL PRINTS (VIEWS OF CITIES) I. N. Phelps Stokes*
AMERICAN GRAPHIC HUMOR William Murrell* (2 vols.)
AMERICAN WAX PORTRAITS Ethel Stanwood Bolton
AMERICAN SHEET MUSIC (covers) Dichter & Shapiro*
ROGERS GROUPS Chatwood Smith
FINE PRINTS Carl Zigrosser*
GREAT PAINTINGS IN AMERICA Kimball & Venturi*
AMERICAN LITHOGRAPHS Helen Comstock*
BIRTH OF THE AMERICAN TRADITION IN ART Oskar Hagen*
AMERICAN FOLK ART IN WOOD, METAL & STONE Jean Lipman*
BITS & PIECES OF AMERICAN HISTORY Irving S. Olds

ARCHITECTURE

DOMESTIC ARCHITECTURE OF THE EARLY AMERICAN REPUBLIC Howard Major

DOMESTIC ARCHITECTURE OF AMERICAN COLONIES & EARLY REPUBLIC Fisk Kimball

CHARLES BULFINCH Charles A. Place
EARLY DOMESTIC ARCHITECTURE OF CONNECTI- CUT J. Frederick Kelly
DUTCHESS COUNTY (N.Y.) DOORWAYS Helen W. Reynolds
OLD PHILADELPHIA COLONIAL DETAILS Sims & Willing
SOME HISTORIC HOUSES John C. Fitzpatrick
A TREASURY OF EARLY AMERICAN HOMES Richard Pratt*
ARCHITECTURE THROUGH THE AGES Hamlin*
HISTORIC HOUSES OF THE HUDSON VALLEY Eberlein & Hubbard
HISTORIC HOUSES OF EARLY AMERICA Elsie Lathrop
EARLY DOMESTIC ARCHITECTURE OF PENNSYL- VANIA Eleanor Raymond
MEASURED DRAWINGS; COLONIAL ARCHITECTURE IN DISTRICT OF COLUMBIA Cunningham, Younger & Smith*
NEW ENGLAND GEORGIAN ARCHITECTURE Kingman*
ALEXANDRIA HOUSES, 1750–1830 Davis, Dorsey & Hall*
ANTE-BELLUM MANSIONS OF ALABAMA Hammond*
ARCHITECTURE & TOWN PLANNING IN COLO- NIAL CONNECTICUT Garvin*

COLONIAL HOUSES, PHILADELPHIA, PRE-REVOLU- TIONARY Wallace*
EARLY DOMESTIC ARCHITECTURE OF CONNECTI- CUT J. F. Kelly
GATEWAYS & DOORWAYS OF CHARLESTON Curtis*
GEORGETOWN HOUSES OF THE FEDERAL PERIOD Davis, Dorsey & Hall*
L'ENFANT & WASHINGTON Elizabeth Kite
MCINTIRE ROOMS FROM PEABODY, MASS. E. J. Hipkiss*
DOMESTIC ARCHITECTURE OF AMERICAN REPUB- LIC, GREEK REVIVAL Howard Major
MOLDINGS OF THE WREN & GEORGIAN PERIOD Small & Woodbridge
INTERIOR ARCHITECTURE & DECORATION A.I.D.A.
EARLY AMERICAN DOORWAYS Frary
EARLY HOMES OF OHIO J. F. Frary
HOUSES OF THE WREN & EARLY GEORGIAN PERI- ODS Small & Woodbridge
AMERICAN ARCHITECTURE Fisk Kimball
THE STORY OF ARCHITECTURE IN AMERICA Thomas Tallmadge
THE LOG CABIN MYTH Harold R. Shurtleff*
SPANISH INFLUENCE ON AMERICAN ARCHITEC- TURE & DECORATION R. W. Sexton

CRAFTS

Home and Shop, Amateur and Professional

DECORATIVE CRAFTS: BARBOLA, WAX, GESSO, STENCIL, ETC. E. T. Black*
PIQUÉ, A BEAUTIFUL MINOR ART Herbert Dent
FOLK ART OF RURAL PENNSYLVANIA Lichten*
PENNSYLVANIA DUTCH STUFF Robacker
TRADES & TRADESMEN IN ESSEX COUNTY (Mass.) H. W. Belknap
OHIO IN HOMESPUN & CALICO I. T. Frary
SEAT WEAVING Perry*
CANDLEMAKING Klenke*
THE CANDLE BOOK L. M. A. Roy* (see also Lighting)

HANDICRAFTS OF THE SOUTHERN HIGHLANDS Allen H. Eaton*
EVERYDAY LIFE IN THE MASSACHUSETTS BAY COLONY George F. Dow
ARTS & CRAFTS IN PHILADELPHIA, MARYLAND & SOUTH CAROLINA A. C. Prime
EVERYDAY THINGS IN AMERICAN LIFE, 1607– 1776 (1st vol.), 1776–1863 (2nd vol.) William C. Langdon
ARTS & CRAFTS IN NEW ENGLAND, 1704–1775 George F. Dow
ARTS & CRAFTS IN NEW YORK Rita Gottesman*

CERAMICS

The fictile arts, including pottery, china, porcelain, faïence, delft, and majolica

THE ART OF THE OLD ENGLISH POTTER L. M. Solon
THE BOOK OF POTTERY & PORCELAIN Warren E. Cox* (2 vols.)
GENERAL HISTORY OF PORCELAIN William Burton
SALT GLAZE L. M. Solon
POTTERY & PORCELAIN E. Hannover
HISTORY OF ENGLISH PORCELAIN L. M. Solon
THE ART OF THE POTTER W. B. Honey
ENGLISH POTTERY Rackham & Read
PRACTICAL BOOK OF CHINAWARE Eberlein & McClure*
ITALIAN MAJOLICA L. M. Solon
ANGLO-AMERICAN HISTORICAL CHINA Mabel Woods Smith
BLUE & WHITE SPODE Sydney B. Williams*
THE OLD CHINA BOOK N. Hudson Moore
THE BOOK OF FAMILLE ROSE George C. Williamson
THE BRIC-A-BRAC COLLECTOR Lewer & Percival
STAFFORDSHIRE POTTERY Wedgwood & Ormsbee

THE SHENANDOAH POTTERY Rice & Stoudt
BLUE & WHITE PORCELAIN OF 18TH CENTURY Stanley Fisher*
DELFTER FAYENCE Dr. Ferrand Hudig
DICTIONNAIRE DES MARQUES DE L'ANCIENNE FAÏENCE DE DELFT R. Delenne*
POTTERY & PORCELAIN Frederick Litchfield*
TRANSFER PRINTING William Turner
WORCESTER PORCELAIN R. L. Hobson
WILLIAM ADAMS, OLD ENGLISH POTTER William Turner
BOW PORCELAIN F. Hurlbutt
OLD DERBY PORCELAIN Frank Hurlbutt
LIVERPOOL TRANSFER DESIGNS ON ANGLO- AMERICAN POTTERY R. H. McCauley*
HANDBOOK OF MARKS ON POTTERY & PORCELAIN Burton & Hobson
BRISTOL PORCELAIN Frank Hurlbutt
WORCESTER CHINA, 1852–1897 R. W. Binns
WEDGWOOD Graham & Wedgwood*
FIRST CENTURY OF ENGLISH PORCELAIN W. M. Binns

POTTERY & PORCELAIN OF THE UNITED STATES Edwin Atlee Barber
L'ART FABRIQUER LA PORCELAINE F. B.-Daudenart
AMERICAN POTTERS & POTTERY John Ramsay
19TH CENTURY ENGLISH CERAMIC ART J. H. Blacker
WARES OF THE MING DYNASTY R. L. Hobson
NEW HALL PORCELAIN George Eyre Stringer
OUR PIONEER POTTERS A. W. Clement*
ENGLISH DELFT POTTERY Major R. G. Mundy
BLUE CHINA BOOK Ada Camehl
BLUE CHINA BOOK Hudson Moore
CHELSEA PORCELAIN TOYS G. E. Bryant
AMERICAN HISTORICAL VIEWS ON STAFFORD-SHIRE CHINA Ellouise Baker Larsen*
THE POTTERS & POTTERIES OF CHESTER COUNTY, Pa. Arthur E. James
BLUE DASH CHARGERS E. A. Downman
ORIENTAL LOWESTOFT J. Lloyd Hyde
CHINA COLLECTING IN AMERICA Alice Morse Earle
COLLECTING OLD ENGLISH LUSTRE Jeanette R. Hodgdon
OLD ENGLISH LUSTRE POTTERY John & Baker*
MARKS & MONOGRAMS ON EUROPEAN & ORIENTAL POTTERY & PORCELAIN Chaffers*
PINK LUSTRE POTTERY Atwood Thorne
PORTRAITS IN POTTERY Albert Lee
ENGLISH POTTERY FIGURES Reginald Haggar*
COLOUR PICTURES ON POT LIDS & OTHER STAFFORDSHIRE POTTERY Clarke & Wrench
STAFFORDSHIRE POTTERY FIGURES Herbert Read
ENGLISH PORCELAIN FIGURES William Ruscoe*
HANDBOOK OF OLD POTTERY & PORCELAIN MARKS Jordan Thorn*

DRESDEN CHINA W. B. Honey*
LADY CHARLOTTE SCHREIBER'S JOURNALS Montague J. Guest, ed.
THE EARTHENWARE COLLECTOR G. W. Rhead
CHATS ON OLD ENGLISH TOBACCO JARS Reginald Myer
THE POTTERY & PORCELAIN OF SWANSEA & NANTGARW E. Morton Nance
POURING VESSEL VAGARIES Dudley L. Pickman*
PORCELAIN AS AN ART & MIRROR OF FASHION Robert Schmidt
LIVERPOOL & HER POTTERS H. B. Lancaster
OLD ENGLISH PORCELAIN W. B. Honey*
ENGLISH POTTERY & PORCELAIN W. B. Honey*
EARLY ENGLISH FIGURE POTTERY Sir Harold Mackintosh
STANDARD CATALOG OF ANGLO-AMERICAN CHINA S. Laidacker*
KERAMIC GALLERY W. Chaffers
ENGLISH POTTERY, WITH APPENDIX ON WROTHAM Rackham, Read & Glaizher
CHELSEA PORCELAIN William King
MAJOLICA Larry Freeman*
THEATRICAL FIGURES IN PORCELAIN Sitwell*
THE BOOK OF SNUFF & TOBACCO BOXES Curtis*
EARLY NEW ENGLAND POTTERS & THEIR WARES Lura Woodside Watkins*
HAVILAND-LIMOGES Wood*
FRENCH PORCELAIN OF 18TH CENTURY W. B. Honey*
WEDGWOOD WARE W. B. Honey*
PRACTICAL BOOK OF CHINA WARE Roberts & Beard
19TH CENTURY ENGLISH POTTERY Bemrose*

CLOCKS, WATCHES, AND OTHER TIMEPIECES

AMERICAN CLOCKS & CLOCKMAKERS Carl W. Drepperd*
OLD CLOCK BOOK N. Hudson Moore
THE CLOCK BOOK Wallace Nutting; 2nd ed., Nutting & Palmer*
CONNECTICUT CLOCKMAKERS OF 18TH CENTURY Penrose Hoopes
FURNITURE TREASURY, VOL. III Wallace Nutting*
TIME & TIMEKEEPERS Willis Milham*
OLD CLOCKS & WATCHES & THEIR MAKERS F. J. Britten*
WATCHMAKERS & CLOCKMAKERS OF THE WORLD G. H. Baillie*

RUDIMENTARY TREATISE ON CLOCKS, WATCHES & BELLS Edward Beckett
TIME & TIME TELLERS J. W. Benson
CHATS ON OLD CLOCKS Allan Lloyd*
THE ENGLISH DOMESTIC CLOCK Allan Lloyd
THE WETHERSFIELD COLLECTION OF ENGLISH CLOCKS Arthur S. Vernay
TIMEPIECES (4 parts) Dr. John Lowry Ruth, ed.
SUNDIALS Newton & Margaret Mayall
SUNDIALS & ROSES OF YESTERDAY Alice Morse Earle
TRAIT DE L'HORLOGERIE Thiou l'Aine
MANUEL DE L'HORLOGER L. S. Normand
TRAITÉ D'HORLOGERIE M. J. A. Lepaute

FURNITURE

FURNITURE OF OUR FOREFATHERS Esther Singleton
COLONIAL FURNITURE IN NEW ENGLAND Irving W. Lyon
COLONIAL FURNITURE IN AMERICA Luke Vincent Lockwood
FURNITURE OF THE PILGRIM CENTURY Wallace Nutting
FURNITURE TREASURY Wallace Nutting
AMERICAN ANTIQUE FURNITURE Edgar G. Miller*
HARTFORD CABINETMAKER'S PRICE BOOK, 1792
PHILADELPHIA CABINET & CHAIRMAKER'S PRICE BOOK, 1794
REGULATIONS & PRICES FOR JOINERS & CABINETMAKERS OF HATFIELD (Mass.), 1796
JOURNEYMAN CABINET & CHAIRMAKER'S NEW YORK PRICE BOOK, 1796

PITTSBURGH CABINETMAKER'S PRICE BOOK, 1830
CINCINNATI CABINETMAKER'S PRICE BOOKS, 1830, 1836
MANUSCRIPT DESIGN BOOK OF JACOB BACHMAN & HIS SON, 1768–1798
FURNITURE OF THE OLDEN TIME Frances Carey Morse
COLONIAL FURNITURE Shea & Wenger
EARLY AMERICAN FURNITURE C. O. Cornelius
THE HADLEY CHEST Dr. Clair Franklin Luther
THE STORY OF AMERICAN FURNITURE Thomas H. Ormsbee*
SOUTHERN ANTIQUES Paul H. Burroughs
THE ROCKING CHAIR Walter Dyer & Esther Fraser
AMERICAN WINDSORS Wallace Nutting
HANDBOOK OF ANTIQUE CHAIRS Carl W. Drepperd*

EARLY AMERICAN FURNITURE MAKERS
  Thomas H. Ormsbee
NEW GEOGRAPHY OF AMERICAN ANTIQUES
  Drepperd & Guild*
SHAKER FURNITURE Edward & Faith Andrews
MEASURED DRAWINGS OF EARLY AMERICAN
  FURNITURE B. & B. Osborn
THE PINE FURNITURE OF EARLY NEW ENGLAND
  Russel H. Kettell
DUNCAN PHYFE & THE ENGLISH REGENCY
  Nancy McClelland
FURNITURE MASTERPIECES BY DUNCAN PHYFE
  Charles O. Cornelius
BLUE BOOK, PHILADELPHIA FURNITURE
  William McP. Hornor
AMERICAN FURNITURE Joseph Downs*
THE PRACTICAL BOOK OF PERIOD FURNITURE
  Eberlein & McClure
AMERICAN FURNITURE & DECORATION
  Edward Stratton Holloway
DOMESTIC ARCHITECTURE & OLD FURNITURE
  Murray Adams-Acton
PERIOD FURNITURE FOR EVERYMAN
  W. G. Menzies
DICTIONARY OF ENGLISH FURNITURE
  Macquoid & Edwards
ENGLISH PERIOD FURNITURE F. Gordon Roe
FURNITURE DESIGNS OF CHIPPENDALE, HEPPLE-
  WHITE & SHERATON (facsimiles) WITH
  ESSAYS & INTRODUCTION Stow & Hayden
ANTIQUE FURNITURE OF WALNUT PERIOD
  Symonds & Ormsbee*
ENGLISH FURNITURE John C. Rogers
OLD ENGLISH WALNUT & LACQUER FURNITURE
  R. W. Symonds
ENGLISH FURNITURE, CHARLES II TO GEORGE II
  R. W. Symonds
OLD ENGLISH FURNITURE FOR THE SMALL COL-
  LECTOR Blake & Hopkins*
ENGLISH FURNITURE OF THE CABRIOLE PERIOD
  H. A. Tipping
ENCYCLOPEDIA OF FURNITURE Aaronson*
FRENCH PROVINCIAL FURNITURE
  Lognon & Huard
FRENCH FURNITURE UNDER LOUIS XIV
  Roger deFelice

THE EVOLUTION OF FURNITURE
  Lucretia Cotchett
OLD ENGLISH FURNITURE Harris & Sons
VENEERED WALNUT FURNITURE
  R. W. Symonds*
ANTIQUE FURNITURE FOR MODERN ROOMS
  Edward Wenham*
FIELD GUIDE TO EARLY AMERICAN FURNITURE
  Thomas H. Ormsbee*
VICTORIAN, THE CINDERELLA OF ANTIQUES
  Carl W. Drepperd*
THE CABINET MAKER'S ASSISTANT John Hall*
CHATS ON COTTAGE & FARMHOUSE FURNITURE
  Arthur Hayden*
THE CABINET & CHAIRMAKER'S REAL FRIEND &
  COMPANION Manwaring*
PRIMITIVE PINE FURNITURE Lazare*
VICTORIAN FURNITURE Larry Freeman*
BOOK OF FURNITURE & DECORATION Aaronson*
ITALIAN FURNITURE A. Pendrini*
ENGLISH PERIOD FURNITURE Hayward*
FINE POINTS OF FURNITURE Sack*
KNOWING, COLLECTING & RESTORING EARLY
  AMERICAN FURNITURE Taylor*
COLLECTORS GUIDE TO FURNITURE DESIGN
  Edward Wenham
AN EXEMPLAR OF ANTIQUE FURNITURE DESIGN
  E. & Verna Cook Salomonsky
MANUAL OF FURNITURE ARTS & CRAFTS
  Johnson & Sironen
ILLUSTRATED HISTORY OF FURNITURE
  Frederick Litchfield
ENGLISH & AMERICAN FURNITURE
  Cescinsky & Hunter
CABINET-MAKER & UPHOLSTERER'S GUIDE
  George Smith
CABINET-MAKER & UPHOLSTERER'S COMPANION
  J. Stokes
DICTIONNAIRE DE L'AMEUBLEMENT ET DE LA
  DÉCORATION, ETC. Henri Havard (4 vols.)
PRIMER OF AMERICAN ANTIQUES
  Carl W. Drepperd*
FIRST READER FOR ANTIQUES COLLECTORS
  Carl W. Drepperd*

FIREARMS AND ARMOR

HAND CANNON TO AUTOMATIC Logan*
SAMUEL COLT Rywell*
U.S. MILITARY MUSKETS, RIFLES & CARBINES
  Rywell*
OUR RIFLES Sawyer*
AMERICAN GUNMAKERS
  Satterlee & Gluckman*
AMERICAN FIREARMS Van Rensselaer*
EARLY AMERICAN FIREARMS Abels*
EARLY AMERICAN GUNSMITHS Kauffman*
RIFLE IN AMERICA P. B. Sharpe*
CONFEDERATE SWORDS Albaugh & Steuart*
GUN COLLECTING Chapel*
HAND FIREARMS, TO END OF 15TH CENTURY
  Clephan*
MUZZLE LOADING RIFLE, THEN AND NOW Cline*

FIREARMS OF THE CONFEDERACY
  Fuller & Steuart*
TREATISE ON THE RIFLE, MUSKET, PISTOL &
  FOWLING PIECE N. Bosworth*
REMARKS ON RIFLE GUNS Ezekiel Baker*
BLACK POWDER SNAPSHOTS Sherlock*
WHITNEY FIREARMS Fuller*
TO ALL SPORTSMEN Colonel Hanger
MASTER FRENCH GUNSMITH'S DESIGN OF MID-
  17TH CENTURY S. V. Grancsay
KRIDER'S SPORTING ANECDOTES Milnor Klapp
HISTORY OF FIREARMS H. B. C. Pollard
GLOSSARY . . . OF ARMS & ARMOR, IN ALL
  COUNTRIES G. C. Stone
RECORD OF EUROPEAN ARMS & ARMOR
  Sir Guy F. Leking

GLASS

200 YEARS OF AMERICAN BLOWN GLASS
  George & Helen McKearin*
SANDWICH GLASS Ruth Webb Lee*
EARLY AMERICAN PRESSED GLASS
  Ruth Webb Lee*
VICTORIAN GLASS Ruth Webb Lee*

PRICE GUIDE TO PATTERN GLASS
  Ruth Webb Lee*
ABC's OF OLD GLASS Carl W. Drepperd*
MILK GLASS Belknap*
STIEGEL GLASS F. W. Hunter*
ENGLISH GLASS W. A. Thorp*

5000 YEARS OF GLASS Rogers & Beard*
OLD GLASS & HOW TO COLLECT IT
  Sidney Lewis*
OLD GLASS PAPERWEIGHTS
  Evangeline Bergstrom*
AMERICAN GLASS M. H. Northend*
SANDWICH, THE TOWN THAT GLASS BUILT
  Barber*
OPAQUE GLASS S. T. Millard*
GOBLETS Millard* (2 vols.)
BITTERS BOTTLES J. H. Thompson*
AMERICAN GLASS Valentine VanTassel*
SWEDISH GLASS Elisa Steenberg*
AMERICAN GLASS CUP PLATES
  Ruth Webb Lee & James H. Rose*
OLD GLASS, EUROPEAN & AMERICAN
  N. Hudson Moore*
THE MAKING OF FINE GLASS Sidney Waugh*
EARLY AMERICAN GLASS
  Rhea Manfield Knittle*
PORTLAND GLASS Frank H. Swan*
CAMBRIDGE GLASS Lura Woodside Watkins*
GLASS W. B. Honey*
IRISH GLASS Dudley Westropp
ENGLISH & IRISH GLASS W. A. Thorpe

COLLECTORS GUIDE TO FLASKS & BOTTLES
  Charles McMurray
MODERN FINE GLASS Leloise Skelley
GLASS Gustavus A. Eisen
BOTTLES Harry Hall White
THE STORY OF OLD ENGLISH GLASS PICTURES
  H. G. Clarke
REMINISCENCES OF GLASSMAKING
  Deming W. Jarves
WHEELING GLASS Josephine Jefferson
GLASER DER EMPIRE UND BIEDERMIERZEIT
  Gustaf V. Pazaurek
SANDWICH GLASS Lenore Wheeler Williams
SALT DISHES C. W. Brown
AMERICAN BOTTLES, OLD & NEW
  W. S. Walbridge
LORE OF OUR LAND IN GLASS
  Bessie M. Lindsay
GLASS CUP PLATES Charles Burns
COLLECTING OLD GLASS Sir James Yoxall
OLD ENGLISH GLASS Albert Hatshorne
OLD IRISH GLASS Mrs. Graydon Stannus
GLASS Edward Dillon
CUT & ENGRAVED GLASS Dorothy Daniel
PITCHER BOOKS (Nos. 1–6)
  Mrs. Watson Kamm

INTERIOR DECORATION

THE HOMES OF THE PILGRIM FATHERS IN ENG-
  LAND & AMERICA Dr. Martin S. Briggs
COLONIAL INTERIORS Edith Sale
FURNISHING THE COLONIAL & FEDERAL HOUSE
  Nancy McClelland
ELEMENTS OF INTERIOR DECORATION
  Sherrill Whiton
WILLIAM MORRIS, DESIGNER G. H. Crow
ENGLISH INTERIORS IN SMALLER HOUSES
  M. Jourdain

DECORATING FOR & WITH ANTIQUES Bjerkoe*
ELEMENTS OF INTERIOR DESIGN & DECORATION
  Sherrill Whiton*
BEYOND NEW ENGLAND THRESHOLDS
  Chamberlain*
BEAUPORT Hollister & Chamberlain*
AMERICAN INTERIOR DESIGN Meyric Rogers*
HOMES OF OUR ANCESTORS Halsey & Tower
LIVING WITH ANTIQUES Alice Winchester*
FURNISHING IN STYLE Walter R. Storey*

BUTTONS

THE COMPLETE BUTTON BOOK
  Lilian Smith Albert & Kathryn Kent*
UNIFORM BUTTONS David Johnson*
WASHINGTON HISTORICAL BUTTONS Albert*
THE BUTTON SAMPLER Albert & Adams*

BUTTON COLLECTOR'S HISTORY
  Grace Horney Ford*
THE BUTTON HANDBOOK
  Florence Zachary Nicholls*

SILVER, BRASS, COPPER, PEWTER, AND IRON

AMERICAN SILVERSMITHS & THEIR MARKS, III
  Stephen G. C. Ensko*
JOHN CONEY, SILVERSMITH
  H. Frederick Clarke
MARYLAND SILVERSMITHS Pleasants & Sill
EARLY AMERICAN SILVER C. Louise Avery
MARKS OF EARLY AMERICAN SILVERSMITHS
  Ernest M. Currier*
THE SILVERSMITHS OF LITTLE REST (R.I.)
  William D. Miller
THREE CENTURIES OF HISTORIC SILVER
  Alfred Coxe Prime
THE BOOK OF OLD SILVER Seymour B. Wyler*
HISTORIC SILVER OF THE COLONIES & ITS
  MAKERS Francis Hill Bigelow
ENGLISH SILVER Stephen G. C. Ensko*
OLD SILVER & OLD SHEFFIELD PLATE
  Howard Pitcher Okie*
OLD SILVER OF EUROPE & AMERICA
  E. Alfred Jones
DOMESTIC SILVER OF GREAT BRITAIN & IRELAND
  Edward Wenham

EARLY OHIO SILVERSMITHS & PEWTERERS
  Rhea Mansfield Knittle
SILVER, BY NEW YORK MAKERS Isabelle Miller
GUIDE TO OLD FRENCH PLATE Louis Carre
SILVERSMITHS OF DELAWARE Jesse Harrington
ENGLISH GOLDSMITHS & THEIR MARKS
  C. J. Jackson*
SOUTH CAROLINA SILVERSMITHS
  E. Milby Burton
NEW YORK STATE SILVERSMITHS G. B. Cutten
NORTH CAROLINA SILVERSMITHS G. B. Cutten
HISTORY OF OLD SHEFFIELD PLATE
  Frederick Bradbury
EARLY AMERICAN WROUGHT IRON
  Albert H. Sonn
FORGES & FURNACES OF PENNSYLVANIA
  Editorial Board, Colonial Dames
EARLY FORGES & FURNACES IN NEW JERSEY
  Charles Boyer
AN ENCYCLOPEDIA OF IRONWORK Otto Hoever*
THE BIBLE IN IRON H. C. Mercer*
PEWTER IN AMERICA Ledlie I. Laughlin

AMERICAN PEWTER H. B. Kerfoot
PEWTER DOWN THE AGES H. H. Cotterell
OLD PEWTER, MAKERS & MARKS OF ENGLAND,
    SCOTLAND & IRELAND H. H. Cotterell

AMERICAN PEWTERERS & THEIR MARKS
    Metropolitan Museum Publication
NEW PEWTER MARKS & OLD PEWTER WARE
    C. A. Markham

LAMPS AND LIGHTING

THE CANDLE BOOK L. M. A. Roy*
COLONIAL LIGHTING Arthur Hayward
THE STORY OF THE LAMP & THE CANDLE
    F. W. Robins*

CANDLEMAKING W. W. Klenke*
NEW LIGHT ON OLD LAMPS Larry Freeman*

TEXTILES, FABRICS, RUGS, ETC.

THE ART OF HOOKED RUG MAKING Batchelder*
CREATING HOOKED RUGS Underhill & Burks*
HANDWEAVING & EDUCATION Mairet*
HANDWEAVING TODAY Mairet*
PRACTICAL BOOK OF ORIENTAL RUGS Lewis*
AMERICAN NEEDLEWORK Georgiana Harbeson*
QUILTS, THEIR STORY & HOW TO MAKE THEM
    Webster*
AMERICAN QUILTS & COVERLETS Florence Peto*
PRACTICAL BOOK OF TAPESTRIES G. L. Hunter*
RARE HOOKED RUGS William Winthrop Kent*
AMERICAN LACE & LACEMAKERS
    Emily Vanderpoel*
WEAVING & DYEING Bronson*
HISTORIC QUILTS Florence Peto*
EARLY AMERICAN TEXTILES Frances D. Little
ROMANCE OF THE PATCHWORK QUILT IN
    AMERICA Hall & Kretsinger*
OLD PATCHWORK QUILTS & THE WOMEN WHO
    MADE THEM Ruth Finley
THE HOOKED RUG William Winthrop Kent
AMERICAN SAMPLERS Ethel Bolton & Eva Coe
HOMESPUN & BLUE (crewelwork) Martha
    Stearns
ORIENTAL RUGS Edna H. Roberts
THE SHUTTLECRAFT BOOK OF AMERICAN HAND-
    WEAVING Mary M. Atwater

HANDMADE RUGS Ella Shannon
COLLECTING HOOKED RUGS Waugh & Foley
THE RUG DICTIONARY C. R. Clifford
THE CHINTZ BOOK M. Percival
HISTORIC TEXTILE FABRICS R. Glazier
PAINTED & PRINTED FABRICS Clouzot & Morris
HISPANIC LACE & LACE MAKING
    Florence L. May
INDIANA COVERLETS & COVERLET WEAVERS
    Kate M. Rabb
SAMPLERS & STITCHES Mrs. Archibald Christie
HISTORY OF BRITISH CARPETS
    C. E. C. Tattersall
SAMPLERS & TAPESTRY EMBROIDERIES
    Marcus B. Huish & Mrs. Head
A BOOK OF HAND WOVEN COVERLETS
    Eliza C. Hall
FANCY WORK FOR PLEASURE & PROFIT
    Addie E. Heron
HEIRLOOMS FROM OLD LOOMS Coverlet Guild
    of America*
HOMESPUN HANDICRAFTS Ella S. Bowles
HOMECRAFT RUGS Lydia Walker
ENGLISH NEEDLEWORK A. F. Kendrick
ORIENTAL RUGS & CARPETS Arthur U. Dilley
BIBLIOGRAPHIE DER MODELBUCHER Arthur Lotz

GENERAL

Subjects not isolated; important volumes noted in capitals

DOMESTIC UTENSILS OF WOOD
    Owen Evan-Thomas
HISTORIC WALL PAPERS
    Nancy McClelland
WALL PAPER, ITS HISTORY, DESIGN & USE
    Phyllis Ackerman
HISTORY OF ENGLISH WALL PAPER
    Sugden & Edmondson
EARLY AMERICAN WALL PAINTINGS
    Edward B. Allen
THE DOMESTIC ENCYCLOPEDIA
    Willich & Mease
THE WHOLE ART OF CONFECTIONERY
    Frederick Nutt
TREATISE ON BREAD & BREADMAKING
    Sylvester Graham
THE FAN BOOK M. Percival
L'ART DU TURNEUR MÉCANICIEN M. Hulot
CANDLE DAYS M. N. Rawson
MEDIEVAL COSTUME & LIFE Dorothy Hartley
EARLY CHINESE JADES U. P. Hennessy
OLD COVERED BRIDGES Albert Jackman
HISTORIC HOUSE MUSEUMS L. V. Coleman

ANTIQUES & THEIR HISTORY
    Buckley of Binghamton
PIONEER AMERICA, ITS FIRST 3 CEN-
    TURIES Carl W. Drepperd*
AMERICA'S PAST Roger Butterfield*
PHILIP HOOKER (architect) E. W. Root
CAVALCADE OF TOYS R. & L. Freeman
THE STORY OF SNUFF & SNUFF BOXES
    M. M. Curtis
WILLIAMSBURG IN COLONIAL TIMES
    J. A. Osborn
EVERYDAY LIFE IN THE MASSACHUSETTS BAY
    COLONY George Francis Dow
OLDTIME SCHOOLS & SCHOOLBOOKS
    Clifton Johnson
AMERICAN FIREMARKS
    Insurance Company of North America
THE HORSE & BUGGY AGE IN NEW ENGLAND
    Edwin V. Mitchell*
HANDBOOK OF THE AMERICAN WING
    Halsey & Cornelius*
AMERICAN INTERIOR DESIGN Meyrick Rogers*
HOMES OF OUR ANCESTORS Halsey & Tower

THE M. & M. KAROLIK COLLECTION OF 18TH CENTURY AMERICAN ARTS
E. J. Hipkiss*

PRIMER OF AMERICAN ANTIQUES
Carl W. Drepperd*

FIRST READER FOR ANTIQUES COLLECTORS Carl W. Drepperd*

COLLECTING IN AMERICA Thomas H. Ormsbee*

HANDBOOK OF POPULAR ANTIQUES
K. M. McClinton*

ENCYCLOPEDIA OF ANTIQUES H. L. Bond

EARLY AMERICAN EPITAPHS
Timothy Alden

FIRE ON THE HEARTH Josephine Pierce*

THE FIRST MAGAZINE C. Tennant

PORTRAIT OF A COLONIAL CITY
Eberlein & Hubbard

THE ODD & QUAINT IN VIRGINIA
Georgia Wardlaw*

THE LADY OF GODEY'S Ruth Finley

STAGE COACH & TAVERN DAYS
Alice Morse Earle

EARLY AMERICAN WOODENWARE
Mary Earle Gould*

PRACTICAL BOOK OF AMERICAN ANTIQUES
Eberlein & McClure

ABOUT ANTIQUES Ella S. Bowles

KNOWING COLLECTING & RESTORING EARLY AMERICAN FURNITURE H. H. Taylor

THE BOOK OF ANTIQUES Horace Shipp

THE LURE OF AMATEUR COLLECTING
G. B. Dexter

ACCOUNT OF THE NEWLY INVENTED PENNSYLVANIA FIREPLACE B. Franklin

ACCESSORIES OF DRESS
Katherine Lester & Viola Oerke

HOW TO RESTORE ANTIQUE FURNITURE
Lorini & Williams*

PENNSYLVANIA DUTCH STUFF E. F. Robacker*

COLONIAL IRONWORK IN OLD PHILADELPHIA
Wallace*

EARLY AMERICAN ADVERTISING ART
C. W. Drepperd

COLLECTION OF HEATING & LIGHTING UTENSILS IN U.S. NATIONAL MUSEUM*

EARLY AMERICAN DECORATION
Esther Stevens Brazer

THE FASCINATING STORY OF DOLLS
Janet Pagter Johl

PUPPEN & PUPPENSPIELE M. V. Boehn

HAWKERS & WALKERS IN EARLY AMERICA
Richardson Wright

WALPOLE SOCIETY ANNUALS, 1912-1940

Other Award Books You'll Be Sure To Enjoy

RELIVE GREAT MOMENTS IN HISTORY WITH THESE DELIGHTFUL AND USEFUL ANTIQUE BOOKS

For the collector . . .
ABC'S OF OLD GLASS
by Carl W. Drepperd

An indispensable guide, containing thousands of simple and concise definitions of names, styles, manufacturing processes, and all types of glassware—including carefully detailed illustrations that show precisely how various pieces look and illuminate the minute differences in designs.   A675-$1.25

HOW TO STAY YOUNG ALL YOUR LIFE
Clement G. Martin, M.D.

Avoid the physical and mental signs of aging. Retain youthful sexual vigor, a slim, firm body, an open, relaxed mind.   A542—illus. 75¢